Beginning
Visual C++ 6

Ivor Horton

Wrox Press Ltd.

Beginning Visual C++ 6

First Published   August 1998
Reprinted   August 1998
Reprinted with Revisions October 1998

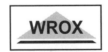

Published by Wrox Press Ltd, 30 Lincoln Road, Olton, Birmingham B27 6PA , UK.
Printed in Canada
3 4 5 TRI 99 98

ISBN 1-861000-88-X

Trademark Acknowledgements

Credits

Author
Ivor Horton

Managing Editor
John Franklin

Editors
Daniel Maharry
Chris Hindley
Ian Nutt
Adrian Young
Victoria Hudgson
Julian Templeman

Technical Reviewers
Claus Loud
Curt Krone
Tim Nelson
Gavin Smyth

Cover/Design/Layout
Andrew Guillaume

Copy Edit
George Briggs
Alex Zoro
Barney Zoro

Index
Seth Maislin

A Note From the Author

In all my *Beginning...* books, my objective is to minimize what, in my judgment, are the three main hurdles the aspiring programmer must face: getting to grips with the jargon that pervades every programming language and environment, understanding the *use* of the language elements (as opposed to what they are), and appreciating how the language is applied in a practical context.

Jargon is an invaluable and virtually indispensable means of communication for the competent amateur as well as the expert professional, so it can't be avoided. My approach is to ensure that the beginner understands what the jargon means and gets comfortable with using it in context. In that way, they can use the documentation that comes along with most programming products more effectively, and can also feel competent to read and learn from the literature that surrounds most programming languages.

Comprehending the syntax and effects of the language elements are obviously essential to learning a language, but I believe illustrating *how* the language features work and *how* they are used are equally important. Rather than just use code fragments, I always try to provide the reader with practical working examples that show the relationship of each language feature to specific problems. These can then be a basis for experimentation, to see at first hand the effects of changing the code in various ways.

The practical context needs to go beyond the mechanics of applying individual language elements. To help the beginner gain the competence and confidence to develop their own applications, I aim to provide them with an insight into how things work in combination and on a larger scale than a simple example with a few lines of code. That's why I like to have at least one working example that builds over several chapters. In that way it's possible to show something of the approach to managing code as well as how language features can be applied together.

Finally, I know the prospect of working through a book of doorstop proportions can be quite daunting. For that reason it's important for the beginner to realize three things that are true for most programming languages. Firstly, there *is* a lot to it, but this means there will be a greater sense of satisfaction when you've succeeded. Secondly, it's great fun, so you really will enjoy it. Thirdly, it's a lot easier than you think, so you positively *will* make it.

Ivor Horton

Beginning
Visual C++
6

Table Of Contents

Chapter 7: A Taste of Old-Fashioned Windows   243

Chapter 8: Structuring Your Data Using Classes   279

Chapter 14: Working With Menus And Toolbars — 561

Chapter 15: Drawing in a Window   593

Chapter 23: ActiveX Controls   959

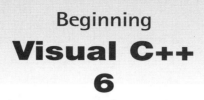

Beginning
Visual C++
6

Introduction

Welcome to *Beginning Visual C++ 6*. With this book you will become a competent C++ and Windows programmer.

I have revised and updated the best-selling *Beginning Visual C++ 5*, to cover what's new in version 6.0 of Visual C++ and to improve the tutorial as a whole, based on the feedback I have received from many readers, for which I'm grateful.

Who's This Book For?

Beginning Visual C++ 6 is designed to teach you how to write useful programs as quickly and as easily as possible using Microsoft's Visual C++ compiler. This is the tutorial for you, if:

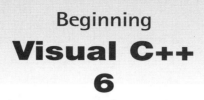 You've done a little bit of programming before, so you understand the concepts behind it — maybe you've used BASIC or Pascal. Now you're keen to learn C++ and develop practical Windows programming skills using the most powerful tools available. This book will give you the solid foundation you're looking for, but will move along fast enough to keep you excited.

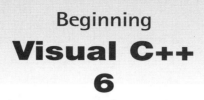 You're a newcomer to programming, but you don't want to mess around with toy languages — you want to plunge straight in at the deep end. That's fine: you need to learn the basics of C++ quickly and then be prepared to work hard to use that knowledge, in real Windows programming. That's exactly what this book does.

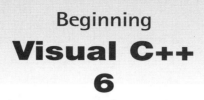 You have some knowledge of C++, but you need a refresher course using a visual development environment. You realize that further progress in computing hinges upon your experience of Windows, MFC and component programming. What you already know will be reinforced, letting you get to the real meat in the sandwich: MFC and Windows.

What's Covered in This Book

Practically everything, to be frank. I've aimed to take you from an introduction to C++ right up to the cutting edge of Windows programming: developing ActiveX controls. The book is actually split into two halves. The first half covers the C++ language, while the second covers Windows programming with Microsoft Foundation Class & Templates (MFC&T).

The first half of the book is a complete tutorial to the C++ programming language. It starts with an introduction to the integrated development environment (IDE) provided with Visual C++, briefly covering the main components of the interface. The next five chapters cover the basics of the C++ language (data types and program flow) before we break for a brief interlude in Chapter 7 where you will write your first Windows program. Chapters 8 to 11 develop the concept and syntax of object-oriented programming with C++, culminating with the design and implementation of a challenging project. Chapter 12, meanwhile, gives you important advice on how to successfully debug your applications. The lessons you learn here provide a solid foundation for the chapters to follow.

In the second half of the book, you'll get to grips with Microsoft Foundation Classes & Templates and Windows programming for real. We'll look at AppWizard and ClassWizard, two tools to speed up your application development. We'll cover building applications with menus, dialogs and scrollbars. Saving and reading data to and from the disk will be discussed, along with how to print documents and write dynamic-link libraries. All these new topics are reinforced through the progressive development of a simple drawing application which grows in functionality as your knowledge increases.

Chapters 20 and 21 demonstrate how to connect to, and interact with, databases using Visual C++, showing you how easy it is to produce a dialog-based database interface using the classes provided by MFC for the purpose.

The last three chapters of the book form an introduction to one of the most important areas of development now and in the future: custom controls. We'll start by explaining the concept of object linking and embedding (OLE), and produce a version of our drawing application which allows you to edit your drawings *inside* other applications — Microsoft Word, for example. After that, we take the next step and use MFC to produce an ActiveX control, which as well as being embeddable inside other applications can also communicate with them. Finally, we use the ATL Object Wizard, newly updated for Visual C++6, to create two more ActiveX controls without MFC.

Every chapter is concluded with a summary and a set of exercises which can form part of a course, or serve simply to consolidate the new things you've learned during the chapter.

What You Need to Use This Book

To use this book you need Visual C++ 6.0, the latest version of Microsoft's best-selling C++ compiler. This version is 32-bit only, so you'll need to install it on Windows 95, Windows 98 or Windows NT 4 (with service pack 3). For Windows 95 and 98, your computer needs to have at least a 486 CPU and a minimum 16Mb of memory. NT4 requires at least a 486 DX4 with 32 Mb of memory.

For Visual C++, you'll need quite a lot of hard disk space — a typical installation is 270 Mb. You can do a minimal installation which takes up around 70 Mb, but this will mean longer compile times as the CD-ROM will be utilized more often.

More importantly however, to get the most out of this book you need a willingness to learn, a desire to succeed and the determination to master the most powerful tool there is to program Windows. You might believe that doing all this is going to be difficult, but I think you'll be surprised by how much you can achieve. I'll help you to start experimenting on your own and, from there, to become a successful programmer.

Conventions Used

We use a number of different styles of text and layout in the book to help differentiate between the different kinds of information. Here are examples of the styles we use and an explanation of what they mean:

> *These boxes hold important, not-to-be forgotten, mission critical details which are directly relevant to the surrounding text.*

 Extra details, For Your Information, come in boxes like this.

Background information, asides and references appear in text like this.

▶ **Important Words** are in a bold type font.

▶ Words that appear on the screen, such as menu options, are in a similar font to the one used on screen, for example, the File menu.

▶ Keys that you press on the keyboard, like *Ctrl* and *Enter*, are in italics.

▶ All filenames are in this style: **Videos.mdb**.

▶ Function names look like this: **main()**.

▶ Code which is new, important or relevant to the current discussion, will be presented like this:

```
void main()
{
    cout << "Beginning Visual C++";
}
```

▶ whereas code you've seen before, or which has little to do with the matter at hand, looks like this:

```
void main()
{
    cout << "Beginning Visual C++";
}
```

Tell Us What You Think

We have tried to make this book as accurate and enjoyable for you as possible, but what really matters is what the book actually does for you. Please let us know your views, whether positive or negative, either by returning the reply card in the back of the book or by contacting us at Wrox Press using either of the following methods:

        E-mail: feedback@wrox.com
        Internet: http://www.wrox.com/

Source Code and Keeping Up-to-date

We try to keep the prices of our books reasonable, even when they're as big as this one, and so to replace an accompanying disk, we make the source code for the book available on our web sites:

http://www.wrox.com/

The code is also available via FTP:

ftp://ftp.wrox.com
ftp://ftp.wrox.co.uk

If you don't have access to the Internet, then we can provide a disk for a nominal fee to cover postage and packing.

Errata & Updates

We've made every effort to make sure there are no errors in the text or the code. However, to err is human and as such we recognize the need to keep you informed of any mistakes as they're spotted and amended.

While you're visiting our web site, please make use of our *Errata* page that's dedicated to fixing any small errors in the book or, offering new ways around a problem and its solution. Errata sheets are available for all our books — please download them, or take part in the continuous improvement of our tutorials and upload a 'fix' or pointer.

For those without access to the net, call us on 1-800 USE WROX and we'll gladly send errata sheets to you. Alternatively, send a letter to:

Wrox Press Inc.,
1512 North Fremont,
Suite 103
Chicago,
Illinois 60622
USA

Wrox Press Ltd,
30, Lincoln Road,
Olton,
Birmingham,
B27 6PA
UK

Programming with Visual C++

Windows programming isn't difficult. In fact, Microsoft Visual C++ Version 6.0 makes it remarkably easy, as you'll see throughout the course of this book. There's just one obstacle in our path: before we get to the specifics of Windows programming, we have to be thoroughly familiar with the capabilities of the C++ programming language, particularly the object-oriented aspects of the language. Object oriented techniques are central to the effectiveness of all the tools provided by Visual C++ for Windows programming, so it's essential that you gain a good understanding of them. That's exactly what this book will provide.

In this chapter, as a base for tackling the C++ language, we're going to take a rapid tour of the the Integrated Development Environment (IDE) that comes with Visual C++. Becoming reasonably fluent with the IDE will make the whole process of developing your applications much easier.

The IDE is very straightforward, and generally intuitive in its operation, so you'll be able to pick up most of it as you go along. The best approach to getting familiar with it is to work through creating, compiling and executing a simple program. You'll get some insight into the philosophy and mechanics of the (IDE) as you use it. We'll take you through this process and beyond, so that by the end of this chapter, you will have learned about:

▶ The principal components of Visual C++

▶ Projects and how you create them

▶ How to create and edit a program

▶ How to compile, link and execute your first C++ program

▶ How to create a basic Windows program

So power up your PC, start Windows, load the mighty Visual C++ and we can begin our journey.

Learning C++ and Windows Programming

With this book, you'll learn how to write programs in C++ and how to write Windows programs. We'll approach the topics in that order, insulating C++ from Windows considerations until you're comfortable with the language. You should find that it's a natural progression from understanding C++ to applying it to the development of Windows applications.

To give you a feel for where we are ultimately headed, we can take look at the characteristics of a typical Windows program. We can also introduce the development context that we will use while you're grappling with C++.

Introducing Windows Programming

Our approach to Windows programming will be to use all the tools that Visual C++ provides. **AppWizard**, which (as you will see) can generate a basic Windows program automatically, will be the starting point for all the Windows examples later in the book, and we'll be using **ClassWizard** in the process of developing what AppWizard produces into something more useful. To get a flavor of how AppWizard works, later in this chapter we'll look at the mechanics of starting a Windows program.

A Windows program has quite a different structure to that of the typical DOS program, and it's rather more complicated. There are two reasons for this. First, in a DOS program you can get input from the keyboard or write to the display directly, whereas a Windows program can only access the input and output facilities of the computer by way of Windows functions; no direct access to these hardware resources is permitted. Since several programs can be active at one time under Windows, Windows has to determine which application a given input is destined for and signal the program concerned accordingly. Windows has primary control of all communications with the user.

Second, the nature of the interface between a user and a Windows application is such that a range of different inputs are possible at any given time. A user may key some data, select any of a number of menu options, or click the mouse somewhere in the application window. A well-designed Windows application has to be prepared to deal with any type of input at any time, because there is no way of knowing in advance which type of input is going to occur.

These user actions are all regarded by Windows as **events**, and will typically result in a particular piece of your program code being executed. How program execution proceeds is therefore determined by the sequence of user actions. Programs that operate in this way are referred to as **event-driven** programs.

Therefore, a Windows program consists primarily of pieces of code that respond to events caused by the action of the user, or by Windows itself. This sort of program structure can be represented as illustrated:

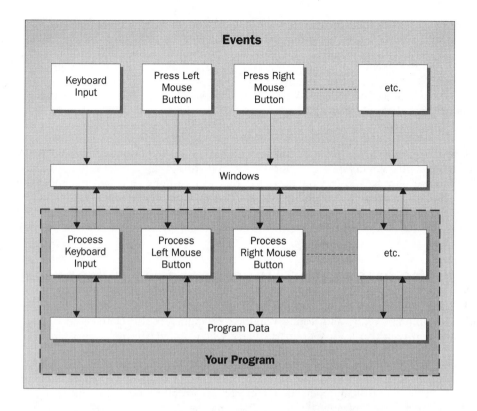

Each block in the illustration represents a piece of code written specifically to deal with a particular event. Although the program may appear to be somewhat fragmented, the primary factor welding the program into a whole is Windows itself. You can think of your Windows program as customizing Windows to provide a particular set of capabilities. Of course, the modules servicing various external events, such as selecting a menu or clicking the mouse, will all typically have access to a common set of application-specific data in a particular program. This application data will contain information that relates to what the program is about — for example, blocks of text in an editor, or player scoring records in a program aimed at tracking how your baseball team is doing — as well as information about some of the events that have occurred during execution of the program. This shared collection of data allows various parts of the program which look independent to communicate and operate in a coordinated and integrated fashion. We will, of course, go into this in much more detail later in the book.

Even an elementary Windows program involves quite a few lines of code, and with AppWizard-based Windows programs, 'quite a few' turns out to be rather a lot. To make the process of understanding how C++ works easy, you really need a context which is as simple as possible. Fortunately, Visual C++ comes with an environment that is ready-made for the purpose.

Console Applications

As well as developing Windows applications, Visual C++ also allows you to write, compile, and test C++ programs that have none of the baggage required for Windows programs — that is, applications that are essentially character-based DOS programs. These programs are called **console applications** in Visual C++ because you communicate with them through the keyboard and the screen in character mode.

Writing console applications might seem as though you are being sidetracked from the main objective, but when it comes to learning C++ (which you do need to do before embarking on Windows-specific programming) it's the best way to proceed. As we said earlier, there's a lot of code in even a simple Windows program, and it's very important not to be distracted by the complexities of Windows when learning the ins and outs of C++. Therefore, in the early chapters of the book where we are concerned with how C++ works, we'll spend time walking with a few lightweight console applications before we get to run with the heavyweight sacks of code in the world of Windows.

While you're learning C++, you'll be able to concentrate on the language features without worrying about the environment in which we're operating. With the console applications that we'll write, we only have a text interface, but this will be quite sufficient for understanding all of C++. There's no graphical capability within the definition of the language. Naturally, we will provide extensive coverage of graphical user interface programming when we come to write programs specifically for Windows using Microsoft Foundation Classes and Templates (**MFC&T**).

What is the Integrated Development Environment?

The IDE that comes with Visual C++ version 6.0 is a completely self-contained environment for creating, compiling, linking and testing Windows programs. It also happens to be a great environment in which to learn C++ (particularly when combined with a great book).

Visual C++ incorporates a range of fully integrated tools designed to make the whole process of writing Windows programs easy. We will see something of these in this chapter, but rather than grind through a boring litany of features and options in the abstract, we will first take a look at the basics to get a view of how the IDE works and then pick up the rest in context as we go along.

Components of the System

The fundamental parts of Visual C++, provided as part of the IDE, are the editor, the compiler, the linker and the libraries. These are the basic tools that are essential to writing and executing a C++ program. Their functions are as follows:

The Editor

The editor provides an interactive environment for creating and editing C++ source code. As well as the usual facilities, such as cut and paste, which you are certainly already familiar with, the editor also provides color cues to differentiate between various language elements. The editor automatically recognizes fundamental words in the C++ language and assigns a color to them according to what they are. This not only helps to make your code more readable, but also provides a clear indicator of when you make errors in keying such words.

The Compiler

The compiler converts your source code into machine language, and detects and reports errors in the compilation process. The compiler can detect a wide range of errors that are due to invalid or unrecognized program code, as well as structural errors, where, for example, part of a program can never be executed. The output from the compiler is known as **object code** and is stored in files called **object files**, which usually have names with the extension `.obj`.

The Linker

The linker combines the various modules generated by the compiler from source code files, adds required code modules from program libraries supplied as part of C++, and welds everything into an executable whole. The linker can also detect and report errors — for example, if part of your program is missing, or a non-existent library component is referenced.

The Libraries

A library supports and extends the C++ language by providing routines to carry out operations that are not part of the language. For example, libraries can contain routines such as calculating a square root, comparing two character strings or obtaining date and time information. There are several kinds of library provided by Visual C++.

The first kind contains routines that aren't platform-specific. There is a basic set of routines common to all C++ compilers which make up the **Standard C++ Library**. There are also extensions to the standard set, which will be supported in many other C++ compilers, but their universality isn't guaranteed. You'll get to know quite a number of these as you develop your knowledge of C++.

The other libraries provided by Visual C++ are collectively known as the **Microsoft Foundation Classes and Templates** library (or **MFC&T**). We'll see a lot more of the MFC&T when we get to the details of Windows programming. For now, it suffices to say that MFC&T is made up of three parts. One of these is the **Microsoft Foundation Class** library (**MFC**), which is the cornerstone of Windows programming with Visual C++. The MFC provides the basis for many of the Windows programs you'll write. The MFC is also referred to as an **application framework** because it provides a set of structured components that provide a ready-made basis for almost any Windows program. The **Active Template Library** (**ATL**) provides structures for writing specialized windows programs; we'll look at the ATL much later in the book. Finally, something called **Object Linking and Embedding DataBase Template Library** (**OLE DB**) comes into play when creating databases; but OLE DB is really beyond the scope of this book.

Other Tools

Visual C++ also includes two important tools which work in a wholly integrated way to help you write Windows programs. These are the **AppWizard** and the **ClassWizard**. They aren't essential to the process of writing Windows programs, but provide such immense advantages in simplifying the development process, reducing the incidence of errors, and shortening the time to completing a program, that we will use them for all of our major examples. Read on for an idea of the services that these tools provide.

AppWizard

The AppWizard automatically generates a basic framework for your Windows program. In fact, the framework is itself a complete, executable Windows program, as we shall see later in this chapter. Of course, you need to add the specific functionality necessary to make the program do what you want, which is an essential part of developing a Windows program.

ClassWizard

Classes are the most important language feature of C++ and are fundamental to Windows programming with Visual C++. The ClassWizard provides an easy means of extending the classes generated by AppWizard as part of your basic Windows program and also helps you to add new classes based on classes in the MFC to support the functionality you want to include in your program. Note that ClassWizard neither recognizes nor deals with classes that are not based on MFC classes.

The Wizard Bar

A further capability for managing, modifying, and extending your code is provided by the Wizard Bar, which is optionally displayed in the toolbar area of the Visual C++ window. It's particularly useful in the context of MFC- and ATL-based Windows programs, so we'll see more of it then. For now, let's just say that its particular forte is adding code to your programs to deal with the Windows events we discussed earlier.

Using the IDE

All our program development and execution will be performed from within the IDE. When you start Visual C++, assuming no project was active when you shut it down last (we'll see what a project is, exactly, in a moment), you will see the window shown below:

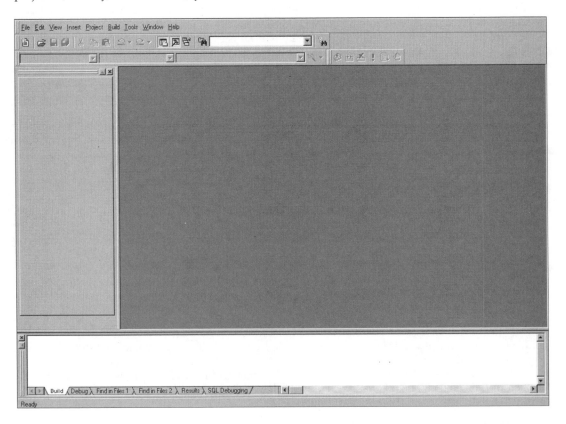

The window to the left is the **project workspace window**, the window to the right is the **editor window**, and the window at the bottom is the **output window**. The workspace window provides access to the on-line documentation and enables you to navigate through your program files, the editor window is where you enter and modify source code and other components of your application, and the output window displays messages that result from compiling and linking your program.

If you're using Visual C++ for the first time, you may find that the output window is missing. Don't worry about that — it will appear the first time you compile a program.

The toolbars below the main menu that you see above, provide icons which act as an instant route to some of the functions available from the main menus. Just clicking on a toolbar icon will directly perform the function that it corresponds to. Visual C++ offers a whole range of dockable and customizable toolbars that you can use.

Toolbar Options

It may be that your Visual C++ window doesn't show the toolbars that appear above. If this is the case, just right click with the mouse in the toolbar area. You will see a pop-up with a list of toolbars, some of which have check marks alongside:

This is where you decide which toolbars are visible at any one time. You can make your set of toolbars the same as those shown by making sure the Output, Workspace, Standard, Build MiniBar and WizardBar menu items are checked.

You needn't clutter up the application window with all the toolbars you think you might need at some time. Other toolbars will appear automatically when required, so you'll probably find the default toolbar selections are perfectly adequate most of the time. As you develop your applications, from time to time you might think it would be more convenient to have access to toolbars that aren't displayed. You can change the set of toolbars that are visible whenever it suits you by right clicking in the toolbar area and choosing from the pop-up.

> *Like many other Windows applications, the toolbars that make up Visual C++ come complete with tooltips. Just let the mouse pointer linger over a button for a second or two and a little white label will provide you with the function and shortcut key combination of that button.*

Dockable Toolbars

A **dockable** toolbar is one that you can drag around with the mouse to position it at a convenient place in the window. When it is placed in any of the four borders of the application, it is said to be *docked* and will look like the toolbars that you see at the top of the application window. The toolbar on the upper line of toolbar buttons which contains the disk icons and the text box to the right of a pair of binoculars is the Standard toolbar. You can drag this away from the toolbar by placing the cursor on it and dragging it with the mouse while you hold down the left mouse button. It will then appear as a separate window that you can position anywhere.

If you drag any dockable toolbar away from its docked position, it will look like the Standard toolbar that you see above, enclosed in a little window — but, of course, with a different caption. In this state, it is called a **floating toolbar**. All the toolbars that you see above are dockable and can be floating, so you can experiment with dragging any of them around. You can position them in docked positions where they will revert to their normal toolbar appearance. You can dock a dockable toolbar at any side of the main window.

You'll be familiar with many of the toolbar icons that Visual C++ uses from other Windows applications, but you may not appreciate exactly what these icons do in the context of Visual C++, so we'll describe them as we use them.

Since we'll use a new project for every program we develop, looking at what exactly a project is, and understanding how the mechanism for defining a project works, is a good place to start finding out about Visual C++.

Documentation

There will be plenty of occasions when you will want to find out more information about Visual C++. If you're new to C++, then it's handy to have a ready reference for checking syntax (apart from this book, of course!). If you are using Visual C++ for the first time, you'll probably want to learn about the facilities and capabilities offered by Visual C++, the tools offered and how to make the most of them.

All this and more is offered in the **Microsoft Development Network (MSDN) Library**. When you install Visual C++ onto your machine, there is an option to install part or all of the MSDN documentation. It's highly recommended that you do install the MSDN Library — if Visual C++ is the only part of the Visual Studio you're using, then choose a custom installation, and check only the VC++ Documentation box in the MSDN Library Visual Studio 6.0 – Custom window.

To browse the MSDN Library, you can click on the Search button on the Standard toolbar. As well as offering general guidance, the MSDN Library is a useful tool when dealing with errors in your code, as we shall see later in this chapter.

Projects and Project Workspaces

A **project** is simply a program of some kind — it might be a console program, a Windows program, or some other kind of program. A **project workspace** is a folder in which all the information relating to a project is stored. When you create a project, a project workspace is created automatically, and Visual C++ will maintain all of the source code and other files in the project workspace folder. This folder will also contain other folders, which will store the output from compiling and linking your project. When you have created a project along with its project workspace, you can add further projects to the same workspace. These are referred to as **subprojects** of the original project. Where a project has one or more subprojects, you can work on any of the files for the project or its subprojects.

Any kind of project can be a subproject of another, but you would usually only create a subproject in a project workspace where the subproject depends on the project in some way — for example, sharing source code, or some operational interdependency. Generally, unless you have a good reason to do otherwise, each of your projects should have its own project workspace. This ensures you only access the files that belong to your project within Visual C++, and that there is no possibility of confusion with files for other projects which might have similar names. All the examples we will create will have their own workspace.

Defining a Project

The first step in writing a Visual C++ program is to create a project for it using the File | New... menu option from the main menu. As well as containing files that define and keep track of all the code that goes to make up your program, the project workspace also holds files that record the Visual C++ options you're using. The workspace folder will hold the project definition files and all your source code. A project definition includes:

- A project name
- A list of all the source files
- A definition of what sort of program is to be built from the source files, for example, a Windows **.exe** program, or a console application
- The options set for the editor, the compiler, the linker and other components of Visual C++ that might be involved
- The windows to be displayed in Visual C++ when the project is opened

The basic definition of a project is actually stored on disk in a file with the extension **.dsp** (in some previous versions of Visual C++ this was a **.mak** file). This contains information about how your program is to be created from the files in the project workspace and is produced when you create a project workspace. Your project workspace will also contain a file with the extension **.opt** which contains the settings for the project workspace. This will include information about the appearance of the project workspace so that this can be restored when you open a project you have worked on previously. Another file, with the extension **.dsw**, is used to store further information about the workspace, such as what projects it contains.

All of these files are created and maintained automatically by Visual C++ and the IDE, so you shouldn't attempt to edit or amend them directly yourself. If you want to make any changes — for example, to the options in effect for a program — then you should introduce them using the menus for that purpose in the Visual C++ IDE.

Debug and Release Versions of Your Program

You can set a range of options for a project through the <u>P</u>roject | <u>S</u>ettings... menu. These options determine how your source code is to be processed during the compile and link stages. The set of options that produces a particular executable version of your program is called a **configuration**. When you create a new project workspace, Visual C++ will automatically create configurations for producing two versions of your application. One includes information which will help you to debug the program, and is called the Debug version. With the debug version of your program you can step through the code when things go wrong, checking on the data values in the program. The other, called the Release version, has no debug information included and has the code optimization options for the compiler turned on to provide you with the most efficient executable module. These two configurations will be sufficient for our needs throughout the book, but when you need to add other configurations for an application, you can do so through the <u>B</u>uild | Con<u>f</u>igurations... menu. Note that this menu won't appear if you haven't got a project loaded. This is obviously not a problem, but might be confusing if you're just browsing through the menus to see what's there.

You can choose which configuration of your program to work with by selecting the <u>B</u>uild | Set Active C<u>o</u>nfiguration... menu option:

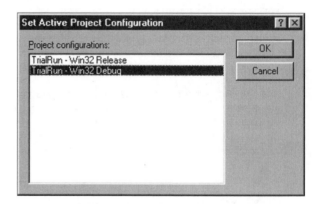

You just select the configuration you want to work with from the list, and click on the OK button. You can display the Build toolbar, which will provide a drop down list box on the toolbar from which you can select a configuration. While you're developing an application, you'll be working with the debug configuration. Once your application has been tested using the debug configuration and appears to be working correctly, you would typically rebuild the program as a release version — since this produces optimized code without the debug and trace capability, which will run faster and occupy less memory.

TRY IT OUT - Creating a New Project

Let's take a look at creating a project for a console application. First select <u>N</u>ew... from the <u>F</u>ile menu to bring up the list of items shown below:

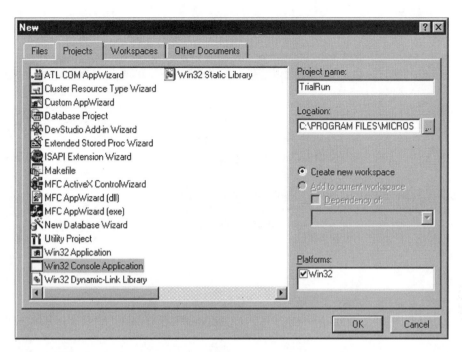

The default tab shown is the Projects tab, which displays the kinds of project that you can create. The selection that you make from the list determines what kind of program you are creating. For many of these options, a basic set of program source modules will be created automatically.

For the project we are creating, you should select Win 32 Console Application as the project's type. This won't generate any code, but will set the options for this kind of application. You can now enter a suitable name for your project by typing into the Project name: edit box — for instance, you could call this one TrialRun, or you can use any other name that takes your fancy. Visual C++ supports long file names, so you have a lot of flexibility.

This dialog also allows you to enter the location for your project, as well as the platforms upon which you'd like it to run, where this is applicable. (We won't need to change the platform setting at all for the examples in this book.) If you simply enter a name for your project, the workspace folder will automatically be set to a folder with that name, with the path shown in the Location: edit box. The folder will be created for you if it doesn't already exist. If you want to specify a different path, just enter it in the Location: edit box.

Alternatively, you can use the 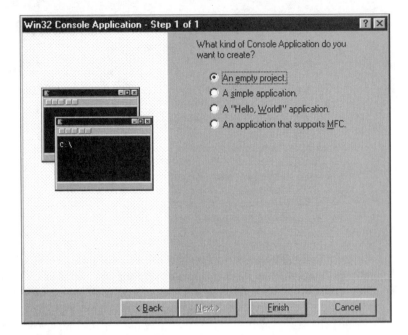 button to select another folder and path for your project's files.

When you click on the
OK button, this list will
appear:

This dialog allows you to select the file support you want in the project. For this project, we will need only the very basic support, so select An **e**mpty project and click on the **F**inish button. You should get an information window, which tells you the specifications of your new project:

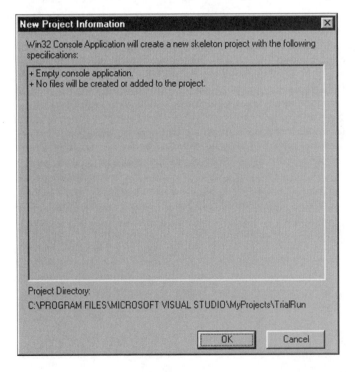

You can confirm that you're happy with the specifications by clicking OK (there's also an option to Cancel, if the specifications aren't what you need). A new project workspace folder will be created in the folder that you have specified as the Location: entry. The folder will have the name that you supplied as the project name and will store all the files making up the project definition. If you use Explorer to look in the project folder, you will see there are just three files initially: the **.dsp** and **.dsw** files that we mentioned earlier, plus the file **TrialRun.ncb**, which stores browse information from your program which is used by several components of Visual C++. So what's browse information? It's information that records where each entity in your program is defined, and where it's used. With the browse information available, you can right click on anything in your source code in the editor window and by selecting the appropriate menu item from the pop-up, go directly to the definition of the item, or find out where it is used in your program.

> *If you're wondering about the* **.opt** *file at this point — Visual C++ creates the* **.opt** *file when you close the project down.*

The new workspace will automatically be opened in Visual C++. You will see that two tabs have been added to the Project Workspace window, showing a ClassView and a FileView for your project. You can switch between these windows by clicking the tab for the window you want to see. The tabs are shown below:

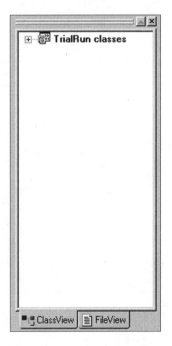
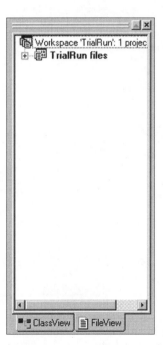

Although these views are looking rather empty at the moment, you'll see later that they provide a quick and convenient way of viewing and accessing various aspects of your project.

The **ClassView** displays the classes defined in your project and will also show the contents of each class. We don't have any classes in this application, so the view is empty. When we get into discussing classes, you will see that you can use ClassView to move around the code relating to the definition and implementation of all your application classes very quickly and easily.

The **FileView** shows the source program files that make up your project. You can display the contents of any of your project files by double clicking on a file name in FileView. This will open a window for the file and automatically invoke an editor to enable you to modify the file contents. At the moment we have no source program files.

Projects for Windows applications will also have a tab to display a **ResourceView** which will display the dialogs, icons, menus and toolbars that are used by the program.

Like most elements of the Visual C++ IDE, the Project Workspace window provides context-sensitive pop-up menus when you right click in the window. If you find that the Project Workspace window gets in your way when writing code, you can hide and show it most easily by using the Project Workspace button provided on the Standard toolbar.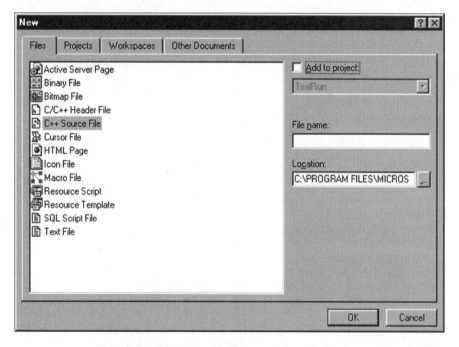

Entering Your First Program

Since a project workspace isn't really a great deal of use without a program file, it's time we entered our first program. Select <u>F</u>ile then <u>N</u>ew... from the main menu again. Visual C++ knows that we've already created a project, and this time offers the Files tab by default:

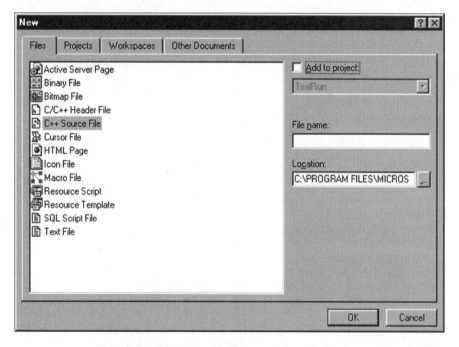

As the name suggests, this dialog lets you choose to create one from a range of different kinds of file. Make your dialog look like the one above, by selecting the type of file from the list as C++ Source File and unchecking the <u>A</u>dd to project: box. Then click on OK. This will open a new editor window to display the file, which will have the default name **Cpp1**.

You'll see that the file name is displayed in the editor window title bar. You can maximize the size of the editor window by clicking on the middle of the three buttons on the editor window title bar — the file name then appears in the Visual C++ title bar at the top. If you type anything into the editor window, then an asterisk will appear following the file name, indicating that the contents of the file displayed in the window have been modified.

Because you chose to open the file as a C++ source file, the editor is already prepared to accept source code, so go right ahead and type in the program code exactly as shown in the window below. Don't worry about what it does. This is a very simple program which outputs some lines of text and is just meant to exercise the Visual C++ facilities.

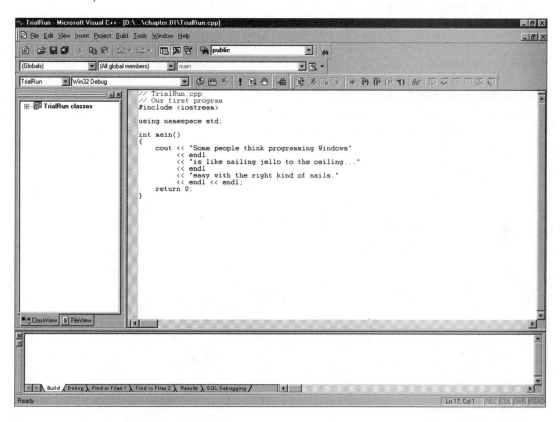

 FYI The keyword `endl` appears four times in the above program. Notice that the last character is the *letter* l, not the *number* 1. It can sometimes be difficult to tell the difference between the two!

Note the automatic indenting that occurs as you type in the code. C++ uses indenting to make programs more readable, and the editor automatically indents each line of code that you enter, based on what was in the previous line. You can also see the syntax color highlighting in action as you type. Some elements of the program are shown in different colors as the editor automatically assigns colors to language elements depending on what they are.

All the executable code is contained between the curly braces. The block of code here is called a **function** and has the name **main**. Every C++ console program has this function, and execution of the program starts at the beginning of **main**. Windows programs, on the other hand, are very different in structure. We will come back to the structure of console programs in the next chapter and will look at the structure of a Windows program in Chapter 7.

Having entered the program, you need to save it with a suitable file name. C++ source programs are usually assigned a name with the extension **.cpp**, so, using the Save option from the File menu (or the corresponding toolbar button), save this file as **TrialRun.cpp**. Files with the extensions **.cpp** or **.cxx** are recognized as C++ source files, whereas files with the extension **.c** are assumed to be C source files. If you don't use one of these extensions, Visual C++ won't recognize the file as a source file. It's best to stick to the **.cpp** extension for C++ as this is most commonly used in the PC environment. You can save a file in any folder that you feel like, but since we intend this file to be part of the TrialRun project that we just created, it's a good idea to store it in the same directory as the project files, which will be the default option.

Adding a Source File to a Project

Now that we have a program source file, we need to add it to our project (saving it in the project directory doesn't do that, it just stores it on disk). The easiest way to do this is to right click in the text file window and select the Insert File into Project item from the pop-up. Alternatively, you could have chosen Add to Project from the Project menu on the main menu bar, selected Files... from the pop-up, and browsed for the file that you wished to add.

```
// TrialRun.cpp
// Our first program
#include <iostream>

using namespace std;

int main()
{
    cout << "Some people think |
         << endl
         << "is like nailing je!
         << endl
         << "easy with the righ
         << endl << endl;
    return 0;
}
```

Menu items:
- Cut
- Copy
- Paste
- Insert File into Project
- Open Document
- List Members
- Type Info
- Parameter Info
- Complete Word
- Go To Definition Of cpp
- Go To Reference To cpp
- Insert/Remove Breakpoint
- Enable Breakpoint
- ClassWizard...
- Properties

You could also have created the file as part of the project at the outset. By selecting Add to Project from the Project menu, and then choosing New... from the pop-up, the C++ file would automatically have been part of the project. In this case you are obliged to supply the name of the file in the New dialog, before Visual C++ creates the file. Once the file is part of the project, the file name appears on the FileView tab in the Project Workspace window, under TrialRun files | Source Files.

Notice that your files are grouped into sub-folders of the **TrialRun** folder: Source Files, Header Files and Resource Files. FileView does this to make it easier for you to access your files; this is a useful facility when you're creating a large console application with a number of files. These three sub-folders aren't real folders, and you won't be able to see them if you view the contents of **TrialRun** through Explorer.

Building a Project

The combined process of compiling the source files in a project to produce object code modules and then linking these to produce an executable file is referred to as **building** a project. The project file with the extension **.dsp** is used by Visual C++ in the build process to set the options for the compiler and linker to create the executable file. You can build a project in a number of ways:

▶ Click the [▦] button on the Build toolbar

▶ Choose the Build item from the menu that appears when you right click the TrialRun files folder in the FileView

▶ Choose the Build TrialRun.exe item from the Build menu on the main menu bar

▶ Press *F7*

> *Note that open source files are automatically saved when a build is performed.*

When you build the executable file, the Output window, which provides you with status and error information about the process, will appear.

```
------------------Configuration: TrialRun - Win32 Debug-------------------
Compiling...
TrialRun.cpp
Linking...

TrialRun.exe - 0 error(s), 0 warning(s)
```
Build / Debug \ Find in Files 1 \ Find in Files 2 \ Results \ SQL Debugging /

Dealing with Errors

Of course, if you didn't type in the program correctly, you'll get errors reported. To show how this works, we could deliberately introduce an error into the program. If you already have errors of your own, you can use those to perform this exercise. Go back to the Text Editor window and delete the semicolon at the end of the second-to-last line and then recompile the source file. The Output window should appear like this:

```
------------------Configuration: TrialRun - Win32 Debug-------------------
Compiling...
TrialRun.cpp
C:\Program Files\Microsoft Visual Studio\MyProjects\TrialRun\TrialRun.cpp(16) : error C2143: syntax error : missing ';' bef
Error executing cl.exe.

TrialRun.exe - 1 error(s), 0 warning(s)
```
Build / Debug \ Find in Files 1 \ Find in Files 2 \ Results \ SQL Debugging /

The error message here is very clear. It specifically states that a semicolon is missing and, if you double click on the error message you will be taken directly to the line in error. You can then correct the error and rebuild the executable file.

Using Help with the Output Window

Sometimes, the cause of an error may not be quite so obvious, in which case some additional information can be very helpful. You can get more information about any error reported by placing the cursor in the output window, anywhere in the line containing the error code (in this case C2143). You can position the cursor just by clicking with the mouse anywhere in the line. If you now press the function key *F1*, you will automatically bring up a help page from the MSDN Library with more information on the particular error in question, often containing examples of the sort of incorrect code that can cause the problem.

The build operation works very efficiently because the project definition keeps track of the status of the files making up the project. During a normal build, Visual C++ only recompiles the files that have changed since the program was last compiled or built. This means that if your project has several source files and you've edited only one of the files since the project was last built, only that file is recompiled before linking to create a new `.exe` file.

You also have the option of rebuilding all files from the start if you want, regardless of when they were last compiled. You just need to use the Rebuild All menu option instead of Build TrialRun.exe (or whatever the name of the executable file is).

Files Created by Building a Console Application

Once the example has been built without error, if you take a look in the project folder, you'll see a new subfolder called Debug. This folder contains the output of the build that you just performed on the project. You will see that this folder contains seven new files.

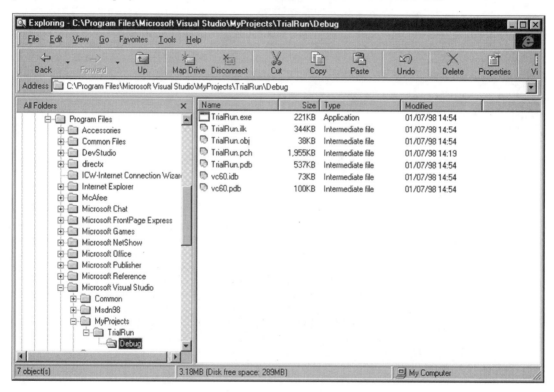

Other than the `.exe` file, which is your program in executable form, you don't need to know much about what's in these files. However, in case you're curious, let's do a quick run-through of what the more interesting ones are for:

File Extension	Description
.exe	This is the executable file for the program. You only get this file if both the compile and link steps are successful
.obj	The compiler produces these object files containing machine code from your program source files. These are used by the linker, along with files from the libraries, to produce your **.exe** file.
.ilk	This file is used by the linker when you rebuild your project. It enables the linker to incrementally link the object files produced from the modified source code into the existing **.exe** file. This avoids the need to re-link everything each time you change your program.
.pch	This is a **pre-compiled header** file. With pre-compiled headers, large tracts of code which are not subject to modification (particularly code supplied by Visual C++) can be processed once and stored in the **.pch** file. Using the **.pch** file substantially reduces the time needed to build your program.
.pdb	This file contains debugging information that is used when you execute the program in debug mode. In this mode, you can dynamically inspect information that is generated during program execution.
.idb	Contains additional debug information

If you have a **.exe** file for the TrialRun project, you can take it for a trial run, so let's see how to do that.

Executing Your First Program

We can, of course, execute the program in the normal way by double-clicking the **.exe** file from Explorer, but we can also execute it without leaving the Visual C++ development environment. You can do this by selecting E̲xecute TrialRun.exe from the B̲uild menu, or by clicking on the toolbar button for this menu item. Our example will produce the output shown:

```
Mc TrialRun
Some people think programming Windows
is like nailing jello to the ceiling...
Easy with the right kind of nails.

Press any key to continue_
```

FYI

The text Press any key to continue **wouldn't normally appear in the console window - you can verify that by double-clicking the** .exe **file. Visual C++ is lending a helping hand by letting you peruse the output from your application at your leisure.**

If we had changed any of the source files since the last build of the executable, or if we hadn't built the executable at all, we would be prompted to rebuild the project when we clicked the Execute Program button.

You could also run your program from a DOS window under Windows 95. You just start a DOS session, change the current directory to the one that contains the `.exe` file for your program, then enter the program name to run it. You can leave the DOS session running while you are working with Visual C++ and just switch back to it when you want to run a console program.

Setting Options in Visual C++

There are two sets of options you can set. First, you can set options that apply to the tools provided by Visual C++, which will apply in every project context. Second, you can set options that are specific to a project, which determine how the project code is to be processed when it is compiled and linked.

Setting Visual C++ Options

Visual C++ options are set through a dialog that's displayed when you select <u>T</u>ools | <u>O</u>ptions... from the main menu.

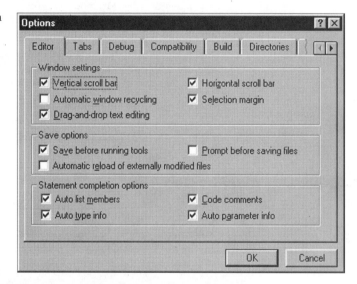

On each tab you'll see a range of options that you can select or deselect by clicking the check boxes. You can get an explanation of any of the options on a tab by clicking on the question mark at top right, and then clicking on the check box you're interested in. You only need concern yourself with a couple of these at this time, but it will be useful to explore the range of options available to you.

If you want to choose a path to be used as a default when you create a new project, select the Directories tab, and then Source files from the drop-down list box on the right. If you then click on the empty line at the bottom of the list of paths that is displayed, you can type in your own path that you want used for new projects.

The Workspace tab allows you to set up which toolbars are dockable and which are not. It also has a range of other options relating to the way a workspace is handled. You may like to check the box for Reload last workspace at startup; then you will automatically pick up precisely where you left off when you closed Visual C++ last.

The <u>T</u>ools | <u>C</u>ustomize... menu option will display a dialog where you can change the contents of the toolbars in Visual C++:

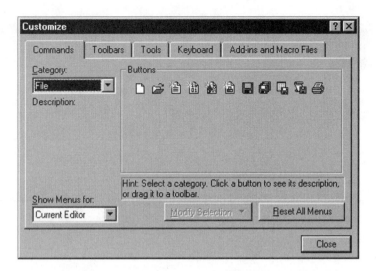

By selecting from the Category: list box on the Commands tab, you can view the toolbar buttons for any of the menus. You can see what any toolbar button on the Commands tab does by clicking it, and you can add any of the buttons shown to any toolbar by dragging it to where you want while holding down the left mouse button. You can also remove a button from an existing toolbar while this dialog is displayed simply by dragging the button that you want to remove off the toolbar.

If you're a keyboard fan, then through the Keyboard tab you can define your own shortcut key for any of the menu options on the main menu.

Setting Project Options

To set the options for a project, you select Project | Settings... from the main menu. This will display another dialog with a variety of tabs. Most of this you can ignore for now, but one thing you'll find very useful for a project of any significant size is to create a browse information file. This will enable you to find out where in your source code any item is used, and where it is defined, just by right clicking it and selecting from the pop-up menu. You can get a browse information file generated by switching to the C/C++ tab.

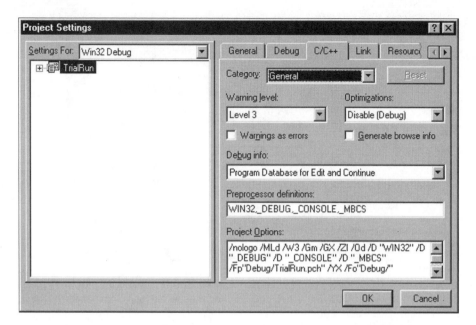

Just click on the Generate browse info check box to get the compiler to generate browse information for each source file. Then switch to the Browse Info tab and click on the Build browse info file check box. This will cause a composite of all the browse information to be assembled into a file with the extension `.bsc`, which will be used when you're browsing your source code. The `.bsc` file is updated when you build your project.

Creating and Executing a Windows Program

Just to show how easy it's going to be, we'll now create a working Windows program, although we'll defer discussion of the program that we generate until we've covered the necessary ground for you to understand it in detail. You will see, though, that the process really is very straightforward.

To start with, if an existing project is active — this will be indicated by the project name appearing in the title bar of the Visual C++ main window — you can select Close Workspace from the File menu. Alternatively, you can just go ahead and create a new project.

To create the Windows program we're going to use AppWizard, so select New... from the File menu, then select the Projects tab in the dialog. Select the project type as MFC AppWizard (exe) and enter TrialWin as the project's name.

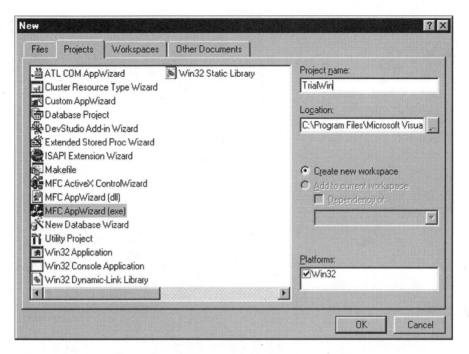

If you didn't close the previous project workspace, you'll need to check the C<u>r</u>eate new workspace radio button, otherwise the project will be created in the current workspace.

When you click on the OK button, the MFC AppWizard window will be displayed. The AppWizard consists of a number of dialog pages with options that let you choose which features you'd like to have included in your application, and we'll get to use most of these in examples later on.

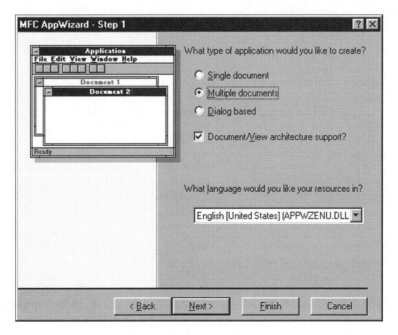

We'll ignore all these options and just accept the default settings, so click the Finish button. Another window will be displayed:

This is to advise you of what AppWizard is about to do and provides you with an opportunity to abort the whole thing if it doesn't seem to be what you want. It defines a list of the classes that it's going to create, and what the basic features of the program are going to be. We won't worry about what all these signify—we'll get to them eventually. It also indicates the folder that it will use to store the project and program files. Just click on the OK button and let AppWizard out of its cage. AppWizard will spend a few moments generating the necessary files and then eventually return to the main window. If you now expand the FileView in the project workspace window, you'll see the file list shown:

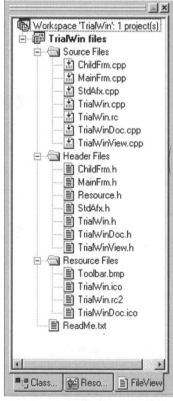

The list shows a large number of files that have been created. You need plenty of space on your hard drive when writing Windows programs! The files with the extension **.cpp** contain executable C++ source code, and the **.h** files contain C++ code consisting of definitions which are used by the executable code. The **.ico** files contain icons. FileView groups the files into the sub-folders you can see for ease of access. These aren't real folders, though, and they won't appear in the project folder on your disk.

If you now take a look at the **TrialWin** folder using Explorer, or whatever else you may have handy for looking at the files on your hard disk, you will see that we have generated a total of 23 files (24, if you've closed the project), four of which are in a sub-folder, **res**. The files in this sub-folder contain the resources used by the program — these are such things as the menus and icons used in the program. We get all this as a result of just entering the name we want to assign to the project. You can see why, with so many files and file names being created automatically, a separate directory for each project becomes more than just a good idea.

One of the files in the **TrialWin** subdirectory, **ReadMe.txt**, provides an explanation of the purpose of each of the files that AppWizard has generated. You can take a look at it if you wish, using Notepad, WordPad, or even the Visual C++ editor. To view it in the editor window just double click on it in FileView.

Executing a Windows Program

Before we can execute our program, we have to compile and link the program modules. You do this in exactly the same way that you did with the console application example. To save time, just select the Execute TrialWin.exe item from the Build menu or the toolbar button:

Since you haven't built the executable yet, you'll be asked whether you want to do so. Click Yes.

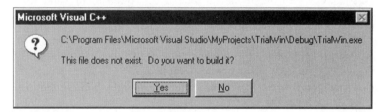

Compiling and linking the project will take a little time, even if you have a fast machine, since we already have quite a complex program. Once the project has been built, the Output window will indicate that there were no errors and the executable will start running. The window for the program we've generated is shown here:

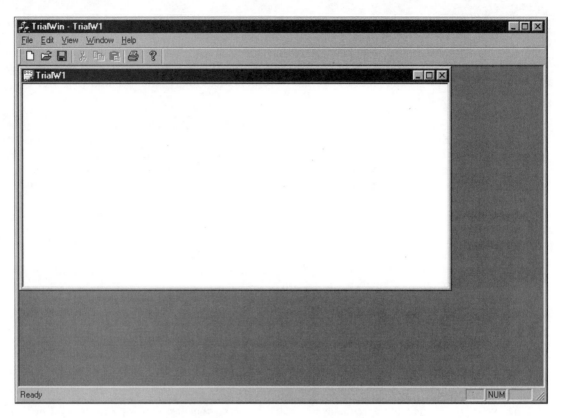

As you see, it's complete with menus and a toolbar. Although there is no specific functionality in the program — that's what we need to add to make it *our* program — all the menus work. You can try them out. You can even create further windows by selecting the New item from the File menu.

I think you'll agree that creating a Windows program with AppWizard hasn't really stressed too many brain cells. We'll need to get a few more ticking away when we come to developing the basic program we have here into a program that does something more interesting, but it won't be that hard. Certainly, for many people, writing a serious Windows program the old-fashioned way, without the aid of Visual C++, required at least a couple of months on a fish diet before making the attempt. That's why so many programmers used to eat sushi. That's all gone now with Visual C++. However, you never know what's around the corner in programming technology. If you like sushi, it's best to continue with it to be on the safe side.

Summary

In this chapter, we've run through the basic mechanics of using Visual C++. We used the Studio to enter and execute a console application program and, with the help of AppWizard, we created a complete Windows program.

Every program should have a project defined for it. The project will store information as to the kind of program it is, what files need to be combined to construct the program and the options in effect for the program. All programs in this book will have a project defined.

Starting with the next chapter, we'll be using console applications extensively throughout the first half of the book. All the examples illustrating how C++ language elements are used will be executed using console applications. We will return to AppWizard as soon as we have finished delving into the secrets of C++.

Exercises

It's not easy to set exercises for this chapter, because we haven't got much new knowledge to exercise yet, so we'll use this opportunity to familiarize ourselves with the basics of the Visual C++.

Ex1-1: List as many different ways as possible to build (i.e. compile and link) a project.

Ex1-2: List the three types of file used to store information about a project and describe the role of each.

Ex1-3: Describe the use of the following file types produced by the Visual C++ compiler: **.obj**, **.pch**, **.pdb**, **.exe**.

Ex1-4: Edit the **TrialRun** program to introduce various errors—miss out or put in the wrong curly braces, misspell names like **main** or **iostream**. Build the project, and use the help system to look at the error messages produced. Don't worry too much for now if you don't understand exactly what they mean; the idea is to get some practice in using the compiler and the help system.

Ex1-5: Read about the IDE in the MSDN Library. A good place to start is under Visual C++ \Visual C++ User's Guide.

Data, Variables and Calculations

In this chapter, we'll get down to the essentials of programming in C++. By the end of the chapter you will be able to write a simple C++ program of the traditional form: input — process — output.

As we explore aspects of the language using working examples, you'll have an opportunity to get some additional practice with the Visual C++ Development Environment. You should create a project for each of the examples before you build and execute them. Remember that when you are defining a project, they are all console applications.

In this chapter you will learn about:

▶ C++ program structure

▶ Namespaces

▶ Variables in C++

▶ Defining variables and constants

▶ Basic input from the keyboard and output to the screen

▶ Performing arithmetic calculations

▶ Casting Operands

▶ Variable scope

The Structure of a C++ Program

Programs which will run as console applications under Visual C++ are text-based MS-DOS programs. All the examples that we'll write to understand how C++ works will be MS-DOS programs, so let's look at how such programs are structured.

A program in C++ consists of one or more **functions**. In Chapter 1, we saw an example consisting simply of the function **main()**, where **main** is the name of the function. This was an MS-DOS program. Every C++ program in the DOS environment contains the function **main()** and all C++ programs of any size consist of several functions. A function is simply a self-contained block of code with a unique name which is invoked by using the name of the function.

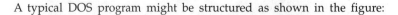
A typical DOS program might be structured as shown in the figure:

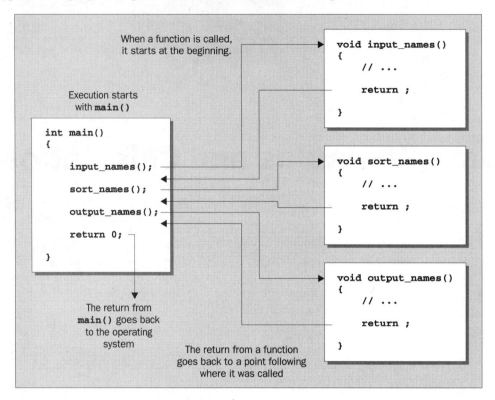

The figure above illustrates that execution of the program shown starts at the beginning of the function **main()**. From **main()**, execution transfers to a function **input_names()** which returns execution to the position immediately following the point where it was called in **main()**. The function **sort_names()** is then called from **main()** and, once control returns to **main()**, the final function **output_names()** is called. Eventually, once output has been completed, execution returns once again to **main()** and the program ends.

Of course, different programs under DOS may have radically different functional structures, but they all start execution at the beginning of **main()**. The principal advantage of having a program broken up into functions is that you can write and test each piece separately. There is a further advantage in that functions written to perform a particular task can be re-used in other programs. The libraries that come with C++ provide a lot of standard functions that you can use in your programs. They can save you a great deal of work.

We'll see more about creating and using functions in Chapter 5.

TRY IT OUT - A Simple Program

Let's look at a simple example to understand the elements of a program a little better. Start by creating a new project from the range of alternatives offered on the Projects tab when you click the New... item in the File menu. When the dialog appears, select Win 32 Console Application and name the project Ex2_01.

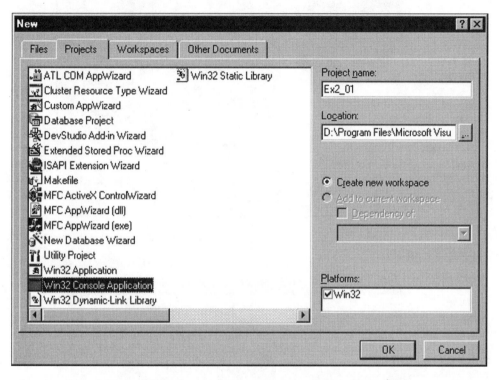

Note that the Create new workspace option is selected by default. A workspace is a directory that can contain one or more projects and in this case it will have the same name as the project. A project corresponds to a single program and is always contained in a workspace.

We could have created a new empty workspace first using the Workspaces tab and given it a name. We could then have added the project to the workspace using the File/New... menu option and supplied a separate name for the project. In this case the workspace directory would have a project sub-directory that would contain the program files for the project. This allows you to have several projects in a single workspace, each of which is a separate program, but will typically be related to the others in some way – part of a suite of programs perhaps.
When you click on OK, the Console Application dialog appears. We'll start from the very basic project structure, so choose An empty project, and click on the Finish button.

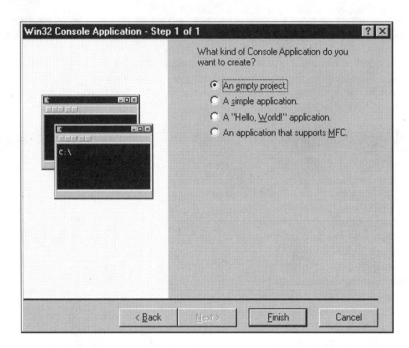

The New Project Information tells you about the project you're about to create; it should look something like this:

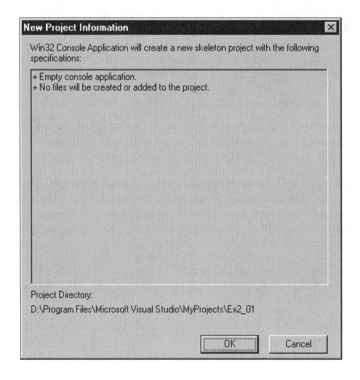

The project directory at the foot of the screen may be slightly different on your machine; everything else should be identical. Once you're happy with it, click on OK.

We'll start by adding a new source file to the project, so select <u>N</u>ew... from the <u>F</u>ile menu (or just press *Ctrl+N*) and select the Files tab. Choose C++ Source File from the list and enter the file name as shown below.

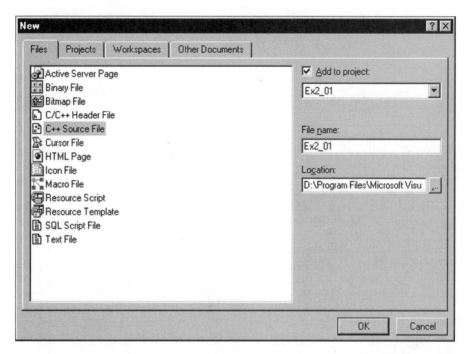

The file will automatically be given the extension **.cpp**, so you don't have to enter it. There is no problem having the name of the file the same as the name of the project. The project file will have the extension **.dsp** so that will differentiate it. Make sure the Add to project checkbox is checked and then click on OK to create the file. You can then type the following code in the editor window:

```cpp
// EX2_01.CPP
// A Simple Example of a Program
#include <iostream>

using namespace std;

int main()
{
   int apples, oranges;       // Declare two integer variables
   int fruit;                 // ...then another one

   apples = 5; oranges = 6;   // Set initial values
   fruit = apples + oranges;  // Get the total fruit

   cout << endl;              // Start output on a new line
   cout << "Oranges are not the only fruit... " << endl
        << "- and we have " << fruit << " fruits in all.";
```

```
    cout << endl;              // Start output on a new line

    return 0;                  // Exit the program
}
```

 FYI The above example is intended to illustrate some of the ways in which you can write C++ statements, rather than to be a model of good programming style.

Since the file is identified by its extension as a file containing C++ code, the keywords in the code that the editor recognizes will be colored their colors. You will be able to see if you have entered **Int** where you should have entered **int**, since the two will be different colors.

If you look at the FileView tab for your new project, you'll see the newly created source file in the FileView. FileView will always show all the files in a project. The **main()** function will appear under the Globals section of the ClassView. We'll consider the meaning of this later.

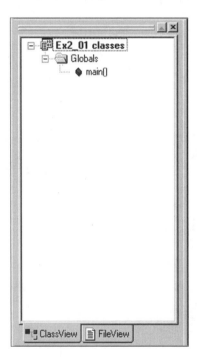

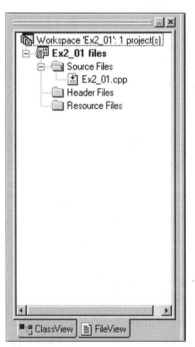

If you now build this program by using the Build button on the Build toolbar, and execute it using the Execute Ex2_01.exe item in the Build menu, you should get the following output:

```
Ex2_01

Oranges are not the only fruit...
- and we have 11 fruits in all.
Press any key to continue
```

Program Comments

The first two lines in the program are **comments**. Comments are an important part of any program, but they're not executable code — they are there simply to help the human reader. All comments are ignored by the compiler. On any line of code, two successive slashes **//** that are not contained within a text string (we shall see what text strings are later) indicate that the rest of the line is a comment.

You can see that several lines of the program contain comments as well as program statements. You can also use an alternative form of comment bounded by **/*** and ***/**. For example, the first line of the program could have been written:

```
/*   EX2_01.CPP   */
```

The comment using **//** only covers the portion of the line following the two successive slashes, whereas the **/*...*/** form defines whatever is enclosed as a comment and can span several lines. For example, we could write:

```
/*
   EX2_01.CPP
   A Simple Program Example
*/
```

All four lines are comments. If you want to highlight some particular comment lines, you can always embellish them with a frame of some description:

```
/*****************************
 *   EX2-01.CPP              *
 *   A Simple Program Example *
 *****************************/
```

As a rule, you should always comment your programs comprehensively. The comments should be sufficient for another programmer, or you at a later date, to understand the purpose of any particular piece of code, and to understand how it works.

The #include Directive — Header Files

Following the comments, we have the **#include** directive,

```
#include <iostream>
```

which makes the compiler insert the contents of the file **iostream** into the program before compilation. This file is called a **header file** because it's usually brought in at the beginning of a program file. This particular header file contains definitions that are necessary for you to be able to use input and output statements in C++. If we didn't include **iostream** in our program, it wouldn't compile because we use output statements that depend on some of the definitions in this file. There are many different header files provided by Visual C++ that cover a wide range of capabilities. We shall be seeing more of them as we progress through the language facilities.

A **#include** statement is one of several **preprocessor directives**. The Visual C++ editor recognizes these and highlights them in blue in your edit window. Preprocessor directives are commands executed by the compiler that generally act on your source code in some way before it is compiled. They all start with the **#** character. We'll be introducing other preprocessor directives as we need them.

The using Directive — Namespaces

As we saw in Chapter 1, the **standard library** is an extensive set of routines which have been written to do many common tasks: for example, dealing with input and output, performing basic mathematical calculations, etc. Since there are a very large number of these routines, it is quite possible that you might accidentally use the same name as one of the library routines for your own purposes. A **namespace** is a mechanism in C++ for avoiding problems that can arise with duplicate names being used in a program. All the names used in code that appears within a namespace also have the namespace name associated with them. All standard library routines are contained within the namespace **std**, so every routine in it has its own name, plus the namespace name, std. This is why we have the line following the **#include** directive for **<iostream>**:

```
using namespace std;
```

This is a **using directive** that tells the compiler that we intend to use names from the namespace **std** without specifying the namespace name - names from the standard library in other words. The compiler will then look out for names from the standard library in the program so the connection with the routine in the standard library can be established. We will discuss namespaces further at the end of this chapter.

The Function main()

The function **main()** in our example consists of the function header defining it as **main()** plus everything from the first opening curly brace (**{**) to the corresponding closing curly brace (**}**). The curly braces enclose the executable statements in the function, which are referred to collectively as the **body** of the function.

As we shall see, all functions consist of a header which defines (amongst other things) the function name, followed by the function body which consists of a number of program statements enclosed between a pair of curly braces. The body of a function may contain no statements at all, in which case it doesn't do anything.

A function that doesn't do anything may seem somewhat superfluous, but when you're writing a large program, you may map out the complete program structure in functions but, initially, leave the code for many of them with empty bodies. Doing this means that you can compile and execute the whole program with all its functions at any time, but add detailed coding for the functions incrementally.

Program Statements

The program statements making up the function body of **main()** are each terminated with a *semicolon*. The program statement is the basic unit in defining what a program does. This is a bit like a sentence in a paragraph of text, where each sentence stands by itself in expressing an action or an idea, but relates to and combines with the other sentences in the paragraph in expressing a more general idea. A statement is a self-contained definition of an action that the computer is to carry out, but which can be combined with other statements to define a more complex action or calculation.

The action of a function is always expressed by a number of statements, each ending with a semicolon. Let's take a quick look at each of the statements in the example that we have just written, just to get a general feel for how it works. We will discuss each type of statement more fully later in this chapter.

The first statement in the program,

```
int apples, oranges;          // Declare two integer variables
```

declares two variables, **apples** and **oranges**. A **variable** is a named bit of computer memory that you can use to store data. A statement introducing the names of variables is called a **variable declaration**. The keyword **int** indicates that the variables are to store values that are whole numbers, or integers. The next statement declares another integer variable, **fruit**. While you can declare several variables in the same statement, as we did for **apples** and **oranges**, it is generally a good idea to declare them separately. This enables you to comment them individually.

In the example, the line

```
apples = 5; oranges = 6;      // Set initial values
```

contains two statements, each terminated by a semicolon. While it isn't obligatory, it's good programming practice to write only one statement on a line. The two statements store the values **5** and **6** in the variables **apples** and **oranges** respectively. These statements are called **assignment statements** because they assign a new value to a variable.

The next statement,

```
fruit = apples + oranges;     // Get the total fruit
```

is also an assignment statement. This one adds the values stored in the variables **apples** and **oranges** and stores the result in the variable **fruit**.

The next three statements are:

```
cout << endl;                     // Start output on a new line
cout << "Oranges are not the only fruit... " << endl
     << "- and we have " << fruit << " fruits in all.";
cout << endl;                     // Start output on a new line
```

These are all output statements. The first sends a newline character, denoted by the word **endl**, to the screen. In C++, a source of input or a destination for output is referred to as a **stream**. The word **cout** specifies the 'standard' output stream, and the operator **<<** indicates that what appears to the right of the operator is to be sent to the output stream, **cout**. The operator **<<** 'points' in the direction that the data flows — from the variable or string on the right to the output destination on the left.

The meaning of the word **cout** and the operator << are defined by the contents of the header file **iostream**, which you'll remember we added to our program code in the **#include** directive at the beginning of the program. **cout** is a name in the standard library, and therefore is within the namespace **std**. Without the **using** directive it would not be recognized. The name **cout** represents your display screen and it is a standard destination for output. Because **cout** has been defined for this purpose, you shouldn't use the word **cout** for other purposes — for example, as a variable in your program.

The second statement sends a text string (defined between quotes) to the screen, followed by another newline character (**endl**), then another text string, followed by the value stored in the variable **fruit**, then finally another text string. There is no problem stringing together a sequence of things that you want to output in this way. The statement executes from left to right, with each item being sent to **cout** in turn. Note that each item is preceded by its own **<<** operator.

The third statement sends another newline character to the screen. These statements produce the output from the program that you see. Note that the second statement runs over two lines. The successive lines are combined into a single statement until the compiler finds the semicolon that defines the end of the statement. This means that if you forget a semicolon for a statement, the compiler will assume the next line is part of the same statement and join them together. This usually results in something the compiler cannot understand, so you'll get an error.

The last statement in our program,

```
return 0;                        // Exit the program
```

stops execution of the program and returns control to the operating system. We will be discussing all of these statements in more detail later on.

The statements in a program are executed in the sequence in which they are written, unless a statement specifically causes the natural sequence to be altered. In Chapter 3, we will look at statements that alter the sequence of execution.

Whitespace

Whitespace is the term used in C++ to describe blanks, tabs, newline characters and comments. A whitespace separates one part of a statement from another and enables the compiler to identify where one element in a statement, such as **int**, ends and the next element begins. Therefore, in the statement,

```
int fruit;                    // ...then another one
```

there must be at least one whitespace character (usually a space) between **int** and **fruit** for the compiler to be able to distinguish them. On the other hand, in the statement

```
fruit = apples + oranges;     // Get the total fruit
```

no whitespace characters are necessary between **fruit** and **=**, or between **=** and **apples**, although you are free to include some if you wish. This is because the **=** is not alphabetic or numeric, so the compiler can separate it from its surroundings. Similarly, no whitespace characters are necessary either side of the **+** sign.

Apart from its use as a separator between elements in a statement that might otherwise be confused, whitespace is ignored by the compiler (except, of course, in a string of characters between quotes). You can therefore include as much whitespace as you like to make your program more readable, as we did when we spread our output statement in the last example over several lines. In some programming languages the end of a statement is at the end of the line, but in C++ the end of a statement is wherever the semicolon occurs.

Since variable names must be made up of single words, you must not put whitespace characters in the middle. If you do, the single variable name won't be seen by the compiler as such, and it won't be interpreted correctly.

Statement Blocks

We can enclose several statements between a pair of curly braces, in which case they become a **block**, or a **compound statement**. The body of a function is an example of a block. Such a compound statement can be thought of as a single statement (as we shall see when we look at the decision making possibilities in C++ in Chapter 3). In fact, wherever you can put a single statement in C++, you could equally well put a block of statements between braces. As a consequence, blocks can be placed inside other blocks. In fact, blocks can be nested, one within another, to any depth.

A statement block also has important effects on variables, but we will defer discussion of this until later in this chapter when we discuss something called variable scope.

Defining Variables

Now that we are beyond our first program, we are going to want to manipulate some meaningful information and get some answers. An essential element in this process is having a piece of memory that we can call our own, that we can refer to using a meaningful name and where we can store an item of data. Each individual piece of memory so specified is called a **variable**.

Each variable will store a particular kind of data that is fixed when we define the variable in our program. One variable might store whole numbers (that is, integers), in which case it couldn't be used to store numbers with fractional values. The value that each variable contains at any point is determined by the instructions in our program and, of course, its value will usually change many times as the program calculation progresses.

Let's look first at the rules for naming a variable when we introduce it into a program.

Naming Variables

The name we give to a variable is called an **identifier**, or more conveniently a **variable name**. Variable names can include the letters A-z (upper or lower case), the digits 0-9 and the underscore character. All other characters are illegal. Variable names must also begin with either a letter or an underscore. Names are usually chosen to indicate the kind of information to be stored.

In Visual C++, variable names can be up to 255 characters long, which gives you a reasonable amount of flexibility. In fact, as well as variables, there are quite a few other things that have names in C++. We shall see that they too can have names of up to 255 characters, with the same definition rules as a variable name. Using names of the maximum length can make your programs a little difficult to read and, unless you have amazing keyboard skills, they are the very devil to type in. A more serious consideration is that not all compilers support such long names. If you anticipate compiling your code in other environments, names with up to 31 characters are usually adequate and will not cause problems in most instances.

Although you can use variable names that begin with an underscore, for example `_this` and `_that`, this is best avoided because of potential clashes with standard system variables which have the same form. You should also avoid using names starting with a double underscore for the same reason.

Examples of good variable names are:

- `Price`
- `discount`
- `pShape`
- `Value_`
- `COUNT`

8_Ball, **7Up**, and **6_pack** are not legal. Neither is **Hash!** or **Mary-Ann**. This last example is a common mistake, although **Mary_Ann** would be quite acceptable. Of course, **Mary Ann** would not be, because blanks are not allowed in variable names. Note that the variable names **republican** and **Republican** are quite different, as upper- and lower-case letters are differentiated.

A convention that is often adopted in C++ is to reserve names beginning with a capital letter for naming classes. We shall discuss classes in Chapter 8.

Keywords in C++

There are reserved words in C++, also called **keywords**, which have special significance within the language. They will be highlighted with a particular color by the Visual C++ editor as you enter your program. If the keywords you type do not appear highlighted, then the keyword has been entered incorrectly.

> *Remember that keywords, like the rest of the C++ language, are case-sensitive.*

For example, the program that you entered earlier in the chapter contained the keywords **int** and **return**. You will see many more as you progress through the book. You must ensure that the names you choose for entities in your program, such as variables, are not the same as any of the keywords in C++. A complete list of keywords used in Visual C++ appears in Appendix A.

Declaring Variables

A variable **declaration** is a program statement which specifies the name of a variable and the sort of data that it can store. For example, the statement,

```
int value;
```

declares a variable with the name **value** that can store integers. The type of data that can be stored in the variable **value** is specified by the keyword **int**. Because **int** is a keyword, you can't use **int** as a name for one of your variables.

> *Note that a declaration always ends with a semicolon.*

A single declaration can specify the names of several variables but, as we have said, it is generally better to declare variables in individual statements, one per line. We will deviate from this from time to time in this book, but only in the interests of not spreading code over too many pages.

A variable name alone can't store anything, so it's not much use on its own. In order to store data (for example, the value of an integer), we need to assign a piece of the computer's memory to the variable. This process is called variable **definition**.

In C++, a variable declaration is also a definition (except in a few special cases, which we shall come across during the book). In the course of a single statement, we introduce the variable name, and also tie it to an appropriately-sized piece of memory. So, the statement

```
int value;
```

is both a declaration and a definition. We use the variable *name* **value** that we declared, to access the piece of the computer's *memory* that we defined.

> *We use the term* declaration *when we introduce a name into our program, with information on what the name will be used for. The term* definition *refers to the allotment of computer memory to the name. In the case of variables, we can declare and define in a single statement, as in the line above.*

You must declare a variable at some point between the beginning of your program and when the variable is used for the first time. In C++, it is good practice to declare variables close to their first point of use.

Initial Values for Variables

When you declare a variable, you can also assign an initial value to it. A variable declaration that assigns an initial value to a variable is called an **initialization**. To initialize a variable when you declare it, you just need to write an equals sign followed by the initializing value after the variable name. We can write the following statements to give each of the variables an initial value:

```
int value = 0;
int count = 10;
int number = 5;
```

In this case, **value** will have the value 0, **count** will have the value **10** and **number** will have the value **5**.

There is another way of writing the initial value for a variable in C++ called **functional notation**. Instead of an equals sign and the value, you can simply write the value in parentheses following the variable name. So we could rewrite the previous declarations as:

```
int value(0);
int count(10);
int number(5);
```

If you don't supply an initial value for a variable, then it will usually contain whatever garbage was left in the memory location it occupies by the previous program you ran (there is an exception to this which we shall see later). Wherever possible, you should initialize your variables when you declare them. If your variables start out with known values, it makes it easier to work out what is happening when things go wrong. And one thing you can be sure of — things *will* go wrong.

Data Types in C++

The sort of information that a variable can hold is determined by its **data type**. All data and variables in your program must be of some defined type. C++ provides you with a range of standard data types, specified by particular keywords. We have already seen the keyword **int** for defining integer variables. As part of the object-oriented aspects of the language, you can also create your own data types, as we shall see later. For the moment, let's take a look at elementary numerical data types that C++ provides.

Integer Variables

As we have said, integer variables are variables that can only have values that are whole numbers. The number of players in a football team is an integer, at least at the beginning of the game. We already know that you can declare integer variables using the keyword **int**. These are variables which occupy 4 bytes in memory and can take both positive and negative values.

The upper and lower limits for the values of a variable of type int correspond to the maximum and minimum signed binary numbers which can be represented by 32 bits. The upper limit for a variable of type int is $2^{31}-1$, and the lower limit is $-(2^{31})$.

In Visual C++, the keyword **short** also defines an integer variable, this time occupying two bytes. The keyword **short** is equivalent to **short int**.

C++ also provides another integer type, **long**, which can also be written as **long int**. In this case, we can write the statement,

```
long bigNumber = 1000000L, largeValue = 0L;
```

where we declare the variables **bigNumber** and **largeValue** with initial values **1000000** and **0** respectively. The letter **L** appended to the end of the values specifies that they are **long** integers. You can also use the small letter **l** for the same purpose, but it has the disadvantage that it is easily confused with the numeral **1**.

> *We don't include commas when writing large numeric values in a program.*

Integer variables declared as **long** occupy 4 bytes and can have values from –2,147,483,648 to 2,147,483,647. This is the same as variables declared as **int** using Visual C++ 6.0.

With other C++ compilers, long and long int may not be the same as int, so if you expect your programs to be compiled in other environments, don't assume that long and int are equivalent. For truly portable code, you should not even assume that an int is 4 bytes (for example, under older 16-bit versions of Visual C++ an int was 2 bytes).

The char Data Type

The **char** data type serves a dual purpose. It specifies a one-byte variable that you can use to store integers, or to store a single **ASCII** character, which is the American Standard Code for Information Interchange.

The ASCII character set appears in Appendix B. We can declare a **char** variable with this statement:

```
char letter = 'A';
```

This declares the variable **letter** and initializes it with the constant **'A'**. Note that we specify a value which is a single character between single quotes, rather than the double quotes which we used previously for defining a string of characters to be displayed. A string of characters is a series of values of type **char**, that are grouped together into a single entity called an **array**. We will discuss arrays and how strings are handled in C++ in Chapter 4.

Because the character **'A'** is represented in ASCII by the decimal value 65 (have a look at Appendix B if you don't believe me), we could have written this:

```
char letter = 65;                // Equivalent to A
```

to produce the same result as the previous statement. The range of integers that can be stored in a variable of type **char** is from −128 to 127.

We can also use hexadecimal constants to initialize **char** variables (and other integer types). A hexadecimal number is written using the standard representation for hexadecimal digits: 0 to 9, and A to F (or a to f) for digits with values from 10 to 15. It's also preceded by 0x (or 0X) to distinguish it from a decimal value. Thus, to get exactly the same result again, we could rewrite the last statement as follows:

```
char letter = 0x41;              // Equivalent to A
```

> *Don't write decimal integer values with a leading zero. The compiler will interpret such values as octal (base 8), so a value written as 065 will be equivalent to 53 in normal decimal notation.*

Integer Type Modifiers

Variables of the integral types **char**, **int**, **short** or **long**, which we have just discussed, contain signed values by default. That is, they can store both positive and negative values, as we have just seen. This is because these types are assumed to have the default **type modifier signed**. So, wherever we wrote **char**, **int**, or **long**, we could have written **signed char**, **signed int**, or **signed long** respectively.

If you are sure that you don't need to store negative values in a variable (for example, if you were recording the number of miles you drive in a week), then you can specify a variable as **unsigned**:

```
unsigned long mileage = 0UL;
```

Here, the minimum value that can be stored in the variable **mileage** is zero, and the maximum value is 4,294,967,295 (that's $2^{32}-1$). Compare this to the range of −2,147,483,648 to 2,147,483,647 for a **signed long**. The bit which is used in a **signed** variable to determine the sign, is used in an **unsigned** variable as part of the numeric value instead. Consequently, an **unsigned** variable has a larger range of positive values, but it can't take a negative value. Note how a **U** (or **u**) is appended to **unsigned** constants. In the above example we also have **L** appended to indicate that the constant is **long**. You can use either upper or lower case for **U** and **L** and the sequence is unimportant, but it's a good idea to adopt a consistent way of specifying such values.

> *Of course, both* **signed** *and* **unsigned** *are keywords, so you can't use them as variable names.*

Floating Point Variables

Values which aren't integral are stored as **floating point** numbers. A floating point number can be expressed as a decimal value such as 112.5, or with an exponent such as 1.125E2 where the decimal part is multiplied by the power of 10 specified after the E (for Exponent). Our example is, therefore, 1.125×10^2, which is 112.5.

> *A floating point constant must contain a decimal point, or an exponent, or both. If you write neither, you have an integer.*

You can specify a floating point variable using the keyword **double**, as in this statement:

```
double in_to_mm = 25.4;
```

A **double** variable occupies 8 bytes of memory and stores values accurate to 15 decimal digits. The range of values stored is much wider than that indicated by the 15 digits accuracy, being from 1.7×10^{-308} to 1.7×10^{308}, positive and negative.

If you don't need 15 digits precision, and you don't need the massive range of values provided by **double** variables, you can opt to use the keyword **float** to declare floating point variables occupying 4 bytes. For example, the statement,

```
float pi = 3.14159f;
```

defines a variable **pi** with the initial value 3.14159. The **f** at the end of the constant specifies it to be a **float** type. Without the **f**, the constant would have been of type **double**. Variables declared as **float** are of 7 decimal digits precision and can have values from 3.4×10^{-38} to 3.4×10^{38}, positive and negative.

FYI You can find a complete summary of the various data types in the MSDN online documentation, provided with Visual C++ 6.0.

Logical Variables

Logical variables can only have two values: a value called **true** and a value called **false**. The type for a logical variable is **bool**, named after George Boole, who developed Boolean algebra. Variables of type **bool** are used to store the results of tests which can be either **true** or **false**, such as whether one value is equal to another.

51

You can declare a variable of type **bool** with the statement:

```
bool testResult;
```

Of course, you can also initialize them when you declare them:

```
bool colorIsRed = true;
```

> *You will find that the values **true** and **false** are used quite extensively with variables of numeric type, and particularly of type **int**. This is a hangover from the time before variables of type **bool** were implemented in C++ when integer variables were typically used to represent logical values. In this case a zero value is treated as false and a non-zero value as true. The symbols **TRUE** and **FALSE** are still used within the MFC where they represent the integers 1 and 0 respectively. Note that **TRUE** and **FALSE** are not keywords in C++, and they are not legal **bool** values.*

Variables with Specific Sets of Values

You will sometimes be faced with the need for variables that have a limited set of possible values which can be usefully referred to by labels — the days of the week, for example, or months of the year. There is a specific facility in C++ to handle this situation, called an **enumeration**. Let's take one of the examples we have just mentioned — a variable that can assume values corresponding to days of the week. We can define this as follows:

```
enum Week {Mon, Tues, Wed, Thurs, Fri, Sat, Sun} this_week;
```

This declares an enumeration type called **Week** and the variable **this_week**, which is an instance of the enumeration type **Week** that can only assume the values specified between the braces. If you try to assign to **this_week** anything other than one of the set of values specified, it will cause an error. The symbolic names listed between the braces are known as **enumerators**. In fact, each of the names of the days will be automatically defined as representing a fixed integer value. The first name in the list, **Mon**, will have the value 0, **Tues** will be 1, and so on.

By default, each successive enumerator is one larger than the value of the previous one, but if you would prefer the implicit numbering to start at a different value, you can just write

```
enum Week {Mon = 1, Tues, Wed, Thurs, Fri, Sat, Sun} this_week;
```

and they will be equivalent to 1 through 7. The enumerators don't even need to have unique values. You could define **Mon** and **Tues** as both having the value 1 for example, with the statement:

```
enum Week {Mon = 1, Tues = 1, Wed, Thurs, Fri, Sat, Sun} this_week;
```

As it's the same as an **int**, the variable **this_week** will occupy four bytes, as will all variables which are of an enumeration type.

Having defined the form of an enumeration, you can define another variable thus:

```
enum Week next_week;
```

This defines a variable **next_week** as an enumeration that can assume the values previously specified. You can also omit the keyword **enum** in declaring a variable, so, instead of the previous statement, you could write:

```
Week next_week;
```

If you wish, you can assign specific values to all the enumerators. For example, we could define this enumeration:

```
enum Punctuation {Comma = ',', Exclamation = '!', Question = '?'} things;
```

Here we have defined the possible values for the variable **things** as the numerical equivalents of the appropriate symbols. If you look in the ASCII table in Appendix B, you will see that the symbols are 44, 33 and 63 respectively in decimal. As you can see, the values assigned don't have to be in ascending order. If you don't specify all the values explicitly, each enumerator will be assigned a value incrementing by 1 from the last specified value, as in our second **Week** example.

You can omit the enumeration type if you don't need to define other variables of this type later. For example:

```
enum {Mon, Tues, Wed, Thurs, Fri, Sat, Sun} thisWeek, nextWeek, lastWeek;
```

Here we have three variables declared that can assume values from **Mon** to **Sun**. Since the enumeration type is not specified we cannot refer to it. Note that you cannot define other variables for this enumeration *at all*, since you would not be permitted to repeat the definition. Doing so would imply that you were redefining values for **Mon** to **Sun**, and this isn't allowed.

Defining Your Own Data Types

The **typedef** keyword enables you to define your own data type specifier. Using **typedef**, you could define the type name **BigOnes** as equivalent to the standard **long int** type with the declaration:

```
typedef long int BigOnes;        // Defining BigOnes as a type name
```

This defines **BigOnes** as an alternative type specifier for **long int**, so you could declare a variable **mynum** as **long int** with the declaration:

```
BigOnes mynum = 0;               // Define a long int variable
```

There's no difference between this declaration and the one using the built-in type name. You could equally well use:

```
long int mynum = 0;              // Define a long int variable
```

for exactly the same result. In fact, if you define your own type name such as **BigOnes**, you can use both type specifiers within the same program for declaring different variables that will end up as having the same type.

Since **typedef** only defines a synonym for an existing type, it may appear to be a bit superficial. We will see later that it can fulfill a very useful role in enabling us to simplify more complex declarations than we have met so far. We will also see later that **classes** provide us with a means of defining completely new data types.

Literals

In C++, fixed values of any kind are referred to as **literals**. Values such as 23, 3.14159 or "Samuel Clemens" are examples of **integer**, **floating point** and **string literals** respectively. You will often need to use a literal within a program, for example, to convert feet into inches, or to specify an error message. However, you should avoid using literals within programs explicitly where their significance is not obvious. It is not necessarily apparent to everyone that when you use the value 2.54, it is the number of centimeters in an inch. It is better to declare a variable with a fixed value corresponding to your literal instead – you might name the variable inchesToCentimeters for example. Then wherever you use inchesToCentimeters in your code it will be quite obvious what it is. We will see how to fix the value of a variable a little later on in this chapter.

Basic Input/Output Operations

Here, we will only look at enough of C++ input and output to get us through learning about C++. It's not that it's difficult — quite the opposite in fact — but for Windows programming we won't need it at all.

C++ input/output revolves around the notion of a data stream, where we can insert data into an output stream or extract data from an input stream. We have already seen that the standard output stream to the screen is referred to as **cout**. The input stream from the keyboard is referred to as **cin**.

Input from the Keyboard

We obtain input from the keyboard through the stream **cin**, using the extractor operator for a stream **>>**. To read two integer values from the keyboard into integer variables **num1** and **num2**, you can write this:

```
cin >> num1 >> num2;
```

The operator 'points' in the direction that data flows — in this case, from **cin** to each of the two variables in turn. Any leading whitespace is skipped and the first integer value you key in is read into **num1**. This is because the input statement executes from left to right. Whitespace following **num1** is ignored and the second integer value that you enter is read into **num2**. There has to be some whitespace between successive values though, so that they can be differentiated. The stream input operation ends when you press the *Enter* key and execution then continues with the next statement. Of course, errors can arise if you key in the wrong data, but we will assume that you always get it right!

Floating point values are read from the keyboard in exactly the same way as integers and, of course, we can mix the two. The stream input and operations automatically deal with variables and data of any of the basic types. For example, in the statements,

```
int num1 = 0, num2 = 0;
double factor = 0.0;
cin >> num1 >> factor >> num2;
```

the last line will read an integer into **num1**, then a floating point value into **factor** and, finally, an integer into **num2**.

TRY IT OUT - Output to the Display

Writing information to the display operates in a complementary fashion to input. The stream is called **cout** and we use the insertion operator **<<**. This also 'points' in the direction of data movement. We have already used this operator to output a text string between quotes. We can demonstrate the process of outputting the value of a variable with a simple program. We'll assume that you've got the hang of creating a new project and a new source file, adding the source file to the project and building it into an executable. Here's the code:

```
// EX2_02.CPP
// Exercising output
#include <iostream>

using namespace std;

int main()
{
   int num1 = 1234, num2 = 5678;
   cout << endl;                    // Start on a new line
   cout << num1 << num2;            // Output two values
   cout << endl;                    // End on a new line
   return 0;                        // Exit program
}
```

How It Works

The first statement in the body of **main()** declares and initializes two integer variables, **num1** and **num2**. This is followed by two output statements, the first of which moves the screen cursor position to a new line. Because output statements execute from left to right, the second output statement displays the value of **num1** followed by the value of **num2**.

When you compile and execute this, you will get the output:

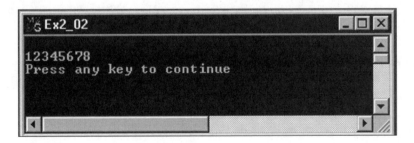

This is correct, but not exactly helpful. We really need the two output values separated by at least one space. The default for stream output is to just output the digits in the output value, which doesn't provide for spacing different values out nicely so they can be differentiated. As it is, we have no way to tell where the first number ends and the second number begins.

TRY IT OUT - Manipulators

We can fix this quite easily, though, just by outputting a space between the two values. We can do this by replacing the following line in our original program:

```
cout << num1 << num2;                          // Output two values
```

with the statement:

```
cout << num1 << ' ' << num2;                   // Output two values
```

Of course, if we had several rows of output that we wanted to align in columns, we would need some extra capability as we do not know how many digits there will be in each value. We can take care of this situation by using what is called a **manipulator**. A manipulator modifies the way in which data output to (or input from) a stream is handled.

Manipulators are defined in the header file **iomanip**, so we need to add an **#include** statement for it. The manipulator that we will use is **setw(n)** which will output the following value right-justified in a field **n** spaces wide, so **setw(6)** puts the output in a field with a width of six spaces. To get something more like the output we want, we can change our program to the following:

```cpp
// EX2_03.CPP
// Exercising output
#include <iostream>
#include <iomanip>

using namespace std;

int main()
{
   int num1 = 1234, num2 = 5678;
   cout << endl;                                // Start on a new line
   cout << setw(6) << num1 << setw(6) << num2;  // Output two values
   cout << endl;                                // Start on a new line
   return 0;                                    // Exit program
}
```

How It Works

The only changes from the last example are the addition of the **#include** statement for the file **iomanip**, and the insertion of the **setw()** manipulator in the output stream preceding each value, to output the values in a field six characters wide. Now we get nice neat output where we can actually separate the two values:

Note that the **setw()** manipulator only works for the single output value immediately following it. We have to insert it into the stream immediately preceding each value that we want to output within a given field width. If we put only one **setw()**, it would apply to the first value to be output after it was inserted. Any following value would be output in the default manner. You could try this out by deleting the second **setw(6)** and its insertion operator in our example.

Escape Sequences

When we write a character string between quotes, we can include special characters called **escape sequences**. They are called escape sequences because they allow characters to be included in a string that otherwise could not be represented. An escape sequence starts with a backslash character, ****. For example, a tab character is written as **\t**, so these two output statements

```
cout << endl << "This is output.";
cout << endl << "\tThis is output after a tab.";
```

will produce these lines:

This is output.
    This is output after a tab.

In fact, instead of using **endl**, we could include the escape sequence for the newline character, **\n**, in each string, so we could rewrite the statements above as follows:

```
cout << "\nThis is output.";
cout << "\n\tThis is output after a tab.";
```

Here are some escape sequences which may be particularly useful:

Escape sequence	What it does
\a	sounds a beep
\n	newline
\'	single quote
\\	backslash
\b	backspace
\t	tab
\"	double quote
\?	question mark

Obviously, if you want to be able to include a backslash or a double quote as a character to be output in a string between quotes, you must use the escape sequences to represent them. Otherwise, the backslash would be interpreted as another escape sequence and a double quote would indicate the end of the character string.

You can also use characters specified by escape sequences in the initialization of **char** variables. For example:

```
char Tab = '\t';                // Initialize with tab character
```

That gives us enough of a toehold in input/output. We will collect a few more bits as and when we need them.

Calculating in C++

This is where we actually start doing something with the data that we enter. We are beginning the 'processing' part of a C++ program. Almost all of the computational aspects of C++ are fairly intuitive, so we should slice through this like a hot knife through butter.

The Assignment Statement

We have already seen examples of the assignment statement. A typical assignment statement would look like this:

```
whole = part1 + part2 + part3;
```

The assignment statement enables you to calculate the value of an expression which appears on the right hand side of the equals sign, in this case the sum of **part1**, **part2** and **part3**, and store the result in the variable specified on the left hand side, in this case **whole**. In this statement, the **whole** is exactly the sum of its parts, and no more.

 Note how the statement, as always, ends with a semicolon.

You can also write repeated assignments such as,

```
A = B = 1;
```

where this is equivalent to assigning the value 1 to **B**, then assigning the value of **B** to **A**.

Understanding Lvalues

An **lvalue** is something that refers to an address in memory, and is so-called because it can appear on the left of an equals sign in an assignment. Most variables are lvalues, since they specify a place in memory. However, as we shall see, there are variables which aren't lvalues and can't appear on the left of an assignment because their values have been defined as constant. The variables **A** and **B** appearing in the preceding paragraph are lvalues, whereas the expression **A+B** would not be, since its result doesn't determine an address in memory where a value might be stored.

Lvalues will pop up at various times throughout the book, sometimes where you least expect them, so keep the idea in mind.

Arithmetic Operations

The basic arithmetic operators we have at our disposal are addition, subtraction, multiplication and division, represented by the symbols **+**, **-**, ***** and **/** respectively. These operate generally as you would expect, with the exception of division which has a slight aberration when working with integer variables or constants, as we'll see. You can write statements such as the following:

```
netPay = hours * rate - deductions;
```

Here, the product of **hours** and **rate** will be calculated, then **deductions** subtracted from the value produced. The multiply and divide operators are executed before addition and subtraction. We will discuss the order of execution more fully later in this chapter. The overall result of the expression will be stored in the variable **netPay**.

The minus sign used in the last statement applies to two operands — it subtracts one from another. This is called a *binary* operation because two values are involved. The minus sign can also be used with one operand to change the sign of its value, in which case it is called a *unary* minus. You could write this:

```
int A = 0;
int B = -5;
A = -B;                          // Changes the sign of the operand
```

Here, **A** will be assigned the value +5 because the unary minus changes the sign of the value of the operand **B**.

Note that an assignment is not the equivalent of the equations you saw in high school algebra. It specifies an action to be carried out rather than a statement of fact. The statement

```
A = A + 1;
```

means, 'add 1 to the current value stored in **A** and then store the result back in **A**'. As a normal algebraic statement it wouldn't make sense.

TRY IT OUT - Exercising Basic Arithmetic

We can exercise basic arithmetic in C++ by calculating how many standard rolls of wallpaper are needed to paper a room. This is done with the following example:

```
// EX2_04.CPP
// Calculating how many rolls of wallpaper are required for a room
#include <iostream>

using namespace std;

int main()
{
```

```
   double height = 0.0, width = 0.0, length = 0.0; // Room dimensions
   double perimeter = 0.0;                          // Room perimeter

   const double rollwidth = 21.0;                   // Standard roll width
   const double rolllength = 12.0*33.0;             // Standard roll length(33ft.)

   int strips_per_roll = 0;                         // Number of strips in a roll
   int strips_reqd = 0;                             // Number of strips needed
   int nrolls = 0;                                  // Total number of rolls

   cout << endl                                     // Start a new line
        << "Enter the height of the room in inches: ";
   cin >> height;

   cout  << endl                                    // Start a new line
        << "Now enter the length and width in inches: ";
   cin >> length >> width;

   strips_per_roll = rolllength / height;     // Get number of strips per roll
   perimeter = 2.0*(length + width);          // Calculate room perimeter
   strips_reqd = perimeter / rollwidth;       // Get total strips required
   nrolls = strips_reqd / strips_per_roll;    // Calculate number of rolls

   cout << endl
        << "For your room you need " << nrolls << " rolls of wallpaper."
        << endl;

   return 0;
}
```

Unless you are more adept than me at typing, chances are there will be a few errors when you compile this for the first time. Once you have fixed the typos, it will run just fine.

How It Works

One thing needs to be clear at the outset. No responsibility is assumed for you running out of wallpaper as a result of using this program! As we shall see, all errors in the estimate of the number of rolls required are due to the way C++ works and to the wastage that inevitably occurs when you hang your own wallpaper — usually 50%+!

We can work through the statements in this example in sequence, picking out the interesting, novel, or even exciting features. The statements down to the start of the body of **main()** are familiar territory by now, so we will take those for granted.

A couple of general points worth noting are about the layout of the program. First, the statements in the body of **main()** are indented to make the extent of the body easier to see and, second, various groups of statements are separated by a blank line to indicate that they are functional groups. Indenting statements is a fundamental technique in laying out program code in C++. You will see that this is applied universally to provide visual cues for various logical blocks in a program.

The const Modifier

We have a block of declarations for the variables used in the program right at the beginning of the body of **main()**. These statements are also fairly familiar, but there are two which contain some new features:

```
const double rollwidth = 21.0;              // Standard roll width
const double rolllength = 12.0*33.0;        // Standard roll length(33ft.)
```

They both start out with a new keyword: **const**. This is a type modifier which indicates that the variables are not just of type **double**, but are also constants. Because we effectively tell the compiler that these are constants, the compiler will check for any statements which attempt to change the values of these variables and, if it finds any, it will generate an error message. This is relatively easy since a variable declared as **const** is not an lvalue and, therefore, can't legally be placed on the left of an assignment operation.

You could check this out by adding, anywhere after the declaration of **rollwidth**, a statement such as:

```
rollwidth = 0;
```

You will find the program no longer compiles, returning 'error C2166: l-value specifies const object'.

It can be very useful defining constants by means of **const** variable types, particularly when you use the same constant several times in a program. For one thing, It is much better than sprinkling literals throughout your program. For another, if you need to change the value of a **const** variable that you are using, you will only need to change its definition at the beginning to ensure that the change automatically appears throughout. We'll see this technique used quite often.

Constant Expressions

The **const** variable **rolllength** is also initialized with an arithmetic expression (**12.0*33.0**). Being able to use constant expressions to initialize variables saves having to work out the value yourself, and can also be more meaningful, as 33 feet times 12 inches is much clearer than simply writing 396. The compiler will generally evaluate constant expressions accurately, whereas if you do it yourself, depending on the complexity of the expression and your ability to number-crunch, there is a finite probability that it may be wrong.

You can use any expression that can be calculated as a constant at compile time, including **const** objects that you have already defined. So, for instance, if it was useful in the program to do so, we could declare the area of a standard roll of wallpaper as:

```
const double rollarea = rollwidth*rolllength;
```

Obviously, this statement would need to be placed after the declarations for the two **const** variables used in the initialization of **rollarea**.

Program Input

After declaring some integer variables, the next four statements in the program handle input:

```
cout << endl                                    // Start a new line
    << "Enter the height of the room in inches: ";
cin >> height;

cout << endl                                    // Start a new line
    << "Now enter the length and width in inches: ";
cin >> length >> width;
```

Here we have used **cout** to prompt for the input required and then read the input from the keyboard using **cin**. We first obtain the room **height** and then read the **length** and **width** successively. In a practical program, we would need to check for errors and possibly make sure that the values that are read are sensible, but we don't have enough knowledge to do that yet!

Calculating the Result

We have four statements involved in calculating the number of standard rolls of wallpaper required for the size of room given:

```
strips_per_roll = rolllength / height;      // Get number of strips in a roll
perimeter = 2.0*(length + width);           // Calculate room perimeter
strips_reqd = perimeter / rollwidth;        // Get total strips required
nrolls = strips_reqd / strips_per_roll;     // Calculate number of rolls
```

The first statement calculates the number of strips of paper with a length corresponding to the height of the room that we can get from a standard roll, by dividing one into the other. So, if the room is 8 feet high, we divide 96 into 396, which would produce the floating point result 4.125. There is a subtlety here, however. The variable where we store the result, **strips_per_roll**, was declared as **int**, so it can only store integer values. Consequently, any floating point value to be stored as an integer is rounded down to the nearest integer, 4 in our case, and this value is stored. This is actually the result that you want here since, although they may fit under a window or over a door, fractions of a strip are best ignored when estimating.

The conversion of a value from one type to another is called **casting**. This particular example is called an **implicit cast**, because the code doesn't explicitly state that a cast is needed, and the compiler has to work it out for itself. You should beware when using implicit casts. The compiler does not always supply a warning that an implicit cast is being made, and if you are assigning a value of one type to a variable of a type with a lesser range of values, then there is a danger that you will lose information. If there are implicit casts in your program which you don't know about, then they may represent bugs that may be difficult to locate.

Where such an assignment is unavoidable, you can specify the conversion explicitly to demonstrate that it is no accident and that you really meant to do it. We do this by making an **explicit cast** of the value on the right of the assignment to **int**, so the statement would become:

```
strips_per_roll = static_cast<int>(rolllength / height);    // Get number of strips
                                                            // in a roll
```

The addition of **static_cast<int>** with the parentheses around the expression on the right tells the compiler explicitly that we want to convert the value of the expression to **int**.

Although this means that we still lose the fractional part of the value, the compiler assumes that we know what we are doing and does not issue a warning. We'll see more about `static_cast<>()`, and other types of explicit casting, later in this chapter.

Note how we calculate the perimeter of the room in the next statement. In order to multiply the sum of the **length** and the **width** by two, we enclose the expression summing the two variables between parentheses. This ensures that the addition is performed first and the result is multiplied by 2.0 to give us the correct value for the perimeter. We can use parentheses to make sure that a calculation is carried out in the order we require since expressions in parentheses are always evaluated first. Where there are nested parentheses, the expressions within the parentheses are evaluated in sequence, from the innermost to the outermost.

The third statement, calculating how many strips of paper are required to cover the room, uses the same effect that we observed in the first statement: the result is rounded down to the nearest integer because it is to be stored in the integer variable, **strips_reqd**. This is not what we need in practice. It would be best to round up for estimating, but we don't have enough knowledge of C++ to do this yet. Once you have read the next chapter you can come back and fix it!

The last arithmetic statement calculates the number of rolls required by dividing the number of strips required (integer) by the number of strips in a roll (also integer). Because we are dividing one integer by another, the result has to be integer and any remainder is ignored. This would still be the case if the variable **nrolls** were floating point. The resulting integer value would be converted to floating point form before it was stored in **nrolls**. The result that we obtain is essentially the same as if we had produced a floating point result and rounded down to the nearest integer. Again, this is not what we want, so if you want to use this, you will need to fix it.

Displaying the Result

The result of the calculation is displayed by the following statement:

```
cout << endl
    << "For your room you need " << nrolls << " rolls of wallpaper."
    << endl;
```

This is a single output statement spread over three lines. It first outputs a newline character, then the text string **"For your room you need "**. This is followed by the value of the variable **nrolls**, and finally the text string **" rolls of wallpaper."**. As you can see, output statements are very easy in C++.

Finally, the program ends when this statement is executed:

```
return 0;
```

The value zero here is a return value which, in this case, will be returned to the operating system. We will see more about return values in Chapter 5.

Calculating a Remainder

We have seen in the last example that dividing one integer value by another produces an integer result which ignores any remainder, so that 11 divided by 4 gives the result 2. Since the remainder after division can be of great interest, particularly when you are dividing cookies amongst children, for example, C++ provides a special operator, **%**, for this. So we can write the statements,

```
int residue = 0, cookies = 19, children = 5;
residue = cookies % children;
```

and the variable **residue** will end up with the value 4, the number left after dividing 19 by 5. To calculate how many each of them received, you just need to use division, as in the statement:

```
each = cookies / children;
```

Modifying a Variable

It's often necessary to modify the existing value of a variable, such as incrementing it or doubling it. We could increment a variable called **count** using the statement:

```
count = count + 5;
```

This simply adds 5 to the current value stored in **count**, and stores the result back in **count**, so if **count** started out at 10, it would end up as 15. You have an alternative, shorthand way of writing the same thing in C++:

```
count += 5;
```

This says, 'Take the value in **count**, add 5 to it and store the result back in **count**'. We can also use other operators with this notation. For example,

```
count *= 5;
```

has the effect of multiplying the current value of **count** by 5 and storing the result back in **count**. In general, we can write statements of the form,

lhs op= rhs;

where **op** is any of the following operators:

+	–	*	/	%
<<	>>	&	^	|

The first five of these we have already met, and the remainder, which are shift and logical operators, we will see later in this chapter. **lhs** stands for any legal expression for the left-hand side of the statement, and is usually (but not necessarily) a variable name. **rhs** stands for any legal expression on the right-hand side of the statement.

The general form of the statement is equivalent to this:

lhs = lhs op (rhs);

This means that we can write statements such as

```
A /= B + C;
```

which will be identical in effect to

```
A = A/(B + C);
```

The Increment and Decrement Operators

We will now take a brief look at some unusual arithmetic operators called the **increment** and **decrement operators**, as we will find them to be quite an asset once we get further into applying C++ in earnest. These are unary operators, which are used to increment or decrement a variable. For example, assuming the variable **count** is of type **int**, the following three statements all have exactly the same effect:

```
count = count + 1;      count += 1;        ++count;
```

They each increment the variable **count** by 1. The last form, using the increment operator, is clearly the most concise. If this action is contained within another expression then the action of the operator is to *first* increment the value of the variable, *then* use the incremented value in the expression. For example, if **count** has the value 5, and the variable **total** is of type **int**, then the statement,

```
total = ++count + 6;
```

results in **count** being incremented to 6, while **total** is then assigned the value 12.

So far, we have written the increment operator, **++**, in front of the variable to which it applies. This is called the **prefix** form. The increment operator also has a **postfix** form, where the operator is written *after* the variable to which it applies; the effect of this is slightly different. The variable to which the operator applies is only incremented *after* its value has been used in context. For example, let's reset **count** to the value 5, and rewrite the previous example as,

```
total = count++ + 6;
```

Then **total** is assigned the value 11, since the initial value of **count** is used to evaluate the expression before the increment by 1 is applied. The statement above is equivalent to the two statements:

```
total = count + 6;
++count;
```

The clustering of '**+**' signs, in the example of the postfix form above, is likely to lead to confusion. Generally, it isn't a good idea to write the increment operator in the way that we have here. It would be clearer to write:

```
total = 6 + count++;
```

Where we have an expression such as **a++ + b**, or even **a+++b**, it becomes less obvious what is meant or what the compiler will do. They are actually the same, but in the second case you might really have meant **a + ++b**, which is different. It evaluates to one more than the other two expressions.

Exactly the same rules that we have discussed in relation to the increment operator apply to the decrement operator, **--**. For example, if **count** has the initial value 5, then the statement,

```
total = --count + 6;
```

results in **total** having the value 10 assigned, whereas,

```
total = 6 + count--;
```

sets the value of **total** to 11. Both operators are usually applied to integers, particularly in the context of **loops**, as we shall see in Chapter 3. We shall also see in later chapters that they can be applied to other data types in C++.

TRY IT OUT - The Comma Operator

The comma operator allows you to specify several expressions where normally only one might occur. This is best understood by looking at an example that demonstrates how it works:

```cpp
// EX2_05.CPP
// Exercising the comma operator
#include <iostream>

using namespace std;

int main()
{
    long num1 = 0, num2 = 0, num3 = 0, num4 = 0;

    num4 = (num1 = 10, num2 = 20, num3 = 30);
    cout << endl
         << "The value of a series of expressions "
         << "is the value of the right most: "
         << num4;
    cout << endl;

    return 0;
}
```

How It Works

If you compile and run this program you will get this output:

```
Ex2_05
The value of a series of expressions is the value of the right most: 30
Press any key to continue
```

which is fairly self-explanatory. The variable **num4** receives the value of the last of the series of three assignments, the value of an assignment being the value assigned to the left-hand side. The parentheses in the assignment for **num4** are essential. You could try executing this without them to see the effect. Without the parentheses, the first expression separated by commas in the series will become:

```
num4 = num1 = 10
```

So, **num4** will have the value 10.

Of course, the expressions separated by the comma operator don't have to be assignments. We could equally well write the following:

```
long num1 = 1, num2 = 10, num3 = 100, num4 = 0;
```

```
num4 = (++num1, ++num2, ++num3);
```

The effect of this assignment would be to increment the variables **num1**, **num2** and **num3** by 1, and to set **num4** to the value of the last expression which will be 101. This example is aimed at illustrating the effect of the comma operator, and is not an example of how to write good code.

The Sequence of Calculation

So far, we haven't talked about how we arrive at the sequence of calculations involved in evaluating an expression. It generally corresponds to what you will have learnt at school when dealing with basic arithmetic operators, but there are many other operators in C++. To understand what happens with these we need to look at the mechanism used in C++ to determine this sequence. It's referred to as **operator precedence**.

Operator Precedence

Operator precedence orders the operators in a priority sequence. In any expression, operators with the highest precedence are always executed first, followed by operators with the next highest precedence, and so on, down to those with the lowest precedence of all. The precedence of the operators in C++ is shown in the following table:

Operators	Associativity
`::`	Left
`()` `[]` `->` `.`	Left
`!` `~` `+`(unary) `-`(unary) `++` `--` `&`(unary)	Right
`*`(unary) `(typecast)` `static_cast`	Right
`const_cast` `dynamic_cast` `reinterpret_cast`	Right
`sizeof` `new` `delete...typeid`	Right
`.*`(unary) `->*`	Left
`*` `/` `%`	Left
`+` `-`	Left
`<<` `>>`	Left
`<` `<=` `>` `>=`	Left

Operators	Associativity
`==` `!=`	Left
`&`	Left
`^`	Left
`|`	Left
`&&`	Left
`||`	Left
`?:` (conditional operator)	Right
`=` `*=` `/=` `%=` `+=` `-=`	Right
`&=` `^=` `|=` `<<=` `>>=`	Right
`,`	Left

There are a lot of operators that you haven't seen yet, but you will know them all by the end of the book. Rather than being spread around, they all appear in the precedence table here so that you can always refer back to it if you are uncertain about the precedence of one operator relative to another.

Operators with the highest precedence appear at the top of the table. The compound operators have casting equal precedence. If there are no parentheses in an expression, operators of equal precedence are executed in a sequence determined by their **associativity**. Thus, if the associativity is 'left', the left-most operator in an expression is executed first, progressing through the expression to the right-most. This means that an expression such as `a + b + c + d` is executed as though it was written `(((a + b) + c) + d)` because binary `+` is left associative.

Note that where an operator has a unary (working with one operand) and a binary (working with two operands) form, the unary form is always of a higher precedence and is, therefore, executed first.

> *You can always override the precedence of operators by using parentheses. Since there are so many operators in C++, it's sometimes hard to be sure what takes precedence over what. It is a good idea to insert parentheses to make sure. A further plus is that parentheses often make the code much easier to read.*

Variable Types and Casting

Calculations in C++ can only be carried out between values of the same type. When you write an expression involving variables or constants of different types, for each operation to be performed the compiler has to convert the type of one of the operands to match that of the other. This conversion process is called **casting**. For example, if you want to add a **double** value to an integer, the integer value is first converted to **double**, after which the addition is carried out. Of course, the variable which contains the value to be cast is itself not changed. The compiler will store the converted value in a temporary memory location which will be discarded when the calculation is finished.

There are rules which govern the selection of the operand to be converted in any operation. Any expression to be calculated breaks down into a series of operations between two operands. For example, the expression **2*3-4+5** amounts to the series **2*3** resulting in **6**, **6-4** resulting in **2**, and finally **2+5** resulting in **7**. Thus, the rules for casting operands where necessary only need to be defined in terms of decisions about pairs of operands. So, for any pair of operands of different types, the following rules are checked in the order that they are written. When one applies, that rule is used.

Rules for Casting Operands

1. If either operand is of type **long double**, the other is converted to **long double**.

2. If either operand is of type **double**, the other is converted to **double**.

3. If either operand is of type **float**, the other is converted to **float**.

4. Any operand of type **char**, **signed char**, **unsigned char**, **short**, or **unsigned short** is converted to type **int**.

5. An enumeration type is converted to the first of **int**, **unsigned int**, **long**, or **unsigned long** that accommodates the range of the enumerators.

6. If either operand is of type **unsigned long**, the other is converted to **unsigned long**.

7. If one operand is of type **long** and the other is of type **unsigned int**, then both operands are converted to type **unsigned long**.

8. If either operand is of type **long**, the other is converted to type **long**.

This looks and reads as though it is incredibly complicated, but the basic principle is to always convert the value that has the type that is of a more limited range to the type of the other value. This maximizes the likelihood of being able to accommodate the result. We could try these rules on a hypothetical expression to see how they work. Let's suppose that we have a sequence of variable declarations as follows:

```
double value = 31.0;
int count = 16;
float many = 2.0f;
char num = 4;
```

Let's also suppose that we have the following rather arbitrary arithmetic statement:

```
value = (value - count)*(count - num)/many + num/many;
```

We can now work out what casts the compiler will apply. The first operation is to calculate **(value - count)**. Rule 1 doesn't apply but Rule 2 does, so the value of **count** is converted to **double** and the **double** result 15.0 is calculated. Next **(count - num)** must be evaluated, and here the first rule in sequence which applies is Rule 4, so **num** is converted from **char** to **int** and the result 12 is produced as a value of type **int**. The next calculation is the product of the first two results, a **double** 15.0 and an **int** 12. Rule 2 applies here and the 12 is converted to 12.0 as **double**, and the **double** result 180.0 is produced. This result now has to be divided by **many**, so Rule 2 applies again and the value of **many** is converted to **double** before generating the **double** result 90.0. The expression **num/many** is calculated next, and here Rule 3 applies to produce the **float** value 2.0f after converting the type of **num** from **char** to **float**. Lastly, the **double** value 90.0 is added to the **float** value 2.0f for which Rule 2 applies, so after converting the 2.0f to 2.0 as **double**, the final result of 92.0 is stored in **value**.

In spite of the last paragraph reading a bit like *The Auctioneer's Song*, I hope you get the general idea.

Casts in Assignment Statements

As we saw in example **Ex2_04.cpp** earlier in this chapter, you can cause an implicit cast by writing an expression on the right-hand side of an assignment that is of a different type to the variable on the left-hand side. This can cause values to be changed and information to be lost. For instance, if you assign a **float** or **double** value to an **int** or a **long** variable, the fractional part of the **float** or **double** will be lost and just the integer part will be stored. (You may lose even more information, if your floating point variable exceeds the range of values available for the integer type concerned.)

For example, after executing the following code fragment,

```
int number = 0;
float decimal = 2.5f;
number = decimal;
```

the value of **number** will be 2. Note the **f** at the end of the constant 2.5. This indicates to the compiler that this constant is single precision floating point. Without the **f**, the default would have been **double**. Any constant containing a decimal point is floating point. If you don't want it to be double precision, you need to append the **f**. A capital **F** would do the job just as well.

Explicit Casts

With mixed expressions involving the basic types, your compiler automatically arranges casting where necessary, but you can also force a conversion from one type to another by using an **explicit cast**. To cast the value of an expression to a given type, you write the cast in the form:

static_cast<*the_type_to_convert_to*>(*expression*)

The keyword **static_cast** reflects the fact that the cast is checked statically — that is, when your program is compiled. No further checks are made when you execute the program to see if this cast is safe to apply. Later, when we get to deal with classes, we will meet **dynamic_cast**, where the conversion is checked dynamically — that is, when the program is executing. There are also two other kinds of cast, **const_cast** for removing the **const**-ness of an expression and **reinterpret_cast**, which is an unconditional cast, but we'll say no more about these here.

The effect of **static_cast** is to convert the value that results from evaluating *expression* to the type that you specify between the angled brackets. The *expression* can be anything from a single variable to a complex expression involving lots of nested parentheses.

Here's a specific example of the use of **static_cast<>()**:

```
double value1 = 10.5;
double value2 = 15.5;
```

```
int whole_number = static_cast<int>(value1) + static_cast<int>(value2);
```

The initializing value for the variable **whole_number** is the sum of the integral parts of **value1** and **value2**, so they are each explicitly cast to type **int**. The variable **whole_number** will therefore have the initial value 25. The casts do *not* affect the values stored in **value1** and **value2**, which will remain as 10.5 and 15.5 respectively. The values 10 and 15 produced by the casts are just stored temporarily for use in the calculation, and then discarded. Although both casts cause a loss of information in the calculation, the compiler will always assume that you know what you are doing when you explicitly specify a cast.

Also, as we described in **Ex2_04.cpp** when relating to assignments with different types, you can always make it clear that you know the cast is necessary by making it explicit:

```
strips_per_roll = static_cast<int>(rolllength / height);    //Get number of strips
                                                            // in a roll
```

You can write an explicit cast for any standard type, but you should be conscious of the possibility of losing information. If you cast a **float** or **double** value to **long**, for example, you will lose the fractional part of the value converted, so if the value started out as less than 1.0, the result will be 0. If you cast **double** to **float**, you will lose accuracy because a **float** variable has only 7 digits precision, whereas **double** variables maintain 15. Even casting between integer types provides the potential for losing data, depending on the values involved. For example, the value of an integer of type **long** can exceed the maximum that you can store in a variable of type **short**, so casting from a **long** value to a **short** may lose information.

In general, you should avoid casting as far as possible. If you find that you need a lot of casts in your program, the overall design of your program may well be at fault. You need to look at the structure of the program and the ways in which you have chosen data types to see whether you can eliminate, or at least reduce, the number of casts in your program.

Old-Style Casts

Prior to the introduction of **static_cast<>()** (and the other casts: **const_cast<>()**, **dynamic_cast<>()** and **reinterpret_cast<>()**, which we'll discuss later in the book) into C++, an explicit cast of the result of an expression to another type was written as:

(*the_type_to_convert_to***)***expression*

The result of ***expression*** is cast to the type between the parentheses. For example, the statement to calculate **strips_per_roll** in our previous example could be written:

```
strips_per_roll = (int)(rolllength / height);       //Get number of strips
                                                    //in a roll
```

Essentially, there are four different kinds of casts, and the old-style casting syntax covers them all. Because of this, code using the old-style casts is more error prone — it is not always clear what you intended, and you may not get the result you expected. Although you will still see the old style of casting used extensively (it's still part of the language and you will see it in MFC code for historical reasons), I strongly recommend that you stick to using only the new casts in your code.

The Bitwise Operators

The bitwise operators treat their operands as a series of individual bits rather than a numerical value. They only work with integer variables or constants as operands, so only data types **short**, **int**, **long** and **char** can be used. They are useful in programming hardware devices, where the status of a device is often represented as a series of individual flags (that is, each bit of a byte may signify the status of a different aspect of the device), or for any situation where you might want to pack a set of on-off flags into a single variable. You will see them in action when we look at input/output in detail, where single bits are used to control various options in the way data is handled.

There are six bitwise operators:

The Six Bitwise Operators		
& bitwise AND	**|** bitwise OR	**^** bitwise exclusive OR
~ bitwise NOT	**>>** shift right	**<<** shift left

Let's take a look at how each of them works.

The Bitwise AND

The bitwise AND, **&**, is a binary operator that combines corresponding bits in its operands. If both corresponding bits are 1, the result is a 1 bit, and if either or both operand bits are 0, the result is a 0 bit.

The effect of a particular binary operator is often shown using what is called a **truth table**. This shows, for various possible combinations of operands, what the result is. The truth table for **&** is as follows:

Bitwise AND	0	1
0	0	0
1	0	1

For each row and column combination, the result of **&** combining the two is the entry at the intersection of the row and column. Let's see how this works in an example:

```
char letter1 = 'A', letter2 = 'Z', result = 0;
result = letter1 & letter2;
```

We need to look at the bit patterns to see what happens. The letters **'A'** and **'Z'** correspond to hexadecimal values 0x41 and 0x5A respectively (see Appendix B for ASCII codes). The way in which the bitwise AND operates on these two values is shown below:

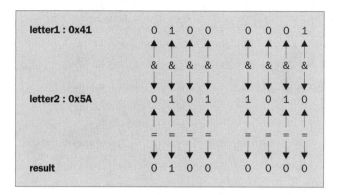

You can confirm this by looking at how corresponding bits combine with **&** in the truth table. After the assignment, **result** will have the value 0x40, which corresponds to the character '**@**'.

Because the **&** produces zero if *either* bit is zero, we can use this operator to make sure that unwanted bits are zero in a variable. We achieve this by creating what is called a 'mask' and combining with the original variable using **&**. We create the mask by putting 1 where we want to keep a bit, and 0 where we want to set a bit to zero. The result will be 0s where the mask bit is 0, and the same value as the original bit in the variable where the mask is 1. Suppose we have a **char** variable **letter** where, for the purposes of illustration, we want to eliminate the high order 4 bits, but keep the low order 4 bits. This is easily done by setting up a mask as 0x0F and combining it with the letter using **&** like this,

```
letter = letter & 0x0F;
```

or, more concisely:

```
letter &= 0x0F;
```

If **letter** started out as 0x41, it would end up as 0x01 as a result of either of these statements. This operation is shown in the illustration below:

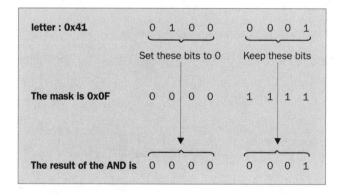

The 0 bits in the mask cause corresponding bits in **letter** to be set to 0, and the 1 bits in the mask cause corresponding bits to be kept.

Similarly, you can use a mask of 0xF0 to keep the 4 high order bits, and zero the 4 low order bits. Therefore, this statement,

```
letter &= 0xF0;
```

will result in the value of **letter** being changed from 0x41 to 0x40.

The Bitwise OR

The bitwise OR, |, sometimes called the **inclusive OR**, combines corresponding bits such that the result is a 1 if either operand bit is a 1, and 0 if both operand bits are 0. The truth table for the bitwise OR is:

Bitwise OR	0	1
0	0	1
1	1	1

We can exercise this with an example of how we could set individual flags packed into a variable of type **int**. Let's suppose that we have a variable called **style**, of type **short**, which contains 16 individual 1-bit flags. Let's suppose further that we are interested in setting individual flags in the variable **style**. One way of doing this is by defining values that we can combine with the OR operator to set particular bits on. To use in setting the rightmost bit, we can define:

```
short vredraw = 0x01;
```

For use in setting the second-to-rightmost bit, we could define the variable **hredraw** as:

```
short hredraw = 0x02;
```

So we could set the rightmost two bits in the variable **style** to 1 with the statement:

```
style = hredraw | vredraw;
```

The effect of this statement is illustrated in the diagram below:

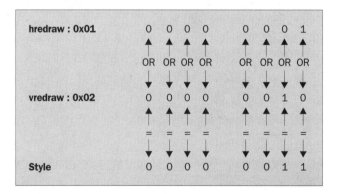

Because the OR operation results in 1 if either of two bits is a 1, ORing the two variables together produces a result with both bits set on.

A very common requirement is to be able to set flags in a variable without altering any of the others which may have been set elsewhere. We can do this quite easily with a statement such as:

```
style |= hredraw | vredraw;
```

This statement will set the two rightmost bits of the variable **style** to 1, leaving the others at whatever they were before the execution of this statement.

The Bitwise Exclusive OR

The **exclusive OR**, ^, is so called because it operates similarly to the inclusive OR but produces 0 when both operand bits are 1. Therefore, its truth table is as follows:

Bitwise EOR	0	1
0	0	1
1	1	0

Using the same variable values that we used with the AND, we can look at the result of the following statement:

```
result = letter1 ^ letter2;
```

This operation can be represented as:

	letter1	0100 0001
	letter2	0101 1010
EORed together produce:		
	result	0001 1011

The variable **result** is set to 0x1B, or 27 in decimal notation.

The ^ operator has a rather surprising property. Suppose that we have two **char** variables, **first** with the value **'A'**, and **last** with the value **'Z'**, corresponding to binary values 0100 0001 and 0101 1010. If we write the statements,

```
first ^= last;      // Result first is 0001 1011
last ^= first;      // Result last is 0100 0001
first ^= last;      // Result first is 0101 1010
```

the result of these is that **first** and **last** have exchanged values without using any intermediate memory location. This works with any integer values.

The Bitwise NOT

The bitwise NOT, ~, takes a single operand for which it inverts the bits: 1 becomes 0, and 0 becomes 1. Thus, if we execute the statement,

```
result = ~letter1;
```

if **letter1** is 0100 0001, the variable **result** will have the value 1011 1110, which is 0xBE, or 190 as a decimal value.

The Bitwise Shift Operators

These operators shift the value of an integer variable a specified number of bits to the left or right. The operator **>>** is for shifts to the right, while **<<** is the operator for shifts to the left. Bits that 'fall off' either end of the variable are lost. The illustration below shows the effect of shifting the 2 byte variable left and right, with the initial value shown.

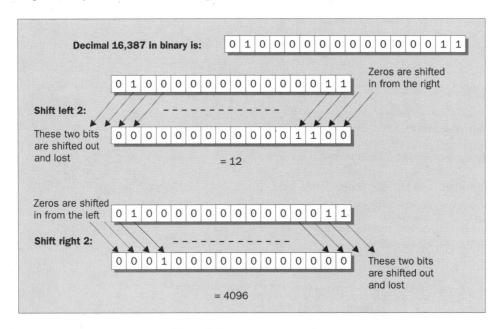

We declare and initialize a variable called **number** with the statement:

```
unsigned int number = 16387U;
```

As we saw earlier in this chapter, we should write unsigned integer literals with a letter **U** or **u** appended to the number. We can shift the contents of this variable with the statement:

```
number <<= 2;              // Shift left two bit positions
```

The left operand of the shift operator is the value to be shifted, and the number of bit positions that the value is to be shifted is specified by the right operand. The illustration shows the effect of the operation. As you can see, shifting the value 16,387 two positions to the left produces the value 12. The rather drastic change in the value is the result of losing the high order bit.

We can also shift the value to the right. Let's reset the value of **number** to its initial value of 16,387. Then we can write:

```
number >>= 2;            // Shift right two bit positions
```

This shifts the value 16,387 two positions to the right, storing the value 4,096. Shifting right two bits is effectively dividing the value by 4 (without remainder). This is also shown in the illustration.

As long as bits are not lost, shifting n bits to the left is equivalent to multiplying the value by 2, n times. In other words, it is equivalent to multiplying by 2^n. Similarly, shifting right n bits is equivalent to dividing by 2^n. But beware: as we saw with the left shift of the variable **number**, if significant bits are lost, the result is nothing like what you would expect. However, this is no different from the multiply operation. If you multiplied the two-byte number by four you would get the same result, so shifting left and multiply are still equivalent. The problem of accuracy arises because the value of the result of the multiplication is outside the range of a two-byte integer.

You might imagine that confusion could arise with the operators that we have been using for input and output. As far as the compiler is concerned, the meaning will always be clear from the context. If it isn't, the compiler will generate a message, but you need to be careful. For example, if you want to output the result of shifting a variable **number** left by two bits, you could write:

```
cout << (number << 2);
```

Here, the parentheses are essential. Without them, the shift operator will be interpreted by the compiler as a stream operator, so you won't get the result that you intended.

In the main, the right shift operation is similar to the left shift. For example, if the variable **number** has the value 24, and we execute the statement,

```
number >>= 2;
```

it will result in **number** having the value 6, effectively dividing by 4. However, the right shift operates in a special way with **signed** integer types that are negative (that is, the sign bit, which is the leftmost bit, is 1). In this case, the sign bit is propagated to the right. For example, let's declare and initialize a variable **number**, of type **char**, with the value -104 in decimal:

```
char number = -104;      // Binary representation is 1001 1000
```

Now we can shift it right 2 bits with the operation:

```
number >>= 2;            // Result 1110 0110
```

The decimal value of the result is -26, as the sign bit is repeated. With operations on **unsigned** integer types, of course, the sign bit is not repeated and zeros appear.

These shift operations can be faster than the regular multiply or divide operations on some computers — on an Intel 80486, for example, a multiply is slower than a shift left by at least a factor of 3. However, you should only use them in this way if you are sure you are not going to lose bits that you can ill afford to be without.

Understanding Scope

All variables have a finite lifetime when your program executes. They come into existence from the point at which you declare them and then, at some point, they disappear — at the latest, when your program terminates. How long a particular variable lasts is determined by a property called its **storage duration**. There are three different kinds of storage duration that a variable can have:

automatic storage duration
static storage duration
dynamic storage duration

Which of these a variable will have depends on how you create it. We will defer discussion of variables with dynamic storage duration until Chapter 4, but we will look into the characteristics of the other two in this chapter.

Another property that variables have is **scope**. The scope of a variable is simply that part of your program in which the variable name is valid. Within a variable's scope, you can legally refer to it, to set its value or use it in an expression. Outside of the scope of a variable, you cannot refer to its name — any attempt to do so will cause a compiler error. Note that a variable may still *exist* outside of its scope, even though you cannot refer to it by name. We will see examples of this situation a little later in this discussion.

All of the variables that we have declared up to now have had automatic storage duration, and are therefore called **automatic variables**. Let's take a closer look at these first.

Automatic Variables

The variables that we have declared so far have been declared within a block — that is, within the extent of a pair of curly braces. These are called **automatic** variables and are said to have **local scope** or **block scope**. An automatic variable is 'in scope' from the point at which it is declared until the end of the block containing its declaration.

An automatic variable is 'born' when it is declared and automatically ceases to exist at the end of the block containing the declaration. This will be at the closing brace matching the first opening brace that precedes the declaration of the variable. Every time the block of statements containing a declaration for an automatic variable is executed, the variable is created anew, and if you specified an initial value for the automatic variable, it will be reinitialized each time it is created.

There is a keyword, **auto**, which you can use to specify automatic variables, but it is rarely used since it is implied by default. Let's put together an example of what we've discussed so far.

TRY IT OUT - Automatic Variables

We can demonstrate the effect of scope on automatic variables with the following example:

```cpp
// EX2_06.CPP
// Demonstrating variable scope
#include <iostream>

using namespace std;

int main()
{                                       // Function scope starts here
   int count1 = 10;
   int count3 = 50;
   cout << endl
        << "Value of outer count1 = " << count1
        << endl;

   {                                    // New scope starts here...
      int count1 = 20;                  // This hides the outer count1
      int count2 = 30;
      cout << "Value of inner count1 = " << count1
           << endl;
      count1 += 3;                      // This affects the inner count1
      count3 += count2;
   }                                    // ...and ends here

   cout << "Value of outer count1 = " << count1
        << endl
        << "Value of outer count3 = " << count3
        << endl;

   // cout << count2 << endl;           // uncomment to get an error

   return 0;
}                                       // Function scope ends here
```

How It Works

The output from this example will be:

```
Value of outer count1 = 10
Value of inner count1 = 20
Value of outer count1 = 10
Value of outer count3 = 80
Press any key to continue
```

79

The first two statements declare and define two integer variables, **count1** and **count3**, with initial values of 10 and 50 respectively. Both these variables exist from this point to the closing brace at the end of the program. The scope of these variables also extends to the closing brace at the end of **main()**.

> *Remember that the lifetime and scope of a variable are two different things. It's important not to get these two ideas confused.*

Following the variable definitions, the value of **count1** is output to produce the first of the lines shown above.

There is then a second curly brace which starts a new block. Two variables, **count1** and **count2**, are defined within this block, with values 20 and 30 respectively. The **count1** declared here is *different* from the first **count1**. The first **count1** still exists, but its name is masked by the second **count1**. Any use of the name **count1** following the declaration within the inner block refers to the **count1** declared within that block.

> *The variable name* **count1** *has been duplicated here only to illustrate what happens. Although this code is legal, it isn't a good approach to programming in general. It's confusing, and it's very easy to hide variables defined in an outer scope accidentally.*

The value shown in the second output line shows that within the inner block, we are using the **count1** in the inner scope — that is, inside the innermost braces:

```
cout << "Value of inner count1 = " << count1
     << endl;
```

Had we still been using the outer **count1**, then this would display the value 10. The variable **count1** is then incremented by the statement:

```
count1 += 3;                          // This affects the inner count1
```

The increment applies to the variable in the inner scope, since the outer one is still hidden. However, **count3**, which was defined in the outer scope, is incremented in the next statement without any problem:

```
count3 += count2;
```

This shows that the variables which were declared at the beginning of the outer scope are accessible from within the inner scope. (Note that if **count3** had been declared *after* the second of the inner pair of braces, then it would still be within the outer scope, but in that case **count3** would not exist when the above statement is executed.)

After the brace ending the inner scope, **count2** and the inner **count1** cease to exist. The variables **count1** and **count3** are still there in the outer scope and the values displayed show that **count3** was indeed incremented in the inner scope.

If you uncomment the line:

```
// cout << count2 << endl;            // uncomment to get an error
```

the program will no longer compile correctly because it attempts to output a non-existent variable. You will get an error message something like,

  d:\program files\microsoft visual studio\myprojects\ex2_06\ex2_06.cpp(29) : error C2065: 'count2' : undeclared identifier

since **count2** is out of scope at this point.

Positioning Variable Declarations

You have great flexibility in where you place the declarations for your variables. The most important aspect to consider is what scope the variables need to have. Beyond that, you should generally place a declaration close to where the variable is to be first used in a program. You should write your programs with a view to making them as easy as possible for another programmer to understand, and declaring a variable at its first point of use can be helpful in achieving that.

It is possible to place declarations for variables outside of all of the functions that make up a program. Let's look what effect that has on the variables concerned.

Global Variables

Variables which are declared outside of all blocks and classes (we will discuss classes later in the book) are called **globals** and have **global scope** (which is also called **global namespace scope** or **file scope**). This means that they are accessible throughout all the functions in the file, following the point at which they are declared. If you declare them at the very top of your program, they will be accessible from anywhere in the file.

Globals also have **static storage duration** by default. Global variables with static storage duration will exist from the start of execution of the program, until execution of the program ends. If you do not specify an initial value for a global variable, it will be initialized with 0 by default. Initialization of global variables takes place before the execution of **main()** begins, so they are always ready to be used within any code that is within the variable's scope.

The illustration below shows the contents of a source file, **Example.cpp**, and the arrows indicate the scope of each of the variables.

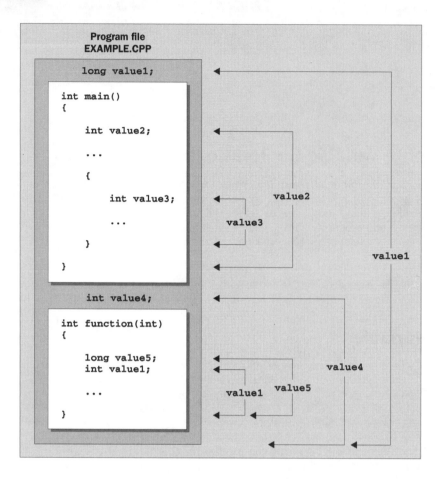

The variable **value1**, which appears at the beginning of the file, is declared at global scope, as is **value4**, which appears after the function **main()**. The scope of each global variable extends from the point at which it is defined to the end of the file. Even though **value4** exists when execution starts, it cannot be referred to in **main()** because **main()** is not within the variable's scope. For **main()** to use **value4**, you would need to move its declaration to the beginning of the file. Both **value1** and **value4** will be initialized with 0 by default, which is not the case for the automatic variables. Note that the local variable called **value1** in **function()** hides the global variable of the same name.

Since global variables continue to exist for as long as the program is running. This might raise the question in your mind, 'Why not make all variables global and avoid this messing about with local variables that disappear?' This sounds very attractive at first, but as with the Sirens of mythology, there are serious side effects which completely outweigh any advantages you may gain.

Real programs are generally composed of a large number of statements, a significant number of functions and a great many variables. Declaring all variables at the global scope greatly magnifies the possibility of accidental erroneous modification of a variable, as well as making the job of naming them sensibly quite intractable. They will also occupy memory for the duration of program execution. By keeping variables local to a function or a block, you can be sure they have almost complete protection from external effects, they will only exist and occupy memory from the point at which they are defined to the end of the enclosing block, and the whole development process becomes much easier to manage.

If you take a look at ClassView for any of the examples that you have created so far, and extend the class tree for the project by clicking on the +, you will see an entry called Globals. If you extend this, you will see a list of everything in your program that has global scope. This will include all the global functions, as well as any global variables that you have declared.

TRY IT OUT - The Scope Resolution Operator

As we have seen, a global variable can be hidden by a local variable with the same name. However, it's still possible to get at the global variable using the **scope resolution operator (::)**, which you saw in Chapter 1 when we were discussing namespaces. We can demonstrate how this works with a revised version of the last example:

```cpp
// EX2_07.CPP
// Demonstrating variable scope
#include <iostream>

using namespace std;

int count1 = 100;                         // Global version of count1

int main()
{                                         // Function scope starts here
   int count1 = 10;
   int count3 = 50;
   cout << endl
        << "Value of outer count1 = " << count1
        << endl;
   cout << "Value of global count1 = " << ::count1        // From outer block
        << endl;

   {                                      // New scope starts here...
      int count1 = 20;                    //This hides the outer count1
      int count2 = 30;
      cout << "Value of inner count1 = " << count1
           << endl;
      cout << "Value of global count1 = " << ::count1        // From inner block
           << endl;

      count1 += 3;                        // This affects the inner count1
      count3 += count2;
   }                                      // ...and ends here.

   cout << "Value of outer count1 = " << count1
        << endl
        << "Value of outer count3 = " << count3
        << endl;

   //cout << count2 << endl;              // uncomment to get an error

   return 0;
}                                         // Function scope ends here
```

83

How It Works

If you compile and run this example, you'll get the following output:

```
Ex2_07                                                    _ □ X
Value of outer count1 = 10
Value of global count1 = 100
Value of inner count1 = 20
Value of global count1 = 100
Value of outer count1 = 10
Value of outer count3 = 80
Press any key to continue
```

The shaded lines indicate the changes we have made to the previous example; we just need to discuss the effects of those. The declaration of **count1** prior to the definition of the function **main()** is global, so in principle it is available anywhere through the function **main()**. This global variable is initialized with the value of 100:

```
int count1 = 100;                                // Global version of count1
```

However, we have two other variables called **count1**, which are defined within **main()**, so throughout the program the global **count1** is hidden by the local **count1** variables. The first new output statement is:

```
cout << "Value of global count1 = " << ::count1      // From outer block
     << endl;
```

This uses the scope resolution operator (**::**) to make it clear to the compiler that we want to reference the global variable **count1**, *not* the local one. You can see that this works from the value displayed in the output.

In the inner block, the global **count1** is hidden behind *two* variables called **count1**: the inner **count1** and the outer **count1**. We can see the global scope resolution operator doing its stuff within the inner block, as you can see from the output generated by the statement we have added there:

```
cout << "Value of global count1 = " << ::count1      // From inner block
     << endl;
```

This outputs the value 100, as before — the long arm of the scope resolution operator used in this fashion always reaches a global variable.

We mentioned namespaces earlier in this chapter, when discussing the namespace *std* — we accessed the namespace *std* by employing the *using* directive. Alternatively, we can access a namespace by using the scope resolution operator — for example, we can write *std::endl* to access the end-of-line operator in the standard library. In the example above, we are using the scope resolution operator to search the **global namespace** for the variable *count1*. By not specifying a namespace in front of the operator, the compiler knows that it must search the **global namespace** for the name that follows it.

We'll be seeing a lot more of this operator when we get to talking about object-oriented programming, in which context it is used extensively. We'll also talk further about namespaces, including how to create your own, in Chapter 6.

Static Variables

It's conceivable that you might want to have a variable that's defined and accessible locally, but which also continues to exist after exiting the block in which it is declared. In other words, you need to declare a variable within a block scope, but to give it **static storage duration**. The **static** specifier provides you with the means of doing this, and the need for this will become more apparent when we come to deal with functions in Chapter 5.

In fact, a static variable will continue to exist for the life of a program even though it is declared within a block and only available from within that block (or its sub-blocks). It still has block scope, but it has static storage duration. To declare a static integer variable called **count** you would write:

```
static int count;
```

If you don't provide an initial value for a static variable when you declare it, then it will be initialized for you. The variable **count** declared here will be initialized with 0. The default initial value for a static variable is always 0, converted to the type applicable to the variable. Remember that this is *not* the case with automatic variables.

> *If you don't initialize your automatic variables, they will contain junk values left over from the program that last used the memory they occupy.*

Namespaces

We have mentioned namespaces several times, so it's time we got a better idea of what they are about. They are a new and important addition to the C++ language so you need to have an idea of how they work. They are not used in MFC so far, so you won't see much of them in this book, but it is probable that they will be used within MFC at some point.

You know already that all the names used in the standard library are defined in the namespace **std**. This means that all the names used in the standard library have an additional qualifying name, **std**, so **cout** for example is really **std::cout**. We could show this with a trivial example. This will use a variable at global scope only because we want to see how namespaces work:

```
// EX2_08.CPP
// Demonstrating namespace names
#include <iostream>

int value = 0;

int main()
{
```

```
        std::cout << "enter an integer: ";
        std::cin  >> value;
        std::cout << "\nYou entered " << value
                  << std:: endl;
        return 0;
    }
```

Note the absence of the **using** directive for **std**. It isn't necessary here because we are fully qualifying the names we are using from the namespace **std**. It would be silly to do so, but we could use **cout** as the name of our integer variable here and there would be no confusion because **cout** by itself is different from **std::cout**. Thus namespaces provide a way to separate the names used in one part of a program from those used in another. This is invaluable with large project involving several teams of programmers working on different parts of the program. Each team can have its own namespace name, and worries about two teams accidentally using the same name for different functions disappears.

Of course, you can define your own namespace that has your own namespace name. Let's see how that's done.

Declaring a Namespace

You use the keyword **namespace** to declare a namespace – like this:

```
namespace myStuff
{
    // Code that I want to have in the namespace myStuff...
}
```

You can't declare a namespace inside a function, it's intended to be used the other way round. you use it to contain functions, variables, and other entities in your program. You mustn't put main in a namespace though. The function **main()** where execution starts must always be at global namespace scope, otherwise the compiler won't recognize it.

We could put the variable **value** in the previous example in a namespace:

```
// EX2_09.CPP
// Declaring a namespace
#include <iostream>

namespace myStuff
{
    int value = 0;
}

int main()
{
    std::cout << "enter an integer: ";
    std::cin  >> myStuff::value;
    std::cout << "\nYou entered " << myStuff::value
              << std:: endl;
    return 0;
}
```

The **myStuff** namespace defines a scope and everything within the namespace scope is qualified with the namespace name. To refer to a name declared within a namespace from outside, you must qualify it with the namespace name. Inside the namespace scope any of the names declared within it can be referred to without qualification – they are all part of the same family. Now we must qualify the name value with **myStuff**, the name of our namespace. If not the program will not compile. The function **main()** now refers to names in two different namespaces, and in general you can have as many namespaces in your program as you need. We could remove the need to qualify **value**, by adding a **using** directive:

```
// EX2_10.CPP
// Using a using directive
#include <iostream>

namespace myStuff
{
  int value = 0;
}

using namespace myStuff;               // Make all the names in myStuff available

int main()
{
  std::cout << "enter an integer: ";
  std::cin  >> value;
  std::cout << "\nYou entered " << value
            << std:: endl;
  return 0;
}
```

You could also have a **using** directive for **std** as well, so you wouldn't need to qualify standard library names either, but this is defeating the whole point of namespaces. Generally, if you use namespaces in your program, you should not add **using** directives all over your program since you might as well not bother with namespaces in the first place. Having said that, we will add a **using** directive for **std** in all our examples to keep the code less cluttered and easier for you to read. When you are starting out with a new programming language you can do without clutter, no matter how useful it is in practice.

Multiple Namespaces

A real-world program is likely to involve multiple namespaces. You can have multiple declarations of a namespace with a given name and the contents of the block for each namespace with a given name is within the same namespace. For example, you might have a program file with two namespaces:

```
namespace sortStuff
{
   // Everything in here is within sortStuff namespace
}

namespace calculateStuff
{
  // Everthing in here is within calculateStuff namespace
  // To refer to names from sortStuff they must be qualified
}
```

```
namespace sortStuff
{
  // This is a continuation of the namespace sortStuff
  // so from here you can refer to names in the first sortStuff namespace
  // without qualifying the names
}
```

A second declaration of a namespace with a given name is just a continuation of the first, so you can reference names in the first namespace block from the second without having to qualify them. They are all in the same namespace. Of course, you would not usually organize a source file in this way deliberately, but in can arise quite naturally with header files that you include into a program. For example, you might have something like this:

```
#include <iostream>      // Contents in namespace std
#include "myheader.h"    // Contents in namespace myStuff
#include <string>        // Contents in namespace std

// and so on...
```

We'll explain the different **#include** directives later in the book. Here, **iostream** and **string** are standard library headers, and **myheader.h** represents a header file that contains our program code. We have a situation with the namespaces that is an exact parallel of the previous illustration.

This has given you a basic idea of how namespaces work. There is a lot more to namespaces than we have discussed here, but if you grasp this bit you should be able to find out more about it without difficulty, if the need arises.

Summary

In this chapter, we have covered the basics of computation in C++. We have learnt about all of the elementary types of data provided for in the language, and all the operators that manipulate these types directly. The essentials of what we have discussed up to now are as follows:

- A DOS program in C++ consists of at least one function called **main()**.

- The executable part of a function is made up of statements contained between curly braces.

- A statement in C++ is terminated by a semicolon.

- Named objects in C++, such as variables or functions, can have names that consist of a sequence of letters and digits, the first of which is a letter, and where an underscore is considered to be a letter. Upper and lower case letters are distinguished.

- All the objects, such as variables, that you name in your program must not have a name that coincides with any of the reserved words in C++. The full set of reserved words in Visual C++ appears in Appendix A.

- All constants and variables in C++ are of a given type. The basic types are **char**, **int**, **long**, **float**, and **double**.

▶ The name and type of a variable is defined in a declaration statement ending with a semicolon. Variables may also be given initial values in a declaration.

▶ You can protect the value of a variable of a basic type by using the modifier **const**. This will prevent direct modification of the variable within the program and give you compiler errors everywhere that a constant's value is altered.

▶ By default, a variable is automatic, which means that it only exists from the point at which it is declared to the end of the scope in which it is defined, indicated by the corresponding closing brace after its declaration.

▶ A variable may be declared as **static**, in which case it continues to exist for the life of the program. It can only be accessed within the scope in which it was defined.

▶ Variables can be declared outside of all blocks within a program, in which case they have global namespace scope. Variables with global namespace scope are accessible throughout a program, except where a local variable exists with the same name as the global variable. Even then, they can still be reached by using the scope resolution operator.

▶ The Standard Library contains functions and operators which you can use in your program. They are contained in the namespace **std**. This namespace is usually accessed with the **using** directive; individual objects in the namespace can be accessed by using the scope resolution operator.

▶ A namespace defines a scope where each of the names declared within it are qualified by the namespace name. Referring to names from outside a namespace requires the names to be qualified.

▶ An lvalue is an object that can appear on the left-hand side of an assignment. Non-**const** variables are examples of lvalues.

▶ You can mix different types of variables and constants in an expression, but they will be automatically converted to a common type where necessary. Conversion of the type of the right hand side of an assignment to that of the left-hand side will also be made where necessary. This can cause loss of information when the left-hand side type can't contain the same information as the right-hand side: **double** converted to **int**, or **long** converted to **short**, for example.

▶ You can explicitly cast the value of an expression to another type. You should always make an explicit cast to convert a value when the conversion may lose information. There are also situations where you need to specify an explicit cast in order to produce the result that you want.

The keyword **typedef** allows you to define synonyms for other types.

Although we have discussed all the basic types, don't be misled into thinking that's all there is. There are more complex types based on the basic set as we shall see, and eventually you will be creating original types of your own.

Exercises

Ex2-1: Write a program which asks the user to enter a number and then prints it out, using an integer as a local variable. We'll build on this example in chapters to come, so save it as [Prg1].

Ex2-2: Write a program which inputs a variable of type **int**, and uses one of the bitwise operators (i.e. not the **%** operator!) to determine the positive remainder when divided by 8. For example, 29 = (3x8)+5 and -14 = (-2x8)+2 have positive remainder 5 and 2 respectively.

Ex2-3: Fully parenthesize the following expressions, in order to show the precedence and associativity:

```
1 + 2 + 3 + 4

16 * 4 / 2 * 3

a > b? a: c > d? e: f

a & b && c & d
```

Ex2-4: Suppose we try to calculate the aspect ratio of our computer screen, given the width and height in pixels:

```
int width = 640;
int height = 480;

double aspect = width / height;
```

What answer will we get? Is it satisfactory — and if not, how could you modify the code, without adding any more variables?

Ex2-5: (Advanced) Without running it, can you work out what the following code is going to print, and why?

```
unsigned s = 555;

int i = (s >> 4) & ~(~0 << 3);
cout << i;
```

Decisions and Loops

In this chapter, we will look at how to add decision-making capabilities to your C++ programs. You will also learn how to make your programs repeat a set of actions until a specific condition is met. This will enable you to handle variable amounts of input, as well as make validity checks on the data that you read in. You will also be able to write programs that can adapt their actions depending on the input data, and to deal with problems where logic is fundamental to the solution. By the end of this chapter you will have learnt:

▶ How to compare data values

▶ How to alter the sequence of program execution based on the result

▶ What logical operators and expressions are and how you can apply them

▶ How to deal with multiple choice situations

▶ How to write and use loops in your programs

We will start with one of the most powerful programming tools: the ability to compare variables and expressions with other variables and expressions and, based on the outcome, execute one set of statements or another.

Comparing Values

Unless we want to make decisions on a whim for the rest of our lives, we need a mechanism for comparing things. This involves some new operators called **relational operators**. Because all information in your computer is ultimately represented by numerical values (we saw in the last chapter how character information is represented by numeric codes), comparing numerical values is the essence of practically all decision making. We have six fundamental operators for comparing two values:

<	less than	<=	less than or equal to
>	greater than	>=	greater than or equal to
==	equal to	!=	not equal to

> *The 'equal to' comparison operator has two successive '=' signs. This is **not** the same as the assignment operator, which only consists of a single '=' sign. It's a pretty common mistake to use the assignment operator instead of the comparison operator, so watch out for this potential cause of confusion.*

Each of these operators compares two values and returns one of the two possible Boolean values: **true** if the comparison is true, or **false** if it is not. We can see how this works by having a look at a few simple examples of comparisons. Suppose we have integer variables **i** and **j** with the values 10 and -5 respectively. Then the expressions,

```
i > j         i != j       j > -8        i <= j + 15
```

all return the value **true**.

Let's further assume that we have the following variables defined:

```
char first = 'A', last = 'Z';
```

We can now write some examples of comparisons using character variables. Take a look at these:

```
first == 65       first < last       'E' <= first       first != last
```

All four of these involve comparing ASCII code values. The first expression returns **true** since **first** was initialized with **'A'**, which is the equivalent of decimal 65. The second expression checks whether the value of **first**, which is **'A'**, is less than the value of **last**, which is **'Z'**. If you check the ASCII codes for these characters in Appendix B, you will see that the capital letters are represented by an ascending sequence of numerical values from 65 to 90, 65 representing **'A'** and 90 representing **'Z'**, so this comparison will also return the value **true**. The third expression returns the value **false**, since **'E'** is greater than the value of **first**. The last expression returns **true**, since **'A'** is definitely not equal to **'Z'**.

Let's consider some slightly more complicated numerical comparisons. With variables defined by the statements,

```
int i = -10, j = 20;
double x = 1.5, y = -0.25E-10;
```

take a look at the following:

```
-1 < y            j < (10 - i)        2.0*x >= (3 + y)
```

As you can see, we can use expressions resulting in a numerical value as operands in comparisons. If you check with the precedence table that we saw in Chapter 2, you will see that none of the parentheses are strictly necessary, but they do help to make the expressions clearer. The first comparison is true and so returns the **bool** value **true**. The variable **y** has a very small negative value, -0.000000000025, and so is greater than -1. The second comparison returns the value **false**. The expression **10 - i** has the value 20 which is the same as **j**. The third expression returns **true** since the expression **3 + y** is slightly less than 3.

We can use relational operators to compare values of any of the basic types, so all we need now is a practical way of using the results of a comparison to modify the behavior of a program. Let's look into that right now.

The if Statement

The basic **if** statement allows your program to execute a single statement, or a block of statements enclosed within curly braces, if a given condition returns the value **true**. This is illustrated in this figure:

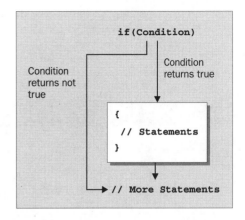

A simple example of an **if** statement is:

```
if(letter == 'A')
   cout << "The first capital, alphabetically speaking.";
```

The condition to be tested appears in parentheses immediately following the keyword, **if**. Note the position of the semicolon here. It goes after the statement *following* the **if**; there shouldn't be a semicolon after the condition in parentheses. You can also see how the statement following the **if** is indented, to indicate that it is only executed when the **if** condition returns the value **true**. The indentation is not necessary for the program to execute, but it helps you to recognize the relationship between the **if** condition and the statement that depends on it.

The output statement will only be executed if the variable **letter** has the value **'A'**. We could extend this example to change the value of **letter** if it contains the value **'A'**:

```
if(letter == 'A')
{
   cout << "The first capital, alphabetically speaking.";
   letter = 'a';
}
```

Here we execute the statements in the block only if the condition **(letter == 'A')** returns the value **true**. Without the curly braces, only the first statement would be the subject of the **if**, and the statement assigning the value **'a'** to **letter** would always be executed. Note that there is a semicolon after each of the statements in the block, and not after the closing brace at the end of the block. There can be as many statements as you like within the block. Now, as a result of **letter** having the value **'A'**, we change its value to **'a'** after outputting the same message as before. If the condition returns **false**, then neither of these statements will be executed.

Nested if Statements

The statement that is to be executed when the condition in an **if** statement is true can also be an **if**. This arrangement is called a **nested if**. The condition for the inner **if** is only tested if the condition for the outer **if** is true. An **if** that is nested inside another can also contain a nested **if**. You can generally continue nesting **if**s one inside the other like this for as long as you know what you are doing.

TRY IT OUT - Using Nested Ifs

We can demonstrate the nested **if** with a working example:

```cpp
// EX3_01.CPP
// A nested if demonstration
#include <iostream>

using namespace std;

int main()
{
   char letter = 0;                     // Store input in here

   cout << endl
        << "Enter a letter: ";          // Prompt for the input
   cin >> letter;                       // then read a character

   if(letter >= 'A')                    // Test for 'A' or larger
      if(letter <= 'Z')                 // Test for 'Z' or smaller
      {
         cout << endl
              << "You entered a capital letter."
              << endl;
         return 0;
      }

   if(letter >= 'a')                    // Test for 'a' or larger
      if(letter <= 'z')                 // Test for 'z' or smaller
      {
         cout << endl
              << "You entered a small letter."
              << endl;
         return 0;
      }

   cout << endl << "You did not enter a letter." << endl;
   return 0;
}
```

How It Works

This program starts with the usual comment lines, then the **#include** statement for the header file supporting input/output, and the **using** directive because those input/output routines belong to the namespace **std**. The first action in the body of **main()** is to prompt for a letter to be entered. This is stored in the **char** variable **letter**.

The **if** statement that follows the input checks whether the character entered is **'A'** or larger. Since the ASCII codes for lower case letters (97 to 122) are greater than those for upper case letters(65 to 90), entering a lower case letter causes the program to execute the first **if** block, as **(letter >= 'A')** will return **true** for all letters. In this case, the nested **if**, which checks for an input of **'Z'** or less is executed. If it is **'Z'** or less, we know that we have a capital letter, the message is displayed and we are done, so we execute a **return** statement to end the program. Both statements are enclosed between braces, so they are both executed when the nested **if** condition returns **true**.

The next **if** checks whether the character entered is lower case, using essentially the same mechanism as the first **if**, displays a message and returns.

If the character entered is not a letter, then the output statement following the last **if** block will be executed. This displays a message to the effect that the character entered was not a letter. The **return** is then executed.

You can see that the relationship between the nested **if**s and the output statement is much easier to follow because of the indentation applied to each.

A typical output from this example is:

```
M Ex3_01

Enter a letter: H

You entered a capital letter.
Press any key to continue
```

You could easily arrange to change upper case to lower case by adding just one extra statement to the **if**, checking for upper case:

```
if(letter >= 'A')                    // Test for 'A' or larger
   if(letter <= 'Z')                 // Test for 'Z' or smaller
   {
      cout << endl
           << "You entered a capital letter.";
           << endl;
      letter += 'a' - 'A';           // Convert to lower case
      return 0;
   }
```

This involves adding one additional statement. This statement for converting from upper to lower case increments the **letter** variable by the value **'a' - 'A'**. It works because the ASCII codes for **'A'** to **'Z'** and **'a'** to **'z'** are two groups of consecutive numerical codes, so the expression **'a' - 'A'** represents the value to be added to an upper case letter to get the equivalent lower case letter.

97

You could equally well use the equivalent ASCII values for the letters here, but by using the letters we've ensured that this code would work on computers where the characters were not ASCII, as long as both the upper and lower case sets are represented by a contiguous sequence of numeric values.

There is a library function provided with Visual C++ to convert letters to upper case, so you don't normally need to program for this yourself. It has the name **toupper()** *and appears in the standard library file* **ctype**. *You will see more about standard library facilities when we get to look specifically at how functions are written.*

The Extended if Statement

The if statement that we have been using so far executes a statement if the condition specified returns **true**. Program execution then continues with the next statement in sequence. We also have a version of the **if** which allows one statement to be executed if the condition returns **true**, and a different statement to be executed if the condition returns **false**. Execution then continues with the next statement in sequence. As we saw in Chapter 2, a block of statements can always replace a single statement, so this also applies to these **if**s.

TRY IT OUT - Extending the If

Here's an extended **if** example:

```
// EX3_02.CPP
// Using the extended if
#include <iostream>

using namespace std;

int main()
{
   long number = 0;               // Store input here
   cout << endl
        << "Enter an integer number less than 2 billion: ";
   cin >> number;

   if(number % 2L)                // Test remainder after division by 2
      cout << endl                // Here if remainder 1
           << "Your number is odd." << endl;
   else
      cout << endl                // Here if remainder 0
           << "Your number is even." << endl;
   return 0;
}
```

Typical output from this program is:

How It Works

After reading the input value into **number**, the value is tested by taking the remainder after division by two (using the remainder operator **%** that we saw in the last chapter) and using that as the condition for the **if**. In this case the condition of the **if** statement returns an integer, not a Boolean. The **if** statement interprets a non-zero value returned by the condition as **true**, and interprets zero as **false**. In other words, the **if** statement:

```
if(number % 2L)
```

is interpreted as follows: if the remainder is 1 then the condition is **true**, and the statement immediately following the **if** is executed. If the remainder is 0 then the condition is **false**, and the statement following the **else** keyword is executed.

The relational operators return only the values true **or** false. **In an** if **statement, the condition may also take the form of any of the basic data types that we saw in Chapter 2. In such a case, the** if **statement always interprets a** *non-zero* **value returned by the condition as** true, **and a** *zero* **as** false. **Inversely, the** bool **value** true **has the value 1 when converted to an integer, while** false **has the value 0.**

Since the remainder of a division of an integer by two can only be one or zero, we have commented the code to indicate this fact. After either outcome, the **return** statement is executed to end the program.

> *The **else** keyword is written without a semicolon, similar to the **if** part of the statement. Again, indentation is used as a visible indicator of the relationship between various statements. You can clearly see which statement is executed for a **true** or non-zero result, and which for a **false** or zero result. You should always indent the statements in your programs to show their logical structure.*

The **if-else** combination provides a choice between two options. The general logic of the **if-else** is shown here:

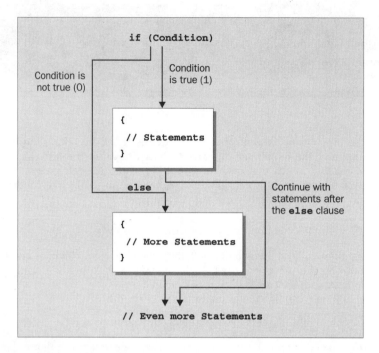

The arrows in the diagram indicate the sequence in which statements are executed, depending on whether the **if** condition returns **true** or **false**.

Nested if-else Statements

As we have seen, you can nest **if** statements within **if** statements. You can also nest **if-else** statements within **if**s, **if**s within **if-else** statements, and **if-else** statements within **if-else** statements. This provides us with considerable room for confusion, so let's look at a few examples. Taking the first case first, an example of an **if-else** nested within an **if** might be:

```
if(coffee == 'y')
   if(donuts == 'y')
      cout << "We have coffee and donuts.";
   else
      cout << "We have coffee, but not donuts";
```

The test for **donuts** is executed only if the result of the test for **coffee** returns **true**, so the messages reflect the correct situation in each case. However, it is easy to get this confused. If we write much the same thing with incorrect indentation, we can be trapped into the wrong conclusion:

```
if(coffee == 'y')
   if(donuts == 'y')
      cout << "We have coffee and donuts.";
else                                    // This else is indented incorrectly
   cout << "We have no coffee...";      // Wrong!
```

This mistake is easy to see here, but with more complicated **if** structures we need to keep in mind the rule about which **if** owns which **else**.

> An **else** *always belongs to the nearest preceding **if** which is not already spoken for by another **else**.*

Whenever things look a bit complicated you can apply this rule to sort things out. When you are writing your own programs you can always use braces to make the situation clearer. It isn't really necessary in such a simple case, but we could write the last example as follows:

```
if(coffee == 'y')
{
   if(donuts == 'y')
      cout << "We have coffee and donuts.";
   else
      cout << "We have coffee, but not donuts";
}
```

and it should be absolutely clear. Now that we know the rules, understanding the case of an **if** nested within an **if-else** becomes easy:

```
if(coffee == 'y')
{
   if(donuts == 'y')
      cout << "We have coffee and donuts.";
}
else
   if(tea == 'y')
      cout << "We have tea, but not coffee";
```

Here the braces are essential. If we leave them out, the **else** would belong to the **if** which is looking out for **donuts**. In this kind of situation, it is easy to forget to include them, and hence create an error which may be hard to find. A program with this kind of error will compile fine, and even produce the right results some of the time.

If we removed the braces in this example, we'd get the right results only as long as **coffee** and **donuts** are both equal to **'y'** so that the **if(tea == 'y')** check wouldn't be executed.

Here we'll look at **if-else** statements nested in **if-else** statements. This can get very messy, even with just one level of nesting. Let's beat the coffee and donuts analysis to death by using it again:

```
if(coffee == 'y')
   if(donuts == 'y')
      cout << "We have coffee and donuts.";
   else
      cout << "We have coffee, but not donuts";
else
   if(tea == 'y')
      cout << "We have no coffee, but we have tea, and maybe donuts...";
   else
      cout << "No tea or coffee, but maybe donuts...";
```

The logic here doesn't look quite so obvious, even with the correct indentation. No braces are necessary, as the rule you saw earlier will verify that this is correct, but it would look a bit clearer if we included them:

```
if(coffee == 'y')
{
   if(donuts == 'y')
      cout << "We have coffee and donuts.";
   else
      cout << "We have coffee, but not donuts";
}
else
{
   if(tea == 'y')
      cout << "We have no coffee, but we have tea, and maybe donuts...";
   else
      cout << "No tea or coffee, but maybe donuts...";
}
```

There are much better ways of dealing with this kind of logic in a program. If you put enough nested **if**s together, you can almost guarantee a mistake somewhere. The following section will help to simplify things.

Logical Operators and Expressions

As we have just seen, using **if**s where we have two or more related conditions can be a bit cumbersome. We have tried our **if** talents on looking for coffee and donuts, but in practice you may want to check much more complex conditions. You could be searching a personnel file for someone who is over 21 but under 35, female with a college degree, unmarried and speaks Hindi or Urdu. Defining a test for this could involve the mother of all **if**s.

Logical operators provide a neat and simple solution. Using logical operators, we can combine a series of comparisons into a single expression, so we end up needing just one **if**, virtually regardless of the complexity of the set of conditions.

We have just three logical operators:

&&	Logical AND
||	Logical OR
!	Logical negation (NOT)

We'll first consider what each of these is used for in general terms, then we'll look at an example.

Logical AND

You would use the AND operator, **&&**, where you have two conditions that must both be **true** for a true result. You want to be rich *and* healthy. For example, you could use the **&&** operator when you are testing a character to determine whether it's an upper case letter. The value being tested must be both greater than or equal to **'A'** AND less than or equal to **'Z'**. Both conditions must return **true** for the value to be a capital letter.

As before, these conditions may return numerical values. Remember that a non-zero value is treated as true, while zero is treated as false.

Taking the example of a value stored in a **char** variable **letter**, we could replace the test using two **if**s for one that uses only a single **if** and the **&&** operator:

```
if((letter >= 'A') && (letter <= 'Z'))
    cout << "This is a capital letter.";
```

The parentheses inside the **if** expression ensure that there is no doubt that the comparison operations are executed first, which makes the statement clearer. Here, the output statement will be executed only if *both* of the conditions combined by the operator **&&** are **true**.

Just as with binary operators in the last chapter, we can represent the effect of a particular logical operator using a truth table. The truth table for **&&** is as follows:

&&	false	true
false	false	false
true	false	true

The row headings of the left and the column headings at the top represent the value of the logical expressions to be combined by the operator **&&**. Thus, to determine the result of combining a **true** condition with a **false** condition, select the row with true at the left and the column with false at the top and look at the intersection of the row and column for the result (false). With the **&&** operation, the result is **true** only if both operands are **true**.

Logical OR

The OR operator, **||**, applies when you have two conditions and you want a **true** result if either or both of them are true. For example, you might be considered creditworthy for a loan from the bank if your income was at least $100,000 a year, or you had $1,000,000 in cash. This could be tested using the following **if**:

```
if((income >= 100000.00) || (capital >= 1000000.00))
    cout << "How much would you like to borrow, Sir (grovel, grovel)?";
```

The ingratiating response emerges when either or both of the conditions are **true**. (A better response might be, "Why do you *want* to borrow?" It's strange how banks will only lend you money if you don't need it.)

We can also construct a truth table for the **||** operator:

||	false	true
false	false	true
true	true	true

As you can see, you only get a **false** result if both conditions are **false**.

Logical NOT

The third logical operator, **!**, takes one operand with a logical value, **true** or **false**, and inverts its value. So if the value of **test** is **true** then **!test** is **false**; and if **test** is **false** then **!test** is **true**. To take the example of a simple expression, if **x** has the value 10, the expression:

```
!(x > 5)
```

is **false**, since **x > 5** is **true**.

We could also apply the **!** operator in an expression that was a favorite of Charles Dickens:

```
!(income > expenditure)
```

If this expression is **true**, the result is misery, at least as soon as the bank starts bouncing your checks.

Finally, we can apply the **!** operator to other basic data types. Suppose we have a variable **rate** of type **float**, which has the value 3.2. For some reason we might want to use the expression:

```
!(rate)
```

The value 3.2 is non-zero, and converts to the Boolean **true**: so the result of this expression is **false**.

TRY IT OUT - Combining Logical Operators

You can combine conditional expressions and logical operators to any degree that you feel comfortable with. For example, we could construct a test for whether a variable contained a letter just using a single **if**. Let's write it as a working example:

```cpp
// EX3_03.CPP
// Testing for a letter using logical operators
#include <iostream>

using namespace std;

int main()
{
   char letter = 0;                               // Store input in here

   cout << endl
        << "Enter a character: ";
   cin >> letter;

   if(((letter >= 'A') && (letter <= 'Z')) ||
      ((letter >= 'a') && (letter <= 'z')))       // Test for alphabetic
      cout << endl
           << "You entered a letter." << endl;
```

```
      else
         cout << endl
              << "You didn't enter a letter." << endl;
      return 0;
   }
```

How It Works

This example starts out in the same way as **Ex3_01.cpp** by reading a character after a prompt for input. The interesting part of the program is in the **if** statement condition. This consists of two logical expressions combined with the || (OR) operator, so that, if either is true, the condition returns **true** and the message:

You entered a letter.

is displayed. If both logical expressions are false, then the **else** statement is executed which displays the message:

You didn't enter a letter.

Each of the logical expressions combines a pair of comparisons with the operator **&&** (AND), so both comparisons must return **true** if the logical expression is to be true. The first logical expression returns **true** if the input is an upper case letter, and the second returns **true** if the input is a lower case letter.

The Conditional Operator

The conditional operator is sometimes called the **ternary operator** because it involves three operands. It is best understood by looking at an example. Suppose we have two variables, **a** and **b**, and we want to assign the maximum of **a** and **b** to a third variable **c**. We can do this with the statement:

```
   c = a > b ? a : b;          // Set c to the maximum of a and b
```

The first argument of the conditional operator is a logical expression, in this case **a > b**. If this expression returns **true** then the second operand — in this case **a** — is selected as the value resulting from the operation. If the first argument returns **false** then the third operand — in this case **b** — is selected as the value. Thus, the result of the conditional expression **a > b ? a : b** is **a** if **a** is greater than **b**, and **b** otherwise. This value is stored in **c**. The use of the conditional operator in this assignment statement is equivalent to the **if** statement:

```
   if(a > b)
      c = a;
   else
      c = b;
```

The conditional operator can be written generally as:

condition ? *expression1* : *expression2*

If the ***condition*** evaluates as **true**, then the result is the value of ***expression1***, and if it evaluates to **false**, then the result is the value of ***expression2***.

TRY IT OUT - Using the Conditional Operator with Output

A common use of the conditional operator is to control output, depending on the result of an expression or the value of a variable. You can vary a message by selecting one text string or another depending on the condition specified.

```cpp
// EX3_04.CPP
// The conditional operator selecting output
#include <iostream>

using namespace std;

int main()
{
   int nCakes = 1;              // Count of number of cakes

   cout << endl
        << "We have " << nCakes << " cake" << ((nCakes > 1) ? "s." : ".")
        << endl;

   ++nCakes;

   cout << endl
        << "We have " << nCakes << " cake" << ((nCakes > 1) ? "s." : ".")
        << endl;
   return 0;
}
```

The output from this program will be:

```
Ex3_04

We have 1 cake.

We have 2 cakes.
Press any key to continue
```

How It Works

First we initialize the **nCakes** variable with the value 1, then perform an output statement that shows us the number of cakes. The part that uses the conditional operator simply tests the variable to determine whether we have a singular cake or plural cakes:

```cpp
((nCakes>1) ? "s." : ".")
```

This expression evaluates to **"s."** if **nCakes** is greater than 1, or **"."** otherwise. This allows us to use the same output statement for any number of cakes. We show this in the example by incrementing the **nCakes** variable and repeating the output statement.

There are many other situations where you can apply this sort of mechanism; selecting between **"is"** and **"are"**, for example.

The switch Statement

The **switch** statement enables you to select from multiple choices based on a set of fixed values for a given expression. It operates like a physical rotary switch in that you can select one of a fixed number of choices; some makes of washing machine provide a means of choosing an operation for processing your laundry in this way. There are a given number of possible positions for the switch, such as cotton, wool, synthetic fiber, and so on, and you can select any one of them by turning the knob to point to the option that you want.

In the **switch** statement, the selection is determined by the value of an expression that you specify. You define the possible **switch** positions by one or more **case values**, a particular one being selected if the value of the **switch** expression is the same as the particular case value. There is one case value for each possible choice in the **switch** — the case values must be distinct.

If the value of the **switch** expression does not match any of the case values, then the **switch** automatically selects the **default** case. You can, if you wish, specify the code for the default case, as we will do below; otherwise, the default is to do nothing.

TRY IT OUT - The Switch Statement

We can examine how the **switch** statement works with the following example:

```cpp
// EX3_05.CPP
// Using the switch statement
#include <iostream>

using namespace std;

int main()
{
   int choice = 0;                        // Store selection value here

   cout << endl
        << "Your electronic recipe book is at your service." << endl
        << "You can choose from the following delicious dishes: "
        << endl
        << endl << "1 Boiled eggs"
        << endl << "2 Fried eggs"
        << endl << "3 Scrambled eggs"
        << endl << "4 Coddled eggs"
        << endl << endl << "Enter your selection number: ";
   cin >> choice;

   switch(choice)
   {
      case 1: cout << endl << "Boil some eggs." << endl;
              break;
      case 2: cout << endl << "Fry some eggs." << endl;
              break;
      case 3: cout << endl << "Scramble some eggs." << endl;
              break;
      case 4: cout << endl << "Coddle some eggs." << endl;
              break;
```

```
           default: cout << endl <<"You entered a wrong number, try raw eggs."
                              << endl;
       }
       return 0;
   }
```

How It Works

After defining your options in the stream output statement, and reading a selection number into the variable **choice**, the **switch** statement is executed with the condition specified as simply **choice** in parentheses, immediately following the keyword **switch**. The possible options in the **switch** are enclosed between braces and are each identified by a **case label**. A case label is the keyword **case**, followed by the value of **choice** that corresponds to this option, and terminated by a colon.

As you can see, the statements to be executed for a particular **case** are written following the colon at the end of the case label, and are terminated by a **break** statement. The **break** transfers execution to the statement after the **switch**. The **break** isn't mandatory, but if you don't include it, all the statements for the cases following the one selected will be executed, which isn't usually what you want. You can demonstrate this by removing the **break** statements from this example and seeing what happens.

If the value of **choice** doesn't correspond with any of the case values specified, the statements preceded by the **default** label are executed. A **default** case isn't essential. In its absence, if the value of the test expression doesn't correspond to any of the cases, the **switch** is exited and the program continues with the next statement after the **switch**.

TRY IT OUT - Sharing a Case

Each of the case constant expressions must be constant and unique. The reason that no two case constants can be the same is that the compiler would have no way of knowing which case statement should be executed for that particular value. However, different cases don't need to have a unique action. Several cases can share the same action, as shown here:

```
// EX3_06.CPP
// Multiple case actions
#include <iostream>

using namespace std;

int main()
{
   char letter = 0;
   cout << endl
        << "Enter a small letter: ";
   cin >> letter;

   switch(letter*(letter >= 'a' && letter <= 'z'))
   {
      case 'a':
      case 'e':
      case 'i':
      case 'o':
```

```
        case 'u': cout << endl << "You entered a vowel.";
                  break;

        case 0: cout << endl << "That is not a small letter.";
                break;

        default: cout << endl << "You entered a consonant.";
    }
    cout << endl;
    return 0;
}
```

How It Works

In this example, we have a more complex expression in the **switch**. If the character entered isn't a lower case letter, then the expression:

```
   (letter >= 'a' && letter <= 'z')
```

will result in the value 0. Then, **letter** is multiplied by this expression, so the **switch** expression would be set to 0 if a lower case letter wasn't entered. This will then cause the statements following the case label **case 0** to be executed.

If a lower case letter was entered, the expression above will result in the value 1. Multiplying **letter** by one results in the **switch** expression having the same value as **letter**. For all values corresponding to vowels, the same output statement is executed since we haven't used **break** statements to separate these case labels. You can see that a single action can be taken for a number of different cases by writing each of the case labels one after the other before the statements to be executed. If a lower case letter that is a consonant is entered as program input, the **default** case label statement is executed.

Unconditional Branching

The **if** statement provides you with the flexibility to choose to execute one set of statements or another, depending on a specified condition, so the statement execution sequence is varied depending on the values of the data in the program. The **goto** statement, in contrast, is a blunt instrument. It enables you to branch to a specified program statement unconditionally. The statement to be branched to must be identified by a statement label which is an identifier defined according to the same rules as a variable name. This is followed by a colon and placed before the statement requiring labeling. Here is an example of a labeled statement:

```
   myLabel: cout << "myLabel branch has been activated" << endl;
```

This statement has the label **myLabel**, and an unconditional branch to this statement would be written as follows:

```
   goto myLabel;
```

Whenever possible, you should avoid using **goto**s in your program. They tend to encourage very convoluted code that can be extremely difficult to follow.

Repeating a Block of Statements

The ability to repeat a group of statements is fundamental to most applications. Without this ability, an organization would need to modify the payroll program every time an extra employee was hired, and you would need to reload Tetris every time you wanted to play another game. So let's first understand how a loop works.

What is a Loop?

A loop executes a sequence of statements until a particular condition is true (or false). We can actually write a loop with the C++ statements that we have met so far. We just need an **if** and the dreaded **goto**. Look at this example:

```
// EX3_07.CPP
// Creating a loop with an if and a goto
#include <iostream>

using namespace std;

int main()
{
   int i = 0, sum = 0;
   const int max = 10;

   i = 1;
loop:
   sum += i;                  // Add current value of i to sum
   if(++i <= max)
      goto loop;              // Go back to loop until i = 11

   cout << endl
        << "sum = " << sum
        << endl
        << "i = " << i
        << endl;
   return 0;
}
```

This example accumulates the sum of integers from 1 to 10. The first time through the sequence of statements, **i** is 1 and is added to **sum** which starts out as zero. In the **if**, **i** is incremented to 2 and, as long as it is less than or equal to **max**, the unconditional branch to **loop** occurs and the value of **i**, now 2, is added to **sum**. This continues with **i** being incremented and added to **sum** each time, until finally, when **i** is incremented to 11 in the **if**, the branch back will not be executed. If you run this example, you will get this output:

```
Ex3_07

sum = 55
i = 11
Press any key to continue
```

This shows quite clearly how the loop works. However, it uses a **goto** and introduces a label into our program, both of which are things we should avoid if possible. We can achieve the same thing, and more, with the next statement which is specifically for writing a loop.

TRY IT OUT - Using the for Loop

We can rewrite the last code fragment as a working example using what is known as a **for** loop:

```cpp
// EX3_08.CPP
// Summing integers with a for loop
#include <iostream>

using namespace std;

int main()
{
   int i = 0, sum = 0;
   const int max = 10;

   for(i = 1; i <= max; i++)          // Loop specification
      sum += i;                       // Loop statement

   cout << endl
        << "sum = " << sum
        << endl
        << "i = " << i
        << endl;
   return 0;
}
```

How It Works

If you compile and run this, you will get exactly the same output as the previous example, but the code is much simpler here. The conditions determining the operation of the loop appear in parentheses after the keyword **for**. There are three expressions that appear within the parentheses:

▶ The first sets **i** to 1

▶ The second determines that the loop statement on the following line is executed as long as **i** is less than or equal to **max**

▶ The third increments **i** each iteration

111

Actually, this loop is not *exactly* the same as the version in **Ex3_07.cpp**. You can demonstrate this if you set the value of **max** to 0 in both programs and run them again. Then, you will find that the value of **sum** is 1 in **Ex3_07.cpp** and 0 in **Ex3_08.cpp**, and the value of **i** differs too. The reason for this is that the **if** version of the program always executes the loop at least once, since we don't check the condition until the end. The **for** loop doesn't do this because the condition is actually checked at the beginning.

The general form of the **for** loop is:

```
for (initializing_expression; test_expression; increment_expression)
loop_statement;
```

Of course, **loop_statement** can be a block between braces. The sequence of events in executing the **for** loop is shown here:

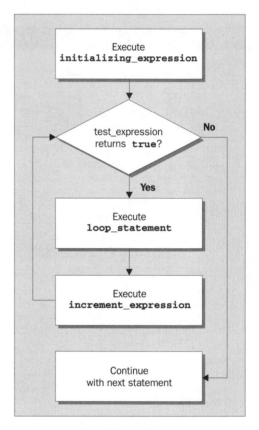

As we have said, the loop statement shown in the diagram can also be a block of statements. The expressions controlling the **for** loop are very flexible. You can even put multiple expressions for each, separated by the comma operator. This gives you a lot of scope in applying the **for** loop.

Variations on the for Loop

Most of the time, the expressions in a **for** loop are used in a fairly standard way: the first for initializing one or more loop counters, the second to test if the loop should continue, and the third to increment or decrement one or more loop counters. However, you are not obliged to use these expressions in this way and quite a few variations are possible.

The initialization expression in a **for** loop can also include a declaration for a loop variable. Using our previous example, we could have written the loop to include the declaration for the loop counter **i**:

```
for(int i = 1; i <= max; i++)        // Loop specification
    sum += i;                        // Loop statement
```

Naturally, the original declaration for **i** would need to be omitted in the program. If you make this change to the last example, you will find that it runs exactly as before, but there is something odd about this. A loop has a scope which extends from the **for** expression to the end of the body of the loop, which of course can be a block of code between braces, as well as just a single statement. The counter **i** is now declared within the loop scope, but we are still able to refer to it in the output statement, which is outside the scope of **i**. This is because a special extension has been allowed for loop counters to extend their scope to the scope enclosing the loop.

In Visual C++ 6.0, a counter which is declared within a for loop expression remains in scope after the loop has finished executing. However, I recommend that you don't write programs that rely on the scope of the counter extending beyond the end of the loop. This is because the recently released ANSI standard for C++ recommends that this should not be supported by future C++ compilers. If you need to use the value in the counter after the loop has executed, then declare the counter *outside* the scope of the loop.

You can also omit the initialization expression altogether. If we initialize **i** appropriately in the declaration, we can write the loop as:

```
int i = 1;
for(; i <= max; i++)                 // Loop specification
    sum += i;                        // Loop statement
```

You still need the semicolon that separates the initialization expression from the test condition for the loop. In fact, both semicolons must be in place. If you omit the first semicolon, the compiler will be unable to decide which expression has been omitted.

This flexibility also applies to the contents of the increment expression. For example, we can place the loop statement in the last example inside the increment expression — the loop becomes:

```
for(i = 1; i <= max; sum += i++);        // The whole loop
```

We still need the semicolon after the closing parentheses, to indicate that the loop statement is now empty. If you omit this, the statement immediately following this line will be interpreted as the loop statement.

TRY IT OUT - Using Multiple Counters

You can use the comma operator to include multiple counters in a **for** loop. We can show this in operation in the following program:

```
// EX3_09.CPP
// Using multiple counters to show powers of 2
#include <iostream>
#include <iomanip>

using namespace std;

int main()
{
   long i = 0, power = 0;
   const int max = 10;

   for(i = 0, power = 1; i <= max; i++, power += power)
      cout << endl
           << setw(10) << i << setw(10) << power;        // Loop statement

   cout << endl;
   return 0;
}
```

How It Works

We initialize two variables in the initialization section of the **for** loop, separated by the comma operator, and increment each of them in the increment section. Clearly, you can put as many expressions as you like in each position.

FYI You can even specify multiple conditions, separated by commas, in the test part of the for loop; but only the right-most condition will affect when the loop ends.

Note that the assignments defining the initial values for **i** and **power** are expressions, not statements. A statement always ends with a semicolon.

For each increment of **i**, the value of the variable **power** is doubled by adding it to itself. This produces the powers of two that we are looking for and so the program will produce the following output:

```
Ex3_09                                    _ □ ×
          0          1
          1          2
          2          4
          3          8
          4         16
          5         32
          6         64
          7        128
          8        256
          9        512
         10       1024
Press any key to continue
```

The **setw()** manipulator that we saw in the previous chapter is used to align the output nicely. We have included **iomanip** so that we can use **setw()**.

TRY IT OUT - The Infinite for Loop

If you omit the test condition then the value is assumed to be **true**, so the loop will continue indefinitely unless you provide some other means of exiting from it. In fact, if you like, you can omit all the expressions in the parentheses after **for**. This may not seem to be very useful, but in fact, quite the reverse is true. You will often come across situations where you want to execute a loop a number of times, but you do not know in advance how many iterations you will need. Have a look at this:

```cpp
// EX3_10.CPP
// Using an infinite for loop to compute an average
#include <iostream>

using namespace std;

int main()
{
   double value = 0.0;                // Value entered stored here
   double sum = 0.0;                  // Total of values accumulated here
   int i = 0;                         // Count of number of values
   char indicator = 'n';              // Continue or not?

   for(;;)                            // Infinite loop
   {
      cout << endl
           << "Enter a value: ";
      cin >> value;                   // Read a value
      ++i;                            // Increment count
      sum += value;                   // Add current input to total

      cout << endl
           << "Do you want to enter another value (enter n to end)? ";
      cin >> indicator;               // Read indicator
      if ((indicator == 'n') || (indicator == 'N'))
        break;                        // Exit from loop
   }

   cout << endl
        << "The average of the " << i
        << " values you entered is " << sum/i << "."
        << endl;
   return 0;
}
```

How It Works

This program will compute the average of an arbitrary number of values. After each value is entered you need to indicate whether you want to enter another value, by entering a single character y or n. Typical output from executing this example is:

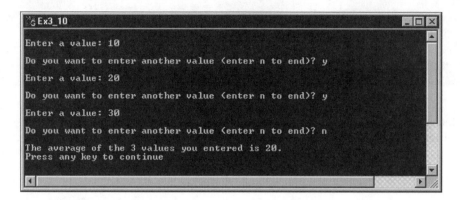

After declaring and initializing the variables that we're going to use, we start a **for** loop with no expressions specified, so there is no provision for ending it here. The block immediately following is the subject of the loop which is to be repeated.

The loop block performs two basic actions:

1 It reads a value

2 It checks whether you want to continue to enter values

The first action within the block is to prompt you for input and then read a value into the variable **value**. The value that you enter is added to **sum** and the count of the number of values, **i**, is incremented. After accumulating the value in **sum**, you are prompted to enter **'n'** if you have finished. The character that you enter is stored in the variable **indicator** for testing against **'n'** or **'N'** in the **if** statement. If neither is found, the loop continues, otherwise a **break** is executed. The effect of **break** in a loop is similar to its effect in the context of the **switch** statement. In this instance, it exits the loop immediately by transferring to the statement following the closing brace of the loop block.

Finally, we output the count of the number of values entered and their average, calculated by dividing **sum** by **i**. Of course, **i** will be promoted to **double** before the calculation, as you will remember from the casting discussion in Chapter 2.

The continue Statement

There is another statement, besides **break**, that is used to affect the operation of a loop: the **continue** statement. This is written simply as:

```
continue;
```

Executing **continue** within a loop starts the next loop iteration immediately, skipping over any statements remaining in the current iteration. We can demonstrate how this works with the following code fragment:

```cpp
#include <iostream>

using namespace std;

int main()
{
    int i = 0, value = 0, product = 1;
    for(i = 1; i <= 10; i++)
    {
        cin >> value;

        if(value == 0)                  // If value is zero
            continue;                   // skip to next iteration

        product *= value;
    }
    cout << "Product (ignoring zeros): " << product
        << endl;

    return 0;                           // Exit from loop
}
```

This loop reads 10 values with the intention of producing the product of the values entered. The **if** checks each value entered, and if it is zero, then the **continue** statement skips to the next iteration. This is so that we don't end up with a zero product if one of the values is zero. Obviously, if a zero value occurred on the last iteration, the loop would end. There are clearly other ways of achieving the same result, but **continue** provides a very useful capability, particularly with complex loops where you may need to skip to the end of the current iteration from various points in the loop.

The effect of the **break** and **continue** statements on the logic of a **for** loop is illustrated here:

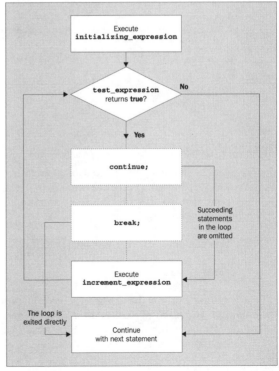

117

Obviously, in a real situation, the **break** and **continue** statements are used with some condition-testing logic to determine when the loop should be exited, or when an iteration of the loop should be skipped. The **break** and **continue** statements can also be used with the other kinds of loop which we'll discuss later on in this chapter, where they work in exactly the same way.

TRY IT OUT - Using Other Types in Loops

So far, we have only used integers to count loop iterations. You are in no way restricted as to what type of variable you use to count iterations. Look at this example:

```cpp
// EX3_11.CPP
// Display ASCII codes for alphabetic characters
#include <iostream>
#include <iomanip>

using namespace std;

int main()
{
   for(char capital = 'A', small = 'a'; capital <= 'Z'; capital++, small++)
      cout << endl
            << "\t" << capital                               // Output capital as
                                                             // character
            << hex << setw(10) << static_cast<int>(capital)  // Output capital as
                                                             // hex
            << dec << setw(10) << static_cast<int>(capital)  // Output capital as
                                                             // decimal
            << "  " << small                                 // Output small as
                                                             // character
            << hex << setw(10) << static_cast<int>(small)    // Output small as
                                                             // hex
            << dec << setw(10) << static_cast<int>(small);   // Output small as
                                                             // decimal

   cout << endl;
   return 0;
}
```

How It Works

The loop in this example is controlled by the **char** variable **capital** which we declare along with the variable **small** in the initializing expression. We also increment both variables in the increment part, so that the value of **capital** varies from **'A'** to **'Z'**, and the value of **small** correspondingly varies from **'a'** to **'z'**.

The loop contains just one output statement spread over seven lines. The first line:

```cpp
cout << endl
```

starts a new line on the screen. On each iteration, after outputting a tab character, the value of **capital** is displayed three times: as a character, as a hexadecimal value and as a decimal value. We insert the manipulator **hex** which causes succeeding data values to be displayed as hexadecimal values for the second output of **capital**, and we then insert the manipulator **dec** to cause succeeding values to be output as decimal once more. We get the **char** variable **capital** to output as a numeric value by casting it to **int**, using the **static_cast<>()** which we saw in the last chapter. The value of **small** is output in a similar way. As a result, the program will generate the following output:

A	41	65	a	61	97
B	42	66	b	62	98
C	43	67	c	63	99
D	44	68	d	64	100
E	45	69	e	65	101
F	46	70	f	66	102
G	47	71	g	67	103
H	48	72	h	68	104
I	49	73	i	69	105
J	4a	74	j	6a	106
K	4b	75	k	6b	107
L	4c	76	l	6c	108
M	4d	77	m	6d	109
N	4e	78	n	6e	110
O	4f	79	o	6f	111
P	50	80	p	70	112
Q	51	81	q	71	113
R	52	82	r	72	114
S	53	83	s	73	115
T	54	84	t	74	116
U	55	85	u	75	117
V	56	86	v	76	118
W	57	87	w	77	119
X	58	88	x	78	120
Y	59	89	y	79	121
Z	5a	90	z	7a	122

You can also use a floating point value as a loop counter. An example of a **for** loop with this kind of counter is:

```
double a = 0.3, b = 2.5;
for(double x = 0.0; x <= 2.0; x += 0.25)
   cout << "\n\tx = " << x
        << "\ta*x + b = " << a*x + b;
```

This calculates the value of **a*x+b** for values of **x** from 0.0 to 2.0 in steps of 0.25. However, you need to take care when using a floating point counter in a loop. Many decimal values are not represented exactly in binary floating point, so discrepancies can build up with accumulative values.

The while Loop

A second kind of loop in C++ is the **while** loop. Where the **for** loop is primarily used to repeat a statement or a block for a prescribed number of iterations, the **while** loop will continue as long as a specified condition is true. The general form of the **while** loop is:

```
while(condition)
   loop_statement;
```

where **loop_statement** will be executed repeatedly as long as the **condition** expression has the value **true**. Once the condition becomes **false**, the program continues with the statement following the loop. Of course, a block of statements between braces could replace the single **loop_statement**. The logic of the **while** loop can be represented like this:

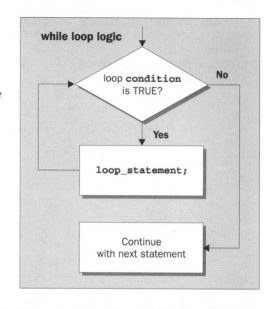

TRY IT OUT - Using the while Loop

We could rewrite our program to compute averages (**Ex3_10.cpp**) to use the **while** loop:

```cpp
// EX3_12.CPP
// Using a while loop to compute an average
#include <iostream>

using namespace std;

int main()
{
   double value = 0.0;            // Value entered stored here
   double sum = 0.0;              // Total of values accumulated here
   int i = 0;                     // Count of number of values
   char indicator = 'y';          // Continue or not?

   while(indicator == 'y')        // Loop as long as y is entered
   {
      cout << endl
           << "Enter a value: ";
      cin >> value;               // Read a value
      ++i;                        // Increment count
      sum += value;               // Add current input to total

      cout << endl
           << "Do you want to enter another value (enter n to end)? ";
      cin >> indicator;           // Read indicator
   }

   cout << endl
        << "The average of the " << i
```

```
             << " values you entered is " << sum/i << "."
             << endl;
        return 0;
    }
```

How It Works

For the same input, this version of the program will produce the same output as before. One statement has been updated, and another has been added — they are highlighted above. The **for** loop statement has been replaced by the **while** statement and the test for **indicator** in the **if** has been deleted, as this function is performed by the **while** condition. You need to initialize **indicator** with **'y'** in place of the **'n'** which appeared previously — otherwise the **while** loop will terminate immediately. As long as the condition in the **while** returns **true**, then the loop continues. You can put any expression resulting in **true** or **false** as the loop condition. The example would be a better program if the loop condition were extended to allow **'Y'** to be entered to continue the loop as well as **'y'**. Modifying the **while** to the following:

```
    while((indicator == 'y') || (indicator == 'Y'))
```

would do the trick.

You can also create an infinite **while** loop by using a condition that is always **true**. This can be written as follows:

```
    while(1)
    {
      ...
    }
```

Here, as elsewhere, the integer value 1 is converted to the **bool** value **true**. Naturally, the same requirement applies here as in the case of the infinite **for** loop: namely, that there must be some way of exiting the loop within the loop block. We'll look at other ways to use the **while** loop in Chapter 4.

The do-while Loop

The **do-while** loop is similar to the **while** loop in that the loop continues as long as the specified loop condition remains **true**. The main difference is that the condition is checked at the end of the loop — in the case of the **while** loop and the **for** loop, the condition is checked at the beginning of the loop. Thus, the **do-while** loop statement is *always* executed at least once. The general form of the **do-while** loop is:

```
    do
    {
       loop_statements;
    }while(condition);
```

The logic of this form of loop is shown here:

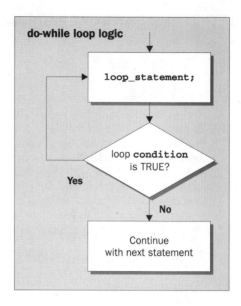

do-while loop logic

loop_statement;

loop **condition** is TRUE?

Yes

No

Continue with next statement

We could replace the **while** loop in the last version of the program to calculate an average with a **do-while** loop:

```
do
{
    cout << endl
        << "Enter a value: ";
    cin >> value;                  // Read a value
    ++i;                           // Increment count
    sum += value;                  // Add current input to total

    cout << "Do you want to enter another value (enter n to end)?";
    cin >> indicator;              // Read indicator
} while((indicator == 'y') || (indicator == 'Y'));
```

There's little to choose between them, except that this version doesn't depend on the initial value set in **indicator** for correct operation. As long as you want to enter at least one value, which is not unreasonable for the calculation in question, this version of the loop is preferable.

Nested Loops

You can nest one loop inside another. In Chapter 4, the usual application of this will become more apparent — it's typically applied to repeating actions at different levels of classification. An example might be calculating the total marks for each student in a class, then repeating the process for each class in a school.

TRY IT OUT - Nested Loops

We can illustrate the effects of nesting one loop inside another by calculating a simple formula. A factorial of an integer is the product of all the integers from 1 to the integer in question; so the factorial of 3, for example, is 1 times 2 times 3, which is 6. The following program will compute the factorial of integers that you enter (until you've had enough):

```cpp
// EX3_13.CPP
// Demonstrating nested loops to compute factorials
#include <iostream>

using namespace std;

int main()
{
   char indicator = 'n';
   long value = 0,
        factorial = 0;

   do
   {
      cout << endl
           << "Enter an integer value: ";
      cin >> value;

      factorial = 1;
      for(int i = 2; i <= value; i++)
         factorial *= i;

      cout << "Factorial " << value << " is " << factorial;
      cout << endl
           << "Do you want to enter another value (y or n)? ";
      cin >> indicator;
   } while((indicator == 'y') || (indicator == 'Y'));

   return 0;
}
```

How It Works

If you compile and execute this example, the typical output produced is:

```
Ex3_13
Enter an integer value: 5
Factorial 5 is 120
Do you want to enter another value (y or n)? y

Enter an integer value: 10
Factorial 10 is 3628800
Do you want to enter another value (y or n)? y

Enter an integer value: 13
Factorial 13 is 1932053504
Do you want to enter another value (y or n)? y

Enter an integer value: 22
Factorial 22 is -522715136
Do you want to enter another value (y or n)? n
Press any key to continue
```

Factorial values grow very fast. In fact, 12 is the largest input value for which this example produces a correct result. The factorial of 13 is actually 6,227,020,800 and not 1,932,053,504 as the program will tell you. If you run it with even larger input values, leading digits will be lost in the result stored in the variable **factorial**, and you may well get negative values for the factorial as you do when you ask for the factorial of 22.

> *This situation doesn't cause any error messages, so it is of paramount importance that you are sure that the values you're dealing with in a program can be contained in the permitted range of the type of variable you're using. You also need to consider the effects of incorrect input values. Errors of this kind, which occur silently, can be very hard to find.*

The outer of the two nested loops is the **do-while** loop which controls when the program ends. As long as you keep entering y or Y at the prompt, the program will continue to calculate factorial values. The factorial for the integer entered is calculated in the inner **for** loop. This is executed **value** times to multiply the variable **factorial** (with an initial value of 1) with successive integers from 2 to **value**.

TRY IT OUT - Another Nested Loop

If you haven't dealt much with nested loops they can be a little confusing, so let's try another example. This program will generate a multiplication table of a given size:

```cpp
// EX3_14.CPP
// Using nested loops to generate a multiplcation table
#include <iostream>
#include <iomanip>

using namespace std;

int main()
{
   const int size = 12;                 // Size of table
   int i = 0, j = 0;                    // Loop counters

   cout << endl                         // Output table title
        << size << " by " << size
        << " Multiplication Table" << endl << endl;

   cout << endl << "     |";
   for(i = 1; i <= size; i++)           // Loop to output column headings
   cout << setw(3) << i << "  ";

   cout << endl;                        // Newline for underlines
   for(i = 0; i <= size; i++)
   cout << "_____";                     // Underline each heading

   for(i = 1; i <= size; i++)           // Outer loop for rows
   {
       cout << endl
            << setw(3) << i << " |";     // Output row label
```

```
        for(j = 1; j <= size; j++)          // Inner loop to output the rest of
                                            // the row
            cout << setw(3) << i*j << "   ";  // End of inner loop

    }                                       // End of outer loop
    cout  << endl;
    return 0;
}
```

How It Works

If you build this example and execute it, you will see the output shown in the figure below. This shows the output window when execution is complete:

```
Ex3_14                                                    _ □ ×

12 by 12 Multiplication Table

       ¦  1    2    3    4    5    6    7    8    9   10   11   12
      _____
    1 ¦  1    2    3    4    5    6    7    8    9   10   11   12
    2 ¦  2    4    6    8   10   12   14   16   18   20   22   24
    3 ¦  3    6    9   12   15   18   21   24   27   30   33   36
    4 ¦  4    8   12   16   20   24   28   32   36   40   44   48
    5 ¦  5   10   15   20   25   30   35   40   45   50   55   60
    6 ¦  6   12   18   24   30   36   42   48   54   60   66   72
    7 ¦  7   14   21   28   35   42   49   56   63   70   77   84
    8 ¦  8   16   24   32   40   48   56   64   72   80   88   96
    9 ¦  9   18   27   36   45   54   63   72   81   90   99  108
   10 ¦ 10   20   30   40   50   60   70   80   90  100  110  120
   11 ¦ 11   22   33   44   55   66   77   88   99  110  121  132
   12 ¦ 12   24   36   48   60   72   84   96  108  120  132  144
Press any key to continue
```

The table title is produced by the first output statement in the program. The next output statement, combined with the loop following it, generates the column headings. Each column will be five characters wide, so the heading value is displayed in a field width of three specified by the **setw(3)** manipulator, followed by two blanks. The output statement preceding the loop outputs four spaces and a vertical bar above the first column which will contain the row headings. A series of underline characters is then displayed beneath the column headings.

The nested loop generates the main table contents. The outer loop repeats once for each row, so **i** is the row number. The output statement,

```
        cout << endl
            << setw(3) << i << " |";       // Output row label
```

goes to a new line for the start of a row and then outputs the row heading given by the value of **i** in a field width of three, followed by a space and a vertical bar.

A row of values is generated by the inner loop:

```
        for(j = 1; j <= size; j++)          // Inner loop to output the rest of
                                            // the row
            cout << setw(3) << i*j << "   ";  // End of inner loop
```

125

This loop outputs values **i*j** corresponding to the product of the current row value **i**, and each of the column values in turn by varying **j** from 1 to **size**. So for each iteration of the outer loop, the inner loop executes **size** iterations. The values are positioned in the same way as the column headings.

When the outer loop is completed, the **return** is executed to end the program.

Summary

In this chapter, we've assembled all of the essential mechanisms for making decisions in C++ programs. We've also gone through all the facilities for repeating a group of statements. The essentials of what we've discussed are as follows:

> ▶ The basic decision-making capability is based on the set of relational operators, which allow expressions to be tested and compared, and yield a **bool** value **true** or **false**.

> ▶ We can also make decisions based on conditions that return non-**bool** values. Any non-zero value will be interpreted as **true** when a condition is tested, while zero is interpreted as **false**.

> ▶ The primary decision-making capability in C++ is provided by the **if** statement. Further flexibility is provided by the **switch** statement, and by the conditional operator.

> ▶ There are three basic methods provided for repeating a block of statements: the **for** loop, the **while** loop and the **do-while** loop. The **for** loop allows the loop to repeat a given number of times. The **while** loop allows a loop to continue as long as a specified condition returns **true**. Finally, **do-while** executes the loop at least once and allows continuation of the loop as long as a specified condition returns **true**.

> ▶ Any kind of loop may be nested within any other kind of loop.

> ▶ The keyword **continue** allows you to skip the remainder of the current iteration in a loop and go straight to the next iteration.

> ▶ The keyword **break** provides an immediate exit from a loop. It also provides an exit from a **switch** at the end of a group of **case** statements.

Exercises

Ex3-1: Write a program which reads numbers from **cin**, and adds them, stopping when 0 has been entered. Construct three versions of this program, using the **while**, **do-while** and **for** loops.

Ex3-2: Write a program to input characters from the keyboard and count the vowels. Stop counting when a Q (or a q) is encountered. Use a combination of an infinite loop to get the characters, and a **switch** statement to count them.

Ex3-3: Write a program to print out the multiplication tables from 2 to 12 in columns.

Ex3-4: Imagine that in a program we want to set a 'file open mode' variable based on two attributes: the file type (text or binary), and the way in which we want to open the file (read, write or append). Using the bitwise operators (**&** and **|**) and a set of flags, devise a method to allow an integer variable to be set to any combination of the two attributes. Write a program which sets such a variable and then decodes it, printing out its settings.

Ex3-5: Take [Prg1], and modify it so that you continue asking the user for numbers and printing them, until zero is entered. Save this as [Prg2].

Arrays, Pointers and References

So far, we've covered all the basic data types of consequence and have accumulated a basic knowledge of how to perform calculations and make decisions in a program. This chapter is about broadening the application of the basic programming techniques that we have covered so far, from using single data elements to working with whole collections of data items. In this chapter, you will learn:

- What an array is and how you can use it
- How to declare and initialize arrays of different types
- How to declare and use multidimensional arrays
- What a pointer is and how you can use it
- How to declare and initialize pointers of different types
- The relationship between arrays and pointers
- What a reference is, how it is declared, and some initial ideas on its uses
- How to create and allocate memory for variables dynamically

Handling Multiple Data Values of the Same Type

We already know how to declare and initialize variables of various types, which each hold a single item of information and which we will refer to as **data elements**. We know how to create a single character in a **char** variable, a single integer in a variable of type **int** or of type **long**, or a single floating point number in a variable of type **float**. The most obvious extension to these ideas is to be able to reference several data elements of a particular type with a single variable name. This would enable you to handle applications of a much broader scope.

Let's think about an example of where you might need this. Suppose that you needed to write a payroll program. Using a separately-named variable for each individual's pay, tax liability, and so on, would be an uphill task to say the least. A much more convenient way to handle such a problem would be to reference an employee by some kind of generic name — **EmployeeName** to take an imaginative example — and to have other generic names for the kinds of data related to each employee, such as **Pay**, **Tax**, and so on. Of course, you would also need some means of picking out a particular employee from the whole bunch, together with the data from the generic variables associated with them. This kind of requirement arises with any collection of like entities that you want to handle in your program, whether they're baseball players or battleships. Naturally, C++ provides you with a way to deal with this.

Arrays

The basis for the solution to all of these problems is provided by the **array** in C++. An array is simply a number of memory locations, each of which can store an item of data of the same data type and which are all referenced through the same variable name. The employee names in a payroll program could be stored in one array, the pay for each employee in another, and the tax due for each employee could be stored in a third array.

Individual items in an array are specified by an index value which is simply an integer representing the sequence number of the elements in the array, the first having the sequence number **0**, the second **1**, and so on. You can also envisage the index value of an array element as an offset from the first element in an array. The first element has an offset of **0** and therefore an index of **0**, and an index value of **3** will refer to the fourth element of an array. For our payroll, we could arrange our arrays so that if an employee's name was stored in the **EmployeeName** array at a given index value, then the arrays **Pay** and **Tax** would store the associated data on pay and tax for the same employee in the array positions referenced by the same index value.

The basic structure of an array is illustrated in the figure below:

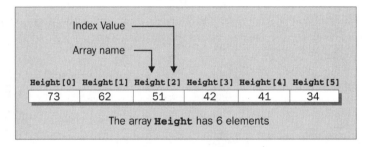

This shows an array, called **Height**, with six elements, each storing a different value. These might be the heights of the members of a family, for instance, recorded to the nearest inch. As there are six elements, the index values run from **0** through **5**. To refer to a particular element, you write the array name, followed by the index value of the particular element between square brackets. The third element is referred to as **Height[2]**, for example. Some people like to think of the index as the offset from the first element, so for example, the fourth element is offset by 3 from the first element.

The amount of memory required to store each element will be determined by its type, and all the elements of an array will be stored in a contiguous block of memory.

Declaring Arrays

You declare an array in essentially the same way as you declared the variables that we have seen up to now, the only difference being that the number of elements in the array is specified between square brackets immediately following the array name. For example, we could declare the integer array **Height**, shown in the previous figure, with the following declaration statement:

```
long Height[6];
```

Since each **long** value occupies 4 bytes in memory, the whole array requires 24 bytes. Arrays can be of any size, subject to the constraints imposed by the amount of memory in the computer that your program will be running on.

You can declare arrays to be of any type. For example, to declare arrays intended to store the capacity and power output of a series of engines, you could write the following:

```
double cubic_inches[10];
double horsepower[10];
```

If auto mechanics are your thing, this would enable you to store the cubic capacity and power output of up to 10 engines, referenced by index values from **0** to **9**. As we have seen before with other variables, you can declare multiple arrays of a given type in a single statement, but in practice it is better to declare variables in separate statements.

TRY IT OUT — Using Arrays

As a basis for an exercise in using arrays, let's imagine that we have kept a record of both the amount of gas we have bought for the car and the odometer reading on each occasion. We can write a program to analyze this data to see how the gas consumption looks on each occasion that we bought gas:

```
// EX4_01.CPP
// Calculating gas mileage
#include <iostream>
#include <iomanip>
using namespace std;

int main()
{
   const int MAX = 20;                   // Maximum number of values
   double gas[ MAX ];                    // Gas quantity in gallons
   long miles[ MAX ];                    // Odometer readings
   int count = 0;                        // Loop counter
   char indicator = 'y';                 // Input indicator

   while( (indicator == 'y' || indicator == 'Y') && count < MAX )
   {
      cout << endl
           << "Enter gas quantity: ";
      cin >> gas[count];                 // Read gas quantity
      cout << "Enter odometer reading: ";
      cin >> miles[count];               // Read odometer value
```

```
    ++count;
        cout << "Do you want to enter another(y or n)? ";
        cin >> indicator;
    }

    if(count <= 1)                              // count = 1 after 1 entry
    {                                           // completed - we need at least 2
        cout << endl
             << "Sorry - at least two readings are necessary.";
        return 0;
    }

    // Output results from 2nd entry to last entry
    for(int i = 1; i < count; i++)
    cout << endl
         << setw(2) << i << "."              // Output sequence number
         << "Gas purchased = " << gas[i] << " gallons" // Output gas
         << " resulted in "                 // Output miles per gallon
         << (miles[i] - miles[i - 1])/gas[i] << " miles per gallon.";

    cout << endl;
    return 0;
}
```

How It Works

Since we need to take the difference between two odometer readings to calculate the miles covered for the gas used, we only use the odometer reading from the first pair of input values — we ignore the gas bought in the first instance. The typical output produced by this example is shown in the figure below:

```
Ex4_01                                                              _ □ X

Enter gas quantity: 12.8
Enter odometer reading: 25032
Do you want to enter another(y or n)? y

Enter gas quantity: 14.9
Enter odometer reading: 25537
Do you want to enter another(y or n)? y

Enter gas quantity: 11.8
Enter odometer reading: 25798
Do you want to enter another(y or n)? n

 1.Gas purchased = 14.9 gallons resulted in 33.8926 miles per gallon.
 2.Gas purchased = 11.8 gallons resulted in 22.1186 miles per gallon.
Press any key to continue
```

During the second period shown in the output, the traffic must have been really bad — or maybe the parking brake was always on.

The dimensions of the two arrays **gas** and **miles** used to store the input data are determined by the value of the constant variable **MAX**. By changing the value of **MAX**, you can change the program to accommodate a different maximum number of input values. This technique is commonly used to make a program flexible in the amount of information that it can handle. Of course, all the program code must be written to take account of the array dimensions, or of any other parameters being specified by **const** variables. However, this presents little difficulty in practice, so there's no reason why you should not adopt this approach. We'll also see later how to allocate memory for storing data as the program executes, so that we don't need to fix the amount of memory allocated for data storage in advance.

Inputting the Data

The data values are read in the **while** loop. Since the loop variable **count** can run from **0** to **MAX - 1**, we haven't allowed the user of our program to enter more values than the array can handle. We initialize the variables **count** and **indicator** to **0** and **'y'** respectively, so that the **while** loop is entered at least once. There's a prompt for each input value required and the value is read into the appropriate array element. The element used to store a particular value is determined by the variable **count**, which is **0** for the first input. The array element is specified in the **cin** statement by using **count** as an index, and **count** is then incremented ready for the next value.

After you enter each value, the program prompts you for confirmation that another value is to be entered. The character entered is read into the variable **indicator** and then tested in the loop condition. The loop will terminate unless **'y'** or **'Y'** is entered and the variable **count** is less than the specified maximum value, **MAX**.

Once the input loop ends (by whatever means), the value of **count** contains one more than the index value of the last element entered in each array. (Remember, we increment it after we enter each new element). This is checked in order to verify that at least two pairs of values were entered. If this wasn't the case, the program ends with a suitable message, since two odometer values are necessary to calculate a mileage value.

Producing the Results

The output is generated in the **for** loop. The control variable **i** runs from **1** to **count-1**, allowing mileage to be calculated as the difference between the current element, **miles[i]** and the previous element, **miles[i - 1]**. Note that an index value can be any expression evaluating to an integer that represents a legal index for the array in question.

If the value of an index expression lies outside of the range corresponding to legitimate array elements, you will be referencing a spurious data location that may contain other data, garbage, or even program code. If the reference to such an element appears in an expression, you will be using some arbitrary data value in the calculation, which will certainly produce a result that you did not intend. If you are storing a result in an array element using an illegal index value, you will overwrite whatever happens to be in that location. When this is part of your program code, the results will be catastrophic. If you use illegal index values, there are no warnings produced either by the compiler or at run-time. The only way to guard against this is to code your program to prevent it happening.

The output is generated by a single **cout** statement for all values entered, except for the first. A line number is also generated for each line of output using the loop control variable **i**. The miles per gallon is calculated directly in the output statement. You can use array elements in exactly the same way as any other variables in an expression.

Initializing Arrays

To initialize an array, the initializing values are enclosed within curly braces in the declaration and placed following an equals sign after the array name. An example of a declaration and initialization of an array would be this:

```
int cubic_inches[5] = { 200, 250, 300, 350, 400 };
```

The values in the initializing list correspond to successive index values of the array, so in this case **cubic_inches[0]** will have the value 200, **cubic_inches[1]** the value 250, **cubic_inches[2]** the value 300, and so on.

You mustn't specify more initializing values than there are elements in the list, but you can include fewer. If there *are* fewer, the values are assigned to successive elements, starting with the first element which has the index **0**. The array elements for which you didn't provide an initial value will be initialized with zero. This isn't the same as supplying no initializing list. Without an initializing list, the array elements will contain junk values. Also, if you include an initializing list, there must be at least one initializing value in it, otherwise the compiler will generate an error message. We can illustrate this with the following, rather limited, example.

TRY IT OUT — Initializing an Array

```
// EX4_02.CPP
// Demonstrating array initialization
#include <iostream>
#include <iomanip>
using namespace std;

int main()
{
    int value[5] = { 1, 2, 3 };
    int Junk [5];

    cout << endl;
    for(int i = 0; i < 5; i++)
        cout << setw(12) << value[i];

    cout << endl;
    for(i = 0; i < 5; i++)
        cout << setw(12) << Junk[i];

    cout << endl;
    return 0;
}
```

In this example we declare two arrays, the first of which, **value**, is initialized in part, and the second, **Junk**, is not initialized at all. The program generates two lines of output which on my computer look like this:

The second line (corresponding to values of **Junk[0]** to **Junk[4]**) may well be different on your computer.

How It Works

The first three values of the array **value** are the initializing values and the last two have the default value of 0. In the case of **Junk**, all the values are spurious since we didn't provide any initial values at all. The array elements will contain whatever values were left there by the program which last used these memory locations.

A convenient way to initialize a whole array to zero is simply to specify a single initializing value as 0. For example, the statement,

```
long data[100] = {0};        // Initialize all elements to zero
```

declares the array **data**, with all one hundred elements initialized with 0.

You can also omit the dimension of an array of numeric type, providing you supply initializing values. The number of elements in the array will be determined by the number of initializing values. For example, the array declaration,

```
int value[] = { 2, 3, 4 };
```

defines an array with three elements which will have the initial values 2, 3, and 4.

Character Arrays and String Handling

An array of type **char** is called a character array and is generally used to store a character string. A character string is a sequence of characters with a special character appended to indicate the end of the string. The string terminating character is defined by the escape sequence **'\0'**, and is sometimes referred to as a **null character**, being a byte with all bits as zero. The representation of a string in memory is shown in the figure below:

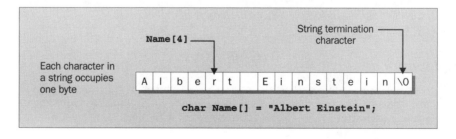

135

This illustrates how a string looks in memory and shows a form of declaration for a string that we will get to in a moment.

> *Each character in the string occupies one byte, so together with the null character, a string requires a number of bytes that is one greater than the number of characters contained in the string.*

We can declare a character array and initialize it with a string literal between quotation marks. For example:

```
char movie_star[15] = "Marilyn Monroe";
```

Note that the terminating `'\0'` will be supplied automatically by the compiler. If you include one explicitly in the string literal, you will end up with two of them. You must, however, include space for the terminating null in the number of elements that you allot to the array.

You can let the compiler work out the length of an initialized array for you, as we saw in the previous illustration. Have a look at the following declaration:

```
char President[] = "Ulysses Grant";
```

Because the dimension is unspecified, the compiler will allocate space for enough elements to hold the initializing string, plus the terminating null character. In this case it allocates 14 elements for the array **President**. Of course, if you want to use this array later for storing a different string, its length (including the terminating null character) must not exceed 14 bytes. In general, it is your responsibility to ensure that the array is large enough for any string you might subsequently want to store.

> *You may well have heard of **Unicode**, or seen references to it in the Visual C++ documentation, so we'll just outline it here so that you know what it refers to. For supporting international character sets, a character type **wchar_t** is supported, which uses 2 bytes for each character. This allows 65,536 different characters to be represented, which makes it possible for all the national character sets to be given unique 16-bit codes, so they can coexist within a single 2-byte character set. This makes creating applications intended for multinational markets much easier.*
>
> *The definition of the 2-byte character set which incorporates all national character sets, as well as all other standard technical and publishing symbols, is called **Unicode**. The MFC provides facilities for using the Unicode character set in your Windows programs. We won't be going into any further detail on Unicode in this book, not because it's difficult — it isn't — but simply because we have to stop somewhere!*

String Input

The header file **iostream** contains definitions of a number of functions for reading characters from the keyboard. The one that we shall look at here is the function **getline()**, which reads a string into a character array. This is typically used with statements such as this:

```
const int MAX = 80;
char name[MAX];
```

```
...
cin.getline(name, MAX, '\n');
```

These statements first declare a **char** array name with **MAX** elements and then read characters from **cin** using the function **getline()**. The source of the data, **cin**, is written as shown, with a period separating it from the function name. The significance of various parts of the input statement is shown below:

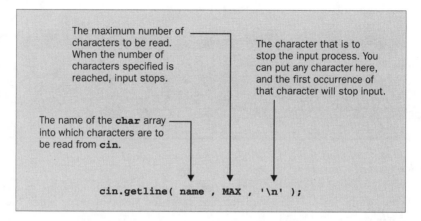

The maximum number of characters to be read. When the number of characters specified is reached, input stops.

The character that is to stop the input process. You can put any character here, and the first occurrence of that character will stop input.

The name of the **char** array into which characters are to be read from **cin**.

```
cin.getline( name , MAX , '\n' );
```

Characters are read from **cin** until the **'\n'** (newline or end line character) character is read, or when **MAX** **-** **1** characters have been read (plus the terminating **'\0'** is appended), whichever occurs first. The **'\n'** character is generated when you press the *Return* key on your keyboard, and is therefore usually the most convenient character to end input. You can, however, specify something else if you wish by changing the last argument. The **'\n'** isn't stored in the input array **name**, but a **'\0'** is added at the end of the input string in the array.

We will learn more about this form of syntax when we discuss classes later on. Meanwhile, we can take it for granted, and use it in an example.

TRY IT OUT — Programming With Strings

We now have enough knowledge to write a simple program to read a string, and then count how many characters it contains.

```cpp
// EX4_03.CPP
// Counting string characters
#include <iostream>
using namespace std;

int main()
{
    const int MAX = 80;                    // Maximum array dimension
    char buffer[MAX];                      // Input buffer
    int count = 0;                         // Character count

    cout << "Enter a string of less than 80 characters:\n";
    cin.getline(buffer, MAX, '\n');        // Read a string until \n

    while(buffer[count] != '\0')           // Increment count as long as
        count++;                           // the current character is not null
```

```
    cout << endl
        << "The string \"" << buffer
        << "\" has " << count << " characters.";

    cout << endl;
    return 0;
}
```

Typical output from this program is illustrated below:

```
Ex4_03                                                    _ □ ✕
Enter a string of less than 80 characters:
Radiation fades your genes

The string "Radiation fades your genes" has 26 characters.
Press any key to continue
```

How It Works

This program declares a character array **buffer** and reads a character string from the keyboard after displaying a prompt for the input. Reading from the keyboard ends when the user presses *Return*, or when **MAX-1** characters have been read.

A **while** loop is used to count the number of characters read. The loop continues as long as the current character referenced with **buffer[count]** is not **'\0'**. This sort of checking on the current character (while stepping through an array) is a common technique in C++. The only action in the loop is to increment **count** for each non-null character.

There is also a library function, **strlen()**, that can save you the trouble of coding it yourself. If you use it, you need to include the **cstring** header file in your program.

Finally in our example, the string and the character count is displayed with a single output statement. Note how we need to use the escape character **'\"'** to output a quote.

Multidimensional Arrays

The arrays that we have defined so far with one index are referred to as **one-dimensional** arrays. An array can also have more than one index value, in which case it is called a **multidimensional** array. Suppose we have a field in which we are growing bean plants in rows of 10, and the field contains 12 such rows (so there are 120 plants in all). We could declare an array to record the weight of beans produced by each plant using the following statement:

```
double beans[12][10];
```

This declares the two-dimensional array **beans**, the first index being the row number, and the second index the number within the row. To refer to any particular element requires two indices. For example, we could set the value of the element reflecting the fifth plant in the third row with the following statement:

```
beans[2][4] = 10.7;
```

Remember that the index values start from zero, so the row index value is **2** and the index for the fifth plant within the row is **4**.

Being successful bean farmers, we might have several identical fields planted with beans in the same pattern. Assuming that we have eight fields, we could use a three-dimensional array, declared thus:

```
double beans[8][12][10];
```

This will record production for all of the plants in each of the fields, the leftmost index referencing a particular field. If we ever get to bean farming on an international scale, we will be able to use a four-dimensional array, with the extra dimension designating the country. Assuming that you're as good a salesman as you are a farmer, growing this quantity of beans to keep up with the demand may start to affect the ozone layer.

Arrays are stored in memory such that the rightmost index value varies most rapidly. You can visualize the array **data[3][4]** as three one-dimensional arrays of four elements each. The arrangement of this array is illustrated below:

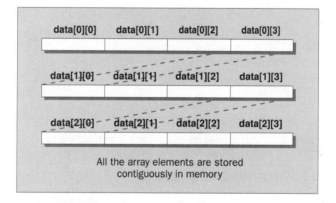

All the array elements are stored
contiguously in memory

Initializing Multidimensional Arrays

To initialize a multidimensional array, you use an extension of the method used for a one-dimensional array. For example, you can initialize a two-dimensional array, **data**, with the following declaration:

```
long data[2][4] = {
                   { 1,  2,  3,  5 },
                   { 7, 11, 13, 17 }
                 };
```

Thus, the initializing values for each row of the array are contained within their own pair of curly braces. Since there are four elements in each row, there are four initializing values in each group, and since there are two rows, there are two groups between braces, each group of initializing values being separated from the next by a comma.

You can omit initializing values in any row, in which case the remaining array elements in the row will be zero. For example, in the declaration:

```
long data[2][4] = {
                     { 1,  2,  3        },
                     { 7, 11           }
                  };
```

the initializing values have been spaced out to show where values have been omitted. The elements **data[0][3]**, **data[1][2]**, and **data[1][3]** have no initializing values and will therefore be zero.

If you wanted to initialize the whole array with zeros you could simply write:

```
long data[2][4] = {0};
```

If you are initializing arrays with even more dimensions, remember that you need as many nested braces for groups of initializing values as there are dimensions in the array.

TRY IT OUT — Storing Multiple Strings

We can use a single two-dimensional array to store several strings. We can see how this works with an example:

```
// EX4_04.CPP
// Storing strings in an array.
#include <iostream>
using namespace std;

int main()
{
   char stars[6][80] = { "Robert Redford",
                         "Hopalong Cassidy",
                         "Lassie",
                         "Slim Pickens",
                         "Boris Karloff",
                         "Oliver Hardy"
                       };
   int dice = 0;

   cout << endl
        << " Pick a lucky star!"
        << " Enter a number between 1 and 6: ";
   cin >> dice;

   if(dice >= 1 && dice <= 6)                // Check input validity
      cout << endl                           // Output star name
           << "Your lucky star is " << stars[dice - 1];
   else
      cout << endl                           // Invalid input
           << "Sorry, you haven't got a lucky star.";

   cout << endl;
   return 0;
}
```

How It Works

Apart from its incredible inherent entertainment value, the main point of interest in this example is the declaration of the array **stars**. It is a two-dimensional **char** array, which can hold up to 6 strings, each of which can be up to 80 characters (including the terminating null character that is automatically added by the compiler). The initializing strings for the array are enclosed between braces and separated by commas.

> *One disadvantage of using arrays in this way is the memory that is almost invariably left unused. All of our strings are less than 80 characters and the surplus elements in each row of the array are wasted.*

You can also let the compiler work out how many strings you have by omitting the first array dimension and declaring it as follows:

```
char stars[][80] = { "Robert Redford",
                     "Hopalong Cassidy",
                     "Lassie",
                     "Slim Pickens",
                     "Boris Karloff",
                     "Oliver Hardy"
                   };
```

This will cause the compiler to define the first dimension to accommodate the number of initializing strings that you have specified. Since we have six the result is exactly the same, but it avoids the possibility of an error. Here you can't omit both array dimensions. The rightmost dimension must always be defined.

> *Note the semicolon at the end of the declaration. It's easy to forget it when there are initializing values for an array.*

Where we need to reference a string for output in the following statement, we need only specify the first index value:

```
cout << endl                            // Output star name
     << "Your lucky star is " << stars[dice - 1];
```

A single index value selects a particular 80-element sub-array, and the output operation will display the contents up to the terminating null character. The index is specified as **dice - 1** as the **dice** values are from **1** to **6**, whereas the index values clearly need to be from **0** to **5**.

Indirect Data Access

The variables that we have dealt with so far provide you with the ability to name a memory location in which you can store data of a particular type. The contents of a variable are either entered from an external source, such as the keyboard, or calculated from other values that are entered. There is another kind of variable in C++ which does not store data that you normally enter or calculate, but greatly extends the power and flexibility of your programs. This kind of variable is called a **pointer**.

What is a Pointer?

Each memory location that you use to store a data value has an address. The address provides the means for your PC hardware to reference a particular data item. A pointer is a variable that stores an address of another variable of a particular type. A pointer has a variable name just like any other variable and also has a type that designates what kind of variables its contents refer to. Note that the type of a pointer variable includes the fact that it's a pointer. A variable that is a pointer, that can contain addresses of locations in memory containing values of type **int**, is of type 'pointer to **int**'.

Declaring Pointers

The declaration for a pointer is similar to that of an ordinary variable, except that the pointer name has an asterisk in front of it to indicate that it's a variable which is a pointer. For example, to declare a pointer **pnumber** of type **long**, you could use the following statement:

```
long* pnumber;
```

This declaration has been written with the asterisk close to the type name. If you wish, you can also write it as:

```
long *pnumber;
```

The compiler won't mind at all. However, the type of the variable **pnumber** is 'pointer to **long**', which is often indicated by placing the asterisk close to the type name.

You can mix declarations of ordinary variables and pointers in the same statement. For example:

```
long* pnumber, number = 99;
```

This declares the pointer **pnumber** of type 'pointer to **long**' as before, and also declares the variable **number**, of type **long**. On balance, it's probably better to declare pointers separately from other variables, otherwise the statement can appear misleading as to the type of the variables declared, particularly if you prefer to place the ***** adjacent to the type name. The following statements certainly look clearer and putting declarations on separate lines enables you to add comments for them individually, making for a program that is easier to read.

```
long number = 99;     // Declaration and initialization of long variable
long* pnumber;        // Declaration of variable of type pointer to long
```

It's a common convention in C++ to use variable names beginning with **p** to denote pointers. This makes it easier to see which variables in a program are pointers, which in turn can make a program easier to follow.

Let's take an example to see how this works, without worrying about what it's for. We will come on to how this is used very shortly. Suppose we have the **long** integer variable **number**, as we declared it above containing the value **99**. We also have the pointer, **pnumber**, of type pointer to **long**, which we could use to store the address of our variable **number**. But how can we obtain the address of a variable?

The Address-Of Operator

What we need is the address-of operator, **&**. This is a unary operator which obtains the address of a variable. It's also called the reference operator, for reasons we will discuss later in this chapter. To set up the pointer that we have just discussed, we could write this assignment statement:

```
pnumber = &number;            // Store address of number in pnumber
```

The result of this operation is illustrated below:

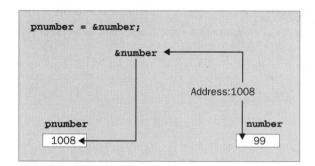

You can use the operator **&** to obtain the address of any variable, but you need a pointer of the same type to store it. If you want to store the address of a **double** variable for example, the pointer must have been declared as **double***, which is type 'pointer to **double**'.

Using Pointers

Taking the address of a variable and storing it in a pointer is all very well, but the really interesting aspect is how you can use it. Fundamental to using a pointer is accessing the data value in the variable to which a pointer points. This is done using the indirection operator, *****.

The Indirection Operator

The indirection **operator**, *****, is used with a pointer to access the contents of the variable pointed to. The name 'indirection operator' stems from the fact that the data is accessed indirectly. It is also called the de-reference operator, and the process of accessing the data in the variable pointed to by a pointer is termed **de-referencing** the pointer.

One aspect of this operator that can seem confusing is the fact that we now have several different uses for the same symbol, *****. It is the multiply operator, the indirection operator, and it is used in the declaration of a pointer. Each time you use *****, the compiler is able to distinguish its meaning by the context. When you multiply two variables, **A*B** for instance, then there's no meaningful interpretation of this expression for anything other than a multiply operation.

Why Use Pointers?

A question that usually springs to mind at this point is, "Why use pointers at all?" After all, taking the address of a variable you already know and sticking it in a pointer so that you can de-reference it seems like an overhead you can do without. There a several reasons why pointers are important.

First of all, as you will see shortly, you can use pointer notation to operate on data stored in an array, which often executes faster than if you use array notation. Secondly, when we get to define our own functions later in the book, you will see that pointers are used extensively for enabling access within a function to large blocks of data, such as arrays, that are defined outside the function. Thirdly and most importantly, you will also see later that you can allocate space for variables dynamically, that is, during program execution. This sort of capability allows your program to adjust its use of memory depending on the input to the program. Since you don't know in advance how many variables you are going to create dynamically, the only way you can do this is by using pointers — so make sure you get the hang of this bit.

TRY IT OUT — *Using Pointers*

We can try out various aspects of pointer operations with an example:

```cpp
//EX4_05.CPP
// Exercising pointers
#include <iostream>
using namespace std;

int main()
{
   long* pnumber = NULL;              // Pointer declaration & initialization
   long number1 = 55, number2 = 99;

   pnumber = &number1;               // Store address in pointer
   *pnumber += 11;                   // Increment number1 by 11
   cout << endl
        << "number1 = " << number1
        << "   &number1 = " << hex << pnumber;

   pnumber = &number2;               // Change pointer to address of number2
   number1 = *pnumber*10;            // 10 times number2

   cout << endl
        << "number1 = " << dec << number1
        << "    pnumber = " << hex << pnumber
        << "    *pnumber = " << dec << *pnumber;

   cout << endl;
   return 0;
}
```

On my computer, this example generates the following output:

```
Ex4_05                                                    _ □ ×

number1 = 66    &number1 = 0012FF78
number1 = 990    pnumber = 0012FF74    *pnumber = 99
Press any key to continue
```

How It Works

There is no input to this example. All operations are carried out with the initializing values for the variables. After storing the address of **number1** in the pointer **pnumber**, the value of **number1** is incremented indirectly through the pointer in this statement:

```
*pnumber += 11;                    // Increment number1 by 11
```

> *Note that when we first declared the pointer pnumber, we intialized it to* **NULL**. *We'll discuss pointer initialization in the next section.*

The indirection operator determines that we are adding 11 to the contents of the variable pointed to, **number1**. If we forgot the *****, we would be attempting to add 11 to the address stored in the pointer.

The values of **number1**, and the address of **number1** stored in **pnumber**, are displayed. We use the **hex** manipulator to generate the address output in hexadecimal notation.

You can obtain the value of ordinary integer variables as hexadecimal output by using the manipulator **hex**. You send it to the output stream in the same way that we have applied **endl**, with the result that all following output will be in hexadecimal notation. If you want the following output to be decimal, you need to use the manipulator **dec** in the next output statement to switch the output back to decimal mode again.

After the first line of output, the contents of **pnumber** are set to the address of **number2**. The variable **number1** is then changed to the value of 10 times **number2**:

```
number1 = *pnumber*10;             // 10 times number2
```

This is calculated by accessing the contents of **number2** indirectly through the pointer. The second line of output shows the results of these calculations

The address values you see in your output may well be different from those shown in the screenshot above since they reflect where the program is loaded in memory, which depends on how your operating system is configured. The **0x** prefixing the address values indicates that they are hexadecimal numbers. Note that the addresses **&number1** and **pnumber** (when it contains **&number2)** differ by four bytes. This shows that **number1** and **number2** occupy adjacent memory locations, as a **long** variable requires four bytes. The output demonstrates that everything is working as we expect.

Initializing Pointers

Just as with arrays, using pointers that aren't initialized is extremely hazardous. If you do this, you can overwrite random areas of memory. The resulting damage just depends on how unlucky you are, so it's more than just a good idea to initialize your pointers. It's very easy to initialize a pointer to the address of a variable that has already been defined. Here you can see that we have initialized the pointer **pnumber** with the address of the variable **number** just by using the operator **&** with the variable name:

```
int number = 0;              // Initialized integer variable
int* pnumber = &number;      // Initialized pointer
```

When initializing a pointer with another variable, remember that the variable must already have been declared prior to the pointer declaration.

Of course, you may not want to initialize a pointer with the address of a specific variable when you declare it. In this case, you can initialize it with the pointer equivalent of zero. For this, Visual C++ provides the symbol **NULL** that is already defined as 0, so you can declare and initialize a pointer using the following statement, rather like we did in the last example:

```
int* pnumber = NULL;          // Pointer not pointing to anything
```

This ensures that the pointer doesn't contain an address that will be accepted as valid, and provides the pointer with a value that you can check in an **if** statement, such as:

```
if(pnumber == NULL)
   cout << endl << "pnumber is null.";
```

Of course, you can also initialize a pointer explicitly with 0, which will also ensure that it is assigned a value that doesn't point to anything. No object can be allocated the address 0, so in effect 0 used as an address indicates that the pointer has no target. In spite of it being arguably somewhat less legible, if you expect to run your code with other compilers, it is preferable to use 0 as an initializing value for a pointer that you want to be null.

> *This is also more consistent with the current 'good practice' in C++, the argument being that if you have an object with a name in C++, it should have a type. However, **NULL** does not have a type — it's an alias for 0.*

To use **0** as the initializing value for a pointer you would simply write:

```
int* pnumber = 0;             // Pointer not pointing to anything
```

To check whether a pointer contains a valid address, you could use the statement:

```
if(pnumber == NULL)           // or pnumber == 0
   cout << endl << "pnumber is null.";
```

Equally well, you could use the statement,

```
if(!pnumber)
   cout << endl << "pnumber is null.";
```

which does exactly the same as the previous example.

Of course, you can also use the form:

```
if(pnumber != 0)
   // Pointer is valid, so do something useful
```

> *The address pointed to by the **NULL** pointer contains a junk value. You should never attempt to de-reference a null pointer as it will cause your program to end immediately.*

Pointers to char

A pointer of type **char*** has the interesting property that it can be initialized with a string literal. For example, we can declare and initialize such a pointer with the statement:

```
char* proverb = "A miss is as good as a mile.";
```

This looks very similar to initializing a **char** array but it's slightly different. This will create a string literal (actually an array of type **const char**) with the character string appearing between the quotes and terminated with **/0**, and store the address of the literal in the pointer **proverb**. The address of the literal will be the address of its first character. This is shown in the figure below:

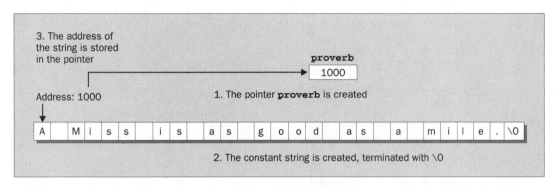

3. The address of the string is stored in the pointer

proverb

1000

Address: 1000

1. The pointer **proverb** is created

| A | | M | i | s | s | | i | s | | a | s | | g | o | o | d | | a | s | | a | | m | i | l | e | . | \0 |

2. The constant string is created, terminated with \0

TRY IT OUT — Lucky Stars With Pointers

We could rewrite our lucky stars example using pointers instead of an array to see how that would work:

```
// EX4_06.CPP
// Initializing pointers with strings
#include <iostream>
using namespace std;

int main()
{
   char* pstr1 = "Robert Redford";
   char* pstr2 = "Hopalong Cassidy";
   char* pstr3 = "Lassie";
   char* pstr4 = "Slim Pickens";
   char* pstr5 = "Boris Karloff";
   char* pstr6 = "Oliver Hardy";
   char* pstr  = "Your lucky star is ";

   int dice = 0;

   cout << endl
        << " Pick a lucky star!"
        << " Enter a number between 1 and 6: ";
   cin >> dice;
```

```
      cout << endl;
      switch(dice)
      {
         case 1: cout << pstr << pstr1;
                 break;

         case 2: cout << pstr << pstr2;
                 break;

         case 3: cout << pstr << pstr3;
                 break;

         case 4: cout << pstr << pstr4;
                 break;

         case 5: cout << pstr << pstr5;
                 break;

         case 6: cout << pstr << pstr6;
                 break;

         default: cout << "Sorry, you haven't got a lucky star.";
      }

      cout << endl;
      return 0;
   }
```

How It Works

The array in **Ex4_04.cpp** has been replaced by the six pointers, **pstr1** to **pstr6**, each initialized with a name. We have also declared an additional pointer, **pstr**, initialized with the phrase that we want to use at the start of a normal output line. Because we have discrete pointers, it is easier to use a **switch** statement to select the appropriate output message than to use an **if** as we did in the original version. Any incorrect values that are entered are all taken care of by the **default** option of the **switch**.

Outputting the string pointed to by a pointer couldn't be easier. As you can see, you simply write the pointer name. It may cross your mind at this point that in **Ex4_05.cpp** we wrote a pointer name in the output statement and the address that it contained was displayed. Why is it different here? The answer lies in the way the output operation views a pointer of type 'pointer to **char**'. It treats a pointer of this type as a string (which is an array of **char**), and so outputs the string itself, rather than its address.

Using pointers has eliminated the waste of memory that occurred with the array version of this program, but the program seems a little long-winded now — there must be a better way. Indeed there is — using an array of pointers.

TRY IT OUT — Arrays of Pointers

With an array of pointers of type **char**, each element can point to an independent string, and the lengths of each of the strings can be different. We can declare an array of pointers in the same way that we declare a normal array. Let's go straight to rewriting the previous example using a pointer array:

```cpp
// EX4_07.CPP
// Initializing pointers with strings
#include <iostream>
using namespace std;

int main()
{
   char* pstr[] =  { "Robert Redford",          // Initializing a pointer array
                     "Hopalong Cassidy",
                     "Lassie",
                     "Slim Pickens",
                     "Boris Karloff",
                     "Oliver Hardy"
                   };
   char* pstart = "Your lucky star is ";

   int dice = 0;

   cout << endl
        << " Pick a lucky star!"
        << " Enter a number between 1 and 6: ";
   cin >> dice;

   cout << endl;
   if(dice >= 1 && dice <= 6)                          // Check input validity
      cout << pstart << pstr[dice - 1];                // Output star name

   else
      cout << "Sorry, you haven't got a lucky star.";  // Invalid input

   cout << endl;
   return 0;
}
```

How It Works

In this case, we are nearly getting the best of all possible worlds. We have a one-dimensional array of **char** pointers declared such that the compiler works out what the dimension should be from the number of initializing strings. The memory usage that results from this is illustrated below:

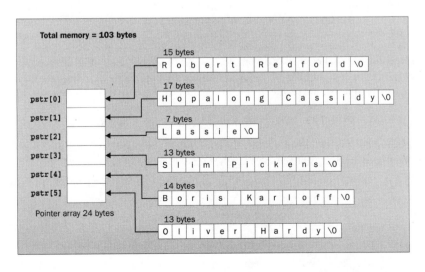

Compared to using a 'normal' array, the pointer array carries less overhead in terms of space. With an array, we would need to make each row the length of the longest string, and six rows of seventeen bytes each is 102 bytes, so by using a pointer array we have saved a whole... -1 bytes! What's gone wrong? The simple truth is that for this small number of relatively short strings, the size of the extra array of pointers is significant. You *would* make savings if you were dealing with more strings that were longer and had more variable lengths.

Space saving isn't the only advantage that you get by using pointers. In a lot of circumstances you save time too. Think of what happens if you want to move 'Oliver Hardy' to the first position and 'Robert Redford' to the end. With the pointer array as above you just need to swap the pointers — the strings themselves stay where they are. If we had stored these simply as strings, as we did in **Ex4_04.cpp**, a great deal of copying would be necessary — we would need to copy the whole string 'Robert Redford' to a temporary location while we copied 'Oliver Hardy' in its place, and then we would need to copy 'Robert Redford' to the end position. This would require significantly more computer time to execute.

Since we are using **pstr** as the array name, the variable holding the start of the output message needs to be different, so we have called it **pstart**. We select the string that we want to output by means of a very simple **if** statement, similar to that of the original version of the example. We either display a star selection, or a suitable message if the user enters an invalid value.

One weakness of the way we have written the program is that the code assumes there are six options, even though the compiler is allocating the space for the pointer array from the number of initializing strings that we supply. So if we add a string to the list, we have to alter other parts of the program to take account of this. It would be nice to be able to add strings and have the program automatically adapt to however many strings there are.

The sizeof Operator

A new operator will help us here. The **sizeof** operator produces an integer constant that gives the number of bytes occupied by its operand. For example, with the variable **dice** from the previous example, the expression,

```
cout << sizeof dice;
```

will output the value **4**, since **dice** was declared as **int** and therefore occupies 4 bytes.

The **sizeof** operator can be applied to an element in an array or to the whole array. When the operator is applied to an array name by itself, it produces the number of bytes occupied by the whole array, whereas when it is applied to a single element with the appropriate index value or values, it results in the number of bytes occupied by that element. Thus, in the last example, we could output the number of elements in the **pstr** array with the expression:

```
cout << (sizeof pstr) / (sizeof pstr[0]);
```

The expression divides the number of bytes occupied by the whole pointer array by the number of bytes occupied by the first element of the array. Since all elements of the array occupy the same amount of memory, the result is the number of elements in the array.

> *Remember that **pstr** is an array of pointers — using the **sizeof** operator on the array or on individual elements will not tell us anything about the memory occupied by the text strings.*

The **sizeof** operator can also be applied to a type name rather than a variable, in which case the result is the number of bytes occupied by a variable of that type. The type name should be enclosed between parentheses. For example, after executing the statement,

```
long_size = sizeof(long);
```

the variable **long_size** will have the value **4**.

The result returned by **sizeof** is obviously an integer and you can always treat it as such. Its precise type is actually **size_t**, which is used for values measured in bytes. The type **size_t**, which will pop up in various contexts from time to time, is defined in various standard libraries in Visual C++ and is equivalent to **unsigned int**.

TRY IT OUT — Using the sizeof Operator

We can use this to amend the last example so that it automatically adapts to an arbitrary number of string values from which to select:

```
// EX4_08.CPP
// Flexible array management using sizeof
#include <iostream>
using namespace std;

int main()
{
   char* pstr[] = { "Robert Redford",          // Initializing a pointer array
                    "Hopalong Cassidy",
                    "Lassie",
                    "Slim Pickens",
                    "Boris Karloff",
                    "Oliver Hardy"
                  };
   char* pstart = "Your lucky star is ";
   int count = (sizeof pstr) / (sizeof pstr[0]);   // Number of array elements

   int dice = 0;

   cout << endl
        << " Pick a lucky star!"
        << " Enter a number between 1 and " << count << ": ";
   cin >> dice;

   cout << endl;
   if(dice >= 1 && dice <= count)               // Check input validity
      cout << pstart << pstr[dice - 1];         // Output star name

   else
      cout << "Sorry, you haven't got a lucky star."; // Invalid input
```

151

```
        cout << endl;
        return 0;
}
```

How It Works

As you can see, the changes required in the example are very simple. We just calculate the number of elements in the pointer array **pstr** and store the result in **count**. Then, wherever the total number of elements in the array was referenced as **6**, we just use the variable **count**. You could now just add a few more names to the list of lucky stars and everything affected in the program will be adjusted automatically.

Constant Pointers and Pointers to Constants

The array **pstr** in the last example is clearly not intended to be modified in the program, and nor are the strings being pointed to, nor the variable **count**. It would be a good idea to ensure that these didn't get modified in error in the program. We could very easily protect the variable **count** from accidental modification by writing this:

```
const int count = (sizeof pstr) / (sizeof pstr[0]);
```

However, the array of pointers deserves closer examination. We declared the array like this:

```
char* pstr[] = { "Robert Redford",    // Initializing a pointer array
                 "Hopalong Cassidy",
                 "Lassie",
                 "Slim Pickens",
                 "Boris Karloff",
                 "Oliver Hardy"
               };
```

Each pointer in the array is initialized with the address of a string literal, "Robert Redford", "Hopalong Cassidy" and so on. The type of a string literal is 'array of **const char**' so we are storing the address of a const array in a non-**const** pointer. The reason the compiler allows us to assign a string literal to an array of **char*** is for reasons of backwards compatibility with existing code. If you try to alter the character array with a statement like this,

```
*pstr[0] = 'X';
```

then the program will crash when you try to run it.

We don't really want to have unexpected behavior like the program crashing at run time, and we can prevent it. A far better way of writing the declaration is as follows:

```
const char* pstr[] = { "Robert Redford",    // Array of pointers
                       "Hopalong Cassidy",  // to constants
                       "Lassie",
                       "Slim Pickens",
                       "Boris Karloff",
                       "Oliver Hardy"
                     };
```

In this case, there is no ambiguity about the **const**-ness of the objects pointed to by the elements of the pointer array. If you now attempt to change these objects, the compiler will flag this as an error at compile time.

However, we could still legally write this statement:

```
pstr[0] = pstr[1];
```

Those lucky individuals due to be awarded Mr. Redford would get Mr. Cassidy instead, since both pointers now point to the same name. Note that this isn't changing the values of the objects pointed to by the pointer array element — it is changing the value of the pointer stored in **pstr[0]**. We should therefore inhibit this kind of change as well, since some people may reckon that good old Hoppy may not have the same sex appeal as Robert. We can do this with the following statement:

```
// Array of constant pointers to constants
const char* const pstr[] = { "Robert Redford",
                             "Hopalong Cassidy",
                             "Lassie",
                             "Slim Pickens",
                             "Boris Karloff",
                             "Oliver Hardy"
                           };
```

To summarize, we can distinguish three situations relating to **const**, pointers and the objects to which they point:

- A pointer to a constant object
- A constant pointer to an object
- A constant pointer to a constant object

In the first situation, the object pointed to cannot be modified but we can set the pointer to point to something else:

```
const char* pstring = "Some text";
```

In the second, the address stored in the pointer can't be changed, but the object pointed to can be:

```
char* const pstring = "Some text";
```

Finally, in the third situation, both the pointer and the object pointed to have been defined as constant and, therefore, neither can be changed:

```
const char* const pstring = "Some text";
```

> *Of course, all this applies to pointers of any type. Type **char** is used here purely for illustrative purposes.*

Pointers and Arrays

Array names can behave like pointers under some circumstances. In most situations, if you use the name of a one-dimensional array by itself, it is automatically converted to a pointer to the first element of the array. Note that this is not the case when the array name is used as the operand of the **sizeof** operator.

If we have these declarations,

```
double* pdata;
double data[5];
```

then we can write this assignment:

```
pdata = data;         // Initialize pointer with the array address
```

This is assigning the address of the first element of the array **data** to the pointer **pdata**. Using the array name by itself refers to the address of the array. If we use the array name **data** with an index value, it refers to the contents of the element corresponding to that index value. So, if we want to store the address of that element in the pointer, then we have to use the address-of operator:

```
pdata = &data[1];
```

Here, the pointer **pdata** will contain the address of the second element of the array.

Pointer Arithmetic

You can perform arithmetic operations with pointers. You are limited to addition and subtraction in terms of arithmetic, but you can also perform comparisons using pointers to produce a logical result. Arithmetic with a pointer implicitly assumes that the pointer points to an array, and that the arithmetic operation is on the address contained in the pointer. For the pointer **pdata** for example, we could assign the address of the third element of the array **data** to a pointer with this statement:

```
pdata = &data[2];
```

In this case, the expression **pdata+1** would refer to the address of **data[3]**, the fourth element of the **data** array, so we could make the pointer point to this element by writing this statement:

```
pdata += 1;           // Increment pdata to the next element
```

This statement has incremented the address contained in **pdata** by the number of bytes occupied by one element of the array **data**. In general, the expression **pdata+n**, where **n** can be any expression resulting in an integer, will add **n*sizeof(double)** to the address contained in the pointer **pdata**, since it was declared to be of type pointer to **double**. This is illustrated below:

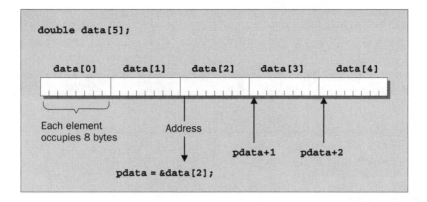

In other words, incrementing or decrementing a pointer works in terms of the type of the object pointed to. Increasing a pointer to **long** by one changes its contents to the next **long** address, and so increments the address by four. Similarly, incrementing a pointer to **short** by one will increment the address by two. The more common notation for incrementing a pointer is using the increment operator. For example, this,

```
pdata++;            // Increment pdata to the next element
```

is equivalent to (and more common than) the **+=** form. However, the **+=** form was used above to make it clear that while the increment value is actually specified as one, the effect is usually an increment greater than one, except in the case of a pointer to **char**.

> *The address resulting from an arithmetic operation on a pointer can be a value ranging from the address of the first element of the array to the address which is one beyond the last element. Outside of these limits, the behavior of the pointer is undefined.*

You can, of course, de-reference a pointer on which you have performed arithmetic (there wouldn't be much point to it otherwise). For example, assuming that **pdata** is still pointing to **data[2]**, then this statement,

```
*(pdata + 1) = *(pdata + 2);
```

is equivalent to this:

```
data[3] = data[4];
```

When you want to de-reference a pointer after incrementing the address it contains, the parentheses are necessary as the precedence of the indirection operator is higher than that of the arithmetic operators, **+** or **-**. If you write the expression ***pdata + 1**, instead of ***(pdata + 1)**, this would add one to the value stored at the address contained in **pdata**, which is equivalent to executing **data[2] + 1**. Since this isn't an lvalue, its use in the assignment statement above would cause the compiler to generate an error message.

We can use an array name as though it were a pointer for addressing elements of an array. If we have the same one-dimensional array as before, declared as

```
long data[5];
```

then using pointer notation, we can refer to the element `data[3]` for example as `*(data + 3)`. This kind of notation can be applied generally so that, corresponding to the elements `data[0]`, `data[1]`, `data[2]`, we can write `*data`, `*(data + 1)`, `*(data + 2)`, and so on.

TRY IT OUT — Array Names as Pointers

We could exercise this aspect of array addressing with a program to calculate prime numbers (a prime number is a number divisible only by itself and one).

```cpp
// EX4_09.CPP
// Calculating primes
#include <iostream>
#include <iomanip>
using namespace std;

int main()
{
   const int MAX = 100;                   // Number of primes required
   long primes[MAX] = { 2,3,5 };          // First three primes defined
   long trial = 5;                        // Candidate prime
   int count = 3;                         // Count of primes found
   int found = 0;                         // Indicates when a prime is found

   do
   {
      trial += 2;                         // Next value for checking
      found = 0;                          // Set found indicator
      for(int i = 0; i < count; i++)      // Try division by existing primes
      {
         found = (trial % *(primes + i)) == 0; // True for exact
                                          // division
            if(found)                     // If division is exact
               break;                     // it's not a prime
      }
      if (found == 0)                     // We got one...
         *(primes + count++) = trial;     // ...so save it in primes array
   }while(count < MAX);

   // Output primes 5 to a line
   for(int i = 0; i < MAX; i++)
   {
      if(i % 5 == 0)                      // New line on 1st, and every 5th line
         cout << endl;
      cout << setw(10) << *(primes + i);
   }
   cout << endl;
   return 0;
}
```

If you compile and execute this example you should get the output shown:

```
Ex4_09                                                    _ □ ×
        2        3        5        7       11
       13       17       19       23       29
       31       37       41       43       47
       53       59       61       67       71
       73       79       83       89       97
      101      103      107      109      113
      127      131      137      139      149
      151      157      163      167      173
      179      181      191      193      197
      199      211      223      227      229
      233      239      241      251      257
      263      269      271      277      281
      283      293      307      311      313
      317      331      337      347      349
      353      359      367      373      379
      383      389      397      401      409
      419      421      431      433      439
      443      449      457      461      463
      467      479      487      491      499
      503      509      521      523      541
Press any key to continue
```

How It Works

We have the usual **#include** statements for **iostream** for input and output, and for **iomanip** since we will be using a stream manipulator to set the field width for output.

We use the constant **MAX** to define the number of primes that we want the program to produce. The **primes** array, which stores the results, has the first three primes already defined to start the process off. All the work is done in two loops, the outer **do-while** loop, which picks the next value to be checked and adds the value to the **primes** array if it is prime, and the inner **for** loop that actually checks the value to see whether it's prime or not.

The algorithm in the **for** loop is very simple and is based on the fact that if a number is not a prime, then it must be divisible by one of the primes found so far — all of which are less than the number in question, since all numbers are either prime or a product of primes. In fact, only division by primes less than or equal to the square root of the number in question need to be checked, so this example isn't as efficient as it might be.

```
found = (trial % *(primes + i)) == 0;   // True for exact division
```

This statement sets the variable **found** to be **1** if there's no remainder from dividing the value in **trial** by the current prime ***(primes + i)** (remember that this is equivalent to **primes[i]**), and **0** otherwise. The **if** statement causes the **for** loop to be terminated if **found** has the value **1**, since the candidate in **trial** can't be a prime in that case.

After the **for** loop ends (for whatever reason), it's necessary to decide whether or not the value in **trial** was prime. This is indicated by the value in the indicator variable **found**.

```
*(primes + count++) = trial;   // ...so save it in primes array
```

If **trial** *does* contain a prime, this statement stores the value in **primes[count]** and then increments **count** through the postfix increment operator.

157

Once **MAX** number of primes have been found, they are output with a field width of 10 characters, 5 to a line, as a result of this statement:

```
if(i % 5 == 0)                          // New line on 1st, and every 5th line
    cout << endl;
```

This starts a new line when **i** has the values **0**, **5**, **10**, and so on.

TRY IT OUT — Counting Characters Revisited

To see how handling strings works in pointer notation, we could produce a version of the program we looked at earlier for counting the characters in a string:

```
// EX4_10.CPP
// Counting string characters using a pointer
#include <iostream>
using namespace std;

int main()
{
    const int MAX = 80;                 // Maximum array dimension
    char buffer[MAX];                   // Input buffer
    char* pbuffer = buffer;             // Pointer to array buffer

    cout << endl                        // Prompt for input
        << "Enter a string of less than "
        << MAX << " characters:"
        << endl;

    cin.getline(buffer, MAX, '\n');     // Read a string until \n

    while(*pbuffer)                     // Continue until \0
        pbuffer++;

    cout << endl
        << "The string \"" << buffer
        << "\" has " << pbuffer - buffer << " characters.";
    cout << endl;
    return 0;
}
```

How It Works

Here the program operates using the pointer **pbuffer** rather than the array name **buffer**. We don't need the **count** variable since the pointer is incremented in the **while** loop until \0 is found. When the \0 is found, **pbuffer** will contain the address of that position in the string. The count of the number of characters in the string entered is therefore the difference between the address stored in the pointer **pbuffer** and the address of the beginning of the array denoted by **buffer**.

We could also have incremented the pointer in the loop by writing the loop like this:

```
while(*pbuffer++);                      // Continue until \0
```

Now the loop contains no statements, only the test condition. This would work adequately, except for the fact that the pointer would be incremented after **\0** was encountered, so the address would be one more than the last position in the string. We would therefore need to express the count of the number of characters in the string as **pbuffer - buffer - 1**.

Note that here we can't use the array name in the same way that we have used the pointer. The expression **buffer++** is strictly illegal since you can't modify an array name — it isn't a pointer.

Using Pointers with Multidimensional Arrays

Using a pointer to store the address of a one-dimensional array is relatively straightforward, but with multidimensional arrays, things can get a little complicated. If you don't intend to do this, you can skip this section as it's a little obscure, but if your previous experience is with C, this section is worth a glance.

If you have to use a pointer with multidimensional arrays, you need to keep clear in your mind what is happening. By way of illustration, we can use an array **beans**, declared as follows:

```
double beans[3][4];
```

We can declare and assign a value to the pointer **pbeans** as follows:

```
double* pbeans;
pbeans = &beans[0][0];
```

Here we are setting the pointer to the address of the first element of the array, which is of type **double**. We could also set the pointer to the address of the first row in the array with the statement:

```
pbeans = beans[0];
```

This is equivalent to using the name of a one-dimensional array which is replaced by its address. We used this in the earlier discussion. However, because **beans** is a two-dimensional array, we cannot set an address in the pointer with the following statement:

```
pbeans = beans;          // Will cause an error!!
```

The problem is one of type. The type of the pointer you have defined is **double***, but the array is of type **double[3][4]**. A pointer to store the address of this array must be of type **double*[4]**. C++ associates the dimensions of the array with its type and the statement above is only legal if the pointer has been declared with the dimension required. This is done with a slightly more complicated notation than we have seen so far:

```
double (*pbeans)[4];
```

The parentheses here are essential, otherwise you would be declaring an array of pointers. Now the previous statement is legal, but this pointer can only be used to store addresses of an array with the dimensions shown.

Pointer Notation with Multidimensional Arrays

You can use pointer notation with an array name to reference elements of the array. You can reference each element of the array **beans** that we declared earlier, which had three rows of four elements, in two ways:

> Using the array name with two index values.

> Using the array name in pointer notation

Therefore, the following two statements are equivalent:

```
beans[i][j]
*(*(beans + i) + j)
```

Let's look at how these work. The first line uses normal array indexing to refer to the element with offset **j** in row **i** of the array.

We can determine the meaning of the second line by working from the inside, outwards. **beans** refers to the address of the first row of the array, so **beans + i** refers to row **i** of the array. The expression ***(beans + i)** is the address of the first element of row **i**, so ***(beans + i) + j** is the address of the element in row **i** with offset **j**. The whole expression therefore refers to the value of that element.

If you really want to be obscure — and it isn't recommended that you do so — the following two statements, where we have mixed array and pointer notation, are also legal references to the same element of the array:

```
*(beans[i] + j)
(*(beans + i))[j]
```

There is yet another aspect to the use of pointers which is really the most important of all: the ability to create variables dynamically. We will look into that next.

Dynamic Memory Allocation

Working with a fixed set of variables in a program can be very restrictive. The need often arises within an application to decide the amount of space to be allocated for storing different types of variables at execution time, depending on the input data for the program. With one set of data it may be appropriate to use a large integer array in a program, whereas with a different set of input data, a large floating point array may be required. Obviously, since any dynamically allocated variables can't have been defined at compile time, they can't be named in your source program. When they are created, they are identified by their address in memory which is contained within a pointer. With the power of pointers and the dynamic memory management tools in Visual C++, writing your programs to have this kind of flexibility is quick and easy.

The Free Store, Alias the Heap

In most instances, when your program is executed there is unused memory in your computer. This unused memory is called the **heap** in C++, or sometimes the **free store**. You can allocate space within the free store for a new variable of a given type using a special operator in C++ which returns the address of the space allocated. This operator is **new**, and it's complemented by the operator **delete**, which de-allocates memory previously allocated by **new**.

You can allocate space in the free store for some variables in one part of a program, and then release the allocated space and return it to the free store once you have finished with the variables concerned. This makes the memory available for reuse by other dynamically allocated variables, later in the same program.

You would want to use memory from the free store whenever you need to allocate memory for items that can only be determined at run time. One example of this might be allocating memory to hold a string entered by the user of your application. There is no way you can know in advance how large this string will need to be, so you would allocate the memory for the string at run time, using the **new** operator. Later, we'll look at an example of using the free store to dynamically allocate memory for an array, where the dimensions of the array are determined by the user at run time.

This can be a very powerful technique; it enables you to use memory very efficiently, and in many cases, it results in programs that can handle much larger problems, involving considerably more data than otherwise might be possible.

The Operators new and delete

Suppose that we need space for a **double** variable. We can define a pointer to type **double** and then request that the memory be allocated at execution time. We can do this using the operator **new** with the following statements:

```
double* pvalue = NULL;    // Pointer initialized with null
pvalue = new double;      // Request memory for a double variable
```

This is a good moment to recall that *all pointers should be initialized*. Using memory dynamically typically involves a number of pointers floating around, so it's important that they should not contain spurious values. You should try to arrange that if a pointer doesn't contain a legal address value, it is set to **0**.

The **new** operator in the second line of code above should return the address of the memory in the free store allocated to a **double** variable, and this address will be stored in the pointer **pvalue**. We can then use this pointer to reference the variable using the indirection operator as we have seen. For example:

```
*pvalue = 9999.0;
```

However, using a dynamic variable as shown here is very risky. The memory may not have been allocated, because the free store had been used up. Alternatively, it could be that the free store is fragmented by previous usage, meaning that there isn't a sufficient number of contiguous bytes to accommodate the variable for which you want to obtain space. In this case, the operator

new will return a **NULL** pointer value, so before using it we should always test for a valid address being returned and stored in our pointer. We could have done this by writing the following:

```
if(!(pvalue = new double))
{
   cout << endl
        << "Out of memory.";
   exit(1);
}
```

Here, we have called for the space to be allocated and the address to be stored in the pointer, **pvalue**, all within the **if** statement. If a **NULL** pointer value was returned, the **if** expression will be **true**, so the message will be displayed and the **exit()** function called to end the program. The **exit()** function is used when you want to terminate a program abnormally. The value between the parentheses is an integer (**int**) value that can be used to indicate the circumstances under which the program was terminated. If you use the **exit()** function, you should include the header file **cstdlib** into your program.

You can also initialize a variable created by **new**. Taking our example of the **double** variable which was allocated by **new** and the address stored in **pvalue**, we could have set the value to 999.0 as it was created with this statement:

```
pvalue = new double(999.0);   // Allocate a double and initialize it
```

When you no longer need a variable that has been dynamically allocated, you can free up the memory that it occupies in the free store with the **delete** operator:

```
delete pvalue;                // Release memory pointed to by pvalue
```

This ensures that the memory can be used subsequently by another variable. If you don't use **delete**, and subsequently store a different address value in the pointer **pvalue**, it will be impossible to free up the memory or to use the variable that it contains, since access to the address will have been lost.

Allocating Memory Dynamically for Arrays

Allocating memory for an array dynamically is very straightforward. If we wanted to allocate an array of type **char**, assuming **pstr** is a pointer to **char**, we could write the following statement:

```
pstr = new char[20];       // Allocate a string of twenty characters
```

This allocates space for a **char** array of 20 characters and stores its address in **pstr**.

To remove the array that we have just created in the free store, we must use the **delete** operator. The statement would look like this:

```
delete [] pstr;            // Delete array pointed to by pstr
```

> *Note the use of square brackets to indicate that what we are deleting is an array. When removing arrays from the free store, you should always include the square brackets or the results will be unpredictable. Note also that you do not specify any dimensions here, simply* [].

TRY IT OUT — Using Free Store

We can see how this works in practice by rewriting our program to calculate an arbitrary number of primes, but this time using memory in the free store to store them.

```cpp
// EX4_11.CPP
// Calculating primes using dynamic memory allocation
#include <iostream>
#include <iomanip>
#include <cstdlib>                 // For the exit function
using namespace std;

int main()
{
   long* pprime = 0;              // Pointer to prime array
   long trial = 5;                // Candidate prime
   int count = 3;                 // Count of primes found
   int found = 0;                 // Indicates when a prime is found
   int max = 0;                   // Number of primes required

   cout << endl
        << "Enter the number of primes you would like (at least 4): ";
   cin >> max;                    // Number of primes required

   if(max < 5)                    // Test the user input, and if less than 5
      max = 4;                    // change it to at least 4

   if(!(pprime = new long[max]))
   {
      cout << endl
           << "Memory allocation failed.";
      exit(1);                    // Terminate program
   }

   *pprime = 2;                   // Insert three
   *(pprime + 1) = 3;             // seed primes
   *(pprime + 2) = 5;

   do
   {
      trial += 2;                              // Next value for checking
      found = 0;                               // Set found indicator
      for(int i = 0; i < count; i++)           // Division by existing primes
      {
         found =(trial % *(pprime + i)) == 0;  // True for exact division
         if(found)                             // If division is exact
            break;                             // it's not a prime
      }
      if (found == 0)                          // We got one...
         *(pprime + count++) = trial;          // ...so save it in primes array
```

```
      } while(count < max);

      // Output primes 5 to a line
      for(int i = 0; i < max; i++)
      {
         if(i % 5 == 0)                          // New line on 1st, and every 5th line
            cout << endl;
         cout << setw(10) << *(pprime + i);
      }
      delete [] pprime;                          // Free up memory
      cout << endl;
      return 0;
   }
```

How It Works

Apart for the prompt for the number of primes required, the output from this example is the same as the previous version (assuming that the same number of primes is being generated), so we won't reproduce it again here.

In fact, the program is very similar to the previous version. We have an extra **#include** statement for **cstdlib** because we are using the function **exit()** if we run out of memory. After receiving the number of primes required in the **int** variable **max**, we allocate an array of that size in the free store using the operator **new**. Note that we've made sure that **max** can be no less than 4. This is because the program requires space to be allocated in the free store for at least the three seed primes, plus one new one. We specify the size of the array required by putting the variable **max** between the square brackets following the array type specification. The pointer value, returned by **new** and stored in the pointer **pprime**, is validated in the **if** statement. If it turns out to be **NULL**, a message is displayed and the program is exited.

```
   if(!(pprime = new long[max]))
   {
      cout << endl
           << "Memory allocation failed.";
      exit(1);                        // Terminate program
   }
```

Assuming that the memory allocation is successful, the first three array elements are set to the values of the first three primes.

> *We can't specify initial values for elements of an array allocated dynamically. We have to use explicit assignment statements if we want to set initial values for elements of the array.*

The calculation of the prime numbers is exactly as before; the only change is that the name of the pointer we have here, **pprime**, is substituted for the array name **primes**, used in the previous version. Equally, the output process is the same. Acquiring space dynamically is really not a problem at all. Once it has been allocated, it in no way affects how the computation is written.

Once we have finished with the array, we remove it from the free store using the **delete** operator, not forgetting to include the square brackets to indicate that it is an array we are deleting.

```
delete [] pprime;                    // Free up memory
```

Dynamic Allocation of Multidimensional Arrays

Allocating memory in the free store for a multidimensional array involves using the operator **new** in only a slightly more complicated form than that for a one-dimensional array. Assuming that we have already declared the pointer **pbeans** appropriately, to obtain the space for our array **beans[3][4]** that we used earlier in this chapter, we could write this:

```
pbeans = new double [3][4];          // Allocate memory for a 3x4 array
```

Allocating space for a three-dimensional array simply requires the extra dimension specified with **new**, as in this example:

```
pBigArray = new double [5][10][10];   // Allocate memory for a 5x10x10 array
```

However many dimensions there are in the array that has been created, to destroy it and release the memory back to the free store you write the following:

```
delete [] pBigArray;                 // Release memory for array
```

You use just one pair of square brackets regardless of the dimensionality of the array with which you are dealing.

We have already seen that we can use a variable as the specification of the dimension of a one-dimensional array to be allocated by **new**. This extends to two or more dimensions only in that the leftmost dimension may be specified by a variable. All the other dimensions must be constants or constant expressions. So we could write this,

```
pBigArray = new double[max][10][10];
```

where **max** is a variable. However, specifying a variable for any other dimension will cause an error message to be generated by the compiler.

Using References

A **reference** appears to be similar to a pointer in many respects, which is why we've introduced it here, but it isn't the same thing at all. Its real significance will only become apparent when we get to discuss its use with functions, particularly in the context of object-oriented programming. Don't be misled by its simplicity and what might seem to be a trivial concept. As you will see later, references provide some extraordinarily powerful facilities, and in some contexts it will enable you to achieve results that would be impossible without using them.

What is a Reference?

A reference is an alias for another variable. It has a name that can be used in place of the original variable name. Since it is an alias, and not a pointer, the variable for which it is an alias has to be specified when the reference is declared, and unlike a pointer, a reference can't be altered to represent another variable.

Declaring and Initializing References

If we have a variable declared as follows,

```
long number = 0;
```

we can declare a reference for this variable using the following declaration statement:

```
long& rnumber = number;      // Declare a reference to variable number
```

The ampersand following the type **long** and preceding the name **rnumber**, indicates that a reference is being declared and the variable name it represents, **number**, is specified as the initializing value following the equals sign. Therefore, **rnumber** is of type 'reference to **long**'. The reference can now be used in place of the original variable name. For example, this statement:

```
rnumber += 10;
```

has the effect of incrementing the variable **number** by 10.

Let's contrast the reference **rnumber** with the pointer **pnumber**, declared in this statement:

```
long* pnumber = &number;      // Initialize a pointer with an address
```

This declares the pointer **pnumber**, and initializes it with the address of the variable **number**. This then allows the variable number to be incremented with a statement such as:

```
*pnumber += 10;               // Increment number through a pointer
```

You should see a significant distinction between using a pointer and using a reference. The pointer needs to be de-referenced and whatever address it contains is used to access the variable to participate in the expression. With a reference there is no need for de-referencing. In some ways, a reference is like a pointer that has already been de-referenced, although it can't be changed to reference another variable. The reference is the complete equivalent of the variable for which it is a reference. A reference may seem like just an alternative notation for a given variable, and here it certainly appears to behave like that. However, we shall see when we come to discuss functions in C++ that this is not quite true, and that it can provide some very impressive extra capabilities.

Summary

You are now familiar with all of the basic types of values in C++, how to create and use arrays of those types and how to create and use pointers. You have also been introduced to the idea of a reference. However, we have not exhausted all of these topics. We'll come back to arrays, pointers and references again later in the book. The important points that we have discussed in this chapter are:

▶ An array allows you to manage a number of variables of the same type using a single name. Each dimension of an array is defined between square brackets following the array name in the declaration of the array.

▶ Each dimension of an array is indexed starting from zero. Thus the fifth element of a one-dimensional array will have the index value 4.

▶ Arrays can be initialized by placing the initializing values between curly braces in the declaration.

▶ A pointer is a variable that contains the address of another variable. A pointer is declared as a 'pointer to *type*', and may only be assigned addresses of variables of the given type.

▶ A pointer can point to a constant object. Such a pointer can be reassigned to another object. A pointer may also be defined as **const**, in which case it can't be reassigned.

▶ A reference is an alias for another variable, and can be used in the same places as the variable it references. A reference must be initialized in its declaration.

▶ A reference can't be reassigned to another variable.

▶ The operator **sizeof** returns the number of bytes occupied by the object specified as its argument. Its argument may be a variable or a type name between parentheses.

▶ The operator **new** allocates memory dynamically in the free store. When memory has been assigned as requested, it returns a pointer to the beginning of the memory area provided. If memory cannot be assigned for any reason, a **NULL** pointer will be returned. Memory allocated by **new** can only be freed using the **delete** operator with the address originally returned by **new** as an argument.

The pointer mechanism is sometimes a bit confusing because it can operate at different levels within the same program. Sometimes it is operating as an address, and at other times it can be operating with the value stored at an address. It's very important that you feel at ease with the way pointers are used, so if you find that they are in any way unclear, try them out with a few examples of your own until you feel confident about applying them.

Exercises

Ex4-1: Given the following declarations,

```
int   i = 3;
int&  j = i;
int*  pi;
int   array[10];
```

what are the types of the following expressions?

a) `i`
b) `j`
c) `&i`
d) `pi`
e) `*pi`
f) `array`
g) `*array`
h) `pi[3]`
i) `pi + 3`

Ex4-2: Take [Prg2], and modify it so that it now has a 15-character string called **name** as a local variable, in addition to an integer. Modify the loop to ask for and print a number and a string. Save your solution as [Prg3].

Ex4-3: Declare a character array, and initialize it to a suitable string. Use a loop to change every other character to upper case.

Hint: in the ASCII character set, values for upper case characters are 32 less than their lower-case counterparts.

Ex4-4: Given the following code,

```
char c[] = "hello world!";
char* pc = &c[2];
```

what would you expect the following statements to produce?

a) `cout << c;`
b) `cout << c[3];`
c) `cout << pc;`
d) `cout << *(pc - 2);`
e) `cout << *pc - 2;`

Ex4-5: (Advanced) In the following declaration,

```
int** ppi;
```

what type is **ppi**? (Its name is a clue!) From what you know of the relationship between pointers and arrays, can you think of a way to construct a two-dimensional array using **ppi**?

Introducing Structure Into Your Programs

Up to now we haven't really been able to structure our program code in a modular fashion, since we've only been able to construct a program as a single function, **main()**; but we *have* been using library functions of various kinds. Whenever you write a C++ program, you should have a modular structure in mind from the outset and, as we shall see, a good understanding of how to implement functions is essential to object-oriented programming in C++. In this chapter, you'll learn:

- How to declare and write your own C++ functions
- What function arguments are, and how they are defined and used
- How arrays can be passed to and from a function
- What pass-by-value means
- How to pass pointers to functions
- How to use references as function arguments, and what pass-by-reference means
- How the **const** modifier affects function arguments
- How to return values from a function
- What recursion is and how it can be used

There's quite a lot to structuring your C++ programs, so to avoid indigestion, we won't try to swallow the whole thing in one gulp. Once we've chewed over and gotten the full flavor of the morsels listed above, we'll move on to the next chapter, where we shall get further into the meat of the topic.

Understanding Functions

First let's look at the broad principles of how a function works. A function is a self-contained block of code with a specific purpose. A function has a name that both identifies it and is used to call it for execution in a program. The name of a function is global, but is not necessarily unique in C++, as we shall see in the next chapter. However, functions which perform different actions should generally have different names.

The name of a function is governed by the same rules as those for a variable. A function name is, therefore, a sequence of letters and digits, the first of which is a letter, and where an underscore counts as a letter. The name of a function should generally reflect what it does, so for example, you might call a function that counts beans **CountBeans()**.

You pass information to a function by means of **arguments** specified when you invoke it. These arguments need to correspond with **parameters** appearing in the definition of the function. The arguments that you specify replace the parameters used in its definition when the function is executed. The code in the function then executes as though it was written using your argument values. The relationship between arguments in the function call and its parameters is illustrated below:

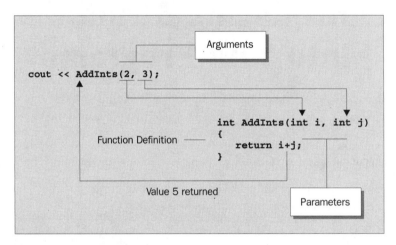

In this example, the function returns the sum of the two arguments passed to it. In general, a function returns either a single value to the point in the program where it was called, or nothing at all, depending on how the function is defined. You might think that returning a single value from a function is a constraint, but the single value returned can be a pointer which might contain the address of an array, for example. We will see more about how data is returned from a function a little later in this chapter.

Why Do You Need Functions?

One major advantage that a function offers is that it can be executed as many times as necessary from different points in a program. Without the ability to package a block of code into a function, programs would end up being much larger, since you would typically need to replicate the same code at various points in them. But the real reason that you need functions is to break up a program into easily manageable chunks.

Imagine a really big program, a million lines of code let's say. A program of this size would be virtually impossible to write without functions. Functions allow a program to be segmented so that it can be written piecemeal, and each piece tested independently before bringing it together with the other pieces. It also allows the work to be divided among members of a programming team, with each team member taking responsibility for a tightly specified piece of the program, with a well defined functional interface to the rest of the code.

Structure of a Function

As we have seen when writing the function **main()**, a function consists of a function header which identifies the function, followed by the body of the function between curly braces containing the executable code for the function. Let's look at an example. We could write a function to raise a value to a given power, that is, compute x^n:

```
double power(double x, int n)        // Function header
{                                    // Function body starts here...
   double result = 1.0;              // Result stored here
   for(int i = 1; i <= n; i++)
      result *= x;
   return result;
}                                    // ...and ends here
```

The Function Header

Let's first examine the function header in this example. This is the first line of the function:

```
double power(double x, int n)        // Function header
```

It consists of three parts:

▶ The type of the **return value** (**double** in this case)

▶ The name of the function, **power**

▶ The parameters of the function enclosed between parentheses

The return value is returned to the calling function when the function is executed, so when the function is called, it will have a value of type **double** in the expression in which it appears.

Our function has two parameters: **x**, the value to be raised to a given power which is of type **double**, and the value of the power, **n**, which is of type **int**. The computation that the function performs is written using these parameter variables together with another variable, **result**, declared in the body of the function.

> *No semicolon is required at the end of the function header.*

The General Form of a Function Header

The general form of a function header can be written as follows:

return_type FunctionName(parameter_list)

The ***return_type*** can be any legal type. If the function does not return a value, the return type is specified by the keyword **void**. The keyword **void** is also used to indicate the absence of parameters, so a function that has no parameters and doesn't return a value would have this header:

```
void MyFunction(void)
```

An empty parameter list also indicates that a function takes no arguments, so you could omit the keyword **void** between the parentheses as follows:

```
void MyFunction()
```

> *A function with a return type specified as **void** should not be used in an expression in the calling program. Because it doesn't return a value, it can't sensibly be part of an expression, so using it in this way will cause the compiler to generate an error message.*

The Function Body

The desired computation in a function is performed by the statements in the function body following the function header. The first of these in our example declares a variable **result** which is initialized with the value 1.0. The variable **result** is local to the function, as are all automatic variables declared within a function body. This means that the variable **result** ceases to exist after the function has completed execution.

The calculation is performed in the **for** loop. A loop control variable **i** is declared in the **for** loop which will assume successive values from **1** to **n**. The variable **result** is multiplied by **x** once for each loop iteration, so this occurs **n** times to generate the required value. If **n** is **0**, the statement in the loop won't be executed at all because the loop continuation condition will immediately fail, and so **result** will be left as 1.0.

As we've said, all the variables declared within the body of a function, as well as the parameters, are local to the function. There is nothing to prevent you from using the same names for variables in other functions for quite different purposes. Indeed, it's just as well this is so, because it would be extremely difficult to ensure variables' names were always unique within a program containing a large number of functions, particularly if the functions were not all written by the same person.

The scope of variables declared within a function is determined in the same way that we have already discussed. A variable is created at the point at which it is defined and ceases to exist at the end of the block containing it. There is one type of variable that is an exception to this — variables declared as **static**. We'll discuss static variables a little later in this chapter.

> *Be careful about masking global variables with local variables of the same name. We discussed this situation back in Chapter 2 and saw how we could use the scope resolution operator **::** to avoid any problems.*

The return Statement

The **return** statement returns the value of **result** to the point where the function was called. What might immediately strike you is that we just said **result** ceases to exist on completing execution of the function — so how is it returned? The answer is that a copy of the value being returned is made automatically, and this copy is available to the return point in the program.

The general form of the return statement is as follows,

```
return expression;
```

where ***expression*** must evaluate to a value of the type specified in the function header for the return value. The expression can be any expression you want, as long as you end up with a value of the required type. It can include function calls — even a call of the same function in which it appears, as we shall see later in this chapter.

If the type of return value has been specified as **void**, there must be no expression appearing in the **return** statement. It must be written simply as:

```
return;
```

Using a Function

At the point at which you use a function in a program, the compiler must know something about it. It needs enough information to be able to identify the function, and to verify that you are using it correctly. Unless the definition of the function that you intend to use appears earlier in the same source file, you must declare the function using a statement called a **function prototype**.

Function Prototypes

A prototype of a function provides the basic information that the compiler needs to check that a function is used correctly. It specifies the parameters to be passed to the function, the function name, and the type of the return value — essentially, it contains the same information as appears in the function header, with the addition of a semicolon. Clearly, the number of parameters and their types must be the same in the function prototype as they are in the function header in the definition of the function.

The prototypes for the functions called from within another function must appear before the statements doing the calling, and are usually placed at the beginning of the program source file. The header files that we've been including for standard library functions contain the prototypes of the functions provided by the library, amongst other things.

For our **power()** example, we could write the prototype as follows:

```
double power(double value, int index);
```

> *Don't forget that a semicolon is required at the end of a function prototype. Without it, you will get error messages from the compiler.*

Note that we have specified different names for the parameters in the function prototype to those we used in the function header when we defined the function. This is just to indicate that it's possible. Most often, the same names are used in the prototype and in the function header in the definition of the function, but this doesn't *have* to be so. The parameter names in the function prototype can be selected to aid understanding of the significance of the parameters.

If you like, you can even omit the names altogether in the prototype, and just write the following:

```
double power(double, int);
```

This is enough for the compiler to do its job. However, it's better practice to use some meaningful name in a prototype, since it aids readability and, in some cases, makes all the difference between clear code and confusing code. If you have a function with two parameters of the same type (suppose our index was also of type **double** in the function **power()** for example), the use of suitable names can indicate which parameter appears first and which second.

TRY IT OUT - Using a Function

We can see how all this goes together in an example exercising our **power()** function:

```
// EX5_01.CPP
// Declaring, defining, and using a function
#include <iostream>
using namespace std;

double power(double x, int n);      // Function prototype

int main(void)
{
   int index = 3;                   // Raise to this power
   double x = 3.0;                  // Different x from that in function power
   double y = 0.0;

   y = power(5.0, 3);               // Passing constants as arguments
   cout << endl
       << "5.0 cubed = " << y;

   cout << endl
       << "3.0 cubed = "
       << power(3.0, index);        // Outputting return value

   x = power(x, power(2.0, 2.0));   // Using a function as an argument
   cout << endl                     // with auto conversion of 2nd parameter
       << "x = " << x;

   cout << endl;
   return 0;
}

// Function to compute integral powers of a double value
// First argument is value, second argument is power index
double power(double x, int n)
{                                   // Function body starts here...
   double result = 1.0;            // Result stored here
   for(int i = 1; i <= n; i++)
      result *= x;
   return result;
}                                   // ...and ends here
```

This shows some of the ways in which we can use the function **power()**, specifying the arguments in a variety of ways. If you run this example, you'll get the following output:

```
Ex5_01                                                        _ □ ×
5.0 cubed = 125
3.0 cubed = 27
x = 81
Press any key to continue_
```

How It Works

After the usual **#include** statement for input/output and the **using** directive, we have the prototype for the function **power()**. If you tried deleting this and recompiling the program, the compiler wouldn't be able to process the calls to the function in **main()** and would instead generate two errors: error C2065: 'power' : undeclared identifier and error C2373: 'power' : redefinition; different type modifiers

In a change to previous examples, we've used the new keyword **void** in the function **main()** where the parameter list would usually appear to indicate that no parameters are to be supplied. Previously, we left the parentheses enclosing the parameter list empty, which is also interpreted in C++ as indicating that there are no parameters; but it's better to specify the fact by using the keyword **void**. As we saw, the keyword **void** can also be used as the return type for a function to indicate that no value is returned. If you specify the return type of a function as **void**, you must not place a value in any **return** statement within the function — otherwise you'll get an error message from the compiler.

You'll have gathered from some of our previous examples that using a function is very simple. To use the function **power()** to calculate 5.0^3 and store the result in a variable **y** in our example, we've written this:

```
y = power(5.0, 3);
```

The values 5.0 and 3 here are called **arguments**. They happen to be constants, but any expression can be used as an argument, as long as a value of the correct type is ultimately produced. The arguments substitute for the parameters **x** and **n**, which were used in the definition of the function. The computation is performed using these values, then a copy of the result, 125, will be returned to the calling function, **main()**, which will then be stored in **y**. You can think of the function as having this value in the statement or expression in which it appears. We then output the value of **y** to the screen:

```
cout << endl
     << "5.0 cubed = " << y;
```

The next call of the function is used within the output statement,

```
cout << endl
     << "3.0 cubed = "
     << power(3.0, index);        // Outputting return value
```

so the value returned is transferred directly to the output stream. Since we haven't stored the returned value anywhere, it is otherwise unavailable to us. The first argument in the call of the function here is a constant, while the second argument is a variable.

The function **power()** is next used in this statement:

```
x = power(x, power(2.0, 2.0));    // Using a function as an argument
```

Here the function will be called twice. The first call to the function will be the rightmost in the expression, appearing as an argument to the leftmost call. Although the arguments are both specified as 2.0, the function will actually be called with the first argument as 2.0 and the second argument as 2. The compiler will convert the **double** value specified for the second argument to **int**, because it knows from the function prototype (shown again below) that the type of the second parameter has been specified as **int**.

```
double power(double x, int n);        // Function prototype
```

There's a possible loss of data in converting from a double to an int and the compiler has instituted this conversion. This is a dangerous programming practice, and it is not at all obvious from the code that this conversion is intended. It is far better to be explicit in your code, and to pass the argument as an int in the first place, if that is the type that the function requires.

The **double** result 4.0 will be returned, and after converting this to **int**, the compiler will insert this value as the second argument in the next call of the function, with **x** as the first argument. Since **x** has the value 3.0, the value of 3.0^4 will be computed and the result, 81.0, stored in **x**. This sequence of events is illustrated below:

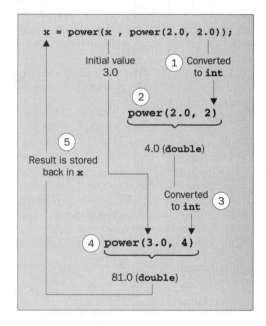

Again, this involves an implicit conversion by the compiler from a **double** to an **int**. We could write this code using **static_cast** to make absolutely clear that this conversion is intended:

```
x = power(x, static_cast<int>(power(2.0, static_cast<int>2.0)));
```

Using **static_cast** does not remove the possibility of losing data in the conversion of data types. Since we specify it, though, it is clear that we recognize that data loss might occur.

Passing Arguments to a Function

It's very important to understand how arguments are passed to a function, as it will affect how you write functions and how they will ultimately operate. There are also a number of pitfalls to be avoided, so we'll look at the mechanism for this quite closely.

The arguments specified when a function is called should usually correspond in type and sequence to the parameters appearing in the definition of the function. As we saw in the last example, if the type of an argument specified in a function call doesn't correspond with the type of parameter in the function definition, then (where possible) it will be converted to the required type, obeying the same rules as those for casting operands that we discussed in Chapter 2. If this proves not to be possible, you will get an error message from the compiler. However, even if the conversion is possible and the code compiles, it could well result in the loss of data (for example from type **long** to **short**) and should therefore be avoided.

There are two mechanisms used generally in C++ to pass parameters to functions. The first mechanism applies when you specify the parameters in the function definition as ordinary variables (*not* references). This is called the **pass-by-value** method of transferring data to a function so let's look into that first of all.

The Pass-by-value Mechanism

With this mechanism, the variables or constants that you specify as arguments are not passed to a function at all. Instead, copies of the arguments are created and these copies are used as the values to be transferred. We can show this in a diagram using the example of our function **power()**:

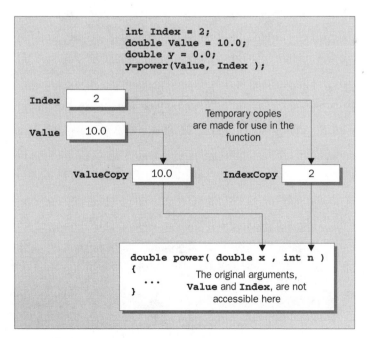

Each time you call the function **power()**, the compiler arranges for copies of the arguments that you specify to be stored in a temporary location in memory. During execution of the functions, all references to the function parameters will be mapped to these temporary copies of the arguments.

Purely to help your understanding of the diagram, we have used pseudo-names for the copies generated in the illustration. In reality, they do not exist in this form.

TRY IT OUT - Passing-by-value

One consequence of the pass-by-value mechanism is that a function can't directly modify the arguments passed. We can demonstrate this by deliberately trying to do so in an example:

```cpp
// EX5_02.CPP
// A futile attempt to modify caller arguments
#include <iostream>
using namespace std;

int incr10(int num);              // Function prototype

int main(void)
{
   int num = 3;

   cout << endl
           << "incr10(num) = " << incr10(num)
           << endl
           << "num = " << num;

   cout << endl;
   return 0;
}

// Function to increment a variable by 10
int incr10(int num)              // Using the same name might help...
{
   num += 10;                    // Increment the caller argument - hopefully

   return num;                   // Return the incremented value
}
```

How It Works

Of course, this program is doomed to failure. If you run it, you will get this output:

```
Ex5_02

incr10(num) = 13
num = 3
Press any key to continue_
```

This confirms that the original value of **num** remains untouched. The incrementing occurred on the copy of **num** that was generated, and was eventually discarded on exiting from the function.

Clearly, the pass-by-value mechanism provides you with a high degree of protection from having your caller arguments mauled by a rogue function, but it is conceivable that we might actually want to arrange to modify caller arguments. Of course, there is a way to do this. Didn't you just know that pointers would turn out to be incredibly useful?

Pointers as Arguments to a Function

When you use a pointer as an argument, the pass-by-value mechanism still operates as before. However, a pointer is an address of another variable, and if you take a copy of this address, the copy still points to the same variable. This is how specifying a pointer as a parameter enables your function to get at a caller argument.

TRY IT OUT - Pass-by-pointer

We can change the last example to use a pointer to demonstrate the effect:

```cpp
// EX5_03.CPP
// A successful attempt to modify caller arguments
#include <iostream>
using namespace std;

int incr10(int* num);                    // Function prototype

int main(void)
{
   int num = 3;
   int* pnum = &num;                     // Pointer to num

   cout << endl
        << "Address passed = " << pnum;

   cout << endl
        << "incr10(pnum) = " << incr10(pnum);

   cout << endl
        << "num = " << num;

   cout << endl;
   return 0;
}

// Function to increment a variable by 10
int incr10(int* num)                     // Function with pointer argument
{
   cout << endl
        << "Address received = " << num;

   *num += 10;                           // Increment the caller argument
                                         // confidently
   return *num;                          // Return the incremented value
}
```

How It Works

In this example, the principal alterations from the previous version relate to passing a pointer, **pnum**, in place of the original variable, **num**. The prototype for the function now has the parameter type specified as a pointer to **int**, and the **main()** function has the pointer **pnum** declared and initialized with the address of **num**. The function **main()**, and the function **incr10()**, output the address sent and the address received respectively, to verify that the same address is indeed being used in both places.

If you run this program, you'll get output similar to this:

```
Ex5_03

Address passed = 0012FF7C
Address received = 0012FF7C
incr10(pnum) = 13
num = 13
Press any key to continue_
```

The address values produced by your computer may be different from those shown above, but the two values should be identical to each other.

The output shows that this time the variable **num** has been incremented and has a value that's now identical to that returned by the function.

In the rewritten version of the function **incr10()**, both the statement incrementing the value passed to the function, and the **return** statement, now need to de-reference the pointer in order to use the value stored.

Passing Arrays to a Function

You can also pass an array to a function, but in this case the array is not copied, even though a pass-by-value method of passing arguments still applies. The array name is converted to a pointer, and a copy of the pointer to the beginning of the array is passed by value to the function. This is quite advantageous, as copying large arrays could be very time consuming. However, as you may have worked out, elements of the array may be changed within a function and thus an array is the only type that cannot be passed by value.

TRY IT OUT - Passing Arrays

We can illustrate the ins and outs of this by writing a function to compute the average of a number of values that are passed to a function in an array.

```
// EX5_04.CPP
// Passing an array to a function
#include <iostream>
using namespace std;

double average(double array[], int count);      //Function prototype
```

```
int main(void)
{
   double values[] = { 1.0, 2.0, 3.0, 4.0, 5.0, 6.0, 7.0, 8.0, 9.0, 10.0 };

   cout << endl
        << "Average = "
        << average(values, (sizeof values)/(sizeof values[0]));

   cout << endl;
   return 0;
}

// Function to compute an average
double average(double array[], int count)
{
   double sum = 0.0;                    // Accumulate total in here
   for(int i = 0; i < count; i++)
      sum += array[i];                  // Sum array elements

   return sum/count;                    // Return average
}
```

How It Works

The function **average()** is designed to work with an array of any length. As you can see from the prototype, it accepts two arguments: the array and a count of the number of elements. Since we want it to work with arrays of arbitrary length, the array parameter appears without a dimension specified.

The function is called in **main()** in this statement,

```
   cout << endl
        << "Average = "
        << average(values, (sizeof values)/(sizeof values[0]));
```

with the first argument as the array name, **values**, and the second argument as an expression which evaluates to the number of elements in the array.

> *You'll recall this expression, using the operator **sizeof**, from when we looked at arrays in Chapter 4.*

Within the body of the function, the computation is expressed in the way you would expect. There's no significant difference between this and the way we would write the same computation if we implemented it directly in **main()**.

If you run the example, it will produce the following output:

```
MS
 S  Ex5_04

Average = 5.5
Press any key to continue
```

183

This confirms that everything works as we anticipated.

TRY IT OUT - Using Pointer Notation When Passing Arrays

However, we haven't exhausted all the possibilities here. As we determined at the outset, the array name is passed as a pointer — in fact, as a copy of a pointer, so within the function we needn't necessarily deal with the data as an array at all. We could modify the function in the example to work with pointer notation throughout, in spite of the fact that we are using an array.

```cpp
// EX5_05.CPP
// Handling an array in a function as a pointer
#include <iostream>
using namespace std;

double average(double* array, int count);        //Function prototype

int main(void)
{
    double values[] = { 1.0, 2.0, 3.0, 4.0, 5.0, 6.0, 7.0, 8.0, 9.0, 10.0 };

    cout << endl
        << "Average = "
        << average(values, (sizeof values)/(sizeof values[0]));

    cout << endl;
    return 0;
}

// Function to compute an average
double average(double* array, int count)
{
    double sum = 0.0;                     // Accumulate total in here
    for(int i = 0; i < count; i++)
        sum += *array++;                  // Sum array elements

    return sum/count;                     // Return average
}
```

How It Works

As you can see, the program needed very few changes to make it work with the array as a pointer. The prototype and the function header have been changed, although neither change is absolutely necessary. If you change both back to the original version with the first parameter specified as a **double** array, and leave the function body written in terms of a pointer, it will work just as well. The most interesting aspect of this version is the **for** loop statement:

```cpp
    sum += *array++;                  // Sum array elements
```

Here we apparently break the rule about not being able to modify an address specified as an array name, because we are incrementing the address stored in **array**. In fact, we aren't breaking the rule at all. Remember that the pass-by-value mechanism makes a copy of the original array address and passes that, so we are just modifying the copy here — the original array address will be quite unaffected. As a result, whenever we pass a one-dimensional array to a function, we are free to treat the value passed as a pointer in every sense, and change the address in any way we wish.

Naturally, this version produces exactly the same output as the original.

Passing Multidimensional Arrays to a Function

Passing a multidimensional array to a function is quite straightforward. The following line declares a two dimensional array, **beans**:

```
double beans[2][4];
```

You could then write the prototype of a hypothetical function, **yield()**, like this:

```
double yield(double beans[2][4]);
```

> *You may be wondering how the compiler can know that this is defining an array of the dimensions shown as an argument, and not a single array element. The answer is simple — you can't write a single array element as a parameter in a function definition or prototype, although you can pass one as an argument when you call a function. For a parameter accepting a single element of an array as an argument, the parameter would have just a variable name. The array context doesn't apply.*

When you are defining a multidimensional array as a parameter, you can also omit the first dimension value. Of course, the function will need some way of knowing the extent of the first dimension. For example, you could write this:

```
double yield(double beans[][4], int index);
```

Here, the second parameter would provide the necessary information about the first dimension. Here the function can operate with a two-dimensional array with any value for the first dimension, but with the second dimension fixed at 4.

TRY IT OUT - Passing Multi-Dimensional Arrays

We define such a function in the following example:

```
// EX5_06.CPP
// Passing a two-dimensional array to a function
#include <iostream>
using namespace std;

double yield(double array[][4], int n);

int main(void)
{
    double beans[3][4] = {   { 1.0,  2.0,  3.0,  4.0 },
                             { 5.0,  6.0,  7.0,  8.0 },
                             { 9.0, 10.0, 11.0, 12.0 }   };
```

```
        cout << endl
            << "Yield = " << yield(beans, sizeof beans/sizeof beans[0]);

        cout << endl;
        return 0;
    }

    // Function to compute total yield
    double yield(double beans[][4], int count)
    {
        double sum = 0.0;
        for(int i = 0; i < count; i++)      // Loop through number of rows
            for(int j = 0; j < 4; j++)      // Loop through elements in a row
                sum += beans[i][j];
        return sum;
    }
```

How It Works

Here, we have used different names for the parameters in the function header from those in the prototype, just to remind you that this is possible — but in this case, it doesn't really improve the program at all. The first parameter is defined as an array of an arbitrary number of rows, each row having four elements. We actually call the function using the array **beans** with three rows. The second argument is specified by dividing the total size of the array in bytes by the size of the first row. This will evaluate to the number of rows in the array.

The computation in the function is simply a nested **for** loop with the inner loop summing elements of a single row and the outer loop repeating this for each row. For what it's worth, the program will display this result:

Using a pointer in a function rather than a multidimensional array as an argument doesn't really apply particularly well. When the array is passed, it passes an address value which points to an array of four elements (a row). This doesn't lend itself to an easy pointer operation within the function. We would need to modify the statement in the nested **for** loop to the following,

```
    sum += *(*(beans + i) + j);
```

so the computation is probably clearer in array notation.

References as Arguments to a Function

We now come to the second of the two mechanisms for passing arguments to a function. Specifying a parameter to a function as a reference changes the method of passing data for that parameter. The method used is not pass-by-value, where an argument is copied before being transferred to the function, but **pass-by-reference** where the parameter acts as an alias for the argument passed. This eliminates any copying and allows the function to access the caller argument directly. It also means that the de-referencing, which is required when passing and using a pointer to a value, is also unnecessary.

TRY IT OUT - Pass-by-reference

Let's go back to a revised version of a very simple example, **Ex5_03.cpp**, to see how it would work using reference parameters:

```cpp
// EX5_07.CPP
// Using a reference to modify caller arguments
#include <iostream>
using namespace std;

int incr10(int& num);                  // Function prototype

int main(void)
{
   int num = 3;
   int value = 6;

   cout << endl
        << "incr10(num) = " << incr10(num);

   cout << endl
        << "num = " << num;

   cout << endl
        << "incr10(value) = " << incr10(value);

   cout << endl
        << "value = " << value;

   cout << endl;
   return 0;
}

// Function to increment a variable by 10
int incr10(int& num)                   // Function with reference argument
{
   cout << endl
        << "Value received = " << num;

   num += 10;                          // Increment the caller argument
                                       //  - confidently
   return num;                         // Return the incremented value
}
```

How It Works

You should find the way this works quite remarkable. This is essentially the same as **Ex5_03.cpp**, except that the function uses a reference as a parameter. The prototype has been changed to reflect this. When the function is called, the argument is specified just as though it was a pass-by-value operation, so it's used in the same way as the earlier version. The argument value isn't passed to the function. Here, the function parameter is *initialized* with the address of the argument, so whenever the parameter **num** is used in the function, it accesses the caller argument directly.

Just to reassure you that there's nothing fishy about the use of the identifier **num** in **main()** as well as in the function, the function is called a second time with the variable **value** as the argument. At first sight this may give you the impression that it contradicts what we said was a basic property of a reference — that once declared and initialized, it couldn't be reassigned to another variable. The reason it isn't contradictory is that a reference as a function parameter is created and initialized when the function is called, and destroyed when the function ends, so we get a completely new reference each time we use the function.

Within the function, the value received from the calling program is displayed on the screen. Although the statement is essentially the same as the one used to output the address stored in a pointer, because **num** is now a reference, we obtain the data value rather than the address.

> *This clearly demonstrates the difference between a reference and a pointer. A reference is an alias for another variable, and therefore can be used as an alternative way of referring to it. It is equivalent to using the original variable name.*

The output from this example is as follows:

```
Ex5_07

Value received = 3
incr10(num) = 13
num = 13
Value received = 6
incr10(value) = 16
value = 16
Press any key to continue_
```

This shows that the function **incr10()** is directly modifying the variable passed as a caller argument.

You will find that if you try to use a numeric value, such as 20, as an argument to **incr10()**, the compiler will output an error message. This is because the compiler recognizes that a reference parameter can be modified within a function, and the last thing you want is to have your constants changing value now and again. This would introduce a kind of excitement into your programs that you could probably do without.

This security is all very well, but if the function didn't modify the value, we wouldn't want the compiler to create all these error messages every time we pass a reference argument that was a constant. Surely there ought to be some way to accommodate this? As Ollie would have said, 'There most certainly is, Stanley!'

Use of the const Modifier

We can use the **const** modifier with a parameter to a function to tell the compiler that we don't intend to modify it in any way. This will cause the compiler to check that your code indeed does not modify the argument, and there will be no error messages when you use a constant argument.

TRY IT OUT - Passing a const

We can modify the previous program to show how the **const** modifier changes the situation.

```
// EX5_08.CPP
// Using a reference to modify caller arguments
#include <iostream>
using namespace std;

int incr10(const int& num);        // Function prototype

int main(void)
{
    const int num = 3;             // Declared const to test for temporary
                                   // creation
    int value = 6;

    cout << endl
        << "incr10(num) = " << incr10(num);

    cout << endl
        << "num = " << num;

    cout << endl
        << "incr10(value) = " << incr10(value);

    cout << endl
        << "value = " << value;

    cout << endl;
    return 0;
}

// Function to increment a variable by 10
int incr10(const int& num)         // Function with const reference argument
{
    cout << endl
        << "Value received = " << num;

//    num += 10;                   // this statement would now be illegal
    return num+10;                 // Return the incremented value
}
```

How It Works

We declare the variable **num** in **main()** as **const** to show that when the parameter to the function **incr10()** is declared as **const**, we no longer get a compiler message when passing a **const** object.

It has also been necessary to comment out the statement which increments **num** in the function **incr10()**. If you uncomment this line, you'll find the program will no longer compile, because the compiler won't allow **num** to appear on the left-hand side of an assignment. When you specified **num** as **const** in the function header and prototype, you promised not to modify it, and so the compiler checks that you kept your word.

Everything works as before, except that the variables in **main()** are no longer changed in the function, so the program produces the following output:

```
Ex5_08

Value received = 3
incr10(num) = 13
num = 3
Value received = 6
incr10(value) = 16
value = 6
Press any key to continue
```

Now, by using reference arguments, we have the best of both worlds. On one hand, we can write a function that can access caller arguments directly, and avoid the copying that is implicit in the pass-by-value mechanism. On the other hand, where we don't intend to modify an argument, we can get all the protection against accidental modification we need by using a **const** modifier with a reference.

Returning Values from a Function

All the example functions that we have created have returned a single value. Is it possible to return anything other than a single value? Well, not directly, but as we said earlier, the single value returned needn't be a numeric value; it could also be an address, which provides the key to returning any amount of data. You simply use a pointer. Unfortunately, here is where the pitfalls start, so you need to keep your wits about you for the adventure ahead.

Returning a Pointer

Returning a pointer value is very easy. A pointer value is just an address, so if you want to return the address of some variable **value**, you can just write the following:

```
return &value;                        // Returning an address
```

As long as the function header and function prototype indicate the return type appropriately, we have no problem — or at least no apparent problem. Assuming that the variable **value** is of type **double**, the prototype of a function called **treble**, which might contain the above **return** statement, could be as follows:

```
double* treble(double data);
```

The parameter list has been defined arbitrarily here.

So let's look at a function that will return a pointer. It's only fair that I warn you in advance — this function doesn't work. Let's assume that we need a function which will return a pointer to three times its argument value. Our first attempt might look like this:

```
// Function to treble a value - mark 1
double* treble(double data)
{
   double result = 0.0;

   result = 3.0*data;
   return &result;
}
```

TRY IT OUT - Returning a Bad Pointer

We could create a little test program to see what happens (remember that the **treble** function won't work as expected):

```
//EX5_09.CPP
#include <iostream>
using namespace std;

double* treble(double);                   // Function prototype

int main(void)
{
   double num = 5.0;                      // Test value
   double* ptr = 0;                       // Pointer to returned value

   ptr = treble(num);

   cout << endl
       << "Three times num = " << 3.0*num;

   cout << endl
       << "Result = " << *ptr;            // Display 3*num

   cout << endl;
   return 0;
}

// Function to treble a value - mark 1
double* treble(double data)
{
   double result = 0.0;

   result = 3.0*data;
   return &result;
}
```

How It Works (or Why It Doesn't)

The function **main()** calls the function **treble()** and stores the address returned in the pointer **ptr**, which should point to a value which is three times the argument, **num**. We then display the result of computing three times **num**, followed by the value at the address returned from the function.

On my computer, I get this output:

```
Ex5_09

Three times num = 15
Result = 1.78923e-307
Press any key to continue
```

Clearly, the second line doesn't reflect the correct value of 15, but where's the error? Well, it's not exactly a secret, since the compiler gives fair warning of the problem with the message Warning C4172: returning address of local variable or temporary.

The error arises because the variable **result** in the function **treble()** is created when the function begins execution, and is destroyed on exiting from the function — so the memory that the pointer is pointing to no longer contains the original variable value. The memory previously allocated to **result** becomes available for other purposes, and here it has evidently been used for something else.

A Cast Iron Rule for Returning Addresses

There is an absolutely cast iron rule for returning addresses:

> *Never return the address of a local automatic variable from a function.*

Now that we have a function that doesn't work, we need to think about what to do to rectify that. We could use a reference and modify the original variable, but that's not what we set out to do. We are trying to return a pointer to some useful data so that, ultimately, we can return more than a single item of data. One answer lies in dynamic memory allocation (we saw this in action in the last chapter). With the operator **new**, we can create a new variable in the free store, which will continue to exist until it is eventually destroyed by **delete** — or until the program ends. The function would then look like this:

```
// Function to treble a value - mark 2
double* treble(double data)
{
   double* result = new double(0.0);
   if(!result)
   {
     cout << "Memory allocation failed.";
     exit(1);
   }

   *result = 3.0*data;
   return result;
}
```

Rather than declaring **result** as of type **double**, we now declare it as **double*** and store in it the address returned by the operator **new**. We then have the necessary check that we received a valid address, and exit the program if anything is wrong.

Since the result is a pointer, the rest of the function is changed to reflect this, and the address contained in the result is finally returned to the calling program. You could exercise this by replacing the function in the last working example with this version.

You need to remember that with dynamic memory allocation from within a function like this, more memory is allocated each time the function is called. The onus is on the calling program to delete the memory when it's no longer required. It's easy to forget to do this in practice, with the result that the free store is gradually eaten up until, at some point, it is exhausted and the program will fail. This sort of problem is often referred to as a **memory leak**.

Here you can see how the function would be used. The two changes that we needed to make to the original code, once the function was replaced, were to include the standard library header file **<cstdlib>** for access to the **exit()** function and to use **delete** to free the memory as soon as we finished with the returned pointer.

```cpp
#include <iostream>
#include <cstdlib>                       // This is for the exit()
                                         // function

double* treble(double);                  // Function prototype

int main(void)
{
   double num = 5.0;                     // Test value
   double* ptr = 0;                      // Pointer to returned value

   ptr = treble(num);

   cout << endl
        << "Three times num = " << 3.0*num;

   cout << endl
        << "Result = " << *ptr;          // Display 3*num
   delete ptr;                           // Don't forget to free the memory

   cout << endl;
   return 0;
}

// Function to treble a value - mark 2
double* treble(double data)
{
   double* result = new double(0.0);
   if(!result)
   {
     cout << "Memory allocation failed.";
     exit(1);
   }

   *result = 3.0*data;
   return result;
}
```

Returning a Reference

You can also return a reference from a function. This is just as fraught with potential errors as returning a pointer, so you need to take care with this too. Because a reference has no existence in its own right (it's always an alias for something else), you must ensure that the object it refers to still exists after the function completes execution. It's very easy to forget this when you use references in a function, because they appear to be just like ordinary variables.

References as return types are of primary significance in the context of object-oriented programming. As you will see later in the book, they will enable you to do things that would be impossible without them. (This particularly applies to 'operator overloading' which we'll come to in Chapter 9.) The principal characteristic of a reference-type return value is that it's an lvalue. This means that you can use the result of a function on the left-hand side of an assignment statement.

TRY IT OUT - Returning a Reference

Let's look at one example which illustrates the use of reference return types, and also demonstrates how a function can be used on the left of an assignment operation when it returns an lvalue. We will assume that we have an array containing a mixed set of values. Whenever we want to insert a new value into the array, we want to replace the lowest value.

```cpp
// EX5_10.CPP
// Returning a reference
#include <iostream>
#include <iomanip>
using namespace std;

double& lowest(double A[], int len);        // Prototype of function
                                            // returning a reference

int main(void)
{
   double array[] = { 3.0, 10.0, 1.5, 15.0, 2.7, 23.0,
                      4.5, 12.0, 6.8, 13.5, 2.1, 14.0};
   int len = sizeof array/sizeof array[0];  // Initialize to number
                                            // of elements

   cout << endl;
   for(int i = 0; i < len; i++)
      cout << setw(6) << array[i];

   lowest(array, len) = 6.9;                // Change lowest to 6.9
   lowest(array, len) = 7.9;                // Change lowest to 7.9

   cout << endl;
   for(i = 0; i < len; i++)
      cout << setw(6) << array[i];

   cout << endl;
   return 0;
}
```

```
double& lowest(double A[], int len)
{
   int j = 0;                            // Index of lowest element
   for(int i = 1; i < len; i++)
      if(A[j] > A[i])                    // Test for a lower value...
         j = i;                          // ...if so update j
   return A[j];                          // Return reference to lowest
                                         // element

}
```

How It Works

Let's first take a look at how the function is implemented. The prototype for the function **lowest()** uses **double&** as the specification of the return type, which is therefore of type 'reference to **double**'. You write a reference type return value in exactly the same way as we've already seen for variable declarations, appending the **&** to the data type. The function has two parameters specified: a one-dimensional array **A** of type **double**, and an **int** parameter **len**, which should specify the length of the array.

The body of the function has a straightforward **for** loop to determine which element of the array passed contains the lowest value. The index, **j**, of the array element with the lowest value is arbitrarily set to 0 at the outset, and then modified within the loop if the current element, **A[i]**, is less than **A[j]**. Thus, on exit from the loop, **j** will contain the index value corresponding to the array element with the lowest value. The **return** statement is as follows:

```
   return A[j];                  // Return reference to lowest element
```

In spite of the fact that this looks identical to the statement which would return a value, because the return type was declared as a reference, this returns a reference to **A[j]** rather than the value that the element contains. The address of **A[j]** is used to initialize the reference to be returned. This reference is created by the compiler, because the return type was declared as a reference.

Don't confuse returning **&A[j]** with returning a reference. If you write **&A[j]** as the return value, you are specifying the address of **A[j]**, which is a *pointer*. If you do this after having specified the return type as a *reference*, you will get an error message from the compiler. Specifically, you'll get this: error C2440: 'return' : cannot convert from 'double *' to 'double &'. A reference that is not to 'const' cannot be bound to a non-lvalue

The function **main()**, which exercises our function **lowest()**, is very simple. An array of type **double** is declared and initialized with 12 arbitrary values, and an **int** variable **len** is initialized to the length of the array. The initial values in the array are output for comparison purposes.

> *Again, we've used the stream manipulator **setw()** to space the values uniformly, requiring the #include statement for **iomanip***

The function **main()** then calls the function **lowest()** on the left side of an assignment to change the lowest value in the array. This is done twice to show that it does actually work and is not an accident. The contents of the array are then output to the display again, with the same field width as before, so corresponding values line up. If you run this example, you should see the following output:

```
Ex5_10                                                                    _ □ ✕
      3     10    1.5    15    2.7    23    4.5    12    6.8   13.5    2.1    14
      3     10    6.9    15    2.7    23    4.5    12    6.8   13.5    7.9    14
Press any key to continue
```

As you can see, with the first call to **lowest()**, the third element of the array, **array[2]**, contained the lowest value, so the function returned a reference to it and its value was changed to 6.9. Similarly, on the second call, **array[10]** was changed to 7.9.

This demonstrates quite clearly that returning a reference allows the use of the function on the left side of an assignment statement. The effect is as if the variable specified in the **return** statement appeared on the left of the assignment.

Of course, if you want to, you can also use it on the right side of an assignment, or in any other suitable expression. If we had two arrays, **X** and **Y**, with **lenX** and **lenY** elements respectively, we could set the lowest element in the array **X** to twice the lowest element in the array **Y** with this statement:

```
lowest(X, lenX) = 2.0*lowest(Y, lenY);
```

This statement would call our function **lowest()** twice, once with arguments **Y** and **lenY** in the expression on the right side of the assignment, and once with arguments **X** and **lenX** to obtain the address where the result of the right-hand expression is to be stored.

A Teflon-Coated Rule: Returning References

A similar rule to the one concerning the return of a pointer from a function also applies to returning references:

> *Never return a reference to a local variable from a function.*

We'll leave the topic of returning a reference from a function for now, but we haven't finished with it yet. We'll come back to it again in the context of user-defined types and object-oriented programming, when we shall unearth a few more magical things that we can do with references.

Static Variables in a Function

There are some things you can't do with automatic variables within a function. You can't count how many times a function is called, for example, because you can't accumulate a value from one call to the next. There's more than one way to get around this if you need to. For instance, you could use a reference parameter to update a count in the calling program, but this wouldn't help if the function was called from lots of different places within a program. You could use a global variable which you incremented from within the function, but globals are risky things to use as they can be accessed from anywhere in a program, which makes it very easy to change them accidentally.

For a general solution, you can declare a variable within a function as **static**. You use exactly the same form of declaration for a **static** variable that we saw in Chapter 2. For example, to declare a variable **count** as **static** you could use this statement:

```
static int count = 0;
```

This also initializes the variable to zero.

> *Initialization of a static variable within a function only occurs the first time that the function is called. In fact, on the first call of a function, the static variable is created and initialized. It then continues to exist for the duration of program execution, and whatever value it contains when the function is exited is available when the function is next called.*

TRY IT OUT - Using Static Variables in Functions

We can demonstrate how a static variable behaves in a function with the following simple example:

```cpp
// EX5_11.CPP
// Using a static variable within a function
#include <iostream>
using namespace std;

void record(void);        // Function prototype, no arguments or return value

int main(void)
{
   record();

   for(int i = 0; i <= 3; i++)
      record();

   cout << endl;
   return 0;
}

// A function that records how often it is called
void record(void)
{
   static int count = 0;
   cout << endl
        << "This is the " << ++count;
   if((count > 3) && (count < 21))       // All this....
      cout <<"th";
   else
      switch(count%10)                    // is just to get...
      {
         case 1: cout << "st";
                 break;
         case 2: cout << "nd";
                 break;
         case 3: cout << "rd";
                 break;
```

```
            default: cout << "th";          // the right ending for...
        }                                    // 1st, 2nd, 3rd, 4th, etc.
    cout << " time I have been called";
    return;
}
```

Our function here serves only to record the fact that it was called. If you build and execute it you will get this output:

```
Ex5_11
This is the 1st time I have been called
This is the 2nd time I have been called
This is the 3rd time I have been called
This is the 4th time I have been called
This is the 5th time I have been called
Press any key to continue
```

How It Works

The static variable **count** is initialized with 0, and is incremented in the first output statement in the function. Because the increment operation is prefixed, the incremented value is displayed by the output statement. It will be 1 on the first call, 2 on the second, and so on. Because the variable **count** is static, it continues to exist and retain its value from one call of the function to the next.

The remainder of the function is concerned with working out when **'st'**, **'nd'**, **'rd'**, or **'th'** should be appended to the value of **count** that is displayed. It's surprisingly irregular. (I guess 101 should be 101st rather than 101th, shouldn't it?)

> Note the **return** statement. Because the return type of the function is **void**, to include a value would cause a compiler error. You don't actually need to put a **return** statement in this particular case as running off the closing brace for the body of the function is equivalent to the **return** statement without a value. The program would compile and run without error even if you didn't include the **return**.

Recursive Function Calls

When a function contains a call to itself it's referred to as a **recursive function**. A recursive function call can also be indirect, where a function **fun1** calls a function **fun2**, which in turn calls **fun1**.

Recursion may seem to be a recipe for an infinite loop, and if you aren't careful it certainly can be. An infinite loop will lock up your machine and require *Ctrl-Alt-Del*, which is always a nuisance. A prerequisite for avoiding an infinite loop is that the function contains some means of stopping the process.

Unless you have come across the technique before, the sort of things to which recursion may be applied may not be obvious. In physics and mathematics there are many things which can be thought of as involving recursion. A simple example is the factorial of an integer which for a given integer N, is the product 1x2x3x...xN. This is very often the example given to show recursion in operation. However, we shall look at something even simpler.

TRY IT OUT - A Recursive Function

At the start of the chapter (see **Ex5_01.cpp**) we produced a function to compute the integral power of a value, that is, to compute x^n. This is equivalent to x multiplied by itself n times. We'll implement this as a recursive function as an elementary illustration of recursion in action.

```cpp
// EX5_12.CPP (based on EX5_01.CPP)
// A recursive version of x to the power n
#include <iostream>
#include <cstdlib>                    // This is for the exit() function
using namespace std;

double power(double x, int n);     // Function prototype

int main(void)
{
   int index = 3;                  // Raise to this power
   double x = 3.0;                 // Different x from that in function power
   double y = 0.0;

   y = power(5.0, 3);             // Passing constants as arguments
   cout << endl
        << "5.0 cubed = " << y;

   cout << endl
        << "3.0 cubed = "
        << power(3.0, index);     // Outputting return value

   x = power(x, power(2.0, 2.0)); // Using a function as an argument
   cout << endl                   // with auto conversion of 2nd parameter
        << "x = " << x;


   cout << endl;
   return 0;
}
// Recursive function to compute integral powers of a double value
// First argument is value, second argument is power index
double power(double x, int n)
{
   if(n < 0)
   {
      cout << endl
           << "Negative index, program terminated.";
      exit(1);
   }
   if(n)
      return x*power(x, n-1);
   else
```

```
        return 1.0;
}
```

The function **main()** is exactly the same as the previous version so the output is also the same:

```
Ex5_12

5.0 cubed = 125
3.0 cubed = 27
x = 81
Press any key to continue
```

We have added the **#include** statement for **cstdlib**, because we use the **exit()** function in our revised function **power()**. Let's now look at how the function works.

How It Works

We only intend to support positive powers of **x**, so the first action is to check that the value for the power that **x** is to be raised to, **n**, is not negative. With a recursive implementation this is essential, otherwise we could get an infinite loop with a negative value for **n** because of the way the rest of the function is written. The **if** statement provides for the value 1.0 being returned if **n** is zero, and in all other cases it returns the result of the expression, **x*power(x, n-1)**. This causes a further call to the function **power()** with the index value reduced by 1.

Clearly, within the function **power()**, if the value of **n** is greater than zero, a further call to the function **power()** will occur. In fact, for any given value of **n** greater than 0, the function will call itself **n** times. The mechanism is illustrated in the figure below, assuming the value 3 for the index argument.

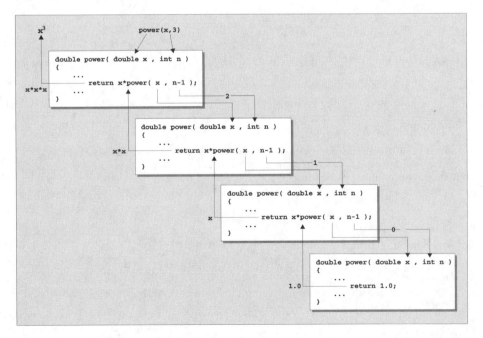

As you see, we need a total of four calls to the **power()** function to generate x^3.

Using Recursion

Unless you have a problem which particularly lends itself to using recursive functions, or if you have no obvious alternative, it's generally better to use a different approach, such as a loop. This will be much more efficient than using recursive function calls. Think about what happens with our last example to evaluate a simple product, **x*x*...x, n** times. On each call, the compiler will generate copies of the two arguments to the function, and also has to keep track of the location it must return to when each **return** is executed. It's also necessary to arrange to save the contents of various registers in your computer so that they can be used within the function **power()**, and of course these will need to be restored to their original state at each return from the function. With a quite modest depth of recursive call, the overhead can be considerably greater than if you use a loop.

This is not to say you should never use recursion. Where the problem suggests the use of recursive function calls as a solution, it can be an immensely powerful technique, greatly simplifying the code. We'll see an example where this is the case in the next chapter.

Summary

In this chapter, you've learned about the basics of program structure. You should have a good grasp of how functions are defined, how data can be passed to a function, and how results are returned to a calling program. Functions are fundamental to programming in C++, so everything we do from here on will involve using multiple functions in a program. The key points that you should keep in mind about writing your own functions are these:

▶ Functions should be compact units of code with a well-defined purpose. A typical program will consist of a large number of small functions, rather than a small number of large functions.

▶ Always provide a function prototype for each function defined in your program, positioned before you call that function.

▶ Passing values to a function using a reference can avoid the copying implicit in the call-by-value transfer of arguments. Parameters which are not modified in a function, should be specified as **const**.

▶ When returning a reference or a pointer from a function, ensure that the object being returned has the correct scope. Never return a pointer or a reference to an object which is local to a function.

The use of references as arguments is a very important concept, so make sure you are confident about using them. We'll see a lot more about references as arguments to functions when we look into object-oriented programming.

Exercises

Ex5-1: The **factorial** of 4 (written as 4!) is 4*3*2*1 = 24, and 3! is 3*2*1 = 6, so it follows that 4! = 4*3!, or more generally:

fact(n) = n*fact(n - 1)

The limiting case is when n is 1, in which case 1! = 1. Write a recursive function which calculates factorials, and test it.

Ex5-2: Write a function which swaps two integers, using pointers as arguments. Write a program which uses this function, and test that it works correctly.

Ex5-3: The trigonometry functions (**sin()**, **cos()** and **tan()**) in the standard math library take arguments in radians. Write three equivalent functions, called **sind()**, **cosd()** and **tand()**, which takes arguments in degrees. All arguments and return types should be **double**s.

Ex5-4: Take [Prg3], and split the code into three, so that the data entry is done in one function, and the printing in another. Keep the data in the main program. Think about how you are going to pass the data between functions—by value, by pointer, or by reference? The result of your efforts will be [Prg4].

Ex5-5: (Advanced) Write a function which, when passed a string consisting of words separated by single spaces, will return the first word; calling it again with an argument of **NULL** will return the second word, and so on, until the string has been processed completely, when **NULL** will be returned. This is a simplified version of the way the run-time library routine **strtok()** works. So, when passed the string **'one two three'**, the function will return you **'one'**, then **'two'**, and finally **'three'**. Passing it a new string results in the current string being discarded before the function starts on the new string.

More About Program Structure

In the previous chapter, you learned about the basics of defining functions and the various ways in which data can be passed to a function. You also saw how results are returned to a calling program.

In this chapter, we will cover the further aspects of how functions can be put to good use, including:

▶ What a pointer to a function is

▶ How to define and use pointers to functions

▶ How to define and use arrays of pointers to functions

▶ What an exception is, and how to write exception handlers that deal with them.

▶ How to write multiple functions with a single name to handle different kinds of data automatically

▶ What function templates are and how you define and use them

▶ How to write a substantial program example using several functions

Pointers to Functions

A pointer stores an address value which, up to now, has been the address of another variable with the same basic type as the pointer. This has provided considerable flexibility in allowing us to use different variables at different times through a single pointer. A pointer can also point to the address of a function. This enables you to call a function through a pointer, which will be the function at the address that was last assigned to the pointer.

Obviously, a pointer to a function must contain the memory address of the function that you want to call. To work properly, however, the pointer must also maintain information about the parameter list for the function it points to, as well as the return type. Therefore, when you declare a pointer to a function, you have to specify the parameter types and the return type of the functions that it can point to, in addition to the name of the pointer. Clearly, this is going to restrict what you can store in a particular pointer to a function. If you have declared a pointer to functions that accept one argument of type **int** and return a value of type **double**, then you can only store the address of a function that has exactly the same form. If you want to store the address of a function that accepts two arguments of type **int** and returns type **char**, then you must define another pointer with these characteristics.

Declaring Pointers to Functions

Let's declare a pointer **pfun** that we can use to point to functions that take two arguments, of type **char*** and **int**, and return a value of type **double**. The declaration would be as follows:

```
    double (*pfun)(char*, int);           // Pointer to function declaration
```

The parentheses may make this look a little weird at first. This declares a pointer, **pfun**, which can point to functions which accept two arguments of type pointer to **char** and of type **int**, and which return a value of type **double**. The parentheses around the pointer name, **pfun**, and the asterisk, are necessary: without them, it would be a function declaration rather than a pointer declaration. In this case, it would look like this:

```
    double *pfun(char*, int);             // Prototype for a function
                                          // returning type double*
```

This is a prototype for a function **pfun()** which has two parameters, and returns a pointer to a **double** value. Since we were looking to declare a pointer, this is clearly not what we want at the moment.

The general form of a declaration of a pointer to a function is given here:

return_type **(****pointer_name***)(***list_of_parameter_types***);**

> *The pointer can only point to functions with the same* **return_type** *and* **list_of_parameter_types** *specified in the declaration.*

This shows that the declaration breaks down into three components:

▶ The return type of the functions that can be pointed to

▶ The pointer name preceded by an asterisk to indicate it is a pointer

▶ The parameter types of the functions that can be pointed to

> *If you attempt to assign a function to a pointer that does not conform to the types in the pointer declaration, the compiler generates an error message.*

You can initialize a pointer to a function with the name of a function within the declaration of the pointer. This is what it might look like:

```
    long sum(long num1, long num2);       // Function prototype
    long (*pfun)(long, long) = sum;       // Pointer to function points to sum()
```

Here, the pointer can be set to point to any function that accepts two arguments of type **long**, and also returns a value of type **long**.

Of course, you can also initialize a pointer to a function by using an assignment statement. Assuming the pointer **pfun** has been declared as above, we could set the value of the pointer to a different function with these statements:

```
long product(long, long);              // Function prototype
...
pfun = product;                        // Set pointer to function product()
```

As with pointers to variables, you must ensure that a pointer to a function is initialized before you use it to call a function. Without initialization, catastrophic failure of your program is guaranteed.

TRY IT OUT - Pointers to Functions

To get a proper feel for these newfangled pointers and how they perform in action, let's try one out in a program:

```
// EX6_01.CPP
// Exercising pointers to functions
#include <iostream>
using namespace std;

long sum(long a, long b);              // Function prototype
long product(long a, long b);          // Function prototype

int main(void)
{
   long (*pdo_it)(long, long);         // Pointer to function declaration

   pdo_it = product;
   cout << endl
        << "3*5 = " << pdo_it(3, 5);   // Call product thru a pointer

   pdo_it = sum;                       // Reassign pointer to sum()
   cout << endl
        << "3*(4 + 5) + 6 = "
        << pdo_it(product(3, pdo_it(4, 5)), 6);  // Call thru a pointer,
                                                 // twice
   cout << endl;
   return 0;
}

// Function to multiply two values
long product(long a, long b)
{
   return a*b;
}

// Function to add two values
long sum(long a, long b)
{
   return a + b;
}
```

How It Works

This is hardly a useful program, but it does show very simply how a pointer to a function is declared, assigned a value, and subsequently used to call a function.

After the usual preamble, we declare a pointer to a function, **pdo_it**, which can point to either of the other two functions that we have defined, **sum()** or **product()**. The pointer is given the address of the function **product()** in this assignment statement:

```
pdo_it = product;
```

When initializing an ordinary pointer, the name of the function is used in a similar way to that of an array name in that no parentheses or other adornments are required. The function name is automatically converted to an address which is stored in the pointer.

The function **product()** is then called indirectly through the pointer **pdo_it** in the output statement.

```
cout << endl
     << "3*5 = " << pdo_it(3, 5);        // Call product thru a pointer
```

The name of the pointer is used just as if it were a function name, and is followed by the arguments between parentheses exactly as they would appear if the original function name were being used directly.

Just to show that we can do it, we change the pointer to point to the function **sum()**. We then use it again in a ludicrously convoluted expression to do some simple arithmetic. This shows that a pointer to a function can be used in exactly the same way as the function that it points to. The sequence of actions in the expression is shown here:

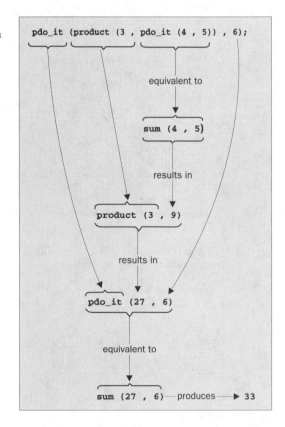

A Pointer to a Function as an Argument

Since 'pointer to a function' is a perfectly reasonable type, a function can also have a parameter that is a pointer to a function. The function can then call the function pointed to by the argument. Since the pointer can be made to point at different functions in different circumstances, this allows the particular function that is to be called from inside a function to be determined in the calling program. In this case, you can pass a function explicitly as an argument.

TRY IT OUT - Passing a Function Pointer

We can look at this with an example. Suppose we need a function that will process an array of numbers by producing the sum of the squares of each of the numbers on some occasions, and the sum of the cubes on other occasions. One way of achieving this is by using a pointer to a function as an argument.

```cpp
//EX6_02.CPP
// A pointer to a function as an argument
#include <iostream>
using namespace std;

// Function prototypes
double squared(double);
double cubed(double);
double sumarray(double array[], int len, double (*pfun)(double));

int main(void)
{
   double array[] = { 1.5, 2.5, 3.5, 4.5, 5.5, 6.5, 7.5 };
   int len = sizeof array/sizeof array[0];

   cout << endl
        << "Sum of squares = "
        << sumarray(array, len, squared);

   cout << endl
        << "Sum of cubes = "
        << sumarray(array, len, cubed);

   cout << endl;
   return 0;
}

// Function for a square of a value
double squared(double x)
{
   return x*x;
}

// Function for a cube of a value
double cubed(double x)
{
   return x*x*x;
}
```

```
// Function to sum functions of array elements
double sumarray(double array[], int len, double (*pfun)(double))
{
    double total = 0.0;                    // Accumulate total in here

    for(int i = 0; i < len; i++)
        total += pfun(array[i]);

    return total;
}
```

If you compile and run this code, you should see the following output:

Ex6_02

```
Sum of squares = 169.75
Sum of cubes = 1015.88
Press any key to continue
```

How It Works

The first statement of interest is the prototype for the function **sumarray()**. Its third parameter is a pointer to a function which has a parameter of type **double**, and returns a value of type **double**.

```
double sumarray(double array[], int len, double (*pfun)(double));
```

The function **sumarray()** processes each element of the array passed as its first argument with whatever function is pointed to by its third argument. The function then returns the sum of the processed array elements.

We call the function **sumarray()** twice in **main()**, the first time with **squared** as the third argument, and the second time using **cubed**. In each case, the address corresponding to the function name used as an argument, will be substituted for the function pointer in the body of the function **sumarray()**, so the appropriate function will be called within the **for** loop.

There are obviously easier ways of achieving what this example does, but using a pointer to a function provides you with a lot of generality. You could pass any function to **sumarray()** that you care to define as long as it takes one **double** argument and returns a value of type **double**.

Arrays of Pointers to Functions

In the same way as with regular pointers, you can declare an array of pointers to functions. You can also initialize them in the declaration. An example of declaring an array of pointers would be:

```
double sum(double, double);              // Function prototype
double product(double, double);          // Function prototype
double difference(double, double);       // Function prototype
double (*pfun[3])(double,double) =
            { sum, product, difference }; // Array of function pointers
```

Each of the elements in the array is initialized by the corresponding function address appearing in the initializing list between braces. To call the function **product()** using the second element of the pointer array, you would write:

```
pfun[1](2.5, 3.5);
```

The square brackets which select the function pointer array element appear immediately after the array name and before the arguments to the function being called. Of course, you can place a function call through an element of a function pointer array in any appropriate expression that the original function might legitimately appear in, and the index value selecting the pointer can be any expression producing a valid index value.

Initializing Function Parameters

With all the functions we have used up to now, we have had to take care to provide an argument corresponding to each parameter in a function call. It can be quite handy to be able to omit one or more arguments in a function call, and have some default values for the arguments that you leave out supplied automatically. You can arrange this by initializing the parameters to a function in its prototype.

For example, let's suppose that we write a function to display a message, where the message to be displayed is to be passed as an argument. Here is the definition of such a function:

```
void showit(const char message[])
{
   cout << endl
        << message;
   return;
}
```

We can initialize the parameter to this function by specifying the initializing string value in the function prototype, as follows:

```
void showit(const char message[] = "Something is wrong.");
```

Here, the parameter **message** is initialized with the string (literal) shown. If you've initialized a parameter to a function in the prototype, and if you leave out that argument when you call the function, the initializing value is used in the call.

TRY IT OUT - Omitting Function Arguments

Leaving out the function argument when you call the function will execute it with the default value. If you supply the argument, it will replace the default value. We can use the previous function to output a variety of messages.

```
//EX6_03.CPP
// Omitting function arguments
#include <iostream>
using namespace std;
```

```cpp
void showit(const char message[] = "Something is wrong.");

int main(void)
{
   const char mymess[] = "The end of the world is nigh.";

   showit();                               // Display the basic message
   showit("Something is terribly wrong!"); // Display an alternative
   showit();                               // Display the default again
   showit(mymess);                         // Display a predefined message

   cout << endl;
   return 0;
}

void showit(const char message[])
{
   cout << endl
        << message;
   return;
}
```

If you execute this example, it will produce the following apocalyptic output:

How It Works

As you can see, we get the default message specified in the function prototype whenever the argument is left out. Otherwise, the function behaves normally.

If you have a function with several arguments, you can provide initial values for as many of them as you like. If you want to omit more than one argument to take advantage of a default value, all arguments to the right of the leftmost argument that you omit must also be left out. For example, if you have this function,

```cpp
int do_it(long arg1 = 10, long arg2 = 20, long arg3 = 30, long arg4 = 40);
```

and you want to omit one argument in a call to it, you can omit only the last one, **arg4**. If you want to omit **arg3**, you must also omit **arg4**. If you omit **arg2**, **arg3** and **arg4** must also be omitted, and if you want to use the default value for **arg1**, you have to omit all of the arguments in the function call.

You can conclude from this that you need to put the arguments which have default values in the function prototype together in sequence at the end of the parameter list, with the argument most likely to be omitted appearing last.

Exceptions

If you've had a go at the exercises we've left at the end of the chapters so far, you're more than likely to have come across compiler errors and warnings, as well as errors that occur while the program is running. **Exceptions** are a way of flagging errors or unexpected conditions that have occurred in your C++ programs.

So far, we have typically handled error conditions by using an **if** statement to test some expression, and then executing some specific code to deal with the error. C++ also provides another, more general mechanism for handling errors that allows you to separate the code that deals with these conditions from the code that executes when such conditions do not arise. It is important to realize that exceptions are not intended to be used as an alternative to the normal data checking and validating that you might do in a program. The code that is generated when you use exceptions carries quite a bit of overhead with it, so exceptions are really intended to be applied in the context of exceptional, near catastrophic conditions that might arise, but are not normally expected to occur in the normal course of events. An error reading from a disk might be something that you use exceptions for. An invalid data item being entered is not a good candidate for using exceptions.

The exception mechanism uses three new keywords:

- ▶ **try** — identifies a code block in which an exception can occur
- ▶ **throw** — causes an exception condition to be originated
- ▶ **catch** — identifies a block of code in which the exception is handled

Let's see how they work in practice.

TRY IT OUT - Throwing and Catching Exceptions

We can see how exception handling operates by working through an example. Let's use a very simple context for this. Suppose we write a program to read the height of a person in inches, and then display the height in meters. Let's also suppose that we want to validate the height entered so that we won't accept any values greater than 100 inches, or less than 9 inches. This is contrary to what was said earlier about the situations in which exceptions fit, but we need something simple and reproducible just to show the mechanism. Looking for a disk read error wouldn't cut it.

We could code this using exception handling as follows:

```
// EX6_04.CPP  Using exception handling
#include <iostream>
using namespace std;

int main(void)
{
    int Height = 0;
    const double InchesToMeters = 0.0254;
    char ch = 'y';
```

```
        while(ch == 'y' || ch == 'Y')
        {
           cout << "Enter a height in inches: ";
           cin >> Height;                            // Read the height to be
                                                      // converted

           try                                        // Defines try block in which
           {                                          // exceptions may be thrown
              if(Height > 100)
                 throw "Height exceeds maximum";      // Exception thrown
              if(Height < 9)
                 throw "Height below minimum";        // Exception thrown

                 cout << static_cast<double>(Height)* InchesToMeters << " meters"
                      << endl;

                 cout << "Do you want to continue (y or n)?";
                 cin >> ch;
           }

           catch(const char aMessage[])               // Start of catch block which
           {                                           // catches exceptions of type
                                                       // const char[]
              cout << aMessage << endl;
           }
        }
        return 0;
     }
```

If you run this example, typical output will be as shown below:

```
Ex6_04
Enter a height in inches: 23
0.5842 meters
Do you want to continue (y or n)?y
Enter a height in inches: 2
Height below minimum
Enter a height in inches: 457
Height exceeds maximum
Enter a height in inches: _
```

How It Works

The code in the **try** block is executed in the normal sequence. The **try** block serves to define where an exception can be raised. You can see from the output that when an exception is thrown, the **catch** block is executed, and execution continues with the statement following the **catch** block. When no exception is thrown, the **catch** block is not executed. Because the **try** block encloses the statement to output the converted value of **Height** and read a value for **ch**, and because these follow the **throw** statements, they are not executed when an exception is thrown. When a throw statement is executed, control passes immediately to the first statement in the **catch** block.

Throwing Exceptions

Exceptions can be thrown anywhere within a **try** block. In our example, we throw two exceptions in the **throw** statements that you see. The operand of the **throw** statements determines a type for the exception — both the exceptions thrown here are string literals and therefore of type **const char[]**. The operand following the **throw** keyword can be any expression and the type of the result of the expression determines the type of exception thrown.

Exceptions can also be thrown in functions called from within a **try** block and caught by a **catch** block following the **try** block. You could add a function to the previous example to demonstrate this, with the definition:

```
void TestThrow(void)
{
    throw "An exception from within a function!";
}
```

If you place a call to this function after the statement reading the value for **ch**, this exception will be thrown and caught by the **catch** block on every iteration when no other exception is thrown. Don't forget the function prototype if you add the definition of **TestThrow()** to the end of the source code.

Catching Exceptions

The **catch** block following the **try** block in our example catches any exception of type **const char[]**. This is determined by the exception declaration that appears in parentheses following the keyword **catch**. You must supply at least one **catch** block for a **try** block, and the **catch** blocks must immediately follow the **try** block. A **catch** block will catch all exceptions (of the correct type) that occur anywhere in the code in the immediately preceding **try** block, including those thrown in any functions that are called directly or indirectly within the **try** block.

If you want to specify that a **catch** block is to handle any exception that is thrown in a **try** block, you must put an ellipsis, **...**, between the parentheses enclosing the exception declaration:

```
catch (...)
{
    // code to handle any exception
}
```

This **catch** block must appear last if you have other **catch** blocks defined for the **try** block.

TRY IT OUT - Nested try Blocks

You can nest **try** blocks one within another. With this situation, if an exception is thrown from within an inner **try** block which is not followed by a **catch** block corresponding to the type of exception thrown, the catch handlers for the outer **try** block will be searched. You can demonstrate this by modifying the previous example as follows:

```
// EX6_05.cpp
// Nested try blocks
#include <iostream>
using namespace std;
```

```
    int main(void)
    {
        int Height = 0;
        const double InchesToMeters = 0.0254;
        char ch = 'y';

        try                                     // Outer try block
        {
            while(ch == 'y'||ch =='Y')
            {
                cout << "Enter a height in inches: ";
                cin >> Height;                  // Read the height to be converted

                try                             // Defines try block in which
                {                               // exceptions may be thrown
                    if(Height > 100)
                        throw "Height exceeds maximum"; // Exception thrown
                    if(Height < 9)
                        throw Height;           // Exception thrown

                    cout << static_cast<double>(Height)*InchesToMeters
                        << " meters" << endl;

                    cout << "Do you want to continue(y or n)?";
                    cin >> ch;
                }

                catch(const char aMessage[])    // start of catch block which
                {                               // catches exceptions of type
                    cout << aMessage << endl;   // const char[]
                }
            }
        }
        catch(int BadHeight)
        {
            cout << BadHeight << " inches is below minimum" << endl;
        }
        return 0;
    }
```

Here, there is an extra **try** block enclosing the **while** loop and the second exception thrown in the inner **try** block has been changed to throw the value of **Height** when this value is below the minimum. If you run this version of the program, the exception of type **const char[]** is caught by the **catch** block in the inner **try** block. The exception of type **int** has no catch handler for exceptions of this type, so the catch handler in the outer try block is executed. In this case, the program ends immediately because the statement following the **catch** block is a **return**.

Exception Handling in the MFC

This is a good point to raise the question of MFC and exceptions, since they are used to some extent. If you are browsing the documentation that came with Visual C++, you may come across **TRY**, **THROW**, and **CATCH** in the index These are macros defined within MFC that were created before exception handling was implemented in the C++ language. They mimic the operation of **try**, **throw** and **catch** in the C++ language, but the language facilities for exception handling really obsolete these so you should not use them. However, they are still there for two reasons. Firstly, there are large numbers of programs still around that use these macros, and it is important to ensure that old code still compiles as far as possible. Secondly, most of the MFC that throws exceptions was implemented in terms of these macros. In any event, any new programs should use the **try**, **throw** and **catch** keywords in C++ since they will work with the MFC.

There is one slight anomaly you need to keep in mind when we come to using MFC functions that throw exceptions. The MFC functions that throw exceptions, generally throw exceptions of class types – you will find out about class types before we get to using the MFC. Even though the exception that an MFC function throws is of a given class type – **CDBException** say, you need to catch the exception as a pointer, not as the type of the exception. So with the exception thrown being of type **CDBException**, the type that would appear as the **catch** block parameter would be **CBDException***. We will see examples where this is the case in context later in the book.

Handling Memory Allocation Errors

When we used the operator **new** to allocate memory for our variables (as we saw in Chapters 4 and 5), we had to test the value of the pointer returned for **NULL**, since **new** returns **NULL** if the memory was not allocated. If the memory wasn't allocated, we used the **exit()** function to quit the execution of our program. This is quite adequate in most situations, as having no memory left is usually a terminal condition for a program. However, there can be circumstances where you might be able to do something about it if you had the chance. For instance, you might be allocating several blocks of memory for different purposes, and if the program ran out, you could conceivably delete one of the blocks to allow the program to stagger on for a bit. Under these circumstances there is something you can do which depends on the ability to define a pointer to a function.

Visual C++ supplies a function called **_set_new_handler()** which accepts a pointer to a function as an argument. The function name begins with an underscore, which is used to distinguish system functions in Visual C++. This enables you to avoid naming functions that clash with system functions — all you need to do is ensure that the names of your own functions do not begin with an underscore. The pointer argument to **_set_new_handler()** should point to a function that you supply, which will handle the problem of the operator **new** not being able to allocate memory . This is how the function gets its name. The function that you write will then be called whenever **new** fails to allocate the memory requested. Once you have called the function **_set_new_handler()** with a pointer to your function as an argument, the problem of dealing with the failure of **new** to work properly is fixed for the entire program, assuming that the action in your function is effective. To use the function **_set_new_handler()**, you must include the header file **<new>** into your program.

The function that you supply to handle out-of-memory conditions must have a prototype of the form:

```
    int mem_error(size_t space);        // Function to handle memory depletion
```

You can give the function any name you like, but the parameter list and return type must correspond to that shown above. The argument passed to your function will be a count of the number of bytes required. Its type, **size_t,** is defined in the **new** header file and, as we saw in Chapter 4, is the same as that of values returned by the operator **sizeof**. It is generally used for values which are a count of a number of bytes. With this value available, you may have a chance to scrape up enough memory to carry on. The statement to set the function **mem_error()** to be called when memory is exhausted might be:

```
_set_new_handler(mem_error);
```

The function **_set_new_handler()** actually returns a pointer to the previous handler (which would be the default function if you haven't called **_set_new_handler()** previously). Most of the time, you'll find that it's a good idea to store the pointer returned by the function in a variable so that you can restore the old handler when you no longer need your handler to be active. You can do this by calling **_set_new_handler()** once more, using the pointer to the old handler as the argument.

The header file, **new**, also defines a type **_PNH** (for **P**ointer to **N**ew **H**andler) which you can use to declare a pointer to store the address of the previous handler. So, the statement,

```
_PNH pOldHandler = _set_new_handler(mem_error);
```

declares the pointer **pOldHandler**, sets **mem_error()** as the function to handle out of memory conditions, and stores the address of the old handler in the pointer **pOldHandler**. If you want to restore the old handler, you just call **_set_new_handler()** once more:

```
_set_new_handler(pOldHandler);
```

Having done whatever you feel is necessary to free up memory in your **mem_error** function, you may want to try again to allocate the memory which previously caused a failure. To do this, you should return a positive value from your function, in which case the **new** operator will automatically retry the failed memory allocation. Of course, if it fails again, it will call your function again. To avoid this, you should make sure that your function doesn't keep returning positive values if it hasn't freed up enough memory. Otherwise, you risk being trapped in an infinite loop. If you return zero from your function, the operator **new** will terminate.

To implement a function to handle the out-of-memory situations with some positive effect, clearly you must have some means of returning memory to the free store. This implies that some dynamically allocated memory must be accessible at the global scope in order that you can make sure that the function is able to release it using **delete**. In most practical cases, this involves some serious work on the program to manage memory, unless you're just setting some memory aside for a rainy day.

Function Overloading

Suppose we have a function which generates the maximum value of an array of values of type **double**:

```
// Function to generate the maximum value in an array of type double
double maxdouble(double array[], int len)
{
   double max = array[0];

   for(int i = 1; i < len; i++)
```

```
        if(max < array[i])
            max = array[i];

    return max;
}
```

We now want to create a function which produces the maximum value from an array of type **long**, so we write another function very similar to the first, with this prototype:

```
long maxlong(long array[], int len);
```

We now have to be careful to choose the appropriate function name to match the particular task in hand. We may also need the same function for other types of argument. It seems a pity that we have to keep inventing new names. Ideally, we would want to use the function **max()** for whatever type, and have the appropriate version executed.

The mechanism which enables you to do this is called **function overloading**.

What is Function Overloading?

Function overloading allows you to use the same name in different functions and, in each instance, to have the compiler choose the correct version for the job. There has to be a clear method for the compiler to decide which function is to be called in any particular instance. The key to this is the parameter list. A series of functions with the same name, but differentiated by their parameter lists, is a set of overloaded functions. So, following on from our **max()** function example, we could have overloaded functions with the following prototypes:

```
int max(int array[], int len);          // Prototypes for
long max(long array[], int len);        // a set of overloaded
double max(double array[], int len);    // functions
```

Each of the functions that share a common name must have a different parameter list. Note that a different return type does not distinguish a function adequately. You can't add the function,

```
double max(long array[], int len);
```

to the above set as it would clash with this prototype,

```
long max(long array[], int len);
```

causing the compiler to complain with error C2556: 'long __cdecl max(long array[], int len)' : overloaded function differs only by return type from 'double __cdecl max(long array[], int len)' and the program not to compile. This may seem slightly unreasonable, until you remember that you can write statements such as these:

```
long numbers[] = {1, 2, 3, 3, 6, 7, 11, 50, 40};
int len = sizeof numbers/sizeof numbers[0];
...
max(numbers, len);
```

If the return type were permitted as a distinguishing feature, the version of **max()** taking a **long** array as an argument and returning a **double** value would be allowed, along with the original three. In the instance of the code above, the compiler would be unable to decide

219

whether to choose the version with a **long** return type or a **double** return type. You could however *replace* the **long** function with the **double** function in the set, as the parameter list for each function in the set would still be unique.

Each function in a set of overloaded functions is sometimes said to have a unique **signature**, which is determined by the parameter list.

TRY IT OUT - Using Overloaded Functions

We can exercise the overloading capability with the function **max()** that we have already defined. Let's try an example that includes the three versions for **int**, **long** and **double** arrays.

```cpp
// EX6_06.CPP
// Using overloaded functions
#include <iostream>
using namespace std;

int max(int array[], int len);              // Prototypes for
long max(long array[], int len);            // a set of overloaded
double max(double array[], int len);        // functions

int main(void)
{
   int small[] = {1, 24, 34, 22};
   long medium[] = {23, 245, 123, 1, 234, 2345};
   double large[] = {23.0, 1.4, 2.456, 345.5, 12.0, 21.0};

   int lensmall = sizeof small/sizeof small[0];
   int lenmedium = sizeof medium/sizeof medium[0];
   int lenlarge = sizeof large/sizeof large[0];

   cout << endl << max(small, lensmall);
   cout << endl << max(medium, lenmedium);
   cout << endl << max(large, lenlarge);

   cout << endl;
   return 0;
}

// Maximum of ints
int max(int x[], int len)
{
   int max = x[0];
   for(int i = 1; i < len; i++)
      if(max < x[i])
         max = x[i];
   return max;
}

// Maximum of longs
long max(long x[], int len)
{
   long max = x[0];
   for(int i = 1; i < len; i++)
      if(max < x[i])
```

```
        max = x[i];
    return max;
}

// Maximum of doubles
double max(double x[], int len)
{
 double max = x[0];
    for(int i = 1; i < len; i++)
        if(max < x[i])
            max = x[i];
    return max;
}
```

How It Works

We have three prototypes for the three overloaded versions of the function **max()**. In each of the three output statements, the appropriate version of the function **max()** is selected by the compiler based on the argument list types. The example works as expected and produces this output:

```
MS Ex6_06

34
2345
345.5
Press any key to continue
```

When to Overload Functions

Function overloading provides you with the means of ensuring that a function name describes the function being performed, and is not confused by extraneous information such as the type of data being processed. This is akin to what happens with basic operations in C++. To add two numbers you use the same operator, regardless of the types of the operands. Our overloaded function **max()** has the same name, regardless of the type of data being processed. This helps to make the code more readable and makes these functions easier to use.

> *The intent of function overloading is clear: to enable the same operation to be performed with different operands using a single function name. So, whenever you have a series of functions that do essentially the same thing, but with different types of arguments, you should overload them and use a common function name.*

221

Function Templates

The last example was somewhat tedious in that we had to repeat essentially the same code for each function, but with different variable and parameter types. We also have the possibility of having a recipe for automatically generating functions of various types. The code to do this for a particular group of functions is called a **function template**.

The functions generated by a function template all have the same basic code, but have one or more types defined as parameters to the template. As you use a particular form of a template function, a version is automatically generated to support the type of arguments that you use. We can demonstrate this by defining a function template for the function **max()** in the previous example.

Using a Function Template

We can define a template for the function **max()** as follows:

```
template<class T> T max(T x[], int len)
{
    T max = x[0];
    for(int i = 1; i < len; i++)
        if(max < x[i])
            max = x[i];
    return max;
}
```

The **template** keyword identifies this as a template definition. The angled brackets following the **template** keyword enclose the type parameters that are used to create a particular instance of the function. The keyword **class** before the **T** indicates that the **T** is the type parameter for this template, **class** being the generic term for type. We shall see later in the book that defining a class is essentially defining your own data type. Consequently, you have basic types in C++, such as **int** and **char**, and you also have the types that you define yourself.

Wherever **T** appears in the definition of the template, it is to be replaced by a specific type, such as **long**, when an instance of the template is created. If you try this out manually, you'll see that this will generate a perfectly satisfactory function for calculating the maximum value from an array of type **long**. The creation of a particular function instance is referred to as **instantiation**. In our case, we have just one type parameter, **T**, but in general, there can be more.

Each time you use the function **max()** in your program, the compiler will check to see if a function corresponding to the type of arguments that you have used in the function call already exists. If the function required does not exist, the compiler will create one by substituting the argument type that you have used in place of the parameter **T** throughout the source code in the template definition. You could exercise this template with the same function **main()** that we used in the previous example:

```
// EX6_07.CPP
// Using function templates
#include <iostream>
using namespace std;
```

```
// Template for function to compute the maximum element of an array
template<class T> T max(T x[], int len)
{
   T max = x[0];
   for(int i = 1; i < len; i++)
      if(max < x[i])
         max = x[i];
   return max;
}

int main(void)
{
   int small[] = { 1, 24, 34, 22};
   long medium[] = { 23, 245, 123, 1, 234, 2345};
   double large[] = { 23.0, 1.4, 2.456, 345.5, 12.0, 21.0};

   int lensmall = sizeof small/sizeof small[0];
   int lenmedium = sizeof medium/sizeof medium[0];
   int lenlarge = sizeof large/sizeof large[0];

   cout << endl << max(small, lensmall);
   cout << endl << max(medium, lenmedium);
   cout << endl << max(large, lenlarge);

   cout << endl;
   return 0;
}
```

If you run this program, it will produce exactly the same output as the previous example. For each of the statements outputting the maximum value in an array, a new version of **max()** is instantiated using the template. Of course, if you add another statement calling the function **max()** with one of the types used previously, no new version of the code is generated.

Note that using a template doesn't reduce the size of your compiled program in any way. A version of the source code is generated for each function that you require. In fact, using templates can generally increase the size of your program, as functions can be created automatically even though an existing version might satisfactorily be used by casting the argument accordingly. You can force the creation of particular instances of a template by explicitly including a declaration for it. For example, if you wanted to ensure that an instance of the template for the function **max()** was created corresponding to the type **float**, you could place the following declaration after the definition of the template:

```
float max(float, int);
```

This will force the creation of this version of the function template. It does not have much value in the case of our program example, but it can be useful when you know that several versions of a template function might be generated, but you want to force the generation of a subset that you plan to use with arguments cast to the appropriate type where necessary.

An Example Using Functions

We have covered a lot of ground in C++ up to now, and a lot on functions in this chapter alone. After wading through a varied menu of language capabilities, it's not always easy to see how they relate to one another. Now would be a good point to see how some of this goes together to produce something with more meat than a simple demonstration program.

Let's work through a more realistic example to see how a problem can be broken down into functions. The process will involve defining the problem to be solved, analyzing the problem to see how it can be implemented in C++, and finally writing the code. The approach here is aimed at illustrating how various functions go together to make up the final result, rather than a tutorial on how to develop a program.

Implementing a Calculator

Suppose we need a program that will act as a calculator; not one of these fancy devices with lots of buttons and gizmos designed for those who are easily pleased, but one for people who know where they are going, arithmetically speaking. We can really go for it and enter a calculation from the keyboard as a single arithmetic expression, and have the answer displayed immediately. An example of the sort of thing that we might enter is:

        2*3.14159*12.6*12.6 / 2 + 25.2*25.2

To avoid unnecessary complications for the moment, we won't allow parentheses in the expression and the whole computation must be entered in a single line. However, to allow the user to make the input look attractive, we *will* allow blanks to be placed anywhere. The expression entered may contain the operators multiply, divide, add, and subtract represented by *, /, + and – respectively, and should be evaluated with normal arithmetic rules, so that multiplication and division take precedence over addition and subtraction.

The program should allow as many successive calculations to be performed as required, and should terminate if an empty line is entered. It should also have helpful and friendly error messages.

Analyzing the Problem

A good place to start is with the input. The program will read in an arithmetic expression of any length on a single line, which can be any construction within the terms given. Since nothing is fixed about the elements making up the expression, we will have to read it as a string of characters and then work out within the program how it's made up. We can decide arbitrarily that we will handle a string of up to 80 characters, so we could store it in an array declared within these statements:

```
const int MAX = 80;          // Maximum expression length including '\0'
char buffer[MAX];            // Input area for expression to be evaluated
```

To change the maximum length of the string processed by the program, we will only need to alter the initial value of **MAX**.

We need to determine the basic structure of the information in the input string, so let's break it down step-by-step.

The first thing to do is to make sure that it is as uncluttered as possible, so before we start analyzing, we will get rid of all the blanks in the input string. Let's call the function we use to do this **eatspaces()**. This can work by moving through the input buffer — which will be the array **buffer[]** — using two indexes to it, **i** and **j**, and shuffling elements up to overwrite any blank characters. The indexes **i** and **j** start out at the beginning of the buffer, and we store element **j** at position **i**. As we progress through the elements, each time we find a blank we don't increment **i**, so it will get overwritten by the next element. We can illustrate the logic of this in the following figure:

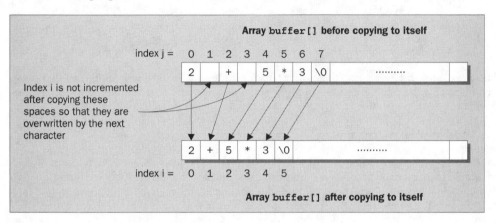

This process is one of copying the contents of the array **buffer[]** to itself, but not copying any blanks. The diagram shows the array buffer before the copying process and after it has been completed.

The next thing we need to do is to evaluate the expression. We will define the function **expr()** which will return the value of the whole expression in the input buffer. To decide what goes on inside the function, we need to look into the structure of the input in more detail. The add and subtract operators have the lowest precedence and so are evaluated last. We can envisage the string as one or more terms, each of which we can refer to as a **term**, connected by operators which can be either the operator **+** or the operator **-**. We can refer to either operator as an **addop**. With this terminology, we can represent the general expression like this:

>   *expression: term addop term ... addop term*

The expression will contain at least one **term** and can have an arbitrary number of following **addop term** combinations. In fact, assuming that we've removed all the blanks, there are only three legal possibilities for the character following each **term**:

▶   The next character is **'\0'**, so we are at the end of the string

▶   The next character is **'-'**, in which case we should subtract the next **term** from the value accrued for the expression up to this point

▶   The next character is **'+'**, in which case we should add the value of the next **term** to the value of the expression accumulated so far

If anything else follows a **term**, the string is not what we expect, so we'll display a message and exit from the program. The structure of an expression is illustrated here:

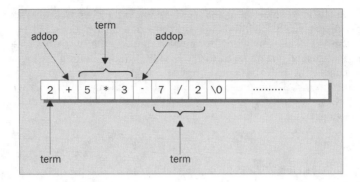

The next thing that we need to know about an input expression is a more detailed and precise definition of a **term**. A **term** is simply a series of numbers that are connected by either the operator ***** or the operator **/**. Therefore, a **term** (in general) will look like this:

```
term: number multop number ... multop number
```

By **multop** we mean either multiply or divide. What we need is a function **term()** to return the value of a **term**. This will need to progress through the string first by finding a number and then looking for a **multop** followed by another number. If a character is found that isn't a **multop**, we'll assume that it is an **addop** and return the value that we have found up to that point.

The last thing that we need to understand before writing the program is what a number is. To avoid unnecessary complications, we'll only allow a number to be unsigned. Therefore, a number consists of a series of digits that may be followed by a decimal point and some more digits. To determine the value of a number we move through the buffer finding digits. If we find anything that isn't a digit, we check whether it's a decimal point. If it's not a decimal point it has nothing to do with a number, so we return what we have got. If it is a decimal point, we look for more digits. As soon as we find anything that's not a digit, we have the complete number and we return that. Imaginatively, we'll call the function to sort this out **number()**.

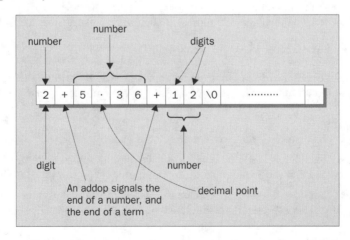

We now have enough understanding of the problem to write some code. We can work through the functions we need, then write a **main()** function to tie them all together. The first and perhaps easiest function to write is **eatspaces()** which is going to eliminate the blanks from the input string.

Eliminating Blanks from a String

We can write the prototype for **eatspaces()** as follows:

```
void eatspaces(char* str);                    // Function to eliminate blanks
```

It doesn't need to return any value since the blanks can be eliminated from the string *in situ*, modifying the original string directly through the pointer provided as an argument. The process for eliminating blanks is a very simple one. We need to copy the string to itself, but overwriting any blanks as we saw earlier in this chapter.

We can define the function to do this as follows:

```
// Function to eliminate blanks from a string
void eatspaces(char* str)
{
   int i = 0;                                 // 'Copy to' index to string
   int j = 0;                                 // 'Copy from' index to string

   while((*(str + i) = *(str + j++)) != '\0') // Loop while character
                                              // copied is not \0
      if(*(str + i) != ' ')                   // Increment i as long as
         i++;                                 // character is not a blank
   return;
}
```

How the Function Functions

All the action is in the **while** loop. The loop condition copies the string by moving the character at position **j** to the character at position **i**, and then increments **j** to the next character. If the character copied was **'\0'**, we have reached the end of the string, and we're done.

The only action in the loop statement is to increment **i** to the next character if the last character copied was not a blank. If it *is* a blank, **i** will not be incremented and the blank will therefore be overwritten by the character copied on the next iteration.

That wasn't hard, was it? Next, we can try writing the function providing the result of evaluating the expression.

Evaluating an Expression

The function **expr()** needs to return the value of the expression specified in the string that is supplied as an argument, so we can write its prototype as follows:

```
double expr(char* str);                       // Function evaluating an expression
```

The function declared here accepts a string as an argument and returns the result as type **double**. Based on the structure for an expression that we worked out earlier, we can draw a logic diagram for the process of evaluating an expression as shown below:

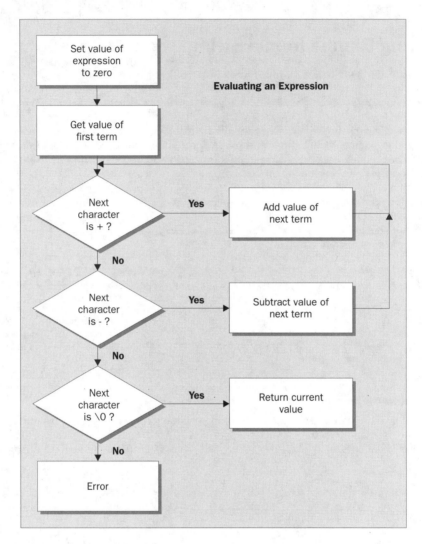

Using this basic definition of the logic, we can now write the function:

```
// Function to evaluate an arithmetic expression
double expr(char* str)
{
    double value = 0.0;        // Store result here
    int index = 0;             // Keeps track of current character position

    value = term(str, index);  // Get first term

    for(;;)                    // Infinite loop, all exits inside
    {
```

```
          switch(*(str + index++)) // Choose action based on current character
          {
            case '\0':                    // We're at the end of the string
              return value;               // so return what we have got

            case '+':                     // + found so add in the
              value += term(str, index);  // next term
              break;

            case '-':                     // - found so subtract
              value -= term(str, index);  // the next term
              break;

            default:                      // If we reach here the string
              cout << endl                // is junk
                   << "Arrgh!*#!! There's an error"
                   << endl;
              exit(1);
          }
        }
      }
```

How the Function Functions

Considering this function is analyzing any arithmetic expression that you care to throw at it (as long as it uses our operator subset), it's not a lot of code. We define a variable **index** of type **int**, which is intended to keep track of the current position in the string where we're working, and we initialize it to 0 which corresponds to the index position of the first character in the string. We also define a variable **value** of type **double** in which we'll accumulate the value of the expression passed to the function in the **char** array **str**.

Since an expression must have at least one term, the first action in the function is to get the value of the first term by calling the function **term()**, which we have yet to write. This actually places three requirements on the function **term()**:

1 It should accept a **char*** pointer and an **int** variable as parameters, the second parameter being an index to the first character of the term in the string supplied.

2 It should update the index value passed to position it at the character following the last character of the term found.

3 It should return the value of the term as type **double**.

The rest of the program is an infinite **for** loop. Within the loop, the action is determined by a **switch** statement which is controlled by the current character in the string. If it is a **'+'**, we call the function **term()** to get the value of the next term in the expression and add it to the variable **value**. If it is a **'-'**, we subtract the value returned by **term()** from the variable value. If it is a **'\0'**, we are at the end of the string, so we return the current contents of the variable **value** to the calling program. If it is any other character, it shouldn't be there, so after remonstrating with the user we end the program!

If either a `'+'` or a `'-'` was found, the loop continues. Each call to `term()` will have moved the value of the variable `index` to the next character after the last term, which should be either another `'+'` or `'-'`, or the end of string character `'\0'`. Thus, the function either terminates normally when `'\0'` is reached, or abnormally by calling `exit()`. We need to remember the `#include` for `cstdlib` to provide the prototype for the function `exit()` when we come to put the whole program together.

It would also be possible to analyze an arithmetic expression using a recursive function. If we think about the definition of an expression slightly differently, we could specify it as being either a term, or a term followed by an expression. The definition here is recursive (i.e. the definition involves the item being defined), and this approach is very common in defining programming language structures. This definition provides just as much flexibility as the first, but using it as the base concept, we could arrive at a recursive version of `expr()` instead of using a loop as we did in the implementation above. You might wish to try this alternative approach as an exercise, once we have completed the first version.

Getting the Value of a Term

The function `term()` needs to return a `double` value and receive two arguments: the string being analyzed and an index to the current position in the string. There are other ways of doing this, but this arrangement is quite straightforward. We can, therefore, write the prototype of the function `term()` as follows:

```
double term(char* str, int& index);        // Function analyzing a term
```

We've specified the second parameter as a reference. This is because we want the function to modify the value of the variable `index` in the calling program to position it at the character following the last character of the term found in the input string. We could return `index` as a value but then we would need to return the value of the term in some other way, so the arrangement we've chosen seems quite natural.

The logic for analyzing a term is going to be similar in structure to that for an expression. It is a number, potentially followed by one or more combinations of a multiply or a divide operator and another number. We can write the definition of the function `term()` as follows:

```cpp
// Function to get the value of a term
double term(char* str, int& index)
{
   double value = 0.0;                        // Somewhere to accumulate
                                              // the result

   value = number(str, index);               // Get the first number in the term

   // Loop as long as we have a good operator
   while((*(str + index) == '*') || (*(str + index) == '/'))
   {

      if(*(str + index) == '*')              // If it's multiply,
         value *= number(str, ++index);      // multiply by next number

      if(*(str + index) == '/')              // If it's divide,
         value /= number(str, ++index);      // divide by next number
```

```
      }
      return value;                         // We've finished, so return what
                                            // we've got
   }
```

How the Function Functions

We first declare a local **double** variable value in which we'll accumulate the value of the current term. Since a term must contain at least one number, the first action in the function is to obtain the value of the first number by calling the function **number()** and storing the result in the variable **value**. We implicitly assume that the function **number()** will accept the string and an index to the string as arguments, and will return the value of the number found. Since the function **number()** must also update the index to the string to the position after the number that was found, we'll again specify the second parameter as a reference when we come to define that function.

The rest of the function is a **while** loop, which continues as long as the next character is `'*'` or `'/'`. Within the loop, if the character found at the current position is `'*'`, we increment the variable **index** to position it at the beginning of the next number, call the function **number()** to get the value of the next number, and then multiply the contents of the variable **value** by the value returned. In a similar manner, if the current character is `'/'`, we increment the variable **index** and divide the contents of **value** by the value returned from **number()**. Since the function **number()** automatically alters the value of the variable index to the character following the number found, **index** is already set to select the next available character in the string on the next iteration.

The loop terminates when a character other than a multiply or divide operator is found, whereupon the current value of the term accumulated in the variable **value** is returned to the calling program.

The last analytical function that we require is **number()**, which needs to determine the numerical value of any number appearing in the string.

Analyzing a Number

Based on the way we've used the function **number()** within the function **term()**, we need to declare it with this prototype:

```
   double number(char* str, int& index);    // Function to recognize a number
```

The specification of the second parameter as a reference will allow the function to update the argument in the calling program directly, which is what we require.

We can make use of a function provided in a standard C++ library here. The header file **cctype** provides declarations for a range of functions for testing single characters. These functions return values of type **int** – positive values (corresponding to **true**) or zero (**false**). Four of these functions are shown below:

Functions in cctype for Testing Single Characters	
`int isalpha(int c)`	Returns **true** if the argument is alphabetic, **false** otherwise.
`int isupper(int c)`	Returns **true** if the argument is an upper case letter, **false** otherwise.
`int islower(int c)`	Returns **true** if the argument is a lower case letter, **false** otherwise.
`int isdigit(int c)`	Returns **true** if the argument is a digit, **false** otherwise.

There are also a number of other functions provided by **cctype**, but we won't grind through all the detail. If you're interested, you can look them up in the MSDN Library Help. Simply do a search on 'is routines' or look at Visual C++ Documentation\Using Visual C++\Visual C++ Programmer's Guide\Run-Time Library Reference\Alphabetic Function Reference\I Through K for a fuller listing.

We only need the last of the functions shown above in our program. Remember that **isdigit()** is testing a character, such as the character **'9'** (ASCII character 57 in decimal notation) for instance, not a numeric 9, because the input is a string.

We can define the function **number()** as follows:

```
// Function to recognize a number in a string
double number(char* str, int& index)
{
    double value = 0.0;                  // Store the resulting value

    while(isdigit(*(str + index)))       // Loop accumulating leading digits
        value = 10*value + (*(str + index++) - 48);

                                         // Not a digit when we get to here
    if(*(str + index) != '.')            // so check for decimal point
        return value;                    // and if not, return value

    double factor = 1.0;                 // Factor for decimal places
    while(isdigit(*(str + (++index))))   // Loop as long as we have digits
    {
        factor *= 0.1;                   // Decrease factor by factor of 10
        value = value + (*(str + index) - 48)*factor;   // Add decimal place
    }

    return value;                        // On loop exit we are done
}
```

How the Function Functions

We declare the local variable **value** as **double** which will hold the value of the number. We initialize it with 0.0 because we will add in the digit values as we go along.

As the number in the string is a series of digits as ASCII characters, the function will walk through the string accumulating the value of the number digit by digit. This will occur in two steps, accumulating digits before the decimal point, and then if we find a decimal point, accumulating the digits after it.

The first step is in the **while** loop that continues as long as the current character selected by the variable **index** is a digit. The value of the digit is extracted and added to the variable **value** in the loop statement:

```
value = 10*value + (*(str + index++) - 48);
```

The way this is constructed bears a closer examination. A digit character will have an ASCII value between 48, corresponding to the digit 0, and 57 corresponding to the digit 9. Thus, if we subtract 48 from the ASCII code for a digit, we will convert it to its equivalent numeric value, which is the actual digit. We have put parentheses around the sub-expression ***(str + index++) - 48** to make what's going on a little clearer. The contents of the variable **value** are multiplied by 10 in order to shift the value one decimal place to the left before adding in the digit, since we'll find digits from left to right—that is, the most significant digit first. This process is illustrated here:

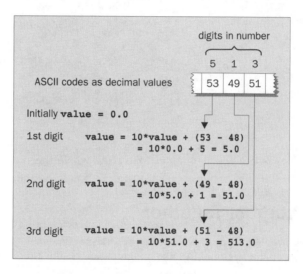

As soon as we come across something other than a digit, it is either a decimal point, or something else. If it's not a decimal point, we've finished, so we return the current contents of the variable **value** to the calling program. If it is a decimal point, we accumulate the digits corresponding to the fractional part of the number in the second loop. In this loop, we use the variable **factor**, which has the initial value 1.0, to set the decimal place for the current digit, and consequently it is multiplied by 0.1 for each digit found. Thus, the first digit after the decimal point will be multiplied by 0.1, the second by 0.01, the third by 0.001, and so on. This process is illustrated here:

digits in number

| 5 | 1 | 3 | · | 6 | 0 | 8 |

ASCII codes as decimal values

| 53 | 49 | 51 | 46 | 54 | 48 | 56 |

Before the decimal point `value = 513.0`
`factor = 1.0`

After the decimal point:

1st digit   `factor = 0.1*factor`
                          `= 0.1`
            `value = value + factor*(54 - 48)`
                      `= 513.0 + 0.1*6 = 513.6`

2nd digit   `factor = 0.1*factor`
                          `= 0.01`
            `value = value + factor*(48 - 48)`
                      `= 513.6 + 0.01*0 = 513.60`

3rd digit   `factor = 0.1*factor`
                          `= 0.001`
            `value = value + factor*(56 - 48)`
                      `= 513.60 + 0.01*8 = 513.608`

As soon as we find a non-digit character, we are done, so after the second loop we return the value of the variable **value**. We now almost have the whole thing. We just need a **main()** function to read the input and drive the process.

Putting the Program Together

The first thing we need to do is to collect the **#include** statements together and assemble the function prototypes at the beginning of the program for all the functions used in this program:

```
// EX6_08.CPP
// A program to implement a calculator

#include <iostream>              // For stream input/output
#include <cstdlib>               // For the exit() function
#include <cctype>                // For the isdigit() function
using namespace std;

void eatspaces(char* str);       // Function to eliminate blanks
double expr(char* str);          // Function evaluating an expression
double term(char* str, int& index);   // Function analyzing a term
double number(char* str, int& index); // Function to recognize a number

const int MAX = 80;              // Maximum expression length,
                                 // including '\0'
```

We've also defined a global variable **MAX**, which is the maximum number of characters in the expression processed by the program (including the terminating **NULL**).

Now all we need to define is the function **main()** and our program is complete. It needs to read a string and exit if it is empty, otherwise call the function **expr()** to evaluate the input and display the result. This process should repeat indefinitely. That doesn't sound too difficult, so let's give it a try.

```
int main()
{
   char buffer[MAX] = {0};              // Input area for expression to be evaluated

   cout << endl
        << "Welcome to your friendly calculator."
        << endl
        << "Enter an expression, or an empty line to quit."
        << endl;

   for(;;)
   {
      cin.getline(buffer, sizeof buffer);    // Read an input line
      eatspaces(buffer);                      // Remove blanks from input

      if(!buffer[0])                          // Empty line ends calculator
         return 0;

      cout << "\t= " << expr(buffer)          // Output value of expression
           << endl << endl;
   }
}
```

How the Function Functions

In **main()**, we set up the **char** array **buffer** to accept an expression up to 80 characters long (including the terminating **NULL**). The expression is read within the infinite **for** loop using the input function **getline()**, and after obtaining the input, blanks are eliminated from the string by calling the function **eatspaces()**.

The only other things that the function **main()** provides for are within the loop. They are to check for an empty string which will consist of just the null character, **'\0'**, in which case the program ends, and to output the value of the string produced by the function **expr()**.

Once you've typed in all the functions, you should get output similar to that shown here:

```
MS Ex6_08

Welcome to your friendly calculator.
Enter an expression, or an empty line to quit.
22/7
         = 3.14286

2*3 +4 - 0.35*6
         = 7.9

2.5*3.5/1.4 + 7.8*.76/7
         = 7.09686

1/2 + 1/3 + 1/4 + 1/5 + 1/6 + 1/7
         = 1.59286

1/3 + 1/5 + 1/7 + 1/9
         = 0.787302


Press any key to continue_
```

You can enter as many calculations as you like, and when you are fed up with it you just press *Enter* to end the program.

Extending the Program

Now that we've got a working calculator, we can start to think about extending it. Wouldn't it be nice to be able to handle parentheses in an expression? It can't be that difficult, can it? Let's give it a try. We need to think about the relationship between something in parentheses which might appear in an expression, and the kind of expression analysis that we have made so far. Let's look at an example of the kind of expression we want to handle:

$$2*(3 + 4) / 6 - (5 + 6) / (7 + 8)$$

The first thing to notice is that the expressions in parentheses always form part of a **term** in our original parlance. Whatever sort of computation you come up with, this is always true. In fact, if we could substitute the value of the expressions within parentheses back into the original string, we would have something that we can already deal with. This indicates a possible approach to handling parentheses. Why don't we treat an expression in parentheses as just another number, and modify the function **number()** to sort out the value of whatever appears between the parentheses?

That sounds like a good idea, but 'sorting out' the expression in parentheses requires a bit of thought: the clue to success is in our terminology. The expression that appears within parentheses is a minute replica of a full-blown expression, and we already have a function **expr()** which will return the value of an expression. All we need to do is to get the function **number()** to work out what the contents of the parentheses are and extract those from the string to be passed to the function **expr()**, so recursion really simplifies the problem. What's more, we don't need to worry about nested parentheses. Since any set of parentheses will contain what we've defined as an expression, they will be taken care of automatically. Recursion wins again.

Let's have a stab at rewriting the function **number()** to recognize an expression between parentheses.

```
// Function to recognize an expression in parentheses
// or a number in a string
double number(char* str, int& index)
{
   double value = 0.0;                  // Store the resulting value

   if(*(str + index) == '(')           // Start of parentheses
   {
      char* psubstr = 0;               // Pointer for substring
      psubstr = extract(str, ++index); // Extract substring in brackets
      value = expr(psubstr);           // Get the value of the substring
      delete[]psubstr;                 // Clean up the free store
      return value;                    // Return substring value
   }

   while(isdigit(*(str + index)))      // Loop accumulating leading digits
      value = 10*value + (*(str + index++) - 48);
                                       // Not a digit when we get to here
   if(*(str + index)!= '.')            // so check for decimal point
      return value;                    // and if not, return value

   double factor = 1.0;                // Factor for decimal places
```

```
    while(isdigit(*(str + (++index))))  // Loop as long as we have digits
    {
        factor *= 0.1;                   // Decrease factor by factor of 10
        value = value + (*(str + index) - 48)*factor;  // Add decimal place
    }

    return value;                        // On loop exit we are done
}
```

How the Function Functions

Look how little has changed to support parentheses. I suppose it is a bit of a cheat, since we use a function (**extract()**) that we haven't written yet, but for one extra function you get as many levels of nested parentheses as you want. This really is icing on the cake, and it's all down to the magic of recursion!

The first thing that the function **number()** does now is to test for a left parenthesis. If it finds one, it calls another function, **extract()** to extract the substring between the parentheses from the original string. The address of this new substring is stored in the pointer **psubstr**, so we then apply the function **expr()** to the substring by passing this pointer as an argument. The result is stored in **value**, and after releasing the memory allocated on the free store in the function **extract()** (as we will eventually implement it), we return the value obtained for the substring as though it were a regular number. Of course, if there is no left parenthesis to start with, the function **number()** continues exactly as before.

Extracting a Substring

We now need to write the function **extract()**. It's not difficult, but it's also not trivial. The main complication comes from the fact that the expression within parentheses may also contain other sets of parentheses, so we can't just go looking for the first right parenthesis we can find. We need to watch out for more left parentheses as well, and for every one we find, ignore the corresponding right parenthesis. We can do this by maintaining a count of left parentheses as we go along, adding one to the count for each left parenthesis we find, and if the count is not zero, subtracting one for each right parenthesis. Of course, if the count is zero, and we find a right parenthesis, we're at the end of the substring. The mechanism is illustrated in the following figure:

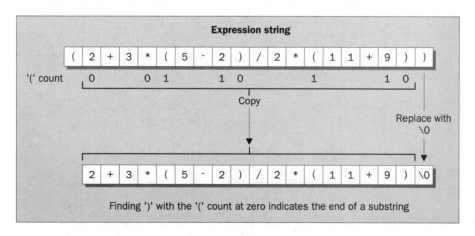

Finding ')' with the '(' count at zero indicates the end of a substring

Since the string extracted here contains sub-expressions enclosed within parentheses, eventually `extract()` will be called again to deal with those.

The function `extract()` will also need to allocate memory for the substring and return a pointer to it. Of course, the index to the current position in the original string will need to end up selecting the character following the substring, so the parameter for that will need to be specified as a reference. The prototype of `extract()` will, therefore, be as follows:

```cpp
char* extract(char* str, int& index); //Function to extract a substring
```

We can now have a shot at the definition of the function.

```cpp
// Function to extract a substring between parentheses
// (requires cstring)
char* extract(char* str, int& index)
{
   char buffer[MAX];                    // Temporary space for substring
   char* pstr = 0;                      // Pointer to new string for return
   int numL = 0;                        // Count of left parentheses found
   int bufindex = index;                // Save starting value for index

   do
   {
     buffer[index - bufindex] = *(str + index);
     switch(buffer[index - bufindex])
     {
        case ')':
          if(numL == 0)
          {
            buffer[index - bufindex] = '\0';  // Replace ')' with '\0'
            ++index;
            pstr = new char[index - bufindex];
            if(!pstr)
            {
               cout << "Memory allocation failed,"
                    << " program terminated.";
               exit(1);
            }
            strcpy(pstr, buffer);    // Copy substring to new memory
            return pstr;             // Return substring in new memory
          }
          else
            numL--;                  // Reduce count of '(' to be matched
          break;

        case '(':
          numL++;                    // Increase count of '(' to be
                                     // matched
          break;
     }
   } while(*(str + index++) != '\0');  // Loop - don't overrun end of string

   cout << "Ran off the end of the expression, must be bad input."
        << endl;
   exit(1);
   return pstr;
}
```

How the Function Functions

We declare a **char** array to hold the substring temporarily. We don't know how long the substring will be, but it can't be more than **MAX** characters. We can't return the address of **buffer** to the calling function, because it is local and will be destroyed on exit from the function. Therefore, we will need to allocate some memory on the free store when we know how long the string is. We do this by declaring a variable, **pstr**, of type 'pointer to **char**', which we will return by value when we have the substring safe and sound in the free store memory.

We also declare a counter **numL**, to keep track of left parentheses in the substring (as we discussed earlier). The initial value of **index** (when the function begins execution) is stored in the variable **bufindex**. This will be used in combination with incremented values of **index** to index the array **buffer**.

The executable part of the function is basically one big **do-while** loop. Within the loop, the substring is copied from **str** to **buffer** one character at each iteration, with a check for left or right parentheses each cycle. If a left parenthesis is found, **numL** is incremented, and if a right parenthesis is found and **numL** is non-zero, it is decremented. When we find a right parenthesis and **numL** is zero, we have found the end of the substring. The **')'** in the substring in **buffer** is then replaced by **'\0'**, and sufficient memory is obtained on the free store to hold the substring. The substring in **buffer** is then copied to the memory obtained through the operator **new** by using the function **strcpy()**, which is defined in the header file **cstring**. This function copies the string specified by the second argument, **buffer**, to the address specified by the first argument, **pstr**.

If we fall through the bottom of the loop, it means that we hit the **NULL** at the end of the expression in **str** without finding the complementary right bracket, so we display a message and terminate the program.

Running the Modified Program

After replacing the function **number()** in the old version of the program, adding the **#include** statement for **cstring**, and incorporating the prototype and the definition for the new **extract()** function we have just written, you're ready to roll with an all-singing, all-dancing calculator. If you have assembled all that without error, you will get output something like this:

```
Ex6_08A

Welcome to your friendly calculator.
Enter an expression, or an empty line to quit.
1/(1+1/(1+1/(1+1)))
        = 0.6

(1/2 - 1/3)*(1/3 - 1/4)*(1/4 - 1/5)
        = 0.000694444

2.5*(1.5 - 3/(1.3-2*1.5))-1
        = 7.16176

2.5 - 28

Arrrgh!*#!! There's an error
Press any key to continue
```

The friendly and informative error message in the last output line is due to the use of the comma instead of the decimal point in the expression above it, in what should be 2.5. As you can see, we get nested parentheses to any depth with a relatively simple extension of the program, all due to the amazing power of recursion.

Summary

You now have a reasonably comprehensive knowledge of writing and using functions. You've used a pointer to a function in a practical context for handling out-of-memory conditions in the free store, and you have used overloading to implement a set of functions providing the same operation with different types of parameters. We'll see more about overloading functions in the following chapters.

The important bits that you learned in this chapter are:

> A pointer to a function stores the address of a function, plus information about the number and types of parameters and return type for a function.

> You can use a pointer to a function to store the address of any function with the appropriate return type, and number and types of parameters.

> You can use a pointer to a function to call the function at the address it contains. You can also pass a pointer to a function as a function argument.

> An exception is a way of signaling an error in a program so that the error handling code can be separated from the code for normal operations.

> You throw an exception with a statement that uses the keyword **throw**.

> Code that may throw exceptions should be placed in a **try** block, and the code to handle a particular type of exception is placed in a **catch** block immediately following the try block. There can be several **catch** blocks following a **try** block, each catching a different type of exception.

> Overloaded functions are functions with the same name, but with different parameter lists.

> When you call an overloaded function, the function to be called is selected by the compiler based on the number and types of the arguments that you specify.

> A function template is a recipe for generating overloaded functions automatically.

> A function template has one or more arguments that are type variables. An instance of the function template — that is, a function definition — will be created by the compiler for each function call that corresponds to a unique set of type arguments for the template.

> You can force the compiler to create a particular instance from a function template by specifying the function you want in a prototype declaration.

You also got some experience of using several functions in a program by working through the calculator example. But remember that all the uses of functions up to now have been in the context of a traditional procedural approach to programming. When we come to look at object-oriented programming, we will still use functions extensively, but with a very different approach to program structure, and to the design of a solution to a problem.

Exercises

Ex6-1: Consider the following function:

```
int ascVal(int i, const char* p)
{
   // print the ASCII value of the char
   if (!p || i > strlen(p))
       return -1;
   else
       return static_cast<int>p[i];
}
```

Write a program which will call this function through a pointer and verify that it works. You'll need to include **<cstring>** in your program in order to use **strlen()**.

Ex6-2: Write a family of overloaded functions called **equal()**, which take two arguments of the same type, returning true if they are equal, and false otherwise. Provide versions having **char**, **int**, **double** and **char*** arguments. (Use the **strcmp()** function from the runtime library to test for equality of strings. If you don't know how to use **strcmp()**, search for it in the online help. You'll need to include **<cstring>** in your program.) Write test code to verify that the correct versions are called.

Ex6-3: At present, when the calculator hits an invalid input character, it prints an error message, but doesn't show you where the error was in the line. Write an error routine which will print out the input string, putting a caret (^) below the offending character, like this:

12 + 4,2*3
        ^

Ex6-4: Add an exponentiation operator, ^, to the calculator, fitting it in alongside * and /. What are the limitations of implementing it in this way, and how can you overcome them?

Ex6-5: (Advanced) Extend the calculator so it can handle trig and other math functions, allowing you to input expressions such as

2 * sin(0.6)

The math library functions all work in radians; provide versions of the trig functions so that the user can use degrees, e.g.

2 * sind(30)

A Taste of Old-Fashioned Windows

In this chapter, we're going to take a break from delving into C++ language features. Instead, we're going to take a look at the nuts and bolts of a Windows program to see how you can put one together without the assistance of the AppWizard and MFC.

In later chapters, you will be using MFC for your Windows application development, so that you can take advantage of its object-oriented approach and have the application framework set up for you by the AppWizard. In this chapter, you'll see how Windows operates behind the scenes — knowledge that will be useful to you even when you are developing applications using MFC.

Believe it or not, you can almost write a Windows program with the knowledge that you have of C++ so far. However, before we can go any further in our quest for Windows enlightenment, there is one other feature of the language that you need to understand: the **struct**. So, after first taking a look at how to define and use a **struct**, we will write a simple Windows program to display text in a window.

By the end of this chapter you will have learnt:

- What a **struct** is and how it is used in Windows programming
- What the basic structure of a window is
- What the Windows API is and how it is used
- What Windows messages are and how you deal with them
- What notation is commonly used in Windows programs
- What the basic structure of a Windows program is

The struct in C++

Before we start programming in Windows, there is one language feature that we need to understand because it is used so extensively in the programming interface to Windows. It is called a structure and is defined using the keyword **struct**. The **struct** is something of a hangover from the C language, and C++ incorporates and expands on the C **struct**, which is functionally replaceable by a class. However, because Windows was written in C before C++

became widely used, the **struct** appears pervasively in Windows programming. We'll take a look at (C-style) **struct**s in this chapter, and examine some of the additional capabilities offered by C++, in the form of classes, in the next chapter.

What is a struct?

All the variables and data types that we have seen up to now have consisted of a single type of entity — a number of some kind, a character, or a string. Life, the universe and everything are usually a bit more complicated than that, unless you are among those who believe that the answer is 42, in which case all you ever need is an **int**.

Describing virtually anything requires you to define several values, in order that the description is of practical use in a program. Think about the information that might be needed to describe something as simple as a book. You might consider title, author, publisher, date of publication, number of pages, price, topic or classification and ISBN number just for starters, and you can probably come up with a few more without too much difficulty. You could specify separate variables to contain each of the parameters that you need to describe a book, but ideally you would want to have a single data type, **BOOK** say, which embodied all of these parameters. I'm sure you won't be surprised to hear that this is exactly what a **struct** can do for you.

Defining a struct

Let's stick with the notion of a book, and suppose that we just want to include the title, author, publisher and year of publication within our definition of a book. We could declare a structure to accommodate this as follows:

```
struct BOOK
{
   char Title[80];
   char Author[80];
   char Publisher[80];
   int Year;
};
```

This doesn't define any variables, but it actually creates a new variable type, called **BOOK**. The keyword **struct** defines **BOOK** as such, and the elements making up a **struct** of this type are defined within the curly braces. Note that each line defining an element in the **struct** is terminated by a semicolon, and that a semicolon also appears after the closing brace. The elements of a **struct** can be of any type, except the same type as the **struct** being defined. We couldn't have an element of type **BOOK** included in the structure definition for **BOOK**, for example. You may think this to be a limitation, but note that we could include a pointer to a variable of type **BOOK**, as we shall see a little later on.

The elements **Title**, **Author**, **Publisher**, and **Year** enclosed between the braces in the definition above may also be referred to as members or fields of the structure **BOOK**. Each variable of type **BOOK** will contain the members **Title**, **Author**, **Publisher**, and **Year**. We can now create variables of type **BOOK** in exactly the same way that we create variables of any other type:

```
BOOK Novel;                      // Declare variable Novel of type BOOK
```

This declares a variable **Novel** which we can now use to store information about a book. All we need now is to understand how we get data into the various members that make up a variable of type **BOOK**.

Initializing a struct

The first way to get data into the members of a **struct** is to define initial values in the declaration. Suppose we wanted to initialize the variable **Novel** to contain the data for one of my favorite books, *Paneless Programming*, published in 1981 by the Gutter Press. This is a story of a guy performing heroic code development while living in an igloo, and as you probably know, inspired the famous Hollywood box office success, *Gone with the Window*. It was written by I.C. Fingers, who is also the author of that seminal three volume work, *The Connoisseur's Guide to the Paper Clip*. With this wealth of information we can write the declaration for the variable **Novel** as:

```
BOOK Novel =
{
   "Paneless Programming",       // Initial value for Title
   "I.C. Fingers",               // Initial value for Author
   "Gutter Press",               // Initial value for Publisher
   1981                          // Initial value for Year
};
```

The initializing values appear between braces, separated by commas, in much the same way that we defined initial values for members of an array. As with arrays, the sequence of initial values obviously needs to be the same as the sequence of the members of the **struct** in its definition. Each member of the structure **Novel** will have the corresponding value assigned to it, as indicated in the comments.

Accessing the Members of a struct

To access individual members of a **struct**, you can use the **member selection operator**, sometimes referred to as the **member access operator,** which is a period. To refer to a particular member, you write the **struct** variable name, followed by a period, followed by the name of the member that you want to access. To change the member **Year** of our structure, **Novel**, we could write,

```
Novel.Year = 1988;
```

which would set the value of this particular member to 1988. You can use a member of a structure in exactly the same way as any other variable of the same type as the member. To increment the member **Year** by two, for example, we can write:

```
Novel.Year += 2;
```

This increments the value of the member **Year** just like any other variable.

TRY IT OUT - *Using structs*

Let's use another console application example to exercise a little further how referencing the members of a **struct** works. Suppose we want to write a program to deal with some of the things you might find in a yard, such as those that are illustrated in the professionally landscaped yard below:

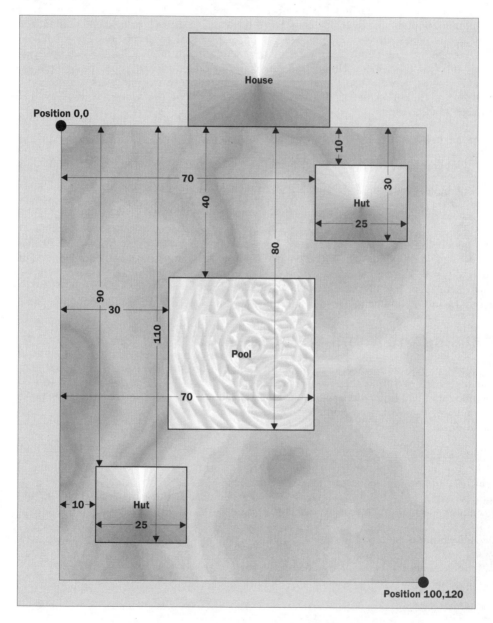

We have arbitrarily assigned the coordinates 0,0 to the top left corner of the yard. The bottom right corner has the coordinates 100,120. Thus, the first coordinate value is a measure of the horizontal position relative to the top left corner, with values increasing from left to right, and the second coordinate is a measure of the vertical position from the same reference point, with values increasing from top to bottom. The illustration also shows the position of the pool and that of the two huts relative to the top left-hand corner of the yard. Since the yard, the huts and the pool are all rectangular, we could define a **struct** which will be convenient for us to use in their representation:

```
struct RECTANGLE
{
   int Left;                        // Top left point
   int Top;                         // coordinate pair

   int Right;                       // Bottom right point
   int Bottom;                      // coordinate pair
};
```

The first two members of the **RECTANGLE** structure type correspond to the coordinates of the top left point of a rectangle, and the next two to the coordinates of the bottom right point. We can use this in an elementary example dealing with the objects in the yard as follows:

```
// EX7_01.CPP
// Exercising structures in the yard
#include <iostream>
using namespace std;

// Definition of a struct to represent rectangles
struct RECTANGLE
{
   int Left;                        // Top left point
   int Top;                         // coordinate pair

   int Right;                       // Bottom right point
   int Bottom;                      // coordinate pair
};

// Prototype of function to calculate the area of a rectangle
long Area(RECTANGLE& aRect);

// Prototype of a function to move a rectangle
void MoveRect(RECTANGLE& aRect, int x, int y);

int main(void)
{
   RECTANGLE Yard = { 0, 0, 100, 120 };
   RECTANGLE Pool = { 30, 40, 70, 80 };
   RECTANGLE Hut1, Hut2;

   Hut1.Left = 70;
   Hut1.Top = 10;
   Hut1.Right = Hut1.Left + 25;
   Hut1.Bottom = 30;

   Hut2 = Hut1;                     // Define Hut2 the same as Hut1
   MoveRect(Hut2, 10, 90);          // Now move it to the right position
```

```
        cout << endl
            << "Coordinates of Hut2 are "
            << Hut2.Left << "," << Hut2.Top << " and "
            << Hut2.Right << "," << Hut2.Bottom;

        cout << endl
            << "The area of the yard is "
            << Area(Yard);

        cout << endl
            << "The area of the pool is "
            << Area(Pool)
            << endl;

        return 0;
    }

    // Function to calculate the area of a rectangle
    long Area(RECTANGLE& aRect)
    {
        return (aRect.Right - aRect.Left)*(aRect.Bottom - aRect.Top);
    }

    // Function to Move a Rectangle
    void MoveRect(RECTANGLE& aRect, int x, int y)
    {
        int length = aRect.Right - aRect.Left;   // Get length of rectangle
        int width = aRect.Bottom - aRect.Top;    // Get width of rectangle

        aRect.Left = x;                          // Set top left point
        aRect.Top = y;                           // to new position
        aRect.Right = x + length;                // Get bottom right point as
        aRect.Bottom = y + width;                // increment from new position

        return;
    }
```

How It Works

Note that the **struct** definition appears at global scope in this example. You'll be able to see it in the ClassView of the Project Workspace window. This allows us to declare a variable of type **RECTANGLE** anywhere in our **.cpp** file of source code. In a program with a more significant amount of code, such definitions are normally stored in a **.h** file and then added to each **.cpp** file where necessary by using a **#include** directive.

We have defined two functions to process **RECTANGLE** objects. The function **Area()** calculates the area of a **RECTANGLE** passed as a reference argument as the product of the length and the width, where the length is the difference between the horizontal positions of the defining points, and the width is the difference between the vertical positions of the defining points. By passing a reference, the code runs a little faster because the argument is not copied. The function **MoveRect()** modifies the defining points of a **RECTANGLE** object to position it at the coordinates **x**, **y** which are passed as arguments. The position of a **RECTANGLE** object is assumed to be the position of the **Left**, **Top** point. Since the **RECTANGLE** variable is passed as a reference, the function is able to modify the members of the **RECTANGLE** object directly. After calculating the length and width of the **RECTANGLE** object passed, the **Left** and **Top** members are set to **x** and **y** respectively, and the new **Right** and **Bottom** members are calculated by incrementing **x** and **y** by the length and width of the original **RECTANGLE** object.

In the function **main()**, we initialize the **Yard** and **Pool RECTANGLE** variables with their coordinate positions as shown in the illustration. The variable **Hut1** represents the hut at the top right in the illustration and its members are set to the appropriate values using assignment statements. The variable **Hut2**, corresponding to the hut at the bottom left of the yard, is first set to be the same as **Hut1** in the assignment statement

```
Hut2 = Hut1;                            // Define Hut2 the same as Hut1
```

This statement results in copying the values of the members of **Hut1** to the members of **Hut2**. You can only assign a **struct** of a given type to another of the same type. You can't increment a **struct** directly, or use a **struct** in an arithmetic expression.

To alter the position of **Hut2** to its place at the bottom left of the yard, we call the **MoveRect()** function with the coordinates of the required position as arguments. This roundabout way of getting the coordinates of **Hut2** is totally unnecessary and serves only to show how we can use a **struct** as an argument to a function.

After displaying the coordinates of the final version of **Hut2**, we display the area of the **RECTANGLE** objects **Yard** and **Pool** using the function **Area()**. If you build and execute this example, you should see the output shown below:

```
Ex7_01

Coordinates of Hut2 are 10,90 and 35,110
The area of the yard is 12000
The area of the pool is 1600
Press any key to continue_
```

The values displayed are what you would expect from the positions and dimensions shown in the illustration of the yard.

Intellisense Assistance with Structures

You may already have noticed that the editor in Visual C++ is quite intelligent – it knows the types of variables for instance. If you hover the mouse cursor over a variable name in the editor window, it will pop-up a little box showing its definition. It also can help a lot with structures (and classes, as we will see) since, not only does it know the types of ordinary variables, it knows the members that belong to a variable of a particular structure type. If your PC is reasonably fast, as you type the member selection operator following a structure variable name, the editor will pop up a window showing the list of members. If you click on one of the members, it will show the comment that appeared in the original definition of the structure, so you know what it is. This is shown below using a fragment of the previous example.

```
aRect.Left = x;                        // Set top left point
aRect.Top = y;                         // to new position
aRect.Right = x + length;              // Get bottom right point as
aRect.
```

Bottom	coordinate pair
Left	
Right	
Top	

Now there's a real incentive to add comments, and to keep them short and to the point. If you double click on a member in the list, it will be automatically\ inserted after the member selection operator, thus eliminating one source of typos in your code. Great, isn't it?

You can turn this off if you want to via the Tools/Options... menu item, but I guess the only reason you would want to is if your machine is too slow to make it useful. If you turn it off, you can still call it up when you want too, either through the Edit menu or through the keyboard. Pressing *Ctrl+Alt+T* will pop-up the members for an object under the cursor. The editor will also show the parameter list for a function when you are typing the code to call it – it pops up as soon as you enter the left parenthesis for the argument list. This is particularly helpful with library functions as its tough to remember the parameter list for all of them. Of course, the **#include** directive for the header file must already be there in the source code for this to work. Without it the editor will have no idea what the library function is. You will see more things that the editor can help with as you learn more about classes.

After that interesting little diversion, let's get back to structures.

The struct RECT

Rectangles are used a great deal in Windows programs. For this reason, there is a **RECT** structure predefined in the header file **windows.h**. Its definition is essentially the same as the structure that we defined in the last example:

```
struct RECT
{
    int left;                          // Top left
    int top;                           // coordinates

    int right;                         // Bottom right
    int bottom;                        // coordinates
};
```

As we shall see, this **struct** is usually used to define rectangular areas on your display for a variety of purposes. Since **RECT** is used so extensively, **windows.h** also contains prototypes for a number of functions to manipulate and modify rectangles. For example, **windows.h** provides the function **InflateRect()** to increase the size of a rectangle and the function **EqualRect()** to compare two rectangles. MFC also defines a class called **CRect**, which is the equivalent of a **RECT** structure. Once we understand classes, we will be using this in preference to the **RECT** structure. The **CRect** class provides a very extensive range of functions for manipulating rectangles, and you will be using a number of these when we are writing Windows programs using MFC. You can find the complete list of functions for manipulating **RECT** structures by looking up Platform SDK\Graphics and Multimedia Services\GDI\Rectangles in the help contents.

Using Pointers with a struct

As you might expect, you can create a pointer to a variable of a structure type. In fact, many of the functions declared in **windows.h** that work with **RECT** objects require pointers to a **RECT** as arguments because this avoids the copying of the whole structure when a **RECT** argument is passed to a function. To define a pointer to a **RECT** object for example, the declaration is what you might expect:

```
RECT* pRect = NULL;                    // Define a pointer to RECT
```

Assuming that we have defined a **RECT** object, **aRect**, we can set our pointer to the address of this variable in the normal way, using the address-of operator:

```
pRect = &aRect;                        // Set pointer to the address of aRect
```

As we saw when we introduced the idea of a **struct**, a **struct** can't contain a member of the same type as the **struct** being defined, but it can contain a pointer to a **struct**, including a pointer to a **struct** of the same type. For example, we could define the structure:

```
struct ListElement
{
   RECT aRect;                          // RECT member of structure
   ListElement* pNextListElement;       // Pointer to a list element
};
```

The first element of the **ListElement** structure is of type **RECT**, and the second element is a pointer to a structure of type **ListElement** — the same type as that being defined. (Remember that this element isn't of type **ListElement**, it's of type 'pointer to **ListElement**'.) This allows elements to be daisy-chained together, where each element of type **ListElement** can contain the address of the next **ListElement** object in a chain, the last in the chain having the pointer as zero. This is illustrated in the diagram:

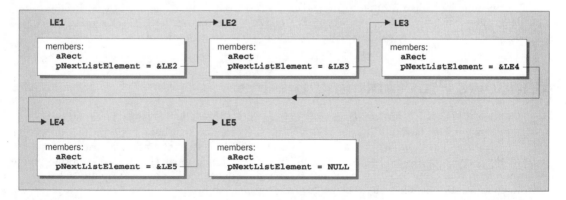

Each box in the diagram represents an object of type **ListElement**. This kind of arrangement is usually referred to as a **linked list**. It has the advantage that as long as you know the first element in the list, you can find all the others. This is particularly important when variables are created dynamically, since a linked list can be used to keep track of them all. Every time a new one is created, it's simply added to the end of the list. We will see this sort of thing in operation in a Windows programming example later on.

Accessing Elements Through a Pointer

Consider the following statements:

```
RECT aRect = { 0, 0, 100, 100 };
RECT* pRect = &aRect;
```

The first declares and defines the **RECT** object, **aRect**, with the first pair of members initialized to (0, 0) and the second pair to (100, 100). The second statement declares the pointer to **RECT**, **pRect**, and initializes it with the address of **aRect**. We can now access the members of **aRect** through the pointer with a statement such as:

```
(*pRect).Top += 10;                    // Increment the Top member by 10
```

The parentheses to de-reference the pointer here are essential since the member access operator takes precedence over the de-referencing operator. Without the parentheses, we would be attempting to treat the pointer as a **struct** and to de-reference the member, so the statement would not compile. After executing this statement, the **Top** member will have the value 10 and, of course, the remaining members will be unchanged.

The Indirect Member Selection Operator

The method that we used to access the member of a **struct** through a pointer looks rather clumsy. Since this kind of operation crops up very frequently in C++, the language includes a special operator to enable you to express the same thing in a much more readable and intuitive form. It is specifically for accessing members of a **struct** through a pointer and is called the **indirect member selection operator**, also referred to as the **indirect member access operator**. We could use it to rewrite the statement to access the **Top** member of **aRect** through the pointer **pRect**, as follows:

```
pRect->Top += 10;                      // Increment the Top member by 10
```

The operator looks like a little arrow and is formed from a minus sign followed by the symbol for 'greater than'. It's much more expressive of what is going on, isn't it? This operator is also used with classes, and we'll be seeing a lot more of it throughout the rest of the book.

Windows Programming Basics

Now that we've seen how **structs** can be used in C++, let's move on to Windows programming. You have already created a Windows program in Chapter 1 with the aid of the AppWizard and without writing a single line of code. The user interface that was created was actually very sophisticated — we are going to create a much more elementary window for our example in this chapter — but we'll use the window generated by our example in Chapter 1 to illustrate the various elements that go to make up a window.

Elements of a Window

You will inevitably be familiar with most, if not all, of the principal elements of the user interface to a Windows program. However, we will go through them anyway, since we will be concerned with programming them as elements rather than just using them. The best way for us to understand what the elements of a window can be is to look at one. An annotated version of the window displayed by the example that we saw in Chapter 1 is shown below:

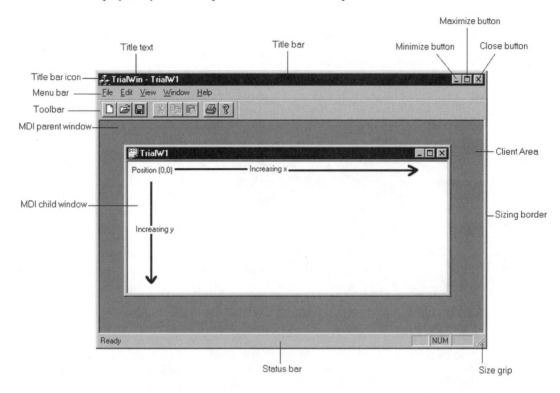

The example actually generated two windows. The larger window with the menu and the tool bars is the main, or **parent window**, and the smaller window is a **child window** of the parent. If you ran the example you will have seen that, while the child window can be closed by double-clicking the title bar icon without closing the parent window, closing the parent window automatically closes the child window as well. This is because the child window is owned by, and dependent upon, the parent window. In general, a parent window may have a number of child windows, as we shall see.

The most fundamental parts of a typical window are its **border**, the **title bar icon**, the **title bar** showing the name that you give to the window, and the **client area** (the area in the center of the window not used by the title bar or borders). We can get all of these for free in a Windows program. As you will see, all we have to do is provide some text for the title bar.

The border defines the boundary of a window and may be fixed or sizable. If the border is sizable, you can drag it to alter the size of the window. The window may also possess a size grip, which you can use to alter the size of a window while maintaining its aspect ratio — the ratio of the width to the height. When we define a window, if we need to, we can modify how the border behaves and appears. Most windows will also have the maximize, minimize and close buttons in the top right corner of the window. These allow the window to be increased to full screen size, reduced to an icon or closed.

When you click on the title bar icon with the left mouse button, it provides a standard menu for altering or closing the window called the 'system menu' or 'control menu'. The system menu also appears when you right-click on the title bar of a window. While it is optional, it's a good idea always to include the title bar icon in any main windows that your program generates. It can be a very convenient way of closing the program when things don't work as you anticipated.

The client area is the part of the window where you will usually want your program to write text or graphics. You address the client area for this purpose in exactly the same way as the yard that we saw in the example earlier in this chapter. The top left corner of the client area has the coordinates (0, 0), with x increasing from left to right, and y increasing from top to bottom.

The menu bar is optional, but is probably the most common way to control an application. The contents of a menu and the physical appearance of many objects that are displayed in a window, such as the icons on the toolbar that appear above, the cursor and many others, are defined by a **resource file**. We will see a lot more of resource files when we get to write some more sophisticated Windows programs.

The toolbar provides a set of icons that usually act as alternatives to the menu options that you use most often. Because they give a pictorial clue to the function provided, they can often make a program easier and faster to use.

A little note about terminology before we move on. One tends to think of a window as the thing that appears on the screen with a border round it, and of course it is, but it is only one kind of window. However, in Windows a window is a generic term covering a whole range of entities. In fact almost any entity that is displayed is a window – for example, a dialog is a window and each button is also a window. We will generally use terminology to refer to objects that describe what they are, buttons, dialogs, and so on, but you need to have tucked in the back of your mind that they are windows too, because you can do things to them that you can do with a regular window – you can draw on a button for instance.

Comparing DOS and Windows Programs

When you write a program for DOS, the operating system is essentially subservient. When you want some service to be provided, you call an operating system function. You can even bypass the operating system and provide your own function to communicate with your PC hardware if you want. You can address any of the hardware in your machine directly, and for some application areas where the ultimate performance is required — games programs, for example — this is how programs are regularly implemented.

With Windows, it's all quite different. Here your program is subservient and Windows is in control. You must not deal directly with the hardware and all communications with the outside must pass through Windows. When you use a Windows program you are interacting primarily with Windows, which then communicates with the application program on your behalf. Your Windows program is the tail, Windows is the dog, and your program wags only when Windows tells it to.

There are a number of reasons why this is so. First and foremost, since you are potentially always sharing the computer with other programs that may be executing at the same time, Windows has to have primary control in order to manage the sharing of machine resources. If one application was allowed to have primary control in a Windows environment this would inevitably make programming more complicated because of the need to provide for the possibility of other programs, and information intended for other applications could be lost. A second reason for Windows being in control is that Windows embodies a standard user interface and needs to be in charge to enforce that standard. You can only display information on the screen using the tools that Windows provides, and then only when authorized.

Event-driven Programs

We have already seen, in Chapter 1, that a Windows program is event-driven. A significant part of the code required for a Windows application is dedicated to processing events caused by external actions of the user. Activities that are not directly associated with your application can nonetheless require that bits of your program code are executed. For example, if the user drags the window of another application that is active alongside yours, and this action uncovers part of the client area of the window devoted to your application, your application will need to redraw that part of the window.

Windows Messages

Events are occurrences such as the user clicking the mouse or pressing a key, or a timer reaching zero. Windows records every event in a message and places the message in a message queue for the program for which the message is intended. If your program is properly organized, then by sending a message Windows can tell it that something needs to be done, or that some information has become available, or that an event such as a mouse click has occurred. There are many different kinds of messages and they can occur very frequently — many times per second when the mouse is being dragged, for example.

A Windows program must contain a function specifically for handling these messages. The function is often called **WndProc()** or **WindowProc()**, although it doesn't have to be, since Windows accesses the function through a pointer to a function that you supply. So the sending of a message to your program boils down to Windows calling a function that you provide, typically called **WindowProc()**, and passing any necessary data to your program by means of arguments to this function. Within your **WindowProc()** function it is up to you to work out what the message is from the data supplied and what to do about it.

Fortunately, you don't need to write code to process every message. You can filter out those that are of interest in your program, deal with those in whatever way you want, and pass the rest back to Windows. Passing a message back to Windows is done by calling a standard function provided by Windows called **DefWindowProc()**, which provides default message processing.

The Windows API

All of the communications between a Windows application and Windows itself use the Windows application programming interface, otherwise known as the **Windows API**. This consists of literally hundreds of functions that are provided as standard with Windows to be used by your applications. Structures are often used for passing some kinds of data between Windows and your program, which is why we needed to look at them first.

The Windows API covers all aspects of the dialog necessary between Windows and your application. Because there is such a large number of functions, using them in the raw can be very difficult — just understanding what they all are is a task in itself. This is where Visual C++ comes in. Visual C++ packages the Windows API in a way that structures the functions in an object-oriented manner, and provides an easier way to use the interface with more default functionality. This takes the form of the Microsoft Foundation Classes (MFC).

Visual C++ also provides an application framework in the form of code generated by the AppWizard, which includes all of the boilerplate code necessary for a Windows application, leaving you just to customize this for your particular purposes. The example in Chapter 1 illustrated how much functionality Visual C++ is capable of providing without any coding effort at all on our part. We will discuss this in much more detail when we get to write some examples using AppWizard.

Before we go any further however, you should note that MFC defines many more variable types on top of the basic types we have seen so far in this book. For example, MFC has its own Boolean variable type **BOOL**. A variable of type **BOOL** contains one of the values **TRUE** or **FALSE**. This is different from a variable containing either the value **true** or **false**, as it would do if it were of type **bool**, one of the standard C++ types, which you have already met. MFC also introduces **handles** and **long pointers**, both of which we'll meet in a few pages time.

Notation in Windows Programs

In many Windows programs, variable names have a prefix which indicates what kind of value the variable holds and how it is used. There are quite a few prefixes and they are often used in combination. For example, the prefix **lpfn** signifies a **l**ong **p**ointer to a **f**unction. A sample of the prefixes you might come across is:

Prefix	Meaning
b	a logical variable of type **BOOL**, equivalent to **int**
by	type unsigned char; a **byte**
c	type char
dw	type **DWORD**, which is **unsigned long**
fn	a function
h	a handle, used to identify something (usually an **int** value)
i	type **int**
l	type **long**
lp	**long** pointer
n	type **int**
p	a pointer
s	a string
sz	a zero terminated string
w	type **WORD**, which is **unsigned short**

This use of these prefixes is called **Hungarian notation**. It was introduced to minimize the possibility of misusing a variable by interpreting it differently from how it was defined or intended to be used. Such misinterpretation was easily done in the C language, a precursor of C++. With C++ and its stronger type checking, to avoid such problems you don't need to make such a special effort with your notation. The compiler will always flag an error for type inconsistencies in your program, and many of the kinds of bugs that plagued earlier C programs can't occur with C++.

On the other hand, Hungarian notation can still help to make programs easier to understand, particularly when you are dealing with a lot of variables of different types that are arguments to Windows API functions. Since a lot of Windows programs are still written in C, and of course since parameters for Windows API functions are still defined using Hungarian notation, the method is still widely used.

You can make up your own mind as to the extent to which you want to use Hungarian notation; it is by no means obligatory. You may choose not to use it at all, but in any event, if you have an idea of how it works, you will find it easier to understand what the arguments to the Windows API functions are. There is a small caveat, however. As Windows has developed, the types of some of the API function arguments have changed slightly, but the variable names that are used remain the same. As a consequence, the prefix may not be quite correct in specifying the variable type.

The Structure of a Windows Program

For a minimal Windows program, written using just the Windows API, we will write two functions. These will be a **WinMain()** function, where execution of the program begins and basic program initialization is carried out, and a **WindowProc()** function, which will be called by Windows to process messages for the application. Usually, the **WindowProc()** part of a Windows program is the larger portion because this is where most of the application-specific code will be, responding to messages caused by user input of one kind or another.

While these two functions make up a complete program, they are not directly connected. **WinMain()** does not call **WindowProc()**, Windows does. In fact, Windows also calls **WinMain()**. This is illustrated in the diagram:

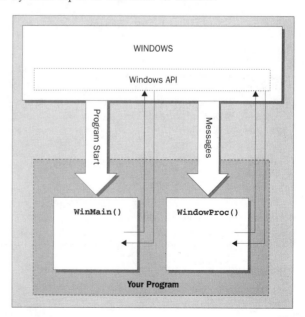

The function **WinMain()** communicates with Windows by calling some of the Windows API functions. The same applies to **WindowProc()**. The integrating factor in your Windows program is Windows itself, which links to both **WinMain()** and **WindowProc()**. We will take a look at what the pieces are that make up **WinMain()** and **WindowProc()**, and then assemble the parts into a working example of a simple Windows program.

The WinMain() Function

The **WinMain()** function is the equivalent of the **main()** function in a DOS (console) program. It's where execution starts and where the basic initialization for the rest of the program is carried out. To allow Windows to pass data to it, **WinMain()** has four parameters and a return value of type **int**. Its prototype is:

```
int WINAPI WinMain(HINSTANCE hInstance,
                   HINSTANCE hPrevInstance,
                   LPSTR lpCmdLine,
                   int nCmdShow
                   );
```

Following the return type specifier, **int**, we have a specification for the function, **WINAPI**, which is new to us. This is a Windows-defined specifier that causes the function name and the arguments to be handled in a special way, which happens to correspond to the way that a function is handled in the Pascal and Fortran languages, which is different from the way functions are normally handled in C++. The precise details are unimportant — this is simply the way Windows requires things to be, so we need to put the **WINAPI** specifier in front of the names of functions called by Windows.

You may wonder why there are types, such as **HINSTANCE** and others, defined by Windows. This is to provide for implementations of Windows in different machine environments. By defining its own, specific Windows types, Windows can control how these types are interpreted and how they can be adjusted to suit the needs of different computers. All the types used by Windows, as well as the prototypes of the Windows API functions, are contained in the header file **windows.h**, so we will need to include this header file when we put our basic Windows program together.

The four arguments passed by Windows to your **WinMain()** function contain important data. The first argument, **hInstance**, is of type **HINSTANCE** which is a handle to an instance, an instance here being a running program. A **handle** is a 32-bit integer value which identifies an object of some kind — in this case the instance of the application. The actual integer value of a handle is not important. The **hInstance** handle allows for the possibility of multiple copies of a Windows program being active simultaneously and individually identifiable. As we will see shortly, handles are also used to identify all sorts of other things. Of course, all handles in a particular context — application instance handles for example — need to be different from one another.

With DOS, only one program can be executed at one time; with Windows, on the other hand, there can be several. This raises the possibility of several copies of the same application being active at once, and this needs to be recognized. Hence, the **hInstance** handle needs to identify a particular copy. If you start more than one copy of the program, each one will have its own unique **hInstance** value.

The next argument, **hPrevInstance**, is a legacy from 16-bit days. Under Windows 3.*x*, this parameter gave you the handle to the previous instance of the program, if there was one. If **hPrevInstance** was **NULL**, you knew that there was no previous instance of the program, so this must be the only copy of the program executing (at the moment, anyway). This information was necessary in many cases, because programs running under Windows 3.*x* share the same address space and multiple copies of a program executing simultaneously could cause complications. For this reason, programmers often limited their applications to only one running instance at a time, and having the **hPrevInstance** argument passed to **WinMain()** allowed them to provide for this very easily by testing it in an **if** statement.

Under 32-bit systems (Windows 95 and Windows NT) the **hPrevInstance** parameter is completely irrelevant since each application runs in its own address space, and one application has no direct knowledge of the existence of another that is executing concurrently. This parameter is always **NULL**, even if another instance of an application is running.

The next argument, **lpCmdLine**, is a pointer to a string containing the command line that started the program. For instance, if you started it using the Run... command from the Start button menu of Windows 95, the string will contain everything that appears in the Open box. Having this pointer allows you to pick up any parameter values that may appear in the command line. The type **LPSTR** is another Windows type, specifying a 32-bit (long) pointer to a string.

The last argument, **nCmdShow**, indicates how the window is to look when it is created. It could be displayed normally or it might need to be minimized; for example, the shortcut for the program might specify that the program should be minimized when it starts. This argument can take one of a fixed set of values that are defined by symbolic constants such as **SW_SHOWNORMAL** and **SW_SHOWMINNOACTIVE**. There are a number of other constants like these which define the way a window is to be displayed and they all begin **SW_**. Other examples are **SW_HIDE** or **SW_SHOWMAXIMIZED**. You don't usually need to examine the value of **nCmdShow**. You typically pass it directly to the Windows API function responsible for displaying your application window.

If you want to know what all the other constants are that specify how a window will be displayed, you can find a complete list of the ten possible values if you search on WinMain in the MSDN Library. The function reference can be found at Platform SDK/User Interface Services/ Windowing/Windows/Window Reference/Window Functions/WinMain

The function **WinMain()** in our Windows program needs to do three things:

▶ Tell Windows what kind of window the program requires

▶ Create and initialize the program window

▶ Retrieve Windows messages intended for the program

Let's take a look at each of these in turn, and then create a complete **WinMain()** function.

Specifying a Program Window

The first step in creating a window is to define just what sort of window it is that we want to create. Windows defines a special **struct** called **WNDCLASS** to contain the data specifying a window. This data defines a window class, which determines the type of window. Do not confuse this with a C++ class, which we will learn about in the next chapter. We need to create a variable from the **struct**, **WNDCLASS**, and give values to each of its members (just like filling in a form). Once we've filled in the variables, we can pass it to Windows (via a function that we'll see later) in order to register the class. When that's been done, whenever we want to create a window of that class, we can tell Windows to look up the class that we've already registered.

The definition of the **WNDCLASS** structure is as follows:

```
struct WNDCLASS
{
    UINT style;                  // Window style
    WNDPROC lpfnWndProc;         // Pointer to message processing function
    int cbClsExtra;              // Extra byte after the window class
    int cbWndExtra;              // Extra bytes after the window instance
    HINSTANCE hInstance;         // The application instance handle
    HICON hIcon;                 // The application icon
    HCURSOR hCursor;             // The window cursor
    HBRUSH hbrBackground;        // The brush defining the background color
    LPCTSTR lpszMenuName;        // A pointer to the name of the menu resource
    LPCTSTR lpszClassName;       // A pointer to the class name
};
```

The **style** member of the **struct** determines various aspects of the window's behavior, in particular, the conditions under which the window should be redrawn. You can select from a number of options for this member's value, each defined by a symbolic constant beginning **CS_**.

You'll find the eleven possible constant values for **style** if you search for **WNDCLASS** in the MSDN Library. Alternatively, the information can be found under Platform SDK/User Interface Services/ Windowing/Window Classes/Window Class Reference/Window Class Structures/ WNDCLASS

Where two or more options are required, the constants can be combined to produce a composite value using the bitwise OR operator, |. For example, assuming that we have declared the variable **WindowClass** of type **WNDCLASS**, we could write:

```
WindowClass.style = CS_HREDRAW | CS_VREDRAW;
```

The option **CS_HREDRAW** indicates to Windows that the window is to be redrawn if its horizontal width is altered, and **CS_VREDRAW** indicates that it is to be redrawn if the vertical height of the window is changed. In the statement above we have elected to have our window redrawn in either case. As a result, Windows will send a message to our program indicating that we should redraw the window whenever the width or height of the window is altered by the user. Each of the possible options for the window style is defined by a unique bit in a 32-bit word being set to 1. That's why the bitwise OR is used to combine them. These bits indicating a particular style are usually called **flags**. Flags are used very frequently, not only in Windows, but also in C++, because they are a very efficient way of representing and processing features that are either there or not, or parameters that are either true or false.

The member **lpfnWndProc** stores a pointer to the function in your program which will handle messages for the window that we will create. The prefix to the name signifies that this is a **long** pointer to a function. If you followed the herd and called the function to handle messages for the application **WindowProc()**, you would initialize this member with the statement:

```
WindowClass.lpfnWndProc = WindowProc;
```

The next two members, **cbClsExtra** and **cbWndExtra**, allow you to ask for some extra space internal to Windows for your own use. An example of this could be when you want to associate additional data with each instance of a window to assist in message handling for each window instance. Normally you won't need extra space allocated for you, in which case you must set the **cbClsExtra** and **cbWndExtra** members to zero.

The **hInstance** member holds the handle for the current application instance, so you should set this to the **hInstance** value passed to **WinMain()** by Windows.

The members **hIcon**, hCursor and **hbrBackground**, are handles which in turn define the icon that will represent the application when minimized, the cursor the window is to use and the background color of the client area of the window. (As we saw earlier, a handle is just a 32-bit integer used as an ID to represent something.) These are set using Windows API functions. For example:

```
WindowClass.hIcon = LoadIcon(0, IDI_APPLICATION);
WindowClass.hCursor = LoadCursor(0, IDC_ARROW);
WindowClass.hbrBackground = static_cast<HBRUSH>(GetStockObject(GRAY_BRUSH));
```

All three members are set to standard Windows values by these function calls. The icon is a default provided by Windows and the cursor is the standard arrow cursor used by the majority of Windows applications. A brush is a Windows object which is used to fill an area, in this case the client area of the window. The function **GetStockObject()** returns a generic type for all stock objects, so we need to cast it to type **HBRUSH**. In the example above, it returns a handle to the standard gray brush, and the background color for our window is thus set to gray. This function can also be used to obtain other standard objects for a window, such as fonts for example.

The **lpszMenuName** member is set to the name of a resource defining the window menu, or to zero if there is no menu for the window. We will be looking into creating and using menu resources when we use the AppWizard.

The last member of the **struct** is **lpszClassName**. This member stores the name that you supply to identify this particular class of window. You would usually use the name of the application for this. You need to keep track of this name, because you will need it again when a window is created. This member would therefore be typically set with the statements:

```
static char szAppName[] = "OFWin";      // Define window class name
WindowClass.lpszClassName = szAppName;   // Set class name
```

In fact, the **WNDCLASS** structure has been obsoleted by another structure **WNDCLASSEX**. The new structure adds a couple of members over those in WNDCLASS, one of which stores the size of the structure in bytes, and the other is a pointer to an icon that is used to represent the application window when it is minimized. Messing with icons is more complication than we really need here, since we just want to understand the basic structure of a Windows program, so we'll stick with the old-fashioned structure in our example.

Creating and Initializing a Program Window

After all the members of your **WNDCLASS** structure have been set to the values required, the next step is to tell Windows about it. You do this using the Windows API function **RegisterClass()**.

Assuming that our structure is **WindowClass**, the statement to do this would be:

```
RegisterClass(&WindowClass);
```

Easy, wasn't it? The address of the **struct** is passed to the function, and Windows will extract and squirrel away all the values that you have set in the structure members. This process is called **registering** the window class. The term *class* here is used in the sense of classification and is not the same as the idea of a **class** in C++, so don't confuse the two. Each instance of the application must make sure that it registers the window classes that it needs. If we were using the **WNDCLASSEX** structure that we just discussed, we would have to use a different function here, **RegisterClassEx()**.

Once Windows knows the characteristics of the window that we want, and the function that is going to handle messages for it, we can go ahead and create it. You use the function **CreateWindow()** for this. The window class that we've already created determines the broad characteristics of a window, and further arguments to the function **CreateWindow()** add additional characteristics. Since an application may have several windows in general, the function **CreateWindow()** returns a handle to the window created, which you can store to enable you to refer to that particular window later. There are a lot of API calls that will require you to specify the window handle as a parameter if you want to use them. We will just look at a typical use of the **CreateWindow()** function at this point. This might be:

```
HWND hWnd;                              // Window handle
...
hWnd = CreateWindow(
        szAppName,                      // the window class name
        "A Basic Window the Hard Way",  // The window title
        WS_OVERLAPPEDWINDOW,            // Window style as overlapped
        CW_USEDEFAULT,                  // Default screen position of upper left
        CW_USEDEFAULT,                  // corner of our window as x,y...
        CW_USEDEFAULT,                  // Default window size, width...
        CW_USEDEFAULT,                  // ...and height
        0,                              // No parent window
        0,                              // No menu
        hInstance,                      // Program Instance handle
        0                               // No window creation data
    );
```

The variable **hWnd** of type **HWND**, is a 32-bit integer handle to a window. We'll use this variable to record the value that identifies the window, returned from the function **CreateWindow()**. The first argument that we pass to the function is the class name. This is used by Windows to identify the **WNDCLASS struct** that we passed to it previously, in the **RegisterClass()** function call, so that the information from this **struct** can be used in the window creation process.

The second argument to **CreateWindow()** defines the text that is to appear on the title bar. The third argument specifies the style that the window will have once it is created. The option specified here, **WS_OVERLAPPEDWINDOW**, actually combines several options. It defines the window as having the **WS_OVERLAPPED**, **WS_CAPTION**, **WS_SYSMENU**, **WS_THICKFRAME**, **WS_MINIMIZEBOX** and **WS_MAXIMIZEBOX** styles. This results in an overlapped window, which is a window intended to be the main application window, with a title bar and a thick frame, which has a title bar icon, system menu and maximize and minimize buttons. A window specified as having a thick frame has borders that can be resized.

The following four arguments determine the position and size of the window on the screen. The first pair are the screen coordinates of the top left corner of the window, and the second pair define the width and height of the window. The value **CW_USEDEFAULT** indicates that we want Windows to assign the default position and size for the window. This tells Windows to arrange successive windows in cascading positions down the screen. **CW_USEDEFAULT** only applies to windows specified as **WS_OVERLAPPED**.

The next argument value is zero, indicating that the window being created is not a child window (a window that is dependent on a parent window). If we wanted it to be a child window, we would set this argument to the handle of the parent window. The next argument is also zero, indicating that no menu is required. We then specify the handle of the current instance of the program which was passed to the program by Windows, and the last argument for window creation data is zero.

The window now exists but is not yet displayed on the screen. We need to call another Windows API function to get it displayed:

```
ShowWindow(hWnd, nCmdShow);              // Display the window
```

Only two arguments are required here. The first identifies the window and is the handle returned by the function **CreateWindow()**. The second is the value **nCmdShow** which was passed to **WinMain()**, and which indicates how the window is to appear on screen.

Initializing the Client Area of the Window

After calling the function **ShowWindow()**, the window will appear on screen but will still have no application content, so let's get our program to draw in the client area of the window. We could just put together some code to do this directly in the **WinMain()** function, but this would be most unsatisfactory: the contents of the client area cannot be considered to be permanent — we can't afford to output what we want and forget about it. Any action on the part of the user which modifies the window in some way, such as dragging a border or dragging the whole window, will typically require that the window *and* its client area are redrawn.

When the client area needs to be redrawn for any reason, Windows will send a particular message to our program and our **WindowProc()** function will need to respond by reconstructing the client area of the window. Therefore, the best way to get the client area drawn in the first instance is to get Windows to send the message requesting this to our program. Indeed, whenever we know in our program that the window should be redrawn, when we change something for example, we just need to tell Windows to send a message back to this effect.

We can do this by calling another Windows API function, **UpdateWindow()**. The statement to accomplish this is:

```
UpdateWindow(hWnd);                  // Cause window client area to be drawn
```

This function only requires one argument: the window handle **hWnd**, which identifies our particular program window. (In general there can be several windows in an application.) The result of the call is that Windows will send a message to our program requesting that the client area be redrawn.

Dealing with Windows Messages

The last task that **WinMain()** needs to address is dealing with the messages that Windows may have queued for our application. This may seem a bit odd, since we said earlier that we needed the function **WindowProc()** to deal with messages.

Queued and Non-Queued Messages

There are, in fact, two kinds of Windows messages. Firstly, there are **queued messages**, which Windows places in a queue and which the **WinMain()** function needs to extract from the queue for processing. The code in **WinMain()** that does this is called the **message loop**. Queued messages include those arising from user input from the keyboard, moving the mouse and clicking the mouse buttons. Messages from a timer and the Windows message to request that a window be repainted are also queued.

Secondly, there are **non-queued messages** which result in the **WindowProc()** function being called directly by Windows. A lot of the non-queued messages arise as a consequence of processing queued messages. What we are doing in the message loop in **WinMain()** is retrieving a message that Windows has queued for our application and then asking Windows to invoke our function **WindowProc()** to process it. Why can't Windows just call **WindowProc()** whenever necessary? Well it could, but it just doesn't work this way. The reasons are to do with how Windows manages multiple applications executing simultaneously.

The Message Loop

Retrieving messages from the message queue is done using a standard mechanism in Windows programming called the message loop. The code for this would be:

```
MSG msg;                                // Windows message structure
while(GetMessage(&msg, 0, 0, 0) == TRUE) // Get any messages
{
    TranslateMessage(&msg);             // Translate the message
    DispatchMessage(&msg);              // Dispatch the message
}
```

This involves three steps in dealing with each message:

▶ **GetMessage()** — retrieves a message from the queue.

▶ **TranslateMessage()** — performs any conversion necessary on the message retrieved.

▶ **DispatchMessage()** — causes Windows to call the **WindowProc()** function in our application to deal with the message

The operation of **GetMessage()** is important since it has a significant contribution to the way Windows works with multiple applications. Let's look into it in a little more detail.

The **GetMessage()** function will retrieve a message queued for our application window and will store information about the message in the variable **msg**, pointed to by the first argument. The variable **msg**, which is a **struct** of type **MSG**, contains a number of different members which we will not be accessing here. Still, for completeness, the definition of the structure is:

```
struct MSG
{
   HWND    hwnd;          // Handle for the relevant window
   UINT    message;       // The message ID
   WPARAM wParam;         // Message parameter (32-bits)
   LPARAM lParam;         // Message parameter (32-bits)
   DWORD   time;          // The time when the message was queued
   POINT   pt;            // The mouse position
};
```

The **wParam** member is an example of a slightly misleading Hungarian notation prefix that we mentioned was now possible. You might assume that it was of type **WORD** (which is **int**), which used to be true in earlier Windows versions, but now it is of type **WPARAM**, which is a 32-bit integer value.

The exact contents of the members **wParam** and **lParam** are dependent on what kind of message it is. The message ID in the member **message** is an integer value and can be one of a set of values that are predefined in the header file, **windows.h**, as symbolic constants. They all start with **WM_** and typical examples are **WM_PAINT** to redraw the screen and **WM_QUIT** to end the program. The function **GetMessage()** will always return **TRUE** unless the message is **WM_QUIT** to end the program, in which case the value returned is **FALSE**, or unless an error occurs, in which case the return value is **-1**. Thus, the **while** loop will continue until a quit message is generated to close the application or until an error condition arises. In either case, we would then need to end the program by passing the **wParam** value back to Windows in a **return** statement.

The second argument in the call to **GetMessage()** is the handle of the window for which we want to get messages. This parameter can be used to retrieve messages for one window separately from another. If this argument is 0, as it is here, **GetMessage()** will retrieve all messages for an application, so this is an easy way of retrieving all messages for an application regardless of how many windows it has. It is also the safest way, since you are sure of getting all the messages for your application. When the user of your Windows program closes the application window, for example, the window is closed before the **WM_QUIT** message is generated. Consequently, if you only retrieve messages by specifying a window handle to the **GetMessage()** function, you will not retrieve the **WM_QUIT** message and your program will not be able to terminate properly.

The last two arguments to **GetMessage()** are integers that hold minimum and maximum values for the message IDs you want to retrieve from the queue. This allows messages to be retrieved selectively. A range is usually specified by symbolic constants. Using **WM_MOUSEFIRST** and **WM_MOUSELAST** as these two arguments would select just mouse messages, for example. If both arguments are zero, as we have them here, all messages are retrieved.

Multitasking

If there are no messages queued, the **GetMessage()** function will not come back to our program. Windows will allow execution to pass to another application and we will only get a value returned from calling **GetMessage()** when a message appears in the queue. This mechanism is fundamental in enabling multiple applications to run under Windows 3.x, and is referred to as **cooperative multitasking** because it depends on concurrent applications giving up their control of the processor from time to time. Once your program calls **GetMessage()**, unless there is a message for your program, another application will be executed and your program will only get another opportunity to do something if the other application releases the processor, perhaps by a call to **GetMessage()** when there are no messages queued for it, but this is not the only possibility.

With Windows 3.*x*, a program that does not call **GetMessage()**, or includes code for a heavy computation that does not make provision for returning control to Windows from time to time, can retain use of the processor indefinitely. With Windows 95, the operating system can interrupt an application after a period of time and transfer control to another application. This is called **pre-emptive multitasking**. However, you still need to program the message loop in **WinMain()** using **GetMessage()** as before, and make provision for relinquishing control of the processor to Windows from time to time in a long running calculation (this is usually done using the **PeekMessage()** API function). If you don't do this, your application may be unable to respond to messages to repaint the application window when these arise. This can be for reasons that are quite independent of your application — when an overlapping window for another application is closed, for example.

The conceptual operation of the **GetMessage()** function is illustrated below:

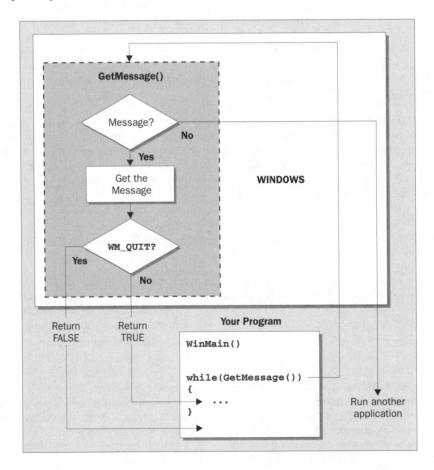

Within the **while** loop, the first function call to **TranslateMessage()** requests Windows to do some conversion work for keyboard related messages. Then the call to the function **DispatchMessage()** causes Windows to dispatch the message, or in other words, to call the **WindowProc()** function in our program to process the message. The return from **DispatchMessage()** will not occur until **WindowProc()** has finished processing the message. The **WM_QUIT** message indicates that the program should end, so this results in **FALSE** being returned to the application, which stops the message loop.

A Complete WinMain() Function

We have looked at all the bits that need to go into the function **WinMain()**. So now let's assemble them into a complete function:

```
// Listing OFWIN_1
int WINAPI WinMain(HINSTANCE hInstance, HINSTANCE hPrevInstance,
                   LPSTR lpCmdLine, int nCmdShow)
{
   WNDCLASS WindowClass;                   // Structure to hold our window's attributes

   static char szAppName[] = "OFWin"; // Define window class name
   HWND hWnd;                              // Window handle
   MSG msg;                                // Windows message structure

   // Redraw the window if the size changes
   WindowClass.style   = CS_HREDRAW | CS_VREDRAW;

   // Define our procedure for message handling
   WindowClass.lpfnWndProc = WindowProc;

   WindowClass.cbClsExtra = 0;         // No extra bytes after the window class
   WindowClass.cbWndExtra = 0;         // structure or the window instance

   WindowClass.hInstance = hInstance; // Application instance handle

   // Set default application icon
   WindowClass.hIcon = LoadIcon(0, IDI_APPLICATION);

   // Set window cursor to be the standard arrow
   WindowClass.hCursor = LoadCursor(0, IDC_ARROW);

   // Set gray brush for background color
   WindowClass.hbrBackground = static_cast<HBRUSH>(GetStockObject(GRAY_BRUSH));

   WindowClass.lpszMenuName = 0;       // No menu, so no menu resource name

   WindowClass.lpszClassName = szAppName;    // Set class name

   // Now register our window class
   RegisterClass(&WindowClass);

   //  Now we can create the window
   hWnd = CreateWindow(
         szAppName,                         // the window class name
         "A Basic Window the Hard Way",     // The window title
         WS_OVERLAPPEDWINDOW,               // Window style as overlapped
         CW_USEDEFAULT,                     // Default screen position of  upper left
         CW_USEDEFAULT,                     // corner of our window as x,y...
```

```
            CW_USEDEFAULT,              // Default window size
            CW_USEDEFAULT,              // ....
            0,                          // No parent window
            0,                          // No menu
            hInstance,                  // Program Instance handle
            0                           // No window creation data
        );

    ShowWindow(hWnd, nCmdShow);         // Display the window
    UpdateWindow(hWnd);                 // Cause window client area to be drawn

    // The message loop
    while(GetMessage(&msg, 0, 0, 0) == TRUE)    // Get any messages
    {
       TranslateMessage(&msg);                  // Translate the message
       DispatchMessage(&msg);                   // Dispatch the message
    }

    return msg.wParam;                           // End, so return to Windows
}
```

How It Works

After declaring the variables we need in the function, all the members of the **WindowClass** structure are initialized and the window is registered.

The next step is to call the **CreateWindow()** function to create the data for the physical appearance of the window, based on the arguments passed and the data established in the **WindowClass** structure that was previously passed to Windows using the **RegisterClass()** function. The call to **ShowWindow()** causes the window to be displayed according to the mode specified by **nCmdShow**, and the **UpdateWindow()** function signals that a message to draw the window client area should be generated.

Finally, the message loop will continue to retrieve messages for the application until a **WM_QUIT** message is obtained, whereupon the **GetMessage()** function will return **FALSE** and the loop will end. The value of the **wParam** member of the **msg** structure is passed back to Windows in the **return** statement.

Message Processing Functions

The function **WinMain()** contained nothing that was application-specific beyond the general appearance of the application window. All of the code that will make the application behave in the way that we want is going to be included in the message processing part of the program. This is the function **WindowProc()** that we identified to Windows in the **WindowClass** structure. Windows will call this function each time a message for our main application window is dispatched.

Our example is going to be very simple, so we will be putting all the code to process messages in the one function, **WindowProc()**. More generally though, the **WindowProc()** function would be responsible for analyzing what a given message was and which window it was destined for, and then calling one of a whole range of functions, each of which would be geared to handling a particular message in the context of the particular window concerned. However, the overall sequence of operations, and the way in which the function **WindowProc()** analyses an incoming message, will be much the same in most application contexts.

The WindowProc() Function

The prototype of our **WindowProc()** function is:

```
long CALLBACK WindowProc(HWND hWnd, UINT message, WPARAM wParam, LPARAM lParam);
```

Since the function will be called by Windows through a pointer (we set the pointer up in **WinMain()** in the **WNDCLASS** structure), we need to qualify the function as **CALLBACK**. This is another specifier defined by Windows that determines how the function arguments are handled. The four arguments that are passed provide information about the particular message causing the function to be called. The meaning of each of these arguments is described in the table below:

Argument	Meaning
HWND hWnd	A handle to the window in which the event causing the message occurred.
UINT message	The message ID, which is a 32-bit value indicating the type of message.
WPARAM wParam	A 32-bit value containing additional information depending on what sort of message it is.
LPARAM lParam	A 32-bit value containing additional information depending on what sort of message it is. Note — **lparam** has some slightly different uses to **wparam**, but for our purposes the difference is negligible - so don't worry about it.

The window that the incoming message relates to is identified by the first argument, **hWnd**, that is passed to the function. In our case, we only have one window, so we can ignore it.

Messages are identified by the value **message** that is passed to **WindowProc()**. You can test this value against predefined symbolic constants, each of which relates to a particular message. They all begin with **WM_**, and typical examples are **WM_PAINT**, which corresponds to a request to redraw part of the client area of a window, and **WM_LBUTTONDOWN**, which indicates that the left mouse button was pressed. You can find the whole set of these by searching for WM_ in the MSDN Library.

Decoding a Windows Message

The process of decoding the message that Windows is sending is usually done using a **switch** statement in the **WindowProc()** function, based on the value of **message**. Selecting the message types that you want to process is then just a question of putting a **case** statement for each case in the **switch**. The typical structure of such a **switch** statement, with arbitrary cases included, is as follows:

```
switch(message)
{
   case WM_PAINT:
      // Code to deal with drawing the client area
      break;

   case WM_LBUTTONDOWN:
      // Code to deal with the left mouse button being pressed
      break;
```

```
     case WM_LBUTTONUP:
        // Code to deal with the left mouse button being released
        break;

     case WM_DESTROY:
        // Code to deal with a window being destroyed
        break;

     default:
        // Code to handle any other messages
  }
```

Every Windows program will have something like this somewhere, although it will be hidden from sight in the Windows programs that we will write later using MFC. Each case corresponds to a particular value for the message ID and provides suitable processing for that message. Any messages that a program does not want to deal with individually are handled by the default statement, which should hand the messages back to Windows by calling **DefWindowProc()**. This is the Windows API function providing default message handling.

In a complex program dealing specifically with a wide range of possible Windows messages, this **switch** statement can become very large and rather cumbersome. When we get to use AppWizard, we won't have to worry about this, because it is all taken care of for us and we will never see the **WindowProc()** function. All we will need to do is to supply the code to process the particular messages that we are interested in.

Drawing the Window Client Area

To signal that the client area of an application should be redrawn, Windows sends a **WM_PAINT** message to the program. So in our example, we will need to draw the text in the window in response to the **WM_PAINT** message.

We can't go drawing in the window willy nilly. Before we can write to our window, we need to tell Windows that we want to do so, and get Windows' authority to go ahead. We do this by calling the Windows API function **BeginPaint()**, which should only be called in response to a **WM_PAINT** message. It is used as follows:

```
   HDC hDC;                          // A display context handle
   PAINTSTRUCT PaintSt;              // Structure defining area to be redrawn

   hDC = BeginPaint(hWnd, &PaintSt);  // Prepare to draw in the window
```

The type **HDC** defines what is called a **display context**, or more generally a **device context**. A device context provides the link between the device-independent Windows API functions for outputting information to the screen or a printer, and the device drivers which support writing to the specific devices attached to your PC. You can also regard a device context as a token of authority which is handed to you on request by Windows and grants you permission to output some information. Without a device context, you simply can't generate any output.

The **BeginPaint()** function provides us with a display context as a return value and requires two arguments to be supplied. The window to which we want to write is identified by the window handle, **hWnd**, which we pass as the first argument. The second argument is the address of a **PAINTSTRUCT** variable **PaintSt**, in which Windows will place information about the area to be redrawn in response to the **WM_PAINT** message. We will ignore the details of this since we are not going to use it. We will just redraw the whole of the client area. We can obtain the coordinates of the client area in a **RECT** structure with the statements:

```
    RECT aRect;                             // A working rectangle
    GetClientRect(hWnd, &aRect);
```

The **GetClientRect()** function supplies the coordinates of the upper-left and lower-right corners of the client area for the window specified by the first argument. These coordinates will be stored in the **RECT** structure **aRect**, which is passed through the second argument as a pointer. We can then use this definition of the client area for our window when we write the text to the window using the **DrawText()** function. Because our window has a gray background, we should alter the background of the text to be transparent, to allow the gray to show through, otherwise the text will appear against a white background. We can do this with the API function call:

```
    SetBkMode(hDC, TRANSPARENT);           // Set text background mode
```

The first argument identifies the device context and the second sets the background mode. The default option is **OPAQUE**.

We can now write the text with the statement:

```
    DrawText(hDC,                          // Device context handle
             "But, soft! What light through yonder window breaks?",
             -1,                           // Indicate null terminated string
             &aRect,                       // Rectangle in which text is to be drawn
             DT_SINGLELINE|                // Text format - single line
             DT_CENTER|                    //              - centered in the line
             DT_VCENTER                    //              - line centered in aRect
    );
```

The first argument is our certificate of authority, the display context **hDC**. The next argument is the text string that we want to output. We could equally well have defined this in a variable and passed the pointer to the text as the second argument in the function call. The next argument, with the value -1, signifies our string is terminated with a null character. If it weren't, we would put the count of the number of characters in the string here. The fourth argument is a pointer to a **RECT** structure defining a rectangle in which we want to write the text. In our case it is the whole client area defined in **aRect**. The last argument defines the format for the text in the rectangle. Here we have combined three specifications with a bitwise OR (|). Our string will be a single line, with the text centered on the line and the line centered vertically within the rectangle. This will place it nicely in the center of the window. There are also a number of other options, which include the possibility to place text at the top or the bottom of the rectangle, and to left or right justify it.

Once we have output all the text we want, we must tell Windows that we have finished drawing the client area. For every **BeginPaint()** function call, there must be a corresponding **EndPaint()** function call. Thus, to end processing the **WM_PAINT** message, we need the statement:

```
    EndPaint(hWnd, &PaintSt);              // Terminate window redraw operation
```

The **hWnd** argument identifies our program window, and the second argument is the address of the **PAINTSTRUCT** structure that was filled in by the **BeginPaint()** function.

Ending the Program

You might assume that closing the window will close the application, but to get this behavior we actually have to add some code. The reason that our application won't close when the window is closed is that we may need to do some clearing up. It is also possible that the application may have more than one window. When the user closes the window by double-clicking the title bar icon or clicking the close button, this causes a **WM_DESTROY** message to be generated. Therefore, in order to close the application we need to process the **WM_DESTROY** message in our **WindowProc()** function. We do this by generating a **WM_QUIT** message with the following statement:

```
PostQuitMessage(0);
```

The argument here is an exit code. This Windows API function does exactly what its name suggests — it posts a **WM_QUIT** message in the message queue for our application. This will result in the **GetMessage()** function in **WinMain()** returning **FALSE** and ending the message loop, so ending the program.

A Complete WindowProc() Function

We have covered all the elements necessary to make up the complete **WindowProc()** function for our example. The code for the function is as follows:

```
// Listing OFWIN_2
long WINAPI WindowProc(HWND hWnd, UINT message, WPARAM wParam,
                       LPARAM lParam)
{
   HDC hDC;                         // Display context handle
   PAINTSTRUCT PaintSt;             // Structure defining area to be drawn
   RECT aRect;                      // A working rectangle

   switch(message)                  // Process selected messages
   {
      case WM_PAINT:                           // Message is to redraw the window
         hDC = BeginPaint(hWnd, &PaintSt);// Prepare to draw the window

         // Get upper left and lower right of client area
         GetClientRect(hWnd, &aRect);

         SetBkMode(hDC, TRANSPARENT);     // Set text background mode

         // Now draw the text in the window client area
         DrawText(
            hDC,                     // Device context handle
            "But, soft! What light through yonder window breaks?",
            -1,                      // Indicate null terminated string
            &aRect,                  // Rectangle in which text is to be drawn
            DT_SINGLELINE|           // Text format - single line
            DT_CENTER|               //             - centered in the line
            DT_VCENTER);             //             - line centered in aRect

         EndPaint(hWnd, &PaintSt); // Terminate window redraw operation
         return 0;
```

```
        case WM_DESTROY:                 // Window is being destroyed
           PostQuitMessage(0);
           return 0;

        default:                         // Any other message - we don't
                                         // want to know, so call
                                         // default message processing
           return DefWindowProc(hWnd, message, wParam, lParam);
    }
}
```

How It Works

The function consists wholly of a **switch** statement. A particular **case** will be selected, based on the message ID passed to our function in the parameter **message**. Because our example is very simple, we only need to process two different messages: **WM_PAINT** and **WM_DESTROY**. We hand all other messages back to Windows by calling the **DefWindowProc()** function in the **default** case for the **switch**. The arguments to **DefWindowProc()** are those that were passed to our function, so we are just passing them back as they are. Note the **return** statement at the end of processing each message type. For the messages we handle, a zero value is returned.

A Simple Windows Program

Since we have written **WinMain()** and **WindowProc()** to handle messages, we have enough to create a complete source file for our Windows program. The complete source file will simply consist of an **#include** statement for the Windows header file, a prototype for the **WindowProc** function and the **WinMain** and **WindowProc** functions that we've already seen:

```
// OFWIN.CPP   Native windows program to display text in a window
#include <windows.h>

long WINAPI WindowProc(HWND hWnd, UINT message, WPARAM wParam, LPARAM lParam);

   // Insert code for WinMain() here (Listing OFWIN_1)

   // Insert code for WindowProc() here (Listing OFWIN_2)
```

Of course, you'll need to create a project for this program, but instead of choosing Win32 Console Application as you've done up to now, you should create this project as a Win32 Application.

> Note that if you mistakenly create it as a *Win32 Console Application*, then when you try to link the code, you'll see the error:
>
> LIBCD.lib(crt0.obj) : error LNK2001: unresolved external symbol _main

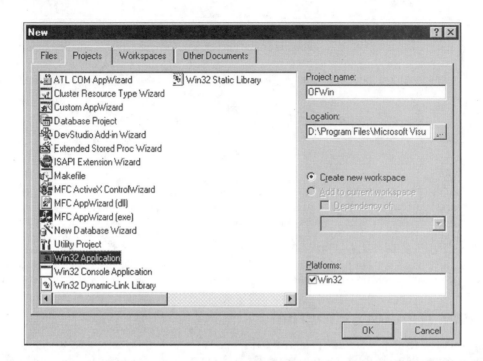

TRY IT OUT - Old-Fashioned Windows

If you build and execute the example, it will produce the window shown below:

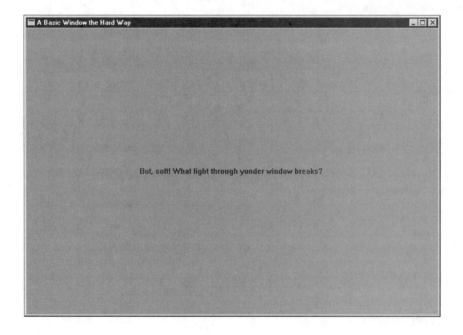

Note that the window has a number of properties provided by Windows that require no programming effort on our part to manage. The boundaries of the window can be dragged to resize it, and the whole window can be moved about on the screen. The maximize and minimize buttons also work. Of course, all of these actions do affect the program. Every time you modify the position or size of the window, a **WM_PAINT** message will be queued and our program will have to redraw the client area, but all the work of drawing and modifying the window itself is done by Windows.

The system menu and close button are also standard features of our window because of the options that we specified in the **WindowClass** structure. Again, Windows takes care of the management. The only additional effect on our program arising from this is the passing of a **WM_DESTROY** message if you close the window, as we have previously discussed.

Summary

In this chapter, we have described the idea of a **struct**, because Windows uses structures for passing data. However, all the capabilities of a **struct** are provided by a **class** in C++, which we'll discuss in the next chapter. Since we can always use a **class** instead of a **struct**, , we won't be elaborating on the **struct** any further. For the remainder of the book, we'll just use classes.

The example that we developed in this chapter was designed to introduce you to the basic mechanics of operating a program under Windows. As we said at the beginning of the chapter, we don't actually need to know about this when using the full capabilities of Visual C++, because all the details of creating and displaying a window, the message loop, and analyzing messages passed to an application are all submerged in the code that Visual C++ can provide automatically. However, you should find that the operation of programs generated by the AppWizard is much easier to understand if you have plowed through the material in this chapter, and this should make the AppWizard even easier to apply.

You may also be like me — never quite comfortable with taking things on trust, and not happy about using things without understanding how they really work. This has its downside of course. It can take a while to get comfortable with using something as mundane as a microwave oven, or even taking a plane. With the latter, understanding the theory still doesn't make sitting in a metal tube seven miles above the earth feel like a secure and natural thing to be doing!

We are back to C++ in the next chapter, this time looking into the basis for object-oriented programming — the class.

Exercises

Ex7-1: Define a struct **X** which contains two integer data items. Write a program which declares two **X**s, called **a** and **b**. Fill in the data items for **a**, and then check that you can copy it into **b** by simple assignment.

Ex7-2: Add a **char*** member to struct **X**, called **sptr**. When you fill in the data for **a**, dynamically create a string buffer and make **a.sptr** point to it. Copy **a** into **b**. What happens when you change the contents of the character buffer in **a** and then print it from **b**? Explain what is happening. How would you get around this?

Ex7-3: Create a function which takes a pointer to an **X** as an argument, and which prints out the members of any **X** passed to it. Test this function using your existing program.

Ex7-4: Take [Prg4], and create a struct, **item**, to hold the **name** and the number. Modify the program to work with **item**s. Now you have [Prg5].

Ex7-5: Code up the **OFWin** program from this chapter, and make sure it runs correctly. Can you now modify it so that the program's main window is exactly in the center of your screen, and measures 300 by 200 pixels? (Hint: look up the **GetSystemMetrics()** API call in the help system to get the size of the screen.)

Structuring Your Data Using Classes

This chapter is about creating your own data types to suit your particular problem. This will go far beyond the notion of collecting related variables together in a data structure that we saw in the last chapter. It's also about creating objects, the building blocks of object-oriented programming. An object can seem a bit mysterious to the uninitiated but, as we shall see in this chapter, an object is just an instance of one of your own data types.

In this chapter you will learn about:

▶ Classes and how they are used

▶ The basic components of a class and how a class is declared

▶ Creating and using objects of a class

▶ Controlling access to members of a class

▶ Constructors and how to create them

▶ The default constructor

▶ References in the context of classes

▶ The copy constructor and how it is implemented

Data Types, Objects, Classes and Instances

Before we get into the language, syntax and programming techniques of classes, we'll start by considering how our existing knowledge relates to the concept of classes.

So far, we've learnt that C++ lets you create variables which can be any of a range of basic data types: **int**, **long**, **double** and so on. In the previous chapter, you saw how you could use the **struct** keyword to define a structure which, in turn, defined a variable representing a composite of several other variable types.

The variables of the basic types don't allow you to model real-world objects (or even imaginary objects) adequately. It's hard to model a box in terms of an **int**, for example. However, as we saw in the previous chapter, you could use the members of a **struct** to define extended attributes of your object. You could define variables, **length**, **breadth** and **height** to represent the dimensions of the box and bind them together as members of a **Box** structure, as follows:

```
struct Box
{
   double length;
   double breadth;
   double height;
};
```

With this definition of a new data type called **Box**, you can go ahead and define variables of this type just as you did with variables of the basic types. You can then create, manipulate and destroy as many **Box** objects as you need to in your program. This means that you can model objects using **struct**s and write your programs around them. So — that's object-oriented programming all wrapped up then?

Well, not quite. You see, object-oriented programming (OOP) is based on a number of foundations (famously *encapsulation*, *polymorphism* and *inheritance*) and what we have seen so far doesn't quite fit the bill. Don't worry about what these terms mean for the moment — we'll be exploring that in the rest of this chapter and throughout the book.

The notion of a **struct** in C++ goes far beyond the **struct** in C — it incorporates the object-oriented notion of a **class**. This idea of classes, from which you can create your own data types and use them just like the native types, is fundamental to C++, and the new keyword **class** was introduced to describe this concept. The keywords **struct** and **class** are almost identical in C++, except for the access control to the members, which we will find out more about later in this chapter. The keyword **struct** is maintained for backwards compatibility with C.

We saw a little of what **struct**s can do in the last chapter. In this chapter, we'll be looking at classes, and we'll see how much more we can do. Let's look at how we'd define a class for boxes:

```
class CBox
{
   public:
      double m_Length;
      double m_Breadth;
      double m_Height;
};
```

Just like when we defined the **Box** structure, when we define **CBox** as a class we are essentially defining a new data type. The only differences here are the use of the keyword **class** instead of **struct**, and the use of the keyword **public** followed by a colon that precedes the definition of the members of the class. These are called **data members** of the class, since they are variables that store data.

We have also called the class **CBox** instead of **Box**. We could have called the class **Box**, but MFC adopts the convention of using the prefix **C** for all class names, so we might as well get into the habit now. MFC also prefixes data members of classes with **m_** to distinguish them from other variables, so we'll use this convention too.

The **public** keyword is a clue as to the difference between a structure and a class. It just defines the members of the class as being generally accessible, in the same way as the members of the structures that we used in the last chapter were. The members of a **struct**, however, are public by default. As you'll see a little later in the chapter, though, it's also possible to place restrictions on the accessibility of the class members.

We can declare a variable, **bigBox** say, that is an instance of the **CBox** class like this:

```
CBox bigBox;
```

This is exactly the same as declaring a variable for a **struct**, or indeed for any other variable type. Once we've defined the class **CBox**, the declaration of variables of this type is quite standard. The variable **bigBox** here is also referred to as an **object** or an **instance** of the class **CBox**.

First Class

The notion of class was invented by an Englishman to keep the general population happy. It derives from the theory that people who knew their place and function in society would be much more secure and comfortable in life than those who did not. The famous Dane, Bjarne Stroustrup, who invented C++, undoubtedly acquired a deep knowledge of class concepts while at Cambridge University in England and appropriated the idea very successfully for use in his new language.

Class in C++ is similar to the English concept, in that each class usually has a very precise role and a permitted set of actions. However, it differs from the English idea, because class in C++ has largely socialist overtones, concentrating on the importance of working classes. Indeed, in some ways it is the reverse of the English ideal, because, as we shall see, working classes in C++ often live on the backs of classes that do nothing at all.

Operations on Classes

In C++ you can create new data types as classes to represent whatever kinds of objects you like. As you'll come to see, classes (and structures) aren't limited to just holding data; you can also define member functions or even operations that act between objects of your classes using the standard C++ operators. You can define the class **CBox**, for example, so that the following statements work and have the meanings you want them to have:

```
CBox box1;
CBox box2;

if(box1 > box2)            // Fill the larger box
   box1.fill();
else
   box2.fill();
```

You could also implement operations as part of the **CBox** class for adding, subtracting or even multiplying boxes — in fact, almost any operation to which you could ascribe a sensible meaning in the context of boxes.

We're talking about incredibly powerful medicine here and it constitutes a major change in the approach that we can take to programming. Instead of breaking down a problem in terms of what are essentially computer-related data types (integer numbers, floating point numbers and so on) and then writing a program, we're going to be programming in terms of problem-related data types, in other words classes. These classes might be named **CEmployee**, or **CCowboy**, or **CCheese**, or **CChutney**, each defined specifically for the kind of problem that you want to solve, complete with the functions and operators that are necessary to manipulate instances of your new types.

Program design now starts with deciding what new application-specific data types you need to solve the problem in hand and writing the program in terms of operations on the specifics that the problem is concerned with, be it **CCoffins** or **CCowpokes**.

Terminology

Let's summarize some of the terminology that we will be using when discussing classes in C++:

> A **class** is a user-defined data type.

> **Object-oriented programming** is the programming style based on the idea of defining your own data types as classes.

> Declaring an object of a class is sometimes referred to as **instantiation** because you are creating an **instance** of a class.

> Instances of a class are referred to as **objects**.

> The idea of an object containing the data implicit in its definition, together with the functions that operate on that data, is referred to as **encapsulation**.

When we get into the detail of object-oriented programming, it may seem a little complicated in places, but getting back to the basics of what you're doing can often help to make things clearer, so always keep in mind what objects are really about. They are about writing programs in terms of the objects that are specific to the domain of your problem. All the facilities around classes in C++ are there to make this as comprehensive and flexible as possible. Let's get down to the business of understanding classes.

Understanding Classes

A class is a data type that you define. It can contain data elements which can either be variables of the basic types in C++, or other user-defined types. The data elements of a class may be single data elements, arrays, pointers, arrays of pointers of almost any kind, or objects of other classes, so you have a lot of flexibility in what you can include in your data type. A class can also contain functions which operate on objects of the class by accessing the data elements that they include. So, a class combines both the definition of the elementary data that makes up an object and the means of manipulating the data belonging to individual objects of the class.

The data and functions within a class are called **members** of the class. Funnily enough, the members of a class that are data items are called **data members** and the members that are functions are called **function members** or **member functions**. The member functions of a class are also sometimes referred to as **methods**, but we will not use this term in this book.

When you define a class, you define a blueprint for a data type. This doesn't actually define any data but it does define what the class name means, that is, what an object of the class will consist of and what operations can be performed on such an object. It's much the same as if you wrote a description of the basic type **double**. This wouldn't be an actual variable of type **double**, but a definition of how it's made up and how it operates. To create a variable of a basic data type, you need to use a declaration statement. It's exactly the same with classes, as you will see.

Defining a Class

Let's look again at the class we started talking about at the start of the chapter — a class of boxes. We defined the **CBox** data type using the keyword **class** as follows:

```
class CBox
{
public:
   double m_Length;           // Length of a box in inches
   double m_Breadth;          // Breadth of a box in inches
   double m_Height;           // Height of a box in inches
};
```

The name that we've given to our class appears following the keyword and the three data members are defined between the curly braces. The data members are defined for the class using the declaration statements that we already know and love and the whole class definition is terminated with a semicolon. The names of all the members of a class are local to a class. You can therefore use the same names elsewhere in a program without causing any problems.

Access Control in a Class

The keyword **public** looks a bit like a label, but in fact it is more than that. It determines the access attributes of the members of the class that follow it. Specifying the data members as **public** means that these members of an object of the class can be accessed anywhere within the scope of the class object. You can also specify the members of a class as **private** or **protected**. In fact, if you omit the access specification altogether, the members have the default attribute, **private**. (This is the only difference between a class and a struct in C++ — the default access specifier for a struct is **public**.) We shall look into the effect of these keywords in a class definition a bit later.

Remember that all we have defined so far is a class, which is a data type. We haven't declared any objects of the class. When we talk about accessing a class member, say **m_Height**, we're talking about accessing the data member of a particular object, and that object needs to be declared somewhere.

Declaring Objects of a Class

We declare objects of a class with exactly the same sort of declaration that we use to declare objects of basic types. We saw this at the beginning of the chapter. So, we could declare objects of our class **CBox** with these statements:

```
CBox box1;                // Declare box1 of type CBox
CBox box2;                // Declare box2 of type CBox
```

Both of the objects **box1** and **box2** will, of course, have their own data members. This is illustrated here:

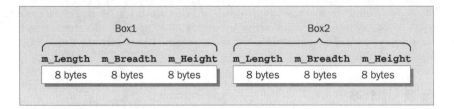

The object name **box1** embodies the whole object, including its three data members. They are not initialized to anything, however — the data members of each object will simply contain junk values, so we need to look at how we can access them for the purpose of setting them to some specific values.

Accessing the Data Members of a Class

The data members of objects of a class can be referred to using the **direct member selection operator** that we used to access members of a **struct**. So, to set the value of the data member **m_Height** of the object **box2** to, say, 18.0, we could write this assignment statement:

```
box2.m_Height = 18.0;              // Setting the value of a data member
```

We can only access the data member in this way, in a function outside the class, because the member **m_Height** was specified as having **public** access. If it wasn't defined as **public**, this statement would not compile. We'll see more about this shortly.

TRY IT OUT - Your First Use of Classes

Let's first verify that we can use our class in the same way as the structure. We'll try it out in the following console application:

```
// EX8_01.CPP
// Creating and using boxes
#include <iostream>
using namespace std;

class CBox                                // Class definition at global scope
{
   public:
      double m_Length;                    // Length of a box in inches
      double m_Breadth;                   // Breadth of a box in inches
      double m_Height;                    // Height of a box in inches
};

int main()
{
   CBox box1;                             // Declare box1 of type CBox
   CBox box2;                             // Declare box2 of type CBox

   double boxVolume = 0.0;                // Store the volume of a box here
```

```
    box1.m_Height = 18.0;                    // Define the values
    box1.m_Length = 78.0;                    // of the members of
    box1.m_Breadth = 24.0;                   // the object box1

    box2.m_Height = box1.m_Height - 10;      // Define box2
    box2.m_Length = box1.m_Length/2.0;       // members in
    box2.m_Breadth = 0.25*box1.m_Length;     // terms of box1

    // Calculate volume of box1
    boxVolume = box1.m_Height*box1.m_Length*box1.m_Breadth;

    cout << endl
        << "Volume of box1 = " << boxVolume;

    cout << endl
        << "box2 has sides which total "
        << box2.m_Height+ box2.m_Length+ box2.m_Breadth
        << " inches.";

    cout << endl                             // Display the size of a box in memory
        << "A CBox object occupies "
        << sizeof box1 << " bytes.";

    cout <<endl;
    return 0;
}
```

As you type in the code for **main()**, you should see the editor prompting you with a list of member names whenever you enter a member selection operator following the name of a class object. You can then select the member you want from the list by double clicking it. Hovering the mouse cursor for a moment over any of the variables in your code will result in the type being displayed.

How It Works

We're back to console application examples again for the moment, so the project should be defined accordingly. Everything here works as we would have expected from our experience with structures. The definition of the class appears outside of the function **main()** and, therefore, has global scope. This enables objects to be declared in any function in the program and causes the class to show up in the ClassView once the program has been compiled.

We've declared two objects of type **CBox** within the function **main()**, **box1** and **box2**. Of course, as with variables of the basic types, the objects **box1** and **box2** are local to **main()**. Objects of a class obey the same rules with respect to scope as variables declared as one of the basic types (such as the variable **boxVolume** used in this example).

The first three assignment statements set the values of the data members of **box1**. We define the values of the data members of **box2** in terms of the data members of **box1** in the next three assignment statements.

We then have a statement which calculates the volume of **box1** as the product of its three data members. This value is then output to the screen. Next, we output the sum of the data members of **box2** by writing the expression for the sum of the data members directly in the output statement. The final action in the program is to output the number of bytes occupied by **box1**, which is produced by the operator **sizeof**.

If you run this program, you should get this output:

```
Ex8_01

Volume of box1 = 33696
box2 has sides which total 66.5 inches.
A CBox object occupies 24 bytes.
Press any key to continue
```

The last line shows that the object **box1** occupies 24 bytes of memory, which is a result of having 3 data members of 8 bytes each. The statement which produced the last line of output could equally well have been written like this:

```cpp
cout << endl                        // Display the size of a box in memory
     << "A CBox object occupies "
     << sizeof (CBox) << " bytes.";
```

Here, we've used the type name between parentheses, rather than a specific object name. You'll remember that this is standard syntax for the **sizeof** operator, as you saw in Chapter 4.

This example has demonstrated the mechanism for accessing the **public** data members of a class. It also shows that they can be used in exactly the same way as ordinary variables. We're now ready to break new ground by taking a look at member *functions* of a class.

Member Functions of a Class

A member function of a class is a function that has its definition or its prototype within the class definition. It operates on any object of the class of which it is a member, and has access to all the members of a class for that object.

TRY IT OUT - Adding a Member Function to CBox

To see how accessing the members of the class works, let's create an example extending the **CBox** class to include a member function.

```cpp
// EX8_02.CPP
// Calculating the volume of a box with a member function
#include <iostream>
using namespace std;

class CBox                              // Class definition at global scope
{
   public:
      double m_Length;                  // Length of a box in inches
      double m_Breadth;                 // Breadth of a box in inches
      double m_Height;                  // Height of a box in inches

      // Function to calculate the volume of a box
      double Volume()
      {
         return m_Length*m_Breadth*m_Height;
      }
};
```

```
int main()
{
   CBox box1;                               // Declare box1 of type CBox
   CBox box2;                               // Declare box2 of type CBox

   double boxVolume = 0.0;                  // Store the volume of a box here

   box1.m_Height = 18.0;                    // Define the values
   box1.m_Length = 78.0;                    // of the members of
   box1.m_Breadth = 24.0;                   // the object box1

   box2.m_Height = box1.m_Height - 10;      // Define box2
   box2.m_Length = box1.m_Length/2.0;       // members in
   box2.m_Breadth = 0.25*box1.m_Length;     // terms of box1

   boxVolume = box1.Volume();               // Calculate volume of box1
   cout << endl
        << "Volume of box1 = " << boxVolume;

   cout << endl
        << "Volume of box2 = "
        << box2.Volume();

   cout << endl
        << "A CBox object occupies "
        << sizeof box1 << " bytes.";

   cout << endl;
   return 0;
}
```

How It Works

The new code that we've added to the class definition is shaded. It's just the definition of the function **Volume()**, which is a member function of the class. It also has the same access attribute as the data members: **public**. This is because every class member declared following an access attribute will have that access attribute, until another one is specified within the class definition. The function **Volume()** returns the volume of a **CBox** object as a value of type **double**. The expression in the **return** statement is just the product of the three data members of the class.

> *There's no need to qualify the names of the class members in any way when accessing them in member functions. The unqualified member names automatically refer to the members of the object that is current when the member function is executed.*

The member function **Volume()** is used in the highlighted statements in **main()**, after initializing the data members (as in the first example). Using the same name for a variable in **main()** causes no conflict or problem. You can call a member function of a particular object by writing the name of the object to be processed, followed by a period, followed by the member function name. As we noted above, the function will automatically access the data members of the object for which it was called, so the first use of **Volume()** calculates the volume of **box1**. Using only the name of a member will always refer to the member of the object for which the member function has been called.

The member function is used a second time directly in the output statement to produce the volume of **box2**. If you execute this example, it will produce this output:

```
Ex8_02

Volume of box1 = 33696
Volume of box2 = 6084
A CBox object occupies 24 bytes.
Press any key to continue
```

Note that the **CBox** object is still the same number of bytes. Adding a function member to a class doesn't affect the size of the objects. Obviously, a member function has to be stored in memory somewhere, but there's only one copy regardless of how many class objects have been declared, and it isn't counted when the operator **sizeof** produces the number of bytes that an object occupies.

The names of the class data members in the member function automatically refer to the data members of the specific object used to call the function, and the function can only be called for a particular object of the class. In this case, this is done by using the direct member access operator with the name of an object.

> *If you try to call a member function without specifying an object name, your program will not compile.*

Positioning a Member Function Definition

A member function definition need not be placed inside the class definition. If you want to put it outside the class definition, you need to put the prototype for the function inside the class. If we rewrite the previous class with the function definition outside, then the class definition looks like this:

```
class CBox                          // Class definition at global scope
{
   public:
      double m_Length;              // Length of a box in inches
      double m_Breadth;             // Breadth of a box in inches
      double m_Height;              // Height of a box in inches
      double Volume(void);          // Member function prototype
};
```

Now we need to write the function definition, but there has to be some way of telling the compiler that the function belongs to the class **CBox**. This is done by prefixing the function name with the name of the class and separating the two with the **scope resolution operator**, **::**, which is formed from two successive colons. The function definition would now look like this:

```
// Function to calculate the volume of a box
   double CBox::Volume()
   {
      return m_Length*m_Breadth*m_Height;
   }
```

It will produce the same output as the last example. However, it isn't exactly the same program. In the second case, all calls to the function are treated in the way that we're already familiar with. However, when we defined the function within the definition of the class in **Ex8_02.cpp**, the compiler implicitly treated the function as an **inline function**.

Inline Functions

With an inline function, the compiler tries to expand the code in the body of the function in place of a call to the function. This avoids much of the overhead of calling the function and, therefore, speeds up your code. This is illustrated here:

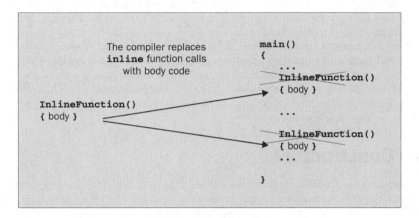

Of course, the compiler takes care of ensuring that expanding a function inline doesn't cause any problems with variable names or scope.

The compiler may not always be able to insert the code for a function inline (such as with recursive functions or functions for which you have obtained an address), but generally it will work. It's best used for very short, simple functions, such as our function **Volume()**, because they will execute faster and will not significantly increase the size of the executable module.

With the function definition outside of the class definition, the compiler treats the function as a normal function and a call of the function will work in the usual way. However, it's also possible to tell the compiler that, if possible, we would like the function to be considered as inline. This is done by simply placing the keyword **inline** at the beginning of the function header. So, for our function, the definition would be as follows:

```
// Function to calculate the volume of a box
inline double CBox::Volume()
{
    return m_Length*m_Breadth*m_Height;
}
```

With this definition for the function, the program would be exactly the same as the original. This allows you to put the member function definitions outside of the class definition, if you so choose, and still retain the speed benefits of inlining.

You can apply the keyword **inline** to ordinary functions in your program that have nothing to do with classes and get the same effect. However, remember that it's best used for short, simple functions.

We now need to understand a little more about what happens when we declare an object of a class.

Class Constructors

In the program above, we declared our **CBox** objects, **box1** and **box2**, and then laboriously worked through each of the data members for each object in order to assign an initial value to it. This is unsatisfactory from several points of view. First of all, it would be easy to overlook initializing a data member, particularly with a class which had many more data members than our **CBox** class. Initializing the data members of several objects of a complex class could involve pages of assignment statements. The final constraint on this approach arises when we get to defining data members of a class that don't have the attribute **public** — we won't be able to access them from outside the class anyway. There has to be a better way, and of course there is — it's known as the class **constructor**.

What is a Constructor?

A class constructor is a special function in a class which is called when a new object of the class is declared. It therefore provides the opportunity to initialize objects as they are created and to ensure that data members only contain valid values.

You have no leeway in naming a class constructor — it always has the same name as the class in which it is defined. The function **CBox()**, for example, is a constructor for our class **CBox**. It also has no return type. It's wrong to specify a return type for a constructor; you must not even write it as **void**. The primary function of a class constructor is to assign initial values to the data elements of the class, and no return type is necessary or permitted.

TRY IT OUT - Adding a Constructor to the CBox class

Let's extend our **CBox** class to incorporate a constructor.

```
// EX8_03.CPP
// Using a constructor
#include <iostream>
using namespace std;

class CBox                              // Class definition at global scope
{
   public:
      double m_Length;                  // Length of a box in inches
      double m_Breadth;                 // Breadth of a box in inches
      double m_Height;                  // Height of a box in inches
```

```
        CBox(double lv, double bv, double hv)   // Constructor definition
        {
           cout << endl << "Constructor called.";
           m_Length = lv;                        // Set values of
           m_Breadth = bv;                       // data members
           m_Height = hv;
        }

     // Function to calculate the volume of a box
     double Volume()
     {
        return m_Length* m_Breadth* m_Height;
     }
};

int main()
{
   CBox box1(78.0,24.0,18.0);                 // Declare and initialize box1
   CBox cigarBox(8.0,5.0,1.0);                // Declare and initialize cigarBox

   double boxVolume = 0.0;                     // Store the volume of a box here

   boxVolume = box1.Volume();                  // Calculate volume of box1
   cout << endl
        << "Volume of box1 = " << boxVolume;

   cout << endl
        << "Volume of cigarBox = "
        << cigarBox.Volume();

   cout << endl;
   return 0;
}
```

How It Works

The constructor **CBox()** has been written with three parameters of type **double**, corresponding to the initial values for the **m_Length**, **m_Breadth** and **m_Height** members of a **CBox** object. The first statement in the constructor outputs a message so that we can tell when it's been called. You wouldn't do this in production programs, but, since it's very helpful in showing when a constructor is called, it's often used when testing a program. We'll use it regularly for the purposes of illustration. The code in the body of the constructor is very simple. It just assigns the arguments passed to the corresponding data members. If necessary, we could also include checks that valid, non-negative arguments are supplied and, in a real context, you probably would want to do this, but our primary interest here is in seeing how the mechanism works.

Within **main()**, we declare the object **box1** with initializing values for the data members **m_Length**, **m_Breadth**, and **m_Height**, in sequence. These are in parentheses following the object name. This uses the functional notation for initialization which, as we saw in Chapter 2, can also be applied to initializing ordinary variables of basic types. We also declare a second object of type **CBox**, called **cigarBox**, which also has initializing values.

The volume of **box1** is calculated using the member function **Volume()** as in the previous example and is then displayed on the screen. We also display the value of the volume of **cigarBox**. The output from the example is:

```
Ex8_03

Constructor called.
Constructor called.
Volume of box1 = 33696
Volume of cigarBox = 40
Press any key to continue
```

The first two lines are output from the two calls of the constructor **CBox()**, once for each object declared. The constructor that we've supplied in the class definition is automatically called when a **CBox** object is declared, so both **CBox** objects are initialized with the initializing values appearing in the declaration. These are passed to the constructor as arguments, in the sequence that they are written in the declaration. As you can see, the volume of **box1** is the same as before and **cigarBox** has a volume looking suspiciously like the product of its dimensions, which is quite a relief.

The Default Constructor

Try modifying the last example by adding the declaration for **box2** that we had previously:

```
CBox box2;                    // Declare box2 of type CBox
```

Here, we've left **box2** without initializing values. When you rebuild this version of the program, you'll get the error message:

error C2512: 'CBox': no appropriate default constructor available

This means that the compiler is looking for a default constructor for **box2**, either one that needs no arguments, because none are specified in the constructor definition, or one whose arguments are all optional, because we haven't supplied any initializing values for the data members. Well, this statement was perfectly satisfactory in **Ex8_02.cpp**, so why doesn't it work now?

The answer is that the previous example used a default constructor that was supplied by the compiler, because we didn't supply one. Since in this example we *did* supply a constructor, the compiler assumed that we were taking care of everything and didn't supply the default. So, if you still want to use declarations for **CBox** objects which aren't initialized, you have to include the default constructor yourself. What exactly does the default constructor look like? In the simplest case, it's just a constructor that accepts no arguments, it doesn't even need to do anything:

```
CBox()                        // Default constructor
{}                            // Totally devoid of statements
```

TRY IT OUT - Supplying a Default Constructor

Let's add our version of the default constructor to the last example, along with the declaration for **box2**, plus the original assignments for the data members of **box2**. We must enlarge the default constructor just enough to show that it is called. Here is the next version of the program:

```cpp
// EX8_04.CPP
// Supplying and using a default constructor
#include <iostream>
using namespace std;

class CBox                                  // Class definition at global scope
{
   public:
      double m_Length;                      // Length of a box in inches
      double m_Breadth;                     // Breadth of a box in inches
      double m_Height;                      // Height of a box in inches

      CBox(double lv, double bv, double hv) // Constructor definition
      {
         cout << endl << "Constructor called.";
         m_Length = lv;                     // Set values of
         m_Breadth = bv;                    // data members
         m_Height = hv;
      }

      // Default constructor definition
      CBox()
      { cout << endl << "Default constructor called."; }

      // Function to calculate the volume of a box
      double Volume()
      {
         return m_Length*m_Breadth*m_Height;
      }
};

int main()
{
   CBox box1(78.0,24.0,18.0);              // Declare and initialize box1
   CBox box2;                              // Declare box2 - no initial values
   CBox cigarBox(8.0, 5.0, 1.0);          // Declare and initialize cigarBox

   double boxVolume = 0.0;                 // Store the volume of a box here

   boxVolume = box1.Volume();             // Calculate volume of box1
   cout << endl
        << "Volume of box1 = " << boxVolume;

   box2.m_Height = box1.m_Height - 10;    // Define box2
   box2.m_Length = box1.m_Length / 2.0;   // members in
   box2.m_Breadth = 0.25*box1.m_Length;   // terms of box1

   cout << endl
        << "Volume of box2 = "
        << box2.Volume();

   cout << endl
        << "Volume of cigarBox = "
        << cigarBox.Volume();

   cout << endl;
   return 0;
}
```

How It Works

Now that we have included our own version of the default constructor, there are no error messages from the compiler and everything works. The program produces this output:

```
Ex8_04

Constructor called.
Default constructor called.
Constructor called.
Volume of box1 = 33696
Volume of box2 = 6084
Volume of cigarBox = 40
Press any key to continue_
```

All that our default constructor does is to display a message. Evidently, it was called when we declared the object **box2**. We also get the correct value for the volumes of all three **CBox** objects, so the rest of the program is working as it should.

One aspect of this example that you may have noticed is that we now know we can overload constructors just as we overloaded functions in Chapter 6. We've just run an example with two constructors that differ only in their parameter list. One has three parameters of type **double** and the other has no parameters at all.

Assigning Default Values in a Constructor

When we discussed functions in C++, we saw how we could specify default values for the parameters to a function in the function prototype. We can also do this for class member functions, including constructors. If we put the definition of the member function inside the class definition, we can put the default values for the parameters in the function header. If we only include the prototype of a function in the class definition, the default parameter value should go in the prototype.

If we decided that the default size for a **CBox** object was a unit box with all sides of length 1, we could alter the class definition in the last example to this:

```
class CBox                              // Class definition at global scope
{
   public:
      double m_Length;                  // Length of a box in inches
      double m_Breadth;                 // Breadth of a box in inches
      double m_Height;                  // Height of a box in inches

      // Constructor definition
      CBox(double lv = 1.0, double bv = 1.0, double hv = 1.0)
      {
         cout << endl << "Constructor called.";
         m_Length = lv;                 // Set values of
         m_Breadth = bv;
         m_Height = hv;                 // data members
      }

      // Default constructor definition
      CBox()
      { cout << endl << "Default constructor called."; }
```

```
      // Function to calculate the volume of a box
      double Volume()
      {
          return m_Length*m_Breadth*m_Height;
      }
};
```

If we make this change to the last example, what happens? We get another error message from the compiler, of course. We get these useful comments:

warning C4520: 'CBox': multiple default constructors specified
error C2668: 'CBox::CBox': ambiguous call to overloaded function

This means that the compiler can't work out which of the two constructors to call — the one for which we have set default values for the parameters or the constructor that doesn't accept any parameters. This is because the declaration of **box2** requires a constructor without parameters and either constructor can now be called without parameters. The immediately obvious solution to this is to get rid of the constructor that accepts no parameters. This is actually beneficial. Without this constructor, any **CBox** object that is declared without being explicitly initialized will automatically have its members initialized to 1.

TRY IT OUT - Supplying Default Values for Constructor Arguments

We can demonstrate this with the following simplified example:

```
// EX8_05.CPP
// Supplying default values for constructor arguments
#include <iostream>
using namespace std;

class CBox                                  // Class definition at global scope
{
   public:
        double m_Length;                    // Length of a box in inches
        double m_Breadth;                   // Breadth of a box in inches
        double m_Height;                    // Height of a box in inches

        // Constructor definition
        CBox(double lv = 1.0, double bv = 1.0, double hv = 1.0)
        {
          cout << endl << "Constructor called.";
          m_Length = lv;                    // Set values of
          m_Breadth = bv;                   // data members
          m_Height = hv;
        }

        // Function to calculate the volume of a box
        double Volume()
        {
          return m_Length*m_Breadth*m_Height;
        }
};
```

```
int main()
{
   CBox box2;                              // Declare box2 - no initial values

   cout << endl
        << "Volume of box2 = "
        << box2.Volume();

   cout << endl;
   return 0;
}
```

How It Works

We only declare a single uninitialized **CBox** variable, **box2**, because that's all we need for demonstration purposes. This version of the program produces the following output:

```
Ex8_05
Constructor called.
Volume of box2 = 1
Press any key to continue_
```

This shows that the constructor with default parameter values is doing its job of setting the values of objects that have no initializing values specified.

You shouldn't assume from this that this is the only, or even the recommended, way of implementing the default constructor. There will be many occasions where you won't want to assign default values in this way, in which case you'll need to write a separate default constructor. There will even be times when you don't want to have a default constructor operating at all, even though you have defined another constructor. This would ensure that all declared objects of a class must have initializing values explicitly specified in their declaration.

Using an Initialization List in a Constructor

Previously, we initialized the members of an object in the class constructor using explicit assignment. We could also have used a different technique, using what is called an **initialization list**. We can demonstrate this with an alternative version of the constructor for the class **CBox**:

```
// Constructor definition using an initialisation list
CBox(double lv = 1.0, double bv = 1.0, double hv = 1.0): m_Length(lv),
                                                          m_Breadth(bv),
                                                          m_Height(hv)
{
   cout << endl << "Constructor called.";
}
```

Now the values of the data members are not set in assignment statements in the body of the constructor. As in a declaration, they are specified as initializing values using functional notation and appear in the initializing list as part of the function header. The member **m_Length** is initialized by the value of **lv**, for example. This can be rather more efficient than using assignments as we did in the previous version. If you substitute this version of the constructor in the previous example, you will see that it works just as well.

Note that the initializing list for the constructor is separated from the parameter list by a colon and each of the initializers is separated by a comma. This technique for initializing parameters in a constructor is important, because, as we shall see later, it's the only way of setting values for certain types of data members of an object.

Private Members of a Class

Having a constructor that sets the values of the data members of a class object, but still admits the possibility of any part of a program being able to mess with what are essentially the guts of an object, is almost a contradiction in terms. To draw an analogy, once you have arranged for a brilliant surgeon such as Dr. Kildare, whose skills were honed over years of training, to do things to your insides, letting the local plumber, bricklayer or the folks from Hill Street Blues have a go hardly seems appropriate. We need some protection for our class data members.

We can get it by using the keyword **private** when we define the class members. Class members which are **private** can, in general, only be accessed by member functions of a class. There's one exception, but we'll worry about that later. A normal function has no direct means of accessing the **private** members of a class. This is shown here:

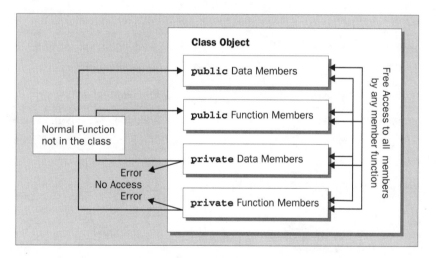

Having the possibility of specifying class members as **private** also enables you to separate the interface to the class from its internal implementation. The interface to a class is composed of the **public** members and the **public** member functions in particular, since they can provide indirect access to all the members of a class, including the **private** members. By keeping the internals of a class **private**, you can later modify them, to improve performance for example, without necessitating modifications to the code that uses the class through its public interface. To keep them safe from unnecessary meddling, it's good practice to declare data and function members of a class that don't need to be exposed as **private**. Only make **public** what is essential to the use of your class.

TRY IT OUT - Private Data Members

We can rewrite the **CBox** class to make its data members **private**.

```cpp
// EX8_06.CPP
// A class with private members
#include <iostream>
using namespace std;

class CBox                                  // Class definition at global scope
{
   public:

      // Constructor definition using an initialisation list
      CBox(double lv = 1.0, double bv = 1.0, double hv = 1.0): m_Length(lv),
                                                               m_Breadth(bv),
                                                               m_Height(hv)
   {
      cout << endl << "Constructor called.";
   }

      // Function to calculate the volume of a box
      double Volume()
      {
         return m_Length*m_Breadth*m_Height;
      }

   private:
      double m_Length;                      // Length of a box in inches
      double m_Breadth;                     // Breadth of a box in inches
      double m_Height;                      // Height of a box in inches
};

int main()
{
   CBox match(2.2, 1.1, 0.5);              // Declare match box
   CBox box2;                             // Declare box2 - no initial values

   cout << endl
        << "Volume of match = "
        << match.Volume();

// Uncomment the following line to get an error
// box2.m_Length = 4.0;

   cout << endl
        << "Volume of box2 = "
        << box2.Volume();

   cout << endl;
   return 0;
}
```

How It Works

The definition of the class **CBox** now has two sections. The first is the **public** section containing the constructor and the member function **Volume()**. The second section is specified as **private** and contains the data members. Now the data members can only be accessed by the member functions of the class. We don't have to modify any of the member functions — they can access all the data members of the class anyway. However, if you uncomment the statement in the function **main()**, assigning a value to the member **m_Length** of the object **box2**, you'll get a compiler error message confirming that the data member is inaccessible.

> *A point to remember is that using a constructor or a member function is now the only way to get a value into a **private** data member of an object. You have to make sure that all the ways in which you might want to set or modify **private** data members of a class are provided for through member functions.*

We could also put functions into the **private** section of a class. In this case, they can only be called by other member functions. If you put the function **Volume()** in the **private** section, you will get a compiler error from the statements that attempt to use it in the function **main()**. If you put the constructor in the **private** section, you won't be able to declare any members of the class.

The above example generates this output:

```
Ex8_06

Constructor called.
Constructor called.
Volume of match = 1.21
Volume of box2 = 1
Press any key to continue
```

This demonstrates that the class is still working satisfactorily, with its data members defined as having the access attribute **private**. The major difference is that they are now completely protected from unauthorized access and modification.

> *If you don't specify otherwise, the default access attribute which applies to members of a class is **private**. You could, therefore, put all your **private** members at the beginning of the class definition and let them default to **private** by omitting the keyword. However, it's better to take the trouble to explicitly state the access attribute in every case, so there can be no doubt about what you intend.*

Of course, you don't have to make all your data members **private**. If the application for your class requires it, you can have some data members defined as **private** and some as **public**. It all depends on what you're trying to do. If there's no reason to make members of a class **public**, it is better to make them **private** as it makes the class more secure. Ordinary functions won't be able to access any of the **private** members of your class.

Accessing private Class Members

On reflection, declaring the data members of a class as **private** is rather extreme. It's all very well protecting them from unauthorized modification, but that's no reason to keep their values a secret. What we need is a Freedom of Information Act for **private** members.

You don't need to start writing to your state senator to get it — it's already available to you. All you need to do is to write a member function to return the value of a data member. Look at this member function for the class **CBox**:

```
inline double CBox::GetLength()
{
    return m_Length;
}
```

Just to show how it looks, this has been written as a member function definition which is external to the class. We've specified it as **inline**, since we'll benefit from the speed increase without increasing the size of our code too much. Assuming that you have the declaration of the function in the **public** section of the class, you can use it by writing this statement:

```
len = box2.GetLength();              // Obtain data member length
```

All you need to do is to write a similar function for each data member that you want to make available to the outside world, and their values can be accessed without prejudicing the security of the class. Of course, if you put the definitions for these functions within the class definition, they will be **inline** by default.

The friend Functions of a Class

There may be circumstances when, for one reason or another, you want certain selected functions which are not members of a class to, nonetheless, be able to access all the members of a class — a sort of elite group with special privileges. Such functions are called **friend functions** of a class and are defined using the keyword **friend**. You can either include the prototype of a friend function in the class definition, or you can include the whole function definition. Functions which are friends of a class and are defined within the class definition are also by default **inline**.

> *Friend functions are not members of the class, and therefore the access attributes do not apply to them. They are just ordinary global functions with special privileges.*

Let's suppose that we wanted to implement a friend function in the **CBox** class to compute the surface area of a **CBox** object.

TRY IT OUT - Using a friend to Calculate the Surface Area

We can see how this works in the following example:

```
// EX8_07.CPP
// Creating a friend function of a class
```

```cpp
#include <iostream>
using namespace std;

class CBox                                       // Class definition at global scope
{
   public:

      // Constructor definition
      CBox(double lv = 1.0, double bv = 1.0, double hv = 1.0): m_Length(lv),
                                                               m_Breadth(bv),
                                                               m_Height(hv)
      {
         cout << endl << "Constructor called.";
      }

      // Function to calculate the volume of a box
      double Volume()
      {
         return m_Length*m_Breadth*m_Height;
      }

   private:
      double m_Length;                           // Length of a box in inches
      double m_Breadth;                          // Breadth of a box in inches
      double m_Height;                           // Height of a box in inches

   //Friend function
   friend double BoxSurface(CBox aBox);

};

// friend function to calculate the surface area of a Box object
double BoxSurface(CBox aBox)
{
   return 2.0*(aBox.m_Length*aBox.m_Breadth +
               aBox.m_Length*aBox.m_Height +
               aBox.m_Height*aBox.m_Breadth);
}

int main()
{
   CBox match(2.2, 1.1, 0.5);                    // Declare match box
   CBox box2;                                    // Declare box2 - no initial values

   cout << endl
        << "Volume of match = "
        << match.Volume();

   cout << endl
        << "Surface area of match = "
        << BoxSurface(match);

   cout << endl
        << "Volume of box2 = "
        << box2.Volume();

   cout << endl
        << "Surface area of box2 = "
        << BoxSurface(box2);
```

```
        cout << endl;
        return 0;
    }
```

How It Works

We declare the function **BoxSurface()** as a friend of the **CBox** class by writing the function prototype with the keyword **friend** at the front. Since the **BoxSurface()** function itself is a global function, it makes no difference where we put the **friend** declaration within the definition of the class, but it's a good idea to be consistent when you position this sort of declaration. You can see that we have chosen to position ours after all the **public** and **private** members of the class. Remember that a **friend** function isn't a member of the class, so access attributes don't apply.

The definition of the function follows that of the class. Note that we specify access to the data members of the object within the definition of **BoxSurface()**, using the **CBox** object passed to the function as a parameter. Because a **friend** function isn't a class member, the data members can't be referenced just by their names. They each have to be qualified by the object name in exactly the same way as they might in an ordinary function, except, of course, that an ordinary function can't access the **private** members of a class. A **friend** function is the same as an ordinary function except that it can access all the members of a class without restriction.

The example produces this:

```
Ex8_07
Constructor called.
Constructor called.
Volume of match = 1.21
Surface area of match = 8.14
Volume of box2 = 1
Surface area of box2 = 6
Press any key to continue_
```

This is exactly what you would expect. The **friend** function is computing the surface area of the **CBox** objects from the values of the **private** members.

Placing friend Function Definitions Inside the Class

We could have combined the definition of the function with its declaration as a friend of the **CBox** class within the class definition and the code would run as before. However, this has a number of disadvantages relating to the readability of the code. Although the function would still have global scope, this wouldn't be obvious to readers of the code, since the function would be hidden in the body of the class definition, and particularly since the function would no longer show up in the ClassView.

The Default Copy Constructor

Suppose we declare and initialize a **CBox** object **box1** with this statement:

```
CBox box1(78.0, 24.0, 18.0);
```

We now want to create another **CBox** object, identical to the first. We would like to initialize the second **CBox** object with **box1**.

TRY IT OUT - Copying Information Between Instances

We can try this out with the **main()** function which follows:

```
// EX8_08.CPP
// Initializing an object with an object of the same class
#include <iostream>
using namespace std;

class CBox                                    // Class definition at global scope
{
   public:

      // Constructor definition
      CBox(double lv = 1.0, double bv = 1.0, double hv = 1.0): m_Length(lv),
                                                               m_Breadth(bv),
                                                               m_Height(hv)

      {
         cout << endl << "Constructor called.";
      }

      // Function to calculate the volume of a box
      double Volume()
      {
         return m_Length*m_Breadth*m_Height;
      }

   private:
      double m_Length;                    // Length of a box in inches
      double m_Breadth;                   // Breadth of a box in inches
      double m_Height;                    // Height of a box in inches

};

int main()
{
   CBox box1(78.0, 24.0, 18.0);
   CBox box2 = box1;                         // Initialize box2 with box1

   cout << endl
        << "box1 volume = " << box1.Volume()
        << endl
        << "box2 volume = " << box2.Volume();

   cout << endl;
   return 0;
}
```

How It Works

This example will produce this:

```
Ex8_08

Constructor called.
box1 volume = 33696
box2 volume = 33696
Press any key to continue
```

Clearly, the program is working as we would want, with both boxes having the same volume. However, as you can see from the output, our constructor was called only once for the creation of **box1**. The question is, how was **box2** created? The mechanism is similar to the one that we experienced when we had no constructor defined and the compiler supplied a default constructor to allow an object to be created. In this case, the compiler generates a default version of what is referred to as a **copy constructor**.

A copy constructor does exactly what we're doing here — it creates an object of a class by initializing it with an existing object of the same class. The default version of the copy constructor creates the new object by copying the existing object, member by member.

This is fine for simple classes such as **CBox**, but for many classes — classes that have pointers or arrays as members for example — it won't work properly. Indeed, with such classes it can create serious errors in your program. In these cases, you need to create your own class copy constructor. This requires a special approach which we'll look into more fully towards the end of this chapter, and again in the next chapter.

The Pointer this

In our class **CBox**, we wrote the function **Volume()** in terms of the class member names in the definition of the class. Of course, every object of type **CBox** that we create contains these members, so there has to be a mechanism for the function to refer to the members of the particular object for which the function is called.

When any member function executes, it automatically contains a hidden pointer with the name **this**, which points to the object used with the function call. Therefore, when the member **m_Length** is accessed in the function **Volume()** during execution, it's actually referring to **this->m_Length**, which is the fully-specified reference to the object member that is being used. The compiler takes care of adding the necessary pointer name **this** to the member names in the function.

If you need to, you can use the pointer **this** explicitly within a member function. You might, for example, want to return a pointer to the current object.

TRY IT OUT - Explicit Use of this

We could add a public function to our class **CBox** to compare the volume of two **CBox** objects.

```cpp
// EX8_09.CPP
// Using the pointer this
#include <iostream>
using namespace std;

class CBox                                     // Class definition at global scope
{
   public:
      // Constructor definition
      CBox(double lv = 1.0, double bv = 1.0, double hv = 1.0): m_Length(lv),
                                                               m_Breadth(bv),
                                                               m_Height(hv)
      {
         cout << endl << "Constructor called.";
      }

      // Function to calculate the volume of a box
      double Volume()
      {
         return m_Length*m_Breadth*m_Height;
      }

      // Function to compare two boxes which returns true (1)
      // if the first is greater than the second, and false (0)
      // otherwise
      int Compare(CBox xBox)
      {
         return this->Volume() > xBox.Volume();
      }

   private:
      double m_Length;                         // Length of a box in inches
      double m_Breadth;                        // Breadth of a box in inches
      double m_Height;                         // Height of a box in inches

};

int main()
{
   CBox match(2.2, 1.1, 0.5);                  // Declare match box
   CBox cigar(8.0, 5.0,1.0);                   // Declare cigar box

   if(cigar.Compare(match))
      cout << endl
           << "match is smaller than cigar";
   else
      cout << endl
           << "match is equal to or larger than cigar";

   cout << endl;
   return 0;
}
```

How It Works

The member function **Compare()** returns **true** if the prefixed **CBox** object in the function call has a greater volume than the **CBox** object specified as an argument, and **false** if it doesn't. In the **return** statements, the prefixed object is referred to through the pointer **this**, used with the indirect member access operator, **->**, that we saw in the previous chapter.

> *Remember that you use the direct member access operator . when dealing with objects and the indirect member access operator -> when dealing with pointers to objects.* **this** *is a pointer.*

The operator **->** works the same for pointers to class objects as it did when we were dealing with a **struct**. Here, using the pointer **this** demonstrates that it exists and *does* work, but it's quite unnecessary to use it explicitly in this case. If you change the **return** statement in the **Compare()** function to be,

```
return Volume() > xBox.Volume();
```

you'll find that it works just as well. Any references to unadorned member names are automatically assumed to be the members of the object pointed to by **this**.

The **Compare()** function is used in **main()** to check the relationship between the volumes of the objects **match** and **cigar**. The output from the program is:

```
Ex8_09

Constructor called.
Constructor called.
match is smaller than cigar
Press any key to continue_
```

This confirms that the **cigar** object is larger than the **match** object.

It also wasn't essential to write the **Compare()** function as a class member. We could just as well have written it as an ordinary function with the objects as arguments. Note that this isn't true of the function **Volume()**, since it needs to access the **private** data members of the class. Of course, if the function **Compare()** was implemented as an ordinary function, it wouldn't have the pointer **this**, but it would still be very simple:

```
// Comparing two CBox objects - ordinary function version
int Compare(CBox B1, CBox B2)
{
    return B1.Volume() > B2.Volume();
}
```

This has both objects as arguments and returns **true** if the volume of the first is greater than the last. You would use this function to perform the same function as in the last example with this statement:

```
      if(Compare(cigar, match))
         cout << endl
              << "match is smaller than cigar";
      else
         cout << endl
              << "match is equal to or larger than cigar";
```

If anything, this looks slightly better and easier to read than the original version. However, there's a much better way to do this, which we shall see before the end of the next chapter.

const Objects of a Class

The **Volume()** function that we defined for our **CBox** class does not alter the object for which it is called, neither does a function such as **getHeight()** that returns the value of the **m_Height** member. Likewise, the **Compare()** function in the previous example didn't change the class objects at all. This may seem at first sight to be a mildly interesting but largely irrelevant observation, but it isn't, it's quite important. Let's think about it.

We will undoubtedly want to have object of classes that are fixed from time to time, just like values such as **pi** or **inchesPerFoot** that you might declare as **const double**. Suppose we wanted to declare a **CBox** object as **const** – because it was a very important standard sized box for instance. We might declare it as:

```
const CBox standard(3.0, 5.0, 8.0);
```

Now that we have defined our standard box having dimensions 3x5x8, we don't want it messed about with. In particular, we don't want to allow the values stored in its data members to be altered. How can we be sure they won't be?

Well we already are. If you declare an object of a class as **const**, the compiler will not allow any member function to be called for it that might alter it. You can demonstrate this quite easily by modifying the declaration for the object, **cigar**, in the previous example to:

```
const CBox cigar(8.0, 5.0, 1.0);                    // Declare cigar box
```

If you try recompiling the program with this change, it won't compile. You will see the error message:

error C2662: 'compare' : cannot convert 'this' pointer from 'const class CBox' to 'class CBox &'
Conversion loses qualifiers

This is produced for the **if** statement that calls the **Compare()** member of cigar. An object that you declare as **const** will always have a **this** pointer that is **const**, so the compiler will not allow any member function to be called that does not assume the **this** pointer that is passed to it is **const**. We need to find out how to make the **this** pointer in a member function **const**.

const Member Functions of a Class

To make the this pointer in a member function **const**, you need to declare the function as **const** within the class definition. Let's look at how we do that with the **Compare()** member of **CBox**. The class definition needs to be modified to the following:

```
class CBox                              // Class definition at global scope
{
    public:
        // Constructor definition
    CBox(double lv = 1.0, double bv = 1.0, double hv = 1.0): m_Length(lv),
                                                             m_Breadth(bv),
                                                             m_Height(hv)

        {
            cout << endl << "Constructor called.";
        }

        // Function to calculate the volume of a box
        double Volume()
        {
            return m_Length*m_Breadth*m_Height;
        }

        // Function to compare two boxes which returns true (1)
        // if the first is greater than the second, and false (0)
        // otherwise
        int Compare(CBox xBox) const
        {
            return this->Volume() > xBox.Volume();
        }

    private:
        double m_Length;                // Length of a box in inches
        double m_Breadth;               // Breadth of a box in inches
        double m_Height;                // Height of a box in inches
};
```

We just append the keyword **const** to the function header. Note that you can only do this with class member functions, not with ordinary global functions. Declaring a function as **const** is only meaningful in the case of a function that is a member of a class. The effect is to make the **this** pointer in the function **const**, which in turn means that you cannot write a data member of the class on the left of an assignment within the function definition. It will be flagged as an error by the compiler. A **const** member function cannot call a non-**const** member function of the same class, since this would potentially modify the object.

When you declare an object as **const**, the member functions that you call for it must be declared as **const**, otherwise the program will not compile.

Member Function Definitions Outside the Class

When the definition of a **const** member function appears outside the class, the header for the definition must have the keyword **const** added, just as the declaration within the class does. In fact, you should always declare all member functions that do not alter the class object for which they are called as **const**. With this in mind, our **CBox** class could be defined as:

```
class CBox                                // Class definition at global scope
{
  public:
    // Constructor
    CBox(double lv = 1.0, double bv = 1.0, double hv = 1.0): m_Length(lv),
                                                             m_Breadth(bv),
                                                             m_Height(hv)

    double Volume() const;                // Calculate the volume of a box
    int Compare(CBox xBox) const;         // Compare two boxes

  private:
    double m_Length;                      // Length of a box in inches
    double m_Breadth;                     // Breadth of a box in inches
    double m_Height;                      // Height of a box in inches
};
```

This assumes all function members are defined separately, including the constructor. Both the **Volume()** and **Compare()** members have been declared as **const**. The **Volume()** function would now be defined outside the class as:

```
double CBox::Volume() const
{
  return m_Length*m_Breadth*m_Height;
}
```

The **Compare()** function definition will be:

```
int CBox::Compare(CBox xBox) const
{
  return this->Volume() > xBox.Volume();
}
```

As you can see, the **const** modifier appears in both definitions. If you leave it out the code will not compile. A function with a **const** modifier is a different function from one without, even though the name and parameters are exactly the same. Indeed you can have both **const** and non-**const** versions of a function in a class, and sometimes this can be very useful.

With the class declared as above, the constructor also needs to be defined separately, like this:

```
CBox(double lv = 1.0, double bv = 1.0, double hv = 1.0): m_Length(lv),
                                                         m_Breadth(bv),
                                                         m_Height(hv)

{
  cout << endl << "Constructor called.";
}
```

Arrays of Objects of a Class

We can declare an array of objects of a class in exactly the same way that we have declared an ordinary array where the elements were one of the built-in types. Each element of an array of class objects causes the default constructor to be called.

TRY IT OUT - Arrays of Class Objects

We can use the class definition of **CBox** from the last example, but modified to include a specific default constructor:

```cpp
// EX8_10.CPP
// Using an array of class objects
#include <iostream>
using namespace std;

class CBox                                      // Class definition at global scope
{
   public:
      // Constructor definition
      CBox(double lv, double bv = 1.0, double hv = 1.0): m_Length(lv),
                                                         m_Breadth(bv),
                                                         m_Height(hv)
      {
         cout << endl << "Constructor called.";
      }

      CBox()                                    // Default constructor
      {
         cout << endl
              << "Default constructor called.";
         m_Length = m_Breadth = m_Height = 1.0;
      }

      // Function to calculate the volume of a box
      double Volume() const
      {
         return m_Length*m_Breadth*m_Height;
      }

   private:
      double m_Length;                          // Length of a box in inches
      double m_Breadth;                         // Breadth of a box in inches
      double m_Height;                          // Height of a box in inches
};

int main()
{
   CBox boxes[5];                               // Array of CBox objects declared
   CBox cigar(8.0, 5.0, 1.0);                   // Declare cigar box

   cout << endl
        << "Volume of boxes[3] = " << boxes[3].Volume()
        << endl
        << "Volume of cigar = " << cigar.Volume();

   cout << endl;
   return 0;
}
```

How It Works

We have modified the constructor accepting arguments so that only two default values are supplied, and we have added a default constructor which initializes the data members to 1 after displaying a message that it was called. We will now be able to see *which* constructor was called *when*. The constructors now have quite distinct parameter lists, so there's no possibility of the compiler confusing them. The program produces this:

```
Ex8_10
Default constructor called.
Default constructor called.
Default constructor called.
Default constructor called.
Default constructor called.
Constructor called.
Volume of boxes[3] = 1
Volume of cigar = 40
Press any key to continue_
```

We can see that the default constructor was called five times, once for each element of the array **boxes**. The other constructor was called to create the object **cigar**. It's clear from the output that the default constructor initialization is working satisfactorily, as the volume of the array element is 1.

Static Members of a Class

Both data members and function members of a class can be declared as static. Because the context is a class definition, there's a little more to it than the effect of the keyword **static** outside of a class, so let's look at static data members.

Static Data Members of a Class

When we declare data members of a class as static, the effect is that the static data members are defined only once and are shared between all objects of the class. Each object gets its own copies of each of the ordinary data members of a class, but only one instance of each static data member exists, regardless of how many class objects have been defined.

```
class CBox
{
    public:
    static int ObjectCount;
        ...
    private:
        double m_Length;
        double m_Breadth;
        double m_Height;
        ...
};
```

Object1	Object2	Object3
m_Length	m_Length	m_Length
m_Breadth	m_Breadth	m_Breadth
m_Height	m_Height	m_Height
...	...	...

One copy of each static member is shared between all objects of a class.

```
ObjectCount
```

One use for a static data member is to count how many objects actually exist. We could add a static data member to the public section of the **CBox** class by adding the following statement to the previous class definition:

```
static int objectCount;              // Count of objects in existence
```

We now have a problem. How do we initialize the static data member? We can't put it in the class definition — that's simply a blueprint for an object, and initializing values are not allowed. We don't want to initialize it in a constructor, because we want to increment it every time the constructor is called. We can't initialize it in another member function since a member function is associated with an object, and we want it initialized before any object is created. The answer is to write the initialization outside of the class definition with this statement:

```
int CBox::ObjectCount = 0;           // Initialize static member of class CBox
```

> Notice that the keyword **static** is not included here. However, we do need to qualify the member name by using the class name and the scope resolution operator so that the compiler understands that we're referring to a static member of the class. Otherwise, we would simply create a global variable that was nothing to do with the class.

TRY IT OUT - Counting Instances

Let's add the **static** data member and the object counting capability to the last example.

```cpp
// EX8_11.CPP
// Using a static data member in a class
#include <iostream>
using namespace std;

class CBox                                // Class definition at global scope
{
   public:
      static int objectCount;             // Count of objects in existence

      // Constructor definition
      CBox(double lv, double bv = 1.0, double hv = 1.0): m_Length(lv),
                                                         m_Breadth(bv),
                                                         m_Height(hv)
      {
         cout << endl << "Constructor called.";
         objectCount++;
      }

      CBox()                              // Default constructor
      {
         cout << endl
              << "Default constructor called.";
         m_Length = m_Breadth = m_Height = 1.0;
         objectCount++;
      }
```

```
        // Function to calculate the volume of a box
        double Volume() const
        {
            return m_Length*m_Breadth*m_Height;
        }

    private:
        double m_Length;                    // Length of a box in inches
        double m_Breadth;                   // Breadth of a box in inches
        double m_Height;                    // Height of a box in inches

    };
```

```
int CBox::objectCount = 0;                  // Initialize static member of
                                            // class CBox
```

```
int main()
{
```
```
    CBox boxes[5];                          // Array of CBox objects declared
    CBox cigar(8.0, 5.0, 1.0);              // Declare cigar box

    cout << endl << endl
        << "Number of objects (through class) = "
        << CBox::objectCount;

    cout << endl
        << "Number of objects (through object) = "
        << boxes[2].objectCount;
```
```
    cout << endl;
    return 0;
}
```

How It Works

This example will produce the output:

```
Ex8_11

Default constructor called.
Default constructor called.
Default constructor called.
Default constructor called.
Default constructor called.
Constructor called.

Number of objects (through class) = 6
Number of objects (through object) = 6
Press any key to continue
```

This code shows that it doesn't matter how we refer to the static member **ObjectCount** (whether through the class itself or any of the objects of that class). The value is the same and it is equal to the number of objects of that class that have been created. The six objects are obviously the five elements of the **Boxes** array, plus the object **cigar**. It's interesting to note that **static** members of a class exist even though there may be no members of the class in existence. This is evidently the case, since we initialized the **static** member **ObjectCount** before any class objects were declared.

> *Static data members are automatically created when your program begins, and they will be initialized with 0 unless you initialize them with some other value. Thus you only need to initialize static data members of a class if you want them to start out with a value other than 0.*

Static Function Members of a Class

By declaring a function member as **static**, you make it independent of any particular object of the class. Referencing members of the class from within a static function must be done using qualified names (as you would do with an ordinary global function accessing a public data member). The static member function has the advantage that it exists, and can be called, even if no objects of the class exist. In this case, only static data members can be used, since they are the only ones that exist. Thus, you can call a static function member of a class to examine static data members, even when you do not know for certain that any objects of the class exist. You could, therefore, use a static member function to determine whether some objects of the class have been created or, indeed, how many have been created.

Of course, once the objects have been defined, a static member function can access **private** as well as **public** members of class objects. A static function might have this prototype:

```
static void Afunction(int n);
```

A static function can be called in relation to a particular object by a statement such as the following,

```
aBox.Afunction(10);
```

where **aBox** is an object of the class. The same function could also be called without reference to an object. In this case, the statement would take the following form,

```
CBox::Afunction(10);
```

where **CBox** is the class name. Using the class name and the scope resolution operator serves to tell the compiler to which class the function **Afunction()** belongs.

Pointers and References to Class Objects

Using pointers, and particularly references to class objects, is very important to object-oriented programming. Class objects can involve considerable amounts of data, so using a pass-by-value mechanism by specifying objects as parameters can be very time consuming and inefficient. There are also some techniques involving the use of references which are essential to some operations with classes. As we shall see, you can't write a copy constructor without using a reference parameter.

Pointers to Class Objects

You declare a pointer to a class object in the same way that you declare other pointers. For example, a pointer to objects of the class **CBox** is declared in this statement:

```
CBox* pBox = 0;                      // Declare a pointer to CBox
```

You can now use this to store the address of a **CBox** object in an assignment in the usual way, using the address operator:

```
pBox = &cigar;                       // Store address of CBox object cigar in pBox
```

As we saw when we used the **this** pointer in the definition of the member function **Compare()**, you can call a function using a pointer to an object. We can call the function **Volume()** for the pointer **pBox** in this statement:

```
cout << pBox->Volume();              // Display volume of object pointed to by pBox
```

Again, this uses the indirect member selection operator. This is the typical notation used by most programmers for this kind of operation, so from now on we'll use it universally.

TRY IT OUT - Pointers to Classes

Let's try exercising the indirect member access operator a little more. We will use the example **Ex8_09.cpp** as a base, but change it a little.

```cpp
// EX8_12.CPP
// Exercising the indirect member access operator
#include <iostream>
using namespace std;

class CBox                                          // Class definition at global scope
{
   public:
      // Constructor definition
      CBox(double lv = 1.0, double bv = 1.0, double hv = 1.0): m_Length(lv),
                                                               m_Breadth(bv),
                                                               m_Height(hv)
      {
         cout << endl << "Constructor called.";
      }

      // Function to calculate the volume of a box
      double Volume() const
      {
         return m_Length*m_Breadth*m_Height;
      }

      // Function to compare two boxes which returns true (1)
      // if the first is greater that the second, and false (0)
      // otherwise
      int Compare(CBox* pBox) const
      {
         return this->Volume() > pBox->Volume();
      }

   private:
      double m_Length;                              // Length of a box in inches
      double m_Breadth;                             // Breadth of a box in inches
```

```
        double m_Height;                    // Height of a box in inches
};

int main()
{
    CBox boxes[5];                          // Array of CBox objects declared
    CBox match(2.2, 1.1, 0.5);              // Declare match box
    CBox cigar(8.0, 5.0, 1.0);              // Declare cigar Box
    CBox* pB1 = &cigar;                     // Initialize pointer to cigar object
                                            // address
    CBox* pB2 = 0;                          // Pointer to CBox initialized to null

    cout << endl
        << "Address of cigar is " << pB1            // Display address
        << endl
        << "Volume of cigar is " << pB1->Volume();  // Volume of object
                                                    // pointed to

    pB2 = &match;
    if(pB2->Compare(pB1))                           // Compare via pointers
        cout << endl
            << "match is greater than cigar";
    else
        cout << endl
            << "match is less than or equal to cigar";

    pB1 = boxes;                            // Set to address of array
    boxes[2] = match;                       // Set 3rd element to match
    cout << endl                            // Now access thru pointer
        << "Volume of boxes[2] is " << (pB1 + 2)->Volume();

    cout << endl;
    return 0;
}
```

How It Works

The only change to the class definition isn't one of great substance. We've only modified the **Compare()** function to accept a pointer to a **CBox** object as an argument, and now we know about **const** member functions we declare it as **const**, since it doesn't alter the object. The function **main()** merely exercises pointers to **CBox** type objects in various, rather arbitrary, ways.

Within the function **main()**, after declaring an array **Boxes**, and the **CBox** objects **cigar** and **match**, we declare two pointers to **CBox** objects. The first, **pB1**, is initialized with the address of the object **cigar**, and the second, **pB2**, is initialized to **NULL**. All of this uses the pointer in exactly the same way you would when you're applying a pointer to a basic type. The fact that we're using a pointer to a type that we have defined ourselves makes no difference.

We use **pB1** with the indirect member access operator to generate the volume of the object pointed to, and the result is displayed. We then assign the address of **match** to **pB2** and use both pointers in calling the compare function. Because the argument of the function **Compare()** is a pointer to a **CBox** object, the function uses the indirect member selection operator in calling the **Volume()** function for the object.

To demonstrate that we can use address arithmetic on the pointer **pB1** when using it to select the member function, we set **pB1** to the address of the first element of the array of type **CBox**, **boxes**. In this case, we select the third element of the array and calculate its volume. This is the same as the volume of **match**.

If you run the example, the output window will look something like that shown below:

```
Ex8_12

Constructor called.
Constructor called.
Constructor called.
Constructor called.
Constructor called.
Constructor called.
Constructor called.
Address of cigar is 006AFD50
Volume of cigar is 40
match is less than or equal to cigar
Volume of boxes[2] is 1.21
Press any key to continue_
```

*Of course, the value of the address for the object **cigar** may well be different on your PC.*

You can see that there were seven calls of the constructor for **CBox** objects: five due to the array **Boxes**, plus one each for the objects **cigar** and **match**.

Overall, there's virtually no difference between using a pointer to a class object and using a pointer to a basic type, such as **double**.

References to Class Objects

References really come into their own when they are used with classes. As with pointers, there is virtually no difference between the way you declare and use references to class objects and the way in which we've already declared and used references to variables of basic types. To declare a reference to the object **cigar**, for instance, we would write this:

```
CBox& rcigar = cigar;              // Define reference to object cigar
```

To use a reference to calculate the volume of the object **cigar**, you would just use the reference name where the object name would otherwise appear:

```
cout << rcigar.Volume();           // Output volume of cigar thru a reference
```

As you may remember, a reference acts as an alias for the object it refers to, so the usage is exactly the same as using the original object name.

Implementing a Copy Constructor

The importance of references is really in the context of arguments and return values in functions, particularly class member functions. Let's return to the question of the copy constructor as a first toe in the water. For the moment, we'll sidestep the question of *when* you need to write your own copy constructor and concentrate on the problem of *how* you can write one. We'll use the class **CBox** just to make the discussion more concrete.

The copy constructor is a constructor which creates an object by initializing it with an object of the same class, which has been created previously. It therefore needs to accept an object of the class as an argument. We might consider writing the prototype like this:

```
CBox(CBox initB);
```

Let's now consider what happens when this constructor is called. If we write this declaration,

```
CBox myBox = cigar;
```

this will generate a call of the copy constructor as follows:

```
CBox::CBox(cigar);
```

This seems to be no problem, until you realize that the argument is passed by value. So, before the object **cigar** can be passed, the compiler needs to arrange to make a copy of it. Therefore, it calls the copy constructor to make a copy of the argument for the call of the copy constructor. Unfortunately, since it is passed by value, this call also needs a copy of its argument to be made, so the copy constructor is called... and so on and so on. We end up with an infinite number of calls to the copy constructor.

The solution, as I'm sure you have guessed, is to use a **const** reference parameter. We could write the prototype of the copy constructor like this:

```
CBox(const CBox& initB);
```

Now, the argument to the copy constructor doesn't need to be copied. It will be used to initialize the reference parameter, so no copying takes place. As you will remember from our discussion on references, if a parameter to a function is a reference, no copying of the argument occurs when the function is called. The function accesses the argument variable in the caller function directly. The **const** qualifier ensures that the argument can't be modified in the function.

> *This is another important use of the qualifier* **const**. *You should always declare a reference parameter of a function as* **const** *unless the function will modify it.*

We could implement the copy constructor as follows:

```
CBox::CBox(const CBox& initB)
{
   m_Length = initB.m_Length;
   m_Breadth = initB.m_Breadth;
   m_Height = initB.m_Height;
}
```

This definition of the copy constructor assumes that it appears outside of the class definition. The name is therefore qualified with the class name using the scope resolution operator. Each data member of the object being created is initialized with the corresponding member of the object passed as an argument. Of course, we could equally well use the initialization list to set the values of the object.

This case is not an example of when we need to write a copy constructor. As we have seen, the default copy constructor works perfectly well with **CBox** objects. We will get to *why* and *when* we need to write our own copy constructor in the next chapter.

Summary

You now understand the basic ideas behind classes in C++. We're going to see more and more about using classes throughout the rest of the book. The key points to keep in mind from this chapter are:

> A **class** provides a means of defining your own data types. They can reflect whatever types of **objects** your particular problem requires.

> A class can contain **data members** and **function members**. The function members of a class always have free access to the data members of the same class.

> Objects of a class are created and initialized using functions called **constructors**. These are automatically called when an object declaration is encountered. Constructors may be overloaded to provide different ways of initializing an object.

> Members of a class can be specified as **public**, in which case they are freely accessible by any function in a program. Alternatively, they may be specified as **private**, in which case they may only be accessed by member functions or **friend** functions of the class.

> Members of a class can be defined as **static**. Only one instance of each static member of a class exists, which is shared amongst all instances of the class, no matter how many objects of the class are created.

> Every non-static member of a class contains the pointer **this**, which points to the current object for which the function was called.

> A member function that is declared as **const** has a **const this** pointer, and therefore cannot modify data members of the class object for which it is called. It also cannot call another member function that is not **const**.

> You can only call **const** member functions for a class object declared as **const**.

> Using references to class objects as arguments to function calls can avoid substantial overheads in passing complex objects to a function.

> A copy constructor, which is a constructor for an object that is initialized with an existing object of the same class, must have its parameter specified as a **const** reference.

Exercises

Ex8-1: Modify [Prg5], so that instead of using the struct, **item**, it uses a class, **CRecord**. Make sure that the data is **private**, and make the data entry and printing routines member functions of your new class. Edit the code so it works with **CRecord** objects. Find a suitable way to signal to the main program that zero has been entered as the number. Save your new code as [Prg6].

Ex8-2: Write a class called **CTrace** which you can use to show you at run time when code blocks have been entered and exited, by producing output like this:

```
function 'f1' entry
'if' block entry
'if' block exit
function 'f1' exit
```

Ex8-3: Can you think of a way to automatically control the indentation in the last exercise, so that the output looks like this?

```
function 'f1' entry
    'if' block entry
    'if' block exit
function 'f1' exit
```

Ex8-4: Write a class to represent a **push-down stack** of integers. A stack is a list of items which only permits adding ('pushing') or removing ('popping') items from one end. For example, if our stack contained [10 4 16 20], then **Pop()** would return 10, and the stack would then contain [4 16 20]; a subsequent **Push(13)** would leave the stack as [13 4 16 20]. We can't get at an item without first popping the ones above it. Your class should implement **Push()** and **Pop()** functions, plus a **Print()** function so that you can check the stack contents. Store the list internally as an array, for now. Write a test program to verify the correct operation of your class.

Ex8-5: What happens if you try to **Pop()** more items than you've pushed, or save more items than you've space for? Can you think of a robust way to trap this? Sometimes you might want to look at the number at the top of the stack without removing it; implement a **Peek()** function to do this.

More on Classes

In this chapter, you will extend your knowledge of classes by understanding how to make your class objects work more like the basic types in C++. You will learn:

 What a class destructor is and when and why it is necessary

 How to implement a class destructor

 How to allocate data members of a class in the free store and how to delete them when they are no longer required

 When you must write a copy constructor for a class

 What a union is and how it can be used

 How to make objects of your class work with C++ operators such as **+** or *****

 What class templates are and how you define and use them

 How to use classes in a practical example

Class Destructors

Although this section heading refers to destructors, it's also about dynamic memory allocation. Allocating memory in the free store for class members can only be managed with the aid of a destructor, in addition to a constructor of course, and, as you'll see, using dynamically allocated class members will require you to write your own copy constructor.

What is a Destructor?

A **destructor** is a function that destroys an object when it is no longer required or when it goes out of scope. It's called automatically when an object goes out of scope. Destroying an object involves freeing the memory occupied by the data members of the object (except for static members which continue to exist even when there are no class objects in existence). The destructor for a class is a member function with the same name as the class, preceded by a tilde ~ . The class destructor doesn't return a value and doesn't have parameters defined. For the class **CBox**, the prototype of the class destructor is:

```
~CBox();                 // Class destructor prototype
```

> *It's an error to specify a return value or parameters for a destructor.*

The Default Destructor

All the objects that we have been using up to now have been destroyed automatically by the default destructor for the class. This is generated by the compiler in the absence of any explicit destructor being provided with a class. The default destructor doesn't delete objects or object members that have been allocated in the free store by the operator **new**. You must explicitly use the **delete** operator to destroy objects that have been created using the operator **new**, just as you would with ordinary variables. If you decide to allocate memory for members of an object dynamically, you must use the operator **delete** to implement a class destructor which frees any memory that was allocated by the operator **new**.

TRY IT OUT - A Simple Destructor

We need some practice in writing our own destructor. First, to show when the destructor is called, we can include a destructor in the class **CBox**. The class definition in this example is based on the last example in the previous chapter, **Ex8_12.cpp**.

```
// EX9_01.CPP
// Class with an explicit destructor
#include <iostream>
using namespace std;

class CBox                      // Class definition at global scope
{
   public:
      // Destructor definition
      ~CBox()
      { cout << "Destructor called." << endl; }

      // Constructor definition
      CBox(double lv = 1.0, double bv = 1.0, double hv = 1.0):
            m_Length(lv), m_Breadth(bv), m_Height(hv)
      {
         cout << endl << "Constructor called.";
      }

      // Function to calculate the volume of a box
      double Volume() const
      {
         return m_Length*m_Breadth*m_Height;
      }

      // Function to compare two boxes which returns true
      // if the first is greater that the second, and false otherwise
      int compare(CBox* pBox) const
      {
         return this->Volume()  >  pBox->Volume();
      }
```

```
    private:
        double m_Length;            // Length of a box in inches
        double m_Breadth;           // Breadth of a box in inches
        double m_Height;            // Height of a box in inches
    };

    int main()
    {
        CBox boxes[5];              // Array of CBox objects declared
        CBox cigar(8.0, 5.0, 1.0);  // Declare cigar box
        CBox match(2.2, 1.1, 0.5);  // Declare match box
        CBox* pB1 = &cigar;         // Initialize pointer to cigar object address
        CBox* pB2 = 0;              // Pointer to CBox initialized to null
```

```
        cout << endl
            << "Volume of cigar is "
            << pB1->Volume();        // Volume of obj. pointed to

        pB2 = boxes;                 // Set to address of array
        boxes[2] = match;            // Set 3rd element to match
        cout << endl                 // Now access thru pointer
            << "Volume of boxes[2] is " << (pB2 + 2)->Volume();
```

```
        cout << endl;
        return 0;
    }
```

How It Works

The only thing that our destructor does is to display a message showing that it was called. The output is:

We get one call of the destructor at the end of the program for each of the objects that exist. For each constructor call that occurred, there's a matching destructor call. We don't need to call the destructor explicitly here. When an object of a class goes out of scope, the compiler will arrange for the destructor for the class to be called automatically. In our example, the destructors are called after **main()** has finished executing, so if there's an error in a destructor, it's quite possible for a program to crash after **main()** has safely terminated.

Destructors and Dynamic Memory Allocation

You will find that you often want to allocate memory for class data members dynamically. We can use the operator **new** in a constructor to allocate space for an object member. In such a case, we must assume responsibility for deleting the space by providing a suitable destructor. Let's first define a simple class where we can do this.

Suppose we want a class where each object is a message of some description, for example, a text string. We want the class to be as memory efficient as possible so, rather than defining a data member as a **char** array big enough to hold the maximum length string that we might require, we'll allocate memory in the free store for a message when an object is created. Here's the class definition:

```
//Listing 09_01
class CMessage
{
   private:
      char* pmessage;                              // Pointer to object text string

   public:

      // Function to display a message
      void ShowIt() const
      {
         cout << endl << pmessage;
      }

      // Constructor definition
      CMessage(const char* text = "Default message")
      {
         pmessage = new char[strlen(text) + 1];    // Allocate space for text
         strcpy(pmessage, text);                   // Copy text to new memory
      }

      ~CMessage();                                 // Destructor prototype
};
```

This class has only one data member defined, **pmessage**, which is a pointer to a text string. This is defined in the **private** section of the class, so that it can't be accessed from outside the class.

In the **public** section, we have a function **ShowIt()** which will output a **CMessage** object to the screen. We also have the definition of a constructor and we have the prototype for the class destructor, **~CMessage()**, which we'll come to in a moment.

The constructor for the class requires a string as an argument, but if none is passed, it uses the default value specified. The constructor obtains the length of the string supplied as an argument, excluding the terminating **NULL**, using the function **strlen()**. For the constructor to use this library function, there must be a **#include** statement for the header file **cstring**. By adding **1** to the value that the function **strlen()** returns, the constructor defines the number of bytes of memory necessary to store the string in the free store.

*We're assuming that we have our own function to handle out-of-memory conditions as sparked off by **_set_new_handler**, so we don't bother to test the pointer returned for **NULL**. (See Chapter 6 for information on handling out-of-memory conditions.)*

Having obtained the memory for the string using the operator **new**, we use the **strcpy()** function, which is also declared in the header file **cstring**, to copy the string supplied as an argument into the memory allocated for it. This function copies the string specified by the second pointer argument to the address contained in the first pointer argument.

We now need to write a class destructor that will free up the memory allocated for a message. If we don't provide this, there's no way to delete the memory allocated for an object. If we use this class in a program, where a large number of **CMessage** objects are created, the free store will be gradually eaten away until the program fails. It's easy for this to happen almost invisibly. For example, if you create a temporary **CMessage** object in a function which is called many times in a program, you might assume that the objects are being destroyed at the return from the function. You'd be right about that, of course, but the free store memory will not be released.

The code for the destructor is as follows:

```
// Listing 09_02
// Destructor to free memory allocated by new
CMessage::~CMessage()
{
    cout << "Destructor called."        // Just to track what happens
         << endl;
    delete[] pmessage;                   // Free memory assigned to pointer
}
```

Because we're defining it outside of the class definition, we need to qualify the name of the destructor with the class name, **CMessage**, and the scope resolution operator. All the destructor does is to display a message so that we can see what's going on and use the operator **delete** to free the memory pointed to by the member **pmessage**. Note that we must include the square brackets with **delete** because we're deleting an array (of type **char**).

TRY IT OUT - Using the Message Class

We can exercise this class with a little example:

```
// EX9_02.CPP
// Using a destructor to free memory
#include <iostream>              // For stream I/O
#include <cstring>              // For strlen() and strcpy()
using namespace std;

// Put the CMessage class definition here (Listing 09_01)

// Put the destructor definition here (Listing 09_02)

int main()
{
    // Declare object
    CMessage motto("A miss is as good as a mile.");
```

```
    // Dynamic object
    CMessage* pM = new CMessage("A cat can look at a queen.");

    motto.ShowIt();              // Display 1st message
    pM->ShowIt();                // Display 2nd message
    cout << endl;

    // delete pM;                // Manually delete object created with new
    return 0;
}
```

How It Works

At the beginning of **main()**, we declare and define an initialized **CMessage** object, **motto**, in the usual manner. In the second declaration we define a pointer to a **CMessage** object, **pM**, and allocate memory for the **CMessage** object pointed to by using the operator **new**. The call to **new** invokes the **CMessage** class constructor, which has the effect of calling **new** again to allocate space for the message text pointed to by the data member **pmessage**. If you build and execute this example, it will produce this:

```
Ex9_02

A miss is as good as a mile.
A cat can look at a queen.
Destructor called.
Press any key to continue
```

We have only one destructor call, even though we created two message objects. We said earlier that the compiler doesn't take responsibility for objects created in the free store. The compiler arranged to call our destructor for the object **motto** because this is a normal automatic object, even though the memory for the data member was allocated in the free store by the constructor. The object pointed to by **pM** is different. We allocated memory for the *object* in the free store, so we have to use **delete** to remove it. You need to uncomment the statement,

```
    // delete pM;                // Manually delete object created with new
```

which appears just before the **return** statement in **main()**. If you run the code now, it will produce this:

```
Ex9_02

A miss is as good as a mile.
A cat can look at a queen.
Destructor called.
Destructor called.
Press any key to continue
```

Now we get an extra call of our destructor. This is surprising in a way. Clearly, **delete** is only dealing with the memory allocated by the call to **new** in the function **main()**. It only freed the memory pointed to by **pM**. Since our pointer to **pM** is a pointer to a **CMessage** object (for which a destructor has been defined), **delete** also calls our destructor to allow us to clean up the details of the members of the object. So when you use **delete** for an object created dynamically with **new**, it will always call the destructor for the object allocated on the free store.

Implementing a Copy Constructor

When you allocate space for class members dynamically, there are demons lurking in the free store. For our class **CMessage**, the default copy constructor is woefully inadequate. If we have these statements,

```
CMessage motto1("Radiation fades your genes.");
CMessage motto2(motto1);
```

the effect of the default copy constructor will be to copy the address in the pointer member from **motto1** to **motto2**. Consequently, there will be only one text string shared between the two objects, as illustrated in the diagram below:

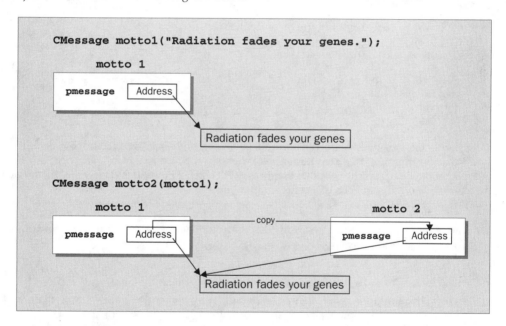

If the string is changed from either of the objects, it will be changed for the other as well. If **motto1** is destroyed, the pointer in **motto2** will be pointing at a memory area which may now be used for something else, and chaos will surely ensue. Of course, the same problem arises if **motto2** is deleted; **motto1** would then contain a member pointing to a nonexistent string.

The solution is to supply a class copy constructor to replace the default version. This could be implemented in the **public** section of the class as follows:

```
CMessage(const CMessage& initM)          // Copy Constructor definition
{
    // Allocate space for text
    pmessage = new char[ strlen(initM.pmessage) + 1 ];
```

```
    // Copy text to new memory
    strcpy(pmessage, initM.pmessage);
}
```

You will remember from the previous chapter that, to avoid an infinite spiral of calls to the copy constructor, the parameter must be specified as a **const** reference. This copy constructor first allocates enough memory to hold the string in the object **initM**, storing the address in the data member of the new object, and then copies the text string from the initializing object. Now, our new object will be identical to, but quite independent of, the old one.

Just because you don't initialize one **CMessage** class object with another, don't think that you're safe and need not bother with the copy constructor. Another monster lurks in the free store. Consider the following statements,

```
CMessage thought("Eye awl weighs yews my spell checker.");
DisplayMessage(thought);       // Call a function to output a message
```

where the function **DisplayMessage()** is defined as:

```
void DisplayMessage(CMessage localMsg)
{
    cout << endl << "The message is: ";
    localMsg.ShowIt();
    return;
}
```

Looks simple enough doesn't it? What could be wrong with that? A catastrophic error, that's what! What the function **DisplayMessage()** does is actually irrelevant. The problem lies with the argument. The argument is a **CMessage** object which is passed by value. With the default copy constructor, the sequence of events is as follows:

1 The object **thought** is created with the space for the message **"Eye awl weighs yews my spell checker"** allocated in the free store.

2 The function **DisplayMessage()** is called and, because the argument is passed by value, a copy, **localMsg**, is made using the default copy constructor. Now the pointer in the copy points to the same string in the free store as the original object.

3 At the end of the function, the local object goes out of scope, so the destructor for the **CMessage** class is called. This deletes the local object (the copy) by deleting the memory pointed to by the pointer **pmessage**.

4 On return from the function **DisplayMessage()**, the pointer in the original object, **thought**, still points to the memory area that has just been deleted. Next time you try to use the original object (or even if you don't, since it will need to be deleted sooner or later) your program will behave in weird and mysterious ways.

Any call to a function that passes by value an object of a class that has a member defined dynamically will cause problems. So, out of this, we have an absolutely 100 percent, 24 carat golden rule:

> *If you allocate space for a class member dynamically, always implement a copy constructor.*

Sharing Memory Between Variables

As a relic of the days when 64K was quite a lot of memory, we have a facility in C++ which allows more than one variable to share the same memory (but obviously not at the same time). This is called a **union**, and there are four basic ways in which you can use one:

▶ First, you can use it so that a variable **A** occupies a block of memory at one point in a program, which is later occupied by another variable **B** of a different type, because **A** is no longer required. I recommend that you don't do this. It's not worth the risk of error that is implicit in such an arrangement. You can achieve the same effect by allocating memory dynamically.

▶ Alternatively, you could have a situation in a program where a large array of data is required, but you don't know in advance of execution what the data type will be — it will be determined by the input data. I also recommend that you don't use unions in this case, since you can achieve the same result using a couple of pointers of different types and again allocating the memory dynamically.

▶ A third possible use for a union is the one that you may need now and again — when you want to interpret the same data in two or more different ways. This could happen when you have a variable that is of type **long**, and you want to treat it as two values of type **short**. Windows will sometimes package two **short** values in a single parameter of type **long** passed to a function. Another instance arises when you want to treat a block of memory containing numeric data as a string of bytes, just to move it around.

▶ Lastly you can use a union as a means of passing an object or a data value around where you don't know in advance what its type is going to be. The union can provide for storing any one of the possible range of types that you might have.

Defining Unions

A union is defined using the keyword **union**. It is best understood by taking an example of a definition:

```
union shareLD                    // Sharing memory between long and double
{
    double dval;
    long lval;
};
```

This defines a union type **shareLD** which provides for the variables of type **long** and **double** to occupy the same memory. The union type name is usually referred to as a **tag name**. This statement is rather like a class definition, in that we haven't actually defined a union instance yet, so we don't have any variables at this point. Once it has been defined, we can declare instances of a union in a declaration. For example:

```
shareLD myUnion;
```

This declares an instance of the union, **shareLD**, that we defined previously. We could also have declared **myUnion** by including it in the union definition statement:

```
union shareLD              // Sharing memory between long and double
{
   double dval;
   long lval;
} myUnion;
```

If we want to refer to a member of the union, we use the direct member selection operator (the period) with the union instance name, just as we have done when accessing members of a class. So, we could set the long variable **lval** to 100 in the union instance **MyUnion** with this statement:

```
myUnion.lval = 100;        // Using a member of a union
```

Using a similar statement later in a program to initialize the double variable **dval** will overwrite **lval**. The basic problem with using a union to store different types of values in the same memory is that, because of the way a union works, you also need some means of determining which of the member values is current. This is usually achieved by maintaining another variable which acts as an indicator of the type of value stored.

A union is not limited to sharing between two variables. If you wish, you can share the same memory between several variables. The memory occupied by the union will be that which is required by its largest member. For example, if we define this union,

```
union shareDLF
{
   double dval;
   long lval;
   float fval;
} uinst = {1.5};
```

it will occupy 8 bytes, as illustrated in the figure here:

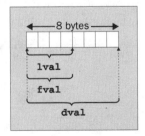

In the example, we defined an instance of the union, **uinst**, as well as the tag name for the union. We also initialized it with the value 1.5.

> *You can only initialize the first member of the union when you declare an instance.*

Anonymous Unions

You can define a union without a union type name, in which case an instance of the union is automatically declared. For example, if we define a union like this,

```
union
{
   char* pval;
   double dval;
   long lval;
};
```

it defines both a union with no name and an instance of the union with no name. Consequently, the variables that it contains may be referred to just by their names, as they appear in the union definition. This can be more convenient than a normal union with a type name, but you need to be careful that you don't confuse the members with ordinary variables. The members of the union will still share the same memory. As an illustration of how the anonymous union above works, to use the **double** member, you could write this statement:

```
dval = 99.5;                    // Using a member of an anonymous union
```

As you can see, there's nothing to distinguish the variable **dval** as a union member. If you need to use anonymous unions, you could use a naming convention to make the members more obvious.

Unions in Classes

You can include an instance of a union in a class. If you intend storing different types of value at different times, this usually necessitates maintaining a class data member to indicate what kind of value is stored in the union. There isn't usually a great deal to be gained by using unions as class members.

Operator Overloading

Operator overloading enables you to make standard operators, such as **+**, **-**, ***** and so on, work with objects of your own data types. It allows you to write a function which redefines a particular operator so that it performs a particular action when it's used with objects of a class. For example, you could redefine the operator **>** so that, when it was used with objects of the class **CBox** (which we saw earlier), it would return **true** if the first **CBox** argument had a greater volume than the second.

Operator overloading doesn't allow you to invent new operators, nor can you change the precedence of an operator, so your overloaded version of an operator will have the same priority in the sequence of evaluating an expression as the original base operator. The operator precedence table can be found both in Chapter 2 of this book and in the MSDN Library.

Although you can't overload all the operators, the restrictions aren't particularly oppressive. These are the operators that you can't overload:

The scope resolution operator,   `::`

The conditional operator,   `?:`

The direct member selection operator,   `.`

The size-of operator,   **`sizeof`**

The de-reference pointer to class member operator,   `.*`

Anything else is fair game, which gives you quite a bit of scope. Obviously, it's a good idea to ensure that your versions of the standard operators are reasonably consistent with their normal usage, or at least reasonably intuitive in their operation. It wouldn't be a very sensible approach to produce an overloaded **+** operator for a class that performed the equivalent of a multiply on class objects. The best way to understand how operator overloading works is to work through an example, so let's implement what we just referred to, the greater than operator, **>**, for the **CBox** class.

Implementing an Overloaded Operator

If we want to implement an overloaded operator for a class, we have to write a special function. Assuming that it is a member of the class **CBox**, the declaration for the function to overload the **>** operator within the class definition will be as follows:

```
class CBox
{
  public:
    bool operator>(CBox& aBox) const;            // Overloaded 'greater than'
  // Rest of the class definition...
};
```

The word **operator** here is a keyword. Combined with an operator, in this case, **>**, it defines an operator function. The function name in this case is **operator>()**. You can write an operator function with or without a space between the keyword **operator** and the operator itself, as long as there's no ambiguity. The ambiguity arises with operators using normal letters such as **new** or **delete**. If they are written without a space, **operatornew** and **operatordelete**, they are legal names for ordinary functions, so for operator functions with these operators, you must leave a space between the keyword **operator** and the operator itself. Note that we declare the function as **const** since it doesn't modify the data members of the class.

With our operator function **operator>()**, the right operand of the operator is that which is defined between parentheses. The left operand will be defined implicitly by the pointer **this**. So, if we have the following **if** statement,

```
if(box1 > box2)
    cout << endl << "box1 is greater than box2";
```

then the expression between parentheses in the **if** will call our operator function. It is equivalent to this function call:

```
box1.operator>(box2);
```

The correspondence between the **CBox** objects in the expression and the operator function parameters is illustrated here:

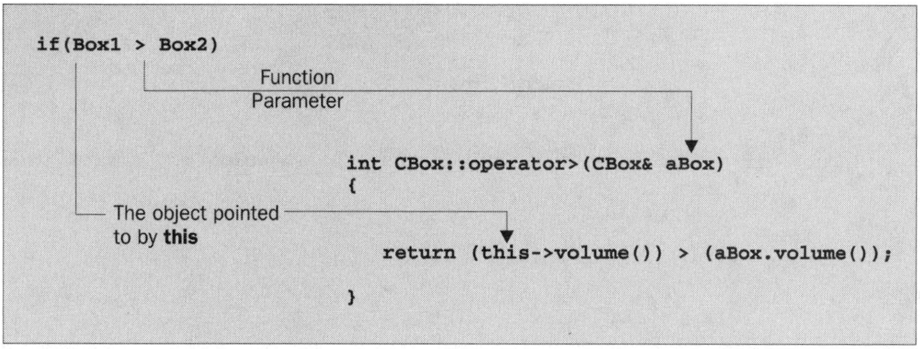

```
if(Box1 > Box2)
                          Function
                          Parameter

              int CBox::operator>(CBox& aBox)
              {
    The object pointed
    to by this
                          return (this->volume()) > (aBox.volume());

              }
```

Let's look at how the code for the **operator>()** function works:

```
// Operator function for 'greater than' which
// compares volumes of CBox objects.
bool CBox::operator>(const CBox& aBox) const
{
   return this->Volume() > aBox.Volume();
}
```

We use a reference parameter to the function to avoid unnecessary copying when the function is called. Since the function does not alter the object for which it is called, we can declare it as **const**. If we don't do this, we could not use the operator to compare **const** objects of type **CBox** at all.

The **return** expression uses the member function **Volume()** to calculate the volume of the **CBox** object pointed to by **this**, and compares the result, using the basic operator **>** , with the volume of the object **aBox**. **>** itself returns an **int** (not a bool) and thus, **1** is returned if the **CBox** object pointed to by the pointer **this** has a larger volume than the object **aBox** passed as a reference argument, and **0** otherwise.

TRY IT OUT - Operator Overloading

We can exercise this function with an example:

```
//EX9_03.CPP
// Exercising the overloaded 'greater than' operator
#include <iostream>                        // For stream I/O
using namespace std;

class CBox                                 // Class definition at global scope
{
   public:
      // Constructor definition
      CBox(double lv = 1.0, double bv = 1.0, double hv = 1.0):
          m_Length(lv), m_Breadth(bv), m_Height(hv)
      {
```

```
            cout << endl << "Constructor called.";
        }

        // Function to calculate the volume of a box
        double Volume() const
        {
            return m_Length*m_Breadth*m_Height;
        }
```

```
        bool operator>(const CBox& aBox) const;   // Overloaded 'greater than'
```

```
        // Destructor definition
        ~CBox()
        { cout << "Destructor called." << endl; }

    private:
        double m_Length;                      // Length of a box in inches
        double m_Breadth;                     // Breadth of a box in inches
        double m_Height;                      // Height of a box in inches
};
```

```
// Operator function for 'greater than' that
// compares volumes of CBox objects.
bool CBox::operator>(const CBox& aBox) const
{
    return this->Volume() > aBox.Volume();
}

int main()
{
    CBox smallBox(4.0, 2.0, 1.0);
    CBox mediumBox(10.0, 4.0, 2.0);
    CBox bigBox(30.0, 20.0, 40.0);

    if(mediumBox > smallBox)
        cout << endl
            << "mediumBox is bigger than smallBox";

    if(mediumBox > bigBox)
        cout << endl
            << "mediumBox is bigger than bigBox";
    else
        cout << endl
            << "mediumBox is not bigger than bigBox";

    cout << endl;
    return 0;
}
```

How It Works

The prototype of the operator function **operator>()** appears in the **public** section of the class. As the function definition is outside the class definition, it won't default to **inline**. This is quite arbitrary. We could just as well have put the definition in place of the prototype in the class definition. In this case, we wouldn't need to qualify the function name with **CBox::** in front of it. As you'll remember, this is needed in order to tell the compiler that the function is a member of the class **CBox**.

The function **main()** has two **if** statements using the operator **>** with class members. These automatically invoke our overloaded operator. If you wanted to get confirmation of this, you could add an output statement to the operator function. The output from this example is:

```
Ex9_03

Constructor called.
Constructor called.
Constructor called.
mediumBox is bigger than smallBox
mediumBox is not bigger than bigBox
Destructor called.
Destructor called.
Destructor called.
Press any key to continue_
```

The output demonstrates that the **if** statements work fine with our operator function, so being able to express the solution to **CBox** problems directly in terms of **CBox** objects is beginning to be a realistic proposition.

Implementing Full Support for an Operator

With our operator function **operator>()**, there are still lots of things that you can't do. Specifying a problem solution in terms of **CBox** objects might well involve statements such as the following:

```
if(aBox > 20.0)
```

Our function won't deal with that. If you try to use an expression comparing a **CBox** object with a numerical value, you'll get an error message. In order to support this, we would need to write another version of the function **operator>()**, as an overloaded function.

We can quite easily support the type of expression that we've just seen. The declaration of the member function within the class would be:

```
// Compare a CBox object with a constant
bool operator>(const double& value) const;
```

This would appear in the definition of the class. The **CBox** object will be passed as the implicit pointer **this**.

The implementation is also easy. It's just one statement in the body of the function:

```
// Function to compare a CBox object with a constant
bool CBox::operator>(const double& value) const
{
   return this->Volume() > value;
}
```

This couldn't be much simpler, could it? But we still have a problem with the operator **>** with **CBox** objects. We may well want to write statements such as this:

```
if(20.0 > aBox)
    ...                         // do something
```

You might argue that this could be done by implementing the operator function **operator<()** and rewriting the statement above to use it, which is quite true. Indeed, the < operator is likely to be a requirement for comparing **CBox** objects anyway, but an implementation of support for an object type shouldn't artificially restrict the ways in which you can use the objects in an expression.

The use of the objects should be as natural as possible. The problem is how to do it. A member operator function always provides the left argument as the pointer **this**. Since the left argument, in this case, is of type **double**, we can't implement it as a member function. That leaves us with two choices: an ordinary function or a **friend** function. Since we don't need to access the **private** members of the class it doesn't need to be a friend function, so we can implement it as an ordinary function. The prototype, placed outside the class definition of course since it isn't a member, would need to be:

```
bool operator>(const double& value, const CBox& aBox);
```

The implementation would be this:

```
// Function comparing a constant with a CBox object
bool operator>(const double& value, const CBox& aBox)
{
    return value > aBox.Volume();
}
```

As we've seen already, an ordinary function (and a **friend** function too for that matter) accesses the members of an object by using the direct member selection operator and the object name. Of course, an ordinary function only has access to the public members. The member function **Volume()** is **public**, so there's no problem using it here.

If the class didn't have the **public** function **Volume()**, we could either use a **friend** function that could access the **private** data members directly, or we could provide a set of member functions to return the values of the **private** data members and use those in an ordinary function to implement the comparison.

TRY IT OUT - Complete Overloading of the > Operator

We can put all this together in an example to show how it works:

```
//EX9_04.CPP
// Implementing a complete overloaded 'greater than' operator
#include <iostream>                   // For stream I/O
using namespace std;

class CBox                            // Class definition at global scope
{
    public:
        // Constructor definition
        CBox(double lv = 1.0, double bv = 1.0, double hv = 1.0):
            m_Length(lv), m_Breadth(bv), m_Height(hv)
```

```
      {
         cout << endl << "Constructor called.";
      }

      // Function to calculate the volume of a box
      double Volume() const
      {
         return m_Length*m_Breadth*m_Height;
      }
```

```
      // Operator function for 'greater than' that
      // compares volumes of CBox objects.
      bool operator>(const CBox& aBox) const
      {
         return this->Volume() > aBox.Volume();
      }

      // Function to compare a CBox object with a constant
      bool operator>(const double& value) const
      {
         return this->Volume() > value;
      }
```

```
      // Destructor definition
      ~CBox()
      { cout << "Destructor called." << endl;}

   private:
      double m_Length;              // Length of a box in inches
      double m_Breadth;             // Breadth of a box in inches
      double m_Height;              // Height of a box in inches
};
```

```
int operator>(const double& value, const CBox& aBox); // Function prototype
```

```
int main()
{
   CBox smallBox(4.0, 2.0, 1.0);
   CBox mediumBox(10.0, 4.0, 2.0);

   if(mediumBox > smallBox)
      cout << endl
           << "mediumBox is bigger than smallBox";
```

```
   if(mediumBox > 50.0)
      cout << endl
           << "mediumBox capacity is more than 50";
   else
      cout << endl
           << "mediumBox capacity is not more than 50";

   if(10.0 > smallBox)
      cout << endl
           << "smallBox capacity is less than 10";
   else
      cout << endl
           << "smallBox capacity is not less than 10";
```

```
        cout << endl;
        return 0;
}
```

```
    // Function comparing a constant with a CBox object
    int operator>(const double& value, const CBox& aBox)
    {
        return value > aBox.Volume();
    }
```

How It Works

Note the position of the prototype for the ordinary function version of **operator>()**. It needs to follow the class definition, because it refers to a **CBox** object in the parameter list. If you place it before the class definition, the example will not compile.

There is a way to place it at the beginning of the program file following the **#include** statement: use an **incomplete class declaration**. This would precede the prototype and would look like this:

```
    class CBox;                                   // Incomplete class declaration
    int operator>(const double& value, CBox& aBox);   // Function prototype
```

The incomplete class declaration identifies **CBox** to the compiler as a class and is sufficient to allow the compiler to process the prototype for the function properly, since it now knows that **aBox** is a variable of a user-defined type to be specified later.

This mechanism is also essential in circumstances such as those where you have two classes, each of which has a pointer to an object of the other class as a member. They will each require the other to be declared first. It's possible to resolve such an impasse through the use of an incomplete class declaration.

The output from the example is:

```
Ex9_04
Constructor called.
Constructor called.
mediumBox is bigger than smallBox
mediumBox capacity is more than 50
smallBox capacity is less than 10
Destructor called.
Destructor called.
Press any key to continue_
```

After the constructor messages due to the declarations of the objects **smallBox** and **mediumBox**, we have the output lines from the three **if** statements, each of which is working as we expected. The first of these is calling the operator function that is a class member and works with two **CBox** objects. The second is calling the member function that has a parameter of type **double**. The expression in the third **if** statement calls the operator function that we implemented as an ordinary function.

As it happens, we could have made both the operator functions which are class members ordinary functions, since they only need access to the member function **Volume()**, which is **public**.

> *Any comparison operator can be implemented in much the same way as we have implemented these. They would only differ in the minor details and the general approach to implementing them would be exactly the same.*

Overloading the Assignment Operator

If you don't provide an overloaded assignment operator function for your class, the compiler will provide a default. The default version will simply provide a member-by-member copying process, similar to that of the default copy constructor. However, don't confuse the default copy constructor with the default assignment operator. The default copy constructor is called by a declaration of a class object that's initialized with an existing object of the same class, or by passing an object to a function by value. The default assignment operator, on the other hand, is called when the left hand side and the right hand side of an assignment statement are objects of the same class.

For our **CBox** class, the default assignment operator works with no problem, but for any class which has space for members allocated dynamically, you need to look carefully at the requirements of the class in question. There may be considerable potential for chaos in your program if you leave the assignment operator out under these circumstances.

For a moment, let's return to our message class that we used when talking about copy constructors. You'll remember it had a member, **pmessage**, that was a pointer to a string. Now consider the effect that the default assignment operator could have. Suppose we had two instances of the class, **motto1** and **motto2**. We could try setting the members of **motto2** equal to the members of **motto1** using the default assignment operator, as follows:

```
motto2 = motto1;                    // Use default assignment operator
```

The effect of using the default assignment operator for this class is essentially the same as using the default copy constructor: disaster will result! Since each object will have a pointer to the same string, if the string is changed for one object, it's changed for both. There's also the problem that when one of the instances of the class is destroyed, its destructor will free the memory used for the string and the other object will be left with a pointer to memory that may now be used for something else.

What we need the assignment operator to do is to copy the text to a memory area owned by the destination object.

Fixing the Problem

We can fix this with our own assignment operator, which we will assume is defined within the class definition:

```
// Overloaded assignment operator for CMessage objects
CMessage& operator=(const CMessage& aMess)
{
```

```
// Release memory for 1st operand
delete[] pmessage;
pmessage = new char[ strlen(aMess.pmessage) + 1];

// Copy 2nd operand string to 1st
strcpy(this->pmessage, aMess.pmessage);

// Return a reference to 1st operand
return *this;
}
```

An assignment might seem very simple, but there's a couple of subtleties need further investigation. First of all, note that we return a reference from the assignment operator function. It may not be immediately apparent why this is so – after all, the function does complete the assignment operation entirely, and the object on the right of the assignment will be copied to that on the left. Superficially this would suggest that we don't need to return anything, but we need to think a little more about how the operator might be used.

There is a possibility that we might need to use the result of the assignment operator on the right hand side of an expression. Consider a statement such as,

```
motto1 = motto2 = motto3;
```

Because the assignment operator is right associative, the assignment of **motto3** to **motto2** will be carried out first, so this will translate into,

```
motto1 = (motto2.operator=(motto3));
```

The result of the operator function call here is on the right of the equals sign, so the statement will finally become this:

```
motto1.operator=(motto2.operator=(motto3));
```

If this is to work, we certainly have to return something. The **operator=()** between the parentheses must return an an object that can be used as an argument to the other **operator=()** call. In this case a return type of either **CMessage** or **CMessage&** would do it, so a reference is not mandatory in this situation, but we must at least return a **CMessage** object.

However, consider the following example:

```
(motto1 = motto2) = motto3;
```

This is perfectly legitimate code – the parentheses serve to make sure the leftmost assignment is carried out first. This translates into,

```
(motto1.operator=(motto2)) = motto3;
```

and ultimately becomes:

```
(motto1.operator=(motto2)).operator=(motto3);
```

Now we have a situation where the object returned from **operator=()** is used to call the **operator=()** member. If the return type is just **CMessage**, this will not be legal because a temporary copy of the original object is actually returned, and the compiler will not allow a member function call using a temporary object. In other words, the return value, when the return type is **Cmessage**, is not an lvalue. The only way to ensure this sort of thing will compile and work correctly is to return a reference, which is an lvalue, so the only possible return type is **CMessage&.**

Note that the C++ language does not enforce any restrictions on the accepted parameter or return types for the assignment operator, but it makes sense to declare the operator in the way just described, if you want your assignment operator functions to support normal C++ usage of assignment.

The second subtlety you need to remember is that each object already has memory for a string allocated, so the first thing that the operator function has to do is to delete the memory allocated to the first object and reallocate sufficient memory to accommodate the string belonging to the second object. Once this is done, the string from the second object can be copied to the new memory now owned by the first.

There's still a defect in this operator function. What if we were to write the following statement?

```
motto1 = motto1;
```

Obviously, you wouldn't do anything as stupid as this directly, but it could easily be hidden behind a pointer, for instance, as in the following statement,

```
Motto1 = *pMess;
```

where the pointer **pMess** points to **motto1**. In this case, the operator function as it stands would delete the memory for **motto1**, allocate some more memory based on the length of the string that has already been deleted and try to copy the old memory which, by then, could well have been corrupted. We can fix this with a check at the beginning of the function, so now it would become this:

```
// Overloaded assignment operator for CMessage objects
CMessage& operator=(const CMessage& aMess)
{
    if(this == &aMess)                    // Check addresses, if equal
        return *this;                     // return the 1st operand
    // Release memory for 1st operand
    delete[] pmessage;
    pmessage = new char[ strlen(aMess.pmessage) +1];

    // Copy 2nd operand string to 1st
    strcpy(this->pmessage, aMess.pmessage);

    // Return a reference to 1st operand
    return *this;
}
```

This assumes that the definition appears within the class definition.

TRY IT OUT - Overloading the Assignment Operator

Let's put this together in a working example. We'll add a function, called **Reset()**, to the class at the same time. This just resets the message to a string of asterisks.

```
// EX9_05.CPP
// Overloaded copy operator perfection
#include <iostream>
#include <cstring>
using namespace std;

class CMessage
{
   private:
      char* pmessage;                          // Pointer to object text string

   public:
      // Function to display a message
      void ShowIt() const
      {
         cout << endl << pmessage;
      }

      //Function to reset a message to *
      void Reset()
      {
         char* temp = pmessage;
         while(*temp)
            *(temp++) = '*';
      }

      // Overloaded assignment operator for CMessage objects
      CMessage& operator=(const CMessage& aMess)
      {
         if(this == &aMess)                  // Check addresses, if equal
            return *this;                    // return the 1st operand

         // Release memory for 1st operand
         delete[] pmessage;
         pmessage = new char[ strlen(aMess.pmessage) +1];

         // Copy 2nd operand string to 1st
         strcpy(this->pmessage, aMess.pmessage);

         // Return a reference to 1st operand
         return *this;
      }

      // Constructor definition
      CMessage(const char* text = "Default message")
      {
         pmessage = new char[ strlen(text) +1 ]; // Allocate space for text
         strcpy(pmessage, text);                 // Copy text to new memory
      }
```

```
        // Destructor to free memory allocated by new
        ~CMessage()
        {
            cout << "Destructor called."      // Just to track what happens
                 << endl;
            delete[] pmessage;                 // Free memory assigned to pointer
        }
};
```

```
int main()
{
   CMessage motto1("The devil takes care of his own");
   CMessage motto2;

   cout << "motto2 contains - ";
   motto2.ShowIt();
   cout << endl;

   motto2 = motto1;                            // Use new assignment operator

   cout << "motto2 contains - ";
   motto2.ShowIt();
   cout << endl;

   motto1.Reset();                             // Setting motto1 to * doesn't
                                               // affect motto2

   cout << "motto1 now contains - ";
   motto1.ShowIt();
   cout << endl;

   cout << "motto2 still contains - ";
   motto2.ShowIt();
   cout << endl;

   return 0;
}
```

You can see from the output of this program that everything works exactly as required, with no linking between the messages of the two objects, except where we explicitly set them equal.

```
Ex9_05
motto2 contains -
Default message
motto2 contains -
The devil takes care of his own
motto1 now contains -
*********************************
motto2 still contains -
The devil takes care of his own
Destructor called.
Destructor called.
Press any key to continue
```

So let's have another golden rule out of all of this:

> *Always implement an assignment operator if you allocate space dynamically for a data member of a class.*

Having implemented the assignment operator, what happens with operations such as **+=**? Well, they don't work unless you implement them. For each form of **op=** that you want to use with your class objects, you need to write another operator function.

Overloading the Addition Operator

Let's look at overloading the addition operator for our **CBox** class. This is interesting because it involves creating and returning a new object. The new object will be the sum (whatever we define that to mean) of the two **CBox** objects that are its operands.

So what do we want the sum to mean? Let's define the sum of two **CBox** objects as a **CBox** object which is large enough to contain the other two boxes stacked on top of each other. We can do this by making the new object have an **m_Length** member which is the larger of the **m_Length** members of the objects being added, and an **m_Breadth** member derived in a similar way. The **m_Height** member will be the sum of the **m_Height** members of the two operand objects, so that the resultant **CBox** object can contain the other two **CBox** objects. This isn't necessarily an optimal solution, but it will be sufficient for our purposes. By altering the constructor, we'll also arrange that the **m_Length** member of a **CBox** object is always greater than or equal to the **m_Breadth** member.

The addition operation is easier to explain graphically, so it's illustrated below:

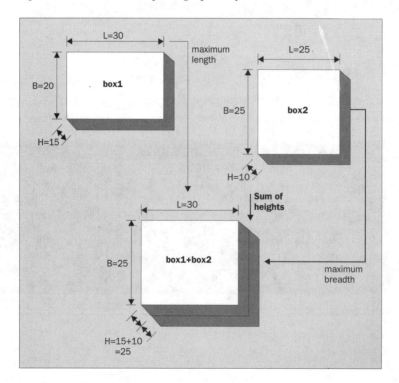

Since we need to get at the members of an object directly, we will make the **operator+()** a member function. The declaration of the function member within the class definition will be this:

```
CBox operator+(const CBox& aBox) const;        // Function adding two CBox objects
```

We define the parameter as a reference to avoid unnecessary copying of the right argument when the function is called, and we make it a **const** reference because the function does not modify the argument. If you don't declare the parameter as a **const** reference, the compiler will not allow a const object to be passed to the function, so the right operand of **+** could not be a **const CBox** object. We also declare the function as **const** as it doesn't change the object for which it is called. Without this, the left operand of **+** could not be a **const CBox** object.

The **operator+()** function definition would now be as follows:

```
// Function to add two CBox objects
CBox CBox::operator+(const CBox& aBox) const
{
    // New object has larger length and breadth, and sum of heights
    return CBox(m_Length > aBox.m_Length? m_Length:aBox.m_Length,
            m_Breadth > aBox.m_Breadth? m_Breadth:aBox.m_Breadth,
            m_Height + aBox.m_Height);
}
```

A local **CBox** object is constructed from the current object(***this**) and the object passed as an argument, **aBox**. Remember that the return process will make a temporary copy of the local object and that is what is passed back to the calling function.

TRY IT OUT - Exercising Our Addition

We can see how this works in an example:

```
// EX9_06.CPP
// Adding CBox objects
#include <iostream>                          // For stream I/O
using namespace std;

class CBox                                   // Class definition at global
scope
{
    public:
        // Constructor definition
        CBox(double lv = 1.0, double bv = 1.0, double hv = 1.0): m_Height(hv)
        {
            m_Length = lv > bv? lv: bv;           // Ensure that
            m_Breadth = bv < lv? bv: lv;          // length >= breadth
        }

        // Function to calculate the volume of a box
        double Volume() const
        {
            return m_Length*m_Breadth*m_Height;
        }
```

```
            // Operator function for 'greater than' which
            // compares volumes of CBox objects.
            int CBox::operator>(const CBox& aBox) const
            {
                return this->Volume() > aBox.Volume();
            }

            // Function to compare a CBox object with a constant
            int operator>(const double& value) const
            {
                return Volume() > value;
            }

            // Function to add two CBox objects
            CBox operator+(const CBox& aBox) const
            {
                // New object has larger length & breadth, and sum of heights
                return CBox(m_Length > aBox.m_Length? m_Length:aBox.m_Length,
                          m_Breadth > aBox.m_Breadth? m_Breadth:aBox.m_Breadth,
                          m_Height + aBox.m_Height);
            }

            // Function to show the dimensions of a box
            void ShowBox() const
            {
                cout << m_Length << " " << m_Breadth << " " << m_Height
                     << endl;
            }

        private:
            double m_Length;                    // Length of a box in inches
            double m_Breadth;                   // Breadth of a box in inches
            double m_Height;                    // Height of a box in inches
    };

    int operator>(const double& value, const CBox& aBox); // Function prototype

    int main()
    {
        CBox smallBox(4.0, 2.0, 1.0);
        CBox mediumBox(10.0, 4.0, 2.0);
        CBox aBox;
        CBox bBox;

        aBox = smallBox + mediumBox;
        cout << "aBox dimensions are ";
        aBox.ShowBox();

        bBox = aBox + smallBox + mediumBox;
        cout << "bBox dimensions are ";
        bBox.ShowBox();

        return 0;
    }
```

```
// Function comparing a constant with a CBox object
int operator>(const double& value, const CBox& aBox)
{
    return value > aBox.Volume();
}
```

How It Works

In this example we've changed the **CBox** class members a little. The destructor has been deleted as it isn't necessary for this class, and the constructor has been modified to ensure that the **m_Length** member isn't less than the **m_Breadth** member. Knowing that the length of a box is always at least as big as the breadth makes the add operation a bit easier. We've also added the function **ShowBox()** to output the dimensions of a **CBox** object. This will enable us to verify that our overloaded add operation is working as we expect.

The output from this program is:

```
Ex9_06

aBox dimensions are 10 4 3
bBox dimensions are 10 4 6
Press any key to continue
```

This seems to be consistent with the notion of adding **CBox** objects that we have defined and, as you can see, the function also works with multiple add operations in an expression. For the computation of **bBox**, the overloaded addition operator will be called twice.

We could equally well have implemented the add operation for the class as a **friend** function. Its prototype would then be this:

```
friend CBox operator+(const CBox& aBox, const CBox& bBox);
```

The method to produce the result would be much the same, except that you'd need to use the direct member selection operator to obtain the members for both the arguments to the function. It would work just as well as the first version of the operator function.

Class Templates

We saw back in Chapter 6 that we could define a function template which would automatically generate functions varying in the type of arguments accepted, or in the type of value returned. C++ has a similar mechanism for classes. A **class template** is not in itself a class, it's a sort of 'recipe' for a class. As you can see from the diagram, it's like the function template — you determine the class that you want generated by specifying your choice of type for the variable parameter (**T** in this case) that appears between the angled brackets in the template. Doing this generates a particular class that is referred to as an **instance** of the class template. The process of creating a class from a template is described as **instantiating** the template.

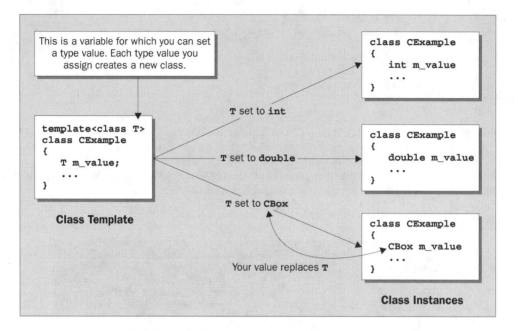

An appropriate class definition is generated when you instantiate an object of a template class for a particular type, so you can generate any number of different classes from one class template. We can see how this works in practice by looking at an example.

Defining a Class Template

We'll choose a simple example to illustrate how you define and use a class template, and we won't complicate things by worrying too much about possible errors that can arise if it's misused. Let's suppose we want to define classes which can store a number of data samples of some kind, and each class is to provide a **Max()** function to calculate the maximum sample of those stored. This function will be similar to the one we saw in the function template discussion in Chapter 6. We can define a class template, which will generate a class **CSamples** for whatever type we want:

```
template <class T>
class CSamples
{
   public:
      // Constructor definition to accept an array of samples
      CSamples(const T values[], int count)
      {
         m_Free = count < 100? count:100;      // Don't exceed the array
         for(int i = 0; i < m_Free; i++)
            m_Values[i] = values[i];           // Store count number of samples
      }

      // Constructor to accept a single sample
      CSamples(const T& value)
      {
         m_Values[0] = value;                  // Store the sample
         m_Free = 1;                           // Next is free
      }
```

```
        // Default constructor
        CSamples(){ m_Free = 0 }                      // Nothing stored, so first is free

        // Function to add a sample
        bool Add(const T& value)
        {
          bool OK = m_Free < 100;                     // Indicates there is a free place
          if(OK)
            m_Values[m_Free++] = value;               // OK true, so store the value
          return OK;
        }

        // Function to obtain maximum sample
        T Max() const
        {
          T theMax = m_Free ? m_Values[0] : 0; // Set first sample or 0 as maximum
          for(int i = 1; i < m_Free; i++)             // Check all the samples
          if(m_Values[i] > theMax)
            theMax = m_Values[i];                     // Store any larger sample
          return theMax;
        }

    private:
        T m_Values[100];                              // Array to store samples
        int m_Free;                                   // Index of free location in
  m_Values
  };
```

To indicate that we are defining a template rather than a straightforward class definition, we insert the keyword **template** and the type parameter, **T**, between angled brackets, just before the keyword **class** and the class name, **CSamples**. This is the same syntax that we used to define a function template back in Chapter 6. The parameter **T** is the type variable that you'll replace by a specific type when you declare a class object. Wherever the parameter **T** appears in the class definition, it will be replaced by the type that you specify in your object declaration; this creates a class definition corresponding to this type. You can specify any type (a basic data type or a class type), but it has to make sense in the context of the class template, of course. Any class type that you use to instantiate a class from a template must have all the operators defined that the member functions of the template will use with such objects. If your class hasn't implemented **operator>()**, for example, it will not work with our class template above. In general, you can specify multiple parameters in a class template if you need them. We'll come back to this possibility a little later in the chapter.

Getting back to our example, the type of the array in which to store the samples is specified as **T**. The array will therefore be an array of whatever type you specify for **T** when you declare a **CSamples** object. As you can see, we also use the type **T** in two of the constructors for the class, as well as in the **Add()** and **Max()** functions. Each of these occurrences will also be replaced when you instantiate a class object. The constructors we've defined support the creation of an empty object, an object with a single sample, and an object initialized with an array of samples. The **Add()** function allows samples to be added to an object one at a time. You could also overload this function to add an array of samples. The class template includes some elementary provision to prevent the capacity of the **m_Values** array being exceeded in the **Add()** function, and in the constructor that accepts an array of samples.

351

As we said earlier, in theory you can create objects of **CSamples** classes that will handle any data type: **int**, **double**, or any class type that you've defined. In practice, this doesn't mean it will necessarily compile and work as you expect. It all depends on what the template definition does, and usually a template will only work for a particular range of types. For example, the **Max()** function implicitly assumes that the **>** operator is available for whatever type is being processed. If it isn't, your program will not compile. Clearly, you'll usually be in the position of defining a template that works for some types but not others, but there's no way you can restrict what type is applied to a template.

Template Member Functions

You may want to place the definition of a class template member function outside of the template definition. The syntax for this isn't particularly obvious, so let's look at how you do it. The function declaration appears in the class template definition in the normal way. For instance:

```
template <class T>
class CSamples
{
   // Rest of the template definition...
   T Max() const;          // Function to obtain maximum sample
   // Rest of the template definition...
}
```

This declares the **Max()** function as a member of the class template but doesn't define it. You now need to create a separate function template for the definition of the member function. You must use the template class name plus the parameters in angled brackets to identify the class template to which the function template belongs:

```
template<class T>
T CSamples<T>::Max() const
{
   T theMax = m_Values[0];            // Set first sample as maximum

   for(int i = 1; i < m_Free; i++)    // Check all the samples
      if(m_Values[i] > theMax)
         theMax = m_Values[i];        // Store any larger sample
   return theMax;
}
```

You saw the syntax for a function template back in Chapter 6. Since this function template is for a member of the class template with the parameter **T**, the function template definition here should have the same parameters as the class template definition. There's just one in this case — **T** — but in general there can be several; a case we'll come to in a few pages time. If the class template had two or more parameters, then so would each template defining a member function.

Note how you only put the parameter name, **T**, along with the class name before the scope resolution operator. This is necessary — the parameters are fundamental to the identification of the class to which a function, produced from the template, belongs. The type will be **CSamples<T>** with whatever type you assign to **T** when you create an instance of the class template. Your type is plugged into the class template to generate the class definition, and into the function template to generate the definition for the **Max()** function for the class. Each class that's produced from the class template needs to have its own definition for the function **Max()**.

Defining a constructor or a destructor outside of the class template definition is very similar. We could write the definition of the constructor accepting an array as:

```
template<class T>
CSamples<T>::CSamples(T values[], int count)
{
   m_Free = count < 100? count:100;     // Don't exceed the array

   for(int i = 0; i < m_Free; i++)
      m_Values[i] = values[i];          // Store count number of samples
}
```

The class to which the constructor belongs is specified in the template in the same way as for an ordinary member function. Note that the constructor name doesn't require the parameter specification – it's just **CSamples**, but it needs to be qualified by the class template type **CSamples<T>**. You only use the parameter with the class template name *preceding* the scope resolution operator.

Creating Objects from a Class Template

When we used a function defined by a function template, the compiler was able to generate the function from the types of the arguments used. The type parameter for the function template was implicitly defined by the specific use of a particular function. Class templates are a little different. To create an object based on a class template, you must always specify the type parameter following the class name in the declaration.

For example, to declare a **CSamples** object to handle samples of type **double**, you could write the declaration as:

```
CSamples<double> myData(10.0);
```

This defines an object of type **CSamples<double>** that can store samples of type **double**, and the object is created with one sample stored with the value 10.0.

TRY IT OUT - Class Templating

You could create an object from our template that stores **CBox** objects. This will work because the **CBox** class implements the **operator>()** function to overload the greater-than operator. We could exercise the class template with the **main()** function in the following listing:

```
// EX9_07.cpp
// Trying out a class template
#include <iostream>
using namespace std;

// Put the CBox class definition here

// CSamples class template definition
template <class T> class CSamples
{
   public:
      // Constructors
```

```
      CSamples(const T values[], int count);
      CSamples(const T& value);
      CSamples(){ m_Free = 0; }

      bool Add(const T& value);              // Insert a value
      T Max() const;                         // Calculate maximum

   private:
      T m_Values[100];                       // Array to store samples
      int m_Free;                            // Index of free location in m_Values
};

// Constructor template definition to accept an array of samples
template<class T> CSamples<T>::CSamples(const T values[], int count)
{
   m_Free = count < 100? count:100;          // Don't exceed the array
   for(int i = 0; i < m_Free; i++)
      m_Values[i] = values[i];               // Store count number of samples
}

// Constructor to accept a single sample
template<class T> CSamples<T>::CSamples(const T& value)
{
   m_Values[0] = value;                      // Store the sample
   m_Free = 1;                               // Next is free
}

// Function to add a sample
template<class T> bool CSamples<T>::Add(const T& value)
{
   bool OK = m_Free < 100;                   // Indicates there is a free place
   if(OK)
     m_Values[m_Free++] = value;             // OK true, so store the value
   return OK;
}

// Function to obtain maximum sample
template<class T> T CSamples<T>::Max() const
{
   T theMax = m_Free ? m_Values[0] : 0;      // Set first sample or 0 as maximum
   for(int i = 1; i < m_Free; i++)           // Check all the samples
     if(m_Values[i] > theMax)
        theMax = m_Values[i];                // Store any larger sample
    return theMax;
}

int main()
{
   CBox boxes[] = {                          // Create an array of boxes
                   CBox(8.0, 5.0, 2.0),      // Initialize the boxes...
                   CBox(5.0, 4.0, 6.0),
                   CBox(4.0, 3.0, 3.0)
                  };

   // Create the CSamples object to hold CBox objects
   CSamples<CBox> myBoxes(boxes, sizeof boxes / sizeof CBox);

   CBox maxBox = myBoxes.Max();              // Get the biggest box
```

```
    cout << endl                               // and output its volume
         << "The biggest box has a volume of "
         << maxBox.Volume()
         << endl;
    return 0;
}
```

You should replace the comment with the **CBox** class definition from **EX9_06.cpp**. With the exception of the default constructor, all the member functions of the template are defined by separate function templates, just to show you a complete example of how it's done.

In **main()** we create an array of three **CBox** objects and then use this array to initialize a **CSamples** object that can store **CBox** objects. The declaration of the **CSamples** object is basically the same as it would be for an ordinary class, but with the addition of the type parameter in angled brackets following the template class name.

The program will generate the following output:

Note that when you create an instance of a class template, it does not follow that instances of the function templates for function members will also be created. The compiler will only create instances of templates for member functions that you actually call in your program. In fact, your function templates can even contain coding errors, and as long as you don't call the member function that the template generates, the compiler will not complain. You can test this out with the example. Try introducing a few errors into the template for the **Add()** member. The program will still compile and run since it doesn't call **Add()**.

You could try modifying the example and perhaps seeing what happens when you instantiate classes by using the template with various other types.

> *You might be surprised at what happens if you add some output statements to the class constructors. The constructor for the **CBox** is being called 103 times! Look at what we are doing in **main()**. First we create an array of 3 **CBox** objects, so that's 3 calls. We then create a **CSamples** object to hold them, but a **CSamples** object contains an array of 100 variables of type **CBox**, so we call the default constructor another 100 times, once for each element in the array. Of course, the **maxBox** object will be created by the default copy constructor supplied by the compiler.*

Class Templates with Multiple Parameters

Using multiple type parameters in a class template is a straightforward extension of the example using a single parameter, which we have just seen. You can use each of the type parameters wherever you want in the template definition. For example, you could define a class template with two type parameters:

```
template<class T1, class T2>
class CExampleClass
{
       // Class data members
   private:
      T1 m_Value1;
      T2 m_Value2;

       // Rest of the template definition...
};
```

The types of the two class data members shown will be determined by the types you supply for the parameters when you instantiate an object.

The parameters in a class template aren't limited to types. You can also use parameters that require constants or constant expressions to be substituted in the class definition. In our **CSamples** template, we arbitrarily defined the **m_Values** array with 100 elements. We could, however, let the user of the template choose the size of the array when the object is instantiated, by defining the template as:

```
template <class T, int Size> class CSamples
{
    private:
      T m_Values[Size];                    // Array to store samples
      int m_Free;                          // Index of free location in m_Values

    public:
      // Constructor definition to accept an array of samples
      CSamples(const T values[], int count)
      {
         m_Free = count < Size? count:Size;   // Don't exceed the array

         for(int i = 0; i < m_Free; i++)
            m_Values[i] = values[i];          // Store count number of samples
      }

      // Constructor to accept a single sample
      CSamples(const T& value)
      {
         m_Values[0] = value;              // Store the sample
         m_Free = 1;                       // Next is free
      }

      // Default constructor
      CSamples()
      {
         m_Free = 0;                       // Nothing stored, so first is free
      }

      // Function to add a sample
      int Add(const T& value)
      {
         int OK = m_Free < Size;           // Indicates there is a free place
         if(OK)
         m_Values[m_Free++] = value;       // OK true, so store the value
         return OK;
      }
```

```
      // Function to obtain maximum sample
      T Max() const
      {
         T theMax = m_Free ? m_Values[0] : 0; // Set first sample or 0 as maximum
         for(int i = 1; i < m_Free; i++)       // Check all the samples
            if(m_Values[i] > theMax)
               theMax = m_Values[i];           // Store any larger sample
         return theMax;
      }
};
```

The value supplied for **Size** when you create an object will replace the appearance of the parameter throughout the template definition. Now we can declare the **CSamples** object from the previous example as:

```
CSamples<CBox, 3> MyBoxes(boxes, sizeof boxes / sizeof CBox);
```

Since we can supply *any* constant expression for the **Size** parameter, we could also have written this as:

```
CSamples<CBox, sizeof boxes / sizeof CBox>
MyBoxes(boxes, sizeof boxes / sizeof CBox);
```

The example is a poor use of a template though – the original version was much more usable. A consequence of making **Size** a template parameter is that instances of the template that store the same types of objects but have different size parameter values are totally different classes and cannot be mixed. For instance, an object of type **CSamples<double, 10>** cannot be used in an expression with an object of type **CSamples<double, 20>**.

You need to be careful with expressions that involve comparison operators when instantiating templates. A statement such as:

```
CSamples<aType, x > y? 10:20> MyType();       // Wrong!
```

will not compile correctly because the **>** in the expression will be interpreted as a right angled bracket. Instead, you should write this as:

```
CSamples<aType, (x > y? 10:20)> MyType();     // OK
```

The parentheses make sure that the expression for the second template argument doesn't get mixed up with the angled brackets.

Using Classes

We've touched on most of the basic aspects of defining a class, so maybe we should look at how a class might be used to solve a problem. We'll need to keep the problem simple in order to keep this book down to a reasonable number of pages, so we'll consider problems in which we can use an extended version of the **CBox** class.

The Idea of a Class Interface

The implementation of an extended **CBox** class should incorporate the notion of a **class interface**. What we're going to provide is a tool kit for anyone wanting to work with **CBox** objects, so we need to assemble a set of functions that represents the interface to the world of boxes. Since the interface will represent the only way to deal with **CBox** objects, it needs to be defined to adequately cover the likely things one would want to do with a **CBox** object, and be implemented, as far as possible, in a manner that protects against misuse or accidental errors.

The first question that we need to consider is the nature of the problem we intend to solve and, from that, derive the kind of functionality we need to provide in the class interface.

Defining the Problem

The principal function of a box is to contain objects of one kind or another so, in a word, our problem is *packaging*. We'll attempt to provide a class that eases packaging problems in general and then see how it might be used. We'll assume that we'll always be working on packing **CBox** objects into other **CBox** objects since, if you want to pack candy in a box, you could always represent each of the pieces of candy as an idealized **CBox** object. The basic operations that we might want to provide for our **CBox** class include:

- Calculate the volume of a **CBox**. This is a fundamental characteristic of a **CBox** object and we have an implementation of this already.

- Compare the volumes of two **CBox** objects to determine which is the larger. We probably should support a complete set of comparison operators for **CBox** objects. We already have a version of the **>** operator.

- Compare the volume of a **CBox** object with a specified value and vice versa. We also have an implementation of this for the **>** operator, but we will also need the other comparison operators.

- Add two **CBox** objects to produce a **CBox** object which will contain both the original objects. Thus, the result will be at least the sum of the volumes, but may be larger. We have a version of this already by overloading the **+** operator.

- Multiply a **CBox** object by an integer (and vice versa) to provide a **CBox** object which will contain a specified number of the original objects. This is effectively designing a carton.

- Determine how many **CBox** objects of a given size can be packed in another **CBox** object of a given size. This is effectively division, so we could overload the **/** operator.

- Determine the volume of space remaining in a **CBox** object after packing it with the maximum number of **CBox** objects of a given size.

We had better stop right there! There are undoubtedly other functions that would be very useful but, in the interest of saving trees, we'll consider the set complete, apart from ancillaries such as accessing dimensions, for example.

Implementing the CBox Class

We really need to consider the degree of error protection that we want to build into the **CBox** class. The basic class that we defined to illustrate various aspects of classes is a starting point, but we should also consider some points a little more deeply. The constructor is a little weak in that it doesn't ensure that we have valid dimensions for a **CBox**, so perhaps the first thing we should do is to ensure we always have valid objects. We could redefine the basic class as follows:

```
class CBox                              // Class definition at global scope
{
  public:
    // Constructor definition
    CBox(double lv = 1.0, double bv = 1.0, double hv = 1.0)
    {
       lv = lv <= 0? 1.0: lv;           // Ensure positive
       bv = bv <= 0? 1.0: bv;           // dimensions for
       hv = hv <= 0? 1.0: hv;           // the object

       m_Length = lv > bv? lv: bv;      // Ensure that
       m_Breadth = bv < lv? bv: lv;     // length >= breadth
       m_Height = hv;
    }

    // Function to calculate the volume of a box
    double Volume() const
    {
       return m_Length*m_Breadth*m_Height;
    }

    // Function providing the length of a box
    double GetLength() const { return m_Length; }

    // Function providing the breadth of a box
    double GetBreadth() const { return m_Breadth; }

    // Function providing the height of a box
    double GetHeight() const { return m_Height; }

  private:
     double m_Length;                   // Length of a box in inches
     double m_Breadth;                  // Breadth of a box in inches
     double m_Height;                   // Height of a box in inches
};
```

Our constructor is now secure, since any dimension that the user of the class tries to set to a negative number or zero will be set to 1 in the constructor. You might also consider displaying a message for a negative or zero dimension, since there's obviously an error when this occurs, and arbitrarily and silently setting a dimension to 1 might not be the best solution.

The default copy constructor is satisfactory for our class, since we have no dynamic memory allocation for data members, and the default assignment operator will also work as we would like. The default destructor also works perfectly well in this case so we don't need to define it. Perhaps now we should consider comparisons of objects of our class.

Comparing CBox Objects

We should include support for `>`, `>=`, `==`, `<` and `<=` to operate between two **CBox** objects, as well between a **CBox** object and a value of type **double**. We should implement these as ordinary global functions, since they don't need to be member functions. We can also write the functions to compare the volumes of two **CBox** objects in terms of the functions to compare the volume of a **CBox** object with a **double** value, so let's start with the latter. We can repeat the **operator>()** function that we had before:

```
// Function for testing if a constant is > a CBox object
int operator>(const double& value, const CBox& aBox)
{
   return value > aBox.Volume();
}
```

We can now write the **operator<()** function in a similar way:

```
// Function for testing if a constant is < CBox object
int operator<(const double& value, const CBox& aBox)
{
   return value < aBox.Volume();
}
```

The implementation of the same operators, but with the arguments reversed, can now be specified using these two functions:

```
// Function for testing if CBox object is > a constant
int operator>(const CBox& aBox, const double& value)
{ return value < aBox; }

// Function for testing if CBox object is < a constant
int operator<(const CBox& aBox, const double& value)
{ return value > aBox; }
```

We just use the appropriate overloaded operator function that we wrote before, with the arguments from the call to the new function switched.

`>=` and `<=` will be the same as the first two functions but with the `<=` operator replacing each use of `<`, and `>=` instead of `>`; there's little point in reproducing them at this stage. The **operator==()** functions are also very similar:

```
// Function for testing if constant is == the volume of a CBox object
int operator==(const double& value, const CBox& aBox)
{
   return value == aBox.Volume();
}

// Function for testing if CBox object is == a constant
int operator==(const CBox& aBox, const double& value)
{
   return value == aBox;
}
```

We now have a complete set of comparison operators for **CBox** objects. Keep in mind that these will also work with expressions as long as the expressions result in objects of the required type, so we will be able to combine them with the use of other overloaded operators.

Combining CBox Objects

Now we come to the question of overloading the operators **+**, *****, **/**, and **%**. We will take them in order. The add operation that we already have from **Ex9_06.cpp** has this prototype:

```
CBox operator+(const CBox& aBox);            // Function adding two CBox objects
```

Although our original implementation of this isn't an ideal solution, we'll use it to avoid overcomplicating our class. A better version would need to see if the operands had any faces with the same dimensions and join along those faces, but coding that could get a bit messy. Of course, if this were a practical application, a better add operation could be developed later and substituted for the existing version, and any programs written using the original would still run without change. The separation of the interface to a class from its implementation is crucial to good C++ programming.

You'll have noticed that we conveniently forgot the subtraction operator. This is a judicious oversight to avoid the complications inherent in implementing this. If you're really enthusiastic about it, and you think it's a sensible idea, you can give it a try — but you need to decide what to do when the result has a negative volume. If you allow the concept, you need to resolve which box dimension, or dimensions, are to be negative, and how such a box is to be handled in subsequent operations.

The multiply operation is very easy. It represents the process of creating a box to contain **n** boxes, where **n** is the multiplier. The simplest solution would be to take the **m_Length** and **m_Breadth** of the object to be packed and multiply the height by **n** to get the new **CBox** object. We'll make it a little cleverer by checking whether or not the multiplier is even and, if it is, stacking the boxes side by side by doubling the **m_Breadth** value and only multiplying the **m_Height** value by half of **n**. This is illustrated here:

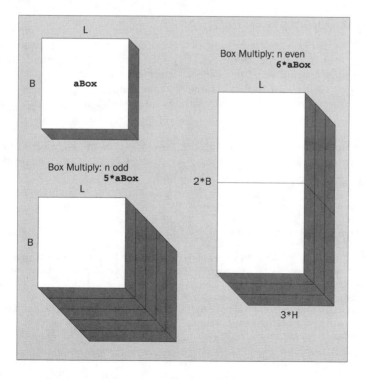

Of course, we don't need to check which is the larger of the length and breadth for the new object, since the constructor will sort it out automatically for us. We'll write the version of the operator function, **operator*()**, as a member function, with the left operand as a **CBox** object:

```
// CBox multiply operator this*n
CBox operator*(int n) const
{
   if(n % 2)
      return CBox(m_Length, m_Breadth, n*m_Height);        // n odd
   else
      return CBox(m_Length, 2.0*m_Breadth, (n/2)*m_Height);   // n even
}
```

Here, we use the **%** operator to determine whether **n** is even or odd. If **n** is odd, the value of **n % 2** is 1 and the **if** statement is **true**. If it's even, **n % 2** is 0 and the statement is **false**.

We can now use the function we've just written in the implementation of the version with the left operand as an integer. We can write this as a non-member function:

```
// CBox multiply operator n*aBox
CBox operator*(int n, const CBox& aBox)
{
   return aBox*n;
}
```

This version of the multiply operation simply reverses the order of the operands so as to use the previous version of the function directly. That completes the set of combinatorial operators for **CBox** objects that we defined. We can finally look at the two analytical operator functions, **operator/()** and **operator%()**.

Analyzing CBox Objects

As we've said, the division operation will determine how many **CBox** objects, given by the right operand can be contained in the **CBox** object specified by the left operand. To keep it relatively simple, we'll assume that all the **CBox** objects are packed the right way up, that is, with the height dimensions vertical. We'll also assume that they are all packed the same way round, so that their length dimensions are aligned. Without these assumptions, it can get rather complicated.

The problem will then amount to determining how many of the right-operand objects can be placed in a single layer, and then deciding how many layers we can get inside the left-operand **CBox**.

We'll code this as a member function as follows:

```
int operator/(const CBox& aBox)
{
   int tc1 = 0;        // Temporary for number in horizontal plane this way
   int tc2 = 0;        // Temporary for number in a plane that way

   tc1 = static_cast<int>((m_Length / aBox.m_Length))*
         static_cast<int>((m_Breadth / aBox.m_Breadth)); // to fit this way
   tc2 = static_cast<int>((m_Length / aBox.m_Breadth))*
         static_cast<int>((m_Breadth / aBox.m_Length));  // and that way
```

```
    //Return best fit
    return static_cast<int>((m_Height / aBox.m_Height)*(tc1 > tc2? tc1:tc2));
}
```

This function first determines how many of the right-operand **CBox** objects can fit in a layer with their lengths aligned with the length dimension of the left-operand **CBox**. This is stored in **tc1**. We then calculate how many can fit in a layer with the lengths of the right-operand **CBox**es lying in the breadth direction of the left-operand **CBox**. We then multiply the larger of **tc1** and **tc2** by the number of layers we can pack in, and return that value. This process is illustrated here:

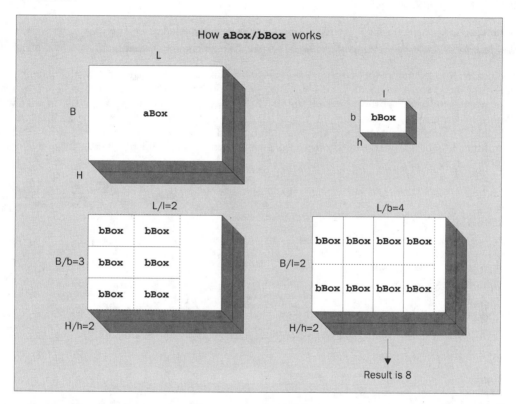

We look at two possibilities: fitting **bBox** into **aBox** with the length aligned with that of **aBox**, and then with the length of **bBox** aligned with the breadth of **aBox**. You can see from the illustration that the best packing results from rotating **bBox** so that the breadth divides into the length of **aBox**.

The other analytical operator function, **operator%()**, for obtaining the free volume in a packed **aBox** is easier, since we can use the operator we've just written. We can write it as an ordinary global function, since we don't need access to the **private** members of the class.

```
// Operator to return the free volume in a packed box
double operator%(const CBox& aBox, const CBox& bBox)
{
   return aBox.Volume() - ((aBox / bBox) * bBox.Volume());
}
```

This computation falls out very easily using existing class functions. The result is the volume of the big box, **aBox**, minus the volume of the **bBox** boxes in it. The number of **bBox** objects packed is given by the expression **aBox / bBox**, which uses the previous overloaded operator. We multiply this by the volume of **bBox** objects to get the volume to be subtracted from the volume of the large box, **aBox**.

That completes our class interface. Clearly, there are many more functions that might be required for a production problem solver but, as an interesting working model demonstrating how we can produce a class for solving a particular kind of problem, it will suffice. Now we should go ahead and try it out on a real problem.

TRY IT OUT - A Multifile Project Using the CBox Class

Before we can actually start writing the code to *use* our **CBox** class and its overloaded operators, the first thing we need to do is to assemble the definition for the class into a coherent whole. We're going to take a rather different approach from what you've seen previously, in that we're going to write multiple files for our project. We're also going to start using the facilities that Visual C++ provides for creating and maintaining code for our classes. This will mean that you do rather less of the work, but it will also mean that the code will be slightly different in places.

Start by creating a new project for a console application called **Ex9_08**. You'll see the left hand window shown here:

This appears on the ClassView tab, which shows a view of all the classes in a project. The other tab is the FileView tab, which presents the files that go to make up the project. Although there are no classes defined — or anything else for that matter — Visual C++ has already made provision for including some. We can use Visual C++ to create a skeleton for our **CBox** class, and the files that relate to it too. Right click anywhere on Ex9_08 classes in ClassView, and select **N**ew Class... from the pop-up menu that appears. You will then be able to enter the name of the class that we want to create, **CBox**, in the New Class dialog as shown here.

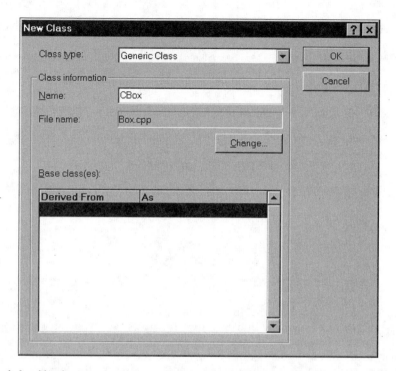

The name of the file that's indicated on the dialog, **Box.cpp**, will be used to contain the **class implementation**, which consists of the definitions for the function members of the class. This is the executable code for the class. You can change the name of this file by selecting the Change... button if you want, but **Box.cpp** looks like a good name for the file in this case. The class definition will be stored in a file called **Box.h**. This is the standard way of structuring a program. Code which consists of class definitions is stored in files with the extension **.h**, and code which defines functions is stored in files with the extension **.cpp**. Usually, each class definition goes in its own **.h** file, and each class implementation goes in its own **.cpp** file.

When you click on the OK button in the dialog several things will happen:

1 A file **Box.h** will be created containing a skeleton definition for the class **CBox**

2 A file **Box.cpp** will be created containing a skeleton implementation for the class

3 The Wizard bar will be activated

The Wizard bar should already be displayed, but if it isn't, right click in the menu area of the window and click on Wizard Bar in the pop-up. The Wizard Bar is used like this:

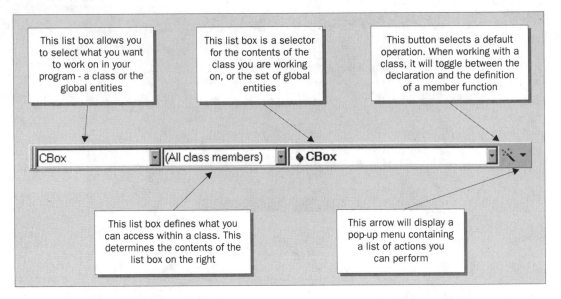

As you can see, the Wizard Bar provides a range of tools for accessing and modifying your code. You can add classes, you can add members to classes, and you can switch between the definition and the implementation of member functions. You can also get any global entity in your program displayed in the editor window. Of course, you should only use the Wizard Bar when it's convenient to do so — you always have the option of displaying a file and modifying your source code directly in the editor window.

Let's start developing our **CBox** class based on what Visual C++ has provided automatically for us.

Defining the CBox Class

If you click on the + to the left of `Ex9_08 classes` in the ClassView, the tree will be expanded and you will see that **CBox** is now defined for the project. All the classes in a project are displayed in this tree. We can view the source code supplied for the definition of the class by double clicking the class name in the tree, or by clicking on the button in the Wizard Bar. The code is as follows:

```
// Box.h: interface for the CBox class.
//
//////////////////////////////////////////////////////////////////////

#if !defined(AFX_BOX_H__EDB99605_15DB_11D2_B72E_CAA50F4F7106__INCLUDED_)
#define AFX_BOX_H__EDB99605_15DB_11D2_B72E_CAA50F4F7106__INCLUDED_

#if _MSC_VER > 1000
#pragma once
#endif // _MSC_VER > 1000

class CBox
{
public:
```

```
    CBox();
    virtual ~CBox();

    };

#endif // !defined(AFX_BOX_H__EDB99605_15DB_11D2_B72E_CAA50F4F7106__INCLUDED_)
```

After the comment lines, there are some preprocessor directives. The first is a test whether the symbol beginning **AFX_BOX_H__**... has not been defined — **#if !defined** is a directive that implements an 'if not defined' test, and works rather like an ordinary **if** statement. If the symbol in the directive doesn't already exist, all the text lines down to the **#endif** directive will be included, including the **#define** directive. If the symbol has been defined, the lines down to the **#endif** directive will be skipped.

The effect of this arrangement is to prevent the code in the file from being included into a file more than once. The first time the code is included, the symbol beginning **AFX_BOX_H**__... gets defined, thus preventing any further inclusions of the same code. This is pretty much standard procedure in **.h** files, and you should write all your **.h** files with this sort of protection built in to avoid the problems that duplicate definitions cause. Visual C++ will always include it automatically in the files for class definitions that it creates. Don't worry that numbers and letters in the symbol are different on your machine; this is done to make absolutely sure the symbol is unique.

The second pair of **#if** — **#endif** directives performs a similar function, but one which is only available on more recent compilers — that's what **_MSC_VER** denotes. If the compiler is sufficiently recent (and Visual C++ 6 most certainly is!), the **#pragma once** directive is executed, which means that this file doesn't even have to be *opened* again. You can see that this is faster than opening the file and testing the symbol every time the compiler comes across a **#include** for it.

Within the code we have an outline class definition including the default class constructor and the destructor. The destructor has been declared as **virtual**, but we'll defer discussion of what that means until the next chapter. You could delete the keyword if you want, as it isn't needed here, but it will do no harm if you leave it in.

Note that the button on the Wizard Bar has changed. Clicking on the button while the class definition is displayed will switch to the **.cpp** file. In fact, it does better than that, although the full benefit isn't clear while your files are as short as they are at this stage. The button switches you to the position in the **.cpp** file which contains the definition of the function at the current cursor position, with the function header highlighted. Clicking on it again will toggle back to the class definition.

Adding Data Members

First, we'll add the private data members **m_Length**, **m_Breadth**, and **m_Height**. Right click on ⬚CBox (in class view) and select Add Member Variable... from the pop-up menu. You can then specify the first data member that we want to add to the class in the dialog.

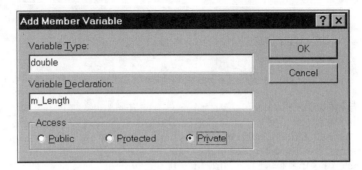

The variable type appears in the upper edit box, and the access specifier is selected from the three radio buttons at the bottom of the dialog. When you click on the OK button, the variable will be added to the class definition. Repeat the process for the other two class data members. You can then add comments to these directly in the editor window if you wish:

```
// Box.h: interface for the CBox class.
//
//////////////////////////////////////////////////////////////////////

#if !defined(AFX_BOX_H__EDB99605_15DB_11D2_B72E_CAA50F4F7106__INCLUDED_)
#define AFX_BOX_H__EDB99605_15DB_11D2_B72E_CAA50F4F7106__INCLUDED_

#if _MSC_VER > 1000
#pragma once
#endif // _MSC_VER > 1000

class CBox
{
public:
    CBox();
    virtual ~CBox();

private:
    double m_Breadth;                   // Breadth of a box in inches
    double m_Height;                    // Height of a box in inches
    double m_Length;                    // Length of a box in inches
};

#endif // !defined(AFX_BOX_H__EDB99605_15DB_11D2_B72E_CAA50F4F7106__INCLUDED_)
```

Of course, you're quite free to enter the declarations for these members manually, directly into the code, if you want.

Defining the Constructor

We want to change the declaration of the constructor in the class definition, so modify it to:

```
CBox(double lv = 1.0, double bv = 1.0, double hv = 1.0);
```

Now we're ready to implement it. Open the file **Box.cpp** if it isn't open already and modify the constructor definition to:

```
CBox::CBox(double lv, double bv, double hv)
{
   lv = lv <= 0.0? 1.0:lv;               // Ensure positive
   bv = bv <= 0.0? 1.0:bv;               // dimensions for
   hv = hv <= 0.0? 1.0:hv;               // the object

   m_Length = lv > bv? lv:bv;            // Ensure that
   m_Breadth = bv < lv? bv:lv;           // length >= breadth
   m_Height = hv;
}
```

Remember that the initializers for the parameters to a member function should only appear in the member declaration in the class definition, not in the definition of the function. If you put them in the function definition, your code will not compile. We've seen this code already, so we won't discuss it again. It would be a good idea to save the file at this point by clicking on the Save toolbar button. Get into the habit of saving the file you're editing before you switch to something else. If we need to edit the constructor again, we can get to it easily by either double clicking its entry in the ClassView window or by selecting it from the right hand drop down menu in the Wizard Bar.

Another useful trick to learn at this stage is to get from a function's definition in a **.cpp** file to its declaration in a **.h** file which we can get to in two ways.

> With the class definition displayed in the editor window, position the cursor on the line declaring the function and click on the magic wand button ⬛ in the Wizard Bar. You should find yourself looking at the function's definition. This works in the opposite direction as well and applies to any function of any class, provided the function header reads the same in both files.

> In the ClassView window, right click on the function name you want to access. Clicking on Go to Definition will place the cursor next to the function header in the relevant `.cpp` file and clicking on Go to Declaration will take position the cursor at the top of the function's header in the relevant **.h** file.

Adding Function Members

We need to add all the functions you saw earlier to the **CBox** class. Previously, we defined several function members within the class definition, so that these functions were automatically inline. However, if we just add code to the body of each function definition in the **.cpp** file, the functions won't be inline, and for those that are very short, such as **Volume()**, **GetLength()**, **GetBreadth()**, and **GetHeight()**, it really would be much better if they were.

You might think it was simply a question of adding the keyword **inline** to the function definitions, but the problem here is that inline functions end up not being 'real' functions. Because the code from the body of each function has to be inserted directly at the position it is called, the definitions of the functions need to be available when the file containing calls to the functions is compiled. If they're not, you'll get linker errors and your program will not run. If you want member functions to be inline, you must include the function definitions in the **.h** file for the class. They can be defined either within the class definition, or immediately following it in the **.h** file. You should put any global inline functions you need into a **.h** file, and **#include** that file into any **.cpp** file that uses them. We'll put the definitions for the functions we want to make inline in the **CBox** class definition, so modify it to:

```
class CBox
{
public:
    double GetHeight() const { return m_Height; }    // Get box height
    double GetBreadth() const { return m_Breadth; }  // Get box breadth
    double GetLength() const { return m_Length; }    // Get box length
    double Volume() const                            // Calculate volume
    { return m_Length*m_Breadth*m_Height; }

    CBox(double lv = 1.0, double bv = 1.0, double hv = 1.0);
    virtual ~CBox();

private:
    double m_Height;        // Height of a box in inches
    double m_Breadth;       // Breadth of a box in inches
    double m_Length;        // Length of a box in inches
};
```

You could enter the other member functions we need directly in the editor window, but you can also use the Wizard Bar to do it, and the practice will be useful. Click on the down arrow in the Wizard Bar and select Add Member Function... from the pop-up. You can then enter the details of the first function we want to add in the dialog that appears:

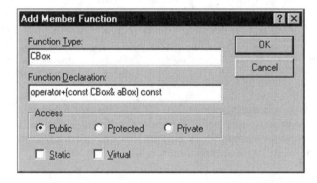

Here we've defined the **operator+()** function as **public** with a return type of **CBox**. Note the options to declare a function as **static** or **virtual**. As you know, a static member function exists independently of any objects of a class. We'll get to virtual functions in Chapter 10. When you click on OK, the declaration for the function will be added to the class definition in the **Box.h** file, and a skeleton definition for the function will be added to the **Box.cpp** file.

You need to repeat this process for each of the other member functions of **CBox**, so the class definition will look like this:

```
class CBox
{
public:
    int operator/(const CBox& aBox) const;          // Divide one box into another
    CBox operator*(int n) const;                     // Multiply a box by an integer
    CBox operator+(const CBox& aBox) const;          // Add two boxes
    double GetHeight() const { return m_Height; }    // Get box height
    double GetBreadth() const { return m_Breadth; }  // Get box breadth
    double GetLength() const { return m_Length; }    // Get box length
    double Volume() const                            // Calculate volume
    { return m_Length*m_Breadth*m_Height; }
```

```
   CBox(double lv = 1.0, double bv = 1.0, double hv = 1.0);
   virtual ~CBox();

private:
   double m_Height;
   double m_Breadth;
   double m_Length;
};
```

Of course, the comments were added manually here. The skeleton implementations of these three functions have been placed in **Box.cpp**. Switch to the **.cpp** file for the class by clicking on the button in the Wizard Bar, and define the functions with the implementations we've already discussed. The **.cpp** file should then contain the following code (where the shaded areas indicate the code that you need to add yourself):

```
// Box.cpp: implementation of the CBox class.
//
//////////////////////////////////////////////////////////////////////

#include "Box.h"

//////////////////////////////////////////////////////////////////////
// Construction/Destruction
//////////////////////////////////////////////////////////////////////

CBox::CBox(double lv, double bv, double hv)
{
   lv = lv <= 0.0? 1.0:lv;                    // Ensure positive
   bv = bv <= 0.0? 1.0:bv;                    // dimensions for
   hv = hv <= 0.0? 1.0:hv;                    // the object

   m_Length = lv > bv? lv:bv;                 // Ensure that
   m_Breadth = bv < lv? bv:lv;                // length >= breadth
   m_Height = hv;
}

CBox::~CBox()
{

}

CBox CBox::operator +(const CBox& aBox) const
{
   // New object has larger length and breadth of the two,
   // and sum of the two heights
   return CBox(m_Length > aBox.m_Length? m_Length:aBox.m_Length,
               m_Breadth > aBox.m_Breadth? m_Breadth:aBox.m_Breadth,
               m_Height + aBox.m_Height);
}

CBox CBox::operator *(int n) const
{
   if(n%2)
      return CBox(m_Length, m_Breadth, n*m_Height);          // n odd
   else
      return CBox(m_Length, 2.0*m_Breadth, (n/2)*m_Height);  // n even
}
```

```
int CBox::operator /(const CBox& aBox) const
{
    // Temporary for number in horizontal plane this way
    int tc1 = 0;
    // Temporary for number in a plane that way
    int tc2 = 0;

    tc1 = static_cast<int>((m_Length / aBox.m_Length))*
        static_cast<int>((m_Breadth / aBox.m_Breadth));     // to fit
                                                            // this way

    tc2 = static_cast<int>((m_Length / aBox.m_Breadth))*
        static_cast<int>((m_Breadth / aBox.m_Length));      // and that way

    //Return best fit
    return static_cast<int>((m_Height / aBox.m_Height))*(tc1 > tc2? tc1:tc2);
}
```

The very short functions, particularly those that just return the value of a data member, have their definitions within the class definition so that they are **inline**. If you take a look at ClassView by clicking on the tab, and then click on the + beside the **CBox** class name, you'll see that all the members of the class are shown.

This completes the **CBox** class, but we still need to define the global functions that implement operators to compare the volume of a **CBox** object with a numerical value.

Adding Global Functions

We need to create a **.cpp** file containing the definitions for the global functions supporting operations on **CBox** objects. Click on the File/New... menu item, select the file type and enter the file name on the Files tab, as shown below.

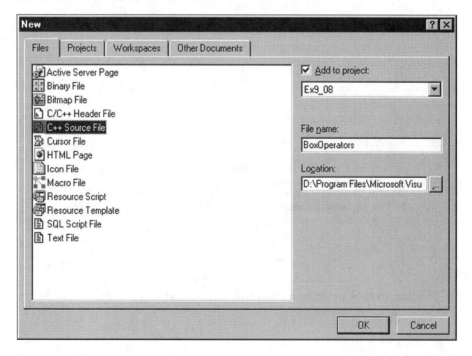

When you click on OK the new empty file will be opened in the editor window, so you can enter the following code:

```
// BoxOperators.cpp
// CBox object operations that don't need to access private members
#include "Box.h"

// Function for testing if a constant is > a CBox object
bool operator>(const double& value, const CBox& aBox)
{ return value > aBox.Volume(); }

// Function for testing if a constant is < CBox object
bool operator<(const double& value, const CBox& aBox)
{ return value < aBox.Volume(); }

// Function for testing if CBox object is > a constant
bool operator>(const CBox& aBox, const double& value)
{ return value < aBox; }

// Function for testing if CBox object is < a constant
bool operator<( const CBox& aBox, const double& value)
{ return value > aBox; }

// Function for testing if a constant is >= a CBox object
bool operator>=(const double& value, const CBox& aBox)
{ return value >= aBox.Volume(); }

// Function for testing if a constant is <= CBox object
bool operator<=(const double& value, const CBox& aBox)
{ return value <= aBox.Volume(); }

// Function for testing if CBox object is >= a constant
bool operator>=( const CBox& aBox, const double& value)
{ return value <= aBox; }

// Function for testing if CBox object is <= a constant
bool operator<=( const CBox& aBox, const double& value)
{ return value >= aBox; }

// Function for testing if a constant is == CBox object
bool operator==(const double& value, const CBox& aBox)
{ return value == aBox.Volume(); }

// Function for testing if CBox object is == a constant
bool operator==(const CBox& aBox, const double& value)
{ return value == aBox; }

// CBox multiply operator n*aBox
CBox operator*(int n, const CBox& aBox)
{ return aBox * n; }

// Operator to return the free volume in a packed CBox
double operator%( const CBox& aBox, const CBox& bBox)
{ return aBox.Volume() - (aBox / bBox) * bBox.Volume(); }
```

We have a `#include` directive for `Box.h` because the functions refer to the `CBox` class. When you have completed this, the Wizard Bar will show the global functions in the right-hand drop-down list box, and you can move between function definitions by selecting from this list. They will also appear under the Globals folder in ClassView.

You have seen all these function definitions earlier in the chapter, so we won't discuss their implementations again. When we want to use them in another `.cpp` file, we'll need to be sure that we declare all the functions so the compiler will recognize them. We can achieve this by putting a set of declarations in a header file. Select the File/New..: menu item again, but this time choose the file type as C/C++ Header File, and enter the name as `BoxOperators`. After clicking OK, an empty header file will be added to the project, and you can add the following code in the editor window:

```
// BoxOperators.h - Declarations for global box operators

bool operator>(const double& value, const CBox& aBox);
bool operator<(const double& value, const CBox& aBox);
bool operator>(const CBox& aBox, const double& value);
bool operator<(const CBox& aBox, const double& value);
bool operator>=(const double& value, const CBox& aBox);
bool operator<=(const double& value, const CBox& aBox);
bool operator>=(const CBox& aBox, const double& value);
bool operator<=(const CBox& aBox, const double& value);
bool operator==(const double& value, const CBox& aBox);
bool operator==(const CBox& aBox, const double& value);
CBox operator*(int n, const CBox aBox);
double operator%(const CBox& aBox, const CBox& bBox);
```

Header files need some preprocessor directives to prevent them from being accidentally included into a source file more than once. You can enter it yourself, but there is a macro in Visual C++ that will do it for you. Select the Tools/Macro... menu option and select the OneTimeInclude macros from the list.

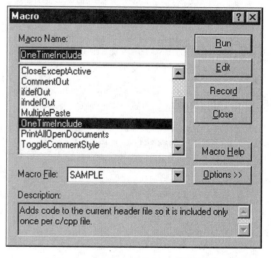

When you click on Run, the macros will insert the preprocessor directives that you need in the current editor window.

We're now ready to start applying these functions, along with the `CBox` class, to a specific problem in the world of boxes.

Using Our CBox Class

Let's suppose that we need to package candies. They are on the big side, real jaw breakers, occupying an envelope 1.5 inches long by 1 inch wide by 1 inch high. We have access to a standard candy box that is 4.5 inches by 7 inches by 2 inches, and we want to know how many candies fit in the box so that we can set the price. We also have a standard carton that is 2 feet 6 inches long, by 18 inches wide and 18 inches deep, and we want to know how many boxes of candy it can hold and how much space we're wasting.

In case the standard candy box isn't a good solution, we would also like to know what custom candy box would be suitable. We know that we can get a good price on boxes with a length from 3 inches to 7 inches, a breadth from 3 inches to 5 inches and a height from 1 inch to 2.5 inches, where each dimension can vary in steps of half an inch. We also know that we need to have at least 30 candies in a box, because this is the minimum quantity consumed by our largest customers at a sitting. Also, the candy box should not have empty space, because the complaints from customers who think they are being cheated goes up. Further, ideally we want to pack the standard carton completely so the candies don't rattle around. We don't want to be too stringent about this, so let's say we have no wasted space if the free space in the packed carton is less than the volume of a single candy box.

With our **CBox** class, the problem becomes almost trivial; the solution is represented by the following **main()** function. Add a new C++ source file, Ex9_08 to the project, then type in the code shown here:

```cpp
// EX9_08.CPP
// A sample packaging problem
#include <iostream>
#include "Box.h"
#include "BoxOperators.h"
using namespace std;

int main()
{
   CBox candy(1.5, 1.0, 1.0);          // Candy definition
   CBox candyBox(7.0, 4.5, 2.0);       // Candy box definition
   CBox carton(30.0, 18.0, 18.0);      // Carton definition

   // Calculate candies per candy box
   int numCandies = candyBox / candy;

   // Calculate candy boxes per carton
   int numCboxes = carton / candyBox;

   // Calculate wasted carton space
   double space = carton % candyBox;

   cout << endl
        << "There are " << numCandies
        << " candies per candy box"
        << endl
        << "For the standard boxes there are " << numCboxes
        << " candy boxes per carton " << endl << "with "
        << space << " cubic inches wasted.";

   cout << endl << endl << "CUSTOM CANDY BOX ANALYSIS (No Waste)";
```

```
      // Try the whole range of custom candy boxes
   for(double length = 3.0; length <= 7.5; length += 0.5)
     for(double breadth = 3.0; breadth <= 5.0; breadth += 0.5)
        for(double height = 1.0; height <= 2.5; height += 0.5)
        {
           // Create new box each cycle
           CBox tryBox(length, breadth, height);

           if(carton%tryBox < tryBox.Volume() &&
                          tryBox % candy == 0.0 && tryBox / candy >= 30)
             cout << endl << endl
                 << "Trial Box L = " << tryBox.GetLength()
                 << " B = " << tryBox.GetBreadth()
                 << " H = " << tryBox.GetHeight()
                 << endl
                 << "Trial Box contains " << tryBox / candy << " candies"
                 << " and a carton contains " << carton / tryBox
                 << " candy boxes.";
        }
   cout << endl;
   return 0;
}
```

We should first look at how our program is structured. We've divided it into a number of files, which is common when writing in C++. You should be able to see them if you look at the FileView:

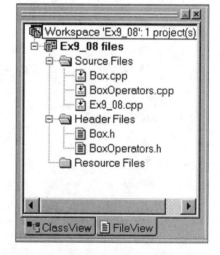

The file **Ex9_08.cpp** contains our function **main()** and a **#include** directive for the file **BoxOperators.h**, which contains the prototypes for the functions in **BoxOperators.cpp** (which aren't class members). It also has a **#include** directive for the definition of the class **CBox** in **Box.h**. So, a C++ console program is usually divided into a number of files that each fall into one of three basic categories:

1 **.h** files containing library **#include** commands, global constants and variables, class definitions and function prototypes — in other words, everything except executable code. They also contain inline function definitions. Where a program has several class definitions, they are often placed in separate **.h** files.

2 `.cpp` files containing the executable code for the program, plus **#include** commands for all the definitions required by the executable code.

3 Another `.cpp` file containing the function **main()**.

The code in our function **main()** really doesn't need a lot of explanation — it's almost a direct expression of the definition of the problem in words, because the operators in the class interface perform problem-oriented actions on **CBox** objects.

The solution to the question of the use of standard boxes is in the declaration statements, which also compute the answers we require as initializing values. We then output these values with some explanatory comments.

The second part of the problem is solved using the three nested **for** loops iterating over the possible ranges of **m_Length**, **m_Breadth** and **m_Height** so that we evaluate all possible combinations. We could output them all as well, but since this would involve 200 combinations, of which we might only be interested in a few, we have an **if** which defines the options that we're actually interested in. The **if** expression is only **true** if there's no space wasted in the carton *and* the current trial candy box has no wasted space *and* it contains at least 30 candies.

Here's the output from this program:

```
Ex9_08                                                    _ □ ✕

There are 42 candies per candy box
For the standard boxes there are 144 candy boxes per carton
with 648 cubic inches wasted.

CUSTOM CANDY BOX ANALYSIS (No Waste)

Trial Box L = 5 B = 4.5 H = 2
Trial Box contains 30 candies and a carton contains 216 candy boxes.

Trial Box L = 5 B = 4.5 H = 2
Trial Box contains 30 candies and a carton contains 216 candy boxes.

Trial Box L = 6 B = 4.5 H = 2
Trial Box contains 36 candies and a carton contains 180 candy boxes.

Trial Box L = 6 B = 5 H = 2
Trial Box contains 40 candies and a carton contains 162 candy boxes.

Trial Box L = 7.5 B = 3 H = 2
Trial Box contains 30 candies and a carton contains 216 candy boxes.
Press any key to continue_
```

We have a duplicate solution due to the fact that, in the nested loop, we evaluate boxes that have a length of 5 and a breadth of 4.5, as well as boxes that have a length of 4.5 and a breadth of 5. Because our class constructor ensures that the length is not less than the breadth, these two are identical. We could include some additional logic to avoid presenting duplicates, but it hardly seems worth the effort. You could treat it as a small exercise if you like.

377

Organizing your Program Code

In this last example, we distributed the code among several files for the first time. Not only is this common practice with C++ applications generally, but with Windows programming it is essential. The sheer volume of code involved in even the simplest program necessitates dividing it into workable chunks.

As we discussed in the previous section, there are basically two kinds of source code file in a C++ program, **.h** files and **.cpp** files. This is illustrated in this diagram:

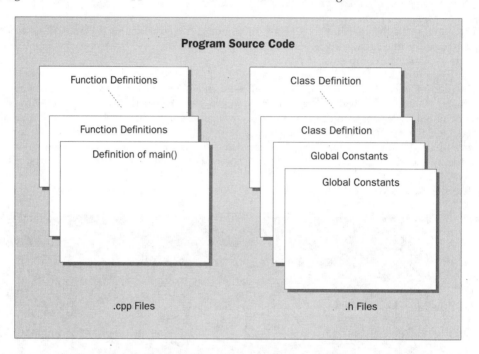

First of all, there's the executable code which corresponds to the definitions of the functions that make up the program. Second, there are definitions of various kinds that are necessary for the executable code to compile correctly. These are global constants and variables, data types which include classes, structures, and unions, and function prototypes. The executable source code is stored in files with the extension **.cpp**, and the definitions are stored in files with the extension **.h**.

From time to time, you might want to use code from existing files in a new project. In this case you only have to add the **.cpp** files to the project, which you can do by using the Project | Add To Project menu option, or by right-clicking in the editor window displaying a **.cpp** file and selecting from the pop-up menu to add the file to your project. You don't need to add **.h** files to your project, although you can if you want them to be shown in FileView immediately. The code from **.h** files will be added at the beginning of the **.cpp** files that require them as a result of the **#include** directives that you specify. You need **#include** directives for header files containing standard library functions and other standard definitions, as well as for your own header files. Visual C++ automatically keeps track of all these files, and enables you to view them in FileView. As you saw in the last example, you can also view the class definitions and global constants and variables in ClassView.

In a Windows program, there are other kinds of definitions for the specification of such things as menus and toolbar buttons. These are stored in files with extensions like **.rc** and **.ico**. Just like **.h** files, these do not need to be explicitly added to a project as they are tracked automatically by Visual C++.

Naming Program Files

As we've already said, for classes of any complexity, it's usual to store the class definition in a **.h** file with a filename based on the class name, and to store the implementation of the function members of the class that are defined outside the class definition in a **.cpp** file with the same name. On this basis, the definition of our **CBox** class appeared in a file with the name **Box.h**. Similarly, the class implementation was stored in the file **Box.cpp**. We didn't follow this convention in the earlier examples in the chapter because the examples were very short, and it was easier to reference the examples with names derived from the chapter number and the sequence number of the example within the chapter.

Segmenting a C++ program into **.h** and **.cpp** files is a very convenient approach, as it makes it easy for you to find the definition or implementation of any class, particularly if you're working in a development environment that doesn't have all the tools that Visual C++ provides. As long as you know the class name, you can go directly to the file you want. This isn't a rigid rule, however. It's sometimes useful to group the definitions of a set of closely-related classes together in a single file and assemble their implementations similarly. However you choose to structure your files, the ClassView will still display all the individual classes, as well as all the members of each class, as you can see here:

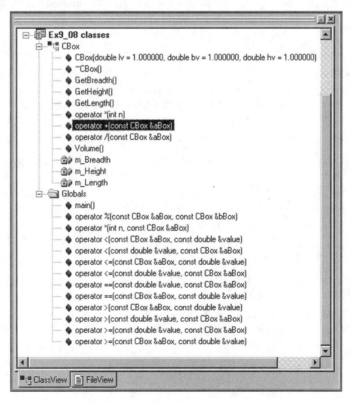

Here, you can see the details of the classes and globals for the last example. As I've mentioned before, double-clicking on any of the entries in the tree will take you directly to the relevant source code.

Summary

In this chapter, we've laid the foundations for object-oriented programming and the basis for understanding how the Microsoft Foundation Classes (MFC) that are provided as part of Visual C++ work, since MFC is based on a set of classes specially designed to make programming Windows easy. In the same way as we defined a **CBox** class interface for working with **CBox** objects, MFC implements a set of classes providing an easy-to-use set of tools for programming Windows. You'll also be applying classes to the application-specific parts of your Windows programs. For example, classes become extremely useful for managing application data that subsequently needs to be displayed in response to a **WM_PAINT** message. The next chapter will complete the knowledge of classes that you will need to understand how to apply classes to your own applications, and how to use MFC.

The key points to keep in mind from this chapter are:

▶ Objects are destroyed using functions called **destructors**. It is essential to define a destructor to destroy objects that contain members that are allocated by **new**, as the default constructor will not do this.

▶ The compiler will supply a default copy constructor for your class if you do not define one. The default copy constructor will not deal correctly with objects of classes that have data members allocated on the free store.

▶ When you define your own copy constructor, you must use a reference parameter.

▶ If you do not define an assignment operator for your class, the compiler will supply a default version. As with the copy constructor, the default assignment operator will not work correctly with classes that have data members allocated on the free store.

▶ It is essential that you provide a destructor, a copy constructor and an assignment operator for classes that have members allocated by **new**.

▶ A union is a mechanism that allows two or more variables to occupy the same location in memory.

▶ Most basic operators can be overloaded to provide actions specific to objects of a class. You should only implement operator functions for your classes that are consistent with the normal interpretation of the basic operators.

▶ A class template is a pattern that you can use to create classes with the same structure, but which support different data types.

▶ You can define a class template that has multiple parameters, including parameters that can assume constant values rather than types.

▶ You should put definitions for your program in **.h** files, and executable code — function definitions — in **.cpp** files. You can then incorporate **.h** files into your **.cpp** files by using **#include** directives.

▶ By using the Visual C++ IDE and the Wizard Bar you can automate a lot of the work in accessing and modifying your program code.

Exercises

Ex9-1: Create a class to represent an estimated integer, such as 'about 40'. These are integers whose value may be regarded as exact or estimated, so the class needs to have as data members a value and an 'estimation' flag. The state of the estimation flag affects arithmetic operations, so that '2 * about 40' is 'about 80'. The state of variables should be switchable between 'estimated' and 'exact'.

Provide one or more constructors for such a class. Overload the + operator so that these integers can be used in arithmetic expressions. Do you want the + operator to be a global or a member function? Do you need an assignment operator? Provide a **Print()** member function so that they can be printed out, using a leading 'E' to denote that the 'estimation' flag is set. Write a program to test the operation of your class, checking especially that the operation of the estimation flag is correct.

Ex9-2: Implement a very simple string class, which holds a **char*** and an integer length as **private** data members. Provide a constructor which takes a **const char***, and implement the copy constructor, assignment and destructor functions. Verify that your class works. You will find it easiest to use the string functions from the **cstring** header file.

Ex9-3: What other constructors might you want to supply for your string class? Make a list, and code them up.

Ex9-4: (Advanced) Does your class correctly deal with cases such as this?

```
string s1;
...
s1 = s1;
```

If not, how should it be modified?

Ex9-5: (Advanced) Overload the + and += operators of your class for concatenation.

Ex9-6: Modify the stack example from the last chapter so that the size of the stack is specified in the constructor and dynamically allocated. What else will you need to add? Test the operation of your new class.

Class Inheritance

In this chapter, we're going to look into a topic that lies at the heart of object-oriented programming and that will enable you to use the facilities of MFC and AppWizard to program Windows applications: **inheritance**. Simply put, inheritance is the means by which you can define a new class in terms of one you already have. You will use this when programming for Windows by redefining the classes provided by MFC to suit your own particular needs, so it's important that you understand how inheritance works.

In this chapter you will learn about:

- How inheritance fits into the idea of object-oriented programming
- Defining a new class in terms of an existing one
- The use of the keyword **protected** to define a new access specification for class members
- How a class can be a friend to another class
- Virtual functions and how you can use them
- Pure virtual functions
- Abstract classes
- Virtual destructors and when to use them
- Multiple inheritance

Basic Ideas of OOP

As we have seen, a class is a data type that you define to suit your own application requirements. Classes in object-oriented programming also define the objects to which your program relates. You program the solution to a problem in terms of the objects that are specific to the problem, using operations that work directly with those objects. You can define a class to represent something abstract, such as a complex number, which is a mathematical concept, or a truck, which is decidedly physical (especially if you run into one on the highway). So, as well as being a data type, a class can also be a definition of a real-world object, at least to the degree necessary to solve a given problem.

You can think of a class as defining the characteristics of a particular group of things that are specified by a common set of parameters and share a common set of operations that may be performed on them. The operations that are possible are defined by the class interface contained in the **public** section of the class definition. The **CBox** class that we used in the last chapter is a good example — it defined a box in the most elementary terms.

Of course, in the real world there are many different kinds of box: there are cartons, coffins, candy boxes and cereal boxes, and you will certainly be able to come up with many others. You can differentiate boxes by the kinds of things they hold, the materials they are made of, and in a multitude of other ways, but even though there are many different kinds of box, they share some common characteristics — the essence of boxiness perhaps — and, therefore, you can still visualize them as actually being related to one another even though they have many differentiating features. You could define a particular kind of box as having the generic characteristics of all boxes — perhaps just a length, a breadth and a height — plus some additional parameters which serve to differentiate your kind of box from the rest. You may also find that there are new things you can do with your particular kind of box that you can't do with other boxes.

Equally, some objects may be the result of combining a particular kind of box with some other kind of object: a box of candy, or a crate of beer for example. You can, of course, define one kind of box as a generic box plus some additional characteristics, and then specify another sort of box as a further specialization of that. An example of the kinds of relationships you might define between different sorts of boxes is illustrated below.

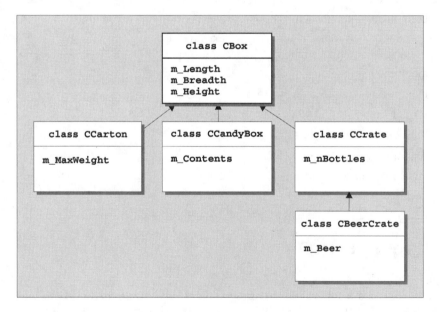

The boxes become more specialized as you move down the diagram. In this case, we have defined three different kinds of box, based on the generic type. We also have beer crates defined as a further refinement of crates designed to hold bottles.

You could deduce from this that a good way to approximate the real world relatively well, using classes in C++, would be through the ability to define classes that are interrelated. A candy box can be considered to be a box with all the characteristics of a basic box, plus a few characteristics of its own. This precisely illustrates the relationship between classes in C++ when one class is defined based on another, and is shown in the diagram above. Let's look at how this works in practice.

Inheritance in Classes

When one class is defined based on another class (or more generally, based on several others), the former is referred to as a **derived class**. A derived class automatically contains all the data members of the class or classes which are used to define it and, with some restrictions, the function members as well. The class is said to **inherit** the data members and function members of the classes on which it is based.

The only members of a base class which are not inherited by a derived class are the destructor, the constructors and any member functions overloading the assignment operator. All other function members, together with all the data members of a base class, will be inherited by a derived class. Of course, the reason for certain base members not being inherited is that a derived class will always have its own constructors and destructor. If the base class has an assignment operator, the derived class provides a version of its own. When we say these functions are not inherited, we mean that they don't exist as members of a derived class object. However, they still exist for the base class part of an object, as we will see.

What is a Base Class?

A base class is any class that is used in the definition of another class. When, for example, a class **B** is defined directly in terms of a class **A**, **A** is said to be a **direct base class** of **B**. In the previous diagram, the class **CCrate** was a direct base class of **CBeerCrate**. When a class such as **CBeerCrate** is defined in terms of another class **CCrate**, **CBeerCrate** is said to be derived from **CCrate**. Because **CCrate** is itself defined in terms of the class **CBox**, **CBox** is said to be an **indirect base class** of **CBeerCrate**. We shall see how this is expressed in the class definition in a moment. The relationship between a derived class and a base class is illustrated in the following figure:

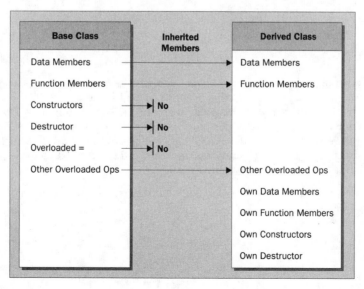

Just because function members are inherited, doesn't mean that you won't want to replace them in the derived class with new versions, and of course, you can do that when necessary.

Deriving Classes from a Base Class

Let's go back to the original **CBox** class with **public** data members that we had at the beginning of the last chapter:

```
// Listing 10_01-01
class CBox
{
   public:
      double m_Length;
      double m_Breadth;
      double m_Height;

      CBox(double lv = 1.0, double bv = 1.0, double hv = 1.0):
            m_Length(lv), m_Breadth(bv), m_Height(hv){}
};
```

We have included a constructor in the class so that we can initialize objects when we declare them. Suppose we now need another class **CCandyBox**, which is the same as a **CBox** object, but also has another data member — a pointer to a text string. We can define **CCandyBox** as a derived class with the class **CBox** as the base class, as follows:

```
// Listing 10_01-02
class CCandyBox: CBox
{
   public:
      char* m_Contents;

      CCandyBox(char* str = "Candy")                  // Constructor
      {
        m_Contents = new char[ strlen(str) + 1 ];
        strcpy(m_Contents, str);
      }

      ~CCandyBox()                                    // Destructor
      { delete[] m_Contents; };
};
```

The base class, **CBox**, appears after the class name for the derived class **CCandyBox** and is separated from it by a colon. In all other respects, it looks like a normal class definition. We have added the new member, **m_Contents**, and, since it is a pointer to a string, we need a constructor to initialize it and a destructor to release the memory for the string. We have also put a default value for the string describing the contents of a **CCandyBox** object in the constructor. Objects of the class **CCandyBox** contain all the members of the base class, **CBox**, plus the additional data member, **m_Contents**.

TRY IT OUT - Using a Derived Class

We can see how our derived class works in an example. Although we used the Wizard Bar to manage our classes in the previous chapter, we will hold off doing that for the most part in this chapter, because we are often combining fragments that we have been developing in discussion. However, if you feel comfortable using the Wizard Bar to put the examples together, it would be good experience to do it that way. In any event we will be using it extensively in later chapters. Here is the code for our first example using a derived class:

```cpp
// EX10_01.CPP
// Using a derived class
#include <iostream>                              // For stream I/O
#include <cstring>                               // For strlen() and strcpy()
using namespace std;

// Insert CBox definition (Listing 10_01-01)

// Insert CCandyBox definition (Listing 10_01-02)

int main()
{
   CBox myBox(4.0, 3.0, 2.0);                    // Create CBox object
   CCandyBox myCandyBox;
   CCandyBox myMintBox("Wafer Thin Mints");      // Create CCandyBox object

   cout << endl
        << "myBox occupies " << sizeof myBox     // Show how much memory
        << " bytes" << endl                      // the objects require
        << "myCandyBox occupies " << sizeof myCandyBox
        << " bytes" << endl
        << "myMintBox occupies " << sizeof myMintBox
        << " bytes";

   cout << endl
        << "myBox length is " << myBox.m_Length;

   myBox.m_Length = 10.0;

   // myCandyBox.m_Length = 10.0;                // uncomment this for an error

   cout << endl;
   return 0;
}
```

How It Works

After declaring a **CBox** object and two **CCandyBox** objects, we output the number of bytes occupied by each object. Let's look at the output:

```
Ex10_01

myBox occupies 24 bytes
myCandyBox occupies 32 bytes
myMintBox occupies 32 bytes
myBox length is 4
Press any key to continue
```

The first line is what we would expect from our discussion in the last chapter. A **CBox** object has three data members of type **double**, each of which will be 8 bytes, making 24 bytes in all. Both our **CCandyBox** objects are the same size: 32 bytes. The length of the string doesn't affect the size of an object, as the memory to hold the string is allocated in the free store. The 32 bytes are made up of 24 bytes for the three **double** members inherited from the base class **CBox**, plus 4 bytes for the pointer member **m_Contents**, which makes 28 bytes... so where did the other 4 bytes come from? This is due to the compiler aligning members at addresses that are multiples of 8 bytes. You should be able to demonstrate this by adding an extra member of type **int**, say, to the class **CCandyBox**. You will find that the size of a class object is still 32 bytes.

We also output the value of the **m_Length** member of the **CBox** object **myBox**. Even though we have no difficulty accessing this member of the **CBox** object, if you uncomment the following statement in the function **main()**,

```
//  myCandyBox.m_Length = 10.0;                    // uncomment this for an error
```

the program will no longer compile. The compiler will generate a message,

error C2248: 'm_Length': cannot access public member declared in class 'CBox'

which means that the **m_Length** member from the base class is not accessible. In the derived class, the member **m_Length** has become **private**.

The reason for this is that there is a default access specifier of **private** for a base class — it's as if the first line of our class definition had been,

```
class CCandyBox: private CBox
```

There always has to be an access specification for a base class which will determine the status of the inherited members in the derived class. Omitting an access specification when specifying a base class causes the compiler to assume that it's **private**. If we change the definition of the class **CCandyBox** to the following,

```
class CCandyBox: public CBox
{
    // Contents the same as in Listing 10_01-02
};
```

then the member **m_Length** in the derived class will be inherited as **public** and will be accessible in the function **main()**. With the access specifier **public** for the base class, all the inherited members originally specified as **public** in the base class will have the same access level in the derived class.

Access Control Under Inheritance

The whole question of the access of inherited members in a derived class needs to be looked at more closely. Firstly, we should consider the **private** members of a base class in a derived class.

There was a good reason for choosing the version of the class **CBox** with **public** data members, rather than the later, more secure version with **private** data members that we looked at. The reason was that although **private** data members of a base class are also members of a derived class, they remain **private** to the base class in the derived class so member functions added to the derived class cannot access them. They are only accessible in the derived class through function members of the base class that are not in the **private** section of the base class. You can demonstrate this very easily by changing all the **CBox** class data members to **private** and putting a function **Volume()** in the derived class **CCandyBox**, so that the class definitions become as follows:

```
// Version of the classes that will not compile
class CBox
{
   public:
       CBox(double lv = 1.0, double bv = 1.0, double hv = 1.0):
       m_Length(lv), m_Breadth(bv), m_Height(hv){}

   private:
       double m_Length;
       double m_Breadth;
       double m_Height;
};

class CCandyBox: public CBox
{
   public:
       char* m_Contents;

       // Function to calculate the volume of a CCandyBox object
       double Volume() const                   // Error - members not accessible
       { return m_Length*m_Breadth*m_Height; }

       CCandyBox(char* str = "Candy")          // Constructor
       {
           m_Contents = new char[ strlen(str) + 1 ];
           strcpy(m_Contents, str);
       }

       ~CCandyBox()                            // Destructor
       { delete[] m_Contents; }
};
```

A program using these classes will not compile. The function **Volume()** in the class **CCandyBox** attempts to access the **private** members of the base class, which is not legal.

TRY IT OUT - Accessing Private Members of the Base Class

It is, however, legal to use the **Volume()** function in the base class, so if you move the definition of the function **Volume()** to the **public** section of the base class, **CBox**, not only will the program compile but you can use the function to obtain the volume of a **CCandyBox** object:

```
// EX10_02.CPP
// Using a function inherited from a base class
#include <iostream>                           // For stream I/O
```

```
#include <cstring>                    // For strlen() and strcpy()
using namespace std;

class CBox
{
   public:
      CBox(double lv = 1.0, double bv = 1.0, double hv = 1.0):
       m_Length(lv), m_Breadth(bv), m_Height(hv){}

      //Function to calculate the volume of a CBox object
      double Volume() const
      { return m_Length*m_Breadth*m_Height; }

   private:
      double m_Length;
      double m_Breadth;
      double m_Height;
};

class CCandyBox: public CBox
{
   // Contents the same as in Listing 10_01-02
};

int main()
{
   CBox myBox(4.0,3.0,2.0);                            // Create CBox object
   CCandyBox myCandyBox;
   CCandyBox myMintBox("Wafer Thin Mints");            // Create CCandyBox
                                                       // object

   cout << endl
        << "myBox occupies " << sizeof  myBox          // Show how much memory
        << " bytes" << endl                            // the objects require
        << "myCandyBox occupies " << sizeof myCandyBox
        << " bytes" << endl
        << "myMintBox occupies " << sizeof myMintBox
        << " bytes";
   cout << endl
        << "myMintBox volume is " << myMintBox.Volume(); // Get volume of a
                                                         // CCandyBox object
   cout << endl;
   return 0;
}
```

How It Works

This example will produce the following output:

```
myBox occupies 24 bytes
myCandyBox occupies 32 bytes
myMintBox occupies 32 bytes
myMintBox volume is 1
Press any key to continue_
```

The interesting additional output is the last line. This shows the value produced by the function **Volume()**, which is now in the **public** section of the base class. Within the derived class, it operates on the members of the derived class that are inherited from the base. It is a full member of the derived class, so it can be used freely with objects of the derived class.

The value for the volume of the derived class object is 1 because, in creating the **CCandyBox** object, the default constructor **CBox()** was called first to create the base class part of the object, and this sets default **CBox** dimensions to 1.

Constructor Operation in a Derived Class

Although we said the base class constructor is not inherited in the base class, it still exists for the base part of the derived class object. This is because creating the base class part of a derived class object is really the business of a base class constructor, not the derived class constructor. After all, we have seen that private members of a base class are inaccessible in a derived class object, even though they are inherited.

The default constructor for the base part of the derived class object was called automatically in the last example, but this doesn't have to be the case. We can arrange to call a particular base class constructor from the derived class constructor. This will enable us to initialize the base class data members with a constructor other than the default, or indeed to choose one or other base class constructor, depending on the data supplied to the derived class constructor.

TRY IT OUT - Calling Constructors

We can demonstrate this in action using a modified version of the last example. To make the class usable, we really need to provide a constructor for the derived class which allows you to specify the dimensions of the object. We can produce an additional constructor in the derived class to do this, and call the base class constructor explicitly to set the values of the data members inherited from the base class.

```cpp
// EX10_03.CPP
// Calling a base constructor from a derived class constructor
#include <iostream>              // For stream I/O
#include <cstring>               // For strlen() and strcpy()
using namespace std;

class CBox
{
  public:
    // Base class constructor
    CBox(double lv = 1.0, double bv = 1.0, double hv = 1.0):
                     m_Length(lv), m_Breadth(bv), m_Height(hv)
    { cout << endl << "CBox constructor called";  }

    //Function to calculate the volume of a CBox object
    double Volume() const
    { return m_Length*m_Breadth*m_Height; }

  private:
    double m_Length;
    double m_Breadth;
```

```
        double m_Height;
};

class CCandyBox: public CBox
{
  public:
      char* m_Contents;

      // Constructor to set dimensions and contents
      // with explicit call of CBox constructor
      CCandyBox(double lv, double bv, double hv, char* str = "Candy")
                                                    :CBox(lv, bv, hv)

      {
          cout << endl <<"CCandyBox constructor2 called";
          m_Contents = new char[ strlen(str) + 1 ];
          strcpy(m_Contents, str);
      }

      // Constructor to set contents
      // calls default CBox constructor automatically
      CCandyBox(char* str = "Candy")
      {
          cout << endl << "CCandyBox constructor1 called";
          m_Contents = new char[ strlen(str) + 1 ];
          strcpy(m_Contents, str);
      }

      ~CCandyBox()                              // Destructor
      { delete[] m_Contents; }
};

int main()
{
    CBox myBox(4.0, 3.0, 2.0);
    CCandyBox myCandyBox;
    CCandyBox myMintBox(1.0, 2.0, 3.0, "Wafer Thin Mints");

    cout << endl
         << "myBox occupies " << sizeof  myBox    // Show how much memory
         << " bytes" << endl                       // the objects require
         << "myCandyBox occupies " << sizeof myCandyBox
         << " bytes" << endl
         << "myMintBox occupies " << sizeof myMintBox
         << " bytes";
    cout << endl
         << "myMintBox volume is "                // Get volume of a
         << myMintBox.Volume();                   // CCandyBox object
    cout << endl;
    return 0;
}
```

How It Works

As well as adding the additional constructor in the derived class, we have put an output statement in each constructor so we will know when either gets called. The explicit call of the constructor for the **CBox** class appears after a colon in the function header of the derived class constructor. You will have perhaps noticed that the notation is exactly the same as what we have been using for initializing members in a constructor anyway:

```
// Calling the base class constructor
CCandyBox(double lv, double bv, double hv, char* str= "Candy"): CBox(lv, bv, hv)
{
...
}
```

This is perfectly consistent with what we are doing here, since we are essentially initializing a **CBox** sub-object of the derived class object. In the first case, we are explicitly calling the default constructor for the **double** types **m_Length**, **m_Breadth** and **m_Height** in the initialization list. In the second instance, we are calling the constructor for **CBox**. This causes the specific **CBox** constructor we have chosen to be called before the **CCandyBox** constructor is executed.

If you build and run this example, it will produce the output shown below:

The calls to the constructors are explained in the table below:

Screen output	Object being constructed
CBox constructor called	**myBox**
CBox constructor called	**myCandyBox**
CCandyBox constructor1 called	**myCandyBox**
CBox constructor called	**myMintBox**
CCandyBox constructor2 called	**myMintBox**

The first line of output is due to the **CBox** class constructor call, originating from the declaration of the **CBox** object, **myBox**. The second line of output arises from the automatic call of the base class constructor caused by the declaration of the **CCandyBox** object **myCandyBox**.

> *Notice how the base class constructor is always called before the derived class constructor.*

The following line is due to our version of the default derived class constructor being called for the object **myCandyBox**. This constructor is invoked because the object is not initialized. The fourth line of output arises from the explicit identification of the **CBox** class constructor to be called in our new constructor for **CCandyBox** objects. The argument values specified for the dimensions of the **CCandyBox** object are passed to the base class constructor. Next comes the output from the new derived class constructor itself, so constructors are again called for the base class first, followed by the derived class.

393

It should be clear from what we have seen up to now, that when a derived class constructor is executed, a base class constructor is always called to construct the base part of the derived class object. If you don't specify the base class constructor to be used, the compiler will call the default.

The last line in the table shows that the initialization of the base part of the object **myMintBox** is working as it should, with the **private** members having been initialized by the **CBox** class constructor.

Having the **private** members of a base class only accessible to function members of the base class isn't always convenient. There will be many instances where we want to have **private** members of a base class that *can* be accessed from within the derived class. As you will surely have anticipated by now, C++ provides a way to do this.

Declaring Protected Members of a Class

In addition to the **public** and **private** access specifiers for members of a class, you can also declare members of a class as **protected**. Within the class, the keyword **protected** has the same effect as the keyword **private**: members of a class that are **protected** can only be accessed by member functions of the class, and by friend functions of the class (also by member functions of a class that is declared as a **friend** of the class — we will look into friend classes later in this chapter). Using the keyword **protected**, we could redefine our class **CBox** as follows:

```
// Listing 10_04-01
class CBox
{
   public:
      // Base class constructor
      CBox(double lv = 1.0, double bv = 1.0, double hv = 1.0):
                      m_Length(lv), m_Breadth(bv), m_Height(hv)
      {  cout << endl << "CBox constructor called";  }

      // CBox destructor - just to track calls
      ~CBox()
      { cout << "CBox destructor called" << endl; }

   protected:
      double m_Length;
      double m_Breadth;
      double m_Height;
};
```

Now the data members are still effectively **private**, in that they can't be accessed by ordinary global functions, but they'll still be accessible to member functions of a derived class.

TRY IT OUT - Using Protected Members

We can demonstrate the use of **protected** data members by using this version of the class **CBox** to derive a new version of the class **CCandyBox**, which will access the members of the base class through its own member function, **Volume()**.

```
// EX10_04.CPP
// Using the protected access specifier
#include <iostream>              // For stream I/O
#include <cstring>               // For strlen() and strcpy()
using namespace std;

// Insert CBox class definition here (Listing 10_04-01)

class CCandyBox: public CBox
{
   public:
      char* m_Contents;

      // Derived class function to calculate volume
      double Volume() const
      { return m_Length*m_Breadth*m_Height; }

      // Constructor to set dimensions and contents
      // with explicit call of CBox constructor
      CCandyBox(double lv, double bv, double hv, char* str = "Candy")
                                    :CBox(lv, bv, hv)  // Constructor
      {
         cout << endl <<"CCandyBox constructor2 called";
         m_Contents = new char[ strlen(str) + 1 ];
         strcpy(m_Contents, str);
      }

      // Constructor to set contents
      // calls default CBox constructor automatically
      CCandyBox(char* str = "Candy")                        // Constructor
      {
         cout << endl << "CCandyBox constructor1 called";
         m_Contents = new char[ strlen(str) + 1 ];
         strcpy(m_Contents, str);
      }

      ~CCandyBox()                                          // Destructor
      {
         cout << "CCandyBox destructor called" << endl;
         delete[] m_Contents;
      }
};

int main()
{
   CCandyBox myCandyBox;
   CCandyBox myToffeeBox(2, 3, 4, "Stickjaw Toffee");

   cout << endl
        << "myCandyBox volume is " << myCandyBox.Volume()
        << endl
        << "myToffeeBox volume is " << myToffeeBox.Volume();

   // cout << endl << myToffeeBox.m_Length;     // Uncomment this for an error

   cout << endl;
   return 0;
}
```

How It Works

In this example, the volumes of the two **CCandyBox** objects are calculated by invoking the function **Volume()**, which is a member of the derived class. This function accesses the inherited members **m_Length**, **m_Breadth**, and **m_Height** to produce the result. The members were declared as **protected** in the base class and remain **protected** in the derived class. The program produces the output shown below:

```
Ms Ex10_04

CBox constructor called
CCandyBox constructor1 called
CBox constructor called
CCandyBox constructor2 called
myCandyBox volume is 1
myToffeeBox volume is 24
CCandyBox destructor called
CBox destructor called
CCandyBox destructor called
CBox destructor called
Press any key to continue_
```

This shows that the volume is being calculated properly for both **CCandyBox** objects. The first object has the default dimensions produced by calling the default **CBox** constructor, so the volume is 1, and the second object has the dimensions defined as initial values in its declaration.

The output also shows the sequence of constructor and destructor calls, and you can see how each derived class object is destroyed in two steps.

> *Destructors for a derived class object are called in the reverse order to the constructors for the object. This is a general rule that always applies. Constructors are invoked starting with the base class constructor and then the derived class constructor, whereas the destructor for the derived class is called first when an object is destroyed, followed by the base class destructor.*

You can demonstrate that the **protected** members of the base class remain **protected** in the derived class by uncommenting the statement preceding the **return** statement in the function **main()**. If you do this, you will get the following error message from the compiler,

error C2248: 'm_Length': cannot access protected member declared in class 'CBox'

which indicates quite clearly that the member **m_Length** is inaccessible.

The Access Level of Inherited Class Members

We know that if we have no access specifier for the base class in the definition of a derived class, the default specification is **private**. This has the effect of causing the inherited **public** and **protected** members of the base class to become **private** in the derived class. The **private** members of the base class remain **private** to the base and therefore inaccessible to member functions of the derived class. In fact, they remain **private** to the base class regardless of how the base class is specified in the derived class definition.

We have also used **public** as the specifier for a base class. This leaves the members of the base class with the same access level in the derived class as they had in the base, so **public** members remain **public** and **protected** members remain **protected**.

The last possibility is to declare a base class as **protected**. This has the effect of making the inherited **public** members of the base **protected** in the derived class. The **protected** (and **private**) inherited members retain their original access level in the derived class.

This is summarized in the following illustration:

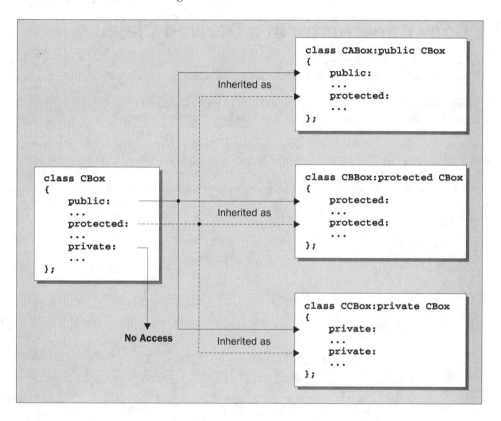

This may look a little complicated, but you can reduce it to the following three points about the inherited members of a derived class:

▶ Members of a base class that are declared as **private** are never accessible in a derived class

▶ Defining a base class as **public** doesn't change the access level of its members in the derived class

▶ Defining a base class as **protected** changes its **public** members to **protected** in the derived class

397

Being able to change the access level of inherited members in a derived class gives you a degree of flexibility, but remember that you can only make the access level more stringent. In no way can you relax the level specified in the base class, which suggests that your base classes need to have **public** members if you want to be able to vary the access level in derived classes. This may seem to run contrary to the idea of encapsulating data in a class in order to protect it from unauthorized access, but, as we shall see, it will often be the case that we construct base classes in such a manner that their only purpose is to act as a base for other classes, and they aren't intended to be used for instantiating objects in their own right.

The Copy Constructor in a Derived Class

You will remember that the copy constructor is called automatically when you declare an object which is initialized with an object of the same class. Look at these statements:

```
CBox myBox(2.0, 3.0, 4.0);        // Calls constructor
CBox copyBox(myBox);              // Calls copy constructor
```

The first will call the constructor, accepting three **double** arguments, and the second will call the copy constructor. If you don't supply your own copy constructor, the compiler will supply one that copies the initializing object member by member to the corresponding members of the new object. So that we can see what is going on during execution, let's add our own version of a copy constructor to the class **CBox**. We can then use this class as a base for defining the class **CCandyBox**.

```
// Listing 10_05-01
class CBox                     // Base class definition
{
   public:
      // Base class constructor
      CBox(double lv = 1.0, double bv = 1.0, double hv = 1.0):
                     m_Length(lv), m_Breadth(bv), m_Height(hv)
      {  cout << endl << "CBox constructor called";  }

      // Copy constructor
      CBox(const CBox& initB)
      {
         cout << endl << "CBox copy constructor called";
         m_Length = initB.m_Length;
         m_Breadth = initB.m_Breadth;
         m_Height = initB.m_Height;
      }

      // CBox destructor - just to track calls
      ~CBox()
      { cout << "CBox destructor called" << endl; }

   protected:
      double m_Length;
      double m_Breadth;
      double m_Height;
};
```

You'll also recall that the copy constructor needs to have its parameter specified as a reference in order to avoid an infinite number of calls to itself, caused by the need to copy an argument that is transferred by value. When the copy constructor in our example is invoked, it will output a message to the screen, so we'll be able to see from the output when this is happening.

We will use the **CCandyBox** class from **Ex10_04.cpp**, shown again here:

```
// Listing 10_05-02
class CCandyBox: public CBox
{
   public:
      char* m_Contents;

      // Derived class function to calculate volume
      double Volume() const
      { return m_Length*m_Breadth*m_Height; }

      // Constructor to set dimensions and contents
      // with explicit call of CBox constructor
      CCandyBox(double lv, double bv, double hv, char* str = "Candy")
                                        :CBox(lv, bv, hv)    // Constructor
      {
         cout << endl <<"CCandyBox constructor2 called";
         m_Contents = new char[ strlen(str) + 1 ];
         strcpy(m_Contents, str);
      }

      // Constructor to set contents
      // calls default CBox constructor automatically
      CCandyBox(char* str = "Candy")                         // Constructor
      {
         cout << endl << "CCandyBox constructor1 called";
         m_Contents = new char[ strlen(str) + 1 ];
         strcpy(m_Contents, str);
      }

      ~CCandyBox()                                           // Destructor
      {
         cout << "CCandyBox destructor called" << endl;
         delete[] m_Contents;
      }
};
```

This doesn't have a copy constructor added yet, so we'll rely on the compiler-generated version.

TRY IT OUT - The Copy Constructor in Derived Classes

We can exercise the copy constructor that we have just defined with the following example:

```
// EX10_05.CPP
// Using a derived class copy constructor
#include <iostream>              // For stream I/O
#include <cstring>              // For strlen() and strcpy()
using namespace std;
```

```
// Insert CBox class definition here (Listing 10_05-01)

// Insert CCandyBox class definition here (Listing 10_05-02)

int main()
{
   CCandyBox chocBox(2.0, 3.0, 4.0, "Chockies");       // Declare and initialize
   CCandyBox chocolateBox(chocBox);                    // Use copy constructor

   cout << endl
        << "Volume of chocBox is " << chocBox.Volume()
        << endl
        << "Volume of chocolateBox is " << chocolateBox.Volume()
        << endl;

   return 0;
}
```

How It Works (or why it doesn't)

When you run this example, in addition to the expected output, you'll see the following message:

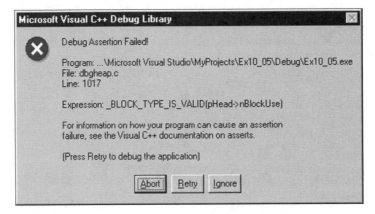

Press **Abort** to clear the dialog and you'll see the output in the console window that you might expect. The output shows that the compiler-generated copy constructor for the derived class automatically called the copy constructor for the base class.

However, as you've probably realized, all is not as it should be. In this particular case, the compiler-generated copy constructor causes problems because the memory pointed to by the **m_Contents** member of the derived class in the second object declared will point to the same memory as the one in the first object. When one object is destroyed (when it goes out of scope at the end of **main()**), it releases the memory occupied by the text. When the second object is destroyed, the destructor attempts to release some memory that has already been freed by the destructor call for the previous object.

The way to fix this is to supply a copy constructor for the derived class that will allocate some additional memory for the new object.

TRY IT OUT - Fixing the Copy Constructor Problem

We can do this by adding the following code for the copy constructor to the **public** section of the derived class:

```
// Derived class copy constructor
CCandyBox(const CCandyBox& initCB)
{
    cout << endl << "CCandyBox copy constructor called";

    // Get new memory
    m_Contents = new char[ strlen(initCB.m_Contents) + 1 ];

    // Copy string
    strcpy(m_Contents, initCB.m_Contents);
}
```

We can now run this new version of the last example with the same function **main()** to see how our copy constructor works.

How It Works

Now when we run the example, it behaves rather better and produces the output shown in the screen below:

```
Ex10_05

CBox constructor called
CCandyBox constructor2 called
CBox constructor called
CCandyBox copy constructor called
Volume of chocBox is 24
Volume of chocolateBox is 1
CCandyBox destructor called
CBox destructor called
CCandyBox destructor called
CBox destructor called
Press any key to continue_
```

However, there is still something wrong. The third line of output shows that the default constructor for the **CBox** part of the object **chocolateBox** is called, rather than the copy constructor. As a consequence, the object has the default dimensions rather than the dimensions of the initializing object, so the volume is incorrect. The reason for this is that when you write a constructor for an object of a derived class, you are responsible for ensuring that the members of the derived class object are properly initialized. This includes the inherited members.

The fix for this is to call the copy constructor for the base part of the class in the initialization list for the copy constructor for the **CCandyBox** class. The copy constructor would then become:

```
// Derived class copy constructor
CCandyBox(const CCandyBox& initCB) : CBox(initCB)
{
    cout << endl << "CCandyBox copy constructor called";

    // Get new memory
    m_Contents = new char[ strlen(initCB.m_Contents) + 1 ];
```

401

```
        // Copy string
        strcpy(m_Contents, initCB.m_Contents);
    }
```

Now, the **CBox** class copy constructor is called with the **initCB** object. Only the base part of the object will be passed to it, so everything will work out. If you modify the last example by adding the base copy constructor call, the output will be as shown:

```
Ex10_05
CBox constructor called
CCandyBox constructor2 called
CBox copy constructor called
CCandyBox copy constructor called
Volume of chocBox is 24
Volume of chocolateBox is 24
CCandyBox destructor called
CBox destructor called
CCandyBox destructor called
CBox destructor called
Press any key to continue_
```

The output shows that all the constructors and destructors are called in the correct sequence and the copy constructor for the **CBox** part of **chocolateBox** is called before the **CCandyBox** copy constructor. The volume of the object **chocolateBox** of the derived class is now the same as that of its initializing object, which is as it should be.

We have, therefore, another golden rule to remember:

> *If you write any kind of constructor for a derived class, you are responsible for the initialization of all members of the derived class object, including all its inherited members.*

Class Members as friends

We saw in Chapter 8 how a function could be declared as a friend of a class. This gave the friend function the privilege of free access to any of the class members. Of course, there is no reason why a friend function cannot be a member of another class.

Suppose we define a class **CBottle** to represent a bottle:

```
class CBottle
{
   public:
      CBottle(double height, double diameter)
      {
         m_Height = height;
         m_Diameter = diameter;
      }

   private:
      double m_Height;          // Bottle height
      double m_Diameter;        // Bottle diameter
};
```

We now need a class to represent the packaging for a dozen bottles, that will automatically have custom dimensions to accommodate a particular kind of bottle. We could define this as:

```
class CCarton
{

   public:
      CCarton(const CBottle& aBottle)
      {
         m_Height = aBottle.m_Height;             // Bottle height
         m_Length = 4.0*aBottle.m_Diameter;       // Four rows of ...
         m_Breadth = 3.0*aBottle.m_Diameter;      // ...three bottles
      }

   private:
      double m_Length;          // Carton length
      double m_Breadth;         // Carton breadth
      double m_Height;          // Carton height
};
```

The constructor here sets the height to be the same as that of the bottle it is to accommodate, and the length and breadth are set based on the diameter of the bottle so that twelve will fit in the box.

As you know by now, this won't work. The data members of the **CBottle** class are private, so the **CCarton** constructor cannot access them. As you also know, a **friend** declaration in the **CBottle** class will fix it:

```
class CBottle
{
   public:
      CBottle(double height, double diameter)
      {
         m_Height = height;
         m_Diameter = diameter;
      }

   private:
      double m_Height;          // Bottle height
      double m_Diameter;        // Bottle diameter

   // Let the carton constructor in
      friend CCarton::CCarton(const CBottle& aBottle);
};
```

The only difference between the **friend** declaration here, and what we saw in Chapter 8 is that we must put the class name and the scope resolution operator with the friend function name to identify it. For this to compile correctly, the compiler needs to have information about the **CCarton** class constructor, so (if you were using multiple files) you would need to put an **#include** statement for the file containing the **CCarton** class definition before the definition of the **CBottle** class.

Friend Classes

You can also allow all the function members of one class to have access to all the data members of another by declaring it as a **friend class**. We could define the **CCarton** class as a friend of the **CBottle** class by writing a friend declaration in the **CBottle** class definition:

```
friend CCarton;
```

All function members of the **CCarton** class will now have free access to all the data members of the **CBottle** class.

Limitations on Class Friendship

Class friendship is not reciprocated. Making the **CCarton** class a friend of the **CBottle** class does not mean that the **CBottle** class is a friend of the **CCarton** class. If you want this to be so you must add a friend declaration for the **CBottle** class to the **CCarton** class.

Class friendship is also not inherited. If you define another class with **CBottle** as a base, members of the **CCarton** class will not have access to its data members, not even those that are inherited from **CBottle**.

Virtual Functions

We need to look more closely at the behavior of inherited member functions and their relationship with derived class member functions. Let's add a function to the class **CBox** to output the volume of a **CBox** object. The simplified class would then become:

```
// Listing 10_06-01
class CBox                   // Base class
{
   public:

      // Function to show the volume of an object
      void ShowVolume() const
      {
         cout << endl
            << "CBox usable volume is " << Volume();
      }

      // Function to calculate the volume of a CBox object
      double Volume() const
      { return m_Length*m_Breadth*m_Height; }

      // Constructor
      CBox(double lv = 1.0, double bv = 1.0, double hv = 1.0)
                        :m_Length(lv), m_Breadth(bv), m_Height(hv) {}

   protected:
      double m_Length;
      double m_Breadth;
      double m_Height;
};
```

Now we can output the usable volume of a **CBox** object just by calling the **ShowVolume()** function of any object for which we require it. The constructor sets the data member values in the initialization list, so no statements are necessary in the body of the function. The data members are as before and are specified as **protected**, so they will be accessible to the member functions of any derived class.

Now, let's suppose we want to derive a class for a different kind of box called **CGlassBox**, to hold glassware. The contents are fragile, and because packing material is added to protect them, the capacity of the box is less than the capacity of a basic **CBox** object. We therefore need a different **Volume()** function to account for this, so we add it to the derived class:

```
// Listing 10_06-02
class CGlassBox: public CBox          // Derived class
{
   public:

       // Function to calculate volume of a CGlassBox
       // allowing 15% for packing
       double Volume() const
       { return 0.85*m_Length*m_Breadth*m_Height; }

       // Constructor
       CGlassBox(double lv, double bv, double hv): CBox(lv, bv, hv){}
};
```

There could conceivably be other additional members of the derived class, but we'll keep it simple and concentrate on how the inherited functions work for the moment. The constructor for the derived class objects just calls the base class constructor in its initialization list to set the data member values. No statements are necessary in its body. We've included a new version of the function **Volume()** to replace the version from the base class, the idea being that we can get the inherited function **ShowVolume()** to call the derived class version of the member function **Volume()** when we call it for an object of the class **CGlassBox**.

TRY IT OUT - Using an Inherited Function

Now we should see how our derived class works in practice. We can try this out very simply by creating an object of the base class and an object of the derived class with the same dimensions, and then verifying that the correct volumes are being calculated. The **main()** function to do this would be as follows:

```
// EX10_06.CPP
// Behavior of inherited functions in a derived class
#include <iostream>
using namespace std;

// Insert CBox class definition (Listing 10_06-01)

// Insert CGlassBox class definition (Listing 10_06-02)

int main()
{
   CBox myBox(2.0, 3.0, 4.0);                 // Declare a base box
   CGlassBox myGlassBox(2.0, 3.0, 4.0);       // Declare derived box - same size
```

```
    myBox.ShowVolume();                    // Display volume of base box
    myGlassBox.ShowVolume();               // Display volume of derived box

    cout << endl;
    return 0;
}
```

How It Works

If you run this example, it will produce the following output:

```
Ex10_06

CBox usable volume is 24
CBox usable volume is 24
Press any key to continue_
```

This isn't only dull and repetitive, it's also disastrous. It isn't working the way we want at all, and the only interesting thing about it is why. Evidently, the fact that the second call is for an object of the derived class **CGlassBox** is not being taken into account. We can see this from the incorrect result in the output. The volume of a **CGlassBox** object should definitely be less than that of a basic **CBox** with the same dimensions.

The reason for the incorrect output is that the call of the function **Volume()** in the function **ShowVolume()** is being set once and for all by the compiler as the version defined in the base class. This is called **static resolution** of the function call since the function call is fixed before the program is executed. This is also sometimes called **early binding** because the particular **Volume()** function chosen is bound to the call from the function **ShowVolume()** during the compilation of the program.

> *The function **Volume()** here in the derived class actually hides the base class version from the view of derived class functions. If you wanted to call the base version of **Volume()** from a derived class function, you would need to use the scope resolution operator to refer to the function as **CBox::Volume()**.*

What we were hoping for in this example was that the question of which **Volume()** function call to use in any given instance would be resolved when the program was executed. This sort of operation is referred to as **dynamic linkage**, or **late binding**. We want the actual version of the function **Volume()** called by **ShowVolume()** to be determined by the kind of object being processed, and not arbitrarily fixed by the compiler before the program is executed.

No doubt you'll be less than astonished that C++ does, in fact, provide us with a way to do this, since this whole discussion would have been futile otherwise! We need to use something called a **virtual function**.

What's a Virtual Function?

A virtual function is a function in a base class that is declared using the keyword **virtual**. Defining in a base class a virtual function that has another version in a derived class signals to the compiler that we don't want static linkage for this function. What we *do* want is the selection of the function to be called at any given point in the program to be based on the kind of object for which it is called.

TRY IT OUT - Fixing the CGlassBox

To make our example work as we originally hoped, we just need to add the keyword **virtual** to the definitions of the **Volume()** functions:

```
// EX10_07.CPP (based on Ex10_06.cpp)
// Using a virtual function
#include <iostream>
using namespace std;

class CBox                // Base class
{
    public:
...
        // Function to calculate the volume of a CBox object
        virtual double Volume() const
        { return m_Length*m_Breadth*m_Height; }
...

};

class CGlassBox: public CBox
{
    public:
...
        // Function to calculate volume of a CGlassBox
        // allowing 15% for packing
        virtual double Volume() const
        { return 0.85*m_Length*m_Breadth*m_Height; }
...

};

int main()
{
...
}
```

How It Works

If you run this version of the program with just the little word **virtual** added to the definitions of **Volume()**, it will produce this output:

```
Ex10_07

CBox usable volume is 24
CBox usable volume is 20.4
Press any key to continue
```

This is now clearly doing what we wanted in the first place. The first call to the function **ShowVolume()** with the **CBox** object **myBox** calls the base version of **Volume()**. The second call with the **CGlassBox** object **myGlassBox** calls the version defined in the derived class.

Note that, although we have put the keyword **virtual** in the derived class definition of the function **Volume()**, it's not essential to do so. The definition of the base version of the function

407

as **virtual** is sufficient. However, I recommend that you *do* specify the keyword for virtual functions in derived classes since it makes it clear to anyone reading the derived class definition that they are virtual functions and that they will be selected dynamically.

In order for a function to behave as virtual, it must have the same name, parameter list, and return type in any derived class as the function has in the base class, and if the base class function is **const**, the derived class function must be too. If you try to use different parameters or return types, or declare one as **const** and the other not, the virtual function mechanism won't work. The function will operate with static linkage established and fixed at compile time.

The operation of virtual functions is an extraordinarily powerful mechanism. You may have heard the term **polymorphism** in relation to object-oriented programming, and this refers to the virtual function capability. Something that is polymorphic can appear in different guises, like a werewolf, or Dr. Jekyll, or a politician before and after an election for example. Calling a virtual function will produce different effects depending on the kind of object for which it is being called.

Using Pointers to Class Objects

Using pointers with objects of a base class and of a derived class is a very important technique. A pointer to a base class object can be assigned the address of a derived class object as well as that of the base. We can thus use a pointer of the type 'pointer to base' to obtain different behavior with virtual functions, depending on what kind of object the pointer is pointing to. We can see how this works more clearly by looking at an example.

TRY IT OUT - Pointers to Base and Derived Classes

Let's use the same classes as in the previous example, but make a small modification to the function **main()** so that it uses a pointer to a base class object.

```
// EX10_08.CPP
// Using a base class pointer to call a virtual function
#include <iostream>
using namespace std;

class CBox                              // Base class
{
   public:

      // Function to show the volume of an object
      void ShowVolume() const
      {
         cout << endl
            << "CBox usable volume is " << Volume();
      }

      // Function to calculate the volume of a CBox object
      virtual double Volume() const
      { return m_Length*m_Breadth*m_Height; }

      // Constructor
      CBox(double lv = 1.0, double bv = 1.0, double hv = 1.0)
                        :m_Length(lv), m_Breadth(bv), m_Height(hv) {}
```

```
    protected:
        double m_Length;
        double m_Breadth;
        double m_Height;
    };

    class CGlassBox: public CBox              // Derived class
    {
        public:

            // Function to calculate volume of a CGlassBox
            // allowing 15% for packing
            virtual double Volume() const
            { return 0.85*m_Length*m_Breadth*m_Height; }

            // Constructor
            CGlassBox(double lv, double bv, double hv): CBox(lv, bv, hv){}
    };

    int main()
    {
        CBox myBox(2.0, 3.0, 4.0);              // Declare a base box
        CGlassBox myGlassBox(2.0, 3.0, 4.0);    // Declare derived box of same size
        CBox* pBox = 0;                         // Declare a pointer to base class
                                                // objects

        pBox = &myBox;                          // Set pointer to address of base object
        pBox->ShowVolume();                     // Display volume of base box
        pBox = &myGlassBox;                     // Set pointer to derived class object
        pBox->ShowVolume();                     // Display volume of derived box

        cout << endl;
        return 0;
    }
```

How It Works

The classes are the same as in example **Ex10_07.cpp**, but the function **main()** has been altered to use a pointer to call the function **ShowVolume()**. Because we are using a pointer, we use the indirect member selection operator, **->**, to call the function. The function **ShowVolume()** is called twice, and both calls use the same pointer to base class objects, **pBox**. On the first occasion, the pointer contains the address of the base object, **myBox**, and on the occasion of the second call, it contains the address of the derived class object, **myGlassBox**.

The output produced is as follows:

```
Ex10_08

CBox usable volume is 24
CBox usable volume is 20.4
Press any key to continue_
```

This is exactly the same as that from the previous example where we used explicit objects in the function call.

We can conclude from this example that the virtual function mechanism works just as well through a pointer to a base class, with the specific function being selected based on the type of object being pointed to. This is illustrated in the following figure.

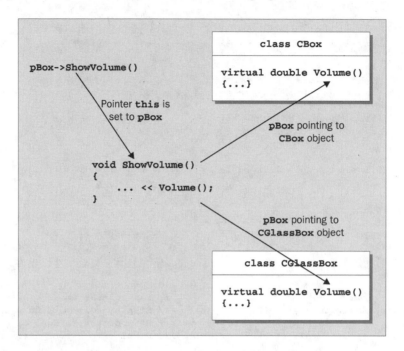

This means that, even when we don't know the precise type of the object pointed to by a base class pointer in a program (when a pointer is passed to a function as an argument, for example), the virtual function mechanism will ensure that the correct function is called. This is an extraordinarily powerful capability, so make sure you understand it. Polymorphism is a fundamental mechanism in C++ that you will find yourself using again and again.

Using References With Virtual Functions

If you define a function with a reference to a base class as a parameter, you can pass an object of a derived class to it as an argument. When your function executes, the appropriate virtual function for the object passed will be selected automatically. We could show this happening by modifying the function **main()** in the last example to call a function that has a reference as a parameter.

TRY IT OUT - Using References with Virtual Functions

Let's move the call to **ShowVolume()** to a separate function, and call that separate function from **main()**:

```
// EX10_09.CPP
// Using a reference to call a virtual function
#include <iostream>
using namespace std;
```

```
    class CBox;          // Incomplete class definition required for prototype

    void Output(const CBox& aBox);          // Prototype of function

  // Insert class definitions for CBox and CGlassBox (as in Ex10_08.cpp)

  int main()
  {
     CBox myBox(2.0, 3.0, 4.0);          // Declare a base box
     CGlassBox myGlassBox(2.0, 3.0, 4.0);  // Declare derived box of same size

     Output(myBox);                       // Output volume of base class object
     Output(myGlassBox);                  // Output volume of derived class object

     cout << endl;
     return 0;
  }

  // Function to output a volume via a virtual function call using a reference
  void Output(const CBox& aBox)
  {
     aBox.ShowVolume();
  }
```

How It Works

At the beginning of the program, we have an incomplete definition of the class **CBox**. This is included so that the compiler will know of the existence of **CBox** as a class when it gets to the prototype of the function **Output()**. Without this, the prototype would cause an error message to be generated. We could have put the prototype for **Output()** after the definition of the **CBox** class, but then you wouldn't be reminded about the use of the incomplete class definition.

The function **main()** now basically consists of two calls of the function **Output()**, the first with an object of the base class as an argument and the second with an object of the derived class. Because the parameter is a reference to the base class, **Output()** accepts objects of either class as an argument and the appropriate version of the virtual function **Volume()** is called, depending on the object that is initializing the reference.

The program produces exactly the same output as the previous example, demonstrating that the virtual function mechanism does indeed work through a reference parameter.

Pure Virtual Functions

It's possible that you'd want to include a virtual function in a base class so that it may be redefined in a derived class to suit the objects of that class, but that there is no meaningful definition you could give for the function in the base class.

For example, we could conceivably have a class **CContainer**, which could be used as a base for defining our **CBox** class, or a **CBottle** class, or even a **CTeapot** class. The **CContainer** class wouldn't have data members, but you might want to provide a virtual member function **Volume()** for any derived classes. Since the **CContainer** class has no data members, and therefore no dimensions, there is no sensible **Volume()** definition that we can write. We can still define the class, however, including the member function **Volume()**, as follows:

```
// Listing 10_10-01
class CContainer          // Generic base class for specific containers
{
   public:

      // Function for calculating a volume - no content
      // This is defined as a 'pure' virtual function, signified by '= 0'
      virtual double Volume() const = 0;

      // Function to display a volume
      virtual void ShowVolume() const
      {
         cout << endl
              << "Volume is " << Volume();
      }
};
```

The statement for the virtual function **Volume()** defines it as having no content by placing the equals sign and zero in the function header. This is called a **pure virtual function**. Any class derived from this class must either define the **Volume()** function or redefine it as a pure virtual function. Since we have declared **Volume()** as **const**, its implementation in any derived class must also be **const**. Remember that **const** and non-**const** varieties of a function with the same name and parameter list are different functions. In other words you can overload a function using **const**.

The class also contains the function **ShowVolume()**, which will display the volume of objects of derived classes. Since this is declared as **virtual**, it can be replaced in a derived class, but if it isn't, the base class version that you see here will be called.

Abstract Classes

A class containing a pure virtual function is called an **abstract class**. It's called abstract because you can't define objects of a class containing a pure virtual function. It exists only for the purpose of defining classes which are derived from it. If a class derived from an abstract class still defines a pure virtual function of the base as pure, it too is an abstract class.

You should not conclude, from the example of the **CContainer** class above, that an abstract class can't have data members. An abstract class can have both data members and function members. The presence of a pure virtual function is the only condition that determines that a given class is abstract. In the same vein, an abstract class can have more than one pure virtual function. In this case, a derived class must have definitions for every pure virtual function in its base, otherwise it too will be an abstract class. If you forget to make the derived class version of the **Volume()** function **const**, then the derived class will still be abstract since it will contain the pure virtual **Volume()** member function that is **const**, as well as the non-**const Volume()** function.

TRY IT OUT - An Abstract Class

We could implement a **CCan** class, representing beer or cola cans perhaps, together with our original **CBox** class. Both are derived from the **CContainer** class. The definitions of these two classes would be as follows:

```
// Listing 10_10-02
class CBox: public CContainer          // Derived class
{
    public:

        // Function to show the volume of an object
        virtual void ShowVolume() const
        {
            cout << endl
                << "CBox usable volume is " << Volume();
        }

        // Function to calculate the volume of a CBox object
        virtual double Volume() const
        { return m_Length*m_Breadth*m_Height; }

        // Constructor
        CBox(double lv = 1.0, double bv = 1.0, double hv = 1.0)
                            :m_Length(lv), m_Breadth(bv), m_Height(hv){}

    protected:
        double m_Length;
        double m_Breadth;
        double m_Height;
};
```

```
// Listing 10_10-03
class CCan: public CContainer
{
    public:

        // Function to calculate the volume of a can
        virtual double Volume() const
        { return 0.25*PI*m_Diameter*m_Diameter*m_Height; }

        // Constructor
        CCan(double hv = 4.0, double dv = 2.0): m_Height(hv), m_Diameter(dv){}

    protected:
        double m_Height;
        double m_Diameter;
};
```

The **CBox** class is essentially as we had it in the previous example, except this time we have specified that it is derived from the **CContainer** class. The **Volume()** function is fully defined within this class (as it must be if this class is to be used to define objects). The only other option would be to specify it as a pure virtual function, since it is pure in the base class, but then we couldn't create **CBox** objects.

The **CCan** class also defines a **Volume()** function based on the formula $h\pi r^2$, where h is the height and r is the radius of the cross-section of a can. This is essentially the height multiplied by the area of the base, to produce the volume. The expression in the function definition assumes a global constant **PI** is defined, so we'll need to remember that. You will also notice that we have redefined the **ShowVolume()** function in the **CBox** class, but not in the **CCan** class. We will see what effect this has when we get some program output.

413

We can exercise these classes with the following **main()** function:

```
// EX10_10.CPP
// Using an abstract class
#include <iostream>                    // For stream I/O
using namespace std;

const double PI= 3.14159265;          // Global definition for PI

// Insert definition of CContainer class (Listing 10_10-01)
// Insert definition of CBox class       (Listing 10_10-02)
// Insert definition of CCan class       (Listing 10_10-03)

int main(void)
{
   // Pointer to abstract base class
   // initialized with address of CBox object
   CContainer* pC1 = new CBox(2.0, 3.0, 4.0);

   // Pointer to abstract base class
   // initialized with address of CCan object
   CContainer* pC2 = new CCan(6.5, 3.0);

   pC1->ShowVolume();                 // Output the volumes of the two
   pC2->ShowVolume();                 // objects pointed to
   cout << endl;

   delete pC1;                        // Now clean up the free store
   delete pC2;                        // ....

   return 0;
}
```

How It Works

In this program, we declare two pointers to the base class, **CContainer**. Although we can't define **CContainer** objects (because **CContainer** is an abstract class), we can still define a pointer to a **CContainer**, which we can then use to store the address of a derived class object. The pointer **pC1** is assigned the address of a **CBox** object created in the free store by the operator **new**. The second pointer is assigned the address of a **CCan** object in a similar manner.

> *Of course, because the derived class objects were created dynamically, we need to use the operator **delete** to clean up the free store when we have finished with them.*

The output produced by this example is as follows:

```
Ex10_10

CBox usable volume is 24
Volume is 45.9458
Press any key to continue
```

Because we have defined **ShowVolume()** in the **CBox** class, the derived class version is called for the **CBox** object. We did not define this function in the **CCan** class, so the base class version that the **CCan** class inherits is invoked for the **CCan** object. Since **Volume()** is a virtual function that is implemented in both derived classes (necessarily, because it is a pure virtual function in the base class), the call to it is resolved when the program is executed by selecting the version belonging to the class of the object being pointed to. Thus, for the pointer **pC1**, the version from the class **CBox** is called and, for the pointer **pC2**, the version in the class **CCan** is called. In each case, therefore, we obtain the correct result.

We could equally well have used just one pointer and assigned the address of the **CCan** object to it (after calling the **Volume()** function for the **CBox** object). A base class pointer can contain the address of *any* derived class object, even when several different classes are derived from the same base class, and so we can have automatic selection of the appropriate virtual function across a whole range of derived classes. Impressive stuff, isn't it?

Indirect Base Classes

At the beginning of this chapter, we said that one class's base could in turn be derived from another, 'more' base class. A small extension of the last example will provide us with an illustration of this, as well as demonstrating the use of a virtual function across a second level of inheritance.

TRY IT OUT - More than One Level of Inheritance

All we need to do is add the class **CGlassBox** to the classes we have from the previous example. The relationship between the classes we now have is illustrated below.

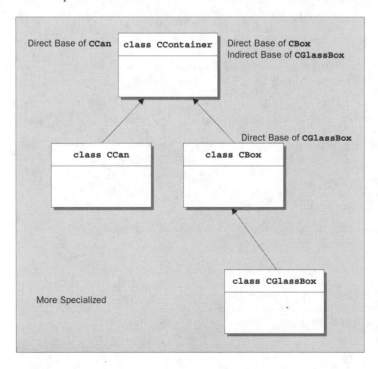

The class **CGlassBox** is derived from the **CBox** class exactly as before, but we will omit the derived class version of **ShowVolume()** to show that the base class version still propagates through the derived classes. With the class hierarchy shown above, the class **CContainer** is an indirect base of the class **CGlassBox**, and a direct base of the classes **CBox** and **CCan**.

Our new example, with an updated function **main()** to use the additional class in the hierarchy, will be as follows:

```cpp
// EX10_11.CPP
// Using an abstract class with multiple levels of inheritance
#include <iostream>                         // For stream I/O
using namespace std;

const double PI = 3.14159265;               // Global definition for PI

class CContainer                            // Generic base class for
{                                           // specific containers
   public:

      // Function for calculating a volume - no content
      // This is defined as a 'pure' virtual function, signified by '= 0'
      virtual double Volume() const = 0;

      // Function to display a volume
      virtual void ShowVolume() const
      {
         cout << endl
            << "Volume is " << Volume();
      }
};

class CBox: public CContainer              // Derived class
{
   public:

      // Function to calculate the volume of a CBox object
      virtual double Volume() const
      { return m_Length*m_Breadth*m_Height; }

      // Constructor
      CBox(double lv = 1.0, double bv = 1.0, double hv = 1.0)
                        :m_Length(lv), m_Breadth(bv), m_Height(hv){}

   protected:
      double m_Length;
      double m_Breadth;
      double m_Height;
};

class CCan: public CContainer
{
   public:

      // Function to calculate the volume of a can
      virtual double Volume() const
      { return 0.25*PI*m_Diameter*m_Diameter*m_Height; }
```

```
        // Constructor
        CCan(double hv = 4.0, double dv = 2.0): m_Height(hv), m_Diameter(dv){}

    protected:
        double m_Height;
        double m_Diameter;
};
```

```
class CGlassBox: public CBox                    // Derived class
{
    public:

        // Function to calculate volume of a CGlassBox
        // allowing 15% for packing
        virtual double Volume() const
        { return 0.85*m_Length*m_Breadth*m_Height; }

        // Constructor
        CGlassBox(double lv, double bv, double hv): CBox(lv, bv, hv){}
};

int main()
{
    // Pointer to abstract base class initialized with CBox object address
    CContainer* pC1 = new CBox(2.0, 3.0, 4.0);

    CCan myCan(6.5, 3.0);                       // Define CCan object
    CGlassBox myGlassBox(2.0, 3.0, 4.0);        // Define CGlassBox object

    pC1->ShowVolume();                          // Output the volume of CBox
    delete pC1;                                 // Now clean up the free store

    // initialized with address of CCan object
    pC1 = &myCan;                               // Put myCan address in pointer
    pC1->ShowVolume();                          // Output the volume of CCan

    pC1 = &myGlassBox;                          // Put myGlassBox address in pointer
    pC1->ShowVolume();                          // Output the volume of CGlassBox

    cout << endl;
    return 0;
}
```

How It Works

We have the three-level class hierarchy shown in the previous illustration, with **CContainer** as an abstract base class, because it contains the pure virtual function, **Volume()**. The function **main()** now calls the function **ShowVolume()** three times, using the same pointer to the base class, but with the pointer containing the address of an object of a different class each time. Since **ShowVolume()** is not defined in any of the derived classes we have here, the base class version is called in each instance. A separate branch from the base **CContainer** defines the derived class **CCan**.

```
Ex10_11

Volume is 24
Volume is 45.9458
Volume is 20.4
Press any key to continue_
```

The example produces the output above, showing that we execute the three different versions of the function **Volume()** according to the type of object involved.

> *Note that we need to delete the **CBox** object from the free store before we assign another address value to the pointer. If we don't do this, we wouldn't be able to clean up the free store, because we would have no record of the original address. This is an easy mistake to make when reassigning pointers and using the free store.*

Virtual Destructors

One problem that arises when dealing with objects of derived classes by using a pointer to the base class is that the correct destructor may not be called. We can show this effect by modifying the last example.

TRY IT OUT - Calling the Wrong Destructor

We just need to add destructors to each of the classes so that we can track which destructor is called when the objects are destroyed. Therefore, the program would be as follows:

```cpp
// EX10_12.CPP
// Destructor calls with derived classes
// using objects via a base class pointer
#include <iostream>                        // For stream I/O
using namespace std;

const double PI = 3.14159265;              // Global definition for PI

class CContainer                           // Generic base class for containers
{
    public:

        // Destructor
        ~CContainer()
        { cout << "CContainer destructor called" << endl; }

        // Insert other members of CContainer as in EX10_11.CPP
};

class CBox: public CContainer              // Derived class
{
    public:
```

```
      // Destructor
      ~CBox()
      { cout << "CBox destructor called" << endl; }

      // Insert other members of CBox as in EX10_11.CPP
};

class CCan: public CContainer
{
   public:

      // Destructor
      ~CCan()
      { cout << "CCan destructor called" << endl; }

      // Insert other members of CCan as in EX10_11.CPP
};

class CGlassBox: public CBox                    // Derived class
{
   public:

      // Destructor
      ~CGlassBox()
      { cout << "CGlassBox destructor called" << endl; }

      // Insert other members of CGlassBox as in EX10_11.CPP
};

int main()
{
   // Pointer to abstract base class initialized with CBox object address
   CContainer* pC1 = new CBox(2.0, 3.0, 4.0);

   CCan myCan(6.5, 3.0);                        // Define CCan object
   CGlassBox myGlassBox(2.0, 3.0, 4.0);         // Define CGlassBox object

   pC1->ShowVolume();                           // Output the volume of CBox
   cout << endl << "Delete CBox" << endl;
   delete pC1;                                  // Now clean up the free store

   pC1 = new CGlassBox(4.0, 5.0, 6.0);          // Create CGlassBox dynamically
   pC1->ShowVolume();                           // ...output its volume...
   cout << endl << "Delete CGlassBox" << endl;
   delete pC1;                                  // ...and delete it

   pC1 = &myCan;                                // Get myCan address in pointer
   pC1->ShowVolume();                           // Output the volume of CCan

   pC1 = &myGlassBox;                           // Get myGlassBox address in pointer
   pC1->ShowVolume();                           // Output the volume of CGlassBox

   cout << endl;
   return 0;
}
```

How It Works

Apart from adding a destructor to each class, which outputs a message to the effect that it was called, the only other change is a couple of additions to the function **main()**. There are additional statements to create a **CGlassBox** object dynamically, output its volume and then delete it. There is also a message displayed to indicate when the dynamically created **CBox** object is deleted. The output generated by this example is shown below:

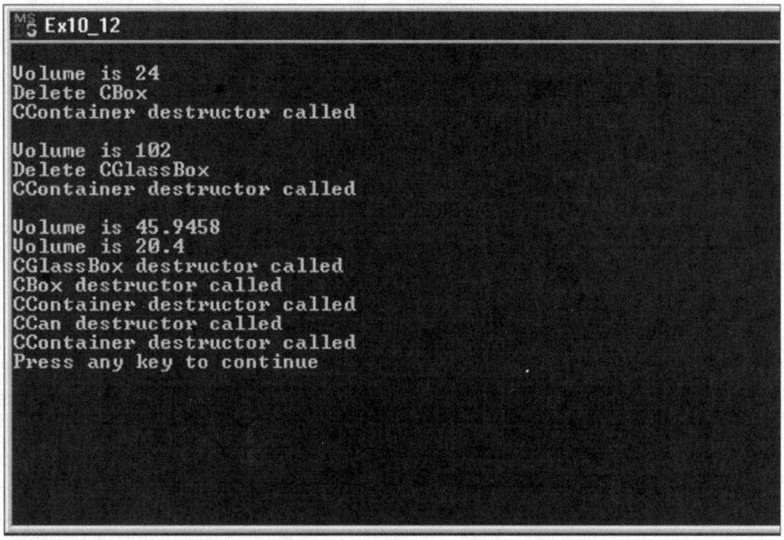

```
Ex10_12

Volume is 24
Delete CBox
CContainer destructor called

Volume is 102
Delete CGlassBox
CContainer destructor called

Volume is 45.9458
Volume is 20.4
CGlassBox destructor called
CBox destructor called
CContainer destructor called
CCan destructor called
CContainer destructor called
Press any key to continue
```

You can see from this that, when we delete the **CBox** object pointed to by **pC1**, the destructor for the base class **CContainer** is called but there is no call of the **CBox** destructor recorded. Similarly, when the **CGlassBox** object that we added is deleted, again the destructor for the base class **CContainer** is called but not the **CGlassBox** or **CBox** destructors. For the other objects, the correct destructor calls occur with the derived class constructor being called first, followed by the base class constructor. For the first **CGlassBox** object created in a declaration, three destructors are called: first, the destructor for the derived class, followed by the direct base destructor and, finally, the indirect base destructor.

All the problems are with objects created in the free store. In both cases, the wrong destructor is called. The reason for this is that the linkage to the destructors is resolved statically, at compile time. For the automatic objects there is no problem — the compiler knows what they are and arranges for the correct destructors to be called.

With objects created dynamically and accessed through a pointer, things are different. The only information that the compiler has when the **delete** operation is executed is that the pointer type is a pointer to the base class. The type of object the pointer is actually pointing to is unknown. The compiler then simply ensures that the **delete** operation is set up to call the base class destructor. In a real application, this can cause a lot of problems, with bits of objects left strewn around the free store and possibly more serious problems, depending on the nature of the objects involved.

The solution is simple. We need the calls to be resolved dynamically as the program is executed. We can organize this by using **virtual destructors** in our classes. As we said when we first discussed virtual functions, it's sufficient to declare the base class function as virtual to ensure that all functions in any derived classes with the same name, parameter list and return type are virtual as well. This applies to destructors just as it does to ordinary member functions. We need to add the keyword **virtual** to the definition of the destructor in the class **CContainer**, so that it becomes as follows:

```
class CContainer                    // Generic base class for containers
{
   public:

      // Destructor
      virtual ~CContainer()
      { cout << "CContainer destructor called" << endl; }

      // Insert other members of CContainer as in Listing 10_10-01
};
```

Now the destructors in all the derived classes are automatically virtual, even though you don't explicitly specify them as such. Of course, you're free to specify them as virtual, if you want the code to be absolutely clear.

If you rerun the example with this modification, it will produce the following output:

As you can see, all the objects are now destroyed with a proper sequence of destructor calls. Destroying the dynamic objects produces the same sequence of destructor calls as the automatic objects of the same type in the program.

The question may arise in your mind at this point, can constructors be declared as virtual? The answer is no – only destructors and other member functions.

> *It's a good idea always to declare your base class destructor as* **virtual** *as a matter of course when using inheritance. There is a small overhead in the execution of the class destructors, but you won't notice it in the majority of circumstances. Using virtual destructors ensures that your objects will be properly destroyed and avoids potential program crashes that might otherwise occur.*

Multiple Inheritance

This is the last major topic before we get to writing some Windows programs, so we are nearly finished with C++ language specifics. This discussion is included because you are certain to become aware of multiple inheritance but, in fact, we don't need to know about it to write Windows programs using Visual C++, and we won't be using it in any of the examples in the book. Multiple inheritance can get you into quite deep water, so we'll just outline the basic considerations here.

All our derived classes so far have had a single direct base class, but we aren't limited to that. In fact, a derived class can have several base classes; this is referred to as **multiple inheritance**. This means, of course, that multiple indirect bases are also possible.

Multiple Base Classes

It's quite difficult to come up with an example of a class with multiple base classes that is based on relationships in the real world. Defining a class, such as **CBox**, in terms of the class **CContainer** reflects the real-world relationship between a box and a container. A box is a form of container, so we are defining a more specific object from a more general one. With most real-world objects, this unidirectional specialization pattern applies. Multiple base classes are often used in practice for the convenience of implementation rather than to reflect any particular relationships between objects.

However, we could consider the example of a **CPackage**, which might be a combination of a **CContainer**, or some specialized form of container such as a **CBox**, together with the contents of the container defined by a class **CContents**. We could define the class **CPackage** as derived from both the class **CBox** and the class **CContents**. This could be represented like so:

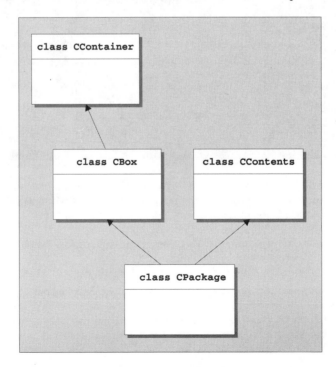

The definition of the class would look like this:

```
class CPackage: public CBox, public CContents
{
    ...
};
```

The class **CPackage** will now inherit all the members of both classes, with the same access specifiers as appear in the definitions of the base classes, since they are defined as **public** base classes. There is no access to members of the base class declared as private, however; the access limitations for inherited class members, which we discussed earlier in this chapter, apply equally well to classes with multiple bases.

Things can get a little more complicated now. For example, it's conceivable that both base classes could have a **public** member function, **Show()**, to display the contents of an object. If so, a statement such as,

```
myPackage.Show();
```

where **myPackage** is an object of the class **CPackage**, will be ambiguous, since the class **CPackage** contains two members with the same name, **Show()**, one inherited from each of the base classes. The compiler has no way of knowing which one should be called, so this will result in an error message. If you need to call one or the other, you have to use the scope resolution operator to specify which of the two functions you want to invoke. For example, you could write this,

```
myPackage.CContents::Show();
```

which makes it quite clear that you want to call the function that is inherited from the class **CContents**.

Virtual Base Classes

A further complication can arise with multiple inheritance if the direct base classes are themselves derived from another class or classes. The possibility arises that both base classes could be derived from a common class. For instance, the classes **CContents** and **CBox**, which we used in the definition of the class package, could be derived from another base called **CRockBottom**. Their definitions could then be something like this:

```
class CContents: public CRockBottom
{
    ...
};

class CBox: public CRockBottom
{
    ...
};
```

Now the class **CPackage** will contain two copies of the members of the class **CRockBottom**, as illustrated here:

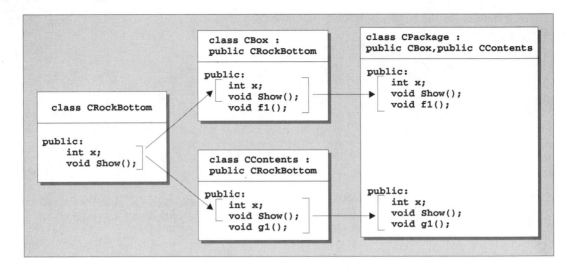

In the class **CPackage**, we end up with two data members called **x**, and two function members **Show()**. The duplication of the members of the indirect base can at best be confusing, and at worst it can cause a lot of problems. However, it's easy to avoid by simply modifying the definitions of the base classes **CBox** and **CContents** such that the class **CRockBottom** is specified as a **virtual base class**. Their definitions in outline would then be as follows:

```
class CContents: public virtual CRockBottom
{
...
};

class CBox: public virtual CRockBottom
{
...
};
```

Now there will be only one instance of the members of the base class **CRockBottom** in any class derived from these two classes, and any problems with the original definition of the class **CPackage** disappear. Specifying the base class as virtual instructs the compiler to make sure that the data members are not duplicated in a derived class, even where there are multiple occurrences of the class as an indirect base.

Summary

In this chapter, we've covered all of the principal ideas involved in using inheritance. The fundamentals that you should keep in mind are these:

▶ A derived class inherits all the members of a base class except for constructors, the destructor and the overloaded assignment operator.

▶ Members of a base class which are declared as **private** in the base class are not accessible in any derived class. To obtain the effect of the keyword **private** but allow access in a derived class, you should use the keyword **protected** in place of **private**.

▶ A base class can be specified for a derived class with the keyword **public**, **private**, or **protected**. If none is specified, the default is **private**. Depending on the keyword specified for a base, the access level of the inherited members may be modified.

▶ If you write a derived class constructor, you must arrange for data members of the base class to be initialized properly, as well as those of the derived class.

▶ A function in a base class may be declared as **virtual**. This allows other definitions of the function appearing in derived classes to be selected at execution time, depending on the type of object for which the function call is made.

▶ You should declare the destructor in a base class containing a virtual function as **virtual**. This will ensure correct selection of a destructor for dynamically-created derived class objects.

▶ A class may be designated as a **friend** of another class. In this case, all the function members of the **friend** class may access all the members of the other class. If class **A** is a **friend** of **B**, class **B** is not a **friend** of **A** unless it has been declared as such.

▶ A virtual function in a base class can be specified as pure by placing **= 0** at the end of the function declaration. The class will then be an abstract class for which no objects can be created. In any derived class, all the pure virtual functions must be defined; if not, it too becomes an abstract class.

▶ A class may be derived from multiple base classes, in which case it inherits members from all of its bases, with the exception of destructors, constructors and overloaded assignment operator functions.

▶ An indirect base class should be specified as **virtual** for derived classes when using multiple inheritance, in order to avoid duplicate occurrences of its data members in a class with multiple bases, two or more of which are derived from the indirect base.

You have now gone through all of the important language features of C++ and it's important that you feel comfortable with the mechanisms for defining and deriving classes and the process of inheritance. With the exception of multiple inheritance, Windows programming with Visual C++ will involve extensive use of all these concepts. If you have any doubts, go back over the last three chapters and try playing around with the source code of the examples related to the areas that you are unsure about. Just to make sure, the next chapter is devoted to a sizable complete example using class inheritance. After that, we will be focusing solely on programming for Windows.

Exercises

Ex10-1: What's wrong with the following code?

```
class CBadClass
{
private:
    int len;
    char* p;
public:
    CBadClass(const char* str): p(str), len(strlen(p)) {}
    CBadClass(){}
};
```

Ex10-2: Suppose we have a class **CBird**, as shown below, which we want to use as a base class for deriving a hierarchy of bird classes:

```
class CBird
{
protected:
    int wingSpan;
    int eggSize;
    int airSpeed;
    int altitude;
public:
    virtual void fly() { altitude = 100; }
};
```

Is it reasonable to create a **CHawk** by deriving from **CBird**? How about a **COstrich**? Justify your answers. Derive an avian hierarchy which can cope with both of these birds.

Ex10-3: Given the following class:

```
class CBase
{
protected:
    int m_anInt;
public:
    CBase(int n): m_anInt(n) { cout << "Base constructor\n"; }
    virtual void Print() const = 0;
};
```

What sort of class is **CBase**, and why? Derive a class from **CBase** which sets its inherited integer value, **m_anInt**, when constructed, and prints it on request. Write a test program to verify that your class is correct.

Ex10-4: Create two classes **CBase_A** and **CBase_B**. **CBase_A** should contain two public member functions **fA()** and **fCommon()**, while **CBase_B** contains **fB()** and **fCommon()**. Each of these functions should do nothing but announce that it has been called. Now create a class **CMulti**, which inherits publicly from both **CBase_A** and **CBase_B**. Write a test program to demonstrate that **CMulti** inherits from both classes. What syntax would you use to call the **fCommon()** function?

Ex10-5: Now change the way in which **CMulti** inherits from its bases from **public** to **private**. Try your test program — how can you make it work as it did before? Can you think of a use for this technique?

An Example Using Classes

In this chapter, we're going to develop an application using a class-based approach to programming. This will provide you with some insight into how to approach a problem from an object-oriented point of view. The example we'll use is that of a calculator like the one we developed in Chapter 6, but this time we're going to build it from an object-oriented perspective.

Although this isn't a perfect candidate for an object-oriented program, having two versions of the calculator will give you a feel for the differences in approach to program design. You'll also see how an object-oriented program looks in comparison to the same problem developed in a traditional way. Our implementation here isn't necessarily ideal, since the objective is to exercise the techniques that we've learnt in the previous chapters in a practical context. It is, however, reasonably efficient and you can get some additional practice by trying out your own ideas on how it should work or by adding functionality to it.

Using Classes

Before we can begin creating our calculator program, we need to decide what objects our problem is concerned with and how they need to behave. Based on that, we'll decide what classes to define to implement the calculator and what operations they'll need to support. Before we get to that stage, however, and well before we get into coding at all, we need to make sure that we have a clear understanding of the problem.

Defining the Problem

We'll aim to create a calculator with the same capabilities as our previous version. It should handle any arithmetic expression involving the operators *, /, + and -, and also allow parentheses to any depth. The only limitation on the complexity of an expression will be that it must be entered on a single input line. Numerical values can be entered with or without a decimal point. A typical expression which the calculator should handle might be:

```
3.5*(2.45*7.1 - 4.7/1.25)*(3+1.5*(8.2-7*125/88.9)/5.7)
```

Spaces can appear anywhere in an expression, and an expression is terminated by pressing the *Enter* key.

We'll also make sure that the calculator will act like a real calculator in that, once a result has been computed, it is retained in the display. When one value has been calculated and displayed, we can then just enter,

`*3`

for example, to multiply it by 3.

Solely for the sake of brevity, we'll also assume that the expressions entered are well formed, so we won't do any error checking. It's not that it's difficult, but it does tend to inflate the number of lines of source code, and we'll have quite a few anyway.

> *Leaving out error checking is the last thing you would do in a real application. Dealing with error conditions is as important as the rest of the program code.*

Analyzing the Problem

Deciding what objects and classes suit a particular problem isn't a clear-cut process; there are no hard and fast rules. Indeed, for many problems, there may be a number of alternative object sets possible, each with their own advantages and disadvantages. However, we can set down some general points about the process which might help:

> ▶ You're not only looking for objects and classes, but also for relationships between them. Representing class and object relationships in a diagram can be very helpful.

> ▶ Approach the problem top-down. Decide what candidates there are for the objects the problem is concerned with and then break these down into their constituents.

> ▶ You can define the outlines of classes as you go along, but you need to be prepared to go back and modify existing classes from time to time, as getting to a final set of classes will often be an iterative process.

> ▶ Remember that classes will not all be representative of physical objects. You may find that quite abstract ideas can be conveniently expressed as a class. Sometimes, the most difficult thing to do is to start. Don't worry about making mistakes. Get some initial ideas down, even if you know they are not quite right. It will give you something to modify and improve.

> ▶ You may find it helpful, as a first pass, to describe the problem and its solution by writing down sentences. You'll often find that the nouns can give you a guide to the classes needed, while the verbs help define the functionality required from the classes.

When you use this approach, you may need to alter your thinking slightly. For example, our particular problem is not so much to perform calculations, but more to model a calculating machine that will perform calculations for us.

Let's begin by modeling our classes on a real calculator. Using a top-down approach, we might start by breaking a calculator into its constituent parts. The most obvious of these are a keyboard for input, a logic unit for processing the input and a display for outputting the results of the calculation. The logic unit will undoubtedly need to use registers, and it will process operations of the kind supported by the calculator. Let's consider these as the initial set of things we need to deal with in our problem. It may not turn out to be the final set, or even that all these are included, but they constitute a reasonable base that we should be able to evolve into something more solid. As mentioned above, developing an application is often an iterative process.

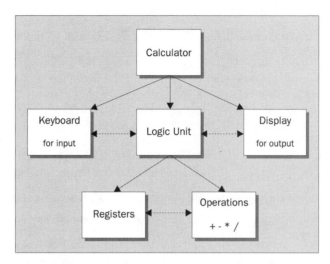

Here you can see a diagram representing our initial thoughts. The blocks represent the main elements of a calculator. Most of them will certainly translate into classes. We can envisage a **CCalculator** class for the whole thing, a **CKeyboard** class, a **CDisplay** class and a **CLogicUnit** class. 'Operations' doesn't seem a likely candidate for a class at the moment, as those sound like actions rather than physical things, but we can't really be certain at this point so let's wait and see. 'Registers' does look like a good prospect for a **CRegister** class, though.

The solid arrows in the diagram indicate an ownership relationship modeled on the real world. A calculator has a keyboard, a logic unit and a display, so we'll give our **CCalculator** class a member of type **CKeyboard**, one of type **CLogicUnit** and one of type **CDisplay**. The dashed arrows indicate a communications requirement, so objects of type **CKeyboard** will need to pass information to objects of type **CLogicUnit**, which in turn will need to communicate with **CDisplay** objects. We'll see how we might take account of this when we get into the detail of the classes.

Deciding Between Class Membership and Class Inheritance

Getting your classes defined with the proper relationships, and deciding when to define classes in an inheritance hierarchy, rather than using class members to create an ownership hierarchy, is of fundamental importance to good object-oriented programs. Unfortunately, this is not always easy and there are no hard and fast rules which will guarantee the desired result. However, we can identify some general guidelines that will help in many cases.

Generally, you should try to reflect the intent of the relationship between a base class and a derived class. A derived class usually represents an object that is a form of the object described by the base class so that, in deriving one class from another, you're going from the general to the particular. In our example, a calculator isn't a type of logic unit, a type of keyboard, or even a type of display, but rather has these things as components, so class derivation isn't appropriate.

Usually, if you can say that one object *is* a version of another, as a chicken is a type of bird, for example, you have a situation where deriving one class from another is appropriate. You could derive a class **CChicken** from a base class **CBird**. An object of class **CChicken**, **Chukkie**, for example, would then be a particular instance of a chicken. You might want to differentiate between birds that can fly, such as owls and eagles, and ones that can't, such as ostriches or penguins. In this case, you could derive two classes, **CFlyingBird** and **CNonFlyingBird**, from the more general class **CBird**, and then derive classes for types of birds from either of these, depending on whether they can fly or not. Objects of each derived class then represent a subset of the objects represented by the base class.

Where an object has another object as a component, as with a chicken having wings, for example, you have a situation where defining objects as members of another class is appropriate. So, a **CChicken** class might contain the member variables **m_LeftWing** and **m_RightWing** of class **CWing**, for example.

This can be summarized by using the *'is a'* versus *'has a'* test:

▶ A chicken *is a* bird, so it's reasonable to derive **CChicken** from the base class **CBird**

▶ A chicken *has a* wing, so it makes sense for **CChicken** to have a member of type **CWing** (and even more sense for it to have two!)

The *'is a'* versus *'has a'* test is quite a good way of deciding which way you should go in defining your classes, particularly when you're starting out with C++. However, it's not a universal or a cast iron method. Sometimes you may need to derive a class from more than one base class, particularly when you're dealing with abstract and complex objects that don't have the simple physical reality of birds. Experience is probably the single most important factor in enhancing your ability to design effective classes in such circumstances.

Let the Coding Commence

It's time to get ourselves into a position where we can actually enter some code, so start a new project workspace for a console application called **Ex11_01**, and we can begin.

We'll be storing the definition of each of our classes in a **.h** file, and the implementation of each class in a **.cpp** file. Remember that in general we add the **.cpp** file to the project and then incorporate the **.h** files into the program by using **#include** directives in the **.cpp** files as necessary. This approach isn't as simple as it sounds with complicated projects, because the sequence of the **#include** directives can affect whether your project compiles successfully.

Where a **.h** file refers directly to another class, you can **#include** the **.h** file for the class required. This can reduce the number of errors arising from class definitions being omitted or **#include** directives being in the wrong sequence, but it can bring problems of its own. By putting **#include** directives in **.h** files, you can very easily have two **.h** files that include each other, and this can cause compilation to fail. It's important that you keep clear in your mind what's being included where in your project if you want to avoid these problems. On balance, the best strategy for keeping your **#include** operations and your files straight involves doing three things:

▶ Always put an incomplete class declaration in your **.h** files for each class that's referenced within the class definition in the **.h** file

▶ Always use the OneTimeInclude macro with your header files that you create yourself to get protection against multiple copies of the header being included in a source file. (The macro adds an **#ifndef/#endif** combination of preprocessor directives that guarantees that the contents of the header will only appear once in a source file. Note that ClassWizard provides this in .h files automatically.

▶ Always put your **#include** directives in the **.cpp** files in a sequence which ensures that each class definition that's included is *preceded* by the **.h** files for any dependent classes; these will be the classes for which you added incomplete class declarations

We'll be developing the code for our application incrementally, so for much of the time the project files will be incomplete. We can create the outline code for a class and its implementation as soon as we have a sufficiently clear view of how it's going to work, and then extend and modify it as we go along. We'll also look at the question of what to include in a file as the project progresses.

Defining the CCalculator Class

One kind of object that we definitely need is a calculator object, so **CCalculator** will be the first class that we will define. Add this class to the project by selecting the menu item Insert | New Class..., and entering the class name in the dialog as shown here.

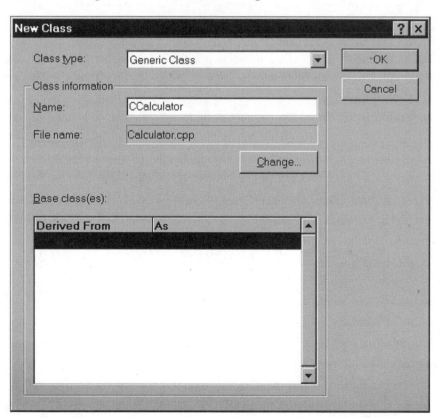

When you click on the OK button, a new source file containing the skeleton class definition will be created and saved in the project directory as **Calculator.h**. You'll also get **Calculator.cpp** created and saved in the same directory, and automatically added to the project. You can see that both of these are there if you switch to FileView by clicking on the tab. You can see the contents of **Calculator.h** if you double click on the filename:

```
// Calculator.h: interface for the CCalculator class.
//
//////////////////////////////////////////////////////////////////////

#if !defined(AFX_CALCULATOR_H__FA599AA3_17DF_11D2_B731_BD7D79977406__INCLUDED_)
#define AFX_CALCULATOR_H__FA599AA3_17DF_11D2_B731_BD7D79977406__INCLUDED_

#if _MSC_VER > 1000
#pragma once
#endif // _MSC_VER > 1000

class CCalculator
{
public:
 CCalculator();
 virtual ~CCalculator();

};

#endif //
!defined(AFX_CALCULATOR_H__FA599AA3_17DF_11D2_B731_BD7D79977406__INCLUDED_)
```

You can see that we've been provided with a comment describing the function of the file and a definition for the **CCalculator** class that includes a constructor and the destructor. The preprocessor commands surrounding the code (the lines beginning with **#**) will ensure that we don't include duplicate definitions of this class; we saw these directives in action back in Chapter 9. The destructor has been declared as **virtual** to cover the possibility that we might use this as a base class. You will recall that if a base class does not have its destructor declared as **virtual**, derived class objects may not be destroyed properly.

Double click on the filename **Calculator.cpp** to take a look at the contents of that:

```
// Calculator.cpp: implementation of the CCalculator class.
//
//////////////////////////////////////////////////////////////////////

#include "Calculator.h"

//////////////////////////////////////////////////////////////////////
// Construction/Destruction
//////////////////////////////////////////////////////////////////////

CCalculator::CCalculator()
{

}

CCalculator::~CCalculator()
{

}
```

Here we have a ready-made **.cpp** file for the class already in the project. It contains a comment describing the function of the file, an **#include** statement for the class's header file, and skeleton definitions for a destructor and the constructor. With the class definition in a **.h** file and the definitions of the member functions in a **.cpp** file, we can make a clear separation between the definition of the class and its implementation.

The class members specified as **public** within the **.h** file form the class interface. The members not declared as **public** will comprise encapsulated data members of the class and functions that are internal to the class's implementation, and therefore not for public consumption. The **.cpp** file will contain the definitions of the function members of the class that aren't defined within the class itself. Usually, only the function members that you want to make inline are defined within the class. All the rest go in the **.cpp** file. Remember that functions you explicitly declare as **inline** must have their definitions in the **.h** file if you are to avoid linker errors.

Communicating Between Classes

Now we need to give a little more thought to the structure of the **CCalculator** class and how we might use objects created from it. As shown in our diagram, a real calculator can be thought of as containing a logic unit to perform individual calculations and control what goes on, a keyboard for input, and a display to show results. We could implement our model from this perspective, but there's something else we need to consider. The logic unit, the display and the keyboard objects need to communicate with one another. We need to devise a way in which information can be passed between the objects that the **CCalculator** owns.

One way in which we can do this is to use the **CCalculator** object itself as the link between the objects it owns. We can store pointers to the objects that are the main components of the calculator, and then create the objects dynamically in the calculator class constructor.

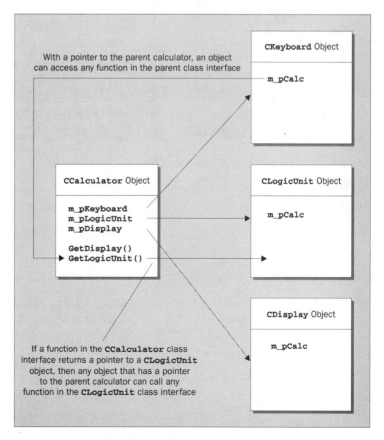

This will allow us to pass to the display, logic unit, and keyboard objects a pointer to the parent calculator, when these objects are created. Any of the objects can then obtain a pointer to any of the other objects through member functions of the **CCalculator** class. To implement this, we'll need three member variables in the **CCalculator** class:

▶ **m_pDisplay** — a pointer to an object of class **CDisplay**

▶ **m_pLogicUnit** — a pointer to an object of class **CLogicUnit**

▶ **m_pKeyboard** — a pointer to an object of class **CKeyboard**.

Adding Data Members to CCalculator

We'll add these variables using the context menu for **CCalculator** provided by the ClassView, so right-click on the class icon for **CCalculator** in the ClassView: ■▪ .This will bring up a menu with many useful options relating to classes. You can ignore most of these for now; just select Add Member Variable... from the menu.

This will bring up the Add Member Variable dialog, which allows you to add variables to your classes easily. Start by adding the variable **m_pDisplay** by setting the dialog options as you see below:

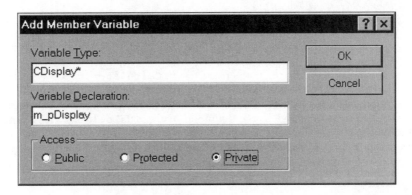

Note that you should set the Access for this variable to **private** by selecting the Private option, since it won't need to be accessible from outside the **CCalculator** class. Now repeat the process to add the pointer variables **m_pLogicUnit** and **m_pKeyboard**, both of which should also be specified as **private**. You'll be able to see the fruits of your labor if you expand the view of the **CCalculator** class in ClassView. Double-clicking on any of the icons for the member variables ![icon] will take you to the corresponding declaration for the variable in **Calculator.h**.

Since we've added member variables of other classes, we need to ensure that the compiler is aware of those classes when it processes this class definition. We can do this by adding an incomplete class declaration for each of the classes we reference in **Calculator.h**. So, double-click on the **CCalculator** class name in ClassView and modify the **.h** file as follows:

```
// Calculator.h: interface for the CCalculator class.
//
//////////////////////////////////////////////////////////////////////

#if !defined(AFX_CALCULATOR_H__FA599AA3_17DF_11D2_B731_BD7D79977406__INCLUDED_)
#define AFX_CALCULATOR_H__FA599AA3_17DF_11D2_B731_BD7D79977406__INCLUDED_

#if _MSC_VER > 1000
#pragma once
#endif // _MSC_VER > 1000

class CDisplay;
class CLogicUnit;
class CKeyboard;

class CCalculator
{
public:
 CCalculator();
 virtual ~CCalculator();

private:
 CKeyboard* m_pKeyboard;
 CLogicUnit* m_pLogicUnit;
 CDisplay* m_pDisplay;
};

#endif //
!defined(AFX_CALCULATOR_H__FA599AA3_17DF_11D2_B731_BD7D79977406__INCLUDED_)
```

You don't get any comments with the Add Member Variable dialog; if you want some you must add them yourself. We've decided that our **CCalculator** class will own a **CKeyboard** object, a **CLogicUnit** object, and a **CDisplay** object, and we'll create these in the class constructor.

You can switch to the definition of the constructor in **Calculator.cpp** by clicking on the + adjacent to the **CCalculator** class name in ClassView, and then double-clicking the constructor name in the extended tree. We also need to add the **#include** directives to **Calculator.cpp** for the classes that are referenced in the definition of the **CCalculator** class. Since **CCalculator** depends on these classes, we should add the includes before the existing **#include** directive for **Calculator.h**. With the definition of the constructor and the **#include** directives added, **Calculator.cpp** will contain:

```
// Calculator.cpp: implementation of the CCalculator class.
//
//////////////////////////////////////////////////////////////////////

#include "Keyboard.h"
#include "LogicUnit.h"
#include "Display.h"
#include "Calculator.h"

//////////////////////////////////////////////////////////////////////
// Construction/Destruction
//////////////////////////////////////////////////////////////////////

CCalculator::CCalculator()
{
    m_pDisplay = new CDisplay(this);        // Create the display
    m_pLogicUnit = new CLogicUnit(this);    // Create the logic unit
    m_pKeyboard = new CKeyboard(this);      // Create the keyboard
}

CCalculator::~CCalculator()
{

}
```

Here we call the constructors for the **CDisplay**, **CLogicUnit** and **CKeyboard** classes, and pass the **this** pointer to each of them. The **this** pointer points to the current object, which will be the **CCalculator** object that is being constructed.

Since we're allocating memory dynamically here, it would be a good time to make sure we delete it properly when we've finished with it, so add the following to the definition of the destructor:

```
CCalculator::~CCalculator()
{
    // Free up memory allocated in the constructor
    delete m_pDisplay;
    delete m_pLogicUnit;
    delete m_pKeyboard;
}
```

Note that it's not necessary to test for a null pointer before using the **delete** operator. Applying the **delete** operator to a null pointer is always harmless. This is perhaps the only situation in C++ where you don't need to worry about the possibility of a pointer being null.

Outlining the CDisplay, CKeyboard, and CLogicUnit Classes

Because of our assumptions about the implementation of the **CCalculator** class, we know that the display, keyboard and logic unit implementation classes must each have a data member to store the pointer to the parent calculator object, and a constructor that accepts such a pointer value as a parameter.

Add the **CLogicUnit** class in the same way as you added the **CCalculator** class. You can then add a constructor to the class by right-clicking the class name in ClassView, selecting Add Member Function... from the pop-up, and completing the dialog as shown:

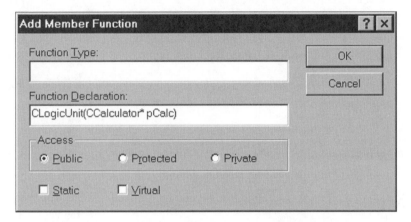

This will add a constructor that accepts a pointer to a **CCalculator** object as an argument. We omit the Function Type: entry here altogether — it's an error to specify a return type for a constructor.

We can also add a data member to the class to store the pointer. Right click on the **CLogicUnit** class name in ClassView and select Add Member Variable... from the pop-up. You can then complete the dialog as shown:

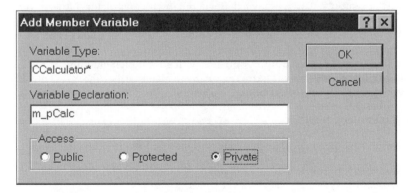

Here we're declaring the member **m_pCalc** as type 'pointer to **CCalculator**', and it's specified **private** as data members normally should be.

Since we've added our own constructor, and we don't really want the default constructor to be used to create objects, we should delete the default constructor from the class definition. We also need to delete its definition in the **LogicUnit.cpp** file. While we're about it we can also add some comments to document the code a little. We can introduce the **CCalculator** class name with an incomplete declaration in the header file. Modify the definition of **CLogicUnit** to:

```
// LogicUnit.h: interface for the CLogicUnit class.
//
//////////////////////////////////////////////////////////////////////

#if !defined(AFX_LOGICUNIT_H__FA599AA6_17DF_11D2_B731_BD7D79977406__INCLUDED_)
#define AFX_LOGICUNIT_H__FA599AA6_17DF_11D2_B731_BD7D79977406__INCLUDED_

#if _MSC_VER > 1000
#pragma once
#endif // _MSC_VER > 1000

class CCalculator;

class CLogicUnit
{
public:
        // Default constructor declaration deleted
  CLogicUnit(CCalculator* pCalc);        // Constructor
  virtual ~CLogicUnit();

  private:
  CCalculator* m_pCalc;                  // Pointer to the parent calculator

};

#endif //
!defined(AFX_LOGICUNIT_H__FA599AA6_17DF_11D2_B731_BD7D79977406__INCLUDED_)
```

Here we have defined our constructor with a pointer to a **CCalculator** object as a parameter. The private data member **m_pCalc** will store the pointer to the parent calculator for use in the member functions of the class. By removing the default constructor, we prevent its use since the compiler will not supply it if we have defined our own constructor. Now if you forget the pointer argument when calling our new constructor, you will get an error message from the compiler. We've also added an incomplete declaration for the **CCalculator** class.

You can now update the **LogicUnit.cpp** file with the implementation of the new constructor, plus the **#include** directive for **Calculator.h**. Remember that the **CCalculator** definition also involves **CDisplay** and **CKeyboard**, so we need to add includes for those files too:

```
// LogicUnit.cpp: implementation of the CLogicUnit class.
//
//////////////////////////////////////////////////////////////////////

#include "Calculator.h"
#include "Display.h"
#include "Keyboard.h"
```

```
#include "LogicUnit.h"

//////////////////////////////////////////////////////////////////////
// Construction/Destruction
//////////////////////////////////////////////////////////////////////

// Default constructor definition deleted

CLogicUnit::~CLogicUnit()
{

}

CLogicUnit::CLogicUnit(CCalculator* pCalc): m_pCalc(pCalc)
{
}
```

All we have at the moment is the constructor, which stores the pointer to the parent calculator, but you can be sure that we'll be adding a lot more member functions as we develop our calculator model.

We can add the **CDisplay** class to the project and update the **Display.h** file similarly to the **CLogicUnit** class:

```
// Display.h: interface for the CDisplay class.
//
//////////////////////////////////////////////////////////////////////

#if !defined(AFX_DISPLAY_H__FA599AA7_17DF_11D2_B731_BD7D79977406__INCLUDED_)
#define AFX_DISPLAY_H__FA599AA7_17DF_11D2_B731_BD7D79977406__INCLUDED_

#if _MSC_VER > 1000
#pragma once
#endif // _MSC_VER > 1000

class CCalculator;

class CDisplay
{
public:
    // Default constructor declaration deleted
    CDisplay(CCalculator* pCalc);    // Constructor
    virtual ~CDisplay();


private:
    CCalculator* m_pCalc;            // Pointer to the parent calculator
};

#endif // !defined(AFX_DISPLAY_H__FA599AA7_17DF_11D2_B731_BD7D79977406__INCLUDED_)
```

You should then amend the **Display.cpp** file so that it contains:

```
// Display.cpp: implementation of the CDisplay class.
//
//////////////////////////////////////////////////////////////////////
```

```
#include "Calculator.h"
#include "Keyboard.h"
#include "LogicUnit.h"
#include "Display.h"

//////////////////////////////////////////////////////////////////////
// Construction/Destruction
//////////////////////////////////////////////////////////////////////

// Default constructor definition dleted

CDisplay::~CDisplay()
{

}
```

```
CDisplay::CDisplay(CCalculator* pCalc): m_pCalc(pCalc)
{

}
```

When you've saved this file you can add the **CKeyboard** class, which will be virtually identical to the other two at this stage. The **.h** file should end up as:

```
// Keyboard.h: interface for the CKeyboard class.
//
//////////////////////////////////////////////////////////////////////

#if !defined(AFX_KEYBOARD_H__FA599AA8_17DF_11D2_B731_BD7D79977406__INCLUDED_)
#define AFX_KEYBOARD_H__FA599AA8_17DF_11D2_B731_BD7D79977406__INCLUDED_

#if _MSC_VER > 1000
#pragma once
#endif // _MSC_VER > 1000

class CCalculator;

class CKeyboard
{
public:
   // Default constructor declaration deleted
   CKeyboard(CCalculator* pCalc);
   virtual ~CKeyboard();

private:
   CCalculator* m_pCalc;       // Pointer to the parent Calculator
};

#endif //
!defined(AFX_KEYBOARD_H__FA599AA8_17DF_11D2_B731_BD7D79977406__INCLUDED_)
```

and **Keyboard.cpp**:

```
// Keyboard.cpp: implementation of the CKeyboard class.
//
//////////////////////////////////////////////////////////////////////
```

```
#include "Calculator.h"
#include "Display.h"
#include "LogicUnit.h"
#include "Keyboard.h"

////////////////////////////////////////////////////////////////////
// Construction/Destruction
////////////////////////////////////////////////////////////////////

// Default constructor definition deleted

CKeyboard::~CKeyboard()
{

}
```

```
CKeyboard::CKeyboard(CCalculator* pCalc):m_pCalc(pCalc)
{

}
```

All the constructors in these classes are very short, so you could equally well have included their definitions within the class definitions; they would then be inline functions.

We now have a stake in the ground for the objects that make up the calculator, but we need to come back to the **CCalculator** class to deal with a very important aspect of its definition.

Making the CCalculator Class Safe to Use

We have created the three objects owned by the **CCalculator** object on the free store. We've also added code to the class destructor to make sure they are deleted properly when a **CCalculator** object is destroyed. Without this, the memory allocated would not be released when a **CCalculator** object is destroyed and we would have a memory leak. However, this isn't enough to ensure our class is safe to use.

We need to recall our golden rules for classes that allocate memory dynamically. We've implemented the destructor, but we must also implement a copy constructor and the assignment operator. We can't afford to allow the possibility of the default versions that the compiler will supply being used, so we should add them now to make sure our class will be safe. Since we don't anticipate needing them, we can just add them as private members of the class. Then there is no possibility of them being called from outside the class, and we don't have to worry about implementing them.

We can add the copy constructor by right-clicking the class name in ClassView, selecting Add Member Function... again, and entering the declaration as **CCalculator(const CCalculator& rCalculator)**. You should make sure the Private radio button is checked.

We can add the assignment operator function to the class in the same way as we did the copy constructor, selecting Private as the Access option:

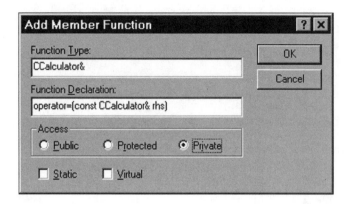

We don't need to add the implementation since it can no longer be used outside of the class.

What we need now is a feel for what the internal operations are. In other words, how exactly is our calculator going to work? We could start by thinking about how to start the calculator.

Starting the Calculator

Execution of our program is going to start in the function **main()**, where two things will need to happen. A calculator must be created, and once created it will need to be switched on. So, **main()** will need to create a **CCalculator** object, and then call a function member of the object to start it going. We could call this function member **Run()** because it runs the calculator. Add a C++ source file to the project with the name **Ex11_01** that will contain **main()**. The function **main()** is going to consist of at least:

```
// EX11_01.CPP - the main() function
#include "Calculator.h"

int main()
{
    CCalculator myCalculator;        // Create a calculator
    myCalculator.Run();              // ...then run it
    return 0;
}
```

For the moment at least we'll assume that everything else that needs to be done in the calculator program will be handled within the function members of our classes.

The **Run()** function in the **CCalculator** class that start things off will need to signal the keyboard to start the input process, but we can't say much more about it at this point. We can add the **Run()** function to the class definition, though: just use the Wizard Bar to do it. The class definition will then be:

```
class CCalculator
{
public:
    void Run() const;
    CCalculator();
    virtual ~CCalculator();
```

```
private:
    CCalculator(const CCalculator& rCalculator);
    CCalculator& operator=(const CCalculator& rhs);

    CKeyboard* m_pKeyboard;         // Pointer to the keyboard
    CLogicUnit* m_pLogicUnit;       // Pointer to the logic unit
    CDisplay* m_pDisplay;           // Pointer to the display
};
```

The **Run()** function is **public**, of course, so we need to specify it as such. We can't define the detail of the implementation of **Run()** yet, but we have a skeleton definition in the **.cpp** file. We may well have to modify its arguments or its return type when we are a little clearer on how it will work. Before we can make progress on that, we need to understand more about what happens in the other classes, so let's start by digging a little into how the keyboard will work.

Calculator Input

The most obvious thing the keyboard object will do is read input from the keyboard of your computer. Since the calculator is supposed to respond to the usual calculator keys, the **CKeyboard** object will need to identify and respond to these appropriately. The keys that need to be recognized are shown in the table below:

Purpose	Keys
For numerical values:	digits 0 to 9, and a decimal point
For operations:	the operators **+ - * /**
For sub-expressions:	left and right parentheses
For end of input:	*Enter* key
To clear the calculator:	The letters *C* or *c*
To quit the calculator:	The letters *Q* or *q*

So what is an appropriate response? As the logic unit has overall responsibility for the operation of the calculator, the **CKeyboard** object will need to send a message to the **CLogicUnit** object indicating which key has been pressed.

We can handle this by having a function in the **CKeyboard** class that gets called by the **Run()** function that starts the calculator. We can call this function **GetKey()**, on the basis that it will get input from the keyboard one key press at a time. As well as reading input from the keyboard, this function will need to signal the logic unit each time a legal calculator key is pressed. The logic unit will then process each key entry appropriately.

We can deduce a couple of things relevant to the internals of our classes from this. The **CLogicUnit** object must have a set of function members to receive the signals from the **CKeyboard** object when different kinds of keys are pressed, and the **CKeyboard** object will need to know about the **CLogicUnit** object that's owned by the **CCalculator** object.

Linking the Keyboard to the Logic Unit

Since we pass a pointer to the parent calculator to the keyboard object when it is created, we just need a function in the **CCalculator** class that will return a pointer to the **CLogicUnit** object. We can call this function **GetLogicUnit()**. Right-click on the **CCalculator** class name in ClassView and select Add Member Function... from the context menu again. Complete the dialog as shown here:

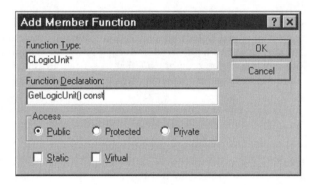

The return type is 'pointer to **CLogicUnit**' and no parameters are necessary. Of course, it needs to have **public** access. We also should declare it as **const** as it doesn't change anything. When you select the OK button you will be able to complete the code for the implementation of the function:

```
CLogicUnit* CCalculator::GetLogicUnit() const
{
    return m_pLogicUnit;                     // Return pointer to the logic unit
}
```

There's not a lot to it — it just returns the address stored in the **m_pLogicUnit** member. We can use this in the **CKeyboard** function that will handle input for the calculator.

Handling Keyboard Input

Add the **GetKey()** function to the **CKeyboard** class using the context menu in ClassView. You can specify a **void** return type and an empty parameter list for the moment, and the function should have **public** access. Since it won't change any data members of **CKeyboard**, you can declare it as **const**. We know what keys the keyboard is supposed to deal with, and that for each kind of key press detected, the **GetKey()** function will need to send a message to the **CLogicUnit** class.

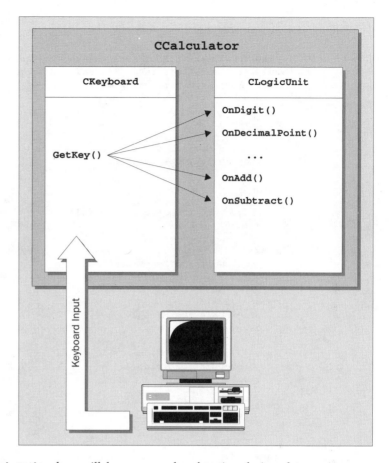

Here, you can see the relationship between the classes:

We can assume that the **CLogicUnit** class will have a member function designed to process each of the possible kinds of input. The **GetKey()** function will need to read one character at a time and send a message to the logic unit appropriate to that character; we can store the character read in a variable **chKey**. We'll continue reading characters in a loop until **'q'** or **'Q'** is entered, so we'll use a flag variable **bExit** to control when to end the loop. On this basis, we can implement **GetKey()** as:

```cpp
// Keyboard manager function
void CKeyboard::GetKey() const
{
    // Get a pointer to the logic unit
    CLogicUnit* pLogicUnit = m_pCalc->GetLogicUnit();

    char chKey = 0;                 // Key press stored here
    bool bExit = false;             // Flag to end calculator operation

    while(!bExit)                   // Get key presses until there's
    {                               // a reason not to...
        chKey = cin.get();          // Get a key depression

        switch (chKey)              // Test key press
        {
```

```
        case ' ':                               // For blank...
          break;                                // ...do nothing

        case '0': case '1': case '2': case '3': case '4':
        case '5': case '6': case '7': case '8': case '9':
          // For any digit send numeric value of digit to the logic unit
          pLogicUnit->OnDigit(chKey - '0');
          break;

        case '.':
          // Send decimal point to the logic unit
          pLogicUnit->OnDecimalPoint();
          break;

        case '(':                               // Left parenthesis
          pLogicUnit->OnLeftParenthesis();
          break;

        case ')':                               // Right parenthesis
          pLogicUnit->OnRightParenthesis();
          break;

        case '*':
          pLogicUnit->OnMultiply();              // Send a multiply message
          break;

        case '/':
          pLogicUnit->OnDivide();                // Send a divide message
          break;

        case '+':
          pLogicUnit->OnAdd();                   // Send an add message
          break;

        case '-':
          pLogicUnit->OnSubtract();              // Send a subtract message
          break;

        case 'Q': case 'q':                      // Quit key pressed
          bExit = true;                          // So set flag to exit
          break;

        case 'c': case 'C':                      // Clear key pressed
          pLogicUnit->Reset();                   // so reset the logic unit
          break;

        case '\n':                               // Enter key pressed
          pLogicUnit->OnEnter();                 // Send Enter message
          break;

        default:                                 // Wrong key pressed
          bExit = true;                          // so set flag to exit
    }
  }
  return;
}
```

This looks like a lot of code, but it's actually very simple. The whole thing is a **while** loop containing a big **switch**. The loop will continue until a **'Q'** or **'q'** is entered to quit the calculator. The first line of the while loop,

```
chKey = cin.get();                    // Get a key depression
```

extracts a single character from the input stream and stores it in the variable **chKey**. Within the **while** loop, the **switch** statement analyses this character and calls a corresponding function member of the logic unit object, using the address that we store locally in **pLogicUnit** for that purpose.

When a legal key is pressed, the appropriate **case** statements are executed, we break out of the **switch** statement, and go to another cycle of the **while** loop. Each of the **case**s simply calls the relevant function of the **CLogicUnit** class, which will then do the real processing. If the character read is a space, it's ignored and another character is read. For any digit key that's pressed, the numeric value (not the ASCII value) is passed to the **OnDigit()** function of the **CLogicUnit** object. We get the numeric value by subtracting the ASCII value of zero from the digit character. A decimal point causes the **OnDecimalPoint()** function to be invoked. We call a separate function for each arithmetic operation key that's pressed, and we also call separate functions for left and right parentheses. If **'C'** or **'c'** is entered, then we want to clear the calculator by calling the **Reset()** function.

When **'Q'** or **'q'** is entered, we set **bExit** to **true** to end the loop and return from the function. Remember that the **GetKey()** function is called from the **Run()** member function of **CCalculator**, which in turn is called from **main()**, so returning from **GetKey()** will eventually get back to **main()** and the program will end. We will reach the **default** case in the **switch** if any key other than the keys we recognize is pressed. For the moment we just set **bExit** to **true** so that the loop terminates and the function returns as if the quit key was pressed, but we will come back and look at this again later.

You need to add an **#include** directive to the top of the file,

```
#include <iostream>
```

and the using directive:

```
using namespace std;
```

This is to get access to the input capability we need in the function. We could dispense with the **using** directive if we wrote the statement to read a character as:

```
chKey = std::cin.get();              // Get a key depression
```

So that we don't forget it, we can add a statement to the definition of **Run()** in **Calculator.cpp** to call **GetKey()**:

```
void CCalculator::Run()const
{
    m_pKeyboard->GetKey();               // Start keyboard input
}
```

This uses the pointer to the **CKeyboard** object to call its **GetKey()** member.

449

Implementing the Logic Unit

From our efforts with the **GetKey()** member of **CKeyboard**, we have established quite a lot of the functionality required in **CLogicUnit**. You can add all the functions we assumed to be available in **CLogicUnit** when we wrote the **GetKey()** function. The class definition will then be:

```
class CLogicUnit
{
public:
    // Process messages from the keyboard
    void Reset();
    void OnEnter();
    void OnAdd();
    void OnSubtract();
    void OnDivide();
    void OnMultiply();
    void OnDecimalPoint();
    void OnDigit(int digit);
    void OnLeftParenthesis();
    void OnRightParenthesis();
    CLogicUnit(CCalculator* pCalc);      // Constructor
    virtual ~CLogicUnit();               // Destructor

private:
    CCalculator* m_pCalc;                // Pointer to the parent Calculator
};
```

You can either add these functions by using the context menu for **CLogicUnit**, or by using the down arrow on the Wizard Bar. Either method will also add skeleton definitions for the functions to the **.cpp** file. The **OnDigit()** function is the only one here that requires an argument — this will communicate the digit that was entered.

> *Remember to add comments to your code to help you understand the code at a later date,*
> *particularly when you use ClassView's context menus or the Wizard Bar to add members,*
> *as it's easy to forget them when using these mechanisms.*

Logic Unit Registers

We're obviously going to need somewhere to store values as they are passed to the logic unit, so that means we need some member variables for the class. In order to maintain correspondence with our conceptual model of a calculator, we won't implement these member variables as simple data types; we'll give them their own functionality by creating them as objects of a new class: **CRegister**.

What registers are we likely to need? We need a display register to hold the value of any result that will appear on the display, and also at least two others. When we discussed arithmetic expressions in the context of the previous calculator implementation in Chapter 6, we determined that an expression breaks down into a series of terms connected by addition or subtraction operators. The terms themselves are a series of numbers or parenthesized expressions connected by multiply or divide operators. This suggests that we'll need a multiply register to hold the value of a term, and an add register to hold any intermediate result that's a combination of one or more terms. We can illustrate how these three registers will be used by considering how an expression such as 2*3/4+5 would be evaluated:

Expression	Action	Registers
*2 * 3 / 4 + 5 Enter*	Put the operand in the display register	Display = 2 Multiply = 0 Add = 0
*2 * 3 / 4 + 5 Enter*	Remember the multiply operation Execute any previous multiply or divide Save the display register in the multiply register	Display = 2 Multiply = 2 Add = 0
*2 * 3 / 4 + 5 Enter*	Put the operand in the display register	Display = 3 Multiply = 2 Add = 0
*2 * 3 / 4 + 5 Enter*	Remember the divide operation Execute the previous multiply — result in display register Save the display register in the multiply register	Display = 6 Multiply = 6 Add = 0
*2 * 3 / 4 + 5 Enter*	Put the operand in the display register	Display = 4 Multiply = 6 Add = 0
*2 * 3 / 4 + 5 Enter*	Remember the add operation Execute the previous divide — result in display register Execute any outstanding add or subtract Save the display register in the add register	Display = 1.5 Multiply = 1.5 Add = 1.5
*2 * 3 / 4 + 5 Enter*	Put the operand in the display register	Display = 5 Multiply = 1.5 Add = 1.5
*2 * 3 / 4 + 5 **Enter***	Execute any outstanding multiply or divide Execute any previous add—result in display register	Display = 6.5 Multiply = 1.5 Add = 6.5

As there is never more than one add/subtract and one multiply/divide operation outstanding, three registers will be sufficient for any expression that doesn't involve parentheses. We'll worry about parentheses as soon as we have simple arithmetic expressions working. We could call the three registers we need in the **CLogicUnit** class **m_DisplayReg**, **m_MultiplyReg**, and **m_AddReg** respectively.

A register is an electronic store for data, and is a component of a logic unit. Since a logic unit *'has a'* register, defining **CRegister** objects as members of the **CLogicUnit** class, rather than relating them by inheritance, is consistent with reality. You can add the three data members representing the registers as variables of type **CRegister**, and make them **private** members of the class. You'll need to add the data members to the **CLogicUnit** class definition using the class context menu, and a partial definition of the **CRegister** class to the top of the file. You'll also need to add an **#include** directive for the file that will contain the definition of **CRegister** at the beginning of **LogicUnit.cpp**. Here's the current state of **LogicUnit.h**:

```
// LogicUnit.h: interface for the CLogicUnit class.
//
//////////////////////////////////////////////////////////////////////

#if !defined(AFX_LOGICUNIT_H__FA599AA6_17DF_11D2_B731_BD7D79977406__INCLUDED_)
#define AFX_LOGICUNIT_H__FA599AA6_17DF_11D2_B731_BD7D79977406__INCLUDED_

#if _MSC_VER > 1000
#pragma once
#endif // _MSC_VER > 1000

class CCalculator;
class CRegister;

class CLogicUnit
{
public:
    // Process messages from the keyboard
    void Reset();
    void OnEnter();
    void OnAdd();
    void OnSubtract();
    void OnDivide();
    void OnMultiply();
    void OnDecimalPoint();
    void OnDigit(int digit);
    void OnLeftParenthesis();
    void OnRightParenthesis();
    CLogicUnit(CCalculator* pCalc);      // Constructor
    virtual ~CLogicUnit();

private:
    CRegister m_DisplayReg;              // Value to be displayed
    CRegister m_AddReg;                  // Result of add or subtract
    CRegister m_MultiplyReg;             // Result of divide or multiply
    CCalculator* m_pCalc;                // Pointer to the parent calculator

};

#endif //
    !defined(AFX_LOGICUNIT_H__FA599AA6_17DF_11D2_B731_BD7D79977406__INCLUDED_)
```

Of course, we'll need to define the **CRegister** class, but in order to understand what capabilities the class should provide, we should first investigate what the functions that handle the keyboard messages for digits and a decimal point in **CLogicUnit** are going to do, since these originate the initial content for a register. When we've done that, we can come back to **CRegister** with a clearer idea of what is required.

A good thing to do at this point is to consider where we've included the **CLogicUnit** class definition into other **.cpp** files, because we'll need an **#include** directive for **Register.h** in each of them. The files affected are **Calculator.cpp**, **Keyboard.cpp**, and **Display.cpp**. The **#include** for **Register.h** must precede the **#include** for **LogicUnit.h**, otherwise the code won't compile. We're adding actual **CRegister** objects to the logic unit (rather than just pointers to them), so the compiler needs to know exactly what they comprise before it can process the **CLogicUnit** files.

Handling Digits

The **OnDigit()** function member of **CLogicUnit** will need to send the digit to the display register, as that's normally how a calculator operates. It would be reasonable to assume that the **CRegister** class will contain a function to accept a digit from somewhere, so we could write this function as:

```
// Send a digit to the display register
void CLogicUnit::OnDigit(int digit)
{
    m_DisplayReg.OnDigit(digit);
}
```

This function receives the digit as a reference and passes it on to the **OnDigit()** member function of the **m_DisplayReg** object. The object will have responsibility for assembling the input value from a succession of digits (and possibly a decimal point) that are passed to it. There's no problem with having a function called **OnDigit()** in both the **CRegister** class and the **CLogicUnit** class; they can only be called in the context of a particular object which will be a member of one class or the other, so there's no risk of confusion. It's also reasonable to give them the same name, since they do much the same sort of thing in context.

Handling a Decimal Point

To handle a decimal point in the **CLogicUnit** class, we can implement the function **OnDecimalPoint()** so that it simply passes the message on to the appropriate **CRegister** object. We can call the **CRegister** class function by the same name here as well:

```
// Send a point to display register
void CLogicUnit::OnDecimalPoint()
{
    m_DisplayReg.OnDecimalPoint();
}
```

This function and the previous one cover everything necessary in the **CLogicUnit** class to handle numeric input. Because these functions are very simple, you could declare them as inline to make the program run a little faster. This would mean adding an **inline** keyword and transferring these definitions to the **LogicUnit.h** file, or putting the function definitions within the class definition itself.

Since the onus is on the register to sort out the value of the input from a sequence of digits and a decimal point, this perhaps is a good point for us to digress into the **CRegister** class. We'll come back and fill in the rest of the detail of the **CLogicUnit** class later.

The CRegister Class

We've already identified two functions that we need a **CRegister** object to have, so we can put a stake in the ground with a first stab at a definition for the class. You can add the class to the project using the down arrow on the Wizard Bar and selecting New Class... from the menu. Next, make sure that **CRegister** is displayed in the leftmost drop-down list box; you can then use the Add Member Function... option from the down arrow menu to add the **OnDigit()** and **OnDecimalPoint()** members. Your class definition should then look like:

```
// Register.h: interface for the CRegister class.
//
//////////////////////////////////////////////////////////////////////

#if !defined(AFX_REGISTER_H__FA599AA9_17DF_11D2_B731_BD7D79977406__INCLUDED_)
#define AFX_REGISTER_H__FA599AA9_17DF_11D2_B731_BD7D79977406__INCLUDED_

#if _MSC_VER > 1000
#pragma once
#endif // _MSC_VER > 1000

class CRegister
{
public:
    void OnDecimalPoint();              // Function to handle a decimal point
    void OnDigit(int digit);            // Function to handle a keyed digit
    CRegister();
    virtual ~CRegister();

};

#endif //
!defined(AFX_REGISTER_H__FA599AA9_17DF_11D2_B731_BD7D79977406__INCLUDED_)
```

A register will need somewhere to store a numeric value, so we can add a member **m_Store** of type **double** using the class context menu. There's no reason to put the **m_Store** data member in the public domain, so we'll put it in the **private** section of the class. Consequently, all references to it and operations on it will be through interface functions in the **public** section. Accepting a digit will involve doing different things depending on whether the digit precedes or follows a decimal point. We should, therefore, first consider how we handle a decimal point.

Handling a Decimal Point in CRegister

The effect of receiving a decimal point is to change the way that a digit is handled. Before a decimal point is received, processing a digit will involve multiplying the value of the **m_Store** member by 10 (freeing up the 'units' position in the number), then adding the digit value to **m_Store**. We're essentially adding the new digit at the right hand end of the number we are creating.

After a decimal point is received, we still add the digit on the right, but we need to keep track of the current decimal place. For the first digit after the decimal point, we should multiply the digit value by 0.1 before adding it to the member **m_Store**. For the second digit after a decimal point, we multiply the digit by 0.01 before adding it to **m_Store**. For each additional digit after the decimal point, the value that multiplies the digit before adding it to **m_Store** decreases by a factor of 10.

To implement this process, we can declare a data member **m_Factor** of type **double** in the **CRegister** class, which will act both as an indicator that we have received a decimal point and as a factor by which to multiply a digit once a decimal point has been received. We'll initially set **m_Factor** to zero. As long as it remains zero, we know that no decimal point has been received. As soon as a decimal point *is* received, we'll set **m_Factor** to 1.0. For each successive digit received after that, we'll multiply **m_Factor** by 0.1 before using it as a multiplier for the digit received.

We also need to take account of the case when a decimal point is the first key press sent to a **CRegister** object. This will necessitate using a **bool** indicator that we can name as **m_bBeginValue**, which will signal when we're starting to enter a new value into a register. We'll also use this to mark when we have come to the end of a value in a register by indicating that a new value is being started. Initially, when the **CRegister** object is created, we'll set **m_bBeginValue** to **true** to indicate that we're starting a new value. The first valid character passed to a register will set the **m_bBeginValue** indicator to **false**, and the value in **m_Store** to 0.0. When the end of an input value is found, **m_bBeginValue** will be set back to **true** again.

Once you've added **m_Factor** of type **double**, and **m_bBeginValue** of type **bool** to the class as **private** members, you can add code to the **OnDecimalPoint()** function to set the data member **m_Factor** when a decimal point is keyed:

```
// Handle a decimal point
void CRegister::OnDecimalPoint()
{
    if(m_bBeginValue)              // Check if we are starting a new number
    {
        m_bBeginValue = false;     // If so, set the indicator to false
        m_Store = 0.0;             // and reset the value in the member m_Store
    }

    m_Factor = 1.0;                // Set the decimal point indicator
}
```

This function will be called by the **CLogicUnit** object when a decimal point is signaled to it by the **CKeyboard** object. The function first checks the **m_bBeginValue** flag. This could be set if the decimal point was the first key pressed when entering a number, as would be the case in an expression such as **2*.75**. If so, it sets the **m_bBeginValue** flag to zero and resets the member **m_Store**. In any event, it will set the value of the data member **m_Factor** to 1.0, which will trigger correct processing of digits to the right of a decimal point in the function **OnDigit()** in the **CRegister** class.

Handling a Digit in CRegister

We can show the logic for handling a digit in the form of a flow chart. This is shown here:

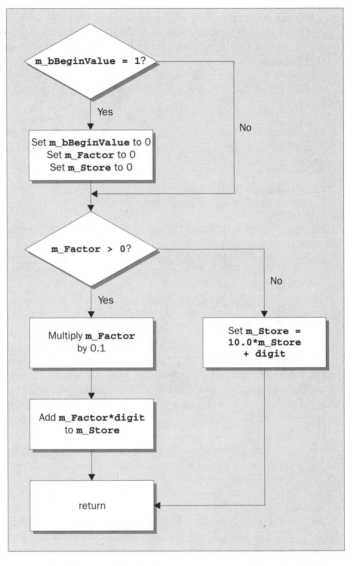

The first action is to test the **m_bBeginValue** flag, to check if we're starting a new value. If we are, the flag is reset and the values of **m_Store** and **m_Factor** are reset to zero. Otherwise, we go straight to checking whether **m_Factor** is positive, which would indicate that we have previously received a decimal point. If we have, we're adding the digit as the last decimal place to the right of the decimal point. If we haven't, we're adding the digit at the 'units' position, after multiplying the current value in **m_Store** by 10.

So, from the flowchart, the code for the **OnDigit()** function in the **CRegister** class will be:

```cpp
// Function to accept a keyed digit
void CRegister::OnDigit(int digit)
{
    if(m_bBeginValue)                    // Check if we are at the start of a number,
    {                                    // if so reset the CRegister components
        m_bBeginValue = false;           // Reset begin flag
        m_Store = 0.0;                   // Reset storage
        m_Factor = 0.0;                  // Reset decimal point factor
    }

    if(m_Factor > 0.0)                   // Test decimal point factor,
    {                                    // positive value indicates decimals
        m_Factor *= 0.1;                 // Shift decimal place
        m_Store += digit*m_Factor;           // Add digit to storage
    }
    else
        m_Store = 10.0 * m_Store + digit;        // Add digit to storage
}
```

This is a straightforward implementation of the logic shown in the flowchart, so we won't spend any more time on it. Just add the shaded lines to the function definition in the **.cpp** file for **CRegister**.

Service Functions for a Register

We'll need interface functions to get and set the value of **m_Store**, as well as a 'set' capability for the **m_bBeginValue** flag. The **Get()**/**Set()** combination of member functions — sometimes in the form **GetValue()**/**SetValue()** when there are several data members — comes up quite frequently in classes. Functions that return and set the values of class variables are named in this way by convention. Data members accessed in this way are also referred to as **class properties**. Since in general it is desirable to keep data members **private**, these functions make the value of a data member accessible from outside the class. You might think there's a bit of a contradiction in allowing the value of a **private** member to be set — after all, you could just make the data member that can be altered from outside the class **public** — but by using a **Set()** function to change it, you also have an opportunity to do some validity checking on a new value.

We could also include a **Reset()** function in the **CRegister** class to reset the **m_Factor** and **m_bBeginValue** members, as well as **m_Store**. A constructor that resets everything is also a fairly fundamental requirement. We would also need to reset the registers if the user presses **'c'** or **'C'** to clear the calculator. We can extend the **CRegister** class by adding a **Get()**/ **Set()** pair of functions to operate on the **m_Store** member and a **SetBeginValue()** function to set the value of **m_bBeginValue**. With these capabilities added, the class definition will be:

```cpp
class CRegister
{
public:
    void Reset();                        // Reset the data members
    void SetBeginValue();                // Set the m_BeginValue flag
    double Get() const;                  // Get the value of m_Store
    void Set(const double& value);       // Set the value of m_Store
    void OnDecimalPoint();               // Function to handle a decimal point
    void OnDigit(const int& digit);      // Function to handle a keyed digit
    CRegister();
    virtual ~CRegister();
```

```
private:
   int m_bBeginValue;                  // New value flag
   double m_Factor;                    // Factor for digits after a decimal point
   double m_Store;                     // Register value
};
```

You can now complete the function member definitions in the **.cpp** file. If you used the context menu or the Wizard Bar to add the new functions to the class, you will just need to add the code to the body of each function:

```
// Constructor
CRegister::CRegister()
{
   Reset();                           // Initialize the data members
}
```

```
// Initialize the flag indicating a new number
void CRegister::SetBeginValue()
{
   m_bBeginValue = true;
}
```

```
// Reset the register
void CRegister::Reset()
{
   m_Store = 0.0;
   m_Factor = 0.0;
   m_bBeginValue = true;
}
```

```
// Set the register value
void CRegister::Set(const double& value)
{
   m_Store = value;
}
```

```
// Get the register value
double CRegister::Get() const
{
   return m_Store;
}
```

All the functions that we have implemented here are very simple, so they too are candidates to be inline. Rather than duplicate perfectly good code, we use the **Reset()** function to provide the initialization required in the constructor. Since we have no dynamically allocated members, we don't need to worry about the destructor, or about writing a copy constructor.

Arithmetic Operations on Registers

A fundamental capability that we need to consider is arithmetic operations on **CRegister** objects. The arithmetic operations in our calculator will always be between two **CRegister** objects, with the result being placed in one of the **CRegister** objects, so we could implement all of them as overloaded **op=** operators. You need to add four operator functions to the **public** section of the class definition:

```
    CRegister& operator-=(const CRegister& rhs);
    CRegister& operator+=(const CRegister& rhs);
    CRegister& operator/=(const CRegister& rhs);
    CRegister& operator*=(const CRegister& rhs);
```

Use either the class context menu or the Wizard Bar to add these. The prototypes of all these functions are much the same; you'll be getting quite familiar with how they look by the time we've finished this example!

You can switch to the **.cpp** file to fill out the code for these members. The definition of the **+=** operator function is:

```
// += operation
CRegister& CRegister::operator+=(const CRegister& rhs)
{
    m_Store += rhs.m_Store;
    return *this;
}
```

This has a **const** reference parameter to avoid copying of the argument and, out of necessity, returns a reference. You'll remember that returning a reference is essential if you want to be able to use the result on the left of another assignment operation, because doing so returns an lvalue. This is a model for all of the **op=** operator functions.

> *It's not required here, but if you needed to implement a function such as **operator+()**, for example, you could use the **operator+=()** function to do it very neatly, as follows:*

```
// Addition operator function using += operator function
CRegister operator+(const CRegister& reg1, const CRegister& reg2)
{
    CRegister temp(reg1);      // Temporary object
                               // initialized with R1
    return temp += reg2;       // Return R1+R2
}
```

> *This will call the default copy constructor to create the object **temp**. If any data member of* **CRegister** *was created dynamically, you would need to implement the copy constructor yourself.*

With the arithmetic operators for **CRegister** objects added, our class will be finished. The three remaining functions you need to add are:

```
// -= operation
CRegister& CRegister::operator-=(const CRegister& rhs)
{
  m_Store -= rhs.m_Store;
  return *this;
}
```

```
// /= operation
CRegister& CRegister::operator/=(const CRegister& rhs)
{
  m_Store /= rhs.m_Store;
  return *this;
}
```

```
// *= operation
CRegister& CRegister::operator*=(const CRegister& rhs)
{
  m_Store *= rhs.m_Store;
  return *this;
}
```

Now we need to come back to the **CLogicUnit** class for our calculator and decide how arithmetic operations are going to be executed.

Handling Arithmetic Operations

The obvious approach to implementing arithmetic operations might seem to be to add a set of interface functions to the **CLogicUnit** class to do them, but it isn't that straightforward. If we consider what happens when an operation key is pressed, and the table we produced when we first discussed the register class, we'll get a better idea of what's required. Look at the position in the diagram here:

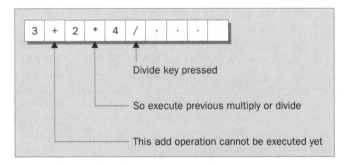

When the divide key is pressed, we can't actually execute a divide, as we haven't yet got the right-hand operand value. At this point, we must execute the previous multiply or divide operation (whichever it was), and then save the operation just entered. Note that we can't execute any previous add or subtract at this time; that can only be triggered by the user pressing another add or subtract key, or the *Enter* key. This situation is illustrated here:

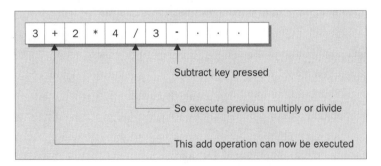

A simple set of functions won't really hack it, since an operation is always deferred. There's more than one way to deal with this, but we could use inheritance and polymorphism. So how would that work?

If we define an arithmetic operation as an object of a derived class, we could save the current operation in a pointer, ready to be executed when the next triggering operation comes along. Since we will be triggering the execution of an operation some time after the object was created, we won't know what it was, but we can use a virtual function call through a pointer to sort it out when the operation is ultimately executed. We'll need to add two data members to the **CLogicUnit** class: one to be used to store an add or subtract operation object, and the other a multiply or divide operation object. But let's look first at the classes that we need to define the operations.

Defining a Base Class for Arithmetic Operations

The classes will represent arithmetic operations as objects. A base class for arithmetic operations really only needs a **virtual** member function to execute an operation. Since an operation will act on **CRegister** objects, an operation class won't need any data members at all. The function to execute an operation will be redefined in each of the derived classes, corresponding to a specific operation in each case.

First, create a new class, **COperation**, using the Wizard Bar. We want the function to execute operations to be a pure virtual function in the base class, since there's no sensible implementation here. Add the function by using the context menu with the dialog data entered as shown here.

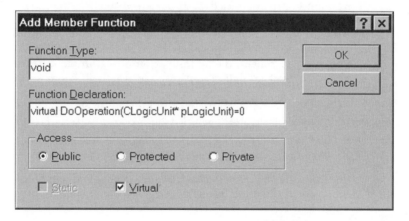

Clicking on the Virtual checkbox will insert the **virtual** keyword in the declaration, and since you entered **=0** after the parameter list, the generation of an implementation in the **.cpp** file will be suppressed. A basic assumption we're making here is that the registers that an operation will act on are owned by a **CLogicUnit** object. Because an operation object will need to know about the **CLogicUnit** object involved, a pointer will be passed as an argument to the **DoOperation()** function to identify the **CLogicUnit** object in question.

After adding a partial definition and a comment, the **.h** file for the base class for arithmetic operations will contain the following:

```
// Operation.h: interface for the COperation class.
//
//////////////////////////////////////////////////////////////////////

#if !defined(AFX_OPERATION_H__FA599AAA_17DF_11D2_B731_BD7D79977406__INCLUDED_)
#define AFX_OPERATION_H__FA599AAA_17DF_11D2_B731_BD7D79977406__INCLUDED_
```

```
#if _MSC_VER > 1000
#pragma once
#endif // _MSC_VER > 1000

class CLogicUnit;

class COperation
{
public:
 //Pure virtual function
 virtual void DoOperation(CLogicUnit* pLogicUnit) = 0;
 COperation();
 virtual ~COperation();

};

#endif //
!defined(AFX_OPERATION_H__FA599AAA_17DF_11D2_B731_BD7D79977406__INCLUDED_)
```

This is an abstract base class for the classes which will represent add, subtract, multiply and divide operations. It's abstract because it contains a pure virtual function, and therefore objects of this class can't be constructed.

The **DoOperation()** function will be used by the relevant interface function in the **CLogicUnit** class (**OnAdd()**, **OnDivide()**, etc.) when an arithmetic operation is actually carried out. Since it's declared as **virtual**, the derived class versions can be selected through a pointer to this base class. Although we can't create objects of an abstract base class, we *can* create pointers to it. The pointer will contain the address of an object of one of the derived classes that will represent an add, a subtract, a multiply or a divide. This will allow us to save any operation in a pointer and execute it properly later, without remembering explicitly what it was. Since the **DoOperation()** function is specified as pure, it must be redefined in the derived classes. They would otherwise be abstract, which would prevent objects being created from them. However, since the function **DoOperation()** will be the only member of each derived class, we're unlikely to overlook it!

The destructor in the **COperation** class is automatically declared as **virtual** to ensure that the correct derived class destructor is called when dynamically created objects of the derived classes are deleted. As we noted in the discussion on inheritance, it's always a good idea to declare the destructor for a base class as **virtual**.

You need to add **#include** directives for **Register.h** and **LogicUnit.h** to **Operation.cpp**.

Deriving Classes for Arithmetic Operations

The derived classes are going to be very simple — they will each just define their own version of the **virtual** function **DoOperation()**. You can add these class definitions using the Wizard Bar. Let's start with multiply. You need to enter the name of the base class in the New Class dialog. Just click on the space below the Derived From heading in the dialog box and key it in.

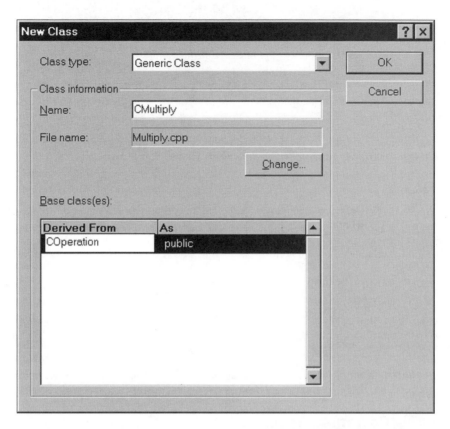

Notice how you get the access specifier for the base class set as **public** by default. That's fine in this case, but if you did want to change it, clicking on the keyword will change the keyword entry to a drop down list box from which you can select the other access specifiers.

When you've created the class, you can add the **DoOperation()** function using the class context menu or the Wizard Bar. Complete the dialog as shown here:

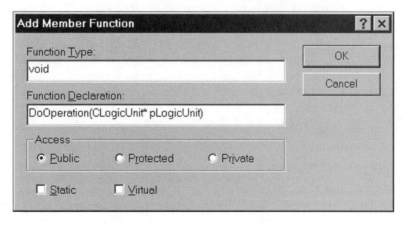

Because we intend this to be a virtual function, the parameter list must be the same as that of the base class function. You can check the Virtual box if you want, but it isn't essential — declaring the base class function as **virtual** is sufficient to get polymorphism working. We'll need an incomplete declaration of **CLogicUnit** before the class definition and we'll also need **#include** directives for **Register.h** and **LogicUnit.h** in the **.cpp** file.

You need to repeat the whole process in exactly the same way for the classes **CDivide**, **CAdd**, and **CSubtract**, with each having **COperation** as a base class plus the member **DoOperation()**. Don't forget the **#include** directives for **Register.h** and **LogicUnit.h** that you need in each of the **.cpp** files for the derived operation classes.

Making Friends

Of course, the **DoOperation()** function will need access to the **CRegister** objects that are members of the **CLogicUnit** object to which the operation is being applied. We can make these accessible to the classes derived from **COperation** by specifying the classes as **friend**s of **CLogicUnit**. Add the following statements to the **CLogicUnit** class definition, just before the closing brace:

```
// Operations classes need to be friends
friend class CMultiply;
friend class CDivide;
friend class CAdd;
friend class CSubtract;
```

Of course, although any of the function members of these classes can access any member of the **CLogicUnit** class, the converse is not true. In C++, friendship is a one-way relationship.

Implementing Operation Execution

We can now go back to complete the implementation of the **DoOperation()** function for **CMultiply** in **Multiply.cpp**, as follows:

```
void CMultiply::DoOperation(CLogicUnit* pLogicUnit)
{
    pLogicUnit->m_MultiplyReg *= pLogicUnit->m_DisplayReg;
    pLogicUnit->m_DisplayReg = pLogicUnit->m_MultiplyReg;
}
```

The **DoOperation()** function is passed a pointer to the **CLogicUnit** object belonging to a calculator. The right operand for the multiply will have been stored in the display register **m_DisplayReg**. This could be the last numeric value entered, or perhaps the result of a parenthesized expression (although we have yet to figure out how parenthesized expressions are going to work). The left operand will be in the register **m_MultiplyReg**. This could be the result of a previous line of input, a parenthesized expression, or a numeric value that was keyed in.

Because the register **m_DisplayReg** should always hold the last value generated, the product of the values in the two registers is generated in **m_MultiplyReg**, and then copied to the display register, **m_DisplayReg**. We could generate the result directly in **m_DisplayReg**, but we still need to maintain a copy of the result in case another multiply or divide operation is following. The left operand of another multiply or divide operation will be assumed to be in **m_MultiplyReg**, and the next value entered or calculated will replace the value in **m_DisplayReg**.

The implementation of **DoOperation()** for **CDivide** is almost identical to that of the **CMultiply** class; the only difference is that the divide operation is used instead of multiply. The derived classes for addition and subtraction operations are also very similar to one another (and to those for multiplication and division), but this time it's the **m_AddReg** member we combine with **m_DisplayReg**. A separate register is used to keep the left operand for an add or subtract operation, since the triggering of add or subtract is separate from that of multiply or divide, and it's quite possible to have a situation where left operands for both multiply/divide and add/subtract operations are stored simultaneously.

The implementation of the **DoOperation()** member of **CAdd** will be:

```
void CAdd::DoOperation(CLogicUnit* pLogicUnit)
{
    pLogicUnit->m_AddReg += pLogicUnit->m_DisplayReg;
    pLogicUnit->m_DisplayReg = pLogicUnit->m_AddReg;
}
```

The function in the **CSubtract** class is the same except that **-=** replaces the **+=** that appears here. We're now ready to add the final touches to **CLogicUnit**.

Completing the CLogicUnit Class

We'll need two data members in the **CLogicUnit** class to store the operations objects — in other words, objects of the classes we derived from **COperation**. If we declare these members as pointers to base class objects, which is type **COperation***, we can use them to store the address of *any* derived class object. We can add them as **private** members of the class using the class context menu; this will add the following two lines to the class definition:

```
    COperation* m_pMultiplyDivide;    // Pointer to CMultiply or CDivide
    COperation* m_pAddSubtract;       // Pointer to CAdd or CSubtract
```

The comments are added manually, of course. Because we now reference the **COperation** class, we need to add an incomplete declaration for the class in the **LogicUnit.h** file and an **#include** directive for **Operation.h** to **LogicUnit.cpp**. We'll be able to use these new pointers to call the corresponding version of the virtual function **DoOperation()** in the derived operations classes, so the kind of operation that is to be executed will be sorted out automatically. The function member of the **CAdd** class will be called for a **CAdd** object, the function member of the **CMultiply** class will be called for a **CMultiply** object, and so on.

We should initialize these pointers in the constructor for **CLogicUnit**. Way back in this chapter, we put the default constructor in the **private** section of the class, and specified the **public** constructor as accepting a pointer to a calculator as a parameter. We can add to the **public** constructor in **LogicUnit.cpp** like this:

```
// Constructor
CLogicUnit::CLogicUnit(CCalculator* pCalc): m-pCalc(pCalc)
{
    m_pMultiplyDivide = 0;      // Initialize pointer to NULL
    m_pAddSubtract = 0;         // Initialize pointer to NULL'
    Reset();                    // Reset the logic unit
}
```

The `Reset()` function should reset the entire logic unit — this includes the registers as well as the pointers to the queued arithmetic operations. Add the following implementation to the skeleton function we created earlier:

```
// Reset the logic unit
void CLogicUnit::Reset()
{
   // Reset all the registers
   m_MultiplyReg.Reset();
   m_AddReg.Reset();
   m_DisplayReg.Reset();

   // Avoid memory leak when the user presses 'C' to clear the calculator
   delete m_pMultiplyDivide;
   delete m_pAddSubtract;

   // Set operations pointers to null
   m_pMultiplyDivide = 0;
   m_pAddSubtract = 0;
}
```

Any memory associated with pointers stored in **m_pMultiplyDivide** or **m_pAddSubtract** should be deleted when the operations are executed, but if the user presses **'C'** or **'c'** to clear the calculator, then this may not necessarily occur. We should therefore call delete on these pointers here in the **Reset()** function to make sure that this memory is released. Similarly, we could add **delete** operations to the destructor:

```
CLogicUnit::~CLogicUnit()
{
   // Just to be on the safe side...
   delete m_pAddSubtract;
   delete m_pMultiplyDivide;
}
```

If these pointers are already null at this point, it won't cause a problem. As we've said, applying **delete** to a null pointer is always harmless.

We've already written the functions **OnDigit()** and **OnDecimalPoint()** for the **CLogicUnit** class. Now we need to complete the functions for each of the arithmetic operations we're supporting, and a function to deal with the *Enter* key.

Handling Multiply and Divide

To reiterate our discussion, when the user presses a key for a multiply or divide operation, two things must be done. Any queued multiply or divide needs to be executed, and the current operation should be saved so that it can be executed when the right-hand operand has been received. We can implement the multiply operation to do this as follows:

```
// Process a multiply message
void CLogicUnit::OnMultiply()
{
   if(m_pMultiplyDivide)                    // Check for previous
   {                                        // multiply or divide.
      m_pMultiplyDivide->DoOperation(this); // If so, do it.
```

```
        delete m_pMultiplyDivide;              // Now delete the
    }                                          // operation object.
    else
        // No previous operation queued so save the display register
        m_MultiplyReg = m_DisplayReg;

    m_pMultiplyDivide = new CMultiply();       // Queue a new operation.

    // Signal start of value in display
    m_DisplayReg.SetBeginValue();
}
```

The first check is for a previous operation stored in the pointer **m_pMultiplyDivide**. If the pointer is not **NULL**, there is an operation waiting, so the pointer is used to call the corresponding **DoOperation()** function member of the derived operation class object. This will carry out the operation on the registers of the **CLogicUnit** object. The pointer **this** contains the address of the current object, so it is passed to **DoOperation()** to identify the **CLogicUnit** object. The **DoOperation()** function will store the result in the **m_MultiplyReg** data member as the left operand for the operation just received. When execution is complete, the queued operation is deleted.

If there is no operation waiting, the display register **m_DisplayReg** must contain the left operand for the operation just received, so this is saved in **m_MultiplyReg**. We do this to free up the display register, since it will be used to store the next operand value.

Finally, a new **CMultiply** object is created in the free store and its address is saved in **m_pMultiplyDivide** for next time around. Since receiving any operation key indicates the end of an input value, the flag is set for the display register to record that this is the case.

The function to process division is virtually identical to the function above, so we won't explain it again. The implementation of the **OnDivide()** member of **CLogicUnit** is:

```
// Process a divide message
void CLogicUnit::OnDivide()
{
    if(m_pMultiplyDivide)                       // Check for previous
    {                                           // multiply or divide.
        m_pMultiplyDivide->DoOperation(this);   // If so, do it.
        delete m_pMultiplyDivide;               // Now delete the
    }                                           // operation object.
    else
        // No previous operation queued so save the display register
        m_MultiplyReg = m_DisplayReg;

    m_pMultiplyDivide = new CDivide();          // Queue a new operation.

    // Signal start of value in display
    m_DisplayReg.SetBeginValue();
}
```

Of course, because we're creating objects of the **CDivide** and **CMultiply** classes, we must now add **#include** directives for **Multiply.h** and **Divide.h** to the beginning of **LogicUnit.cpp**.

467

Handling Add and Subtract

Processing addition is slightly more complicated than dealing with a multiply operation, because it's possible that two previous operations may be queued: a multiply or a divide, as well as an add or a subtract. The code for the function to handle an addition operator is as follows:

```
// Process an add message
void CLogicUnit::OnAdd()
{
    if(m_pMultiplyDivide)                  // m_pMultiplyDivide is a pointer
    {                                      // to any previous * or / object
        // Execute * or / first if it exists
        m_pMultiplyDivide->DoOperation(this);
        delete m_pMultiplyDivide;          // Now delete the object
        m_pMultiplyDivide = 0;             // and set pointer in logic unit
    }                                      // to null

    if(m_pAddSubtract)                     // m_pAddSubtract is a pointer to
    {                                      // any previous + or - object
        m_pAddSubtract->DoOperation(this); // Execute previous + or -
        delete m_pAddSubtract;             // Now delete object
    }
    else
        // If there was none, save the display register
        m_AddReg = m_DisplayReg;

    // Create a new operation object & signal start of value in display
    m_pAddSubtract = new CAdd();
    m_DisplayReg.SetBeginValue();
}
```

Like the last function, we check for a queued multiply or divide operation, and if we find one, we set the pointer **m_pMultiplyDivide** to zero after the operation has been executed. We then look for a previous add or subtract operation, and, if one is queued, we execute that too. We don't need to set the pointer **m_pAddSubtract** to zero, because we will store the address of the new operation to be queued in it. We finally set the flag in **m_DisplayReg** to indicate the end of an input value, as we did in the previous member function.

Again, the process for handling subtraction is almost identical to that for addition, so we won't go through it here. Only one line in the body of the function is different from that in the **OnAdd()** function:

```
// Process a subtract message
void CLogicUnit::OnSubtract()
{
    if(m_pMultiplyDivide)                  // m_pMultiplyDivide is a pointer
    {                                      // to any previous * or / object
        // Execute * or / first if it exists
        m_pMultiplyDivide->DoOperation(this);
        delete m_pMultiplyDivide;          // Now delete the object and set
        m_pMultiplyDivide = 0;             // pointer in logic unit to null
    }

    if(m_pAddSubtract)                     // m_pAddSubtract is a pointer to
    {                                      // any previous + or - object
```

```
            m_pAddSubtract->DoOperation(this);   // Execute previous + or -
            delete m_pAddSubtract;               // Now delete object
    }
    else
        // If there was none, save the display register
        m_AddReg = m_DisplayReg;

    // Create a new operation object & signal start of value in display
    m_pAddSubtract = new CSubtract();
    m_DisplayReg.SetBeginValue();
}
```

We now need to enlarge the growing list of **#include** directives in **LogicUnit.cpp** with includes for **Add.h** and **Subtract.h**.

Handling the Enter Key

The last key we must handle to get the **CLogicUnit** class to evaluate arithmetic expressions is the *Enter* key, which will be transmitted at the end of an input line. The code for this is as follows:

```
// Process an Enter message
void CLogicUnit::OnEnter()
{
    if(m_pMultiplyDivide)                      // m_pMultiplyDivide is a pointer
    {                                          // to any previous * or / object
        m_pMultiplyDivide->DoOperation(this);  // Execute previous * or /
        delete m_pMultiplyDivide;              // Now delete the object
        m_pMultiplyDivide = 0;                 // and set pointer in logic
    }                                          // unit to null

    if(m_pAddSubtract)                         // m_pAddSubtract is a pointer to
    {                                          // any previous + or - object
        m_pAddSubtract->DoOperation(this);     // Execute previous + or -
        delete m_pAddSubtract;                 // Now delete object
        m_pAddSubtract = 0;                    // Set pointer to null
    }

    // Show result in display
    m_pCalc->GetDisplay()->ShowRegister(m_DisplayReg);
    m_DisplayReg.SetBeginValue();              // Set start of value flag
}
```

When the *Enter* key is received, all outstanding operations need to be executed and the final result displayed on the screen. The function checks the pointers **m_pMultiplyDivide** and **m_pAddSubtract**, performs any queued operations through the **DoOperation()** function, and ensures the pointers are reset to **NULL**.

The message signaling that the *Enter* key was pressed is the only way that output is generated. The value in the display register, **m_DisplayReg**, is output to the screen by sending it to the **CDisplay** object using the function **ShowRegister()**. We will need to define the **CDisplay** class so that this function outputs the value stored in the **CRegister** object that is passed to it. The function is called in the statement:

```
    m_pCalc->GetDisplay()->ShowRegister(m_DisplayReg);
```

The pointer **m_pCalc** was initialized in the class constructor and points to the parent **CCalculator** object. It's used to call the **GetDisplay()** member function of **CCalculator**, which operates analogously to the **GetLogicUnit()** function we implemented earlier, in that it returns a pointer to the **CDisplay** object that belongs to the calculator. This pointer to the **CDisplay** object is then used to call the **ShowRegister()** function.

You can use the context menu to add the **GetDisplay()** function as a **const** member of the **CCalculator** class with **public** access and returning type **CDisplay***. This will add the following line to the class definition:

```
CDisplay* GetDisplay() const;
```

The implementation of **GetDisplay()** in **Calculator.cpp** will be simply:

```
CDisplay* CCalculator::GetDisplay() const
{
    return m_pDisplay;
}
```

Finally in the **OnEnter()** function, the flag in **m_DisplayReg** is set to indicate the start of a new input value. The value displayed will still be retained in **m_DisplayReg** so that the next line entered can be applied to this value.

Using the Registers

Just to make sure that we understand what happens between registers when the calculator operates, let's look at how a simple expression, 1+2*3+4, affects the contents of the registers one step at a time. We can best understand this with a table, as shown below:

Key	Action	Contents of m_DisplayReg	Contents of m_AddReg	Contents of m_MultiplyReg
1	Store in m_DisplayReg	1	-	-
+	Copy m_DisplayReg to m_AddReg	1	1	-
2	Store in m_DisplayReg	2	1	-
*	Copy m_DisplayReg to m_MultiplyReg	2	1	2
3	Store in m_DisplayReg	3	1	2
+	m_DisplayReg * m_MultiplyReg	3	1	6
	Copy m_MultiplyReg to m_DisplayReg	6	1	6
	m_DisplayReg + m_AddReg	6	7	6
	Copy m_AddReg to m_DisplayReg	7	7	6
4	Store in m_DisplayReg	4	7	6
Enter	m_DisplayReg + m_AddReg	4	11	6
	Copy m_AddReg to m_DisplayReg	11	11	6

Each of the numeric values is just stored in the display register, **m_DisplayReg**. You should be able to relate the **CLogicUnit** function members that we have just discussed to the actions corresponding to the arithmetic operators. You can see how the receipt of each operator frees up the display register for the next operand.

To get our calculator into basic operational shape, we just need to define the class for the display.

Completing the CDisplay Class

The **CDisplay** class will be relatively simple, since all it needs is the capability to display the result of a calculation. We already decided that this is to work through the member function called **ShowRegister()** that we used in the **OnEnter()** member of the **CLogicUnit** class. The function will accept one parameter of type **CRegister**, which we can make a reference, and the return type will be **void**. The function will display the result on the standard output device for a console application, the screen.

Add this function to the class using the Wizard Bar. After adding a comment and an incomplete declaration for **CRegister**, the contents of the file **Display.h** will be as follows:

```
// Display.h: interface for the CDisplay class.
//
///////////////////////////////////////////////////////////////////

#if !defined(AFX_DISPLAY_H__FA599AA7_17DF_11D2_B731_BD7D79977406__INCLUDED_)
#define AFX_DISPLAY_H__FA599AA7_17DF_11D2_B731_BD7D79977406__INCLUDED_

#if _MSC_VER > 1000
#pragma once
#endif // _MSC_VER > 1000

class CCalculator;

class CDisplay
{
public:
    void ShowRegister(CRegister& rReg) const;
    CDisplay(CCalculator* pCalc);      // Constructor
    virtual ~CDisplay();

private:
    CCalculator* m_pCalc;                // Pointer to the parent calculator
};

#endif // !defined(AFX_DISPLAY_H__FA599AA7_17DF_11D2_B731_BD7D79977406__INCLUDED_)
```

The implementation of the **ShowRegister()** function in **Display.cpp** will be:

```
// Function to display calculated value
void CDisplay::ShowRegister (CRegister& rReg) const
{
    cout << endl << setw(12) << rReg.Get() << endl;
}
```

There is little to say about the detail here. The constructor saves the pointer to the parent calculator, and the **ShowRegister()** function outputs the value stored in **rReg** with a field width of 12. The value is obtained from the **CRegister** object by calling its **Get()** member. We need to add **#include** directives to **Display.cpp** for the standard headers **iostream** and **iomanip** for the output and the 'set width' capabilities. We also need to add the **using** directive for the standard namespace, **std**.

The **CDisplay** class only supports output of values of type **double**, since that's all we'll be using in our calculator program for the moment. If we needed to support output for other types, it would be a simple matter of overloading the **ShowRegister()** member function to accept different types of arguments.

Running the Calculator

If everything has been put together correctly, you should have a calculator which will handle any expression that does not contain parentheses. So far, we have left the implementation of the **LeftParenthesis()** and **RightParenthesis()** members of **CLogicUnit** as the empty skeletons generated by the context menu for the class, so they do nothing at present. Nevertheless, try the program out with a few expressions to see that it works.

The next step is to consider how we can support expressions containing parentheses (which may also be nested).

Handling Parentheses

As it stands, the calculator will evaluate any properly formed arithmetic expression that doesn't contain parentheses. What exactly is the content of a pair of parentheses? It's one of two things. It's either a properly formed arithmetic expression, or it's a properly formed arithmetic expression that contains a parenthesized expression. So if it's the former, our existing calculator can handle it.

That's a very good clue as to how we can deal with parentheses. All we need to do when we find a left parenthesis is to create a new calculator to handle the expression between the parentheses. When the new calculator finds a right parenthesis, it's done, so it should end and return the value of the expression. But what if the expression between parentheses contains another pair of parentheses? The new calculator will take care of it, of course! We just said what a calculator does when it finds a left parenthesis: it creates a new calculator to handle the expression between parentheses...

The sequence of events in evaluating an arbitrary expression is illustrated here.

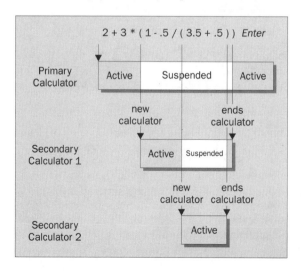

Each left parenthesis causes a new calculator to take over processing while the currently active calculator is suspended, and each right parenthesis ends the currently active calculator.

All we need to do to make this mechanism work is:

▶ Make the calculator return the value in the display register when it ends

▶ Implement the **OnLeftParenthesis()** member of **CLogicUnit** to create a new calculator

▶ Implement the **OnRightParenthesis()** member of **CLogicUnit** to return the value in the display register and end the calculator

The *Enter* key should never be recognized in a secondary calculator handling a parenthesized expression, since a right parenthesis should be found, and this should end the calculator. If the *Enter* key is recognized, it indicates we have an unmatched left parenthesis, so we could use this event to identify the error in this case.

Returning a Calculator Value

We started a calculator running by calling its **Run()** member, so a calculator ends when this function returns. This function should therefore return the value of the display register for the calculator. We need to modify its declaration in **Calculator.h** to:

```
double Run() const;                    // Starts the calculator
```

We then need to modify its implementation in **Calculator.cpp** to:

```
double CCalculator::Run() const
{
    return m_pKeyboard->GetKey();       // Start keyboard input
}
```

This implies that the **GetKey()** member of **CKeyboard** must return the value of the display register. We can alter the declaration in **Keyboard.h** for the function to return type **double**, and we can modify its implementation to:

```
// Keyboard manager function
double CKeyboard::GetKey() const
{
    // Get a pointer to the logic unit
    CLogicUnit* pLogicUnit = m_pCalc->GetLogicUnit();

    char chKey = 0;                     // Key press stored here
    bool bExit = false;                 // Flag to end calculator
                                        // operation
    while(!bExit)                       // Get key presses until there is
    {                                   // a reason not to...
        chKey = cin.get();              // Get a key depression

        switch (chKey)                  // Test key press
        {
            case ' ':                   // For blank...
                break;                  // ...do nothing
```

```
            case '0': case '1': case '2': case '3': case '4':
            case '5': case '6': case '7': case '8': case '9':
                // For any digit send numeric value of digit to the logic unit
                pLogicUnit->OnDigit(chKey - '0');
                break;

            case '.':
                // Send decimal point to the logic unit
                pLogicUnit->OnDecimalPoint();
                break;

            case '(':                               // Left parenthesis
                pLogicUnit->OnLeftParenthesis();
                break;

            case ')':                               // Right parenthesis
                return pLogicUnit->OnRightParenthesis();

            case '*':
                pLogicUnit->OnMultiply();       // Send a multiply message
                break;

            case '/':
                pLogicUnit->OnDivide();         // Send a divide message
                break;

            case '+':
                pLogicUnit->OnAdd();            // Send an add message
                break;

            case '-':
                pLogicUnit->OnSubtract();       // Send a subtract message
                break;

            case 'Q': case 'q':                 // Quit key pressed
                bExit = true;                   // So set flag to exit
                break;

            case 'c': case 'C':                 // Clear key pressed
                pLogicUnit->Reset();            // so reset the logic unit
                break;

            case '\n':                          // Enter key pressed
                pLogicUnit->OnEnter();          // Send Enter message
                break;

            default:                            // Wrong key pressed
                bExit = true;                   // so set flag to exit
        }
    }
    return pLogicUnit->GetDisplayValue();    // Return current display value
}
```

Apart from the declaration, there are just two lines changed here. First, the **case** in the **switch** for **')'** has been altered. The **OnRightParenthesis()** member of **CLogicUnit** is assumed to return the value of the display register so that the **GetKey()** function can return it to the **Run()** function for the **CCalculator** object. Second, when the **while** loop terminates, the

`GetKey()` function now returns the value in the display register by calling a function `GetDisplayValue()` that we need to add to `CLogicUnit`.

You can add this function using the context menu for `CLogicUnit`. It should return a value of type **double**, so it will be declared in the **public** section of the class as:

```
double GetDisplayValue() const;
```

You can add the one line required in its implementation:

```
double CLogicUnit::GetDisplayValue() const
{
    return m_DisplayReg.Get();
}
```

Handling a Right Parenthesis

When a right parenthesis is signaled to the logic unit, all outstanding operations must be executed to produce the value of the expression. The implementation of the `OnRightParenthesis()` member of `CLogicUnit` will therefore be:

```
double CLogicUnit::OnRightParenthesis()
{
    if(m_pMultiplyDivide)                    // m_pMultiplyDivide is a pointer
    {                                         // to any previous * or / object
        m_pMultiplyDivide->DoOperation(this);// Execute previous * or /
        delete m_pMultiplyDivide;            // Now delete the object
        m_pMultiplyDivide = 0;               // and set pointer in LU to null
    }

    if(m_pAddSubtract)                       // m_pAddSubtract is a pointer to
    {                                         // any previous + or - object
        m_pAddSubtract->DoOperation(this);   // Execute previous + or -
        delete m_pAddSubtract;               // Now delete object
        m_pAddSubtract = 0;                  // Set pointer to null
    }

    return m_DisplayReg.Get();               // Return the register value
}
```

This is essentially the same code as that for the **OnEnter()** function, but without outputting the result through the **CDisplay** object. When all operations are complete, the value stored in **m_DisplayReg** is returned. Don't forget to amend the declaration in the **LogicUnit.h** file so that the function returns type **double**!

Handling a Left Parenthesis

The function member of the **CLogicUnit** class that processes a left parenthesis is the last piece we need to put in place to handle any expression. It is remarkably simple. All it needs to do is to create a new calculator and run it. The implementation for this will be:

```
// Process a left parenthesis message
void CLogicUnit::OnLeftParenthesis()
{
    CCalculator* pCalc = new CCalculator();    // Create a calculator
```

```
    // Run the calculator and set the result in the display register
    m_DisplayReg.Set(pCalc->Run());
    delete pCalc;                          // Destroy the calculator
}
```

The new calculator is created dynamically and started using its **Run()** member. The new calculator will process input until the corresponding right parenthesis is met, which will cause the value of the expression between parentheses to be returned from the **Run()** function. This value is passed as an argument to the **Set()** function of the display register for the current calculator. Finally, the new calculator is deleted from the free store.

TRY IT OUT - Exercising the Calculator

You can now recompile the program and try some more complicated expressions. Some examples that I tried it out on are shown here:

```
Ex11_01
2.5-(1.25/17+2.65*7.3)*(1+3.5/14.5*.0023-7/15)/2

      -2.68366
*15/100

      -0.40255
c

            0
1+1/(1+1/(1+1/(1+1/(1+1))))

      1.625
Q
```

The organization of this version of a calculator is quite different to that of our procedural programming example. It seems like a lot more code too, but much of it is concerned with class definitions and the house keeping around that. Generally, object-oriented programs may well involve more lines of code than a procedural approach, but if the classes have been properly designed, the program should be easier to extend to include new capability. Once you've built the classes as a base for the kind of problem you want to solve, applying them to a variety of problems should then be very easy.

Extending the Calculator

This example provides a lot of opportunities for you to exercise your C++ skills further if you think you need it, or even just for fun. The first thing you might try is to build in some error detection and recovery. Handling invalid characters is easy. You just need to change the **GetKey()** member of the **CKeyboard** class. Replace the code for the **default** case in the **switch** statement to display a suitable message (through the display object ideally), reset the logic unit, then break to continue the loop. The reset is necessary to prevent spurious values being left in the registers.

Detecting unmatched parentheses shouldn't be too difficult either. Remember that a calculator will never meet a second left parenthesis, so too many left parentheses will result in one of the secondary calculators processing the *Enter* key. Too many right parentheses will cause the primary calculator to process a right parenthesis — an event which should never occur. All you need to be able to sort these out is to distinguish between the primary calculator and any secondaries that are created. A static member of **CCalculator** that counts how many objects are around would do it.

Don't forget the possibility of a zero divisor. You could also add other operators, such as remainder and exponentiation. Adding trigonometric function capability would also be interesting.

Summary

In this chapter, we've exercised some of the principal ideas involved in using inheritance. The discussion of the problem solution here is not a very precise reflection of how you would work in practice. You wouldn't usually write all the code and then attempt to execute it. Building the classes in an incremental fashion, adding and testing member functions one at a time would be a more practical and productive approach, but space prohibits an exhaustive description of this process.

Some of the key points we've covered in this chapter are:

▶ When approaching a problem for the first time, try to sort out what the principle kinds of objects are that the problem deals with.

▶ Map out the relationships between the problem classes. Determine where inheritance is appropriate versus ownership — try the '*is a*' versus the '*has a*' test.

▶ Be prepared to go back and modify classes. In most instances you won't get the design right first time around.

▶ Don't forget to keep polymorphism in mind. This can often greatly simplify a problem.

▶ When you implement a class that allocates memory on the free store, always implement a destructor and a copy constructor, otherwise you will have memory leaks. Consider whether you also need to implement the assignment operator.

▶ Make sure the constructor initializes all the data members in a class. Uninitialized data members can cause a lot of problems in unexpected places.

▶ If a class object should always be created with a constructor that requires arguments, then define the default constructor in the **private** section of the class to prevent its accidental use.

If you've followed along with the example in this chapter without major difficulty, you are ready to try your hand at Windows programming. The programs in the remainder of the book get a bit larger, but none of them are more difficult than the example we have just completed. We have just one more topic before we get into Windows programming, and that's debugging.

Exercises

This chapter hasn't introduced anything new; we have been concentrating on a class-based version of the calculator. For that reason, the exercises in this chapter are all aimed at extending and improving the calculator application.

Ex11-1: Add an exponentiation operator, using the caret (^) as the operator symbol.

Ex11-2: Modify the calculator code so that it traps any attempt to divide by zero, displaying a suitable error message.

Ex11-3: How can you arrange for such an error to cause the rest of the current input string to be thrown away and the accumulator set to zero, so that processing can commence again with a new command? What is the main drawback with this method?

Debugging

If you have been doing the examples in the previous chapters, you will certainly have been battling with bugs in your code. In this chapter we will explore how the basic debugging capabilities built into Visual C++ can help with this. We will also investigate some additional tools that you can use to find and eliminate errors from your programs. We will also see some of the ways in which you can equip your programs with specific code to check for errors.

In this chapter you will learn:

▶ How to run your program under the control of the Visual C++ debugger.

▶ How to step through your program a statement at a time.

▶ How to monitor or change the values of variables in your programs.

▶ How to monitor the value of an expression in your program.

▶ What the call stack is.

▶ What an assertion is and how to use assertions to check your code.

▶ How to add debugging specific code to a program.

▶ How to detect memory leaks in a program.

Understanding Debugging

Bugs are errors in your program and **debugging** is the process of finding and eliminating them. You are undoubtedly aware by now that debugging is an integral part of the programming process — it goes with the territory as they say. The bald facts about bugs in your programs are rather depressing:

▶ Every program that you write that is more than trivial will contain bugs that you will need to try to expose, find, and eliminate if your program is to be reliable and effective. Note the three phases here — a program bug is not necessarily apparent; even when it is apparent you may not know where it is in your source code; and even when you know roughly where it is, it may not be easy to determine what exactly is causing the problem and thus eliminate it.

▶ Many programs that you write will contain bugs even after you think you have fully tested them.

▶ Program bugs can remain hidden in a program that is apparently operating correctly — sometimes for years. They generally become apparent at the most inconvenient moment.

▶ Programs beyond a certain size and complexity will always contain bugs, no matter how much time and effort you expend testing them. (The measure here is not precisely defined, but Visual C++ and your operating system certainly come into this category!)

It would be unwise to dwell on this last point if are of a nervous disposition. Try not to think about it if, for example, you fly a lot or are regularly in the position where a computer error could cause you some harm. Such systems usually have a series of trusted tests for new code to probe for errors. Of course, these tests could have bugs and then...

Many potential bugs will be eliminated during the compile and link phases, but there will still be quite a few left even after you manage to produce an executable module for your program. Unfortunately, despite the fact that program bugs are as inevitable as death and taxes, debugging is not an exact science. However, you can still adopt a structured approach to eliminating bugs. There are four broad strategies you can adopt to make debugging as painless as possible:

▶ Don't re-invent the wheel. Understand and use the library facilities provided as part of Visual C++ (or other commercial software components you have access to) so that your program uses as much pre-tested code as possible.

▶ Develop and test your code incrementally. By testing each significant class and function individually, and gradually assembling separate code components after testing them, you will make the development process much easier, with fewer obscure bugs occurring along the way.

▶ Code defensively — which means writing code to guard against potential errors. For example, declare member functions that don't modify an object as **const**. Use **const** parameters where appropriate. Don't use 'magic numbers' in your code — define **const** objects with the required values.

▶ Include debugging code that checks and validates data and conditions in your program from the outset. This is something we will be looking at in detail later in this chapter.

Because of the importance of ending up with programs that are as bug-free as is humanly possible, Visual C++ provides you with a powerful armory of tools for finding bugs. The sad truth though is that you may still end up beating your head against a wall trying to find that elusive bug. A fresh set of eyes on the problem may spot the problem immediately, so don't feel obliged to keep your bugs to yourself. Before we get into the detailed mechanics, let's look a little closer at how bugs arise.

Program Bugs

Of course, the primary cause for bugs in your program is you and the mistakes you make. These mistakes will range from simple typos — just pressing the wrong key — to getting the logic completely wrong. I too find it hard to believe that I can make such silly mistakes so often, but no-one has yet managed to come up with a credible alternative as to how bugs get into your code — so it must be true! Humans are creatures of habit so you will probably find yourself making some mistakes time and time again. Frustratingly, many errors will be glaringly obvious to others, but invisible to you — this is just your computer's way of teaching you a bit of humility. Of course, there are bugs in the system environment that you are using (Visual C++ included) but this should be the last place you suspect when your program doesn't work. Even when you do conclude that it *must* be the compiler or the operating system, nine times out of ten you will be wrong. However, there are certainly bugs in Visual C++ and if you want to keep up with those identified to date, together with any fixes available, you can search the information provided on the Microsoft web site related to Visual C++ (**http://www.microsoft.com/visualc/**). Better still, if you can afford a subscription to Microsoft Developer Network, you will get quarterly updates on the latest bugs and fixes.

From the nature of programming, bugs are virtually infinite in their variety, but there are some kinds that are particularly common. You may well be aware of most of these, but let's take a quick look at them anyway.

Common Bugs

A useful way of cataloguing bugs is to relate them to the symptoms they cause, since this is how you will experience them in the first instance. The following list of five common symptoms is by no means exhaustive, and you will certainly be able to add to it as you gain programming experience:

Symptom	Possible Causes
Data corrupted	Failure to initialize variable Exceeding integer type range Invalid pointer Error in array index expression Loop condition error Error in size of dynamically allocated array. Failing to implement class copy constructor, assignment operator, or destructor.
Unhandled exceptions	Invalid pointer or reference Missing catch handler
Program hangs or crashes	Failure to initialize variable Infinite loop Invalid pointer Freeing the same free store memory twice Failure to implement, or error in, class destructor
Stream input data incorrect	Reading using the extraction operator and the `getline()` function.
Incorrect results	Typographical error: `-=` instead of `==`, or `i` instead of `j` etc. Failure to initialize variable Exceeding integer type range Invalid pointer Omitting break in switch statement

Look at how many different kinds of errors can be caused by invalid pointers and the myriad symptoms that bad pointers can generate. This is possibly the most frequent cause of those bugs that are hard to find, so always double check your pointer operations. If you are conscious of the ways in which bad pointers arise, you will avoid many of the pitfalls. The common ways in which bad pointers arise are:

▶ Failing to initialize a pointer when you declare it.

▶ Failing to set a pointer to free store memory to null when you delete the space allocated.

▶ Returning the address of a local variable from a function.

▶ Failing to implement the copy constructor and assignment operator for classes that allocate free store memory.

Even if you do all this, there will still be bugs in your code, so let's look at the tools that Visual C++ provides to assist debugging.

Basic Debugging Operations

So far, although we have been creating debug versions of our programs, we haven't been using the **debugger**. The debugger is a program that controls the execution of your program in such a way that you can step through the source code one line at a time, or run to a particular point in the program. At each point in your code where the debugger stops, you can inspect or even change the values of variables before continuing. You can also change the source code, recompile and then restart the program from the beginning. You can even change the source code in the middle of stepping through a program. When you move to the next step after modifying the code, the debugger will automatically recompile before executing the next statement.

To understand the basic debug capabilities of Visual C++, let's use the debugger on a program that we are sure works. Then we can just pull the levers to see how things operate. We will take a simple example that uses pointers from back in Chapter 4:

```
// EX4_05.CPP
// Exercising pointers
#include <iostream>
using namespace std;

int main()
{
   long* pnumber = NULL;                 // Pointer declaration & initialization
   long number1 = 55;
   long number2 = 99;

   pnumber = &number1;                   // Store address in pointer
   *pnumber += 11;                       // Increment number1 by 11
   cout << endl
        << "number1 = " << number1
        << "   &number1 = " << hex << pnumber;
```

```
        pnumber = &number2;            // Change pointer to address of number2
        number1 = *pnumber*10;         // 10 times number2

        cout << endl
            << "number1 = " << dec << number1
            << "    pnumber = " << hex << pnumber
            << "    *pnumber = " << dec << *pnumber;

        cout << endl;
        return 0;
    }
```

If you have this example on your system then just open the project, otherwise you will need to enter it again.

When you have written a program that doesn't behave as it should, the debugger enables you to inspect work through a program one step at a time to find out where and how it's going wrong. It also allows you to inspect the state of your program's data at any time during execution. We will arrange to execute our example one statement at a time and to monitor the contents of the variables that we are interested in. In this case we want to look at **pnumber**, the contents of the location pointed to by **pnumber** (which is ***pnumber**), **number1**, and **number2**.

First we need to be sure that the build configuration for the example is set to Win32 Debug rather than Win32 Release (it will be unless you've changed it). The build configuration selects the set of project settings for the build operation on your program that you can see when you select the <u>P</u>roject/<u>S</u>ettings... menu option. The current build configuration in effect is shown in the drop-down list on the full Build toolbar (only the MiniBar is shown by default). To display it, select <u>T</u>ools | <u>C</u>ustomize... and choose the Toolbars tab, or just right click on the toolbar. Check the box against Build, and uncheck Build MiniBar. The Build toolbar looks like this:

You can change the build configuration by extending the drop-down list and choosing an alternative to Win32 Debug. Alternatively, you can use the Build/Set Active <u>C</u>onfiguration... menu option.

If you find that the drop down list box showing the build configuration is using too much space in the toolbar area, you can reduce its width. With the customize dialog displayed just click on the right hand end of the list box. You will then be able to drag that side to the left to reduce it to a more convenient width. You can find out what the toolbar buttons are for by letting the mouse cursor linger over a toolbar button. A tooltip for that button will appear that identifies its function and the status line will show a fuller description of what the button does.

The 'debug' configuration in a project causes additional information to be included in your executable program so that the debugging facilities can be used. This extra information is stored in the **.pdb** file that will be in the **Debug** folder for your project. The 'release' configuration omits this information as it represents overhead that you wouldn't want in a fully tested program. With the Professional or Enterprise versions of Visual C++, the compiler will also optimize the code when compiling the release version of a program. Optimization is inhibited when the debug version is compiled because the optimization process can involve resequencing code to make it more efficient, or even omitting redundant code altogether. Since this destroys the one to one mapping between the source code and corresponding blocks of machine code, this would make stepping through a program potentially confusing to say the least.

Right click on the toolbar again and select Debug to display the debugging toolbar. This will appear automatically when the debugger is operating, but we should take a look at what it contains before we get to start the debugger. The debug toolbar looks like this.

If you inspect the tooltips for the buttons on this toolbar you will get a preliminary idea of what they do — we will be using some of them shortly. With the example from Chapter 4, we won't use all the debugging facilities available to us, but we will consider some of the more important features. Once we are familiar with stepping through a program using the debugger, we will explore more of the features with a program that has bugs.

The debugger has two primary modes of operation — it works through the code by single stepping (which is essentially executing one statement at a time), or runs to a particular point in the source code. The point in the source where the debugger is to stop is determined either by where you have placed the cursor or, more usefully, a designated stopping point called a **breakpoint**. Let's see how we define breakpoints.

Setting Breakpoints

A **breakpoint** is a point in your program where the debugger will suspend execution automatically. You can specify multiple breakpoints so that you can run your program, stopping at points of interest that you select along the way. At each breakpoint you can look at variables within the program and change them if they don't have the values they should. We are going to execute our program one statement at a time, but with a large program this would be impractical. Usually, you will only want to look at a particular area of the program where you think there might be an error. Consequently, you would usually set breakpoints where you think the error is and run the program so that it halts at the first breakpoint. You can then single step from that point if you wish, where a single step implies executing a single source code statement.

To set a breakpoint at the beginning of a line of source code, you simply place the cursor in the statement where you want execution to stop and click the Insert/Remove Breakpoint button, , on the Build toolbar, press *F9*, or right click in the left margin and select from the pop-up.

When debugging, you would normally set several breakpoints, each chosen to show when the variables that you think are causing a problem are changing. Execution will stop *before* the statement indicated by the breakpoint is executed. A breakpoint is indicated by a large circle at the start of a line of code, as you can see from this screen shot:

```
//EX4_05.CPP
// Exercising pointers
#include <iostream>
using namespace std;

int main()
{
    long* pnumber = NULL;              // Pointer declaration & initialization
    long number1 = 55, number2 = 99;

    pnumber = &number1;               // Store address in pointer
    *pnumber += 11;                    // Increment number1 by 11
    cout << endl
         << "number1 = " << number1
         << "   &number1 = " << hex << pnumber;

    pnumber = &number2;               // Change pointer to address of number2
    number1 = *pnumber*10;            // 10 times number2

    cout << endl
         << "number1 = " << dec << number1
         << "   pnumber = " << hex << pnumber
         << "   *pnumber = " << dec << *pnumber;

    cout << endl;
    return 0;
}
```

You can set breakpoints by placing the cursor anywhere in a line of code, but the compiler can only break before a complete statement and not halfway through it. The breakpoint is set at the beginning of the line in which you have placed the cursor, so execution will stop before the line is executed. If you place a cursor in a line that doesn't contain any code (for example, the line above the one in the picture), the breakpoint will be set on that line, and the program will stop at the beginning of the next executable line.

You can remove a breakpoint by positioning the cursor anywhere in the same line as an existing breakpoint and clicking the Insert/Remove Breakpoint button (or pressing *F9*) again. Alternatively, you can remove all the breakpoints in the active project by selecting the Remove All button on the Edit | Breakpoints... dialog, or by pressing *Ctrl-Shift-F9*. Note that this will remove breakpoints from all files in the project, even if they're not currently open in Visual C++.

Advanced Breakpoints

A more advanced way of specifying breakpoints is provided through a dialog you can pop up by selecting the Edit/Breakpoints... menu option. As well as setting a breakpoint at a location other than the beginning of a statement, you can set a breakpoint when a particular Boolean expression evaluates to true. This is a powerful tool but it does introduce very substantial overhead in a program as the expression needs to be re-evaluated continuously. Consequently, execution will slow to a crawl, even on the fastest machines.

The dialog also allows a breakpoint to be set when a particular type of Windows message occurs. This is very useful in Windows programs where you might suspect a problem withhandling a particular kind of message.

Starting Debugging

There are four ways of starting your application in debug mode, which you can see if you look at the options under Start Debug in the Build menu.

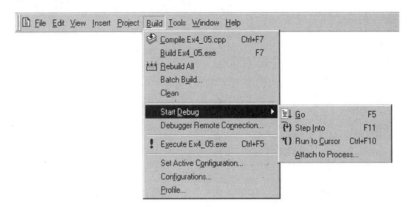

1   The Go option (*F5* or press on the Build toolbar) simply executes a program up to the first breakpoint (if any) where execution will halt. After you've examined all you need to at a breakpoint, selecting Go again will continue execution up to the next breakpoint. In this way, you can move through a program from breakpoint to breakpoint, and at each halt in execution have a look at critical variables, changing their values if you need to. If there are no breakpoints, starting the debugger in this way will execute the entire program without stopping.

Of course, just because you started debugging using Go doesn't mean that you have to continue using it; at each halt in execution you can choose any of the possible ways of moving through your code.

2   Step Into (*F11* or press on the Debug toolbar) executes your program one statement at a time, stepping into every code block — which includes every function that is called. This would be something of a nuisance if we used it throughout the debugging process because, for example, it would also execute all the code in the library functions for stream output — we're not really interested in this, as we didn't write it. Quite a few of the library functions are written in Assembler language — including some of those supporting stream input/output. Assembler language functions will execute one machine instruction at a time, which can be rather time consuming as you might imagine, so to avoid having to step through all that code, we'll use the Step Over facility (*F10* or press on the Debug toolbar) once we are at the beginning of `main()`. This will simply execute the statements in our function `main()` one at a time, and run all the code used by the stream operations (or any other functions that might be called within a statement) without stopping.

3 Run to <u>C</u>ursor (*Ctrl+F10* or press [▣] on the Debug toolbar) does exactly what it says — it executes the program up to the statement where you left the text cursor in the Text Editor window. In this way you can set the position where you want the program to stop as you go along.

4 Finally, the <u>A</u>ttach to Process... option on the Start <u>D</u>ebug menu enables you to debug a program that is already running. This option will display a list of the processes that are running on your machine and you can select the process you want to debug. This is really for advanced users and you should avoid experimenting with it unless you are quite certain that you know what you are doing. You can easily lock up your machine or cause other problems if you interfere with critical operating system processes.

First, we'll start the program with Step <u>I</u>nto, so click the [▣] button or press *F11* to begin.

After a short pause (assuming that you've already built the project), Visual C++ will switch to debugging mode. The configuration of the windows and which windows appear when the debugger is started can be customized. The complete list of windows is shown on the View Debug Windows menu dropdown, and the set you have active and their arrangement when you close the debugger will be remembered for the next session. In the default configuration, when you start the debugger the Project Workspace will disappear and two new windows will appear below the editor window. The Variables window on the left shows values for variables in the context of the function that is currently executing, and the Watch window on the right of the screen monitors values of variables selected by you. The <u>B</u>uild menu will be replaced by the <u>D</u>ebug menu and the Debug toolbar will appear, even if it was not enabled previously. This may pop up as a window, in which case you can dock it in the toolbar area if you wish. If you look at the <u>D</u>ebug menu, you'll see that it contains an option for Step <u>O</u>ver as well as a number of other functions that are available as buttons on the Debug toolbar, plus some that are not. We will not be going into all of these as some of them are applicable to advanced programming techniques that are beyond the scope of this book.

In the Text Editor window you'll see that the opening brace of our `main()` function is highlighted by an arrow to indicate that this is the current point in the program's execution.

Arrow Marker   **[break]** *in title bar*   *Debug Toolbar*

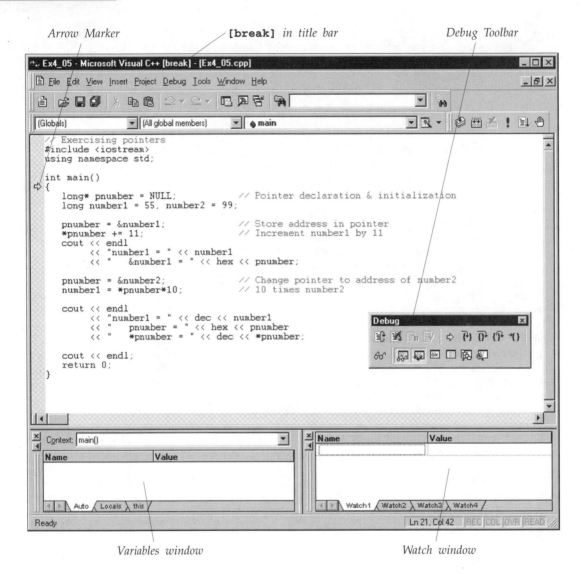

Variables window   *Watch window*

At this point in the program, we can't choose any variables to look at because none exist at present. Until a declaration of a variable has been executed, you cannot look at its value or change it.

There is also a Call Stack window. If this isn't displayed, you can activate it from the View/Debug Windows menu, or by pressing *Alt+7*. The Call Stack window displays a list of the functions or calls that are currently executing — in other words, functions that have been entered but have not yet executed a return statement. The most recently called function is at the top — **main()**. The others are system functions that execute prior to **main()**. We will see more on the Call Stack window later.

Inspecting Variable Values

Defining a variable that you want to inspect is referred to as **setting a watch** for the variable. Before we set any watches, we should get some variables declared in the program. We can execute the declaration statements by invoking Step Over three times. Use the Step Over menu item, the toolbar icon, or press *F10* three times so that the arrow now appears at the start of the line:

```
pnumber = &number1;            // Store address in pointer
```

If you look at the Auto tab in the Variables window now, you should see the following (although the value for **&number1** may be different on your system as it represents a memory location). Note that the values for **&number1** and **pnumber** are not equal to each other since the line in which **pnumber** is set to the address of **number1** (the line that the arrow is pointing at) hasn't yet been executed. We initialized **pnumber** as a **null pointer** in the first line of the function, which is why the address it contains is zero. If we had not initialized the pointer, it would contain a junk value — whatever was left by the last program to use these particular four bytes of memory. Of course, this could be zero but it is basically a random value.

Context: main()	
Name	**Value**
⊞ &number1	0x0012ff78
number1	55
number2	99
⊞ pnumber	0x00000000

Auto / Locals / this /

The Variables window has three tabs, each representing a different view of some of the variables in use in your program:

▶ The Auto tab shows the automatic variables in use in the current statement and its immediate predecessor (in other words, the statement pointed to by the arrow in the Editor Window and the one before it).

▶ The Locals tab shows the values of the variables local to the current function. In general, new variables will come into scope as you trace through a program and then go out of scope as you exit the block in which they are defined. In our case, this window will always show values for **number1**, **number2** and **pnumber** as we only have one function, **main()**, consisting of a single code block.

▶ The this tab shows information about the current **this** pointer that contains the address of the current object when a non-static class member function is executing. We will use this a little later in this chapter.

You'll have noticed that **&number1** and **pnumber** both have plus signs next to their names in the Variables window. Plus signs will appear for any variable for which additional information can be displayed, such as for an array, or a pointer, or a class object. In our case you can expand the view for each of the pointer variables by clicking the plus signs. If you press *F10* once more and click on the + adjacent to ·**pnumber**, the debugger will display the value stored at the memory address contained in the pointer, as shown below.

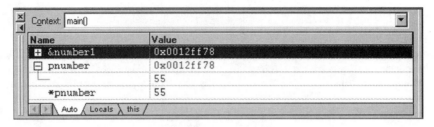

Integer values can be displayed as decimal or hexadecimal. To toggle between the two, right click anywhere on the Auto tab and select (or deselect) Hexadecimal Display from the pop-up menu. You can view the variables that are local to the current function by selecting the Locals tab. There are also other ways that we can inspect variables using the debugging facilities of Visual C++.

Viewing Variables in the Edit Window

If we need to look at the value of a single variable, and that variable is visible in the Text Editor window, the easiest way to look at its value is to position the cursor over the variable for a second. A tooltip will pop up showing the current value of the variable. You can also look at more complicated expressions by highlighting them and resting the cursor over the highlighted area. Again a tooltip will pop up to display the value. Try highlighting the expression ***pnumber*10** a little lower down. Hovering the cursor over the highlighted expression will result in the current value of the expression being displayed. Note that this won't work if the expression is not complete — if you miss the ***** that dereferences **pnumber** out of the highlighted text for instance, or you just highlight ***pnumber***, the value won't be displayed.

Unfortunately, this method won't show the extended information that appears in the Variables window, such as the data stored at the address contained in a pointer, but like all things in the IDE, we can configure the debugger to show it. The key is a small file named **autoexp.dat** which can be found in the **Common\MSDev98\Bin** directory of your Visual C++ installation. This contains all the templates for expanding data within the data tips, watch and variable windows and instructions on how to create your own. You can add rules for your types or change the predefined rules as you wish.

Alternatively, there is yet another way to get at this information.

Watching Variables' Values

To instantly set a watch for the pointer **pnumber**, first position the cursor in the Text Editor window in the middle of the pointer name, **pnumber**, then click on the Debug toolbar icon,

You should see this window:

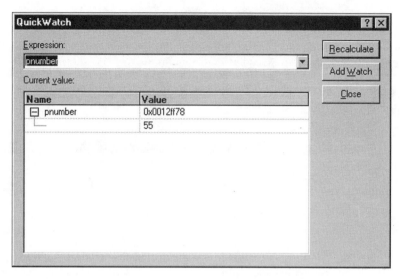

This is called the QuickWatch window because it is a quick way of displaying the value of a variable or an expression. You could enter an expression in place of **pnumber**, pnumber+10 say, click on the Recalculate button, and the new value will be displayed.

The QuickWatch window can only show a single variable or expression, and since the dialog is modal, we can't continue stepping through our code while it is displayed. You must close the dialog in order to continue stepping through your code. If you want to monitor the value of variables or expressions on an ongoing basis, it is better to use the Watch window. You can transfer the expression in the QuickWatch window to the Watch window by clicking on the Add Watch button. Alternatively you can set a permanent watch directly by dragging a highlighted variable or expression from the TextEditor window to the Watch window using the mouse.

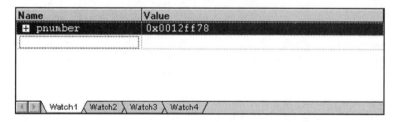

In the QuickWatch and Watch windows, as well as in the Variables window, the variable **pnumber** is automatically displayed in hexadecimal notation, because this is usually the most convenient form for an address. The values for other variables and expressions will be displayed in a notation appropriate to their type. As we said earlier in the context of the Variables window, if you want integer values displayed as hexadecimal, you can right click anywhere in the window, and select the hexadecimal option from the pop-up menu. This will set how integers are displayed in both windows, as well as in the edit window when you hover mouse cursor over a variable. You can also add variables or expressions to the Watch window by typing the name of the variable or the expression into the Name field of a line in the Watch window.

Try expanding the entry for **pnumber** in the Watch window by clicking the plus sign. Now, type ***pnumber** into the Name field of the last blank line. Since ***pnumber** is the value stored at the address given by **pnumber**, the last two lines will always have the same value throughout the execution of the program.

Name	Value
⊟ pnumber	0x0012ff78
	55
*pnumber	55

Watch1 / Watch2 \ Watch3 \ Watch4 /

You could have achieved exactly the same result by highlighting the line under **pnumber** in the Variables window (the line that is shown when you click the plus sign) and dragging it into the Watch window. You could also highlight a variable or expression in the Edit window and drag it to the Watch window. Now try adding the rest of the variables shown by dragging them from either the Auto tab of the Variables window or from the Edit Window into the Watch window. Remember to start your drag by clicking in the Name field of the Variables window, otherwise you'll just drag the value. You can remove items from the Watch window by highlighting the line that they're on and pressing the *Delete* key.

Name	Value	
⊟ pnumber	0x0012ff78	▲
	55	
*pnumber	55	
⊞ &number1	0x0012ff78	
number1	55	
number2	99	▼

Watch1 / Watch2 \ Watch3 \ Watch4 /

Now you can step through each line of code in the program using Step Over so that you don't have to step through all the stream output code. If you do accidentally step into some code that you don't recognize, you can always step out of it again by using the Step Out item from the Debug menu, hitting *Shift+F11* or clicking the 🔲 button on the Debug toolbar. This will complete execution of that code and halt at the beginning of the next statement.

At each stage, you can see that everything operates as described by looking at the values of the variables in the Watch window. The program will end as soon as the last line of code has been executed, but if you wish you can end debugging before that by choosing the Stop Debugging item from the Debug menu, pressing Shift+F5 or hitting the 🔲 button on the Debug toolbar.

There are various options for watching variables that you can experiment with. You can use any of the ways of stepping through a program in any combination, and when debugging a program for real, this is exactly what you would do. Don't forget to try the Help menu if you get stuck.

Changing the Value of a Variable

Using Watch windows also allows you to change the values of the variables you are watching. You would use this in situations where a value displayed is clearly wrong, perhaps because there are bugs in your program, or maybe all the code is not there yet. If you set the 'correct' value, your program will stagger on so that you can test out more of it and perhaps pick up a few more bugs. If your code involves a loop with a large number of iterations, say 30000, you could set the loop counter to 29995 to step through the last few to verify that the loop terminates correctly. It sure beats pressing *F10* 30000 times! Another useful application of the ability to set values for variable during execution is to set values that cause errors. This will enable you to check out the error handling code in your program — something that is almost impossible otherwise.

To change the value of a variable in a Watch window you double-click the variable value shown, and type the new value. If the variable you want to change is an array element, you need to expand the array by clicking on the + box alongside the array name, then change the element value. To change the value for a variable displayed in hexadecimal notation, you can either enter a hexadecimal number, or enter a decimal value prefixed by 0n (zero followed by n), so you could enter a value as A9, or as 0n169. If you just enter 169 it will be interpreted as a hexadecimal value. Naturally, you should be cautious about flinging new values into your program willy-nilly. Unless you are sure you know what effect your changes are going to have, you may end up with a certain amount of erratic program behavior, which is unlikely to get you closer to a working program.

You'll probably find it useful to run a few more of the examples we have seen in previous chapters in debug mode. It will enable you to get a good feel for how the debugger operates under various conditions. Monitoring variables and expressions is a considerable help in sorting out problems with your code, but there's a great deal more assistance available for seeking out and destroying bugs. Let's look at how we can add code to a program that will provide more information about when and why things go wrong.

Adding Debugging Code

For a program involving a significant amount of code, you will certainly need to add code that is aimed at highlighting bugs wherever possible, and providing tracking output to help you pin down where the bugs are. You don't want to be in the business of single stepping through code before you have any idea of what bugs there are, or which part of the code is involved. Code that does this sort of thing is only required while you are testing a program. You won't need it once you believe the program is fully working, and you won't want to carry the overhead of executing it or the inconvenience of seeing all the output in a finished product. For this reason, code that you add for debugging only operates in the debug version of a program, not in the release version — provided you implement it in the right way, of course.

The output produced by debug code should provide clues as to what is causing a problem, and if you have done a good job of building debug code into your program, it will give you a good idea of which part of your program is in error. You can then use the debugger to find the precise nature and location of the bug, and fix it.

The first way of checking the behavior of your program that we will look at is provided by a C++ library function.

Using Assertions

The standard library header **<cassert>** declares a function **assert()** that you can use to check logical conditions within your program when a special preprocessor symbol, **NDEBUG**, is not defined. The function is declared as:

```
void assert(int expression);
```

The argument to the function specifies the condition to be checked, but the effect of the **assert()** function is suppressed if a special preprocessor symbol, **NDEBUG**, is defined. The symbol **NDEBUG** is automatically defined in the release version of a program, but not in the debug version. Thus an assertion will check its argument in the debug version of a program but will do nothing in a release version. If you want to switch off assertions in the debug version of a program, you can define **NDEBUG** explicitly yourself using a **#define** directive. To be effective, you must place the **#define** directive for **NDEBUG** preceding the **#include** directive for the **<cassert>** header in the source file:

```
#define NDEBUG              // Switch off assertions in the code
#include <cassert>          // Declares assert()
```

If the expression passed as an argument to **assert()** is non-zero (i.e. **true**) the function does nothing. If the expression is 0 (**false** in other words) and **NDEBUG** is not defined, a diagnostic message is output showing the expression that failed, the source file name, and the line number in the source file where the failure occurred. After displaying the diagnostic message, the **assert()** function calls **abort()** to end the program. Here's an example of an assertion used in a function:

```
char* append(char* pStr, const char* pAddStr)
{
  // Verify non-null pointers
  assert(pStr != 0);
  assert(pAddStr != 0);

  // Code to append pAddStr to pStr...
}
```

Calling the **append()** function above with a null pointer argument in a simple program produced the following diagnostic message on my machine:

Assertion failed: pStr != 0, file d:\program files\microsoft visual studio\myprojects\ex4_05\debug\ex4_05.exe, line 10

The assertion also displays a message box offering you the three options shown below:

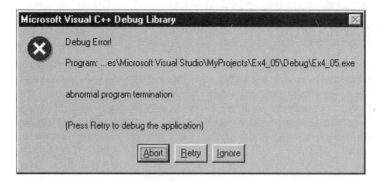

Selecting the <u>A</u>bort button will end the program immediately. The <u>R</u>etry button will start the Visual C++ debugger so you can step through the program to find out more about why the assertion failed. Note that this will start a separate copy of Visual C++ running on your machine, in addition to the original from which you started program execution. In principle, the <u>I</u>gnore button allows the program to continue in spite of the error, but this is usually an unwise choice as the results are likely to be unpredictable.

Where the assertion diagnostic output appears depends on the kind of program you are running. With a console program the message will be passed to **stderr**. If the program is executing under control of Visual C++ it will appear in the console output window as well as in the message box we saw above. If you are running the program in a separate MSDOS session, the message will appear on the DOS command line. With Windows programs — and we will be writing these throughout the remaining chapters of the book — the diagnostic message will be displayed in a Windows message box with three buttons as we saw earlier with our console program run from within Visual C++.

You can use any kind of logical expression as an argument to **assert()**. You can compare values, check pointers, validate object types, or whatever is a useful check on the correct operation of your code. Getting a message when some logical condition fails helps a little, but in general we will need considerably more assistance than that to detect and fix bugs. Let's look at how we can add diagnostic code of a more general nature.

Adding your own Debugging Code

Using preprocessor directives, you can arrange to add any code you like to your program so that it is only compiled and executed in the debug version. Your debug code will be omitted completely from the release version, so it will not affect the efficiency of the tested program at all. You could use the absence of the **NDEBUG** symbol as the control mechanism for the inclusion of debugging code — that's the symbol used to control the **assert()** function operation in the standard library, as we discussed in the last section. Alternatively, for a better and more positive control mechanism, you can use another preprocessor symbol, **_DEBUG**, that is always defined automatically in Visual C++ in the debug version of a program, but is not defined in the release version. You simply enclose code that you only want compiled and executed when you are debugging between a preprocessor **#ifdef**/**#endif** pair of directives, with the test applied to the **_DEBUG** the symbol, as follows:

```
#ifdef _DEBUG

  // Code for debugging purposes...

#endif // _DEBUG
```

The code between the **#ifdef** and the **#endif** will only be compiled if the symbol **_DEBUG** is defined. This means that once your code is fully tested, you can produce the release version completely free of any overhead from your debugging code. The debug code can do anything that is helpful to you in the debugging process, from simply outputting a message to trace the sequence of execution (each function might record that it was called for example) to providing additional calculations to verify and validate data, or calling functions providing debug output.

Of course, you can have as many blocks of debug code like this in a source file as you wish. You also have the possibility of using your own preprocessor symbols to provide more selectivity as to what debug code is included. One reason for doing this is if some of your debug code produced voluminous output, so you would only want to generate this when it was really necessary. Another is to provide a high level of granularity into your debug output, so you can pick and choose which output will be produced on each run. But even in these instances it is still a good idea to use the **_DEBUG** symbol to provide overall control, since this automatically ensures that the release version of a program is completely free of the overhead of debugging code.

Let's consider a simple case. Suppose you used two symbols of your own to control debug code — **MYDEBUG** that managed 'normal' debugging code, and **VOLUMEDEBUG** that you use to control code that produced a lot more output, and that you only wanted some of the time. You can arrange that these symbols are only defined if **_DEBUG** is defined:

```
#ifdef _DEBUG

#define MYDEBUG
#define VOLUMEDEBUG

#endif
```

To prevent volume debugging output you just need to comment out the definition of **VOLUMEDEBUG**, and neither symbol will be defined if **_DEBUG** is not defined. Where your program has several source files, you will probably find it convenient to place your debug control symbols together in a header file, and then **#include** the header into each file that contains debugging code.

Of course, when there is a lot of debugging output, having it directed to the console window will be quite inconvenient. One problem with this is that you can't browse the output afterwards. A useful facility for console programs is provided on the Debug tab of the Project Settings dialog. You can pop this up by right clicking on the project name in FileView (when the debugger is not active) and selecting Settings..., or you can select Settings... from the Project menu or just press *Alt+F7*. You can specify how output is to be redirected with a Program arguments: entry as shown below.

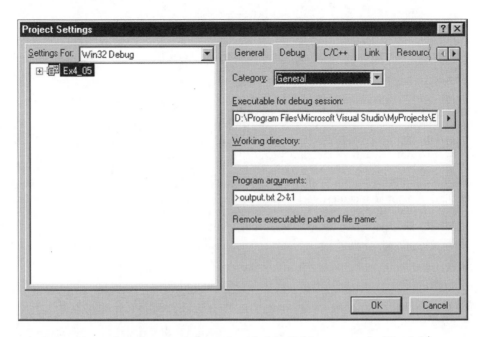

The > symbol is the redirection symbol used with MS_DOS commands. The left argument for > is the source of data and the right argument is the destination. If the left argument is omitted, the default source is **stdout**, the destination for output from your program. Thus, >output.txt redirects the standard output stream, **stdout**, to a file, **output.txt**, which will be created in the current directory.

You can use the digits 1 and 2 to specify a data source to be redirected they correspond to **stdout** and **stderr** respectively. Specifying a destination as &1 or &2 redirects data to the same destination as the current **stdout** or **stderr**, respectively. Thus the second part, 2>&1, redirects the standard error stream, **stderr**, to the same destination as **stdout**. You might also find it useful to read input from a text file that you have prepared in advance. You can redirect input from the standard input stream, **stdin** to be read from a file **input.txt** say, by entering <input.txt here. A further possibility is to append data to an existing stream using the >> operator. If you append the data sent to **stdout** to a file with the entry >>output.txt, you will accumulate output from successive program runs in the same file.

Let's look at a simple example to see how adding debugging code to a program might work in practice.

TRY IT OUT - Adding Code for Debugging

In order to explore these and some general debugging approaches, we will take an example of a program that, while simple, still contains quite a few bugs that we can find and eliminate. Thus you must regard all the code in the remainder of this chapter as suspect, particularly since it will not necessarily reflect good programming practice.

For experimenting with debugging operations, we will start by defining a class that represents a person's name, and then proceed to test it in action. There will be a lot wrong with this code, so resist the temptation to fix the obviously erroneous code here — the idea is to exercise the debugging operations to find them. However, in practice a great many bugs are very evident as soon as you run a program. You don't necessarily need the debugger or additional code to spot them.

First of all we will create an empty console application. You can disable the pre-compiled headers for this project since the example will be small. You do this on the **C/C++** tab in the **Project Settings** dialog — look for precompiled headers in the **Category:** drop down list. Next, let's add a header file, **Name.h**, containing the definition of the **Name** class. We will represent a name by two data members that are pointers to strings storing a person's first and second names. If we want to be able to declare arrays of **Name** objects we must provide a default constructor in addition to any other constructors. We will want to be able to compare **Name** objects, so we should include overloaded operators in the class to do this. We will also want to be able to retrieve the complete name as a single string for convenience. We can add a definition of the **Name** class to the **Name.h** file with these capabilities as follows:

```
// Name.h - Definition of the Name class
#ifndef NAME_H
#define NAME_H

// Class defining a person's name
class Name
{
  public:
    Name();                                        // Default constructor
    Name(const char* pFirst, const char* pSecond);   // Constructor

    char* getName(char* pName) const;        // Get the complete name
    int getNameLength() const;               // Get the complete name length

  // Comparison operators for names
    bool operator<(const Name& name) const;
    bool operator==(const Name& name) const;
    bool operator>(const Name& name) const;

  private:
    char* pFirstname;
    char* pSurname;
};

#endif //NAME_H
```

We can now add a **.cpp** file to the project to hold the definitions for the member functions of **Name**. The constructor definitions are shown below:

```
// Name.cpp - Implementation of the Name class
#include "Name.h"          // Name class definitions
#include "DebugStuff.h"    // Debugging code control
#include <cstring>         // For C-style string functions
#include <cassert>         // For assertions
#include <iostream>
using namespace std;
```

```
  // Default constructor
Name::Name()
{
#ifdef CONSTRUCTOR_TRACE
  // Trace constructor calls
  cerr << "\nDefault Name constructor called.";
#endif
  pFirstname = pSurname = "\0";
}


  // Constructor
Name::Name(const char* pFirst, const char* pSecond):pFirstname(pFirst),
                                                    pSurname(pSecond)

{
  // Verify that arguments are not null
  assert(pFirst != 0);
  assert(pSecond != 0);

#ifdef CONSTRUCTOR_TRACE
  // Trace constructor calls
  cout << "\nName constructor called.";
#endif
}
```

Of course, we don't particularly want to have **Name** objects that have null pointers as members, so the default constructor assigns empty strings for the names. We have used our own debug control symbol, **CONSTRUCTOR_TRACE**, which controls output that traces constructor calls. We will add the definition of this symbol to the header, **DebugStuff.h** a little later. We could put anything at all as debug code here, such as displaying argument values, but it is usually best to keep it as simple as your debugging requirements will allow, otherwise your debug code may introduce further bugs. Here we just identify the constructor when it is called.

We have two assertions in the constructor to check for null pointers being passed as arguments. We could have combined these into one, but by using a separate assertion for each argument we can identify which pointer is null — unless they both are, of course.

You might also want to check that the strings are not empty in an application, by counting the characters prior to the terminating `'\0'` for instance. However, you should not use an assertion to flag this. This sort of thing could arise as a result of user input, so ordinary program checking code should be added to deal with errors that may arise in the normal course of events. It is important to recognize the difference between bugs — errors in the code — and error conditions that can be expected to arise during normal operation of a program. The constructor should never be passed a null pointer, but a zero length name could easily arise under normal operating conditions — from keyboard input for example. In this case it would probably be better if the code reading the names were to check for this before calling the **Name** class constructor. You want errors that will arise during normal use of a program to be handled within the release version of the code.

The **getName()** function requires the caller to supply the address of an array that will accommodate the name:

```
// Return a complete name as a string containing first name, space, surname
// The argument must be the address of a char array sufficient to hold the name
char* Name::getName(char* pName) const
```

```
{
  assert(pName != 0);                                   // Verify non-null argument

#ifdef FUNCTION_TRACE
  // Trace function calls
  cout << "\nName::getName() called.";
#endif

  strcpy(pName, pFirstname);                            // copy first name
  pName[strlen(pName)] = ' ';                           // Append a space
  return strcpy(pName+strlen(pName)+1, pSurname);       // Append second name and
                                                        // return total
}
```

Here we have an assertion to check that the pointer argument passed is not null. Note that we have no way to check that the pointer is to an array with sufficient space to hold the entire name. We must rely on the calling function to do that. We also have debug code to trace when the function is called. Having a record of the complete sequence of calls up to the point where catastrophe strikes can sometimes provide valuable insights as to why and how the problem arose.

The **getNameLength()** member is a helper function that will enable the user of a **Name** object to determine how much space must be allocated to accommodate a complete name:

```
// Returns the total length of a name
int Name::getNameLength() const
{
#ifdef FUNCTION_TRACE
  // Trace function calls
  cout << "\nName::getNameLength() called.";
#endif
  return strlen(pFirstname)+strlen(pSurname);
}
```

A function that intends to call **getName()** will be able use the value returned by **getNameLength()** to determine how much space is needed to accommodate a complete name. We also have trace code in this member function.

In the interests of developing our class incrementally, we can omit the definitions for the overloaded comparison operators. Definitions are only required for member functions that you actually use in your program, and in our initial test program we will keep it very simple.

We can define the preprocessor symbols control whether or not the debug code is executed in the **DebugStuff.h** header:

```
// DebugStuff.h - Debugging control
#ifndef DEBUGSTUFF_H
#define DEBUGSTUFF_H

#ifdef _DEBUG

#define CONSTRUCTOR_TRACE          // Output constructor call trace
#define FUNCTION_TRACE             // Trace function calls
```

```
    #endif

    #endif //DEBUGSTUFF_H
```

Our control symbols will only be defined if **_DEBUG** is defined, so none of the debug code will be included in a release version of the program.

We can now try out the **Name** class with the following **main()** function:

```
// Ex12_1.cpp : Including debug code in a program

#include <iostream>
using namespace std;
#include "Name.h"

int main(int argc, char* argv[])
{
  Name myName("Ivor", "Horton");                   // Try a single object

  // Retrieve and store the name in a local char array
  char theName[10];
  cout << "\nThe name is " << myName.getName(theName);

  // Store the name in an array in the free store
  char* pName = new char[myName.getNameLength()];
  cout << "\nThe name is " << myName.getName(pName);

  cout << endl;
  return 0;
}
```

Now that all the code has been entered, double-checked, and is completely correct, all we have to do is run it to make sure. Hardly seems necessary really...

How It Works

Well it doesn't — it doesn't even compile, does it? The problem is the **Name** constructor. The parameters are **const** — as they should be, but the data members are not. We could declare the data members as **const**, but anyway, we should be copying the name strings, not just copying the pointers. Let's amend the constructor definition to:

```
// Constructor
Name::Name(const char* pFirst, const char* pSecond)
{
  // Verify that arguments are not null
  assert(pFirst != 0);
  assert(pSecond != 0);

#ifdef CONSTRUCTOR_TRACE
  // Trace constructor calls
  cout << "\nName constructor called.";
#endif
  pFirstname = new char[strlen(pFirst)+1];
  strcpy(pFirstname, pFirst);
  pFirstname = new char[strlen(pSecond)+1];
  strcpy(pSurname, pSecond);
}
```

Now we are copying the strings so we should be OK now, shouldn't we?

Rebuild and rerun the program and it gets as far as execution, but fails at the second hurdle. This time we have a message box telling us that the program has performed an illegal operation. You can see from the console window that we got a message from the constructor, so we know roughly how far the execution went. Select the Debug button in the dialog (Cancel if you're running Windows NT) and we will see what happened. This starts a debug session with our example that is separate from the original Visual C++ session.

Debugging a Program

When the debugger starts, we get another message box indicating we have an unhandled exception. In the debugger, we have a comprehensive range of facilities for stepping through our code and tracing the sequence of events. Click on OK in the dialog that indicates there is an unhandled exception, and on the Cancel button in the dialog that follows asking the whereabouts of **STRCAT.ASM** — we really don't want to get into assembler code at this point, and certainly not that of the library function **strcat()**.

The program is at the point where the exception occurred and the code currently executing is in the editor window. The exception is caused by referring to a memory location way outside the realm of the program, so a rogue pointer in our program is the immediate suspect.

The Call Stack

The call stack stores information about functions that have been called and are still executing because they have not returned yet. As we saw earlier, the Call Stack window shows the sequence of function calls outstanding at the current point in the program. Remember that if it's not visible, pressing *Alt+7* will display it.

```
Call Stack                                    ⊠
⇨ strcat() line 169
   Name::Name(const char * 0x0043002c ??_C@_
   main(int 1, char * * 0x00790b60) line 14
   mainCRTStartup() line 206 + 25 bytes
   KERNEL32! bff88e93()
   KERNEL32! bff88d41()
   KERNEL32! bff87759()
```

If you're running Windows NT, the internal workings of the operating system and its kernel mean that you should see a different set of entries in the call stack window to that above and indeed to those variable windows that are used to illustrate the rest of this chapter. However the differences are not so major that you will be unable to follow the remainder of this chapter through. For example, in Windows NT, the current Call Stack window should look like this:

```
Call Stack                                    ⊠
⇨ strcat() line 169
   Name::Name(const char * 0x00430144 ??_C@_
   main(int 1, char * * 0x00440e70) line 14
   mainCRTStartup() line 206 + 25 bytes
   KERNEL32! 77f1b304()
```

The sequence of function calls outstanding runs from the most recent call at the top, the library function **strcat()**, down to the **KERNEL32** calls at the bottom. Each function was called directly or indirectly by the one below it, and none of those displayed have yet executed a return. The bottom four lines (two for NT) are both system routines that start executing prior to our **main()** function. Our interest is the role of our code in this, and you can see from the second line down in the window that the **Name** class constructor was still in execution (had not returned) when the exception was thrown. If you double click on that line, the editor window will display the code for that function, and place the cursor on the line in the source code being executed when the problem arose, which should be the line below:

```
strcpy(pSurname, pSecond);
```

This call caused the unhandled exception to be thrown, but why? The original problem is not necessarily here — it just became apparent here. This is typical of errors involving pointers. Take a look at the window showing the values in the variables in the context of the **Name** constructor at the bottom left.

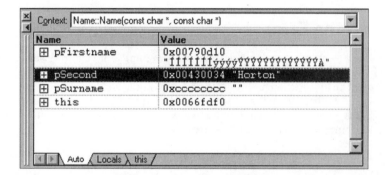

Because the context is a function that is a member of the **Name** class, the Variable window displays the **this** pointer that contains the address of the current object. The pointer, **pSurname** contains a weird address, 0xcccccccc, that corresponds to 3435973836 in decimal! Since I have rather less than 3 billion bytes of memory, it looks a bit unlikely, so **pSurname** has got to be the rogue pointer. If you look at **pFirstname**, this is also in a mess. At the point where we are in the code (copying the surname) the first name should already have been copied, but the contents are rubbish.

The culprit is in the preceding line. Hasty copying of code has resulted in allocating memory for **pFirstname** for a second time, instead of allocating space for **pSurname**. The copy is to a junk address, and this causes the exception to be thrown. Don't you wish you had checked what you did, properly? The line should be:

```
pSurname = new char[strlen(pSecond)+1];
```

It is typically the case that the code causing a bad pointer address is not the code where the error makes itself felt. In general it may be very far away. Just examining the pointer or pointers involved in the statement causing the error can often lead you directly to the problem, but sometimes it can involve a lot of searching. You could always add more debug code if you get really stuck.

You can go right ahead and change the statement in the editor window to what it should be. To recompile the project with the change included, you can select the 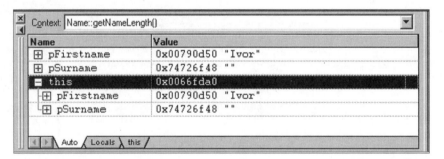 button on the Debug toolbar, or just press *Alt+F10*.

We can restart the program inside the debugger once it has been recompiled by clicking on the button on the Debug toolbar, but surprise, surprise — we get another unhandled exception. This undoubtedly means more pointer trouble, and you can see from the output in the console window that the last function call was to **getNameLength()**:

```
Name constructor called.
Name::getName() called.
The name is Horton
Name::getNameLength() called.
```

The output for the name is definitely not right. However, we don't know where exactly the problem is. Restarting and stepping through the program once more should provide some clues.

Step over to the Error

In the Call Stack window you can see that the program is in the **getNameLength()** function member, which merely calls the **strlen()** library function to get the overall length of the name. The **strlen()** function is unlikely to be at fault, so this must mean that there is something wrong with part of the object. If you double click the **getNameLength()** function in the Call Stack window, the window showing the variables in the context of this function shows that the current object has been corrupted.

The current object is pointed to by **this**, and by clicking on the plus symbol, you can see the data members. It's the **pSurname** member that is the problem. The address it contains should refer to the string "Horton" but it clearly doesn't.

On the assumption that this kind of error does not originate at the point where you experience the effect, we can go back, restart the program and single step through, looking for where the **Name** object gets messed up. You can select in the debug window to restart the application, and single step through the statements by pressing *F10*. After executing the statement that defines the **myName** object, the Variable window for the **main()** function shows that it has been constructed successfully, as you can see below.

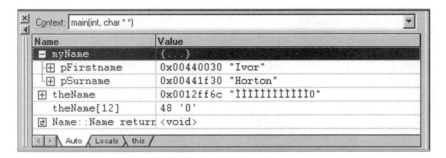

Executing the next statement that outputs the name corrupts the object, **myName**. You can see that this is the case from the Variables window for **main()**.

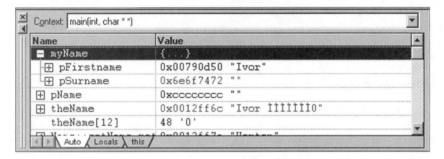

On the reasonable assumption that the stream output operations work OK, it must be our **getName()** member doing something it shouldn't.

If you restart the debugger once more, but this time use [] when execution reaches the output statement, you can step through the statement's **getName()** function. Watch the context window as you progress through the function.

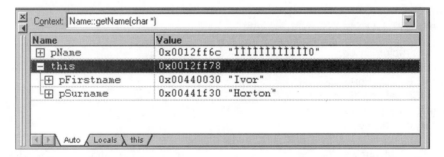

You will see that everything is fine until you execute the statement:

```
return strcpy(pName+strlen(pName)+1, pSurname);        // Append second name after
                                                        // the space
```

This statement causes the corruption of **pSurname** for the current object, pointed to by **this**. You can see this in the Variables window below.

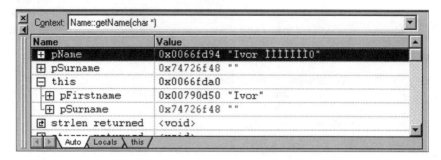

How can copying from the object to another array corrupt the object, especially since **pSurname** is passed as an argument for a **const** parameter? You need to look at the address stored in **pName** for a clue. Compare it with the address contained in the **this** pointer. The difference is only 12 bytes — they could hardly be closer really! The address calculation for the position in **pName** is incorrect, simply because we forgot that copying a space to overwrite the terminating **'\0'** in the **pName** array means that **strlen(pName)** can no longer calculate the correct length of **pName**. The whole problem is caused by the statement:

```
pName[strlen(pName)] = ' ';                    // Append a space
```

This is overwriting the **'\0'** and thus making the subsequent call to **strlen()** produce an invalid result. This code is unnecessarily messy anyway – using the library function **strcat()** to catenate a string is much better than using **strcpy()**, as it renders all this pointer modification unnecessary. We should rewrite the statement as:

```
strcat(pName, " ");                            // Append a space
```

Of course, the subsequent statement also needs to be changed to:

```
return strcat(pName, pSurname);                // Append second name and return total
```

With these changes we can recompile and give it another go. The program appears to run satisfactorily as you can see from the output:

Name constructor called.
Name::getName() called.
The name is Ivor Horton
Name::getNameLength() called.
Name::getName() called.
The name is Ivor Horton

Getting the right output does not always mean that all is well — and it certainly isn't in this case.

```
int main(int argc, char* argv[])
{
  Name myName("Ivor", "Horton");                     // Try a single object

  // Retrieve and store the name in a local char array
  char theName[10];
  cout << "\nThe name is " << myName.getName(theName);
```

```
   // Store the name in an array in the free store
   char* pName = new char[myName.getNameLength()];
   cout << "\nThe name is " << myName.getName(pName);

   cout << endl;
   return 0;
}
```

Both the shaded lines are in error. The first shaded line provides an array of 10 characters to store the name. In fact 12 are required — 10 for the two names, one for the space, and one for `'\0'` at the end. The more serious problem is in the definition **getNameLength()** member of the class. It omits to add 1 for the space between the first and second names, so the value returned will always be one short. The definition should be:

```
int Name::getNameLength() const
{
#ifdef FUNCTION_TRACE
   // Trace function calls
   cout << "\nName::getNameLength() called.";
#endif
   return strlen(pFirstname)+strlen(pSurname)+1;
}
```

That's not the end of it by any means. You may have already spotted that our class still has serious errors, but let's press on with testing to see if they come out in the wash.

Testing the Extended Class

Based on the output, everything is working, so it's time to add the definitions for the overloaded comparison operators to the **Name** class. To implement these we can use the comparison functions declared in the **<cstring>** header. Let's start with the 'less than' operator:

```
// Less than operator
bool Name::operator<(const Name& name) const
{
   int result = strcmp(pSurname, name.pSurname);
   if(result < 0)
     return true;
   if(result == 0 && strcmp(pFirstname, name.pFirstname) < 0)
     return true;
   else
     return false;
}
```

We can now define the `>` operator very easily in terms of the `<` operator:

```
// Greater than operator
bool Name::operator>(const Name& name) const
{
   return name > *this;
}
```

For determining equal names we use the **strcmp()** function from the standard library again:

```
// Equal to operator
bool Name::operator==(const Name& name) const
{
  if(strcmp(pSurname, name.pSurname) == 0 &&
                              strcmp(pFirstname, name.pFirstname) == 0)
    return true;
  else
    return false;
}
```

We must now extend the test program. We can create an array of **Name** objects, initialize them in some arbitrary way, and then compare the elements of the array using our comparison operators for a **Name** object. Here's **main()** along with a function, **init()**, to initialize a **Name** array:

```
// Ex12_2.cpp : Extending the test operation

#include <iostream>
using namespace std;
#include "Name.h"

// Function to initialize an array of random names
void init(Name* names, int count)
{
  char* firstnames[] = { "Charles", "Mary", "Arthur", "Emily", "John"};
  int firstsize = sizeof (firstnames)/sizeof(firstnames[0]);
  char* secondnames[] = { "Dickens", "Shelley", "Miller", "Bronte", "Steinbeck"};
  int secondsize = sizeof (secondnames)/sizeof(secondnames[0]);
  char* first = firstnames[0];
  char* second = secondnames[0];

  for(int i = 0 ; i<count ; i++)
  {
    if(i%2)
      first = firstnames[i%firstsize];
    else
      second = secondnames[i%secondsize];

    names[i] = Name(first, second);
  }
}

int main(int argc, char* argv[])
{
  Name myName("Ivor", "Horton");                    // Try a single object

  // Retrieve and store the name in a local char array
  char theName[12];
  cout << "\nThe name is " << myName.getName(theName);

  // Store the name in an array in the free store
  char* pName = new char[myName.getNameLength()+1];
  cout << "\nThe name is " << myName.getName(pName);
```

```
      const int arraysize = 10;
      Name names[arraysize];                             // Try an array

      // Initialize names
      init(names, arraysize);

   // Try out comparisons
      char* phrase = 0;                                  // Stores a comparison phrase
      char* iName = 0;                                   // Stores a complete name
      char* jName = 0;                                   // Stores a complete name

      for(int i = 0; i < arraysize ; i++)                // Compare each element
      {
        iName = new char[names[i].getNameLength()+1];    // Array to hold first name
        for(int j = i+1 ; j<arraysize ; j++)             // with all the others
        {
          if(names[i] < names[j])
            phrase = " less than ";
          else if(names[i] > names[j])
            phrase = " greater than ";
          else if(names[i] == names[j])                  // Superfluous - but it calls
            phrase = " equal to ";                       // the operator function
          jName = new char[names[j].getNameLength()+1];  // Array to hold second name
          cout << endl << names[i].getName(iName) << " is" << phrase
               << names[j].getName(jName);
        }
      }

   cout << endl;
   return 0;
}
```

The **init()** function picks successive combinations of first and second names from the array of names to initialize the array **Name** objects. Names will be repeated after 25 have been generated, but we only need 10 here.

Finding the Next Bug

It fails again. What's more there's a lot of output. With each element in the array being compared with each of the others, we are going to get 45 lines of output just from that. We could reduce the size of the array, but let's direct the output for the project to a file, as we discussed earlier. Just specify >output.txt 2>&1 as the Program arguments: on the Debug tab of the Project Settings dialog.

The Call Stack window tells you what is wrong. We have successive calls of the **operator>()** function so it must be calling itself. If you look at the code you can see why — a typo. The single line in the body of the function should be:

```
return name < *this;
```

We can fix that, recompile, and try again. This time it works correctly but unfortunately the class is still defective. Don't forget that all the output is now saved to a file called **output.txt**

output.txt in your project directory. It has a memory leak that exhibits no symptoms here, but in another context could cause mayhem. Memory leaks are hard to detect ordinarily, but we can get some extra help from Visual C++.

Debugging Dynamic Memory

Allocating memory dynamically is a potent source of bugs and perhaps the most common bugs in this context are memory leaks. Just to remind you, a memory leak arises when you use the new operator to allocate memory, but you never use the **delete** operator to free it again when you are done with it. Apart from just forgetting to delete memory that you have allocated, you should particularly be aware that non-virtual destructors in a class hierarchy can also cause the problem — since it can cause the wrong destructor to be called when an object is destroyed, as we have seen. Of course, when your program ends, all the memory is freed, but while it is running it remains allocated to your program. Memory leaks present no obvious symptoms much of the time, maybe never in some cases, but it is detrimental to the performance of your machine since memory is being occupied to no good purpose. Sometimes, it can result in a catastrophic failure of the program when all available memory has been allocated.

For checking your program's use of the free store, Visual C++ provides a range of diagnostic routines — these use a special debug version of the free store. These are declared in the header **crtdbg.h**. All calls to these routines are automatically removed from the release version of your program, so you don't need to worry about adding preprocessor controls for them.

Functions Checking the Free Store

Let's get an overview of what's involved in checking free store operations and then see how memory leaks can be detected. The functions declared in **ctrdbg.h** check the free store using a record of its status stored in a structure of type **_CrtMemState**. This structure is relatively simple, and is defined as:

```
typedef struct _CrtMemState
{
  struct _CrtMemBlockHeader* pBlockHeader;    // Pointer to the most recently
                                              // allocated block
  unsigned long lCounts[_MAX_BLOCKS];         // Counter for each of the types of
                                              // block
  unsigned long lSizes[_MAX_BLOCKS];          // Total bytes allocated in each
                                              // block type
  unsigned long lHighWaterCount;              // The most bytes allocated at a time
                                              // up to now
  unsigned long lTotalCount;                  // The total bytes allocated at
                                              // present
} _CrtMemState;
```

We won't be concerned directly with the details of the state of the free store because we will be using functions that present the information in a more readable form. There are quite a few functions involved in tracking free store operations but we will only look at the five most interesting ones.

These provide you with the following capabilities:

- ▶ To record the state of the free store at any point
- ▶ To determine the difference between two states of the free store.
- ▶ To output state information.
- ▶ To output information about objects in the free store.
- ▶ To detect memory leaks.

Here are the declarations of these functions together with a brief description of what they do:

```
void _CrtMemCheckpoint(_CrtMemState* state);
```

This stores the current state of the free store in a **_CrtMemState** structure. The argument you pass to the function is a pointer to a **_CrtMemState** structure in which the state is to be recorded.

```
int _CrtMemDifference(_CrtMemState* stateDiff,
                      const _CrtMemState* oldState,
                      const _CrtMemState* newState);
```

This function compares the state specified by the third argument, with a previous state that you specify in the second argument. The difference is stored in a **_CrtMemState** structure that you specify in the first argument. If the states are different, the function returns a non-zero value (**true**), otherwise 0 (**false**) is returned.

```
void _CrtMemDumpStatistics(const _CrtMemState* state);
```

This dumps information about the free store state specified by the argument to an output stream. The state structure pointed to by the argument can be a state that you recorded using **_CrtMemCheckpoint()** or the difference between two states produced by **_CrtMemDifference()**.

```
void _CrtMemDumpAllObjectsSince(const _CrtMemState* state);
```

This function dumps information on objects allocated in the free store since the state of the free store specified by the argument — this will have been recorded by an earlier call in your program to **_CrtMemCheckpoint()**. If you pass null to the function, it dumps information on all objects allocated since the start of execution of your program.

```
int _CrtDumpMemoryLeaks();
```

This is the function we need for our example as it checks for memory leaks and dumps information on any leak that is detected. You can call this function at any time, but a very useful mechanism can cause the function to be called automatically when your program ends. If you enable this mechanism, you will get automatic detection of any memory leaks that occurred during program execution, so let's see how we can do that.

Controlling Free Store Debug Operations

You control free store debug operations by setting a flag, **_crtDbgFlag**, which is of type **int**. This flag incorporates five separate control bits, including one to enable automatic memory leak checking. You specify these control bits using the following identifiers:

Bit field	Description
_CRTDBG_ALLOC_MEM_DF	When this bit is on it turns on debug allocation so the free store state can be tracked.
_CRTDBG_DELAY_FREE_MEM_DF	When this is on it prevents memory from being freed by delete, so that you can determine what happens under low-memory conditions.
_CRTDBG_CHECK_ALWAYS_DF	When this is on it causes the **_CrtCheckMemory()** function to be called automatically at every new and delete operation. This function verifies the integrity of the free store, checking, for example, that blocks have not been overwritten by storing values beyond the range of an array. A report is output if any defect is discovered. This slows execution, but catches errors quickly.
_CRTDBG_CHECK_CRT_DF	When this is on, the memory used internally by the run-time library is tracked in debug operations.
_CRTDBG_LEAK_CHECK_DF	Causes leak checking to be performed at program exit by automatically calling **_CrtDumpMemoryLeaks()**. You only get output from this if your program has failed to free all the memory that it allocated.

By default, the **_CRTDBG_ALLOC_MEM_DF** bit is on, and all the others are off. You must use the bitwise operators to set and unset combinations of these bits. To set the **_crtDbgFlag** flag you pass a flag of type **int** to the **_CrtDbgFlag()** function that implements the combination of indicators that you require. This puts your flag into effect and returns the previous status of **_CrtDbgFlag**. One way to set the indicators you want is to first obtain the current status of the **_crtDbgFlag** flag. You would do this by calling the **_CrtSetDbgFlag()** function with the argument **_CRTDBG_REPORT_FLAG** as follows:

```
int flag = _CrtSetDbgFlag(_CRTDBG_REPORT_FLAG);          // Get current flag
```

You can then set or unset the indicators by combining the identifiers for the individual indicators with this flag using bitwise operators. To set an indicator on, you OR the indicator identifier with the flag. For example, to set the automatic leak checking indicator on, in the flag, you could write:

```
flag |= _CRTDBG_LEAK_CHECK_DF;
```

To turn an indicator off, you must AND the negation of the identifier with the flag. For example, to turn off tracking of memory that is used internally by the library, you could write:

```
flag &= ~_CRTDBG_CHECK_CRT_DF;
```

To put your new flag into effect, you just call **_CrtSetDbgFlag()** with your flag as the argument:

```
_CrtSetDbgFlag(flag);
```

Alternatively, you can OR all the identifiers for the indicators that you want, together, and pass the result as the argument to **_CrtSetDbgFlag()**. If we just want to leak check when the program exits, we could write:

```
_CrtSetDbgFlag(_CRTDBG_LEAK_CHECK_DF|_CRTDBG_ALLOC_MEM_DF);
```

If you need to set a particular combinations of indicators, rather than setting or unsetting bits at various points in your program, this is the easiest way to do it. We are almost at the point where we can apply the dynamic memory debugging facilities to our example. We just need to look at how we determine where free store debugging output goes.

Free Store Debugging Output

The destination of the output from the free store debugging functions is not the standard output stream by default; they go to the debug message window. If we want to see the output on **stdout** we must set this up. There are two functions involved in this, **_CrtSetReportMode()** which sets the general destination for output, and **_CrtSetReportFile()** which specifies a stream destination specifically. The **_CrtSetReportMode()** function is declared as:

int _CrtSetReportMode(int reportType, int reportMode);

There are three kinds of output produced by the free store debugging functions. Each call to the **_CrtSetReportMode()** function sets the destination specified by the second argument for the output type specified by the first argument. You specify the report type by one of the following identifiers:

Report Type	Description
_CRT_WARN	Warning messages of various kinds. The output when a memory leak is detected is a warning.
_CRT_ERROR	Catastrophic errors that report unrecoverable problems.
_CRT_ASSERT	Output from assertions (not that from the **assert()** function that we discussed earlier).

The **crtdbg.h** header defines two macros, **ASSERT** and **ASSERTE**, that work in much the same way as the **assert()** function in the standard library. The difference between these two macros is that **ASSERTE** reports the assertion expression when a failure occurs, whereas the **ASSERT** macro does not.

You specify the report mode by a combination of the following identifiers:

Report Mode	`_CrtDbgReport` Behavior
`_CRTDBG_MODE_DEBUG`	This is the default mode, which sends output to a debug string that you will see in the debug window when running under control of the debugger.
`_CRTDBG_MODE_FILE`	Output is to be directed to an output stream.
`_CRTDBG_MODE_WNDW`	Output is presented in a message box.
`_CRTDBG_REPORT_MODE`	If you specify this, the `_CrtSetReportMode()` function just returns the current report mode.

To specify more than one destination, you simply OR the identifiers using the | operator. You set the destination for each output type with a separate call of the `_CrtSetReportMode()` function. To direct the output when a leak is detected to a file stream, we can set the report mode with the following statement:

```
CrtSetReportMode(_CRT_WARN, _CRTDBG_MODE_FILE);
```

This just sets the destination generically as a file stream. We still need to call the `_CrtSetReportFile()` function to specify the destination specifically.

The `_CrtSetReportFile()` function is declared as:

```
_HFILE _CrtSetReportFile(int reportType, _HFILE reportFile);
```

The second argument here can either be a pointer to a file stream (of type `_HFILE`), which we will not go into further, or can be one of the following identifiers:

Report File	`_CrtDbgReport` Behavior
`_CRTDBG_FILE_STDERR`	Output is directed to the standard error stream, **stderr**.
`_CRTDBG_FILE_STDOUT`	Output is directed to the standard output stream, **stdout**.
`_CRTDBG_REPORT_FILE`	If you specify this argument, the `_CrtSetReportFile()` function will just return the current destination.

To set the leak detection output to the standard output stream, we can write:

```
_CrtSetReportFile(_CRT_WARN, _CRTDBG_FILE_STDOUT);
```

We now have enough knowledge of the free store debug routines to try out leak detection in our example.

TRY IT OUT - Memory Leak Detection

Even though we have set the project settings to direct the standard output stream to a file, it would be as well to reduce the volume of output, so we will reduce the size of the names array to 5 elements. Here's the new version of **main()** to use the free store debug facilities in general and leak detection in particular:

```
int main(int argc, char* argv[])
{
  // Turn on free store debugging and leak-checking bits
  _CrtSetDbgFlag( _CRTDBG_LEAK_CHECK_DF|_CRTDBG_ALLOC_MEM_DF );

  // Direct warnings to stdout
  _CrtSetReportMode(_CRT_WARN, _CRTDBG_MODE_FILE);
  _CrtSetReportFile(_CRT_WARN, _CRTDBG_FILE_STDOUT);

  Name myName("Ivor", "Horton");                     // Try a single object

  // Retrieve and store the name in a local char array
  char theName[12];
  cout << "\nThe name is " << myName.getName(theName);

  // Store the name in an array in the free store
  char* pName = new char[myName.getNameLength()+1];
  cout << "\nThe name is " << myName.getName(pName);

  const int arraysize = 5;
  Name names[arraysize];                             // Try an array

  // Initialize names
  init(names, arraysize);

  // Try out comparisons
  char* phrase = 0;                                  // Stores a comparison phrase
  char* iName = 0;                                   // Stores a complete name
  char* jName = 0;                                   // Stores a complete name

  for(int i = 0; i < arraysize ; i++)                // Compare each element
  {
    iName = new char[names[i].getNameLength()+1];    // Array to hold first name
    for(int j = i+1 ; j<arraysize ; j++)             // with all the others
    {
      if(names[i] < names[j])
        phrase = " less than ";
      else if(names[i] > names[j])
        phrase = " greater than ";
      else if(names[i] == names[j])                  // Superfluous - but it calls
                                                     // the operator function
        phrase = " equal to ";
      jName = new char[names[j].getNameLength()+1];  // Array to hold second name
      cout << endl << names[i].getName(iName) << " is" << phrase
       << names[j].getName(jName);
    }
  }
  cout << endl;
  return 0;
}
```

You need to add an **#include** directive for **crtdbg.h** to the file of course. To reduce output further we could switch off the trace output by commenting out our control symbols in the **DebugStuff.h** header:

```
// DebugStuff.h - Debugging control
#ifndef DEBUGSTUFF_H
#define DEBUGSTUFF_H

#ifdef _DEBUG

//#define CONSTRUCTOR_TRACE        // Output constructor call trace
//#define FUNCTION_TRACE           // Trace function calls
#endif

#endif //DEBUGSTUFF_H
```

You can recompile the example and run it again.

How It Works

It works just as expected. We get a report that our program does indeed have memory leaks, and we get a list of the objects in the free store at the end of the program. The output generated by the free store debug facility starts with:

```
Detected memory leaks!
Dumping objects ->
{55} normal block at 0x007A1FE0, 16 bytes long.
 Data: <                > CD CD CD CD CD CD CD CD CD CD CD CD CD CD CD CD
{54} normal block at 0x007A0030, 16 bytes long.
 Data: <Emily Steinbeck > 45 6D 69 6C 79 20 53 74 65 69 6E 62 65 63 6B 00
{53} normal block at 0x007A0070, 13 bytes long.
 Data: <Emily Miller > 45 6D 69 6C 79 20 4D 69 6C 6C 65 72 00
...
```

and ends with:

```
...
{32} normal block at 0x007A05B0, 8 bytes long.
 Data: <Dickens > 44 69 63 6B 65 6E 73 00
{31} normal block at 0x007A0C90, 8 bytes long.
 Data: <Charles > 43 68 61 72 6C 65 73 00
{30} normal block at 0x007A0CD0, 12 bytes long.
 Data: <Ivor Horton > 49 76 6F 72 20 48 6F 72 74 6F 6E 00
{27} normal block at 0x007A0F00, 7 bytes long.
 Data: <Horton > 48 6F 72 74 6F 6E 00
{26} normal block at 0x007A0F40, 5 bytes long.
 Data: <Ivor > 49 76 6F 72 00
Object dump complete.
```

The objects reported as being left in the free store are presented with the most recently allocated first, and the earliest last. It is obvious from the output that the **Name** class is allocating memory for its data members, and never releasing it. The last three objects dumped correspond to the **pName** array allocated in main(), and the data members of the object,

myName. The blocks for the complete names are allocated in **main()**, and they too are left laying about. The problem our class has is that we forgot the fundamental rules relating to classes that allocate memory dynamically — they should always define a destructor, a copy constructor, and the assignment operator. Our class should be declared as:

```
class Name
{
  public:
    Name();                                       // Default constructor
    Name(const char* pFirst, const char* pSecond); // Constructor
    Name(const Name& rName);                       // Copy constructor

    ~Name();                                       // Destructor

    char* getName(char* pName) const;              // Get the complete name
    int getNameLength() const;                      // Get the complete name
                                                   // length

  // Comparison operators for names
    bool operator<(const Name& name) const;
    bool operator==(const Name& name) const;
    bool operator>(const Name& name) const;

    Name& operator=(const Name& rName);            // Assignment operator

  private:
    char* pFirstname;
    char* pSurname;
};
```

We can define the copy constructor as:

```
Name:: Name(const Name& rName)
{
  pFirstname = new char[strlen(rName.pFirstname)+1]; // Allocate space for first
                                                     // name
  strcpy(pFirstname, rName.pFirstname);              // and copy it.
  pSurname = new char[strlen(rName.pSurname)+1];      // Same for the surname...
  strcpy(pSurname, rName.pSurname);
}
```

The destructor just needs to release the memory for the two data members:

```
Name::~Name()
{
  delete[] pFirstname;
  delete[] pSurname;
}
```

In the assignment operator we must make the usual provision for the left and right hand sides being identical:

```
Name& Name::operator=(const Name& rName)
{
  if(this == &rName)                               // If lhs equals rhs
    return *this;                                  // just return the object
```

```
      delete[] pFirstname;
      pFirstname = new char[strlen(rName.pFirstname)+1];  // Allocate space for first
                                                          // name
      strcpy(pFirstname, rName.pFirstname);               // and copy it.
      delete[] pSurname;
      pSurname = new char[strlen(rName.pSurname)+1];       // Same for the surname...
      strcpy(pSurname, rName.pSurname);
      return *this;
   }
```

We also should make the default constructor work properly. If the default constructor doesn't allocate memory in the free store, we have the possibility that the destructor will erroneously attempt to delete memory that was not allocated in the free store. We need to modify it to:

```
Name::Name()
{
#ifdef CONSTRUCTOR_TRACE
   // Trace constructor calls
   cout << "\nDefault Name constructor called.";
#endif

   // Allocate array of 1 for empty strings
   pFirstname = new char[1];
   pSurname = new char[1];

   pFirstname[0] = pSurname[0] = '\0';                     // Store null character
}
```

If you add statements to **main()** to delete the memory that is allocated dynamically there, the program should run without any messages relating to memory leaks.

Summary

Debugging is a big topic and Visual C++ provides many debugging facilities beyond what we have discussed here. If you are comfortable with what we have covered in this chapter, you should have little trouble expanding your knowledge of the debug capabilities through the Visual C++ documentation. Searching on 'debugging' should generate a rich list of further information.

The essential points we introduced in this chapter were:

> You can use the **assert()** library function declared in the **<cassert>** header to check logical conditions in your program that should always be **true**. You should not use assertion to check conditions that may be false in normal program operation.

> The preprocessor symbol, **_NDEBUG**, is automatically defined in the debug version of a program. It is not defined in the release version.

> You can add your own debugging code by enclosing it between an **#ifdef/#endif** pair of directives testing for **_NDEBUG**. Your debug code will then only be included in the debug version of the program.

> The **crtdbg.h** headers supplies declarations for functions to provide debugging of free store operations.

> By setting the **_crtDbgFlag** appropriately, you can enable automatic checking of your program for memory leaks.

> To direct output messages from the free store debugging functions, you call the **_CrtSetReportMode()** and **_CrtSetReportFile()** functions.

With the basics of debugging added to your knowledge of C++, you are ready for the big one — Windows programming!

Understanding Windows Programming

This chapter is an overview of using Visual C++ for Windows programming. We'll look at how to use Visual C++ to generate a Windows program, and how that program is organized. By the end of this chapter, you will understand:

- What the Microsoft Foundation Classes are
- The basic elements of an MFC-based program
- Single Document Interface (SDI) applications and Multiple Document Interface (MDI) applications
- What the AppWizard is and how to use it to generate SDI and MDI programs
- What files are generated by the AppWizard and what their contents are
- How an AppWizard-generated program is structured
- The key classes in an AppWizard-generated program, and how they are interconnected
- What the principal source files of an AppWizard program contain
- The general approach to customizing an AppWizard-generated program

We'll expand the AppWizard programs that we generate in this chapter by adding features and code incrementally in subsequent chapters. By the end of the book, you should end up with a sizable, working Windows program that incorporates the basic user interface programming techniques.

The Essentials of a Windows Program

In Chapter 7, we saw an elementary Windows program which displayed a short quote from the Bard. It was unlikely to win any awards, being completely free of any useful functionality, but it did serve to illustrate the two essential components of a Windows program: providing initialization and setup, and servicing Windows messages. These are illustrated here:

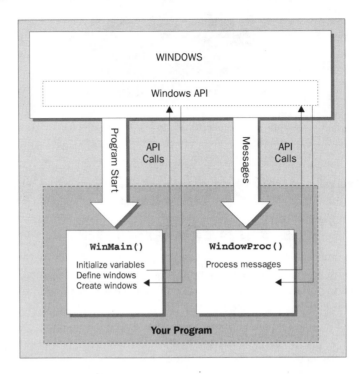

This structure is at the heart of *all* Windows programs. You can see the two essential pieces of a Windows program: the function **WinMain()**, which is called by Windows at the start of execution of the program, and a window procedure for each window class you've defined, often referred to as **WndProc()** or **WindowProc()**, which will be called by the operating system whenever a message is to be passed to your application's window.

The function **WinMain()** does any initialization that's necessary and sets up the window or windows that will be the primary interface to the user. It also contains the message loop for retrieving messages that have been queued for the application.

The function **WindowProc()** handles all the messages that aren't queued: this includes those messages that were initiated in the message loop in **WinMain()**. **WindowProc()**, therefore, ends up handling both kinds of messages. This is because the code in the message loop will sort out what kind of message it has retrieved from the queue, and then dispatch it for processing by **WindowProc()**. **WindowProc()** is where you code your application-specific response to each Windows message: **WindowProc()** should handle all the communications with the user by processing the Windows messages generated by user actions, such as moving or clicking the mouse, or entering information at the keyboard.

The queued messages are largely those caused by user input from either the mouse or the keyboard. The non-queued messages for which Windows calls your **WindowProc()** function directly are either messages that your program created (typically as a result of obtaining a message from the queue and then dispatching it), or messages that are concerned with window management (such as handling menus and scrollbars, or resizing the window).

524

The Windows API

The example that you saw in Chapter 7 used the **Windows Application Programming Interface** (or **Windows API**). The Windows API comes as part of every copy of Windows, and consists of a large set of functions that provide all the services and communications with Windows that are necessary for producing an application that is to run in the Windows environment. The API actually contains over a thousand functions.

All the interactions between a program and the user are handled by Windows. Your program will receive information from the user second-hand, through Windows messages. Every Windows program uses the Windows API, regardless of how it is produced. All the programs we will write using Visual C++ will ultimately use the Windows API, so there's no getting away from it. Fortunately, we don't need to know very much about the Windows API in detail—as MFC does a terrific job of packaging it up into a much more organized and friendly form.

Visual C++ and the Windows API

Remember that the Windows API was not written with Visual C++ in mind, or even considering C++ in general, since it was written before C++ came into general use. Naturally, the Windows API needs to be usable in programs written in a variety of languages, most of which aren't object-oriented. The API functions don't handle or recognize class objects but, as we shall soon see, MFC encapsulates the API in a way that makes using it a piece of cake.

Visual C++ lets you develop a Windows program in two stages. First, you use Visual C++'s set of tools to generate code for a program automatically; then you modify and extend the code to suit your needs. As the basis for doing this, Visual C++ uses a hierarchy of classes called the **Microsoft Foundation Classes** (although they can also be used independently of the development tools in Visual C++).

The Microsoft Foundation Classes

The Microsoft Foundation Classes, usually abbreviated to **MFC**, are a set of predefined classes upon which Windows programming with Visual C++ is built. These classes represent an object-oriented approach to Windows programming that encapsulates the Windows API. The process of writing a Windows program involves creating and using MFC objects, or objects of classes derived from MFC. In the main, we'll derive our own classes from MFC—we'll have considerable assistance from the specialized tools in Visual C++ that make this even easier. The objects created will incorporate member functions for communicating with Windows, for processing Windows messages, and for sending messages to each other.

These derived classes will, of course, inherit all of the members of their base classes. These inherited functions do practically all of the general grunt work necessary for a Windows application to work. All we need to do is add the data and function members that customize the classes; in this way, we can provide the application-specific functionality that we need in our program. In doing this, we'll be applying most of the techniques that we've been grappling with in the preceding chapters, particularly those involving class inheritance and virtual functions.

MFC Notation

All the classes in MFC have names beginning with **C**, such as **CDocument** or **CView**. If you use the same convention when defining your own classes or deriving them from those in the MFC library, your programs will be easier to follow. Data members of an MFC class are prefixed with **m_**. We'll also follow this convention in the examples, just as we've been doing throughout the book.

You'll find that MFC uses Hungarian notation for many variable names, particularly those that originate in the Windows API. As you will recall, this involves using a prefix of **p** for a pointer, **n** for an **int**, **l** for **long**, **h** for a handle, and so on. The name **m_lpCmdLine**, for example, would refer to a data member of a class (because of the **m_** prefix) that is of type 'pointer to **long**'. This practice of explicitly showing the type of a variable in its name was important in the C environment because of the lack of type checking; since you could determine the type from the name, you had a fair chance of not using or interpreting its value incorrectly. The downside is that the variable names can become quite cumbersome, making the code look more complicated than it really is. Since C++ has strong type checking, it will pick up the sort of misuse that used to happen regularly in C; consequently this kind of notation isn't essential, so we won't use it for our own variables in our examples in the book. However, we will retain the **p** prefix for pointers, and some of the other simple type denotations, since this helps to make the code more readable.

How an MFC Program is Structured

We know from Chapter 1 that we can produce a Windows program using the AppWizard without writing a single line of code. Of course, this uses the MFC library, but it's quite possible to write a Windows program which uses MFC without using AppWizard. If we first scratch the surface by constructing the minimum MFC-based program, we can get a clear idea of the fundamental elements involved.

The simplest program that we can produce using MFC is slightly less sophisticated than the example that we wrote in Chapter 7, using the raw Windows API. The example we'll produce here will have a window but no text displayed in it. This will be sufficient to show the fundamentals, so let's try it out.

TRY IT OUT - An MFC Application Without AppWizard

First, create a new project workspace using the File | New... menu option, as you've done many times before. We won't use AppWizard here, so select the type of project as Win32 Application, as shown below:

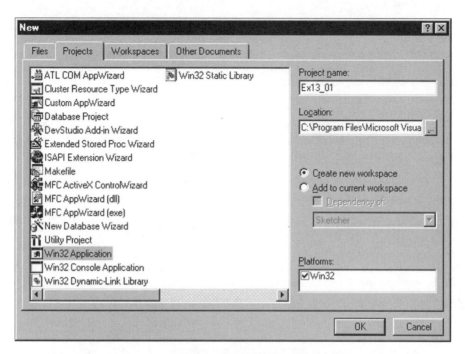

After entering this information, the following dialog will appear:

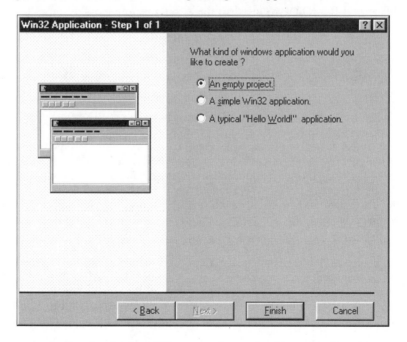

We're going to create the simplest possible type of program here, so select An empty project, and then hit Finish. The New Project Information dialog will confirm that you've chosen an empty application; hit OK to confirm your choice.

With this choice of project type, we must ensure that the linker knows that we intend to use MFC classes. If we don't do this, the wrong link options will be set and we will get some obscure linker errors. Use the Project | Settings... menu item to bring up the Project Settings dialog. Go to the General tab and make sure that the Microsoft Foundation Classes: option is showing Use MFC in a Shared DLL.

Now you can create a new source file — call it **Ex13_01.cpp** — and insert it into the project. So that you can see all the code for the program in one place, we'll put the class definitions we need together with their implementations in this file. To achieve this, we won't use the Wizard Bar; we'll just add the code manually — there isn't very much of it.

To begin with, add a statement to include the header file **afxwin.h**, as this contains the definitions for many MFC classes. This will allow us to derive our own classes from MFC.

```
#include <afxwin.h>                    // For the class library
```

To produce the complete program, we'll only need to derive two classes from MFC: an **application class** and a **window class**. We won't even need to write a **WinMain()** function, as we did in the example in Chapter 7, because this is automatically provided by the MFC library behind the scenes. Let's look at how the two classes that we need are defined.

The Application Class

The class **CWinApp** is fundamental to any Windows program written using MFC. An object of this class includes everything necessary for starting, initializing, running and closing the application. The first thing that we need to do to produce our application is to derive our own application class from **CWinApp**. We will be defining a specialized version of the class to suit our application needs. The code for this is as follows:

```
class COurApp: public CWinApp
{
   public:
      virtual BOOL InitInstance();
};
```

As you might expect for a simple example, there isn't a great deal of specialization necessary in this case. We've only included one member in the definition of our class: the function **InitInstance()**. This function is defined as a virtual function in the base class, so it's not a new function in our derived class. We're redefining the base class function for our application class. All the other data and function members that we need in our class will be inherited from **CWinApp** without changes.

Our application class will be endowed with quite a number of data members that are defined in the base, many of which correspond to variables used as arguments in Windows API functions. For example, the member **m_pszAppName** stores a pointer to a string that defines the name of the application. The member **m_nCmdShow** specifies how the application window is to be shown when the application starts up. Don't panic: we don't need to go into the inherited data members now. We'll see how they are used as the need arises in developing our application-specific code.

In deriving our own application class from **CWinApp**, we must override the virtual function **InitInstance()**. Our version will be called by the version of **WinMain()** that's provided for us, and we'll include code in the function to create and display our application window.

However, before we write **InitInstance()**, we need to look at a class, from the MFC library, that defines a window.

The Window Class

Our MFC application will need a window as the interface to the user, referred to as a **frame window**. We will derive a window class for our application from the MFC class **CFrameWnd**, which is designed specifically for this purpose. Since **CFrameWnd** provides everything for creating and managing a window for our application, all we need to add to our derived window class is a constructor. This will allow us to specify a title bar for our window, to suit the application context:

```
class COurWnd: public CFrameWnd
{
   public:
      // Class constructor
      COurWnd()
      {
         Create(0, "Our Dumb MFC Application");
      }
};
```

The **Create()** function, which we call in our class constructor, is inherited from the base class and will create the window and attach it to the **COurWnd** object being created. Note that the **COurWnd** object is not the same thing as the window that will be displayed by Windows — the class object and the physical window are distinct entities.

The first argument value for the **Create()** function, 0, specifies that we want to use the base class default attributes for the window — you'll recall that we needed to define window attributes in our example in Chapter 7. The second argument specifies the window name which will be used in the window title bar. You won't be surprised to learn that there are other parameters to the function **Create()**, but they all have default values which will be quite satisfactory, so we can afford to ignore them here.

Completing the Program

Having defined a window class for our application, we can write the **InitInstance()** function in our **COurApp** class:

```
BOOL COurApp::InitInstance(void)
{
   // Construct a window object in the free store
   m_pMainWnd = new COurWnd;
   m_pMainWnd->ShowWindow(m_nCmdShow);        // ...and display it
   return TRUE;
}
```

This will override the virtual function defined in the base class **CwinApp**, and (as we've already mentioned) will be called by the **WinMain()** function that's automatically supplied by the MFC library. The function **InitInstance()** constructs a main window object for our application in the free store by using the operator **new**. We store the address returned in the variable **m_pMainWnd**, which is an inherited member of our class **COurApp**. The effect of this is that the window object will be owned by the application object. We don't even need to worry about freeing the memory for the object we've created — the supplied **WinMain()** function will take care of any clean-up necessary.

The only other item we need for a complete, albeit rather limited, program is to define an application object. An instance of our application class, **COurApp**, must exist before **WinMain()** is executed, so we should declare it at global scope with the statement:

```
COurApp AnApplication;      // Define an application object
```

The reason that this object needs to exist at global scope is that it is the application object — the application must exist before it can start executing. The **WinMain()** function, provided by MFC, calls the **InitInstance()** function member of the application object to construct the window object, and thus implicitly assumes that the application object already exists.

The Finished Product

Now that you've seen all the code, you can add it to the project. In a Windows program, the classes are usually defined in **.h** files, and the member functions not appearing within the class definitions are defined in **.cpp** files. Our application is so short, though, that you may as well put it all in a single **.cpp** file. The merit of this is that you can view the whole lot together. The program code is structured as follows:

```cpp
// EX13_01.CPP
// An elementary MFC program
#include <afxwin.h>                          // For the class library

// Application class definition
class COurApp:public CWinApp
{
   public:
      virtual BOOL InitInstance();
};

// Window class definition
class COurWnd:public CFrameWnd
{
   public:
      // Class constructor
      COurWnd()
      {
         Create(0, "Our Dumb MFC Application");
      }
};

// Function to create an instance of the main window
BOOL COurApp::InitInstance(void)
{
   // Construct a window object in the free store
   m_pMainWnd = new COurWnd;
   m_pMainWnd->ShowWindow(m_nCmdShow);      // ...and display it
   return TRUE;
}


// Application object definition at global scope
COurApp AnApplication;                       // Define an application object
```

That's all we need. It looks a bit odd because no **WinMain()** function appears but, as we noted above, the **WinMain()** function is supplied by the MFC library.

Now we're ready to roll, so build and run the application. Select the Build | Build Ex13_01.exe menu item, click on the appropriate toolbar button, or just press *F7* to build the project. You should end up with a clean compile and link, in which case you can select Build | Execute Ex13_01.exe or press *Ctrl-F5* to run it. Our minimum MFC program will appear as shown:

We can resize the window by dragging the border, we can move the whole thing around, and we can also minimize and maximize it in the usual ways. The only other function that the program supports is 'close', for which you can use the system menu, the close button at the top right of the window, or just key *Alt-F4*. It doesn't look like much but, considering that there are so few lines of code, it's quite impressive — particularly when you think of how much code is needed to achieve something like this in the old DOS world.

FYI   **If you find that the linker throws some errors about the symbols** `__beginthreadex` **and** `__endthreadex`, **then you need to change the Microsoft Foundation Classes: list box on the General tab of the Project Settings dialog to use MFC, either statically or with the DLL. The Project Settings dialog is accessed by selecting the Project | Settings... menu item, or by pressing *Alt-F7*.**

The Document/View Concept

When you write applications using MFC, it implies acceptance of a specific structure for your program, with application data being stored and processed in a particular way. This may sound restrictive, but it really isn't for the most part — in fact, you gain benefits in speed and ease of implementation that far outweigh any conceivable disadvantages. The structure of an MFC program incorporates two application-oriented entities — a document and a view. Let's look at what they are and how they're used.

What is a Document?

A **document** is the name given to the collection of data in your application with which the user interacts. Although the word 'document' seems to imply something of a textual nature, a document isn't limited to text. It could be the data for a game, a geometric model, a text file, a collection of data on the distribution of orange trees in California or, indeed, anything you want. The term 'document' is just a convenient label for the application data in your program, treated as a unit.

531

You won't be surprised to hear that a document in your program will be defined as an object of a document class. Your document class will be derived from the class **CDocument** in the MFC library, and you'll add your own data members to store items that your application requires, and member functions to support processing of that data.

Handling application data in this way enables standard mechanisms to be provided within MFC, for managing a collection of application data as a unit, and for storing and retrieving data contained in document objects to and from disk. These mechanisms will be inherited by your document class from the base class defined in the MFC library, so you will get a broad range of functionality built in to your application automatically, without having to write any code.

Document Interfaces

You have a choice as to whether your program deals with just one document at a time, or with several. The **Single Document Interface**, referred to as **SDI**, is supported by the MFC library for programs that require only one document to be open at a time. A program using this interface is referred to as an **SDI application**.

For programs that need several documents to be open at one time, you use the **Multiple Document Interface**, which is usually referred to as **MDI**. With the MDI, as well as being able to open multiple documents of one type, your program can also be organized to handle documents of different types simultaneously. Of course, you will need to supply the code to deal with processing whatever different kinds of documents you intend to support.

What is a View?

A **view** always relates to a particular document object. As we've seen, a document contains a set of application data in your program: a view is an object which provides a mechanism for displaying some or all of the data stored in a document. It defines how the data is to be displayed in a window and how the user can interact with it. Similar to the way that you define a document, you'll define your own view class by deriving it from the MFC class **CView**. Note that a view object and the window in which it is displayed are distinct. The window in which a view appears is called a **frame window**. A view is actually displayed in its own window that exactly fills the client area of a frame window. The general relationship between a document, a view and a frame window is illustrated here:

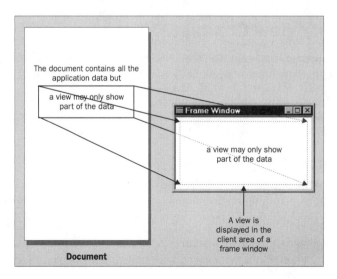

In this illustration, the view displays only part of the data contained in the document, although a view can display all of the data in a document if that is what's required.

A document object can have multiple view objects associated with it. Each view object can provide a different presentation or subset of the same document data. If you were dealing with text, for example, different views could be displaying independent blocks of text from the same document. For a program handling graphical data, you could display all of the document data at different scales in separate windows, or in different formats, such as a textual representation of the elements that form the image.

Linking a Document and its Views

MFC incorporates a mechanism for integrating a document with its views, and each frame window with a currently active view. A document object automatically maintains a list of pointers to its associated views, and a view object has a data member holding a pointer to the document that it relates to. Also, each frame window stores a pointer to the currently active view object. This is similar to the mechanism we used to link objects in our calculator program. The coordination between a document, a view and a frame window is established by another MFC class of objects called document templates.

Document Templates

A **document template** manages the document objects in your program, as well as the windows and views associated with each of them. There will be one document template for each different kind of document that you have in your program. If you have two or more documents of the same type, you only need one document template to manage them.

To be more specific about the use of a document template: document objects and frame window objects are created by a document template object. A view is created by a frame window object. The document template object itself is created by the application object that is fundamental to any MFC application, as we saw in the last example. You can see a graphical representation of these interrelationships here:

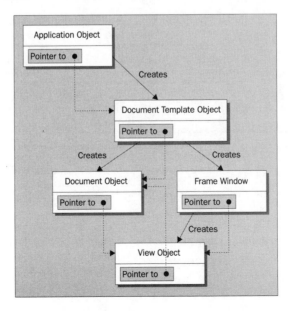

The diagram uses dashed arrows to show how pointers are used to relate objects. These pointers enable function members of one class object to access the **public** data or function members in the interface of another object.

Document Template Classes

MFC has two classes for defining document templates. For SDI applications, the MFC library class **CSingleDocTemplate** is used. This is relatively straightforward, since an SDI application will have only one document and usually just one view. MDI applications are rather more complicated. They have multiple documents active at one time, so a different class, **CMultiDocTemplate**, is needed to define the document template. We'll see more of these classes as we progress into developing application code.

Your Application and MFC

MFC covers a lot of ground and involves a lot of classes. It provides classes that, taken together, are a complete framework for your applications, only requiring the customization necessary to make your programs do what you want them to do. It would be fruitless to try to go through a laundry list of all the classes that are provided; we can learn about them much more easily and naturally by exploring their capabilities as we use them.

However, it's worth taking a look at how the fundamental classes in an SDI application relate to MFC. This is illustrated in the diagram below:

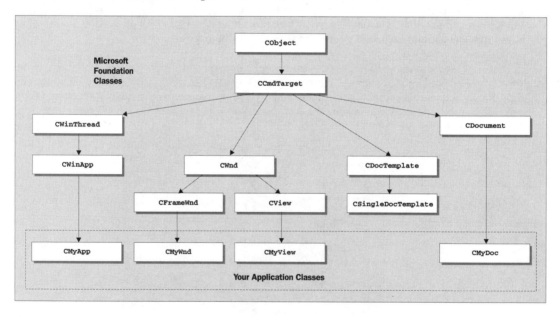

This shows the four basic classes that are going to appear in virtually all your Windows applications:

▶ The application class, **CMyApp**.

▶ The frame window class, **CMyWnd**.

▶ The view class, **CMyView**, which will define how data contained in **CMyDoc** is to be displayed in the client area of a window created by a **CMyWnd** object.

▶ The document class, **CmyDoc**, defining a document to contain the application data.

The actual names for these classes will be specific to a particular application, but the derivation from MFC will be much the same — although there can be alternative base classes, particularly with the view class. As we'll see a bit later, MFC provides several variations of the view class that provide a lot of functionality pre-packaged for you, saving you lots of coding. The class defining a document template for your application will (typically) not need to be extended, so the standard MFC class **CSingleDocTemplate** will usually suffice in an SDI program. When you're creating an MDI program, your document template class will be **CMultiDocTemplate**, which is also derived from **CDocTemplate**.

Each arrow in the diagram points from a derived class to its base class. The MFC library classes shown here form quite a complex inheritance structure, but in fact these are just a very small part of the complete MFC structure. You need not be concerned about the details of the complete MFC hierarchy in the main; however, it is important to have a general appreciation of the hierarchy if you want to understand what the inherited members of your classes are. You will not see any of the definitions of the base classes in your program, but the inherited members of a derived class in your program will be accumulated from the direct base class, as well as from each of the indirect base classes in the MFC hierarchy. To determine what members one of your program's classes has, you therefore need to know from which classes it inherits. Once you know that, you can look up its members using the Help facility.

Another thing you don't need to worry about is remembering what classes you need to have in your program and what base classes to use in their definition. As you'll see next, all of this is taken care of for you by Visual C++.

Windows Programming with Visual C++

You'll be using three tools in the development of your Windows programs:

1 **AppWizard** — for creating the basic program code. You use this when you create a project.

2 **ClassWizard** — for extending and customizing the classes in your programs. You access this through the Wizard Bar, or the context menu for a class from ClassView, or the View | ClassWizard menu item.

3 **Resource Editor** — for creating or modifying such things as menus and toolbars.

There are, in fact, several resource editors; in any given situation, the resource editor used is dependent on the kind of resource that you're editing. We'll look at editing resources in the next chapter, but for now let's take a look at what AppWizard can do for us.

What is the AppWizard?

AppWizard is a programming tool that creates a complete skeleton Windows program using the MFC library. We'll be using AppWizard for the rest of the examples in the book. It's an extraordinarily powerful aid to Windows programming since, in order to produce your application, all you have to do is customize a ready-made program. AppWizard automatically defines all of the classes needed by your program that we have discussed. It even provides hooks and explanations on where you should add your application-specific code.

As we've already seen, you can invoke AppWizard when you create a new project workspace by selecting MFC AppWizard (exe) as the project type. Do this now and name the project **TextEditor**, as shown here:

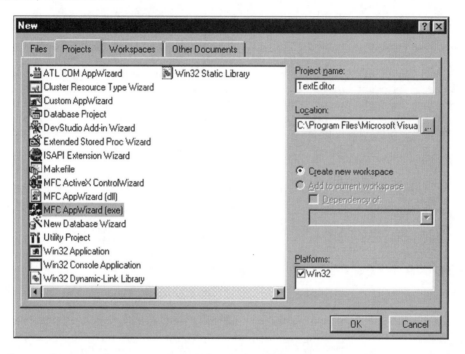

As you know, the name that you assign to the project (**TextEditor** in this case) will be used as the name of the folder which will contain all the project files, but it will also be used as a basis for creating names for classes generated in the application by AppWizard. When you click on OK, you'll find yourself at the first step in the AppWizard dialog that helps you to create the application. Initially, AppWizard allows you to choose an SDI, an MDI or a dialog-based application. Let's concentrate on the first two options. We'll generate both an SDI and an MDI application and see what the resulting programs look like.

Using AppWizard to Create an SDI Application

When you're in the AppWizard dialog, you can always go back to the previous step by clicking on the button labeled < Back. Try it out now. If you felt like it, you could now rename the project and then click on OK again to return to Step 1 of the AppWizard dialog.

Step 1

In this step we choose our application type: SDI, MDI or dialog-based. The default option selected is MDI, and the appearance of an MDI application is shown so that you'll know what to expect. Select the SDI option — the representation for the application shown (top left) will change to a single window, as shown here:

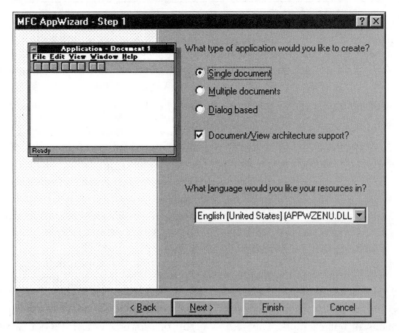

The drop-down list box shows the default language supported. Other languages will only appear in the list if your Visual C++ installation has been set up to support them.

To move on to the next step in the dialog, you should click on Next >.

Step 2

Step 2 gives you choices about the database support in your application. We don't need any in this application, so we'll stick with the default setting, None, and click on Next > once again to move on.

Step 3

This step gives you a range of choices relating to OLE (Object Linking and Embedding), under the label of compound document support. OLE enables you to write programs that can import objects from other programs, or to import your program into another application. We'll see more about this in Chapter 22. There is also a default selection for the ActiveX Controls option. This means that AppWizard will include code that allows the possibility of using ActiveX controls in our application if we want. An ActiveX control is a reusable program component that you can apply in a program or in an Internet web page. We won't be using ActiveX controls in this case, but the option will do no harm. We will see more about OLE and ActiveX controls towards the end of the book. For now, we'll accept the default set of choices and move to the next step.

Step 4

This step offers you a range of functions that can be included in your application by the AppWizard — we'll split these choices up into two groups. The first group contains five functions that relate to menu and toolbar options. Let's take a brief look at them.

Feature	Meaning
Docking toolbar	The toolbar provides a standard range of buttons that are alternatives to using menu options. A docking toolbar can be dragged to the sides or the bottom of the application window, so you can put it wherever is most convenient. We'll see how to add buttons to the toolbar in Chapter 14.
Initial status bar	The status bar appears at the bottom of the application window. It comes with fully implemented standard functions including indicators for the *Num Lock*, *Caps Lock*, and *Scroll Lock* keys, as well as a message line to display prompts for menu options and toolbar selections.
Printing and print preview	This adds the standard Page Setup..., Print Preview, and Print... options to the File menu. The AppWizard will also provide code to support these functions.
Context-sensitive Help	Enabling this option results in a basic set of facilities to support context-sensitive help. You'll obviously need to add the specific contents of the help files if you want to use this feature.
3D controls	This option results in controls that appear in the application — such as buttons — being shaded to give them a 3D appearance.

All of the above, except Context-sensitive Help, are default selections, and we'll keep the default set of options in our example. The second group of choices concern **WOSA**, which is **W**indows **O**pen **S**ervices **A**rchitecture. This is only relevant if your program is to implement communications with other computers. It provides two options for communications support in your program:

Feature	Meaning
MAPI (Messaging API)	This option will cause AppWizard to include support that allows you to send and receive messages.
Windows Sockets	This provides you with the ability to implement TCP/IP capability within your program. This is particularly relevant to applications that support the transfer of files over the Internet.

We will not be getting into either of these options, as they are beyond the scope of this book, so we'll leave them unchecked.

This step also allows you to choose between traditional-style toolbars and IE4-style rebars. For this simple application, we'll choose the default, Normal.

Towards the bottom of the dialog, you can vary the number file entries that will appear in the recently-used file list at the end of the File menu. You can set this to any value from 0 to 16.

Clicking the Advanced... button brings up a range of options for your application, grouped under two tabs, which we'll look at now. The first of these is the Document Template Strings tab:

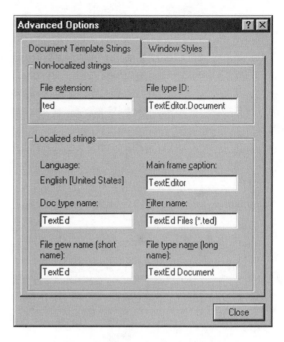

The tab shown allows you to choose the file extension which will identify files that are generated by your application and are to be associated with it. In this instance, we've associated `.ted` with our application. You'll notice that, when you fill in the file extension, the Filter name: box is automatically filled in for you — we'll be getting to what that does in a moment. From this tab, you can also modify the File Type ID: which is used to label the file type for your application in the system registry. The registry associates files with a given unique extension with a particular application.

AppWizard has already decided on a caption for the title bar in your application window — it's shown in the Main frame caption: entry. However, like all the strings shown here, you can change it if you don't like it. For example, it might look better with a space between Text and Editor, or you might want to personalize it in some way.

The Doc type name: entry is a default name for a document. When you create a new document, MFC will use what is entered here as a basis for naming it. The Filter name: will be used to describe files associated with your application in the List Files of Type: box in the File | Open... and File | Save As... menu dialogs although, if you haven't specified a file extension for files produced by your application, this will do nothing. If you want to specify the filter name entry, you should put something descriptive to clearly identify the particular document type — dgm if your document is a diagram, for example.

The option headed File new name (short name): is important if your application will support more than one type of document. This would mean that you had more than one document template implemented in your program. In that case, what you put here will be used to identify the document template in the File | New... menu dialog. Along with the option adjacent to it, it's also applicable if you're writing a program which is an ActiveX server (which used to be known as an OLE server). We'll see rather more about this towards the end of the book.

The Windows Styles tab is shown here:

The bottom area is grayed out because the options here only apply to MDI applications. The Main frame styles area enables you to tailor your application window. Here, the Thick frame option is checked by default. It provides you with a window border that can be dragged to resize the window. The Minimize box, Maximize box, and System menu options, which are also checked by default, provide the three standard buttons that appear at the top of a window. The two unchecked options for Minimized and Maximized frame styles do not apply to Windows 95 programs, so you can ignore them.

We can now move to Step 5 by closing the Advanced Options dialog and clicking on Next >.

Step 5

This step offers three options for your consideration. First, you can choose the style of project that you want: a Windows Explorer-style program features a split window, with a tree view in the left pane. For our simple program we'll favor the default standard style over the Explorer-style.

Second, you can choose whether or not comments are to be included in the source code generated by AppWizard. In most instances, you will want to keep the default option of having them included, so that you can better understand the code generated for you.

The final option relates to how MFC library code is used in your program. The default choice of using the MFC library as a shared DLL (Dynamic Link Library) means that your program will link to MFC library routines at run time. This can reduce the size of the executable file that you'll generate, but requires the MFC DLL to be on the machine that's running it. The two programs together (`.exe` and `.dll`) may be bigger than if you had statically linked the MFC library. If you opt for static linking, the routines will be included in the executable module for your program when it is built. Generally, it's preferable to keep the default option of using MFC as a shared DLL. With this option, several programs running simultaneously using the dynamic link library can all share a single copy of the library in memory.

Step 6

The last step presents you with a list of the classes, that AppWizard will be generating in your program code:

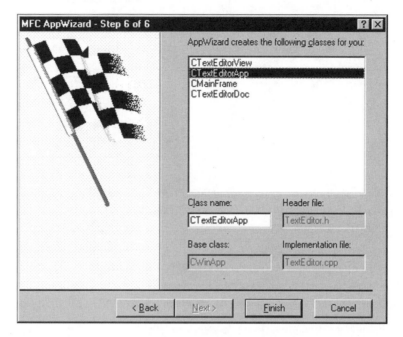

When you highlight a class in the list, the boxes beneath show the name given to the class, the name of the header file in which the definition will be stored, the base class used and the name of the file containing the implementation of member functions in the class. The class definition is always contained in a **.h** file, and the member function source code is always included in a **.cpp** file.

In the case of the class **CTextEditorApp** (shown above), the only thing that you can alter is the class name and, since it's already a good choice, we'll leave it as it is. Try clicking on the other classes in the list. For **CMainFrame** and **CTextEditorDoc**, the wizard will allow you to alter everything except the base class; and for the class **CTextEditorView**, you can change the base class as well.

There is one adjustment to the default that we will make here. Select **CTextEditorView** from the list, and then click the down arrow on the Base class box to display the list of other classes that you can have as a base class:

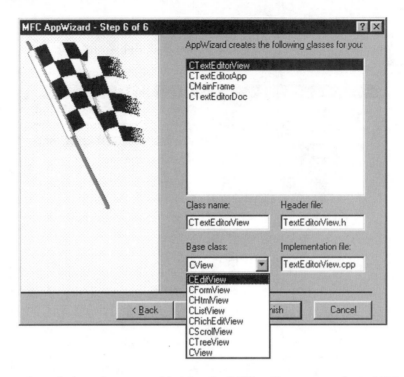

There are a variety of view classes provided by the MFC with a range of capabilities, and the capability built into your view class will depend on which base class you select. Since we've called the application TextEditor, with the notion that it will be able to edit text, choose **CEditView** to get basic editing capability provided automatically.

If you click on Finish, you will see a summary of what AppWizard will include in your project. Just click on OK to have the program files containing a fully working base program generated by AppWizard, using the options you've chosen.

The Output from AppWizard

All the output from AppWizard is stored in the folder **TextEditor**. Visual C++ provides several ways for you to view the information in the project folder:

Tab	View	How project is viewed
ClassView	Class View	Viewed by class and function member name, plus the global entities in your program
ResourceView	Resource View	Viewed by resource type
FileView	File View	Viewed by file name

Each of these is selected using the appropriate tab at the bottom of the Project Workspace window in the IDE.

Viewing Project Files

If you select FileView (by clicking on the third tab) and expand the list by clicking on the + for TextEditor files, then on the ones for Source Files, Header Files and Resource Files, you'll see the complete list of files for the project, as shown here:

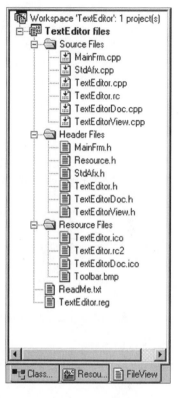

As you can see, there are a total of 18 files in the list. You can view any of the files simply by double-clicking on the filename. The contents of the file selected will be displayed in the right-hand window. Try it out with the **ReadMe.txt** file. You'll see that it contains a brief explanation of the contents of each of the files that make up the project. We won't repeat the descriptions of the files here, as they are very clearly summarized in **ReadMe.txt**.

Viewing Classes

As you may have started to see in Chapter 11, ClassView is often much more convenient than FileView, since classes are the basis for the organization of the application. When you want to look at the code, it's typically the definition of a class or the implementation of a member function that you'll want to see, and from ClassView you can go directly to either. On occasions, however, FileView will come in handy. If you want to check the **#include** directives in a **.cpp** file, you can use FileView to open the file you're interested in directly.

If you click the ClassView tab, you can expand the TextEditor classes item to show the classes defined for the application. Clicking on + for any of the classes will expand the class to show the members of that class.

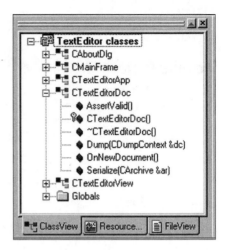

In the window shown below, the **CTextEditorDoc** class
has been expanded:

The icons simply code the various kinds of things that you can display:

▶ Classes are dark blue:

▶ Function members are purple:

▶ Data members are light blue:

▶ A key indicates that the member is **protected**:

▶ A padlock indicates that the member is **private**:

You can see that we have the four classes we discussed earlier that are fundamental to an MFC
application: **CTextEditorApp** for the application, **CMainFrame** for the application frame
window, **CTextEditorDoc** for the document and **CTextEditorView** for the view. We also have
a class **CaboutDlg**, which defines objects that support the dialog that appears when you select
the menu item Help | About... in the application. If you expand Globals, you'll see that it only
contains one definition: the application object **theApp**.

You'll remember from Chapter 11 that to view the code for a class definition, you just double-
click the class name in the tree. To view the code for a member function, double-click the
function name. Note that you can drag the edge of the Project Workspace window to the left or
the right in order to view its contents or your code more easily. However, it's usually convenient
to leave the left window fairly narrow — if you leave the cursor over any line that is partially
obscured, the complete contents of the line will be shown. You can hide or show the Project
Workspace window by clicking the Workspace button, which you'll find on the standard
toolbar.

The Class Definitions

We won't examine the classes in complete detail here — we'll just get a feel for how they look and pick out a few important aspects. If you double-click the name of a class in the ClassView, the code defining the class will be displayed.

CTextEditorApp

Let's take a look at the application class, **CTextEditorApp** first. The definition for this class is shown below:

```
class CTextEditorApp : public CWinApp
{
public:
   CTextEditorApp();

// Overrides
   // ClassWizard generated virtual function overrides
   //{{AFX_VIRTUAL(CTextEditorApp)
   public:
   virtual BOOL InitInstance();
   //}}AFX_VIRTUAL

// Implementation
   //{{AFX_MSG(CTextEditorApp)
   afx_msg void OnAppAbout();
      // NOTE - the ClassWizard will add and remove member functions here.
      //    DO NOT EDIT what you see in these blocks of generated code !
   //}}AFX_MSG
   DECLARE_MESSAGE_MAP()
};
```

It may look complicated at first sight, but there isn't much to it. It's derived from **CWinApp** and includes a constructor, a virtual function **InitInstance()**, a function **OnAppAbout()**, and a macro **DECLARE_MESSAGE_MAP()**.

A macro is not C++ code. It's a name defined by a #define **pre-processor directive that will be replaced by some text that will normally be C++ code, but could also be constants or symbols of some kind.**

The **DECLARE_MESSAGE_MAP()** macro is concerned with defining which Windows messages are handled by which function members of the class. The macro will appear in the definition of any class that may process Windows messages. Of course, our application class will inherit a lot of functions and data members from the base class, and we will be looking further into these as we expand our program examples.

The rest of the **CTextEditorApp** class definition is comments. However, they are very important comments. They include a note indicating where the ClassWizard will make changes to the code. Don't be tempted to delete or alter any of the comments, because some will be used as markers to enable the ClassWizard to find where changes to the class definition should be made. Modifying them may prevent ClassWizard from working properly with this project ever again!

If you take a look at the beginning of the **.h** file containing the class definition, you will notice the directives that prevent the file being included more than once: they look very much like the ones we've seen previously. Again, the long strings of letters and numbers will be differ from class to class.

CMainFrame

The application frame window for our SDI program will be created by an object of the class **CMainFrame**, which is defined by the code shown here:

```
class CMainFrame : public CFrameWnd
{

protected: // create from serialization only
   CMainFrame();
   DECLARE_DYNCREATE(CMainFrame)

// Attributes
public:

// Operations
public:

// Overrides
   // ClassWizard generated virtual function overrides
   //{{AFX_VIRTUAL(CMainFrame)
   virtual BOOL PreCreateWindow(CREATESTRUCT& cs);
   //}}AFX_VIRTUAL

// Implementation
public:
   virtual ~CMainFrame();
#ifdef _DEBUG
   virtual void AssertValid() const;
   virtual void Dump(CDumpContext& dc) const;
#endif

protected:  // control bar embedded members
   CStatusBar  m_wndStatusBar;
   CToolBar    m_wndToolBar;

// Generated message map functions
protected:
   //{{AFX_MSG(CMainFrame)
   afx_msg int OnCreate(LPCREATESTRUCT lpCreateStruct);
      // NOTE - the ClassWizard will add and remove member functions here.
      //    DO NOT EDIT what you see in these blocks of generated code!
   //}}AFX_MSG
   DECLARE_MESSAGE_MAP()
};
```

This class is derived from **CFrameWnd**, which provides most of the functionality required for our application frame window. The derived class includes two protected data members, **m_wndStatusBar** and **m_wndToolBar**, which are instances of the MFC classes **CStatusBar** and **CToolBar** respectively. These objects will create and manage the status bar that will appear at the bottom of the application window, and the toolbar which will provide buttons to access standard menu functions.

CTextEditorDoc

The definition of the **CTextEditorDoc** class supplied by AppWizard is:

```
class CTextEditorDoc : public CDocument
{
protected: // create from serialization only
    CTextEditorDoc();
    DECLARE_DYNCREATE(CTextEditorDoc)

// Attributes
public:

// Operations
public:

// Overrides
    // ClassWizard generated virtual function overrides
    //{{AFX_VIRTUAL(CTextEditorDoc)
    public:
    virtual BOOL OnNewDocument();
    virtual void Serialize(CArchive& ar);
    //}}AFX_VIRTUAL

// Implementation
public:
    virtual ~CTextEditorDoc();
#ifdef _DEBUG
    virtual void AssertValid() const;
    virtual void Dump(CDumpContext& dc) const;
#endif

protected:

// Generated message map functions
protected:
    //{{AFX_MSG(CTextEditorDoc)
        // NOTE - the ClassWizard will add and remove member functions here.
        //    DO NOT EDIT what you see in these blocks of generated code !
    //}}AFX_MSG
    DECLARE_MESSAGE_MAP()
};
```

As with the previous classes, most of the meat comes from the base class and is therefore not apparent here. There are also a lot of comments, some of which are for you, and some are to help ClassWizard out.

The macro **DECLARE_DYNCREATE()**, which appears after the constructor (and which was also used in the **CMainFrame** class), enables an object of the class to be created dynamically by synthesizing it from data read from a file. When you save an SDI document object, the frame window that contains the view is saved along with your data. This allows everything to be restored when you read it back. Reading and writing a document object to a file is supported by a process called **serialization**. In the examples that we develop, we will see how to write our own documents to file using serialization, and then reconstruct them from the file data.

The document class also includes the macro **DECLARE_MESSAGE_MAP()** in its definition to enable Windows messages to be handled by class member functions if necessary.

CTextEditorView

The view class in our SDI application is defined as:

```
class CTextEditorView : public CEditView
{
protected: // create from serialization only
    CTextEditorView();
    DECLARE_DYNCREATE(CTextEditorView)

// Attributes
public:
    CTextEditorDoc* GetDocument();

// Operations
public:

// Overrides
    // ClassWizard generated virtual function overrides
    //{{AFX_VIRTUAL(CTextEditorView)
    public:
    virtual void OnDraw(CDC* pDC);  // overridden to draw this view
    virtual BOOL PreCreateWindow(CREATESTRUCT& cs);
    protected:
    virtual BOOL OnPreparePrinting(CPrintInfo* pInfo);
    virtual void OnBeginPrinting(CDC* pDC, CPrintInfo* pInfo);
    virtual void OnEndPrinting(CDC* pDC, CPrintInfo* pInfo);
    //}}AFX_VIRTUAL

// Implementation
public:
    virtual ~CTextEditorView();
#ifdef _DEBUG
    virtual void AssertValid() const;
    virtual void Dump(CDumpContext& dc) const;
#endif

protected:

// Generated message map functions
protected:
    //{{AFX_MSG(CTextEditorView)
        // NOTE - the ClassWizard will add and remove member functions here.
        //    DO NOT EDIT what you see in these blocks of generated code !
    //}}AFX_MSG
    DECLARE_MESSAGE_MAP()
};
```

As we specified in the AppWizard dialog, the view class is derived from the class **CEditView**, which already includes basic text handling facilities. The **GetDocument()** function returns a pointer to the document object corresponding to the view, and you will be using this to access data in the document object when you add your own extensions to the view class.

Comments in AppWizard-Generated Code

You will probably have noticed a variety of comments in the class definitions created by AppWizard — things like **// Operations** and **// Implementation**. They can seem a little confusing when you start adding your own class members, and you're trying to work out where things fit. So before we get into adding our own code to that which AppWizard provides, let's look at what they these comments mean.

First of all, the comments are there as guidelines. They don't enforce anything on you as to where you should put your code. The only exceptions to this are the comments which quite clearly recommend against modifying code that was inserted by AppWizard. If you change or add code in such a section, you're on your own! The significance of the principal AppWizard comments within class definitions are as follows:

Comment	Meaning
// Implementation	This indicates that everything following it isn't guaranteed to be the same in the next release of Visual C++. Anything can be included in here — data members as well as function members. You can't rely on this code being the same when you move to another version of Visual C++. Of course, you can add your own code here if you want; the comment is just for information.
// Attributes	This indicates that the statements following it define properties of objects of the class — typically these will be data members of the class, but they can also be **Get()**/**Set()** types of functions that supply information about the class but don't change anything.
// Operations	The code following this comment will declare function members that act on the data members of the class, so they change the attributes of a class object in some way.
// Overrides	This defines a section of the class which declares function members that you can override in a derived class. Pure virtual functions will also appear in this section.
// Constructors	Obviously, the section headed by this comment will house the class constructor declarations, but other functions that are used in the initialization of class members will also appear here.

When you're modifying AppWizard-supplied classes, you can choose to add your own sections to accommodate your code. You're under no obligation to put it in the sections designated by the existing comments. We will endeavor to add code within the appropriately commented section in the remaining chapters, but it won't necessarily always fit.

Creating an Executable Module

To compile and link the program, click on Build | Build TextEditor.exe, press *F7*, or click on the build icon.

There are two implementations of the view class member function **GetDocument()** in the code generated by AppWizard. The one in the **.cpp** file for the **CEditView** class is used for the debug version of the program. You will normally use this during program development, since it provides validation of the pointer value stored for the document. (This is stored in the inherited data member **m_pDocument** in the view class.) The version that applies to the release version of your program you can find after the class definition in the **TextEditorView.h** file. This version is declared as **inline** and it does not validate the document pointer.

You will be using the **GetDocument()** function just like the **GetLogicUnit()** member of **CCalculator** in Chapter 11. It provides a link to the document object. Using the pointer to the document, you can call any of the functions in the interface to the document class.

By default, you will have debug capability included in your program. As well as the special version of **GetDocument()**, there are lots of checks in the MFC code that are included in this case. If you want to change this, you can use the drop-down list box in the Build toolbar to choose the release configuration, which doesn't contain all the debug code.

> When compiling your program with debug switched on, the compiler doesn't detect uninitialized variables, so it can be helpful to do the occasional release build even while you are still testing your program.

Precompiled Header Files

The first time you compile and link a program, it will take some time. The second and subsequent times, the compilation should be quite a bit faster; this is because of a feature of Visual C++ called **precompiled headers**. During the initial compilation, the compiler compiles the header files and saves the output in a special file with the extension **.pch**. On subsequent builds, this file is reused (provided the source code in the headers has not changed), thus saving the compilation time for the headers.

You can determine whether or not precompiled headers are used and control how they are handled. Choose Project | Settings... and then select the C/C++ tab. From the Category: drop-down list box, select Precompiled Headers, and you'll see the dialog shown here.

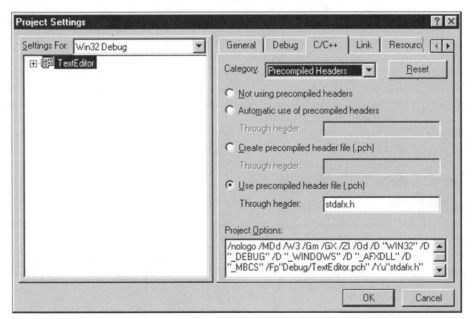

The option for Automatic use of precompiled headers shown here is the easiest to apply. The **.pch** file will be generated if there isn't one, and used if there is. The option to create a **.pch** file does exactly that. The ability to specify the last header file to be included allows you to control what's included in the precompiled header. The option to Use precompiled header file presumes that one already exists. You can get more information on this through the button in the dialog. **?**

Running the Program

To execute the program, press *Ctrl-F5*, or select the Execute option in the Build menu. Because we chose **CEditView** as the base class for our class **CTextEditorView**, the program is a fully functioning, simple text editor. You can enter text in the window as shown below.

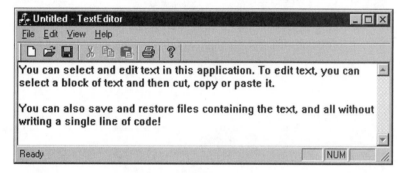

Note that the application has scroll bars for viewing text outside the visible area within the window, and of course you can resize the window by dragging the boundaries. When you save a document, it will automatically be given the extension **.ted**. All the options under the File menu are fully operational. As you move the cursor over the toolbar buttons or the menu options, prompts appear in the status bar describing the function that will be invoked, and if you let the cursor linger on a toolbar button, a tooltip will be displayed showing its purpose.

How the Program Works

As in the trivial MFC example we looked at earlier in this chapter, the application object is created at global scope in our SDI program. You can see this if you expand the Globals item in the ClassView, and then double-click on theApp. In the right part of the project workspace window you'll see this statement:

```
CTextEditorApp theApp;
```

This declares the object **theApp** as an instance of our application class **CTextEditorApp**. The statement is in the file **TextEditor.cpp**, which also contains member function declarations for the application class, and the definition of the **CAboutDlg** class.

Once the object **theApp** has been created, the MFC-supplied **WinMain()** function is called. This in turn calls two member functions of the **theApp** object. First it calls **InitInstance()**, which provides for any initialization of the application that is necessary, and then **Run()**, which provides initial handling for Windows messages. Let's have a look at those two functions now.

551

The Function InitInstance()

You can access the code for this function by double-clicking its entry in the ClassView after expanding the **CTextEditorApp** class in the left pane of the Project Workspace window — or if you're in a hurry you can just look at the code immediately following the line defining the **theApp** object. The version created by AppWizard is as follows:

```
BOOL CTextEditorApp::InitInstance()
{
    AfxEnableControlContainer();

    // Standard initialization
    // If you are not using these features and wish to reduce the size
    //  of your final executable, you should remove from the following
    //  the specific initialization routines you do not need.

#ifdef _AFXDLL
    Enable3dControls();         // Call this when using MFC in a shared DLL
#else
    Enable3dControlsStatic();   // Call this when linking to MFC statically
#endif

    // Change the registry key under which our settings are stored.
    // TODO: You should modify this string to be something appropriate
    // such as the name of your company or organization.
    SetRegistryKey(_T("Local AppWizard-Generated Applications"));

    LoadStdProfileSettings();   // Load standard INI file options (including MRU)

    // Register the application's document templates.  Document templates
    // serve as the connection between documents, frame windows and views.

    CSingleDocTemplate* pDocTemplate;
    pDocTemplate = new CSingleDocTemplate(
        IDR_MAINFRAME,
        RUNTIME_CLASS(CTextEditorDoc),
        RUNTIME_CLASS(CMainFrame),       // main SDI frame window
        RUNTIME_CLASS(CTextEditorView));
    AddDocTemplate(pDocTemplate);

    // Enable DDE Execute open
    EnableShellOpen();
    RegisterShellFileTypes(TRUE);

    // Parse command line for standard shell commands, DDE, file open
    CCommandLineInfo cmdInfo;
    ParseCommandLine(cmdInfo);

    // Dispatch commands specified on the command line
    if (!ProcessShellCommand(cmdInfo))
        return FALSE;

    // The one and only window has been initialized, so show and update it.
    m_pMainWnd->ShowWindow(SW_SHOW);
    m_pMainWnd->UpdateWindow();

    // Enable drag/drop open
    m_pMainWnd->DragAcceptFiles();
```

```
    return TRUE;
  }
```

The string passed to the **SetRegistryKey()** function will be used to define a registry key under which program information will be stored. You can change this to whatever you want. If I changed the argument to **"Horton"**, information about our program would be stored under the registry key

HKEY_CURRENT_USER\Software\Horton\TextEditor

All the application settings will be stored under this key, including the list of files most recently used by the program. The call to the function **LoadStdProfileSettings()** loads the application settings that were saved last time around. Of course, the first time you run the program, there aren't any.

A document template object is created dynamically within **InitInstance()** by the statement:

```
    pDocTemplate = new CSingleDocTemplate(
        IDR_MAINFRAME,
        RUNTIME_CLASS(CTextEditorDoc),
        RUNTIME_CLASS(CMainFrame),          // main SDI frame window
        RUNTIME_CLASS(CTextEditorView));
```

The first parameter to the **CSingleDocTemplate** constructor is a symbol, **IDR_MAINFRAME**, which defines the menu and toolbar to be used with the document type. The following three parameters define the document, main frame window and view class objects that are to be bound together within the document template. Since we have an SDI application here, there will only ever be one of each in the program, managed through one document template object. **RUNTIME_CLASS()** is a macro that enables the type of a class object to be determined at runtime.

There's a lot of other stuff here for setting up the application instance that we need not worry about. You can add any initialization of your own that you need for the application to the **InitInstance()** function.

The Function Run()

The function **Run()**, in the class **CTextEditorApp**, is inherited from the application base class **CWinApp**. Because it is declared as **virtual**, you can replace the base class version of the function **Run()** with one of your own, but this is not usually necessary so you don't need to worry about it.

Run() acquires all the messages from Windows destined for the application and ensures that each message is passed to the function in the program designated to service it, if one exists. Therefore, this function continues executing as long as the application is running. It terminates when you close the application.

Thus, you can boil the operation of the application down to four steps:

1 Creating an application object, **theApp**.

2 Executing **WinMain()**, which is supplied by MFC.

3 `WinMain()` calling `InitInstance()`, which creates the document template, the main frame window, the document, and the view.

4 `WinMain()` calling `Run()`, which executes the main message loop to acquire and dispatch Windows messages.

Using AppWizard to Create an MDI Application

Now let's create an MDI application using AppWizard. Let's give it the project name **Sketcher**, as we will be expanding it into a sketching program during subsequent chapters. You should have no trouble with this procedure, as there are only three things that we need to do differently from the process that we have just gone through for the SDI application:

▶ In Step 1, you should leave the default option, MDI, rather than changing to the SDI option.

▶ Under the Advanced... button in Step 4, you should specify the file extension as **ske**.

▶ In Step 6, you should leave the base class for the class **CSketcherView** as **CView**.

▶ In Step 6, which is shown below, we get an extra class derived from MFC for our application:

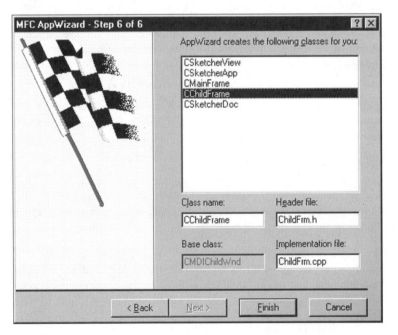

The extra class is **CChildFrame**, which is derived from the MFC class **CMDIChildWnd**. This class provides a frame window for a view of the document that will appear *inside* the application window created by a **CMainFrame** object. With an SDI application there is a single document with a single view, so the view is displayed in the client area of the main frame window. In an MDI application, we can have multiple documents open, and each document can have multiple views. To accomplish this, each view of a document in our program will have its own child frame window created by an object of the class **CChildFrame**. As we saw earlier, a view will be displayed in what is actually a separate window, but one which exactly fills the client area of a frame window.

Running the Program

You can build the program in exactly the same way as the previous example. Then, if you execute it, you will get the application window shown here:

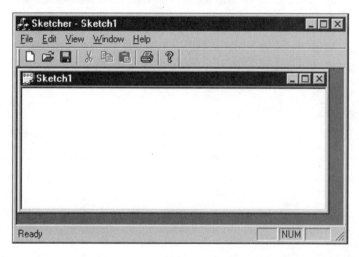

In addition to the main application window, we have a separate document window with the caption Sketch1. **Sketch1** is the default name for the initial document, and it will have the extension **.ske** if you save it. You can create additional views for the document by selecting the Window | New Window menu option. You can also create a new document by selecting File | New, so that there will be two active documents in the application. The situation with two documents active, each with two views open, is shown here:

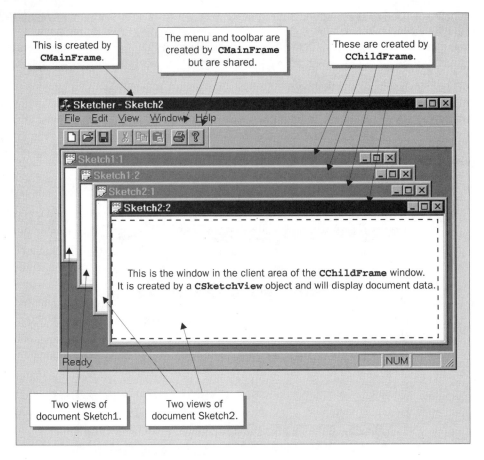

This is created by **CMainFrame**.

The menu and toolbar are created by **CMainFrame** but are shared.

These are created by **CChildFrame**.

This is the window in the client area of the **CChildFrame** window. It is created by a **CSketchView** object and will display document data.

Two views of document Sketch1.

Two views of document Sketch2.

You can't yet actually create any data in the application, since we haven't added any code to do that, but all the code for creating documents and views has already been included by AppWizard.

Using the ClassWizard

We've mentioned the ClassWizard several times in this chapter, and we used some of its basic facilities back in Chapter 11. Since most of the rest of the book will be concerned with using the ClassWizard in various ways, let's make sure we have a good grasp of how we can use it. Once the AppWizard has generated the initial application code, you'll be using the ClassWizard to implement most of the additional code necessary to support your specific application needs, so a good platform for trying out how to use it in practical situations is the Sketcher program we just created.

You've already accessed the ClassWizard through the Wizard Bar, and through the context menu that you get by right-clicking on a class name in ClassView. As you already know how to create classes and add class members by these means we won't repeat them again here, but we should take a look at some of the other things ClassWizard can do. You can invoke the ClassWizard by selecting the <u>V</u>iew | Class<u>W</u>izard... menu option, by pressing *Ctrl-W*, or easiest of all, by clicking on the toolbar button on the menu bar. If the toolbar button for the ClassWizard isn't displayed, you can add it by right-clicking on the menu bar and selecting Customize... from the pop-up. You can then drag the toolbar button from the Customize dialog to the menu bar.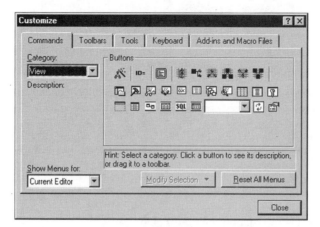

You can get at toolbar buttons for any of the menus by this means. When you have all the toolbar buttons you want, click on the Close button to end the dialog. If you now click on the ClassWizard button with the **Sketcher** application open, you'll get the ClassWizard dialog displayed for the current project. The dialog below shows the **Sketcher** project with the **CSketcherDoc** class selected in the right-hand drop-down list.

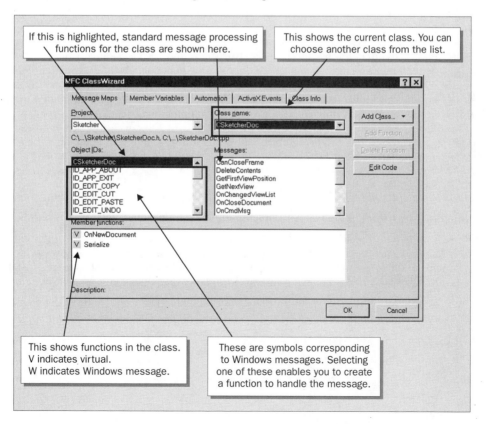

Here you can see the Message Maps tab, where you can add functions to the classes in your application to process specific Windows messages. The name of the current class is shown in the drop-down list box at the top right. For the Object ID highlighted in the left list box, the messages applicable to it are shown in the Messages: list box on the right. You can also edit or delete any of the existing functions in a class. Highlighting one of the existing member functions will enable the grayed out button for Delete Function.

The Add Class... button enables you to derive a new class in your application. This is the same dialog as you get by selecting the down arrow on the Wizard Bar and selecting New Class... from the pop-up menu. However, there's a big difference between the Sketcher program and what we have before. Because Sketcher uses the MFC, the dialog gives you the option of deriving a class from the MFC, in addition to the possibility of creating a generic class, which we used in Chapter 11. The other tabs in the ClassWizard dialog provide a wealth of other facilities for extending your program. We'll be going further into how we actually use the ClassWizard, starting in the very next chapter.

Although there is overlap between the functions accessible through the Wizard Bar, the class context menu, and selecting the ClassWizard toolbar button, you'll find yourself using all three, since they each have some unique abilities. For instance, if you just want to add a variable to a class then the class context menu is the way to go. Of course, none of these options prevent you from modifying your source code directly. Indeed, you should be doing so from time to time, if only to make sure your code is adequately commented.

Summary

In this chapter we've been concerned mainly with the mechanics of using the AppWizard. We have looked at how a Windows program is structured, and we've taken a peek at MFC. We have also seen the basic components of MFC programs generated by the AppWizard. All our examples will be AppWizard-based, so it's a good idea to keep the general structure and broad class relationships in mind. You probably won't feel too comfortable with the detail at this point, but don't worry about that now. You'll find that it becomes much clearer once we have applied the ClassWizard and other Visual C++ tools a few times in the succeeding chapters. They'll be taking care of most of the detail automatically, and an appreciation of what fits where will become quite obvious after a bit of practice.

The key points that we have discussed in this chapter are:

▶   The AppWizard generates a complete, working, framework Windows application for you to customize to your requirements.

▶   The AppWizard can generate single document interface (SDI) applications which work with a single document and a single view, or multiple document interface (MDI) programs which can handle multiple documents and views simultaneously.

▶   The four essential classes in an SDI application that are derived from the foundation classes are:

> The application class
>
> The frame window class

The document class

The view class

▶ A program can have only one application object. This is defined automatically by the AppWizard at global scope.

▶ A document class object stores application-specific data and a view class object displays the contents of a document object.

▶ A document template class object is used to tie together a document, a view and a window. For an SDI application, a **CSingleDocTemplate** class does this, and for an MDI application, the **CMultiDocTemplate** class is used. These are both foundation classes and application-specific versions do not normally need to be derived.

Exercises

It isn't possible to give programming examples for this chapter, as it really just introduces the Windows programming side of the IDE. There aren't solutions to all the exercises, because the reader will either see the answer for themselves on the screen, or be able to check their answer back with the text.

Ex13-1: What is the relationship between a document and a view?

Ex13-2: What is the purpose of the document template in an MFC Windows program?

Ex13-3: Why do you need to be careful, and plan your program structure in advance, when using AppWizard?

Ex13-4: Code up the simple text editor program. Build both debug and release versions, and examine the types and sizes of the files produced in each case.

Ex13-5: Generate the text editor application several times, trying different window styles from the Advanced Options in AppWizard.

Working With Menus And Toolbars

In the last chapter, we saw how a simple framework application generated by the AppWizard is made up and how the parts interrelate. In this chapter, we'll start customizing our MDI framework application, Sketcher, with a view to making it into a useful program. The first step in this process is to understand how menus are defined in Visual C++, and how functions are created to service the application-specific menu items that we add to our program. We'll also see how to add toolbar buttons to the application. By the end of this chapter you'll have learned:

- How an MFC-based program handles messages
- What menu resources are, and how you can create and modify them
- What menu properties are, and how you can create and modify them
- How to create a function to service the message generated when a menu item is selected
- How to add handlers to update menu properties
- How to add toolbar buttons and associate them with existing menu items

Communicating with Windows

As we saw in Chapter 7, Windows communicates with your program by sending messages to it. Most of the drudgery of message handling in a Visual C++ program is taken care of by MFC, so you don't have to worry about providing a **WndProc()** function at all. MFC enables you to provide functions to handle the individual messages that you're interested in and to ignore the rest. These functions are referred to as **message handlers** or just **handlers**. Since your application is MFC-based, a message handler is always a member function of one of your application's classes.

The association between a particular message and the function in your program that is to service it is established by a **message map** — each class in your program that can handle Windows messages will have one. A message map for a class is simply a table of member functions that handle Windows messages. Each entry in the message map associates a particular message with a function; when a given message occurs, the corresponding function will be called. Only the messages that are relevant to a class will appear in the message map for the class.

A message map for a class is created automatically by AppWizard, or by ClassWizard when you add a class that handles messages to your program. Additions to, and deletions from, a message map are mainly managed by ClassWizard, but there are circumstances where you need to modify the message map manually. The start of a message map in your code is indicated by a **BEGIN_MESSAGE_MAP()** macro, and the end is marked by an **END_MESSAGE_MAP()** macro. Let's look into how a message map operates using our Sketcher example.

Understanding Message Maps

A message map is established by AppWizard for each of the main classes in your program. In the instance of our MDI program, Sketcher, a message map will be defined for each of **CSketcherApp**, **CSketcherDoc**, **CSketcherView**, **CMainFrame** and **CChildFrame**. You can see the message map for a class in the **.cpp** file that contains the implementation of the class. Of course, the functions that are included in the message map also need to be declared in the class definition, but they are identified here in a special way. Look at the definition for the **CSketcherApp** class shown here:

```
class CSketcherApp : public CWinApp
{
public:
    CSketcherApp();

// Overrides
    // ClassWizard generated virtual function overrides
    //{{AFX_VIRTUAL(CSketcherApp)
    public:
    virtual BOOL InitInstance();
    //}}AFX_VIRTUAL

// Implementation
    //{{AFX_MSG(CSketcherApp)
    afx_msg void OnAppAbout();
        // NOTE - the ClassWizard will add and remove member functions here.
        //    DO NOT EDIT what you see in these blocks of generated code !
    //}}AFX_MSG
    DECLARE_MESSAGE_MAP()
};
```

You can see the comments that indicate the start (**//{{AFX_MSG(CSketcherApp)**) and end (**//}}AFX_MSG**) of the lines in the class definition where ClassWizard will add declarations for the message handlers that you define in the class. The functions appearing here will also appear in a message map in the class implementation in the **.cpp** file for the class. In **CSketcherApp**, only one message handler is declared (namely **OnAppAbout()**). The word **afx_msg** at the beginning of the line is just to distinguish a message handler from other member functions in the class. It will be converted to whitespace by the preprocessor, so it has no effect when the program is compiled.

The macro **DECLARE_MESSAGE_MAP()** indicates that the class can contain function members that are message handlers. In fact, any class that you derive from the MFC class **CCmdTarget** can potentially have message handlers, so such classes will have this macro included as part of the class definition by AppWizard or ClassWizard, depending on which was responsible for creating it. The diagram below shows the MFC classes derived from **CCmdTarget** that have been used in our examples so far:

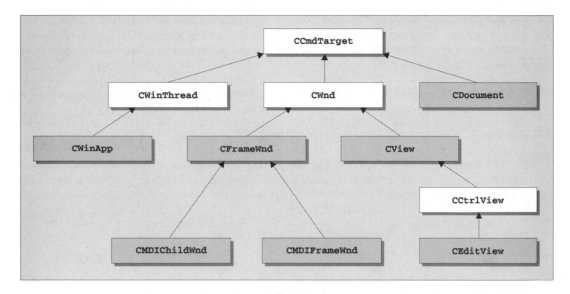

In this diagram, each arrow points from a derived class to its base class. The classes that have been used directly, or as a direct base for our own application classes, are shown shaded. Thus, our class **CSketcherApp** has **CCmdTarget** as an indirect base class and, therefore, will always include the **DECLARE_MESSAGE_MAP()** macro. All of the view (and other) classes derived from **CWnd** will also have it.

If you are adding your own members to a class directly, it's best to leave the **DECLARE_MESSAGE_MAP()** macro as the last line in the class definition. If you do add members after **DECLARE_MESSAGE_MAP()**, you'll also need to include an access specifier for them: **public**, **protected** or **private**.

Message Handler Definitions

If a class definition includes the macro **DECLARE_MESSAGE_MAP()**, the class implementation must include the macros **BEGIN_MESSAGE_MAP()** and **END_MESSAGE_MAP()**. If you look in **Sketcher.cpp**, you'll see the following code as part of the implementation of **CSketcherApp**:

```
BEGIN_MESSAGE_MAP(CSketcherApp, CWinApp)
    //{{AFX_MSG_MAP(CSketcherApp)
    ON_COMMAND(ID_APP_ABOUT, OnAppAbout)
        // NOTE - the ClassWizard will add and remove mapping macros here.
        //      DO NOT EDIT what you see in these blocks of generated code!
    //}}AFX_MSG_MAP
    // Standard file based document commands
    ON_COMMAND(ID_FILE_NEW, CWinApp::OnFileNew)
    ON_COMMAND(ID_FILE_OPEN, CWinApp::OnFileOpen)
    // Standard print setup command
    ON_COMMAND(ID_FILE_PRINT_SETUP, CWinApp::OnFilePrintSetup)
END_MESSAGE_MAP()
```

This is a message map. The **BEGIN_MESSAGE_MAP()** and **END_MESSAGE_MAP()** macros define the boundaries of the message map, and each of the message handlers in the class will appear between these macros. In the case above, the code is handling only one category of message, namely the type of **WM_COMMAND** message called a **command message**, which is generated when the user selects a menu option or accelerator keys. (If that seems clumsy, it's because there's another kind of **WM_COMMAND** message called a **control notifications message**, as we shall see later in this chapter.)

The message map knows which menu or key is pressed, by the identifier (or ID) that's included in the message. There are four **ON_COMMAND** macros in the code above — one for each of the command messages to be handled. The first argument to this macro is an ID that is associated with one particular command, and the **ON_COMMAND()** macro ties the function name to the command specified by the ID. Thus, when a message corresponding to the identifier **ID_APP_ABOUT** is received, the function **OnAppAbout()** will be called. Similarly, for a message corresponding to the **ID_FILE_NEW** identifier, the function **OnFileNew()** will be called. This handler is actually defined in the base class, **CWinApp**, as are the two remaining handlers.

The **BEGIN_MESSAGE_MAP()** macro has two arguments. The first argument identifies the current class name for which the message map is defined and the second provides a connection to the base class for finding a message handler. If a handler isn't found in the class defining the message map, the message map for the base class is then searched.

Note that command IDs such as **ID_APP_ABOUT** are standard IDs defined in MFC. These correspond to messages from standard menu items and toolbar buttons. The prefix **ID_** is used to identify a command associated with a menu item or a toolbar button, as we'll see when we discuss resources later. For example, **ID_FILE_NEW** is the ID that corresponds to the File | New menu item being selected, and **ID_APP_ABOUT** corresponds to the Help | About menu option.

There are more symbols besides **WM_COMMAND** that Windows uses to identify standard messages. Each of them is prefixed with **WM_** for Windows Message. These symbols are defined in **Winuser.h**, which is included in **Windows.h**. If you want to look at them, you'll find **Winuser.h** in the **include** folder, which is in the **VC** folder containing your Visual C++ system.

FYI   There's a nice shortcut for viewing a .h file. If the name of the file appears in the editor window, you can just right click on it, and select the menu item Open Document "*Filename*.h" from the pop-up.

Windows messages often have additional data values that are used to refine the identification of a particular message specified by a given ID. The message **WM_COMMAND**, for instance, is sent for a whole range of commands, including those originating from selecting a menu item or a toolbar button.

Note that you should not map a message (or in the case of command messages, a command ID) to more than one message handler in a class. If you do, it won't break anything, but the second message handler will never be called. Since one of the major uses of the ClassWizard is to define message handlers and make appropriate entries in the message maps in your program, this situation should not arise if you stick to using the ClassWizard. Only when you need to make message map entries manually will you need to take care not to assign more than one handler to a message.

Message Categories

There are three categories of messages that your program may be dealing with, and the category to which a message belongs will determine how it is handled. The message categories are:

Message category	Explanation
Windows messages	These are standard Windows messages that begin with the **WM_** prefix (with the exception of **WM_COMMAND** messages, which we shall come to in a moment). Examples of Windows messages are **WM_PAINT**, which indicates that you need to redraw the client area of a window, and **WM_LBUTTONUP**, which signals that the left mouse button has been released.
Control notification messages	These are **WM_COMMAND** messages which are sent from controls (such as a list box) to the window that created the control, or from a child window to a parent window. Parameters associated with a **WM_COMMAND** message enable messages from the controls in your application to be differentiated.
Command messages	These are also **WM_COMMAND** messages that originate from the user interface elements, such as menu items and toolbar buttons. MFC defines unique identifiers for standard menu and toolbar command messages.

The standard Windows messages in the first category will be identified by the **WM_**-prefixed IDs that Windows defines. We'll be writing handlers for some of these messages in the next chapter. The messages in the second category are a particular group of **WM_COMMAND** messages that we'll see in Chapter 17 when we work with dialogs. We'll deal with the last category, messages originating from menus and toolbars, in this chapter. In addition to the message IDs defined by MFC for the standard menus and toolbars, you can define your own message IDs for the menus and toolbar buttons that you add to your program. If you don't supply IDs for these items, MFC will automatically generate IDs for you, based on the menu text.

Handling Messages in Your Program

You can't put a handler for a message anywhere you like. The permitted sites for a handler depend on what kind of message is to be processed. The first two categories of message that we saw above (that is, standard Windows messages and control notification messages) are always handled by objects of classes derived from **CWnd**. Frame window classes and view classes, for example, are derived from **CWnd**, so they can have member functions to handle Windows messages and control notification messages. Application classes, document classes and document template classes are not derived from **CWnd**, so they can't handle these messages.

Using the ClassWizard solves the headache of remembering where to place handlers, as it will only give you the options that are allowed. For example, if you select **CSketcherDoc** as the Class name:, you won't be offered any of the **WM_** messages.

For standard Windows messages, the class **CWnd** provides default message handling. Thus, if your derived class doesn't include a handler for a standard Windows message, it will be processed by the default handler defined in the base class. If you do provide a handler in your class, you'll sometimes still need to call the base class handler as well, so that the message will be processed properly. When you're creating your own handler, ClassWizard will provide a skeleton implementation of it, which will include a call to the base handler where necessary.

Handling command messages is much more flexible. You can put handlers for these in the application class, the document and document template classes, and of course in the window and view classes in your program. So, what happens when a command message is sent to your application, bearing in mind there are a lot of options as to where it is handled?

How Command Messages are Processed

All command messages are sent to the main frame window for the application. The main frame window then tries to get the message handled by routing it in a specific sequence to the classes in your program. If one class can't process the message, it passes it on to the next.

For an SDI program, the sequence in which classes are offered an opportunity to handle a command message is:

1 The view object

2 The document object

3 The document template object

4 The main frame window object

5 The application object

The view object is given the opportunity to handle a command message first and, if no handler has been defined, the next class object has a chance to process it. If none of the classes has a handler defined, default Windows processing takes care of it, essentially throwing the message away.

For an MDI program, things are only a little more complicated. Although we have the possibility of multiple documents, each with multiple views, only the active view and its associated document are involved in the routing of a command message. The sequence for routing a command message in an MDI program is:

1 The active view object

2 The document object associated with the active view

3 The document template object for the active document

4 The frame window object for the active view

5 The main frame window object

6 The application object

It's possible to alter the sequence for routing messages, but this is so rarely necessary that we won't go into it in this book.

Extending the Sketcher Program

We're going to add code to the Sketcher program we created in the last chapter to implement the functionality we need to create sketches. We'll provide code for drawing lines, circles, rectangles and curves with various colors and line thickness, and for adding annotations to a sketch. The data for a sketch will be stored in a document, and we'll also allow multiple views of the same document at different scales.

It will take us several chapters to add everything we need, but a good starting point would be to add menu items to deal with the types of elements that we want to be able to draw, and to select a color for drawing. We'll make both the element type and color selection persistent in the program, which means that having selected a color and an element type, both of these will remain in effect until we change one or other of them.

The steps that we'll work through to add menus to Sketcher are:

▶ Define the menu items that will appear on the main menu bar and in each of the menus.

▶ Decide which of the classes in our application should handle the message for each menu item.

▶ Add message handling functions to the classes for our menu messages.

▶ Add functions to the classes to update the appearance of the menus to show the current selection in effect.

▶ Add a toolbar button complete with tooltips for each of our menu items.

Elements of a Menu

We'll be looking at two aspects of dealing with menus in Visual C++:

▶ The creation and modification of the menu as it appears in your application

▶ The processing that is necessary when a particular menu item is selected—the definition of a message handler for it

We will look at creating the menu items first.

Creating and Editing Menu Resources

Menus are defined external to the program code in a **resource file** and the specification of the menu is referred to as a **resource**. There are several other kinds of resources that you can include in your application, such as dialogs, toolbars and icons. You'll be seeing more on these as we extend our application.

Having a menu defined in a resource allows the physical appearance of the menu to be changed without affecting the code that processes menu events. For example, you could change your menu items from English to French, or Norwegian, or whatever, without having to modify or recompile the program code. The code to handle the message created when the user selects a menu item doesn't need to be concerned with how the menu looks, only with the fact that it was selected. Of course, if you *add* items to the menu, you'll need to add some code for each of them to ensure that they actually do something!

The Sketcher program already has a menu, which means that it already has a resource file. We can access the resource file contents for the Sketcher program by selecting the ResourceView in the workspace window, or if you have the FileView displayed, by double-clicking **Sketcher.rc**. This will switch you to the ResourceView and display the resources. If you expand the Menu resource, you'll see that there are two menus defined, indicated by the identifiers **IDR_MAINFRAME** and **IDR_SKETCHTYPE**. The first of these applies when there are no documents open in the application, and the second when we have one or more documents open. MFC uses the prefix **IDR_** to identify a resource which defines a complete menu for a window.

We're only going to be modifying the menu which has the identifier **IDR_SKETCHTYPE**. We don't need to look at **IDR_MAINFRAME**, because our new menu items will only be relevant when a document is open. You can invoke a resource editor for the menu by double-clicking its menu ID. If you do this for **IDR_SKETCHTYPE**, you'll see the window shown here:

These are the types of resource in Sketcher.rc

You can add a menu item here. You can also drag it around.

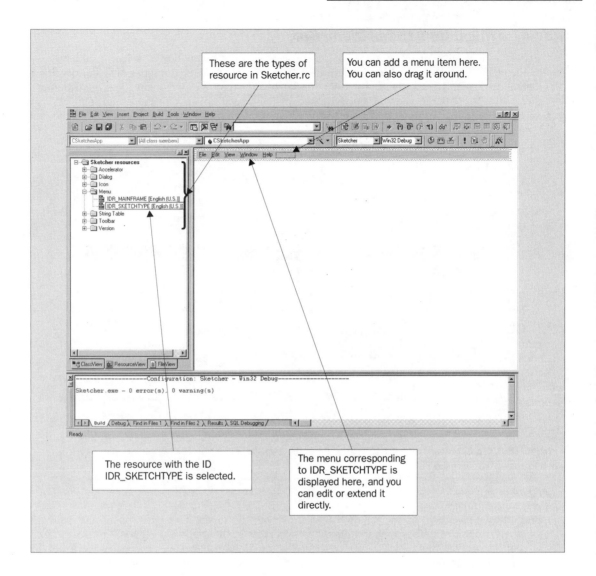

The resource with the ID IDR_SKETCHTYPE is selected.

The menu corresponding to IDR_SKETCHTYPE is displayed here, and you can edit or extend it directly.

Adding a Menu Item to the Menu Bar

To add a new menu item, you can just click on the empty menu box to select it and type in the menu name. If you insert **&** in front of a letter in the menu item, the letter will be identified as a shortcut key to invoke the menu from the keyboard. Type the first menu item as **E&lement**. This will select l (L) as the shortcut letter, so that the user can invoke the menu item by typing *Alt-l*. (We can't use E because it's already used by E̲dit.) As soon as you begin typing, the Menu Item Properties box will appear, as shown here:

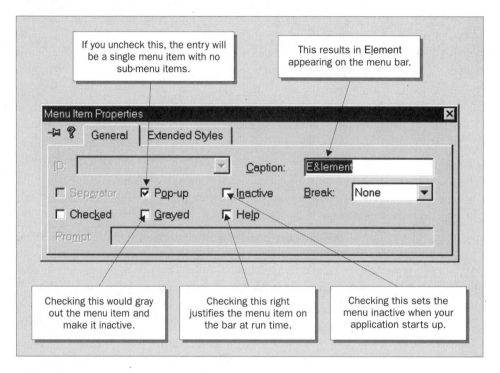

Properties are simply parameters that determine how the menu item will appear and behave. Since we want to create a menu containing the list of elements that we'll have in our program, we can leave everything as it is, so you can just press *Enter*. No ID is necessary for a pop-up menu item, since selecting it just displays the menu beneath. Note that you get a new blank menu box for the first item of the new menu, as well as one on the main menu bar.

It would be better if the E̲lement menu appeared between the V̲iew and W̲indow items, so place the cursor on the E̲lement menu item and, with the left mouse button pressed, drag it to a position between the V̲iew and W̲indow items. Then release the left mouse button. After positioning the new E̲lement menu item, the next step is to add items to the menu beneath it.

Adding Items to the Element Menu

Select the first (currently empty) item in the E̲lement menu by clicking on it, then type &Line as the C̲aption: in the Menu Item Properties dialog, as shown here:

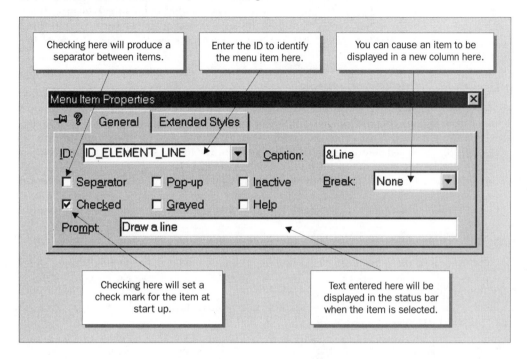

The properties modify the appearance of the menu item and also specify the ID of the message that will be passed to your program when the menu item is selected. Don't press *Enter* just yet: we'll run through the properties that you need to set in a moment.

Because this item is part of a pop-up menu, it isn't identified as a pop-up item by default; however, you could make it into another pop-up with a further list of items, in which case you would need to check the P̲op-up box. Don't you love the way pop-ups pop up all over the place?

Defining Menu Item Properties

You can enter an ID for the menu item in the I̲D: box, as shown above. If you don't, then MFC will generate it for you automatically, based on the menu item name. Sometimes, though, it's convenient to specify the ID yourself — for example, when the generated ID is too long or its meaning is unclear. If you do choose to define your own ID, you should use the MFC convention of prefixing it with **ID_** to indicate that it's a command ID for a menu item. We can use the same format for each of the E̲lement menu item IDs, in this case starting the ID with **ID_ELEMENT_**. The ID will identify the message created when the user selects the menu item, so you'll see it as an entry in the message map for the class handling the messages from the E̲lement menu items.

In the Prompt: box, you can enter a text string that will appear in the status bar of your application when the menu item is highlighted. If you leave it blank, nothing is displayed in the status bar. We want the default element selected in the application at start up to be a line, so we can check the Checked box to get a check mark against the menu item to indicate this. We'll have to remember to add code to update check marks for the menu items when a different selection is made. The Break: entry can alter the appearance of the pop-up by shifting the item into a new column. We don't need that here, so leave it as it is. Press *Enter* to move to the next menu item.

Modifying Existing Menu Items

If you think that you may have made a mistake and want to change an existing menu item, or even if you just want to verify that you have set the properties correctly, it's very easy to go back to an item. Just double-click the item you're interested in, and the properties box for that item will be displayed. (You can achieve the same result by right-clicking on the item and selecting Properties from the menu.) You can then change the properties in any way that you want and press *Enter* when you're done. If the item you want to access is in a pop-up menu that isn't displayed, just click on the relevant item on the menu bar — this will display the pop-up.

Completing the Menu

Now go through the remaining Element menu items we need: &Rectangle, &Circle, and Cur&ve. Of course, none of these should have the Checked box checked. We can't use C as the hotkey for the last item, as hotkeys must be unique and we've already assigned C to the menu item for a circle. You can use the default IDs **ID_ELEMENT_RECTANGLE**, **ID_ELEMENT_CIRCLE**, and **ID_ELEMENT_CURVE** for these.

We also need a Color menu on the menu bar, with items for Black, Red, Green, and Blue. You can create these, starting at the empty menu entry on the menu bar, using the same procedure that we just went through. Set Black as checked, as that will be the default color. You can use the default IDs (**ID_COLOR_BLACK**, etc.) as the IDs for the menu items. You can also add the status bar prompt (for example, Draw in black) for each. When you've finished that, drag Color so that it's just to the right of Element. Then the menu should appear as shown here:

Note that you need to take care not to use the same letter more than once as a shortcut in the pop-up — or in the main menu for that matter. There's no check made as you create new menu items, but if you click the right mouse button with the cursor on the menu when you've edited it, you'll get a pop-up which contains an item Check Mnemonics. Selecting this will verify that you have no duplicate shortcut keys. It's a good idea to do this every time you edit a menu because it's very easy to create duplicates by accident.

That completes extending the menu for elements and colors. Don't forget to save the file to make sure that the additions are safely stored away. Next, we need to decide in which classes we want to deal with messages from our menu items, and add member functions to handle each of the messages. For that, we'll use the ClassWizard.

Using ClassWizard for Menu Messages

You're spoilt for choice when starting ClassWizard. You can invoke it from where we are (the Resource Editor for menus) by right-clicking in the right-hand pane and selecting ClassWizard... from the pop-up. Alternatively, you can enter *Ctrl-W* from the keyboard, or you can select it from the View menu. You'll see the ClassWizard window as shown here:

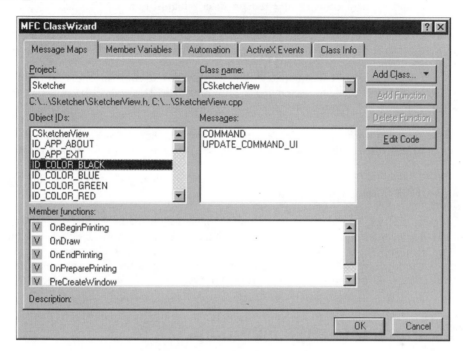

We'll concentrate on Message Maps, so ignore the other tabs for the moment. The contents of the five boxes on this tab are fairly self-explanatory:

Control	Use
Project:	Identifies the current project
Class name:	Identifies the class that we're currently working on
Object IDs:	Lists the IDs for which we can add handlers to the current class
Messages:	Identifies the message types available for a particular object ID. (In the screenshot above, we've selected a command ID, so we have the option of choosing COMMAND or UPDATE_COMMAND_UI. We'll see the difference between these two message types later in this chapter.)
Member functions:	Lists the message handlers already defined in the current class

You can see that the IDs we assigned to our menu items appear in the Object IDs: box. If you change to any of the other classes in the program by selecting from the drop-down list in the Class name: box, you'll see that the IDs for our new menu items appear there too. Because the menu items result in command messages, we can choose to handle them in any of the classes that are currently defined in the application. So how do we decide where we should process the messages?

573

Choosing a Class to Handle Menu Messages

Before we can decide which class should handle the messages for the menu items we've added, we must know what we want to do with the messages, so let's consider that.

We want the element type and the element color to be modal — that is, whatever is set for the element type and element color should remain in effect until one or other is changed. This will allow you to create as many blue circles as you want, and when you want red circles, you just change the color. We have two basic possibilities for handling the setting of a color and the selection of an element type: setting them by view or by document. We could set them by view, in which case, if there's more than one view of a document, each view will have its own color and element set. This would mean that we might draw a red circle in one view, switch to another view, and find that we're drawing a blue rectangle. This would be rather confusing, and in conflict with how we want them to work.

It would be better, therefore, to have the current color and element selection apply to a document. We can then switch from one view to another and continue drawing the same elements in the same color. There might be other differences between the views that we might implement — such as the scale at which the document is displayed, perhaps — but the drawing operation will be consistent across multiple views.

This suggests that we should store the current color and element in the document object. These could then be accessed by any view object associated with the document object. Of course, if we had more than one document active, each document would have its own color and element type settings. It would, therefore, be sensible to handle the messages for our new menu items in the **CSketcherDoc** class and to store information about the current selections in an object of this class.

Creating Menu Message Functions

Switch the class shown in the ClassWizard Class ̲name: box to CSketcherDoc and click on ID_COLOR_BLACK in the Object IDs: list. The window should appear as shown here:

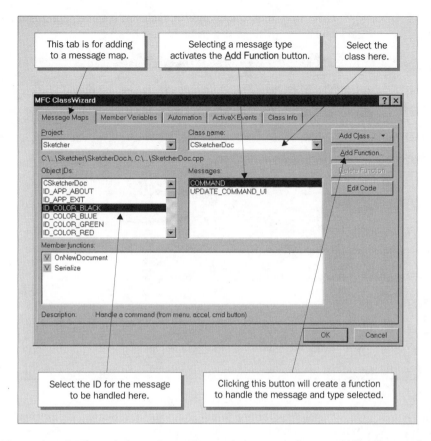

This tab is for adding to a message map.

Selecting a message type activates the Add Function button.

Select the class here.

Select the ID for the message to be handled here.

Clicking this button will create a function to handle the message and type selected.

The Messages: box in the window above shows, for a particular menu ID, the two kinds of message that can arise. They serve distinct purposes in dealing with a menu item:

Message	When Issued
COMMAND	This is issued when a particular menu item has been selected. The handler should provide the action appropriate to the menu item being selected — for example, setting the current color in the document object.
UPDATE_COMMAND_UI	This is issued when the menu should be updated — checked or unchecked, for example — depending on its status. This message occurs before a pop-up menu is displayed so you can set the appearance of the menu item before the user sees it.

The way these work is quite simple. When you click on a menu item in the menu bar, an UPDATE_COMMAND_UI message is sent for each item in that menu *before* the menu is displayed. This provides the opportunity to do any necessary updating of the menu items' properties. When these messages have been handled and any changes to the items' properties have been completed, the menu is drawn. When you then click on one of the items in the menu, a COMMAND message for that menu item is sent. We'll deal with the COMMAND messages for now, and come back to the UPDATE_COMMAND_UI messages a little later in this chapter.

With the ID_COLOR_BLACK object highlighted and COMMAND selected in the Messages: box, click on the button Add Function.... This is the window you'll see:

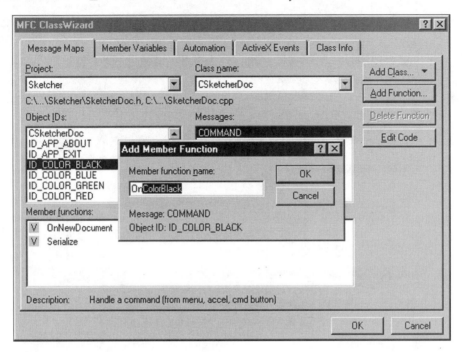

Here, the ClassWizard is about to generate a handler function in the class **CSketcherDoc** with the name shown. You have an opportunity to alter the function name, but this is a good choice so click on the OK button to accept it. This function will be added to the Member functions: box, and the message ID and the type of message that this handler will deal with will also be shown.

In the same way, add COMMAND message handlers for the other color menu IDs and all the element menu IDs. You can create each of the handler functions for the menu items with just four mouse clicks.

ClassWizard will have added the handlers to the class definition, which will now look like this:

```
class CSketcherDoc : public CDocument
{
...
protected:

// Generated message map functions
protected:
   //{{AFX_MSG(CSketcherDoc)
   afx_msg void OnColorBlack();
   afx_msg void OnColorBlue();
   afx_msg void OnColorGreen();
   afx_msg void OnColorRed();
   afx_msg void OnElementCircle();
   afx_msg void OnElementCurve();
   afx_msg void OnElementLine();
```

```
        afx_msg void OnElementRectangle();
    //}}AFX_MSG
    DECLARE_MESSAGE_MAP()
};
```

A declaration has been added for each of the handlers that we've specified in the ClassWizard dialog. Each of the function declarations has been prefixed with **afx_msg** to indicate that it is a message handler.

The ClassWizard also automatically updates the message map in your **CSketcherDoc** class with the new message handlers. If you take a look in the file **SketcherDoc.cpp**, you'll see the message map is as shown below:

```
BEGIN_MESSAGE_MAP(CSketcherDoc, CDocument)
    //{{AFX_MSG_MAP(CSketcherDoc)
    ON_COMMAND(ID_COLOR_BLACK, OnColorBlack)
    ON_COMMAND(ID_COLOR_BLUE, OnColorBlue)
    ON_COMMAND(ID_COLOR_GREEN, OnColorGreen)
    ON_COMMAND(ID_COLOR_RED, OnColorRed)
    ON_COMMAND(ID_ELEMENT_CIRCLE, OnElementCircle)
    ON_COMMAND(ID_ELEMENT_CURVE, OnElementCurve)
    ON_COMMAND(ID_ELEMENT_LINE, OnElementLine)
    ON_COMMAND(ID_ELEMENT_RECTANGLE, OnElementRectangle)
    //}}AFX_MSG_MAP
END_MESSAGE_MAP()
```

The ClassWizard has added an **ON_COMMAND()** macro for each of the handlers that you have identified. This associates the handler name with the message ID, so, for example, the member function **OnColorBlack()** will be called to service a COMMAND message for the menu item with the ID **ID_COLOR_BLACK**.

Each of the handlers generated by ClassWizard is just a skeleton. For example, take a look at the code provided for **OnColorBlack()**. This is also defined in the file **SketcherDoc.cpp**, so you can scroll down to find it, or go directly to it by switching to the ClassView and double-clicking the function name after expanding the tree for the class **CSketcherDoc** (make sure that the file is saved first):

```
void CSketcherDoc::OnColorBlack()
{
    // TODO: Add your command handler code here

}
```

As you can see, the handler takes no arguments and returns nothing. It also does nothing at the moment, but this is hardly surprising since ClassWizard has no way of knowing what you want to do with these messages!

Coding Menu Message Functions

Let's consider what we should do with the COMMAND messages for our new menu items. We said earlier that we want to record the current element and color in the document, so we need a data member added to the **CSketcherDoc** class for each of these.

Adding Members to Store Color and Element Mode

You can add the data members that we need to the 'Attributes' section of the **CSketcherDoc** class definition, just by editing the class definition directly. Display the class definition by double-clicking the class name in the ClassView, then insert the code shown here:

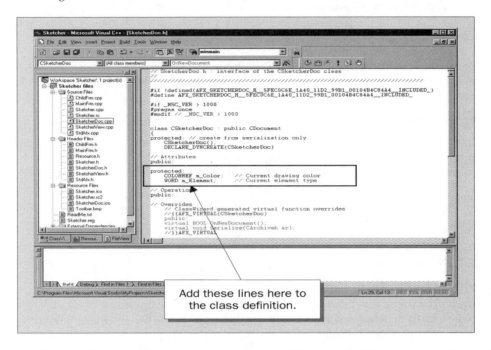

Add these lines here to the class definition.

The new data members are **m_Color** and **m_Element**. We've prefixed their names with **m_** to show that they are members of a class. The member **m_Element** is declared to be of type **WORD**, which is equivalent to **unsigned int**. We'll see why this is a good choice when we come to look into how to save a document in a file. The type for **m_Color** is **COLORREF**, a Windows-defined type that is used to represent color values. It's a 32-bit integer. We'll be able to use this value directly to set the color when we get to draw elements in a view. Both the new data members are **protected** because there is no need for them to be **public**. As we saw when we discussed classes, data members shouldn't be declared as **public** unless it's absolutely necessary, as this undermines the security of the class.

You could also have added these data members by right-clicking the class name in ClassView and selecting Add Member Variable... from the pop-up. You can add the information necessary to define these data members in the dialog box that is displayed. Of course, if you want to add comments — and it's a good idea to do so — you must still go back to the class definition to insert them.

Initializing the New Class Data Members

We need to decide how to represent a color and an element. We could just set them to numeric values, but this would introduce 'magic numbers' into the program, the significance of which would be less than obvious to anyone else looking at the code. A better way would be to define a set of constants that we can use to set values for the two member variables we have added. In this way, we can use a standard mnemonic to refer to a given type of element. We could define the element types with the following statements:

```
// Element type definitions
// Each type value must be unique
const WORD LINE = 101U;
const WORD RECTANGLE = 102U;
const WORD CIRCLE = 103U;
const WORD CURVE = 104U;
```

The constants initializing the element types are arbitrary unsigned integers. You can choose different values if you like, as long as they are all distinct. If we want to add further types in the future, it will obviously be very easy to add definitions here.

For the color values, it would be a good idea if we used constant variables that are initialized with the values that Windows uses to define the color in question. We can do this with the following lines of code:

```
// Color values for drawing
const COLORREF BLACK = RGB(0,0,0);
const COLORREF RED = RGB(255,0,0);
const COLORREF GREEN = RGB(0,255,0);
const COLORREF BLUE = RGB(0,0,255);
```

Each constant is initialized by **RGB()**, which is a standard macro defined in the file **Wingdi.h**, included as part of **Windows.h**. The three arguments define the red, green and blue components of the color value respectively. Each parameter is an integer between 0 and 255, where these limits correspond to no color component and the maximum color component. **RGB(0,0,0)** corresponds to black, since there are no components of red, green or blue. **RGB(255,0,0)** creates a color value with a maximum red component, and no green or blue contribution. Other colors can be created by combining red, green and blue components.

We need somewhere to put these constants, so let's create a new header file and call it **OurConstants.h**. You can create a new file by using the File | New menu option in the Visual C++ IDE, then entering the constant definitions as shown here:

```
//Definitions of constants

#ifndef OurConstants_h
#define OurConstants_h

  // Element type definitions
  // Each type value must be unique
  const WORD LINE = 101U;
  const WORD RECTANGLE = 102U;
  const WORD CIRCLE = 103U;
  const WORD CURVE = 104U;
  /////////////////////////////////

  // Color values for drawing
  const COLORREF BLACK = RGB(0,0,0);
  const COLORREF RED = RGB(255,0,0);
  const COLORREF GREEN = RGB(0,255,0);
  const COLORREF BLUE = RGB(0,0,255);
  /////////////////////////////////

#endif //!defined(OurConstants.h)
```

As you'll recall, the pre-processor directive **#if!defined** is there to ensure that the definitions aren't included more than once. The block of statements down to **#endif** will only be included if **OurConstants_h** hasn't been defined previously.

After saving the file, you can add the following **#include** statement to the beginning of the file **Sketcher.h**, as shown by the shaded line below:

```
////////////////////////////////////////////////////////////////////////////
// CSketcherApp:
// See Sketcher.cpp for the implementation of this class
//

#include "OurConstants.h"

class CSketcherApp : public CWinApp
{
...
};
```

Sketcher.h is included into the other **.cpp** files in the program, so our constants will be available to any of them. To ensure the Visual C++ IDE displays the new file in FileView, you need to add the file to the header files folder. Right click on Header Files in FileView and select Add Files to Folder... from the pop-up. Then enter the name **OurConstants.h** in the dialog, and click on OK.

Modifying the Class Constructor

It's important that we make sure that the data members we have added to the **CSketcherDoc** class are initialized when a document is created. You can add the code to do this to the class constructor as shown here:

```
CSketcherDoc::CSketcherDoc()
{
    // TODO: add one-time construction code here
    m_Element = LINE;    // Set initial element type
    m_Color = BLACK;     // Set initial drawing color
}
```

The element type is initialized with **LINE** and the color with **BLACK**, consistent with the initial check marks that we specified for the menus.

Now we're ready to add the code for the handler functions that we created. We can do this with the ClassView. Double click on the name of the first handler function, **OnColorBlack()**. We just need to add one line to the function, so the code for it becomes:

```
void CSketcherDoc::OnColorBlack()
{
    m_Color = BLACK;         // Set the drawing color to black
}
```

The only job that the handler has to do is to set the appropriate color. In the interests of conciseness, the new line replaces the comment provided by ClassWizard. You can go through and add one line to each of the Color menu handlers.

The element menu handlers are much the same. The handler for the E|ement | L|ine menu item will be:

```
void CSketcherDoc::OnElementLine()
{
    m_Element = LINE;          // Set element type as a line
}
```

With this model, it's not too difficult to write the other handlers for the E|ement menu. That's eight message handlers completed. Let's rebuild the example and see how it works.

Running the Extended Example

Assuming that there are no typos, the compiled and linked program should run without error. When you run the program you should see the window shown here:

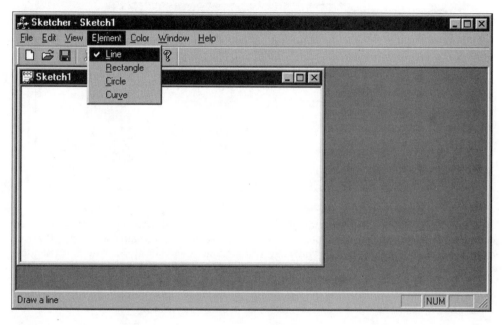

Our new menus are in place on the menu bar, and you can see that the items we have added in the E|ement menu are all there, as is the message in the status bar that we provided in the properties box. You could also verify that *Alt-C* and *Alt-l* work as well. The things that don't work are the check marks for the currently selected color and element, which remain firmly stuck to their initial defaults. Let's look at how we can fix that.

Adding Message Handlers to Update the User Interface

To set the check mark correctly for the new menus, we need to add the second kind of message handler, UPDATE_COMMAND_UI (or update command user interface), for each of the new menu items. This sort of message handler is specifically aimed at updating the menu item properties before the item is displayed.

Let's go back to the ClassWizard. Make sure that the Class name: box shows CSketcherDoc first, then select ID_COLOR_BLACK in the Object IDs: box and UPDATE_COMMAND_UI in the Messages: box. You'll be able to click on the Add Function... button and see the window shown below:

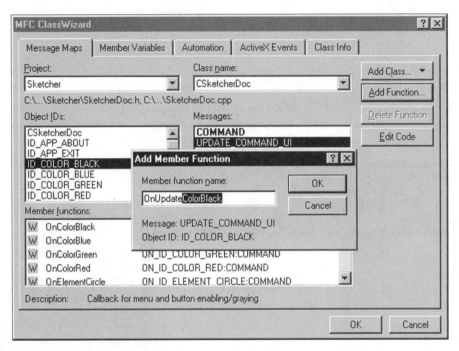

You can see the description of the purpose of the function below the Member functions: box. This description fits our requirement precisely. The name for an update function has been generated, **OnUpdateColorBlack()**, and since this seems a reasonable name for the function we want, click on the OK button and have ClassWizard generate it. As well as generating the skeleton function definition in **SketcherDoc.cpp**, its declaration will be added to the class definition. An entry for it will also be made in the message map:

```
ON_UPDATE_COMMAND_UI(ID_COLOR_BLACK, OnUpdateColorBlack)
```

This uses the macro **ON_UPDATE_COMMAND_UI()**, which identifies the function you have just generated as the handler to deal with update messages corresponding to the ID shown. You can now add command update handlers for each of the seven other menu items.

Coding a Command Update Handler

You can access the code for the handler, **OnUpdateColorBlack()**, by selecting the appropriate line in the Member functions box of the ClassWizard, and then clicking the Edit Code button. This is the skeleton code for the function **OnUpdateColorBlack()**:

```
void CSketcherDoc::OnUpdateColorBlack(CCmdUI* pCmdUI)
{
    // TODO: Add your command update UI handler code here

}
```

The argument passed to the handler is a pointer to an object of the **CCmdUI** class. This is an MFC class that is only used with update handlers. The pointer points to an object that identifies the particular menu item originating the update message and can be used to access members of the class object. The class has five member functions that act on user interface items. The purpose of each of these is described below:

Method	Purpose
`ContinueRouting()`	Pass the message on to the next priority handler.
`Enable()`	Enable or disable the relevant interface item.
`SetCheck()`	Set a check mark for the relevant interface item.
`SetRadio()`	Set a button in a radio group on or off.
`SetText()`	Set the text for the relevant interface item.

We'll use the third function, **SetCheck()**, as that seems to do what we want. The function is declared in the **CCmdUI** class as:

```
virtual void SetCheck(int nCheck = 1);
```

This function will set a menu item as checked if the argument passed is 1, and set it unchecked if the argument passed is 0. The parameter has a default value of 1, so if you just want to set a check mark for a menu item regardless, you can call this function without specifying an argument.

In our case, we want to set a menu item as checked if it corresponds with the current color. We can, therefore, write the update handler for **OnUpdateColorBlack()** as:

```
void CSketcherDoc::OnUpdateColorBlack(CCmdUI* pCmdUI)
{
    // Set menu item Checked if the current color is black
    pCmdUI->SetCheck(m_Color==BLACK);
}
```

The first part of the statement, **pCmdUI->SetCheck**, calls the **SetCheck()** function of the Color | Black menu item, while the comparison **m_Color==BLACK** results in 1 if **m_Color** is **BLACK**, or 0 otherwise. The effect, therefore, is to check the menu item only if the current color stored in **m_Color** is **BLACK**, which is precisely what we want.

Since the update handlers for all the menu items in a menu are always called before the menu is displayed, you can code the other handlers in the same way to ensure that only the item corresponding to the current color (or the current element) will be checked:

```
void CSketcherDoc::OnUpdateColorBlue(CCmdUI* pCmdUI)
{
    // Set menu item Checked if the current color is blue
    pCmdUI->SetCheck(m_Color==BLUE);
}
```

```
void CSketcherDoc::OnUpdateColorGreen(CCmdUI* pCmdUI)
{
    // Set menu item Checked if the current color is green
    pCmdUI->SetCheck(m_Color==GREEN);
}


void CSketcherDoc::OnUpdateColorRed(CCmdUI* pCmdUI)
{
    // Set menu item Checked if the current color is red
    pCmdUI->SetCheck(m_Color==RED);
}
```

A typical Element menu item update handler will be coded as:

```
void CSketcherDoc::OnUpdateElementCircle(CCmdUI* pCmdUI)
{
    // Set Checked if the current element is a circle
    pCmdUI->SetCheck(m_Element==CIRCLE);
}
```

You can now code all the other update handlers in a similar manner:

```
void CSketcherDoc::OnUpdateElementCurve(CCmdUI* pCmdUI)
{
    // Set Checked if the current element is a curve
    pCmdUI->SetCheck(m_Element==CURVE);
}


void CSketcherDoc::OnUpdateElementLine(CCmdUI* pCmdUI)
{
    // Set Checked if the current element is a line
    pCmdUI->SetCheck(m_Element==LINE);
}


void CSketcherDoc::OnUpdateElementRectangle(CCmdUI* pCmdUI)
{
    // Set Checked if the current element is a rectangle
    pCmdUI->SetCheck(m_Element==RECTANGLE);
}
```

Once you get the idea, it's easy, isn't it?

Exercising the Update Handlers

When you've added the code for all the update handlers, you can build and execute the Sketcher application again. Now, when you change a color or an element type selection, this will be reflected in the menu, as shown below:

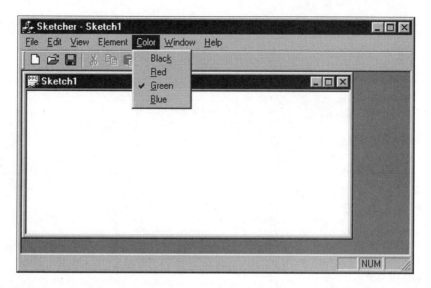

We've completed all the code that we need for our menu items. Make sure that you have saved everything before embarking on the next stage. These days, toolbars are a must in any Windows program of consequence, so we should now take a look at how we can add toolbar buttons to support our new menus.

Adding Toolbar Buttons

Select the ResourceView and extend the Toolbar resource. You'll see that it has the same ID as the main menu, **IDR_MAINFRAME**. If you double-click this ID, the Resource Editor window will be as shown below:

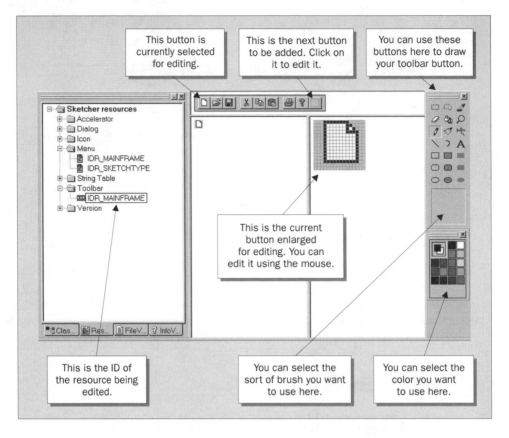

A toolbar button is a 16x15 array of pixels which contains a pictorial representation of the function it operates. You can see above that the resource editor provides an enlarged view of a toolbar button so that you can see and manipulate individual pixels. If you click on the new button at the right-hand end of the row as indicated, you'll be able to draw this button. Before starting the editing, drag the new button about half a button width to the right. It will separate from its neighbor on the left to start a new block.

We should keep the toolbar button blocks in the same sequence as the items on the menu bar, so we'll create the element type selection buttons first. We'll be using the following editing buttons provided by the resource editor:

Pencil for drawing individual pixels

Eraser for erasing individual pixels

Fill an area with the current color

Zoom the view of the button

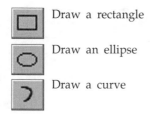 Draw a rectangle

Draw an ellipse

Draw a curve

Make sure that the black color is selected and use the pencil tool to draw a diagonal line in the enlarged image of the new toolbar button. In fact, if you want it a bit bigger, you can use the 'zoom' editing button to enlarge it up to eight times its actual size. If you make a mistake, you can change to the eraser editing button, but you need to make sure that the color selected corresponds to the background color for the button you are editing. You can also erase individual pixels by clicking on them using the right mouse button, but again you need to be sure that the background color is set correctly when you do this. To set the background color, just click on the appropriate color using the right mouse button. Using the left mouse button selects the foreground color. Once you're happy with what you've drawn, the next step is to edit the toolbar button properties.

Editing Toolbar Button Properties

Double-clicking your new button in the toolbar will bring up its properties window:

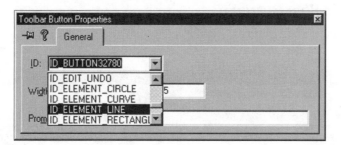

The properties box will show a default ID for the button, but we want to associate the button with the menu item Element | Line that we've already defined, so select ID_ELEMENT_LINE from the drop-down box. You'll find that this will also cause the relevant status bar caption to appear in the Prompt: box, because it is recorded along with the ID. You can press *Enter* to complete the button definition.

You can now go on to designing the other three element buttons. You can use the rectangle editing button to draw a rectangle and the ellipse button to draw a circle. You can draw a curve using the pencil to set individual pixels, or use the curve button. You need to associate each button with the ID corresponding to the equivalent menu item that we defined earlier.

Now add the buttons for the colors. You should also drag the first button for selecting a color to the right, so that it starts a new group of buttons. You could keep the color buttons very simple and just color the whole button with the color it selects. You can do this by selecting the appropriate foreground color, then selecting the 'fill' editing button and clicking on the enlarged button image. Again you need to use **ID_COLOR_BLACK**, **ID_COLOR_RED**, etc., as IDs for the buttons. The toolbar editing window should look like the one shown here:

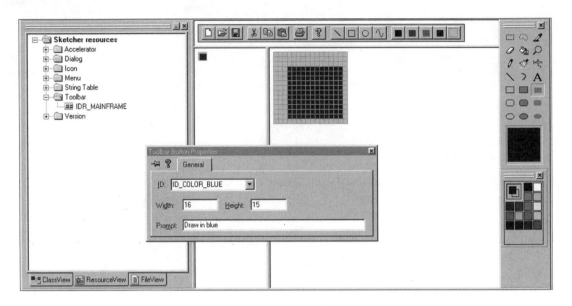

That's all we need for the moment, so save the resource file and give Sketcher another spin.

Exercising the Toolbar Buttons

Build the application once again and execute it. You should see the application window shown below:

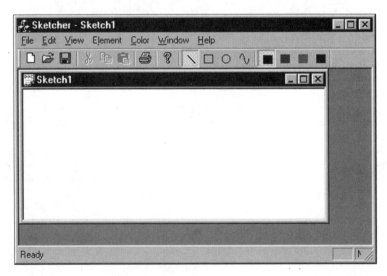

There are some amazing things happening here. The toolbar buttons that we added already reflect the default settings that we defined for the new menu items. If you let the cursor linger over one of the new buttons, the prompt for the button will appear in the status bar. The new buttons work as a complete substitute for the menu items and any new selection made, using either the menu or the toolbar, is reflected by showing the toolbar button depressed, as well as the check against the menu item.

If you close the document view window, Sketch1, you'll see that our toolbar buttons are automatically grayed and disabled. If you open a new document window, they will be automatically enabled once again. You can also try dragging the toolbar with the cursor. You can move it to either side of the application window, or have it free-floating. You can also enable or disable it through the View | Toolbar menu option. We got all this without writing a single additional line of code!

Adding Tooltips

There's one further tweak that we can add to our toolbar buttons which is remarkably easy: adding **tooltips**. A tooltip is a small box that appears adjacent to the toolbar button when you let the cursor linger on the button. The tooltip contains a text string which is an additional clue as to the purpose of the toolbar button.

To add tooltips, select the ResourceView and, after expanding the resource list, double-click on the String Table resource. This contains the IDs and prompt strings associated with menu items and toolbar buttons. You should see the IDs for the menus that we added earlier. Double-click on ID_ELEMENT_LINE to cause the String Properties dialog to be displayed. To add a tooltip, you just need to add **\n**, followed by the tooltip text, to the end of the prompt text. For this ID, you could add **\nLine**, for example.

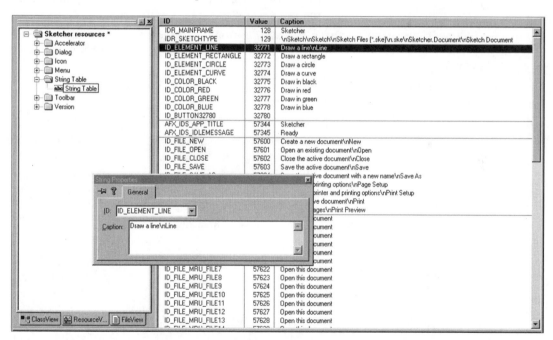

If you press *Enter*, the new prompt string with the tooltip text appended will be recorded against the ID. You can now go through the other menu IDs for elements and colors adding similar tooltips.

That's all you have to do. After saving the String Table resource, you can now rebuild the application and execute it. Placing the cursor over one of the new toolbar buttons will cause the tooltip to be displayed after a second or two.

589

Summary

In this chapter, you've learned how MFC connects a message with a class member function to process it, and you've written your first message handlers. Much of the work in writing a Windows program is writing message handlers, so it's important to have a good grasp of what happens in the process. When we get to consider other message handlers, you'll see that the process for adding them is just the same.

You have also extended the standard menu and the toolbar in the AppWizard-generated program, which provides a good base for the application code that we will add in the next chapter. Although there's no functionality under the covers yet, the menu and toolbar operation looks very professional, courtesy of the AppWizard-generated framework and ClassWizard.

The important points that we've seen in this chapter are:

▶ MFC defines the message handlers for a class in a message map which appears in the **.cpp** file for the class.

▶ Command messages which arise from menus and toolbars can be handled in any class that's derived from **CCmdTarget**. These include the application class, the frame and child frame window classes, the document class and the view class.

▶ Messages other than command messages can only be handled in a class derived from **CWnd**. This includes frame window and view classes, but not application or document classes.

▶ MFC has a predefined sequence for searching the classes in your program to find a message handler for a command message.

▶ You should always use ClassWizard to add message handlers to your program.

▶ The physical appearances of menus and toolbars are defined in resource files, which are edited by the built-in resource editor within the Visual C++ IDE.

▶ Items in a menu that can result in command messages are identified by a symbolic constant with the prefix **ID_**. These IDs are used to associate a handler with the message from the menu item.

▶ To associate a toolbar button with a particular menu item, you give it the same ID as that of the menu item.

▶ To add a tooltip for a toolbar button corresponding to a menu item, you add the tooltip text to the entry for the menu item's ID in the String Table resource. The tooltip text is separated from the menu prompt text by **\n**.

In the next chapter, you'll be adding the code necessary to draw elements in a view and, using the menus and toolbar buttons that we have created here, to select what is to be drawn and in which color. This is where the Sketcher program begins to live up to its name.

Exercises

Ex14-1: Add a menu item Ellipse to the Element pop-up.

Ex14-2: Implement the command and command update handlers for it in the document class.

Ex14-3: Add a toolbar button corresponding to the Ellipse menu item and add a tooltip for the button.

Ex14-4: Modify the command update handlers for the color menu items so that the currently selected item is displayed in upper case, and the others are displayed in lower case.

Drawing in a Window

In this chapter, we'll add some meat to our Sketcher application. We'll concentrate on understanding how you get graphical output displayed in the application window. Although we'll be able to draw all but one of the elements for which we have added menu items, we'll leave the problem of how to store them in a document until the next chapter. In this chapter, you will learn:

- What coordinate systems Windows provides for drawing in a window
- What a device context is and why it is necessary
- How and when your program draws in a window
- How to define handlers for mouse messages
- How to define your own shape classes
- How to program the mouse to draw your shapes in a window
- How to get your program to capture the mouse

Basics of Drawing in a Window

Before we go into drawing using MFC, it's useful to get an idea of what is happening under the covers of the Windows operating system. Like any other operation under Windows, writing to a window on your display screen is achieved through using Windows API functions. There's slightly more to it than that though; the situation is somewhat complicated by the way Windows works.

For a start, you can't just write to a window and forget it. There are many events that occur which mean that you must redraw the window—if the user resizes the window that you're drawing in, for instance, or if part of your window is exposed by the user moving another window.

Fortunately, you don't need to worry about the details of such occurrences because Windows actually manages all these events for you, but it does mean that you can only write permanent data to a window when your application receives a specific Windows message requesting that you do so. It also means that you need to be able to reconstruct everything that you've drawn in the window at any time.

When all, or part, of a window needs to be redrawn, Windows sends a **WM_PAINT** message to your application. This is intercepted by MFC, which passes the message to a function member of one of your classes. You'll see how to handle this a little later in this chapter.

The Window Client Area

A window doesn't have a fixed position on the screen, or even a fixed visible area, because a window can be dragged around using the mouse and resized by dragging its borders. So how do you know where to draw on the screen?

Fortunately, you don't need to. Because Windows provides you with a consistent way of drawing in a window, you don't have to worry about where it is on the screen. Otherwise, drawing in a window would be inordinately complicated. Windows does this by maintaining a coordinate system for the client area of a window that is local to the window. It always uses the top left corner of the client area (rather than, say, the top left corner of the screen) as its reference point. All points within the client area are defined relative to this point, as shown here:

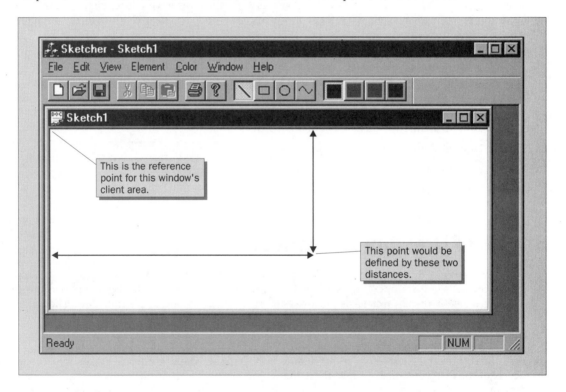

The horizontal and vertical distances of a point from the top left corner of the client area will always be the same, regardless of where the window is on the screen, or how big it is. Of course, Windows will need to keep track of where the window is, and when you draw something at a point in the client area, it will need to figure out where that actually is on the screen.

The Windows Graphical Device Interface

The final constraint Windows imposes is that you don't actually write data to the screen in any direct sense. All output to your display screen is graphical, regardless of whether it is lines and circles, or text. Windows insists that you define this output using the **Graphical Device Interface** (**GDI**). The GDI enables you to program graphical output independently of the hardware on which it will be displayed, meaning that your program will work on different machines with different display hardware. In addition to display screens, the Windows GDI also supports printers and plotters, so outputting data to a printer or a plotter involves essentially the same mechanisms as displaying information on the screen.

What is a Device Context?

When you want to draw something on a graphical output device such as the display screen, you must use a **device context**. A device context is a data structure that's defined by Windows, and which contains information that allows Windows to translate your output requests (which are in the form of device-independent GDI function calls) into actions on the particular physical output device being used. A pointer to a device context is obtained by calling a Windows API function.

A device context provides you with a choice of coordinate systems called **mapping modes**, which will be automatically converted to client coordinates. You can also alter many of the parameters that affect the output to a device context by calling GDI functions; such parameters are called **attributes**. Examples of attributes that you can change are the drawing color, the background color, the line thickness to be used when drawing and the font for text output. There are also GDI functions that will provide information about the physical device you're working with. For example, you may need to be certain that the display on the computer executing your program can support 256 colors, or that a printer can support the output of bitmaps.

Mapping Modes

Each **mapping mode** in a device context is identified by an ID, in a manner similar to what we saw with Windows messages. Each symbol has the prefix **MM_** to indicate that it defines a mapping mode. The mapping modes provided by Windows are:

Mapping Mode	Definition
MM_TEXT	A logical unit is one device pixel with positive x from left to right, and positive y from top to bottom of the window client area.
MM_LOENGLISH	A logical unit is 0.01 inches with positive x from left to right, and positive y from the top of the client area upwards.
MM_HIENGLISH	A logical unit is 0.001 inches with the x and y directions as in **MM_LOENGLISH**.
MM_LOMETRIC	A logical unit is 0.1 millimeters with the x and y directions as in **MM_LOENGLISH**.
MM_HIMETRIC	A logical unit is 0.01 millimeters with the x and y directions as in **MM_LOENGLISH**.
MM_ISOTROPIC	A logical unit is of arbitrary length, but the same along both the x and y axes. The x and y directions are as in **MM_LOENGLISH**.

Mapping Mode	Definition
MM_ANISOTROPIC	This mode is similar to **MM_ISOTROPIC**, but allows the length of a logical unit on the *x* axis to be different from that of a logical unit on the *y* axis.
MM_TWIPS	A logical unit is 0.05 of a point, which is 6.9×10^{-4} of an inch. (A **point** is a unit of measurement for fonts). The *x* and *y* directions are as in **MM_LOENGLISH**.

We're not going to be using all of these mapping modes in this book. However, the ones we will be using form a good cross-section of those available, so you won't have any problem using the others when you need to.

MM_TEXT is the default mapping mode for a device context. If you need to use a different mapping mode, you'll have to take steps to change it. Note that the direction of the positive *y* axis in the **MM_TEXT** mode is opposite to what you will have seen in high school coordinate geometry, as you can see in the following drawing:

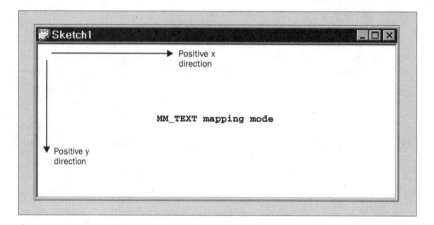

By default, the point at the top left corner of the client area has the coordinates (0,0) in *every* mapping mode, although it's possible to move the origin away from the top left corner of the client area if you want to. With the origin at the top left corner in **MM_TEXT** mode, a point 50 pixels from the left border and 100 pixels down from the top of the client area will have the coordinates (50,100). The units are pixels; so of course, the point will be nearer the top left corner of the client area if your monitor is using the 800x600 SVGA resolution than if it's working with the 640x480 VGA resolution. An object drawn in this mapping mode will be smaller at the SVGA resolution than it would be at the VGA resolution.

Coordinates are always 16-bit signed integers in Windows 95, which is the same as in earlier 16-bit versions of Windows. (It's slightly different under Windows NT, where coordinates can be 32 bits, but we won't go into that here.) This limits the *x* and *y* values to ± 32768. The maximum physical size of the total drawing varies with the physical length of a coordinate unit, which is determined by the mapping mode.

The directions of the *x* and *y* coordinate axes in **MM_LOENGLISH** and all the remaining mapping modes are the same as each other, but different from **MM_TEXT**. While positive *y* is consistent with what you learned in high school (*y* values increase as you move up the screen), **MM_LOENGLISH** is still slightly odd because the origin is at the top left corner of the client area, so for points within the visible client area, *y* is always negative.

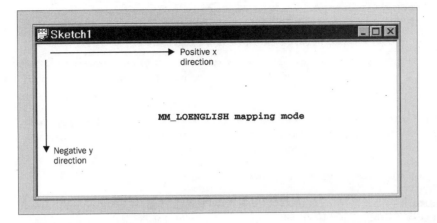

In the **MM_LOENGLISH** mapping mode, the units along the axes are 0.01 inches apiece, so a point at the position (50, -100) will be half an inch from the left border and one inch down from the top of the client area. An object will be the same size in the client area, regardless of the resolution of the monitor on which it is displayed. If you draw anything in the **MM_LOENGLISH** mode with negative *x* or positive *y* coordinates, it will be outside the client area and therefore invisible, since the reference point (0,0) is the top left hand corner by default. However, it's possible to move the position of the reference point, by calling the Windows API function **SetViewportOrg()** (or the **SetViewportOrg()** member of the **CDC** MFC class, which we'll come to shortly).

The Drawing Mechanism in Visual C++

MFC encapsulates the Windows interface to your screen and printer and relieves you of the need to worry about much of the detail involved in programming graphical output. As we saw in Chapter 13, your AppWizard-generated application will already contain a class derived from the MFC class **CView** that's specifically designed to display document data on the screen.

The View Class in Your Application

AppWizard generated the class **CSketcherView** to display information from a document in the client area of a document window. The class definition includes overrides for several virtual functions, but the one we're particularly interested in here is the function **OnDraw()**, because this will be called whenever the client area of the document window needs to be redrawn. It's the function that's called by the application framework when a **WM_PAINT** message is received in your program.

The OnDraw() Member Function

The implementation of the **OnDraw()** member function that's created by AppWizard looks like this:

```
void CSketcherView::OnDraw(CDC* pDC)
{
   CSketcherDoc* pDoc = GetDocument();
```

```
        ASSERT_VALID(pDoc);
        // TODO: add draw code for native data here
}
```

A pointer to an object of the class **CDC** is passed to the **OnDraw()** member of the view class. This object has member functions that call the Windows API functions which allow you to draw in a device context.

Since you'll put all the code to draw the document in this function, the AppWizard has included a declaration for the pointer **pDoc** and initialized it using the function **GetDocument()**, which returns the address of the document object related to the current view:

```
        CSketcherDoc* pDoc = GetDocument();
```

GetDocument() actually retrieves the pointer to the document from **m_pDocument**, an inherited data member of the view object. The function performs the important task of casting the pointer stored in this data member to the type corresponding to the document class in the application, **CSketcherDoc**. This is so that the compiler will have access to the members of the document class that you've defined. Otherwise, the compiler would only be able to access the members of the base class. Thus, **pDoc** will point to the document object in your application associated with the current view, and you will be using it to access the data that you've stored in the document object when you want to draw it.

The following line:

```
        ASSERT_VALID(pDoc);
```

just makes sure that the pointer **pDoc** contains a valid address.

The object of the **CDC** class pointed to by the **pDC** argument that's passed to the **OnDraw()** function is the key to drawing in a window. It provides a device context, plus the tools we need to write graphics and text to it, so we clearly need to look at it in more detail.

The CDC Class

You should do all the drawing in your program using members of the **CDC** class. All objects of this class and classes derived from it contain a device context and the member functions you need for sending graphics and text to your display and your printer. There are also member functions for retrieving information about the physical output device that you are using.

Because **CDC** class objects can provide almost everything you're likely to need by way of graphical output, there are a lot of member functions of this class — in fact, well over a hundred. Therefore, we'll only look at the ones we're going to use in the Sketcher program here in this chapter, and go into others as we need them later on.

Note that MFC includes some more specialized classes for graphics output that are derived from **CDC**. For example, we'll be using objects of **CClientDC** which, because it is derived from **CDC**, also contains all the members we will discuss at this point. The advantage that **CClientDC** has over **CDC** is that it always contains a device context that represents only the client area of a window, and this is precisely what you want in most circumstances.

Displaying Graphics

In a device context, you draw entities such as lines, circles and text relative to a **current position**. A current position is a point in the client area that was set either by the previous entity that was drawn, or by calling a function to set it. For example, we could extend the **OnDraw()** function to set the current position as follows:

```
void CSketcherView::OnDraw(CDC* pDC)
{
    CSketcherDoc* pDoc = GetDocument();
    ASSERT_VALID(pDoc);

    pDC->MoveTo(50, 50);     // Set the current position as 50,50
}
```

The shaded line calls the function **MoveTo()** for the **CDC** object pointed to by **pDC**. This member function simply sets the current position to the *x* and *y* coordinates specified as arguments. As we saw earlier, the default mapping mode is **MM_TEXT**, so the coordinates are in pixels and the current position will be set to a point 50 pixels from the inside left border of the window, and 50 pixels down from the top of the client area.

The **CDC** class overloads the **MoveTo()** function to provide flexibility over how you specify the position that you want to set as the current position. There are two versions of the function, declared in the **CDC** class as:

```
CPoint MoveTo(int x, int y);     // Move to position x,y
CPoint MoveTo(POINT aPoint);     // Move to position defined by aPoint
```

The first version accepts the *x* and *y* coordinates as separate arguments. The second accepts one argument of type **POINT**, which is a structure defined as:

```
typedef struct tagPOINT
{
    LONG x;
    LONG y;
} POINT;
```

The coordinates are members of the **struct** and are of type **LONG**. You may prefer to use a class instead of a structure, in which case you can use objects of the class **CPoint** anywhere that a **POINT** object can be used. The class **CPoint** has data members **x** and **y** of type **LONG** (which is a 32-bit signed integer), and using **CPoint** objects has the advantage that the class also defines member functions that operate on **CPoint** and **POINT** objects. This may seem weird, since **CPoint** would seem to make **POINT** objects obsolete, but remember that the Windows API was built before MFC was around, and **POINT** objects are used in the Windows API and have to be dealt with sooner or later. We'll use **CPoint** objects in our examples, so you'll have an opportunity to see some of the member functions in action.

The return value from the **MoveTo()** function is a **CPoint** object that specifies the current position as it was *before* the move. You might think this a little odd, but consider the situation where you want to move to a new position, draw something, and then move back. You may not know the current position before the move, and once the move occurs it would be lost, so returning the position before the move makes sure it's available to you if you need it.

Drawing Lines

We can follow the call to **MoveTo()** in the **OnDraw()** function with a call to the function **LineTo()**, which will draw a line in the client area from the current position to the point specified by the arguments to the **LineTo()** function, as illustrated here:

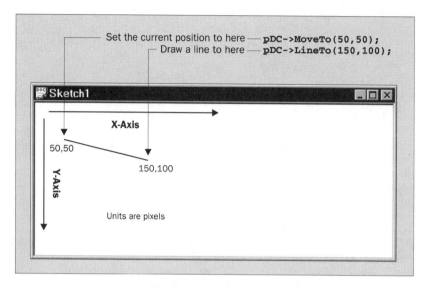

The class **CDC** also defines two versions of the **LineTo()** function with the prototypes:

```
BOOL LineTo(int x, int y); // Draw a line to position x,y
BOOL LineTo(POINT aPoint); // Draw a line to position defined by aPoint
```

This offers you the same flexibility in specifying the argument to the function as **MoveTo()**. You can use a **CPoint** object as an argument to the second version of the function. The function returns **TRUE** if the line was drawn, and **FALSE** otherwise.

When the **LineTo()** function is executed, the current position is changed to the point specifying the end of the line. This allows you to draw a series of connected lines by just calling the **LineTo()** function for each line. Look at the following version of the **OnDraw()** function:

```
void CSketcherView::OnDraw(CDC* pDC)
{
    CSketcherDoc* pDoc = GetDocument();
    ASSERT_VALID(pDoc);

    pDC->MoveTo(50,50);           // Set the current position
    pDC->LineTo(50,200);          // Draw a vertical line down 150 units
    pDC->LineTo(150,200);         // Draw a horizontal line right 100 units
    pDC->LineTo(150,50);          // Draw a vertical line up 150 units
    pDC->LineTo(50,50);           // Draw a horizontal line left 100 units
}
```

If you plug this into the Sketcher program and execute it, it will display the document window shown here:

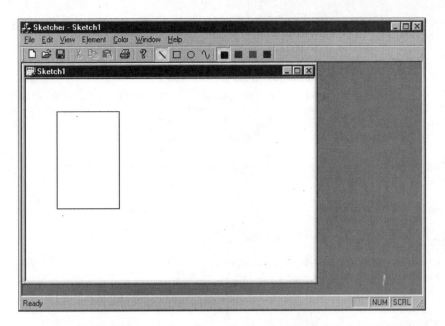

The four calls to the **LineTo()** function draw the rectangle shown counterclockwise, starting with the top left corner. The first call uses the current position set by the **MoveTo()** function; the succeeding calls use the current position set by the previous **LineTo()** function call. You can use this to draw any figure consisting of a sequence of lines, each connected to the previous line. Of course, you are also free to use **MoveTo()** to change the current position at any time.

Drawing Circles

You have a choice of several function members in the class **CDC** for drawing circles, but they're all designed to draw ellipses. As you will know from high school geometry, a circle is a special case of an ellipse, with the major and minor axes equal. You can, therefore, use the member function **Ellipse()** to draw a circle. Like other closed shapes supported by the **CDC** class, the **Ellipse()** function fills the interior of the shape with a color that you set. The interior color is determined by a **brush** that is selected into the device context. The current brush in the device context determines how any closed shape will be filled.

MFC provides a class **CBrush** which you can use to define a brush. You can set the color of a **CBrush** object and also define a pattern to be produced when filling a closed shape. If you want to draw a closed shape that isn't filled, you can use a null brush, which leaves the interior of the shape empty. We'll come back to brushes a little later in this chapter.

Another way to draw circles that aren't filled is to use the **Arc()** function, which doesn't involve brushes. This has the advantage that you can draw any arc of an ellipse, rather than the complete curve. There are two versions of this function in the **CDC** class, declared as:

```
BOOL Arc(int x1, int y1, int x2, int y2, int x3, int y3, int x4, int y4);
BOOL Arc(LPCRECT lpRect, POINT StartPt, POINT EndPt);
```

In the first version, (**x1,y1**) and (**x2,y2**) define the top left and bottom right corners of a rectangle enclosing the complete curve. If you make these coordinates into the corners of a square, the curve drawn will be a segment of a circle. The points (**x3,y3**) and (**x4,y4**) define the start and end points of the segment to be drawn. The segment is drawn counterclockwise. If you make (**x4,y4**) identical to (**x3,y3**), you'll generate a complete, apparently closed curve.

In the second version of **Arc()**, the enclosing rectangle is defined by a **RECT** object, and a pointer to this object is passed as the first argument. The function will also accept a pointer to an object of the class **CRect**, which has four public data members: **left**, **top**, **right**, and **bottom**. These correspond to the x and y coordinates of the top left and bottom right points of the rectangle respectively. The class also provides a range of function members which operate on **CRect** objects, and we shall be using some of these later.

The **POINT** objects **StartPt** and **EndPt** in the second version of **Arc()** define the start and end of the arc to be drawn.

Here's some code that exercises both versions of the **Arc()** function:

```
void CSketcherView::OnDraw(CDC* pDC)
{
   CSketcherDoc* pDoc = GetDocument();
   ASSERT_VALID(pDoc);

   pDC->Arc(50,50,150,150,100,50,150,100);  // Draw the 1st (large) circle

   // Define the bounding rectangle for the 2nd (smaller) circle
   CRect* pRect = new CRect(250,50,300,100);
   CPoint Start(275,100);                    // Arc start point
   CPoint End(250,75);                       // Arc end point
   pDC->Arc(pRect,Start, End);               // Draw the second circle
   delete pRect;
}
```

Note that we used a **CRect** class object instead of a **RECT** structure to define the bounding rectangle, and that we used **CPoint** class objects instead of **POINT** structures. We'll also be using **CRect** objects later, but they have some limitations, as you'll see. The **Arc()** function doesn't require a current position to be set, as the position and size of the arc are completely defined by the arguments you supply. The current position is unaffected by drawing an arc — it remains exactly wherever it was before the arc was drawn. Although coordinates can be ± 32K, the maximum width or height of the rectangle bounding a shape is 32,767 because this is the maximum positive value that can be represented in a signed 16-bit integer.

Now try running Sketcher with this code in the **OnDraw()** function. You should get the results shown here:

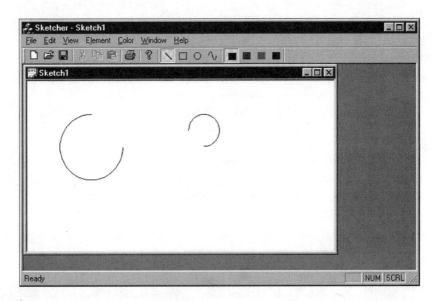

Try re-sizing the borders. The client area is automatically redrawn as you cover or uncover the arcs in the picture. Remember that screen resolution will affect the scale of what is displayed. If you're using a VGA screen at 640x480 resolution, the arcs will be larger and further from the top left corner of the client area.

Drawing in Color

Everything that we've drawn so far has appeared on the screen in black. Drawing implies using a **pen object** which has a color and a thickness, and we've been using the default pen object that is provided in a device context. You're not obliged to do this, of course—you can create your own pen with a given thickness and color. MFC defines the class **CPen** to help you do this.

All closed curves that you draw are filled with the current brush in the device context. As we mentioned earlier, you can define a brush as an instance of the class **CBrush**. Let's take a look at some of the features of **CPen** and **CBrush** objects.

Creating a Pen

The simplest way to create a pen object is first to declare an object of the **CPen** class:

```
CPen aPen;                   // Declare a pen object
```

This object now needs to be initialized with the properties you want. You do this using the class member function **CreatePen()**, which is declared in the **CPen** class as:

```
BOOL CreatePen (int aPenStyle, int aWidth, COLORREF aColor);
```

The function returns **TRUE** as long as the pen is successfully initialized, and **FALSE** otherwise. The first argument defines the line style that you want to use when drawing. You must specify it with one of the predefined symbolic values:

603

Pen Style	Meaning
`PS_SOLID`	The pen draws a solid line.
`PS_DASH`	The pen draws a dashed line. This line style is valid only when the pen width is specified as 1.
`PS_DOT`	The pen draws a dotted line. This line style is valid only when the pen width is specified as 1.
`PS_DASHDOT`	The pen draws a line with alternating dashes and dots. This line style is valid only when the pen width is specified as 1.
`PS_DASHDOTDOT`	The pen draws a line with alternating dashes and double dots. This line style is valid only when the pen width is specified as 1.
`PS_NULL`	The pen doesn't draw anything.
`PS_INSIDEFRAME`	The pen draws a solid line, but unlike `PS_SOLID`, the points that specify the line occur on the edge of the pen rather than in the center, so that the drawn object never extends beyond the enclosing rectangle.

PS_SOLID   PS_INSIDEFRAME

The second argument to the **CreatePen()** function defines the line width. If **aWidth** has the value 0, the line drawn will be 1 pixel wide, regardless of the mapping mode in effect. For values of 1 or more, the pen width is in the units determined by the mapping mode. For example, a value of 2 for **aWidth** in **MM_TEXT** mode will be 2 pixels, while in **MM_LOENGLISH** mode the pen width will be 0.02 inches.

The last argument specifies the color to be used when drawing with the pen, so we could initialize a pen with the statement:

```
aPen.CreatePen(PS_SOLID, 2, RGB(255,0,0));  // Create a red solid pen
```

Assuming that the mapping mode is **MM_TEXT**, this pen will draw a solid red line which is 2 pixels wide.

Using a Pen

In order to use a pen, you must select it into the device context in which you are drawing. To do this, you use the **CDC** class member function **SelectObject()**. To select the pen you want to use, you call this function with a pointer to the pen object as an argument. The function returns a pointer to the previous pen object being used, so that you can save it and restore the old pen when you have finished drawing. A typical statement selecting a pen is:

```
CPen* pOldPen = pDC->SelectObject(&aPen);     // Select aPen as the pen
```

To restore the old pen when you're done, you simply call the function again, passing the pointer returned from the original call:

```
pDC->SelectObject(pOldPen);                    // Restore the old pen
```

We can demonstrate this in action by amending the previous version of the **OnDraw()** function in our view class to:

```
void CSketcherView::OnDraw(CDC* pDC)
{
    CSketcherDoc* pDoc = GetDocument();
    ASSERT_VALID(pDoc);

    // Declare a pen object and initialize it as
    // a red solid pen drawing a line 2 pixels wide
    CPen aPen;
    aPen.CreatePen(PS_SOLID, 2, RGB(255, 0, 0));

    CPen* pOldPen = pDC->SelectObject(&aPen); // Select aPen as the pen

    pDC->Arc(50,50,150,150,100,50,150,100);   // Draw the 1st circle

    // Define the bounding rectangle for the 2nd circle
    CRect* pRect = new CRect(250,50,300,100);
    CPoint Start(275,100);                      // Arc start point
    CPoint End(250,75);                         // Arc end point
    pDC->Arc(pRect,Start, End);                 // Draw the second circle
    delete pRect;

    pDC->SelectObject(pOldPen);                 // Restore the old pen
}
```

If you build and execute the Sketcher application with this version of the **OnDraw()** function, you will get the same arcs drawn as before, but this time the lines will be thicker and they'll be red. You could usefully experiment with this example by trying different combinations of arguments to the **CreatePen()** function and seeing their effects. Note that we have ignored the **BOOL** value returned from the **CreatePen()** function, so we run the risk of the function failing and the failure remaining undetected by the program. It doesn't matter here, since the program is still trivial; but as we develop the program it will become important to check for failures of this kind.

Creating a Brush

An object of the **CBrush** class encapsulates a Windows brush. You can define a brush to be solid, hatched, or patterned. A brush is actually an 8x8 block of pixels that's repeated over the region to be filled.

605

To define a brush with a solid color, you can specify the color when you create the brush object. For example,

```
CBrush aBrush(RGB(255,0,0));        // Define a red brush
```

which defines a red brush. The value passed to the constructor must be of type **COLORREF**, which is the type returned by the **RGB()** macro, so this is a good way to specify the color.

Another constructor is available to define a hatched brush. It requires two arguments to be specified, the first defining the type of hatching, and the second specifying the color, as before. The hatching argument can be any of the following symbolic constants:

Hatching Style	Meaning
HS_HORIZONTAL	Horizontal hatching
HS_VERTICAL	Vertical hatching
HS_BDIAGONAL	Downward hatching from left to right at 45 degrees
HS_FDIAGONAL	Upward hatching from left to right at 45 degrees
HS_CROSS	Horizontal and vertical crosshatching
HS_DIAGCROSS	Crosshatching at 45 degrees

So, to obtain a red, 45-degree crosshatched brush, you could define the **CBrush** object with the statement:

```
CBrush aBrush(HS_DIAGCROSS, RGB(255,0,0));
```

You can also initialize a **CBrush** object in a similar manner to that for a **CPen** object, by using the **CreateSolidBrush()** member function of the class for a solid brush, and the **CreateHatchBrush()** member for a hatched brush. They require the same arguments as the equivalent constructors. For example, we could create the same hatched brush as before, with the statements:

```
CBrush aBrush;                      // Define a brush object
aBrush.CreateHatchBrush(HS_DIAGCROSS, RGB(255,0,0));
```

Using a Brush

To use a brush, you select the brush into the device context by calling the **SelectObject()** member of the **CDC** class in a parallel fashion to that used for a pen. This member function is overloaded to support selecting brush objects into a device context. To select the brush we defined previously, you would simply write:

```
pDC->SelectObject(&aBrush);         // Select the brush into the device context
```

There are a number of standard brushes available. Each of the standard brushes is identified by a predefined symbolic constant, and there are seven that you can use. They are the following:

```
GRAY_BRUSH          LTGRAY_BRUSH          DKGRAY_BRUSH
BLACK_BRUSH         WHITE_BRUSH
HOLLOW_BRUSH        NULL_BRUSH
```

606

The names of these brushes are quite self-explanatory. To use one, you call the **SelectStockObject()** member of the **CDC** class, passing the symbolic name for the brush that you want to use as an argument. To select the null brush, which will leave the interior of a closed shape unfilled, you could write:

```
pDC->SelectStockObject(NULL_BRUSH);
```

Here, **pDC** is a pointer to a **CDC** object, as before. You can also use one of a range of standard pens through this function. The symbols for standard pens are **BLACK_PEN**, **NULL_PEN** (which doesn't draw anything), and **WHITE_PEN**. The **SelectStockObject()** function returns a pointer to the object being replaced in the device context. This is to enable you to save it for restoring later when you have finished drawing.

Because the function works with a variety of objects — we've seen pens and brushes in this chapter, but it also works with fonts — the type of the pointer returned is **CGdiObject***. The **CGdiObject** class is a base class for all the graphic device interface object classes and thus a pointer to this class can be used to store a pointer to any object of these types. However, you need to cast the pointer value returned to the appropriate type so that you can select the old object back to restore it. This is because the **SelectObject()** function you use to do this is overloaded for each of the kinds of object that can be selected. There's no version of **SelectObject()** that accepts a pointer to a **CGdiObject** as an argument, but there are versions that accept an argument of type **CBrush***, **CPen***, and pointers to other GDI objects.

The typical pattern of coding for using a stock brush and later restoring the old brush when you're done is:

```
CBrush* pOldBrush = static_cast<CBrush*>(pDC->SelectStockObject(NULL_BRUSH));

// draw something

pDC->SelectObject(pOldBrush);                    // Restore the old brush
```

We'll be using this in our example later in the chapter.

Drawing Graphics in Practice

We now know how to draw lines and arcs, so it's about time we considered how the user is going to define what they want drawn. In other words, we need to decide how the user interface is going to work.

Since this program is to be a sketching tool, we don't want the user to worry about coordinates. The easiest mechanism for drawing is using just the mouse. To draw a line, for instance, the user could position the cursor and press the left mouse button where they wanted the line to start, and then define the end of the line by moving the cursor with the left button held down. It would be ideal if we could arrange that the line was continuously drawn as the cursor was moved with the left button down (this is known as 'rubber-banding' to graphic designers). The line would be fixed when the left mouse button was released. This process is illustrated in the diagram below:

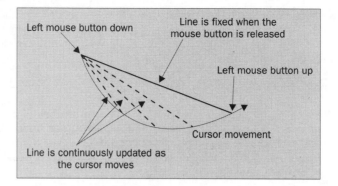

We could allow circles to be drawn in a similar fashion. The first press of the left mouse button would define the center and, as the cursor was moved with the button down, the program would track it. The circle would be continuously redrawn, with the current cursor position defining a point on the circumference of the circle. As with drawing a line, the circle would be fixed when the left mouse button was released. We can see this in the diagram here:

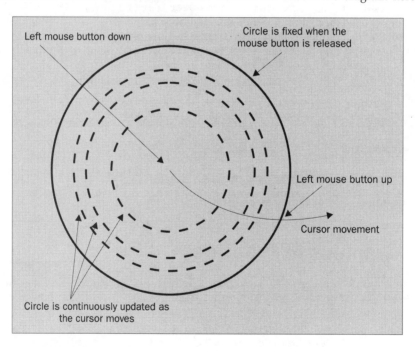

We can draw a rectangle as easily as we draw a line, as illustrated here:

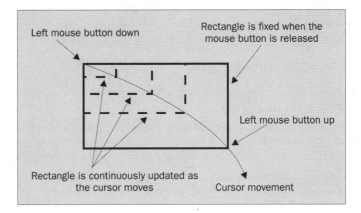

The first point is defined by the position of the cursor when the left mouse button is pressed. This is one corner of the rectangle. The position of the cursor when the mouse is moved with the left button held down defines the diagonally opposite corner of the rectangle. The rectangle actually stored is the last one defined when the left mouse button is released.

A curve will be somewhat different. A curve may be defined by an arbitrary number of points. The mechanism we'll use is illustrated below:

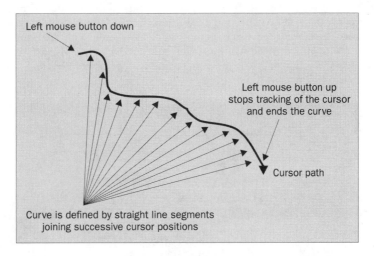

As with the other shapes, the first point is defined by the cursor position when the left mouse button is pressed. Successive positions recorded when the mouse is moved are connected by straight line segments to form the curve, so the mouse track defines the curve to be drawn.

Now we know how the user is going to define an element, clearly our next step in understanding how to implement this is to get a grip on how the mouse is programmed.

Programming the Mouse

To be able to program the drawing of shapes in the way we've discussed, we need to know various things about the status of the mouse. Specifically, we need to know:

- When a mouse button is pressed, since this signals the start of a drawing operation

- Where the cursor is when a button is pressed, because this defines a reference point for the shape

- When the mouse moves, and where the cursor moves to when it does. A mouse movement after detecting that a mouse button has been pressed is a cue to draw a shape, and the cursor position provides a defining point for the shape

- When the mouse button is released, and the cursor position at that instant, because this signals that the final version of the shape should be drawn

As you may have guessed, all this information is provided by Windows in the form of messages sent to your program. The implementation of the process for drawing lines and circles will consist almost entirely of writing message handlers.

Messages from the Mouse

When the user of our program is drawing a shape, they will be interacting with a particular document view. The view class is, therefore, the obvious place to put the message handlers for the mouse. Fire up the ClassWizard and take a look at the Message Maps tab for the **CSketcherView** class. We don't want the messages associated with **ID_**-specified objects; we need to get to the standard Windows messages sent to the class, which have IDs prefixed with **WM_**. You can see these if you select the class name in the Object IDs: box and scroll down the Messages: list, as shown here:

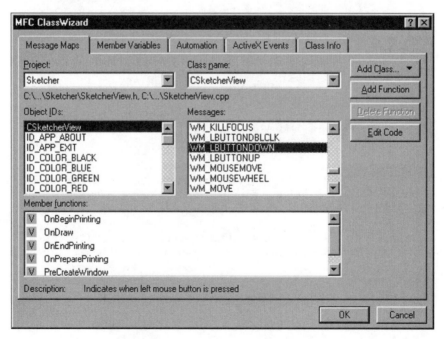

We're interested in three mouse messages at the moment:

Message	Occurs...
WM_LBUTTONDOWN	when the left mouse button is pressed.
WM_LBUTTONUP	when the left mouse button is released.
WM_MOUSEMOVE	when the mouse is moved.

These messages are quite independent of one another and are being sent to the document views in your program even if you haven't supplied handlers for them. It's quite possible for a window to receive a **WM_LBUTTONUP** message without having previously received a **WM_LBUTTONDOWN** message. This can happen if the button is pressed with the cursor over another window and then moved to your view window before being released.

If you scroll the Messages: box, you'll see there are other mouse messages that can occur. You can choose to process any or all of the messages, depending on your application requirements. Let's define in general terms what we want to do with the three messages that we're currently interested in, based on the process for drawing shapes that we saw earlier:

WM_LBUTTONDOWN

This starts the process of drawing an element. So we will:

1 Note that the element drawing process has started.

2 Record the current cursor position as the first point for defining an element.

WM_MOUSEMOVE

This is an intermediate stage where we want to create and draw a temporary version of the current element, but only if the left mouse button is down, so:

1 Check that the left button is down.

2 If it isn't, then exit.

3 If it is, delete any previous version of the current element that was drawn.

4 Record the current cursor position as the second defining point for the current element.

5 Cause the current element to be drawn using the two defining points.

WM_LBUTTONUP

This indicates that the process for drawing an element is finished, so all we need to do is:

1 Store the final version of the element defined by the first point recorded, together with the position of the cursor when the button is released for the second point.

2 Record the end of the process of drawing an element.

Let's now use ClassWizard to generate handlers for these three mouse messages.

Mouse Message Handlers

You can create the handlers for the mouse messages in the same way as you created the menu message handlers. Just open the ClassWizard dialog and click on the **Add** Function button with the message highlighted in the **Messages:** list box. Alternatively, you can use the Wizard Bar. If you display **CSketcherView** in the list box on the left, and then select the down arrow on the right, you'll see the following pop-up menu: contains an option:

If you click on **Add** Windows Message Handler... you'll see the dialog shown here.

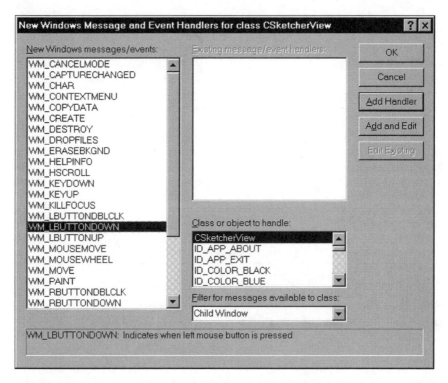

You select the message that you want to add a handler for from the list box on the left, and click on the **Add Handler** button. All the handlers defined for the class will be shown in the list box on the right. You can select any of these when you want to edit the implementation of a handler. Just double-click on the message, or click on the **Edit Existing** button with the appropriate message highlighted.

The functions generated will be **OnLButtonDown()**, **OnLButtonUp()** and **OnMouseMove()**. You don't get the option of changing the names of these functions because you're replacing versions that are already defined in the base class for your **CSketcherView** class. Let's look at how we implement these handlers.

The ClassWizard Generated Code

We can start by looking at the **WM_LBUTTONDOWN** message handler. Make sure that it's highlighted and click on the **Edit Existing** button. This is the skeleton code that's generated:

```
void CSketcherView::OnLButtonDown(UINT nFlags, CPoint point)
{
    // TODO: Add your message handler code here and/or call default

    CView::OnLButtonDown(nFlags, point);
}
```

You can see that ClassWizard has put a call to the base class handler in the skeleton version. This ensures that the base handler is called if you don't add any code here. In this case you don't need to call the base class handler when you handle the message yourself, although you can if you want to. Whether you need to call the base class handler for a message depends on the circumstances.

Generally, the comment indicating where you should add your own code is a good guide. Where it suggests, as in the present instance, that calling the base class handler is optional, you can omit it when you add your own message handling code. Note that the position of the comment in relation to the call of the base class handler is also important, as sometimes you must call the base class message handler before your code, and at other times, afterwards. The comment indicates where your code should appear in relation to the base class message handler call.

The handler in your class is passed two arguments: **nFlags**, which is of type **UINT** and contains a number of status flags indicating whether various keys are being pressed, and the **CPoint** object **point**, which defines the cursor position when the left mouse button was pressed. The type **UINT** is a portable unsigned integer which corresponds to a 32-bit unsigned integer in Windows 95.

The value of **nFlags** which is passed to the function can be any combination of the following symbolic values:

Flag	Meaning
MK_CONTROL	Corresponds to the *Ctrl* key being pressed.
MK_LBUTTON	Corresponds to the left mouse button being down.
MK_MBUTTON	Corresponds to the middle mouse button being down.
MK_RBUTTON	Corresponds to the right mouse button being down.
MK_SHIFT	Corresponds to the *Shift* key being pressed.

Being able to detect if a key is down in the message handler allows you to support different actions, depending on what you find. The value of **nFlags** may contain more than one of these indicators, each of which corresponds to a particular bit in the word, so you can test for a particular key using the bitwise AND operator. For example, to test for the *Ctrl* key being pressed, you could write:

```
if(nFlags & MK_CONTROL)
    // Do something...
```

The expression **nFlags & MK_CONTROL** will only have the value **TRUE** if the **nFlags** variable has the bit defined by **MK_CONTROL** set. In this way, you can have different actions when the left mouse button is pressed, depending on whether the *Ctrl* key is also pressed. We use the bitwise AND operator here, so corresponding bits are ANDed together. Don't confuse this with the logical AND, **&&**, which would not do what we want here.

The arguments passed to the other two message handlers are the same as those for the **OnLButtonDown()** function; the code generated by the ClassWizard for them is:

```
void CSketcherView::OnLButtonUp(UINT nFlags, CPoint point)
{
    // TODO: Add your message handler code here and/or call default

    CView::OnLButtonUp(nFlags, point);
}
```

```
void CSketcherView::OnMouseMove(UINT nFlags, CPoint point)
{
    // TODO: Add your message handler code here and/or call default

    CView::OnMouseMove(nFlags, point);
}
```

Apart from the function names, the skeleton code is the same for each. With an understanding of the information passed to the message handlers, we can start adding our own code.

Drawing Using the Mouse

For the **WM_LBUTTONDOWN** message, we want to record the cursor position as the first point defining an element. We also want to record the position of the cursor after a mouse move. The obvious place to store these cursor positions is in the **CSketcherView** class, so we can add data members to the attributes section of the class for them as follows:

```
class CSketcherView : public CView
{
protected: // create from serialization only
    CSketcherView();
    DECLARE_DYNCREATE(CSketcherView)

// Attributes
public:
    CSketcherDoc* GetDocument();

protected:
    CPoint m_FirstPoint;       // First point recorded for an element
    CPoint m_SecondPoint;      // Second point recorded for an element

    ...
```

As you've seen in previous chapters, another way of adding a new variable to a class is to right-click on the class name in the ClassView and select Add Variable... from the context menu. You can then fill in the details of the variable in the dialog. However, there will be no comments explaining the new data member unless you add them separately.

If you take a look a little further down the listing, you'll see that ClassWizard has added these three function declarations:

```
// Generated message map functions
protected:
    //{{AFX_MSG(CSketcherView)
    afx_msg void OnLButtonDown(UINT nFlags, CPoint point);
    afx_msg void OnLButtonUp(UINT nFlags, CPoint point);
    afx_msg void OnMouseMove(UINT nFlags, CPoint point);
    //}}AFX_MSG
    DECLARE_MESSAGE_MAP()
};
```

The new data members are **protected** to prevent direct modification of them from outside the class. Both of the new data members need to be initialized, so you should add code to the class constructor to do this, as follows:

```
// CSketcherView construction/destruction

CSketcherView::CSketcherView()
{
    // TODO: add construction code here
    m_FirstPoint = CPoint(0,0);          // Set 1st recorded point to 0,0
    m_SecondPoint = CPoint(0,0);         // Set 2nd recorded point to 0,0
}
```

We can now implement the handler for the **WM_LBUTTONDOWN** message as:

```
void CSketcherView::OnLButtonDown(UINT nFlags, CPoint point)
{
    // TODO: Add your message handler code here and/or call default
    m_FirstPoint = point;                // Record the cursor position
}
```

All it does is to note the coordinates passed by the second argument. We can ignore the first argument in this situation altogether.

We can't complete this function yet, but we can have a stab at writing the code for the **WM_MOUSEMOVE** message handler in outline:

```
void CSketcherView::OnMouseMove(UINT nFlags, CPoint point)
{
    // TODO: Add your message handler code here and/or call default
    if(nFlags & MK_LBUTTON)
    {
        m_SecondPoint = point;               // Save the current cursor position

        // Test for a previous temporary element
        {
            // We get to here if there was a previous mouse move
            // so add code to delete the old element
        }

        // Add code to create new element
        // and cause it to be drawn
    }
}
```

The first thing that the handler does (after verifying the left mouse button is down) is to save the current cursor position. This will be used as the second defining point for an element. The rest of the logic is clear in general terms, but there are major gaps in our knowledge of how to complete the function. We have no means of defining an element — we need to be able to define an element as an object of a class. Even if we could, we don't know how to delete an element or get one drawn when we have a new one. A brief digression is called for.

Getting the Client Area Redrawn

As we've already discovered, the client area gets drawn by the **OnDraw()** member function of the **CSketcherView** class, which is called when a **WM_PAINT** message is received. Along with the basic message to repaint the client area, Windows supplies information about the part of the client area that needs to be redrawn. This can save a lot of time when you're displaying complicated images, because only the area specified actually needs to be redrawn, which may be a very small proportion of the total area.

You can tell Windows that a particular area should be redrawn by calling the **InvalidateRect()** function, which is an inherited member of your view class. The function accepts two arguments, the first of which is a pointer to a **RECT** or **CRect** object that defines the rectangle in the client area to be redrawn. Passing **NULL** for this parameter causes the whole client area to be redrawn. The second parameter is a **BOOL** value which is **TRUE** if the background to the rectangle is to be erased, and **FALSE** otherwise. This argument has a default value of **TRUE** since you normally want the background erased before the rectangle is redrawn, so you can ignore it most of the time.

A typical situation in which you'd want to cause an area to be redrawn would be where something has changed which necessitates the contents of the area being recreated — moving a displayed entity might be an example. In this case, you want to erase the background to remove the old representation of what was displayed, before you draw the new version. When you want to draw on top of an existing background, you just pass **FALSE** as the second argument to **InvalidateRect()**.

The **InvalidateRect()** function doesn't directly cause any part of the window to be redrawn; it just communicates to Windows the rectangle that you would like to have it redraw at some time. Windows maintains an **update region** — actually a rectangle — which identifies the area in a window that needs to be redrawn. The area specified in your call to **InvalidateRect()** is added to the current update region, so the new update region will enclose the old region plus the new rectangle you have indicated as invalid. Eventually a **WM_PAINT** message will be sent to the window and the update region will be passed to the window along with it. When processing of the **WM_PAINT** message is complete, the update region is reset to the empty state.

Thus, all you have to do to get a newly-created shape drawn is:

1 Make sure that the **OnDraw()** function in your view includes the newly-created item when it redraws the window.

2 Call **InvalidateRect()** with a pointer to the rectangle bounding the shape to be redrawn passed as the first argument.

Similarly, if you want a shape removed from the client area of a window, you need to do the following:

1 Remove the shape from the items that the **OnDraw()** function will draw.

2 Call **InvalidateRect()** with the first argument pointing to the rectangle bounding the shape that is to be removed.

Since the background to the rectangle specified is automatically erased, as long as the **OnDraw()** function doesn't draw the shape again, the shape will disappear. Of course, this means that we need to be able to obtain the rectangle bounding any shape that we create, so we'll include a function to provide this as a member of our classes that define the elements that can be drawn by Sketcher.

Defining Classes for Elements

Thinking ahead a bit, we'll need to store elements in a document in some way, and to be able to perform file operations with them. We'll deal with the details of file operations later on, but for now it's enough to know that the MFC class **CObject** includes the tools for us to do this, so we'll use **CObject** as a base class for our element classes.

We'll also have the problem that we don't know in advance what sequence of element types the user will create. Our program must be able to handle any sequence of elements. This suggests that using a base class pointer for selecting a particular element class function might simplify things a bit. For example, we won't need to know what an element is in order to draw it. As long as we're accessing the element through a base class pointer, we can always get an element to draw itself by using a virtual function. This is another example of the polymorphism we talked about when we discussed virtual functions. All we need to do to achieve this is to make sure that the classes defining specific elements share a common base class, and that in this class we declare as **virtual** all the functions we want to be selected automatically at run time. This indicates that our class structure should be like that shown in the diagram below:

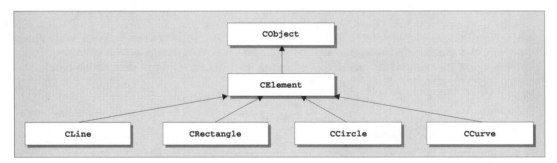

The arrows in the diagram point towards the base class in each case. If we need to add another element type, all we need to do is derive another class from **CElement**. Since these classes are closely related, we'll be putting the definitions for all these classes in a single new **.h** file that we can call **Elements.h**. Create a new source file and add the following skeleton code:

```
#if !defined(Elements_h)
#define Elements_h

// Generic element class
class CElement : public CObject
{
    // Add virtual function declarations here
};
```

```
// Class defining a line object
class CLine : public CElement
{
   // Add class definition here
};

// Class defining a rectangle object
class CRectangle : public CElement
{
   // Add class definition here
};

// Class defining a circle object
class CCircle : public CElement
{
   // Add class definition here
};

// Class defining a curve object
class CCurve : public CElement
{
   // Add class definition here
};

#endif //!defined(Elements_h)
```

You can save the file in the **Sketcher** folder as **Elements.h**. If you then add the file to the Header Files folder in FileView (right-click on Header Files to get the pop-up), the new classes will be displayed in ClassView. We've added the standard **#if !defined** command to protect against having the definitions for our element classes included more than once. Since we haven't involved the ClassWizard in this process, no **.cpp** file for any of these classes exists yet.

From time to time you might see the directive #ifndef in place of #if !defined. The two are completely equivalent, except that the label doesn't require brackets in the former case (e.g. #ifndef Elements_h).

Storing a Temporary Element in the View

When we discussed how shapes would be drawn, it was evident that as the mouse was dragged after pressing the left mouse button, a series of temporary element objects would be created and drawn. Now that we know that the base class for all the shapes is **CElement**, we can add a pointer to the view class to store the address of the temporary element. The class definition will become:

```
class CSketcherView : public CView
{
// other bits of the class definition as before...

// Attributes
public:
   CSketcherDoc* GetDocument();
```

```
protected:
   CPoint m_FirstPoint;          // First point recorded for an element
   CPoint m_SecondPoint;         // Second point recorded for an element
   CElement* m_pTempElement;     // Pointer to temporary element

// other bits of the class definition as before...
};
```

Of course, we should ensure that this is initialized when the view object is constructed, so we need to add the following line to the **CSketcherView** class constructor:

```
CSketcherView::CSketcherView()
{
   // TODO: add construction code here
   m_FirstPoint = CPoint(0,0);          // Set 1st recorded point to 0,0
   m_SecondPoint = CPoint(0,0);         // Set 2nd recorded point to 0,0
   m_pTempElement = NULL;               // Set temporary element pointer to 0
}
```

We'll be able to use this pointer in the **WM_MOUSEMOVE** message handler as a test for previous temporary elements.

We'll be creating **CElement** class objects in the view class member functions, and we refer to the **CElement** class in defining the data member that points to a temporary element. Therefore, we should ensure that the definition of the **CElement** class is included before the **CSketcherView** class definition, wherever **SketcherView.h** is included into a **.cpp** file. You can do this for **CSketcherView** by adding a **#include** directive for **Elements.h** to the **SketcherView.cpp** file before the **#include** directive for **SketcherView.h**:

```
#include "Elements.h"
```

Sketcher.cpp also has a **#include** directive for **SketcherView.h**, so you should add a **#include** for **Elements.h** to this file too.

The CElement Class

We need to fill out the element class definitions. We'll be doing this incrementally as we add more and more functionality to the Sketcher application, but what do we need right now? Some data members, such as color, are clearly common to all types of element; we'll put those in the **CElement** class so that they will be inherited in each of the derived classes. However, the data members in the classes which define specific element properties will be quite disparate, so we'll declare these members in the particular derived class to which they belong.

The **CElement** class will then only contain virtual functions that will be replaced in the derived classes, plus data and function members which are the same in all the derived classes. The virtual functions will be those that are selected automatically for a particular object through a pointer. For now, we can define the **CElement** class as:

```
class CElement : public CObject
{
protected:
   COLORREF m_Color;                          // Color of an element
```

```
public:
    virtual ~CElement(){}                       // Virtual destructor

    // Virtual draw operation
    virtual void Draw(CDC* pDC) const {}        // Virtual draw operation
    CRect GetBoundRect() const;                 // Get the bounding rectangle for an
element

protected:
    CElement(){}                                // Default constructor
};
```

The members to be inherited by the derived classes are:

▶ Data member **m_Color**, which stores the color

▶ Function member **GetBoundRect()**, which calculates the rectangle bounding an element. This function returns a value of type **CRect** which will be the rectangle bounding the shape

We also have a virtual destructor — necessary to ensure that derived class objects are destroyed properly — and a virtual **Draw()** function which, in the derived classes, will draw the particular object in question. The default constructor is in the **protected** section of the class to ensure that it can't be used externally. The **Draw()** function will need a pointer to a **CDC** object passed to it in order to provide access to the drawing functions that we saw earlier.

You might be tempted to declare the **Draw()** member as a pure virtual function in the **CElement** class — after all, it can have no meaningful content in this class. This would also force it to be defined in any derived class. Normally you would do this, but our class inherits a facility from **CObject** called **serialization**, that we'll use later for storing objects in a file, and this will require that an instance of our class be created. A class with a pure virtual function member is an abstract class, and instances of an abstract class can't be created. If you want to use MFC's serialization capability for storing objects, your classes mustn't be abstract.

You might also be tempted to declare the **GetBoundRect()** function as returning a *pointer* to a **CRect** object — after all, we're going to pass a pointer to the **InvalidateRect()** member function in the view class. However, this could lead to problems. You'll be creating the **CRect** object as local to the function, so the pointer would be pointing to a nonexistent object on return from the **GetBoundRect()** function. You could get around this by creating the **CRect** object on the heap, but then you'd need to take care that it's deleted after use, otherwise you'd be filling the heap with **CRect** objects — a new one for every call of **GetBoundRect()**. A further possibility is that you could store the bounding rectangle for an element as a class member and generate it when the element is created. This is a reasonable alternative, but if you changed an element subsequently — by moving it, for instance — you would need to ensure that the bounding rectangle was recalculated.

The CLine Class

We'll define the **CLine** class as:

```
class CLine : public CElement
{
public:
    virtual void Draw(CDC* pDC) const; // Function to display a line

    // Constructor for a line object
    CLine(const CPoint& Start, const CPoint& End, const COLORREF& Color);

protected:
    CPoint m_StartPoint;                // Start point of line
    CPoint m_EndPoint;                  // End point of line

    CLine(){}                           // Default constructor - should not be used
};
```

The data members that define a line are **m_StartPoint** and **m_EndPoint**, both of which are **protected**. The class has a **public** constructor which has parameters for the values that define a line, and a default constructor declared as **protected** to prevent its use externally.

Implementing the CLine Class

We can place the implementation of the member functions in a new file called **Elements.cpp** that we can define in outline as:

```
// Implementations of the element classes
#include "stdafx.h"

#include "OurConstants.h"
#include "Elements.h"

// Add definitions for member functions here
```

We need the file **stdafx.h** to be included into this file to gain access to the definitions of the standard system header files. The other two files we've included are the ones we created containing definitions for our constants and for the classes we're implementing here. We may need to add **#include** statements for the files containing definitions for AppWizard-generated classes if we use any in our code.

We also need to add the **Elements.cpp** file to the Sketcher project, so once you have saved this file, you need to select the Project | Add To Project... menu item and add the file to the project. You can achieve the same result by right clicking in the editor window and selecting from the pop-up menu.

Of course, we'll have to add each of the member function definitions to this file manually, since ClassWizard wasn't involved in defining the classes. We're now ready to add the constructor for the **CLine** class to the **Elements.cpp** file.

The CLine Class Constructor

The code for this will be:

```
// CLine class constructor
CLine::CLine(const CPoint& Start, const CPoint& End, const COLORREF& Color)
{
   m_StartPoint = Start;        // Set line start point
   m_EndPoint = End;            // Set line end pcint
   m_Color = Color;             // Set line color
}
```

There's nothing too intellectually taxing here. We just store each of the values passed to the constructor in the appropriate data member.

Drawing a Line

The **Draw()** function isn't too difficult either, although we do need to take account of the color and pen width to be used when the line is drawn:

```
// Draw a CLine object
void CLine::Draw(CDC* pDC) const
{
   // Create a pen for this object and
   // initialize it to the object color and line width
   CPen aPen;
   if(!aPen.CreatePen(PS_SOLID, m_Pen, m_Color))
   {
      // Pen creation failed. Abort the program
      AfxMessageBox("Pen creation failed drawing a line", MB_OK);
      AfxAbort();
   }

   CPen* pOldPen = pDC->SelectObject(&aPen);  // Select the pen

   // Now draw the line
   pDC->MoveTo(m_StartPoint);
   pDC->LineTo(m_EndPoint);

   pDC->SelectObject(pOldPen);                // Restore the old pen
}
```

We create a pen as we saw earlier, only this time we make sure that the creation works. If it doesn't, the most likely cause is that we're running out of memory, which is a serious problem. This will almost invariably be caused by an error in the program, so we have written the function to call **AfxMessageBox()**, which is a global function to display a message box, and then call **AfxAbort()** to terminate the program. The first argument to **AfxMessageBox()** specifies the message that is to appear, and the second specifies that it should have an OK button. You can get more information from the MSDN library on either of these functions by placing the cursor within the function name in the editor window and then pressing *F1*.

The argument **m_pen** in the call to **CreatePen()** is a variable defining the pen width. We will add this to the **CElement** class definition in a moment.

After selecting the pen, we move the current position to the start of the line, defined in the **m_StartPoint** data member, and then draw the line from this point to the point **m_EndPoint**. Finally, we restore the old pen and we are done.

623

Creating Bounding Rectangles

At first sight, obtaining the bounding rectangle for a shape looks trivial. For example, a line is always a diagonal of its enclosing rectangle, and a circle is *defined* by its enclosing rectangle, but there are a couple of slight complications. Firstly, the shape must lie *completely* inside the rectangle, so we must allow for the thickness of the line used to draw the shape when we create the bounding rectangle. Secondly, how you work out adjustments to the coordinates defining the rectangle depends on the mapping mode, so we must take that into account too.

Look at the illustration below, relating to obtaining the bounding rectangle for a line and a circle:

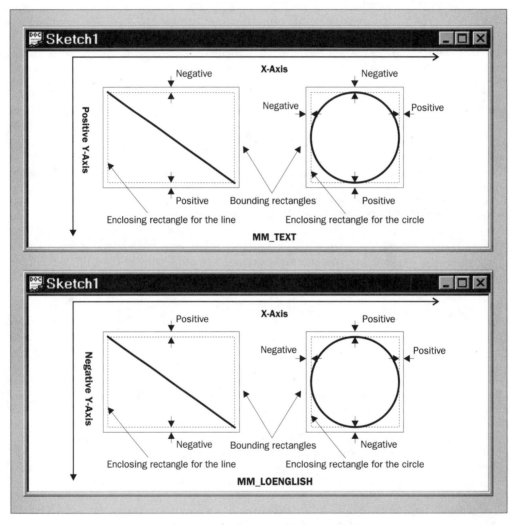

We'll use the term 'enclosing rectangle' for the rectangle that is used to draw a shape, while the term 'bounding rectangle' shall refer to the rectangle which takes into account the width of the pen. The illustration shows the shapes with their enclosing rectangles, and their bounding rectangles offset by the line thickness. This is obviously exaggerated here so you can see what's happening.

In different mapping modes, there are differences in how you calculate the coordinates for the bounding rectangle — but these only concern the y coordinates. To get the corners of the bounding rectangle in the **MM_TEXT** mapping mode, subtract the line thickness from the y coordinate of the top left corner of the enclosing rectangle, and add it to the y coordinate of the bottom right corner. However, in **MM_LOENGLISH** (and all the other mapping modes), the y axis increases in the opposite direction; so you need to *add* the line thickness to the y coordinate of the top left corner of the enclosing rectangle, and *subtract* it from the y coordinate of the bottom right corner. For all the mapping modes, you subtract the line thickness from the x coordinate of the top left corner of the enclosing rectangle, and add it to the x coordinate of the bottom right corner.

To implement our element types as consistently as possible, we can store an enclosing rectangle for each shape in a data element in the base class. This will need to be calculated when a shape is constructed. The job of the **GetBoundRect()** function in the base class will then be to calculate the bounding rectangle by offsetting the enclosing rectangle by the pen width. We can amend the **CElement** class definition by adding the following data members:

```
class CElement : public CObject
{
protected:
    COLORREF m_Color;                       // Color of an element
    CRect m_EnclosingRect;                  // Rectangle enclosing an element
    int m_Pen;                              // Pen width

public:
    virtual ~CElement(){}                   // Virtual destructor

    // Virtual draw operation
    virtual void Draw(CDC* pDC) const {}    // Virtual draw operation
    CRect GetBoundRect() const;             // Get the bounding rectangle for an element

protected:
    CElement(){}                            // Default constructor
};
```

We must update the **CLine** constructor so that it has the correct pen width:

```
// CLine class constructor
CLine::CLine(const CPoint& Start, const CPoint& End, const COLORREF& Color)
{
    m_StartPoint = Start;               // Set line start point
    m_EndPoint = End;                   // Set line end point
    m_Color = Color;                    // Set line color
    m_Pen = 1;                          // Set pen width
}
```

You can add this by right clicking on the class name and selecting Add Member Variable... from the pop-up, or you can add the statement directly in the editor window along with the comment.

We can now implement the **GetBoundRect()** member of the base class, assuming the **MM_TEXT** mapping mode:

```
// Get the bounding rectangle for an element
CRect CElement::GetBoundRect() const
{
```

```
    CRect BoundingRect;                // Object to store bounding rectangle
    BoundingRect = m_EnclosingRect;    // Store the enclosing rectangle

    // Increase the rectangle by the pen width
    BoundingRect.InflateRect(m_Pen, m_Pen);

    return BoundingRect;               // Return the bounding rectangle
}
```

This will return the bounding rectangle for any derived class object. We define the bounding rectangle by modifying the coordinates of the enclosing rectangle stored in the base class data member so that it is enlarged all round by the pen width, using the **InflateRect()** method of the **CRect** class.

The **CRect** class provides an operator, **+** , for rectangles, which we could have used instead. For example, we could have written the statement before the **return** as:

```
    BoundingRect = m_EnclosingRect + CRect(m_Pen, m_Pen, m_Pen, m_Pen);
```

Equally, we could have simply added (or subtracted) the pen width to each of the x and y values that make up the rectangle. We could have replaced the assignment with the following statements:

```
    BoundingRect = m_EnclosingRect;
    BoundingRect.top -= m_Pen;
    BoundingRect.left -= m_Pen;
    BoundingRect.bottom += m_Pen;
    BoundingRect.right += m_Pen;
```

As a reminder, the individual data members of a CRect object are left and top (storing the x and y coordinates of the top left corner) and right and bottom (storing the coordinates of the bottom right corner). These are all public members, so we can access them directly. A commonly made mistake, especially by me, is to write the coordinate pair as (top,left) instead of in the correct order (left,top).

The hazard with both this and the **InflateRect()** option is that there is a built-in assumption that the mapping mode is **MM_TEXT**, which means that the positive y axis is assumed to run from top to bottom. If you change the mapping mode, neither of these will work properly, although it's not immediately obvious that they won't.

Normalized Rectangles

The **InflateRect()** function works by subtracting the values that you give it from the **top** and **left** members of the rectangle and adding the values to the **bottom** and **right**. This means that you may find your rectangle actually decreasing in size if you don't make sure that the rectangle is **normalized**. A normalized rectangle has a **left** value that is less than or equal to the **right** value, and a **top** value that is less than or equal to the **bottom** value. You can make sure that a **CRect** object is normalized by calling the **NormalizeRect()** member of the object. Most of the **CRect** member functions will require the object to be normalized in order for them to work as expected, so we need to make sure that when we store the enclosing rectangle in **m_EnclosingRect**, it is normalized.

Calculating the Enclosing Rectangle for a Line

All we need now is code in the constructor for a line to calculate the enclosing rectangle:

```
CLine::CLine(const CPoint& Start, const CPoint& End, const COLORREF& Color)
{
    m_StartPoint = Start;           // Set line start point
    m_EndPoint = End;               // Set line end point
    m_Color = Color;                // Set line color
    m_Pen = 1;                      // Set pen width

    // Define the enclosing rectangle
    m_EnclosingRect = CRect(Start, End);
    m_EnclosingRect.NormalizeRect();
}
```

This simply calculates the coordinates of the top left and bottom right points, defining the rectangle from the start and end points of the line. We need to take care, though, that the bounding rectangle has the **top** value less than the **bottom** value, regardless of the relative positions of the start and end points of the line, so we call the **NormalizeRect()** member of the **m_EnclosingRect** object.

The CRectangle Class

Although we'll be defining a rectangle object by the same data we used to define a line, we don't need to store the defining points. The enclosing rectangle in the data member inherited from the base class completely defines the shape, so we don't need any data members:

```
// Class defining a rectangle object
class CRectangle : public CElement
{
public:
    virtual void Draw(CDC* pDC) const; // Function to display a rectangle

    // Constructor for a rectangle object
    CRectangle(const CPoint& Start, const CPoint& End, const COLORREF& Color);

protected:
    CRectangle(){}                          // Default constructor - should not be used
};
```

The definition of the rectangle becomes very simple — just a constructor, the virtual **Draw()** function, and the default constructor in the **protected** section of the class.

The CRectangle Class Constructor

The code for the class constructor is somewhat similar to that for a **CLine** constructor:

```
// CRectangle class constructor
CRectangle:: CRectangle(const CPoint& Start, const CPoint& End, const COLORREF&
Color)
{
    m_Color = Color;                // Set rectangle color
    m_Pen = 1;                      // Set pen width

    // Define the enclosing rectangle
    m_EnclosingRect = CRect(Start, End);
    m_EnclosingRect.NormalizeRect();
}
```

627

Since we created the class definition manually, there will be no skeleton definition for the constructor, so you need to add the definition directly to **Elements.cpp**.

This is cheap code. Some minor alterations to a subset of the **CLine** constructor, fix the comments, and we have a new constructor for **CRectangle**. It just stores the color and pen width and computes the enclosing rectangle from the points passed as arguments.

Drawing a Rectangle

There is a member of the class **CDC** to draw a rectangle, called **Rectangle()**. This draws a closed figure and fills it with the current brush. You may think that this isn't quite what we want, since we want to draw rectangles as outlines only, but by selecting a **NULL_BRUSH** this is exactly what we'll draw. Just so you know, there's also a function **PolyLine()**, which draws shapes consisting of multiple line segments from an array of points, or we could have used **LineTo()** again, but the easiest approach for us is to use the **Rectangle()** function:

```
// Draw a CRectangle object
void CRectangle::Draw(CDC* pDC) const
{
    // Create a pen for this object and
    // initialize it to the object color and line width
    CPen aPen;
    if (!aPen.CreatePen(PS_SOLID, m_Pen, m_Color))
    {
        // Pen creation failed
        AfxMessageBox("Pen creation failed drawing a rectangle", MB_OK);
        AfxAbort();
    }

    // Select the pen
    CPen* pOldPen = pDC->SelectObject(&aPen);
    // Select the brush
    CBrush* pOldBrush = static_cast<CBrush*>(pDC->SelectStockObject(NULL_BRUSH));

    // Now draw the rectangle
    pDC->Rectangle(m_EnclosingRect);

    pDC->SelectObject(pOldBrush);              // Restore the old brush
    pDC->SelectObject(pOldPen);                // Restore the old pen
}
```

After setting up the pen and the brush, we can simply pass the whole rectangle directly to the **Rectangle()** function to get it drawn. All that then remains to do is to clear up after ourselves and restore the device context's old pen and brush.

The CCircle Class

The interface of the **CCircle** class is no different from that of the **CRectangle** class. We can define a circle solely by its enclosing rectangle, so the class definition will be:

```
// Class defining a circle object
class CCircle : public CElement
{
public:
    virtual void Draw(CDC* pDC) const;          // Function to display a circle
```

```
    // Constructor for a circle object
    CCircle(const CPoint& Start, const CPoint& End, const COLORREF& Color);

protected:
    CCircle(){}           // Default constructor - should not be used
};
```

We have defined a public constructor, and the default constructor is declared as **protected** again.

Implementing the CCircle Class

As we discussed earlier, when you create a circle, the point where you press the left mouse button will be the center, and after moving the cursor with the left button held down, the point where you release the cursor is a point on the circumference of the final circle. The job of the constructor will be to convert these points into the form used in the class to define a circle.

The CCircle Class Constructor

The point at which you release the left mouse button can be anywhere on the circumference, so the coordinates of the points specifying the enclosing rectangle need to be calculated, as illustrated below:

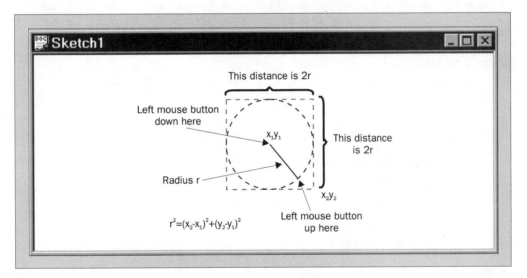

From this diagram, you can see that we can calculate the coordinates of the top left and bottom right points of the enclosing rectangle relative to the center of the circle (x_1, y_1), which is the point we record when the left mouse button is pressed. Assuming that the mapping mode is **MM_TEXT**, for the top left point we just subtract the radius from each of the coordinates of the center. Similarly, the bottom right point is obtained by adding the radius to the x and y coordinates of the center. We can, therefore, code the constructor as:

```
// Constructor for a circle object
CCircle::CCircle(const CPoint& Start, const CPoint& End, const COLORREF& Color)
{
```

```
// First calculate the radius
// We use floating point because that is required by
// the library function (in math.h) for calculating a square root.
long Radius =
    static_cast<long>(sqrt(static_cast<double>((End.x - Start.x)*
                      (End.x - Start.x) + (End.y - Start.y)*(End.y - Start.y))));

// Now calculate the rectangle enclosing
// the circle assuming the MM_TEXT mapping mode
m_EnclosingRect = CRect(Start.x - Radius, Start.y - Radius,
                        Start.x + Radius, Start.y + Radius);

m_Color = Color;          // Set the color for the circle
m_Pen = 1;                // Set pen width
}
```

To use the **sqrt()** function, you should add the line:

```
#include <math.h>
```

to the beginning of the file, after the include for **stdafx.h**. The maximum coordinate values are 16 bits, and the **CPoint** members **x** and **y** are declared as **long**, so evaluating the argument to the **sqrt()** function can safely be carried out as an integer. The result of the square root calculation will be of type **double**, so we cast it to **long** because we want to use it as an integer.

Drawing a Circle

We've already seen how to draw a circle using the **Arc()** function in the **CDC** class, so let's use the **Ellipse()** function here. The **Draw()** function in the **CCircle** class will be:

```
// Draw a circle
void CCircle::Draw(CDC* pDC) const
{
   // Create a pen for this object and
   // initialize it to the object color and line width
   CPen aPen;
   if (!aPen.CreatePen(PS_SOLID, m_Pen, m_Color))
   {
      // Pen creation failed
      AfxMessageBox("Pen creation failed drawing a circle", MB_OK);
      AfxAbort();
   }

   CPen* pOldPen = pDC->SelectObject(&aPen);  // Select the pen

   // Select a null brush
   CBrush* pOldBrush = static_cast<CBrush*>(pDC->SelectStockObject(NULL_BRUSH));

   // Now draw the circle
   pDC->Ellipse(m_EnclosingRect);

   pDC->SelectObject(pOldPen);               // Restore the old pen
   pDC->SelectObject(pOldBrush);             // Restore the old brush
}
```

After selecting a pen of the appropriate color and a null brush, the circle is drawn by calling the **Ellipse()** function. The only argument is a **CRect** object which encloses the circle to be drawn. This is another example of code that's almost for free, as it's very similar to the code we wrote earlier to draw a rectangle.

The CCurve Class

The **CCurve** class is different from the others in that it needs to handle a variable number of defining points. This necessitates maintaining a list of some kind, and since we will look at how MFC can help with lists in the next chapter, we'll defer defining the detail of this class until then. For now, we'll include a class definition that provides dummy member functions so we can compile and link code that contains calls to them. In **Elements.h**, you should have:

```
// Class defining a curve object
class CCurve : public CElement
{
public:
   virtual void Draw(CDC* pDC) const; // Function to display a curve

   // Constructor for a curve object
   CCurve(const COLORREF& Color);

protected:
   CCurve(){}              // Default constructor - should not be used
};
```

And in **Elements.cpp**:

```
// Constructor for a curve object
CCurve::CCurve(const COLORREF& Color)
{
   m_Color = Color;                      // Store the color
   m_EnclosingRect = CRect(0,0,0,0);
   m_Pen = 1;                            // Set pen width
}

// Draw a curve
void CCurve::Draw(CDC* pDC) const
{
}
```

Neither the constructor nor the **Draw()** member function does anything useful yet, and we have no data members to define a curve. The constructor just sets the color, sets **m_EnclosingRect** to an empty rectangle, and sets the pen width. We'll expand the class into a working version in the next chapter.

Completing the Mouse Message Handlers

We can now come back to the **WM_MOUSEMOVE** message handler and fill out the detail. You can get to it through the ClassWizard or by expanding **CSketcherView** in the ClassView and double-clicking the handler name, **OnMouseMove()**.

This handler will only be concerned with drawing a succession of temporary versions of an element as you move the cursor, because the final element will be created when you release the left mouse button. We can therefore treat the drawing of temporary elements to provide rubber-banding as being entirely local to this function, leaving the final version of the element being created to be drawn by the **OnDraw()** function member of the view. This approach will result in the drawing of the rubber-banded elements being reasonably efficient, as we won't involve the **OnDraw()** function, which ultimately will be responsible for drawing the entire document.

We can do this best with the help of a member of the **CDC** class that is particularly effective in rubber-banding operations: **SetROP2()**.

Setting the Drawing Mode

The **SetROP2()** function sets the **drawing mode** for all subsequent output operations in the device context associated with a **CDC** object. The 'ROP' bit of the function name stands for **R**aster **OP**eration, because the setting of drawing modes only applies to raster displays. In case you're wondering, "What's SetROP1() then?" — there isn't one. The function name represents 'Set Raster OPeration **to**', not 2!

There are other kinds of graphic displays, called vector displays or directed beam displays, for which this mechanism does not apply, but you are unlikely to meet them these days — they have been largely rendered obsolete by raster displays.

The drawing mode determines how the color of the pen that you use for drawing is to combine with the background color to produce the color of the entity you are displaying. You specify the drawing mode with a single argument to the function which can be any of the following values:

Drawing Mode	Effect
R2_BLACK	All drawing is in black.
R2_WHITE	All drawing is in white.
R2_NOP	Drawing operations do nothing.
R2_NOT	Drawing is in the inverse of the screen color. This ensures the output will always be visible, since it prevents drawing in the same color as the background.
R2_COPYPEN	Drawing is in the pen color. This is the default drawing mode if you don't set it.
R2_NOTCOPYPEN	Drawing is in the inverse of the pen color.
R2_MERGEPENNOT	Drawing is in the color produced by ORing the pen color with the inverse of the background color.
R2_MASKPENNOT	Drawing is in the color produced by ANDing the pen color with the inverse of the background color.
R2_MERGENOTPEN	Drawing is in the color produced by ORing the background color with the inverse of the pen color.
R2_MASKNOTPEN	Drawing is in the color produced by ANDing the background color with the inverse of the pen color.
R2_MERGEPEN	Drawing is in the color produced by ORing the background color with the pen color.

Drawing Mode	Effect
R2_NOTMERGEPEN	Drawing is in the color that is the inverse of the **R2_MERGEPEN** color.
R2_MASKPEN	Drawing is in the color produced by ANDing the background color with the pen color.
R2_NOTMASKPEN	Drawing is in the color that is the inverse of the **R2_MASKPEN** color.
R2_XORPEN	Drawing is in the color produced by exclusive ORing the pen color and the background color.
R2_NOTXORPEN	Drawing is in the color that is the inverse of the **R2_XORPEN** color.

Each of these symbols is predefined and corresponds to a particular drawing mode. There are a lot of options here, but the one that can work some magic for us is the last of them, **R2_NOTXORPEN**.

When we set the mode as **R2_NOTXORPEN**, the first time you draw a particular shape on the default white background, it will be drawn normally in the pen color you specify. If you draw the same shape again, overwriting the first, the shape will disappear, because the color that the shape will be drawn in corresponds to that produced by exclusive ORing the pen color with itself. The drawing color that results from this will be white. You can see this more clearly by working through an example.

White is formed from equal proportions of the 'maximum' amounts of red, blue, and green. For simplicity, we can represent this as 1,1,1—the three values represent the RGB components of the color. In the same scheme, red is defined as 1,0,0. These combine as follows:

	R	G	B	
Background — white	1	1	1	
Pen — red	1	0	0	
XORed	0	1	1	
NOT XOR	1	0	0	which is red

So, the first time we draw a red line on a white background, it comes out red. If we draw the same line a second time, overwriting the existing line, the background pixels we are writing over are red. The resultant drawing color works out as follows:

	R	G	B	
Background —red	1	0	0	
Pen — red	1	0	0	
XORed	0	0	0	
NOT XOR	1	1	1	which is white

Since the rest of the background is white, the line will disappear.

You need to take care to use the right background color here. You should be able to see that drawing with a white pen on a red background is not going to work too well, as the first time you draw something it will be red, and therefore invisible. The second time it will appear as white. If you draw on a black background, things will appear and disappear, as on a white background, but they will not be drawn in the pen color you choose.

Coding the OnMouseMove() Handler

Let's start by adding the code that creates the element after a mouse move message. Since we are going to draw the element from the handler function, we need to create an object for the device context. The most convenient class to use for this is **CClientDC**, which is derived from **CDC**. As we said earlier, the advantage of using this class rather than **CDC** is that it will automatically take care of creating the device context for us and destroying it when we are done. The device context that it creates corresponds to the client area of a window, which is exactly what we want. Add the following code to the outline handler that we defined:

```
void CSketcherView::OnMouseMove(UINT nFlags, CPoint point)
{
    // Define a Device Context object for the view
    CClientDC aDC(this);
    aDC.SetROP2(R2_NOTXORPEN);                // Set the drawing mode
    if(nFlags & MK_LBUTTON)
    {
        m_SecondPoint = point;                // Save the current cursor position
        // Test for a previous temporary element
        {
            // We get to here if there was a previous mouse move
            // so add code to delete the old element
        }

        // Create a temporary element of the type and color that
        // is recorded in the document object, and draw it
        m_pTempElement = CreateElement();     // Create a new element
        m_pTempElement->Draw(&aDC);           // Draw the element
    }
}
```

The first new line of code creates a local **CClientDC** object. The **this** pointer that we pass to the constructor identifies the current view object, so the **CClientDC** object will have a device context that corresponds to the client area of the current view. As well as the characteristics we mentioned, this object has all the drawing functions we need, as they are inherited from the class **CDC**. The first member function we use is **SetROP2()**, which sets the drawing mode to **R2_NOTXORPEN**.

To create a new element, we save the current cursor position in the data member **m_SecondPoint**, and then call a view member function **CreateElement()**. (We'll define the **CreateElement()** function as soon as we have finished this handler.) This function should create an element using the two points stored in the current view object, with the color and type specification stored in the document object, and return the address of the element. We save this in **m_pTempElement**.

Using the pointer to the new element, we call its **Draw()** member to get the object to draw itself. The address of the **CClientDC** object is passed as an argument. Since we defined the **Draw()** function as virtual in the base class **CElement**, the function for whatever type of element **m_pTempElement** is pointing to will automatically be selected. The new element will be drawn normally with the **R2_NOTXORPEN** because we are drawing it for the first time on a white background.

We can use the pointer **m_pTempElement** as an indicator of whether a previous temporary element exists. The code for this part of the handler will be:

```
void CSketcherView::OnMouseMove(UINT nFlags, CPoint point)
{
    // Define a Device Context object for the view
    CClientDC aDC(this);                        // DC is for this view
    aDC.SetROP2(R2_NOTXORPEN);                  // Set the drawing mode
    if(nFlags&MK_LBUTTON)
    {
        m_SecondPoint = point;                  // Save the current cursor position

        if(m_pTempElement)
        {
            // Redraw the old element so it disappears from the view
            m_pTempElement->Draw(&aDC);
            delete m_pTempElement;              // Delete the old element
            m_pTempElement = 0;                 // Reset the pointer to 0
        }

        // Create a temporary element of the type and color that
        // is recorded in the document object, and draw it
        m_pTempElement = CreateElement();       // Create a new element
        m_pTempElement->Draw(&aDC);             // Draw the element
    }
}
```

A previous temporary element exists if the pointer **m_pTempElement** is not zero. We need to redraw the element it points to in order to remove it from the client area of the view. We then delete the element and reset the pointer to zero. The new element will then be created and drawn by the code that we added previously. This combination will automatically rubber-band the shape being created, so it will appear to be attached to the cursor position as it moves. We must remember to reset the pointer **m_pTempElement** back to 0 in the **WM_LBUTTONUP** message handler after we create the final version of the element.

Creating an Element

We need to add the **CreateElement()** function to the 'Operations' section of the **CSketcherView** class, as a **protected** member:

```
class CSketcherView : public CView
{

// Rest of the class definition as before...

// Operations
public:

protected:
    CElement* CreateElement(); // Create a new element on the heap
```

```
    // Rest of the class definition as before...

    };
```

To do this you can either amend the
class definition directly by adding the
line shown above, or you can right-click
on the class name, **CSketcherView**, in
ClassView, and select Add Member
Function... from the menu. This will
open the following dialog:

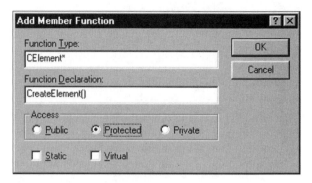

Add the specifications of the function, as shown, and click on OK; then a declaration for the
function member will be added to the class definition, and you will be taken directly to a
skeleton for the function in **SketcherView.cpp**. If you added the declaration to the class
definition manually, you'll need to add the complete definition for the function to the **.cpp** file.
This is:

```cpp
// Create an element of the current type
CElement* CSketcherView::CreateElement()
{
    // Get a pointer to the document for this view
    CSketcherDoc* pDoc = GetDocument();
    ASSERT_VALID(pDoc);                    // Verify the pointer is good

    // Now select the element using the type stored in the document
    switch(pDoc->GetElementType())
    {
        case RECTANGLE:
            return new CRectangle(m_FirstPoint, m_SecondPoint,
                              pDoc->GetElementColor());

        case CIRCLE:
            return new CCircle(m_FirstPoint, m_SecondPoint,
                            pDoc->GetElementColor());

        case CURVE:
            return new CCurve(pDoc->GetElementColor());

        case LINE:
            return new CLine(m_FirstPoint, m_SecondPoint,
                          pDoc->GetElementColor());

        default:
            // Something's gone wrong
            AfxMessageBox("Bad Element code", MB_OK);
            AfxAbort();
            return NULL;
    }
}
```

The lines that aren't shaded are those that will have been supplied automatically if you added the function to the class using the Add Member Function dialog. The first thing we do here is to get a pointer to the document by calling **GetDocument()**, as we've seen before. For safety, the **ASSERT_VALID()** macro is used to ensure that a good pointer is returned. In the debug version of MFC that's used in the debug version of your application, this macro calls the **AssertValid()** member of the object which is specified as the argument to the macro. This checks the validity of the current object, and if the pointer is **NULL** or the object is defective in some way, an error message will be displayed. In the release version of MFC, the **ASSERT_VALID()** macro does nothing.

The **switch** statement selects the element to be created based on the type returned by a function in the document class, **GetElementType()**. Two more functions in the document class are used to obtain the current element color and pen width. We can add the definitions for both these functions directly to the **CSketcherDoc** class definition, because they are very simple:

```
class CSketcherDoc : public CDocument
{
// Rest of the class definition as before...

// Operations
public:
    WORD GetElementType() const              // Get the element type
    { return m_Element; }

    COLORREF GetElementColor() const         // Get the element color
    { return m_Color; }

    // Rest of the class definition as before...
};
```

Each of the functions returns the value stored in the corresponding data member. Remember that putting a member function definition in the class definition is equivalent to a request to make the function **inline**, so as well as being simple, these should be fast.

Dealing with WM_LBUTTONUP Messages

The **WM_LBUTTONUP** message completes the process of creating an element. The job of this handler is to pass the final version of the element that was created to the document object, and then clean up the view object data members. You can access and edit the code for this handler in the same way as you did for the last one. Add the following lines to the function:

```
void CSketcherView::OnLButtonUp(UINT nFlags, CPoint point)
{
    // Make sure there is an element
    if(m_pTempElement)
    {
        // Call a document class function to store the element
        // pointed to by m_pTempElement in the document object

        delete m_pTempElement;                  // This code is temporary
        m_pTempElement = 0;                     // Reset the element pointer
    }
}
```

The **if** statement will test that **m_pTempElement** is not zero. It's always possible that the user could press and release the left mouse button without moving the mouse, in which case no element would have been created. As long as there is an element, the pointer to the element will be passed to the document object; we'll add the code for this in the next chapter. In the meantime, we'll just delete the element here so as not to pollute the heap. Finally, the **m_pTempElement** pointer is reset to 0, ready for the next time the user draws an element.

Exercising Sketcher

Before we can run the example with the mouse message handlers, we need to update the **OnDraw()** function in the **CSketcherView** class implementation to get rid of any old code that we added earlier.

To make sure that the **OnDraw()** function is clean, go to ClassView and double-click on the function name to take you to its implementation in **SketcherView.cpp**. Delete any old code that you added, but leave in the first two lines that AppWizard provided to get a pointer to the document object. We'll need this later to get to the elements when they're stored in the document. The code for the function should now be:

```
void CSketcherView::OnDraw(CDC* pDC)
{
   CSketcherDoc* pDoc = GetDocument();
   ASSERT_VALID(pDoc);
}
```

Since we have no elements in the document as yet, we don't need to add anything to this function at this point. When we start storing data in the document in the next chapter, we'll need to add code here to draw the elements in response to a **WM_PAINT** message. Without it, the elements will just disappear whenever you resize the view, as you'll see.

Running the Example

After making sure that you have saved all the source files, build the program. If you haven't made any mistakes entering the code, you'll get a clean compile and link, so you can execute the program. You can now draw lines, circles and rectangles in any of the four colors the program supports. A typical window is shown below:

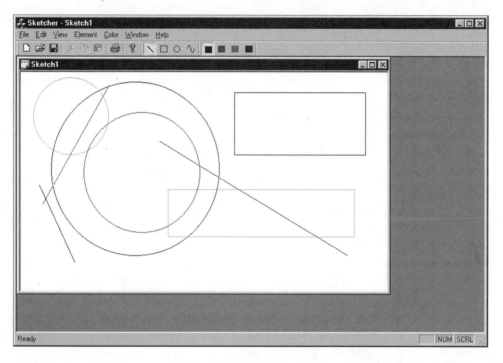

Try experimenting with the user interface. Note that you can move the window around, and that the shapes stay in the window as long as you don't move it so far that they're outside the borders of the application window. If you do, the elements do not reappear after you move it back. This is because the existing elements are never redrawn. When the client area is covered and uncovered, Windows will send a **WM_PAINT** message to the application, which will cause the **OnDraw()** member of the view object to be called. As you know, the **OnDraw()** function for the view doesn't do anything at present. We'll fix this when we use the document to store the elements.

When you resize the view window, the shapes disappear immediately, but when you move the whole view around, they remain (as long as they don't slide beyond the application window border). How come? Well, when you resize the window, Windows invalidates the whole client area and expects your application to redraw it in response to the **WM_PAINT** message. If you move the view around, Windows takes care of relocating the client area as it is. You can demonstrate this by moving the view so that a shape is partially obscured. When you slide it back, you still have a partial shape, with the bit that was obscured erased.

If you try drawing a shape while dragging the cursor outside the client view area, you'll notice some peculiar effects. Outside the view window, we lose track of the mouse, which tends to mess up our rubber-banding mechanism. What's going on?

Capturing Mouse Messages

The problem is caused by the fact that Windows is sending the mouse messages *to the window under the cursor*. As soon as the cursor leaves the client area of our application view window, the **WM_MOUSEMOVE** messages are being sent elsewhere. We can fix this by using some inherited members of **CSketcherView**.

Our view class inherits a function, **SetCapture()**, which tells Windows that we want our window to get *all* the mouse messages until such time as we say otherwise (that is, by calling another inherited function in our view class, **ReleaseCapture()**). We can capture the mouse as soon as the left button is pressed by modifying the handler for the **WM_LBUTTONDOWN** message:

```
void CSketcherView::OnLButtonDown(UINT nFlags, CPoint point)
{
   // TODO: Add your message handler code here and/or call default
   m_FirstPoint = point;              // Record the cursor position
   SetCapture();                      // Capture subsequent mouse messages
}
```

Now we must call the **ReleaseCapture()** function in the **WM_LBUTTONUP** handler. If we don't do this, other programs will not be able to receive any mouse messages as long as our program continues to run. Of course, we should only release the mouse if we've captured it earlier. The function **GetCapture()**, which our view class inherits, will return a pointer to the window that has captured the mouse, and this gives us a way of telling whether or not we have captured mouse messages. We just need to add the following to the handler for **WM_LBUTTONUP**:

```
void CSketcherView::OnLButtonUp(UINT nFlags, CPoint point)
{
   if(this == GetCapture())
      ReleaseCapture();              // Stop capturing mouse messages

   // Make sure there is an element
   if(m_pTempElement)
   {
      // Call a document class function to store the element
      // pointed to by m_pTempElement in the document object

      delete m_pTempElement;         // This code is temporary
      m_pTempElement = 0;            // Reset the element pointer
   }
}
```

If the pointer returned by the **GetCapture()** function is equal to the pointer **this**, our view has captured the mouse, so we release it.

The final alteration we should make is to modify the **WM_MOUSEMOVE** handler so that it only deals with messages that have been captured by our view. We can do this with one small change:

```
void CSketcherView::OnMouseMove(UINT nFlags, CPoint point)
{
   // Rest of the handler as before...

   if((nFlags & MK_LBUTTON) && (this == GetCapture()))
```

```
    {
        // Rest of the handler as before...
    }
}
```

The handler will now only process the message if the left button is down *and* the left button down handler for our view has been called, so that the mouse has been captured by our view window.

If you rebuild Sketcher with these additions, you'll find that the problems which arose earlier when the cursor was dragged off the client area no longer occur.

Summary

After completing this chapter, you should have a good grasp of how to write message handlers for the mouse, and how to organize drawing operations in your Windows programs. The important points that we have covered in this chapter are:

▶ By default, Windows addresses the client area of a window using a client coordinate system with the origin in the top left corner of the client area. The positive x direction is from left to right, and the positive y direction is from top to bottom.

▶ You can only draw in the client area of a window by using a device context.

▶ A device context provides a range of logical coordinate systems called mapping modes for addressing the client area of a window.

▶ The default origin position for a mapping mode is the top left corner of the client area. The default mapping mode is **MM_TEXT** which provides coordinates measured in pixels. The positive x axis runs from left to right in this mode, and the positive y axis from top to bottom.

▶ Your program should always draw the permanent contents of the client area of a window in response to a **WM_PAINT** message, although temporary entities can be drawn at other times. All the drawing for your application document should be controlled from the **OnDraw()** member function of a view class. This function is called when a **WM_PAINT** message is received by your application.

▶ You can identify the part of the client area that you want to have redrawn by calling the **InvalidateRect()** function member of your view class. The area passed as an argument will be added by Windows to the total area to be redrawn when the next **WM_PAINT** message is sent to your application.

▶ Windows sends standard messages to your application for mouse events. You can create handlers to deal with these messages by using ClassWizard.

▶ You can cause all mouse messages to be routed to your application by calling the **SetCapture()** function in your view class. You must release the mouse when you're finished with it by calling the **ReleaseCapture()** function. If you fail to do this, other applications will be unable to receive mouse messages.

▶ You can implement rubber-banding when creating geometric entities by drawing them in the message handler for mouse movements.

▶ The **SetROP2()** member of the **CDC** class enables you to set drawing modes. Selecting the right drawing mode greatly simplifies rubber-banding operations.

Exercises

Ex15-1: Add the menu item and toolbar button for an element of type ellipse, as in the exercises from Chapter 14, and define a class to support drawing ellipses defined by two points on opposite corners of their enclosing rectangle.

Ex15-2: Which functions now need to be modified to support drawing an ellipse? Modify the program to draw an ellipse.

Ex15-3: Which functions must you modify in the example from the previous exercise so that the first point defines the center of the ellipse, and the current cursor position defines a corner of the enclosing rectangle? Modify the example to work this way (Hint — look up the **CPoint** class members in Help).

Ex15-4: Add a new menu pop-up to the **IDR_SKETCHTYPE** menu for Pen Style, to allow solid, dashed, dotted, dash-dotted, and dash-dot-dotted lines to be specified.

Ex15-5: Which parts of the program need to be modified to support the operation of the menu, and the drawing of elements in these line types?

Ex15-6: Implement support for the new menu pop-up and drawing elements for any of the line types.

Creating the Document and Improving the View

In this chapter, we'll look into the facilities offered by MFC for managing collections of data items. We'll use these to complete the class definition and implementation for the curve element that we left open in the last chapter. We'll also extend the Sketcher application to store data in a document, and make the document view more flexible, introducing several new techniques in the process.

In this chapter, you'll learn:

▶ What collections are, and what you can do with them

▶ How to use a collection to store point data for a curve

▶ How to use a collection to store document data

▶ How to implement drawing a document

▶ How to implement scrolling in a view

▶ How to create a pop-up menu at the cursor

▶ How to highlight the element nearest the cursor to provide feedback to the user for moving and deleting elements

▶ How to program the mouse to move and delete elements

What are Collection Classes?

By the nature of Windows programming, you'll frequently need to handle collections of data items where you have no advance knowledge of how many items you will need to manage, or even what particular type they are going to be. This is clearly illustrated by our Sketcher application. The user can draw an arbitrary number of elements which can be lines, rectangles, circles and curves, and in any sequence. MFC provides a group of **collection classes** designed to handle exactly this sort of problem — a **collection** being an aggregation of an arbitrary number of data items organized in a particular way.

Types of Collection

MFC provides you with a large number of collection classes for managing data. We'll use just a couple of them in practice, but it would be helpful to understand the types of collections available. MFC supports three kinds of collections, differentiated by the way in which the data items are organized. The way a collection is organized is referred to as the **shape** of the collection. The three types of organization, or shape, are:

Shape	How information is organized
Array	An array in this context is just like the array we have seen in the C++ language. It's an ordered arrangement of elements, where any element is retrieved by using an integer index value. An array collection can automatically grow to accommodate more data items. However, one of the other collection types is generally preferred, since array collections can be rather slow in operation.
List	A list collection is an ordered arrangement of data items, where each item has two pointers associated with it which point to the next and previous items in the list. We saw a linked list in Chapter 7, when we discussed structures. The list we have here is called a **doubly linked** list, because it has both backward and forward-pointing links. It can be searched in either direction and, like an array, a list collection grows automatically when required. A list collection is easy to use, and fast when it comes to adding items. Searching for an item can be slow, though, if there are a lot of data items in the list.
Map	A map is an unordered collection of data items, where each item is associated with a key that is used to retrieve the item from the map. A key is usually a string, but it can also be a numeric value. Maps are fast at storing data items and at searching, since a key will take you directly to the item you need. This sounds as though maps are always the ideal choice, and this is often the case, but for sequential access arrays will be faster. You also have the problem of choosing a key for your object that's unique to each item in the list.

MFC collection classes provide two approaches to implementing each type of collection. One approach is based on the use of class templates and provides you with **type-safe** handling of data in a collection. Type-safe handling means that the data passed to a function member of the collection class will be checked to ensure that it's of a type that can be processed by the function.

The other approach makes use of a range of collection classes (rather than templates), but these perform no data checking. If you want your collection classes to be type-safe, you have to include code yourself to ensure this. These latter classes were available in older versions of Visual C++ under Windows, but the template collection classes were not. We'll concentrate on the template-based versions, since these will provide the best chance of avoiding errors in our application.

The Type-safe Collection Classes

The template-based type-safe collection classes support collections of objects of any type, and collections of pointers to objects of any type. Collections of objects are supported by the template classes **CArray**, **CList** and **CMap**, and collections of pointers to objects are supported by the template classes **CTypedPtrArray**, **CTypedPtrList** and **CTypedPtrMap**. We won't go into the detail of all of these, just the two that we'll use in the Sketcher program. One will store objects and the other will store pointers to objects, so you'll get a feel for both sorts of collection.

Collections of Objects

The template classes for defining collections of objects are all derived from the MFC class **CObject**. They are defined this way so that they inherit the properties of the **CObject** class which are particularly useful for a number of things, including the file input and output operations (**serialization**, which we'll look at in Chapter 18).

These template classes can store and manage any kind of object, including all the C++ basic data types, plus any classes or structures that you or anybody else might define. Because these classes store objects, whenever you add an element to a list, an array, or a map, the class template object will need to make a copy of your object. Consequently, any class type that you want to store in any of these collections must have a copy constructor. The copy constructor for your class will be used to create a duplicate of the object that you wish to store in the collection.

Let's look at the general properties of each of the template classes providing type-safe management of objects. This is not an exhaustive treatment of all the member functions provided. Rather, it's intended to give you a sufficient flavor of how they work to enable you to decide if you want to use them or not. You can get information on all of the member functions by using <u>H</u>elp to get to the template class definition.

The CArray Template Class

You can use this template to store any kind of object in an array and have the array automatically grow to accommodate more elements when necessary. An array collection is illustrated below:

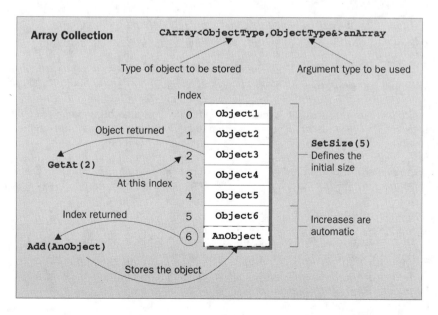

As with the arrays that we've seen in C++, elements in array collections are indexed from 0. The declaration of an array collection takes two arguments. The first argument is the type of the object to be stored; so, if your array collection is to store objects of type **CPoint**, for example, you specify **CPoint** as the first argument. The second argument is the type to be used in member function calls. To avoid the overhead in copying objects when passed by value, this is usually a reference, so an example of an array collection declaration to hold **CPoint** objects is:

```
CArray<CPoint, CPoint&> PointArray;
```

This defines the array collection class object, **PointArray**, which will store **CPoint** objects. When you call function members of this object, the argument is a reference, so to add a **CPoint** object, you would write

```
PointArray.Add(aPoint);
```

and the argument **aPoint** will be passed as a reference.

If you declare an array collection, it's important to call the **SetSize()** member function to fix the initial number of elements that you require before you use it. It will still work if you don't do this, but the initial allocation of elements and subsequent increments will be small, resulting in inefficient operation and frequent reallocation of memory for the array. The initial number of elements that you should specify depends on the typical size of array you expect to need, and how variable the size is. If you expect the minimum your program will require to be of the order of 400 to 500 elements, for example, but with expansion up to 700 or 800, an initial size of 600 should be suitable.

To retrieve the contents of an element, you can use the **GetAt()** function, as shown in the diagram above. To store the third element of **PointArray** in a variable **aPoint**, you would write:

```
aPoint = PointArray.GetAt(2);
```

The class also overloads the **[]** operator, so you could retrieve the third element of **PointArray** by using **PointArray[2]**. For example, if **aPoint** is a variable of type **CPoint**, you could write:

```
aPoint = PointArray[2];          // Store a copy of the third element
```

For array collections that are not **const**, this notation can also be used instead of the **SetAt()** function to set the contents of an existing element. The following two statements are, therefore, equivalent:

```
PointArray.SetAt(3,NewPoint);    // Store NewObject in the 4th element
PointArray[3] = NewPoint;        // Same as previous line of code
```

Here, **NewPoint** is an object of the type used to declare the array. In both cases, the element must already exist. You cannot extend the array by this means. To extend the array, you can use the **Add()** function shown in the diagram, which adds a new element to the array. There is also a function **Append()** to add an *array* of elements to the end of the array.

Helper Functions

Whenever you call the **SetSize()** function member of an array collection, a global function, **ConstructElements()**, is called to allocate memory for the number of elements you want to store in the array collection initially. This is called a **helper function**, as it helps in the process of setting the size of the array collection. The default version of this function sets the contents of the allocated memory to zero and doesn't call a constructor for your object class, so you'll need to supply your own version of this helper function if this action isn't appropriate for your objects. This will be the case if space for data members of objects of your class is allocated dynamically, or if there is other initialization required. **ConstructElements()** is also called by the member function **InsertAt()**, which inserts one or more elements at a particular index position within the array.

Members of the **CArray** collection class that remove elements call the helper function **DestructElements()**. The default version does nothing; so, if your object construction allocates any memory on the heap, you must override this function to release the memory properly.

The **CList** collection template makes use of a helper function when searching the contents of a list for a particular object. We'll discuss this further in the next section. Another helper function, **SerializeElements()**, is used by the array, list and map collection classes, but we'll discuss this when we come to look into how we can write a document to file.

The CList Template Class

A list collection is very flexible; you're likely to find yourself using lists more often than you use either arrays or maps. Let's look at the list collection template in some detail, as we'll apply it in our Sketcher program. The parameters to the **CList** collection class template are the same as those for the **CArray** template:

```
CList<ObjectType, ObjectType&> aList;
```

You need to supply two arguments to the template when you declare a list collection: the type of object to be stored, and the way an object is to be specified in function arguments. The example shows the second argument as a reference, since this is used most frequently. It doesn't necessarily have to be a reference, though — you could use a pointer, or even the object type (so objects would be passed by value), but this would be slow.

We can use a list to manage a curve in the Sketcher program. We could declare a list collection to store the points specifying a curve object with the statement:

```
CList<CPoint, CPoint&> PointList;
```

This declares a list called **PointList** that stores **CPoint** objects, which are passed to functions in the class by reference. We'll come back to this when we fill out more detail of the Sketcher program in this chapter.

Adding Elements to a List

You can add objects at the beginning or at the end of the list by using the **AddHead()** or **AddTail()** member functions, as shown in the following diagram:

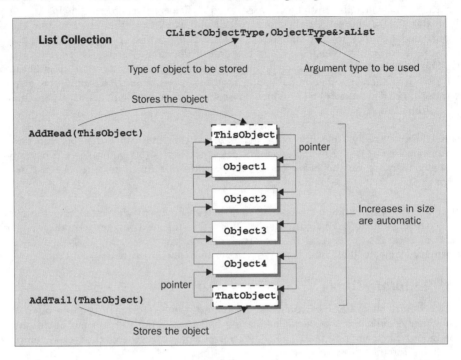

The diagram shows backward and forward pointers for each list element, which 'glue' the objects in the list together. These are internal links that you can't access in any direct way, but you can do just about anything you want by using the functions provided in the public interface to the class.

To add the object **aPoint** to the tail of the list **PointList**, you would write:

```
PointList.AddTail(aPoint);     // Add an element to the end
```

As new elements are added, the size of the list will increase automatically.

Both the **AddHead()** and **AddTail()** functions return a value of type **POSITION**, which specifies the position of the inserted object in the list. The way in which a variable of type **POSITION** is used is shown in the next diagram:

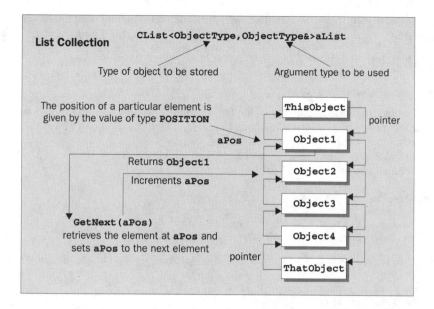

You can use a value of type **POSITION** to retrieve the object at a given position in the list by using the **GetNext()** function. Note that you can't perform arithmetic on values of type **POSITION** — you can only modify a position value through member functions of the list object. Furthermore, you can't set a position value to a specific numerical value. **POSITION** variables can only be set through member functions of the list object.

As well as returning the object, the **GetNext()** function increments the position variable passed to it, so that it points to the next object in the list. You can, therefore, use repeated calls to **GetNext()** to step through a list element by element. The position variable is set to **NULL** if you use **GetNext()** to retrieve the last object from the list, so you can use this to control your loop operation. You should always make sure that you have a valid position value when you call member functions of a list object.

You can insert an element in a list at a specific position as long as you have a **POSITION** value. To insert the object **ThePoint** in the list **PointList** immediately *before* an element at the position **aPosition**, you can use the statement:

```
PointList.InsertBefore(aPosition, ThePoint)
```

The function **InsertBefore()** will also return the position of the new object. To insert an element after the object at a given position, the function **InsertAfter()** is provided. These functions are often used with a list containing geometric elements to be displayed. Elements will be drawn on the screen in the sequence that you traverse the list. Elements that appear later in the list will overlay elements that are positioned earlier, so the order of elements determines what overlays what. You can therefore determine which of the existing elements a new element overlays by entering it at an appropriate position in the list.

When you need to set an existing object in a list to a particular value, you can use the function **SetAt()**, as long as you know the position value for the object:

```
PointList.SetAt(aPosition, aPoint);
```

There is no return value for this function. You must ensure that the **POSITION** value you pass to the function is valid. An invalid value will cause an error. You should, therefore, only pass a **POSITION** value to this function that was returned by one of the other member functions, and you must have verified that it isn't **NULL**.

Iterating through a List

If you want to get the **POSITION** value for the beginning or the end of the list, the class provides the member functions **GetHeadPosition()** and **GetTailPosition()**. Starting with the **POSITION** value for the head of the list, you can iterate through the complete list by calling **GetNext()** until the position value is **NULL**. We can illustrate the typical code to do this using the list of **CPoint** objects that we declared earlier:

```
CPoint CurrentPoint(0,0);

// Get the position of the first list element
POSITION aPosition = PointList.GetHeadPosition();

while(aPosition)                    // Loop while aPosition is not NULL
{
   CurrentPoint = PointList.GetNext(aPosition);
   // Process the current object...
}
```

You can work through the list backwards by using another member function, **GetPrev()**, which retrieves the current object and then decrements the position indicator. Of course, in this case, you would start out by calling **GetTailPosition()**.

Once you know a position value for an object in a list, you can retrieve the object with the member function **GetAt()**. You specify the position value as an argument and the object is returned. An invalid position value will cause an error.

Searching a List

You can find the position of an element that's stored in a list by using the member function **Find()**:

```
POSITION aPosition = PointList.Find(ThePoint);
```

This searches for the object specified as an argument by calling a global template function **CompareElements()** to compare the objects in the list with the argument. This is the helper function we referred to earlier, that aids the search process. The default implementation of this function compares the address of the argument with the address of each object in the list. This implies that if the search is to be successful, the argument must actually be an element in the list — not a copy. If the object is found in the list, the position of the element is returned. If it isn't found, **NULL** is returned. You can specify a second argument to define a position value where the search should begin.

If you want to search a list for an object that is *equal* to another object, you must implement your own version of **CompareElements()** that performs a proper comparison. The function template is of the form:

```
template<class TYPE, class ARG_TYPE> BOOL CompareElements(
                const TYPE* pElement1, const ARG_TYPE* pElement2);
```

where **pElement1** and **pElement2** are pointers to the objects to be compared. For the **PointList** collection class object, the prototype of the function generated by the template would be:

```
BOOL CompareElements(CPoint* pPoint1, CPoint* pPoint2);
```

To compare the **CPoint** objects, you could implement this as:

```
BOOL CompareElements(CPoint* pPoint1, CPoint* pPoint2)
  { return *pPoint1 == *pPoint2; }
```

This uses the **operator==()** function implemented in the **CPoint** class. In general you would need to implement the **operator==()** function for your own class in this context. You could then use it to implement the helper function **CompareElements()**.

You can also obtain the position of an element in a list by using an index value. The index works in the same way as for an array, with the first element being at index 0, the second at index 1, and so on. The function **FindIndex()** takes an index value of type **int** as an argument and returns a value of type **POSITION** for the object at the index position in the list. If you want to use an index value, you are likely to need to know how many objects there are in a list. The **GetCount()** function will return this for you:

```
int ObjectCount = PointList.GetCount();
```

Here, the integer count of the number of elements in the list will be stored in the variable **ObjectCount**.

Deleting Objects from a List

You can delete the first element in a list using the member function **RemoveHead()**. The function will then return the object that has just been removed from the head of the list. To remove the last object, you can use the function **RemoveTail()**. Both of these functions require that there should be at least one object in the list, so you should use the function **IsEmpty()** first, to verify that the list is not empty. For example:

```
if(!PointList.IsEmpty())
   PointList.RemoveHead();
```

The function **IsEmpty()** returns **TRUE** if the list is empty, and **FALSE** otherwise.

If you know the position value for an object that you want to delete from the list, you can do this directly:

```
PointList.RemoveAt(aPosition);
```

There's no return value from this function. It's your responsibility to ensure that the position value you pass as an argument is valid. If you want to delete the entire contents of a list, you use the member function **RemoveAll()**:

```
PointList.RemoveAll();
```

This function will also free the memory that was allocated for the elements in the list.

Helper Functions for a List

We have already seen how the **CompareElements()** helper function is used by the **Find()** function for a list. Both the **ConstructElements()** and **DestructElements()** global helper functions are also used by members of a **CList** template class. These are template functions which will be declared using the object type you specify in your **CList** class declaration. The template prototypes for these functions are:

```
template< class TYPE > void ConstructElements(
                                    TYPE* pElements, int nCount);
template< class TYPE > void DestructElements(
                                    TYPE* pElements, int nCount);
```

To obtain the function that's specific to your list collection, you just plug in the type for the objects you are storing. For example, the prototypes for the **PointList** class for these will be:

```
void ConstructElements(CPoint* pPoint, int PointCount);
void DestructElements(CPoint* pPoint, int PointCount);
```

Note that the parameters here are pointers. We mentioned earlier that arguments to the **PointList** member functions would be references, but this doesn't apply to the helper functions. The parameters to both functions are the same: the first is a pointer to an array of **CPoint** objects, and the second is a count of the number of objects in the array.

The **ConstructElements()** function is called whenever you enter an object in the list, and the **DestructElements()** function is called when you remove an object. As for the **CArray** template class, you need to implement your versions of these functions if the default operation is not suitable for your object class.

The CMap Template Class

Because of the way they work, maps are particularly suited to applications where your objects obviously have a relatively dissimilar key associated with them, such as a customer class where each customer will have an associated customer number, or a name and address class where the name might be used as a key. The organization of a map is shown below:

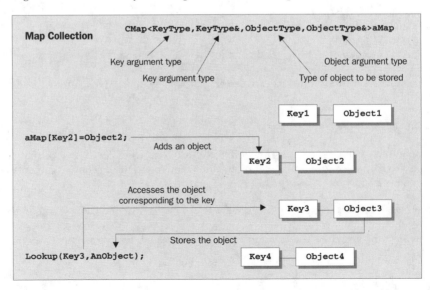

A map stores an object and key combination. The key is used to determine where, within the block of memory allocated to the map, the object is to be stored. The key, therefore, provides a means of going directly to an object stored, as long as the key is unique. The process of converting a key to an integer that can be used to calculate the address of an entry in a map is called **hashing**.

The hashing process applied to a key produces an integer called a **hash value**. This hash value is typically used as an offset to a base address to determine where to store the key and its associated object in the map. If the memory allocated to the map is at address **Base**, and each entry requires **Length** bytes, the entry producing the hash value **HashValue** will be stored at **Base+HashValue*Length**.

The hashing process may not produce a unique hash value from a key, in which case an element — the key together with the associated object — will be entered and linked to whatever element or elements were previously stored with the same hashed key value (often as a list). Of course, the fewer unique hash values that are generated, the less efficient the retrieval process from your map will be, because searching will typically be required to retrieve elements that have the same hash value.

There are four arguments necessary when you declare a map:

```
CMap<LONG, LONG&, CPoint, CPoint&> PointMap;
```

The first two specify the key type and how it is passed as an argument. Usually, it will be passed as a reference. The second pair of arguments specify the object type and how the object is passed as an argument, as we have seen previously.

You can store an object in a map by using the **[]** operator, as shown in the diagram above. You can also use a member function **SetAt()** to store an object, where you supply the key value and the object as arguments. Note that you cannot use the **[]** operator on the right-hand side of an assignment to retrieve an object, as this version of the operator is not implemented in the class.

To retrieve an object, you use the member function, **Lookup()**, as shown in the diagram. This will retrieve the object corresponding to the key specified; the function returns **TRUE** if the object was found, and **FALSE** otherwise. You can also iterate through all the objects in a map using a variable of type **POSITION**, although the sequence in which objects are retrieved is unrelated to the sequence in which they were added to the map. This is because objects are stored in a map in locations determined by the hash value, not by the sequence in which they were entered.

Helper Functions used by CMap

As well as the helper functions that we have discussed in the context of arrays and lists, map collection classes also use a global function **HashKey()**, which is defined by this template:

```
template<class ARG_KEY>
   UINT HashKey(ARG_KEY key);
```

This function converts your key value to a hash value of type **UINT**. The default version does this by simply shifting your key value right by 4 bit positions. You need to implement your own version of this function if the default operation isn't suited to your key type.

There are different techniques used for hashing which vary depending on the type of data being used as a key, and the number of elements you are likely to want to store in your map. The likely number of elements to be stored indicates the number of unique hash values you need. A common method for hashing a numeric key value is to compute the hash value as the value of the key modulo N (that is, the remainder after dividing the number by N), where N is the number of different values you want. For reasons it would take too long to explain here, N needs to be prime for this to work well. Didn't you just know that our program to calculate primes would turn out to be useful after all?

We can, perhaps, understand the principles of the mechanism used here with a simple example. Suppose you expect to store up to 100 different entries in a map using a key value, **Key**. You could hash the key with the statement:

```
HashValue = Key%101;
```

This will result in values for the **HashValue** between 0 and 100, which is exactly what you need to calculate the address for an entry. Assuming your map is stored at some location in memory, **Base**, and the memory required to store the object along with its key is **Length** bytes, then you can store an entry that produces the hash value **HashValue** at the location **Base+HashValue*Length**. With the hashing process as above, we can accommodate up to 101 entries at unique positions in the map.

Where a key is a character string, the hashing process is rather more complicated, particularly with long or variable strings. However, a method that is commonly used involves using numerical values derived from characters in the string. This typically involves assigning a numerical value to each character, so if your string contained lower case letters plus spaces, you could assign each character a value between 0 and 26, with *space* as 0, *a* as 1, *b* as 2, and so on. The string can then be treated as the representation of a number to some base, 32 say. The numerical value for the string 'fred', for instance, would then be

$$6*32^3+18*32^2+5*32^1+4*32^0$$

and, assuming you expected to store 500 strings, you could calculate the hashed value of the key as:

$$6*32^3+18*32^2+5*32^1+4*32^0 \bmod 503$$

The value of 503 for N is the smallest prime greater than the likely number of entries. The base chosen to evaluate a hash value for a string is usually a power of 2 that corresponds to the minimum value that is greater than or equal to the number of possible different characters in a string. For long strings, this can generate very large numbers, so special techniques are used to compute the value modulo N. Detailed discussion of this is beyond the scope of this book.

The Typed Pointer Collections

The typed pointer collection class templates store pointers to objects, rather than objects themselves. This is the primary difference between these class templates and the template classes we have just discussed. We'll look at how the **CTypedPtrList** class template is used, because we'll use this as a basis for managing elements in our document class, **CSketcherDoc**.

The CTypedPtrList Template Class

You can declare a typed pointer list class with a statement of the form:

```
CTypedPtrList<BaseClass, Type*> ListName;
```

The first argument specifies a base class that must be one of two pointer list classes defined in MFC, either **CObList** or **CPtrList**. Your choice will depend on how your object class has been defined. Using the **CObList** class creates a list supporting pointers to objects derived from **CObject**, while **CPtrList** supports lists of **void*** pointers. Since the elements in our Sketcher example have **CObject** as a base class, we'll concentrate on how **CObList** is used.

The second argument to the template is the type of the pointers to be stored in the list. In our example, this is going to be **CElement***, since all our shapes have **CElement** as a base and **CElement** is derived from **CObject**. Thus, the declaration of a class for storing shapes is:

```
CTypedPtrList<CObList, CElement*> m_ElementList;
```

We could have used **CObList*** types to store the pointers to our elements, but then the list could contain an object of any class that has **CObject** as a base. The declaration of **m_ElementList** ensures that only pointers to objects of the class **CElement** can be stored. This provides a greatly increased level of security in the program.

CTypedPtrList Operations

The functions provided in the **CTypedPtrList**-based classes are similar to those supported by **CList**, except of course that all operations are with pointers to objects rather than with objects, so let's tabulate them. They fall into two groups: those that are defined in **CTypedPtrList**, and those that are inherited from the base class — **CObList** in this case.

Defined in **CTypedPtrList**:

Function	Remarks
GetHead()	Returns the pointer at the head of the list. You should use **IsEmpty()** to verify that the list is not empty before calling this function.
GetTail()	Returns the pointer at the tail of the list. You should use **IsEmpty()** to verify that the list is not empty before calling this function.
RemoveHead()	Removes the first pointer in the list. You should use **IsEmpty()** to verify that the list is not empty before calling this function.
RemoveTail()	Removes the last pointer in the list. You should use **IsEmpty()** to verify that the list is not empty before calling this function.
GetNext()	Returns the pointer at the position indicated by the variable of type **POSITION** passed as a reference argument. The variable is updated to indicate the next element in the list. When the end of the list is reached, the position variable is set to **NULL**. This function can be used to iterate forwards through all the pointers in the list.

Function	Remarks
GetPrev()	Returns the pointer at the position indicated by the variable of type **POSITION** passed as a reference argument. The variable is updated to indicate the previous element in the list. When the beginning of the list is reached, the position variable is set to **NULL**. This function can be used to iterate backwards through all the pointers in the list.
GetAt()	Returns the pointer stored at the position indicated by the variable of type **POSITION** passed as an argument, which isn't changed. The function returns a reference, so as long as the list is not defined as **const** — this function can be used on the left of an assignment operator to modify a list entry.

Inherited from **CObList**:

Function	Remarks
AddHead()	Adds the pointer passed as an argument to the head of the list and returns a value of type **POSITION** that corresponds to the new element. There is another version of this function which can add another *list* to the head of the list.
AddTail()	Adds the pointer passed as an argument to the tail of the list and returns a value of type **POSITION** that corresponds to the new element. There is another version of this function which can add another *list* to the tail of the list.
RemoveAll()	Removes all the elements from the list. Note that this doesn't delete the objects pointed to by elements in the list. You need to take care of this yourself.
GetHeadPosition()	Returns the position of the element at the head of the list.
GetTailPosition()	Returns the position of the element at the tail of the list.
SetAt()	Stores the pointer specified by the second argument at the position in the list defined by the first argument. An invalid position value will cause an error.
RemoveAt()	Removes the pointer from the position in the list specified by the argument of type **POSITION**. An invalid position value will cause an error.
InsertBefore()	Inserts a new pointer specified by the second argument before the position specified by the first argument. The position of the new element is returned.
InsertAfter()	Inserts a new pointer specified by the second argument after the position specified by the first argument. The position of the new element is returned.
Find()	Searches for a pointer in the list that is identical to the pointer specified as an argument. Its position is returned if it is found. **NULL** is returned otherwise.

Function	Remarks
`FindIndex()`	Returns the position of a pointer in the list specified by a zero-based integer index argument.
`GetCount()`	Returns the number of elements in the list.
`IsEmpty()`	Returns **TRUE** if there are no elements in the list, and **FALSE** otherwise.

We'll see some of these member functions in action a little later in this chapter in the context of implementing the document class for the Sketcher program.

Using the CList Template Class

We can make use of the **CList** collection template in the definition of the curve object in our Sketcher application. A curve is defined by two or more points, so storing these in a list would be a good method of handling them. We first need to define a **CList** collection class object as a member of the **CCurve** class. We'll use this collection to store points. We've looked at the **CList** template class in some detail, so this should be easy.

The **CList** template class has two parameters, so the general form of declaring a collection class of this type is:

```
CList<YourObjectType, FunctionArgType> ClassName;
```

The first argument, **YourObjectType**, specifies the type of object that you want to store in the list. The second argument specifies the argument type to be used in function members of the collection class when referring to an object. This is usually specified as a reference to the object type to minimize copying of arguments in a function call. So let's declare a collection class object to suit our needs in the **CCurve** class as:

```
class CCurve : public CElement
{
public:
    virtual void Draw(CDC* pDC) const;          // Function to display a curve

    // Constructor for a curve object
    CCurve(const COLORREF& Color);

protected:
    // CCurve data members to go here
    CList<CPoint, const CPoint&> m_PointList; // Type safe point list

    CCurve(){}                       // Default constructor - should not be used
};
```

The rest of the class definition is omitted here, since we're not concerned with it for now. The collection declaration is shaded. It declares the collection **m_PointList** which will store **CPoint** objects in the list, and its functions will use constant reference arguments to **CPoint** objects.

The **CPoint** class doesn't allocate memory dynamically, so we won't need to implement **ConstructElements()** or **DestructElements()**, and we don't need to use the **Find()** member function, so we can forget about **CompareElements()** as well.

Drawing a Curve

Drawing a curve is different from drawing a line or a circle. With a line or a circle, as we move the cursor with the left button down, we are creating a succession of different line or circle elements that share a common reference point — the point where the left mouse button was pressed. This is not the case when we draw a curve, as shown in the diagram:

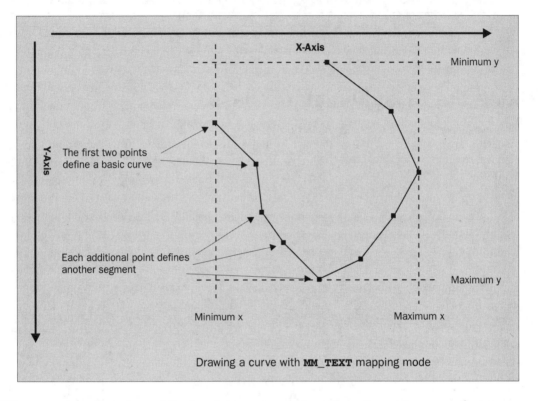

Drawing a curve with **MM_TEXT** mapping mode

When we move the cursor while drawing a curve, we're not creating a sequence of new curves, but extending the same curve, so each successive point adds another segment to the curve's definition. We therefore need to create a curve object as soon as we have the two points from the **WM_LBUTTONDOWN** message and the first **WM_MOUSEMOVE** message. Points defined with subsequent mouse move messages then define additional segments to the existing curve object. We'll need to add a function **AddSegment()** to the **CCurve** class to extend the curve once it has been created by the constructor.

A further point to consider is how we are to calculate the enclosing rectangle. This is defined by getting the minimum *x* and minimum *y* pair from all the defining points to establish the top left corner of the rectangle, and the maximum *x* and maximum *y* pair for the bottom right. This involves going through all the points in the list. We will, therefore, compute the enclosing rectangle incrementally in the **AddSegment()** function as points are added to the curve.

Defining the CCurve Class

With these features added, the complete definition of the **CCurve** class will be:

```
class CCurve : public CElement
{
public:
    virtual void Draw(CDC* pDC) const;          // Function to display a curve

// Constructor for a curve object
    CCurve(const CPoint& FirstPoint, const CPoint& SecondPoint, const COLORREF&
Color);

    void AddSegment(const CPoint& Point);        //Add a segment to the curve

protected:
    // CCurve data members to go here
    CList<CPoint, const CPoint&> m_PointList;  // Type safe point list

    CCurve(){}               // Default constructor - should not be used
};
```

You should modify the definition of the class in **Elements.h** to correspond with the above. The constructor has the first two defining points and the color as parameters, so it only defines a curve with one segment. This will be called in the **CreateElement()** function, invoked by the **OnMouseMove()** function in the view class, the first time a **WM_MOUSEMOVE** message is received for a curve. Consequently, you must remember to modify the **CreateElement()** function to call the constructor with the correct arguments. The statement using the **CCurve** constructor in the **switch** in this function should be changed to:

```
        case CURVE:
            return new CCurve(m_FirstPoint, m_SecondPoint, pDoc->GetElementColor());
```

After the constructor has been called, all subsequent **WM_MOUSEMOVE** messages will result in the **AddSegment()** function being called to add a segment to the existing curve, as shown in the diagram below:

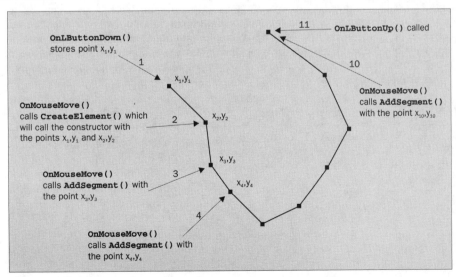

This shows the complete sequence of message handler calls for a curve comprised of nine segments. The sequence is indicated by the numbered arrows. The code for the **OnMouseMove()** function in **CSketcherView** needs to be updated as follows:

```
void CSketcherView::OnMouseMove(UINT nFlags, CPoint point)
{
    // Define a Device Context object for the view
    CClientDC aDC(this);
    aDC.SetROP2(R2_NOTXORPEN);                      // Set the drawing mode
    if((nFlags & MK_LBUTTON) && (this == GetCapture()))
    {
        m_SecondPoint = point;                      // Save the current cursor position

        if(m_pTempElement)
        {
            if(CURVE == GetDocument()->GetElementType())    // Is it a curve?
            {  // We are drawing a curve
               // so add a segment to the existing curve
               (static_cast<CCurve*>(m_pTempElement))->AddSegment(m_SecondPoint);
               m_pTempElement->Draw(&aDC);          // Now draw it
               return;                              // We are done
            }

            aDC.SetROP2(R2_NOTXORPEN);              // Set drawing mode

            // Redraw the old element so it disappears from the view
            m_pTempElement->Draw(&aDC);
            delete m_pTempElement;                  // Delete the old element
            m_pTempElement = 0;                     // Reset the pointer to 0
        }

        // Create a temporary element of the type and color that
        // is recorded in the document object, and draw it
        m_pTempElement = CreateElement();           // Create a new element
        m_pTempElement->Draw(&aDC);                 // Draw the element
    }
}
```

We have to treat an element of type **CURVE** as a special case once it has been created. This is because, on all subsequent calls of the **OnMouseMove()** handler, we want to call the **AddSegment()** function for the existing element, rather than construct a new one in place of the old. We don't need to set the drawing mode, since we don't need to erase the previous curve each time. We take care of this by moving the call to **SetROP2()** to a position after the code processing a curve.

Adding the curve segment and drawing the extended curve is taken care of within the **if** we have added. Note that we must cast the **m_pTempElement** pointer to type **CCurve*** in order to use it to call **AddSegment()** for the old element, because **AddSegment()** is not a virtual function. If we don't add the cast, we'll get an error, because the compiler will try to resolve the call statically to a member of the **CElement** class.

Implementing the CCurve Class

Let's first write the code for the constructor. This should be added to **Elements.cpp** in place of the temporary constructor that we used in the last chapter. It needs to store the two points passed as arguments in the **CList** data member, **m_PointList**:

```
CCurve::CCurve(const CPoint& FirstPoint, const CPoint& SecondPoint, const
COLORREF& Color)
{
    m_PointList.AddTail(FirstPoint);      // Add the 1st point to the list
    m_PointList.AddTail(SecondPoint);     // Add the 2nd point to the list
    m_Color = Color;                      // Store the color
    m_Pen = 1;                            // Set pen width

    // Construct the enclosing rectangle assuming MM_TEXT mode
    m_EnclosingRect = CRect(FirstPoint, SecondPoint);
    m_EnclosingRect.NormalizeRect();
}
```

The points are added to the list, **m_PointList**, by calling the **AddTail()** member of the **CList** template class. This function adds a copy of the point passed as an argument to the end of the list. The enclosing rectangle is defined in exactly the same way as we defined it for a line.

The next function we should add to **Elements.cpp** is **AddSegment()**. This function will be called when additional curve points are recorded, after the first version of a curve object has been created. This member function is very simple:

```
void CCurve::AddSegment(const CPoint& Point)
{
    m_PointList.AddTail(Point);                      // Add the point to the end

    // Modify the enclosing rectangle for the new point
    m_EnclosingRect = CRect( min(Point.x, m_EnclosingRect.left),
                             min(Point.y, m_EnclosingRect.top),
                             max(Point.x, m_EnclosingRect.right),
                             max(Point.y, m_EnclosingRect.bottom) );
}
```

The **min()** and **max()** functions we use here are standard macros that are the equivalent of using the conditional operator for choosing the minimum or maximum of two values. The new point is added to the tail of the list in the same way as in the constructor. It's important that each new point is added to the list in a way that is consistent with the constructor, because we'll draw the segments using the points in sequence, from the beginning to the end of the list. Each line segment will be drawn from the end point of the previous line to the new point. If the points are not in the right sequence, the line segments won't be drawn correctly. After adding the new point, the enclosing rectangle for the curve is redefined, taking account of the new point.

The last member function we need to define for the interface to the **CCurve** class is **Draw()**:

```
void CCurve::Draw(CDC* pDC) const
{
    // Create a pen for this object and
    // initialize it to the object color and line width of 1 pixel
    CPen aPen;
    if (!aPen.CreatePen(PS_SOLID, m_Pen, m_Color))
    {
        // Pen creation failed. Close the program
        AfxMessageBox("Pen creation failed drawing a curve", MB_OK);
        AfxAbort();
    }

    CPen* pOldPen = pDC->SelectObject(&aPen);  // Select the pen

    // Now draw the curve
    // Get the position in the list of the first element
    POSITION aPosition = m_PointList.GetHeadPosition();

    // As long as it's good, move to that point
    if(aPosition)
        pDC->MoveTo(m_PointList.GetNext(aPosition));

    // Draw a segment for each of the following points
    while(aPosition)
        pDC->LineTo(m_PointList.GetNext(aPosition));

    pDC->SelectObject(pOldPen);                // Restore the old pen
}
```

To draw the **CCurve** object, we need to iterate through all the points in the list from the beginning, drawing each segment as we go. We get a **POSITION** value for the first element by using the function **GetHeadPosition()** and then use **MoveTo()** to set the first point as the current position in the device context. We then draw line segments in the **while** loop as long as **aPosition** is not **NULL**. The **GetNext()** function, which appears as the argument to the **LineTo()** function, returns the current point and simultaneously increments **aPosition** to refer to the next point in the list.

Exercising the CCurve Class

With the changes we've just discussed added to the Sketcher program, we have implemented all the code necessary for the element shapes in our menu. In order to make use of the collection class templates, though, we must include the file **afxtempl.h**. The best place to put the **#include** statement would be in **StdAfx.h**, so that it will be added to the precompiled header file. Go to **StdAfx.h** in file mode and add the line shown below:

```
// stdafx.h : include file for standard system include files,
// or project specific include files that are used frequently, but
// are changed infrequently
//

#if !defined(AFX_STDAFX_H__5FEC0C68_1A40_11D2_99B1_00104B4C84A4__INCLUDED_)
#define AFX_STDAFX_H__5FEC0C68_1A40_11D2_99B1_00104B4C84A4__INCLUDED_
```

```
#if _MSC_VER > 1000
#pragma once
#endif // _MSC_VER > 1000

#define VC_EXTRALEAN           // Exclude rarely-used stuff from Windows headers

#include <afxwin.h>            // MFC core and standard components
#include <afxext.h>            // MFC extensions
#include <afxtempl.h>          // Collection templates
#include <afxdisp.h>           // MFC Automation classes
#include <afxdtctl.h>          // MFC support for Internet Explorer 4 Common Controls
#ifndef _AFX_NO_AFXCMN_SUPPORT
#include <afxcmn.h>            // MFC support for Windows Common Controls
#endif // _AFX_NO_AFXCMN_SUPPORT


//{{AFX_INSERT_LOCATION}}
// Microsoft Visual C++ will insert additional declarations immediately before the
previous line.

#endif // !defined(AFX_STDAFX_H__5FEC0C68_1A40_11D2_99B1_00104B4C84A4__INCLUDED_)
```

With the file included here, it will also be available to the implementation of **CSketcherDoc**
when we get to use a collection class template there.

You can now build the Sketcher program once more, and execute it. You should be able to
create curves in all four colors. A typical application window is shown below:

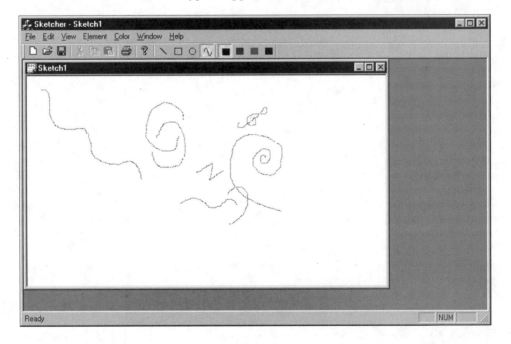

Of course, like the other elements you can draw, the curves are not persistent. You'll notice that they look more like dashes than continuous lines, with the lengths of the dashes dependent on how quickly you move your mouse across the screen. Also, as soon as you cause a **WM_PAINT** message to be sent to the application, by resizing the view for instance, they will disappear. This is because the curves are drawn in relation to mouse movements, and stored temporarily.

Once we can store the curves in the document object for the application, they will be a bit more permanent, and they'll look smoother — so let's take a look at that next.

Creating the Document

The document in the Sketcher application needs to be able to store an arbitrary collection of lines, rectangles, circles and curves in any sequence, and an excellent vehicle for handling this is a list. Because all the element classes that we've defined include the capability for the objects to draw themselves, drawing the document is easily accomplished by stepping through the list.

Using a CTypedPtrList Template

We can declare a **CTypedPtrList** that will store pointers to instances of our shape classes as **CElement** pointers. We just need to add the list declaration as a data member in the **CSketcherDoc** class definition:

```
class CSketcherDoc : public CDocument
{
protected: // create from serialization only
    CSketcherDoc();
    DECLARE_DYNCREATE(CSketcherDoc)

// Attributes
public:

protected:
    COLORREF m_Color;                            // Current drawing color
    WORD m_Element;                              // Current element type
    CTypedPtrList<CObList, CElement*> m_ElementList;  // Element list

// Operations
public:
    WORD GetElementType() const                  // Get the element type
    { return m_Element; }

    COLORREF GetElementColor() const             // Get the element color
    { return m_Color; }

// Rest of the class as before...
};
```

The **CSketcherDoc** class now refers to the **CElement** class. We need to make sure that all **#include** directives for **CSketcherDoc** in the **.cpp** files are preceded by a **#include** for **Elements.h** — so you'll need to add a **#include** for **Elements.h** to **SketcherDoc.cpp**, and make sure the **#include** statements in **Sketcher.cpp** and **SketcherView.cpp** are in the right order.

We'll also need a member function to add an element to the list. **AddElement()** would be a good, if unoriginal, name for this. We create shape objects on the heap, so we can just pass a pointer to the function and, since all it does is add an element, we might just as well put the implementation in the class definition:

```
class CSketcherDoc : public CDocument
{

// Rest of the class as before...

// Operations
public:
    WORD GetElementType() const              // Get the element type
    { return m_Element; }

    COLORREF GetElementColor() const         // Get the element color
    { return m_Color; }

    void AddElement(CElement* pElement)       // Add an element to the list
    { m_ElementList.AddTail(pElement); }

// Rest of the class as before...

};
```

Adding an element to the list requires just a single statement, which calls the **AddTail()** member function. That's all we need to create the document, but we need to consider what happens when a document is closed. We need to make sure that the list of pointers, and all the elements they point to, are destroyed properly. To do this, we need to add code to the destructor for **CSketcherDoc** objects.

Implementing the Document Destructor

In the destructor, we'll need to go through the list deleting the element pointed to by each entry. Once that is complete, we must delete the pointers from the list. The code to do this will be:

```
CSketcherDoc::~CSketcherDoc()
{
    // Get the position at the head of the list
    POSITION aPosition = m_ElementList.GetHeadPosition();

    // Now delete the element pointed to by each list entry
    while(aPosition)
        delete m_ElementList.GetNext(aPosition);

    m_ElementList.RemoveAll();    // Finally delete all pointers
}
```

We use the **GetHeadPosition()** function to obtain the position value for the entry at the head of the list, and initialize the variable **aPosition** with this value. We then use **aPosition** in the **while** loop to walk through the list and delete the object pointed to by each entry. The function **GetNext()** returns the current pointer entry and updates the **aPosition** variable to refer to the next entry. When the last entry is retrieved, **aPosition** will be set to **NULL** by the **GetNext()** function and the loop will end. Once we have deleted all the element objects pointed to by the pointers in the list, we just need to delete the pointers themselves. We can delete the whole lot in one go by calling the **RemoveAll()** function for our list object.

> *In fact, the call to* **RemoveAll()** *isn't strictly necessary in this case, because* **RemoveAll()** *is automatically called by the list's destructor. However, it doesn't do any harm here, and it would be useful if we needed to reuse the list.*

You should add this code to the definition of the destructor in **SketcherDoc.cpp**. You can go directly to the code for the destructor through the ClassView.

Drawing the Document

As the document owns the list of elements, and the list is **protected**, we can't use it directly from the view. The **OnDraw()** member of the view does need to be able to call the **Draw()** member for each of the elements in the list, though, so we need to consider how best to do this. Let's look at our options:

▶ We could make the list **public**, but this would rather defeat the object of maintaining protected members of the document class, as it would expose all the function members of the list object.

▶ We could add a member function to return a pointer to the list, but this would effectively make the list **public** and also incur overhead in accessing it.

▶ We could add a **public** function to the document which would call the **Draw()** member for each element. We could then call this member from the **OnDraw()** function in the view. This wouldn't be a bad solution, as it would produce what we want and would still maintain the privacy of the list. The only thing against it is that the function would need access to a device context, and this is really the domain of the view.

▶ We could make the **OnDraw()** function a friend of **CSketcherDoc**, but this would expose all of the members of the class, which isn't desirable, particularly with a complex class.

▶ We could add a function to provide a **POSITION** value for the first list element, and a second member to iterate through the list elements. This wouldn't expose the list, but it would make the element pointers available.

The last option looks to be the best choice, so let's go with that. We can extend the document class definition to:

```
class CSketcherDoc : public CDocument
{

// Rest of the class as before...

// Operations
public:
    WORD GetElementType() const          // Get the element type
    { return m_Element; }
```

```
    COLORREF GetElementColor() const        // Get the element color
    { return m_Color; }

    void AddElement(CElement* pElement)      // Add an element to the list
    { m_ElementList.AddTail(pElement); }

    POSITION GetListHeadPosition() const     // Return list head POSITION value
    { return m_ElementList.GetHeadPosition(); }

    CElement* GetNext(POSITION& aPos) const  // Return current element pointer
    { return m_ElementList.GetNext(aPos); }

  // Rest of the class as before...

  };
```

By using the two functions that we have added to the document class, the **OnDraw()** function for the view will be able to iterate through the list, calling the **Draw()** function for each element. Notice that the parameter type of the **CSketcherDoc::GetNext()** function is a reference; this is because **CTypedPointerList::GetNext()** also takes a reference. The reason that **CTypedPointerList::GetNext()** takes a reference is that it modifies the value of the position passed to it so that it points to the **POSITION** value of the next entry in the list. This enables you to write simple loops to move through the list calling **GetNext()** each time.

The implementation of **OnDraw()** to do this will be:

```
    void CSketcherView::OnDraw(CDC* pDC)
    {
        CSketcherDoc* pDoc = GetDocument();
        ASSERT_VALID(pDoc);

        POSITION aPos = pDoc->GetListHeadPosition();
        while(aPos)                               // Loop while aPos is not null
        {
            pDoc->GetNext(aPos)->Draw(pDC);       // Draw the current element
        }
    }
```

If we implement it like this, the function will always draw all the elements contained in the document. The statement in the **while** loop first gets a pointer to an element from the document with the expression **pDoc->GetNext()**. The pointer that is returned is used to call the **Draw()** function for that element. The statement works this way without parentheses because of the left to right associativity of the **->** operator. The **while** loop plows through the list from beginning to end. We can do it better, though, and make our program more efficient.

Frequently, when a **WM_PAINT** message is sent to your program, only part of the window needs to be redrawn. When Windows sends the **WM_PAINT** message to a window, it also defines an area in the client area of the window, and only this area needs to be redrawn. The **CDC** class provides a member function, **RectVisible()**, which checks whether a rectangle that you supply to it as an argument overlaps the area that Windows requires to be redrawn. We can use this to make sure we only draw the elements that are in the area Windows wants redrawn, thus improving the performance of the application:

```
void CSketcherView::OnDraw(CDC* pDC)
{
   CSketcherDoc* pDoc = GetDocument();
   ASSERT_VALID(pDoc);

   POSITION aPos = pDoc->GetListHeadPosition();
   CElement* pElement = 0;                 // Store for an element pointer
   while(aPos)                             // Loop while aPos is not null
   {
      pElement = pDoc->GetNext(aPos);   // Get the current element pointer
      // If the element is visible...
      if(pDC->RectVisible(pElement->GetBoundRect()))
         pElement->Draw(pDC);             // ...draw it
   }
}
```

We get the position for the first entry in the list and store it in **aPos**. This controls the loop, which retrieves each pointer entry in turn. The bounding rectangle for each element is obtained using the **GetBoundRect()** member of the object and is passed to the **RectVisible()** function in the **if** statement. As a result, only elements that overlap the area that Windows has identified as invalid will be drawn. Drawing on the screen is a relatively expensive operation in terms of time, so checking for just the elements that need to be redrawn, rather than drawing everything each time, will improve performance considerably.

Adding an Element to the Document

The last thing we need to do to have a working document in our program is to add the code to the **OnLButtonUp()** handler in the **CSketcherView** class to add the temporary element to the document:

```
void CSketcherView::OnLButtonUp(UINT nFlags, CPoint point)
{
   if(this == GetCapture())
      ReleaseCapture();         // Stop capturing mouse messages

   // If there is an element, add it to the document
   if(m_pTempElement)
   {
      GetDocument()->AddElement(m_pTempElement);
      InvalidateRect(0);           // Redraw the current window
      m_pTempElement = 0;          // Reset the element pointer
   }
}
```

Of course, we need to check that there really is an element before we add it to the document. The user might just have clicked the left mouse button without moving the mouse. After adding the element to the list in the document, we call **InvalidateRect()** to get the client area for the current view redrawn. The argument of 0 invalidates the whole of the client area in the view. Because of the way the rubber-banding process works, some elements may not be displayed properly if we don't do this. If you draw a horizontal line, for instance, and then rubber-band a rectangle with the same color so that its top (or bottom) edge overlaps the line, the overlapped bit of line will disappear. This is because the edge being drawn is XORed with the line underneath, so you get the background color back. We must also reset the pointer **m_pTempElement** to avoid confusion when another element is created.

Exercising the Document

After saving all the modified files, you can build the latest version of Sketcher and execute it. You'll now be able to produce art such as 'the happy programmer' shown below.

The program is now working more realistically. It stores a pointer to each element in the document object, so they're all automatically redrawn as necessary. The program also does a proper clean-up of the document data when it's deleted.

There are still some limitations in the program that we need to address. For instance:

▶ You can open another view window by using the <u>W</u>indow | <u>N</u>ew Window menu option in the program. This capability is built in to an MDI application and opens a new view to an existing document (i.e. not a new document). However, if you draw an element in one window, the element does not *immediately* appear in the other window — and will not appear in the second window until there is some other reason for redrawing the area that the element occupies.

▶ We can only draw in the client area we can see. It would be nice to be able to scroll the view and draw over a bigger area.

▶ Neither can we delete an element, so if you make a mistake, you either live with it or start over with a new document.

These are all quite serious deficiencies which, together, make the program fairly useless as it stands. We'll overcome all of them before the end of this chapter.

Improving the View

The first item that we can try to fix is the updating of all the document windows that are displayed when an element is drawn. The problem arises because only the view in which an element is drawn knows about the new element. Each view is acting independently of the others and there is no communication between them. We need to arrange for any view that adds an element to the document to let all the other views know about it, and they need to take the appropriate action.

Updating Multiple Views

The document class conveniently contains a function **UpdateAllViews()** to help with this particular problem. This function essentially provides a means for the document to send a message to all its views. We just need to call it from the **OnLButtonUp()** function in the **CSketcherView** class, whenever we have added a new element to the document:

```
void CSketcherView::OnLButtonUp(UINT nFlags, CPoint point)
{
    if(this == GetCapture())
        ReleaseCapture();        // Stop capturing mouse messages

    // If there is an element, add it to the document
    if(m_pTempElement)
    {
        GetDocument()->AddElement(m_pTempElement);
        GetDocument()->UpdateAllViews(0,0,m_pTempElement);
                                 // Tell all the views
        m_pTempElement = 0;      // Reset the element pointer
    }
}
```

When the **m_pTempElement** pointer is not **NULL**, the specific action of the function has been extended to call the **UpdateAllViews()** member of our document class. This function communicates with the views by causing the **OnUpdate()** member function in each view to be called. The three arguments to **UpdateAllViews()** are described below:

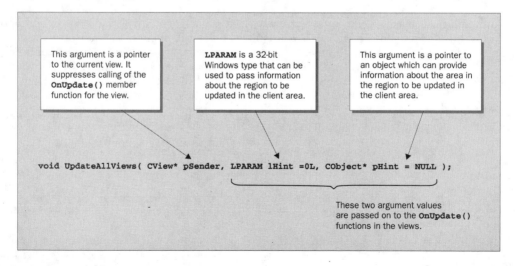

This argument is a pointer to the current view. It suppresses calling of the **OnUpdate()** member function for the view.

LPARAM is a 32-bit Windows type that can be used to pass information about the region to be updated in the client area.

This argument is a pointer to an object which can provide information about the area in the region to be updated in the client area.

```
void UpdateAllViews( CView* pSender, LPARAM lHint =0L, CObject* pHint = NULL );
```

These two argument values are passed on to the **OnUpdate()** functions in the views.

The first argument to the **UpdateAllViews()** function call will often be the **this** pointer for the current view. This suppresses the call of the **OnUpdate()** function for the current view. This is a useful feature when the current view is already up-to-date. In our case, because we are rubber-banding, we want to get the current view redrawn as well, so by specifying the first argument as 0, we get the **OnUpdate()** function called for all the views, including the current view. This removes the need to call **InvalidateRect()** as we did before.

We don't use the second argument to **UpdateAllViews()** here, but we do pass the pointer to the new element through the third argument. Passing a pointer to the new element will allow the views to figure out which bit of their client area needs to be redrawn.

In order to catch the information passed to the **UpdateAllViews()** function, we need to add the **OnUpdate()** member function to our view class. You can do this by opening ClassWizard and looking at the Message Maps tab for **CSketcherView**. If you select **CSketcherView** in the Object IDs: box, you'll be able to find OnUpdate in the Messages: box. Click on the Add Function button, then the Edit Code button. You only need to add the highlighted code below to the function definition:

```
void CSketcherView::OnUpdate(CView* pSender, LPARAM lHint, CObject* pHint)
{
    // Invalidate the area corresponding to the element pointed to
    // if there is one, otherwise invalidate the whole client area
    if(pHint)
        InvalidateRect(static_cast<CElement*>(pHint)->GetBoundRect());
    else
        InvalidateRect(0);
}
```

The three arguments passed to the **OnUpdate()** function in the view class correspond to the arguments that we passed in the **UpdateAllViews()** function call. Thus, **pHint** will contain the address of the new element. However, we can't assume that this is always the case. The **OnUpdate()** function is also called when a view is first created, but with a **NULL** pointer for the third argument. Therefore, the function checks that the **pHint** pointer isn't **NULL** and only then gets the bounding rectangle for the element passed as the third argument. It invalidates this area in the client area of the view by passing the rectangle to the **InvalidateRect()** function. This area will be redrawn by the **OnDraw()** function in this view when the next **WM_PAINT** message is sent to the view. If the **pHint** pointer is **NULL**, the whole client area is invalidated.

You might be tempted to consider redrawing the new element in the **OnUpdate()** function. This isn't a good idea. You should only do permanent drawing in response to the Windows **WM_PAINT** message. This means that the **OnDraw()** function in the view should be the only place that's initiating any drawing operations for document data. This ensures that the view is drawn correctly whenever Windows deems it necessary.

If you build and execute Sketcher with the new modifications included, you should find that all the views will be updated to reflect the contents of the document.

Scrolling Views

Adding scrolling to a view looks remarkably easy at first sight; the water is in fact deeper and murkier than at first it appears, but let's jump in anyway. The first step is to change the base class for **CSketcherView** from **CView** to **CScrollView**. This new base class is derived from **CView**, and has the scrolling functionality built in, so you can alter the definition of the **CSketcherView** class to:

```
class CSketcherView : public CScrollView
{
    // Class definition as before...
};
```

You must also modify two lines of code at the beginning of the **SketcherView.cpp** file which refer to the base class for **CSketcherView**. You need to replace **CView** with **CScrollView** as the base class:

```
IMPLEMENT_DYNCREATE(CSketcherView, CScrollView)

BEGIN_MESSAGE_MAP(CSketcherView, CScrollView)
```

However, this is still not quite enough. The new version of our view class needs to know some things about the area that we are drawing on, such as the size and how far the view is to be scrolled when you use the scroller. This information has to be supplied before the view is first drawn. We can put the code to do this in the **OnInitialUpdate()** function in our view class.

We supply the information that is required by calling a function inherited from the **CScrollView** class: **SetScrollSizes()**. The arguments to this function are shown in the following diagram:

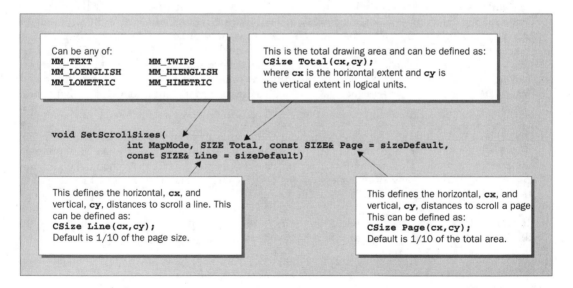

Scrolling a distance of one line occurs when you click on the up or down arrow on the scroll bar; a page scroll occurs when you click on the scrollbar itself. We have an opportunity to change the mapping mode here. **MM_LOENGLISH** would be a good choice for our application, but let's first get scrolling working in **MM_TEXT**, as there are still some difficulties to be uncovered.

To add the code to call **SetScrollSizes()**, you need to override the default version of the **OnInitialUpdate()** function in the view. Use ClassWizard to add the function to **CSketcherView** by double-clicking OnInitialUpdate in the Messages: box, and then clicking Edit Code. The version generated will call the default version in **CScrollView**. We just add our code to the function where indicated by the comment:

```
void CSketcherView::OnInitialUpdate()
{
    CScrollView::OnInitialUpdate();

    // Define document size
    CSize DocSize(20000,20000);

    // Set mapping mode and document size.
    SetScrollSizes(MM_TEXT,DocSize);
}
```

This maintains the mapping mode as **MM_TEXT** and defines the total extent that we can draw on as 20000 pixels in each direction.

This is enough to get the scrolling mechanism working. Build the program and execute it with these additions and you'll be able to draw a few elements and then scroll the view. However, although the window scrolls OK, if you try to draw more elements with the view scrolled, things don't work as they should. The elements appear in a different position from where you draw them and they're not displayed properly. What's going on?

Logical Coordinates and Client Coordinates

The problem is the coordinate systems that we're using — and that plural is deliberate. We've actually been using two coordinate systems in all our examples up to now, although you may not have noticed. As we saw in the previous chapter, when we call a function such as **LineTo()**, it assumes that the arguments passed are **logical coordinates**. The function is a member of the **CDC** class which defines a device context, and the device context has its own system of logical coordinates. The mapping mode, which is a property of the device context, determines what the unit of measurement is for the coordinates when you draw something.

The coordinate data that we receive along with the mouse messages, on the other hand, has nothing to do with the device context or the **CDC** object — and outside of a device context, logical coordinates don't apply. The points passed to our **OnLButtonDown()** and **OnMouseMove()** handlers have coordinates that are always in device units, that is, pixels, and are measured relative to the top left corner of the client area. These are referred to as **client coordinates**. Similarly, when we call **InvalidateRect()**, the rectangle is assumed to be defined in terms of client coordinates.

In **MM_TEXT** mode, the client coordinates and the logical coordinates in the device context are both in units of pixels, and so they're the same *as long as you don't scroll the window*. In all our previous examples there was no scrolling, so everything worked without any problems. With

675

the latest version, it all works fine until you scroll the view, whereupon the logical coordinates origin (the 0,0 point) is moved by the scrolling mechanism, and so it's no longer in the same place as the client coordinates origin. The *units* for logical coordinates and client coordinates are the same here, but the *origins* for the two coordinate systems are different. This situation is illustrated below:

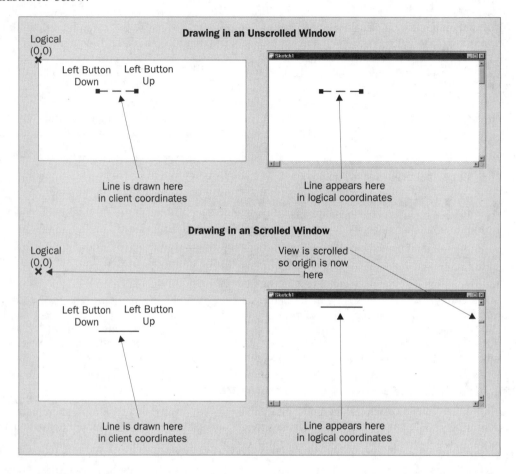

The left-hand side shows the position in the client area where you draw, and the points that are the mouse positions defining the line. These are recorded in client coordinates. The right-hand side shows where the line will actually be drawn. Drawing is in logical coordinates, but we have been using client coordinate values. In the case of the scrolled window, the line appears displaced, due to the logical origin being relocated.

This means that we are actually using the wrong values to define elements in our program, and when we invalidate areas of the client area to get them redrawn, the rectangles passed to the function are also wrong. Hence the weird behavior of our program. With other mapping modes it gets worse: not only are the units of measurement in the two coordinate systems different, but also the *y* axes may be in opposite directions!

Dealing with Client Coordinates

Let's consider what we need to do to fix the problem. There are two things we may have to address:

1 We need to convert the client coordinates that we obtained from mouse messages to logical coordinates before we can use them to create our elements.

2 We need to convert a bounding rectangle that we created in logical coordinates back to client coordinates if we want to use it in a call to **InvalidateRect()**.

This amounts to making sure we always use logical coordinates when using device context functions, and always use client coordinates for other communications about the window. The functions we will have to apply to do the conversions are associated with a device context, so we need to obtain a device context whenever we want to convert from logical to client coordinates, or vice versa. We can use the coordinate conversion functions of the **CDC** class that are inherited by **CClientDC** to do the work.

The new version of the **OnLButtonDown()** handler incorporating this will be:

```
// Handler for left mouse button down message
void CSketcherView::OnLButtonDown(UINT nFlags, CPoint point)
{
    CClientDC aDC(this);              // Create a device context
    OnPrepareDC(&aDC);                // Get origin adjusted
    aDC.DPtoLP(&point);               // convert point to Logical
    m_FirstPoint = point;             // Record the cursor position
    SetCapture();                     // Capture subsequent mouse messages
}
```

We obtain a device context for the current view by creating a **CClientDC** object and passing the pointer **this** to the constructor. The advantage of **CClientDC** is that it automatically releases the device context when the object goes out of scope. It's important that device contexts are not retained, as there are a limited number available from Windows and you could run out of them. If you use **CClientDC**, you're always safe.

As we're using **CScrollView**, the **OnPrepareDC()** member function inherited from that class must be called to set the origin for the logical coordinate system in the device context to correspond with the scrolled position. Once the origin is set by this call, the function **DPtoLP()**, which converts from **D**evice **P**oints **to** **L**ogical **P**oints, is used to convert the **point** value that's passed to the handler to logical coordinates. We then store the converted value, ready for creating an element in the **OnMouseMove()** handler.

The new code for the **OnMouseMove()** handler will be as follows:

```
void CSketcherView::OnMouseMove(UINT nFlags, CPoint point)
{
    // Define a Device Context object for the view
    CClientDC aDC(this);
    OnPrepareDC(&aDC);                // Get origin adjusted
```

677

```
        if((nFlags & MK_LBUTTON) && (this == GetCapture()))
        {
            aDC.DPtoLP(&point);           // convert point to Logical
            m_SecondPoint = point;        // Save the current cursor position

            // Rest of the function as before
        }
    }
```

The code for the conversion of the point value passed to the handler is essentially the same as in the previous handler, and that's all we need here for the moment. The last function that we must change is one that's easy to overlook: the **OnUpdate()** function in the view class. This needs to be modified to:

```
    void CSketcherView::OnUpdate(CView* pSender, LPARAM lHint, CObject* pHint)
    {
        // Invalidate the area corresponding to the element pointed to
        // if there is one, otherwise invalidate the whole client area
        if(pHint)
        {
            CClientDC aDC(this);          // Create a device context
            OnPrepareDC(&aDC);            // Get origin adjusted

            // Get the enclosing rectangle and convert to client coordinates
            CRect aRect = static_cast<CElement*>(pHint)->GetBoundRect();
            aDC.LPtoDP(aRect);
            InvalidateRect(aRect);        // Get the area redrawn
        }
        else
            InvalidateRect(0);            // Invalidate the client area
    }
```

The modification here just creates a **CClientDC** object and uses the **LPtoDP()** function member to convert the rectangle for the area that's to be redrawn to client coordinates.

You may have noticed that, in the code fragments above, the calls to **LPtoDP()** are slightly different in one interesting respect. We used **LPtoDP()** to convert a point like this:

```
    aDC.DPtoLP(&point);
```

However, we used **LPtoDP()** to convert a rectangle like this:

```
    aDC.LPtoDP(aRect);
```

In the first of these we pass the parameter by reference, and in the second we pass by value. This is explained by a difference in the **CRect** and **CPoint** classes. The definition of the **CRect** class contains a couple of member functions, **LPRECT()** and **LPCRECT()**. These are casting operators — they return a **LPRECT** or **LPCRECT** from a **CRect** object.

> *We've seen the **LP** notation before. For example, **CRect** and **CPoint** are derived from their Win32 equivalents, **RECT** and **POINT**—so if you want to get an **LPRECT** (i.e. a **RECT***), you can take the address of a **CRect**, and if you want to get an **LPPOINT** (i.e. a **POINT***), you can take the address of a **CPoint**.*

These casting operators can be invoked explicitly if you choose, or implicitly by the compiler. In this case, the statement **aDC.LPtoDP(aRect);** causes the compiler to invoke the conversion implicitly, by using **LPRECT()** to convert **aRect** from a **CRect** object into an **LPRECT**. This happens whenever you pass a **CRect** object to a function that takes an **LPRECT** argument. (In case you're wondering, the **LPCRECT()** operator casts from **CRect** to **LPCRECT**, which is a pointer to a constant **RECT** structure.)

There aren't any similar casting operators in the **CPoint** class, so we always have to remember to take the address of the object explicitly when passing a **CPoint** object as an **LPPOINT**.

If you now compile and execute Sketcher with the modifications we have discussed and are lucky enough not to have introduced any typos, it will work correctly, regardless of the scroller position.

Using MM_LOENGLISH Mapping Mode

Let's now look into what we need to do to use the **MM_LOENGLISH** mapping mode. This will provide drawings in logical units of 0.01 inches, and will also ensure that the drawing size is consistent on displays at different resolutions. This will make the application much more satisfactory from the users' point of view.

We can set the mapping mode in the call to **SetScrollSizes()**, which is made from the **OnInitialUpdate()** function in the view class. We also need to specify the total drawing area, so, if we define it as 3000 by 3000, this will provide a drawing area of 30 inches by 30 inches, which should be adequate for our needs. The default scroll distances for a line and a page will be satisfactory, so we don't need to specify those. You can use ClassView to get to the **OnInitialUpdate()** function and then change it to that shown below:

```
void CSketcherView::OnInitialUpdate()
{
    CScrollView::OnInitialUpdate();

    // Define document size as 30x30ins in MM_LOENGLISH
    CSize DocSize(3000,3000);

    // Set mapping mode and document size.
    SetScrollSizes(MM_LOENGLISH, DocSize);
}
```

We just alter the arguments in the call to **SetScrollSizes()** for the mapping mode and document the size that we want. That's all we need to enable the view to work in **MM_LOENGLISH**, but we still need to fix our dealings with rectangles.

Note that you are not limited to setting the mapping mode once and for all. You can change the mapping mode in a device context at any time and draw different parts of the image to be displayed using different mapping modes. A function **SetMapMode()** is used to do this, but we won't be going into this any further here. We'll stick to getting our application working just using **MM_LOENGLISH**. Whenever we create a **CClientDC** object for the view and call **OnPrepareDC()**, the device context that it owns will have the mapping mode that we've set for the view.

The problem we have with rectangles is that our element classes all assume **MM_TEXT**, and in **MM_LOENGLISH** these will be upside-down because of the reversal of the y axis. When we apply **LPtoDP()** to a rectangle, it is assumed to be oriented properly with respect to the **MM_LOENGLISH** axes. Because ours are not, the function will mirror our rectangles in the x axis. This creates a problem when we call **InvalidateRect()** to invalidate an area of a view, as the mirrored rectangle in device coordinates will not be recognized by Windows as being inside the visible client area.

We have two options for dealing with this. We can modify the element classes so that the enclosing rectangles are the right way up for **MM_LOENGLISH**, or we can re-normalize the rectangle that we intend to pass to the **InvalidateRect()** function. The easiest course is the latter, since we only need to modify one member of the view class, **OnUpdate()**:

```
void CSketcherView::OnUpdate(CView* pSender, LPARAM lHint, CObject* pHint)
{
    // Invalidate the area corresponding to the element pointed to
    // if there is one, otherwise invalidate the whole client area
    if(pHint)
    {
        CClientDC aDC(this);              // Create a device context
        OnPrepareDC(&aDC);                // Get origin adjusted

        // Get the enclosing rectangle and convert to client coordinates
        CRect aRect = static_cast<CElement*>(pHint)->GetBoundRect();
        aDC.LPtoDP(aRect);
        aRect.NormalizeRect();
        InvalidateRect(aRect);            // Get the area redrawn
    }
    else
        InvalidateRect(0);               // Invalidate the client area
}
```

That should do it for the program as it stands. If you rebuild Sketcher, you should have scrolling working, with support for multiple views. We'll need to remember to re-normalize any rectangle that we convert to device coordinates for use with **InvalidateRect()** in the future. Any reverse conversion will also be affected.

Deleting and Moving Shapes

Being able to delete shapes is a fundamental requirement in a drawing program. One question relating to this that we'll need to find an answer for is how you're going to select the element you want to delete. Of course, once we decide how to select an element, this will apply equally well if you want to move an element, so we can treat moving and deleting elements as related problems. But let's first consider how we're going to bring move and delete operations into the program.

A neat way of providing move and delete functions would be to have a pop-up **context menu** appear at the cursor position when you click the right mouse button. We could then put Move and Delete as items on the menu. A pop-up that works like this is a very handy facility that you can use in lots of different situations.

How should the pop-up be used? The standard way that context menus work is that the user moves the mouse over a particular object and right-clicks on it. This selects the object and pops up a menu containing a list of items which relate to actions that can be performed on that object. This means that different objects can have different menus. You can see this in action in the Visual C++ IDE itself. When you right-click on a class icon in ClassView, you get a menu that's different to the one you get if you right-click on the icon for a member function. The menu that appears is sensitive to the context of the cursor, hence the term 'context menu'. We have two contexts to consider in Sketcher. You could right click with the cursor over an element, and you could right click when there is no element under the cursor.

So, how will we implement this functionality in the Sketcher application? We can do it simply by creating two menus: one for when we have an element under the cursor, and one for when we don't. We can check whether there's an element under the cursor when the user presses the right mouse button. If there *is* an element under the cursor, we can highlight the element so that the user knows exactly which element the context pop-up is referring to.

Let's first take a look at how we can create a pop-up at the cursor and, once that works, come back to how we are going to implement the detail of the move and delete operations.

Implementing a Context Menu

The first step is to create a menu containing two pop-ups: one containing Move and Delete as items, the other a combination of the Element and Color menu items. So, change to ResourceView and expand the list of resources. Right-click on the Menu folder to bring up a context menu — another demonstration of what we are trying to create in our application. Select Insert Menu to create a new menu. This will have a default name **IDR_MENU1** assigned, but you can change this by right-clicking the new menu name and selecting Properties. You could change it to something more suitable, such as **IDR_CURSOR_MENU**, in the ID: box.

To add menu items to the menu, double-click **IDR_CURSOR_MENU**. Now create two new items on the menu bar. These can have any old caption, since they won't actually be seen by the user. They will represent the two context menus that we will provide with Sketcher, so we have named them element and no element, according to the situation in which the context menu will be used. Now you can add the Move and Delete items to the element pop-up.

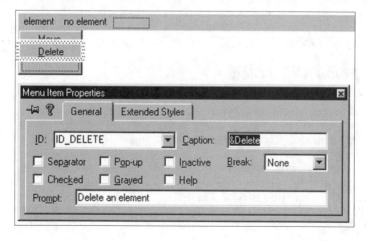

Make sure that you type sensible IDs rather than allowing the default, which is to use the junk name on the menu bar. Here, we have entered **ID_MOVE** and **ID_DELETE** as the IDs for the two items in the pop-up. The illustration shows the properties box for the Delete menu item.

The second menu contains the list of available elements and colors, separated by a Separator. The IDs used should be the same as we applied to the **IDR_SKETCHTYPE** menu: for example, **ID_ELEMENT_LINE** and **ID_COLOR_BLACK**. The handler for a menu is associated with the menu ID. Menu items with the same ID will use the same handlers, so the same handler will be used for the Line menu item regardless of whether it's invoked from the main menu pop-up or from the context menu. To insert the separator, just double click on the empty menu item so the dialog is displayed.

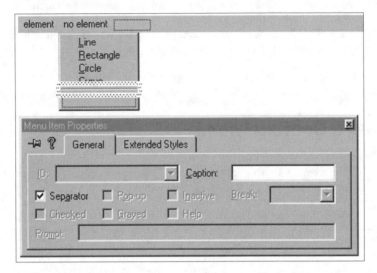

You can then click on the Separator check box and close the dialog without entering anything else.

Close the properties box and save the resource file. At the moment, all we have is the definition of the menu in a resource file. It isn't connected to the code in the Sketcher program. We now need to associate this menu and its ID, **IDR_CURSOR_MENU**, with our view class. This will enable us to create command handlers for the menu items in the pop-up corresponding to the IDs **ID_MOVE** and **ID_DELETE**.

Associating a Menu with a Class

To associate the new menu with the view class in Sketcher, you can use ClassWizard. With the cursor on the menu bar of our new menu, click the right mouse button and select ClassWizard from the pop-up. This will bring up a dialog which will ask whether you want to Create or Select a class. We want to Select an existing class, which is the default option, so just click OK. This will bring up a second dialog with a list of available classes to associate with the menu. Select CSketcherView from the Class list: and click the Select button.

Once you've done that, you'll be back to ClassWizard's standard window. Now, select ID_MOVE in the Object IDs: box, COMMAND in the Messages: box, and click the Add Function... button to create a handler for the menu item. Do the same for ID_DELETE and then close the ClassWizard dialog.

We don't have to do anything for the second context menu, as we already have handlers written for them in the document class. These will take care of the messages from the pop-up items automatically. We're now ready to write the code to allow the pop-up to be displayed.

Displaying a Pop-up at the Cursor

MFC provides a class called **CMenu** for managing and processing menus. Whenever you want to do something with a new menu, you can create a local object of this class and use its member functions to do what you want. We want to be able to display the pop-up menu when the user presses (or more specifically, releases) the right mouse button, so clearly we need to add the code to do this to the handler for **WM_RBUTTONUP** in **CSketcherView**. You can add the handler for this message using ClassWizard in the same way that you added the handlers for the other mouse messages. Just fire up ClassWizard again and select the WM_RBUTTONUP message in the Messages: box for **CSketcherView**. Then create the handler and click the Edit Code button. The code you need to add is:

```
void CSketcherView::OnRButtonUp(UINT nFlags, CPoint point)
{
    // Create the cursor menu
    CMenu aMenu;
    aMenu.LoadMenu(IDR_CURSOR_MENU);    // Load the cursor menu
    ClientToScreen(&point);             // Convert to screen coordinates

    // Display the pop-up at the cursor position
    aMenu.GetSubMenu(0)->TrackPopupMenu(TPM_LEFTALIGN|TPM_RIGHTBUTTON,
                                        point.x, point.y, this);
}
```

We don't need to keep the call to the handler in the base class **CScrollView** that ClassWizard supplied. That was there to ensure that the message would be handled in the base class, even if you didn't add code to deal with it. As we said before, the comment left by ClassWizard to indicate where you should add your code is a clue to the fact that you can omit it in this case.

The handler first creates a local **CMenu** object, **aMenu**, then uses its member function **LoadMenu()** to load the menu that we have just created. The cursor position when the user presses the right button is passed to the handler in the argument **point**, which is in client coordinates. When we display the menu, we must supply the coordinates of where the menu is to appear in **screen coordinates**. Screen coordinates are in pixels and have the top left corner of the screen as position 0,0. As in the case of client coordinates, the positive y axis is from top to bottom. The inherited function **ClientToScreen()** in **CSketcherView** does the conversion for us.

To display the menu, we call two functions. The **GetSubMenu()** member of the object **aMenu** returns a pointer to a **CMenu** object. This object contains the pop-up from the menu owned by **aMenu**, which is the **IDR_CURSOR_MENU** menu that we loaded previously. The argument to **GetSubMenu()** is an integer index specifying the pop-up, with index 0 referring to the first pop-up. The function **TrackPopupMenu()** for the **CMenu** object returned is then called. The arguments to **TrackPopupMenu()** are shown below:

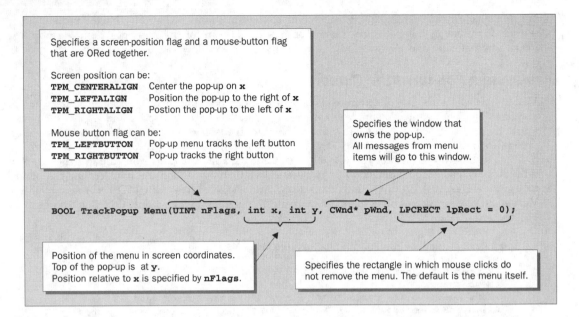

In our case, we have specified the pop-up as being associated with the right mouse button, and displayed it with the left side of the pop-up at the *x* coordinate passed to the function. The coordinates are the *x* and *y* coordinates of the cursor position specified by the **point** object after conversion to screen coordinates. The **this** pointer is used to specify the current view as the owning window.

We don't specify the fifth argument, so it defaults to 0. The rectangle is, therefore, the pop-up itself, so, if you click outside the pop-up, it will close the menu without selecting an item or causing a message to be sent to the view. Of course, if you click on a menu item, it will still close, but will also cause a message to be sent corresponding to the item clicked.

Choosing a Context Menu

At the moment, the **OnRButtonUp()** handler will only display the first context pop-up, no matter where the right button is clicked in the view. This isn't really what we want it to do. The first context menu applies specifically to an element, whereas the second context menu applies in general. We want to display the first menu if there is an element under the cursor, and to display the second menu if there isn't.

We need two things to fix this up. First, we need a mechanism to find out which (if any) element is at the current cursor position, and second, we need to save the address of this element somewhere so we can use it in the **OnRButtonUp()** handler. Let's deal with saving the address of the element first, as this is the easier bit.

When we find out which element is under the cursor, we'll store its address in a data member, **m_pSelected**, of the view class. This will be available to the right mouse button handler, since that's in the same class. You can add the declaration for this variable to the **protected** section of the **CSketcherView** class:

```
class CSketcherView: public CScrollView
{
// Rest of the class as before...

protected:
   CPoint m_FirstPoint;          // First point recorded for an element
   CPoint m_SecondPoint;         // Second point recorded for an element
   CElement* m_pTempElement;     // Pointer to temporary element
   CElement* m_pSelected;        // Currently selected element

// Rest of the class as before...
};
```

Alternatively, you can right-click on the class name and select Add Member Variable... from the pop-up to open the dialog for adding a data member. It is, however, usually a good idea to go back and add some comments.

You also need to initialize this element in the class constructor, so add the code shown below:

```
CSketcherView::CSketcherView()
{
   // TODO: add construction code here
   m_FirstPoint = CPoint(0,0);     // Set 1st recorded point to 0,0
   m_SecondPoint = CPoint(0,0);    // Set 2nd recorded point to 0,0
   m_pTempElement = NULL;          // Set temporary element pointer to 0
   m_pSelected = NULL;             // No element selected initially
}
```

We'll figure out how to decide when an element is under the cursor in a moment, but in the meantime we can use the **m_pSelected** member of the view in the implementation of the **OnRButtonUp()** handler:

```
void CSketcherView::OnRButtonUp(UINT nFlags, CPoint point)
{
// Find the element under the cursor
   m_pSelected = SelectElement(point);

   // Create the cursor menu
   CMenu aMenu;
   aMenu.LoadMenu(IDR_CURSOR_MENU);     // Load the cursor menu
   ClientToScreen(&point);              // Convert to screen coordinates

   // Display the pop-up at the cursor position
   if(m_pSelected)
      aMenu.GetSubMenu(0)->TrackPopupMenu(TPM_LEFTALIGN|TPM_RIGHTBUTTON,
                                          point.x, point.y, this);
   else
      aMenu.GetSubMenu(1)->TrackPopupMenu(TPM_LEFTALIGN|TPM_RIGHTBUTTON,
                                          point.x, point.y, this);
}
```

To get things going, we first store the address of the element at the cursor position (if there is one) by calling the function **SelectElement()**, which accepts a **CPoint** object as an argument to indicate the current cursor position, and returns a pointer to the element at that position, or **NULL** if there isn't one. We'll implement this function in a moment. We will also come back a little later to consider whether this is the best place to find an element at the cursor, bearing in mind that you really can't be sure whether an element will be selected or not when you click the right mouse button.

We have used the data member **m_pSelected** to choose which context menu to display. If the address stored is not **NULL** we'll display the first context menu with the <u>M</u>ove and <u>D</u>elete menu items. If **m_pSelected** is **NULL**, there's no element under the cursor, and so we display the second context menu with the color and element type choices.

Identifying a Selected Element

To find which element is selected, we need to implement the function **SelectElement()** to examine the elements in the document to see whether any of them are at the cursor position. We can add a function member to the view class called **SelectElement()**, which will have a **CPoint** object as a parameter containing the current cursor position in client coordinates.

A simple method we can use to decide whether a particular element is at the cursor position is to see if the current cursor position is inside the bounding rectangle for the element. We can use the functions that we added to the document class to iterate through the list of elements. As we retrieve the pointer to each element in turn, we can check whether the current cursor position is within the bounding rectangle for the element.

First, add the declaration of **SelectElement()** to the **protected** section of **CSketcherView** as follows:

```
// Operations
public:

protected:
   CElement* CreateElement();                  // Create a new element on the heap
   CElement* SelectElement(CPoint aPoint);     // Select an element
```

There's no reason for the function to be **public** since it's only used internally. You can add the implementation of the function to **SketcherView.cpp**, like this:

```
// Find the element at the cursor
CElement* CSketcherView::SelectElement(CPoint aPoint)
{
   // Convert parameter aPoint to logical coordinates
   CClientDC aDC(this);
   OnPrepareDC(&aDC);
   aDC.DPtoLP(&aPoint);

   CSketcherDoc* pDoc=GetDocument();           // Get a pointer to the document
   CElement* pElement = 0;                      // Store an element pointer
   CRect aRect(0,0,0,0);                        // Store a rectangle
   POSITION aPos = pDoc->GetListTailPosition(); // Get last element position

   while(aPos)                                  // Iterate through the list
   {
      pElement = pDoc->GetPrev(aPos);
      aRect = pElement->GetBoundRect();
      // Select the first element that appears under the cursor
```

```
        if(aRect.PtInRect(aPoint))
          return pElement;
    }
    return 0;                                  // No element found
}
```

We first get a device context so that we can convert the parameter **aPoint** from client coordinates to logical coordinates, since all our element data is stored in logical coordinates. We then store a pointer to the document in **pDoc**, which we can use to call the document functions to retrieve elements. We declare local variables, **pElement** and **aRect**, which we will use to store an element pointer and the bounding rectangle for an element, respectively.

To find the element at the cursor we iterate through the list backwards, so we'll search from the most recently added element to the oldest. We get the **POSITION** value corresponding to the last element in the list by calling the function **GetListTailPosition()**, and store this value in **aPos**. We use this to run through the elements in the list by calling the function **GetPrev()** for the document. For each position value, we check whether the bounding rectangle for the corresponding element encloses the current cursor position that was passed in the parameter **aPoint**.

We determine whether **aPoint** is within the rectangle bounding an element in the **if** statement using the **PtInRect()** member of the **CRect** class. This function requires the rectangle to be normalized, which, of course, all ours are because we created them to be so. The function returns **TRUE** if the **CPoint** value passed as an argument is within the **aRect** object, and **FALSE** otherwise. As soon as we find a rectangle that encloses **aPoint**, we exit the function, returning the pointer to the corresponding element. If we manage to walk through the entire list without finding an element, which occurs when the cursor is not over an element, we return 0.

For **SelectElement()** to compile, we must add the **GetListTailPosition()** and **GetPrev()** functions to the document class. These are very similar to the **GetListHeadPosition()** and **GetNext()** functions we already have in **CSketcherDoc**. You can add the code for these to the class definition as follows:

```
    POSITION GetListTailPosition() const     // Return list tail POSITION value
    { return m_ElementList.GetTailPosition(); }

    CElement* GetPrev(POSITION& aPos) const  // Return current element pointer
    { return m_ElementList.GetPrev(aPos); }
```

The code is now in a state where we can test the context menus.

Exercising the Pop-ups

We have added all the code we need to make the pop-ups operate, so you can build and execute Sketcher to try it out. If there are no elements under the cursor, the second context pop-up appears, allowing you to change the element type and color. These options work because they generate exactly the same messages as the main menu options and because we have already written handlers for them.

If there is an element under the cursor, the first context menu will appear with Move and Delete on it. It won't do anything at the moment, as we've yet to handle the messages it generates. Try right button clicks outside of the view window. Messages for these are not passed to the document view window in our application, so the pop-up is not displayed.

687

Note that the context menu to select elements and colors isn't quite right — the check marks are not set properly. The document class handles the messages from the menu, but the **UPDATE_COMMAND_UI** messages don't apply to the context menu — they only work with the **IDR_SKETCHTYPE** menu. How do we fix that?

Checking the Context Menu Items

The **CMenu** class has a function designed to do exactly what we want. Its prototype is:

```
UINT CheckMenuItem(UINT nIDCheckItem, UINT nCheck);
```

This function will check or uncheck any item in the context menu. The first parameter selects which entry in the context pop-up is to be checked or unchecked; the second parameter is a combination of two flags, one of which determines how the first parameter specifies which item is to be checked, and the other specifies whether the menu item is to be checked or unchecked. Because each flag is a single bit in a **UINT** value, you combine the two using the bitwise OR.

The flag to determine how the item is identified can be one of two possible values:

MF_BYPOSITION   The first parameter is an index where 0 specifies the first item, 1 the second, and so on.

MF_BYCOMMAND   The first parameter is a menu ID.

We will use **MF_BYCOMMAND**, so we don't have to worry about the sequence in which the menu items appear in the pop-up, or even in which sub-menu they appear.

The possible flag values to check or uncheck an item are **MF_CHECKED** and **MF_UNCHECKED**, respectively.

The code for checking or unchecking a menu item will be essentially the same for all the menu items in the second context pop-up. Let's see how we can set the check for the menu item Black correctly. The first argument to the **CheckMenuItem()** function will be the menu ID, **ID_COLOR_BLACK**. The second argument will be **MF_BYCOMMAND** combined with either **MF_CHECKED** or **MF_UNCHECKED**, depending on the current color selected. We can obtain the current color from the document using the **GetElementColor()** function, with the following statement:

```
COLORREF Color = GetDocument()->GetElementColor();
```

We can use the **Color** variable to select the appropriate flag using the conditional operator, and then combine the result with the **MF_BYCOMMAND** flag to obtain the second argument to the **CheckMenuItem()** function, so the statement to set the check for the item will be:

```
aMenu.CheckMenuItem(ID_COLOR_BLACK,
                (BLACK==Color?MF_CHECKED:MF_UNCHECKED)|MF_BYCOMMAND);
```

We don't need to specify the sub-menu here, since the menu item is uniquely defined in the menu by its ID. You just need to change the ID and the color value in this statement to obtain the statement to set the flags for each of the other color menu items.

Checking the element menu items is essentially the same. To check the <u>L</u>ine menu item we can write:

```
WORD ElementType = GetDocument()->GetElementType();
aMenu.CheckMenuItem(ID_ELEMENT_LINE,
               (LINE==ElementType?MF_CHECKED:MF_UNCHECKED)|MF_BYCOMMAND);
```

The complete code for the **OnRButtonUp()** handler will therefore be:

```
void CSketcherView::OnRButtonUp(UINT nFlags, CPoint point)
{
// Find the element under the cursor
   m_pSelected = SelectElement(point);

   // Create the cursor menu
   CMenu aMenu;
   aMenu.LoadMenu(IDR_CURSOR_MENU);        // Load the cursor menu
   ClientToScreen(&point);                 // Convert to screen coordinates

   // Display the pop-up at the cursor position
   if(m_pSelected)
     aMenu.GetSubMenu(0)->TrackPopupMenu(TPM_LEFTALIGN|TPM_RIGHTBUTTON,
                                              point.x, point.y, this);
   else
   {
      // Check color menu items
      COLORREF Color = GetDocument()->GetElementColor();
      aMenu.CheckMenuItem(ID_COLOR_BLACK,
                  (BLACK==Color?MF_CHECKED:MF_UNCHECKED)|MF_BYCOMMAND);
      aMenu.CheckMenuItem(ID_COLOR_RED,
                    (RED==Color?MF_CHECKED:MF_UNCHECKED)|MF_BYCOMMAND);
      aMenu.CheckMenuItem(ID_COLOR_GREEN,
                  (GREEN==Color?MF_CHECKED:MF_UNCHECKED)|MF_BYCOMMAND);
      aMenu.CheckMenuItem(ID_COLOR_BLUE,
                  (BLUE==Color?MF_CHECKED:MF_UNCHECKED)|MF_BYCOMMAND);

      // Check element menu items
      WORD ElementType = GetDocument()->GetElementType();
      aMenu.CheckMenuItem(ID_ELEMENT_LINE,
              (LINE==ElementType?MF_CHECKED:MF_UNCHECKED)|MF_BYCOMMAND);
      aMenu.CheckMenuItem(ID_ELEMENT_RECTANGLE,
          (RECTANGLE==ElementType?MF_CHECKED:MF_UNCHECKED)|MF_BYCOMMAND);
      aMenu.CheckMenuItem(ID_ELEMENT_CIRCLE,
            (CIRCLE==ElementType?MF_CHECKED:MF_UNCHECKED)|MF_BYCOMMAND);
      aMenu.CheckMenuItem(ID_ELEMENT_CURVE,
             (CURVE==ElementType?MF_CHECKED:MF_UNCHECKED)|MF_BYCOMMAND);

      // Display the context pop-up
      aMenu.GetSubMenu(1)->TrackPopupMenu(TPM_LEFTALIGN|TPM_RIGHTBUTTON,
                                             point.x, point.y, this);

   }
}
```

Highlighting Elements

Ideally, the user will want to know which element is under the cursor *before* they right-click to get the context menu. When you want to delete an element, you want to know which element you are operating on. Equally, when you want to use the other context menu — to change color, for example — you need to be sure that no element is under the cursor. To show precisely which element is under the cursor, we need to highlight it in some way before a right button click occurs.

We can do this in the **Draw()** member function for an element. All we need to do is pass an argument to the **Draw()** function to indicate when the element should be highlighted. If we pass the address of the currently-selected element that we save in the **m_pSelected** member of the view to the **Draw()** function, then we can compare it to the **this** pointer to see if it is the current element.

Highlights will all work in the same way, so we'll take the **CLine** member as an example. You can add similar code to each of the classes for the other element types. Before we start changing **CLine**, we must first amend the definition of the base class **CElement**:

```
class CElement : public CObject
{
protected:
   COLORREF m_Color;                        // Color of an element
   CRect m_EnclosingRect;                   // Rectangle enclosing an element
   int m_Pen;                               // Pen width

public:
   virtual ~CElement(){}                    // Virtual destructor

   // Virtual draw operation
   virtual void Draw(CDC* pDC, const CElement* pElement = 0) const {}
   CRect GetBoundRect() const;              // Get the bounding rectangle for an
                                            //element

protected:
   CElement(){}                             // Default constructor
};
```

The change is to add a second parameter to the virtual **Draw()** function. This is a pointer to an element. The reason for initializing the second parameter to zero is to allow the use of the function with just one argument; the second will be supplied as 0 by default.

You need to modify the declaration of the **Draw()** function in each of the classes derived from **CElement** (that's **CLine**, **CRectangle**, **CCircle** and **CCurve**) in exactly the same way. For example, you should change the **CLine** class definition to:

```
class CLine : public CElement
{
public:
   // Function to display a line
   virtual void Draw(CDC* pDC, const CElement* pElement = 0) const;

   // Constructor for a line object
   CLine(const CPoint& Start, const CPoint& End, const COLORREF& Color);
```

```
protected:
   CPoint m_StartPoint;          // Start point of line
   CPoint m_EndPoint;            // End point of line

   CLine(){}                     // Default constructor - should not be used
};
```

The implementations for each of the **Draw()** functions for the classes derived from **CElement** all need to be extended in the same way. The function for the **CLine** class will be:

```
void CLine::Draw(CDC* pDC, const CElement* pElement) const
{
   // Create a pen for this object and
   // initialize it to the object color and line width
   CPen aPen;
   COLORREF aColor = m_Color;                 // Initialize with element color
   if (this == pElement)                      // This element selected?
      aColor = SELECT_COLOR;                  // Set highlight color
   if (!aPen.CreatePen(PS_SOLID, m_Pen, aColor))
   {
      // Pen creation failed. Abort the program
      AfxMessageBox("Pen creation failed drawing a line", MB_OK);
      AfxAbort();
   }

   CPen* pOldPen = pDC->SelectObject(&aPen); // Select the pen

   // Now draw the line
   pDC->MoveTo(m_StartPoint);
   pDC->LineTo(m_EndPoint);

   pDC->SelectObject(pOldPen);                // Restore the old pen
}
```

This is a very simple change. We set the new local variable **aColor** to the current color stored in **m_Color**, and the **if** statement will reset the value of **aColor** to **SELECT_COLOR** when **pElement** is equal to **this** — which will be the case when the current element and the selected element are the same. You also need to add the definition for **SELECT_COLOR** to the **OurConstants.h** file:

```
// Element type definitions
// Each type value must be unique
const WORD LINE = 101U;
const WORD RECTANGLE = 102U;
const WORD CIRCLE = 103U;
const WORD CURVE = 104U;
////////////////////////////////////

// Color values for drawing
const COLORREF BLACK = RGB(0,0,0);
const COLORREF RED = RGB(255,0,0);
const COLORREF GREEN = RGB(0,255,0);
const COLORREF BLUE = RGB(0,0,255);
const COLORREF SELECT_COLOR = RGB(255,0,180);
////////////////////////////////////
```

We have nearly implemented the highlighting. The derived classes of the **CElement** class are now able to draw themselves as selected — we just need a mechanism to cause an element to *be* selected. So where should we do this? As we said, ideally, we want to have the element under the cursor always highlighted by default. We need to find a handler in the view that can take care of this all the time.

Is there a handler that always knows where the cursor is? **OnMouseMove()** would seem to fit the bill, since it will be called automatically whenever the cursor moves. We can put code in here to ensure that if there is an element under the cursor, it will always be highlighted. The amendments to this function are indicated below:

```
void CSketcherView::OnMouseMove(UINT nFlags, CPoint point)
{

// Rest of the function as before

        // Create a temporary element of the type and color that
        // is recorded in the document object, and draw it
        m_pTempElement = CreateElement();  // Create a new element
        m_pTempElement->Draw(&aDC);        // Draw the element
    }
    else        // We are not drawing an element...
    {           // ...so do highlighting
      CRect aRect;
      CElement* pCurrentSelection = SelectElement(point);

      if(pCurrentSelection!=m_pSelected)
      {
        if(m_pSelected)                // Old elemented selected?
        {                              // Yes, so draw it unselected
          aRect = m_pSelected->GetBoundRect(); // Get bounding rectangle
          aDC.LPtoDP(aRect);                    // Conv to device coords
          aRect.NormalizeRect();                // Normalize
          InvalidateRect(aRect, FALSE);         // Invalidate area
        }
        m_pSelected = pCurrentSelection;       // Save elem under cursor
        if(m_pSelected)                        // Is there one?
        {                                      // Yes, so get it redrawn
          aRect = m_pSelected->GetBoundRect(); // Get bounding rectangle
          aDC.LPtoDP(aRect);                    // Conv to device coords
          aRect.NormalizeRect();                // Normalize
          InvalidateRect(aRect, FALSE);         // Invalidate area
        }
      }
    }
  }
}
```

We only want to deal with highlighting elements when we aren't in the process of creating a new element. All the highlighting code can thus be added in an **else** clause for the main **if**. It starts by calling **SelectElement()** with the current cursor position as the argument, and stores the result in a local variable, **pCurrentSelection**. The remaining code is then only executed if the element under the cursor is different from the one that was there last time this function was called; there's no point changing the highlighting if the cursor has only moved within an element.

The remaining code does two things. If there is an element already highlighted, it invalidates the area it occupies to get it redrawn. Having done that, it stores the element now under the cursor in **m_pSelected** and (provided that there *is* an element) invalidates the bounding rectangle to get it redrawn. Notice how the calls to **InvalidateRect()** in this function are given a second parameter, **FALSE**. This parameter is optional and specifies that when we update the rectangle, we don't want to update the background as well. This is safe here because nothing is ever moved in this function, and will mean less flicker and faster update times — try omitting **FALSE** and you'll see what I mean.

Since we now do the highlighting here, you can delete the following lines from the **OnRButtonUp()** handler:

```
// Find the element under the cursor
   m_pSelected = SelectElement(point);
```

Drawing Highlighted Elements

We still need to arrange that the highlighted element is actually drawn highlighted. Somewhere, the **m_pSelected** pointer must be passed to the draw function for each element. The only place to do this is in the **OnDraw()** function in the view:

```
void CSketcherView::OnDraw(CDC* pDC)
{
   CSketcherDoc* pDoc = GetDocument();
   ASSERT_VALID(pDoc);

   POSITION aPos = pDoc->GetListHeadPosition();
   CElement* pElement = 0;                      // Store for an element pointer
   while(aPos)                                  // Loop while aPos is not null
   {
      pElement = pDoc->GetNext(aPos);           // Get the current element pointer
      // If the element is visible...
      if(pDC->RectVisible(pElement->GetBoundRect()))
         pElement->Draw(pDC, m_pSelected);      // ...draw it
   }
}
```

We only need to change one line. The **Draw()** function for an element has the second argument added to communicate the address of the element to be highlighted.

Exercising the Highlights

This is all that's required for the highlighting to work all the time. You can build and execute Sketcher to try it out. Any time there is an element under the cursor, the element is drawn in magenta. This makes it obvious which element the context menu is going to act on before you right click the mouse, and means that you know in advance which context menu will be displayed.

Servicing the Menu Messages

The next step is to provide handlers for the <u>M</u>ove and <u>D</u>elete menu items by adding some code to the skeleton functions we created back when we designed the pop-up menus. We'll add the code for <u>D</u>elete first, as that's the simpler of the two.

Deleting an Element

The code that you need to delete a selected element is very simple:

```
void CSketcherView::OnDelete()
{
    if(m_pSelected)
    {
        CSketcherDoc* pDoc = GetDocument();      // Get the document pointer
        pDoc->DeleteElement(m_pSelected);        // Delete the element
        pDoc->UpdateAllViews(0);                 // Redraw all the views
        m_pSelected = 0;                         // Reset selected element ptr
    }
}
```

The code to delete an element is only executed if **m_pSelected** contains a valid address, indicating that there is an element to be deleted. We get a pointer to the document and call the function **DeleteElement()** for the document object; we'll add this member to the **CSketcherDoc** class in a moment. When the element has been removed from the document, we call **UpdateAllViews()** to get all the views redrawn without the deleted element. Finally, we set **m_pSelected** to zero to indicate that there isn't an element selected.

You should add a declaration for **DeleteElement()** as a **public** member of the **CSketcherDoc** class:

```
void DeleteElement(CElement* pElement);        // Delete an element
```

It accepts a pointer to the element to be deleted as an argument and returns nothing. You can implement it as:

```
void CSketcherDoc::DeleteElement(CElement* pElement)
{
    if(pElement)
    {
        // If the element pointer is valid,
        // find the pointer in the list and delete it
        POSITION aPosition = m_ElementList.Find(pElement);
        m_ElementList.RemoveAt(aPosition);
        delete pElement;                         // Delete the element from the heap
    }
}
```

You shouldn't have any trouble with this. After making sure that we have a non-null pointer, we find the **POSITION** value for the pointer in the list using the **Find()** member of the list object. We use this with the **RemoveAt()** member to delete the pointer from the list, then we delete the element pointed to by the parameter **pElement** from the heap.

That's all we need to delete elements. You should now have a Sketcher program in which you can draw in multiple scrolled views, and delete any of the elements in your sketch from any of the views.

Moving an Element

Moving the selected element is a bit more involved. As the element must move along with the mouse cursor, we must add code to the **OnMouseMove()** method to account for this behavior. As this function is also used to draw elements, we need a mechanism for indicating when we're in 'move' mode. The easiest way to do this is to have a flag in the view class, which we can call **m_MoveMode**. If we make it of type **BOOL**, we can use the value **TRUE** for when move mode is on, and **FALSE** for when it's off.

We'll also need to keep track of the cursor during the move, so we need another data member in the view for this. We can call it **m_CursorPos**, and it will be of type **CPoint**. Another thing we should provide for is the possibility of aborting a move. To do this we must remember the first position of the cursor, so we can move the element back. This will be another member of type **CPoint**, and we can call it **m_FirstPos**. Add the three new members to the **protected** section of the view class:

```
class CSketcherView: public CScrollView
{
// Rest of the class as before...

// Attributes
public:
   CSketcherDoc* GetDocument();

protected:
   CPoint m_FirstPoint;       // First point recorded for an element
   CPoint m_SecondPoint;      // Second point recorded for an element
   CElement* m_pTempElement;  // Pointer to temporary element
   CElement* m_pSelected;     // Currently selected element
   BOOL m_MoveMode;           // Move element flag
   CPoint m_CursorPos;        // Cursor position
   CPoint m_FirstPos;         // Original position in a move

// Rest of the class as before...
};
```

We need to initialize these in the constructor for **CSketcherView** by adding the following statements:

```
CSketcherView::CSketcherView()
{
   // TODO: add construction code here
   m_FirstPoint = CPoint(0,0);    // Set 1st recorded point to 0,0
   m_SecondPoint = CPoint(0,0);   // Set 2nd recorded point to 0,0
   m_pTempElement = NULL;         // Set temporary element pointer to 0
   m_pSelected = NULL;            // No element selected initially
   m_MoveMode = FALSE;            // Set move mode off
   m_CursorPos = CPoint(0,0);     // Initialize as zero
   m_FirstPos = CPoint(0,0);      // Initialize as zero
}
```

The element move process starts when the <u>M</u>ove menu item from the context menu is selected. Now we can add the code to the message handler for the <u>M</u>ove menu item to set up the conditions necessary for the operation:

```
void CSketcherView::OnMove()
{
    CClientDC aDC(this);
    OnPrepareDC(&aDC);                  // Set up the device context
    GetCursorPos(&m_CursorPos);         // Get cursor position in screen coords
    ScreenToClient(&m_CursorPos);       // Convert to client coords
    aDC.DPtoLP(&m_CursorPos);           // Convert to logical
    m_FirstPos = m_CursorPos;           // Remember first position
    m_MoveMode = TRUE;                  // Start move mode
}
```

We are doing four things in this handler:

1 Getting the coordinate of the current position of the cursor, since the move operation starts from this reference point.

2 Converting the cursor position to logical coordinates, because our elements are defined in logical coordinates.

3 Remembering the initial cursor position in case the user wants to abort the move later.

4 Setting the move mode on, as a flag for the **OnMouseMove()** handler to recognize.

The **GetCursorPos()** function is a Windows API function that will store the current cursor position in **m_CursorPos**. Note that we pass a pointer to this function. The cursor position will be in screen coordinates — that is, coordinates relative to the top left hand corner of the screen. All operations with the cursor are in screen coordinates. We need the position in logical coordinates, so we must do the conversion in two steps. The **ScreentoClient()** function (which is an inherited member of the view class) converts from screen to client coordinates, and then we apply the **DPtoLP()** function member of the **aDC** object to the result in order to convert to logical coordinates.

After saving the initial cursor position in **m_FirstPos**, we set **m_MoveMode** to **TRUE** so that the **OnMouseMove()** handler can deal with moving the element.

Now we have set the move mode flag, it's time to update the mouse move message handler to deal with moving an element.

Modifying the WM_MOUSEMOVE Handler

Moving an element only occurs when move mode is on and the cursor is being moved. Therefore, all we need to do in **OnMouseMove()** is to add code to handle moving an element in a block which only gets executed when **m_MoveMode** is **TRUE**. The new code to do this is as follows:

```
void CSketcherView::OnMouseMove(UINT nFlags, CPoint point)
{
   // Define a Device Context object for the view
   CClientDC aDC(this);
   OnPrepareDC(&aDC);              // Get origin adjusted

   // If we are in move mode, move the selected element and return
   if(m_MoveMode)
   {
      aDC.DPtoLP(&point);          // Convert to logical coordinatess
      MoveElement(aDC, point);     // Move the element
      return;
   }

   // Rest of the mouse move handler as before...
}
```

This addition doesn't need much explaining really, does it? The **if** verifies that we're in move mode and then calls a function **MoveElement()**, which does what is necessary for the move. All we need to do now is to implement this function.

Add the declaration for **MoveElement()** as a **protected** member of the **CSketcherView** class by adding the following at the appropriate point in the class definition:

```
void MoveElement(CClientDC& aDC, const CPoint& point);  // Move an element
```

As always, you can also right-click on the class name in ClassView to do this if you want to. The function will need access to the object owning a device context for the view, **aDC**, and the current cursor position, **point**, so both of these are reference parameters. The implementation of the function in the **.cpp** file will be:

```
void CSketcherView::MoveElement(CClientDC& aDC, const CPoint& point)
{
   CSize Distance = point - m_CursorPos;   // Get move distance
   m_CursorPos = point;          // Set current point as 1st for next time

   // If there is an element selected, move it
   if(m_pSelected)
   {
      aDC.SetROP2(R2_NOTXORPEN);
      m_pSelected->Draw(&aDC,m_pSelected); // Draw the element to erase it
      m_pSelected->Move(Distance);         // Now move the element
      m_pSelected->Draw(&aDC,m_pSelected); // Draw the moved element
   }
}
```

The distance to move the element currently selected is stored locally as a **CSize** object, **Distance**. The **CSize** class is specifically designed to represent a relative coordinate position and has two public data members, **cx** and **cy**, which correspond to the x and y increments. These are calculated as the difference between the current cursor position, stored in **point**, and the previous cursor position saved in **m_CursorPos**. This uses the – operator, which is overloaded in the **CPoint** class. The version we are using here returns a **CSize** object, but there is also a version which returns a **CPoint** object. You can usually operate on **CSize** and **CPoint** objects combined. We save the current cursor position in **m_CursorPos** for use the next time this function is called, which will occur if there is a further mouse move message during the current move operation.

Moving an element in the view is going to be implemented using the **R2_NOTXORPEN** drawing mode, because it's easy and fast. This is exactly the same as what we've been using during the creation of an element. We redraw the selected element in its current color (the selected color) to reset it to the background color, and then call the function **Move()** to relocate the element by the distance specified by **Distance**. We'll add this function to the element classes in a moment. When the element has moved itself, we simply use the **Draw()** function once more to display it highlighted at the new position. The color of the element will revert to normal when the move operation ends, as the **OnLButtonUp()** handler will redraw all the windows normally by calling **UpdateAllViews()**.

Getting the Elements to Move Themselves

We need to add the **Move()** function as a virtual member of the base class, **CElement**. Modify the class definition to:

```
class CElement : public CObject
{
protected:
    COLORREF m_Color;                          // Color of an element
    CRect m_EnclosingRect;                     // Rectangle enclosing an element
    int m_Pen;                                 // Pen width

public:
    virtual ~CElement(){}                      // Virtual destructor

    // Virtual draw operation
    virtual void Draw(CDC* pDC, const CElement* pElement = 0) const {}
    virtual void Move(const CSize& Size) {}    // Move an element
    CRect GetBoundRect() const;                // Get the bounding rectangle for an element

protected:
    CElement(){}                               // Default constructor
};
```

As we discussed before in relation to the **Draw()** member, although an implementation of the **Move()** function here has no meaning, we can't make it a pure virtual function because of the requirements of serialization.

We need to add a declaration for the **Move()** function as a **public** member of each of the four classes derived from **CElement**. It will be the same in each:

```
virtual void Move(const CSize& aSize);         // Function to move an element
```

Now we can look at how we implement the **Move()** function in the **CLine** class:

```
void CLine::Move(const CSize& aSize)
{
    m_StartPoint += aSize;                     // Move the start point
    m_EndPoint += aSize;                       // and the end point
    m_EnclosingRect += aSize;                  // Move the enclosing rectangle
}
```

This is very easy because of the overloaded **+=** operators in the **CPoint** and **CRect** classes. They all work with **CSize** objects, so we just add the relative distance specified by **aSize** to the start and end points for the line, and to the enclosing rectangle.

Moving a **CRectangle** object is even easier:

```
void CRectangle::Move(const CSize& aSize)
{
    m_EnclosingRect+= aSize;            // Move the rectangle
}
```

Because the rectangle is defined by the **m_EnclosingRect** member, that's all we need to move it.

The **Move()** member of **CCircle** is identical:

```
void CCircle::Move(const CSize& aSize)
{
    m_EnclosingRect+= aSize;            // Move rectangle defining the circle
}
```

Moving a **CCurve** object is a little more complicated because it's defined by an arbitrary number of points. You can implement the function as follows:

```
void CCurve::Move(const CSize& aSize)
{
    m_EnclosingRect += aSize;          // Move the rectangle

    // Get the 1st element position
    POSITION aPosition = m_PointList.GetHeadPosition();

    while(aPosition)
       m_PointList.GetNext(aPosition) += aSize; // Move each pt in the list
}
```

There's still not a lot to it. We first move the enclosing rectangle stored in **m_EnclosingRect**, using the overloaded **+=** operator for **CRect** objects. We then iterate through all the points defining the curve, moving each one in turn with the overloaded **+=** operator in **CPoint**.

Dropping the Element

All that remains now is to drop the element into position once the user has finished moving it, or to abort the whole move. To drop the element in its new position, the user will click the left mouse button, so we'll manage this operation in the **OnLButtonDown()** handler. To abort the operation, the user will click the right mouse button — so we can add a handler for **OnRButtonDown()** to deal with this.

Let's deal with the left mouse button first. We need to provide for this as a special action when move mode is on. The changes are highlighted below:

```
void CSketcherView::OnLButtonDown(UINT nFlags, CPoint point)
{
    CClientDC aDC(this);               // Create a device context
    OnPrepareDC(&aDC);                 // Get origin adjusted
    aDC.DPtoLP(&point);                // convert point to Logical
```

```
        if(m_MoveMode)
        {
            // In moving mode, so drop the element
            m_MoveMode = FALSE;                  // Kill move mode
            m_pSelected = 0;                     // De-select the element
            GetDocument()->UpdateAllViews(0);    // Redraw all the views
        }
        else
        {
            m_FirstPoint = point;                // Record the cursor position
            SetCapture();                        // Capture subsequent mouse messages
        }
    }
```

The code is pretty simple. We must first make sure that we're in move mode. If this is the case, we just set the move mode flag back to **FALSE** and then de-select the element. This is all that's required because we've been tracking the element with the mouse, so it's already in the right place. Finally, to tidy up all the views of the document, we call the document's **UpdateAllViews()** function, causing all the views to be redrawn.

Add a handler for the **WM_RBUTTONDOWN** message to **CSketcherView** using ClassWizard. The implementation for this must do two things: move the element back to where it was, and then turn off move mode. The code to do this is:

```
void CSketcherView::OnRButtonDown(UINT nFlags, CPoint point)
{
    if(m_MoveMode)
    {
        // In moving mode, so drop element back in original position
        CClientDC aDC(this);
        OnPrepareDC(&aDC);                       // Get origin adjusted
        MoveElement(aDC, m_FirstPos);            // Move element to orig position
        m_MoveMode = FALSE;                      // Kill move mode
        m_pSelected = 0;                         // De-select element
        GetDocument()->UpdateAllViews(0);        // Redraw all the views
        return;                                  // We are done
    }
}
```

We first create a **CClientDC** object for use in the **MoveElement()** function. We then call the **MoveElement()** function to move the currently selected element the distance from the current cursor position to the original cursor position that we saved in **m_FirstPos**. Once the element has been repositioned, we just turn off move mode, deselect the element, and get all the views redrawn.

Exercising the Application

Everything is now complete for the context pop-ups to work. If you build Sketcher, you can select the element type and color from one context menu, or if your cursor is over an element, then you can move or delete that element from the other context menu.

Dealing with Masked Elements

There's still a limitation that you might want to get over. If the element you want to move or delete is enclosed by the rectangle of another element that is drawn after the element you want, you won't be able to highlight it because the `SelectElement()` function will always find the outer element first. The outer element completely masks the element it encloses. This is a result of the sequence of elements in the list. You could fix this by adding a Send to Back item to the context menu that would move an element to the beginning of the list.

Add a separator and a menu item to the element drop down in the **IDR_CURSOR_MENU** resource as shown.

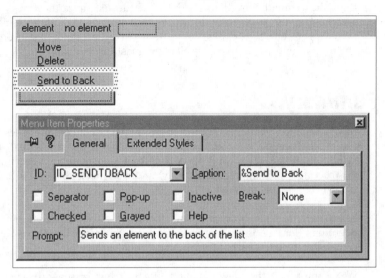

Once you've assigned a suitable ID, close the properties dialog and double click on the new menu item while holding down the *Ctrl* key. You can then add a handler for the item to the view class. We need to handle it in the view because that's where we record the selected element. We can implement the handler as:

```
void CSketcherView::OnSendtoback()
{
    GetDocument()->SendToBack(m_pSelected);        // Move element in list
}
```

We're going to get the document to do the work by passing the currently selected element pointer to a function **SendToBack()** that we will implement in the **CSketcherDoc** class. Add it to the **public** section of the class definition with a **void** return type, and a parameter of type **CElement***. We can implement this function as:

```
void CSketcherDoc::SendToBack(CElement* pElement)
{
    if(pElement)
    {
        // If the element pointer is valid,
        // find the pointer in the list and remove the element
        POSITION aPosition = m_ElementList.Find(pElement);
        m_ElementList.RemoveAt(aPosition);
```

```
        m_ElementList.AddHead(pElement);   // Put it back to the beginning
    }
}
```

Once we have the **POSITION** value corresponding to the element, we remove the element from the list by calling **RemoveAt()**. Of course, this does not delete the element from memory, it just removes the pointer to it from the list. Then we add the element pointer back at the beginning of the list using the **AddHead()** function.

With the element moved to the head of the list, it cannot mask any of the others because we search from the end. We will always find one of the other elements first if the applicable bounding rectangle encloses the current cursor position. The Send to Back menu option will always be able to resolve any element masking problem in the view.

Summary

In this chapter, you've seen how to apply MFC collection classes to the problems of managing objects and managing pointers to objects. Collections are a real asset in programming for Windows because the application data that you store in a document often originates in an unstructured and unpredictable way, and you need to be able traverse the data whenever a view needs to be updated.

You have also seen how to create document data and manage it in a pointer list in the document, and — in the context of the Sketcher application — how the views and the document communicate with each other.

We've improved the view capability in Sketcher in several ways. We've added scrolling to the views using the MFC class **CScrollView**, and we've introduced a pop-up at the cursor for moving and deleting elements. We've also implemented an element highlighting feature to provide the user with feedback when moving or deleting elements.

We have covered quite a lot of ground in this chapter, and some of the important points you need to keep in mind are:

▶ If you need a collection class to manage your objects or pointers, the best choice is one of the template-based collection classes, since they provide type-safe operation in most cases.

▶ When you draw in a device context, coordinates are in logical units that depend on the mapping mode set. Points in a window that are supplied along with Windows mouse messages are in client coordinates. The two coordinate systems are usually not the same.

▶ Coordinates that define the position of the cursor are in screen coordinates which are measured in pixels relative to the top left corner of the screen.

▶ Functions to convert between client coordinates and logical coordinates are available in the **CDC** class.

▶ Windows requests that a view is redrawn by sending a **WM_PAINT** message to your application. This causes the **OnDraw()** member of the affected view to be called.

▶ You should always do any permanent drawing of a document in the **OnDraw()** member of the view class. This will ensure that the window is drawn properly when required by Windows.

▶ You can make your **OnDraw()** implementation more efficient by calling the **RectVisible()** member of the **CDC** class to check whether an entity needs to be drawn.

▶ To get multiple views updated when you change the document contents, you can call the **UpdateAllViews()** member of the document object. This causes the **OnUpdate()** member of each view to be called.

▶ You can pass information to the **UpdateAllViews()** function to indicate which area in the view needs to be redrawn. This will make redrawing the views faster.

▶ You can display a context menu at the cursor position in response to a right mouse click. This menu is created as a normal pop-up.

Exercises

Ex16-1: Implement the **CCurve** class so that points are added to the head of the list instead of the tail.

Ex16-2: Implement the **CCurve** class in the Sketcher program using a typed pointer list, instead of a list of objects, to represent a curve.

Ex16-3: Look up the **CArray** template collection class in Help, and use it to store points in the **CCurve** class in the Sketcher program.

Working with Dialogs and Controls

Dialogs and controls are basic tools for user communications in the Windows environment. In this chapter, you'll learn how to implement dialogs and controls by applying them to extend the Sketcher program. As you do so, you'll see:

▶ What a dialog is and how you can create dialog resources

▶ What controls are and how to add them to a dialog

▶ What basic varieties of controls are available to you

▶ How to create a dialog class to manage a dialog

▶ How to program the creation of a dialog box and how to get information back from the controls in it

▶ What is meant by modal and modeless dialogs

▶ How to implement and use direct data exchange and validation with controls

Understanding Dialogs

Of course, dialogs are not new to you. Most Windows programs of consequence use dialogs to manage some of their data input. You click a menu item and up pops a **dialog box** with various **controls** that you use for entering information. Just about everything that appears in a dialog box is a control. A dialog box is actually a window and, in fact, each of the controls in a dialog is also a specialized window. Come to think of it, most things you see on the screen under Windows are windows!

Although controls have a particular association with dialog boxes, you can also create and use them in other windows if you want to. A typical dialog box is illustrated below:

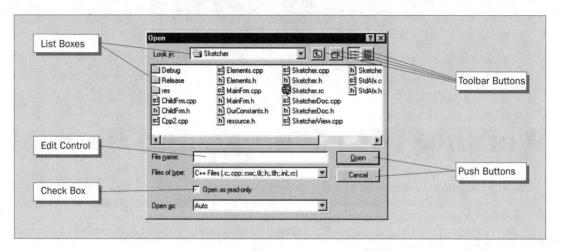

This is the File | Open... dialog in Visual C++. The annotations show the variety of controls that are used, which combine to provide a very intuitive interface for selecting a file to be opened. This makes the dialog very easy to use, even though there's a whole range of possibilities here.

There are two things needed to create and use a dialog box in an MFC program. The physical appearance of the dialog box, which is defined in a resource file, and a dialog class object that's used to manage the operation of the dialog and its controls. MFC provides a class called **CDialog** for you to use, once you have defined your dialog resource.

Understanding Controls

There are many different controls available to you in Windows, and in most cases there's quite a bit of flexibility in how they look and operate. Most of them fall into one of six categories. We'll take a look at these and, for each category, see what a typical control looks like and what it does.

Type	Appearance	What they do
Static Controls	This is a static control	These provide static information, such as titles or instructions, or simply provide decoration in a dialog in the form of an icon or a filled rectangle.
Button Controls	○ A radio button	Buttons allow communication to the application with a single mouse button click. Radio buttons, named after the old car radios which used push buttons to select predefined stations, are usually grouped so that if one is checked, the others are unchecked.
	☐ A check box	Check boxes, on the other hand, can be individually checked, so more than one can be checked at one time.
	A push button	Push buttons, such as OK and Cancel buttons, are typically used to close a dialog.
Scroll Bars	◄ █ ►	We have already seen scroll bars attached to the edge of our view window. Scroll bar controls can be free-standing and are used inside a dialog box.
List Boxes	Items / Listbox / Sample	This presents a list from which you can choose predefined items. The scroll bar need not appear in a short list. The list can also have multiple columns, and can be scrolled horizontally. A version of the list box is available that can display icons as well as text.
Edit Controls	You can edit this	In its simplest form, you can enter and edit a line of text. An edit control can be extended to allow sophisticated editing of multiple lines of text.
Combo Boxes	Choose this item / Or choose this item / Or enter one yourself	These combine the capability of a list box with the option of modifying a line or entering a complete line yourself. This is used to present a list of files in the Save As dialog.

A control may or may not be associated with a class object. Static controls don't do anything directly, so an associated class object may seem superfluous, but there's an MFC class, **CStatic**, that provides functions to enable you to alter the appearance of static controls. Button controls can also be handled by the dialog object in many cases, but again MFC provides the **CButton** class for use in situations where you need a class object to manage a control. MFC also provides a full complement of classes to support the other controls. Since a control is a window, they are all derived from **CWnd**.

Common Controls

The set of standard controls that are supported by MFC and the Resource Editor under 32-bit versions of Windows are called **common controls**. Common controls include all of the controls we have just seen, as well as other, more complex controls. Examples of these include the **animate control** which has the capability to play an AVI (**A**udio **V**ideo **I**nterleaved) file, and the **tree control** which can display a hierarchy of items in a tree. The tree control is used in Explorer in Windows 95 to display your files and folders in a hierarchy, but it can be used to display anything you like that can usefully be· represented by a tree.

Another useful control in the set of common controls is the **spin button**. You can use this to increment or decrement values in an associated edit control. To go into all of the possible controls that you might use is beyond the scope of this book, so we'll just take a few illustrative examples (including an example that uses a spin button) and implement them in the Sketcher program.

Creating a Dialog Resource

Let's take a concrete example. We can add a dialog to Sketcher to provide a choice of pen widths for drawing elements. This will ultimately involve modifying the current pen width in the document, as well as in **CElement**, and adding or modifying functions to deal with pen widths. We'll deal with all that, though, once we've got the dialog together.

First, change to the ResourceView, expand the resource tree for Sketcher and right-click on the Dialog folder in the tree. You'll see the pop-up shown here:

If you click on Insert Dialog, a new dialog resource is displayed with a default ID assigned. You can edit the ID by right-clicking on it and selecting Properties from the pop-up. Change the ID to something more meaningful, such as **IDD_PENWIDTH_DLG**. To the right of the ResourceView, you'll see a basic dialog box which already has an OK button and a Cancel button.

There is also a Controls palette from which you can select the controls to be added. (If the palette doesn't appear immediately, you can call it up by right-clicking on the menu bar and selecting Controls from the pop-up menu.) The palette includes 26 buttons, 24 of which select a Windows 95 common control.

Adding Controls to a Dialog Box

To provide a mechanism for entering a pen width, we're going to change the basic dialog that's initially displayed to the one shown below:

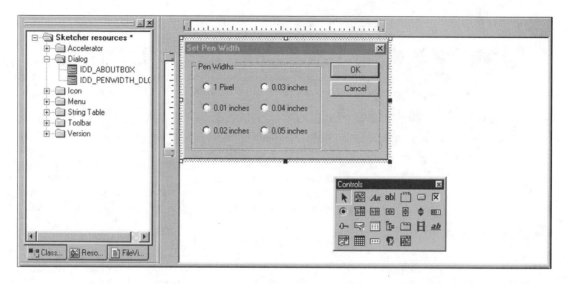

The dialog has six radio buttons which provide the pen width options. These are enclosed within a **group box** with the caption Pen Widths. Each radio button has an appropriate label to identify it.

The first step is to change the text in the title bar of the dialog box:

Make sure that the select button is active in the Controls window, as shown on the left. You can now right-click on the dialog box and select Properties from the pop-up list to display the dialog's properties box. Modify the caption text to Set Pen Width, as shown above. Each of the controls in a dialog will have their own set of properties that you can access and modify in the same way as for the dialog box itself.

The next step is to add the group box:

We'll use the group box to enclose the radio buttons that will be used to select a pen width. The group box serves to associate the radio buttons in a group from an operational standpoint, and to provide a caption and a boundary for the group of buttons. Where you need more than one set of radio buttons, a means of grouping them is essential if they are to work properly.

Select the button corresponding to the group box from the common controls palette (as shown on the left) by clicking it with the left mouse button. Then move the cursor to the approximate position in the dialog box where you want the center of the group box to be and press the left mouse button once more. This will place a group box of default size on to the dialog. You can then drag the borders of the group box to enlarge it to accommodate the six radio buttons that we will add. To set the caption for the group box, you can just type the caption you want. In this case, type Pen Widths. The properties box will open automatically.

The last step is to add the radio buttons:

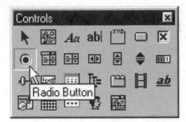

Select the radio button control as shown. You can now position the mouse cursor at the point where you want to position a radio button within the group box and click the left mouse button. Do the same for all six radio buttons. For each button, just type in the caption to change it; this will open the properties box as before—the width of the radio button will increase to accommodate the text. You can also drag the border of the button to set its size. You can change the ID for each radio button in the properties dialog to correspond better with its purpose: **IDC_PENWIDTH0** for the 1 pixel pen width, **IDC_PENWIDTH1** for the 0.01 inch width pen, **IDC_PENWIDTH2** for the 0.02 inch pen, and so on.

You can position individual controls by dragging them around with the mouse when the selection tool is active in the Controls window. You can also select a group of controls by selecting successive controls with the *Shift* key pressed, or by dragging the cursor with the left button pressed to create a rectangle enclosing them. To align a group of controls, select an item from the Layout menu, or use the toolbar which appeared at the bottom of the window when you opened this resource for editing. This toolbar is dockable, so you can drag it into the main window if you like.

Testing the Dialog

The dialog resource is now complete. You can test it by selecting the Layout | Test menu option, pressing *Ctrl-T*, or by using the leftmost dialog edit toolbar button that appears at the bottom of the Visual C++ IDE window. This will display a dialog window with the basic operations of the controls available, so you can try clicking on the radio buttons. When you have a group of radio buttons, only one can be selected, so, as you select one, any other that was previously selected is reset. Click on the OK or Cancel button in the dialog to end the test. Once you have saved the dialog resource, we're ready to add some code to support it.

Programming for a Dialog

There are two aspects to programming for a dialog: getting it displayed and handling the effects of its controls. Before we can display the dialog corresponding to the resource we've just created, we first need to define a dialog class for it. ClassWizard will help us with this.

Adding a Dialog Class

With the cursor on the dialog box that we've just created, press the right mouse button and select ClassWizard... from the pop-up at the cursor. ClassWizard will then take you through a process to associate a class with the dialog. The first ClassWizard dialog will ask whether you want to associate the new resource with a new class or an existing class. We'll define a new dialog class derived from the MFC class **CDialog**, which you can call **CPenDialog** in the following dialog. Just click OK to bring it up.

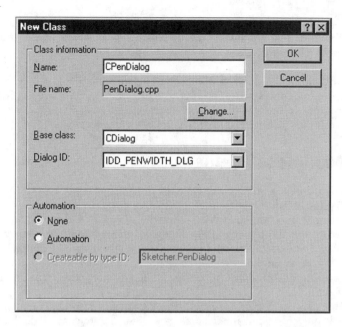

In the New Class dialog, type in **CPenDialog** in the Name: box. The Base Class: drop-down list will automatically show **CDialog**, which is fine for us. You may have to select the Dialog ID:, just make sure that it shows **IDD_PENWIDTH_DLG**. You can now click OK to create the new class, and click OK again to exit ClassWizard.

The **CDialog** class is a window class (derived from the MFC class **CWnd**) that's specifically for displaying and managing dialogs. The dialog resource that we've created will automatically be associated with an object of our **CPenDialog** class, since the class definition includes a definition of a member **IDD** which is initialized with the ID of the dialog resource:

```
class CPenDialog : public CDialog
{
// Construction
public:
    CPenDialog(CWnd* pParent = NULL);   // standard constructor

// Dialog Data
    //{{AFX_DATA(CPenDialog)
    enum { IDD = IDD_PENWIDTH_DLG };
        // NOTE: the ClassWizard will add data members here
    //}}AFX_DATA

    // Plus the rest of the class definition...
};
```

The highlighted statement defines **IDD** as a symbolic name for the dialog ID in the enumeration. Incidentally, using an enumeration is the *only* way you can get an initialized data member into a class definition. If you try putting an initial value for any regular data member declaration it won't compile. You will get an error message about illegal use of pure syntax. It works here because an **enum** defines a symbolic name for an **int**. Unfortunately, you can only define values of type **int** in this way. It's not strictly necessary here, since the initialization for **IDD** could be done in the constructor, but this is how ClassWizard chose to do it. This technique is more commonly used to define a symbol for the dimension of an array which is a member of a class, in which case using an enumeration is your only option.

Having our own dialog class derived from **CDialog** also enables us to customize the dialog class by adding data members and functions to suit our particular needs. You'll often want to handle messages from controls within the dialog class, although you can also choose to handle them in a view or a document class if this is more convenient.

Modal and Modeless Dialogs

There two different types of dialog, which work in quite distinct ways. These are termed **modal** and **modeless** dialogs. While a modal dialog remains in effect, all operations in the other windows in the application are suspended until the dialog box is closed, usually by clicking on an OK or Cancel button. With a modeless dialog, you can move the focus back and forth between the dialog box and other windows in your application just by clicking on them with the mouse, and you can continue to use the dialog box at any time until you close it. ClassWizard is an example of a modal dialog, while the properties window is modeless.

A modeless dialog box is created by calling the **Create()** function defined in the **CDialog** class, but as we'll only be using modal dialogs in our example, we call the **DoModal()** function in the dialog object, as you'll see shortly.

Displaying a Dialog

Where you put the code to display a dialog in your program depends on the application. In the Sketcher program, we need to add a menu item which, when it's selected, will result in the pen width dialog being displayed. We'll put this in the **IDR_SKETCHTYPE** menu bar. As both the width and the color are associated with a pen, we'll rename the Color menu as Pen. You do this just by double-clicking the Color menu item to open its properties box and changing the Caption: entry to &Pen.

When we add the menu item Width... to the Pen menu, we should separate it from the colors in the menu. You can add a separator after the last color menu item by double-clicking the empty menu item and selecting the Separator check box. If you close the properties box, you can then enter the new Width... item as the next menu item after the separator. Double-click on the menu to display the menu properties for modification, as shown below:

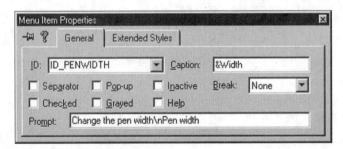

Enter **ID_PENWIDTH** as the ID for the menu item. You can also add a status bar prompt for it and, since we'll also add a toolbar button, you can include text for the tool tip as well. The menu will look like this:

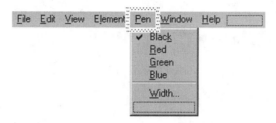

To add the toolbar button, open the toolbar resource by extending Toolbar in the ResourceView and double-clicking on **IDR_MAINFRAME**. You can add a toolbar button to represent a pen width. The one shown below tries to represent a pen drawing a line:

To associate the new button with the menu item that we just added, open the properties box for the button (by pressing *Enter* while the button is active) and specify its ID as **ID_PENWIDTH**, the same as that for the menu item.

Code to Display the Dialog

The code to display the dialog will go in the handler for the Pen | Width... menu item, so in which class should we implement this handler? We could consider the view class as a candidate for dealing with pen widths, but following our previous logic with colors and elements, it would be sensible to have the current pen width selection in the document, so we'll put the handler in the **CSketcherDoc** class. Open ClassWizard and create a function for the COMMAND message handler corresponding to **ID_PENWIDTH** in the **CSketcherDoc** class. Now edit this handler and enter the following code:

```
// Handler for the pen width menu item
void CSketcherDoc::OnPenwidth()
{
    CPenDialog aDlg;                     // Create a local dialog object

    // Display the dialog as modal
    aDlg.DoModal();
}
```

There are just two statements in the handler at the moment. The first creates a dialog object which is automatically associated with our dialog resource. We then display the dialog by calling the function **DoModal()** in the **aDlg** object. When the dialog box is closed, the function returns a value corresponding to the button used to close it. In our dialog, the value returned can be **IDOK** if the OK button is selected to close the dialog, or **IDCANCEL** if the dialog is closed using the Cancel button. We'll add code to use this return value a little later.

Because the handler declares a **CPenDialog** object, you must add a **#include** statement for **PenDialog.h** to the beginning of **SketcherDoc.cpp** (after the **#includes** for **stdafx.h** and **Sketcher.h**), otherwise you'll get compilation errors when you build the program. Once you've done that, you can build Sketcher and try out the dialog. It should appear when you click the toolbar button or the <u>Pen</u> | <u>W</u>idth... menu item. Of course, if the dialog is to do anything, we still have to add the code to support the operation of the controls.

Supporting the Dialog Controls

For our pen dialog, we'll store the selected pen width in a data member, **m_PenWidth**, of the **CPenDialog** class. You can either add the data member by right-clicking the **CPenDialog** class name, or you can add it directly to the class definition as follows:

```
class CPenDialog : public CDialog
{
// Construction
public:
    CPenDialog(CWnd* pParent = NULL);    // standard constructor

// Dialog Data
    //{{AFX_DATA(CPenDialog)
    enum { IDD = IDD_PENWIDTH_DLG };
        // NOTE: the ClassWizard will add data members here
    //}}AFX_DATA

// Data stored in the dialog
public:
    int m_PenWidth;                     // Record the pen width

// Plus the rest of the class definition....

};
```

 If you do use the context menu for the class to add m_PenWidth, **be sure to add a comment to the class definition. This is a good habit to get into, even when the member name looks self-explanatory.**

We'll use the data member **m_PenWidth** to set the radio button corresponding to the current pen width in the document as checked. We'll also arrange that the pen width selected in the dialog is stored in this member, so that we can retrieve it when the dialog closes.

Initializing the Controls

We can initialize the radio buttons by overriding the function **OnInitDialog()** which is defined in the base class, **CDialog**. This function is called in response to a **WM_INITDIALOG** message, which is sent during the execution of **DoModal()**, just before the dialog box is displayed. You can add the function to the class by selecting **WM_INITDIALOG** in the <u>M</u>essages: box in ClassWizard. The implementation for our version of **OnInitDialog()** will be:

```
BOOL CPenDialog::OnInitDialog()
{
    CDialog::OnInitDialog();
```

```
    // Check the radio button corresponding to the pen width
    switch(m_PenWidth)
    {
       case 1:
          CheckDlgButton(IDC_PENWIDTH1,1);
          break;
       case 2:
          CheckDlgButton(IDC_PENWIDTH2,1);
          break;
       case 3:
          CheckDlgButton(IDC_PENWIDTH3,1);
          break;
       case 4:
          CheckDlgButton(IDC_PENWIDTH4,1);
          break;
       case 5:
          CheckDlgButton(IDC_PENWIDTH5,1);
          break;
       default:
          CheckDlgButton(IDC_PENWIDTH0,1);
    }
    return TRUE;   // return TRUE unless you set the focus to a control
                   // EXCEPTION: OCX Property Pages should return FALSE
}
```

You should leave the call to the base class function there, as it does some essential setup for the dialog. The **switch** statement will check one of the radio buttons, depending on the value set in the **m_PenWidth** data member. This implies that we must arrange to set **m_PenWidth** before we execute **DoModal()**, since the **DoModal()** function causes the **WM_INITDIALOG** message to be sent and our version of **OnInitDialog()** to be called.

The **CheckDlgButton()** function is inherited indirectly from **CWnd** through **CDialog**. If the second argument is 1, it checks the button corresponding to the ID specified in the first argument. If the second argument is 0, the button is unchecked. This works with both check boxes and radio buttons.

Handling Radio Button Messages

Once the dialog box is displayed, every time you click on one or other of the radio buttons, a message will be generated and sent to the application. To deal with these messages, we can add handlers to our **CPenDialog** class. Open ClassWizard and create a handler for the **BN_CLICKED** message for each of the radio button IDs, **IDC_PENWIDTH0** through **IDC_PENWIDTH5**. The implementations of all of these are very similar, since each of them just sets the pen width in the dialog object. As an example, the handler for **IDC_PENWIDTH0** will be:

```
void CPenDialog::OnPenwidth0()
{
    m_PenWidth = 0;
}
```

You need to add the code for all six handlers to the **CPenDialog** class implementation, setting **m_PenWidth** to 1 in **OnPenWidth1()**, 2 in **OnPenWidth2()**, and so on.

715

Completing Dialog Operations

We need to modify the **OnPenwidth()** handler in **CSketcherDoc** to make the dialog effective. Add the following code to the function:

```
// Handler for the pen width menu item
void CSketcherDoc::OnPenwidth()
{
    CPenDialog aDlg;        // Create a local dialog object

    // Set the pen width in the dialog to that stored in the document
    aDlg.m_PenWidth = m_PenWidth;

    // Display the dialog as modal
    // When closed with OK, get the pen width
    if(aDlg.DoModal() == IDOK)
        m_PenWidth = aDlg.m_PenWidth;
}
```

The **m_PenWidth** member of the **aDlg** object is passed a pen width stored in the **m_PenWidth** member of the document; we've still to add this member to **CSketcherDoc**. The call of the **DoModal()** function now occurs in the condition of the **if** statement, which will be **TRUE** if the **DoModal()** function returns **IDOK**. In this case, we retrieve the pen width stored in the **aDlg** object and store it in the **m_PenWidth** member of the document. If the dialog box is closed using the Cancel button, **IDOK** won't be returned by **DoModal()** and the value of **m_PenWidth** in the document will not be changed.

Note that even though the dialog box is closed when **DoModal()** returns a value, the **aDlg** object still exists, so we can call its member functions without any problem. The object **aDlg** is destroyed automatically on return from **OnPenwidth()**.

All that remains to do to support variable pen widths in our application is to update the affected classes: **CSketcherDoc**, **CElement**, and the four shape classes derived from **CElement**.

Adding Pen Widths to the Document

We need to add the member **m_PenWidth** to the document, and the function **GetPenWidth()** to allow external access to the value stored. You should add the shaded statements below to the **CSketcherDoc** class definition:

```
class CSketcherDoc : public CDocument
{
// the rest as before...

// Attributes
public:

protected:
    COLORREF m_Color;       // Current drawing color
    WORD m_Element;         // Current element type
    int m_PenWidth;         // Current pen width
    CTypedPtrList<CObList, CElement*> m_ElementList;  // Element list
```

```
    // Operations
    public:
        // the rest as before...

        int GetPenWidth() const                  // Get the current pen width
        { return m_PenWidth; }

        // the rest as before...
    };
```

Because it's trivial, we can define the **GetPenWidth()** function in the definition of the class and gain the benefit of it being implicitly **inline**. We do need to add initialization for **m_PenWidth** to the constructor for **CSketcherDoc**, so add the line,

```
        m_PenWidth = 0;        // Set 1 pixel pen
```

to the constructor definition in **SketcherDoc.cpp**.

Adding Pen Widths to the Elements

We have a little more to do to the **CElement** class and the shape classes derived from it. We already have a member **m_Pen** in **CElement** to store the width to be used when drawing an element, and we must extend each of the constructors for elements to accept a pen width as an argument, and set the member in the class accordingly. The **GetBoundRect()** function in **CElement** must be altered to deal with a pen width of zero. Let's deal with **CElement** first. The new version of **GetBoundRect()** in the **CElement** class will be:

```
    // Get the bounding rectangle for an element
    CRect CElement::GetBoundRect() const
    {
        CRect BoundingRect;                  // Object to store bounding rectangle
        BoundingRect = m_EnclosingRect;      // Store the enclosing rectangle

        // Increase the rectangle by the pen width
        int Offset = m_Pen == 0? 1:m_Pen;    // Width must be at least 1
        BoundingRect.InflateRect(Offset, Offset);
        return BoundingRect;
    }
```

We use the local variable **Offset** to ensure that we pass the **InflateRect()** function a value of 1 if the pen width is zero (a pen width of 0 will always draw a line one pixel wide), and we pass the actual pen width in all other cases.

Each of the constructors for **CLine**, **CRectangle**, **CCircle** and **CCurve** needs to be modified to accept a pen width as an argument, and to store it in the **m_Pen** member of the class. The declaration for the constructor in each class definition needs to be modified to add the extra parameter. For example, in the **CLine** class, the constructor declaration will become,

```
        CLine(const CPoint& Start, const CPoint& End, const COLORREF& Color,
                                              const int& PenWidth);
```

and the constructor implementation should be modified to:

```
CLine::CLine(const CPoint& Start, const CPoint& End, const COLORREF& Color,
                                                   const int& PenWidth)
{
   m_StartPoint = Start;      // Set line start point
   m_EndPoint = End;          // Set line end point
   m_Color = Color;           // Set line color
   m_Pen = PenWidth;          // Set pen width

   // Define the enclosing rectangle
   m_EnclosingRect = CRect(Start, End);
   m_EnclosingRect.NormalizeRect();
}
```

You should modify each of the class definitions and constructors for the shapes in the same way.

Creating Elements in the View

The last change we need to make is to the **CreateElement()** member of **CSketcherView**. Since we've added the pen width as an argument to the constructors for each of the shapes, we must update the calls to the constructors to reflect this. Change the definition of **CSketcherView::CreateElement()** to:

```
CElement* CSketcherView::CreateElement()
{
   // Get a pointer to the document for this view
   CSketcherDoc* pDoc = GetDocument();
   ASSERT_VALID(pDoc);                     // Verify the pointer is good

   // Now select the element using the type stored in the document
   switch(pDoc->GetElementType())
   {
      case RECTANGLE:
         return new CRectangle(m_FirstPoint, m_SecondPoint,
                         pDoc->GetElementColor(), pDoc->GetPenWidth());
      case CIRCLE:
         return new CCircle(m_FirstPoint, m_SecondPoint,
                         pDoc->GetElementColor(), pDoc->GetPenWidth());
      case CURVE:
         return new CCurve(m_FirstPoint, m_SecondPoint,
                         pDoc->GetElementColor(), pDoc->GetPenWidth());
      case LINE:                            // Always default to a line
         return new CLine(m_FirstPoint, m_SecondPoint,
                         pDoc->GetElementColor(), pDoc->GetPenWidth());
      default:
         // Something's gone wrong
         AfxMessageBox("Bad Element code", MB_OK);
         AfxAbort();
         return NULL;
   }
}
```

Each constructor call now passes the pen width as an argument. This is retrieved from the document using the **GetPenWidth()** function that we added to the document class.

Exercising the Dialog

You can now build and run the latest version of Sketcher to see how our dialog works out. Selecting the Pen | Width... menu option will display the dialog box so that you can select the pen width. The following screen is typical of what you might see when the program is executing:

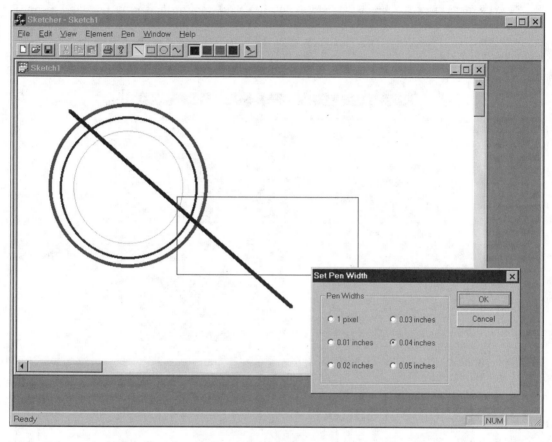

Note that the dialog box is a completely separate window. You can drag it around to position it where you want. You can even drag it outside the Sketcher application window.

Using a Spin Button Control

Now let's move on to looking at how the spin button can help us in the Sketcher application. The spin button is particularly useful when you want to constrain an input within a given integer range. It's normally used in association with another control, called a **buddy control**, which displays the value that the spin button modifies. The associated control is usually an edit control, but it doesn't have to be. We could apply the spin control to managing scaling in a document view. A drawing scale would be a view-specific property, and we would want the element drawing functions to take account of the current scale for a view.

Altering the existing code to deal with view scaling will require rather more work than setting up the control, so let's first look at how we can create a spin button and make it work.

Adding the Scale Menu Item and Toolbar Button

Let's begin by providing a means of displaying the scale dialog. Go to ResourceView and open the **IDR_SKETCHTYPE** menu. We'll add a S&cale... menu item to the end of the View menu. First, add a separator to the end of that menu by checking the Separator check box in the properties window for a new item. Now fill in the properties window for the next item, as shown below. This item will bring up the scale dialog, so we end the caption with an ellipsis (three periods) to indicate that it displays a dialog. This is a standard Windows convention.

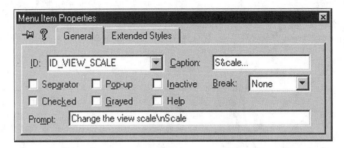

The menu should now look like this:

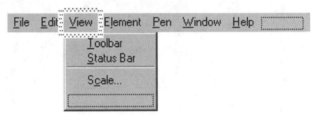

You can also add a toolbar button for this menu item. All you need to do is make sure that the ID for the button is also set to **ID_VIEW_SCALE**.

Creating the Spin Button

We've got the menu item; we'd better have a dialog to go with it. In ResourceView, add a new dialog by right-clicking the Dialog folder on the tree and selecting Insert Dialog. Change the ID to **IDD_SCALE_DLG**.

Click on the spin control in the palette, as shown on the left, and then click on the position in the dialog where you want it to be placed. Next, right-click on the spin control and select Properties from the pop-up. Change its ID to something more meaningful than the default, such as **IDC_SPIN_SCALE.** Now take at look at the Styles tab in the spin button properties. It's shown below:

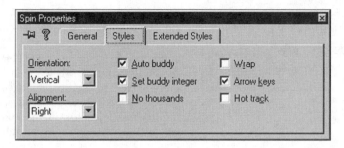

The Arrow keys check box will be automatically selected, enabling you to operate the spin button by using arrow keys on the keyboard. You should also check the box Set buddy integer, which specifies the buddy control value as an integer, and Auto buddy, which provides for automatic selection of the buddy control. The control selected as the buddy will automatically be the previous control defined in the dialog. At the moment, this is the Cancel button, which is not exactly ideal, but we'll see how to change this in a moment. The Alignment: list determines how the spin button will be displayed in relation to its buddy. You should set this to Right so that the spin button is attached to the right edge of its buddy.

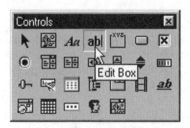

Next, add an edit control at the side of the spin button by selecting the edit control from the palette, as shown on the left, and clicking in the dialog where you want it positioned. Change the ID for the edit control to **IDC_SCALE**.

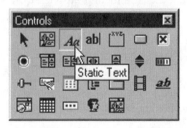

To make the contents of the edit control quite clear, you could add a static control just to the left of the edit control in the palette and enter View Scale: as the caption. You can select all three controls by clicking on them while holding down the *Shift* key. Clicking the right mouse button will pop up a menu at the cursor with options you can use for aligning the controls tidily, or you can use the Layout menu.

If you use *Ctrl-T* to test this now, it won't seem quite right: the spin button seems to have gotten involved with the Cancel button. This will be resolved next, as we look at the controls' tab sequence.

The Controls' Tab Sequence

Controls in a dialog have what is called a **tab sequence**. This is the sequence in which the focus shifts from one control to the next, determined initially by the sequence in which controls are added to the dialog. You can see the tab sequence for the current dialog box by selecting Layout | Tab Order from the main menu, or by pressing *Ctrl-D*.

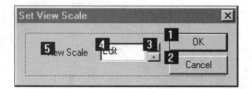

The tab order will be displayed as shown on the left. Because the Cancel button immediately precedes the spin button in sequence, the Auto buddy property for the spin button will select it as the buddy control. We want the edit control to precede the spin button in the tab sequence, so you need to select the controls by clicking on them with the left mouse button in the following sequence: OK button; Cancel button; edit control; spin button; and finally the static control. Now the edit control will be selected as the buddy to the spin button.

Generating the Scale Dialog Class

After saving the resource file, you can click the right mouse button on the dialog and select ClassWizard from the pop-up at the cursor. This will take you through a dialog to define the new class associated with the dialog resource that you have created. You should name the class **CScaleDialog**.

We need to define a variable in the dialog class that will store the value returned from the edit control, so switch to the Member Variables tab in ClassWizard and select the **IDC_SCALE** ID which identifies the edit control. Click on Add Variable... and enter the variable name as **m_Scale**. We'll be storing an integer scale value, so select **int** as the variable type and click OK.

The ClassWizard will display boxes at the bottom of the Member Variables tab where you can enter maximum and minimum values for the variable **m_Scale**. For our application, a minimum of 1 and a maximum of 8 would be good values. Note that this constraint only applies to the edit box; the spin control is independent of it. The definition which ClassWizard will produce when you click on the OK button is as follows:

```
class CScaleDialog : public CDialog
{
// Construction
public:
   CScaleDialog(CWnd* pParent = NULL);   // standard constructor

// Dialog Data
   //{{AFX_DATA(CScaleDialog)
   enum { IDD = IDD_SCALE_DLG };
   int m_Scale;
   //}}AFX_DATA

// Overrides
   // ClassWizard generated virtual function overrides
   //{{AFX_VIRTUAL(CScaleDialog)
   protected:
   virtual void DoDataExchange(CDataExchange* pDX);    // DDX/DDV support
   //}}AFX_VIRTUAL

// Implementation
protected:
```

```
    // Generated message map functions
    //{{AFX_MSG(CScaleDialog)
        // NOTE: the ClassWizard will add member functions here
    //}}AFX_MSG
    DECLARE_MESSAGE_MAP()
};
```

The interesting bits are shaded. The class is associated with the dialog resource through the **enum** statement initializing **IDD** with the ID of the resource. It contains the variable **m_Scale**, which is specified as a **public** member of the class, so we can set and retrieve its value directly.

Dialog Data Exchange and Validation

A virtual function called **DoDataExchange()** has been included in the class by ClassWizard. If you take a look in the **ScaleDialog.cpp** file, you'll find the implementation looks like this:

```
void CScaleDialog::DoDataExchange(CDataExchange* pDX)
{
    CDialog::DoDataExchange(pDX);
    //{{AFX_DATA_MAP(CScaleDialog)
    DDX_Text(pDX, IDC_SCALE, m_Scale);
    DDV_MinMaxInt(pDX, m_Scale, 1, 8);
    //}}AFX_DATA_MAP
}
```

This function is called by the framework to carry out the exchange of data between variables in a dialog and the dialog's controls. This mechanism is called **Dialog Data Exchange**, usually abbreviated to **DDX**. This is a very powerful mechanism that can provide automatic transfer of information between a dialog and its controls in most circumstances, thus saving you the effort of programming to get the data yourself, as we did with the radio buttons in the pen width dialog.

In our scale dialog, DDX handles data transfers between the edit control and the variable **m_Scale** in the **CScaleDialog** class. The variable **pDX** passed to the function controls the direction in which data is transferred. After calling the base class **DoDataExchange()** function, the **DDX_Text()** function is called, which actually moves data between the variable, **m_Scale**, and the edit control.

The call to the **DDV_MinMaxInt()** function verifies that the value transferred is within the limits specified. This mechanism is called **Dialog Data Validation**, or **DDV**. The **DoDataExchange()** function will be called automatically, before the dialog is displayed, to pass the value stored in **m_Scale** to the edit control. When the dialog is closed with the OK button, it will be automatically called again to pass the value in the control back to the variable **m_Scale** in the dialog object. All this is taken care of for you. You only need to ensure that the right value is stored in **m_Scale** before the dialog box is displayed, and arrange to collect the result when the dialog box closes.

Initializing the Dialog

To initialize the dialog, we'll use the **OnInitDialog()** function, just as we did for the pen width dialog. This time we'll use it to set up the spin control. We'll initialize the **m_Scale** member a little later, when we create the dialog in the handler for a Scale... menu item, because we'll want to set it to the value of the scale stored in the view. For now, add the handler for the **WM_INITDIALOG** message to the **CScaleDialog** class, using the same mechanism that you used for the previous dialog, and add code to initialize the spin control as follows:

```
BOOL CScaleDialog::OnInitDialog()
{
   CDialog::OnInitDialog();

   // First get a pointer to the spin control
   CSpinButtonCtrl* pSpin;
   pSpin = (CSpinButtonCtrl*)GetDlgItem(IDC_SPIN_SCALE);

   // If you have not checked the auto buddy option in
   // the spin control's properties, set the buddy control here

   // Set the spin control range
   pSpin->SetRange(1, 8);

   return TRUE;  // return TRUE unless you set the focus to a control
                 // EXCEPTION: OCX Property Pages should return FALSE
}
```

There are only three lines of code added, along with four lines of comments. The first line of code creates a pointer to an object of the MFC class **CSpinButtonCtrl**. This class is specifically for managing spin buttons, and is initialized in the next statement to point to the control in our dialog. The function **GetDlgItem()** is inherited from **CWnd** via **CDialog**, and it will retrieve the address of any control from the ID passed as an argument. Since, as we saw earlier, a control is just a specialized window, the pointer returned is of type **CWnd***, so we have to cast it to the type appropriate to the particular control, which is **CSpinButtonCtrl*** in this case. The third statement that we've added sets the upper and lower limits for the spin button by calling the **SetRange()** member of the spin control object. Although we've set the range limits for the edit control, this doesn't affect the spin control directly. If we don't limit the values in the spin control here, we would be allowing the spin control to insert values in the edit control that were outside the limits, so there would be an error message from the edit control. You can demonstrate this by commenting out the **SetRange()** statement here and trying out Sketcher without it.

If you want to set the buddy control using code rather than using the Auto buddy option in the spin button's properties, the **CSpinButtonCtrl** class has a function member to do this. You would need to add the statement,

```
pSpin->SetBuddy(GetDlgItem(IDC_SCALE));
```

at the point indicated by the comments.

Displaying the Spin Button

The dialog will be displayed when the Scale... menu option (or its associated toolbar button) is selected, so you need to use ClassWizard's Message Maps tab to add a COMMAND handler to the **CSketcherView** class corresponding to the **ID_VIEW_SCALE** message. Then you can select the Edit Code button and add code as follows:

```
void CSketcherView::OnViewScale()
{
    CScaleDialog aDlg;            // Create a dialog object
    aDlg.m_Scale = m_Scale;      // Pass the view scale to the dialog
    if(aDlg.DoModal() == IDOK)
    {
        m_Scale = aDlg.m_Scale;  // Get the new scale
        InvalidateRect(0);       // Invalidate the whole window
    }
}
```

The dialog is created as modal, in the same way as the pen width dialog. Before the dialog box is displayed by the **DoModal()** call, we store the scale value provided by the **CSketcherView** member, **m_Scale**, in the dialog member with the same name, which ensures that the control will display the current scale value when the dialog is displayed. If the dialog is closed with the OK button, we store the new scale from the dialog member **m_Scale**, in the view member **m_Scale**. Since we have changed the view scale, we need to get the view redrawn with the new scale value applied. The call to **InvalidateRect()** will do this for us.

Of course, we must add **m_Scale** to the definition of **CSketcherView**, so add the following line at the end of the other **protected** data members in the class definition:

```
int m_Scale;                 // Current view scale
```

You should also add a line to the **CSketcherView** constructor to initialize **m_Scale** to 1:

```
m_Scale = 1;                 // Set scale to 1:1
```

This will result in a view always starting out with a scale of one to one. If you forget to do this, it's unlikely that your program will work properly.

As we're using the **CScaleDialog** class, we need to add a **#include** statement for **ScaleDialog.h** to the beginning of the **SketcherView.cpp** file. That's all we need to get the scale dialog and its spin control operational. You can build and run Sketcher to give it a trial spin before we add the code to use a view scale factor.

Using the Scale Factor

Scaling with Windows usually involves using one of the scaleable mapping modes, **MM_ISOTROPIC** or **MM_ANISOTROPIC**. By using one or other of these mapping modes, you can get Windows to do most of the work. Unfortunately, it's not as simple as just changing the mapping mode, because neither of these mapping modes is supported by **CScrollView**. However, if we can get around that, we're home and dry. We'll use **MM_ANISOTROPIC**, so let's first understand what's involved in using this mapping mode.

Scaleable Mapping Modes

As we've said, there are two mapping modes that allow the mapping between logical coordinates and device coordinates to be altered. These are **MM_ISOTROPIC** and **MM_ANISOTROPIC**. **MM_ISOTROPIC** has the property that Windows will force the scaling factor for both the *x* and *y* axes to be the same, which has the advantage that your circles will always be circles, but the disadvantage that you can't map a document to fit into a rectangle of a different shape. **MM_ANISOTROPIC**, on the other hand, permits scaling of each axis independently. Because it's the more flexible, we'll use **MM_ANISOTROPIC** for scaling operations in Sketcher.

The way in which logical coordinates are transformed to device coordinates is dependent on the following parameters, which you can set:

Parameter	Description
Window Origin	The logical coordinates of the top left corner of the window. This is set by calling the function **CDC::SetWindowOrg()**.
Window Extent	The size of the window specified in logical coordinates. This is set by calling the function **CDC::SetWindowExt()**.
Viewport Origin	The coordinates of the top left corner of the window in device coordinates (pixels). This is set by calling the function **CDC::SetViewportOrg()**.
Viewport Extent	The size of the window in device coordinates (pixels). This is set by calling the function **CDC::SetViewportExt()**.

The *viewport* referred to here has no physical significance by itself; it serves only as a parameter for defining how coordinates are transformed from logical coordinates to device coordinates.

FYI

Remember that:

Logical coordinates (also referred to as *page coordinates*) are determined by the mapping mode. For example, the MM_LOENGLISH mapping mode has logical coordinates in units of 0.01 inches, with the origin in the top left corner of the client area, and the positive y axis direction running from bottom to top. These are used by the device context drawing functions.

Device coordinates (also referred to as *client coordinates* in a window) are measured in pixels in the case of a window, with the origin at the top left corner of the client area, and with the positive y axis direction from top to bottom. These are used outside of a device context, for example for defining the position of the cursor in mouse message handlers.

Screen coordinates are measured in pixels and have the origin at the top left corner of the screen, with the positive y axis direction from top to bottom. These are used when getting or setting the cursor position.

The formulae that are used by Windows to convert from logical coordinates to device coordinates are:

$$xDevice = (xLogical - xWindowOrg) * \frac{xViewPortExt}{xWindowExt} + xViewportOrg$$

$$yDevice = (yLogical - yWindowOrg) * \frac{yViewPortExt}{yWindowExt} + yViewportOrg$$

With coordinate systems other than **MM_ISOTROPIC** and **MM_ANISOTROPIC**, the window extent and the viewport extent are fixed by the mapping mode and you can't change them. Calling the functions **SetWindowExt()** or **SetViewportExt()** in the **CDC** object to change them will have no effect, although you can still move the position of (0,0) in your logical reference frame by calling **SetWindowOrg()** or **SetViewportOrg()**. However, for a given document size which will be expressed by the window extent in logical coordinate units, we can adjust the scale at which elements are displayed by setting the viewport extent appropriately. By using and setting the window and viewport extents, we can get the scaling done automatically.

Setting the Document Size

We need to maintain the size of the document in logical units in the document object. Add a **protected** data member, **m_DocSize**, to the **CSketcherDoc** class definition:

```
CSize m_DocSize;                        // Document size
```

We will also need to access this data member from the view class, so add a **public** function to the **CSketcherDoc** class definition as follows:

```
CSize GetDocSize() const
   { return m_DocSize; }                // Retrieve the document size
```

We must initialize the **m_DocSize** member in the constructor for the document, so modify the implementation of **CSketcherDoc()** as follows:

```
CSketcherDoc::CSketcherDoc()
{
    // TODO: add one-time construction code here
    m_Element = LINE;            // Set initial element type
    m_Color = BLACK;             // Set initial drawing color
    m_PenWidth = 0;              // Set 1 pixel pen
    m_DocSize = CSize(3000,3000); // Set initial document size 30x30 inches
}
```

We'll be using notional **MM_LOENGLISH** coordinates, so we can treat the logical units as 0.01 inches, and the value set will give us an area of 30 inches square to draw on.

Setting the Mapping Mode

We'll set the mapping mode to **MM_ANISOTROPIC** in the **OnPrepareDC()** member of **CSketcherView**. This is always called for any **WM_PAINT** message, and we've arranged to call it when we draw temporary objects in the mouse message handlers. However, we must do a little more than just set the mapping mode. The implementation of **OnPrepareDC()** will be:

```
void CSketcherView::OnPrepareDC(CDC* pDC, CPrintInfo* pInfo)
{
    CScrollView::OnPrepareDC(pDC, pInfo);
```

```
            CSketcherDoc* pDoc = GetDocument();
            pDC->SetMapMode(MM_ANISOTROPIC);            // Set the map mode
            CSize DocSize = pDoc->GetDocSize();         // Get the document size

            // y extent must be negative because we want MM_LOENGLISH
            DocSize.cy = -DocSize.cy;                   // Change sign of y
            pDC->SetWindowExt(DocSize);                 // Now set the window extent

            // Get the number of pixels per inch in x and y
            int xLogPixels = pDC->GetDeviceCaps(LOGPIXELSX);
            int yLogPixels = pDC->GetDeviceCaps(LOGPIXELSY);

            // Calculate the viewport extent in x and y
            int xExtent = DocSize.cx * m_Scale * xLogPixels / 100;
            int yExtent = DocSize.cy * m_Scale * yLogPixels / 100;

            pDC->SetViewportExt(xExtent, -yExtent);     // Set viewport extent
      }
```

You'll need to create the handler for this before you can add the code. The easiest way is to open the ClassWizard dialog by right clicking in the edit window and selecting ClassWizard... from the pop-up, and then to select OnPrepareDC from the Messages: drop-down list on the Message Maps tab for the **CSketcherView** class. If you click on the Add Function button and then the Edit Code button, you can type the code straight in.

Our override of the base class function is unusual in that we have left the call to **CScrollView::OnPrepareDC()** in, and added our modifications after it. If our class was derived from **CView**, we would replace the call to the base class version because it does nothing, but for **CScrollView** this isn't the case. We need the base class function to set some attributes before we set the mapping mode. Don't make the mistake of calling the base class function at the end though — if you do, scaling won't work.

After setting the mapping mode and obtaining the document extent, we set the window extent with the *y* extent negative. This is just to be consistent with the **MM_LOENGLISH** mode that we were using previously — remember that the origin is at the top, so *y* values in the client area are negative with this mapping mode.

The **CDC** member function **GetDeviceCaps()** supplies information about the device that the device context is associated with. You can get various kinds of information about the device, depending on the argument you pass to the function. In our case, the arguments **LOGPIXELSX** and **LOGPIXELSY** return the number of pixels per logical inch in the *x* and *y* directions. These values will be equivalent to 100 units in our logical coordinates.

We use these values to calculate the *x* and *y* values for the viewport extent, which we store in the local variables **xExtent** and **yExtent**. The document extent along an axis in logical units, divided by 100, gives the document extent in inches. If this is multiplied by the number of logical pixels per inch for the device, we get the equivalent number of pixels for the extent. If we then use this value as the viewport extent, we will get the elements displayed at a scale of 1 to 1. If we simplify the equations for converting between device and logical coordinates by assuming the window origin and the viewport origin are both (0,0), they become:

$$xDevice = xLogical * \frac{xViewPortExt}{xWindowExt} \qquad yDevice = yLogical * \frac{yViewPortExt}{yWindowExt}$$

If we multiply the viewport extent values by the scale (in **m_Scale**), the elements will be drawn according to the value of **m_Scale**. This logic is exactly represented by the expressions for the x and y viewport extents in our code. The simplified equations with the scale included will be:

$$xDevice = xLogical * \frac{xViewPortExt * m\_Scale}{xWindowExt}$$

$$yDevice = yLogical * \frac{yViewPortExt * m\_Scale}{yWindowExt}$$

You should be able the see from this that a given pair of device coordinates will vary in proportion to the scale value. The coordinates at a scale of 3 will be three times the coordinates at a scale of 1. Of course, as well as making elements larger, increasing the scale will also move them away from the origin.

That's all we need to scale the view. Unfortunately, at the moment the scrolling won't work with scaling — the lengths of the scroll bars don't scale appropriately with the rest of the view. Let's see what we can do about that.

Implementing Scrolling with Scaling

CScrollView just won't work with **MM_ANISOTROPIC**, so clearly we must use another mapping mode to set up the scrollbars. The easiest way to do this is to use **MM_TEXT**, because in this case the logical coordinates are the same as the client coordinates — pixels, in other words. All we need to do, then, is to figure out how many pixels are equivalent to our logical document extent for the scale at which we are drawing, which is easier than you might think. We can add a function to **CSketcherView** to take care of the scrollbars and implement everything in there. Right-click on the **CSketcherView** class name and add a **public** function **ResetScrollSizes()** with a **void** return type. Add the code to the implementation, as follows:

```
void CSketcherView::ResetScrollSizes()
{
    CClientDC aDC(this);
    OnPrepareDC(&aDC);                               // Set up the device context
    CSize DocSize = GetDocument()->GetDocSize();     // Get the document size
    aDC.LPtoDP(&DocSize);                            // Get the size in pixels
    SetScrollSizes(MM_TEXT, DocSize);               // Set up the scrollbars
}
```

After creating a local **CClientDC** object for the view, we call **OnPrepareDC()** to set up the **MM_ANISOTROPIC** mapping mode. Because this takes account of the scaling, the **LPtoDP()** member of **aDC** will convert the document size stored in the local variable **DocSize** to the correct number of pixels for the current logical document size and scale. The total document size in pixels defines how large the scrollbars must be in **MM_TEXT** mode—remember **MM_TEXT** logical coordinates are in pixels. Based on this, we can get the **SetScrollSizes()** member of **CScrollView** to set up the scrollbars by specifying **MM_TEXT** as the mapping mode.

It may seem strange that we can change the mapping mode in this way, but it's important to keep in mind that the mapping mode is nothing more than a definition of how logical coordinates are to be converted to device coordinates. Whatever mode (and therefore coordinate conversion algorithm) you've set up will apply to all subsequent device context functions until you change it, and you can change it whenever you want. When you set a new mode, subsequent device context function calls just use the conversion algorithm defined by the new mode. We figure how big the document is in pixels with **MM_ANISOTROPIC**, since this is the only way we can get the scaling into the process, and then switch to **MM_TEXT** to set up the scrollbars because we need units for this in pixels for it to work properly. Simple really, when you know how.

Setting Up the Scrollbars

We must set up the scrollbars initially for the view in the **OnInitialUpdate()** member of **CSketcherView**. Change the previous implementation of the function to:

```
void CSketcherView::OnInitialUpdate()
{
    ResetScrollSizes();                // Set up the scrollbars
    CScrollView::OnInitialUpdate();
}
```

All we need to do is call the function that we just added to the view. This takes care of everything — well, almost. The **CScrollView** object needs an initial extent to be set for **OnPrepareDC()** to work properly, so we need to add one statement to the **CSketcherView** constructor:

```
CSketcherView::CSketcherView()
{
    // TODO: add construction code here
    m_FirstPoint = CPoint(0,0);        // Set 1st recorded point to 0,0
    m_SecondPoint = CPoint(0,0);       // Set 2nd recorded point to 0,0
    m_pTempElement = NULL;             // Set temporary element pointer to 0
    m_pSelected = NULL;                // No element selected initially
    m_MoveMode = FALSE;                // Set move mode off
    m_CursorPos = CPoint(0,0);         // Initialize as zero
    m_FirstPos = CPoint(0,0);          // Initialize as zero
    m_Scale = 1;                       // Set scale to 1:1
    SetScrollSizes(MM_TEXT, CSize(0,0));  // Set arbitrary scrollers
}
```

This just calls **SetScrollSizes()** to an arbitrary extent to get the scrollbars initialized before the view is drawn. When the view is drawn for the first time, the **ResetScrollSizes()** function call in **OnInitialUpdate()** will set up the scrollbars properly.

Of course, each time the view scale changes, we need to update the scrollbars before the view is redrawn. We can take care of this in the **OnViewScale()** handler in **CSketcherView**:

```
void CSketcherView::OnViewScale()
{
    CScaleDialog aDlg;           // Create a dialog object
    aDlg.m_Scale = m_Scale;      // Pass the view scale to the dialog
    if(aDlg.DoModal() == IDOK)
```

```
      {
         m_Scale = aDlg.m_Scale;      // Get the new scale
         ResetScrollSizes();          // Adjust scrolling to the new scale
         InvalidateRect(0);           // Invalidate the whole window
      }
   }
```

Using our function **ResetScrollSizes()**, taking care of the scrollbars isn't complicated. Everything is covered by the one additional line of code.

Now you can build the project and run the application. You'll see that the scrollbars work just as they should. Note that each view maintains its own scale factor, independently of the other views.

Creating a Status Bar

With each view now being scaled independently, it becomes necessary to have some indication of what the current scale in a view is. A convenient way to do this would be to display the scale in a status bar. Windows 95 style conventions indicate that the status bar should appear at the bottom of the window, below the scroll bar if there is one. Also, there tends to be only one status bar attached to the main application window, which you can see in the following screen showing Sketcher at its current stage of development:

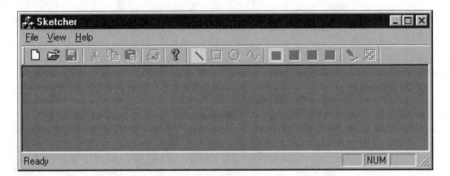

The status bar is divided into segments, called **panes**. The status bar in the previous screen has four panes. The one on the left contains the text Ready, and the other three are the recessed areas on the right. It's possible for you to write to this status bar, but you need to get access to the **m_wndStatusBar** member of **CMainFrame**, as this represents it. As it's a **protected** member of the class, you must add a public member function to modify the status bar. You could add a **public** function member to **CMainFrame** as follows:

```
   void CMainFrame::SetPaneText(int Pane, LPCTSTR Text)
   {
      m_wndStatusBar.SetPaneText(Pane, Text);
   }
```

This function sets the text in the pane specified by **Pane** in the status bar represented by **m_wndStatusBar** to the text, **Text**. The status bar panes are indexed from the left, starting at 0. Now we could write from anywhere outside the **CMainFrame** class:

```
CMainFrame* pFrame = (CMainFrame*)AfxGetApp()->m_pMainWnd;
pFrame->SetPaneText(0, "Goodbye cruel world");
```

This gets a pointer to the main window of the application and outputs the text string you see to the leftmost pane in the status bar. This is fine, but the main application window is no place for a view scale. We may well have several views, so we really want to associate displaying the scale with each view. The answer is to give each child window its own status bar. The **m_wndStatusBar** in **CMainFrame** is an instance of the **CStatusBar** class. We can use the same class to implement our own status bars.

Adding a Status Bar to a Frame

The **CStatusBar** class defines a control bar with multiple panes in which you can display information. Objects of type **CStatusBar** can also provide the same functionality as the Windows common status bar control through a member function **GetStatusBarCtrl()**. There is an MFC class that specifically encapsulates each of the Windows common controls — the one for the common status bar control is **CStatusBarCtrl**. However, using this directly involves quite a bit of work to integrate it with the other MFC classes, as the raw Windows control doesn't connect to MFC. Using **CStatusBar** in our program is easier and safer. The **GetStatusBarCtrl()** function will return a reference to a **CStatusBarCtrl** object that provides all the functionality of the common control, and the **CStatusBar** object will take care of the communications to the rest of the MFC.

The first step towards utilizing it is to add a data member for the status bar to the definition of **CChildFrame**, which is the frame window for a view, so add the following declaration to the **public** section of the class:

```
// Attributes
public:
    CStatusBar m_StatusBar;     // Status bar object
```

A word of advice is required at this point. Status bars should be part of the frame, not part of the view. We don't want to be able to scroll the status bars or draw over them. They should just remain anchored to the bottom of the window. If you added a status bar to the view, it would appear inside the scrollbars and would be scrolled whenever we scrolled the view. Any drawing over the part of the view containing the status bar would cause the bar to be redrawn, leading to an annoying flicker. Having the status bar as part of the frame avoids these problems.

We need to initialize this data member just before the visible view window is displayed. So, using ClassWizard, add a function to the class that will be called in response to the **WM_CREATE** message, which is sent to the application when the window is to be created. Add the following code to the **OnCreate()** handler:

```
int CChildFrame::OnCreate(LPCREATESTRUCT lpCreateStruct)
{
    if (CMDIChildWnd::OnCreate(lpCreateStruct) == -1)
        return -1;
```

```
    // Create the status bar
    m_StatusBar.Create(this);

    // Work out the width of the text we want to display
    CRect textRect;
    CClientDC aDC(&m_StatusBar);
    aDC.SelectObject(m_StatusBar.GetFont());
    aDC.DrawText("View Scale:99", -1, textRect, DT_SINGLELINE|DT_CALCRECT);

    // Setup a part big enough to take the text
    int width = textRect.Width();
    m_StatusBar.GetStatusBarCtrl().SetParts(1, &width);

    // Initialize the text for the status bar
    m_StatusBar.GetStatusBarCtrl().SetText("View Scale:1", 0, 0);

    return 0;
}
```

The ClassWizard generated the code that isn't shaded. It has inserted a call to the base class version of the **OnCreate()** function, which takes care of creating the definition of the view window. It's important not to delete this function call, otherwise the window will not be created.

The actual creation of the status bar is done with the **Create()** function in the **CStatusBar** object. The **this** pointer for the current **CChildFrame** object is passed to the **Create()** function, setting up a connection between the status bar and the window that owns it. Let's look into what's happening in the code that we have added to the **OnCreate()** function.

Defining the Status Bar Parts

A **CStatusBar** object has an associated **CStatusBarCtrl** object with one or more **parts**. Parts and panes in the context of status bars are equivalent terms — **CStatusBar** refers to panes and **CStatusBarCtrl** refers to parts. You can display a separate item of information in each part.

We can define the number of parts and their widths by a call to the **SetParts()** member of the **CStatusBarCtrl** object. This function requires two arguments. The first argument is the number of parts in the status bar, and the second is an array specifying the right-hand edge of each part in client coordinates. If you omit the call to **SetParts()**, the status bar will have one part by default, which stretches across the whole bar. We could use this, but it looks untidy. A better approach is to size the part so that the text to be displayed fits well — we'll do this now.

The first thing we do in the **OnCreate()** function is to create a temporary **CRect** object in which we'll store the enclosing rectangle for the text that we want to display. We then create a **CClientDC** object which will contain a device context with the same extent as the status bar. This is possible because the status bar, like other controls, is just a window.

Next, the font used in the status bar (set up as part of the desktop properties) is selected into the device context by calling the **SelectObject()** function. The **GetFont()** member of **m_StatusBar** returns a pointer to a **CFont** object that represents the current font. Obviously, the particular font will determine how much space the text we want to display will take up.

The **DrawText()** member of the **CClientDC** object is called to calculate the enclosing rectangle for the text we want to display. This function has four arguments:

1 The text string to be drawn. We have passed a string containing the maximum number of characters we would ever want to display, **"View Scale:99"**.

2 The count of the number of characters in the string. We have specified this as -1, which indicates we are supplying a null-terminated string. In this case the function will work out the character count.

3 Our rectangle, **textRect**. The enclosing rectangle for the text will be stored here in logical coordinates.

4 One or more flags controlling the operation of the function.

We have specified a combination of two flags. **DT_SINGLELINE** specifies that the text is to be on a single line, and **DT_CALCRECT** specifies that we want the function to calculate the size of the rectangle required to display the string and store it in the rectangle pointed to by the third argument. The **DrawText()** function is normally used to output text, but in this instance the **DT_CALCRECT** flag stops the function from actually drawing the string. There are a number of other flags that you can use with this function; you can find details of them by looking up this function with Help.

The next statement sets up the parts for the status bar:

```
m_StatusBar.GetStatusBarCtrl().SetParts(1, &width);
```

The expression **m_StatusBar.GetStatusBarCtrl()** returns a reference to the **CStatusBarCtrl** object that belongs to **m_StatusBar**. The reference returned is used to call the function **SetParts()** for the object. The first argument to **SetParts()** defines the number of parts for the status bar — which is 1 in our case. The second argument is typically the address of an array of type **int** containing the *x* coordinate of the right hand edge of each part in client coordinates. The array will have one element for each part in the status bar. Since we have only one part we pass the address of the single variable, **width**, which contains the width of the rectangle we stored in **textRect**. This will be in client coordinates, since our device context uses **MM_TEXT** by default.

Lastly, we set the initial text in the status bar with a call to the **SetText()** member of **CStatusBarCtrl**. The first argument is the text string to be written, the second is the index position of the part which is to contain the text string, and the third argument specifies the appearance of the part on the screen. The third argument can be any of the following:

Style Code	Appearance
0	The text will have a border such that it appears recessed into the status bar.
SBT_NOBORDERS	The text is drawn without borders.
SBT_OWNERDRAW	The text is drawn by the parent window.
SBT_POPOUT	The text will have a border such that it appears to stand out from the status bar.

In our code, we specify the text with a border so that it appears recessed into the status bar. You could try the other options to see how they look.

Updating the Status Bar

If you build and run the code now, the status bars will appear but they will only show a scale factor of 1, no matter what scale factor is actually being used. Not very useful. What we need to do is to change the text each time a different scale is chosen. This means modifying the **OnViewScale()** handler in **CSketcherView** to change the status bar for the frame. We need to add only four lines of code:

```
void CSketcherView::OnViewScale()
{
   CScaleDialog aDlg;                     // Create a dialog object
   aDlg.m_Scale = m_Scale;                // Pass the view scale to the dialog
   if(aDlg.DoModal() == IDOK)
   {
      m_Scale = aDlg.m_Scale;             // Get the new scale

      // Get the frame window for this view
      CChildFrame* viewFrame = static_cast<CChildFrame*>(GetParentFrame());

      // Build the message string
      CString StatusMsg("View Scale:");
      StatusMsg += static_cast<char>('0' + m_Scale);

      // Write the string to the status bar
      viewFrame->m_StatusBar.GetStatusBarCtrl().SetText(StatusMsg, 0, 0);

      ResetScrollSizes();                 // Adjust scrolling to the new scale
      InvalidateRect(0);                  // Invalidate the whole window
   }
}
```

As we refer to the **CChildFrame** object here, you must add a **#include** directive for **ChildFrm.h** to the beginning of **SketcherView.cpp**, after the **#include** for **Sketcher.h**.

The first line calls the **GetParentFrame()** member of **CSketcherView** that's inherited from the **CScrollView** class. This returns a pointer to a **CFrameWnd** object to correspond to the frame window, so it has to be cast to **CChildFrame*** for it to be of any use to us.

The next two lines build the message that is to be displayed in the status bar. The **CString** class is used simply because it is more flexible than using a **char** array. **CString**s will be discussed in greater depth a bit later when we add a new element type to Sketcher. We get the character for the scale value by adding the value of **m_Scale** (which will be from 1 to 8) to the character **'0'**. This will generate characters from **'1'** to **'8'**.

Finally, we use the pointer to the child frame to get at the **m_StatusBar** member that we added earlier. We can then get its status bar control and use the **SetText()** member of the control to change the displayed text. The rest of the **OnViewScale()** function remains unchanged.

That's all we need for the status bar. If you build Sketcher again, you should have multiple, scrolled windows, each at different scales, with the scale displayed in a status bar in each view.

Using a List Box

Of course, you don't have to use a spin button to set the scale. You could also use a list box, for example. The logic for handling a scale factor would be exactly the same, and only the dialog box and the code to extract the value for the scale factor from it would change. If you want to try this out without messing up the development of the Sketcher program, you can copy the complete Sketcher project to another folder and make the modifications to the copy. Deleting part of a ClassWizard managed program can be a bit messy, so it's a useful experience for when you really need to do it.

Removing the Scale Dialog

You first need to delete the definition and implementation of **CScaleDialog** from the new Sketcher project, as well as the resource for the scale dialog. To do this, go to FileView, select **ScaleDialog.cpp** and press *Delete*, and then select **ScaleDialog.h** and press *Delete* to remove them from the project. Then go to ResourceView, expand the Dialog folder, click on IDD_SCALE_DLG and hit *Delete* to remove the dialog resource. Now, delete the **#include** statement for **ScaleDialog.h** from **SketcherView.cpp**. At this stage, all references to the original dialog class will have been removed from the project, but the files are still in your project directory so you must remove or delete them. All done yet? Not by a long chalk. The IDs for the resources are still around. To delete these, select the View | Resource Symbols... menu item, and select and delete **IDC_SCALE** and **IDC_SPIN_SCALE** from the list. If you haven't deleted the resources they represent, then they will still be checked and you won't be able to delete them.

In spite of all the deletions so far, ClassWizard will still think that the **CScaleDialog** class exists. To get around this, you need to start ClassWizard and attempt to choose **CScaleDialog** as the Class name:. After an initial warning, you'll see the following dialog:

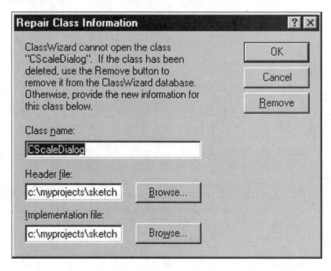

You should select Remove to remove the class from the project completely. You'll need to go through this rigmarole every time that you want to delete a class from an AppWizard-generated project. Believe it or not, we're still not done!

Select the Build | Clean menu item to remove any intermediate files from the project that may contain references to **CScaleDialog**, then close the project workspace by selecting the File | Close Workspace menu item, then re-open it again. Once that's done, we can start by recreating the dialog resource for entering a scale value.

Creating a List Box Control

Right-click on Dialog in ResourceView and add a new dialog with a suitable ID and caption. You could use the same ID as before, **IDD_SCALE_DLG**.

Select the list box button in the controls palette as shown, and click on where you want the list box positioned in the dialog box. You can enlarge the list box and adjust its position in the dialog by dragging it appropriately.

Right-click on the list box and select Properties from the pop-up. You can set the ID to something suitable, such as **IDC_SCALELIST**. Next, select the Styles tab and set it to the options shown below:

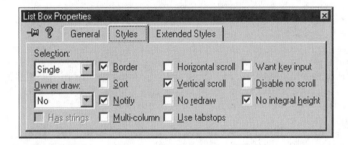

The Sort option box will be checked by default, so make sure you uncheck it. This will mean that strings that we add to the list box will not be automatically sorted. Instead, they'll be appended to the end of the list in the box, and so will be displayed in the sequence in which they are entered. Since we'll use the position in the list of the selected item to indicate the scale, it's important not to have the sequence changed. The list box will have a vertical scroll bar for the list entries by default, which is very useful, and we can ignore the other options. If you want to look into the effects of the other options, you can click the question mark button to display a help screen explaining them.

Now that the dialog is complete you can save it, and you're ready to create the class for the dialog.

Creating the Dialog Class

Right-click on the dialog and select ClassWizard... from the pop-up. Again, you'll be taken through the dialog to create a new class. Give it an appropriate name, such as the one we used before: **CScaleDialog**. Once you've completed that, all you need to do is add a **public** member variable from ClassWizard's Member Variables tab, called **m_Scale**, corresponding to the list box ID, **IDC_SCALELIST**. The default type will be **int**, which is fine. ClassWizard will implement DDX for this data member storing an index to the selected entry, in the list box in it.

We need to add some code to the **OnInitDialog()** member of **CScaleDialog** to initialize the list box, so you'll have to create a handler for **WM_INITDIALOG** using ClassWizard. Add code as follows:

```
BOOL CScaleDialog::OnInitDialog()
{
   CDialog::OnInitDialog();

   CListBox* pListBox = static_cast<CListBox*>(GetDlgItem(IDC_SCALELIST));
   pListBox->AddString("Scale 1");
   pListBox->AddString("Scale 2");
   pListBox->AddString("Scale 3");
   pListBox->AddString("Scale 4");
   pListBox->AddString("Scale 5");
   pListBox->AddString("Scale 6");
   pListBox->AddString("Scale 7");
   pListBox->AddString("Scale 8");
   pListBox->SetCurSel(m_Scale - 1);

   return TRUE;  // return TRUE unless you set the focus to a control
                 // EXCEPTION: OCX Property Pages should return FALSE
}
```

The first line that we have added obtains a pointer to the list box control by calling the **GetDlgItem()** member of the dialog class. This is inherited from the MFC class **CWnd**. It returns a pointer of type **CWnd***, so we need to cast this to the type **CListBox***, which is a pointer to the MFC class defining a list box.

Using the pointer to our dialog's **CListBox** object, we then use the **AddString()** member to add the lines defining the list of scale factors. These will appear in the list box in the order that we enter them, so that the dialog will be displayed as shown below:

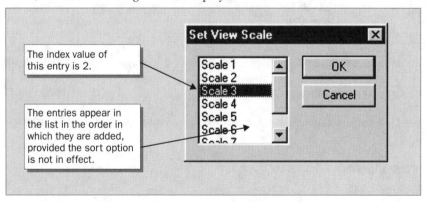

Each entry is associated with a zero-based index value that will be automatically stored in the **m_Scale** member of **CScaleDialog** through the DDX mechanism. Thus, if the third entry in the list is selected, **m_Scale** will be set to 2.

The call to the **SetCurSel()** member selects the string and, if necessary, scrolls it into view—this ensures that one scale option is alreadyhighlighted when you open the dialog.

Displaying the Dialog

The dialog will be displayed by the **OnViewScale()** handler that we added to **CSketcherView** in the previous version of Sketcher. You just need to amend this to deal with the new dialog using a list box. The code for it will be as follows:

```
void CSketcherView::OnViewScale()
{
   CScaleDialog aDlg;                    // Create a dialog object
   aDlg.m_Scale = m_Scale;               // Pass the view scale to the dialog
   if(aDlg.DoModal() == IDOK)
   {
      m_Scale = 1 + aDlg.m_Scale;        // Get the new scale

      // Get the frame window for this view
      CChildFrame* viewFrame = static_cast<CChildFrame*>(GetParentFrame());

      // Build the message string
      CString StatusMsg("View Scale:");
      StatusMsg += static_cast<char>('0' + m_Scale);

      // Write the string to the status bar
      viewFrame->m_StatusBar.GetStatusBarCtrl().SetText(StatusMsg, 0, 0);

      ResetScrollSizes();                // Adjust scrolling to the new scale
      InvalidateRect(0);                 // Invalidate the whole window
   }
}
```

Because the index value for the entry selected from the list is zero-based, we just need to add 1 to it to get the actual scale value to be stored in the view. The code to display this value in the view's status bar is exactly as before. The rest of the code to handle scale factors is already complete and requires no changes. Once you've added back the **#include** statement for **ScaleDialog.h**, you can build and execute this version of Sketcher to see the list box in action.

Using an Edit Box Control

We could use an edit box control to add annotations in Sketcher. We'll need a new element type, **CText**, that will correspond to a text string, and an extra menu item to set a **TEXT** mode for creating elements. Since a text element will only need one reference point, we can create it in the **OnLButtonDown()** handler. We'll also need a new menu item in the Element pop-up to set the **TEXT** mode. We'll add this text capability to Sketcher in the following sequence:

1 Create the dialog box resource and its associated class.

2 Add the new menu item.

3 Add the code to open the dialog for creating an element.

4 Add the support for a **CText** class.

Creating an Edit Box Resource

Create a new dialog resource in ResourceView by right-clicking the Dialog folder and selecting Insert Dialog from the pop-up. Change the ID for the new dialog to **IDD_TEXT_DLG** and the caption text to Enter Text.

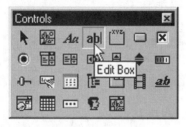

To add an edit box, select the edit box icon from the control palette as shown on the left, and then click the position in the dialog where you want to place it. You can adjust the size of the edit box by dragging its borders, and you can alter its position in the dialog by dragging the whole thing around.

You can display the properties for the edit box by right-clicking it and selecting Properties from the pop-up. You could first change its ID to **IDC_EDITTEXT** (on the General tab), then select the Styles tab, which is shown below:

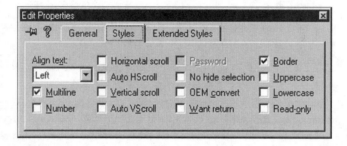

Some of the options here are of interest at this point. First, select the Multiline option. This creates a multi-line edit box, where the text entered can span more than one line. This enables quite a long line of text to be entered and still remain visible in its entirety in the edit box.

The Align text: option determines how the text is to be positioned in the multi-line edit box. Left is fine for us, since we'll be displaying the text as a single line anyway, but you also have the options for Centered and Right.

If you select the Want return option, pressing *Enter* on the keyboard would enter a return character in the text string. This would allow you to analyze the string if you wanted to break it into multiple lines for display. We don't want this effect, so leave it unselected. With this option unselected, pressing *Enter* has the same effect as selecting the default control (which is the OK button), and so will close the dialog.

If Auto HScroll is unselected, there will be an automatic spill to the next line in the edit box when you reach the end of a line of text. However, this is just for visibility in the edit box — it has no effect on the contents of the string.

When you've finished setting the styles for the edit box, you can press *Enter* to close it. You should make sure that the edit box is first in the tab order by selecting the Tab Order menu item from the Layout pop-up. You can then test the dialog by selecting the Test menu item. The dialog is shown below:

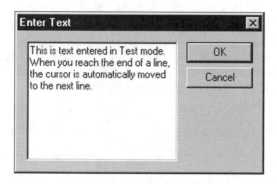

You can even enter text into the dialog in test mode to see how it works. You can press *Enter*, or click on the Cancel or OK button, to close the dialog.

Creating the Dialog Class

After saving the dialog resource, you can go to ClassWizard to create a suitable dialog class corresponding to the resource, which you could call **CTextDialog**. Next, switch to the Member Variables tab in ClassWizard, select the **IDC_EDITTEXT** control ID and click the Add Variable... button. Call the new variable **m_TextString** and select its type as **CString**. We'll take a look at this class once we've finished the dialog class. Having added the variable you can also specify a maximum length for it, as shown here:

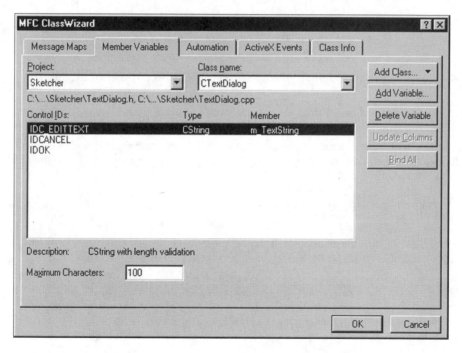

A length of 100 will be more than adequate for our needs. The variable that we have added here will be automatically updated from the data entered into the control by the DDX mechanism. You can click on OK to save the dialog class and close ClassWizard.

The CString Class

The **CString** class provides a very convenient and easy-to-use mechanism for handling strings that you can use just about anywhere a string is required. To be more precise, you can use a **CString** object in place of strings of type **const char[]**, which is the usual type for a character string in C++, or of type **LPCTSTR**, which is a type that comes up frequently in Windows API functions.

The **CString** class provides several overloaded operators which make it easy to process strings:

Operator	Usage
=	Copies one string to another, as in:

	```Str1 = Str2; // Copies contents of Str1 to Str2```
	```Str1 = "A normal string"; // Copies the RHS string to Str1```

+	Concatenates two or more strings, as in:
	```Str1 = Str2 + Str3 + " more"; // Forms Str1 from 3 strings```
+=	Appends a string to an existing **CString** object
==	Compares two strings for equality, as in:
	```if(Str1 == Str2)``` ``` // do something```
< <=	Tests if one string is less than, or less than or equal to, another.
> >=	Tests if one string is greater than, or greater than or equal to, another.

The variables **Str1** and **Str2** above are **CString** objects. **CString** objects automatically grow as necessary, such as when you add an additional string to the end of an existing object. For example, in the statements:

```
CString Str = "A fool and your money ";
Str += "are soon partners.";
```

the first statement declares and initializes the object **Str**. The second statement appends an additional string to **Str**, so the length of **Str** will automatically increase.

> *Generally, you should avoid creating* **CString** *objects on the heap as far as possible. The memory management necessary for growing them means that operations will be rather slow.*

Adding the Text Menu Item

Adding a new menu item should be easy by now. You just need to open the menu resource with the ID **IDR_SKETCHTYPE** by double-clicking it, and add a new menu item Text to the Element menu. The default ID, **ID_ELEMENT_TEXT**, will be fine so you can accept that. You can add a prompt to be displayed on the status bar corresponding to the menu item, and since we'll also want add an additional toolbar button corresponding to this menu item, you can add a tool tip to the end of the prompt line, using \n to separate the prompt and the tool tip.

Don't forget the context menu. You can copy the menu item from **IDR_SKETCHTYPE**. Right click on the Text menu item and select Copy from the pop-up. Open the menu **IDR_CURSOR_MENU**, extend the no element menu, and you can right click on the empty item at the bottom and select Paste. Then, all you need to do is to drag the item to the appropriate position, before the separator, and save the resource file.

Add the toolbar button to the **IDR_MAINFRAME** toolbar and set its ID to the same as that for the menu item, **ID_ELEMENT_TEXT**. You can drag the new button so that it's positioned at the end of the block defining the other types of element. When you've saved the resources, we need to add a handler for the menu item.

Go to ClassWizard and add a COMMAND handler to **CSketcherDoc** corresponding to **ID_ELEMENT_TEXT**. Click the Edit Code button and add code as follows:

```
void CSketcherDoc::OnElementText()
{
    m_Element = TEXT;
}
```

Only one line of code is necessary to set the element type in the document to **TEXT**. You must also add a line to the **OurConstants.h** file:

```
const WORD TEXT = 105U;
```

This statement can be added at the end of the other element type definitions. You also need to add a function to check the menu item if it is the current mode — use ClassWizard to add an **UPDATE_COMMAND_UI** handler corresponding to the **ID_ELEMENT_TEXT** ID, and implement the code for it as follows:

```
void CSketcherDoc::OnUpdateElementText(CCmdUI* pCmdUI)
{
    // Set checked if the current element is text
    pCmdUI->SetCheck(m_Element == TEXT);
}
```

This operates in the same way as the other Element pop-up menu items. We can now define the **CText** class for an object of type **TEXT**.

Defining a Text Element

We can derive the class **CText** from the **CElement** class as follows:

```
class CText : public CElement
{
public:
  // Function to display a text element
  virtual void Draw(CDC* pDC, const CElement* pElement = NULL) const;

  // Constructor for a text element
  CText(const CPoint& Start, const CPoint& End, const CString& String,
                                        const COLORREF& Color);

  virtual void Move(const CSize& Size);      // Move a text element

protected:
  CPoint m_StartPoint;                       // position of a text element
  CString m_String;                          // Text to be displayed
  CText(){}                                  // Default constructor
};
```

You can put this definition at the end of the **Elements.h** file (but before the **#endif** statement, of course). This class definition declares the virtual **Draw()** and **Move()** functions, as the other element classes do. The data member **m_String** of type **CString** stores the text to be displayed, and **m_StartPoint** specifies the position of the string in the client area of a view.

We should now look at the constructor declaration in a little more detail. The **CText** constructor declaration defines four parameters which provide the following essential information:

Argument		Defines
CPoint	Start	The position of the text in logical coordinates
CPoint	End	The corner opposite **Start** that defines the rectangle enclosing the text
CString	String	The text string to be displayed as a **CString** object
COLORREF	Color	The color of the text

The pen width doesn't apply to an item of text, since the appearance is determined by the font. Although we do not need to pass a pen width as an argument to the constructor, the constructor will need to initialize the **m_Pen** member inherited from the base class. This is because it will be used in the computation of the bounding rectangle for the text.

Implementing the CText Class

We have three functions to implement for the **CText** class:

1 The constructor for a **CText** object.

2 The virtual **Draw()** function, to display it.

3 The **Move()** function, to support moving a text object by dragging it with the mouse.

You can add these to the **Elements.cpp** file.

The CText Constructor

The constructor for a **CText** object needs to initialize the class and base class data members:

```
CText::CText(const CPoint& Start, const CPoint& End, const CString& String,
                                        const COLORREF& Color)
{
   m_Pen = 1;                        // Pen width only for bounding rectangle
   m_Color = Color;                  // Set the color for the text
   m_String = String;                // Make a copy of the string
   m_StartPoint = Start;             // Start point for string

   m_EnclosingRect = CRect(Start, End);
   m_EnclosingRect.NormalizeRect();
}
```

This is all standard stuff, just like we've seen before for the other elements.

Drawing a CText Object

Drawing text in a device context is different to drawing a geometric figure. The **Draw()** function for a **CText** object is as follows:

```
void CText::Draw(CDC* pDC, const CElement* pElement) const
{
   COLORREF Color(m_Color);          // Initialize with element color

   if (this == pElement)
      Color = SELECT_COLOR;          // Set selected color

   // Set the text color and output the text
   pDC->SetTextColor(Color);
   pDC->TextOut(m_StartPoint.x, m_StartPoint.y, m_String);
}
```

We don't need a pen to display text. We just need to specify the text color using the **SetTextColor()** function member of the **CDC** object, and then use the **TextOut()** member to output the text string. This will display the string using the default font.

Since the **TextOut()** function doesn't use a pen, it won't be affected by setting the drawing mode of the device context. This means that the raster operations (ROP) method that we use to move the elements will leave temporary trails behind when applied to text. Remember that we used the **SetROP2()** function to specify the way in which the pen would logically combine with the background. By choosing **R2_NOTXORPEN** as the drawing mode, we could cause a previously drawn element to disappear by redrawing it; then it would revert to the background color and thus become invisible. Fonts aren't drawn using a pen, so it won't work with our text elements. We'll see how to fix this problem in the next chapter.

Moving a CText Object

The **Move()** function for a **CText** object is very simple:

```
void CText::Move(const CSize& aSize)
{
   m_StartPoint += aSize;                  // Move the start point
   m_EnclosingRect += aSize;               // Move the rectangle
}
```

All we need to do is alter the point defining the position of the string, and the data member defining the enclosing rectangle, by the distance specified in the **aSize** parameter.

Creating a Text Element

Once the element type has been set to **TEXT**, a text object should be created at the cursor position whenever you click the left mouse button and enter the text you want to display. We therefore need to open the dialog to enter text in the **OnLButtonDown()** handler. Add the following code to this handler in **CSketcherView**:

```
void CSketcherView::OnLButtonDown(UINT nFlags, CPoint point)
{
   CClientDC aDC(this);                    // Create a device context
   OnPrepareDC(&aDC);                      // Get origin adjusted
   aDC.DPtoLP(&point);                     // convert point to Logical

   if(m_MoveMode)
   {
      // In moving mode, so drop the element
      m_MoveMode = FALSE;                  // Kill move mode
      m_pSelected = 0;                     // De-select the element
      GetDocument()->UpdateAllViews(0);    // Redraw all the views
   }
   else
   {
      CSketcherDoc* pDoc = GetDocument();  // Get a document pointer
      if(pDoc->GetElementType() == TEXT)
      {
         CTextDialog aDlg;
         if(aDlg.DoModal() == IDOK)
         {
            // Exit OK so create a text element
            CSize TextExtent = aDC.GetTextExtent(aDlg.m_TextString);

            // Get bottom right of text rectangle - MM_LOENGLISH
            CPoint BottomRt(point.x+TextExtent.cx, point.y-TextExtent.cy);
            CText* pTextElement = new CText(point, BottomRt,
                         aDlg.m_TextString, pDoc->GetElementColor());

            // Add the element to the document
            pDoc->AddElement(pTextElement);

            // Get all views updated
            pDoc->UpdateAllViews(0,0,pTextElement);
         }
         return;
      }
```

```
        m_FirstPoint = point;          // Record the cursor position
        SetCapture();                  // Capture subsequent mouse messages
    }
}
```

The code to be added is shaded. It creates a **CTextDialog** object and then opens the dialog using the **DoModal()** function call. The **m_TextString** member of **aDlg** will be automatically set to the string entered in the edit box, so we can just use this data member to pass the string entered back to the **CText** constructor if the OK button is used to close the dialog. The color is obtained from the document using the **GetElementColor()** member function that we have used previously. The position of the text is the **point** value holding the cursor position that is passed to the handler.

We also need to calculate the opposite corner of the rectangle that bounds the text. Because the size of the rectangle for the block of text depends on the font used in a device context, we use the **GetTextExtent()** function in the **CClientDC** object, **aDC**, to initialize the **CSize** object, **TextExtent**, with the width and height of the text string in logical coordinates.

Calculating the rectangle for the text in this way is a bit of a cheat, which could cause a problem once we start saving documents in a file. Problems could occur because it's conceivable that a document could be read back into an environment where the default font in a device context is larger than that in effect when the rectangle was calculated. This shouldn't arise very often, so we won't worry about it here, but as a hint, if you want to pursue it, you could use an object of the class **CFont** in the **CText** definition to define a specific font to be used. You could then use the characteristics of the font to calculate the enclosing rectangle for the text string.

You could also use **CFont** to change the font size so that the text is zoomed when the scale factor is increased. However, you also need to devise a way to calculate the bounding rectangle based on the font size currently being used, which will vary with the view scale.

The **CText** object is created on the heap because the list in the document only maintains pointers to the elements. We add the new element to the document by calling the **AddElement()** member of **CSketcherDoc**, with the pointer to the new text element as an argument. Finally, **UpdateAllViews()** is called with the first argument 0, which specifies that all views are to be updated.

The Context Menu

In order to make the context menu reflect the selection of a text item we need to add the following shaded line to the **OnRButtonUp()** handler in **CSketcherView.cpp**:

```
aMenu.CheckMenuItem(ID_ELEMENT_LINE,
    (LINE==ElementType?MF_CHECKED:MF_UNCHECKED)|MF_BYCOMMAND);
aMenu.CheckMenuItem(ID_ELEMENT_RECTANGLE,
    (RECTANGLE==ElementType?MF_CHECKED:MF_UNCHECKED)|MF_BYCOMMAND);
aMenu.CheckMenuItem(ID_ELEMENT_CIRCLE,
    (CIRCLE==ElementType?MF_CHECKED:MF_UNCHECKED)|MF_BYCOMMAND);
aMenu.CheckMenuItem(ID_ELEMENT_CURVE,
    (CURVE==ElementType?MF_CHECKED:MF_UNCHECKED)|MF_BYCOMMAND);
aMenu.CheckMenuItem(ID_ELEMENT_TEXT,
    (TEXT==ElementType?MF_CHECKED:MF_UNCHECKED)|MF_BYCOMMAND);
```

Exercising the Edit Box

For the program to compile successfully, you need to add a **#include** statement for **TextDialog.h** to the **SketcherView.cpp** file. You should now be able to produce annotated sketches using multiple scaled and scrolled views, such as the ones shown below:

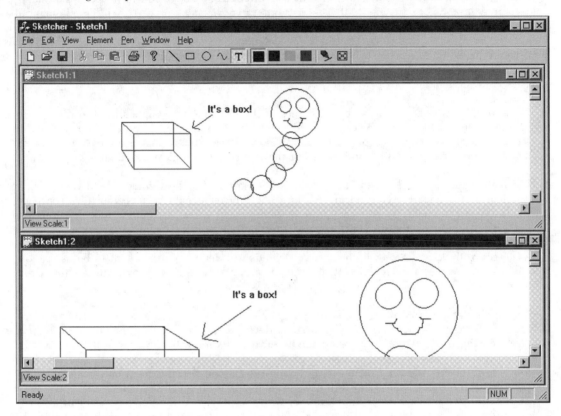

Summary

In this chapter, you've seen several different dialogs using a variety of controls. Although we haven't created dialogs involving several different controls at once, the mechanism for handling them is the same as we have seen, since each control can operate independently of the others.

The most important points that you've seen in this chapter are:

▶ A dialog involves two components: a resource defining the dialog box and its controls, and a class that will be used to display and manage the dialog.

▶ Information can be extracted from controls in a dialog using the DDX mechanism. The data can be validated using the DDV mechanism. To use DDX/DDV you need only to use ClassWizard to define variables in the dialog class associated with the controls.

▶ A modal dialog retains the focus in the application until the dialog box is closed. As long as a modal dialog is displayed, all other windows in an application are inactive.

▶ A modeless dialog allows the focus to switch from the dialog box to other windows in the application and back again. A modeless dialog can remain displayed as long as the application is executing, if required.

▶ Common Controls are a set of standard Windows 95 controls that are supported by MFC and the resource editing capabilities of the Visual C++ IDE.

▶ Although controls are usually associated with a dialog, you can add controls to any window if you want to.

Exercises

Ex17-1: Implement the scale dialog using radio buttons.

Ex17-2: Implement the pen width dialog using a list box.

Ex17-3: Implement the pen width dialog as a combo box with the drop list type selected on the Styles tab in the properties box. (The drop list type allows the user to select from a drop-down list, but not to key alternative entries in the list.)

Storing and Printing Documents

With what we have accomplished so far in our Sketcher program, we can create a reasonably comprehensive document with views at various scales, but the information is transient since we have no means of saving a document. In this chapter, we'll remedy that by seeing how we can store a document on disk. We'll also see how we can output a document to a printer.

In this chapter, you will learn:

> What serialization is and how it works

> What you need to do to make objects of a class serializable

> The role of a **CArchive** object in serialization

> How to implement serialization in your own classes

> How to implement serialization in the Sketcher application

> How printing works with MFC

> What view class functions you can use to support printing

> What a **CPrintInfo** object contains and how it's used in the printing process

> How to implement multi-page printing in the Sketcher application

Understanding Serialization

A document in an MFC-based program is not a simple entity — it's a class object that can be very complicated. It typically contains a variety of objects, each of which may contain other objects, each of which may contain still more objects... and that structure may continue for a number of levels.

We need to be able to save a document in a file, but writing a class object to a file represents something of a problem, as it isn't the same as a basic data item like an integer or a character string. A basic data item consists of a known number of bytes, so to write it to a file only requires that the appropriate number of bytes be written. Conversely, if you know that an **int** was written to a file, then to get it back you just read the appropriate number of bytes.

Writing objects is different. Even if you write away all the data members of an object, that's not enough to be able to get the original object back. Class objects contain function members as well as data members, and all the members, both data and functions, will have access specifiers. Therefore, to record objects in an external file, the information written to the file must contain complete specifications of all the class structures involved. The read process must also be clever enough to synthesize the original objects completely from the data in the file. MFC supports a mechanism called **serialization** to help you to implement input from (and output to disk of) your class objects, with a minimum of time and trouble.

The basic idea behind serialization is that any class that's serializable must take care of storing and retrieving itself. This means that for your classes to be serializable—in the case of the Sketcher application this will include **CElement** and the shape classes we have derived from it—they must be able to write themselves to a file. This implies that for a class to be serializable, all the class types that are used to declare data members must be serializable too.

Serializing a Document

This all sounds like it might be rather tricky, but the basic capability for serializing your document was built into the application by AppWizard right at the outset. The handlers for File | Save, File | Save As..., and File | Open all assume that you want serialization implemented for your document, and they already contain the code to support it. Let's take a look at the parts of the definition and implementation of **CSketcherDoc** that relate to creating a document using serialization.

Serialization in the Document Class Definition

The code in the definition of **CSketcherDoc** that enables serialization of a document object is shown shaded in the following fragment:

```
class CSketcherDoc : public CDocument
{
protected: // create from serialization only
    CSketcherDoc();
    DECLARE_DYNCREATE(CSketcherDoc)

// Rest of the class...

// Overrides
    // ClassWizard generated virtual function overrides
    //{{AFX_VIRTUAL(CSketcherDoc)
    public:
    virtual BOOL OnNewDocument();
    virtual void Serialize(CArchive& ar);
    //}}AFX_VIRTUAL

// Rest of the class...

};
```

There are three items here relating to serializing a document object:

1 The **DECLARE_DYNCREATE()** macro

2 The **Serialize()** member function

3 The default class constructor

DECLARE_DYNCREATE() is a macro which enables objects of the **CSketcherDoc** class to be created dynamically by the application framework during the serialization input process. It's matched by a complementary macro, **IMPLEMENT_DYNCREATE()**, in the class implementation. These macros only apply to classes derived from **CObject**, but as we shall see shortly, they aren't the only pair of macros that can be used in this context. For any class that you want to serialize, **CObject** must be a direct or indirect base, since it adds the functionality that enables serialization to work. This is why we took the trouble to derive our **CElement** class from **CObject**. Almost all MFC classes are derived from **CObject** and, as such, are serializable.

The Hierarchy Chart, which you can find in the MSDN library under Visual C++ Documentation\Reference\MFC Library and Templates, shows those classes which aren't derived from CObject. **Note that** CArchive **is in this list.**

The class definition also includes a declaration for a virtual function **Serialize()**. Every class that's serializable must include this function. It's called to perform both input and output serialization operations on the data members of the class. The object of type **CArchive** that's passed as an argument to this function determines whether the operation that is to occur is input or output. We'll look into this in more detail when we consider the implementation of serialization for the document class.

Note that the class explicitly defines a default constructor. This is also essential for serialization to work, as the default constructor will be used by the framework to synthesize an object when reading from a disk file, which is then filled out with the data from the file to set the values of the data members of the object.

Serialization in the Document Class Implementation

There are two bits of the file containing the implementation of **CSketcherDoc** that relate to serialization. The first is the macro **IMPLEMENT_DYNCREATE()** that complements the **DECLARE_DYNCREATE()** macro:

```
// SketcherDoc.cpp : implementation of the CSketcherDoc class
//

#include "stdafx.h"
#include "Sketcher.h"
#include "PenDialog.h"

#include "Elements.h"
#include "SketcherDoc.h"
```

```
#ifdef _DEBUG
#define new DEBUG_NEW
#undef THIS_FILE
static char THIS_FILE[] = __FILE__;
#endif


/////////////////////////////////////////////////////////////////////////////
// CSketcherDoc

IMPLEMENT_DYNCREATE(CSketcherDoc, CDocument)

// Message maps and the rest of the file...
```

All this macro does is to define the base class for **CSketcherDoc** as **CDocument**. This is required for the proper dynamic creation of a **CSketcherDoc** object, including members inherited from the base class.

The Serialize() Function

The class implementation also includes the definition of the **Serialize()** function:

```
void CSketcherDoc::Serialize(CArchive& ar)
{
   if (ar.IsStoring())
   {
      // TODO: add storing code here
   }
   else
   {
      // TODO: add loading code here
   }
}
```

This function serializes the data members of the class. The argument passed to the function is a reference to an object of the **CArchive** class, **ar**. The **IsStoring()** member of this class object returns **TRUE** if the operation is to store data members in a file, and **FALSE** if the operation is to read back data members from a previously stored document.

Since AppWizard can have no knowledge of what data your document contains, the process of writing and reading this information is up to you, as indicated by the comments. To understand how this is done, we need to look a little more closely at the **CArchive** class.

The CArchive Class

The **CArchive** class is the engine that drives the serialization mechanism. It provides an MFC-based equivalent of the stream operations in C++ that we used for reading from the keyboard, and writing to the screen, in our console program examples. An object of the MFC class **CArchive** provides a mechanism for streaming your objects out to a file, or recovering them again as an input stream, automatically reconstituting the objects of your class in the process.

A **CArchive** object has a **CFile** object associated with it which provides disk input/output capability for binary files, and provides the actual connection to the physical file. Within the serialization process, the **CFile** object takes care of all the specifics of the file input and output operations, and the **CArchive** object deals with the logic of structuring the object data to be written or reconstructing the objects from the information read. You only need to worry about the details of the associated **CFile** object if you are constructing your own **CArchive** object. With our document in Sketcher, the framework has already taken care of it and passes the **CArchive** object **ar**, that it constructs, to the **Serialize()** function in **CSketcherDoc**. We'll be able to use the same object in each of the **Serialize()** functions we add to the shape classes when we implement serialization for them.

CArchive overloads the extraction and insertion operators (**>>** and **<<**) for input and output operations respectively on objects of classes derived from **CObject**, plus a range of basic data types. These overloaded operators will work with the following types of objects:

Type	Definition
float	Standard single precision floating point.
double	Standard double precision floating point.
BYTE	8-bit unsigned integer.
int	16-bit signed integer.
LONG	32-bit signed integer.
WORD	16-bit unsigned integer.
DWORD	32-bit unsigned integer.
CObject*	Pointer to **CObject**.
CString	A **CString** object defining a string.
SIZE and **CSize**	An object defining a size as a **cx**, **cy** pair.
POINT and **CPoint**	An object defining a point as an **x**, **y** pair.
RECT and **CRect**	An object defining a rectangle by its top left and bottom right corners.
CTime	A **CTime** object defines a time and a date.
CTimeSpan	A **CTimeSpan** object contains a time interval in seconds, usually the difference between two **CTime** objects.

For basic data types in your objects, you use the insertion and extraction operators to serialize the data. To read or write an object of a serializable class which you have derived from **CObject**, you can either call the **Serialize()** function for the object, or use the extraction or insertion operator. Whichever way you choose must be used consistently for both input and output, so you mustn't output an object using the insertion operator and then read it back using the **Serialize()** function, or vice versa.

Where you don't know the type of an object when you read it, as in the case of the pointers in the list of shapes in our document, for example, you must *only* use the **Serialize()** function. This brings the virtual function mechanism into play, so the appropriate **Serialize()** function for the type of object pointed to is determined at run time.

A **CArchive** object is constructed either for storing objects or for retrieving objects. The **CArchive** function **IsStoring()** will return **TRUE** if the object is for output, and **FALSE** if the object is for input. We saw this function used in the **if** statement in the **Serialize()** member of the **CSketcherDoc** class.

There are many other member functions of the **CArchive** class which are concerned with the detailed mechanics of the serialization process, but you don't usually need to know about them to use serialization in your programs.

Functionality of CObject-based Classes

There are three levels of functionality available in your classes when they're derived from the MFC class **CObject**. The level you get in your class is determined by which of three different macros you use in the definition of your class:

Macro	Functionality
DECLARE_DYNAMIC()	Support for run-time class information.
DECLARE_DYNCREATE()	Support for run-time class information and dynamic object creation.
DECLARE_SERIAL()	Support for run-time class information, dynamic object creation and serialization of objects.

Each of these requires a complementary macro, named with the prefix **IMPLEMENT_** instead of **DECLARE_**, to be placed in the file containing the class implementation. As the table indicates, the macros provide progressively more functionality, so we'll concentrate on the third macro, **DECLARE_SERIAL()**, since it provides everything that the preceding macros do and more. This is the macro you should use to enable serialization in your own classes. It requires the macro **IMPLEMENT_SERIAL()** to be added to the file containing the class implementation.

You may be wondering why the document class uses **DECLARE_DYNCREATE()** and not **DECLARE_SERIAL()**. The **DECLARE_DYNCREATE()** macro provides the capability for dynamic creation of the objects of the class in which it appears. The **DECLARE_SERIAL()** macro provides the capability for serialization of the class, plus the dynamic creation of objects of the class, so it incorporates the effects of **DECLARE_DYNCREATE()**. Your document class doesn't need serialization, since the framework only has to synthesize the document object and then restore the values of its data members. However, the data members of a document *do* need to be serializable, as this is the process used to store and retrieve them.

The Macros Adding Serialization to a Class

With the **DECLARE_SERIAL()** macro in the definition of your **CObject**-based class, you get access to the serialization support provided by **CObject**. This includes special **new** and **delete** operators that incorporate memory leak detection in debug mode. You don't need to do anything to use this, as it works automatically.

The macro requires the class name to be specified as an argument, so for serialization of the **CElement** class, you would add the following line to the class definition:

```
DECLARE_SERIAL(CElement)
```

> *There's no semicolon required here since this is a macro, not a C++ statement.*

It doesn't matter where you put the macro within the class definition (as long as it's not in a section that ClassWizard maintains), but if you always put it as the first line, then you'll always be able to verify that it's there, even when the class definition involves many lines of code.

The macro **IMPLEMENT_SERIAL()**, which you need to place in the implementation file for your class, requires three arguments to be specified. The first argument is the name of your class, the second is the direct base class, and the third argument is an unsigned 32-bit integer identifying a **schema number**, or version number, for your program. This schema number allows the serialization process to guard against problems that can arise if you write objects with one version of a program and read them with another, in which the classes may be different.

For example, we could add the following line to the implementation of the **CElement** class:

```
IMPLEMENT_SERIAL(CElement, CObject, 1)
```

If we subsequently modified the class definition, we would change the schema number to 2, say. If the program attempts to read data that was written with a different schema number from that in the currently active program, an exception will be thrown. The best place for this macro is as the first line following the **#include**s and any initial comments in the **.cpp** file.

Where **CObject** is an indirect base of a class, as in the case of our **CLine** class, for example, each class in the hierarchy must have the serialization macros added for serialization to work in the top level class. For serialization in **CLine** to work, the macros must also be added to **CElement**.

How Serialization Works

The overall process of serializing a document is illustrated in a simplified form below:

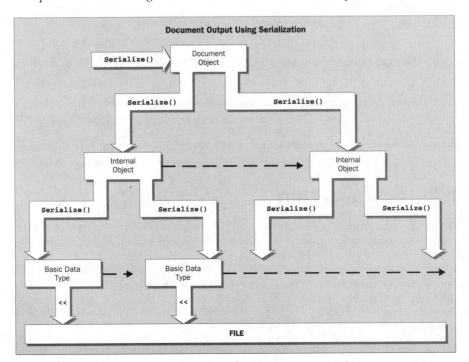

The **Serialize()** function in the document object needs to call the **Serialize()** function (or use an overloaded insertion operator) for each of its data members. Where a member is a class object, the **Serialize()** function for that object will serialize each of its data members in turn, until ultimately basic data types are written to the file. Since most classes in MFC ultimately derive from **CObject**, they contain serialization support, so you can almost always serialize objects of MFC classes.

The data that you'll deal with in the **Serialize()** member functions of your classes and the application document object will, in each case, be just the data members. The structure of the classes involved, and any other data necessary to reconstitute your original objects, is automatically taken care of by the **CArchive** object.

Where you derive multiple levels of classes from **CObject**, the **Serialize()** function in a class must call the **Serialize()** member of its direct base class to ensure that the direct base class data members are serialized. Note that serialization doesn't support multiple inheritance, so there can only be one base class for each class defined in a hierarchy.

How to Implement Serialization for a Class

From the previous discussion, we can summarize the actions that you need to take to add serialization to a class:

1 Make sure that the class is derived directly or indirectly from **CObject**.

2 Add the **DECLARE_SERIAL()** macro to the class definition (and to the direct base class if the direct base is not **CObject**).

3 Declare the function **Serialize()** as a member function of your class.

4 Add the **IMPLEMENT_SERIAL()** macro to the file containing the class implementation.

5 Implement the **Serialize()** function for your class.

Let's now see how we can implement serialization for documents in our Sketcher program.

Applying Serialization

To implement serialization in the Sketcher application, we need to complete the **Serialize()** function in **CSketcherDoc** to deal with all of the data members of that class. We need then to add serialization to each of the classes which specify objects that may be included in a document. Before we start adding serialization to our application classes, let's make some small changes to the program to record when we change the document. This isn't absolutely necessary, but it is highly desirable, since it will enable the program to guard against the document being closed without saving changes.

Recording Document Changes

There's already a mechanism for noting when a document changes; it uses an inherited member of **CSketcherDoc**, **SetModifiedFlag()**. By calling this function consistently whenever the document changes, you record the fact that the document has been altered in a data member of the document class object. This will cause a prompt to be displayed automatically when you try to exit the application without saving the modified document. The argument to the function **SetModifiedFlag()** is a value of type **BOOL**, and the default value is **TRUE**. If you have occasion to specify that the document was unchanged, you can call this function with the argument **FALSE**, although circumstances where this is necessary are rare.

There are only three occasions when we alter a document object:

1 When we call the **AddElement()** member of **CSketcherDoc** to add a new element.

2 When we call the **DeleteElement()** member of **CSketcherDoc** to delete an element.

3 When we move an element.

All three situations are very easy to deal with. All we need to do is add a call to **SetModifiedFlag()** to each of the functions involved in these operations. The definition of **AddElement()** appears in the class definition. You can extend this to:

```
void AddElement(CElement* pElement)      // Add an element to the list
{
   m_ElementList.AddTail(pElement);
   SetModifiedFlag();                    // Set the modified flag
}
```

You can get to the definition of **DeleteElement()** by clicking on its member name in the ClassView. You should add one line to it, as follows:

```
void CSketcherDoc::DeleteElement(CElement* pElement)
{
   if(pElement)
   {
      // If the element pointer is valid,
      // find the pointer in the list and delete it
      SetModifiedFlag();          // Set the modified flag
      POSITION aPosition = m_ElementList.Find(pElement);
      m_ElementList.RemoveAt(aPosition);
      delete pElement;            // Delete the element from the heap
   }
}
```

Note that we must only set the flag if **pElement** is not **NULL**, so you can't just stick the function call anywhere.

In a view object, moving an element occurs in the **MoveElement()** member called by the handler for the **WM_MOUSEMOVE** message, but we only actually change the document when the left mouse button is pressed. If there's a right button click, the element is put back to its original position, so you only need to add a line to the **OnLButtonDown()** function calling the **SetModifiedFlag()** function for the document, as follows:

```
void CSketcherView::OnLButtonDown(UINT nFlags, CPoint point)
{
    CClientDC aDC(this);                // Create a device context
    OnPrepareDC(&aDC);                  // Get origin adjusted
    aDC.DPtoLP(&point);                 // convert point to Logical

    if(m_MoveMode)
    {
        // In moving mode, so drop the element
        m_MoveMode = FALSE;              // Kill move mode
        m_pSelected = 0;                 // De-select element
        GetDocument()->UpdateAllViews(0); // Redraw all the views
        GetDocument()->SetModifiedFlag(); // Set the modified flag
    }
    // Rest of the function as before...
}
```

We just need to call the inherited member of our view class, **GetDocument()**, to get access to a pointer to the document object, and then use this pointer to call the **SetModifiedFlag()** function. We now have all the places where we change the document covered.

If you build and run Sketcher, and modify a document or add elements to it, you'll now get a prompt to save the document when you exit the program. Of course, the File | Save menu option doesn't do anything yet, except to clear the modified flag and save an empty file to disk. We need to implement serialization to get the document written away to disk properly, and that's the next step.

Serializing the Document

The first step is the implementation of the **Serialize()** function for the **CSketcherDoc** class. Within this function, we must add code to serialize the data members of **CSketcherDoc**. The data members that we have declared in the class are as follows:

```
class CSketcherDoc : public CDocument
{
protected: // create from serialization only
    CSketcherDoc();
    DECLARE_DYNCREATE(CSketcherDoc)

// Attributes
public:

protected:
    COLORREF m_Color;                                   // Current drawing color
    WORD m_Element;                                     // Current element type
    CTypedPtrList<CObList, CElement*> m_ElementList;    // Element list
    int m_PenWidth;                                     // Current pen width
    CSize m_DocSize;                                    // Document size
```

```
        // Rest of the class...
    };
```

All we need to do is to insert the statements to store and retrieve these five data members in the **Serialize()** member of the class. We can do this with the following code:

```
void CSketcherDoc::Serialize(CArchive& ar)
{
    m_ElementList.Serialize(ar);        // Serialize the element list

    if (ar.IsStoring())
    {
        ar << m_Color              // Store the current color
           << m_Element            // the current element type,
           << m_PenWidth           // and the current pen width
           << m_DocSize;           // and the current document size
    }
    else
    {
        ar >> m_Color              // Retrieve the current color
           >> m_Element            // the current element type,
           >> m_PenWidth           // and the current pen width
           >> m_DocSize;           // and the current document size
    }
}
```

For four of the data members, we just use the extraction and insertion operators overloaded by **CArchive**. This works for the data member **m_Color**, even though its type is **COLORREF**, because type **COLORREF** is the same as type **long**. We can't use the extraction and insertion operators for **m_ElementList** because its type isn't supported by the operators. However, as long as the **CTypedPtrList** class is defined from the collection class template using **CObList**, as we've done in the declaration of **m_ElementList**, the class will automatically support serialization. We can, therefore, just call the **Serialize()** function for the object.

We don't need to place calls to the **Serialize()** member of the object **m_ElementList** in the **if-else** statement because the kind of operation to be performed will be determined automatically by the **CArchive** argument **ar**. The single statement calling the **Serialize()** member of **m_ElementList** will take care of both input and output.

That's all we need for serializing the document class data members, but serializing the element list, **m_ElementList**, will cause the **Serialize()** functions for the element classes to be called to store and retrieve the elements themselves. Therefore, we also need to implement serialization for those classes.

Serializing the Element Classes

All the shape classes are serializable because we derived them from their base class **CElement**, which in turn is derived from **CObject**. The reason that we specified **CObject** as the base for **CElement** was solely to get support for serialization. We can now add support for serialization to each of the shape classes by adding the appropriate macros to the class definitions and implementations. We must also add code to the **Serialize()** function member of each class to serialize its data members. We can start with the base class, **CElement**, where you need to modify the class definition as follows:

```
class CElement: public CObject
{
DECLARE_SERIAL(CElement)

protected:
    COLORREF m_Color;                       // Color of an element
    CRect m_EnclosingRect;                  // Rectangle enclosing an element
    int m_Pen;                              // Pen width

public:
    virtual ~CElement(){}                          // Virtual destructor

    // Virtual draw operation
    virtual void Draw(CDC* pDC, const CElement* pElement=0) const {}
    virtual void Move(const CSize& aSize){}  // Move an element
    CRect GetBoundRect() const;              // Get bounding rectangle for an element

    virtual void Serialize(CArchive& ar);  // Serialize function for CElement

protected:
    CElement(){}                                   // Default constructor
};
```

We have added the **DECLARE_SERIAL()** macro and a declaration for the virtual function **Serialize()**.

We already had the default constructor defined as **protected** in the class, although in fact it doesn't matter what its access specification is, as long as it appears explicitly in the class definition. It can be **public**, **protected**, or **private**, and serialization will still work. If you forget to include it, though, you'll get an error message when the **IMPLEMENT_SERIAL()** macro is compiled.

You should add the **DECLARE_SERIAL()** macro to each of the classes **CLine**, **CRectangle**, **CCircle**, **CCurve** and **CText**, with the relevant class name as the argument. You should also add a declaration for the **Serialize()** function as a **public** member of each class.

In the file **Elements.cpp**, you must add the following macro at the beginning:

```
IMPLEMENT_SERIAL(CElement, CObject, VERSION_NUMBER)
```

You can define the constant **VERSION_NUMBER** in the **OurConstants.h** file by adding the lines:

```
// Program version number for use in serialization
const UINT VERSION_NUMBER = 1;
```

You can then use the same constant when you add the macro for each of the other shape classes. For instance, for the **CLine** class you should add the line,

```
IMPLEMENT_SERIAL(CLine, CElement, VERSION_NUMBER)
```

and similarly for the other shape classes. When you modify any of the classes relating to the document, all you need to do is change the definition of **VERSION_NUMBER** in the **OurConstants.h** file, and the new version number will apply in all your **Serialize()** functions. You can put all the **IMPLEMENT_SERIAL()** statements at the beginning of the **Elements.cpp** file if you like. The complete set is:

```
IMPLEMENT_SERIAL(CElement, CObject, VERSION_NUMBER)
IMPLEMENT_SERIAL(CLine, CElement, VERSION_NUMBER)
IMPLEMENT_SERIAL(CRectangle, CElement, VERSION_NUMBER)
IMPLEMENT_SERIAL(CCircle, CElement, VERSION_NUMBER)
IMPLEMENT_SERIAL(CCurve, CElement, VERSION_NUMBER)
IMPLEMENT_SERIAL(CText, CElement, VERSION_NUMBER)
```

The Serialize() Functions for the Shape Classes

We need to implement the **Serialize()** member function for each of the shape classes. We can start with the **CElement** class:

```
void CElement::Serialize(CArchive& ar)
{
    CObject::Serialize(ar);          // Call the base class function

    if (ar.IsStoring())
    {
        ar << m_Color                // Store the color,
           << m_EnclosingRect        // and the enclosing rectangle,
           << m_Pen;                 // and the pen width
    }
    else
    {
        ar >> m_Color                // Retrieve the color,
           >> m_EnclosingRect        // and the enclosing rectangle,
           >> m_Pen;                 // and the pen width
    }
}
```

This function is of the same form as the one supplied for us in the **CSketcherDoc** class. All of the data members defined in **CElement** are supported by the overloaded extraction and insertion operators, and so everything is done using those operators. Note that we must call the **Serialize()** member for the **CObject** class to ensure that the inherited data members are serialized.

For the **CLine** class, you can code the function as:

```
void CLine::Serialize(CArchive& ar)
{
    CElement::Serialize(ar);         // Call the base class function

    if (ar.IsStoring())
    {
        ar << m_StartPoint           // Store the line start point,
           << m_EndPoint;            // and the end point
    }
    else
    {
        ar >> m_StartPoint           // Retrieve the line start point,
           >> m_EndPoint;            // and the end point
    }
}
```

Again, the data members are all supported by the extraction and insertion operators of the **CArchive** object **ar**. We call the **Serialize()** member of the base class **CElement** to serialize its data members, and this will call the **Serialize()** member of **CObject**. You can see how the serialization process cascades through the class hierarchy.

The **Serialize()** function member of the **CRectangle** class is very simple:

```
void CRectangle::Serialize(CArchive& ar)
{
    CElement::Serialize(ar);        // Call the base class function
}
```

All it does is to call the direct base class function, since the class has no additional data members.

The **CCircle** class doesn't have additional data members beyond those inherited from **CElement** either, so its **Serialize()** function also just calls the base class function:

```
void CCircle::Serialize(CArchive& ar)
{
    CElement::Serialize(ar);        // Call the base class function
}
```

For the **CCurve** class, we have surprisingly little work to do. The **Serialize()** function is coded as follows:

```
void CCurve::Serialize(CArchive& ar)
{
    CElement::Serialize(ar);        // Call the base class function
    m_PointList.Serialize(ar);      // Serialize the list of points
}
```

After calling the base class **Serialize()** function, we just call the **Serialize()** function for the **CList** object, **m_PointList**. Objects of any of the **CList**, **CArray**, and **CMap** classes can be serialized in this way, as once again, these classes are all derived from **CObject**.

The last class for which we need to add an implementation of **Serialize()** to **Elements.cpp** is **CText**:

```
void CText::Serialize(CArchive& ar)
{
    CElement::Serialize(ar);        // Call the base class function

    if (ar.IsStoring())
    {
        ar << m_StartPoint          // Store the start point
           << m_String;             // and the text string
    }
    else
    {
        ar >> m_StartPoint          // Retrieve the start point
           >> m_String;             // and the text string
    }
}
```

After calling the base class function, we serialize the two data members using the insertion and extraction operators in **ar**. The class **CString**, although not derived from **CObject**, is still fully supported by **CArchive** with these overloaded operators.

Exercising Serialization

That's all we need for storing and retrieving documents in our program! The save and restore menu options in the file menu are now fully operational without adding any more code. If you build and run Sketcher after incorporating the changes we've discussed in this chapter, you'll be able to save and restore files, and be automatically prompted to save a modified document when you try to close it or exit from the program, as shown here:

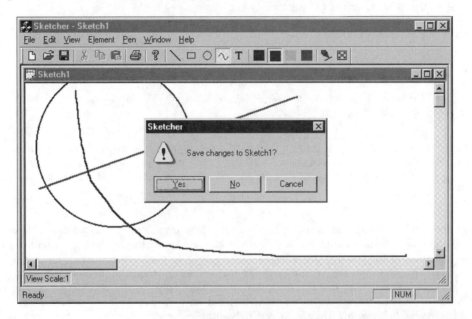

This works because of the **SetModifiedFlag()** calls that we added everywhere we update the document. If you click on the Yes button in the screen above, you'll see the File | Save As... dialog shown here:

This is the standard dialog for this menu item under Windows 95. It's all fully working, supported by code supplied by the framework. The file name for the document has been generated from that assigned when the document was first opened, and the file extension is automatically defined as **.ske**. Our application now has full support for file operations on documents. Easy, wasn't it?

Moving Text

Now it's time to take a brief digression to go back and fix a problem that we created in the last chapter. You'll remember that whenever you try to move a text element, it leaves a trail behind it until the text is positioned on the document again. This is caused by our reliance on ROP drawing in the **MoveElement()** member of the view:

```
void CSketcherView::MoveElement(CClientDC& aDC,const CPoint& point)
{
   CSize Distance = point - m_CursorPos;   // Get move distance
   m_CursorPos = point;             // Set current point as 1st for next time

   // If there is an element, selected, move it
   if(m_pSelected)
   {
      aDC.SetROP2(R2_NOTXORPEN);
      m_pSelected->Draw(&aDC,m_pSelected); // Draw the element to erase it
      m_pSelected->Move(Distance);         // Now move the element
      m_pSelected->Draw(&aDC,m_pSelected); // Draw the moved element
   }
}
```

As we mentioned, setting the drawing mode of the device context to **R2_NOTXORPEN** won't remove the trail left by moving the text. We could get around this by using a method of invalidating the rectangles that are affected by the moving elements so that they redraw themselves. This can, however, cause some annoying flicker when the element is moving fast. A better solution would be to use the invalidation method only for the text elements, and our original ROP method for all the other elements, but how are we to know which class the selected element belongs to? This is surprisingly simple: we can use an **if** statement, as follows:

```
if (m_pSelected->IsKindOf(RUNTIME_CLASS(CText)))
{
   // Code here will only be executed if the selected element is of class CText
}
```

This uses the **RUNTIME_CLASS** macro to get a pointer to an object of type **CRuntimeClass**, then passes this pointer to the **IsKindOf()** member function of **m_pSelected**. This returns a non-zero result if **m_pSelected** is of class **CText**, and returns zero otherwise. The only proviso is that the class we're checking for must be declared using either of the **DECLARE_DYNCREATE** or **DECLARE_SERIAL** macros, which is why we left this fix until now.

The final code for **MoveElement()** will be as follows:

```
void CSketcherView::MoveElement(CClientDC& aDC, const CPoint& point)
{
   CSize Distance = point - m_CursorPos;   // Get move distance
   m_CursorPos = point;             // Set current point as 1st for next time
```

```
            // If there is an element, selected, move it
         if(m_pSelected)
         {
            // If the element is text use this method...
            if (m_pSelected->IsKindOf(RUNTIME_CLASS(CText)))
            {
              CRect OldRect=m_pSelected->GetBoundRect();   // Get old bound rect
              m_pSelected->Move(Distance);                 // Move the element
              CRect NewRect=m_pSelected->GetBoundRect();   // Get new bound rect
              OldRect.UnionRect(&OldRect,&NewRect);        // Combine the bound rects
              aDC.LPtoDP(OldRect);                         // Convert to client coords
              OldRect.NormalizeRect();                     // Normalize combined area
              InvalidateRect(&OldRect);                    // Invalidate combined area
              UpdateWindow();                              // Redraw immediately
              m_pSelected->Draw(&aDC,m_pSelected);         // Draw highlighted

              return;
            }

            // ...otherwise, use this method
            aDC.SetROP2(R2_NOTXORPEN);
            m_pSelected->Draw(&aDC,m_pSelected); // Draw the element to erase it
            m_pSelected->Move(Distance);         // Now move the element
            m_pSelected->Draw(&aDC,m_pSelected); // Draw the moved element
         }
      }
```

You can see that the code for invalidating the rectangles that we need to use for moving the text is much less elegant than the ROP code that we use for all the other elements. It works, though, as you'll be able to see for yourself if you make this modification and build and run the application.

Printing a Document

Now let's look at printing the document. We already have a basic printing capability implemented in the Sketcher program, courtesy of AppWizard and the framework. The File | Print..., File | Print Setup..., and File | Print Preview menu items all work. The File | Print Preview will display a window showing the current Sketcher document on a page, as shown below:

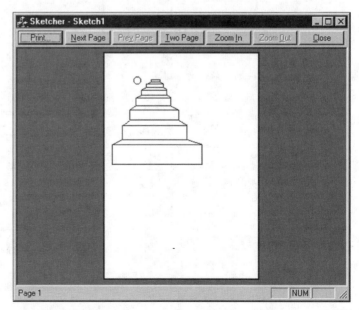

767

Whatever is in the current document is placed on a single sheet of paper at the current view scale. If the document's extent is beyond the boundary of the paper, the section of the document off the paper won't be printed. If you select the <u>P</u>rint... button, this page will be sent to your printer.

As a basic capability which you get for free, it's quite impressive, but it's not adequate for most purposes. A typical document in our program may well not fit on a page, so you would either want to scale the document to fit, or perhaps more conveniently, print the whole document over as many pages as necessary. You can add your own print processing code to extend the capability of the facilities provided by the framework, but to implement this you first need to understand how printing has been implemented in MFC.

The Printing Process

Printing a document is controlled by the current view. The process is inevitably a bit messy, since printing is inherently a messy business, and it potentially involves you in implementing your own versions of quite a number of inherited functions in your view class.

The logic of the process and the functions involved are shown in the diagram below

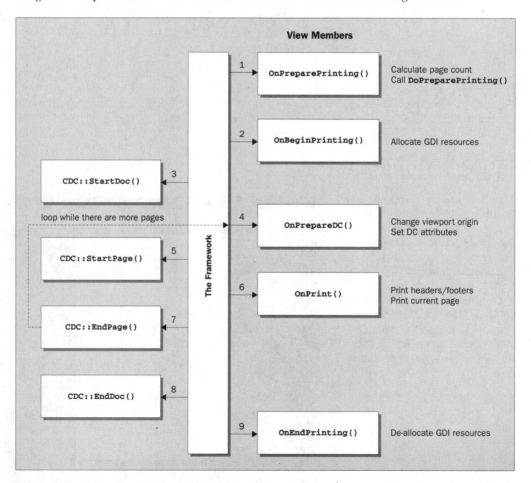

The diagram shows how the sequence of events is controlled by the framework and involves calling five inherited members of your view class, which you may need to override. The **CDC** member functions shown on the left side of the diagram communicate with the printer device driver and are called automatically by the framework.

The typical role of each of the functions in the current view during a print operation is specified in the notes alongside it. The sequence in which they are called is indicated by the numbers on the arrows. In practice, you don't necessarily need to implement all of these functions, only those that you want for your particular printing requirements. Typically, you'll want at least to implement your own versions of **OnPreparePrinting()**, **OnPrepareDC()** and **OnPrint()**. You'll see an example of how these functions can be implemented in the context of the Sketcher program a little later in this chapter.

The output of data to a printer is done in the same way as outputting data to the display— through a device context. The GDI calls that you use to output text or graphics are device-independent, so they work just as well for a printer as they do for a display. The only difference is the device that the **CDC** object applies to.

The **CDC** functions in the process diagram communicate with the device driver for the printer. If the document to be printed requires more than one printed page, the process loops back to call the **OnPrepareDC()** function for each successive new page, as determined by the **EndPage()** function.

All the functions in your view class that are involved in the printing process are passed a pointer to an object of type **CPrintInfo** as an argument. This object provides a link between all the functions that manage the printing process, so let's take a look at the **CPrintInfo** class in more detail.

The CPrintInfo Class

A **CPrintInfo** object has a fundamental role in the printing process, since it stores information about the print job being executed and details of its status at any time. It also provides functions for accessing and manipulating this data. This object is the means by which information is passed from one view function to another during printing, and between the framework and your view functions.

An object of the **CPrintInfo** class is created whenever you select the File | Print... or File | Print Preview menu options. After being used by each of the functions in the current view that are involved in the printing process, it's automatically deleted when the print operation ends.

All the data members of **CPrintInfo** are **public**. They are:

Member	Usage
m_pPD	A pointer to the **CPrintDialog** object: displays the print dialog box
m_bDirect	This is set to **TRUE** by the framework if the print operation is to bypass the print dialog box, and **FALSE** otherwise.
m_bPreview	A member of type **BOOL** which has the value **TRUE** if File	Print Preview was selected, and **FALSE** otherwise.

Member	Usage
m_bContinuePrinting	A member of type **BOOL**. If set to **TRUE**, the framework will continue printing the loop shown in the diagram. If set to **FALSE**, the printing loop will end. You only need to set this variable if you don't pass a page count for the print operation to the **CPrintInfo** object (using the **SetMaxPage()** member function). In this case, you'll be responsible for signaling when you're finished by setting this variable to **FALSE**.
m_nCurPage	A value of type **UINT** which stores the page number of the current page. Pages are usually numbered starting from 1.
m_nNumPreviewPages	A value of type **UINT** which specifies the number of pages displayed in the print preview window. This can be 1 or 2.
m_lpUserData	Of type **LPVOID**. Stores a pointer to an object that you create. Allows you to create an object to store additional information about the printing operation and associate it with the **CPrintInfo** object.
m_rectDraw	**CRect** object: defines usable area of the page in logical coordinates.
m_strPageDesc	**CString** object containing a format string used by the framework to display page numbers during print preview.
m_bDocObject	Set **TRUE** if application prints by **IPrint** interface and **FALSE** otherwise. IPrint interface is outside the scope of this book
m_dwFlags	Only valid if **m_bDocObject** is **TRUE**. A value of type **UINT** that gives the first page offset in a combined **IPrint** job.
m_nOffsetPage	Only valid if **m_bDocObject** is **TRUE**; it's a **DWORD** value that represents the flags passed to **IPrint::Print**.

A **CPrintInfo** object will have the following **public** member functions:

Member Function	Functionality
SetMinPage(UINT nMinPage)	The argument specifies the number of the first page of the document. There is no return value.
SetMaxPage(UINT nMaxPage)	The argument specifies the number of the last page of the document. There is no return value.
GetMinPage() const	Returns the number of the first page as type **UINT**.
GetMaxPage() const	Returns the number of the last page as type **UINT**.
GetFromPage() const	Returns the number of the first page of the document to be printed as type **UINT**. This value would be set through the print dialog.
GetToPage() const	Returns the number of the last page to be printed as type **UINT**. This value would be set through the print dialog.
GetOffsetPage() const	This is only valid if **m_bDocObject** is **TRUE**; when multiple **DocObject** items are being printed, it returns the number of pages preceding the first page of a **DocObject** item being printed, as type **UINT**.

When printing documents containing several pages, you need to figure out how many printed pages the document will occupy, and store this information in the **CPrintInfo** object to make it available to the framework. You can do this in your version of the **OnPreparePrinting()** member of the current view.

To set the number of the first page in the document, you need to call the function **SetMinPage()** in the **CPrintInfo** object, which accepts the page number as an argument of type **UINT**. There's no return value. To set the number of the last page in the document, you call the function **SetMaxPage()**, which also accepts the page number as an argument of type **UINT** and doesn't return a value. If you later need to retrieve these values, you can use the functions **GetMinPage()** and **GetMaxPage()** in the **CPrintInfo** object.

The page numbers that you supply will be stored in the **CPrintDialog** object pointed to by the **m_pPD** member of **CPrintInfo**, and displayed in the dialog box which pops up when you select File | Print... from the menu. The user will then be able to specify the numbers of the first and last pages that are to be printed, which you can retrieve by calling the **GetFromPage()** and **GetToPage()** members of the **CPrintInfo** object. In each case, the values returned are of type **UINT**. The dialog will automatically verify that the numbers of the first and last pages to be printed are within the range you supplied by specifying the minimum and maximum pages of the document.

We now know what functions in our view class we can implement to manage printing for ourselves, with the framework doing most of the work. We also know what information is available through the **CPrintInfo** object passed to the functions concerned with printing. We can get a much clearer understanding of the detailed mechanics of printing if we implement a basic multi-page print capability for Sketcher documents.

Implementing Multipage Printing

In the Sketcher program, we use the **MM_LOENGLISH** mapping mode to set things up and then switch to **MM_ANISOTROPIC**. This means that our shapes and the view extent are measured in terms of hundredths of an inch. Ideally, with the unit of size a fixed physical measure, we will want to print objects at their actual size.

With the document size specified as 3000 by 3000 units, we can create documents up to 30 inches square, which spreads over quite a few sheets of paper if we fill the whole area. It will require a little more effort to work out the number of pages necessary to print a sketch than with a typical text document, because in most instances we'll need a two-dimensional array of pages to print a complete sketch document.

To avoid overcomplicating the problem, let's assume that we're printing on something like a normal sheet of paper (either A4 size or 8½ by 11 inches) and in portrait orientation (which means the long edge is vertical). With either paper size, we'll print the document in a central portion of the paper measuring 6 inches by 9 inches. With these assumptions, we don't need to worry about the actual paper size, we just need to chop the document into 600 by 900 unit chunks. For a document larger than one page, we'll divide up the document as illustrated in the example below:

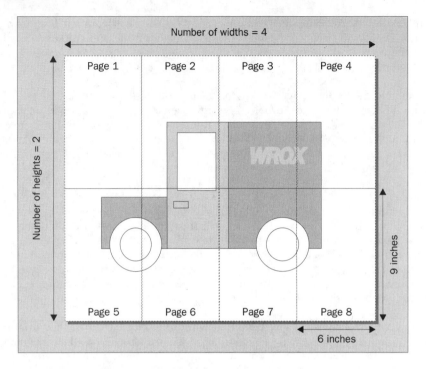

As you can see, we'll be numbering the pages row-wise, so in this case pages 1 to 4 are in the first row and pages 5 to 8 are in the second.

Getting the Overall Document Size

In order to figure out how many pages a particular document occupies, we're going to need to calculate the rectangle that encloses everything in the document. We can do this quite easily by adding a function `GetDocExtent()` to the document class `CSketcherDoc`. Add the following declaration to the `public` interface for `CSketcherDoc`:

```
CRect GetDocExtent() const;  // Get the bounding rectangle for the whole document
```

The implementation is no great problem. The code for it will be:

```
// Get the rectangle enclosing the entire document
CRect CSketcherDoc::GetDocExtent() const
{
   CRect DocExtent(0,0,1,1);     // Initial document extent
   CRect ElementBound(0,0,0,0);  // Space for element bounding rectangle

   POSITION aPosition = m_ElementList.GetHeadPosition();

   while(aPosition)          // Loop through all the elements in the list
   {
      // Get the bounding rectangle for the element
      ElementBound=(m_ElementList.GetNext(aPosition))->GetBoundRect();
```

```
         // Make coordinates of document extent the outer limits
         DocExtent.UnionRect(DocExtent, ElementBound);
      }
   DocExtent.NormalizeRect();
   return DocExtent;
   }
```

You should add this function definition to the **SketcherDoc.cpp** file. The process loops through every element in the document, using the **aPosition** variable to step through the list and getting the bounding rectangle for each element. The **UnionRect()** member of the **CRect** class calculates the smallest rectangle that contains the two rectangles passed as arguments, and puts that value in the **CRect** object for which the function is called. Therefore, **DocExtent** will keep increasing in size until all the elements are contained within it. Note that we have to initialize **DocExtent** with **(0,0,1,1)**, as the **UnionRect()** function doesn't work properly with rectangles that have zero height or width.

Storing Print Data

The **OnPreparePrinting()** function in the view class is called by the application framework to enable you to initialize the printing process for your document. The basic initialization that's required is to provide information about how many pages are in the document for the print dialog that will be displayed. We'll need to store information about the pages that our document requires so that we can use it later in the other view functions involved in the printing process. We'll originate this in the **OnPreparePrinting()** member of the view class, store it in an object of our own class that we'll define for this purpose, and then store a pointer to the object in the **CPrintInfo** object that the framework makes available. This is largely to show you how this mechanism works, since in most cases you'll find it easier just to store the data in your view object, mainly because it makes the notation for referencing the data much simpler.

We'll need to store the number of pages running along the width of the document, **m_nWidths**, and the number of rows of pages down the length of the document, **m_nLengths**. We'll also store the top-left corner of the rectangle enclosing the document data as a **CPoint** object, **m_DocRefPoint**, because we'll use this when we need to work out the position of a page to be printed from its page number. We can also store the file name for the document in a **CString** object, **m_DocTitle**, so that we can add it as a title to each page. The definition of our class to accommodate these will be:

```
class CPrintData
{
   public:
      UINT m_nWidths;        // No. of pages for the width of the document
      UINT m_nLengths;       // No. of pages for the length of the document
      CPoint m_DocRefPoint;  // Top left corner of the document contents
      CString m_DocTitle;    // The name of the document
};
```

You need to create a new file and add the class definition to it. Save the file as **PrintData.h** and add the file to the Header Files folder in FileView by right clicking the folder and selecting from the pop-up.

We don't need an implementation file for this class. The default constructor (which is automatically generated) will be quite adequate here. Since an object of this class is only going to be used transiently, we don't need to use **CObject** as a base, or to consider any other complication.

The printing process starts with a call to the view member **OnPreparePrinting()**, so let's see how we should implement that.

Preparing to Print

AppWizard added versions of **OnPreparePrinting()**, **OnBeginPrinting()** and **OnEndPrinting()** to **CSketcherView** at the outset. The base code provided for **OnPreparePrinting()** calls **DoPreparePrinting()** in the **return** statement, as you can see:

```
BOOL CSketcherView::OnPreparePrinting(CPrintInfo* pInfo)
{
    // default preparation
    return DoPreparePrinting(pInfo);
}
```

The **DoPreparePrinting()** function displays the print dialog using information about the number of pages to be printed that's defined in the **CPrintInfo** object. Whenever possible, you should calculate the number of pages to be printed and store it in the **CPrintInfo** object before this call occurs. Of course, in many circumstances you may need information from the device context for the printer before you can do this—when you're printing a document where the number of pages is going to be affected by the size of font to be used, for example—in which case it won't be possible to get the page count before you call **OnPreparePrinting()**. In this case, you can compute the number of pages in the **OnBeginPrinting()** member, which receives a pointer to the device context as an argument. This function is called by the framework after **OnPreparePrinting()**, so the information entered in the print dialog is available. This means that you can also take account of the paper size selected by the user in the print dialog.

We're assuming that the page size is large enough to accommodate a 6 inch by 9 inch area to draw the document data, so we can calculate the number of pages in **OnPreparePrinting()**. The code for it will be as follows:

```
BOOL CSketcherView::OnPreparePrinting(CPrintInfo* pInfo)
{
    // Create a print data object
    CPrintData* pPrintData;
    pInfo->m_lpUserData = pPrintData = new CPrintData;

    CSketcherDoc* pDoc = GetDocument();     // Get a document pointer

    // Get the whole document area
    CRect DocExtent = pDoc->GetDocExtent();

    // Save the reference point for the whole document
    pPrintData->m_DocRefPoint = CPoint(DocExtent.left, DocExtent.bottom);

    // Get the name of the document file and save it
    pPrintData->m_DocTitle = pDoc->GetTitle();

    // Calculate how many printed page widths of 600 units are required
```

```
    // to accommodate the width of the document
    pPrintData->m_nWidths =
                     (UINT)ceil(static_cast<double>(DocExtent.Width()) / 600.0);

    // Calculate how many printed page lengths of 900 units are required
    // to accommodate the document length
    pPrintData->m_nLengths =
                     (UINT)ceil(static_cast<double>(DocExtent.Height()) / 900.0);

    // Set the first page number as 1 and
    // set the last page number as the total number of pages
    pInfo->SetMinPage(1);
    pInfo->SetMaxPage(pPrintData->m_nWidths * pPrintData->m_nLengths);

    if(!DoPreparePrinting(pInfo))
       {
          delete static_cast<CPrintData*>(pInfo->m_lpUserData);
          return FALSE;
       }

    return TRUE;
}
```

We first create a **CPrintData** object on the heap and store its address in the pointer **m_lpUserData** in the **CPrintInfo** object passed to the function via the pointer **pInfo**. We store the same address in the pointer **pPrintData.** After getting a pointer to the document, we get the rectangle enclosing all of the elements in the document by calling the function **GetDocExtent()** that we added to the document class earlier in this chapter. We then store the corner of this rectangle in the **m_DocRefPoint** member of the **CPrintData** object and put the name of the file containing the document in **m_DocTitle**.

We reference the **CPrintData** object through the pointer in the **CPrintInfo** object, using **pPrintData** as a shorthand. For example:

```
pPrintData->m_DocRefPoint = CPoint(DocExtent.left, DocExtent.bottom);
```

We use this approach for all references to members of the **CPrintData** object. If we put the data in the view class, we would only need to use the name of the data member. Don't forget to add a **#include** directive for **PrintData.h** to the **SketcherView.cpp** file.

The next two lines of code calculate the number of pages across the width of the document, and the number of pages required to cover the length. The number of pages to cover the width is computed by dividing the width of the document by the width of the print area of a page, which is 600 units or 6 inches, and rounding up to the next highest integer using the **ceil()** library function from **math.h**. A **#include** for this file also needs to be added to **SketcherView.cpp**. For example, **ceil(2.1)** will return **3.0**, **ceil(2.9)** will also return **3.0**, and **ceil(-2.1)** will return **-2.0**. A similar calculation to that for the number of pages across the width of a document produces the number to cover the length. The product of these two values is the total number of pages to be printed, and this is the value that we'll supply for the maximum page number.

Finally we call **DoPreparePrinting()** to show the print dialog. We have to check the returned value from this call, just in case the user hits Cancel. If this is the case then we must clean up our **CPrintData**, otherwise we'll leak the memory.

Cleaning Up after Printing

Because we created the **CPrintData** object on the heap, we need to ensure that it's deleted when we're done with it. We do this by adding code to the **OnEndPrinting()** function:

```
void CSketcherView::OnEndPrinting(CDC* /*pDC*/, CPrintInfo* pInfo)
{
    // Delete our print data object
    delete static_cast<CPrintData*>(pInfo->m_lpUserData);
}
```

That's all we need to do for this function in the Sketcher program, but in some cases you'll need to do more. All your one-time final clean up should be done here. Make sure that you remove the comment delimiters (**/*   */**) from the second parameter name, otherwise your function won't compile. The default implementation comments the parameter names out because you may not need to refer to them in your code. Since we use the **pInfo** parameter we must uncomment it, otherwise the compiler will report it as undefined.

We don't need to add anything to the **OnBeginPrinting()** function in the Sketcher program, but you'd need to add code to allocate any GDI resources, such as pens, if they were required throughout the printing process. You would then delete these as part of the clean up process in **OnEndPrinting()**.

Preparing the Device Context

At the moment, our program calls **OnPrepareDC()**, which sets up the mapping mode as **MM_ANISOTROPIC** to take account of the scaling factor. We need to make some additional changes so that the device context is properly prepared in the case of printing:

```
void CSketcherView::OnPrepareDC(CDC* pDC, CPrintInfo* pInfo)
{
    int Scale = m_Scale;                // Store the scale locally
    if(pDC->IsPrinting())
        Scale = 1;                      // If we are printing, set scale to 1

    CScrollView::OnPrepareDC(pDC, pInfo);
    CSketcherDoc* pDoc = GetDocument();
    pDC->SetMapMode(MM_ANISOTROPIC);    // Set the map mode
    CSize DocSize = pDoc->GetDocSize(); // Get the document size

    // y extent must be negative because we want MM_LOENGLISH
    DocSize.cy = -DocSize.cy;           // Change sign of y
    pDC->SetWindowExt(DocSize);         // Now set the window extent

    // Get the number of pixels per inch in x and y
    int xLogPixels = pDC->GetDeviceCaps(LOGPIXELSX);
    int yLogPixels = pDC->GetDeviceCaps(LOGPIXELSY);
```

```
    // Calculate the viewport extent in x and y
    int xExtent = DocSize.cx * Scale * xLogPixels / 100;
    int yExtent = DocSize.cy * Scale * yLogPixels / 100;

    pDC->SetViewportExt(xExtent, -yExtent); // Set viewport extent
}
```

This function is called by the framework for output to the printer as well as to the screen. We need to make sure that when we're printing, a scale of 1 is used to set the mapping from logical coordinates to device coordinates. If you left everything as it was, the output would be at the current view scale, but you'd need to take account of the scale when calculating how many pages you needed, and how you set the origin for each page.

We can determine whether we have a printer device context or not by calling the **IsPrinting()** member of the current **CDC** object, which returns **TRUE** if we are printing. All we need to do when we have a printer device context is to set the scale to 1. Of course, we need to change the statements lower down which use the scale value, so that they use the local variable **Scale**, rather than the **m_Scale** member of the view. The values returned by the calls to **GetDeviceCaps()** with the arguments **LOGPIXELSX** and **LOGPIXELSY** return the number of logical points per inch in the x and y directions for your printer when we're printing, and the equivalent values for your display when we're drawing to the screen, so this automatically adapts the viewport extent to suit the device to which you're sending the output.

Printing the Document

We can write the data to the printer device context in the **OnPrint()** function. This is called once for each page to be printed. You will need to add this function to **CSketcherView**, using ClassWizard. Select OnPrint from the Messages: list on the Message Maps tab.

We can obtain the page number of the current page from the **m_nCurPage** member of the **CPrintInfo** object, and use this value to work out the coordinates of the position in the document that corresponds to the top-left corner of the current page. The way to do this is best understood using an example, so let's suppose that we're printing page seven of an eight-page document, as illustrated in the diagram below:

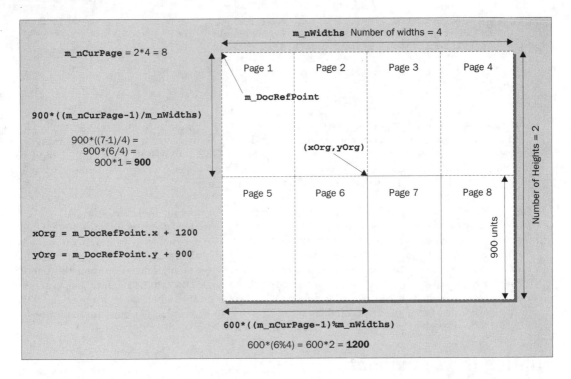

We can get an index to the horizontal position of the page by decrementing the page number by 1 and taking the remainder after dividing by the number of page widths required for the width of the printed area of the document. Multiplying the result by 600 produces the *x* coordinate of the top-left corner of the page, relative to the top-left corner of the rectangle enclosing the elements in the document. Similarly, we can determine the index to the vertical position of the document by dividing the current page number reduced by 1 by the number of page widths required for the horizontal width of the document. By multiplying the remainder by 900 you get the relative *y* coordinate of the top-left corner of the page. We can express this in two statements as follows:

```
CPrintData* pPrintData = static_cast<CPrintData*>(pInfo->m_lpUserData);
...
int xOrg = pPrintData->m_DocRefPoint.x +
           600 * ((pInfo->m_nCurPage - 1)%
              (pPrintData->m_nWidths));
int yOrg = pPrintData->m_DocRefPoint.y -
           900 * ((pInfo->m_nCurPage - 1)/
              (pPrintData->m_nWidths));
```

As in the member function **OnPreparePrinting()**, we access the information stored in our **CPrintData** object through the pointer in the **CPrintInfo** object, storing the address in **pPrintData**.

We want to print the file name of the document at the top of each page, and we want to be sure we don't print the document data over the file name. We also want to center the printed area on the page. We can do this by moving the origin of the coordinate system in the printer device context *after* we have printed the file name. This is illustrated in the diagram opposite:

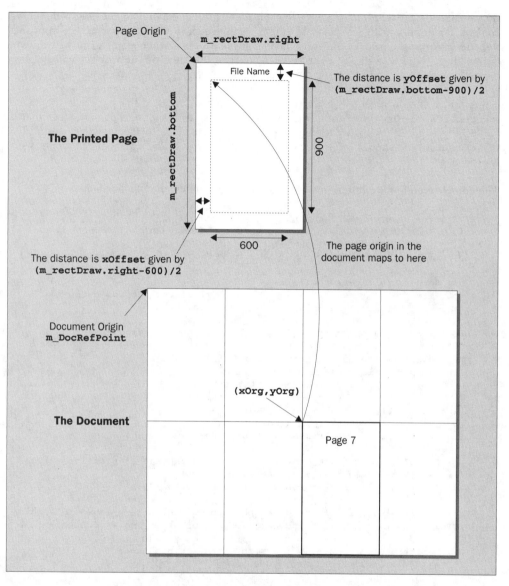

The diagram illustrates the correspondence between the printed page area in the device context and the page to be printed in the reference frame of the document data. Remember that these are in logical coordinates—the equivalent of **MM_LOENGLISH** in Sketcher—so y is increasingly negative from top to bottom. The page shows the expressions for the offsets from the page origin for the 600 by 900 area where we are going to print the page. We want to print the information from the document in the dashed area shown on the page. Consequently we need to map the **xOrg, yOrg** point in the document to the position in the printed page shown, which is displaced from the page origin by the offset values **xOffset** and **yOffset**.

By default, the origin in the coordinate system that we use to define elements in the document is mapped to the origin of the device context, but we can change this. The **CDC** object provides a function **SetWindowOrg()** for this purpose. This enables you to define a point in the document's logical coordinate system that you want to correspond to the origin in the device context. It's important to save the old origin that's returned as a **CPoint** object from the **SetWindowOrg()** function. You must restore the old origin when you've finished drawing the current page, otherwise the **m_rectDraw** member of the **CPrintInfo** object will not be set up correctly when you come to print the next page.

The point in the document that we want to map to the origin of the page has the coordinates **xOrg-xOffset, yOrg+yOffset**. This may not be easy to visualize, but remember that by setting the window origin, we're defining the point that maps to the viewport origin. If you think about it, you should see that the **xOrg, yOrg** point in the document is where we want it on the page.

The complete code for printing a page of the document will be:

```
// Print a page of the document
void CSketcherView::OnPrint(CDC* pDC, CPrintInfo* pInfo)
{
    CPrintData* pPrintData = static_cast<CPrintData*>(pInfo->m_lpUserData);

    // Output the document file name
    pDC->SetTextAlign(TA_CENTER);              // Center the following text
    pDC->TextOut(pInfo->m_rectDraw.right/2, -20,
                    pPrintData->m_DocTitle);
    pDC->SetTextAlign(TA_LEFT);                // Left justify text

    // Calculate the origin point for the current page
    int xOrg = pPrintData->m_DocRefPoint.x +
                600 * ((pInfo->m_nCurPage - 1)%
                    (pPrintData->m_nWidths));
    int yOrg = pPrintData->m_DocRefPoint.y -
                900 * ((pInfo->m_nCurPage - 1)/
                    (pPrintData->m_nWidths));

    // Calculate offsets to center drawing area on page as positive values
    int xOffset = (pInfo->m_rectDraw.right - 600) / 2;
    int yOffset = -(pInfo->m_rectDraw.bottom + 900) / 2;

    // Change window origin to correspond to current page & save old origin
    CPoint OldOrg = pDC->SetWindowOrg(xOrg - xOffset, yOrg + yOffset);

    // Define a clip rectangle the size of the printed area
    pDC->IntersectClipRect(xOrg, yOrg, xOrg + 600, yOrg - 900);

    OnDraw(pDC);                       // Draw the whole document
    pDC->SelectClipRgn(NULL);          // Remove the clip rectangle
    pDC->SetWindowOrg(OldOrg);         // Restore old window origin
}
```

The first step is to output the file name that we squirreled away in the **CPrintInfo** object. The **SetTextAlign()** function member of the **CDC** object allows you to define the alignment of subsequent text output in relation to the reference point that you supply for the text string in the **TextOut()** function. The alignment is determined by the constant passed as an argument to the function. You have three possibilities for specifying the horizontal alignment of the text:

Constant	Alignment
TA_LEFT	The point is at the left of the bounding rectangle for the text, so the text is to the right of the point specified. This is the default alignment.
TA_RIGHT	The point is at the right of the bounding rectangle for the text, so the text is to the left of the point specified.
TA_CENTER	The point is at the center of the bounding rectangle for the text.

We define the x coordinate of the file name on the page as half the page width, and the y coordinate as 20 units, which is 0.2 inches, from the top of the page. After outputting the name of the document file as centered text, we reset the text alignment to the default, **TA_LEFT**, for the text in the document.

The **SetTextAlign()** function also allows you to change the position of the text vertically by ORing a second flag with the justification flag. The second flag can be any of the following:

Constant	Alignment
TA_TOP	Aligns the top of the rectangle bounding the text with the point defining the position of the text. This is the default.
TA_BOTTOM	Aligns the bottom of the rectangle bounding the text with the point defining the position of the text.
TA_BASELINE	Aligns the baseline of the font used for the text with the point defining the position of the text.

The next action in **OnPrint()** uses the method that we've just discussed for mapping an area of the document to the current page. We get the document drawn on the page by calling the **OnDraw()** function that is used to display the document in the view. This potentially draws the entire document, but we can restrict what appears on the page by defining a **clip rectangle**. A clip rectangle encloses a rectangular area in the device context within which output appears. Outside the clip rectangle, output is suppressed. It's also possible to define irregularly shaped areas for clipping called **regions**.

The initial default clipping area defined in the print device context is the page boundary. We define a clip rectangle which corresponds to the 600 by 900 area centered in the page. This ensures that we will only draw in this area, and the file name will not be overwritten.

After the current page has been drawn, we call **SelectClipRgn()** with a **NULL** argument to remove the clip rectangle. If we don't do this, output of the document title is suppressed on all pages after the first because it lies outside the clip rectangle, which would otherwise remain in effect in the print process until the next time **IntersectClipRect()** gets called.

Our final action is to call **SetWindowOrg()** again to restore the window origin to its original location, as we discussed earlier.

Getting a Printout of the Document

To get your first printed Sketcher document, you just need to build the project and execute the program (once you've fixed any typos). If you try File | Print Preview, you should get something similar to the window shown below:

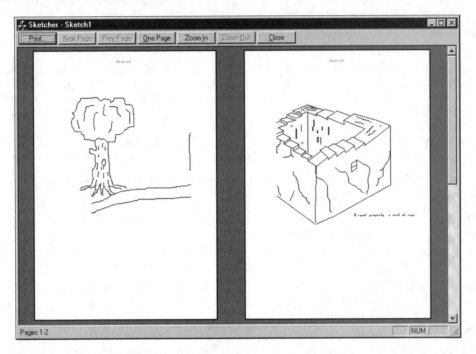

We get print preview functionality completely for free. The framework uses the code that you've supplied for the normal multi-page printing operation to produce page images in the print preview window. What you see in the print preview window should be exactly the same as appears on the printed page.

Summary

In this chapter, we've seen how to get a document stored on disk in a form that allows us to read it back and reconstruct its constituent objects using the serialization process supported by MFC. To implement serialization for classes defining document data, you must:

▶ Derive your class directly or indirectly from **CObject**.

▶ Specify the **DECLARE_SERIAL()** macro in your class definition.

▶ Specify the **IMPLEMENT_SERIAL()** macro in your class implementation.

▶ Implement a default constructor in your class.

▶ Declare the **Serialize()** function in your class.

▶ Implement the **Serialize()** function in your class to serialize all the data members.

The serialization process uses a **CArchive** object to perform the input and output. You use the **CArchive** object passed to the **Serialize()** function to serialize the data members of the class.

Implementing classes for serialization also has the side-effect that it allows us access to run-time class information using the **RUNTIME_CLASS** macro and the **IsKindOf()** function.

We have also seen how MFC supports output to a printer. To add to the basic printing capability provided by default, you can implement your own versions of the view class functions involved in printing a document. The principal roles of each of these functions are:

Function	Role
OnPreparePrinting()	Determine the number of pages in the document and call the view member **DoPreparePrinting()**.
OnBeginPrinting()	Allocate the resources required in the printer device context which are needed throughout the printing process, and determine the number of pages in the document (where this is dependent on information from the device context).
OnPrepareDC()	Set attributes in the printer device context as necessary.
OnPrint()	Print the document.
OnEndPrinting()	Delete any GDI resources created in **OnBeginPrinting()** and do any other necessary clean-up.

Information relating to the printing process is stored in an object of type **CPrintInfo** that's created by the framework. You can store additional information in the view, or in another object of your own. If you use your own class object, you can keep track of it by storing a pointer to it in the **CPrintInfo** object.

Exercises

Ex18-1: Add some code to the **OnPrint()** function so that the page number is printed at the bottom of each page of the document in the form 'Page *n*'. If you use the features of the **CString** class, you can do this with just 3 extra lines!

Ex18-2: As a further enhancement to the **CText** class, change the implementation so that scaling works properly. (Hint—look up the **CreatePointFont()** function in the MSDN library.)

Writing Your Own DLLs

In this chapter, we'll be investigating a different kind of library from the static libraries that contain standard C++ functions such as **sqrt()** or **rand()**. These libraries are called **dynamic-link libraries**, or **DLL**s, and they provide a very powerful way of storing and managing standard library functions that is integral to the Windows environment. They also provide much more flexibility than static libraries.

A complete discussion of DLLs is outside the scope of a beginner's book, but they are important enough to justify including an introductory chapter on them. In this chapter, you will learn:

▶ What a DLL is and how it works

▶ When you should consider implementing a DLL

▶ What varieties of DLL are possible and what they are used for

▶ How you can extend MFC using a DLL

▶ How to define what is accessible in a DLL

▶ How to access the contents of a DLL in your programs

Understanding DLLs

Almost all programming languages support libraries of standard code modules for commonly used functions. In C++ we've been using lots of functions stored in standard libraries, such as the **ceil()** function that we used in the previous chapter, which is declared in the **math.h** header file. The code for this function is stored in a library file with the extension **.lib**, and when the executable module for the Sketcher program was created, the linker retrieved the code for this standard function from the library file and integrated a copy of it into the **.exe** file for the Sketcher program.

If you write another program and use the same function, it too will have its own copy of the **ceil()** function. The **ceil()** function is **statically linked** to each application, and is an integral part of each executable module, as illustrated here:

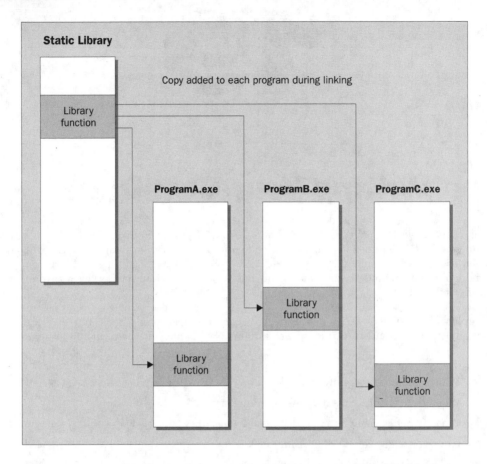

While this is a very convenient way of using standard functions with minimal effort on your part, it does have its disadvantages as a way of sharing common functions in the Windows environment. Since Windows can execute several programs simultaneously, a statically linked standard function being used by more than one program concurrently will be duplicated in memory for each program using it. This may not seem to matter very much for the `ceil()` function, but some functions — input and output, for instance — will invariably be common to most programs and are likely to occupy sizable chunks of memory. Having these statically linked would be extremely inefficient.

Another consideration is that a standard function from a static library may be linked into hundreds of programs in your system, so identical copies of the code for them will be occupying disk space in the `.exe` file for each program. For these reasons, an additional library facility is supported by Windows for standard functions. It's called a **Dynamic Link Library**, and it's usually abbreviated to **DLL**. This allows one copy of a function to be shared among several concurrently executing programs and avoids the need to incorporate a copy of the code for a library function into a program that uses it.

How DLLs Work

A dynamic link library is a file containing a collection of modules that can be used by any number of different programs. The file usually has the extension **.dll**, but this isn't obligatory. When naming a DLL, you can assign any extension that you like, but this can affect how they're handled by Windows. Windows automatically loads dynamic link libraries that have the extension **.dll**. If they have some other extension, you will need to load them explicitly by adding code to do this to your program. Windows itself uses the extension **.exe** for some of its DLLs. You're also likely to have seen the extensions **.vbx** and **.ocx**, which are applied to DLLs containing specific kinds of controls.

You might imagine that you have a choice about whether or not you use dynamic-link libraries in your program, but you don't. The Win32 API is used by every Windows 95 program, and the API is implemented in a set of DLLs. DLLs really are fundamental to Windows programming.

Connecting a function in a DLL to a program is achieved differently from the process used with a statically linked library, where the code is incorporated once and for all when the program is linked to generate the executable module. A function in a DLL is only connected to a program that uses it when the application is run, and this is done on each occasion the program is executed, as illustrated here:

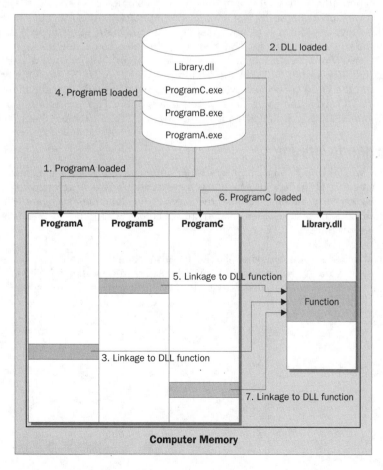

This illustrates what happens when three programs that use a function in a DLL are started successively, and then all execute concurrently. No code from the DLL is included in the executable module of any of the programs. When one of the programs is executed, the program is loaded into memory, and if the DLL it uses isn't already present, it too is loaded separately. The appropriate links between the program and the DLL are then established. If, when a program is loaded, the DLL is already there, all that needs to be done is to link the program to the required function in the DLL.

Note particularly that when your program calls a function in a DLL, Windows will automatically load the DLL into memory. Any program that's subsequently loaded into memory which uses the same DLL can use any of the capabilities provided by the *same copy* of the DLL, since Windows recognizes that the library is already in memory and just establishes the links between it and the program. Windows keeps track of how many programs are using each DLL that is resident in memory so that the library will remain in memory as long as at least one program is still using it. When a DLL is no longer used by any executing program, Windows will automatically delete it from memory.

MFC is provided in the form of a number of DLLs that your program can link to dynamically, as well as a library which your program can link to statically. By default, AppWizard generates programs that link dynamically to the DLL form of MFC.

Having a function stored in a DLL introduces the possibility of changing the function without affecting the programs that use it. As long as the interface to the function in the DLL remains the same, the programs can use a new version of the function quite happily, without the need for re-compiling or re-linking them. Unfortunately, this also has a downside: it's very easy to end up using the wrong version of a DLL with a program. This can be a particular problem with applications that install DLLs in the Windows System folder. Some commercial applications arbitrarily write the DLLs associated with the program to this folder without regard to the possibility of a DLL with the same name being overwritten. This can interfere with other applications you've already installed and, in the worst case, can render them inoperable.

Run-time Dynamic Linking

The DLL that we'll create in this chapter will be automatically loaded into memory when the program that uses it is loaded into memory for execution. This is referred to as **load-time dynamic linking** or **early binding**, because the links to the functions used are established as soon as the program and DLL have been loaded into memory. This kind of operation was illustrated in the previous diagram.

However, this isn't the only choice available. It's also possible to cause a DLL to be loaded after execution of a program has started. This is called **run-time dynamic linking,** or **late binding**. The sequence of operations that occurs with this is illustrated in the following diagram:

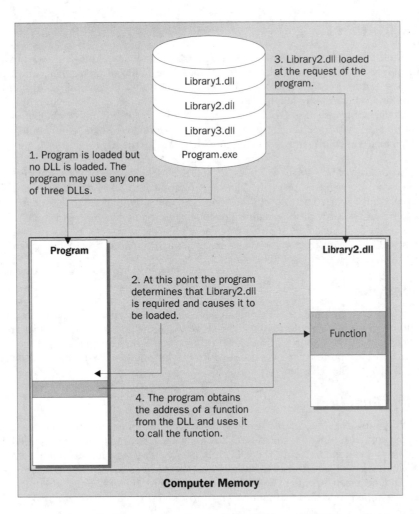

Run-time dynamic linking enables a program to defer linking of a DLL until it's certain that the functions in a DLL are required. This will allow you to write a program that can choose to load one or more of a number of DLLs based upon input to the program, so that only those functions that are necessary are actually loaded into memory. In some circumstances, this can drastically reduce the amount of memory required to run a program.

A program implemented to use run-time dynamic linking calls a function **LoadLibrary()** to load the DLL when it's required. The address of a function within the DLL can then be obtained using a function **GetProcAddress()**. When the program no longer has a need to use the DLL, it can detach itself from the DLL by calling the **FreeLibrary()** function. If no other program is using the DLL, it will be deleted from memory. We won't be going into further details of how this works in this book.

Contents of a DLL

A dynamic-link library isn't limited to storing code for functions. You can also put resources into a DLL, including such things as bitmaps and fonts. The Solitaire game that comes with Windows uses a dynamic-link library called **Cards.dll** which contains all the bitmap images of the cards and functions to manipulate them. If you wanted to write your own card game, you could conceivably use this DLL as a base and save yourself the trouble of creating all the bitmaps needed to represent the cards. Of course, in order to use it, you would need to know specifically which functions and resources are included in the DLL.

You can also define static global variables in a DLL, including C++ class objects, so that these can be accessed by programs using it. The constructors for global static class objects will be called automatically when such objects are created. You should note that each program using a DLL will get its own copy of any static global objects defined in the DLL, even though they may not necessarily be used by a program. For global class objects, this will involve the overhead of calling a constructor for each. You should, therefore, avoid introducing such objects into a DLL unless they are absolutely essential.

The DLL Interface

You can't access just anything that's contained in a DLL. Only items specifically identified as **exported** from a DLL are visible to the outside world. Functions, classes, global static variables and resources can all be exported from a DLL, and those that are make up the **interface** to it. Anything that isn't exported can't be accessed from the outside. We'll see how to export items from a DLL later in this chapter.

The DllMain() Function

Even though a DLL isn't executable as an independent program, it does contain a special variety of the **main()** function, called **DllMain()**. This is called by Windows when the DLL is first loaded into memory to allow the DLL to do any necessary initialization before its contents are used. Windows will also call **DllMain()** just before it removes the DLL from memory to enable the DLL to clean up after itself if necessary. There are also other circumstances where **DllMain()** is called, but these situations are outside the scope of this book.

Varieties of DLL

There are three different kinds of DLL that you can build with Visual C++ using MFC: an MFC extension DLL, a regular DLL with MFC statically linked, and a regular DLL with MFC dynamically linked.

MFC Extension DLL

You build this kind of DLL whenever it's going to include classes that are derived from the MFC. Your derived classes in the DLL effectively extend the MFC. The MFC must be accessible in the environment where your DLL is used, so all the MFC classes are available together with your derived classes — hence the name 'MFC extension DLL'. However, deriving your own classes from the MFC isn't the only reason to use an MFC extension DLL. If you're writing a DLL that includes functions which pass pointers to MFC class objects to functions in a program using it, or which receive such pointers from functions in the program, then you must create it as an MFC extension DLL.

Accesses to classes in the MFC by an extension DLL are always resolved dynamically by linking to the shared version of MFC that is itself implemented in DLLs. An extension DLL is created using the shared DLL version of the MFC, so when you use an extension DLL, the shared version of MFC must be available. An MFC extension DLL can be used by a normal AppWizard generated application. It requires the option Use MFC in a Shared DLL to be selected under the General tab of the project settings, which you access through the Project | Settings... menu option. This is the default selection with an AppWizard-generated program. Because of the fundamental nature of the shared version of the MFC in an extension DLL, an MFC extension DLL can't be used by programs that are statically linked to MFC.

Regular DLL - Statically Linked to MFC

This is a DLL that uses MFC classes which are linked statically. Use of the DLL doesn't require MFC to be available in the environment in which it is used because the code for all the classes it uses will be incorporated into the DLL. This will bulk up the size of the DLL, but the big advantage is that this kind of DLL can be used by any Win32 program, regardless of whether it uses MFC.

Regular DLL - Dynamically Linked to MFC

This is a DLL that uses dynamically linked classes from MFC but doesn't add classes of its own. This kind of DLL can be used by any Win32 program regardless of whether it uses MFC itself, but use of the DLL does require the MFC to be available in the environment.

You can use the AppWizard to build all three types of DLL that use MFC. You can also create a project for a DLL that doesn't involve MFC at all, by selecting the project type as Dynamic-Link Library.

Deciding What to Put in a DLL

How do you decide when you should use a DLL? In most cases, the use of a DLL provides a solution to a particular kind of programming problem, so if you have the problem, a DLL can be the answer. The common denominator is often sharing code between a number of programs, but there are other instances where a DLL provides advantages. The kinds of circumstance where putting code or resources in a DLL provides a very convenient and efficient approach include the following:

▶ You have a set of functions or resources on which you want to standardize and which you will use in several different programs. The DLL is a particularly good solution for managing these, especially if some of the programs using your standard facilities are likely to be executing concurrently.

▶ You have a complex application which involves several programs and a lot of code, but which has sets of functions or resources that may be shared among several of the programs in the application. Using a DLL for common functionality or common resources enables you to manage and develop these with a great deal of independence from the program modules that use them and can simplify program maintenance.

▶ You have developed a set of standard application-oriented classes derived from MFC which you anticipate using in several programs. By packaging the implementation of these classes in an extension DLL, you can make using them in several programs very straightforward, and in the process provide the possibility of being able to improve the internals of the classes without affecting the applications that use them.

▶ You have developed a brilliant set of functions which provide an easy-to-use but amazingly powerful tool kit for an application area which just about everybody wants to dabble in. You can readily package your functions in a regular DLL and distribute them in this form.

There are also other circumstances where you may choose to use DLLs, such as when you want to be able to dynamically load and unload libraries, or to select different modules at run-time. You could even use them to ease the development and updating of your applications generally.

The best way of understanding how to use a DLL is to create one and try it out. Let's do that now.

Writing DLLs

There are two aspects to writing a DLL that we'll look at: how you actually write a DLL, and how you define what's to be accessible in the DLL to programs that use it. As a practical example of writing a DLL, we'll create an extension DLL to add a set of application classes to the MFC. We'll then extend this DLL by adding variables that will be available to programs using it.

Writing and Using an Extension DLL

We can create an MFC extension DLL to contain the shape classes for the Sketcher application. While this will not bring any major advantages to the program, it will demonstrate how you can write an extension DLL without involving you in the overhead of entering a lot of new code.

The starting point is AppWizard, so create a new project workspace by using the File | New... menu option, selecting the Projects tab and choosing MFC AppWizard (dll), as shown here:

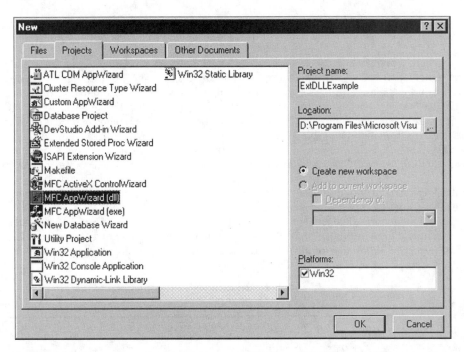

This selection identifies that we are creating an MFC-based DLL and will invoke the AppWizard. The option Win 32 Dynamic-Link Library that you see a little lower down the list is for creating DLLs that don't involve MFC. You need to make sure that the Location: entry corresponds to the folder where you want the folder containing the code for the DLL to be placed. Once this is done, and you've entered a suitable name for the DLL (as shown above), you can click on the OK button to go to the next step:

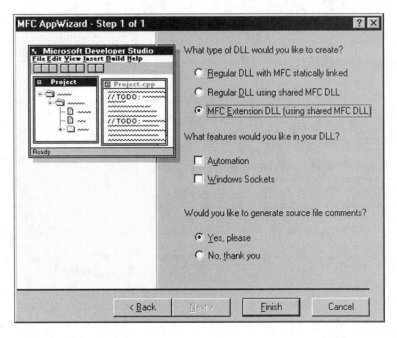

Here, you can see three radio buttons corresponding to the three types of MFC-based DLL that we discussed earlier. You should choose the third option, as shown above.

The two check boxes below the first group of three radio buttons allow you to include code to support A<u>u</u>tomation and <u>W</u>indows Sockets in the DLL. These are both advanced capabilities within a Windows program, so we don't need either of them here. **Automation** provides the potential for hosting objects created and managed by one application inside another, and we'll be taking a tentative look into this before the end of the book. **Windows Sockets** provides classes and functionality to enable your program to communicate over a network, but we won't be getting into this as it's beyond the scope of the book. The default choice to include comments is OK, so you can click on the <u>F</u>inish button and complete creation of the project.

Now that AppWizard has done its stuff, we can look into the code that has been generated on our behalf. If you look at the contents of the project using Windows Explorer, you'll see that AppWizard has generated a total of eleven files in the project folder, including a **.txt** file which contains a description of the other files, and one further resource file in the subfolder **Res**. You can read what they're all for in the **.txt** file, but the following two are the ones of immediate interest in implementing our DLL:

Filename	Contents
ExtDLLExample.cpp	This contains the function **DllMain()** and is the primary source file for the DLL.
ExtDLLExample.def	The information in this file is used by Visual C++ during compilation. It contains the name of the DLL, and you can also add to it the definitions of those items in the DLL that are to be accessible to a program using the DLL. We'll use an alternative and somewhat easier way of identifying such items in our example.

When your DLL is loaded, the first thing that happens is that **DllMain()** is executed, so perhaps we should take a look at that first.

Understanding DllMain()

If you take a look at the contents of **ExtDLLExample.cpp**, you will see that AppWizard has generated a version of **DllMain()** for us, as shown here:

```
extern "C" int APIENTRY
DllMain(HINSTANCE hInstance, DWORD dwReason, LPVOID lpReserved)
{
    // Remove this if you use lpReserved
    UNREFERENCED_PARAMETER(lpReserved);

    if (dwReason == DLL_PROCESS_ATTACH)
    {
        TRACE0("EXTDLLEXAMPLE.DLL Initializing!\n");

        // Extension DLL one-time initialization
        if (!AfxInitExtensionModule(ExtDLLExampleDLL, hInstance))
            return 0;
```

```
        // Insert this DLL into the resource chain
        // NOTE: If this Extension DLL is being implicitly linked to by
        //   an MFC Regular DLL (such as an ActiveX Control)
        //   instead of an MFC application, then you will want to
        //   remove this line from DllMain and put it in a separate
        //   function exported from this Extension DLL.  The Regular DLL
        //   that uses this Extension DLL should then explicitly call that
        //   function to initialize this Extension DLL.  Otherwise,
        //   the CDynLinkLibrary object will not be attached to the
        //   Regular DLL's resource chain, and serious problems will
        //   result.

        new CDynLinkLibrary(ExtDLLExampleDLL);
    }
    else if (dwReason == DLL_PROCESS_DETACH)
    {
        TRACE0("EXTDLLEXAMPLE.DLL Terminating!\n");
        // Terminate the library before destructors are called
        AfxTermExtensionModule(ExtDLLExampleDLL);
    }
    return 1;    // ok
}
```

There are three arguments passed to **DllMain()**. The first argument, **hInstance**, is a handle which has been created by Windows to identify the DLL. Every task under Windows 95 has an instance handle which identifies it uniquely. The second argument, **dwReason**, indicates the reason why **DllMain()** is being called. You can see this argument being tested in the **if** statements in **DllMain()**. The first **if** tests for the value **DLL_PROCESS_ATTACH**, which indicates that a program is about to use the DLL, and the second **if** tests for the value **DLL_PROCESS_DETACH**, which indicates that a program is finished using the DLL. The third argument is a pointer that's reserved for use by Windows, so you can ignore it.

When the DLL is first used by a program, it's loaded into memory and the **DllMain()** function will be executed with the argument **dwReason** set to **DLL_PROCESS_ATTACH**. This will result in the function **AfxInitExtensionModule()** being called to initialize the DLL and an object of the class **CDynLinkLibrary** created on the heap. Windows uses objects of this class to manage extension DLLs. If you need to add initialization of your own, you can add it to the end of this block. Any clean-up you require for your DLL can be added to the block for the second **if** statement.

Adding Classes to the Extension DLL

We're going to use the DLL to contain the implementation of our shape classes, so move the files **Elements.h** and **Elements.cpp** from the folder containing the source for Sketcher to the folder containing the DLL. Be sure that you move rather than copy the files. Since the DLL is going to supply the shape classes for Sketcher, we don't want to leave them in the source code for Sketcher.

You'll also need to remove **Elements.cpp** from the Sketcher project. To do this, simply change to the FileView, highlight Elements.cpp by clicking on the file, then press *Delete*. If you don't do this, Visual C++ will complain that it couldn't find the file when you try to compile the project. Follow the same procedure to get rid of **Elements.h** from the Header Files folder.

The shape classes use the constants that we have defined in the file **OurConstants.h**, so *copy* this file from Sketcher to the folder containing the DLL. Note that the variable **VERSION_NUMBER** is used exclusively by the **IMPLEMENT_SERIAL()** macros in the shape classes, so you could delete it from the **OurConstants.h** file used in the Sketcher program.

We need to add **Elements.cpp** containing the implementation of our shape classes to the extension DLL project, so select the menu option Project | Add To Project | Files… and choose the file **Elements.cpp** from the list box in the dialog, as shown here:

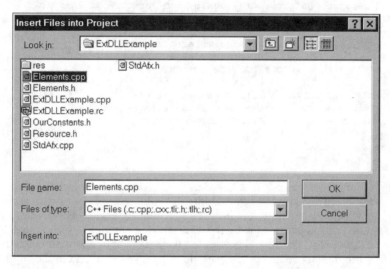

To make sure that the project includes the files containing the definitions of the shape classes and our constants, you need to add these to the project. To add **Elements.h** to the project, right click on Header Files in FileView, and select Add Files to Folder… from the pop-up. You can then select the **.h** file in the dialog. To add **OurConstants.h**, repeat the process, or if you like you can select both files at once by holding down the *Ctrl* key. This will make sure that all the classes are displayed in ClassView.

Exporting Classes from the Extension DLL

The names of the classes that are defined in the DLL and are to be accessible in programs that use it must be identified in some way, so that the appropriate links can be established between a program and the DLL. As we saw earlier, one way of doing this is by adding information to the **.def** file for the DLL. This involves adding what are called **decorated names** to the DLL and associating the decorated name with a unique identifying numeric value called an **ordinal**. A decorated name for a object is a name generated by the compiler, which adds an additional string to the name you gave to the object. This additional string provides information about the type of the object or, in the case of a function for example, information about the types of the parameters to the function. Among other things, it ensures that everything has a unique identifier and enables the linker to distinguish overloaded functions from each other.

Obtaining decorated names and assigning ordinals to export items from a DLL is a lot of work, and isn't the best or the easiest approach with Windows 95. A much easier way to identify the classes that we want to export from the DLL is to modify the class definitions in **Elements.h** to include the keyword **AFX_EXT_CLASS** before each class name, as shown below for the **CLine** class:

```
    // Class defining a line object
    class AFX_EXT_CLASS CLine : public CElement
    {
    DECLARE_SERIAL(CLine)

    public:
        // Function to display a line
        virtual void Draw(CDC* pDC, const CElement* pElement = 0) const;
        virtual void Move(const CSize& aSize);        // Function to move an element

        // Constructor for a line object
        CLine(const CPoint& Start, const CPoint& End, const COLORREF& Color, const int&
    PenWidth);

        virtual void Serialize(CArchive& ar);        // Serialize function for CLine

    protected:
        CPoint m_StartPoint;        // Start point of line
        CPoint m_EndPoint;          // End point of line

        CLine(){}                   // Default constructor - should not be used
    };
```

The keyword **AFX_EXT_CLASS** indicates that the class is to be exported from the DLL. This has the effect of making the complete class available to any program using the DLL and automatically allows access to any of the data and functions in the public interface of the class. The collection of things in a DLL that are accessible by a program using it is referred to as the **interface** to the DLL. The process of making an object part of the interface to a DLL is referred to as **exporting** the object.

You need to add the keyword **AFX_EXT_CLASS** to all of the other shape classes, including the base class **CElement** and the text class **CText**. Why is it necessary to export **CElement** from the DLL? After all, programs will only create objects of the classes derived from **CElement**, and not objects of the class **CElement** itself. The reason is that we have declared **public** members of **CElement** which form part of the interface to the derived shape classes, and which are almost certainly going to be required by programs using the DLL. If we don't export the **CElement** class, functions such as **GetBoundRect()** will not be available.

The final modification needed is to add the directive:

```
    #include <afxtempl.h>
```

to **StdAfx.h** in the DLL project so that the definition of **CList** is available.

We've done everything necessary to add the shape classes to the DLL. All you need to do is compile and link the project to create the DLL.

Building a DLL

You build the DLL in exactly the same way as you build any other project — by using the Build | Build menu option. The output produced is somewhat different, though. You can see the files that are produced in the **Debug** subfolder of the project folder. The executable code for the DLL is contained in the file **ExtDLLExample.dll**. This file needs to be available to execute a program that uses the DLL. The file **ExtDLLExample.lib** is an import library file that contains the definitions of the items that are exported from the DLL, and it must be available to the linker when a program using the DLL is linked.

Using the Extension DLL in Sketcher

We now have no information in the Sketcher program on the shape classes, because we moved the files containing the class definitions and implementations to the DLL project. However, the compiler will still need to know where the shape classes are coming from in order to compile the code for the program. The Sketcher program needs to include a **.h** file defining the classes that are to be imported from the DLL. We can just copy the file **Elements.h** from the DLL project to the folder containing the Sketcher source. It would be a good idea to identify this file as specifying the imports from the DLL in the Sketcher source code. You could do this by changing its name to **DllImports.h**, in which case you'll need to change the **#include** statements that are already in the Sketcher program for **Elements.h** to refer to the new file name (these occur in **Sketcher.cpp**, **SketcherDoc.cpp** and **SketcherView.cpp**).

When the Sketcher source has been recompiled, the linker will need to know where to find the DLL in order to include information that will trigger loading of the DLL when the Sketcher program is executed, and to allow the links to the class implementations in the DLL to be established. We must, therefore, add the location of the DLL to the project settings for the link operation. Select <u>P</u>roject | <u>S</u>ettings..., choose the Link tab of the Project Settings dialog, and enter the name of the **.lib** file for the DLL, **ExtDLLExample.lib** (including the full path to it), as shown here:

Be aware that if the complete path to the **.lib** file contains spaces (as in the example here), you'll need to enclose it within quotation marks for the linker to recognize it correctly.

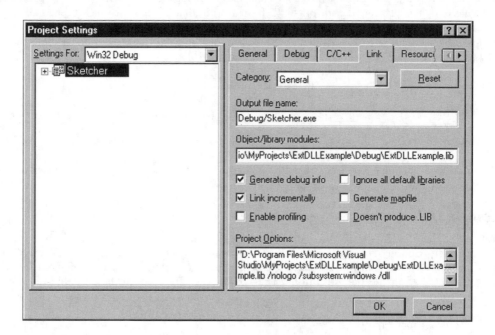

This shows the entry for the debug version of Sketcher. The **.lib** file for the DLL will be in the **Debug** folder within the DLL project folder, as you can see from the entry under Object/ library modules: in the dialog box shown. If you create a release version of Sketcher, you'll also need the release version of the DLL available to the linker, so you'll have to enter the fully qualified name of the **.lib** file for the release version of the DLL, corresponding to the release version of Sketcher. The file to which the Link tab applies is selected in the Settings For: drop-down list box in the dialog above.

You can now build the Sketcher application once more, and everything should compile and link as usual. However, if you try to execute the program, this happens:

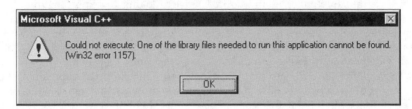

This is one of the less cryptic error messages — it's fairly clear what's gone wrong. To enable Windows to load a DLL for a program, it's usual to place the DLL in your **\Windows\System** folder. Since you probably don't want to clutter up this folder unnecessarily, you can copy **ExtDllExample.dll** from the **Debug** folder of the DLL project to the **Debug** folder for Sketcher. Sketcher should execute exactly as before, except that now it will use the shape classes in the DLL we have created.

Files Required to Use a DLL

From what we've just seen in the context of using the DLL we created in the Sketcher program, we conclude that three files must be available to use a DLL in a program:

Extension	Contents
.h	Defines those items that are exported from a DLL and enables the compiler to deal properly with references to such items in the source code of a program using the DLL. The **.h** file needs to be added to the source code for the program using the DLL.
.lib	Defines the items exported by a DLL in a form which enables the linker to deal with references to exported items when linking a program that uses a DLL.
.dll	Contains the executable code for the DLL which is loaded by Windows when a program using the DLL is executed.

If you plan to distribute program code in the form of a DLL for use by other programmers, you need to distribute all three files in the package. For users, just the **.dll** is required.

Exporting Variables and Functions from a DLL

You've seen how you can export classes from an extension DLL using the **AFX_EXT_CLASS** keyword. You can also export *objects* of classes that are defined in a DLL, as well as ordinary variables and functions. These can be exported from any kind of DLL by using the attribute **dllexport** to identify them. By using **dllexport** to identify class objects, variables or functions that are to be exported from a DLL, you avoid getting involved in the complications of modifying the **.def** file and, as a consequence, you make defining the interface to the DLL a straightforward matter.

Don't be misled into thinking that the approach we're taking to exporting things from our DLL makes the **.def** file method redundant. The **.def** file approach is more complicated — which is why we're taking the easy way out — but it offers distinct advantages in many situations over the approach we're taking. This is particularly true in the context of products that are distributed widely, and are likely to be developed over time. One major plus is that a **.def** file enables you to define the ordinals that correspond to your exported functions. This allows you to add more exported functions later and assign new ordinals to them, so the ordinals for the original set of functions remain the same. This means that someone using a new version of the DLL with a program built to use the old version doesn't have to relink their application.

You must use the **dllexport** attribute in conjunction with the keyword **_declspec** when you identify an item to be exported. For example, the statement

```
_declspec(dllexport) double aValue = 1.5;
```

defines the variable **aValue** of type **double** with an initial value of 1.5, and identifies it as a variable that is to be available to programs using the DLL. To export a function from a DLL, you use the **dllexport** attribute in a similar manner. For example:

```
_declspec(dllexport) CString FindWinner(CString* Teams);
```

This statement exports the function **FindWinner()** from the DLL.

To avoid the slightly cumbersome notation for specifying the **dllexport** attribute, you can simplify it by using a preprocessor directive:

```
#define DLLEXPORT _declspec(dllexport)
```

With this definition, the two previous examples can be written alternatively as:

```
DLLEXPORT double aValue = 1.5;
DLLEXPORT CString FindWinner(CString* Teams);
```

This notation is much more economical, as well as being easier to read, so you may wish to adopt this approach when coding your DLLs.

Obviously, only symbols which represent objects with global scope can be exported from a DLL. Variables and class objects that are local to a function in a DLL cease to exist when execution of a function is completed, in just the same way as in a function in a normal program. Attempting to export such symbols will result in a compile-time error.

Importing Symbols into a Program

The **dllexport** attribute identifies the symbols in a DLL that form part of the interface. If you want to use these in a program, you must make sure that they are correspondingly identified as being imported from the DLL. This is done by using the **dllimport** keyword in declarations for the symbols to be imported in a **.h** file. We can simplify the notation by using the same technique we applied to the **dllexport** attribute. Let's define **DLLIMPORT** with the directive:

```
#define DLLIMPORT _declspec(dllimport)
```

We can now import the **aValue** variable and the **FindWinner()** function with the declarations:

```
DLLIMPORT double aValue;
DLLIMPORT CString FindWinner(CString* Teams);
```

These statements would appear in a **.h** file which would be included into the **.cpp** files in the program that referenced these symbols.

Implementing the Export of Symbols from a DLL

We could extend the extension DLL to make the symbols defining shape types and colors available in the interface to it. We can then remove the definitions that we have in the Sketcher program and import the definitions of these symbols from the extension DLL.

We can first modify the source code for the DLL to add the symbols for shape element types and colors to its interface. To export the element types and colors, they must be global variables. As global variables, it would be better if they appeared in a **.cpp** file, rather than a **.h** file, so move the definitions of these out of the **OurConstants.h** file to the beginning of **Elements.cpp** in the DLL source. You can then apply the **dllexport** attribute to their definitions in the **Elements.cpp** file, as follows:

```
// Definitions of constants and identification of symbols to be exported

#define DLLEXPORT __declspec(dllexport)

// Element type definitions
// Each type value must be unique
DLLEXPORT extern const WORD LINE = 101U;
DLLEXPORT extern const WORD RECTANGLE = 102U;
DLLEXPORT extern const WORD CIRCLE = 103U;
DLLEXPORT extern const WORD CURVE = 104U;
DLLEXPORT extern const WORD TEXT = 105U;
////////////////////////////////////

// Color values for drawing
DLLEXPORT extern const COLORREF BLACK = RGB(0,0,0);
DLLEXPORT extern const COLORREF RED = RGB(255,0,0);
DLLEXPORT extern const COLORREF GREEN = RGB(0,255,0);
DLLEXPORT extern const COLORREF BLUE = RGB(0,0,255);
DLLEXPORT extern const COLORREF SELECT_COLOR = RGB(255,0,180);
////////////////////////////////////
```

Add these to the beginning of **Elements.cpp**, after the **#include** directives. We first define the symbol **DLLEXPORT** to simplify the specification of the variables to be exported, as we saw earlier. We then assign the attribute **dllexport** to each of the element types and colors.

You will notice that the **extern** specifier has also been added to the definitions of these variables. The reason for this is the effect of the **const** modifier, which indicates to the compiler that the values are constants and shouldn't be modified in the program, which was what we wanted. However, by default, it also specifies the variables as having internal linkage, so they are local to the file in which they appear. We want to export these variables to another program, so we have to add the modifier **extern** to override the default linkage specification due to the **const** modifier and ensure that they have external linkage. Symbols that are assigned external linkage are global and so can be exported. Of course, if the variables didn't have the **const** modifier applied to them, we wouldn't need to add **extern**, since they would be global automatically as long as they appeared at global scope.

The **OurConstants.h** file now only contains one definition:

```
// Definitions of constants

#if !defined(OurConstants_h)
#define OurConstants_h

    // Define the program version number for use in serialization
    UINT VERSION_NUMBER = 1;

#endif // !defined(OurConstants_h)
```

Of course, this is still required because it is used in the **IMPLEMENT_SERIAL()** macros in **Elements.cpp**. You can now build the DLL once again, so it's ready to use in the Sketcher program. Don't forget to copy the latest version of the **.dll** file to the Sketcher **Debug** folder.

Using Exported Symbols

To make the symbols exported from the DLL available in the Sketcher program, you need to specify them as imported from the DLL. You can do this by adding the identification of the imported symbols to the file **DllImports.h** which contains the definitions for the imported classes. In this way, we'll have one file specifying all the items imported from the DLL. The statements that appear in this file will be as follows:

```
// Variables defined in the shape DLL ExtDLLExample.dll
#if !defined(DllImports_h)
#define DllImports_h

#define DLLIMPORT __declspec( dllimport )

// Import element type declarations
// Each type value must be unique
DLLIMPORT extern const WORD LINE;
DLLIMPORT extern const WORD RECTANGLE;
DLLIMPORT extern const WORD CIRCLE;
DLLIMPORT extern const WORD CURVE;
DLLIMPORT extern const WORD TEXT;
//////////////////////////////////
```

```
// Import color values for drawing
DLLIMPORT extern const COLORREF BLACK;
DLLIMPORT extern const COLORREF RED;
DLLIMPORT extern const COLORREF GREEN;
DLLIMPORT extern const COLORREF BLUE;
DLLIMPORT extern const COLORREF SELECT_COLOR;
/////////////////////////////////////

// Plus the definitions for the element classes...

#endif // !defined(DllImports_h)
```

This defines and uses the **DLLIMPORT** symbol to simplify these declarations, in the way that
we saw earlier. This means that the **OurConstants.h** file in the Sketcher project is now
redundant, so we can delete it, along with the **#include** for it in **Sketcher.h**. It's a good
idea to close and reopen the project after deleting the file from the project, as Visual C++ can
be a little reluctant to let go of dependencies. This usually forces it to let go, though.

That looks as though we've done everything necessary to use the new version of the DLL with
Sketcher, but we haven't. If you try to recompile Sketcher, you'll get error messages for the
switch statement in the **CreateElement()** member of **CSketcherView**.

The values in the case statements must be constant, but although we've given the element type
variables the attribute **const**, the compiler has no access to these values because they are
defined in the DLL, not in the Sketcher program. The compiler, therefore, can't determine what
these constant case values are, and flags an error. The simplest way round this problem is to
replace the **switch** statement in the **CreateElement()** function by a series of **if** statements,
as follows:

```
// Create an element of the current type
CElement* CSketcherView::CreateElement()
{
    // Get a pointer to the document for this view
    CSketcherDoc* pDoc = GetDocument();
    ASSERT_VALID(pDoc);                         // Verify the pointer is good

    // Now select the element using the type stored in the document
    WORD ElementType = pDoc->GetElementType();
    if(ElementType == RECTANGLE)
        return new CRectangle(m_FirstPoint, m_SecondPoint,
                            pDoc->GetElementColor(), pDoc->GetPenWidth());

    if(ElementType == CIRCLE)
        return new CCircle(m_FirstPoint, m_SecondPoint,
                            pDoc->GetElementColor(), pDoc->GetPenWidth());

    if(ElementType == CURVE)
        return new CCurve(m_FirstPoint, m_SecondPoint,
                            pDoc->GetElementColor(), pDoc->GetPenWidth());
    else
        // Always default to a line
        return new CLine(m_FirstPoint, m_SecondPoint,
                            pDoc->GetElementColor(), pDoc->GetPenWidth());
}
```

We've added a local variable **ElementType** to store the current element type retrieved from the document. This is then tested against the element types imported from the DLL in the series of **if** statements. This does exactly the same job as the **switch** statement, but has no requirement for the element type constants to be known explicitly. If you now build Sketcher with these changes added, it will execute using the DLL, using the exported symbols as well as the exported shape classes.

Summary

In this chapter, you've learned the basics of how to construct and use a dynamic link library. The most important points we've looked at in this context are:

▶ Dynamic link libraries provide a means of linking to standard functions dynamically when a program executes, rather than incorporating them into the executable module for a program.

▶ An AppWizard-generated program links to a version of MFC stored in DLLs by default.

▶ A single copy of a DLL in memory can be used by several programs executing concurrently.

▶ An **extension** DLL is so called because it extends the set of classes in MFC. An extension DLL must be used if you want to export MFC-based classes or objects of MFC classes from a DLL. An extension DLL can also export ordinary functions and global variables.

▶ A **regular** DLL can be used if you only want to export ordinary functions or global variables that aren't instances of MFC classes.

▶ You can export classes from an extension DLL by using the keyword **AFX_EXT_CLASS** preceding the class name in the DLL.

▶ You can export ordinary functions and global variables from a DLL by assigning the **dllexport** attribute to them using the **_declspec** keyword.

▶ You can import the classes exported from an extension DLL by using including the **.h** file from the DLL that contains the class definitions using the **AFX_EXT_CLASS** keyword.

▶ You can import ordinary functions and global variables that are exported from a DLL by assigning the **dllimport** attribute to their declarations in your program by using the **_declspec** keyword.

Exercise

Ex19-1: This is the last time we'll be amending this version of the Sketcher program, so try this. Using the DLL we've just created, implement a Sketcher document viewer—in other words, a program which simply opens a document created by Sketcher and displays the whole thing in a window at once. You needn't worry about editing, scrolling or printing, but you will have to work out the scaling required to make a big picture fit in a little window!

Connecting to Data Sources

In this chapter, we'll show you to how to interface to a database using Visual C++ and MFC. This is by no means a comprehensive discussion of the possibilities, since we'll only address retrieving data, but at least you'll take a few steps down this particular path.

In this chapter you will learn:

▶ What SQL is, and how it is used

▶ How to retrieve data using the SQL **SELECT** operation

▶ What a recordset object is, and how it links to a relational database table

▶ How a recordset object can retrieve information from a database

▶ How a record view can display information from a recordset

▶ How to create a database program using AppWizard

▶ How to add recordsets to your program

▶ How to handle multiple record views

Database Basics

This is not the place for a detailed dissertation on database technology, but we do need to make sure that we have a common understanding of database terminology. Databases come in a variety of flavors, but the majority these days are **relational databases**. It is relational databases that we will be talking about throughout this chapter.

In a database, your data is organized into one or more **tables**. You can think of a database table as being like a spreadsheet table, made up of rows and columns. Each row contains information about a single item, and each column contains the information about the same characteristic from every item.

A **record** is equivalent to a row in the spreadsheet. Each record consists of elements of data that make up that record. These elements of data are known as **fields**. A field is a cell in the table identified by the column heading. The term *field* can also represent the whole column.

We can best see the structure of a table with a diagram:

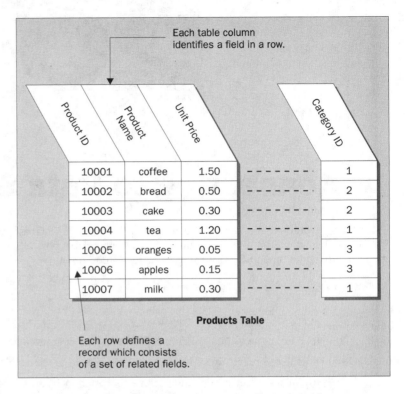

Each table column identifies a field in a row.

Products Table

Each row defines a record which consists of a set of related fields.

Here you can see that this table is being used to store information on a line of products. Unsurprisingly then, the table is called **Products**. Each record in the table, represented by a row in the diagram, contains the data for one product. The description of a product is separated into fields in the table, each storing information about one aspect of a product: **Product Name**, **Unit Price**, and so on.

Although the fields in this table store only relatively simple information (character strings or numeric values), the type of data you decide to put in a particular field can be virtually anything you want. You could store times, dates, pictures or even binary objects in a database.

A table will usually have at least one field that can be used to identify each record uniquely and in the example above the **Product ID** is a likely candidate. A field in a table that serves to identify each record within the table is called a **key**; a key which uniquely identifies each record in a table is referred to as a **primary key**. In some cases, a table may have no single field that uniquely identifies each record. In this circumstance, two or more key fields may be used. A key composed of two or more fields is called a **multivalue key**.

The relational aspect of a database, and the importance of keys, comes into play when you store related information in separate tables. You define relationships between the tables, using keys, and use the relationships to find associated information stored in your database. Note that the tables themselves don't know about relationships, just as the table doesn't understand the bits of data stored in it. It is the program that accesses the data which must use the information in the tables to pull together related data, whether that program is Access 95, SQL Server 6, or your own program written in Visual C++. These are known collectively as **relational database management systems** or **RDBMS**s.

A real-world, well-designed relational database will usually consist of a large number of tables. Each table usually has only several fields and many records. The reason for only having a few fields in each table is to increase query performance. Without going into the details of database optimization, have faith that it's much faster to query many tables with a few fields each than to query a single table with many fields.

We can extend the example shown in the previous diagram to illustrate a relational database with two tables: **Products** and **Categories**.

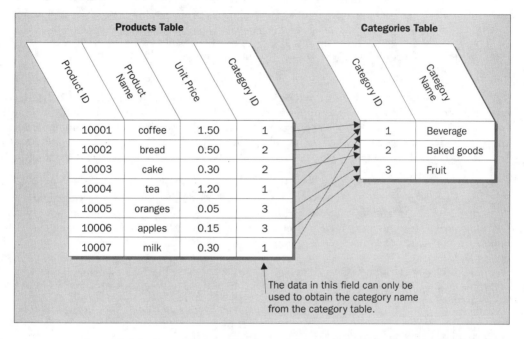

As you can see from the diagram, the **Category ID** field is used to relate the information stored in the two tables. **Category ID** uniquely identifies a category record in the **Categories** table, so it is a primary key for that table. In the **Products** table, the **Category ID** field is used to relate a product record to a category, so the field is termed a **foreign key** for that table.

Relational databases can be created and manipulated in numerous ways. There are a large number of RDBMSs on the market that provide a wide range of facilities for creating and manipulating database information. Obviously, it's possible for you to add and delete records in a database table, and to update the fields in a record, although typically there are controls within the RDBMS to limit such activities, based on the authorization level of the user. As well as accessing information from a single table in a database, you can combine records from two or more tables into a new table, based on their relationships, and retrieve information from that. Combining tables in this way is called a **table join**. To program all these kinds of operations for a relational database, you can use a language known as **SQL**, which is supported by most RDBMSs and programming languages.

A Little SQL

SQL (often pronounced 'sequel') stands for Structured Query Language. It's a relatively simple language, designed specifically for accessing and modifying information in relational databases. It was originally developed at IBM in a mainframe environment, but is now used throughout the computing world. SQL doesn't actually exist as a software package by itself — it's usually hosted by some other environment, whether that's an RDBMS or a programming language, such as COBOL, C or C++. The environment hosting SQL provides for mundane things such as regular I/O and talking to the operating system, while SQL is used to query the database.

MFC support for databases uses SQL to specify queries and other operations on database tables. These operations are provided by a set of specialized classes. You'll see how to use some of these in the example that we'll write later in this chapter.

SQL has statements to retrieve, sort and update records from a table, to add and delete records and fields, to join tables and to compute totals, as well as a lot of other capabilities for creating and managing database tables. We won't be going into all the possible programming options available in SQL, but we'll discuss the details sufficiently to enable you to understand what's happening in the examples that we write, even though you may not have seen any SQL before.

When we use SQL in an MFC-based program, we won't need to write complete SQL statements for the most part because the framework takes care of assembling a complete statement and supplying it to the database engine you're using. Nevertheless, we'll look here at how typical SQL statements are written in their entirety, so that you get a feel for how the language statements are structured.

SQL statements are written with a terminating semicolon (just like C++ statements), and keywords in the language are written in capital letters. Let's take a look at a few examples of SQL statements and see how they work.

Retrieving Data Using SQL

To retrieve data, you use the **SELECT** statement. In fact, it's quite surprising how much of what you want to do with a database is covered by the **SELECT** statement, which operates on one or more tables in your database. The result of executing a **SELECT** statement is always a **recordset**, which is a collection of data produced using the information from the tables you supply in the detail of the statement. The data in the recordset is organized in the form of a table, with named columns that are from the tables you specified in the **SELECT** statement, and rows or records that are selected, based on conditions specified in the **SELECT** statement. The recordset generated by a **SELECT** statement might have only one record, or might even be empty.

Perhaps the simplest retrieval operation on a database is to access all the records in a single table, so given that our database includes a table called **Products**, we can obtain all the records in this table with the following SQL statement:

```
SELECT * FROM Products;
```

The ***** indicates that we want all the fields in the database. The parameter following the keyword **FROM** defines the table from which the fields are to be selected. We haven't constrained the records that are returned by the **SELECT** statement, so we'll get all of them. A little later we'll see how to constrain the records that are selected.

If you wanted all the records, but only needed to retrieve specific fields in each record, you could specify these by using the field names separated by commas in place of the asterisk in the previous example. An example of a statement that would do this is:

```
SELECT ProductID,UnitPrice FROM Products;
```

This statement selects all the records from the **Products** table, but only the **ProductID** and **UnitPrice** fields for each record. This will produce a table having just the two fields specified here.

The field names that we've used don't contain spaces, but they could. Where a name contains spaces, standard SQL says that it has to be written between double quotes. If the fields had the names **Product ID** and **Unit Price**, we would write the **SELECT** statement as:

```
SELECT "Product ID","Unit Price" FROM Products;
```

Using double quotes with names, as we have done here, is a bit inconvenient in the C++ context, as we need to be able to pass SQL statements as strings. In C++, double quotes are already used as character string delimiters, so there would be confusion if we tried to enclose the names of database objects (tables or fields) in double quotes.

For this reason, when you reference database table or field names which include spaces in the Visual C++ environment, you should enclose them within square brackets rather than double quotes. Thus, you would write the field names from the example as **[Product ID]** and **[Unit Price]**. You'll see this notation in action in the database program that we write later in this chapter.

Choosing Records

Unlike fields, records in a table don't have names. The only way to choose particular records is by applying some condition or restriction on the contents of one or more of the fields in a record, so that only records meeting the condition are selected. This is done by adding a **WHERE** clause to the **SELECT** statement. The parameter following the **WHERE** keyword defines the condition that is to be used to select records.

We could select the records in the **Products** table that have a particular value for the **Category ID** field, with the statement:

```
SELECT * FROM Products WHERE [Category ID] = 1;
```

This selects just those records where the **Category ID** field has the value 1, so from the table we illustrated earlier, we would get the records for coffee, tea and milk. Note that a single equals sign is used to specify a check for equality in SQL, not **==** as we use in C++.

You can use other comparison operators, such as **<**, **>**, **<=** and **>=**, to specify the condition in a **WHERE** clause. You can also combine logical expressions with **AND** and **OR**. To place a further restriction on the records selected in the last example, we could write:

```
SELECT * FROM Products WHERE [Category ID] = 1 AND [Unit Price] > 0.5;
```

In this case, the resulting table would just contain two records, because milk would be out as it's too cheap. Only records with a **Category ID** of 1 and a **Unit Price** value greater than 0.5 are selected by this statement.

Joining Tables Using SQL

You can also use the **SELECT** statement to join tables together, although it's a little more complicated than you might imagine. Suppose we have two tables: **Products** with three records and three fields, and **Orders** with three records and four fields. These are illustrated below:

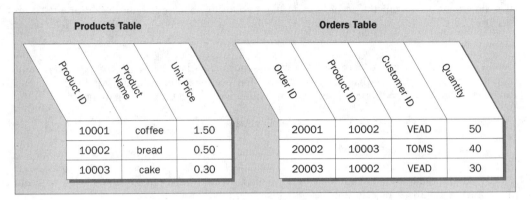

Here, we have a meager product set in the **Products** table, consisting of just coffee, bread and cake, and we have three orders as shown in the **Orders** table — but we haven't managed to sell any coffee.

We could join these tables together with the **SELECT** statement:

```
SELECT * FROM Products,Orders;
```

This statement creates a recordset using the records from both the tables specified. The recordset will have seven fields, three from the **Products** table and four from the **Orders** table, but how many records does it have? The answer is illustrated in the diagram below:

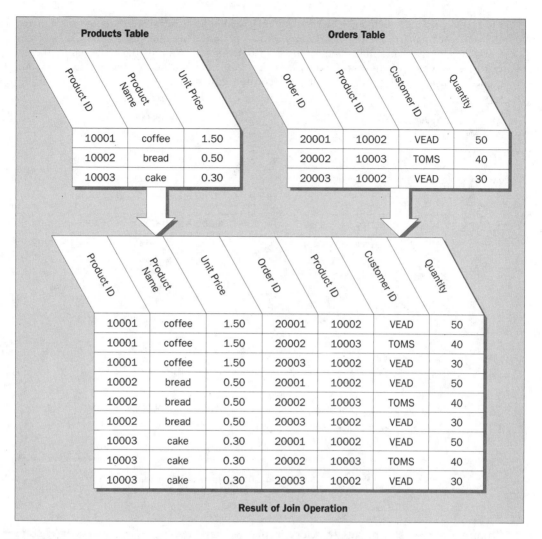

Result of Join Operation

The recordset produced by the **SELECT** statement has nine records that are created by combining each record from the **Products** table with every record from the **Orders** table, so all possible combinations are included. This may not be exactly what is required, or what you expected. Arbitrarily including all combinations of records from one table with another is of limited value. The meaning of a record containing details of the bread product and an order for cake is hard to fathom. You could also end up with an incredibly big table in a real situation. If you combine a table containing 100 products with one containing 500 orders and you don't constrain the join operation, the resulting table will contain 50,000 records!

To get a useful join, you usually need to add a **WHERE** clause to the **SELECT** statement. With the tables we've been using, one condition that would make sense would be to only allow records where the **Product ID** from one table matched the same field in the other table. This would combine each record from the **Products** table with the records from the **Orders** table that related to that product. The statement to do this would be:

```
SELECT * FROM Products,Orders WHERE Products.[Product ID] = Orders.[Product ID];
```

Notice how a specific field for a particular table is identified here. You add the table name as a prefix and separate it from the field name with a period. This qualification of the field name is essential where the same field name is used in both tables. Without the table name, there's no way to know which of the two fields you mean. With this **SELECT** statement and the same table contents we used previously, we'll get the recordset shown here:

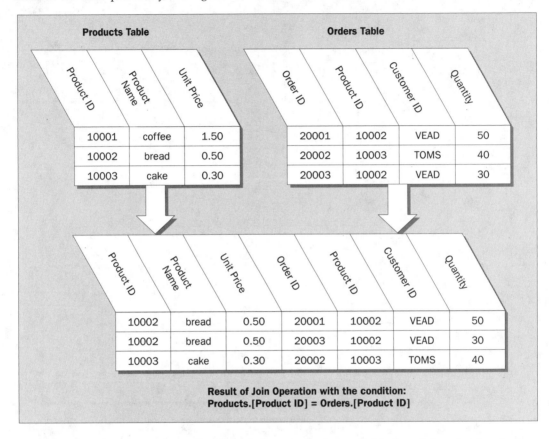

Result of Join Operation with the condition:
Products.[Product ID] = Orders.[Product ID]

Of course, this may still be unsatisfactory in that we have two fields containing the **Product ID**, but you could easily remove this by specifying the field names you want, instead of the ***** in the **SELECT** statement. However, the columns with the same name could be distinguished here by being qualified with the name of their original table when they appear in the recordset.

Sorting Records

When you retrieve data from a database using the **SELECT** statement, you'll often want the records sorted in a particular order. With the previous example, the tables shown are already ordered, but in practice this isn't necessarily the case. You might want to see the output of the last example sorted in a different way, depending on the circumstances. At one time, it might be convenient to have the records ordered by **Customer ID**, and on another occasion perhaps ordered by **Quantity** within **Product ID**. The **ORDER BY** clause added to the **SELECT** statement will do this for you. For example, we could refine the last **SELECT** statement by adding an **ORDER BY** clause:

```
SELECT * FROM Products,Orders WHERE Products.[Product ID] = Orders.[Product ID]
                        ORDER BY [Customer ID];
```

The result of this will be the same records that we obtained with the last example, but with the records arranged so that the **Customer ID** field is in ascending sequence. Since the kind of data stored in a given field is known, the records will be ordered according to the data type applicable to the field. In our case the ordering will be alphabetical.

If you wanted to sort on two fields, **Customer ID** and **Product ID** say, and you wanted the records arranged in descending sequence, you would write:

```
SELECT * FROM Products,Orders
                WHERE Products.[Product ID] = Orders.[Product ID]
                ORDER BY [Customer ID] DESC, Products.[Product ID] DESC;
```

We need to use the qualified name, **Products.[Product ID]**, in the **ORDER BY** clause to avoid ambiguity, as we do in the **WHERE** clause. The keyword **DESC** at the end of each field in the **ORDER BY** statement specifies descending sequence for the sort operation. There's a complementary keyword, **ASC**, for ascending sequence, although this is usually omitted because it is the default condition.

This is by no means all there is to SQL, or even all there is to the **SELECT** statement, but it's enough to get you through the database example that we will write.

FYI | If you need to know more about SQL, there's an excellent book written by Joe Celko and published by Wrox Press entitled *Instant SQL Programming*. ISBN 1-874416-50-8.

Database Support in MFC

You're spoilt for choice when you use MFC for database application development, since two distinct approaches are supported, each of which uses its own set of MFC classes.

One approach is to use **Data Access Objects (DAO)**. These objects provide an interface to the **Jet database engine**. The Jet database engine is a generalized piece of software that provides the ability to store data in, and retrieve data from, a range of database management systems. Jet is the engine used by Microsoft's Access DBMS. Whenever you manipulate a database in Access, you're actually getting Jet to do all the hard work. Jet is optimized for accessing Access (**.mdb**) database files directly, but will also enable you to attach to any database that supports the **O**pen **D**ata**B**ase Connectivity interface, better known as **ODBC**. This allows you to manipulate databases in any format for which you have the appropriate ODBC driver. Databases that you can access using Jet, in addition to Microsoft Access, include Oracle, dBase 5, Btrieve 6.0, and FoxPro 2.6.

The other approach is ODBC-specific, but since ODBC drivers are also available for **.mdb** files, both approaches cover essentially the same range of database formats. How do you choose between them?

The first consideration is whether you're accessing your database in a client/server environment. If you are, you need to use ODBC. If you're not in a client/server situation, perhaps the most significant factor is whether you are going to use your program primarily with `.mdb` databases. If you are, the DAO-based approach will be more efficient than the ODBC approach. On the other hand, if you use the DAO approach with databases other than those in Microsoft Access format, which don't use the Microsoft Jet engine to drive them, you'll be working through the ODBC interface included within the DAO implementation, and this will be less efficient than using the ODBC specific approach directly. The DAO-based classes also provide a more comprehensive range of capabilities than the ODBC classes, so you need to consider this aspect as well.

If you want to take a simplistic view, you could decide on the basis that if you intend to use Microsoft Access databases and you're not in a client/server situation, you should program using DAO, otherwise you use ODBC.

DAO vs ODBC

DAO uses objects for accessing and manipulating a database. There are objects representing tables, queries and the database itself. These objects insulate you from the detail of the specific database system implementation you are concerned with and provide you with a programming interface that is consistent with the object-oriented approach to programming.

ODBC, on the other hand, is a system-independent interface to a database environment that requires an **ODBC driver** to be provided for each database system from which you want to manipulate data. ODBC defines a set of function calls for database operations that are system-neutral. You can only use a database with ODBC if you have the DLL that contains the driver to work with that database application's file format. The purpose of the driver is to interface the standard set of system-independent calls for database operations that will be used in your program to the specifics of a particular database implementation.

While the concept here is rather different from that of DAO, the programming approach in Visual C++ is very similar with both methodologies. MFC packages the ODBC interface in a set of classes that are structured in a very similar way to the classes that apply with DAO. The application of MFC classes for ODBC closely parallels the use of the equivalent DAO classes.

It would be useful now to take a broad view of the classes supporting DAO and ODBC in MFC. We won't go into detail at this point, but will use a programming example to understand the basic mechanics of how the ODBC classes can be used.

Classes Supporting DAO

The following eight classes are used with the DAO approach:

Class	What it does
CDaoWorkspace	An object of this class manages a database session from start to finish. A **CDaoDatabase** object requires a **CDaoWorkspace** object to be available, and if you don't create one, the framework will supply one automatically when your **CDaoDatabase** object is created. A workspace object can contain several database objects.
CDaoDatabase	An object of this class implements a connection to a specific database. An object of this class will always be created when you access a database, but you don't necessarily have to create a database object explicitly. It can be created implicitly when you create a **CDaoRecordset** object.
CDaoRecordset	An object of a class derived from this class represents the result of an SQL **SELECT** operation, which is a set of records. The object makes available one record of the table produced by the **SELECT** at a time, and provides a range of functions to enable you to move backwards and forwards through the records available, and to search for records conforming to a set of search criteria.
CDaoRecordView	An object of a class derived from this class is used to display the current record from an associated recordset object. The record view object uses a child dialog to display data items from the DAO recordset object. There are automatic mechanisms for updating the controls in the dialog with current data from the DAO recordset object.
CDaoFieldExchange	This class supports the exchange of data between your database and a DAO recordset object. You can use objects of this class yourself, but AppWizard and ClassWizard will implement and maintain the use of these objects automatically.
CDaoQueryDef	An object of this class defines a query on your database that is usually predefined in the database. These are typically standard queries that are used frequently in a particular database. A **CDaoQueryDef** object can be used to create a **CDaoRecordset** object that represents a particular **SELECT** statement. An object of this class can also be used to execute SQL statements explicitly, by using its **Execute()** member function.
CDaoTableDef	An object of this class defines a table in your database. It can represent an existing table, or can be used to construct a new table.
CDaoException	An object of this class is constructed when an exception condition arises from a DAO database operation. All DAO errors cause exceptions and result in objects of this class being created. The **CDaoException** class members enable you to determine the cause of the exception.

The most essential classes that you'll use in DAO programming are a **CDaoDatabase** class that will represent your database, one or more classes derived from **CDaoRecordset** that will represent **SELECT** operations on your database, and one or more classes derived from **CDaoRecordView** that will display data made available by your **CDaoRecordset**-based classes.

As we shall see, an ODBC application involves a similar set of basic classes with the same sort of functionality. The **CDaoTableDef** and **CDaoQueryDef** classes provide capability that is not available within MFC support for ODBC.

Classes Supporting ODBC

MFC support for ODBC is implemented through five classes:

Class	What it does
CDatabase	An object of this class represents a connection to your database. This connection must exist before you can carry out any operations on the database. No workspace class is used with an ODBC database.
CRecordset	An object of a class derived from this class represents the result of an SQL **SELECT** operation. This is the same concept that we saw with the **CDaoRecordset** class.
CRecordView	An object of a class derived from this class is used to display current information from an associated recordset object. This is the same concept that we saw with the **CDaoRecordView** class.
CFieldExchange	This class provides for the exchange of data between the database and a recordset object, in the same manner that we saw for DAO databases.
CDBException	Objects of this class represent exceptions that occur within ODBC database operations.

The ODBC classes look very much like a subset of the DAO classes and, in the sense that the interface they provide is similar to that of the equivalent DAO classes, they are. Of course, the underlying process for accessing the database is rather different.

We can best understand how database operations with MFC work by creating an example. We will use the ODBC approach, but apply it to accessing a Microsoft Access database. The database that we'll use is supplied on the Visual C++ CD. It has the merit of containing a considerable variety of tables that are populated by realistic numbers of records. This will give you a lot of scope for experimentation, as well as providing some feel for how well your code will work in practice. It's easy to be lulled into a false sense of security by running your program against a test database where the numbers of tables and records within a table is trivial. It can be quite a surprise to find out how long transactions can take in a real world context.

Creating a Database Application

For our example, we'll show how to use three related tables in the database contained in the **sampdata.mdb** file. You'll find this file in the **\Samples\vc98\mfc\database\daoctl** folder on the MSDN library CD. Copy the file to a suitable folder on your hard disk and make sure that it's no longer set to read-only. (In Windows 95, you can alter this by right-clicking the file, selecting Properties from the pop-up menu and making sure that the Read-only attribute box is unchecked.) Since you'll always have the read-only version of the database on the CD to go back to if something goes wrong, you won't need to worry about messing it up, so feel free to experiment as we go along.

In the first step, we'll create a program to display records from the **Products** table in the database. We'll then add code to allow us to examine all the orders for a given product using two other tables. Finally, we'll access the **Customers** table to enable the customer details for an order to be displayed. Before we can start with the code, we need to identify the database to the operating system.

Registering an ODBC Database

Before you can use an ODBC database, it needs to be registered. You do this through the Control Panel that you access by selecting Settings from the Start menu. In the Control Panel, select the 32bit ODBC icon. The procedure may vary depending on which release of Windows 95 you're using, but if you have a recent version, you should see the dialog shown here:

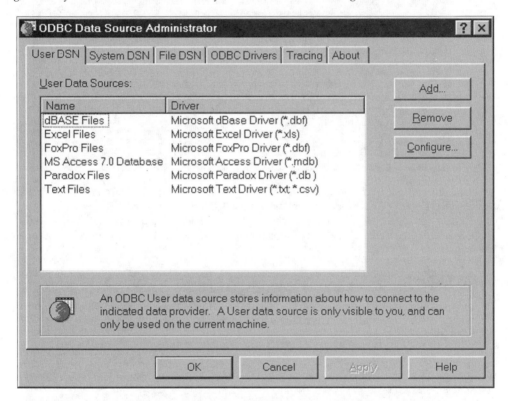

The User DSN tab shows you the data sources you already have configured on your system, which may differ from the ones in the diagram. Click on the Add... button to add a new data source. You should see the next dialog:

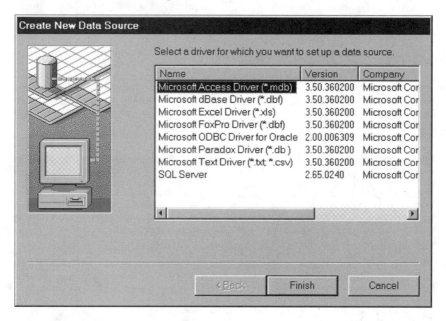

Here you must select from the list of ODBC drivers the one that we're going to use: Microsoft Access Driver(*.mdb). This was automatically installed with the typical setup when you installed Windows. If you don't see this driver, you need to go back to Windows setup to install it. When you've selected the driver, click on the Finish button. This will take you to yet another dialog, as shown:

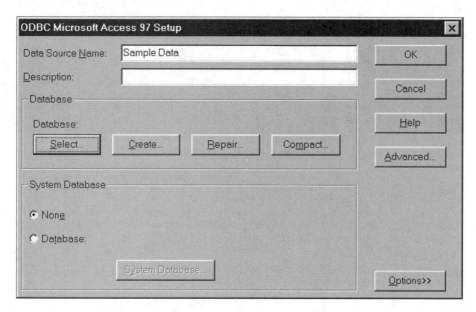

Enter **Sample Data** as the Data Source Name:. We'll use this name to identify the database when we generate our application using AppWizard. You now need to click on the Select... button to go to the final, Select Database dialog, in which you can select the **sampdata.mdb** file in whichever directory it now sits:

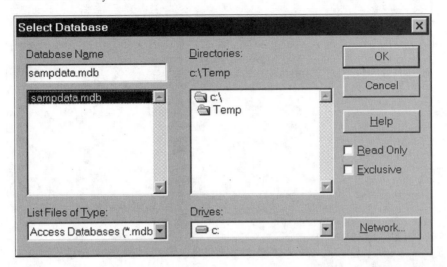

Finally, click on three successive OK buttons, and you've registered the database. If this procedure isn't the same on your PC, you'll need to resort to Help for your operating system, or just experiment with the ODBC option on Control Panel. The truth is in there.

Once you've succeeded, we can go ahead with our database application and, as ever, the starting point is AppWizard.

Using AppWizard to Generate an ODBC Program

Create a new project workspace in the usual way and give it a suitable name, such as **DBSample**. Choose the SDI interface for document support, since that will be sufficient for our needs. The document is somewhat incidental to operations in a database application, since most things are managed by recordset and record view objects. As you'll see, the main use of the document is to store recordset objects, so you won't need more than one of them. Click on the Next > button to move to the next step.

In Step 2 you have a choice as to whether you include file support with the database view option. File support refers to serializing the document, which isn't normally necessary since any database input and output that you need will be taken care of using the recordset objects in your application. Therefore, you should choose the option without file support, as shown here:

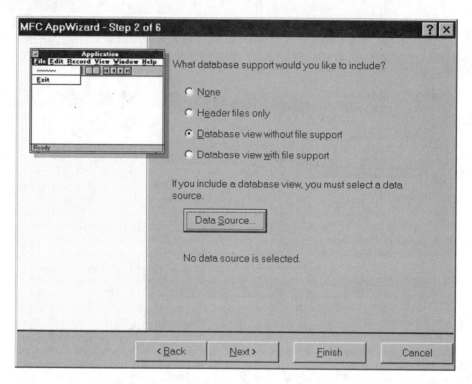

When you select either of the database options, the Data Source... button is activated. You now need to click on this button to specify the database that your application is going to use. This will display the dialog shown here:

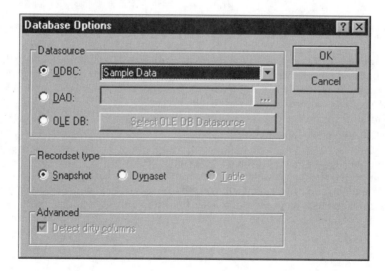

ODBC is already selected as the database option and, if you expand the drop-down list, you should find Sample Data as one of the data sources available to you (provided you've registered it correctly beforehand). In the dialog above, it has already been selected.

AppWizard will automatically equip your program with a recordset class and a record view class, and the dialog also shows a choice for the recordset your program will use. The grayed Table option only applies if you're using DAO. For ODBC, you have a choice between Snapshot and Dynaset for your initial recordset class. There's a significant difference between these options, so let's look at what they mean.

Snapshot vs Dynaset Recordsets

Your recordset object will provide you with the result of a **SELECT** operation on the database. In the case of a **snapshot** recordset, the query is executed once and the result is stored in memory. Your recordset object can then make available to you any of the records in the table that result from the query, so a snapshot is essentially static in nature. Any changes that might occur in the database due to other users updating the database will not be reflected in the data you have obtained with your snapshot recordset. If you need to see changes that may have been made, you'll need to re-run the **SELECT** statement.

There's another feature of snapshot recordsets that depends on whether you're using DAO or ODBC. A DAO snapshot can't be changed by your program — it's read-only. However, an ODBC snapshot can be either read-only or updatable. An updatable snapshot writes any modifications that you make to the table straight back to the underlying database, and your program can see the change. Other programs with a snapshot of the database will not, however, see the changes until they requery the database.

With the **dynaset** option, your recordset object will automatically refresh the current record from the database when you move from one record to another in the table generated by the query for the recordset. As a consequence, the record available in the recordset will reflect the up-to-date status of the database when you accessed the record, not when you first opened the recordset. Be aware that the refresh only occurs when your recordset object accesses a record. If the data in the current record is modified by another user, this will not be apparent in your recordset object unless you move to another record and then return to the original record. A dynaset recordset uses an index to the database tables involved to generate the contents of each record dynamically.

Since we have no other users accessing the Sample Data database, you can choose the Snapshot option for our example. This will be adequate here because we'll only be implementing the retrieval of data from the database. If you want to try to add some update capability yourself, you should use the Dynaset option.

Choosing Tables

Once Snapshot has been chosen, you can click on the OK button to display the dialog which will determine the tables that the recordset class in your application will relate to. Here, you are effectively specifying the tables parameter for the **SELECT** statement that will be applied for the recordset. The dialog is shown here:

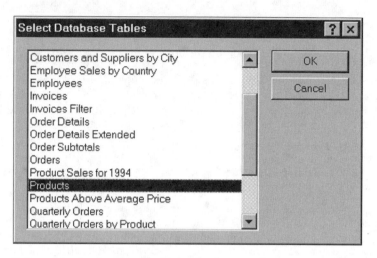

The dialog lists all the tables in the Sample Data database and, as you can see, there are quite a few. You could select several tables to be associated with the recordset by holding down the *Shift* key as you click on entries in the list box, but here we only need one, so just select the Products table, as shown, and then click on the OK button.

You have now specified the operation for the recordset class that AppWizard will generate as:

```
SELECT * FROM Products;
```

The use of * for all fields is determined by the framework. It just uses the table names you choose here to form the SQL operation that will be applied for the recordset.

You can now move through the remaining steps for generating the project workspace without changing any of the options, until you get to the dialog displaying the class and filenames to be used, which is Step 6, as shown here:

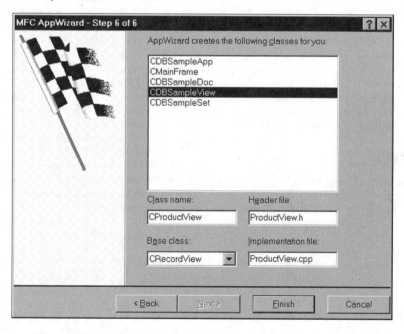

As well as the changes shown above for the **CDBSampleView** class, you should also change the **CDBSampleSet** class name to **CProductSet**, and the associated **.h** and **.cpp** file names to be consistent with the class name. Once that's done, you can click on Finish and generate the program.

Understanding the Program Structure

The basic structure of the program is as we've seen before, comprising an application class **CDBSampleApp**, a frame window class **CMainFrame**, a document class **CDBSampleDoc**, and a view class **CProductView**. A document template object is responsible for creating and relating the frame window, the document and the view objects. This is done in a standard manner in the **InitInstance()** member of the application object.

The document class is quite standard, except that AppWizard has added a data member, **m_productSet** which is an object of the **CProductSet** class. As a consequence, a recordset object will be automatically created when the document object is created in the **InitInstance()** function member of the application object. The significant departures from a non-database program arise in the detail of the **CRecordset** class, and in the **CRecordView** class, so let's take a look at those.

Understanding Recordsets

We can look at the definition of the **CProductSet** class that AppWizard has generated piecemeal and see how each piece works. The bits under discussion are shaded.

Recordset Creation

The first segment of the class definition that is of interest is:

```
class CProductSet : public CRecordset
{
public:
   CProductSet(CDatabase* pDatabase = NULL);
   DECLARE_DYNAMIC(CProductSet)

// Plus more of the class definition...

// Overrides
   // ClassWizard generated virtual function overrides
   //{{AFX_VIRTUAL(CProductSet)
   public:
   virtual CString GetDefaultConnect();    // Default connection string
   virtual CString GetDefaultSQL();        // default SQL for Recordset
   virtual void DoFieldExchange(CFieldExchange* pFX);// RFX support
   //}}AFX_VIRTUAL

// Plus some more standard stuff

};
```

The class has **CRecordset** as a base class and provides the functionality for retrieving data from the database. The constructor for the class accepts a pointer to a **CDatabase** object that is set to **NULL** as a default. The parameter to the constructor allows a **CProductSet** object to be created for a **CDatabase** object that already exists, which allows an existing connection to a database to be reused. Opening a connection to a database is a lengthy business, so it's advantageous to reuse a database connection when you can.

If no pointer is passed to the constructor, as will be the case for the **m_productSet** member of the document class **CDBSampleDoc**, the framework will automatically create a **CDatabase** object for you and call the **GetDefaultConnect()** function member of **CProductSet** to define the connection. The implementation of this function provided by AppWizard is as follows:

```
CString CProductSet::GetDefaultConnect()
{
    return _T("ODBC;DSN=Sample Data");
}
```

This function is a pure virtual function in the base class, and so must always be implemented in a derived recordset class. The implementation provided by AppWizard will return the text string shown to the framework. This identifies our database by name and enables the framework to create a **CDatabase** object to provide the database connection automatically.

In practice, it's usually necessary to supply a user ID and a password before access to a database is permitted. You can add this information to the string returned by the **GetDefaultConnect()** function. Where this is necessary, you specify your user ID by adding **UID=** and your ID following the **DSN=** part of the string, and you specify the password by adding **PWD=** followed by your password. Each piece of the string is separated from the next by a semicolon. For example, if your user ID is Reuben and your password is Hype, you could specify these in the **return** statement from **GetDefaultConnect()** as:

```
return _T("ODBC;DSN=Sample Data;UID=Reuben;PWD=Hype");
```

You can also make the framework pop up a dialog for the user to select the database name from the list of registered database sources by writing the return as:

```
return _T("ODBC;");
```

Querying the Database

The **CProductSet** class includes a data member for each field in the **Products** table. AppWizard obtains the field names from the database and uses these to name the corresponding data members of the class. They appear in the block of code delimited by the **AFX_FIELD** comments in the following:

```
class CProductSet : public CRecordset
{
public:
    CProductSet(CDatabase* pDatabase = NULL);
    DECLARE_DYNAMIC(CProductSet)

// Field/Param Data
    //{{AFX_FIELD(CProductSet, CRecordset)
    long    m_ProductID;
    CString m_ProductName;
    long    m_SupplierID;
    long    m_CategoryID;
    CString m_QuantityPerUnit;
    CString m_UnitPrice;
```

```
    int       m_UnitsInStock;
    int       m_UnitsOnOrder;
    int       m_ReorderLevel;
    BOOL      m_Discontinued;
    //}}AFX_FIELD

// Overrides
    // ClassWizard generated virtual function overrides
    //{{AFX_VIRTUAL(CProductSet)
    public:
    virtual CString GetDefaultConnect();  // Default connection string
    virtual CString GetDefaultSQL();       // default SQL for Recordset
    virtual void DoFieldExchange(CFieldExchange* pFX);  // RFX support
    //}}AFX_VIRTUAL

// Implementation
#ifdef _DEBUG
    virtual void AssertValid() const;
    virtual void Dump(CDumpContext& dc) const;
#endif

};
```

The type of each data member is set to correspond with the field type for the corresponding field in the **Products** table. You may not want all these fields in practice, but you shouldn't delete them willy-nilly in the class definition. As you will see shortly, they are referenced in other places, so always use ClassWizard to delete fields that you don't want. A further caveat is that you must not delete primary keys. If you do, the recordset won't work, so you need to be sure which fields are primary keys before chopping out what you don't want.

The SQL operation which applies to the recordset to populate these data members is specified in the **GetDefaultSQL()** function. The implementation that AppWizard has supplied for this is:

```
CString CProductSet::GetDefaultSQL()
{
    return _T("[Products]");
}
```

The string returned is obviously obtained from the table you selected during the creation of the project. The square brackets have been included to provide for the possibility of the table name containing blanks. If you had selected several tables in ·Step 2 of the project creation process, they would all be inserted here, separated by commas, with each table name enclosed within square brackets.

The **GetDefaultSQL()** function is called by the framework when it constructs the SQL statement to be applied for the recordset. The framework slots the string returned by this function into a skeleton SQL statement with the form:

```
SELECT * FROM < String returned by GetDefaultSQL() >;
```

This looks very simplistic, and indeed it is, but we can add **WHERE** and **ORDER BY** clauses to the operation, as you'll see later.

Data Transfer between the Database and the Recordset

The transfer of data from the database to the recordset, and vice versa, is accomplished by the **DoFieldExchange()** member of the **CProductSet** class. The implementation of this function provided by AppWizard is:

```
void CProductSet::DoFieldExchange(CFieldExchange* pFX)
{
  //{{AFX_FIELD_MAP(CProductSet)
  pFX->SetFieldType(CFieldExchange::outputColumn);
  RFX_Long(pFX, _T("[ProductID]"), m_ProductID);
  RFX_Text(pFX, _T("[ProductName]"), m_ProductName);
  RFX_Long(pFX, _T("[SupplierID]"), m_SupplierID);
  RFX_Long(pFX, _T("[CategoryID]"), m_CategoryID);
  RFX_Text(pFX, _T("[QuantityPerUnit]"), m_QuantityPerUnit);
  RFX_Text(pFX, _T("[UnitPrice]"), m_UnitPrice);
  RFX_Int(pFX, _T("[UnitsInStock]"), m_UnitsInStock);
  RFX_Int(pFX, _T("[UnitsOnOrder]"), m_UnitsOnOrder);
  RFX_Int(pFX, _T("[ReorderLevel]"), m_ReorderLevel);
  RFX_Bool(pFX, _T("[Discontinued]"), m_Discontinued);
  //}}AFX_FIELD_MAP
}
```

This function is called automatically by the framework to store data in and retrieve data from the database. It works in a similar fashion to the **DoDataExchange()** function we have seen with dialog controls, in that the **pFX** parameter determines whether the operation is a read or a write. Each time it's called, it moves a single record to or from the recordset object.

The first function called is **SetFieldType()**, which sets a mode for the **RFX_()** function calls that follow. In this case, the mode is specified as **outputColumn**, which indicates that data is to be exchanged between the database field and the corresponding argument specified in each of the following **RFX_()** function calls.

There are a whole range of **RFX_()** functions for various types of database field. The function call for a particular field will correspond with the data type applicable to that field. The first argument to an **RFX_()** function call is the **pFX** object which determines the direction of data movement. The second argument is the table field name and the third is the data member that is to store that field for the current record.

Understanding the Record View

The purpose of the view class is to display information from the recordset object in the application window, so we need to understand how this works. The bits of the class definition for the **CProductView** class produced by AppWizard that are of primary interest are shaded:

```
class CProductView : public CRecordView
{
protected: // create from serialization only
  CProductView();
  DECLARE_DYNCREATE(CProductView)

public:
  //{{AFX_DATA(CProductView)
  enum{ IDD = IDD_DBSAMPLE_FORM };
  CProductSet* m_pSet;
```

```
        // NOTE: the ClassWizard will add data members here
    //}}AFX_DATA

// Attributes
public:
    CDBSampleDoc* GetDocument();

// Operations
public:

// Overrides
    // ClassWizard generated virtual function overrides
    //{{AFX_VIRTUAL(CProductView)
    public:
    virtual CRecordset* OnGetRecordset();
    virtual BOOL PreCreateWindow(CREATESTRUCT& cs);
    protected:
    virtual void DoDataExchange(CDataExchange* pDX);     // DDX/DDV support
    virtual void OnInitialUpdate(); // called first time after construct
    virtual BOOL OnPreparePrinting(CPrintInfo* pInfo);
    virtual void OnBeginPrinting(CDC* pDC, CPrintInfo* pInfo);
    virtual void OnEndPrinting(CDC* pDC, CPrintInfo* pInfo);
    //}}AFX_VIRTUAL

    // plus implementation and generated message maps
    // that we have seen with standard view classes...
};
```

The view class for a recordset always needs to be derived because the class has to be customized to display the particular fields from the recordset that we want. The base class, **CRecordView**, includes all the functionality required to manage communications with the recordset. All we need to do is use ClassWizard to tailor our record view class to suit our application. We'll get to that in a moment.

Note that the constructor is **protected**. This is because objects of this class are expected to be created from serialization, which is a default assumption for record view classes. When we add further record views to our application, we'll need to change the default access for their constructors to **public** because we'll be creating the views ourselves.

In the block bounded by the comments containing **AFX_DATA**, the enumeration adds the ID **IDD_DBSAMPLE_FORM** to the class. This is the ID for a blank dialog that AppWizard has included in the program. We'll need to add controls to this dialog to display the database fields from the **Products** table that we want displayed. The dialog ID is passed to the base class, **CRecordView**, in the initialization list of the constructor for our view class:

```
CProductView::CProductView() : CRecordView(CProductView::IDD)
{
   //{{AFX_DATA_INIT(CProductView)
      // NOTE: the ClassWizard will add member initialization here
   m_pSet = NULL;
   //}}AFX_DATA_INIT
   // TODO: add construction code here
}
```

829

This action links the view class to the dialog, which is necessary to enable the mechanism which transfers data between the recordset object and the view object to work.

There is also a pointer to a **CProductSet** object, **m_pSet**, in the **AFX_DATA** block of the class definition, which is initialized to **NULL** in the constructor. A more useful value for this pointer is set in the **OnInitialUpdate()** member of the class, which has been implemented as:

```
void CProductView::OnInitialUpdate()
{
    m_pSet = &GetDocument()->m_productSet;
    CRecordView::OnInitialUpdate();
    GetParentFrame()->RecalcLayout();
    ResizeParentToFit();
}
```

This function is called when the record view object is created. The first line sets **m_pSet** to the address of the **m_productSet** member of the document, thus tying the view to the product set object. The second line gives the base class a chance to initialize itself, and the final two lines ensure that the frame window resizes itself properly to fit around the dialog.

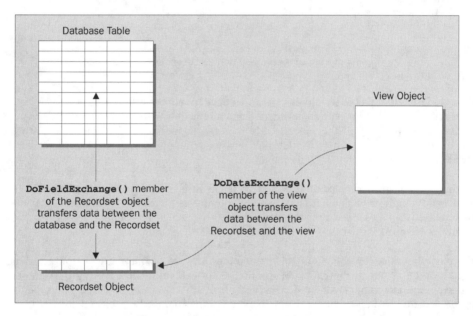

The transfer of data between the data members in the **CProductSet** object that correspond to fields in the **Products** table, and the controls in the dialog associated with the **CProductView** object, will be managed by the **DoDataExchange()** member of **CProductView**. The code in this function to do this isn't in place yet, since we first need to add the controls to the dialog that are going to display the data, and then use ClassWizard to link the controls to the recordset data members. Let's do that next.

Creating the View Dialog

The first step is to place the controls on the dialog, so go to ResourceView, expand the list of Dialog resources and double-click on **IDD_DBSAMPLE_FORM**. You can delete the static text object with the TODO message from the dialog. If you right-click on the dialog, you can choose to view its Properties, as shown here:

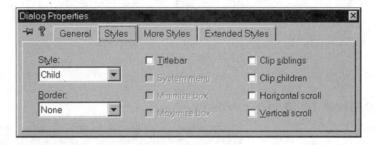

The Style: option has been set to Child because the dialog is going to be a child window and will fill the client area. The Border: option has been set to None because if it fills the client area, the dialog doesn't need a border.

We'll add a static text control to identify each field from the recordset that we want to display, plus an edit control to display it. The tab order of the text control should be such that each static text control immediately precedes the corresponding control displaying the data in sequence. This is because ClassWizard will determine the data member name to be associated with each control that is to display a field from the text in the static control immediately preceding it. The text you choose for the static control is, therefore, most important if this is to work.

You can add each static control, followed immediately by the corresponding edit control, to create the tab order that you want, or you can simply fix the tab order at the end using the Layout | Tab Order menu option.

You can enlarge the dialog by dragging its borders. Then, place controls on the dialog as shown here:

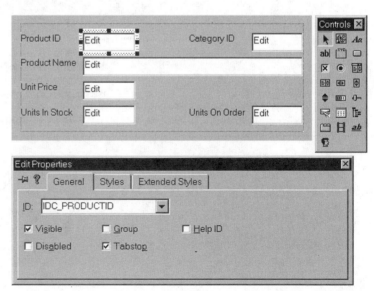

You can add the text to each static control by just typing it as soon as the control has been placed on the dialog. The Properties dialog box will open automatically. As you see, the text for each static control corresponds to the field name in the database. You need to make sure that all the edit controls have different IDs. It's helpful to use the field name as part of the control ID, as shown in the Properties dialog above. You need not worry about the IDs for the static controls, since they aren't referenced in the program. After you have arranged the controls, you should check the tab order to make sure that each static control has a sequence number one less than its corresponding edit control.

You can add other fields to the dialog if you want. The one that is most important for the rest of our example is the **Product ID**, so you *must* include that. Save the dialog and then we can move on to the last step, which is to link the controls to the variables in the recordset class.

Linking the Controls to the Recordset

Linking the controls to the data members of **CProductSet** is simplicity itself. Just double-click on the **Product ID** edit control while holding down the *Ctrl* key and you'll see the dialog box shown here:

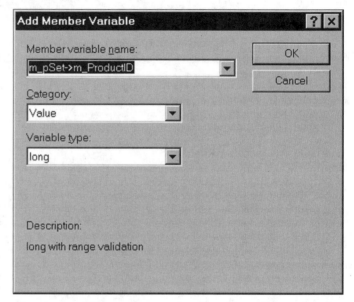

ClassWizard has filled in all the required values for you using the text from the preceding static control and the information from **CProductSet**. All you need to do is to verify that the variable name is correct — it should be if you put the right text in the static control — and click on OK. You then need to repeat this for the other edit controls on your dialog. This will enable ClassWizard to fill out the code for the **DoDataExchange()** function in the **CProductView** class, which will now be implemented as:

```
void CProductView::DoDataExchange(CDataExchange* pDX)
{
    CRecordView::DoDataExchange(pDX);
    //{{AFX_DATA_MAP(CProductView)
    DDX_FieldText(pDX, IDC_PRODUCTID, m_pSet->m_ProductID, m_pSet);
    DDX_FieldText(pDX, IDC_PRODUCTNAME, m_pSet->m_ProductName, m_pSet);
    DDX_FieldText(pDX, IDC_UNITPRICE, m_pSet->m_UnitPrice, m_pSet);
    DDX_FieldText(pDX, IDC_UNITSINSTOCK, m_pSet->m_UnitsInStock, m_pSet);
    DDX_FieldText(pDX, IDC_CATEGORYID, m_pSet->m_CategoryID, m_pSet);
```

```
    DDX_FieldText(pDX, IDC_UNITSONORDER, m_pSet->m_UnitsOnOrder, m_pSet);
    //}}AFX_DATA_MAP
}
```

This function works in the same way you've seen previously with dialog controls. Each **DDX_()** function transfers data between the control and the corresponding data member of the **CProductSet** class, which is accessed through the pointer **m_pSet**.

The complete mechanism for data transfer between the database and the dialog owned by the **CProductView** object is illustrated here:

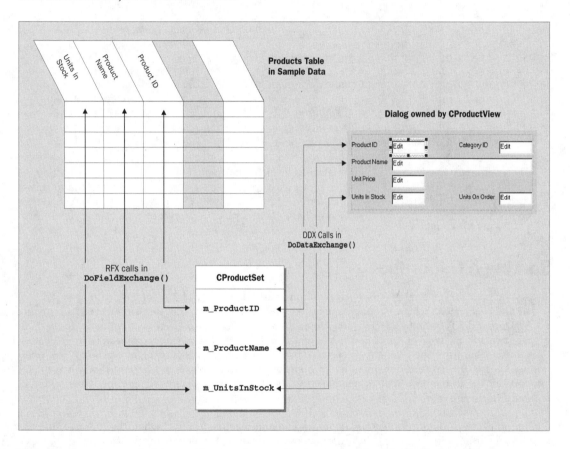

The recordset class and the record view class cooperate to enable data to be transferred between the database and the controls in the dialog. The **CProductSet** class handles transfers between the database and its data members and **CProductView** deals with transfers between the data members of **CProductSet** and the controls in the dialog.

Exercising the Example

Believe it or not, you can now run the example. Just build it in the normal way and then execute it. The application should display a window similar to this one:

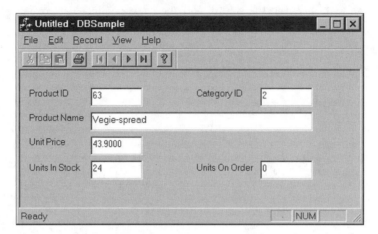

The **CRecordView** base class automatically implements toolbar buttons that step from one record in the recordset to the next or to the previous record. There are also toolbar buttons to move directly to the first or last record in the recordset. You'll notice that the products are not completely in order. It would be nice to have them sorted in **Product ID** sequence, so let's see how we can do that.

Sorting a Recordset

As we saw earlier, the data is retrieved from the database by the recordset, using an SQL **SELECT** statement which is generated by the framework using the **GetDefaultSQL()** member. We can add an **ORDER BY** clause to the statement generated by setting a value in the **m_strSort** member of **CProductSet**, which is inherited from **CRecordSet**. This will cause the output table from the query to be sorted, based on the string stored in **m_strSort**. We only need to set the **m_strSort** member to a string that contains the field name that we want to sort on; the framework will provide the **ORDER BY** keywords. But where should we add the code to do this?

The transfer of data between the database and the recordset occurs when the **Open()** member of the recordset object is called. In our program, the **Open()** function member of the recordset object is called by the **OnInitialUpdate()** member of the base class to our view class, **CRecordView**. We can, therefore, put the code for setting the sort specification in the **OnInitialUpdate()** member of the **CProductView** class, as follows:

```
void CProductView::OnInitialUpdate()
{
   m_pSet = &GetDocument()->m_productSet;
   m_pSet->m_strSort = "[ProductID]";        // Set the sort fields
   CRecordView::OnInitialUpdate();
   GetParentFrame()->RecalcLayout();
   ResizeParentToFit();
}
```

834

We just set **m_strSort** in the recordset to the name of the **ProductID** field. Square brackets are useful, even when there are no blanks in a name, because they differentiate strings containing these names from other strings, so you can immediately pick out the field names. They are, of course, optional if there are no blanks in the field name.

If there was more than one field that you wanted to sort on here, you would just include each of the field names in the string, separated by commas.

Modifying the Window Caption

There's one other thing we could add to this function at this point. The caption for the window would be better if it showed the name of the table being displayed. We can fix this by adding code to set the title in the document object:

```
void CProductView::OnInitialUpdate()
{
    m_pSet = &GetDocument()->m_productSet;
    m_pSet->m_strSort = "[ProductID]";        // Set the sort fields
    CRecordView::OnInitialUpdate();

    // Set the document title to the table name
    if (m_pSet->IsOpen())                      // Verify the recordset is open
    {
        CString strTitle = _T("Table Name"); // Set basic title string
        CString strTable = m_pSet->GetTableName();
        if (!strTable.IsEmpty())               // Verify we have a table name
            strTitle += _T(":") + strTable;    // and add to basic title
        GetDocument()->SetTitle(strTitle);     // Set the document title
    }

    GetParentFrame()->RecalcLayout();
    ResizeParentToFit();
}
```

After checking that the recordset is indeed open, we initialize a local **CString** object with a basic title string. We then get the name of the table from the recordset object by calling its **GetTableName()** member. In general, you should check that you do get a string returned from the **GetTableName()** function. Various conditions can arise that will prevent a table name from being set — for instance, there may be more than one table involved in the recordset. After appending a colon followed by the table name we have retrieved to the basic title in **strTitle**, we set the result as the document title by calling the document's **SetTitle()** member.

If you rebuild the application and run it again, it will work as before, but with a new window caption and with the product IDs in ascending sequence.

Using a Second Recordset Object

Now that we can view all the products in the database, a reasonable extension of the program would be to add the ability to view all the orders for any particular product. To do this, we'll add another recordset class to handle order information from the database, and a complementary view class to display some of the fields from the recordset. We'll also add a button to the **Products** dialog to enable you to switch to the **Orders** dialog when you want to view the orders for the current product. This will enable us to operate with the arrangement shown in the next diagram:

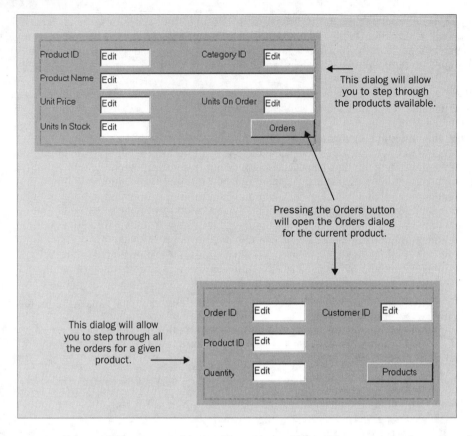

The **Products** dialog will be the starting position. You will be able to step backwards and forwards through all the available products. Clicking the Orders button will switch you to the dialog where you'll be able to view all the orders for the current product. You will be able to return to the **Products** dialog by clicking the Products button.

Adding a Recordset Class

We start by adding the recordset class using ClassWizard, so bring that into view by right clicking in the editor window and selecting from the pop-up. Then, click on the Add Class... button in the ClassWizard dialog and select New... from the pop-up. In the dialog, enter the name of the class as **COrderSet** and select the base class from the drop-down list box, as shown here.

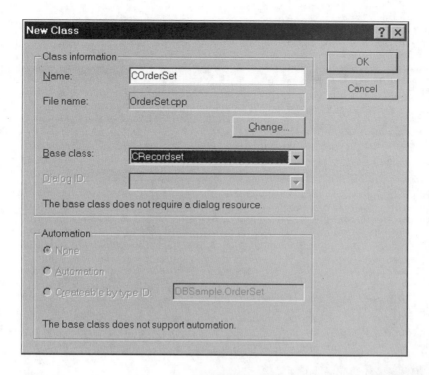

If you now select the OK button, ClassWizard will take you to the dialog to select the database for the recordset class. Select Sample Data from the list box and leave the Recordset type as Snapshot, as before. Then click on the OK button to move to the table selection dialog shown here:

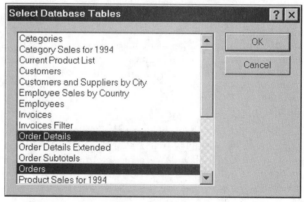

We'll select two tables to associate with the **COrderSet** class, so select the Orders and Order Details table names. You can then click the OK button to complete the process.

You can examine what has been created through ClassWizard. If you switch to the Member Variables tab, you'll see the dialog shown here:

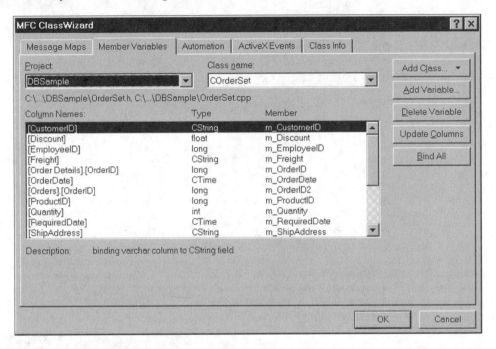

ClassWizard has created a data member for every field in each of the tables. Note that the **OrderID** field appears in both tables, so ClassWizard identifies these by prefixing the field names with the table name in each case. The data member for the **OrderID** field in the **Orders** table is differentiated from the member for the corresponding field in the **Order Details** table by adding a **2** to the name created from the field name.

If you don't want all these fields, you can delete any of them by selecting the appropriate record in the list and then clicking the Delete Variable button. You should, however, take care not to delete any variables that are primary keys. When you delete a data member for a table field, ClassWizard will take care of deleting the initialization for it in the class constructor and the **RFX_()** call for it in the **DoFieldExchange()** member function. The variables that we need are: **m_OrderID**, **m_OrderID2**, **m_ProductID**, **m_Quantity** and **m_CustomerID**.

You can now close ClassWizard by clicking the OK button. To hook the new recordset to the document, you need to add a data member to the definition of the **CDBSampleDoc** class, so right-click the class name in ClassView and select Add Member Variable... from the pop-up. Specify the type as **COrderSet** and the variable name as **m_OrderSet**. You can leave it as a **public** member of the class. After clicking OK to finish adding the data member to the document, you need to be sure the compiler understands that **COrderSet** is a class before it gets to compiling the **CBSampleDoc** class. If you take a look at the definition of **CBDSampleDoc**, you'll see that an **#include** statement has already been added to the top of **DBSampleDoc.h**:

```
#include "OrderSet.h"   // Added by ClassView
...
class CDBSampleDoc : public CDocument
{ // Rest of class definition }
```

Adding a Record View Class

Now you need to create another dialog resource. This must be done before you create the view class so that ClassWizard can automatically connect the dialog to the class for you.

Creating the Dialog Resource

Switch to ResourceView, right-click on the Dialog folder and select Insert Dialog from the pop-up. You can delete both of the default buttons from the dialog. Now change the name and styles for the dialog, so right-click on it and display the Properties box. Change the dialog ID to **IDD_ORDERS_FORM**. You also need to change the dialog style to Child and the border style to None. You do this on the Styles tab, as shown here:

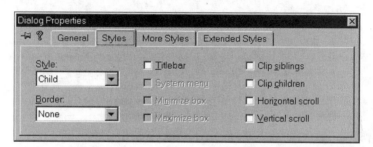

You're now ready to populate the dialog with controls for the fields that you want to display from the **Orders** and **Order Details** tables. If you switch to ClassView and extend the **COrderSet** part of the classes tree, you'll be able to see the names of the variables concerned while you're working on the dialog. Add controls to the dialog as shown here:

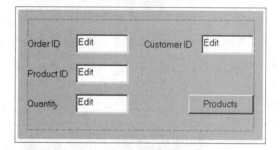

Here, we have four edit controls for the **OrderID**, **CustomerID**, **ProductID**, and **Quantity** fields from the tables associated with the **COrderSet** class, together with static controls to identify them. You can add a few more if you wish. Don't forget to modify the IDs for the edit controls so that they are representative of the purpose of the control. You can use the table field names as we did previously. You also need to check the tab order and verify that each static control immediately precedes the associated edit control in sequence. If they don't, just click on them in the sequence that you want.

The button control labeled Products will be used to return to the **Products** table view, so modify the ID for this button to **IDC_PRODUCTS**. When everything is arranged to your liking, save the dialog resource.

Creating the Record View Class

To create the view class for the recordset, right-click on the dialog and select ClassWizard... from the pop-up. You will then see a dialog offering you two options for identifying a class to associate with the dialog. If you elect to create a new class, you'll see the dialog for creating a New Class.

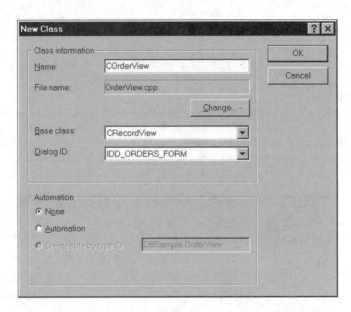

You need to enter the class name as **COrderView** and select the base class from the drop-down list box as **CRecordView**. You also need to select the ID for the dialog you have just created, **IDD_ORDERS_FORM**, from the Dialog ID: list box.

When you click on the OK button, ClassWizard will display a dialog asking you to choose the record set to associate with the view. It should choose **COrderSet** for you, but if it doesn't, select **COrderSet** from the list, and click this OK button as well.

You can see what the characteristics of the **COrderView** class are if you look at the Class Info tab shown here:

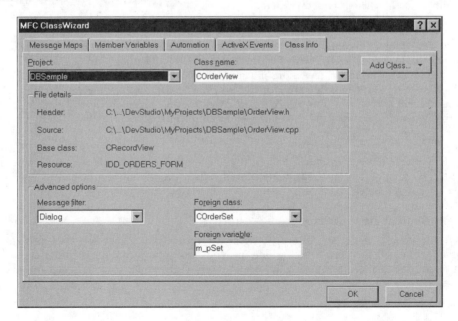

This tells you everything you need to know. The view class, which is derived from **CRecordView**, is hooked to the dialog resource you created with the ID **IDD_ORDERS_FORM** and has the **COrderSet** class associated with it. A data member **m_pSet** has also been added to hold the address of the associated **COrderSet** object. The class **COrderSet** is called a **foreign class** in the dialog above because **DDX** normally links data members of a dialog class and a view class. In this case, a third, 'foreign', class (which is **COrderSet**) is also involved, since this is the source of the data being exchanged.

Check out the destructor for the **COrderView** class, which will have been implemented by ClassWizard with the following code:

```
COrderView::~COrderView()
{
   if (m_pSet)
       delete m_pSet;
}
```

Remove the **if** and the **delete** statement. They aren't necessary in our example because the **COrderSet** object will be created and deleted by the framework, so we shouldn't delete it in the view. If you leave the code in you'll get assertion failures when you close the application, because an attempt will be made to delete the object twice.

Linking the Dialog Controls to the Recordset

To link the controls to the recordset, you follow the same procedure as we did for the **CProductView** class. Go back to the dialog **IDD_ORDERS_FORM** and double-click each edit control while holding down the *Ctrl* key.

Customizing the Record View Class

As it stands, the SQL **SELECT** operation for a **COrderSet** object will produce a table which will contain all combinations of records from the two tables involved. This could be a lot of records, so we must add the equivalent of a **WHERE** clause to the query to restrict the records selected to those that make sense. But there's another problem too: when we switch from the **Products** table display, we don't want to look at just any old orders. We want to see precisely those orders for the product ID we were looking at, which amounts to selecting only those orders that have the same product ID as that contained in the current **CProductSet** record. This is also effected through a **WHERE** clause. In the MFC context, the **WHERE** clause for a **SELECT** operation for a recordset is called a **filter**.

Adding a Filter to the Recordset

Adding a filter to the query is accomplished by assigning a string to the **m_strFilter** member of the recordset object. This member is inherited from the base class, **CRecordSet**. As with the **ORDER BY** clause, which we added by assigning a value to the **m_strSort** member of the recordset, the place to implement this is in the **OnInitialUpdate()** member of the record view class, just before the base class function is called.

We want to set two conditions in the filter. One is to restrict the records generated in the recordset to those where the **OrderID** field in the **Orders** table is equal to the field with the same name in the **Order Details** table. We can write this condition as:

```
[Orders].[OrderID] = [Order Details].[OrderID]
```

841

The other condition we want to apply is that, for the records meeting the first condition, we only want those with a **ProductID** field that is equal to the **ProductID** field in the current record in the recordset object displaying the **Products** table. This means that we need to have the **ProductID** field from the **COrderSet** object compared to a variable value. The variable in this operation is called a parameter, and the condition in the filter is written in a special way:

```
ProductID = ?
```

The question mark represents a parameter value for the filter, and the records that will be selected are those where the **ProductID** field equals the parameter value. The value that is to replace the question mark will be set in the **DoFieldExchange()** member of the recordset. We'll implement this in a moment, but first let's complete the specification of the filter.

We can define the string for the filter variable that incorporates both the conditions that we need with the statement:

```
// Set the filter as Product ID field with equal Order IDs
m_pSet->m_strFilter =
    "[ProductID] = ? AND [Orders].[OrderID] = [Order Details].[OrderID]";
```

We'll insert this into the **OnInitialUpdate()** member of the **COrderView** class, but before that, let's finish setting the parameter for the filter.

Defining the Filter Parameter

We need to add a data member to the **COrderSet** class that will store the current value of the **ProductID** field from the **CProductSet** object, and will also act as the parameter to substitute for the **?** in our filter for the **COrderSet** object. So, right-click on the **COrderSet** class name in ClassView and select Add Member Variable… from the pop-up. The variable type needs to be the same as that of the **m_ProductID** member of the **CProductSet** class, which is **long**, and you can specify the name as **m_ProductIDparam**. You can also leave it as a **public** member. Now we need to initialize this data member in the constructor and set the parameter count, so add the code shown below:

```
COrderSet::COrderSet(CDatabase* pdb) : CRecordset(pdb)
{
  //{{AFX_FIELD_INIT(COrderSet)
  m_OrderID = 0;
  m_ProductID = 0;
  m_Quantity = 0;
  m_OrderID2 = 0;
  m_CustomerID = _T("");
  m_nFields = 5;
  //}}AFX_FIELD_INIT

  m_ProductIDparam = 0L;      // Set initial parameter value
  m_nParams = 1;              // Set number of parameters

  m_nDefaultType = snapshot;
}
```

All of the unshaded code was supplied by ClassWizard to initialize the data members corresponding to the fields in the recordset and to specify the type as **snapshot**. Our code initializes the parameter to zero and sets the count of the number of parameters to 1. The

m_nParams variable is inherited from the base class, **CRecordSet**. Since there is a parameter count, evidently you can have more than one parameter in the filter for the recordset. The application framework requires the count of the number of parameters in your recordset to be set to reflect the number of parameters you're using, otherwise it won't work correctly.

To identify the **m_ProductIDparam** variable in the class as a parameter to be substituted in the filter for the **COrderSet** object, we must also add some code to the **DoFieldExchange()** member of the class:

```
void COrderSet::DoFieldExchange(CFieldExchange* pFX)
{
  //{{AFX_FIELD_MAP(COrderSet)
  pFX->SetFieldType(CFieldExchange::outputColumn);
  RFX_Long(pFX, _T("[Order Details].[OrderID]"), m_OrderID);
  RFX_Long(pFX, _T("[ProductID]"), m_ProductID);
  RFX_Int(pFX, _T("[Quantity]"), m_Quantity);
  RFX_Long(pFX, _T("[Orders].[OrderID]"), m_OrderID2);
  RFX_Text(pFX, _T("[CustomerID]"), m_CustomerID);
  //}}AFX_FIELD_MAP

  // Set the field type as parameter
  pFX->SetFieldType(CFieldExchange::param);
  RFX_Long(pFX, _T("ProductIDParam"), m_ProductIDparam);
}
```

The ClassWizard has provided code to transfer data between the database and the field variables it has added to the class. There is one **RFX_()** function call for each data member of the recordset.

Other than the comment, we only needed to add two lines to the code that ClassWizard has generated to specify **m_ProductIDparam** as a filter. The first line of code calls the **SetFieldType()** member of the **pFX** object to set the mode for the following **RFX_()** calls to **param**. The effect of this is to cause the third argument in any succeeding **RFX_()** calls to be interpreted as a parameter that is to replace a? in the filter for the recordset. If you have more than one parameter, the parameters substitute for the question marks in the **m_strFilter** string in sequence from left to right, so it's important to ensure that the **RFX_()** calls are in the right order. With the mode set to **param**, the second argument in the **RFX_()** call is ignored, so you could put **NULL** here, or some other string if you want.

Initializing the Record View

We now need to add the code to the **OnInitialUpdate()** member of the **COrderView** class. As well as specifying the filter, we can also define a value for **m_strSort** to sort the records in **OrderID** sequence, and add code to change the window caption to match the tables we're dealing with:

```
void COrderView::OnInitialUpdate()
{
  BeginWaitCursor();       // This could take time so start the wait cursor
  CDBSampleDoc* pDoc = (CDBSampleDoc*)GetDocument();   // Get doc pointer
  m_pSet = &pDoc->m_OrderSet;          // Get a pointer to the recordset

  // Use the DB that is open for products recordset
  m_pSet->m_pDatabase = pDoc->m_productSet.m_pDatabase;
```

```
    // Set the current product ID as parameter
    m_pSet->m_ProductIDparam = pDoc->m_productSet.m_ProductID;

    // Set the filter as product ID field
    m_pSet->m_strFilter =
      "[ProductID] = ? AND [Orders].[OrderID] = [Order Details].[OrderID]";

    GetRecordset();                                    // Get the recordset

    // Now fix the caption
    if (m_pSet->IsOpen())
    {
        CString strTitle = "Table Name:";
        CString strTable = m_pSet->GetTableName();     // Get the table name

        //If the recordset uses 2 or more tables, the name will be empty
        if (!strTable.IsEmpty())
            strTitle += _T(":") + strTable;            // It isn't so use the name
        else
            strTitle += _T("Orders - Multiple Tables"); // Use generic name

        GetDocument()->SetTitle(strTitle);             // Set the document title
    }

    CRecordView::OnInitialUpdate();
    EndWaitCursor();
}
```

The version of the **COrderSet** class that has been implemented by ClassWizard doesn't override the **GetDocument()** member because it isn't associated with the document class. As a result, we need to cast the pointer from the base class **GetDocument()** member to a pointer to a **CDBSampleDoc** object. Alternatively, you could add an overriding version of **GetDocument()** to **COrderSet** to do the cast. Clearly, we need a pointer to our document object because we need to access the members of the object.

Because we refer to the **CDBSampleDoc** class, you need to add three **#include** statements to the beginning of the **OrderView.cpp** file:

```
#include "ProductSet.h"
#include "OrderSet.h"
#include "DBSampleDoc.h"
```

The **BeginWaitCursor()** call added by ClassWizard at the start of the **OnInitialUpdate()** function displays the hourglass cursor while this function is executing. The reason for this is that, especially when multiple tables are involved, this function can take an appreciable time to execute. The processing of the query and the transfer of data to the recordset all takes place in here. The cursor is returned to normal by the **EndWaitCursor()** call at the end of the function.

The first thing that our code does is to set the **m_pDatabase** member of the **COrderSet** object to the same as that for the **CProductSet** object. If we don't do this, the framework will re-open the database when the orders recordset is opened. Since the database has already been opened for the products recordset, this would waste a lot of time.

Next, we set the value for the parameter variable to the current value in the **m_ProductID** member of the products recordset. This value will replace the question mark in the filter when the orders recordset is opened and so select the records we want. We then set the filter for the orders recordset to the string we saw earlier.

Next, the **GetRecordSet()** call supplied by ClassWizard is executed. This in turn calls the **OnGetRecordSet()** member, which creates a recordset object if there isn't one — in our case there is one because we added it to the document object — and then calls the **Open()** function for the recordset.

Finally, we have the code we saw earlier to define the caption for the window. The test for an empty table name isn't strictly necessary — we know that the table name will be empty, because the recordset has two tables specified for it. You could just use the code to explicitly define the caption, but the code we've implemented serves to demonstrate that the table name is indeed empty in this case.

Accessing Multiple Tables

Since we have implemented our program with the single document interface, we have one document and one view. The availability of just one view might appear to be a problem, but we can arrange for the frame window object in our application to create an instance of our **COrderView** class, and switch the current window to that when the orders recordset is to be displayed.

We'll need to keep track of what the current window is, which we can do by assigning a unique ID to each of the record view windows in our application. At the moment there are two: the product view and the order view. To do this, create a new file called **OurConstants.h** and add the following code to define the window IDs:

```
// Definition of our constants

#if !defined(OUR_CONSTANTS_H)
#define OUR_CONSTANTS_H

// Arbitrary constants to identify record views
const UINT PRODUCT_VIEW = 1U;
const UINT ORDER_VIEW = 2U;

/////////////////////////////////////////////////////

#endif // !defined(OUR_CONSTANTS_H)
```

We can now use one of these constants to identify each view and to record the ID of the current view in the frame window object. To do this, add a **public** data member to the **CMainFrame** class of type **UINT** and give it the name **m_CurrentViewID**. Once you've done that, you can initialize it in the constructor for **CMainFrame**, by adding code as follows:

```
CMainFrame::CMainFrame()
{
    m_CurrentViewID = PRODUCT_VIEW;        // We always start with this view
}
```

Now add an **#include** statement for **OurConstants.h** to the beginning of **MainFrm.cpp** so that the definition of **PRODUCT_VIEW** is available here.

Switching Views

To enable the view switching mechanism, we're going to add a public function member called **SelectView()** to the **CMainFrame** class, which will have a parameter defining a view ID. This function will switch from the current view to whatever view is specified by the ID passed as an argument.

Right-click on **CMainFrame** and select Add Member Function... from the pop-up. You can enter the return type as **void** and the Function Declaration: entry as **SelectView(UINT ViewID)**. The implementation of the function is as follows:

```
void CMainFrame::SelectView(UINT ViewID)
{
   CView* pOldActiveView = GetActiveView();                // Get current view

   // Get pointer to new view if it exists
   // if it doesn't the pointer will be null
   CView* pNewActiveView = (CView*)GetDlgItem(ViewID);

   // If this is 1st time around for the new view,
   // the new view won't exist, so we must create it
   if (pNewActiveView == NULL)
   {
      switch(ViewID)
      {
         case ORDER_VIEW:                                  // Create an Order view
            pNewActiveView = (CView*)new COrderView;
            break;
         default:
            AfxMessageBox("Invalid View ID");
            return;
      }

      // Switching the views
      // Obtain the current view context to apply to the new view
      CCreateContext context;
      context.m_pCurrentDoc = pOldActiveView->GetDocument();
      pNewActiveView->Create(NULL, NULL, 0L, CFrameWnd::rectDefault,
                                              this, ViewID, &context);
      pNewActiveView->OnInitialUpdate();
   }
   SetActiveView(pNewActiveView);                          // Activate the new view
   pOldActiveView->ShowWindow(SW_HIDE);                    // Hide the old view
   pNewActiveView->ShowWindow(SW_SHOW);                    // Show the new view
   pOldActiveView->SetDlgCtrlID(m_CurrentViewID);          // Set the old view ID
   pNewActiveView->SetDlgCtrlID(AFX_IDW_PANE_FIRST);
   m_CurrentViewID = ViewID;                               // Save the new view ID
   RecalcLayout();
}
```

The operation of the function falls into three distinct parts:

1 Getting pointers to the current view and the new view

2 Creating the new view if it doesn't exist

3 Swapping to the new view in place of the current view

The address of the current active view is supplied by the **GetActiveView()** member of the **CMainFrame** object. To get a pointer to the new view, we call the **GetDlgItem()** member of the frame window object. If a view with the ID specified in the argument to the function exists, it returns the address of the view, otherwise it returns **NULL** and we need to create the new view.

Since we'll create a **COrderView** object on the heap here, we need access to the constructor for the class. The default access specification for the constructor **COrderView()** in the class definition is **protected**, so change it to **public** to make creating the view object legal, as in the following code:

```
class COrderView : public CRecordView
{
public:
    COrderView();              // we changed this to public

protected:
    DECLARE_DYNCREATE(COrderView)

    // rest of class definition
};
```

After creating a view object, we define a **CCreateContext** object, **context**. A **CCreateContext** object is only necessary when you're creating a window for a view that is to be connected to a document. A **CCreateContext** object contains data members that can tie together a document, a frame window and a view, and for MDI applications, a document template as well. When we switch between views, we'll create a new window for the new view to be displayed in. Each time we create a new view window, we will use the **CCreateContext** object to establish a connection between the view and our document object. All we need to do is store a pointer to our document object in the **m_pCurrentDoc** member of **context**. In general you may need to store additional data in the **CCreateContext** object before you create; it depends on the circumstances and the kind of window you're creating.

In the call to the **Create()** member of the view object which creates the window for the new view, we pass the object, **context**, as an argument. This will establish a proper relationship with our document and will validate the document pointer. The argument **this** in the call to **Create()** specifies the current frame as the parent window, and the **ViewID** argument specifies the ID of the window. This ID enables the address of the window to be obtained with a subsequent call to the **GetDlgItem()** member of the parent window.

To make the new view the active view, we call the **SetActiveView()** member of **CMainFrame**. The new view will then replace the current active view. To remove the old view window, we call the **ShowWindow()** member of the view with the argument **SW_HIDE** using the pointer to the old view. To display the new view window, we call the same function with the argument **SW_SHOW** using the pointer to the new view.

```
SetActiveView(pNewActiveView);                   // Activate the new view
pOldActiveView->ShowWindow(SW_HIDE);             // Hide the old view
pNewActiveView->ShowWindow(SW_SHOW);             // Show the new view
pOldActiveView->SetDlgCtrlID(m_CurrentViewID);   // Set the old view ID
pNewActiveView->SetDlgCtrlID(AFX_IDW_PANE_FIRST);
m_CurrentViewID = ViewID;                         // Save the new view ID
```

We restore the ID of the old active view to the ID value that we've defined for it in the **m_CurrentViewID** member of the **CMainFrame** class that we added earlier. We also set the ID of the new view to **AFX_IDW_PANE_FIRST** to identify it as the first window for the application. This is necessary because our application has but one view, so the first view is the only view. Lastly, we save our ID for the new window in the **m_CurrentViewID** member, so it's available the next time the current view is replaced. The call to **RecalcLayout()** causes the view to be redrawn when the new view is selected.

You must add a **#include** statement for the **OrderView.h** file to beginning of the **MainFrm.cpp** file, so that the **COrderView** class definition is available here. Once you have saved **MainFrm.cpp**, we can move on to adding a button control to the **Products** dialog to link to the **Orders** dialog, and adding handlers for this button and its partner on the **Orders** dialog to call the **SelectView()** member of **CMainFrame**.

Enabling the Switching Operation

To implement the view switching mechanism, go back to ResourceView and open the **IDD_DBSAMPLE_FORM** dialog. You need to add a button control to the dialog, as shown here:

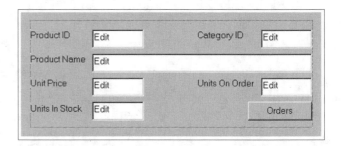

You can set the ID for the button to **IDC_ORDERS**, consistent with the naming for the other controls in the dialog.

After saving the resource, you can create a handler for the button by double-clicking it while holding down the *Ctrl* key. ClassWizard will add the function **OnOrders()** to the **CProductView** class, and this handler will be called when the button is clicked. You only need to add one line of code to complete the handler:

```
void CProductView::OnOrders()
{
    ((CMainFrame*)GetParentFrame())->SelectView(ORDER_VIEW);
}
```

The **GetParentFrame()** member of the view object is inherited from **CWnd**, which is an indirect base class of **CMainFrame**. This function returns a pointer to the parent frame window and we use it to call the **SelectView()** function that we've just added to the **CMainFrame** class. The argument **ORDER_VIEW** will cause the frame window to switch to the **Orders** dialog window. If this is the first time this has occurred, it will create the view object and the window. On the second and subsequent occasions that a switch to the orders view is selected, the existing **Orders** view will be reused.

You must add the following **#include** statements to the beginning of the **ProductView.cpp** file:

```
#include "OurConstants.h"
#include "MainFrm.h"
```

The next task is to add the handler for the button we previously placed on the **IDD_ORDERS_FORM** dialog. Double-click the button with the *Ctrl* key pressed, as before, and add the following code to the **OnProducts()** handler that is generated in the **COrderView** class:

```
void COrderView::OnProducts()
{
    ((CMainFrame*)GetParentFrame())->SelectView(PRODUCT_VIEW);
}
```

This works in the same way as the previous button control handler. Again, you must add **#include** statements for the **OurConstants.h** and **MainFrm.h** files to the beginning of the **.cpp** file, and then save it.

Handling View Activation

When we switch to a view that already exists, we need to ensure that the recordset is refreshed and that the dialog is re-initialized, so that the correct information is displayed. When an existing view is activated or deactivated, the framework calls the **OnActivateView()** member of the class. We need to override this function in each of our view classes. You can do this using the Message Maps tab in the ClassWizard dialog. With the class name selected in the Object IDs list box, extend the Messages list box and double click on OnActivateView. You need to add the handler to both view classes.

You can add the following code to complete the implementation of the function:

```
void COrderView::OnActivateView(BOOL bActivate,
                                CView* pActivateView, CView* pDeactiveView)
{
    if(bActivate)
    {
        // Get a pointer to the document
        CDBSampleDoc* pDoc = (CDBSampleDoc*)GetDocument();

        // Get a pointer to the frame window
        CMainFrame* pMFrame = (CMainFrame*)GetParentFrame();

        // If the last view was the product view, we must re-query
        // the recordset with the product ID from the product recordset
        if(pMFrame->m_CurrentViewID==PRODUCT_VIEW)
        {
```

```
            if(!m_pSet->IsOpen())           // Make sure the recordset is open
                return;
            // Set current product ID as parameter
         m_pSet->m_ProductIDparam = pDoc->m_productSet.m_ProductID;
            m_pSet->Requery();               // Get data from the DB
       }


        // Set the window caption
        CString strTitle = _T("Table Name:");
        CString strTable = m_pSet->GetTableName();
        if(!strTable.IsEmpty())
            strTitle += strTable;
        else
            strTitle += _T("Orders - Multiple Tables");
       pDoc->SetTitle(strTitle);
       CRecordView::OnInitialUpdate(); // Update values in dialog
    }
```

```
    CRecordView::OnActivateView(bActivate, pActivateView, pDeactiveView);
}
```

We only execute our code if the view is being activated; if this is the case, the **bActivate** argument will be **TRUE**. After getting pointers to the document and the parent frame, we verify that the previous view was the product view, before requerying the order set. This check isn't necessary at present, since the previous view is always the product view, but if and when we add another view to our application, this will not always be true, so we might as well put the code in now.

To requery the database, we set the parameter member of **COrderSet**, **m_ProductIDparam**, to the current value of the **m_ProductID** member of the product recordset. This will cause the orders for the current product to be selected. We don't need to set the **m_strFilter** member of the recordset here because that will have been set in the **OnInitialUpdate()** function when the **CRecordView** object was first created. The **IsEOF()** function member of the **COrderSet** object is inherited from **CRecordSet** and will return **TRUE** if the recordset is empty when it is re-queried.

Before continuing, however, we need to perform one check. If there are no orders for a product, then it isn't very useful to show a blank window, and it would be better to display a message box informing the user that there's nothing to display. First, add a member function to the **COrderView** class, like this:

```
BOOL COrderView::HasOrders()
{
  CDBSampleDoc* pDoc = (CDBSampleDoc*)GetDocument();

  // If the dataset isn't open, we can't help
  if (!m_pSet->IsOpen())
    return FALSE;

  m_pSet->m_ProductIDparam = pDoc->m_productSet.m_ProductID;
  m_pSet->Requery();                    // Get data from the DB

  // If we're already at the end, there are no orders here
  if (m_pSet->IsEOF())
    return FALSE;
```

```
  else
    return TRUE;
}
```

We call this function in the **CMainFrame::SelectView()** function, like this:

```
void CMainFrame::SelectView(UINT ViewID)
{
   CView* pOldActiveView = GetActiveView();               // Get current view

   // Get pointer to new view if it exists
   // if it doesn't the pointer will be null
   CView* pNewActiveView = (CView*)GetDlgItem(ViewID);

   // If this is 1st time around for the new view,
   // the new view won't exist, so we must create it
   if (pNewActiveView == NULL)
   {
      switch(ViewID)
      {
         case ORDER_VIEW:                                 // Create an Order view
            pNewActiveView = (CView*)new COrderView;
            break;
         default:
            AfxMessageBox("Invalid View ID");
            return;
      }

      // Switching the views
      // Obtain the current view context to apply to the new view
      CCreateContext context;
      context.m_pCurrentDoc = pOldActiveView->GetDocument();
      pNewActiveView->Create(NULL, NULL, 0L, CFrameWnd::rectDefault,
                                              this, ViewID, &context);
      pNewActiveView->OnInitialUpdate();
   }

   // Check whether there are any orders
   if (ViewID == ORDER_VIEW && !((COrderView*)pNewActiveView)->HasOrders())
   {
      AfxMessageBox("No orders for this product ID");
      return;
   }

   SetActiveView(pNewActiveView);                          // Activate the new view
   pOldActiveView->ShowWindow(SW_HIDE);                    // Hide the old view
   pNewActiveView->ShowWindow(SW_SHOW);                    // Show the new view
   pOldActiveView->SetDlgCtrlID(m_CurrentViewID);          // Set the old view ID
   pNewActiveView->SetDlgCtrlID(AFX_IDW_PANE_FIRST);
   m_CurrentViewID = ViewID;                               // Save the new view ID
   RecalcLayout();
}
```

If there are no orders to be displayed, the function displays a message box and exits. You may be wondering why we couldn't do this in the **OnActivateView()** function itself. The reason is that **OnActivateView()** is called in response to a window getting or losing the focus, and if you do something which interferes with this (such as displaying a message box) you'll get unpredictable and probably undesirable results! For that reason the error checking has to be done outside the `OnActivateView()` function.

You now need to add the `OnActivateView()` function to the **CProductView** class as well, and code it as follows:

```
void CProductView::OnActivateView(BOOL bActivate,
                                  CView* pActivateView, CView* pDeactiveView)
{
    if(bActivate)
    {
        // Update the window caption
        CString strTitle = _T("Table Name");
        CString strTable = m_pSet->GetTableName();
        strTitle += _T(":") + strTable;
        GetDocument()->SetTitle(strTitle);
    }
    CRecordView::OnActivateView(bActivate, pActivateView, pDeactiveView);
}
```

In this case, all we need to do if the view has been activated is to update the window caption. Since the product view is the driving view for the rest of the application, we always want to return the view to its state before it was deactivated. If we do nothing apart from updating the window caption, the view will be displayed in its previous state.

Viewing Orders for a Product

You are now ready to try to build the executable module for the new version of the example. When you run the example, you should be able to see the orders for any product just by clicking the Orders button on the products dialog. A typical view of an order is shown here:

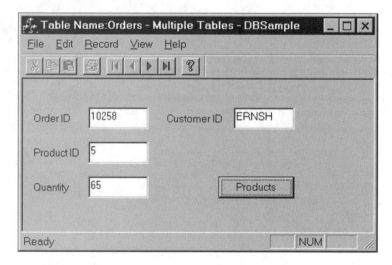

Clicking the Products button will return you to the products dialog, so you can browse further through the products. In this dialog, you can use the toolbar buttons to browse all the orders for the current product.

The Customer ID is a bit cryptic. We could add one more view to display the details of the customer's name and address. It won't be too difficult because we've built the mechanism to switch between views already.

Viewing Customer Details

The basic mechanism that we'll add will work through another button control on the order dialog, which will switch to a new dialog for customer data. As well as controls to display customer data, we'll add two buttons to the customer dialog: one to return to the order view, and the other to return to the product view. We'll need another view ID corresponding to the customer view, which we can add with the following line in the **OurConstants.h** file:

```
const UINT CUSTOMER_VIEW = 3U;
```

Let's now add the recordset for the customer details.

Adding the Customer Recordset

The process is exactly the same as we followed for the **COrderSet** class. You use the Add Class... button in ClassWizard to define the **CCustomerSet** class, with **CRecordset** specified as the base class. You select the database as Sample Data, as before, and select the Customers table for the recordset. The class should then be created with the data members shown here:

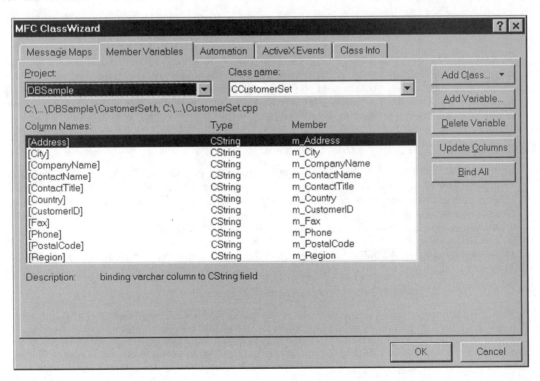

853

You can click on the OK button to store the class. At this point, you could add a **CCustomerSet** member to the document so that it will be created when the document object is created. Right-click on the **CDBSampleDoc** class name in ClassView and add a variable of type **CCustomerSet** with the name **m_CustomerSet**. You can leave the access specifier as **public**.

You will find that ClassView has already added an **#include** directive for **CustomerSet.h** into **DBSampleDoc.h**. After saving all the files you have modified, you can move next to creating the customer dialog resource.

Creating the Customer Dialog Resource

This process is also exactly the same as the one you went through for the orders dialog. Change to ResourceView and create a new dialog resource with the ID **IDD_CUSTOMER_FORM**, not forgetting to set the style to Child and the border to None in the Properties box for the dialog. After deleting the default buttons, add controls to the dialog to correspond to the field names for the **Customers** table, as shown here:

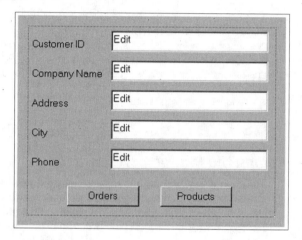

The two buttons enable you to switch to either the Orders dialog, which will be how you got here, or directly back to the Products dialog.

Specify the IDs for the controls, using the field names as a basis. You can get help with this by expanding the list of members of **CCustomerSet** in ClassView and keeping that visible while you work on the dialog. You can set the button IDs as **IDC_ORDERS** and **IDC_PRODUCTS**. Remember to check the tab order is as required and then save the dialog resource. Now we're ready to create the view class for the recordset.

Creating the Customer View Class

Right-click the dialog and select Class<u>W</u>izard... from the pop-up. Create a new class based on **CRecordView** with the name **CCustomerView**, and select the **IDD_CUSTOMER_FORM** as the ID for the dialog to be associated with the class. ClassWizard should automatically choose **CCustomerSet** as the recordset for the view class. Complete the process and click on OK in ClassWizard. You can then associate the edit controls with variables in the recordset.

To tie the controls to the recordset data members, double-click on each edit control in turn with the *Ctrl* key held down. If the tab order for the controls is correct, all the variables should be selected automatically.

You can also process the button controls in the same way to add the **OnOrders()** and **OnProducts()** functions to the class. The code for these is very similar to the corresponding functions in the other views. The code you need to add to **OnOrders()** is:

```
void CCustomerView::OnOrders()
{
   ((CMainFrame*)GetParentFrame())->SelectView(ORDER_VIEW);
}
```

You can add a similar line of code to the **OnProducts()** function:

```
void CCustomerView::OnProducts()
{
   ((CMainFrame*)GetParentFrame())->SelectView(PRODUCT_VIEW);
}
```

Once again, the destructor for **CCustomerView** will contain code to delete the object pointed to by **m_pSet**, as follows:

```
CCustomerView::~CCustomerView()
{
   if (m_pSet)
      delete m_pSet;
}
```

Delete the highlighted lines, since the framework will delete the record set object without our intervention.

We now need to add code to specify a filter for the customer recordset so that we only get the customer details displayed that correspond to the customer ID field from the current order in the **COrderSet** object.

Adding a Filter

We can define the filter in the **OnInitialUpdate()** member of **CCustomerView**. Since we only anticipate one record being returned corresponding to each customer ID, we don't need to worry about sorting. The code you need to add to this function is as follows:

```
void CCustomerView::OnInitialUpdate()
{
   BeginWaitCursor();

   CDBSampleDoc* pDoc = (CDBSampleDoc*)GetDocument();
   m_pSet = &pDoc->m_CustomerSet;                 // Initialize the recordset pointer

   // Set the DB for the customer recordset
   m_pSet->m_pDatabase = pDoc->m_productSet.m_pDatabase;

   // Set the current customer ID as the filter parameter value
   m_pSet->m_CustomerIDparam = pDoc->m_OrderSet.m_CustomerID;
   m_pSet->m_strFilter ="CustomerID = ?";     // Filter on CustomerID field

   GetRecordset();
   CRecordView::OnInitialUpdate();
   if (m_pSet->IsOpen())
   {
      CString strTitle = m_pSet->m_pDatabase->GetDatabaseName();
      CString strTable = m_pSet->GetTableName();
      if (!strTable.IsEmpty())
         strTitle += _T(":") + strTable;
```

```
            GetDocument()->SetTitle(strTitle);
        }
        EndWaitCursor();
    }
```

After getting a pointer to the document, we store the address of the **CCustomerSet** object member of the document in the **m_pSet** member of the view. We know the database is already open, so we can set the database pointer in the customer recordset to that stored in the **CProductSet** object.

The parameter for the filter will be defined in the **m_CustomerIDparam** member of **CCustomerSet**. We'll add this member to the class in a moment. It's set to the current value of the **m_CustomerID** member of the **COrderSet** object owned by the document. The filter is defined in such a way that the customer recordset will only contain the record with the same customer ID as that in the current order.

To handle activation of the customer view, you must add the **OnActivateView()** function using ClassWizard, as before. You can implement it as follows:

```
void CCustomerView::OnActivateView(BOOL bActivate,
                             CView* pActivateView, CView* pDeactiveView)
{
    if(bActivate)
    {
      if(!m_pSet->IsOpen())
         return;
      CDBSampleDoc* pDoc = (CDBSampleDoc*)GetDocument();

      // Set current customer ID as parameter
      m_pSet->m_CustomerIDparam = pDoc->m_OrderSet.m_CustomerID;
      m_pSet->Requery();                // Get data from the DB
      CRecordView::OnInitialUpdate();   // Redraw the dialog

      CString strTitle = _T("Table Name:");
      CString strTable = m_pSet->GetTableName();
      if (!strTable.IsEmpty())
         strTitle += strTable;
      else
         strTitle += _T("Multiple Tables");
      pDoc->SetTitle(strTitle);
    }
    CRecordView::OnActivateView(bActivate, pActivateView, pDeactiveView);
}
```

If this function is called because the view has been activated (rather than deactivated), **bActivate** will have the value **TRUE**. In this case, we set the filter parameter from the order recordset and re-query the database.

The **m_CustomerIDparam** member for the **CCustomerSet** recordset object that's associated with this view object is set to the customer ID from the orders recordset object that's stored in the document. This will be the customer ID for the current order. The call to the **Requery()** function for the **CCustomerSet** object will retrieve records from the database using the filter we've set up. The result will be that the details for the customer for the current order will be stored in the **CCustomerSet** object, and then passed to the **CCustomerView** object for display in the dialog.

We also need to add a function to check that there are customer details to display, just as we did for the order class:

```
BOOL CCustomerView::HasDetails()
{
   if (!m_pSet->IsOpen())
      return FALSE;

   CDBSampleDoc* pDoc = (CDBSampleDoc*)GetDocument();
   m_pSet->m_CustomerIDparam = pDoc->m_OrderSet.m_CustomerID;
   m_pSet->Requery();

   if (m_pSet->IsEOF ())
      return FALSE;
   else
      return TRUE;
}
```

If the dataset isn't open, or if it doesn't contain any records, this function will return **FALSE**.

You will need to add the following **#include** statements to the beginning of the **CustomerView.cpp** file:

```
#include "ProductSet.h"
#include "OrderSet.h"
#include "CustomerSet.h"
#include "DBSampleDoc.h"
#include "OurConstants.h"
#include "MainFrm.h"
```

The first three are required because of classes used in the definition of the document class. We need **DBSampleDoc.h** because of the **CDBSampleDoc** class reference in **OnInitialUpdate()**, and the remaining two **.h** files contain definitions that are referred to in the button handlers in the **CCustomerView** class.

At this point, you can save the current file and return to the definition of the **CCustomerView** class. You'll need to change the constructor from **protected** access specification to **public** because we need to be able to create a customer view object in the **SelectView()** member of **CMainFrame**.

Implementing the Filter Parameter

Add a **public** variable of type **CString** to the **CCustomerSet** class to correspond with the type of the **m_CustomerID** member of the recordset, and give it the name **m_CustomerIDparam**. You can initialize this in the constructor and set the parameter count as follows:

```
CCustomerSet::CCustomerSet(CDatabase* pdb): CRecordset(pdb)
{
   //{{AFX_FIELD_INIT(CCustomerSet)
   m_CustomerID = _T("");
   m_CompanyName = _T("");
   m_ContactName = _T("");
   m_ContactTitle = _T("");
   m_Address = _T("");
```

```
        m_City = _T("");
        m_Region = _T("");
        m_PostalCode = _T("");
        m_Country = _T("");
        m_Phone = _T("");
        m_Fax = _T("");
        m_nFields = 11;
        //}}AFX_FIELD_INIT
        m_CustomerIDparam = _T("");          // Initial customer ID parameter
        m_nParams = 1;                       // Number of parameters
        m_nDefaultType = snapshot;
    }
```

ClassWizard uses the comments containing **AFX_FIELD_INIT** as markers for updating the constructor when data members for table fields are added or deleted, so we add our initialization code outside that block. We set the parameter to an empty string and the parameter count in **m_nParams** to 1.

To set up the parameter, you add statements to the **DoFieldExchange()** member, as before:

```
    void CCustomerSet::DoFieldExchange(CFieldExchange* pFX)
    {
        //{{AFX_FIELD_MAP(CCustomerSet)
        pFX->SetFieldType(CFieldExchange::outputColumn);
        RFX_Text(pFX, _T("[CustomerID]"), m_CustomerID);
        RFX_Text(pFX, _T("[CompanyName]"), m_CompanyName);
        RFX_Text(pFX, _T("[ContactName]"), m_ContactName);
        RFX_Text(pFX, _T("[ContactTitle]"), m_ContactTitle);
        RFX_Text(pFX, _T("[Address]"), m_Address);
        RFX_Text(pFX, _T("[City]"), m_City);
        RFX_Text(pFX, _T("[Region]"), m_Region);
        RFX_Text(pFX, _T("[PostalCode]"), m_PostalCode);
        RFX_Text(pFX, _T("[Country]"), m_Country);
        RFX_Text(pFX, _T("[Phone]"), m_Phone);
        RFX_Text(pFX, _T("[Fax]"), m_Fax);
        //}}AFX_FIELD_MAP
        pFX->SetFieldType(CFieldExchange::param);      // Set parameter mode
        RFX_Text(pFX, _T("CustomerIDParam"), m_CustomerIDparam);
    }
```

After setting the **param** mode by calling the **SetFieldType()** member of the **pFX** object, we call the **RFX_Text()** function to pass the parameter value for substitution in the filter. We use **RFX_Text()** because the parameter variable is of type **CString**. There are various **RFX_()** functions supporting a range of parameter types.

Once you've completed this modification, you can save the **CustomerSet.cpp** file.

Linking the Order Dialog to the Customer Dialog

To permit a switch to the customer dialog, we require a button control on the **IDD_ORDERS_FORM** dialog, so open it in ResourceView and add an extra button, as shown here:

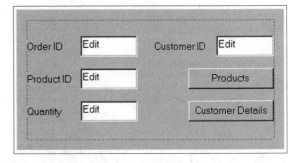

You can define the ID for the new button control as **IDC_CUSTOMER**. After you save the dialog, you can add a handler for the button by double-clicking on it while keeping the *Ctrl* key pressed. The handler only requires one line of code to be added to it, as follows:

```
void COrderView::OnCustomer()
{
    ((CMainFrame*)GetParentFrame())->SelectView(CUSTOMER_VIEW);
}
```

This obtains the address of the frame window and uses it to call the **SelectView()** member of **CMainFrame** to switch to a customer view. The final step to complete the program is to add the code to the **SelectView()** function that will deal with the **CUSTOMER_VIEW** value being passed to it. This requires us to make two changes — we need to add a **CUSTOMER_VIEW** case to the switch statement, and check whether there are any customer details :

```
void CMainFrame::SelectView(UINT ViewID)
{
    CView* pOldActiveView = GetActiveView();           // Get current view

    // Get pointer to new view if it exists
    // if it doesn't the pointer will be null
    CView* pNewActiveView = (CView*)GetDlgItem(ViewID);

    // If this is 1st time around for the new view,
    // the new view won't exist, so we must create it
    if (pNewActiveView == NULL)
    {
        switch(ViewID)
        {
            case ORDER_VIEW:                           // Create an Order view
                pNewActiveView = (CView*)new COrderView;
                break;
            case CUSTOMER_VIEW:                        // Create a customer view
                pNewActiveView = (CView*)new CCustomerView;
                break;
            default:
                AfxMessageBox("Invalid View ID");
                return;
        }

        CCreateContext context;
```

```
            context.m_pCurrentDoc = pOldActiveView->GetDocument();
            pNewActiveView->Create(NULL, NULL, 0L, CFrameWnd::rectDefault,
                                                    this, ViewID, &context);
            pNewActiveView->OnInitialUpdate();
        }

        // Check whether there are any orders
        if (ViewID == ORDER_VIEW && !((COrderView*)pNewActiveView)->HasOrders())
        {
            AfxMessageBox("No orders for this product ID");
            return;
        }

        // Check whether there are any customer details
        if (ViewID == CUSTOMER_VIEW && !((CCustomerView*)pNewActiveView)->HasDetails())
        {
            AfxMessageBox("No details for this customer");
            return;
        }

        SetActiveView(pNewActiveView);                    // Activate the new view
        pNewActiveView->ShowWindow(SW_SHOW);              // Hide the old view
        pOldActiveView->ShowWindow(SW_HIDE);              // Show the new view
        pOldActiveView->SetDlgCtrlID(m_CurrentViewID);    // Set the old view ID
        pNewActiveView->SetDlgCtrlID(AFX_IDW_PANE_FIRST);
        m_CurrentViewID = ViewID;                         // Save the new view ID
        RecalcLayout();
    }
```

The only change necessary is the addition of a **case** statement in the **switch** to create a **CCustomerView** object when one doesn't exist. Each view object will be re-used next time around, so they only get created once. The code to switch between views works with any number of views, so if you want this function to handle more views, you just need to add another **case** in the **switch** for each new view that you want. Although we are creating view objects dynamically here, we don't need to worry about deleting them. Because they are associated with a document object, they will be deleted by the framework when the application closes.

Because we reference the **CCustomerView** class in the **SelectView()** function, you must add an **#include** statement for the **CustomerView.h** file to the block at the beginning of **MainFrm.cpp**.

Exercising the Database Viewer

At this point, the program is complete. You can build the application and execute it. As before, the main view of the database is the products view. Clicking on Orders will, as before, take you to the orders view. The second button on this form should now be active, and clicking on it takes you to the details of the customer:

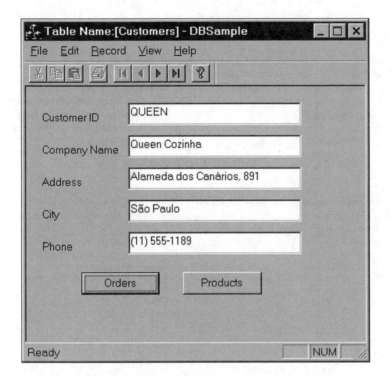

The two buttons take you back to the Orders view or the Products view respectively.

Summary

You should now be comfortable with the basics of how MFC links to your database. The fundamentals of the recordset and the record view are the same, whether you use the DAO or the ODBC classes. Although we haven't covered adding records to tables or deleting them in our example, you should have little difficulty implementing this as the recordset already has the functions you need built-in.

The key points we've seen in this chapter are:

▶ MFC provides DAO and ODBC support for accessing databases.

▶ To use a database with ODBC the database must be registered.

▶ A connection to a database is represented by a **CDatabase** or a **CDaoDatabase** object.

▶ A recordset object represents an SQL **SELECT** statement applied to a defined set of tables. Where necessary, the framework will automatically create a database object representing a connection to a database when a recordset object is created.

▶ A **WHERE** clause can be added for a recordset object through its **m_strFilter** data member.

▶ An **ORDER BY** clause can be defined for a recordset through its **m_strSort** data member.

▶ A record view object is used to display the contents of a recordset object.

Exercises

Ex20-1: Using the **Products** table again, add a 'stock control' dialog to the application. This should be reachable through a button on the products dialog, and must itself contain a button to go back to the products dialog. The fields it should display are the product ID, product name, reorder level, unit price and units in stock. Don't worry about filtering or sorting at the moment; just get the basic mechanism working.

Ex20-2: Refine the above project so that the stock control dialog automatically displays information about the product that was being shown in the products dialog when the button was pressed.

Ex20-3: Implement a system whereby the user of the database is warned in the stock control dialog about the present stock being near or below the reorder level. You'll have noticed by now that some of the stock reorder levels are set to zero; don't display a warning in those cases.

Updating Data Sources

We will build on what we learnt about accessing a database via ODBC in the previous chapter, and try our hand at updating through the same mechanism. We will use the Sample Data database throughout as you are already familiar with some of its contents, and it is a reasonable test database. It also has the advantage that you can always restore the original by copying it from the CD to your hard disk in the event of problems.

By the end of this chapter you will have learnt:

- What database transactions are
- How to update a database using recordset objects
- How data is transferred from a recordset to the database in an update operation
- How to update an existing row in a table
- How to add a new row to a table

Update Operations

When we are just writing code to view information from a database, the only issue is whether we are authorized to access the data. As long as the administration of the database has the right kind of access protection, the data in the database is safe. As soon as we start writing code to update a database, it's another kettle of fish. Since we are altering the contents of the database, such modifications could destroy the integrity of the database and make nonsense of the contents of a table, or even make it unusable. You always need to take great care to test your code properly with a test database, before letting it loose on the real thing.

A database update typically involves modifying one or more fields in a row in an existing table, modifying an order quantity for instance, or adding a new row – a new order perhaps, in the context of the Sample Data database. We will be taking a look at an example of both of these, but first, let's consider the implications.

Most of the complications that can arise with database update operations become apparent in the context of multi-user databases. Without proper control of the update process, concurrent access by several users provides the potential for two kinds of problems. The first arises if one person is allowed to retrieve a record while an update operation is in progress on the same record. The person reading the data can potentially end up with the old data prior to the update, or even a mixture with some fields containing old data and some new. The second problem arises with concurrent update, where one person starts updating a record while another update is already in progress on the same record. In a situation such as this, with a single record in a table, there is potential for an update to be lost. Where records from several tables are involved, the data in the database can end up in an inconsistent state. As you'll come to realize from working with databases for any length of time, working with a set of data that is wrong is far worse than not being able to access it in the first place. The integrity of the data — i.e. its correctness — is paramount. Before we look into how these problems can be handled, let's see how basic update operations on a recordset work.

CRecordset Update Operations

We saw in the previous chapter how the **RFX_()** function calls, in the **DoFieldExchange()** member of the recordset object, retrieved data from the selected fields in the table or tables in the database, and transferred it to the data members of the recordset object. The same functions are also used to update fields in a database table, or to add a completely new row.

There are five member functions of the **CRecordset** class that support update operations:

Function	Description
AddNew()	Call this function to start adding a completely new record. Throws a **CDBException** if a new record cannot be appended to the table.
CancelUpdate()	Cancels any outstanding operation in order to modify an existing record, or to add a new one.
Delete()	Delete the current record by creating and executing an SQL DELETE. Throws a **CDBException** if an error occurs – if the database is read-only for instance. After a **Delete()** operation, all the data members of the recordset will be set to null values — the equivalent of no value set — so you must move to a new record before executing any other operation on the recordset object.
Edit()	Call this function to start updating an existing record. Throws a **CDBException** if the table cannot be updated, and throws a **CMemoryException** if an out of memory condition arises.
Update()	Call this function to complete updating of an existing record or adding a new one. Throws a **CDBException** if a single record was not updated, or an error occurred.

None of the functions have parameters. Four of the functions throw exceptions as detailed above, so you should put them in a **try** block and add a **catch** block if you don't want your program to end abruptly when an error occurs.

To delete the current record for a recordset object, you just call its **Delete()** member. You must then scroll the recordset to a new position before attempting to use any of the functions above, since the values of the data members of the recordset object will be invalid after calling **Delete()**.

The basic sequence of events in updating an existing record or adding a new one is illustrated below.

Updating an Existing Record	Adding a New Record
1. Call **Edit()** for recordset object: · Saves current values from recordset field data members in a buffer.	1. Call **AddNew()** for recordset object: ·Saves current values from recordset field data members in a buffer. ·Sets current values for recordset field data members to **PSEUDO_NULL**.
2. Set field data members to new values.	2. Set new field data member values.
3. Call **Update()** for recordset object: ·Checks for modified fields by comparing with saved values. ·Creates and executes an SQL **INSERT** to update DB for changed fields. ·Discards the buffer containing the old saved values for fields.	3. Call **Update()** for recordset object: ·Checks for non-NULL fields. ·Creates and executes an SQL **INSERT** to update DB for non-NULL fields. ·Restores the old saved values for fields from the buffer.

When you call **AddNew()** for a recordset to start adding a new record to a table, the function saves the current values of all the data members of the recordset object that correspond to field values in a buffer, and then sets the data members to **PSEUDO_NULL**. This is not zero, or null, as in a pointer. It is a value that indicates that the data member has not been set. When you call **Update()** to complete adding a record, the original values of the data members of the recordset before **AddNew()** was called are restored. If you want the recordset to contain the values for the new record, you must call the **Requery()** member of the recordset object. This function returns **TRUE** if the operation was successful. You also call **Requery()** when you want to obtain a different view of the data, where you will retrieve records using a different SQL command, or a different filter for the records.

The transfer of data between the recordset data members and the database always uses the **DoFieldExchange()** member of the recordset object, so the **RFX_()** functions provide a dual capability – writing to the database as well as reading from it.

Checking that Operations are Legal

It is a good idea to confirm that the operation you intend to carry out with your recordset object is legal. It is all too easy to end up with a read-only recordset – just forgetting to reset the read-only attribute on the **SampleData.mdb** file will do it! If you try to update a table that is read-only, an exception will be thrown that is entirely avoidable if you verify that the operation is possible.

The **CanUpdate()** member of **CRecordset** returns **TRUE** if you can modify records in the table represented by the recordset object. When you want to add a new record, you can call the **CanAppend()** member of **CRecordset** beforehand to check. This will return **TRUE** if adding new records to the table is permitted.

Record Locking

Record locking prevents other users from accessing the locked record while a table row is being updated. The extent to which a record is locked during an update is determined by the locking mode set in the recordset object. There are two locking modes defined in **CRecordset**, referred to as **optimistic mode** and **pessimistic mode**:

Mode Name	Description
CRecordset::optimistic	In optimistic locking mode, the record is only locked while the **Update()** member function is executing. This minimizes the time that the record is inaccessible to other users of the database.
CRecordset::pessimistic	In pessimistic locking mode, the record is locked as soon as you call **Edit()**, and it remains locked (and therefore inaccessible to other users) until the completion of the call to **Update()** or until the update operation is aborted. This can obviously severely affect performance when updates are being prepared interactively.

The default mode for a recordset object is optimistic, so you only have to set it if you want pessimistic mode. To set this mode, you call the **SetLockingMode()** member of the recordset object with **CRecordset::pessimistic** as the argument. Of course you can also reset it by calling the function with **CRecordset::optimistic** as the argument.

Transactions

The idea of a **transaction** in the database context is to enable operations to be safely undone when necessary. A transaction packages a well-defined series of one or more modifications to a database into a single operation so that, at any point prior to the completion of the transaction, everything can be reversed (or **rolled back**) if an error occurs. Clearly, if an update were to fail when it was partially completed — due to a hardware problem for instance — it could have a disastrous effect on the integrity of the database. A transaction is not just an update to a single table. It can involve very complex operations on a database involving a series of modifications to multiple tables, and may take an appreciable time to complete. In these situations, support for transactions is virtually a necessity if the integrity of the database is to be assured.

With transaction based operations, the database system manages the processing of the transaction and records recovery information so that anything that the transaction does to the data can be undone in the event of a problem part way through. Thus by basing your database operations on transactions, you can protect the database against errors that might occur during processing. Typically, transaction processing locks records as necessary, along the way, and also ensures that any other database users accessing data that has been modified by the transaction will see the changes immediately.

Transactions are supported by most large commercial database systems on mainframe computers, but this is not the case with many database systems that run on a PC. In spite of this, the **CDatabase** class in MFC does support transactions, and as it happens, so does the Microsoft ODBC support for Access databases, so you can try out transaction processing with the Sample Data database if you want.

CDatabase Transaction Operations

Transactions are managed through those members of your **CDatabase** class object that provide the connection to the database. To determine whether transactions are supported for any given connection, you call the **CanTransact()** member of the **CDatabase** object. This will return **TRUE** if transactions are supported. Incidentally, there is also a **CanUpdate()** member of **CDatabase** that will return **FALSE** if the data source is read-only.

There are three member functions of **CDatabase** involved in transaction processing:

Function	Description
BeginTrans()	Starts a transaction on the database. All subsequent recordset operations are part of the transaction, until either **CommitTrans()** or **Rollback()** is called. The function returns **TRUE** if the transaction start was successful.
CommitTrans()	Commits the transaction so all recordset operations that are part of the transaction are expedited. The function returns **FALSE** if an error occurred, in which case the state of the data source is undefined.
Rollback()	Rolls back all the recordset operations executed since **BeginTrans()** was called, and restores the data source to the condition at the time when **BeginTrans()** was called.

The sequence of events in a transaction is basically very simple:

1 Call **BeginTrans()** to start the transaction.

2 Call **Edit()**, **Update()**, **AddNew()**, for your recordset as necessary.

3 Call **CommitTrans()** to complete the transaction.

Outside of a transaction, **Edit()** or **AddNew()** operations on a recordset are executed when you call **Update()**. Within a transaction they are not executed until you call **CommitTrans()** for the **CDatabase** object. If you need to abort the transaction at any time after calling **BeginTrans()**, you just call **Rollback()**.

Complications can arise due to the effects of **CommitTrans()** and **Rollback()** — the position in the recordset you are operating on can be lost, for instance — so you may need to take some action in your program to recover the situation after completing or aborting a transaction. There are two members of **CDatabase** to help with this. After a **CommitTrans()** call, you need to call the **GetCursorCommitBehavior()** member of **CDatabase**, and, after calling **Rollback()**, you need to call **GetCursorRollbackBehavior()**. Both these functions return one of three values of type **int** that indicate what you should do:

Return Value	Effect on **CRecordset** Objects
SQL_CB_PRESERVE	The recordset's connection to the data source will be unaffected by the commit or rollback operation, so you need do nothing.
SQL_CB_CLOSE	You need to call **Requery()** for the recordset object to restore the current position in the recordset.
SQL_CB_DELETE	You must close the recordset by calling the **Close()** member of the object, and then re-open the recordset if necessary.

There are further complications with using transactions in practice because the particular drivers you are using can affect when you must open the recordset. With some drivers you must open the recordset before you call **BeginTrans()**. With others, and the Microsoft Access ODBC drivers are a case in point, **Rollback()** will not work unless you open your recordset after you call **BeginTrans()**. Therefore you need to understand how the particular drivers you intend to use will behave, before attempting to use transactions in your application.

A Simple Update Example

Let's get some hands on experience with update operations in action, starting with a very basic example. Initially, this will omit most of what we have discussed so far in this chapter, but we will be building on this to apply some of what we have learned. We can create an application to update a database table with minimal effort using the MFC AppWizard. We will be creating a program to allow updating of certain fields in the Order Details table.

Create a project called **DBSimpleUpdate** using the wizard as an SDI program. Select the Database view without file support on step 2, as we did in the previous chapter. We are still going to use the "Sample Data" database through ODBC, but this time choose Dynaset as the recordset type.

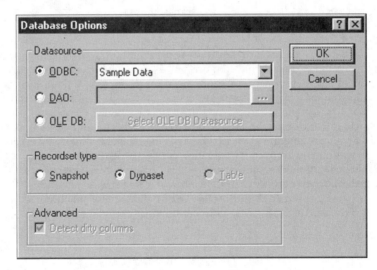

In a multi-user environment, a dynaset will be automatically updated with any changes made to a record while it is accessed by our program. This ensures the data we have in our application is always up to date. For operations to modify an existing record or add new ones you should choose dynaset as the recordset type.

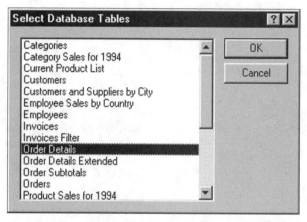

Since we plan to update the database, we must map the recordset to a single data base table. The database classes in MFC do not support updating of recordsets that involve joining two or more tables. Choose the Order Details table for the default recordset, as shown below.

If you select multiple tables here, updating the recordset will be inhibited because the recordset will automatically be made read-only. The database classes only support read-only access to joins of multiple tables, not updating.

You can change the view and recordset class and associated file names to match the table we are dealing with, as illustrated by the window below:

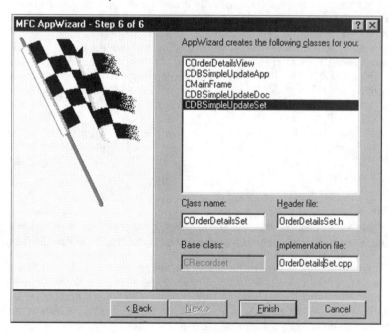

Now all we need to do is customize the dialog to do what we want.

Customizing the Application

The Order Details table contains five columns – Order ID, Product ID, Unit Price, Quantity, and Discount. If you display ClassView, and look at the members of **COrderDetailsSet**, you will see the data members corresponding to these. We need a static text control and an edit control for each of these on the dialog corresponding to the recordset. I arranged them as shown below, but you can arrange them how you like.

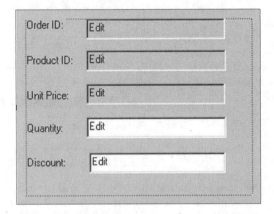

Make sure that the tab order is such that each edit control immediately follows the corresponding static control in sequence. Assign IDs to the edit controls to match the field name as we did in the previous chapter – the last one will be **IDC_DISCOUNT** for example. The default style set for an edit control allows keyboard input, but, on the assumption that we want to limit which recordset fields can be altered, I have set the first three edit controls as read-only, using the styles tab in the Properties dialog. The value displayed in a read-only control can be set in the program, but a value cannot be entered in the control from the keyboard. You can set all these to read-only in a single step by selecting each of the three controls with the *Ctrl* key held down, then right clicking to display the pop-up menu. Whatever you then set in the Properties dialog tabs will be applied to all three. With the dialog arrangement shown, you will only be able to enter data for Quantity and Discount.

The only other thing we need to do is to associate the edit controls with a corresponding data member of the recordset, and as we saw in the previous chapter, you just double click each control while holding down the *Ctrl* key, and select OK in the pop-up window to accept the selection. Having done that, you will have completed the program to update the Order Details table, believe it or not. Let's give it a whirl.

TRY IT OUT - Updating a Database

This should compile right off the bat if you have set up the controls correctly. When the program executes, you will be able to move through the rows in the table using the toolbar buttons. If you enter data for an order into the edit controls for Quantity or Discount, it will be updated when you move backwards or forwards in the recordset. Don't forget, if you haven't already done it, to make sure **sampdata.mdb** is no longer read-only. Unsurprisingly, you can't update a record if it is.

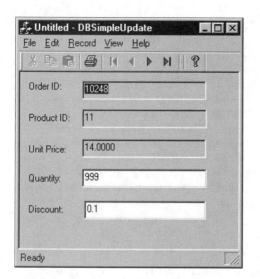

You can see here that I have changed the quantity and discount values for the product with the ID 11, on the order with the ID 10248, to some unlikely values.

How It Works

It is quite remarkable that we have completed our update program with no coding. All the necessary code has been supplied for us. The update is expedited by our **COrderDetailsView** class through functionality that is inherited from the base class.

When you click on one of the toolbar buttons to move to another record, the **OnMove()** handler provided by the default base class, **CRecordView,** is called. This function will write out any changes that have been entered into the recordset before it moves to a new record in the recordset. It moves to a new record by calling the **Move()** member of the **CRecordset** class that is inherited in **COrderDetailsSet**. Remember that there are two levels of data exchange going on here. The **RFX_()** functions called in the **DoFieldExchange()** member of our **COrderDetailsSet** class transfer data between a row in the recordset from the database and the data members of the class. The **DDX_()** functions called in the **DoDataExchange()** member of **COrderDetailsView**, transfer data between the edit controls and the data members of **COrderDetailsSet**. When you change the value in an edit control, the new data is propagated through to the appropriate data member of the recordset object. When you move to the next recordset by clicking a toolbar button, the new data will be written to the database by the **DoFieldExchange()** function.

This example is fine as far as it goes, but having data written to the database without any evident action on the part of the user is a bit disconcerting. We really need a bit more control over what's going on. Let's put together an example where our code has more control of what happens.

Managing the Update Process

We really want a positive action on the part of the user to enable an update rather than allowing it to happen by default. We could start by making all the edit controls read-only, so by default, data entry from the keyboard is inhibited for all the controls. We could then add an Edit Order button to the dialog, which is intended to enable the appropriate edit controls to allow keyboard entry.

Here we will be implementing two notional modes in our program; 'read-only mode' when updating is not possible since the controls will be read-only, and 'edit mode', when keyboard entry for selected controls will be possible so the recordset can be updated. The idea is that when the user clicks the Edit Order button, the edit controls for fields that we want to allow updating on will be enabled for keyboard input, and we will enter our 'edit mode'. Go ahead and add the button to the dialog for our **DBSimpleUpdate** application. You can set the ID for the button as **IDC_EDITORDER**. You can also add a handler for the button to the **COrderDetailsView** class by double clicking the button with the *Ctrl* key held down. ClassWizard will add the **OnEditorder()** function to the class, and add a skeleton implementation in **OrderDetailsView.cpp**.

Ideally, we should inhibit the use of the toolbar buttons or the Record menu items to move to another row in the table when in update mode. This is because we want a button click by the user to end the update operation, not moving the current position of the recordset.

When the Edit Order button is clicked, the read-only status of the controls for quantity and discount should be removed, and there should be a button to be clicked when the update should take place. To accommodate all this, we want the dialog in the application to appear as follows after an Edit Order button click:

Notice that the toolbar buttons to move the current record are disabled. So too are the menu items in the Record menu drop down. The Edit Order button now reads Update, and an extra button has appeared with the label Cancel. Our program is now in 'edit mode'.

We need to add the Cancel button to the dialog, but since we don't want the button displayed initially, we should disable the Visible option on the General tab in the Properties dialog:

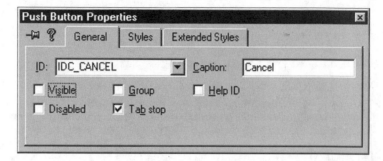

We will also need a handler for the Cancel button, so double click it with the *Ctrl* key pressed to add one now – we will be filling in the code later.

The user enters the data in the enabled fields on the dialog and clicks the Update button to complete the update. The dialog will then return to its original 'read-only mode' state with all the edit controls read-only. The user will click on the Cancel button if he or she does not want to proceed with the update operation.

To achieve this mechanism, and to manage the update process effectively, we will need to do several things after the Edit Order button is clicked:

- Change the text on the Edit Order button to "Update", so it now becomes the button to complete the update operation.

- Cause the Cancel button to appear on the dialog – in other words, make it visible.

- Record in the class that we have entered 'edit mode'. This is necessary because we will use the same button for two purposes, flip-flopping the label between Edit Order and Update.

- Enable keyboard entry for the edit controls that show the fields we want to allow updating on.

Let's explore how we can put the code together so that it will do what we want.

Implementing Update Mode

Let's start by providing for recording whether or not we are in update mode. We can do this by adding a **bool** data member to the **COrderDetailsView** class. Right click on the class name in ClassView and add the data member as shown.

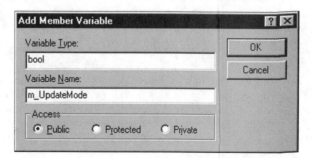

This variable will be **true** when we are in update mode. Since we start out in normal mode, we should add a line to the class constructor to initialize our new variable to **false**:

```
COrderDetailsView::COrderDetailsView()
                    : CRecordView(COrderDetailsView::IDD), m_UpdateMode(false)
{
  //{{AFX_DATA_INIT(COrderDetailsView)
  m_pSet = NULL;
  //}}AFX_DATA_INIT
}
```

We can do the switching of the button label and the program mode in the handler that we added to the view class. In principle an initial version of the function will need to be implemented something like this:

```
void COrderDetailsView::OnEditorder()
{
  if(m_UpdateMode)
  {                                    // When button was clicked we were in edit mode

    // Disable input to edit controls
    // Change the Update button text to Edit Order
    // Make the Cancel button invisible
    // Enable Record menu items and toolbar buttons
    // Complete the update
    // Switch to normal mode
  }
  else
  {                                    // When button was clicked we were in read-only mode

    // Enable input to edit controls
    // Change the Edit Order button text to Update
    // Make the Cancel button visible
    // Disable Record menu items and toolbar buttons
    // Start the update
    // Switch to update mode
  }
  m_UpdateMode = !m_UpdateMode;        // Switch the mode
}
```

We've put the mode switching code in right away, outside of the **if** statement. At the moment all the function does is switch the **m_UpdateMode** member between **true** and **false** to record the current mode. When the variable is **true** we are in edit mode, and **false** indicates read-only mode. The rest of the functionality that we require is simply described in comments. Let's investigate how to implement each of the comment lines in turn.

Enabling and Disabling Edit Controls

To modify the properties of a control, we need to call a function of some kind that relates to the control. This implies that we must have access to an object that represents the control. ClassWizard can do this for us. Right click in the edit window and open ClassWizard. If you look at the Member Variables tab for the view class you will see the IDs for each of the edit controls.

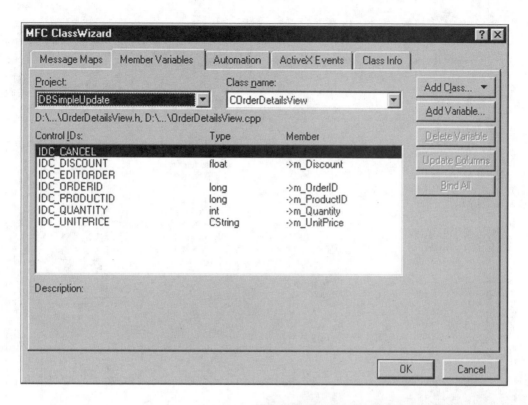

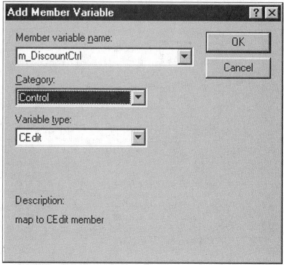

They each have a data member defined that stores the field value, but we can add another data member for a control ID that will give us access to the object representing the control. We will do this for the controls that we want to allow updates on – these correspond to **IDC_QUANTITY** and **IDC_DISCOUNT**. With the line containing the control ID highlighted, **IDC_DISCOUNT** at the moment, select the Add Variable... button.

In the dialog, make sure you select Control in the Category dropdown list box, and enter a suitable name for the data member. Because the data member will correspond to an edit control it will be of type **CEdit**. Click on OK to create the variable, and repeat the process with the **IDC_QUANTITY** ID to add a variable **m_QuantityCtrl**. If you have done this correctly, the ClassWizard will show two data members for each of the two control IDs — the original value variable, and the new control variable.

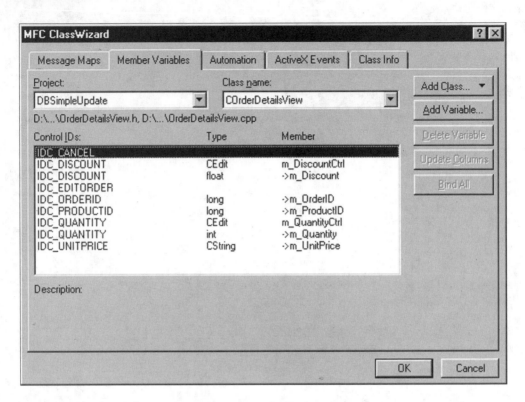

With these two variables we have access to the controls to update their styles, so you can now use ClassWizard (via the **Message Maps** tab) to go to the **OnEditorder()** function, and modify it as follows:

```
void COrderDetailsView::OnEditorder()
{
  if(m_UpdateMode)
  {                               // When button was clicked we were in edit mode
    // Change the button text to Edit Order
    // Make the Cancel button invisible
    // Enable Record menu items and toolbar buttons
    // Complete the update
  }
  else
  {                               // When button was clicked we were in read-only mode
    // Change the button text to Update
    // Make the Cancel button visible
    // Disable Record menu items and toolbar buttons
    // Start the update
  }
  // When m_UpdateMode is true, we are leaving edit mode, so we want to make the
  // controls read-only. Using m_UpdateMode as the argument to SetReadOnly() will
  // set the state as we require.
  m_QuantityCtrl.SetReadOnly(m_UpdateMode);  // Set state of quantity edit control
  m_DiscountCtrl.SetReadOnly(m_UpdateMode);  // Set state of discount edit control
  m_UpdateMode = !m_UpdateMode;              // Switch the mode
}
```

We use the variables that we added to call the **SetReadOnly()** members for the objects corresponding to the edit controls. The **SetReadOnly()** member of the **CEdit** class has a parameter of type **BOOL**, which sets the control to be read-only when the value **TRUE** is passed as an argument. We don't need to modify the state of the controls in the **if** statement as we can use the **m_UpdateMode** value as the argument to **SetReadOnly()**. If this has the value **TRUE**, then we are switching back to read-only mode, so we can just pass the value as the argument to make the controls read-only. The reverse applies when the variable is **FALSE**. Many of the MFC functions have parameters of type **BOOL** that can have values **TRUE** and **FALSE** because they were written before the availability of the **bool** type in C++. You can always use values of type **bool** as arguments for **BOOL** parameters.

Changing the Button Label

We get at the object corresponding to the Edit button by adding a control data member, **m_EditCtrl**, to the view class using ClassWizard in exactly the same way as we did for the edit controls. Just add a control data member for **IDC_EDITORDER** ID. It will be of type **CButton**, which is the MFC class that defines a button. We can use the variable to set the button label in the **OnEditorder()** member, by calling the **SetWindowText()** member that is inherited in the **CButton** class from **CWnd,** as follows:

```
void COrderDetailsView::OnEditorder()
{
  if(m_UpdateMode)
  {                                  // When button was clicked we were in edit mode
    m_EditCtrl.SetWindowText("Edit Order");           // Switch button text
    // Make the Cancel button invisible
    // Enable Record menu items and toolbar buttons
    // Complete the update
  }
  else
  {                                  // When button was clicked we were in read-only mode
    m_EditCtrl.SetWindowText("Update");               // Switch button text
    // Make the Cancel button visible
    // Disable Record menu items and toolbar buttons
    // Start the update
  }
  m_QuantityCtrl.SetReadOnly(m_UpdateMode);  // Set state of quantity edit control
  m_DiscountCtrl.SetReadOnly(m_UpdateMode);  // Set state of discount edit control
  m_UpdateMode = !m_UpdateMode;              // Switch the mode
}
```

Controlling the Visibility of the Cancel Button

To make the Cancel button visible or invisible, we need a control variable available, so using ClassWizard, add **m_CancelCtrl** corresponding to **IDC_CANCEL**, just as you did for the Edit Order button. Since **CButton** is derived from **CWnd**, we can call the inherited **ShowWindow()** member of the **CButton** object to set the button as visible or invisible, as follows:

```
void COrderDetailsView::OnEditorder()
{
  if(m_UpdateMode)
  {                                  // When button was clicked we were in edit mode
    m_EditCtrl.SetWindowText("Edit Order");        // Switch button text
    m_CancelCtrl.ShowWindow(SW_HIDE);              // Hide the Cancel Button
```

```
    // Enable Record menu items and toolbar buttons
    // Complete the update
  }
  else
  {                            // When button was clicked we were in read-only mode
    m_EditCtrl.SetWindowText("Update");        // Switch button text
    m_CancelCtrl.ShowWindow(SW_SHOW);          // Show the Cancel button
    // Disable Record menu items and toolbar buttons
    // Start the update
  }
  m_QuantityCtrl.SetReadOnly(m_UpdateMode);  // Set state of quantity edit control
  m_DiscountCtrl.SetReadOnly(m_UpdateMode);  // Set state of discount edit control
  m_UpdateMode = !m_UpdateMode;              // Switch the mode
}
```

The **ShowWindow()** function inherited from **CWnd** requires an argument of type **int** that must be one of a range of fixed values (see the documentation for the full set). We use the argument value **SW_HIDE** to make the button disappear if **m_UpdateMode** is **true**, and **SW_SHOW** when we are entering edit mode to make the button visible and activate it.

Disabling the Record Menu

We want to disable the menu items in the Record menu when the **m_UpdateMode** member of the view is **true**. We won't do this in the **OnEditorder()** handler after all, as there is an easier and better way as we will now see, so you can remove the comment lines to this effect in the **if**.

We can manage the state of the menu items and toolbar buttons by adding update handlers that are specifically for this purpose in the view class. This is another job for ClassWizard so fire it up and display the tab for the view class. We will add a handler for the **UPDATE_COMMAND_UI** message for each of the IDs for the menu items – starting with **ID_RECORD_FIRST**.

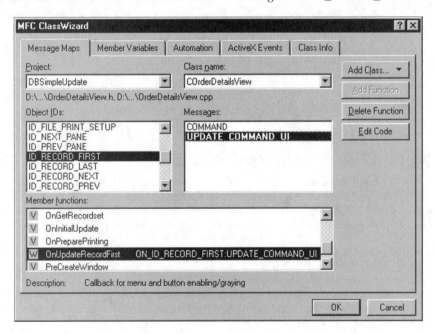

We have already implemented this kind of message handler back in Chapter 17. The description at the bottom of the dialog indicates their prime purpose – exactly what we need. The **CCmdUI** class has a member function, **enable()**, that you can call to enable or disable the item. An argument value of **true** will enable the item and a value of **false** will disable it. We want to disable the menu items and toolbar buttons when **m_UpdateMode** is **true**, but the circumstances when we want to disable them are a little more complicated because of the behavior of the menu items and toolbar buttons before we started messing with them.

The program, as provided by ClassWizard by default, already disabled the menu items and toolbar buttons corresponding to the IDs **ID_RECORD_FIRST** and **ID_RECORD_PREV** when the current record is the first in the recordset. Similarly, when the current record is the last in the recordset, the **ID_RECORD_NEXT** and **ID_RECORD_LAST** items are disabled. We should maintain this behavior when **m_UpdateMode** is **false**. The key to doing this is to use functions inherited in our view class that test whether the current record is the first or the last. We only need to add one line of code to each of these handlers to do what we want. It's exactly the same line of code for **OnUpdateRecordFirst()** and **OnUpdateRecordPrev()**. For example:

```
void COrderDetailsView::OnUpdateRecordFirst(CCmdUI* pCmdUI)
{
    // Disable item if m_UpdateMode is true, enable if false and not the 1st record
    pCmdUI->Enable(!m_UpdateMode && ! IsOnFirstRecord());
}
```

The **IsOnFirstRecord()** function returns **true** if the view is on the first record in the recordset, and **false** otherwise. This will disable the items (the menu item and the corresponding toolbar button) if either **m_UpdateMode** or the value returned by the **IsOnFirstRecord()** member of **COrderDetailsView** is **true**. The items will be enabled if both are **false**. This handler affects both the menu item and the toolbar button because they both have the same ID, **ID_RECORD_FIRST**.

The handlers corresponding to **ID_RECORD_NEXT** and **ID_RECORD_LAST** also require the same line of code:

```
void COrderDetailsView::OnUpdateRecordLast(CCmdUI* pCmdUI)
{
    // Disable item if m_UpdateMode is true, enable if false and not the last record
    pCmdUI->Enable(!m_UpdateMode && !IsOnLastRecord());
}
```

This works in the same way as the previous handler.

Expediting the Update

The last thing we need to do is to actually carry out the update when the Update button is clicked. To update a record, the user first clicks the Edit Order button, so at this point we must call the **Edit()** member of the recordset object to start the process of modifying the recordset. When the Update button is clicked, we need to call the **Update()** member of the recordset object to get the new data written to the record in the database. Using the **m_pSet** member of our view class, we can implement it like this:

```
void COrderDetailsView::OnEditorder()
{
    if(m_pSet->CanUpdate())
    {
```

```
      try
      {
        if(m_UpdateMode)
        {                          // When button was clicked we were in edit mode
          m_EditCtrl.SetWindowText("Edit Order");       // Switch button text
          m_CancelCtrl.ShowWindow(SW_HIDE);             // Hide the Cancel button
          m_pSet->Update();                             // Complete the update
        }
        else
        {                          // When button was clicked we were in read-only mode
          m_EditCtrl.SetWindowText("Update");           // Switch button text
          m_CancelCtrl.ShowWindow(SW_SHOW);             // Show the Cancel button
          m_pSet->Edit();                               // Start the update process
        }
        m_QuantityCtrl.SetReadOnly(m_UpdateMode);            // Set state of
quantity
        m_DiscountCtrl.SetReadOnly(m_UpdateMode);            // & discount edit
control
        m_UpdateMode = !m_UpdateMode;         // Switch the mode
      }
    catch(CException* pEx)
    {
      pEx->ReportError();              // Display error message
    }
  }
  else
    AfxMessageBox("Recordset is not updateable.");
}
```

As we discussed at the beginning of this chapter, the **Edit()** and **Update()** functions can throw an exception if an error occurs, so we put the calls within a **try** block along with the rest of the code. Clearly if we cannot update the recordset, there is no purpose to any of the processing in the **OnEditorder()** function. If an exception is thrown, we call its **ReportError()** function to display an error message. The **catch** block exception parameter is a pointer to **CException**, so the **catch** block will be executed for exception objects of type **CException**, or any class derived from **CException**. We need this in order to accommodate the **CMemoryException** that can be thrown by **Edit()**, as well as the **CDBException** that can be thrown by both **Edit()** and **Update()**. Note the use of the pointer as the catch block parameter. You will recall that this is because these are MFC exceptions thrown using the **THROW** macro, not C++ exceptions thrown using the keyword **throw**. If they were the latter, we would use a reference as the **catch** block parameter type.

We also verify that the recordset is updateable by calling its **CanUpdate()** member. If this returns **false** we display an error message in a message box.

Implementing the Cancel Operation

The Cancel button should abort the update operation. All that is necessary to do this is to call The **CancelUpdate()** member of the **COrderDetailsSet** object. Of course, we have a little housekeeping to do, but this will be exactly the same as if the **Update()** button was pressed, except that we don't call **Edit()**. Here's the code for the **OnCancel()** handler:

```
void COrderDetailsView::OnCancel()
{
   m_pSet->CancelUpdate();                        // Cancel the update operation
   UpdateData(FALSE);                             // Transfer data to controls
   m_EditCtrl.SetWindowText("Edit");              // Switch button text
   m_CancelCtrl.ShowWindow(SW_HIDE);              // Hide the Cancel button
   m_QuantityCtrl.SetReadOnly(m_UpdateMode);      // Set state of quantity and
   m_DiscountCtrl.SetReadOnly(m_UpdateMode);      // discount edit controls
   m_UpdateMode = !m_UpdateMode;                  // Switch the mode
}
```

The **CancelUpdate()** function ends the update operation and restores the recordset object's fields to what they were before **Edit()** was called. Since the Cancel button can only be clicked in edit mode, we can update the buttons and other controls in the same way as in the **OnEditorder()** handler. That's everything we need. We are ready for a trial run.

TRY IT OUT - Controlled Updating

Assuming you have no typos in your code, when you have compile and run the program it should work as we hoped it would. You can only enter data in the Quantity and Discount edit controls after you have clicked the Edit button.

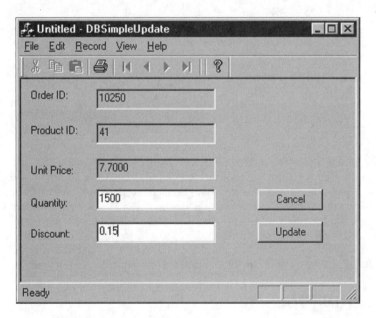

The buttons for moving to a new record are now disabled, as are the menu items for the Record menu. To complete the update after you have entered the new data, you click on the Update button. This will cause the new data to be written to the database, and the application will return to the normal state – all edit controls disabled and the buttons and menu restored to their original status.

Adding Rows to a Table

Let's extend the example to implement the capability to add a new order to the Sample Data database. This will provide insight into some of the practical problems and complexities you will face in this kind of operation.

First of all, an order itself is not a simple record in a table. Two tables are involved in defining a new order. The basic order data is in the Orders table, where information about the customer is stored. For each order there will be one or more records in the Order Details table, one for each product in the order, the link to the record in the Orders table being the Order ID. The relationship between these tables is illustrated below.

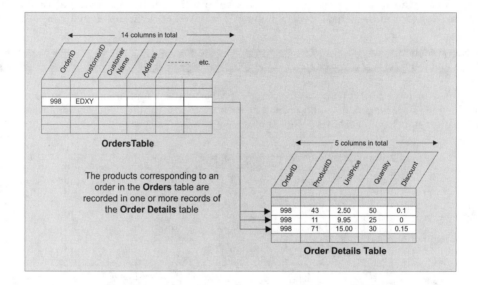

But there's more than these two tables involved. First of all, in creating a new order, we will need to provide a way for the user to select a customer from the Customers table. The Orders table includes a field identifying the employee, which needs to be one of the employees recorded in the Employees table. Once the information required for a new record in the Orders table has been established, one or more products will need to be selected from those defined in the Products table. With all these tables involved, it's going to be a somewhat messy business. We will simplify it slightly by making the Employee ID field 1 by default. This will avoid the need to deal with the Employees table in the example. Let's establish the overall logic first of all.

The Order Entry Process

We will be using two dialogs in addition to the dialog we already have that provides for viewing and editing the details of existing orders. One dialog will deal with the selection of the customer for the order and setting the required delivery date, and the other will take care of entering the details of the products and quantities for the order. The dialog to select the customer will be associated with the Customers table in the database, and the dialog for selecting products will be associated with the Products table. Buttons on the dialog will enable the transition from one dialog to another. The basic logic is shown below.

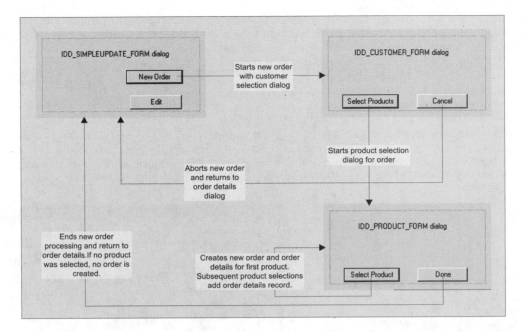

We will hold off creating a new record in the Orders table until we have the first Product Details record entered. That way we will avoid ending up with an order that doesn't order anything. Let's put together the dialog resources we need first of all, and then implement the code to support the operations.

Creating the Resources

We need an additional button on the dialog we have at present to process the creating of a new order, so add a button with the label New Order, and with the ID **IDC_NEWORDER**. Once you have done this, you can place the new button coincident with the Cancel button since only one will be visible at any given time, the Cancel button being visible by default. If you want the New Order button to appear on top when it is in the same position as the Cancel button, you need to make sure it is before the Cancel button in the tab order.

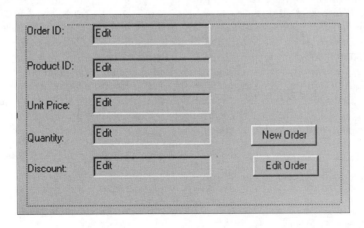

You can add a handler for the new button to **COrderDetailsView** by double clicking the button with the *Ctrl* key pressed. We will add the code for this later. Of course, we could have used the Cancel button here by changing its label and altering the effect of its handler depending on the state of the **m_UpdateMode** member of **COrderDetailsView**, but let's see how we can work with two buttons here.

You can insert both of the new dialog resources we need by right clicking the Dialog folder on the ResourceView tab, and selecting Insert Dialog from the pop-up. Assign the IDs as **IDD_CUSTOMER_FORM** and **IDD_PRODUCT_FORM** respectively. They both need to have Child selected in the Style: list box, and None selected in the Border: list box. You should also make all three dialogs about the same size and a little larger than the original dialog – I made them 30 units high by 60 units wide. You can delete the buttons from both of the new dialogs.

We need to connect the new dialogs to record view classes, so double click on the **IDD_CUSTOMER_FORM** dialog first of all, with the *Ctrl* key held down, assign the class name and then select the base class as shown below.

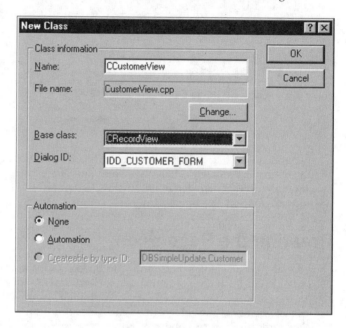

Since we have selected **CRecordView** as the base class, ClassWizard knows that this will be associated with a data source and a recordset class, so it pops the dialog to select the recordset. We need a new recordset class, so click on the New... button. On the New Class dialog, you can enter the class name as **CCustomerSet**. Note that the base class has already been selected to be **CRecordSet**. Of course, on the Database Options dialog which appears once you've pressed OK, the Datasource selection is still ODBC and Sample Data. You can leave the recordset option as Snapshot as we only want to retrieve data from the table. The database table we want is Customers. Go through the same ritual with the **IDD_PRODUCT_FORM** dialog, assigning the view class name as **CProductView** with **CRecordView** as the base class. The recordset class will be **CProductSet**, and the table you need to select is Products. Again, Snapshot recordset type will be fine as we just want to view the data.

We are now ready to populate the dialogs, with the controls we need.

Adding Controls to the Dialog Resources

Although we have only tied the **IDD_CUSTOMER_FORM** dialog into the Customers table, within the process we will need to provide all the information necessary to create a new record in the Orders table. The source of the data for each field of a new Orders record is shown in the diagram below.

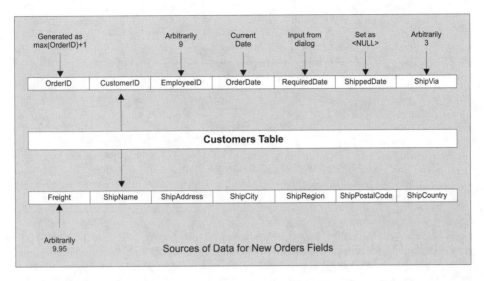

Sources of Data for New Orders Fields

Half of the fields will be drawn from the record in the Customers table that the user selects. Since we are creating a new order, we will need to synthesize a new unique order ID. To do this we can find the largest ID currently in use in the Orders table, and then just add 1 to that value.

To select the customer, the user will just scroll through the recordset until the required customer is displayed. We can then retrieve the data we need to construct the new Orders record from the recordset. We will display the current date in the dialog as the order date, and we will provide a control for selecting the required ship date. The other fields we will assign arbitrary values to, so that we don't overcomplicate our example.

Of course, we don't need to display all the information from the Customers table in our dialog – just the name will be sufficient to identify the customer for selection purposes. We will still need the data in the recordset though. You can place controls on the **IDD_CUSTOMER_FORM** dialog as shown below.

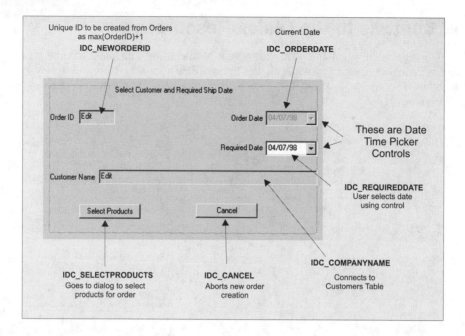

You can see from the diagram how the controls are to be used, and the IDs that you need to assign to them. The date time picker controls allow a date or time to be entered or selected. Whether it selects a date or a time depends on the **Format:** style you choose in the properties. The controls here use Short Date format. The date is chosen by clicking on the down arrow and choosing a date from the calendar that pops up. You can try it out to see how it works.

We can add variables to the **CCustomerView** class to store values from the date time picker controls using ClassWizard. Right click in the edit window and start ClassWizard, and go to the Member Variables tab. Select the line containing the **IDC_ORDERDATE** control ID and click the Add Variable... button. You can enter the name as **m_OrderDate**. Note the type is already set as **CTime**. Objects of this class store date and time values, as we will see. Do the same with **IDC_REQUIREDDATE**, and specify the member name as **m_RequiredDate**.

Both edit controls are read-only as they are there just to display information. The date picker control for the order date is disabled, as this will always be the current date and does not need to be changed. The date picker control for the required ship date will be enabled by default, so leave it like that as we want a date selected in this case. Although this view is associated with a recordset corresponding to the Customers table, in fact only the edit control showing the customer name needs to be connected to the **CCustomerSet** recordset as we are only displaying this field on the dialog.   You can double click on that now with the *Ctrl* key held down to make the connection. Note that we want to connect this control to the **CompanyName** field, so select the variable name from the drop down list accordingly. At this point you can also double click on each of the buttons, with the *Ctrl* key pressed, to add handlers for them. We will fill in the code for these handlers and deal with the rest of the controls later.

The **IDD_PRODUCT_FORM** dialog will select the products to be ordered, once the customer has been selected. We will get to this dialog when the Select Products button is clicked on the customer selection dialog. We need to show sufficient information on the dialog to allow the product to be chosen, and we need to provide for the quantity and discount to be entered. The dialog with its controls is shown below.

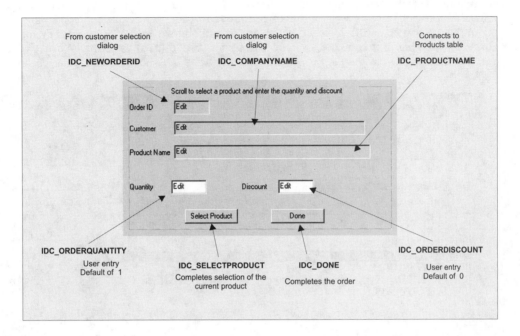

As always, check that the tab order for the controls is correct. The static control should immediately precede the corresponding edit control in the tab order. Note that all the controls here are read-only, except for the edit controls for quantity and discount, since these two values are the only ones the user needs to supply. You can connect the edit control for the Product Name to the recordset by double clicking it with the *Ctrl* key pressed. Add handlers for the buttons in the same way as you did for the previous dialog resource.

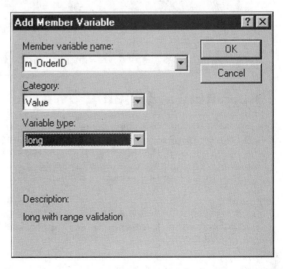

The controls showing the Order ID and the Customer name will be initialized with values that will originate in the previous dialog, so we will need class variables to hold the values for these controls. ClassWizard can help with this. Display the Member Variables tab in ClassWizard for the **CProductView** class. You will see that the IDs for these controls appear in the list. Click on the line containing **IDC_NEWORDERID** and click on the Add Variable... button. Enter the variable name and select the type as shown:

Notice that the default type is **CString** so you must select from the drop down list to make it **long**. Click on OK to accept it, then create a variable **m_CustomerName** corresponding to **IDC_COMPANYNAME**, but leaving it as type **CString** this time.

The user will enter values in the edit controls for quantity and discount, so we will need a variable for each of these as well in the **CProductView** class. Select the line containing **IDC_ORDERQUANTITY** on the Member Variables tab and add a variable, **m_Quantity**, of type **int**. Add a variable, **m_Discount**, of type **float**, for **IDC_ORDERDISCOUNT**. When you have done this the variables in the list on the Member Variables tab should be as shown below.

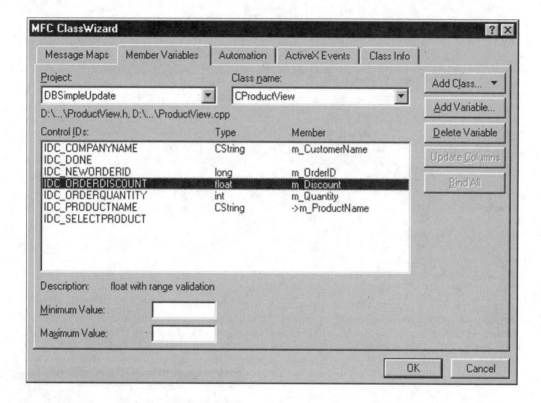

With the dialogs defined we can implement the mechanism to switch between them.

Implementing Dialog Switching

We saw all the basic logic for switching between dialogs in an earlier diagram. A button click is the mechanism for switching from one dialog to the next, so the button handlers will contain code to cause the switch. We will use the same process for switching views that we used in the previous chapter, so we won't go into detailed explanations again – we will just implement the code.

We will need to define view IDs to identify each of the three dialogs, so add a header file, **OurConstants.h**, containing the following code:

```
// Definition of our constants

#ifndef OUR_CONSTANTS_H
#define OUR_CONSTANTS_H

// Arbitrary constants to identify record views
const int ORDERDETAILS_VIEW = 1;
const int NEWORDER_VIEW = 2;
const int SELECTPRODUCT_VIEW = 3;


//////////////////////////////////////////////////

#endif
```

We need a variable of type **int** in the **CMainFrame** class to record the ID of the current view, so add **m_CurrentViewID** by right clicking on **CMainFrame** in ClassView and selecting Add Member Variable... from the pop-up. We need to initialize this, so modify the **CMainFrame** constructor to:

```
CMainFrame::CMainFrame() : m_CurrentViewID(ORDERDETAILS_VIEW)
{
   // TODO: add member initialization code here
}
```

This identifies the view that the application always starts with. Add an **#include** directive for **OurConstants.h** to the **.cpp** file so the definitions for the view IDs are available here.

We also need to add a member function, **SelectView()**, to **CMainFrame** that will perform switching between dialogs, exactly as we did in the previous chapter. The return type is **void** and the single parameter is of type **int** as the argument will be one of our view IDs. The implementation of **SelectView()** is essentially the same as you have seen before:

```
// Enables switching between views. The argument specifies the new view
void CMainFrame::SelectView(int viewID)
{
   CView* pOldActiveView = GetActiveView();            // Get current view

   // Get pointer to new view if it exists
   // if it doesn't the pointer will be null
   CView* pNewActiveView = static_cast<CView*>(GetDlgItem(viewID));

   // If this is first time around for the new view, the new view
   // won't exist, so we must create it
   // The Order Details view is always created first so we don't need
   // to provide for creating that.
   if (pNewActiveView == NULL)
   {
      switch(viewID)
      {
         case NEWORDER_VIEW:              // Create view to add new order
            pNewActiveView = new CCustomerView;
            break;
         case SELECTPRODUCT_VIEW:        // Create view to add product to order
            pNewActiveView = new CProductView;
            break;
         default:
```

```
            AfxMessageBox("Invalid View ID");
            return;
        }


    // Switching the views
    // Obtain the current view context to apply to the new view
    CCreateContext context;
    context.m_pCurrentDoc = pOldActiveView->GetDocument();
    pNewActiveView->Create(NULL, NULL, 0L, CFrameWnd::rectDefault,
                                          this, viewID, &context);

    pNewActiveView->OnInitialUpdate();
    }
    SetActiveView(pNewActiveView);                    // Activate the new view
    pOldActiveView->ShowWindow(SW_HIDE);              // Hide the old view
    pNewActiveView->ShowWindow(SW_SHOW);              // Show the new view
    pOldActiveView->SetDlgCtrlID(m_CurrentViewID);    // Set the old view ID
    pNewActiveView->SetDlgCtrlID(AFX_IDW_PANE_FIRST);
    m_CurrentViewID = viewID;                          // Save the new view ID
    RecalcLayout();
}
```

The code here refers to the **CCustomerView** and **CProductView** classes, so **#include** directives for **CustomerView.h** and **ProductView.h** are necessary in **MainFrm.cpp**. We also call the constructors for **CCustomerView** and **CProductView** and at the moment these are protected. You need to change the access specifier for the constructors in both classes to **public** if this code is to compile.

Switching from the order details dialog to the dialog starting new order creation is done in the handler for **OnNeworder()** in the **COrderDetailsView** class:

```
void COrderDetailsView::OnNeworder()
{
  static_cast<CMainFrame*>(GetParentFrame())->SelectView(NEWORDER_VIEW);
}
```

This gets a pointer to the parent frame for the view — the **CMainFrame** object for our application — and then uses that to call **SelectView()** to select the new order processing dialog. An **#include** directive for **OurConstants.h** is also necessary in this source file since we refer to **NEWORDER_VIEW** here, and we also must add an **#include** for **MainFrm.h** to get at the definition of **CMainFrame**..

The Select Products button handler in the **CCustomerView** class will switch to the dialog for **CProductsView**:

```
void CCustomerView::OnSelectproducts()
{
  static_cast<CMainFrame*>(GetParentFrame())->SelectView(SELECTPRODUCT_VIEW);
}
```

The Cancel button handler in the same class will just switch back to the previous view:

```
void CCustomerView::OnCancel()
{
  static_cast<CMainFrame*>(GetParentFrame())->SelectView(ORDERDETAILS_VIEW);
}
```

We also need **#include** directives for **OurConstants.h** and **MainFrm.h** in **CustomerView.cpp**.

The last switching operation to be implemented is in the **OnDone()** handler in the **CProductView** class:

```
void CProductView::OnDone()
{
  static_cast<CMainFrame*>(GetParentFrame())->SelectView(ORDERDETAILS_VIEW);
}
```

This switches back to the original application view that allows browsing and editing of order details. Of course, you could alternatively switch back to the **CCustomerView** dialog to provide a succession of order entries if you wanted to. Don't forget the **#include** directives for **OurConstants.h** and **MainFrm.h** once more.

We mustn't forget that the switching from the initial dialog for browsing order details to the dialog for editing the details will now have to control the visibility of the New Order button, otherwise the Cancel button will be hidden by the New Order button in the editing dialog. First we will use ClassWizard to add a control variable, **m_NewOrder**, in **COrderDetailsView** corresponding to the **IDC_NEWORDER** ID. Then we can amend the **OnEditorder()** handler to:

```
void COrderDetailsView::OnEditorder()
{
  if(m_pSet->CanUpdate())
  {
    try
    {
      if(m_UpdateMode)
      {                                // When button was clicked we were in edit mode
        m_EditCtrl.SetWindowText("Edit Order");     // Switch button text
        m_CancelCtrl.ShowWindow(SW_HIDE);           // Hide the Cancel button
        m_NewOrder.ShowWindow(SW_SHOW);             // Show the new order button
        m_pSet->Update();                           // Complete the update
      }
      else
      {                                // When button was clicked we were in read-only mode
        m_EditCtrl.SetWindowText("Update");         // Switch button text
        m_NewOrder.ShowWindow(SW_HIDE);             // Hide the new order button
        m_CancelCtrl.ShowWindow(SW_SHOW);           // Show the Cancel button
        m_pSet->Edit();                             // Start the update process
      }
      m_QuantityCtrl.SetReadOnly(m_UpdateMode);     // Set state of quantity &
      m_DiscountCtrl.SetReadOnly(m_UpdateMode);     // discount edit controls
      m_UpdateMode = !m_UpdateMode;                 // Switch the mode
    }
    catch(CException* pEx)
    {
      pEx->ReportError();                           // Display the error message
    }
  }
  else
    AfxMessageBox("Recordset is not updatable.");
}
```

Now we **hide** or **show** the New Order button, depending on whether **m_UpdateMode** is true or **false**. We also must make the button visible in the **OnCancel()** handler:

```
void COrderDetailsView::OnCancel()
{
  m_pSet->CancelUpdate();                          // Cancel the update operation
  m_EditCtrl.SetWindowText("Edit");                // Switch button text
  m_CancelCtrl.ShowWindow(SW_HIDE);                // Hide the Cancel button
  m_NewOrder.ShowWindow(SW_SHOW);                  // Show the New Order button
  m_QuantityCtrl.SetReadOnly(m_UpdateMode);        // Set state of quantity &
  m_DiscountCtrl.SetReadOnly(m_UpdateMode);        // discount edit controls
  m_UpdateMode = !m_UpdateMode;                    // Switch the mode
}
```

What we have done here is to implement the basic view switching mechanism. We will still need to come back and add code to deal with updating the database. However, this is a good point to try compiling and executing what we have in order to shake out any typos or other errors we might have added. Once it works, you should find that you can scroll through the customers and the products. Make sure that you check out all the switching paths.

Creating an Order ID

To create an ID for a new order, we need a recordset for the Orders table. We don't need a view this time, so we can just create a recordset class using ClassWizard. Click on the Add Class... button and select New... from the pop-up. Enter the class name and select the base class as shown below.

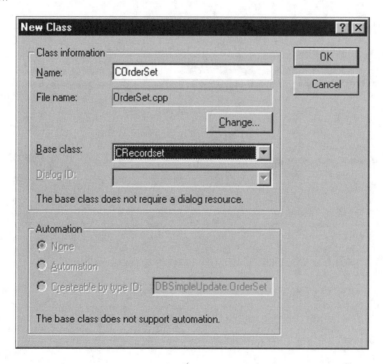

When you click on the OK button, ClassWizard will display the Database Options dialog where you want the ODBC check box and Sample Data to be selected. We will choose the recordset type as Dynaset since we will reuse this recordset when we want to add a new order. Of course, the table you should select is Orders.

Storing the New Order ID

In this section we will go into operations with recordsets in a little more depth. We will need to create a unique order ID whenever we start creating a new order in the **CCustomerView** class, so we need to think about where we can best do this and what the process should be. It really should be a **COrderSet** object's responsibility to create the new ID, even though the ID will be displayed by one of the edit controls in the view represented by the **CCustomerView** object. A good approach would be to add a variable in the **CCustomerView** class that will set the value of the ID in the edit control and that can be set using a function belonging to a **COrderSet** object.

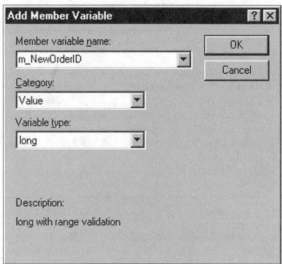

Go to the ClassWizard's Member Variables tab and select the class as **CCustomerView**. Select the ID for the edit control that we are interested in, **IDC_NEWORDERID**, and click on the Add Variable... button. Enter the name and choose the Variable type: as shown:

The type will be **CString** by default so make sure you set it to **long**. The **DDX_Text()** functions that transfer data to and from an edit control come in a number of flavors to accommodate the different data types shown in the drop down list.

Creating the New Order ID

The **COrderSet** object belongs in the document object, so add a **public** data member to the **CDBSimpleUpdateDoc** class with the name **m_OrderSet** to go along with the **m_orderDetailsSet** member created by AppWizard.

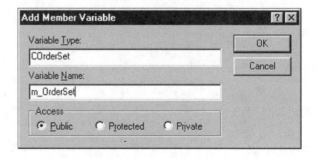

This object will be created automatically when the document object is created. Since we have already created the **COrderSet** class, ClassWizard will automatically add an **#include** directive for **OrderSet.h** to the **DBSimpleUpdate.h** file. With the object for the order set in the document, it will be accessible in any of the view classes that needs it.

We can add a new member function to the **COrderSet** class to generate the unique new order ID. Go to ClassView and add the function, **CreateNewOrderID()**, with a **long** return type and no parameters.

The first thing the **CreateNewOrderID()** function will need to do is check whether the recordset is open:

```
long COrderSet::CreateNewOrderID()
{
  if(!IsOpen())
    Open(CRecordset::dynaset);

  // Rest of the function implementation...
}
```

The **IsOpen()** function that we call in the **if** will return **TRUE** if the recordset is open and **FALSE** otherwise. To open it, we call the **Open()** member that is inherited from **CRecordset**. This runs an SQL query against the database with the recordset type specified by the first argument. We have the first argument specified as **CRecordset::dynaset**, which, as you might expect, **opens** the recordset as a **dynaset**. As it happens, this is unnecessary because if we omitted the argument, the default that we specified when we created the class – **dynaset** – would apply. However, it does provide a cue to mention the other options that you have for this argument:

Argument	Description
CRecordset::snapshot	Recordset is opened as snapshot – we discussed snapshot and dynaset in the previous chapter).
CRecordset::forwardonly	Recordset is opened as read-only and it can only be scrolled forward.(When a recordset is opened, it is positioned at the first record automatically.)
CRecordset::dynamic	Recordset is open with scrolling in both directions, and changes made by other users will be reflected in the recordset fields.
AFX_DB_USE_DEFAULT_TYPE	Recordset is opened with the default recordset type stored in the inherited member, **m_nDefaultType**, that is initialized in the constructor.

There are two further parameters to **Open()** for which we have accepted default argument values. The second parameter is a pointer to a string that can be a table name, an SQL **SELECT** statement, a call of a predefined query procedure, or null, which is the default. If it is null, the string returned by **GetDefaultSQL()** is used. The third parameter is a bit mask that you can use to specify a myriad of options for the connection, including making it read-only, which means that you can't write to it at all, or making it append-only, which prohibits editing or deleting records. You will find more details on this in the documentation for this function.

With the recordset opened, we want to scan through all the records to find the largest value in the OrderID field. We can do that by adding the following code:

```
long COrderSet::CreateNewOrderID()
{
  if(!IsOpen())
    Open(CRecordset::dynaset);

  // Check for no records in recordset
  long newOrderID = 0;
  if(!(IsBOF() && IsEOF()))
  {                                          // We have records
    MoveFirst();                             // so go to the first
    while(!IsEOF())                          // Compare with all the others
    {
      // Save order ID if its larger
      if(newOrderID < m_OrderID)
          newOrderID = m_OrderID;

      MoveNext();                            // Go to next record
    }
  }
  return ++newOrderID;
}
```

The **IsBOF()** and **IsEOF()** members of the recordset class return **TRUE** if you are beyond the beginning or end of the records in the recordset respectively, in which case no record is currently active so you should be using the fields. When a recordset is empty, both functions will return **TRUE**. As long as there are records, we move to the first record by calling the **MoveFirst()** member function. There is also a **MoveLast()** member that will go to the last record in the recordset.

We create a local variable, **newOrderID**, with an initial value of 0 that will eventually store the maximum order ID in the table. The **while** loop moves through each of the records in the recordset using the **MoveNext()** member function, checking for a larger value for the **m_OrderID** member. Before calling any of the move members of a recordset, you must call either **IsEOF()** or **IsBOF()**, depending on which way you are going. If you call a move function when you are beyond the end or beginning of the recordset, the function will throw an exception of type **CDBException**.

In addition to the move functions we have used here, a recordset object also provides you with three others:

Function	Description
MoveLast()	Moves to the last record in the recordset. You must not use this function(or **MoveFirst()**) with forward-only recordset, otherwise an exception of type **CDBException** will be thrown.
MovePrev()	Moves to the record preceding the current record in the recordset. If there isn't one, it will move to one position beyond the first record. After this the recordset fields are not valid and **IsBOF()** will return **TRUE**.
Move()	This is used to move one or more records through a recordset. The first argument, of type **long**, specifies the number of rows to move. The second argument of type **WORD** determines the nature of the move operation. Four values for the second argument make the function equivalent to the other move functions we have seen. You will find more details on this in the Visual C++ documentation.

When the loop ends we have the maximum order ID stored in **newOrderID**, so we just need to increment it by 1 before returning it. The last step is to get the value transferred to the control so it will appear in the dialog. The call to **UpdateData()** with an argument of **FALSE** does this. This function is inherited in the record view class from **CWnd**. An argument of **FALSE** causes the data to be transferred from data member of the view class to the controls in the dialog. A value of **true** will cause data to be retrieved from the controls and stored in the data members. In both cases this is achieved by causing the **DoDataExchange()** member of view to be called by the framework.

Initiating ID Creation

The customer view will need a new order ID to be available when it is first displayed. Add a **public** member function, **SetNewOrderID()**, to the **CCustomerView** class and implement it as follows:

```
void CCustomerView::SetNewOrderID()
{
    // Get a new order ID from the COrderSet object in the document
    m_NewOrderID = static_cast<CDBSimpleUpdateDoc*>(GetDocument())
                                      ->m_OrderSet.CreateNewOrderID();
    UpdateData(FALSE);                        // Transfer data to controls
}
```

The pointer returned by the inherited **GetDocument()** function is of type **CDocument**. We want to use this to access the **m_OrderSet** member of the derived class so we must cast the pointer to **CDBSimpleUpdateDoc***. We then call the member function for the **m_OrderSet** member of the document class that returns the new order ID, and store the result in the **m_NewOrderID** member of the **CCustomerView** class. Calling the inherited **UpdateData()** member of the view transfers the data from the data members of the view to the controls. We must now add an **#include** directive for **DBSimpleUpdateDoc.h** to the source file because we refer to the **CDBSimpleUpdateDoc** class.

Since we only ever create a single **CCustomerView** object and reuse it as necessary, we will want a new ID to be available each time we switch to that view. We deal with switching between dialogs in the **SelectView()** member of the **CMainFrame** object and this is also where a **CCustomerView** object gets created first time around, so that would be a good place to initiate the process for creating the new order ID. All we need to do is to add some code to call the **SetNewOrderID()** member if the view corresponds to the **CCustomerView**. This is quite easy:

```
void CMainFrame::SelectView(int viewID)
{
    CView* pOldActiveView = GetActiveView();       // Get current view

    // Get pointer to new view if it exists
    // if it doesn't the pointer will be null
    CView* pNewActiveView = static_cast<CView*>(GetDlgItem(viewID));

    // If this is first time around for the new view, the new view
    // won't exist, so we must create it
    // The Order Details view is always created first so we don't need
    // to provide for creating that.
    if (pNewActiveView == NULL)
    {
        switch(viewID)
        {
            case NEWORDER_VIEW:          // Create view to add new order
                pNewActiveView = new CCustomerView;
                break;
            case SELECTPRODUCT_VIEW:     // Create view to add product to order
                pNewActiveView = new CProductView;
                break;
             default:
                AfxMessageBox("Invalid View ID");
                return;
        }

        // Switching the views
        // Obtain the current view context to apply to the new view
        CCreateContext context;
        context.m_pCurrentDoc = pOldActiveView->GetDocument();
        pNewActiveView->Create(NULL, NULL, 0L, CFrameWnd::rectDefault,
                                              this, viewID, &context);
        pNewActiveView->OnInitialUpdate();
    }
    SetActiveView(pNewActiveView);                 // Activate the new view
    if(viewID==NEWORDER_VIEW)
      static_cast<CCustomerView*>(pNewActiveView)->SetNewOrderID();

    pOldActiveView->ShowWindow(SW_HIDE);           // Hide the old view
    pNewActiveView->ShowWindow(SW_SHOW);           // Show the new view
    pOldActiveView->SetDlgCtrlID(m_CurrentViewID); // Set the old view ID
    pNewActiveView->SetDlgCtrlID(AFX_IDW_PANE_FIRST);
    m_CurrentViewID = viewID;                      // Save the new view ID
    RecalcLayout();
}
```

899

All we do is check the **viewID** value. If it is **NEWORDER_VIEW** we call the **SetNewOrderID()** member of the new view object. Since **pNewActiveView** is of type **CView**, we must cast it to the actual view type in order to call the member function.

Storing the Order Data

We don't want to create a new entry in the Orders table until we have the first Product Details record for the order, so we need a way to pass the data accumulated in the **CCustomerView** object to the **CProductView** object. A simple way to do this is to define a new class to represent an order. It just needs to have a data member for each data value that we need to stash away. Except for the shipped date field which doesn't sensibly have a value in a new order, the data members will be the same as the data members corresponding to the fields in the **COrderSet** class. Create a new header file, **Order.h**, in the project, and add the following code to it:

```
#ifndef ORDER_H
#define ORDER_H
class COrder
{
    public:
        // Data members same as fields in COrderSet
        long     m_OrderID;
        CString m_CustomerID;
        long     m_EmployeeID;
        CTime    m_OrderDate;
        CTime    m_RequiredDate;
        long     m_ShipVia;
        CString m_Freight;
        CString m_ShipName;
        CString m_ShipAddress;
        CString m_ShipCity;
        CString m_ShipRegion;
        CString m_ShipPostalCode;
        CString m_ShipCountry;

    // Default constructor
    COrder():
        m_OrderID(0),                    // Will be set by CCustomerView object
        m_EmployeeID(1),                 // Arbitrary employee ID assigned
        m_ShipVia(3),                    // Arbitrary shipping company
        m_CustomerID(_T("")),    m_Freight(_T("")),    m_ShipName(_T("")),
        m_ShipAddress(_T("")),   m_ShipCity(_T("")),   m_ShipRegion(_T("")),
        m_ShipPostalCode(_T("")), m_ShipCountry(_T(""))
    {
        SYSTEMTIME Now;
        GetLocalTime(&Now);                          // Get current time
        m_OrderDate = m_RequiredDate = CTime(Now);   // Set time as today
    }
};
#endif //ORDER_H
```

In general it is not good practice to make all the data members of a class **public** like this, but since the recordset classes generated by ClassWizard all have public members, there is little to be gained by making them **private** in our class here.

If we add a data member, **m_Order**, of type **COrder**, to the document class, we will be able to use this to pass the order data to the **CProductView** object. All we have to do is get the **CCustomerView** object to load up the data members when the Select Products button is pressed, ready to be picked up by the **CProductView** object. The button handler in **CCustomerView** will be implemented like this:

```
void CCustomerView::OnSelectproducts()
{
  // Get a pointer to the document
  CDBSimpleUpdateDoc* pDoc = static_cast<CDBSimpleUpdateDoc*>(GetDocument());

  // Set up order field values from CCustomerSet object
  pDoc->m_Order.m_CustomerID = m_pSet->m_CustomerID;
  pDoc->m_Order.m_ShipAddress = m_pSet->m_Address;
  pDoc-> m_Order.m_ShipCity = m_pSet->m_City;
  pDoc-> m_Order.m_ShipCountry = m_pSet->m_Country;
  pDoc-> m_Order.m_ShipName = m_pSet->m_CompanyName;
  pDoc-> m_Order.m_ShipPostalCode = m_pSet->m_PostalCode;
  pDoc-> m_Order.m_ShipRegion = m_pSet->m_Region;


  // Set up order field values from CCustomerView dialog input
  pDoc-> m_Order.m_OrderID = m_NewOrderID;          // Generated new ID
  pDoc-> m_Order.m_OrderDate = m_OrderDate;         // From order date control
  pDoc-> m_Order.m_RequiredDate = m_RequiredDate;   // From required date control

  static_cast<CMainFrame*>(GetParentFrame())->SelectView(SELECTPRODUCT_VIEW);
}
```

This is straightforward stuff. We are just copying values from the recordset and record view objects to the Order object stored in the document object.

Setting Dates

There is a small problem with the date picker controls on the **CCustomerView** dialog. The variables corresponding to these, **m_OrderDate** and **m_RequiredDate** are not initialized at the moment, so the controls will not display sensible values to start with. We want them to display the current date at the outset, so we should add some code to initialize them at the end of the **OnInitialUpdate()** member that is called when the view object is first created:

```
void CCustomerView::OnInitialUpdate()
{
  BeginWaitCursor();
  GetRecordset();
  CRecordView::OnInitialUpdate();
  if (m_pSet->IsOpen())
  {
    CString strTitle = m_pSet->m_pDatabase->GetDatabaseName();
    CString strTable = m_pSet->GetTableName();
    if(!strTable.IsEmpty())
      strTitle += _T(":") + strTable;
  GetDocument()->SetTitle(strTitle);
  }
  EndWaitCursor();
```

```
        // Initialize time values
        SYSTEMTIME Now;
        GetLocalTime(&Now);                        // Get current time
        m_OrderDate = m_RequiredDate = CTime(Now); // Set time as today
    }
```

Here we set both **CTime** variables to the current time, just as we did in the constructor for the **COrder** class.

Now the **CCustomerView** object is in good shape. It displays the right date and it squirrels away all the value for the fields in a row in the Orders table, so we are ready to tackle the production selection process.

Selecting Products for an Order

When the view for selecting a product is displayed, we want to have the variables for the controls that display the order ID and the customer name already set up with appropriate values. We will get these values from the **Order** member of the document object. We can add a function to **CProductView** to do this. We will call it **InitializeView()** and the return type will be **void**. We will arrange to call the function from the **SelectView()** member of the **CMainFrame** object for the application. That way we can ensure that the controls are always initialized before the dialog is displayed.

Before we implement **InitializeView()**, let's consider something else. The new Orders table record will only be added when the Select Product button is clicked to add a product to the order for the first time. Subsequent clicks on the button should just add another product to the order, so we will need a way to determine whether the Orders table has been appended, to or not, when the button is clicked. We can do this by adding a variable, **m_OrderAdded**, of type **bool** to **CProductView**, that will be **false** to start with, and set to **true** by the Select Product button handler. So add this variable to the class. We can initialize it in the **InitializeView()** member that we will implement as follows:

```
void CProductView::InitializeView()
{
    // Get a pointer to the document
    CDBSimpleUpdateDoc* pDoc = static_cast<CDBSimpleUpdateDoc*>(GetDocument());

    m_OrderID = pDoc->m_Order.m_OrderID;
    m_CustomerName = pDoc->m_Order.m_ShipName;
    m_Quantity = 1;                 // Must order at least 1
    m_Discount = 0;                 // No default discount
    m_OrderAdded = false;           // Order not added initially
    UpdateData(FALSE);              // Transfer data to controls
}
```

This initializes the view class members for the order ID and customer name controls by copying values from the appropriate member of the **Order** member of the document. This function is also an opportunity to ensure that the controls for order quantity and discount start with suitable initial values. The order quantity for any product has to be at least 1, and the discount will be 0 by default. Calling the inherited **UpdateData()** member with an argument value **FALSE** causes the data to be transferred from the class variables to the controls, as we saw previously. You will need to add an **#include** directive for **DBSimpleUpdateDoc.h** to the beginning of the source file to make the document class definition available.

To put this into operation, we just need to call **InitializeView()** whenever we switch to the product selection dialog. The obvious place to do this is in the **SelectView()** member of the **CMainFrame** class:

```
void CMainFrame::SelectView(int viewID)
{
   CView* pOldActiveView = GetActiveView();            // Get current view

   // Get pointer to new view if it exists
   // if it doesn't the pointer will be null
   CView* pNewActiveView = static_cast<CView*>(GetDlgItem(viewID));

   // If this is first time around for the new view, the new view
   // won't exist, so we must create it
   // The Order Details view is always created first so we don't need
   // to provide for creating that.
   if (pNewActiveView == NULL)
   {
      switch(viewID)
      {
         case NEWORDER_VIEW:           // Create view to add new order
            pNewActiveView = new CCustomerView;
            break;
         case SELECTPRODUCT_VIEW:      // Create view to add product to order
            pNewActiveView = new CProductView;
            break;
          default:
            AfxMessageBox("Invalid View ID");
            return;
      }

      // Switching the views
      // Obtain the current view context to apply to the new view
      CCreateContext context;
      context.m_pCurrentDoc = pOldActiveView->GetDocument();
      pNewActiveView->Create(NULL, NULL, 0L, CFrameWnd::rectDefault,
                                               this, viewID, &context);
      pNewActiveView->OnInitialUpdate();
   }
   SetActiveView(pNewActiveView);                       // Activate the new view
   if(viewID==NEWORDER_VIEW)
      static_cast<CCustomerView*>(pNewActiveView)->SetNewOrderID();
   else if(viewID == SELECTPRODUCT_VIEW)
      static_cast<CProductView*>(pNewActiveView)->InitializeView();

   pOldActiveView->ShowWindow(SW_HIDE);                 // Hide the old view
   pNewActiveView->ShowWindow(SW_SHOW);                 // Show the new view
   pOldActiveView->SetDlgCtrlID(m_CurrentViewID);       // Set the old view ID
   pNewActiveView->SetDlgCtrlID(AFX_IDW_PANE_FIRST);
   m_CurrentViewID = viewID;                            // Save the new view ID
   RecalcLayout();
}
```

When the **ViewID** variable has the value **SELECTPRODUCT_VIEW**, the **CProductView** class variables for the order ID and customer name controls will be initialized, as will the **bool** variable controlling the creation of a new record in the Orders table.

Adding a New Order

The final piece of our program that we have to put together is the code to add a new order. Adding an order will always be done by the **OnSelectproducts()** member of **CProductView**. The effect of pressing the Select Products button will depend on the value of the data member, **m_OrderAdded**. If it is **false**, the function should add a new record to the Orders table, as well as a new record to the Order Details table. If **m_OrderAdded** is **true**, only the Order Details table should have a new record added as this will be another product for the same order. All the values we need for the new Orders record are stored in the **m_Order** member of the document. We just need to copy them to the members of the **COrderSet** object that is also a member of the document. The document object is in quite a strong position to deal with this, so add a member function, **AddOrder()** to **CDBSimpleUpdateDoc** with a **bool** return type, and implement it as:

```
bool CDBSimpleUpdateDoc::AddOrder()
{
  try
  {
    if(!m_OrderSet.IsOpen())                        // If recordset is not open
        m_OrderSet.Open();                          // open it

     if(m_OrderSet.CanAppend())                     // If we can add a record
     {                                              // then add it
        m_OrderSet.AddNew();                        // Start adding new record
        m_OrderSet.m_CustomerID = m_Order.m_CustomerID;
        m_OrderSet.m_EmployeeID = m_Order.m_EmployeeID;
        m_OrderSet.m_Freight = m_Order.m_Freight;
        m_OrderSet.m_OrderDate = m_Order.m_OrderDate;
        m_OrderSet.m_OrderID = m_Order.m_OrderID;
        m_OrderSet.m_RequiredDate = m_Order.m_RequiredDate;
        m_OrderSet.m_ShipAddress = m_Order.m_ShipAddress;
        m_OrderSet.m_ShipName = m_Order.m_ShipName;
        m_OrderSet.m_ShipPostalCode = m_Order.m_ShipPostalCode;
        m_OrderSet.m_ShipRegion = m_Order.m_ShipRegion;
        m_OrderSet.m_ShipVia = m_Order.m_ShipVia;

        // No value for the Shipped Date field
        m_OrderSet.SetFieldNull(&m_OrderSet.m_ShippedDate);

        m_OrderSet.Update();                        // Complete adding new record
        return true;                               // Return success
     }
     else
        AfxMessageBox("Cannot append to Orders table");  }
  catch(CException* pEx)                            // Catch any exceptions
  {
    pEx->ReportError();                             // Display the error message
  }
  return false;                                     // Here we have failed
}
```

We saw earlier in this chapter that the functions in a recordset object for adding and editing records can throw exceptions, so we put the code in a **try** block and catch any exceptions to avoid aborting the application if this happens.

After ensuring the **COrderSet** recordset is open, we check that the it allows records to be added by calling its **CanAppend()** member. Adding a new record involves three steps:

▶ We first call the **AddNew()** member of the recordset. This starts the process and saves the current values of the data members in the recordset as we will be altering them. It also sets the values of the data members to null. This is nothing to do with null for pointers and it is not zero – null here implies no value has been set for a variable.

▶ We set all the data members for the field values in the recordset to the values required in the record. This is quite straightforward. We just copy the values stored in the members of the **m_Order** object to the members of the recordset object. The **m_ShippedDate** member will be null since we have not set a value for it here.

▶ We call **Update()** to actually get the record written, and this will also restore the original values in the recordset object. It doesn't apply here but if we were displaying the recordset that we were adding to, we would need to call the **Requery()** member of the recordset object to get the new record values displayed.

We can now put in the basic logic for the **OnSelectproduct()** handler for the **CProductView** class. We need to call **UpdateData()** for the view to get the data that was entered in the edit controls transferred to data members of the view object. Here's the outline code for the handler function:

```
void CProductView::OnSelectproduct()
{
    UpdateData(TRUE);                                    // Transfer data from controls

    // Get a pointer to the document
    CDBSimpleUpdateDoc* pDoc = static_cast<CDBSimpleUpdateDoc*>(GetDocument());

    if(!m_OrderAdded)                                    // If order not added
      m_OrderAdded = pDoc->AddOrder();                  // then try to add it
    if(m_OrderAdded)

    // Code to add new Order Details record...
}
```

After calling the **UpdateData()** for the **CProductView** object, we get a pointer to the document object. We need this to call the **AddOrder()** member of the document that will do the work for us. Next we check the **m_OrderAdded** member. We only want to add a record to Orders when this is **false**. The **AddOrder()** member of the document object returns a **bool** value that is **true** if the order was added successfully, and **false** for any failure. We use this value to set the **m_OrderAdded** member of **CProductView**, and as an indicator for whether we can continue to add order details. We don't need to display any message in the case of failure. The **AddOrder()** function will have already done that.

The code to add a record to the Order Details table is also probably best handled by the document object, but the document class member function to do it will need access to four values from members of the **CProductView** and **CProductSet** classes – for the product ID, the order quantity, the unit price, and the applicable discount. The order ID is available in the document class from its **m_Order** member so we don't need to worry about that. We can add a function, **AddOrderDetails()**, to **CDBSimpleUpdateDoc** to add a record to the Order Details table:

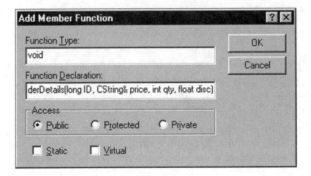

We can now implement this as follows:

```
void CDBSimpleUpdateDoc::AddOrderDetails(long ID, CString& price, int qty, float
disc)
{
  try
  {
    if(!m_orderDetailsSet.IsOpen())             // If recordset is not open
      m_orderDetailsSet.Open();                 // open it

    m_orderDetailsSet.AddNew();                 // Start adding new record

    // Set Product Details recordset data member values
    m_orderDetailsSet.m_OrderID = m_Order.m_OrderID;
    m_orderDetailsSet.m_Quantity = qty;
    m_orderDetailsSet.m_Discount = disc;
    m_orderDetailsSet.m_ProductID = ID;
    m_orderDetailsSet.m_UnitPrice = price;
    m_orderDetailsSet.Update();                 // Complete adding new record
  }
  catch(CException* pEx)                         // Catch any exceptions
  {
    pEx->ReportError();                         // Display the error message
  }
}
```

This sets up the values in the **m_orderDetailsSet** members and then updates the table in essentially the same way as for the Orders table. Again, we need to put the update code in a try block to catch any exceptions that might be thrown by **AddNew()** or **Update()**.

We want to call this function every time the Select Product button handler in the **CProductView** class is called, so we can modify the handler to do this:

```
void CProductView::OnSelectproduct()
{
  UpdateData(TRUE);                             // Transfer data from controls

  // Get a pointer to the document
  CDBSimpleUpdateDoc* pDoc = static_cast<CDBSimpleUpdateDoc*>(GetDocument());
```

906

```
      if(!m_OrderAdded)                         // If order not added
        m_OrderAdded = pDoc->AddOrder();        // then try to add it
      if(m_Order_Added)
      {
          pDoc->AddOrderDetails(m_pSet->m_ProductID,
                                m_pSet->m_UnitPrice,
                                m_Quantity,
                                m_Discount);
          // Now reset the values in the quantity and discount controls
          m_Quantity = 1;
          m_Discount = 0;
          UpdateData(false); // Transfer data to controls
      }
  }
```

We use the **m_OrderDetailsSet** object to update the Order Details table. This was used by the original view in the application, and it is stored in the document object. We get the values for quantity and discount from the data members in the view object corresponding to the edit controls that provide for these values to be entered. The order ID value was set when the dialog was displayed so that it would be displayed for information only. The product ID and unit price values are retrieved from the **CProductSet** object associated with this view. After calling **Update()** to write the record, we reset the values for quantity and discount back to their defaults.

TRY IT OUT - Adding New Orders

After adding a number of other orders, as you might deduce from the order ID, I added the following order:

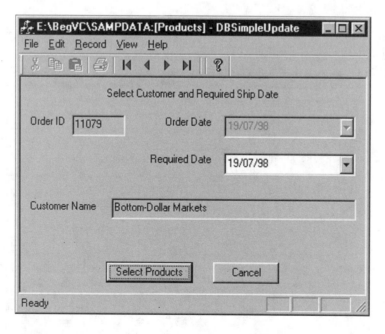

I then clicked on the Select Products button, and selected the product, the quantity and discount as shown below.

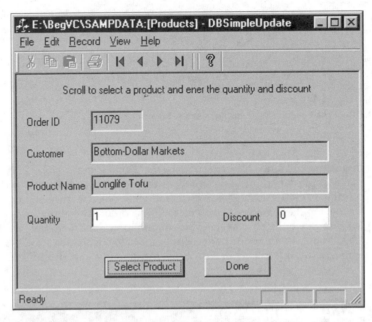

Clicking the Select Product button adds that product to the order for the customer and then allows the selection of another product. Each click of the Select Product button adds a new record to the Order Details table for the current order ID. When the order is complete you just click on the Done button to end the process.

Once you have added an order, you can verify that is was added correctly by moving to the last order in the order details browsing view.

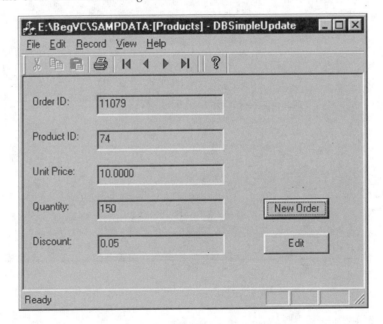

You may notice that the views don't reset to the beginning of the recordset when you finish an order entry operation. Try the first exercise at the end of the chapter to fix this for the customer recordset. You should not find this too difficult.

Summary

In this chapter you have learned how elementary updating works using the ODBC support in MFC. You should have no difficulty in using DAO support in the same way if you need to, as the implementation of the DAO classes is very similar to that of the ODBC classes.

The important points we have covered in this chapter include:

▶ Updating is only possible if a recordset corresponds to a single table. Recordsets corresponding to table joins cannot be updated.

▶ To start editing a record in a recordset you call the **Edit()** member of the recordset object.

▶ To start adding a new record to a recordset, you call the **AddNew()** member of the recordset object.

▶ To complete either modifying an existing record or adding a new one, you must call the **Update()** member of the recordset object.

▶ Before initializing an update of a recordset, you should always ensure that the recordset is open, and that the update operation you intend to perform is legal.

▶ A transaction packages a series of database update operations so that the original state of that database can be restored in the event of an error.

Exercises

Ex21-1: Modify the update application in this chapter so that the dialog for adding a new order always displays the customers in alphabetical order, and the dialog always displays the first customer each time it is displayed.

Ex21-2: Modify the example to display the total value of a new order on the view used to select products for the order (which corresponds to **CProductView**).

Ex21-3: Extend the example in this chapter to enable the employee to be selected from the records in the Employees table.

Ex21-4: Extend the example further to allow the shipped via field in an order to be chosen from the records in the Shippers table.

Understanding OLE Documents

OLE is a complex topic which many would argue is out of place in a beginners' programming book. However, because of the advantages it brings, more and more applications are making the most of OLE, so it's important to have a basic understanding of how it works.

There are whole books dedicated to OLE, so we'll only scratch the surface in this chapter. Fortunately, MFC hides most of the complexity, and with the help you get from AppWizard you shouldn't find it difficult to implement some examples that use OLE. By the end of this chapter you will have learnt:

> What OLE is and how it can be used

> How the OLE mechanism works

> What OLE containers and OLE servers are

> How to write a simple OLE container using AppWizard

> How to write an OLE server using AppWizard

Object Linking and Embedding

Before we launch into writing code, we first need to get the ideas and terminology straight. **Object Linking and Embedding**, perhaps better known as **OLE** (and sometimes pronounced 'olé'), is a mechanism which enables you to write a program — a text editor, say — that will allow other applications to edit data within it that it can't handle itself, like graphics. OLE also allows an application that you write to handle data contained within other applications. This isn't the whole story, but it's what we'll concentrate on.

Once you've allowed your program to contain these data objects, you can have any kind of object you like, and as many of them as you like. This is a pretty incredible capability when you think about it: the program hosting these alien objects has no knowledge of what they are, but you can still edit and manipulate them as though they were handled by the same program. In fact, there's a different program involved for each type of alien object you're working with.

An object from one program can appear in another in two different ways. An object from an external document can be **linked** to the document of another program, in which case the external object isn't stored as part of the document for the current program, but just as a reference allowing it to be retrieved from wherever it is. Alternatively, an external document can be **embedded** in the current document, in which case it's actually stored within it. A document that contains an embedded or linked OLE object is called a **compound document**.

A linked object has the advantage that it can be modified independently of the compound document, so that when you open a document containing a linked object, the latest version of the object will automatically be incorporated. However, if you delete the file containing the linked object, or even move it to another folder, the compound document will not know about this and won't be able to find the linked object. With an embedded object, the object only exists in the context of the compound document and is, therefore, not independently accessible. The compound document with all its embedded OLE objects is a single file, so there's no possibility of the embedded objects getting lost. These provisions aside, to the user there appears to be no difference between the appearances of the compound documents.

Containers and Servers

Clearly, to enable OLE to work, a program must contain special code supporting this sort of functionality. A program that can handle embedded objects is called an **OLE container** and a program that creates objects that can be embedded in an OLE container is referred to as an **OLE server**. OLE servers also come in two flavors. A **full server** can operate as an independent program, or just servicing an object embedded in a compound document. A **mini-server** can't operate in stand-alone mode — its sole function is to support objects in a compound document.

It's possible for an application to be both an OLE server and an OLE container. The AppWizard can generate programs which have OLE container and/or OLE server functionality built in. All you have to do is to choose the appropriate options when creating an OLE project.

Compound Documents

A compound document is illustrated here:

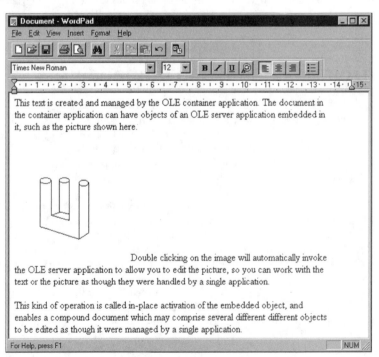

When you work with an embedded object in a program, the code for the application that generated the embedded object can be automatically invoked to allow you to edit the object in the container application window. This is referred to as **in-place activation**. With an OLE server that supports in-place activation, you can edit an embedded object in an OLE container application just by double-clicking it. The menus and toolbars for the container application will then change to incorporate those required to use the server application to edit the object. More than that, if there are several different embedded objects, the menus and toolbars in the container will change to incorporate the menus and toolbars for whatever embedded object you're working with, all completely automatically.

With in-place activation, the appearance of the compound document comprising the natively-supported object and the embedded object or objects is seamless, and generally hides the fact that several different programs may be involved in manipulating what you see in the application window.

If an OLE server doesn't support in-place activation, double-clicking the embedded object will open a separate window for the server application, allowing you to edit the embedded object. When you've finished editing the embedded object, you only need to close the server application window to resume work with the container application. Obviously, in-place activation is a much more attractive way of handling compound documents, as it appears to the user as a single application. Most containers also allow you to edit an embedded object in a server window, even when the server does support in-place activation. Double-clicking an object while holding down the *Ctrl* or the *Alt* key often initiates this mode of server operation. In-place activation is only possible with embedded, not linked, items.

Activating an Embedded Object

Once an object has been embedded in a container, the server supporting it can be in two basic states. When the server has been activated in-place for editing, the object is shown with a shaded border in the client area of the container. If you click once outside the object, the server will be deactivated and the shaded border will not be displayed. You can see both of these states in the following screen:

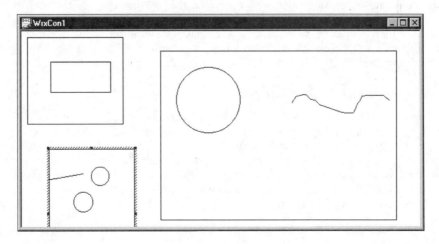

There are three embedded objects here. Only the object at the bottom left is in-place activated, and in fact only one object can be in this state at a time. The user interface is under the control of the server. The other two embedded objects are inactive, and no communication between the container and server is necessary for them. To change an inactive object to the fully in-place activated state, you just double-click on it. With the fully activated object, the server will advise the container each time the area occupied by the embedded object needs to be redrawn. This could be because the contents have changed, or because a larger area is required.

If you *single*-click on an inactive object, the appearance of the object will be as for an inactive object but with resize handles on the borders. In this situation, you can't edit the object, but you can resize the area it occupies by dragging the border. You can also move the object around in the client area. The container signals the server whenever the contents of the object need to be redrawn because of changes to the size or position of the area occupied by the embedded object.

How Does OLE Work?

The communications between an OLE server application for an embedded object and the OLE container application are concerned primarily with the area occupied by the object, when it needs to be redrawn, and the resources the server needs to make available in the container for editing, such as menus and toolbars. The container has no knowledge of what is to be displayed by the server. All it knows is that an area in its view is going to be used by the server and the server is going to sort out what needs to be displayed. Neither does the container know which menus or toolbars are required to use the server — all it does is provide space for them within its own menus and toolbars. It's a bit like the owner of a market hall renting a stall to someone. The person who runs the stall does what they want, within an agreed set of rules. The owner doesn't get involved in what goes on at the stall or what they sell. As long as the rent is paid and the rules are obeyed, everybody's happy.

As you've probably guessed, the communication between an OLE container and the servers supporting the embedded objects uses the Windows operating system as a go-between. Each OLE program uses a common OLE DLL which is part of Windows, and the functions in the DLL provide the means of passing information between them. Thus, the key to the operation of OLE is a **standard interface**. The standard interface that enables OLE to work is specified by the **Component Object Model**, or **COM**. This is essentially a definition of the appearance of an embedded object and how a container communicates with it. COM is a big topic, and we won't be delving into the detail. We'll just be looking close enough to understand the ideas involved.

The OLE Component Object Model

The Component Object Model has sets of standard functions that are used for OLE communications, packaged in named groups called **interfaces**. This is analogous to a C++ class which defines an interface through its **public** function members. A complete discussion of COM is far beyond the scope of this book, but its operation is hidden in the framework that we get with an AppWizard-generated program, so you won't need to deal with the details. However, we'll look far enough into it to give you a feel for what's happening when we implement an OLE container and a server later in this chapter.

For a COM object such as an OLE server, at least one interface (or group of functions), called **IUnknown**, is always implemented. The **IUnknown** interface contains three standard functions:

Function	Usage
`QueryInterface()`	Tests whether a particular interface is supported by the object. If an interface that is queried is supported, a pointer to it is returned. The calling function can then access the functions in the queried interface through the pointer.
`AddRef()`	Increments a count of the number of clients using the interface. This count enables the object owning the interface to know when it is no longer required.
`Release()`	Decrements the count of the number of clients using the interface. When the count is zero, the object knows that it is no longer in use and can remove itself from memory.

You can do almost anything with these three functions. Since the `QueryInterface()` function allows you to ask about other interfaces, you can access any interface that an object supports, as long as you know about it. OLE defines a set of standard interfaces, each identified by an **interface ID**, or **IID**, which is passed as an argument in the `QueryInterface()` call. It's also possible to define your own custom interfaces which will also need to be identified by a unique IID. We won't need to look into the detail of these interface functions, since for the most part MFC takes care of using them.

IUnknown is by no means all there is to the component object model. There are several other interfaces involved, concerned with transferring data, managing memory and so on, but we can create a container and a server without knowing any more about COM, so let's press on.

 FYI   Interface names usually start with 'I', just as class names usually begin with 'C'.

The Registry

In order to use an OLE server, it must be identified in some way. When you run an OLE container, you wouldn't want to be just rummaging around your hard disk to see if any of the applications on your PC might support OLE, so how are OLE programs identified?

An **OLE object** can be a program, a document type, or indeed any kind of object that supports OLE. Each OLE object in your system is identified by a unique 128-bit numeric value, called a **class ID** or **CLSID**. CLSIDs and IIDs are in turn particular types of **globally unique IDs**, or **GUIDs**. The IDs are called 'globally unique' because they are generated by an algorithm that ensures within reason that they are unique throughout the world. Information about every OLE object in your system, including its CLSID, is stored on your hard disk in a database called the **system registry**.

You can look at the registry by executing the program **Regedit.exe**. A typical window is shown here:

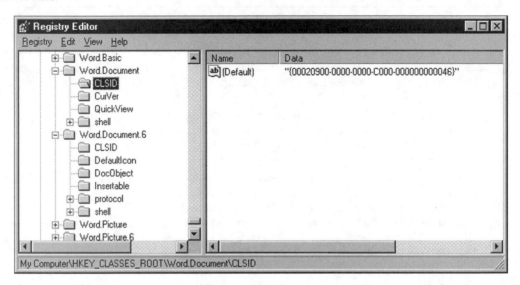

FYI

It's not advisable to start messing around with the values in the registry, as you can very quickly render Windows unusable. The registry is definitely a case for looking with your eyes and not your hands!

This shows the Word.Document entry for the word processing package, Microsoft Word, and its class ID. You can see that there is also a key (it looks like a folder) for Word.Picture, which represents a different document type. Because it is also an OLE object, this also has its own CLSID. An OLE server can't be used until it has been entered in the system registry with all the information necessary to identify it.

MFC Classes Supporting OLE

MFC has a set of classes that represent OLE objects, as well as classes that represent documents that can contain OLE objects. The relationships between these classes are illustrated here:

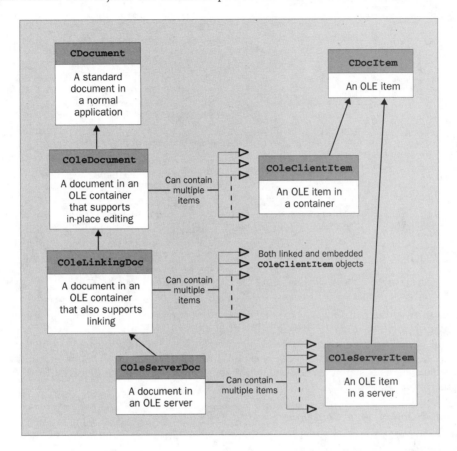

The arrows in the diagram point from a derived class towards a base class, so the **COleServerDoc** class, for example, inherits the functionality of its base class **COleLinkingDoc**, as well as its indirect base classes, which are **CDocument** and **COleDocument**.

OLE Object Classes

The two classes that are shown derived from the class **CDocItem**, **COleClientItem** and **COleServerItem**, represent different perspectives of an OLE object corresponding to the points of view of a container and a server respectively, as shown here:

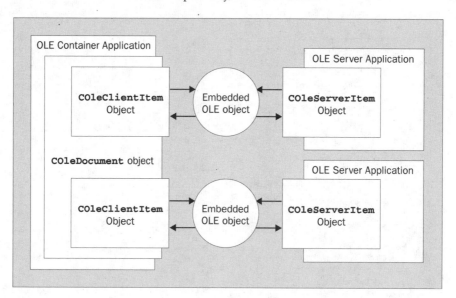

This shows two different OLE objects embedded in a container application. The class objects in the container corresponding to the embedded objects will both be included in the container document object. Each embedded object will have its own server application, and each server will have a **COleServerItem** object corresponding to the object in the container for which it is responsible. This is a simplified representation, since the OLE DLL is involved in the communications.

An Embedded Object in a Container

The class **COleClientItem** provides the interfaces required by a container to manage an embedded item. This involves a large number of functions which enable the object to be queried and manipulated, as well as functions which enable communications between the container and the server. The most important of these are the ones you will need to implement, which are as follows:

Function to implement	Usage
OnChange()	This function is called by the framework when a change to an embedded item is signaled by the item's server. The typical action is to invalidate the embedded object to get it redrawn in the container.
OnGetItemPosition()	This function is called by the framework to obtain the rectangle in the client area of the container where the OLE object is to be displayed.

Function to implement	Usage
`OnChangeItemPosition()`	This function is called by the framework to indicate to the container that the extent of the embedded object has changed during editing.
`Serialize()`	If you add any members to the object in the container, you will need to serialize them in this function.

The drawing of an embedded object and any modifications made by the user is carried out by the server, but the object is displayed in an area in a window that is owned and managed by the container. Thus, the communications between the container and the server are fundamental to proper OLE operation.

An Embedded Object in a Server

An OLE object embedded in a server application is represented by an object of the class `COleServerItem` in the server. The interface supporting a server in `COleServerItem` also involves a large number of functions, but the most important of these are:

Function to implement	Usage
`OnDraw()`	This function is responsible for drawing the embedded object in the container when it's not being edited, so it's essential to implement it. When the object is in-place active, the object is drawn by the `OnDraw()` function in the server's view class. Drawing in the container has to be done by the server because the container has no knowledge of the internals of the embedded object. When the server runs stand-alone, the `OnDraw()` function in the view object is of course also responsible for drawing the object in the normal way.
`Serialize()`	This function is responsible for serializing the embedded object when required to do so by the container. This is usually implemented by calling the `Serialize()` function for the document object in the server.
`OnGetExtent()`	This function is called by the framework to get the actual extent of the embedded object. This is communicated to the container application.
`NotifyChanged()`	This function is called by the server application when it changes the embedded object. This signals the change to the framework which will call the `OnChange()` function in the corresponding `COleClientItem` object in the container.

OLE Document Classes

Specialized document classes are necessary for OLE applications because the documents must include the ability to deal with the added complexity of OLE objects. There are two document classes that are used in OLE container applications: `COleDocument` and `COleLinkingDoc`. `COleDocument` supports embedded objects that are edited in-place by a server. It represents the embedded objects as instances of a class derived from `COleClientItem`. The class `COleLinkingDoc` is derived from `COleDocument` and adds support for linked objects that are stored separately from the container document. The document class in a container application is typically derived from either `COleDocument` or `COleLinkingDoc`. The container example that we'll implement later in this chapter will use the `COleDocument` class as a base.

A document in a server application is derived from the class **COleServerDoc**. When the server is supporting an embedded object, the OLE object is represented by a class derived from the **COleServerItem** class that we saw earlier. Of course, a server document will only include one instance of this class, which will represent the whole document when it is embedded in a container document.

A document class for an OLE server must implement the member **OnGetEmbeddedItem()**, because this is a pure virtual function in the **COleServerDoc** class. If you don't implement it, your code won't compile. This function is called by the framework to get a pointer to the OLE object supported by the server and is used by the framework to call function members of the object.

Implementing an OLE Container

AppWizard makes it very easy to create an OLE container application, so let's try it out. Create a new project of type MFC AppWizard (exe). You could call it something meaningful, like WrxContainer. Select the OK button to create it, then click on the Next > button to accept the default MDI implementation, and another Next > without electing for database support. The next step is shown here:

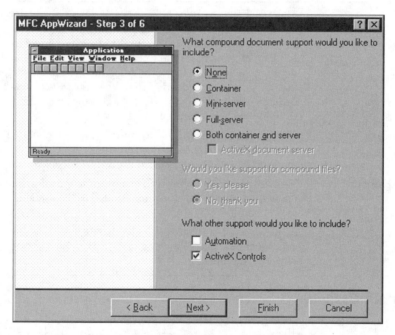

Select the Container radio button here to generate an OLE container. When you click on this, the option for compound files will be activated and selected automatically. The other options on this dialog are all the variations on a server that we referred to earlier: the Mini-server is just a server that can't be used independently of a container; the Full-server can operate as a stand-alone application or as a server to a container. We'll implement a full server a little later in this chapter. The third possibility, Both container and server, generates a program that can run stand-alone, can run as a server and can itself act as a container for other embedded objects. This raises the possibility of an embedded object containing embedded objects.

The other two options, Automation and ActiveX Controls, provide additional levels of functionality. Automation adds a programmable interface to your application so that other applications which have provision for doing so can make use of functions within your application. Selecting ActiveX Controls adds the capability for your program to incorporate and use ActiveX controls. We'll be looking at creating an ActiveX control in the next chapter.

Click on Next > to go to Step 4 and select the Advanced... button. Change the File extension field to con as shown (the Filter name field will adjust automatically).

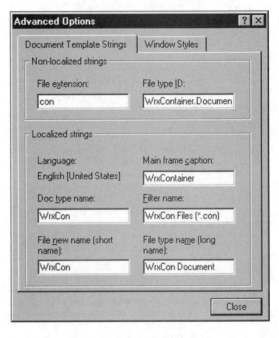

The entry in the File type ID: box, WrxContainer.Document, will appear in the registry.

The only other change to make is on Step 6 when you get to the list of classes that AppWizard plans to generate. Select the class CWrxContainerCntrItem, and shorten it to CWrxContainerItem, and also change the names of the files that this class will live in to WrxContainerItem.h and WrxContainerItem.cpp. This is just for our convenience. You can then proceed to the end and generate the program.

If you look at the classes in the program by selecting the ClassView tab, you'll see that we have the standard set of classes supporting the MFC document/view architecture. If you look at the definition of **CWrxContainerApp**, you'll see that it is perfectly standard. The differences really start to become apparent in the initialization of the application object.

Initializing a Container Application

The initialization is done in the **InitInstance()** member of the application class **CWrxContainerApp**. The code generated for it by AppWizard is as follows:

```
BOOL CWrxContainerApp::InitInstance()
{
    // Initialize OLE libraries
    if (!AfxOleInit())
    {
```

```
            AfxMessageBox(IDP_OLE_INIT_FAILED);
            return FALSE;
      }

   AfxEnableControlContainer();

   // Standard initialization
   // If you are not using these features and wish to reduce the size
   //  of your final executable, you should remove from the following
   //  the specific initialization routines you do not need.

#ifdef _AFXDLL
   Enable3dControls();              // Call this when using MFC in a shared DLL
#else
   Enable3dControlsStatic();        // Call this when linking to MFC statically
#endif

   // Change the registry key under which our settings are stored.
   // You should modify this string to be something appropriate
   // such as the name of your company or organization.
   SetRegistryKey(_T("Local AppWizard-Generated Applications"));

   LoadStdProfileSettings();   // Load standard INI file options (including MRU)

   // Register the application's document templates.  Document templates
   //  serve as the connection between documents, frame windows and views.

   CMultiDocTemplate* pDocTemplate;
   pDocTemplate = new CMultiDocTemplate(
      IDR_WRXCONTYPE,
      RUNTIME_CLASS(CWrxContainerDoc),
      RUNTIME_CLASS(CChildFrame),      // custom MDI child frame
      RUNTIME_CLASS(CWrxContainerView));
   pDocTemplate->SetContainerInfo(IDR_WRXCONTYPE_CNTR_IP);
   AddDocTemplate(pDocTemplate);

   // The rest of the function definition is
   //  as in a normal application that we have seen before...

}
```

This time we've used shading to highlight the differences between this code and that generated in a standard application. We'll just discuss these differences. The call to the global function **AfxOleInit()** initializes the system DLL that supports OLE operations. This establishes the links between the application and the DLL. If the initialization fails for some reason, perhaps because the version of the DLL required by the application is not installed, a message will be displayed and the container will terminate.

The call to the member function **SetContainerInfo()** of the document template object transfers the ID of the menu to be used when an OLE object is embedded and in-place active. The container has three different menu resources that are shown in the diagram below:

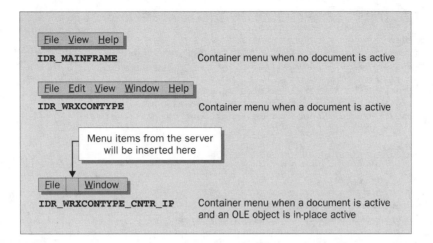

The menu corresponding to the ID passed to the **SetContainerInfo()** function has separator bars to identify where the menu items supplied by the server are to be inserted. The additional menu items are inserted automatically by the framework when the embedded object is active. We'll look at the specific menu items that are inserted when we implement an OLE server, but it is essentially the set required to interact with the in-place object.

The CWrxContainerItem Class

Another differentiating feature of our container application is the class **CWrxContainerItem**, which is derived from **COleClientItem**. As we have seen, an object of this class refers to an embedded OLE object which is supported by a server application. When you introduce an object into the container application, a **CWrxContainerItem** object is constructed and will only be destroyed when the container document is closed or the embedded item it corresponds to is deleted from the container. When a **CWrxContainerItem** is constructed, the constructor requires a pointer to the container's document object, so that the object being constructed is associated with the container document. The definition of the class provided by AppWizard is:

```
class CWrxContainerItem : public COleClientItem
{
   DECLARE_SERIAL(CWrxContainerItem)

// Constructors
public:
   CWrxContainerItem(CWrxContainerDoc* pContainer = NULL);
      // Note: pContainer is allowed to be NULL to enable IMPLEMENT_SERIALIZE.
      //  IMPLEMENT_SERIALIZE requires the class have a constructor with
      //  zero arguments.  Normally, OLE items are constructed with a
      //  non-NULL document pointer.

// Attributes
public:
   CWrxContainerDoc* GetDocument()
      { return (CWrxContainerDoc*)COleClientItem::GetDocument(); }
   CWrxContainerView* GetActiveView()
      { return (CWrxContainerView*)COleClientItem::GetActiveView(); }
```

```
    // ClassWizard generated virtual function overrides
    //{{AFX_VIRTUAL(CWrxContainerItem)
    public:
    virtual void OnChange(OLE_NOTIFICATION wNotification, DWORD dwParam);
    virtual void OnActivate();
    protected:
    virtual void OnGetItemPosition(CRect& rPosition);
    virtual void OnDeactivateUI(BOOL bUndoable);
    virtual BOOL OnChangeItemPosition(const CRect& rectPos);
    //}}AFX_VIRTUAL

// Implementation
public:
    ~CWrxContainerItem();
#ifdef _DEBUG
    virtual void AssertValid() const;
    virtual void Dump(CDumpContext& dc) const;
#endif
    virtual void Serialize(CArchive& ar);
};
```

As the note in the code indicates, the constructor will normally be called with a pointer to a container document as an argument. The default value of **NULL** for the parameter is only there because the serialization mechanism requires a default constructor.

One addition to the **CWrxContainerItem** class definition that we can make straight away is a data member to store the rectangle defining the position of the embedded object. Add the following declaration to the **public** section of the class definition:

```
    CRect m_Rect;                          // Item position in the document object
```

You can do this by right-clicking the class name in ClassView and selecting Add Member Variable... from the pop-up. Now each item can record where it is in the container document. You should also add initialization for the **m_Rect** member to the constructor:

```
CWrxContainerItem::CWrxContainerItem(CWrxContainerDoc* pContainer)
    : COleClientItem(pContainer)
{
    m_Rect.SetRect(10, 10, 100, 100);  // Set initial item position
}
```

The statement initializes **m_Rect** by calling the **SetRect()** member of the **CRect** class. This sets an arbitrary position which will be overridden when an object is added to the container document. Note that the constructor explicitly calls the base class constructor in the initialization list for our constructor and passes the pointer to the document object to it.

We should also arrange to store and retrieve **m_Rect** by adding the following code to the implementation of the **Serialize()** function for the embedded object:

```
void CWrxContainerItem::Serialize(CArchive& ar)
{
    ASSERT_VALID(this);

    // Call base class first to read in COleClientItem data.
    // Since this sets up the m_pDocument pointer returned from
```

```
    //  CWrxContainerItem::GetDocument, it is a good idea to call
    //  the base class Serialize first.
    COleClientItem::Serialize(ar);

    // now store/retrieve data specific to CWrxContainerItem
    if (ar.IsStoring())
    {
        ar << m_Rect;
    }
    else
    {
        ar >> m_Rect;
    }
}
```

The base class **Serialize()** function takes care of everything else, so we don't need to add anything further.

AppWizard has provided an implementation of **GetDocument()** which returns a pointer to the document object, and **GetActiveView()** which returns a pointer to the active view belonging to the document containing the embedded object. The next member function that we're interested in is **OnChange()**, which is called when an embedded object is fully open for editing and is modified in some way.

Reacting to OLE Object Modification

When the server modifies an embedded object, it calls a function to notify the framework that a change has occurred. The framework reacts by calling the **OnChange()** member of the object in the container application. The container owns the window in which the object is displayed, so it's up to the container to do something about the change.

The reason for calling the **OnChange()** function is indicated by the first argument passed, the two arguments being of type **OLE_NOTIFICATION** (nCode) and **DWORD** (dwParam). We need to deal with two possibilities: when **nCode** has the value **OLE_CHANGED**, which indicates that the object has been modified, and when **nCode** has the value **OLE_CHANGED_STATE**, which indicates the object has changed in some other way. You should add the code for this to the implementation of the **OnChange()** member, as follows:

```
    void CWrxContainerItem::OnChange(OLE_NOTIFICATION nCode, DWORD dwParam)
    {
        ASSERT_VALID(this);

        COleClientItem::OnChange(nCode, dwParam);

        // When an item is being edited (either in-place or fully open)
        //   it sends OnChange notifications for changes in the state of the
        //   item or visual appearance of its content.

        switch(nCode)
        {
            case OLE_CHANGED:           // Item appearance has been changed
                InvalidateItem();       // Invalidate the current item
                GetServerSize();        // Update to the size from the server
                break;
            case OLE_CHANGED_STATE:     // Item state has changed
```

925

```
            // Pass a hint to update all views in the document
            InvalidateItem();
            break;
      }
   }
```

Our code replaces the call to **UpdateAllViews()** in the default implementation. We will update selectively, depending on what is happening to the embedded object. Where the value of **nCode** indicates that there was a change to the content of the server, we need to get the object redrawn. We initiate this by calling the function **InvalidateItem()**, which we'll add to the **CWrxContainerItem** class in a moment. We also need to deal with the possibility that the size of the object may be altered by the server, and we may want to record the area it occupies in the **m_Rect** member and resize it in the container document view. This will be done in the second function that we'll add to the **CWrxContainerItem** class, **GetServerSize()**.

The second value of **nCode** reflects a change in state such as occurs when an object is active but not being edited, and the user double-clicks the object in the document view to edit it. In this case, we just need to get the object redrawn by calling the **InvalidateItem()** function. You'll need to add this function, so right-click the CWrxContainerItem class name in ClassView and select the Add Member Function... menu item from the pop-up. Specify the return type as **void** and enter the function name as **InvalidateItem()**. You can leave its access specification as **public**. Click on the OK button, then add the following code to its implementation:

```
void CWrxContainerItem::InvalidateItem()
{
   // Pass a hint to update all views in the document
   GetDocument()->UpdateAllViews(0, HINT_UPDATE_ITEM, this);
}
```

This calls the **UpdateAllViews()** function member of the document object to get all the views redrawn. The second argument value, **HINT_UPDATE_ITEM**, indicates that there is a hint passed in the third argument which is the address of the current object. This will be used when the **OnUpdate()** function in the container document view is called as a consequence of the call to **UpdateAllViews()**. We'll be extending the implementation of the view a little later in this chapter.

We can define the value of the symbol **HINT_UPDATE_ITEM** within the definition file for the **CWrxContainerItem** class. Add it at the beginning of the **WrxContainerItem.h** file with the directive:

```
#define HINT_UPDATE_ITEM 1              // Indicates a hint is present
```

When you have entered this definition, you can add the **GetServerSize()** function next. Just right-click the **CWrxContainerItem** class name again and select Add Member Function... from the pop-up. Enter the return type as **void** and the function name as **GetServerSize()**. You can implement the function as follows:

```
void CWrxContainerItem::GetServerSize()
{
   CSize aSize;                         // Create a size object
   if (GetCachedExtent(&aSize))         // Get the size of the current item
   {
      // Size is specified by OLE in HIMETRIC units
      CClientDC aDC(0);                 // Get a device context
```

926

```
        aDC.HIMETRICtoDP(&aSize); // Convert size to device coordinates

    // Verify that size has changed and item is not in-place active
    if (aSize != m_Rect.Size() && !IsInPlaceActive())
    {
        InvalidateItem();          // Invalidate old item

        // Change the rectangle for the item to the new size
        m_Rect.right = m_Rect.left + aSize.cx;
        m_Rect.bottom = m_Rect.top + aSize.cy;

        InvalidateItem();          // Invalidate the item with the new size
    }
}
}
```

The size of the OLE object is stored in the **aSize** object by the **GetCachedExtent()** member function that is inherited from the base class, **COleClientItem**. If the object is blank, this function will return **FALSE** and we will do nothing.

Whenever size information about an OLE object is passed to or from the framework, it is always in **HIMETRIC** units to ensure that such information is handled uniformly. This provides a standard unit for specifying size information that has more precision than any of the other possible choices, such as **LOMETRIC**, **HIENGLISH** or **LOENGLISH**. This means that whenever you pass size information to the framework, you must convert it from whatever units you're using to **HIMETRIC**. Whenever you receive size information, you need to convert it to whatever units you require, if they are different from **HIMETRIC**. In the container, we need the rectangle to be in device units, which are pixels, so we get a **CClientDC** object which provides a conversion function from **HIMETRIC** to device coordinate units.

After converting **aSize** to pixels, we then check that the size is actually different from that recorded in **m_Rect** for the item and that the object is not still in-place active. We don't want to do anything if the size hasn't changed. If the item *is* in-place active and a change occurs, the framework will call **OnChangeItemPosition()**. We'll come to this shortly, so we don't need to handle that situation here.

The **Size()** member of the **CRect** class returns the size of the rectangle stored in **m_Rect**. The **IsInPlaceActive()** function inherited from **COleClientItem** returns **TRUE** if the object is currently being edited, and **FALSE** otherwise. With a new size, we invalidate the object with its old extent, create a new extent, then invalidate the object with the new extent. We define the new extent corresponding to the new size by leaving the top left point of the rectangle in **m_Rect** in the same position and creating the bottom right point coordinates by adding the **cx** and **cy** components of **aSize** to the top left point coordinates.

Dealing with the Position of an Object in the Container

There are two members of the **CWrxContainerItem** class concerned with the position of the object in the view: **OnGetItemPosition()** and **OnChangeItemPosition**().

As we noted earlier, the function **OnGetItemPosition()** is called by the framework when it needs to know where the object is to be displayed in the document view in the container. This occurs each time an item is in-place activated. A reference to a **CRect** object is passed as an argument, in which you need to store the required information. You can do this quite simply by modifying the default implementation to correspond with the following:

```
void CWrxContainerItem::OnGetItemPosition(CRect& rPosition)
{
    ASSERT_VALID(this);

    rPosition = m_Rect;
}
```

We just set the **rPosition** variable that is passed as a parameter to the value we have in the **m_Rect** member of the object. This replaces the previous line of code . Since we update the rectangle in **m_Rect** whenever we get a change signaled by the server, this will always be the current rectangle appropriate to the object.

The **OnChangeItemPosition()** member is called when you move the embedded object in the view, when you resize the borders of the object in the view, or when the server requests that the size of the object be altered. We therefore need to change the default implementation to the following:

```
BOOL CWrxContainerItem::OnChangeItemPosition(const CRect& rectPos)
{
    ASSERT_VALID(this);

    if (!COleClientItem::OnChangeItemPosition(rectPos))
      return FALSE;

    InvalidateItem();            // Invalidate the item at the old position
    m_Rect = rectPos;            // Set the item rectangle to the new position
    InvalidateItem();            // Invalidate the item in the new position
    GetDocument()->SetModifiedFlag();    // Mark the document as changed

    return TRUE;
}
```

Since we're moving the object or altering its extent, we first invalidate it in its old position. After that, we set **m_Rect** for the object to the new extent passed in the parameter **rectPos**, and then invalidate the object in its new position. Finally, we call the **SetModifiedFlag()** member of the document to indicate that the document in the container has been changed.

Managing Multiple Embedded Objects

The container program generated by AppWizard assumes that there's only one embedded object. To manage more than one, we must add functionality to the **CWrxContainerView** class to enable a user to switch from one embedded object to another. This means keeping track of a current active object, processing a single mouse click in a view to switch to the object at the cursor position, and responding to a double mouse click by activating the object at the cursor position. The view class already contains a data member **m_pSelection** that is a pointer to an embedded item, so we can store the currently active item in this variable. AppWizard has already added statements to set this member to **NULL** in the constructor for the view class and in the **OnInitialUpdate()** member of the view, so we don't need to worry about initializing it.

Let's take a look at how we handle a single mouse click.

Selecting an Object

We need to add a handler for the **WM_LBUTTONDOWN** message to **CWrxContainerView**, so right-click on CWrxContainerView in ClassView and select Add Windows Message Handler.... Now select WM_LBUTTONDOWN in the New Windows messages/events list and click the Add and Edit button. Add code to the handler as follows:

```
void CWrxContainerView::OnLButtonDown(UINT nFlags, CPoint point)
{
    // Get address of item hit
    CWrxContainerItem* pHitItem = HitTestItems(point);
    SelectItem(pHitItem);                          // Now select the item

    if (pHitItem)      // As long as an item was selected
    {
        CRectTracker aTracker;                      // Create a tracker rectangle

        // Set the tracker rectangle to the item selected
        SetupTracker(pHitItem, &aTracker);
        UpdateWindow();                             // Get the window redrawn

        // Enable the rectangle to be resized
        // TRUE is returned from Track() if rectangle is changed
        if (aTracker.Track(this, point))
        {
            pHitItem->InvalidateItem();             // Invalidate the old item

            // Set the item rectangle to the new tracker rectangle
            pHitItem->m_Rect = aTracker.m_rect;
            // Invalidate the item with the new tracker rect
            pHitItem->InvalidateItem();
            GetDocument()->SetModifiedFlag();       // Mark document as changed
        }
    }

    CView::OnLButtonDown(nFlags, point);
}
```

The handler uses several helper functions that we will add once we've discussed how it works in general terms. The first helper function, **HitTestItems()**, is used to initialize the pointer **pHitItem**. This function iterates over all the OLE objects in the container until it finds one that has the **point** object within its bounding rectangle. The **point** object is passed to the handler as an argument and contains the current cursor position, so the item containing it will be the item the user has clicked on. Its address is returned and stored in the local pointer **pHitItem**. If no item was hit, a null pointer will be returned from **HitTestItems()**.

If the user has clicked on an embedded item, we create an object of the class **CRectTracker**. An object of this class is a rectangle called a **tracker** that can be displayed in different ways to provide visual clues to different situations. A tracker can be set to display its border as solid, dotted or hatched. The interior of the tracker can be hatched, and it can also have resize handles. You can use a **CRectTracker** object anywhere you need this kind of capability. The first thing we do with our tracker, **aTracker**, is to initialize it using the helper function **SetupTracker()**. This will set the tracker rectangle to be the same size as the rectangle stored in the embedded object pointed to by **pHitItem** and set its appearance according to the state of the object. Two examples of trackers appear in this window:

929

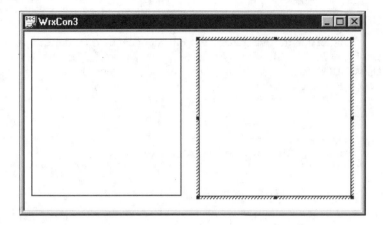

The one on the left represents an inactive object and the one on the right, with the hatched border and the resize handles, represents an active item.

After initializing the tracker, we call the **UpdateWindow()** member function of **CWrxContainerView**. This is a function that is inherited indirectly from the **CWnd** class which causes the window to be redrawn immediately and will result in the tracker being displayed.

In the succeeding **if** statement, the **Track()** member of the tracker object is called. This is quite a sophisticated function that provides for the possibility that this **WM_LBUTTONDOWN** message was triggered by the user re-sizing the border of the embedded object. The arguments are a pointer to the current window and the current cursor position, **point**. The function captures the mouse and allows the user to resize the tracker rectangle by dragging its borders. As the border is dragged, the cursor is tracked and the border updated as long as the left mouse button is held down. The **Track()** function stores the modified rectangle in the tracker object and returns **TRUE** if the tracker was re-sized, and **FALSE** otherwise.

If the tracker rectangle was changed, the current item with its old extent is invalidated to get the area it occupies redrawn. The **m_rect** member of the tracker object contains the new rectangle, which is stored in the **m_Rect** member of the embedded object. Finally, the item with the new extent is invalidated to get it redrawn.

Finding the Object Selected

The helper function **HitTestItems()** searches through the embedded items in the document to find the one the user is clicking on. You can add this function to the class by right-clicking on CWrxContainerView in the ClassView. Specify the **private** function's return type as **CWrxContainerItem***, and the name as **HitTestItems(CPoint aPoint)**. Select the OK button and enter its code as follows:

```
CWrxContainerItem* CWrxContainerView::HitTestItems(CPoint aPoint)
{
    CWrxContainerDoc* pDoc = GetDocument();
    CWrxContainerItem* pItem = 0;              // Place to store an item pointer

    // Get position of the first item
    POSITION aPosition = pDoc->GetStartPosition();
```

```
       while(aPosition)                    // Iterate over items until one is hit
       {
          pItem = (CWrxContainerItem*)pDoc->GetNextItem(aPosition);
          if (pItem->m_Rect.PtInRect(aPoint))
              return pItem;                 // Return pointer to item hit
       }
       return 0;                            // No item hit
    }
```

After getting a pointer to the document object, we create a pointer, **pItem**, to store the address of the item hit. We get a position value for the first item in the document by calling the **GetStartPosition()** member of the document object. The value returned from this function is of type **POSITION** because pointers to the items stored in the document are maintained in a list. This is used in the same way as you've seen with the lists we used in the Sketcher application. We iterate through the list of embedded objects by calling the **GetNextItem()** member of the document object.

In the loop, the **m_Rect** member of each embedded object is tested using the **PtInRect()** member of **CRect** to see whether the **aPoint** object is inside the rectangle. As soon as an object is found where this is the case, the address of the embedded object is returned. If we reach the end of the list, **aPosition** will be zero and the **while** loop will end. In this case we haven't hit an item, so we return a null pointer value. This situation arises when the user clicks on a point in the view that is outside of all the embedded objects. This might be done to deactivate the current object, for instance, so that another object can be embedded in the document.

Setting an Object as Selected

When the user clicks on an item, we must deactivate any active item and activate the new item. This is carried out by the **SelectItem()** helper function that we used in the **OnLButtonDown()** handler. You can add this function by right-clicking on CWrxContainerView in ClassView and selecting Add Member Function... from the pop-up. You can specify the return type as **void** and enter the name as **SelectItem(CWrxContainerItem* pItem)**. You can then add the code for the function as follows:

```
    void CWrxContainerView::SelectItem(CWrxContainerItem * pItem)
    {
       if (m_pSelection != 0 && m_pSelection != pItem)
          m_pSelection->Close();            // De-activate current selected item

       if (m_pSelection != pItem)           // Only update view for a new selection
       {
          if (m_pSelection)                 // Check there is an old selection
             // Update area for the old
             OnUpdate(0, HINT_UPDATE_ITEM, m_pSelection);

          m_pSelection = pItem;             // Set the current selection to the new item
          if (m_pSelection)                 // Check there is a new selection
             // Update area for the new
             OnUpdate(0, HINT_UPDATE_ITEM, m_pSelection);
       }
    }
```

The first **if** statement deactivates the currently selected object (which has its address stored in the **m_pSelection** member of the view) provided there's a current selection that's different from the new item to be selected (which has its address passed in the parameter **pItem**). Note that we won't deactivate the current item if it's the same as the new item.

The next **if** tests whether the address of the new item is different from that of the old. If they are the same, we have nothing further to do. Otherwise, we verify that the address of the current selected item is not zero before using it as the hint argument in the call to the **OnUpdate()** member of the view.

Finally, we store the address of the new embedded object in the **m_pSelection** member of the view. If *it* isn't zero, we use it as a hint in the call to the **OnUpdate()** function once more.

Setting the Tracker Style

The last helper function sets the style for the tracker which determines its appearance. You can add this function in the same way as the others by right-clicking on CWrxContainerView in ClassView. Set the return type as **void** and the name of the function as **SetupTracker(CWrxContainerItem* pItem, CRectTracker* pTracker)**. The code for the function is as follows:

```
void CWrxContainerView::SetupTracker(CWrxContainerItem* pItem,
                                          CRectTracker* pTracker)
{
   pTracker->m_rect = pItem->m_Rect;

   if (pItem == m_pSelection)                  // Check if the item is selected
      pTracker->m_nStyle |= CRectTracker::resizeInside;

   if (pItem->GetType() == OT_LINK)            // Test for linked item
      // Item is linked so dotted border
      pTracker->m_nStyle |= CRectTracker::dottedLine;
   else
      // Item is embedded so solid border
      pTracker->m_nStyle |= CRectTracker::solidLine;

   // If the item server window is open or activated in-place,
   // hatch over the item
   if (pItem->GetItemState() == COleClientItem::openState ||
                 pItem->GetItemState() == COleClientItem::activeUIState)
      pTracker->m_nStyle |= CRectTracker::hatchInside;
}
```

The **m_rect** member of the tracker object stores the rectangle representing the tracker in device coordinates. This is set up by storing the rectangle in the **m_Rect** member of the object, which has its address passed as the parameter **pItem**.

The style of the tracker object is stored in the member **m_nStyle**. This can consist of a number of different flags, so the style is set by ORing flags with **m_nStyle**. The symbols corresponding to possible values for the flags are defined in an enumeration within the definition of the **CRectTracker** class, so you must prefix them with **CRectTracker::**. The symbols defining valid flags are:

Flag	Meaning
solidLine	Specifies the border of the rectangle as solid. This is used for an embedded object that is inactive.
dottedLine	Specifies the border of the rectangle as dotted. This is used to identify a linked object. We won't be dealing with linked objects.
hatchedBorder	Specifies the border of the rectangle as hatched. This identifies an embedded object as active, with the server menus displayed in the container.
resizeInside	Specifies that resize handles appear inside the border.
resizeOutside	Specifies that resize handles appear outside the border.
hatchInside	Specifies that the interior of the rectangle is to be hatched. This is used to identify an object that can't be edited in its present state.

The first **if** statement in the **SetupTracker()** function checks whether the object indicated by **pItem** is actually the current selection. If it is, the **resizeInside** style is set to allow the border to be resized. The next **if** checks whether the item is linked by calling the **GetType()** member of the object. If it is, the flag **dottedLine** is added, otherwise we assume that it is embedded and set the **solidLine** flag. The last **if** statement checks the state of the item by calling its **GetItemState()** member. The states that are tested for reflect conditions under which the item can't be edited, so the **hatchInside** style is set.

Setting the Cursor

Although we've implemented the capability to resize an object by dragging the tracker rectangle, the user has no indication of when this is possible. We really need to ensure that the cursor representation provides a cue for this by switching its appearance to a double arrow to indicate when a border can be dragged, or to a four-way arrow showing that the object can be moved in the view, as is usual for Windows applications.

To do this, we must add a handler for the **WM_SETCURSOR** message. As long as the mouse hasn't been captured, this message is sent to the application whenever the cursor is moved. All we need to do is implement the handler to check where the cursor is in relation to the tracker for the currently selected object.

You can use the ClassView context menu to add the Windows message handler and then code it as follows:

```
BOOL CWrxContainerView::OnSetCursor(CWnd* pWnd, UINT nHitTest, UINT message)
{
    if (pWnd == this && m_pSelection)
    {
        CRectTracker aTracker;                   // Create a tracker rectangle
        SetupTracker(m_pSelection, &aTracker);   // Set the tracker style

        // Change the cursor if it is over the currently selected item
        // Check if the last hit was in the tracker rectangle
        if (aTracker.SetCursor(this, nHitTest))
            return TRUE;                          // and if so return TRUE
    }

    return CView::OnSetCursor(pWnd, nHitTest, message);
}
```

The first parameter passed to the handler is a pointer to the window that currently contains the cursor. The second parameter is a numeric value that identifies the area in the window where the cursor is. The third parameter, which we will ignore, is a mouse message number.

After verifying that the cursor is in the view window and that there is an object selected, we create a **CRectTracker** object and set its style to correspond to the state of the selected object. We then use the **SetCursor()** member of the tracker object, **aTracker**, which will take care of setting the cursor appropriately if it is over the tracker. If the cursor was not set, the **SetCursor()** function will return 0 and the message will be passed to the handler in the **CView** class to give it a chance to set the cursor.

Activating an Embedded Object

An object is activated by double-clicking it, so we need to add a handler for the **WM_LBUTTONDBLCLK** message to **CWrxContainerView**. You can use the ClassView context menu to add the Windows message handler and implement it with the following code:

```
void CWrxContainerView::OnLButtonDblClk(UINT nFlags, CPoint point)
{
    OnLButtonDown(nFlags, point);
    if (m_pSelection)
      m_pSelection->DoVerb((GetKeyState(VK_CONTROL) < 0) ?
                         OLEIVERB_OPEN:OLEIVERB_PRIMARY, this);
    CView::OnLButtonDblClk(nFlags, point);
}
```

Because the left button has been clicked, we first call the **OnLButtonDown()** handler. If **m_pSelection** is not zero, we use the pointer to call the **DoVerb()** member of the embedded item selected.

The word **verb** has been given a special meaning in the context of OLE. A **verb** specifies an action that an embedded object is to take, usually in response to some action by the user. The first argument to the **DoVerb()** function specifies a verb, which in our case is given by:

```
(GetKeyState(VK_CONTROL) < 0) ? OLEIVERB_OPEN:OLEIVERB_PRIMARY
```

This is a conditional expression which will result in the verb **OLEIVERB_OPEN** if the function **GetKeyState()** returns a negative value, and the verb **OLEIVERB_PRIMARY** if it doesn't. The **GetKeyState()** function tests the status of keys, in this case the *Ctrl* key. If the *Ctrl* key is pressed, the function will return a negative value. If you double-click with the *Ctrl* key pressed, the verb **OLEIVERB_OPEN** will be selected, otherwise the other verb will be selected.

The verb **OLEIVERB_OPEN** opens the item for editing in a separate server window, although the object will remain embedded in the container. You will see that the object in the container window will be cross-hatched, because opening the server window modifies the style of the tracker for the object to do this. The verb **OLEIVERB_PRIMARY** activates the server and makes the item available for in-place editing in the container in the normal way. The second argument to **DoVerb()** identifies the current view in the container where the double-click occurred.

Drawing Multiple Embedded Objects

To draw objects in the container document, you must extend the **OnDraw()** handler in **CWrxContainerView**. The version provided by AppWizard assumes that there is only one object. We need it to iterate over all the objects in the document and draw each of them with an appropriate tracker. Change the code to the following:

```
void CWrxContainerView::OnDraw(CDC* pDC)
{
   CWrxContainerDoc* pDoc = GetDocument();
   ASSERT_VALID(pDoc);

   // Get the first item position
   POSITION aPosition = pDoc->GetStartPosition();

   while (aPosition)                            // For each item in the list
   {
      // Get the pointer to the current item
      CWrxContainerItem* pItem =
                     (CWrxContainerItem*)pDoc->GetNextItem(aPosition);
      pItem->Draw(pDC, pItem->m_Rect);          // Now draw the item

      // Now create a suitable tracker for the item
      CRectTracker aTracker;                    // Create a tracker rectangle
      SetupTracker(pItem, &aTracker);           // Set the style for current item
      aTracker.Draw(pDC);                       // Draw the tracker rectangle
   }
}
```

This is very straightforward. We iterate through all the items embedded in the document in the **while** loop, using the **GetNextItem()** function member of the document object that you saw earlier. For each item in the list, we call the **Draw()** function to get it to draw itself, passing the **m_Rect** member of the item as the second argument. This function is inherited from the base class, **COleClientItem**. We didn't implement a **Draw()** function for the **CWrxContainerItem** class; you'll remember that we saw at the beginning of this chapter that the server, not the container, draws embedded objects.

The object will be drawn by the **OnDraw()** member of the OLE object in the server. This drawing operation will generate the picture in an internal format called a **metafile**, which is a way of storing all the function calls you make to draw the image to produce a device-independent representation of the image. This can then be replayed in a specific device context. The **Draw()** function member of **COleClientItem** will access the metafile generated by the server and display it in the device context here.

After drawing an item, we create a tracker with a style based on the state of the current item and get it to draw itself by calling its **Draw()** member. Each time a tracker needs to be displayed for an item, we can just generate a new one because it's only a visual aid to interaction. It doesn't need to be permanently saved with the item.

We have no local data in the container document. If the container application has its own document data, you would need to display that in the **OnDraw()** function as well.

Dealing with Object Insertion

AppWizard already provided the mechanism for handling the insertion of a new object into the container. This is in the implementation of the handler **OnInsertObject()** in the **CWrxContainerView** class. We can make two additions to improve it a little, though. We'll add code to update the rectangle for a new object to that corresponding to the size from the server, and replace the default code that redraws all the views in the container with code that only redraws the area occupied by the new object:

```
void CWrxContainerView::OnInsertObject()
{
    // Invoke the standard Insert Object dialog box to obtain information
    //  for new CWrxContainerItem object.
    COleInsertDialog dlg;
    if (dlg.DoModal() != IDOK)
      return;

    BeginWaitCursor();

    CWrxContainerItem* pItem = NULL;
    TRY
    {
        // Create new item connected to this document.
        CWrxContainerDoc* pDoc = GetDocument();
        ASSERT_VALID(pDoc);
        pItem = new CWrxContainerItem(pDoc);
        ASSERT_VALID(pItem);

        // Initialize the item from the dialog data.
        if (!dlg.CreateItem(pItem))
            AfxThrowMemoryException();          // any exception will do
        ASSERT_VALID(pItem);

        pItem->UpdateLink();                    // Update the item display
        pItem->GetServerSize();                 // Update the item size

        // If item created from class list (not from file) then launch
        //  the server to edit the item.
        if (dlg.GetSelectionType() == COleInsertDialog::createNewItem)
            pItem->DoVerb(OLEIVERB_SHOW, this);

        ASSERT_VALID(pItem);

        // As an arbitrary user interface design, this sets the selection
        //  to the last item inserted.

        // TODO: reimplement selection as appropriate for your application
        SelectItem(pItem);                      // Select last inserted item
        pItem->InvalidateItem();                // then invalidate the item
    }
    CATCH(CException, e)
    {
        if (pItem != NULL)
        {
            ASSERT_VALID(pItem);
            pItem->Delete();
        }
    }
```

```
        AfxMessageBox(IDP_FAILED_TO_CREATE);
    }
    END_CATCH

    EndWaitCursor();
}
```

In the **TRY** block, the default code creates a new **CWrxContainerItem** object associated with the document and stores its address in **pItem**. This is then initialized to the new embedded object through the **CreateItem()** member of the dialog object **dlg**, which manages the selection of the type of object to be embedded. As long as everything works OK, the first two lines of code we've added are executed. The call to the **UpdateLink()** member of the new **CWrxContainerItem** object causes the contents of the embedded object to be drawn. We then call our **SetServerSize()** helper function to update the size to that required for the server.

The next **if** statement in the default code checks for a new embedded item being created, rather than one being loaded from a file. If·it's a new item, it executes the **DoVerb()** member of the object to open it for editing. Our new code follows, which calls our **SelectItem()** function to select the new item and causes the area occupied by the new object to be redrawn. These lines replace the two default lines which set **m_pSelection** and called **UpdateAllViews()**.

Trying Out the OLE Container

The container is ready to run. You can build it in the normal way and, if you haven't made any typos, it should execute. You may well have applications installed on your system which are OLE servers, in which case you'll see a list of them when you select the Edit | Insert New Object... menu option:

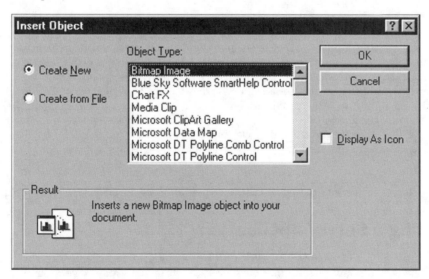

This shows some of the OLE servers that are around in my system. If you want to load a file, you should check the radio button Create from File on the left. Of course, you can add more than one embedded object, as shown in the following screen:

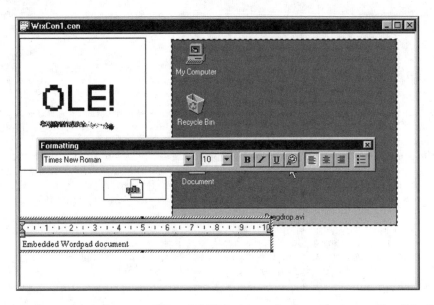

Here you can see inactive bitmap, AVI and MIDI objects, and an in-place active WordPad document towards the bottom. The Formatting toolbar shown here is supplied by the WordPad server application.

Implementing an OLE Server

It would be nice to have the Sketcher application working as a server. If we had chosen the options in AppWizard at the beginning, we would have the basics built in now, but that would have meant carrying a lot of excess baggage around in the early stages, which we really didn't want. However, we can quite quickly reconstruct a skeleton version of Sketcher to act as a full server. For this exercise, we'll just add the bare bones drawing capability that we had in the early versions of Sketcher, plus serialization of the document object. We'll go through the code that you need to add to the AppWizard-generated base program, but you should be able to steal a lot of it from versions of Sketcher that you have already. Of course, if you want to, you can add any of the other functionality that we implemented in earlier chapters, but here we'll just discuss the minimum we need to get an operational server going that we can exercise in our container.

The first step is to recreate the basic Sketcher application as an OLE server using AppWizard.

Generating a Server Application

Create a new project of type MFCAppWizard (exe) and call it Sketcher. Make sure that it's in a different folder from any of the other versions of Sketcher you may have around. The process is almost identical to the one we used to generate the program in the first instance — it should be an MDI application, and the only differences from the default options are in Step 3 and Step 4. In Step 3, make sure that you select the Full-server option as the type of application. In Step 4, select the Advanced button to bring up the Advanced Options dialog, then set the entries as you see here:

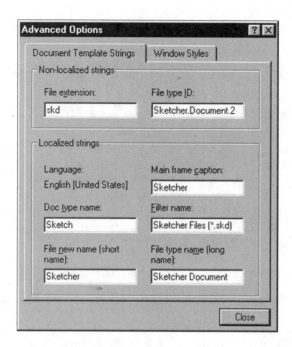

You can see that we have used a different File extension and File type ID for this version of the Sketcher application. Once this information has been filled in, you can click Close and then Finish to create the new project. You may find that you get the following message displayed, in which case, you should click No to ensure that a unique ID is used for your documents.

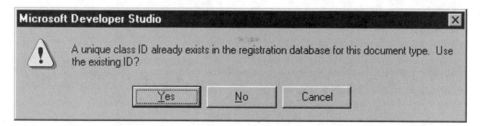

Adding Sketcher Application Functionality

The first step to recreating Sketcher is to copy the **Elements.h**, **Elements.cpp** and **OurConstants.h** files from an earlier version of Sketcher to the folder containing the current version. Make sure that it's a version containing serialization of the elements; the one you had at the end of Chapter 18 will do nicely. Then, add the **Elements.cpp** file to the current project by using the Project | Add To Project | Files... menu option.

We'll attempt to keep the code simple in this version of Sketcher, so we won't implement scrolling, text, different pen widths or the context menu. The only change that you'll need to make to the elements as we used them in Chapter 18 is to remove the **PenWidth** parameter from the constructors, both in the class definitions and in the implementations, and set the **m_Pen** member to 1 in each element constructor. The easiest way to do this is to search for '**PenWidth**' in both the **Elements.h** and **Elements.cpp** files (using the Edit | Find... menu item), and delete any occurences of '**, const int PenWidth**' that you find as a result of this search. Once that's done, go back to the **.cpp** file and replace all remaining occurrences of **PenWidth** with **1**.

You can now follow what should be a well-trodden path to add the basic drawing functionality to the project. You can do it in the following steps:

Document Data and Interface Functions

Add the **protected** data members to the **CSketcherDoc** class:

```
WORD m_Element;
COLORREF m_Color;
CSize m_DocSize;
```

To do this, you can right-click on the class name in ClassView, or just copy the code from an earlier implementation. The third data item is a record of the document size, which we'll use extensively when Sketcher is operating as an OLE server.

Next, you can add the **protected** data member for storing the list of elements:

```
CTypedPtrList<CObList, CElement*> m_ElementList;   // Element list
```

Note that you have to add this explicitly, and that you must remember to add an **#include** for **afxtempl.h** to **StdAfx.h**. (Put it after the **#include** for **afxole.h**).

The first three data members must be initialized in the constructor for the document:

```
CSketcherDoc::CSketcherDoc()
{
   // Use OLE compound files
   EnableCompoundFile();

   // TODO: add one-time construction code here
   m_Element = LINE;                      // Set initial element type
   m_Color = BLACK;                       // Set initial drawing color
   m_DocSize = CSize(200,200);            // Set document size
}
```

Because we refer to the constants that we've defined for the element types and colors, you must add a **#include** directive for **OurConstants.h** to the beginning of **SketcherDoc.cpp**. We must also remember to clean up the **m_ElementList** object in the destructor for the document:

```
CSketcherDoc::~CSketcherDoc()
{
   // Get the position at the head of the list
   POSITION aPosition = m_ElementList.GetHeadPosition();

   // Now delete the element pointed to by each list entry
   while (aPosition)
      delete m_ElementList.GetNext(aPosition);

   m_ElementList.RemoveAll();                  // Finally delete all pointers
}
```

You can copy the **public** interface functions for the document class directly from the Chapter 18 version of Sketcher. The ones that you need are:

```
WORD GetElementType() const                // Get the element type
{ return m_Element; }

COLORREF GetElementColor() const           // Get the element color
{ return m_Color; }

void AddElement(CElement* pElement)         // Add an element to the list
{ m_ElementList.AddTail(pElement); }

POSITION GetListHeadPosition() const        // Return list head POSITION value
{ return m_ElementList.GetHeadPosition(); }

CElement* GetNext(POSITION& aPos) const     // Return current element pointer
{ return m_ElementList.GetNext(aPos); }

CSize GetDocSize() const                    // Retrieve the document size
{ return m_DocSize; }
```

Because we refer to the **CElement** class here, you should add an **#include** statement for **Elements.h** to the **SketcherDoc.h** file.

You also need to implement the **Serialize()** member of the document:

```
void CSketcherDoc::Serialize(CArchive& ar)
{
    m_ElementList.Serialize(ar);           // Serialize the element list
    if (ar.IsStoring())
    {
        ar << m_Color                      // Store the current color
           << m_Element                    // the current element type,
           << m_DocSize;                   // and the document size
    }
    else
    {
        ar >> m_Color                      // Retrieve the current color
           >> m_Element                    // the current element type,
           >> m_DocSize;                   // and the document size
    }
}
```

The reason that you need serialization implemented for your server is that, when an embedded object is deactivated, the framework uses it to save the document. When you reactivate the object, it is restored using serialization. This is necessary because your server may be servicing several embedded objects at one time.

Adding the Menus

Now you need to add the Element and Color menus that we had in earlier versions of Sketcher (Chapter 14 and later). You should add them to the **IDR_SKETCHTYPE** menu, just as we did before. You'll see that this version of Sketcher contains a couple of menu resources in addition to **IDR_SKETCHTYPE** and **IDR_MAINFRAME** which are for use when the program is operating as a server, but ignore these for now — we'll get to them later. For each menu item, use the same IDs and captions that we used before.

There is a shortcut you can use here to transfer your menus across from a previous version of Sketcher. First, close all the open windows in Developer Studio, then open the **.rc** file for the menu you want to copy. Double-click on the **IDR_SKETCHTYPE** menu resource for the newly opened file to display the menu. Open **IDR_SKETCHTYPE** for the current project, then use the Window | Tile Horizontally to view both menus simultaneously. You can copy the menu items that you want by dragging them with the mouse while holding down the *Ctrl* key.

Now you should add the COMMAND and UPDATE_COMMAND_UI handlers for each menu item to the **CSketcherDoc** class, exactly as you did way back in Chapter 14. You can use ClassWizard to add these handlers, then copy the code for the command handlers (**OnColorBlack()**, etc.) and update handlers (**OnUpdateColorBlack()**, etc.) from an earlier version of Sketcher into the current one, or you can just enter the code — the functions are very simple. The typical command handler for an element is:

```
void CSketcherDoc::OnElementLine()
{
    // TODO: Add your command handler code here
    m_Element = LINE;                    // Set element type as a line
}
```

A typical update command handler is:

```
void CSketcherDoc::OnUpdateElementLine(CCmdUI* pCmdUI)
{
    // TODO: Add your command update UI handler code here
    // Set Checked if the current element is a line
    pCmdUI->SetCheck(m_Element==LINE);
}
```

All the command and command update handlers are of a similar form.

Adding the Toolbar Buttons

You can also add the toolbar buttons for the menu items exactly as before. All you need are the buttons for the four element types and the four colors. You add these to the toolbar **IDR_MAINFRAME** and set the IDs to the same as those for the corresponding menu item.

If you like, you can also take a shortcut to this process. In the same way that you did for the menus, display the current project **IDR_MAINFRAME** toolbar and one containing the toolbar buttons you need — any version of Sketcher from the end of Chapter 14 onwards will be OK. You can then drag toolbar buttons from one toolbar to the other by holding down the *Ctrl* key. You only need the four buttons for colors and the four for element types.

Adding the View Application Functionality

The **protected** data items you need in the **CSketcherView** class definition are:

```
CPoint m_FirstPoint;         // First point recorded for an element
CPoint m_SecondPoint;        // Second point recorded for an element
CElement* m_pTempElement;    // Pointer to temporary element
```

Since the class definition uses the **CElement** class, we ought to add an **#include** statement for **Elements.h** to **SketcherView.h**.

The data members must be initialized in the constructor, so add the code to the constructor implementation to do this:

```
CSketcherView::CSketcherView()
{
    m_FirstPoint = CPoint(0,0);          // Set 1st recorded point to 0,0
    m_SecondPoint = CPoint(0,0);         // Set 2nd recorded point to 0,0
    m_pTempElement = 0;                  // Set temporary element pointer to 0
}
```

The only message handling functions you need to add to the view class at this point are the handlers for **WM_LBUTTONDOWN**, **WM_LBUTTONUP** and **WM_MOUSEMOVE**. Add these as before by using ClassWizard or the context menu from ClassView.

You can use simple implementations of the handlers, similar to those from Chapter 16 without the context menu support, but with the proper conversion from client coordinates to logical coordinates. The handler for **WM_LBUTTONDOWN** is:

```
void CSketcherView::OnLButtonDown(UINT nFlags, CPoint point)
{
    CClientDC aDC(this);                 // Create a device context
    OnPrepareDC(&aDC);                   // Prepare the device context
    aDC.DPtoLP(&point);                  // Convert point to Logical
    m_FirstPoint = point;                // Record the cursor position
    SetCapture();                        // Capture subsequent mouse messages
}
```

The implementation of the handler for **WM_LBUTTONUP** messages will be:

```
void CSketcherView::OnLButtonUp(UINT nFlags, CPoint point)
{
    CSketcherDoc* pDoc = GetDocument();        // Get the document pointer

    if (this == GetCapture())
        ReleaseCapture();                       // Stop capturing mouse messages

    // If there is an element, add it to the document
    if (m_pTempElement)
    {
        pDoc->AddElement(m_pTempElement);       // Add the element

        // Tell the other views about it
        pDoc->UpdateAllViews(0, 0, m_pTempElement);
        m_pTempElement = 0;                     // Reset the element pointer
    }
}
```

Finally, the code for the **WM_MOUSEMOVE** handler will be:

```
void CSketcherView::OnMouseMove(UINT nFlags, CPoint point)
{
    // Define a Device Context object for the view
    CClientDC aDC(this);
    OnPrepareDC(&aDC);                          // Prepare the device context
```

```
      if ((nFlags & MK_LBUTTON) && (this == GetCapture()))
      {
        aDC.DPtoLP(&point);                     // Convert point to logical
        m_SecondPoint = point;                  // Save the current cursor position

        if(m_pTempElement)
        {
          if(CURVE == GetDocument()->GetElementType())       // Is it a curve?
          {  // We are drawing a curve
             // so add a segment to the existing curve
             ((CCurve*)m_pTempElement)->AddSegment(m_SecondPoint);
             m_pTempElement->Draw(&aDC);                      // Now draw it
             return;                                          // We are done
          }

          aDC.SetROP2(R2_NOTXORPEN);                          // Set drawing mode

          // Redraw the old element so it disappears from the view
          m_pTempElement->Draw(&aDC);
          delete m_pTempElement;                  // Delete the old element
          m_pTempElement = 0;                     // Reset the pointer to 0
        }

        // Create a temporary element of the type and color that
        // is recorded in the document object, and draw it
        m_pTempElement = CreateElement();         // Create a new element
        m_pTempElement->Draw(&aDC);               // Draw the element
      }
    }
```

All of this should be quite familiar to you now, so these additions shouldn't take very long. We also need the **CreateElement()** function to create elements on the heap. Add a **protected** declaration for this function to the view class and implement it as:

```
CElement* CSketcherView::CreateElement()
{
   // Get a pointer to the document for this view
   CSketcherDoc* pDoc = GetDocument();
   ASSERT_VALID(pDoc);                      // Verify the pointer is good

   // Now select the element using the type stored in the document
   switch (pDoc->GetElementType())
   {
     case RECTANGLE:
       return new CRectangle(m_FirstPoint, m_SecondPoint,
                      pDoc->GetElementColor());
     case CIRCLE:
       return new CCircle(m_FirstPoint, m_SecondPoint,
                      pDoc->GetElementColor());
     case CURVE:
       return new CCurve(m_FirstPoint, m_SecondPoint,
                      pDoc->GetElementColor());
     case LINE:
       return new CLine(m_FirstPoint, m_SecondPoint,
                      pDoc->GetElementColor());
```

```
          default:                                  // Something's gone wrong
            AfxMessageBox("Bad Element code", MB_OK);
            AfxAbort();
            return NULL;
       }
   }
```

This is like the code you've seen in earlier chapters.

Drawing the Document

As you well know by now, we'll draw the document in the **OnDraw()** member of the view class. The implementation is:

```
void CSketcherView::OnDraw(CDC* pDC)
{
   CSketcherDoc* pDoc = GetDocument();
   ASSERT_VALID(pDoc);

   POSITION aPos = pDoc->GetListHeadPosition();
   CElement* pElement = 0;                     // Store for an element pointer
   while (aPos)                                // Loop while aPos is not null
   {
      pElement = pDoc->GetNext(aPos);          // Get the current element pointer
      // If the element is visible...
      if (pDC->RectVisible(pElement->GetBoundRect()))
         pElement->Draw(pDC);                  // ...draw it
   }
}
```

This is identical code to that in earlier versions of Sketcher, so you can copy it from one of those if you like.

We must add the **OnUpdate()** function to respond to the **UpdateAllViews()** call that occurs when we add an element to the document, so add this handler to **CSketcherView** using ClassWizard or the WizardBar. The implementation for it will be:

```
void CSketcherView::OnUpdate(CView* pSender, LPARAM lHint, CObject* pHint)
{
   // Invalidate the area corresponding to the element pointed to
   // if there is one, otherwise invalidate the whole client area
   if (pHint)
   {
      CClientDC aDC(this);                     // Create a device context
      OnPrepareDC(&aDC);                       // Prepare the device context

      // Get the enclosing rectangle and convert to client coordinates
      CRect aRect = static_cast<CElement*>(pHint)->GetBoundRect();
      aDC.LPtoDP(aRect);
      aRect.NormalizeRect();
      InvalidateRect(aRect);                   // Get the area redrawn
   }
   else
      InvalidateRect(0);
}
```

Once again, this is very similar to the code we've used in previous versions of Sketcher. Finally, you need to add an **#include** statement for **OurConstants.h** to **SketcherView.cpp** after the **#include** for **Sketcher.h**.

Now that you've added **OnDraw()**, **OnUpdate()**, the mouse handlers, the **CreateElement()** function and the **#include** statements, you should have a basic working version of Sketcher with the OLE server mechanism built in. You can build it and run it as a stand-alone application to check out all is well. Any omissions or errors should come out during the compilation. When it works stand-alone, you can try it out in the container.

Running Sketcher as a Server

Start the WrxContainer application and select Insert New Object... from the Edit menu. The list of OLE servers available should include Sketcher Document, if that is how you identified the file type name in Step 4 of the AppWizard dialog to create the OLE version of Sketcher. If you select this, a Sketcher object will be loaded ready for editing.

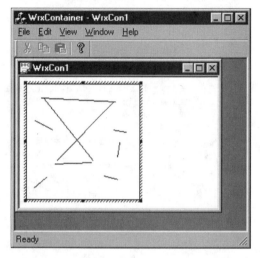

Unfortunately, we have no Sketcher menus or toolbars in the container, but at least you can draw black lines. However, there's another little problem: if you click outside the object to deactivate it, the contents of the object disappear. We clearly have a little more work to do on our server.

Server Resources

Let's go back to the Sketcher server and take a look at the menus. If you extend the Menu part of the resource tree, you'll see that there are two extra menu resources included in the server beyond the two menus that are used when Sketcher is running stand-alone. The contents of these are shown here:

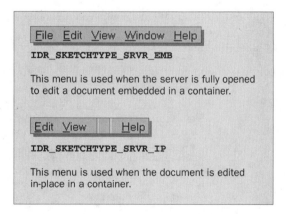

The menu corresponding to **IDR_SKETCHTYPE_SRVR_EMB** is used when you open the server to edit an object embedded in a container by double-clicking the object while holding down the *Ctrl* key. This will appear in a server window separate from the container, so this menu should contain all the items that appear in Sketcher when it's running stand-alone.

The **IDR_SKETCHTYPE_SRVR_IP** menu applies when you're editing an object in-place, which occurs when you just double-click on an object embedded in a container. The server menu will be merged with the menu in the container to enable you to interact with the server during editing, while still providing access to the essential container menus. The segments of the menus in the server and the container that are delineated by the separators will be merged in a predetermined sequence, as we shall see.

If you extend the Toolbar resources in the ResourceView, you'll see that there's also an extra toolbar with the ID **IDR_SKETCHTYPE_SRVR_IP**. This will replace the container's toolbar when you're editing an object in-place. We can copy the menu and toolbar resources that we need in the extra menus from the **IDR_SKETCHTYPE** menu and the **IDR_MAINFRAME** toolbar in the project.

Updating Menu Resources

The first step is to arrange to display the **IDR_SKETCHTYPE** and **IDR_SKETCHTYPE_SRVR_EMB** menus together. The easiest way to do this is to close all the windows in the project, then, with ResourceView displayed in the Project Window, extend the Menu resource tree and double-click on **IDR_SKETCHTYPE** and **IDR_SKETCHTYPE_SRVR_EMB** to open both windows. Finally, select Tile Horizontally from the Window menu.

You can now simply copy each menu that you need in turn from **IDR_SKETCHTYPE** to **IDR_SKETCHTYPE_SRVR_EMB** by dragging it with *Ctrl* held down as we did before. You need to copy the Color and Element menus. That completes the **IDR_SKETCHTYPE_SRVR_EMB** menu, so you can save it. All the links to the handlers for the menu items are already in place because they are the ones that are used normally.

After saving **IDR_SKETCHTYPE_SRVR_EMB**, you can close the window for this menu and open the menu **IDR_SKETCHTYPE_SRVR_IP**. Select Window | Tile Horizontally so that this menu and **IDR_SKETCHTYPE** are both visible. You can then copy the Element and Color menu items from **IDR_SKETCHTYPE** to **IDR_SKETCHTYPE_SRVR_IP**. The new menu should look like this:

The combined menu is now in a state where it will merge with the container menu to provide a composite menu in the container application for in-place editing of a Sketcher object.

How Container and Server Menus are Merged

If we assume the context of the container that we created earlier in this chapter, the menu for our server will be merged into the container's menu, as shown here:

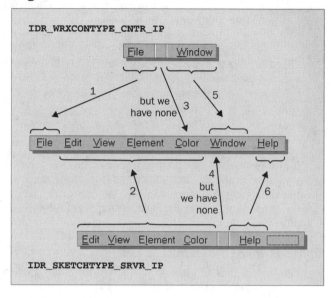

The diagram shows the composite menu in the center that is produced in the container by merging the menus from the container and the server. The numbers on the arrows indicate the sequence in which segments of the two menus are added to form the composite menu. There's actually more scope here than we're using, as we have no items between the separators in either the server or the container. The resulting menu has the File and Window menu items from the container, since a save operation will apply to the container document with its embedded objects, and the window in which the object is displayed is owned by the container application. The application menu items and the Help menu item are contributed by the server.

Updating Toolbar Resources

You need to open both toolbars in the current project corresponding to the IDs **IDR_MAINFRAME** and **IDR_SKETCHTYPE_SRVR_IP** in the same way that you opened the menus previously. Then modify the toolbar with the ID **IDR_SKETCHTYPE_SRVR_IP** as shown here:

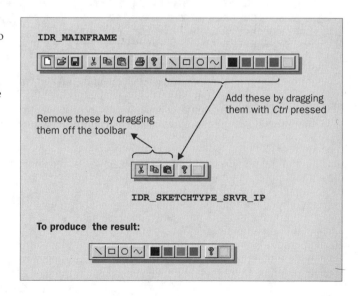

As we saw earlier, you can copy toolbar buttons using the same mechanism that you used for copying menu items. Just drag each button while holding down the *Ctrl* key. We need to remove the buttons indicated because these apply to server editing operations and, in the container context, the container operations will apply. We haven't implemented these functions in Sketcher anyway.

That completes updating the resources for the Sketcher project. Now would be a good time to save the resources if you haven't done so already. You can build Sketcher at this point to see how menu merging works out. If you run the container application and insert an object of the latest version of the Sketcher server, you should get something like the next screen:

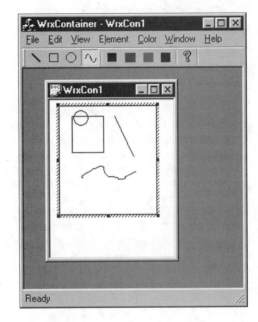

All the menus and toolbar buttons from Sketcher should work OK. You can draw any of the elements in any color. The problem of the picture not staying around when the object is deactivated remains, but we're getting there.

Adding Server Functionality

As we discussed earlier on in this chapter, a server object is an instance of the class **COleServerItem** in the server application. It's this object that's responsible for drawing the embedded item when it isn't active. In Sketcher, AppWizard has provided the class **CSketcherSrvrItem**, which is derived from **COleServerItem**, so this class represents the embedded object in Sketcher. Whenever the embedded object is being edited, the drawing is being done by the **OnDraw()** function in **CSketcherView** and is being transferred to the container to be displayed. When the embedded object isn't active, the container is asking the **CSketcherSrvrItem** object to draw it, but we haven't provided the capability to do this. This is what we need to do now.

Implementing the Embedded Object

A **CSketcherSrvrItem** object has two essential jobs to do. It must draw the object when the object is embedded but isn't being edited in-place, and it must be able to supply the extent of the document when requested by the framework on behalf of the container. Drawing is done by the **OnDraw()** member of the **CSketcherSrvrItem** class and the document extent is supplied by the **OnGetExtent()** member.

Scaleable Mapping Modes

There are some complications arising from Sketcher being a server. We can no longer draw the document in the same way as before. You already know that there are two places in the Sketcher program where an embedded document will be drawn: in the **OnDraw()** function in the view object when it's being edited, and in the **OnDraw()** function of the **CSketcherSrvrItem** object when it isn't. Further complications arise because we'll be drawing the embedded document in a rectangle within a view of a container. This rectangle is inevitably small. After all, the whole point of embedding objects is that they should coexist with other objects. It may also be moved about and varied in size, so we need to use a flexible mapping mode.

There are two mapping modes that allow the mapping between logical coordinates and device coordinates to be altered: **MM_ISOTROPIC** and **MM_ANISOTROPIC**. We discussed these mapping modes back in Chapter 17, but it won't hurt to go over things again. The **MM_ISOTROPIC** mapping mode has the property that Windows will force the scaling factor to be the same for both the x and y axes, which has the advantage that your circles will always be circles, but you can't map a document to fit into a rectangle of a different shape — you will always leave part of the rectangle empty. **MM_ANISOTROPIC**, on the other hand, permits scaling of each axis independently, so that you can map an object to fit exactly into a rectangle of any shape, but, of course, shapes will deform in the process. Because it's the more flexible, we will use **MM_ANISOTROPIC** in our server version of Sketcher. This is necessary in the view class, as well as in the class representing the embedded object.

You'll remember that we saw the following equations which express device coordinates in terms of logical coordinates:

$$xDevice = (xLogical - xWindowOrg) * \frac{xViewPortExt}{xWindowExt} + xViewPortOrg$$

$$yDevice = (yLogical - yWindowOrg) * \frac{yViewPortExt}{yWindowExt} + yViewPortOrg$$

With a bit of algebraic juggling, you'll see that the conversion from device coordinates to logical coordinates will use the formulae:

$$xLogical = (xDevice - xViewPortOrg) * \frac{xWindowExt}{xViewPortExt} + xWindowOrg$$

$$yLogical = (yDevice - yViewPortOrg) * \frac{yWindowExt}{yViewPortExt} + yWindowOrg$$

With coordinate systems other than **MM_ISOTROPIC** and **MM_ANISOTROPIC**, the window extent and the viewport extent are fixed by the mapping mode, and you can't change them. Calling the functions **SetWindowExt()** or **SetViewportExt()** in the **CDC** object to change them will have no effect, although you can still move the position of (0, 0) in your logical reference frame around by calling **SetWindowOrg()** or **SetViewportOrg()**. With **MM_ISOTROPIC** and **MM_ANISOTROPIC**, you can mess everything around to your heart's content.

Updating the View

We need to adjust how the document is drawn by the view to take account of the implications of the server mode of operation. This means using a mapping mode that allows for flexibility in the way the conversion from logical to device coordinates occurs. In other words, we need to work with the **MM_ANISOTROPIC** mode. We can best do this by adding the **OnPrepareDC()** function to **CSketcherView** and setting up the mapping mode there, as we did in Chapter 17.

Changing the Mapping Mode

With the server version of Sketcher, we must define our logical units for drawing in the **MM_ANISOTROPIC** mapping mode so that Windows can determine the mapping to pixels. This is a bit more complicated than it seems at first sight, and requires a little more thought than our Chapter 17 exercise. You must take account of the scaling between the size at which you're drawing a document and the size of the document when it's displayed in the container.

The measure of this scaling between the server and the container is called a **zoom factor**. We'll use this zoom factor to provide true WYSIWYG drawing for embedded objects. If you don't adjust for the zoom factor, the size of a document object will vary depending on whether it's being edited or not. The **GetZoomFactor()** member of **COleDocument** provides a value for the zoom factor that you can use to adjust the viewport extent in the device context to get the correct mapping.

We'll set up the mapping mode and the parameters that determine how our logical coordinates are converted in the **OnPrepareDC()** function member of **CSketcherView**. Of course, you'll need to add the function to the view class using ClassWizard. Its implementation will be as follows:

```
void CSketcherView::OnPrepareDC(CDC* pDC, CPrintInfo* pInfo)
{
    CView::OnPrepareDC(pDC, pInfo);
    CSketcherDoc* pDoc = GetDocument();
    pDC->SetMapMode(MM_ANISOTROPIC);
    CSize DocSize = pDoc->GetDocSize();

    // y extent must be negative because document assumes MM_LOENGLISH
    DocSize.cy = -DocSize.cy;                    // Change sign of y
    pDC->SetWindowExt(DocSize);                  // Now set the window extent

    // Get the zoom factor for the server compared to the container
    // If the server isn't in-place active, zoom factor will be 1 to 1
    CSize SizeNum, SizeDenom;                    // Places to store zoom factors
    pDoc->GetZoomFactor(&SizeNum, &SizeDenom);

    int xLogPixels = pDC->GetDeviceCaps(LOGPIXELSX);
    int yLogPixels = pDC->GetDeviceCaps(LOGPIXELSY);

    int xExtent = (DocSize.cx * xLogPixels * SizeNum.cx) / (100*SizeDenom.cx);
    int yExtent = (DocSize.cy * yLogPixels * SizeNum.cy) / (100*SizeDenom.cy);
    pDC->SetViewportExt(xExtent, -yExtent); // Set viewport extent
}
```

Note that we add our code *after* the call to the base class function that was supplied in the default implementation. After setting the mapping mode to **MM_ANISOTROPIC**, we set the window extent to correspond to the size of the document, not forgetting that the *y* extent must be negative because we're assuming **MM_LOENGLISH** compatibility, with the origin at the top-left corner of the client area. As we saw earlier, the conversion to device coordinates is determined by the ratio of the window extent to the viewport extent, so we need to set the viewport extent to be the number of pixels that are equivalent to the window extent we've specified, adjusted for the zoom factor.

As you've seen previously, the number of pixels in a logical inch is returned by the **GetDeviceCaps()** member of the **CDC** object. By using the argument **LOGPIXELSX** we get the number of pixels in a logical inch on the x axis, and perform a similar operation for the y axis. A logical inch is a Windows invention which is an inch enlarged to make characters readable. For every 100 logical units, we want to set the viewport extent to a logical inch's worth of pixels, so the number of pixels for the viewport's x-extent, before adjustment for the zoom factor, is:

$$\frac{DocSize.cx * xLogPixels}{100}$$

The zoom factor is returned as two **CSize** values — **SizeNum** and **SizeDenom** — corresponding to the numerator and denominator in the factor respectively. The ratio of the **cx** members of these apply to the x-extent for the viewport and the ratio of the **cy** members apply to the y-extent. Thus, the x-extent, for example, is calculated by the expression:

$$\frac{DocSize.cx * xLogPixels * SizeNum.cx}{100 * SizeDenom.cx}$$

This is what we have in the code for the function above.

Drawing the Embedded Object

To draw the embedded object, we need to add code to the **OnDraw()** member of **CSketcherSrvrItem** as follows:

```
BOOL CSketcherSrvrItem::OnDraw(CDC* pDC, CSize& rSize)
{
    // Remove this if you use rSize
    UNREFERENCED_PARAMETER(rSize);

    CSketcherDoc* pDoc = GetDocument();
    ASSERT_VALID(pDoc);

    // TODO: set mapping mode and extent
    //  (The extent is usually the same as the size returned from OnGetExtent)
    pDC->SetMapMode(MM_ANISOTROPIC);
    CSize DocSize = pDoc->GetDocSize();          // Get the current document size

    DocSize.cy = -DocSize.cy;                     // Invert the y axis for MM_LOENGLISH
    pDC->SetWindowOrg(0,0);
    pDC->SetWindowExt(DocSize);

    // TODO: add drawing code here.  Optionally, fill in the HIMETRIC extent.
    //  All drawing takes place in the metafile device context (pDC).
    POSITION aPos = pDoc->GetListHeadPosition();
    CElement* pElement = 0;                       // Store for an element pointer
    while (aPos)                                  // Loop while aPos is not null
    {
        pElement = pDoc->GetNext(aPos);          // Get the current element pointer
```

```
      // If the element is visible...
      if (pDC->RectVisible(pElement->GetBoundRect()))
         pElement->Draw(pDC);                          // ...draw it
   }

      return TRUE;
   }
```

This is relatively straightforward. After setting the mapping mode, we retrieve the size of the document and use this to set the window extent. We make sure that the value for the y extent is negative. All our code in Sketcher assumes **MM_LOENGLISH** with the origin at the top-left corner of the client area. We must, therefore, specify the y extent and set the origin here to be consistent with that assumption. Note that AppWizard already supplied the statement to set the mapping mode to **MM_ANISOTROPIC**. This is the standard approach to drawing an embedded server object.

After setting up the mapping mode and the window extent, we draw the document using the same code we used in the **OnDraw()** function in the view. Drawing here is not directly to the screen. The GDI function calls that create the document image are stored in a metafile, which is a device-independent representation of the image. The viewport extent will be adjusted by the framework to map this metafile into the rectangle in the container view before the metafile is replayed to draw the document. This will result in the image being deformed if the rectangle enclosing the item in the container has been resized. If you want to prevent this, you need to include code here to do so. One possibility is to use **MM_ISOTROPIC** to force consistent scaling of the axes.

We haven't set the value of the second parameter, **rSize**, in the **OnDraw()** function. If you set this value it should be the size of the document in **MM_HIMETRIC** units. If you don't set it (we haven't here), the framework will call the **OnGetExtent()** function in the **COleServerItem** class object to get it from there. We'll implement that next.

Getting the Extent of an Embedded Object

The framework calls the **OnGetExtent()** member of the embedded object class in the server to get the size of the document that is to be displayed in the container. We need to implement this to return the size of the document object in Sketcher. The code to do this is as follows:

```
BOOL CSketcherSrvrItem::OnGetExtent(DVASPECT dwDrawAspect,
                                                CSize& rSize)
{
   // Most applications, like this one, only handle drawing the content
   //  aspect of the item.  If you wish to support other aspects, such
   //  as DVASPECT_THUMBNAIL (by overriding OnDrawEx), then this
   //  implementation of OnGetExtent should be modified to handle the
   //  additional aspect(s).

   if (dwDrawAspect != DVASPECT_CONTENT)
      return COleServerItem::OnGetExtent(dwDrawAspect, rSize);

   // CSketcherSrvrItem::OnGetExtent is called to get the extent in
   //  HIMETRIC units of the entire item.  The default implementation
   //  here simply returns a hard-coded number of units.

   CSketcherDoc* pDoc = GetDocument();
   ASSERT_VALID(pDoc);
```

```
        // TODO: replace this arbitrary size
        rSize = pDoc->GetDocSize();             // Get the document size

        CClientDC aDC(0);                       // Get device context for conversion
        aDC.SetMapMode(MM_ANISOTROPIC);         // Set map mode that is scaleable

        // Set window extent to 1 inch in each direction in MM_LOENGLISH
        aDC.SetWindowExt(100, -100);            // Set window extent with negative y

        // Set viewport extent to the number of pixels in 1 inch
        aDC.SetViewportExt(aDC.GetDeviceCaps(LOGPIXELSX),
                           aDC.GetDeviceCaps(LOGPIXELSY));

        aDC.LPtoHIMETRIC(&rSize);               // Convert document size to HIMETRIC

    return TRUE;
}
```

The comments explain what the framework expects from this function. Here, we take a simplistic approach and just retrieve the document size that is stored in the document. Ideally, the value returned should reflect the physical extent of the object to be drawn, not just the arbitrarily assigned extent for the document, but this will suffice to get our server working. The size must be returned in **HIMETRIC** units because this is the standard unit of measure set by the framework. Our document size is in **LOENGLISH** units, so we need to set up a mapping that will ensure that the logical unit in the device context is equivalent to this. We do this by setting the window extent to 100, which is the equivalent of 1 inch in each direction in **LOENGLISH** units, and then setting the viewport extent to the number of logical pixels per inch in each direction.

The number of logical pixels per inch is obtained by calling the **GetDeviceCaps()** member of the **CClientDC** object with the arguments shown. You will remember we used this in Chapter 17 when we were implementing scaling, and in Chapter 18 to get the number of points per inch for the printer. By using suitable arguments, you can use this function to get at a vast range of parameters that apply to the device context. You can get the complete list of these through the Help menu option. Finally, having set the scaling in the device context appropriately, we call the function **LPtoHIMETRIC()** to convert the document size to **HIMETRIC** units.

Add an **#include** directive for **Elements.h** to the beginning of the **SrvrItem.cpp** file because of the references to the **CElement** class in the **OnDraw()** member function.

Notifying Changes

To communicate to the framework that we've altered the document, we need to call the functions **NotifyChanged()** and **SetModifiedFlag()** whenever we do so. This is because both the container and the server need to know the document has changed. Both functions are members of the document class that is inherited from the base class, **COleDocument**.

We need to call the functions in the **WM_LBUTTONUP** handler in the view class:

```
    void CSketcherView::OnLButtonUp(UINT nFlags, CPoint point)
    {
        CSketcherDoc* pDoc = GetDocument();        // Get the document pointer

        if (this == GetCapture())
            ReleaseCapture();                       // Stop capturing mouse messages
```

```
      // If there is an element, add it to the document
      if (m_pTempElement)
      {
         pDoc->AddElement(m_pTempElement);              // Add the element
         pDoc->SetModifiedFlag();                       // Note the modification
         // Tell the other views about it
         pDoc->UpdateAllViews(0, 0, m_pTempElement);
         m_pTempElement = 0;                            // Reset the element pointer
         pDoc->NotifyChanged();                         // Tell the container...
         pDoc->SetModifiedFlag();                       // ...and the server
      }
   }
```

For the cut-down version of the Sketcher application, this is the only place where we change the document. The two new lines are highlighted in the above code.

Executing the Server

Sketcher should now be ready to run as a server. You can try it out stand-alone first, to make sure nothing has been overlooked. To run as a server, Sketcher needs to be entered in the registry, but this will be done automatically for you when you build the application.

You can run Sketcher with the container we created at the beginning of this chapter. Run the container application and select Edit | Insert New Object... from the menu. Then choose Sketcher Document from the list box in the dialog and click the OK button. You should then get an embedded Sketcher object, ready for editing.

You aren't limited to Sketcher. You can try embedding objects of other server applications. There are sure to be some on your system. Below, you can see an example of the container running with a Paintbrush object and a Sketcher object embedded:

Here, the Sketcher object is in-place active and currently being edited, as you can see from the hatched tracker border and the toolbar and menu items. You may also like to try editing an embedded object in a server window. You'll remember that you do this by double-clicking the object while you hold down the *Ctrl* key.

Summary

In this chapter, we've taken a brief look into how to implement an OLE container and a server based on AppWizard-generated base code. The significant points that we have discussed in this chapter are:

▶ A program that can host OLE objects that are maintained and edited by an independent program is called an **OLE container**. An OLE container can typically accommodate multiple embedded objects of different types.

▶ OLE objects in a container can be **linked**, in which case they are stored separately from the container document, or **embedded**, in which case they are stored within the container document.

▶ A program that can provide an object embedded in an OLE container application is called an **OLE server**. A server can also be a container.

▶ There are two kinds of server that you can create with AppWizard: a **mini-server** which can only operate in support of embedded objects, and a **full server** which can operate as a stand-alone application as well as a server.

▶ Embedded objects in a container are represented by instances of a class derived from the class **COleClientItem**. A server document that is embedded in a container is represented in the server application by an instance of a class derived from **COleServerItem**.

▶ Embedded objects are drawn in the container view by the server application. When an embedded object is being edited, it is drawn by the **OnDraw()** member of the document view object in the server, otherwise it is drawn by the **OnDraw()** member of the class derived from **COleServerItem**.

▶ An object is subjected to a scaling effect when it is displayed embedded in a container. Consequently, the server must use a mapping mode to allow the drawing operation to take account of the effect of this. This typically involves using **MM_ANISOTROPIC** as the mapping mode in the server.

Exercise

Ex22-1: Add a menu item to the Edit menu of WrxContainer that allows you to delete the selected item from the container. (Hint — look in the online documentation at the class members of **COleClientItem**. You'll find the function you need under General Operations.)

ActiveX Controls

ActiveX controls are another powerful innovation and are becoming very important in the development of applications. This chapter, therefore, ventures a few steps into the basic concepts of ActiveX controls and how they work. We'll create a simple ActiveX control example that you'll be able to exercise using the test container provided with Visual C++.

By the end of this chapter, you will have learned:

▶ What OLE controls are

▶ What ActiveX controls are

▶ What properties are and how they are used

▶ What ambient and stock properties are

▶ What methods in an ActiveX control are

▶ What events are and how they are used

▶ How to use Developer Studio to implement an ActiveX control

▶ How to add properties to a control

▶ How to add events to a control

▶ How to provide constants for use with your control

▶ How to embed an ActiveX control in a Web page

ActiveX and OLE

Perhaps the most important point to keep in mind is that OLE and ActiveX are marketing terms. Clearly, they do correspond to things in the real world, but they are subject to change over time. Marketing has always fully embraced the notion, first expressed by Humpty Dumpty, that words mean whatever you want them to mean.

The term OLE, which we discussed in the last chapter, predates ActiveX. OLE originally related just to the ability to embed a document created by one application within a document created by another. The archetypal example of this is an Excel spreadsheet embedded in a Word document. The original concept of OLE changed substantially over time and eventually spawned the notion of the Component Object Model, COM, which we outlined in the last chapter. COM transcends the original OLE concept in that it's a general interface specification for creating software components that you can connect together in virtually any context.

ActiveX is a term coined by Microsoft to identify their technologies that can be applied to the Internet. Since these, like OLE, are COM-based, there is an inevitable overlap between what OLE and ActiveX relate to, to the extent that you will find the terms used interchangeably in many contexts. For the moment there seems to be a distinction between OLE and ActiveX, although this could conceivably be eliminated completely in time. Let's explore what the terms OLE and ActiveX mean when they are applied to controls.

What Are OLE Controls?

Just like the Windows controls that we have seen in previous chapters, an OLE control is a facility for a programmer to use someone else's code. For instance, a Visual Basic programmer could use your C++ control in his code. An OLE control is often referred to as an **OCX**, because the extension to the name of the executable module for an OLE control is usually **.ocx**.

OLE controls provide a way to implement component-based software, and they achieve this by using COM as the means of communication. With the ever-increasing complexity of applications, there's a growing need to be able to assemble applications from sets of components which, although written completely independently of one another, can be slotted together as required. An OLE document server goes a little way along that path, in that an OLE container can use any OLE server that's written to conform to the OLE standard. The primary limitation of an OLE server is that it's anonymous as far as the container is concerned — the container has no knowledge of what the server does and has no real mechanism for communicating with it. An OLE control is different. It can communicate extensively with the container, so a greater degree of integration is possible between the container and the control.

What About ActiveX Controls?

You've almost certainly heard about **ActiveX controls** as part of the huge amount of discussion and interest in ActiveX, but you're probably wondering exactly what they are and how they relate to OLE controls.

An ActiveX control is defined simply as a control which meets two conditions: it must communicate with its container using the COM interface **IUnknown**, and it must be able to create its own entries in the System Registry. We mentioned in the previous chapter that every COM object must implement the interface known as **IUnknown**, so this is the minimum requirement for something to be a COM object, but many COM objects (such as OLE servers and containers) will also implement other interfaces. An ActiveX control, however, is only *required* to implement **IUnknown** to qualify. Therefore, other COM controls that may implement other interfaces are also ActiveX controls, as long as they can create their own Registry entries.

Although we didn't look beneath the MFC code to see what interfaces were necessary to implement an OLE server or container, you can rest assured that each OLE server or container is required to implement a certain set of interfaces that interact with each other in a particular way. Similarly, an OLE control must, by definition, implement a particular set of interfaces. Since

OLE document servers and OLE controls are COM objects, they must (and do) implement **IUnknown**; since they are also able to create their own Registry entries, they qualify as ActiveX controls. Thus we can say that all OLE controls are ActiveX controls, but not all ActiveX controls are OLE controls (because an ActiveX control doesn't have to implement the interfaces necessary to make it an OLE control).

It follows that anywhere you see 'OLE control' in this chapter, you can read it as 'ActiveX control'. Indeed, in the Visual C++ documentation you'll see it stated that OLE controls have been renamed ActiveX controls. We'll still use the term OLE control in this chapter because much of the current documentation, as well as the MFC class names, still uses this terminology.

A detailed discussion of ActiveX is outside the scope of this book, but we'll get far enough into how to create a control to give you a solid base for learning more. In this chapter, the ActiveX control that we'll develop will, in fact, be a full-blown OLE control that supports rather more than the minimum required for an ActiveX control. In the next chapter we'll take a look at how the **Active Template Library** (**ATL**) can be used to create an ActiveX component that's implemented rather differently from this chapter's control.

How OLE Controls Work

First and foremost, an OLE control communicates with the environment that's using it through a set of standard OLE interfaces, specific to OLE controls. The standard for OLE controls is an extension of the standard relating to OLE compound documents that we discussed in Chapter 22. You can easily reuse an OLE control in different application contexts, since a program that is to use an OLE control uses the same interfaces, regardless of what the control does.

A program that uses an OLE control is called an **OLE control container**, which implies that it supports the standard interfaces necessary to communicate with the OLE control. Obviously, an OLE control container is typically an application in its own right, which uses one or more OLE controls in its implementation. Because an OLE control uses the OLE interface, it's extremely portable, in that it can be used in any program designed to act as an OLE control container. An OLE control that you write using Visual C++ can be used in applications implemented in other programming languages, as long as they also support the standard OLE control interface.

The major advantage of an OLE control over an OLE server is its potential for integrating with its container. There are three ways in which an OLE control and its container can interact. As well as being able to accommodate the transfer of data to and from an OLE container, an OLE control supports a programmable interface through which its container can alter the behavior of the control, and the control can send messages to its container. The names for the mechanisms corresponding to these three capabilities are **properties**, **methods** and **events**. Let's take a look at what each of these involves.

Properties

Properties are variables which specify things about an OLE control. Although they have names, properties are specifically identified by integer values called **DispIDs**, which is an abbreviation for **Dispatch IDs**. In the case of **standard properties**, which are properties defined within the OLE standard, the DispIDs are negative values.

There are three kinds of property used in communications between an OLE control and its container:

▶ **Ambient properties**, which specify information about the environment provided by the container.

▶ **Control properties**, which are values determining aspects of the control and are set by the control.

▶ **Extended properties**, which are parameters that affect a control, such as the position where it is displayed, but which are set by the container.

Ambient Properties

Ambient properties are values that the container makes available to a control. A control cannot alter ambient properties, but it can use the values to provide better integration with the container. Through having access to such things as the screen's current background and foreground colors, the control can adjust its appearance to look consistent with that of the current container. More than that, a control may be displayed from various points in the code which goes to make up a container application, and the ambient properties may vary from place to place. The control can be programmed to automatically adapt to the conditions prevailing whenever it is displayed.

In order for ambient properties to be of any use, before you create a control you need to know which ambient properties are likely to be available. If you know what they are, you can incorporate code in your control to react to them. For this reason, there is a standard set of ambient properties. There are eighteen standard ambient properties defined in all, and they all have negative DispID values. MFC defines symbols for these in the **Olectl.h** file. We won't look at them all, but some of the more common ambient properties are:

Ambient Property Symbol	Purpose
BackColor	Specifies the background color, in RGB values, used by the container.
DisplayName	Specifies the name of the control for use in error messages.
Font	Specifies the font used by the container.
ForeColor	Specifies the foreground color, in RGB values, used by the container for the display of text and graphics.
ScaleUnits	Specifies the name of the coordinate units being used by container.
TextAlign	Specifies how the container would like text displayed in a control to be aligned. A value of 0 indicates general alignment, which means text left justified and numbers right justified. A value of 1 is left justified, 2 means text should be centered, 3 means right justified, and 4 is full justification.

These are the ones that you're likely to use most often, but you can get the complete set by looking at the contents of **Olectl.h**. Each of the DispIDs for these is represented by a symbol which is obtained by preceding the name in upper case with **DISPID_AMBIENT_**, so the symbol corresponding to the DispID for **ForeColor** is **DISPID_AMBIENT_FORECOLOR**. You're not obliged to do anything about any of the ambient properties when you write an OLE control, and a container isn't obliged to provide any of them, but your control will look more professional if you react to those that are available and relevant.

Control Properties

Control properties are attributes which are set by, and give information about, the control. They can be any kind of attribute that's relevant to your control, but there's a standard set of these too, corresponding to control parameters that are also of interest to a container. If (as we shall in our example) you create your control using the MFC ActiveX ControlWizard, the base class for your control will be **COleControl**. This class implements nine standard control properties, which are referred to as **stock** properties. They are:

Stock Property	Purpose
BackColor	Specifies the background color for the control in RGB values.
Appearance	Specifies whether the control appears flat (with the value **FALSE**), or has a 3D appearance (with the value **TRUE**).
BorderStyle	Determines whether a control is displayed with a border.
Font	Defines the current font for the control.
ForeColor	Specifies, in RGB values, the foreground color for the control that's used to display text and graphics.
Enabled	When this has the value **TRUE**, it indicates that the control is enabled.
HWnd	Specifies the handle of the control's main window.
Text	Value for a text box, list box, or combo box in the control.
Caption	Defines the caption for the control.

The DispIDs for these properties can be specified by symbols consisting of the name for the property in capital letters with a prefix of **DISPID_**, so the symbol for the font property is **DISPID_FONT**. These symbols are also defined in **Olectl.h**.

It's possible to arrange for a container to be notified automatically when a stock property is modified by a control. It is also possible to arrange that the control seeks permission from the container before a certain stock property is changed. You are under no obligation to implement support for any particular stock property in a control, although it makes sense to support some of the basic stock properties that relate to the control's appearance. The usual approach is to synchronize them with the corresponding ambient properties.

You'll certainly be defining non-standard properties for your control, and these are referred to as **custom properties**. Custom properties can be anything you need to provide as a means of adapting the behavior of your control.

Extended Properties

Extended properties are properties that apply to a control, but which are set by the container for the control. A control is able to access the extended properties defined by the container, but it is not usually necessary to do so. There are only four extended properties defined, with the names, **Visible**, **Parent**, **Cancel**, and **Default**. We won't dwell on these, as we won't be concerned with them in this book, but you should avoid giving your own properties names that are the same as these.

Property Pages

A **property page** is a dialog that's used to display an interface for modifying a group of properties so that the values assigned to them can be altered by the programmer.

With a complicated control, several property pages may be used, with a group of related properties being assigned to each page. A series of property pages like this is organized into a **property sheet**, which has the appearance of a tabbed dialog box. You've used such tabbed dialog boxes many times in Developer Studio, so they'll be nothing new to you.

MFC includes the class **CPropertySheet** to define a property sheet, and the class **CPropertyPage** to define individual tabbed pages within a property sheet. Each property page will use controls such as edit boxes, list boxes or radio buttons for the setting of individual property values. We'll see how to use controls on a property page to set values for properties when we come to implement an ActiveX control later in this chapter.

Methods

In this context, a method is a function in a control that can be invoked to perform some action in response to an external request. There are two stock methods defined by the **COleControl** class:

Method Name	Purpose
Refresh()	Causes the control to be redrawn.
DoClick()	Simulates the control being clicked with the left mouse button.

Of course, you can also add your own custom methods to a control that will execute when some specific action occurs. We'll be adding custom methods to an OLE control example later in this chapter.

The ability of an OLE control to react to ambient properties, and the ability of a container to call control methods which affect the operation of the control, is referred to as **Automation**, although it is not limited to OLE controls. You can, for example, implement Automation in an OLE server to provide a programmable mechanism for a container to interact with the server.

Events

Events are signals that an OLE control sends to a container as a consequence of some action by the user on the control, or when some Windows message is received by the control. A control event can have parameters associated with it that provide additional information about the event. The container needs to implement functions to service these events in an appropriate way. The most common standard OLE control events are:

Event Name	Purpose
`Click`	Occurs when a mouse button is pressed and then released over a control.
`DblClick`	Occurs when the control is double-clicked.
`KeyDown`	Occurs when a key is pressed and the control has the focus.
`KeyPress`	Occurs when a **WM_CHAR** message is received.
`KeyUp`	Occurs when a key is released and the control has the focus.
`MouseDown`	Occurs when a mouse button is pressed while the cursor is over the control.
`MouseMove`	Occurs when the cursor moves over the control.
`MouseUp`	Occurs when a mouse button is released over the control.
`Error`	Signals the container when some kind of error has occurred.

All the standard events noted above are supported by the class **COleControl**.

The Interface to an OLE Control

In order to make the properties, events and methods of a control available to a container program, there needs to be an external description of what they are. Controls developed using the MFC ActiveX ControlWizard in Developer Studio make the external description available in a **type library** file, which has the extension **.tlb**. This file is produced from the definitions of the interface elements expressed in the **Object Description Language**, or **ODL**, which is stored in a source file with the extension **.odl**. ODL is also sometimes referred to as the **Object Definition Language**.

ODL was originated with OLE as a means of defining interfaces, but in the next chapter we'll see that COM interfaces can also be defined using the Interface **Definition Language**, or **IDL** for short. The Microsoft implementation of IDL incorporates ODL, so the Microsoft IDL processor, **MIDL**, will handle either ODL or IDL. IDL is more recent and more general than ODL, and will almost certainly render ODL obsolete in time.

You don't need to worry about the detail of the object description language, since this is all taken care of by ClassWizard when you add properties and other interface elements to your control. In the **.odl** file, you will find statements that associate the DispIDs for particular control properties with the variables in the code for your control which represent them. The same applies to the DispIDs for methods in your control that you make available to a container, and the events that you implement. The appropriate entries will be added to the **.odl** file as you develop the source code for your control, and the type library file for your control will be generated automatically when you build the executable module.

Implementing an ActiveX Control

We can implement a model of a traffic signal as an ActiveX control. We'll expose properties for the period of time for which the stop or go light operates, and for the starting condition of the signal, to make it possible to change these externally.

The starting point for our example is a basic ActiveX (OLE) control that we can create using ControlWizard in Developer Studio.

Creating a Basic ActiveX Control

Create a new project and workspace with the type set to MFC ActiveX ControlWizard, as shown below:

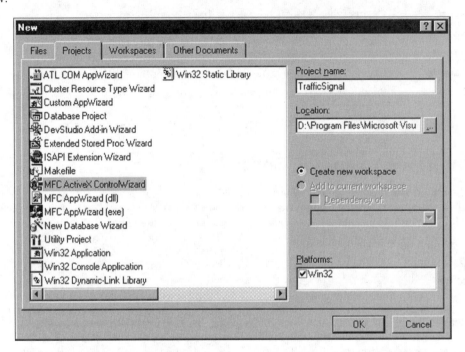

You can name the project as shown, or choose your own name if you wish. ControlWizard will use the name you supply as the name of the directory containing the project files, and as a basis for naming the classes in the project. Now click on the OK button to move to the next step.

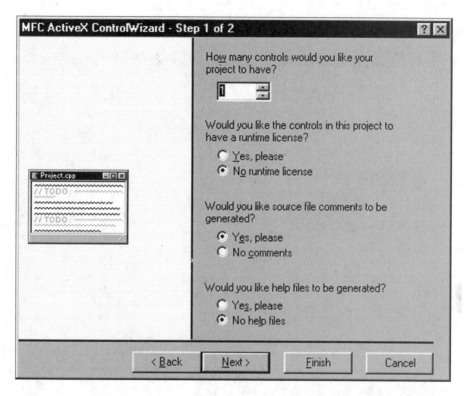

We're going to leave all these options at their default settings, but let's take a brief run-through of what they are.

The first choice allows you to specify up to 99 controls within a single project. This is in case you're developing a package of controls that will be used or distributed as a unit. Since we're just starting out, trying to get one working will provide us with enough entertainment.

Next, you have the option of including a run-time license. This is a program mechanism for controlling where your control can be used. Your control can be used in an application that is licensed — which implies that the application was developed with a suitable **.lic** license file available — but a user of the application won't be able to use your control in another context.

The last two options here hardly need explanation. It goes without saying that we want the code to be commented, and we don't want help files to be generated because we don't need the overhead of creating their contents at this point. For a production control that would be used extensively, the help files would most likely be a must.

The second and final ActiveX ControlWizard step is shown here:

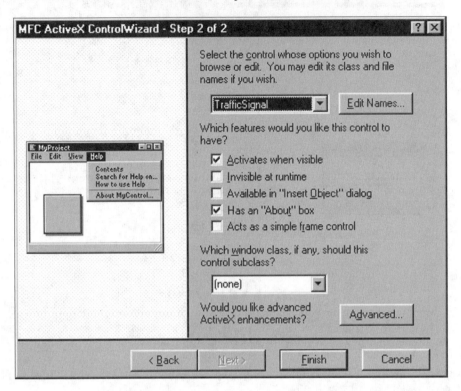

The first option allows you to change the names of files and classes relating to the project, and if you click on the Edit Names... button you can see what you can alter in our project. The Type IDs for the control and the property page classes will be entered in the registry eventually, so you need to avoid conflicts. Before the code is generated, ControlWizard will check for conflicts with the existing registry entries and let you know if there's a potential problem. If you leave everything as it is for the moment, there shouldn't be any.

The control features that are selected by the check boxes are quite straightforward. We do want our control to be activated when it's visible and we might as well have an 'About' box. If you extend the drop-down list box you'll see that you can base the control on an existing Windows control, such as a button or an edit box, but that doesn't apply in our case. The last option here, for advanced ActiveX enhancements, we'll leave unexposed and move on to accept all the default settings on this step. If you click on the Finish button, ControlWizard will go ahead and create all the files for the project.

Structure of the Program

If you look at ClassView and extend the contents, you'll see that we have a new icon used with **_DTrafficSignal** and **_DTrafficSignalEvents**. This icon indicates these are COM interface elements. The green icon used with **AboutBox()** indicates that it's an interface method. All these interface specifications appear in the **TrafficSignal.odl** file. We'll look into this in more detail later in the chapter.

There are just three classes defined: the application class **CTrafficSignalApp**, the control class **CTrafficSignalCtrl**, and the property page class **CTrafficSignalPropPage**.

The Application Class

The application class **CTrafficSignalApp** is very simple, containing just two members: the **InitInstance()** function, in which you can include any initialization code you want to add, and the **ExitInstance()** function, in which you can do any necessary clean-up when the control is terminated.

This external simplicity hides a good deal of internal sophistication. The base class for our application class is **COleControlModule** which in turn is derived from **CWinApp**, which provides all of the functionality of any other Windows application. The default version of the **InitInstance()** function calls the version in **COleControlModule**, which initializes the control.

The Control Class

The class **CTrafficSignalCtrl** is derived from the MFC class **COleControl** and provides the interface to the control container. The definition provided by ControlWizard is as follows:

```
class CTrafficSignalCtrl : public COleControl
{
   DECLARE_DYNCREATE(CTrafficSignalCtrl)

// Constructor
public:
   CTrafficSignalCtrl();
```

```
   // Overrides
      // ClassWizard generated virtual function overrides
      //{{AFX_VIRTUAL(CTrafficSignalCtrl)
      public:
      virtual void OnDraw(CDC* pdc, const CRect& rcBounds, const CRect& rcInvalid);
      virtual void DoPropExchange(CPropExchange* pPX);
      virtual void OnResetState();
      //}}AFX_VIRTUAL

   // Implementation
   protected:
      ~CTrafficSignalCtrl();

      DECLARE_OLECREATE_EX(CTrafficSignalCtrl)    // Class factory and guid
      DECLARE_OLETYPELIB(CTrafficSignalCtrl)      // GetTypeInfo
      DECLARE_PROPPAGEIDS(CTrafficSignalCtrl)     // Property page IDs
      DECLARE_OLECTLTYPE(CTrafficSignalCtrl)      // Type name and misc status

   // Message maps
      //{{AFX_MSG(CTrafficSignalCtrl)
         // NOTE - ClassWizard will add and remove member functions here.
         //     DO NOT EDIT what you see in these blocks of generated code !
      //}}AFX_MSG
      DECLARE_MESSAGE_MAP()

   // Dispatch maps
      //{{AFX_DISPATCH(CTrafficSignalCtrl)
         // NOTE - ClassWizard will add and remove member functions here.
         //     DO NOT EDIT what you see in these blocks of generated code !
      //}}AFX_DISPATCH
      DECLARE_DISPATCH_MAP()

      afx_msg void AboutBox();

   // Event maps
      //{{AFX_EVENT(CTrafficSignalCtrl)
         // NOTE - ClassWizard will add and remove member functions here.
         //     DO NOT EDIT what you see in these blocks of generated code !
      //}}AFX_EVENT
      DECLARE_EVENT_MAP()

   // Dispatch and event IDs
   public:
      enum {
      //{{AFX_DISP_ID(CTrafficSignalCtrl)
         // NOTE: ClassWizard will add and remove enumeration elements here.
         //     DO NOT EDIT what you see in these blocks of generated code !
      //}}AFX_DISP_ID
      };
};
```

You'll need to add application-specific data and function members to this class to customize the control to your requirements.

The **OnDraw()** function is called when a **WM_PAINT** message is sent to the control, so you add the drawing operations for your control to this function.

The **DoPropExchange()** member handles serialization of the properties for the control. ClassWizard will automatically extend this function for stock properties that you add, but if your control requires custom properties, you must add code to serialize these yourself. It may not be immediately obvious why you would want to serialize the properties of a control, but think about what might be involved in setting up a complicated control that you are using in a program. There could be a significant number of properties that you need to set to achieve the behavior that you want, and without serialization someone using your program would need to set every single one each time your application was executed. This could get very tedious very quickly.

The **OnResetState()** member is called by the framework when the control properties need to be set to their default values. The default implementation of this member calls the **DoPropExchange()** function to do this. If your control needs special initialization, you can add it to the **OnResetState()** member.

The group of four macros starting with **DECLARE_OLECREATE_EX()** are included by ControlWizard to set up essential mechanisms required for the operation of an ActiveX control, and we'll mention a little more about them shortly when we discuss the implementation of the class.

This class will eventually include the code to support the specifics of the interface to a container. You can see that there are three blocks at the end of the class, relating to **message maps**, **dispatch maps** and **event maps** definitions, that are maintained by ClassWizard. The message maps are the same as the ones we have seen previously in ordinary Windows programs, providing Windows message handlers for the class. The dispatch maps specify the connection between internal and external names for properties and methods which are accessible by a container. The event maps will include the specification of the class function that's responsible for firing each event that the control can send to its container. Entries in all these maps are all handled automatically by ClassWizard as and when you specify elements of the interface.

Implementation of the Control Class

The default implementation of the control class provided by ControlWizard in **TrafficSignalCtl.cpp** has the definitions of the maps we've just discussed, plus a lot of other stuff that's essential to the operation of the control. With the exception of the list of property pages, all of these are maintained by ClassWizard, so you can safely ignore their detailed contents. We'll just give the briefest indication of what they are, so that you get a basic understanding of what they do.

The maps are followed by the block that contains the list of property pages for the control. There is just one at present, but if you need to add more property pages to your control, then for each page you must add an additional line which applies the **PROPPAGEID()** macro to the property page class name. You must also increase the count of the number of property pages to correspond to the total number of property pages that you have.

The next macro in the implementation of **CTrafficSignalCtrl** is:

```
IMPLEMENT_OLECREATE_EX(CTrafficSignalCtrl,
            "TRAFFICSIGNAL.TrafficSignalCtrl.1",
            0x261d8be5, 0x6938, 0x11d0, 0xab, 0x3a,
            0, 0x20, 0xaf, 0x71, 0xe4, 0x33)
```

The purpose of this macro is to create a **class factory** for the control. A class factory is an object that has the ability to create COM objects and, in this case, the objects it will be able to create are instances of our control. Instances of our control are identified by the CLSID which is specified here in the last eleven arguments to the macro. This is a unique identifier for our control that has been generated automatically by ControlWizard. The class factory object implements another standard COM interface, known as the **IClassFactory** interface, but you need not be concerned with the detailed mechanics of this — it's all handled by the framework.

The **IMPLEMENT_OLETYPELIB()** macro which follows creates a member of the control class that's used to retrieve information about the interface to a container that's supported by the control. The detail of this is also taken care of by the framework.

We then have definitions of two global constants, which are **struct**s that define unique identifiers for the interfaces to a container supported by our control. These identifiers are used to reference the interfaces. They are followed by a global constant which defines miscellaneous characteristics of the control's behavior, and a macro which implements these characteristics.

The definition of **UpdateRegistry()** overrides the base class implementation. The purpose of this member is to cause the control to be entered in the system registry. The control cannot be used until it has been registered. Note that **UpdateRegistry()** is a member of the factory class **CTrafficSignalCtrlFactory**, not **COleControl**. It isn't obvious where the factory class is defined — there's no definition evident in the **.h** files for our control — so where does it come from? If you look back at the definition of **CTrafficSignalCtrl**, you'll see that it contains the line:

```
DECLARE_OLECREATE_EX(CTrafficSignalCtrl)   // Class factory and guid
```

DECLARE_OLECREATE_EX() is a macro that creates a factory class definition for our control class. The class name appearing between the parentheses is used in the macro to create the definition for **CTrafficSignalCtrlFactory**. This is all handled by the preprocessor and the compiler, so you never see the source code for the class definition. Because the definition that's created for the factory class is *nested* within the **CTrafficSignalCtrl** control class, its members must be referenced using fully qualified names. Hence the need for both class names being used as qualifiers when referring to **UpdateRegistry()**.

The remainder of the implementation of **CTrafficSignalCtrl** contains simple default implementations of the class members, some of which we'll extend when we customize the control to behave as we want.

The Property Page Class

The class **CTrafficSignalPropPage** implements the ability to set control properties through property pages. Each property page that is created for your control is managed by an instance of this class. The definition of this class provided by ControlWizard is:

```
class CTrafficSignalPropPage : public COlePropertyPage
{
  DECLARE_DYNCREATE(CTrafficSignalPropPage)
  DECLARE_OLECREATE_EX(CTrafficSignalPropPage)

// Constructor
public:
  CTrafficSignalPropPage();
```

```
    // Dialog Data
       //{{AFX_DATA(CTrafficSignalPropPage)
       enum { IDD = IDD_PROPPAGE_TRAFFICSIGNAL };
          // NOTE - ClassWizard will add data members here.
          //    DO NOT EDIT what you see in these blocks of generated code !
       //}}AFX_DATA

    // Implementation
    protected:
       virtual void DoDataExchange(CDataExchange* pDX);     // DDX/DDV support

    // Message maps
    protected:
       //{{AFX_MSG(CTrafficSignalPropPage)
          // NOTE - ClassWizard will add and remove member functions here.
          //    DO NOT EDIT what you see in these blocks of generated code !
       //}}AFX_MSG
       DECLARE_MESSAGE_MAP()

    };
```

The main activity supported by this class is the transfer of data that is set through a property page to update the variables that represent the properties in your ActiveX control implementation. The data is entered through controls, such as buttons and list boxes that you place on a property page, and the **DoDataExchange()** function handles the exchange of data between the controls collecting the input and the variables in the control.

Implementation of the Property Page Class

If you look in the **TrafficSignalPpg.cpp** file for the property page class, you'll see that it contains code for defining a CLSID and an implementation of the **UpdateRegistry()** member function. This is because each property page is a COM object in its own right and has its own class factory and entry in the system registry.

The class constructor doesn't contain any code at present, but ClassWizard will add code to initialize any properties that we add to the property page. Similarly, the **DoDataExchange()** function will be extended by ClassWizard when we add variables to receive the values for properties from controls on the property page.

Defining a Traffic Signal Object

We can define the basic representation of a traffic signal in a class. To add this class to the project, select New Class... from the Insert menu. Select Generic Class for the Class type and give the class the name **CTrafficSignal**. Now Change... the filenames to be used for the class to **OurTrafficSignal.h** and **OurTrafficSignal.cpp**. Finally, click OK to create the new class.

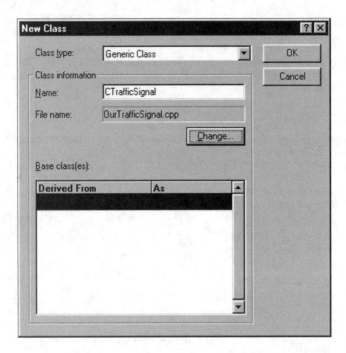

The first thing we should consider is what we want the traffic signal to do. That will give us an idea of what function members we'll need to provide a satisfactory interface to the class.

A traffic signal object will represent the signal in a particular state. The change of state will be triggered externally to the class. We'll need the ability to set the initial state of the signal and step the signal from one state to another, keeping our traffic signal object very simple.

We can build in the ability for the signal to draw itself, but it would be useful if the size of the signal could adapt to the size of the control when it's displayed. If we decide that the signal will be the same height as the control, and will be positioned in the center of it, we can pass sufficient information to a signal such that it can draw itself to fit the control with just two functions in the class interface: one to set the position of the control, the other to set the height. We can calculate a value for the width based on the height.

With these considerations in mind, we can define the traffic signal class as follows. Add the highlighted code to the new class definition in **OurTrafficSignal.h**.

```
class CTrafficSignal
{
public:
   CTrafficSignal();
   virtual ~CTrafficSignal();

   // Class interface
   void SetPosition(CPoint ptPosition)
      { m_ptPosition = ptPosition; }
   void SetHeight(int nHeight)
      { m_nHeight =nHeight; }
   void SetSignalState(int nState)
      { m_nSignalState = nState; }
```

```
      void Draw(CDC* pDC);              // Draw the traffic signal
      int NextState();                 // Change to the next state

   private:
      CPoint m_ptPosition;             // Bottom center of signal
      int m_nHeight;                   // Height of signal
      int m_nSignalState;              // State of signal
   };
```

We have five functions defining the class interface to provide the capability we've just outlined, and three **private** data members for the position of the signal, the height of the signal and the state of the signal, which will determine which light is lit. The reference point for the position is arbitrarily the center point on the bottom edge of the signal.

The only functions that we haven't defined in the class definition are the **Draw()** function which will draw the signal using the **m_ptPosition** and **m_nHeight** values, and the **NextState()** function which will change the signal to the next state in sequence by setting the value of **m_nSignalState** appropriately. All we need to complete the class is to add the definitions for these.

Implementing the NextState() Function

Before we can implement the **NextState()** function, we need to define what we mean by a state. The signal has three different states: it can be at 'stop', at 'go', or it can be at 'get-ready-to-stop'. (British signals have an extra state, 'get-ready-to-go', between stop and go, but we won't implement that.) We can define these states by a set of **const** variables that we can put in another file, so create a new source file and save it in the control project folder as **OurConstants.h**, then add the following code:

```
// Definition of constants

#if !defined(__OURCONSTANTS_H__)
#define __OURCONSTANTS_H__

const int STOP          = 101;
const int GO            = 103;
const int READY_TO_STOP = 104;

#endif // !defined(__OURCONSTANTS_H__)
```

After saving the file, you can add it to the project by right-clicking in the project window and selecting Insert File into Project from the pop-up. The file should then appear in the FileView immediately.

Now add **#include "OurConstants.h"** to the top of **OurTrafficSignal.cpp** just below all the other **#include**s, since we're going to define the **NextState()** function using these constants. Add the following code to the end of **OurTrafficSignal.cpp**.

```
// Change the signal state to the next in sequence
int CTrafficSignal::NextState()
{
   switch (m_nSignalState)
   {
      case STOP:
```

```
            m_nSignalState = GO;
            break;
        case GO:
            m_nSignalState = READY_TO_STOP;
            break;
        case READY_TO_STOP:
            m_nSignalState = STOP;
            break;
        default:
            m_nSignalState = STOP;
            AfxMessageBox("Invalid signal state");
    }
    return m_nSignalState;
}
```

This is very straightforward. The three cases in the **switch** correspond to the three possible states of the signal, and each sets the **m_nSignalState** variable to the next state in sequence. The action for the default case, which would only arise if an invalid state were set somewhere, is to arbitrarily set the signal state to **STOP** and to display a message.

Implementing the Draw() Function

To draw the signal, we need a feel for how the width is set in relation to the height, and the positioning of the lights relative to the reference point **m_ptPosition**. The dimensions determining this are shown in the diagram below:

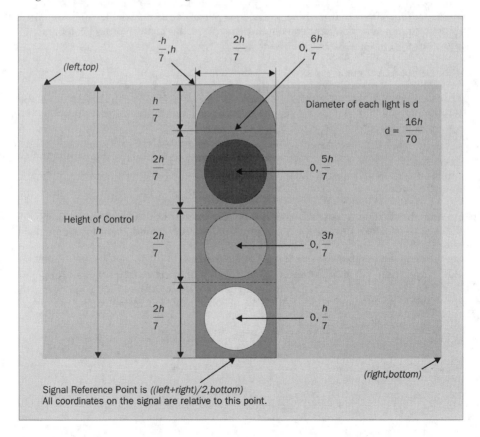

The overall height of the signal is the same as that of the control. All the other dimensions for the signal have been defined in terms of the height to produce a consistently proportioned representation of it. All the coordinates for the centers of the lights and the top semicircular section are defined relative to the reference point for the signal which is set at the center of the base. The reference point is positioned at the midpoint on the bottom edge of the control.

There are several steps to drawing the complete signal, so let's build up the code for the **Draw()** function incrementally. Using the drawing above and the coordinates of the reference point for the signal stored in the data member **m_ptPosition**, we can draw the basic outline of the signal with the following code, which you should add to the **OurTrafficSignal.cpp** file:

```
// Draw the signal
void CTrafficSignal::Draw(CDC* pDC)
{
   // Set the pen and brush to draw the signal
   CBrush* pOldBrush = (CBrush*)pDC->SelectStockObject(GRAY_BRUSH);
   CPen* pOldPen = (CPen*)pDC->SelectStockObject(BLACK_PEN);

   // Define the main body of the signal
   int nLeft = m_ptPosition.x - m_nHeight/7;
   int nTop = m_ptPosition.y - (long)m_nHeight*6L/7L;
   int nRight = m_ptPosition.x + m_nHeight/7;
   int nBottom = m_ptPosition.y;

   pDC->Rectangle(nLeft, nTop, nRight, nBottom);      // Draw the body

   // Define the semi-circular top of the signal
   CRect rect(nLeft, nTop - m_nHeight/7, nRight, nTop + m_nHeight/7);
   CPoint ptStart(nRight, nTop);
   CPoint ptEnd(nLeft, nTop);

   pDC->Chord(rect, ptStart, ptEnd);

   // Code to create brushes for the lights will go here...
   // Code to actually draw the lights will go here...

   pDC->SelectObject(pOldBrush);                      // Put the old brush back
   pDC->SelectObject(pOldPen);                        // Put the old pen back
}
```

We use the **SelectStockObject()** member of the **CDC** class to select a standard gray brush and a standard black pen into the device context, saving the old objects in each case so we can restore them when we're done. The brush is used to fill the interior of any closed shapes we draw subsequently. We need to cast the pointer returned from **SelectStockObject()** to the appropriate type, as it returns a **void*** pointer.

The next step is to calculate the coordinates of the upper left and bottom right corners of the rectangle making up the main body of the signal. We won't change the mapping mode so the default **MM_TEXT** will apply, with positive y from top to bottom, and positive x from left to right. With these coordinates, we draw a closed rectangle with the **Rectangle()** member of the **CDC** class. The interior of the rectangle will automatically be filled with the current brush color.

To draw the semicircle on the top of the signal, we calculate a **CRect** object corresponding to the coordinates of the top left and bottom right corners of the rectangle enclosing a full circle, together with the end points of the semicircular section that we want. The **Chord()** member of

CDC will draw a closed figure corresponding to the segment of the circle from **StartPt** to **EndPt** plus the chord, and fill the interior with the current brush color.

To draw the lights, we'll need to define the colors that we're going to use for them. We can add the definitions for the colors in the **OurConstants.h** file with the following code:

```
const COLORREF RED      = RGB(255, 0, 0);
const COLORREF ORANGE   = RGB(200, 100, 0);
const COLORREF GREEN    = RGB(0, 255, 0);
const COLORREF GRAY     = RGB(100, 100, 100);
```

The red, orange and green colors are the colors for the lights when they are on, and the gray color will be used for a light when it's off. If you don't like the way the colors come out, you can always mess around with the RGB values for them!

For each light, we'll need to create a brush to fill its interior depending on the state of the signal stored in **m_nSignalState**. We can do this by adding code to the **Draw()** function, as follows:

```
// Draw the signal
void CTrafficSignal::Draw(CDC* pDC)
{
    // Drawing code as before...

    // Create brushes for the lights
    CBrush brStop;                          // A brush to fill the stop light
    CBrush brReady;                         // A brush to fill the ready light
    CBrush brGo;                            // A brush to fill the go light

    switch (m_nSignalState)
    {
        case STOP:                          // Red only
            brStop.CreateSolidBrush(RED);
            brReady.CreateSolidBrush(GRAY);
            brGo.CreateSolidBrush(GRAY);
            break;
        case GO:                            // Green only
            brStop.CreateSolidBrush(GRAY);
            brReady.CreateSolidBrush(GRAY);
            brGo.CreateSolidBrush(GREEN);
            break;
        case READY_TO_STOP:                 // Orange only
            brStop.CreateSolidBrush(GRAY);
            brReady.CreateSolidBrush(ORANGE);
            brGo.CreateSolidBrush(GRAY);
            break;
        default:
            brStop.CreateSolidBrush(GRAY);
            brReady.CreateSolidBrush(GRAY);
            brGo.CreateSolidBrush(GRAY);
    }

    // Code to actually draw the lights will go here...

    pDC->SelectObject(pOldBrush);           // Get the old brush back
    pDC->SelectObject(pOldPen);             // Get the old pen back
}
```

We create a **CBrush** object for each light, which we'll use later to fill the interior of the lights. We set the color for each **CBrush** object in the **switch** by calling the **CreateSolidBrush()** member of the object. The colors are determined by the state set in **m_nSignalState**. If **m_nSignalState** doesn't contain a valid state, all the lights will be out.

With the brush colors set, we're ready to draw the three lights. We can do this by adding the following code to the **Draw()** function:

```
// Draw the signal
void CTrafficSignal::Draw(CDC* pDC)
{
    // Code to draw the outline of the signal as before...
    // Code to create brushes for the three lights as before...

    // Define the rectangle bounding the stop light
    int nMargin = (long)m_nHeight * 2L/70L;      // Ten percent of the width
    nLeft += nMargin;                            // Left side of stop light
    nTop += nMargin;                             // Top of stop light
    nRight -= nMargin;                           // Right side of stop light
    int nStep = (long)m_nHeight * 2L/7L;         // Distance between lights
    nBottom = nTop + nStep - 2 * nMargin;        // Bottom of stop light

    // Draw the stop light
    pDC->SelectObject(&brStop);
    pDC->Ellipse(nLeft, nTop, nRight, nBottom);

    // Set the position of the ready light
    nTop += nStep;
    nBottom += nStep;

    // Draw the ready light
    pDC->SelectObject(&brReady);
    pDC->Ellipse(nLeft, nTop, nRight, nBottom);

    // Set the position of the go light
    nTop += nStep;
    nBottom += nStep;

    // Draw the go light
    pDC->SelectObject(&brGo);
    pDC->Ellipse(nLeft, nTop, nRight, nBottom);

    pDC->SelectObject(pOldBrush);                // Get the old brush back
    pDC->SelectObject(pOldPen);                  // Get the old pen back
}
```

To draw the lights, we'll be using the **Ellipse()** member of the class **CDC**. This requires an enclosing rectangle for the figure to be drawn, so we need to construct the coordinates of the top left and bottom right corners of the square enclosing each light. If we construct the square enclosing the red light, we can just displace this down by the appropriate amount to draw the orange light, and again by the same amount for the green light.

The diameter of each light is 20% less than the width of the signal, so we first calculate 10% of the width and store it in the local variable **nMargin**. We'll use this value to decrease the size of the bounding rectangle for a light, all round. At this point, the coordinates stored in **nLeft** and **nTop** are the top left corner of the rectangle defining the main body of the signal. We can offset these by the value of **nMargin** to get the top left corner of the square enclosing the red light. We can obtain the *x* coordinate of the bottom right corner of the square by subtracting the value of **nMargin** from **nRight**; to get the *y* coordinate, we increment **nTop** by the value of **nStep**, which we have set to the width of the signal, and subtract twice the value of **nMargin**, that is, 20% of the width. All we then have to do to draw the red light is select the appropriate brush into the device context and use the **Ellipse()** function with the coordinates we have calculated.

Drawing the orange and green lights is simple. The orange light is the same size as the red one, just displaced in the *y* direction by the width of the signal which we've stored in **nStep**. The green light is displaced from the position of the orange light by a further distance **nStep** in the *y* direction.

Adding a Constructor

We need to add the implementation of the constructor to the file **OurTrafficSignal.cpp**. All this needs to do is to set some default values for the data members of the class:

```
CTrafficSignal::CTrafficSignal()
{
    m_ptPosition = CPoint(0, 0);        // Set arbitrary position
    m_nHeight = 1000;                   // Set arbitrary height
    m_nSignalState = STOP;              // Set initial state to STOP
}
```

All the data member values will eventually be set by the control, so the values given here are arbitrary.

Using a CTrafficSignal Object

To add a traffic signal object to the control, we need to add a **protected** member to the class **CTrafficSignalCtrl**. You can do this either by right-clicking the class name in ClassView and following the dialog after selecting Add Member Variable... from the pop-up, or by adding the following code directly to the class definition in **TrafficSignalCtl.h**:

```
protected:
    CTrafficSignal* m_pSignal;          // Pointer to a traffic signal object
```

The merit of adding the code directly is that you can organize the class definition sensibly. Adding members using the dialog can put members of the class in rather bizarre places in the class definition.

Add a line just before the beginning of the **CTrafficSignalCtrl** class definition to inform the compiler that **CTrafficSignal** is a class:

```
class CTrafficSignal;
```

We now need to create an object in the constructor, so amend the default constructor definition in the file **TrafficSignalCtl.cpp** by adding a line of code to it, as follows:

```
CTrafficSignalCtrl::CTrafficSignalCtrl()
{
    InitializeIIDs(&IID_DTrafficSignal, &IID_DTrafficSignalEvents);

    m_pSignal = new CTrafficSignal;      // Create a signal
}
```

The first line of code in the constructor that was included by ControlWizard passes information to the base class about the interface to a container. This enables properties and events that we add to the control to be properly identified. Since we create a **CTrafficSignal** object on the heap, we should arrange to delete it in the class destructor, so modify the destructor as follows:

```
CTrafficSignalCtrl::~CTrafficSignalCtrl()
{
    delete m_pSignal;                    // Delete the signal
}
```

If we now add some code to the **OnDraw()** function, we can try out the control to make sure that our traffic signal object displays as we expect it to. The default **OnDraw()** function in the control draws an ellipse, so you need to delete that code and add code to draw the traffic signal, like this:

```
void CTrafficSignalCtrl::OnDraw(
          CDC* pdc, const CRect& rcBounds, const CRect& rcInvalid)
{
    pdc->FillRect(rcBounds,
              CBrush::FromHandle((HBRUSH)GetStockObject(WHITE_BRUSH)));

    // Set the height of the signal
    m_pSignal->SetHeight(abs(rcBounds.Height()));

    // The reference point for the signal is the middle of its base
    // so set the position of the signal at the midway point
    // along the bottom of the bound rectangle
    CPoint ptPosition(((long)rcBounds.right + rcBounds.left)/2L, rcBounds.bottom);
    m_pSignal->SetPosition(ptPosition);
    m_pSignal->Draw(pdc);                // Draw the signal
}
```

The first statement in the default version fills the whole rectangle occupied by the control using a white brush. We'll be amending this later to use the background color defined by the ambient property, but for now you can leave it as it is.

The **rcBounds** parameter passed to the function defines the rectangle that the control occupies. We calculate the midpoint of the base of this rectangle and use this to set the position of the reference point in the traffic signal object. We then call the **Draw()** member of the object to get the traffic signal to draw itself.

Finally, we need to add **#include** statements to the beginning of the **TrafficSignalCtl.cpp** file for the **.h** files containing the definition of the **CTrafficSignal** class and the constants we have defined:

```
#include "OurTrafficSignal.h"
#include "OurConstants.h"
```

Testing the Control

If you build the control, it should be ready to run. It won't do much, since we haven't built in any ability to interact with a container, or to sequence the traffic signal, but at least you can verify that it looks like a traffic signal and that it re-sizes itself satisfactorily.

Of course, you need a container to exercise the control and, conveniently, Developer Studio has one available in the Tools menu. Just select the ActiveX Control Test Container option. The control needs to be in the system registry before you can use it, but if it compiled and linked OK, it will have been registered automatically.

Once the test container is running, select Edit | Insert OLE Control..., or click the seventh toolbar button on the left (the one with the 🖼 icon), to bring up a dialog displaying a list of controls that you can use. Select TrafficSignal Control from the list to get our control displayed in the container.

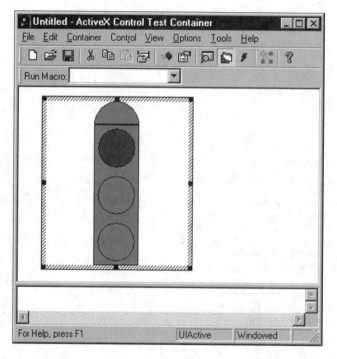

If you want to add another instance of our control, you can just click the same toolbar button again. You can resize the control and the signal should automatically alter its height and width. The hatching around the control indicates that it is currently active. You can render it inactive by clicking anywhere outside it. A single-click in the control will reactivate it again.

Now that the basic drawing code works, we should think about extending the control to add some properties and to get the signal working.

Using Stock and Ambient Properties

We can see how to introduce stock properties into our control by using the **BackColor** property as an example. You use ClassWizard to add stock properties to the control. With the control project open, select View | ClassWizard... in Developer Studio, and select the Automation tab. Make sure that **CTrafficSignalCtrl** is shown in the Class name: list box and click on the Add Property... button.

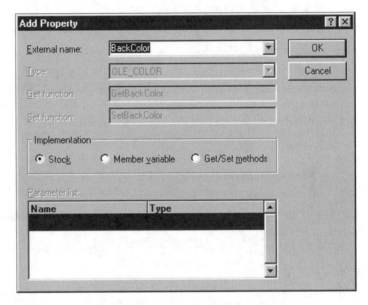

If you extend the External name: list box, you'll see a list of stock properties. When you select BackColor, the other three list boxes will be set to appropriate values and grayed to indicate that you can't change them. The Stock radio button is also selected automatically. The resulting dialog is shown below:

If you now select the OK button, you'll return to the ClassWizard dialog shown below:

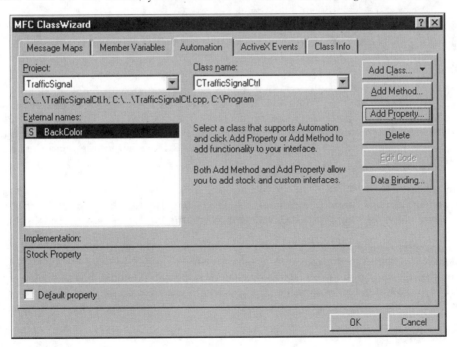

The list of External names: now includes the name BackColor. The prefix S indicates that it's a stock property. Custom properties will be prefixed with C, as you'll see when we add some a little later. If you look in the implementation file for **CTrafficSignalCtrl**, you'll see that the dispatch map has been modified by ClassWizard to become the following:

```
BEGIN_DISPATCH_MAP(CTrafficSignalCtrl, COleControl)
    //{{AFX_DISPATCH_MAP(CTrafficSignalCtrl)
    DISP_STOCKPROP_BACKCOLOR()
    //}}AFX_DISPATCH_MAP
    DISP_FUNCTION_ID(CTrafficSignalCtrl, "AboutBox", DISPID_ABOUTBOX,
                     AboutBox, VT_EMPTY, VTS_NONE)
END_DISPATCH_MAP()
```

This extra line of code ensures that the **BackColor** property is made available to the world outside our control. With this code in place, users will be able to set and retrieve the value for the **BackColor** of our control, but if we don't add any drawing code that actually makes use of this property, there would be little point in having it. We must add some code to the **OnDraw()** function so that our control actually uses the value of the **BackColor** property for its background:

```
void CTrafficSignalCtrl::OnDraw(
        CDC* pdc, const CRect& rcBounds, const CRect& rcInvalid)
{
    // Set the background using the control's BackColor property
    CBrush brBack(TranslateColor(GetBackColor()));
    pdc->FillRect(rcBounds, &brBack);           // Fill the background

    // Set the height of the signal
    m_pSignal->SetHeight(abs(rcBounds.Height()));

    // The reference point for the signal is the middle of its base
    // so set the position of the signal at the midway point
    // along the bottom of the bound rectangle
    CPoint ptPosition(((long)rcBounds.right + rcBounds.left)/2L, rcBounds.bottom);
    m_pSignal->SetPosition(ptPosition);
    m_pSignal->Draw(pdc);                       // Draw the signal
}
```

You should replace the default code that filled the background with the shaded lines of code above. The **GetBackColor()** function, which is inherited from **COleControl**, returns the color stored in the stock property in the control as type **OLE_COLOR**. The **OLE_COLOR** type defines a standard way of representing color values when they are transferred between COM objects. The **OLE_COLOR** value is converted to a **COLORREF** value (RGB value) by the **TranslateColor()** function.

There are functions defined in the **COleControl** class for each of the stock properties that you may include in your control. Examples of these are **GetForeColor()** which returns the foreground color, and **GetScaleUnits()** which returns the type of units used in the container.

The implementation for the stock property provided by **COleControl** uses the ambient **BackColor** property of the container to initialize the **BackColor** property for the control. This means that the background color of the container and control should be the same when the control is first added to the container. If the background color in the container later changes for some reason, the stock property in the container won't be updated. If you want to find out the current background color in the container, you can use the **AmbientBackColor()** function inherited from **COleControl**.

You can easily see the difference between the effects of **GetBackColor()** and **AmbientBackColor()** by trying two versions of the control in the test container. First, build the current version of the control that uses **GetBackColor()** in its drawing code. Start the Test Container by selecting it from the Tools menu. You can load the control by selecting Insert OLE Control... from the Edit menu and selecting the control from the list available in the dialog. There is also a toolbar button that you can use corresponding to this menu item.

You can change the ambient background color by selecting Ambient Properties... from the Container menu, or by selecting the tenth toolbar button from the left (with the 🔲 icon). You can choose the property that you want to set from the drop-down list box in the dialog, as shown:

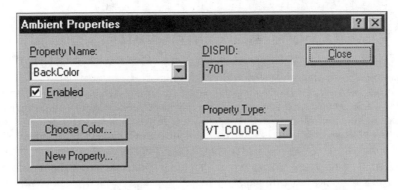

To select a color, click on the Choose Color... button in the dialog. Even though you change it, the new background color will have no effect on the control. However, if you load another instance of the control, it will use the new background color. Once you've added one instance of a control, you can add another just by clicking on the seventh toolbar button (🔲). Note that the visible background of the test container is always white, even when you change the ambient property to another color. Although most containers will keep their actual background color and the ambient background color in synch, it doesn't have to be that way.

Now let's see what happens if we use the ambient background color to draw the background of our control. Change the code in **CTrafficSignalCtrl::OnDraw()** as shown:

```
void CTrafficSignalCtrl::OnDraw(
            CDC* pdc, const CRect& rcBounds, const CRect& rcInvalid)
{
    // Set the background using the control's BackColor property
    // CBrush brBack(TranslateColor(GetBackColor()));
    // Set the background using the container's ambient BackColor property
    CBrush brBack(TranslateColor(AmbientBackColor()));

    pdc->FillRect(rcBounds, &brBack);              // Fill the background

    // Set the height of the signal
    m_pSignal->SetHeight(abs(rcBounds.Height()));

    // The reference point for the signal is the middle of its base
    // so set the position of the signal at the midway point
```

```
                  // along the bottom of the bound rectangle
            CPoint ptPosition(((long)rcBounds.right + rcBounds.left)/2L, rcBounds.bottom);
            m_pSignal->SetPosition(ptPosition);
            m_pSignal->Draw(pdc);                      // Draw the signal
      }
```

If you build the new version of the control and insert it in the Test Container, you'll see the difference in the way the background is drawn. This version of the control will always use the ambient background color, even when you change it in the test container. If you do change the ambient back color of the container, you'll need to get the control to redraw itself — by moving it, for example — in order to see it use the new color.

When you've finished experimenting with the control, comment out the line that uses **AmbientBackColor()** and uncomment the line that uses **GetBackColor()** to get back to the original scheme. Then we can look at adding custom properties to the control.

Adding Custom Properties to the Control

There are actually four different flavors of custom property that you can define for an ActiveX control. They reflect different ways in which the properties can operate:

The simplest variety of custom property is of type **DISP_PROPERTY**. This is represented by a data member of the control class and is usually made available just for information. Because the property is freely accessible, this is referred to as **direct exposure** of the property.

▶ The **DISP_PROPERTY_NOTIFY** type of property is represented by a data member of the control class, and has a function in the control class which is called if the property value is altered. This allows the control to adapt its operation to the new value for the control immediately. The notification function will typically cause the control to be redrawn.

▶ The **DISP_PROPERTY_EX** type of property is supported with functions accessible by a container both to set the value of the property and to retrieve its current value. These are usually referred to as **Get/Set** functions. This type of property is referred to as being **indirectly exposed**.

▶ The **DISP_PROPERTY_PARAM** type of property is similar to the **DISP_PROPERTY_EX** type in that it has **Get/Set** functions to manipulate it, but in addition can involve multiple parameter values stored in an array.

We'll try out custom properties by adding two to our control. One property that we might want to add is the duration of the stop or go period when the signal is running. A real signal might well operate so that the time that the signal was at red and green could vary, depending on traffic conditions. Another property could be the start-up conditions when the signal runs. Let's suppose that we'll allow it to start on either red or green. We can provide the option for the user to set this through a custom property.

Using ClassWizard to Add Custom Properties

First, we'll add the property to define which light is 'on' when the signal runs. We can make this a logical value which will make the signal start on red if the property value is **TRUE**, and green otherwise.

With the control project open, start up ClassWizard and select the Automation tab. Make sure the **CTrafficSignalCtrl** class is shown in the Class name: list box and click on the Add Property... button. You can enter **StartRed** as the External name, **m_bStartRed** as the Variable name and select **BOOL** from the Type: drop-down list box, as shown below:

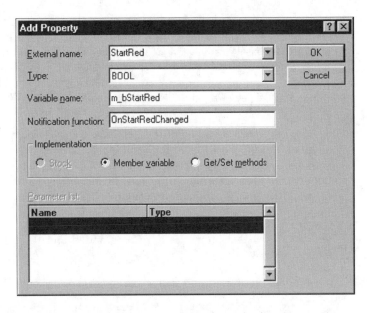

The type of the member variable for a property must be one of those from the list. You can't use your own types here. ClassWizard will generate a variable and a notification function with the names shown, so here our property is of type **DISP_PROPERTY_NOTIFY**. The Member variable radio button has also been selected by default.

You can select the OK button to close this dialog and return to the Automation tab. You'll see that the list of External names now includes StartRed, which is shown with the prefix C because it is a custom property. We can now add the second custom property which will determine the time period for stop and go conditions for the signal, so select the Add Property... button once more.

We'll make this property of type **DISP_PROPERTY_EX**, just for the experience, so select the Get/Set methods radio button. You can enter the external name as **StopOrGoTime**, and select **long** from the Type: drop-down list box. The dialog will appear as shown:

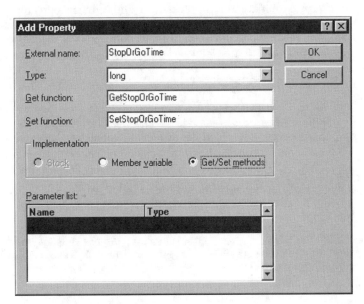

Remember that we have a diminished set of types available, so although **long** isn't the most convenient for a time interval, it will have to do. Note that there are edit boxes showing the names that ClassWizard has assigned to the **Get** and **Set** functions. You can change these if you want, but the defaults seem to be reasonable.

If you were specifying a property of type **DISP_PROPERTY_PARAM**, you would need to specify parameters to the **Get**/**Set** functions in the Parameter list: box at the bottom of the dialog.

You can select the OK button to return to the Automation tab. We now have two custom properties listed in addition to our stock property. The two functions that have been added to **CTrafficSignalCtrl** are also noted, and we could go directly to them by selecting the Edit Code button, but we're not ready to do that yet. We've finished with ClassWizard for the moment, though, so click the OK button.

If you take a look at the dispatch map in the implementation of **CTrafficSignalCtrl**, you'll see that the custom properties have been added and the types have been set based on the options we selected:

```
BEGIN_DISPATCH_MAP(CTrafficSignalCtrl, COleControl)
    //{{AFX_DISPATCH_MAP(CTrafficSignalCtrl)
    DISP_PROPERTY_NOTIFY(CTrafficSignalCtrl, "StartRed", m_bStartRed,
                       OnStartRedChanged, VT_BOOL)
    DISP_PROPERTY_EX(CTrafficSignalCtrl, "StopOrGoTime", GetStopOrGoTime,
                   SetStopOrGoTime, VT_I4)
    DISP_STOCKPROP_BACKCOLOR()
    //}}AFX_DISPATCH_MAP
    DISP_FUNCTION_ID(CTrafficSignalCtrl, "AboutBox", DISPID_ABOUTBOX,
                   AboutBox, VT_EMPTY, VTS_NONE)
END_DISPATCH_MAP()
```

Initializing Custom Properties

We need initial values to be set for both our custom properties, but the **StopOrGoTime** property has no variable defined for it. This is because the **Get**/**Set** functions are the interface between the container and the property, and you must fill in the detail. You can add a data member to the **CTrafficSignalCtrl** class definition directly by including the line:

```
long m_lStopOrGoTime;              // Duration of stop period, or go period
```

You can put this in the **protected** section since there's no reason to make it **public**. We can initialize this property and **m_bStartRed** by adding code to the **DoPropExchange()** member of the control class, which has the job of serializing properties:

```
void CTrafficSignalCtrl::DoPropExchange(CPropExchange* pPX)
{
    ExchangeVersion(pPX, MAKELONG(_wVerMinor, _wVerMajor));
    COleControl::DoPropExchange(pPX);

    // TODO: Call PX_ functions for each persistent custom property.
    PX_Bool(pPX, _T("StartRed"), m_bStartRed, TRUE);
    PX_Long(pPX, _T("StopOrGoTime"), m_lStopOrGoTime, 5000);
```

```
      // Set the signal state from the StartRed property
   if(m_bStartRed)
      m_pSignal->SetSignalState(STOP);
   else
      m_pSignal->SetSignalState(GO);
}
```

There's a global **PX_** function for each data type that can be used. They come in two versions. One version has three parameters and the other has an extra parameter; we're using the latter kind here. The parameters to the functions are, from left to right:

> A pointer to a **CPropExchange** object which determines whether the function is storing or retrieving property values.

> The external name of the property. The **_T()** macro, which is used here, takes care of converting the text if the control is used in an environment using the Unicode character set. It must be used for all literal strings that are to be transferred across the COM interface.

> A reference to the class data member that represents the property.

> A default value for the property which is used if the serialization process fails. The first time you use the control the process will fail, of course, since the properties haven't previously been saved.

The **PX_** function versions with three parameters omit the default value for the property. However, it's usually desirable to ensure that a value is set for all properties, so if you used this method, you'd need to ensure that a value was set elsewhere. Of course, on the second and subsequent times your control is used, the properties will be initialized to the values that were last set. We need the **if** statement following the **PX_** functions that import the property values because the signal state is dependent on the **StartRed** property. This sets the signal state to **STOP** if **m_bStartRed** is **TRUE**, and **GO** otherwise

By default we set **m_bStartRed** to **TRUE** and **m_lStopOrGoTime** to 5000 initially. Time intervals are measured in milliseconds, therefore we're setting the default red and green signal intervals to 5 seconds, so you need to be ready to floor the pedal!

Making the Signal Work

To get the signal running, we need three more data members in our **CTrafficSignalCtrl** class. Add the following lines to the **protected** section of the class definition:

```
   UINT m_nChangeTime;          // Duration of orange period
   BOOL m_bSignalGo;            // TRUE indicates the signal is running
   UINT m_nTimerID;             // Timer event ID
```

The first will define the duration of the transient state of the signal between red and green, the second is a flag which will be **TRUE** when the signal is running and **FALSE** when it is not, and the third is a variable identifying the timer we will use to control stepping the signal from one state to the next.

We can initialize these three members in the class constructor as follows:

```
CTrafficSignalCtrl::CTrafficSignalCtrl()
{
    InitializeIIDs(&IID_DTrafficSignal, &IID_DTrafficSignalEvents);

    m_pSignal = new CTrafficSignal;   // Create a signal
    m_bSignalGo = FALSE;              // Signal not running initially
    m_nChangeTime = 1500U;            // Change over time in milliseconds
    m_nTimerID = 10;                  // Timer ID
}
```

Initially, the signal is not running since we have set **m_bSignalGo** to **FALSE**. The change-over time is set to 1.5 seconds and the timer ID is set to an arbitrary integer value of 10.

Starting and Stopping the Signal

We need some external means of starting and stopping the signal and, for demonstration purposes, a convenient way to do this is using a mouse click. We can get it to operate like a flip-flop, so that clicking the control when the signal is not running will start it, and vice versa.

Add a handler for the **WM_LBUTTONDOWN** message to **CTrafficSignalCtrl** using ClassWizard, and implement it as follows:

```
void CTrafficSignalCtrl::OnLButtonDown(UINT nFlags, CPoint point)
{
    // If the signal is stopped, start it
    // If the signal is running, stop it
    m_bSignalGo = !m_bSignalGo;
    if (m_bSignalGo)
        StartSignal();
    else
        StopSignal();

    COleControl::OnLButtonDown(nFlags, point);
}
```

Since we want mouse clicks in the control to flip its operating state, the first action in the handler is to invert the value stored in **m_bSignalGo**. If this value is now **TRUE**, we call a member function **StartSignal()** to start the signal, and if it is **FALSE**, we invoke the function **StopSignal()** to stop the signal.

Starting the Signal

You can add the **StartSignal()** member by right-clicking the CTrafficSignalCtrl class name in ClassView and selecting Add Member Function... from the context menu. Enter the return type as **void** and the name as **StartSignal()**. The code for this **private** function will be:

```
void CTrafficSignalCtrl::StartSignal()
{
    // Setup a timer with the required interval
    m_nTimerID = SetTimer(m_nTimerID, (UINT)m_lStopOrGoTime, NULL);
    if (!m_nTimerID)
    {
        AfxMessageBox("No Timer!");
        exit(1);
```

```
    }
    InvalidateControl();                         // Get the control redrawn
}
```

We obtain a timer by calling the **SetTimer()** member of our class inherited from **CWnd**. The first argument is an ID for the timer which must be non-zero, and the second argument is the time interval we want, expressed in milliseconds as a **UINT** value. The third argument can be a pointer to a function that will be called when the time interval is up, but if it's **NULL**, as we've specified here, a **WM_TIMER** message will be sent. We'll add a handler for this in a moment.

There are a limited number of timers available, so we need to make sure that we got one. If none are available, the **SetTimer()** function returns **FALSE**, in which case we display a message and end the program. If a timer is available, **SetTimer()** returns the ID of the timer. Once we have a timer, we get the control redrawn so that it always starts with the state determined by the **StartRed** property. This will be set in the notification function for this property which we'll complete shortly.

Stopping the Signal

Add the **StopSignal()** function, which also has a **void** return type, and implement it as follows:

```
void CTrafficSignalCtrl::StopSignal()
{
    KillTimer(m_nTimerID);                       // Destroy the timer
    InvalidateControl();                         // Redraw the control
}
```

The **KillTimer()** function kills the timer event specified by the ID passed as an argument and removes any **WM_TIMER** messages that have been queued for it. The function returns **TRUE** if it finds the specified event, and **FALSE** otherwise, so it copes with a non-existent timer event without any problem. We get the control redrawn to return it to its initial state.

Handling WM_TIMER Messages

Add a handler for the **WM_TIMER** message using ClassWizard. The process is exactly the same as for any other message handler. Add code to the handler as follows:

```
void CTrafficSignalCtrl::OnTimer(UINT nIDEvent)
{
    UINT nInterval = 0;                          // Interval in milliseconds

    // Step to the next state and set the time interval
    // based on the new state
    switch (m_pSignal->NextState())
    {
        case STOP: case GO:
            nInterval = (UINT)m_lStopOrGoTime;   // Stop or Go interval
            break;
        default:
            nInterval = m_nChangeTime;           // Transient interval
    }

    InvalidateControl();                         // Redraw the signal
```

```
    // Make sure the old timer is dead
    KillTimer(m_nTimerID);

    // Set a new timer event
    m_nTimerID = SetTimer(m_nTimerID, nInterval, NULL);
    if (!m_nTimerID)
    {
        AfxMessageBox("No Timer!");
        exit(1);
    }
}
```

The signal is stepped to the next state by calling the **NextState()** member of the **CTrafficSignal** object. The new state is used to select the appropriate time interval for it. Having stored the time interval in the local variable **nInterval**, we call **InvalidateControl()** to get the signal drawn in its new state and start a new timer period.

Implementing the Notify Function for the Control

The notify function, **OnStartRedChanged()** will be called when the **StartRed** property is modified externally, so we must add code to deal with this change, as follows:

```
void CTrafficSignalCtrl::OnStartRedChanged()
{
    // Stop the signal if necessary
    if (m_bSignalGo)
    {
        m_bSignalGo = FALSE;        // Set signal not running
        StopSignal();               // Stop the signal
    }
    // Set the signal object to the appropriate state
    if (m_bStartRed)
        m_pSignal->SetSignalState(STOP);
    else
        m_pSignal->SetSignalState(GO);

    InvalidateControl();            // Get the control redrawn

    SetModifiedFlag();
}
```

Other than at initialization when the control is loaded, this is the only place the **StartRed** property change is acted upon. We need to take account of the possibility that the signal is already running when the property is changed. We first check for this and stop the signal, since we're assuming that the user changed the starting condition because it will be restarted (there would be little point in changing it otherwise). To set the signal state, we use the **SetSignalState()** member of **CTrafficSignal** with a parameter determined by the value of the property. We then call **InvalidateControl()** to get the signal drawn in its latest state.

Implementing the Property Get/Set Functions

The **Get** function for the **StopOrGoTime** property is extremely simple since all we need to do is return the current property value:

```
long CTrafficSignalCtrl::GetStopOrGoTime()
{
    return m_lStopOrGoTime;                    // Return the current interval
}
```

The **Set** function requires a little more work:

```
void CTrafficSignalCtrl::SetStopOrGoTime(long nNewValue)
{
    // Only alter the control if the value is different
    if (m_lStopOrGoTime != nNewValue)
    {
        m_lStopOrGoTime = nNewValue;           // Set the new stop or go time

        OnStartRedChanged();                   // Set the initial state
        SetModifiedFlag();
    }
}
```

The value passed to the function is the new value for the property, but we don't want to do anything drastic unless it's different from the old value. If we have a new value, we store it in the **m_lStopOrGoTime** member that we added for the purpose. We then set the signal state back to its initial starting state, according to the value of the property **StartRed**, by calling **OnStartRedChanged()**.

Using the Property Page

Now let's move on to adding some controls to the property page that ControlWizard conveniently provided for us, to allow us to modify the values of the control's custom properties. To add controls to the property page, you need to be in ResourceView. Extend the Dialog part of the resource set, and double-click on IDD_PROPPAGE_TRAFFICSIGNAL to display the property page dialog. You can remove the static text control that has been added to the dialog by selecting it and pressing the *Delete* key.

We need to add two controls to the property page corresponding to the **StartRed** property, which is Boolean, and the **StopOrGoTime** property, which is a **long** integer. The former we can handle with a check box control and for the latter we can use an edit box.

From the control palette, select a check box and place it at a suitable point on the property page. Bring up its properties and enter the text as Start with Red Light. You may also like to check the Left text check box on the Styles tab. Next, you can add a static text control and place it on the property page. Display its properties and change the text to Stop or Go Period:. Next, add an edit box to the property page and place it to the right of the static text box. Your property page should look something like this:

We've finished laying out the property page, so you can save the resource. Now we need to connect the controls that we've added to the properties in our ActiveX control.

Connecting Controls to Properties

First, we'll connect the check box to the **StartRed** property. Double-click on the check box control with the *Ctrl* key held down. You'll then see the Add Member Variable dialog box. You can complete the name for the variable to be added to the **CTrafficSignalPropPage** class as **m_bStartRed**, and the property name in the bottom list box as **StartRed**. The category and variable type boxes will already have been set as we are using a check box, so the dialog box will be as shown:

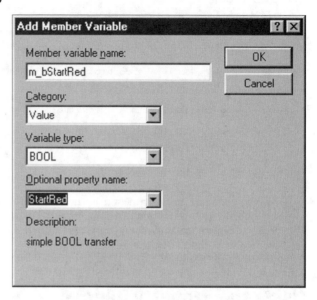

The drop-down list for property names provides stock property names for when you are adding these to a property page. You can click on the OK button to complete the addition of the data member to the class.

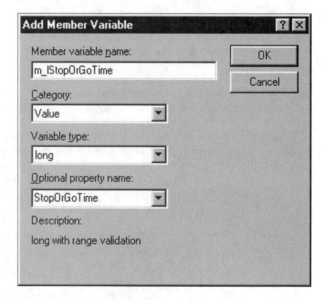

Next, you should double-click the edit box while holding the *Ctrl* key down to add the data member to receive the value of the **StopOrGoTime** property from the control. Enter the information in the dialog box as shown below:

Here you must set the Variable type: to **long** to be consistent with what we have specified previously for this value. Make sure the Category: entry is Value. As well as adding this data member, ClassWizard will make provision for range validation of the value entered, as indicated by the note at the bottom. You can click on the OK button to complete this operation and then save the property page.

In fact, ClassWizard has done rather more than just adding two data members to the **CTrafficSignalPropPage** class. It has also included initialization for them in the class constructor:

```
CTrafficSignalPropPage::CTrafficSignalPropPage() :
    COlePropertyPage(IDD, IDS_TRAFFICSIGNAL_PPG_CAPTION)
{
    //{{AFX_DATA_INIT(CTrafficSignalPropPage)
    m_bStartRed = FALSE;
    m_lStopOrGoTime = 0;
    //}}AFX_DATA_INIT
}
```

However, neither of these are good values for us, so set the initial value for **m_bStartRed** to **TRUE**, and the value for **m_lStopOrGoTime** to 5000.

The transfer of data between the controls and the variables we've added is accomplished using the **DDX** macros in the **DoPropExchange()** member of the property page class. These are exactly the same macros that we have seen used for controls in ordinary dialog boxes. ClassWizard has also added the code to do this, so the function implementation has already been created, as follows:

```
void CTrafficSignalPropPage::DoDataExchange(CDataExchange* pDX)
{
    //{{AFX_DATA_MAP(CTrafficSignalPropPage)
    DDP_Check(pDX, IDC_CHECK1, m_bStartRed, _T("StartRed") );
    DDX_Check(pDX, IDC_CHECK1, m_bStartRed);
    DDP_Text(pDX, IDC_EDIT1, m_lStopOrGoTime, _T("StopOrGoTime") );
    DDX_Text(pDX, IDC_EDIT1, m_lStopOrGoTime);
    //}}AFX_DATA_MAP
    DDP_PostProcessing(pDX);
}
```

The **DDP** macros you see here are specific to properties. They do the job of synchronizing the property values in the control with the values in the data members of the property page class, so all the updating of the property values is taken care of.

The last thing you need to do is to set the range limits for the **m_lStopOrGoTime** value. For this, you can add a **DDV** macro at the end of the block of **DDX** and **DDP** macros in the **DoDataExchange()** member, as follows:

```
void CTrafficSignalPropPage::DoDataExchange(CDataExchange* pDX)
{
    //{{AFX_DATA_MAP(CTrafficSignalPropPage)
    DDP_Check(pDX, IDC_CHECK1, m_bStartRed, _T("StartRed") );
    DDX_Check(pDX, IDC_CHECK1, m_bStartRed);
    DDP_Text(pDX, IDC_EDIT1, m_lStopOrGoTime, _T("StopOrGoTime") );
    DDX_Text(pDX, IDC_EDIT1, m_lStopOrGoTime);
    //}}AFX_DATA_MAP
```

995

```
        DDV_MinMaxUInt(pDX, m_lStopOrGoTime, 1000, 30000);
    DDP_PostProcessing(pDX);
}
```

You should add this line immediately before the **DDP_PostProcessing** macro to prevent values less than 1000 milliseconds or greater than 30000 milliseconds being accepted for the **StopOrGoTime** property. This is the same macro that's used for range checking values for controls in an ordinary dialog box.

Using the Control

You can now build the control once more, and exercise it using the test container. The window shows three instances of the control running in the container, each having a different interval set for the **StopOrGoTime** property:

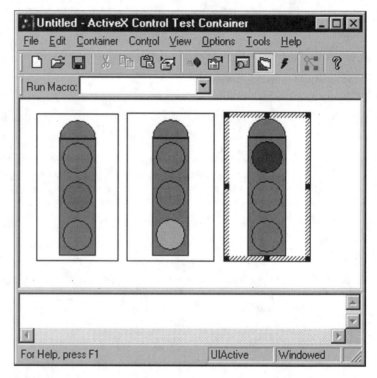

You can bring up the Properties dialog box by using the Edit | Properties... menu item. Try setting the **StopOrGoTime** outside the permitted range. Whenever you set a property value, it only applies to the control that is currently active. An instance of the control which is running will continue to run when it isn't active, so several can run simultaneously.

Adding Events to a Control

You'll recall that events are used to tell a container that something has occurred in an ActiveX control. It might conceivably be useful for a container using our traffic signal control to know when the signal has changed and to know what state the signal has changed to.

You can add events to the control using ClassWizard. Open ClassWizard and select the ActiveX Events tab. After making sure **CTrafficSignalCtrl** is the class name selected, click on the

Add Event... button. Enter the external name for the event as **SignalChanged** and add a parameter called **lNewState** of type **long**. This parameter will indicate to the container the new state of the control.

The drop-down list for the External name: list box contains names for standard events, but we don't need them here because we're creating a custom event. ClassWizard will fill in the internal name field. This will be the name of the function you call when you want to fire the event.

Click the OK button to create the event. The ActiveX Events tab will now show the new custom event. This event will have been entered in **CTrafficSignalCtrl**'s event map and the definition for the function **FireSignalChanged()** will also have been created. All we have to do is to use it.

The best place to fire this event is from the handler for the **WM_TIMER** message, because it is here that we change the state of the signal object. Close ClassWizard by clicking the OK button and switch to the **OnTimer()** function implementation from ClassView. Alter the code in it as follows:

```
void CTrafficSignalCtrl::OnTimer(UINT nIDEvent)
{
   UINT nInterval = 0;                        // Interval in milliseconds

   // Step to the next state and set the time interval
   // based on the new state
   int nNewState = m_pSignal->NextState();
   switch (nNewState)
   {
      case STOP: case GO:
         nInterval = (UINT)m_lStopOrGoTime;   // Stop or Go interval
         break;
      default:
         nInterval = m_nChangeTime;           // Transient interval
   }
```

```
FireSignalChanged(nNewState);

   InvalidateControl();                          // Redraw the signal

   // Make sure the old timer is dead
   KillTimer(m_nTimerID);
   // Set a new timer event
   m_nTimerID = SetTimer(m_nTimerID, nInterval, NULL);
   if (!m_nTimerID)
   {
      AfxMessageBox("No Timer!");
      exit(1);
   }
}
```

Here, we're keeping track of the precise state of the traffic signal and passing it as a parameter to the event. The rest of the handler remains as before.

With the event added, you can compile the control and see how it runs in the test container. You can view the event log by selecting the View | Event log... menu option in the container. The event log is shown below:

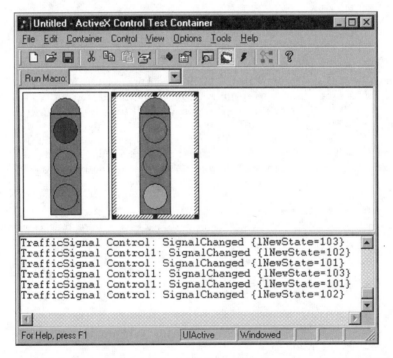

Here, two controls are running with different values assigned for the **StopOrGoTime** property. The individual instances of the control are indicated in the event log by the name of the control (in this case Control and Control1). You can also see the value that is being passed as the parameter to indicate the new state.

Of course, the control will also be usable from more functional control container applications, including Visual Basic or Visual C++ itself. In fact, since Visual Basic is such an important container when writing professional controls, it's a good idea to make your controls as easy as possible to use from that environment. We can enhance the ease in which our control can be used by changing some of the code in the **.odl** file. Remember that the **.odl** file is compiled into a type library that container applications can use to find information about an ActiveX control. We will make some simple changes to the file so that users of the control can use named constants for the values passed to the **SignalChanged** event.

The ODL File

First, open **TrafficSignal.odl** in Developer Studio. This file defines a **type library** for our control using ODL, which we alluded to earlier. The type library defines what's in the control by way of interfaces and data types that can be accessed externally. Although you're probably unfamiliar with ODL and the file may seem a bit confusing at first sight, ODL is actually relatively straightforward. In fact, you should be able to see that the file contains definitions for four items.

```
[ uuid(A833B927-78FF-11D0-9257-00201834E2A3), version(1.0),
  helpfile("TrafficSignal.hlp"),
  helpstring("TrafficSignal ActiveX Control module"),
  control ]
library TRAFFICSIGNALLib
{
    importlib(STDOLE_TLB);
    importlib(STDTYPE_TLB);

    // Primary dispatch interface for CTrafficSignalCtrl

    [ uuid(A833B928-78FF-11D0-9257-00201834E2A3),
      helpstring("Dispatch interface for TrafficSignal Control"), hidden ]
    dispinterface _DTrafficSignal
    {
        properties:
            // NOTE - ClassWizard will maintain property information here.
            //    Use extreme caution when editing this section.
            //{{AFX_ODL_PROP(CTrafficSignalCtrl)
            [id(DISPID_BACKCOLOR), bindable, requestedit] OLE_COLOR BackColor;
            [id(1)] boolean StartRed;
            [id(2)] long StopOrGoTime;
            //}}AFX_ODL_PROP

        methods:
            // NOTE - ClassWizard will maintain method information here.
            //    Use extreme caution when editing this section.
            //{{AFX_ODL_METHOD(CTrafficSignalCtrl)
            //}}AFX_ODL_METHOD

            [id(DISPID_ABOUTBOX)] void AboutBox();
    };

    // Event dispatch interface for CTrafficSignalCtrl

    [ uuid(A833B929-78FF-11D0-9257-00201834E2A3),
      helpstring("Event interface for TrafficSignal Control") ]
```

```
dispinterface _DTrafficSignalEvents
{
    properties:
        //  Event interface has no properties

    methods:
        // NOTE - ClassWizard will maintain event information here.
        //     Use extreme caution when editing this section.
        //{{AFX_ODL_EVENT(CTrafficSignalCtrl)
        [id(1)] void SignalChanged(long lNewState);
        //}}AFX_ODL_EVENT
};


//  Class information for CTrafficSignalCtrl

[ uuid(A833B92A-78FF-11D0-9257-00201834E2A3),
  helpstring("TrafficSignal Control"), control ]
coclass TrafficSignal
{
    [default] dispinterface _DTrafficSignal;
    [default, source] dispinterface _DTrafficSignalEvents;
};


//{{AFX_APPEND_ODL}}
//}}AFX_APPEND_ODL}}
};
```

The definition for the type library, which has the name **TRAFFICSIGNALLib**, is delimited by a pair of braces. The opening brace is immediately after the **library** statement, and the closing brace is at the end of the file. These braces enclose the definitions for three items in the type library: the primary dispatch interface, the event interface and the control. Each definition consists of some information between square brackets followed by a further set of information specific to the type of the item contained between braces. The whole structure looks rather like a set of nested classes.

The two **importlib** statements add all the standard OLE interfaces, types, and dispatch IDs to the type library for our control. Note that each definition in the ODL file is uniquely identified by a **uuid** tag. UUID stands for **u**niversally **u**nique **id**entifier, because it's a number that uniquely identifies the item. The UUID for an item should be different from any other UUID worldwide, so your UUIDs will certainly be different from those shown here.

For the control, the number given after **uuid** is the CLSID. You can see that it's the same number as was used in the ControlWizard-generated **IMPLEMENT_OLECREATE_EX** statement in **TrafficSignalCtl.cpp**.

```
IMPLEMENT_OLECREATE_EX( CTrafficSignalCtrl,
                        "TRAFFICSIGNAL.TrafficSignalCtrl.1",
                        0xa833b92a, 0x78ff, 0x11d0, 0x92, 0x57,
                        0, 0x20, 0x18, 0x34, 0xe2, 0xa3 )
```

Each of the items we've provided in the interface to our control appears within the definitions in the type library. You can use a type library with an object browser, such as the OLE-COM Object Viewer (provided with Visual C++ in the **DevStudio\VC\bin** directory as **Oleview.exe**), to determine what interfaces are supported by a control, and the information provided by a type library can be used to build applications that will use a control. The type library information is recorded in the system registry, including the UUIDs for the library itself and the interface items it defines. Because a UUID, rather than a name, is used to identify an interface, there's no possibility of an interface to one control being confused with that for another.

Adding an Enumeration

We're going to change the ODL file so that it defines an enumeration for the state parameter of the **SignalChanged** event for our control. This will allow Visual Basic users to determine the state of our control in a very simple way. They'll be able to make use of the named constants that we will define to represent the status of the signal after a change has occurred. First, add the following code to the **.odl** file just below the **importlib** statements:

```
importlib(STDTYPE_TLB);
```

```
typedef [ uuid(/* Need to add a valid ID here */),
         helpstring("Signal state constants") ]
    enum { [helpstring ("Stop")] IsStop = 101,
           [helpstring ("Go")] IsGo = 103,
           [helpstring ("Ready to stop")] IsReadyToStop = 104
         } SignalState;
```

```
//  Primary dispatch interface for CTrafficSignalCtrl
```

This code simply defines an enumeration called **SignalState** containing the named constants **IsStop**, **IsGo** and **IsReadyToStop**. These correspond to the values that could be passed via the **SignalChanged** event. It's a common ActiveX control convention to use mixed case constants with a two or three letter prefix to ensure that they're unique.

The one thing that's missing from this definition is a valid ID to use in the **uuid** statement. The ID needs to take a particular form and it needs to be unique, so we can't just type in anything here. Instead, we have to use the GUID generator utility, **Guidgen.exe**, that's supplied with Visual C++; **GUID** stands for **G**lobally **U**nique **ID**. This utility is also known as Uuidgen for obvious reasons, and you'll see references to both Guidgen and Uuidgen in the documentation. The reason that there are two names for the same thing is that there are two groups dealing with it. GUID comes from Microsoft, and UUID comes from the Open Software Foundation.

The easiest way to access Guidgen is through the Components and Controls Gallery, which you can get to by selecting Add to Project | Components and Controls... on the Project menu. You can also make the Components and Controls Gallery available as a toolbar button by right-clicking on one of the Developer Studio toolbars and selecting Customize... from the resulting menu.

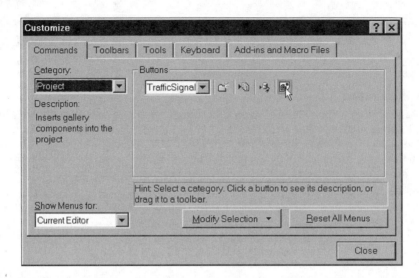

Change the Category to Project and drag the icon shown on to your favorite toolbar or create a new toolbar for it. Now close the Customize dialog and you can use the new toolbar button to display the Components and Controls Gallery.

If you do this now, you'll see a dialog showing a list of folders. Select the folder Visual C++ Components from the list. You'll see the dialog shown:

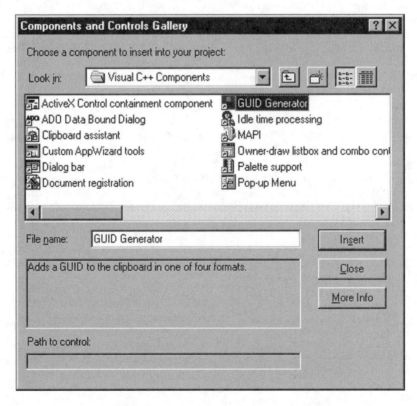

Select GUID Generator from the
list and hit In<u>s</u>ert. Now you'll be
presented with a dialog that
allows you to generate GUIDs in
a variety of formats and copy
them to the clipboard so that
you can paste the results
wherever they are needed:

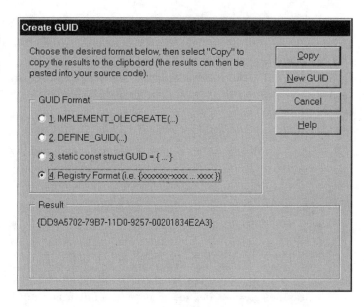

We want an ID in Registry Format, so select the radio button, click <u>C</u>opy to copy the GUID to
the clipboard, then close the Gallery and return to the **.odl** file. Of course, the ID generated
when you run GUID Generator will be different to the one shown here, since the whole point of
the GUID Generator is that it produces unique IDs!

Now paste the generated ID between the parentheses of the **uuid** term in the definition of the
enumeration by keying *Ctrl-V*, and remove the braces from around the ID. The last step to
enable the enumeration to be used for determining the result of the event is to change the type
of the event parameter from **long** to **SignalState**:

```
[ uuid(261D8BE4-6938-11D0-AB3A-0020AF71E433),
               helpstring("Event interface for TrafficSignal Control") ]
dispinterface _DTrafficSignalEvents
{
    properties:
        //  Event interface has no properties

    methods:
        // NOTE - ClassWizard will maintain event information here.
        //     Use extreme caution when editing this section.
        //{{AFX_ODL_EVENT(CTrafficSignalCtrl)
        [id(1)] void SignalChanged(SignalState lNewState);
        //}}AFX_ODL_EVENT
};
```

Now you can compile the control and test it out once more. If you use the test container, you
won't see any differences in the control, but if you use Visual Basic (4 or later), you'll see that
you can make use of the new constants we defined in the enumeration.

```
' Example Visual Basic code
Private Sub TrafficSignal1_SignalChanged(ByVal lNewState As Long)
    If lNewState = IsStop Then
        Print "Stop Light"
```

```
        End If
End Sub
```

The Visual Basic routine shown will be executed each time the **SignalChanged** event is fired by the control. The status stored in **lNewState** is compared with the **IsStop** value defined in the enumeration that we added to the **.odl** file. Whenever the signal state is **IsStop**, a message will be displayed.

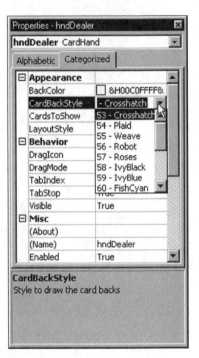

Enumerations like the one we've just defined are even more useful when used in conjunction with properties that should only accept a limited number of specific values. Visual Basic can use the constants defined in an enumeration and offer them to the user through the Properties window that it provides for all controls, as you can see in this sample:

Embedding an ActiveX Control in a Web Page

To get the next section to work, you'll need to have an ActiveX-aware browser installed on your PC. Internet Explorer 3.0 or later from Microsoft will do, or any other browser that supports ActiveX. If you can access the Internet but don't have an ActiveX capable browser, you can download Internet Explorer for free, courtesy of those nice folks at Microsoft. You'll find it on their web site at http://www.microsoft.com. While you're there, you might like to take a look at another freebie: the ActiveX Control Pad. This is a very nice tool that will help you to create web pages and embed ActiveX controls in them.

You define web pages using something called the HyperText Markup Language, commonly known as **HTML**. The elements of a web page are specified by HTML tags, which usually occur in pairs, and are delimited by angled brackets. Fire up the ActiveX Control Pad and you'll see a new, basic document specified with the following HTML tags:

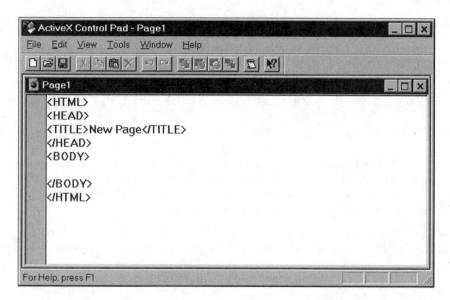

Each pair of tags encloses a particular kind of entity. The Microsoft ActiveX Control Pad creates this for you automatically. To customize it, you could start by changing the title to something more appropriate. If you want some text to appear on the page, you just add it between the **BODY** tags. To add our ActiveX control to the page, we use a pair of **<OBJECT>** tags, as follows:

```
<HTML>
<HEAD>
<TITLE> A Page with a Traffic Signal</TITLE>
</HEAD>
<BODY>
<OBJECT ID="TrafficSignal1" WIDTH=100 HEIGHT=50
 CLASSID="CLSID:A833B92A-78FF-11D0-9257-00201834E2A3">
</OBJECT>
</BODY>
</HTML>
```

Again, inserting an ActiveX control is very easy using Microsoft ActiveX Control Pad. All you have to do is select the control you want from the list presented by the menu item Edit | Insert ActiveX Control… and all the detail is taken care of. ActiveX Control Pad knows about all the controls in your system because they are entered in the registry, so you get the choice of inserting any of them.

In the page definition above, the specification of the name of object to be inserted, and the **CLASSID** for the object which identifies what kind of object it is, both appear in the opening **<OBJECT>** tag along with the width and height of the control. We've specified the **CLASSID** between quotes as the characters **CLSID:**, followed by the hexadecimal digits for the CLSID that appeared in the arguments to the **IMPLEMENT_OLECREATE_EX** macro that we saw earlier in **TrafficSignalCtrl.cpp**. This was:

```
IMPLEMENT_OLECREATE_EX( CTrafficSignalCtrl,
                "TRAFFICSIGNAL.TrafficSignalCtrl.1",
                0xa833b92a, 0x78ff, 0x11d0, 0x92, 0x57,
                0, 0x20, 0x18, 0x34, 0xe2, 0xa3)
```

1005

Note that the sixth argument is a byte, so it actually has two hexadecimal digits, **0x00**.

FYI **Don't worry if you don't have the ActiveX Control Pad. Just save the HTML segment into a file, and provided you make sure the CLSID is correct, the control will be displayed by your browser. The Control Pad doesn't do anything special, it just makes life a little easier.**

That's all you need to include the control in the page, but there are a myriad of other possibilities available to you through HTML. You can assign values to parameters for the control for example, or determine its position on the page when it is displayed. Since we just want to see that it works, we'll ignore these and go with what we've got.

If you save the HTML above in a file with the extension **.htm** — **TrafficSignal.htm**, for example — you should then be able to open it in your web browser to see the control. The **<OBJECT>** tag is relatively new to HTML, and not all web browsers support it, so if the control doesn't appear, it probably isn't your code that's at fault. The page is shown here in a Microsoft Internet Explorer window:

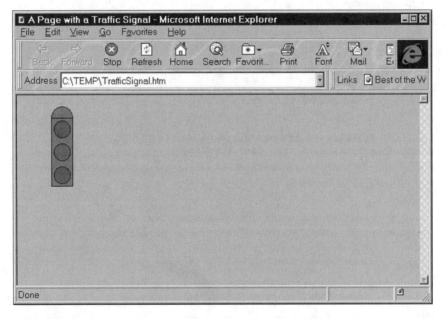

The control works, too. If you click on it, the traffic signal will start operating — amazing isn't it? Now it's up to you to discover what use you can put your new-found knowledge to.

Summary

In this chapter, we've dug a little into the how and why of OLE and ActiveX controls. You should have a good idea now of how a control communicates with its container, and how the basic features of an ActiveX control can be implemented. You also know that an OLE control *is* an ActiveX control.

The important ideas we have explored in this chapter are:

▶ An OLE control is a reusable software component. An OLE control is also an ActiveX control.

▶ ActiveX controls can be executed in any ActiveX container and can be embedded within a Web page.

▶ A control communicates with a container through properties, methods, and events.

▶ There are three kinds of properties for a control: ambient properties, control properties, and extended properties.

▶ A method is a function in a control that can be called from outside the control.

▶ Events are signals that a control sends to a container as a consequence of some action by the user.

▶ You can create an ActiveX control in Visual C++ by using the MFC ActiveX ControlWizard. The controls that it produces are also OLE controls.

▶ You can manipulate the **.odl** file to provide the users of your control with useful constants.

Of course, there is much more to learn about many of the topics we have covered, but we have scratched the surface sufficiently for you to see the gleam of gold underneath. ActiveX controls are an extremely powerful mechanism for reusing and distributing code, and there's no doubt that you will be seeing more and more of them. COM is more general though, and we'll look at that in the next chapter.

Exercises

Ex23-1: Explain the limitations of the **StartRed** property and say how the control could be improved by adding a new **StartState** property to define the starting state of the signal.

Ex23-2: Implement the new **StartState** property and use an enumeration for its possible values.

Ex23-3: (Advanced) Explain what difference it would have made to your implementation if there were already many users of the existing control. How could you ensure compatibility with the existing control? How could you discourage use of legacy functions? (Hints — investigate **CPropExchange::GetVersion()** and **COleControl::ExchangeVersion()**. Also, ODL provides a **hidden** keyword.)

Using the Active Template Library

The **Active Template Library**, known as **ATL**, provides you with another means of creating COM components, including simple and full ActiveX controls, but using a very different approach from that of the previous chapter.

In this chapter you will learn:

▶ More about how COM works

▶ What the Active Template Library is

▶ How to use the ATL Object Wizard

▶ How to implement a simple COM component

▶ How you can use a COM component in Visual Basic

▶ How you can use a COM component in a C++ program

▶ How to implement a full ActiveX control using ATL

More About COM

Using ATL takes you much closer to COM than the example in the previous chapter, so we need to understand a little more about what COM involves. It's cards on the table time: COM is actually quite complicated. When you consider what COM achieves, it was inevitable, wasn't it? Defining a mechanism which allows program modules to be written in almost any language such that they can always be connected together — even when they're on different computers — is no mean achievement. The basic concepts are quite easy, but the devil is in the details. Fortunately, you can get by with an understanding of the basics, at least for the purposes of getting started with using ATL to create simple COM components.

You already know that COM is an interface specification for reusable software components. The COM interface isn't dependent on C++ or any other programming language in particular; provided a programming language has the capability to implement a COM interface, you can use it to create a COM component. COM doesn't require an object-oriented approach and classes aren't necessary to implement COM components, but they do make it easier. As we saw in the last chapter, all ActiveX controls are COM components, because they implement a COM interface.

A COM component is called a **server**, and a program that uses a COM component is called a **client**. A single COM component can be used by several clients simultaneously, rather like a function in a DLL. In fact, as we shall see later, we can store a COM component in a `.dll` file. To use a COM component, a client must create an **instance** of the component. An instance of a component is referred to as a **COM object**, although this term is also used to describe a COM component in general.

A COM interface contains only functions (often referred to as methods). A component can have properties — parameters that can be set for a component or have their values retrieved — as we saw with our TrafficSignal control, but these are accessed through **get** and **put** functions in the interface. A COM component has at least one interface, and can have several.

COM and Interfaces

The basis of COM is the interface called **IUnknown**. All COM component interfaces must support the minimum **IUnknown** capability, since **IUnknown** allows a client to find out what other interfaces the component has. This is the key to unlimited flexibility in what a COM interface can include. The **IUnknown** interface contains three functions:

Function Name	Description
`QueryInterface()`	You call this function to determine whether the component supports a particular interface and to get a pointer to the interface if it does.
`AddRef()`	A COM object that's being shared keeps track of the number of clients that are using the interface. Calling `AddRef()` increments the reference count.
`Release()`	Called by a client when it ceases using a component interface. Calling `Release()` decrements the reference count for an interface. When the interface count is zero, the object knows that there are no clients using the interface.

Since the client and the COM server may be implemented in completely different programming languages — indeed, the server and the client can be running on completely different computers — the interface functions aren't accessed directly by a client. Instead, they're accessed indirectly through a table of pointers to functions.

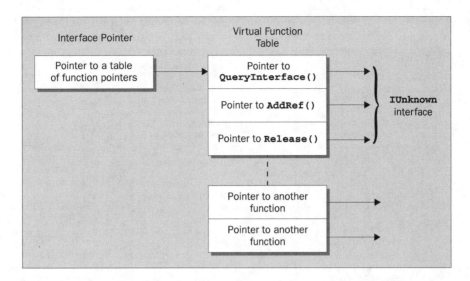

An interface pointer contains the address of a table containing the addresses of the functions in the interface. This table of addresses is called a **virtual function table** (or **vtable**); virtual functions in C++ work through a similar mechanism. An interface function is called indirectly through its address in the table. A particular function is referenced through the base address for the table, plus an offset for the particular entry required. In C++ terms, the entries in the vtable are pointers to functions, and the interface pointer is of type pointer to pointer, usually **void****.

COM defines its own data types. These are independent of C++, but they do of course map to C++ types. The parameters to a COM interface function can only be of the types that COM supports, and there are restrictions on how information is passed to and from an interface function. We shall see more of the detail of this when we come to put a COM component together.

The basic **IUnknown** interface is just a platform — the absolute minimum necessary to get communications working between a COM server and a client. In practice, other interfaces can be added that will be specific to the sort of capability implemented in a component. **IUnknown** provides the means by which a client can find out about these additional interfaces. In C++, **IUnknown** can be represented very easily as a class, and extending it then becomes a matter of deriving a new class that inherits the functions in **IUnknown**. Since the notion of virtual functions is fundamental to C++, accessing a COM interface is a relatively straightforward matter. The way in which **IUnknown** works is not always the most convenient in other environments, and some are just not comfortable with having to work through a virtual function table. An important COM interface that can overcome such difficulties, and that was first defined for use in the Visual Basic environment, is called a **dispatch interface** (or **dispinterface**).

Dispatch Interfaces

A dispatch interface is an interface that's based on a standard interface called **IDispatch**. **IDispatch** inherits the functions from **IUnknown**, and implements additional functions that make calling interface functions easier. In particular, the **IDispatch** interface adds a function called **Invoke()** that you can use to call different functions depending on an argument passed to it. The argument is a positive 32-bit integer value called a **DispID** (**Disp**atch **ID**) that identifies the function. To get the DispIDs for the functions implemented in a dispatch interface you call another function called **GetIDsOfNames()**. You can pass an array of function names to it and get back an array of corresponding DispIDs for the functions.

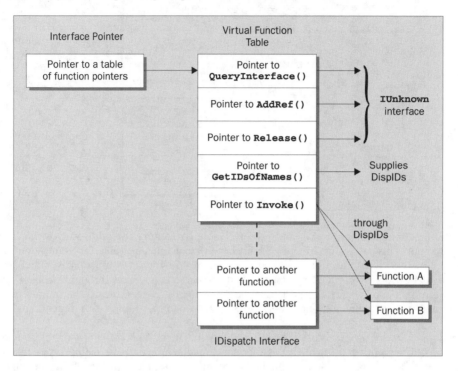

Note that the functions that are part of the dispatch interface and callable through **Invoke()** do not necessarily appear in the virtual function table. When they do, the interface is referred to as a **dual interface**, because the functions can be called through **Invoke()** using DispIDs, or they can be called directly through the virtual function table pointers. Calling functions through the vtable pointers is faster than calling them through **Invoke()**.

COM Interfaces and Class Interfaces

Don't confuse a COM interface with a class interface. Being immersed in C++ classes all the time makes it easy to mix them up, but when you write a COM component in C++ you will be involved with both kinds. The COM interface will be defined in a file using **IDL**, the Interface **D**escription **L**anguage that we referred to in the last chapter. IDL looks quite similar to C++ but it most certainly isn't C++ and there are many differences. Keep in mind that IDL isn't a programming language in the normal sense; it's a language for defining interfaces and other information that will be stored in a type library — that is, in a **.tlb** file. When you build a COM component, the MIDL compiler processes the **.idl** file and the C++ compiler processes the **.cpp** files. The two are interrelated but they aren't the same.

Of course, a COM component will need to be implemented in C++. A C++ class will represent the COM object, and the implementation of the COM interface will require class functions to be declared corresponding to the COM interface functions. Since these are called from outside the COM object, potentially from a client written in another programming language, the declaration and implementation of the interface functions must be made in a special way to accommodate this. The default C++ calling convention for functions isn't acceptable to COM. We'll see how we specify the calling convention to suit COM in an example.

Understanding the Active Template Library

Believe it or not, the Active Template Library is a library of class templates that support ActiveX — in other words, COM components. We saw how class templates work back in Chapter 9, so here we can see them applied in a real-world context. The ATL class templates enable you to create classes that form a basis for an ActiveX component that doesn't involve the overhead implicit in using the MFC. In fact, ATL is completely independent of the MFC. Such a component will therefore require substantially less memory than the MFC-based ActiveX control that we produced in the previous chapter.

Being able to produce a COM component in racing trim by using ATL is a major plus, but where there's a plus, there's often a minus or two. One minus in this case is that if your component needs any kind of visual representation that the user can see or interact with, you must program it yourself. This isn't necessarily as big a problem as it sounds, but it does mean that you'll be calling Windows API functions directly. Another minus is that you can't use ClassWizard with ATL programs — ClassWizard just doesn't support them. It's possible to use the MFC and ATL together, but there's really no point in doing so. If you intend to use the MFC, you don't need ATL at all.

We can deduce from this that ATL is aimed squarely at the development of components that are lightweight in memory requirements, but with the flexibility to add whatever capability you want. One context in which ATL excels is the development of lightweight, invisible controls.

Invisible Controls

'Invisible' and 'lightweight' suggest we could be dealing with vaporware here, but that certainly isn't the case. Why would you want such a component? Well, there are a couple of reasons. Firstly, consider a hypothetical COM component that provides a computation function of some kind. When you need the function it supplies, you can plug it into your application. It doesn't need a visual representation, and the lighter it is on memory requirements, the better. Secondly, we saw in the previous chapter that ActiveX controls can be used in web pages on the Internet. Clearly, the growing requirement for Internet web pages to contain active code implies a need for components in this context, and because Internet communications bandwidth is a critical resource, such components need to be as lightweight as possible. Clumping several heavyweight MFC-based ActiveX controls in your web page would most likely mean that nobody will be prepared to wait for it to download.

This second example is where ATL components come riding to the rescue, although it isn't immediately obvious how. Lightweight components are all very well, but an ATL-based, invisible one doesn't seem right — after all, if you can't see it, how do you know it's there, and what's more, how do you use it? The current facilities you have available to you for defining web pages can help. There are scripting languages such as VBScript and JavaScript that you can use within the description of a web page in HTML. From these scripting languages you can get and set component properties and call functions, so you can use them to interface with invisible components. You can even tie multiple components together so they work in an integrated way.

We can get a clearer idea of how an ATL-based COM component is developed by creating one. After we've done that we can see how to use it. We'll start with the simplest kind (it has no visual appearance implemented), but later we'll see how we can use ATL to implement the traffic signal control we created in the previous chapter without incurring the overhead of MFC.

Using the ATL COM AppWizard

We need something simple as an example of a COM component. Let's create a component that can figure out the maximum refresh rate for a monitor, given the monitor's horizontal scanning frequency. The horizontal scanning frequency is a measure of how many lines your monitor can draw in one second, so if you know how many lines there are on the screen, you can divide this into the scanning frequency to get how many times the screen will be redrawn in a second. The number of lines on the screen is just the vertical resolution, and we can get the component to figure that out. In reality, the refresh rate is also limited by the vertical scan rate that your monitor can sustain, but we'll ignore that for the purposes of this exercise.

Visual C++ 6 provides a special Wizard for projects using ATL, so we can jump right in with that. Start a new ATL COM AppWizard project called **RefreshRate**, as shown here.

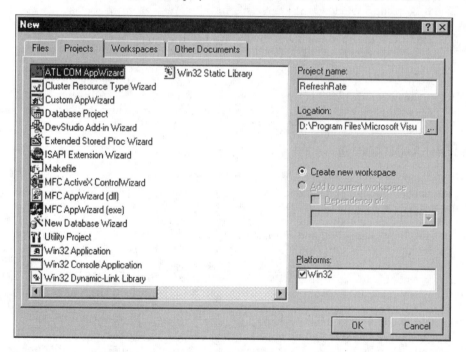

This will generate a new project in a new workspace in the directory shown in the edit box. If you click on the OK button you'll move on to the first (and only) step in the ATL COM AppWizard process:

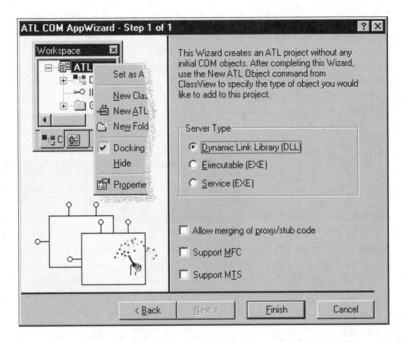

As you see, you can create a component as a DLL or as an **.exe** file. When you think about it, there's no reason why an application in a **.exe** file shouldn't have a COM interface — after all, that's essentially what you're using when you embed an Excel worksheet in a Word document. A COM component in a DLL is called an **in-process server**, because it shares the address space of a client. A COM component implemented in a **.exe** file is called an **out-of-process server** because it runs in its own address space. The default DLL **Server Type** option is what we want for our example.

When your COM component is in one address space and the client program using it is in another, the client clearly can't call the interface functions in the COM component directly. Some extra software is necessary in each process to manage the transfer of data and provide the interface between the client and the component.

The software that sits in the client process is called a **proxy**, because it represents the interface to the COM server component. The client communicates with the proxy, and the proxy communicates with the server process via a piece of software in that process called a **stub**. This calls the interface functions in the component on behalf of the client.

The process the proxy goes through when it gathers the arguments together for an interface function call is called **marshaling**; the process of sorting them out at the component end, which is carried out by the stub, is called **unmarshaling**. The proxy and stub code is generated from the **.idl** file by the MIDL compiler and is usually placed in a separate DLL. We have the option here of including this code within the same DLL as the component, but we'll leave it unchecked.

If you want to use the MFC classes, you can check the Support MFC box. This will add an application class to the project derived from **CWinApp**, and the program will contain an application object. It will also increase the size of the component considerably, but it does mean that you would be able to use *any* of the MFC classes in your project. We don't need it here, so leave this box unchecked as well.

Finally, if you want your ATL COM project to integrate with Microsoft Transaction Server, then you can check the **Support MTS** box. MTS is a back office component of Windows NT that provides a backbone for applications which want to incorporate strict transactions into their workings. If you do check the box, the AppWizard will modify the build script for the project to include two MTS-specific libraries. Again, however, we don't need it here, so leave the box unchecked.

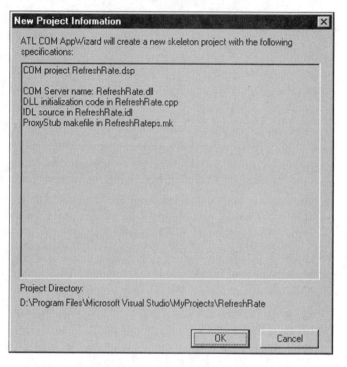

If you click on the Finish button you'll see the last dialog which, as usual, shows you the details of the files that will be generated, and gives you a last chance to back out.

Don't weaken now! Click on the OK button to complete the operation. We can then take a look at the code that's generated for us.

Basic COM AppWizard Code

If you switch to ClassView and extend the tree, you'll see that there's very little there, especially compared with what we've been used to in the last few chapters:

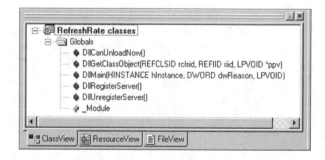

There are no classes defined at all. We have five global functions and a global object, **_Module**, defined. At the moment there's no COM object and no COM interface implemented.

Two of the global functions, **DllRegisterServer()** and **DllUnregisterServer()**, will provide the ability to register and unregister our COM component, as you can probably guess from the function names. The **DllMain()** function is called when the DLL is loaded into memory and, as we saw in Chapter 19, initializes the DLL. The function **DllCanUnloadNow()** determines whether the DLL is still in use, and is called to decide when to remove the DLL from memory. Lastly, the **DllGetClassObject()** function is used to retrieve the COM object from the DLL when you create an instance of the component in a client program. You don't usually call this function directly, though — we'll see how we can create an instance of a COM component later in this chapter.

The global object. **_Module** is an instance of the class **CComModule**, which represents the COM server module we're creating. The COM server module will contain functions to manage all the class objects in the module and provides the mechanism for entering information about the COM components in the system registry. **DllRegisterServer()** and **DllUnregisterServer()** call functions belonging to the **_Module** object to perform the registration and unregistration operations. So where does our COM object implementation come from?

Adding a COM object to the Project

To add a COM object, you can either select the Insert | New ATL Object... menu item, or display the ATL toolbar and click on the button. A dialog will be displayed that gives you a selection of COM objects that you can add to your project:

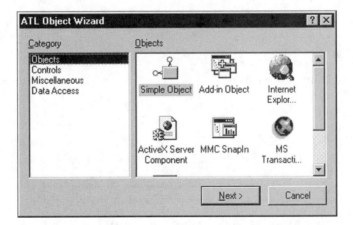

The dialog offers four sets of COM components to choose from: Objects, Controls, Miscellaneous and Data Access. We'll be creating another COM component later in this chapter which will be an ActiveX control, but for now we will just add a Simple Object. Highlight that by clicking it, as shown, and click on the Next> button.

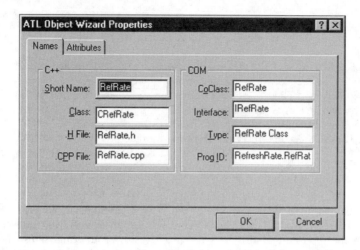

Here you need to enter the name for the COM component, **RefRate**. This is used as the basis for the C++ class name that implements the component, and for the names of the files containing the C++ code. It is also the basis for the names of the CoClass, which is the component class, the name of the interface, **IRefRate**, that the component will support, the type name and the Prog ID that will appear in the registry. Note that the component class is not a C++ class — it's a COM class which identifies the interfaces that the component supports.

The other tab on the dialog provides options as to how the component will be implemented:

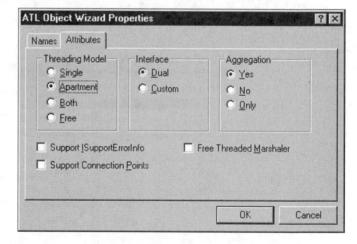

The threading options relate to the degree of concurrency of executing processes within a component and are beyond the scope of this book, so we'll ignore that here. Dual interfaces, on the other hand, we have mentioned previously. This option provides for interface functions to be callable through a dispatch interface (using the **Invoke()** function) as well as through the virtual function table. **Aggregation** refers to the capability of one COM component to make use of another, making the contained component's interfaces available as well as its own. All the defaults are fine for our example, so click on the OK button to add the object to our project. Let's see what we've got now.

ATL Object Code

The ATL-based component is very different from the ActiveX control we saw in the previous chapter. If you extend all the trees in ClassView, you can see that we have one class defined, **CRefRate**, and one interface, **IRefRate**, in addition to the five global functions and the global object **_Module** that we had before:

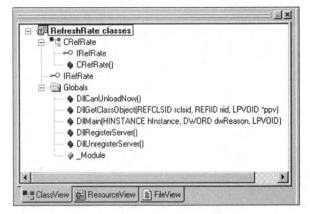

The class **CRefRate** represents our COM object, and **IRefRate** is the definition of the COM interface for this object. **IRefRate** is defined in the **RefreshRate.idl** file, and is implemented by the class **CRefRate**, which has its definition in **RefRate.h** and its implementation in **RefRate.cpp**, as you might expect. If you look at the files in the project in FileView, you will see a file of a type that we haven't met before: **RefRate.rgs**. This contains the information that will be entered in the system registry when we successfully build our COM project.

The COM Object Class

The definition of the class **CRefRate** is short, but there's quite a lot there nonetheless, because it has no less than three base classes. Notice that while MFC relies on single inheritance, ATL capitalizes on using multiple inheritance:

```
class ATL_NO_VTABLE CRefRate :
    public CComObjectRootEx<CComSingleThreadModel>,
    public CComCoClass<CRefRate, &CLSID_RefRate>,
    public IDispatchImpl<IRefRate, &IID_IRefRate, &LIBID_REFRESHRATELib>
{
public:
    CRefRate()
    {
    }

    DECLARE_REGISTRY_RESOURCEID(IDR_REFRATE)

    DECLARE_PROTECT_FINAL_CONSTRUCT()

    BEGIN_COM_MAP(CRefRate)
        COM_INTERFACE_ENTRY(IRefRate)
        COM_INTERFACE_ENTRY(IDispatch)
    END_COM_MAP()

    // IRefRate
public:
};
```

The base classes add the basic COM infrastructure that our COM object needs. As you can see, they're all generated from templates. The first base class, **CComObjectRootEx**, implements the basic COM interface, **IUnknown**. It takes cares of the reference counting through the **AddRef()** and **Release()** functions, and it implements the **QueryInterface()** function. The argument to the template, **CComSingleThreadModel**, makes the generated class applicable to single thread operations. This is a consequence of accepting the default threading model on the Attributes tab of the ATL Object Wizard.

The second base class, **CComCoClass**, defines the factory class for our component. The factory class enables an instance of the COM component to be created. You need to create an instance of a component before you can call any of its interface functions. The template for **CComCoClass** uses the class name, **CRefRate**, and the CLSID for the component as parameters to define the factory class.

The last base class, **IDispatchImpl**, will provide the dual interface for our control. We'll have **IUnknown** by default, plus the **IDispatch** interface functions to allow interface methods to be called using **Invoke()**. The three parameters to the template are our component interface, **IRefRate**, a pointer to the corresponding interface ID, and a pointer to the GUID for the type library. These aren't defined in the C++ code yet, but code will be added to define them when the **.idl** file is processed.

We will be extending the interface **IRefRate** by adding our own functions to the **.idl** file. When we do, we'll also need to add declarations for these functions to the **CRefRate** class definition. These will go after the **public** keyword at the end of the class definition.

The interfaces defined for the class are identified following the **BEGIN_COM_MAP()** macro. We have an entry for **IRefRate** in addition to the standard **IDispatch** interface, since this will contain our application-specific interface functions. The COM map makes the methods in these interfaces accessible to a container through the **QueryInterface()** method in **IUnknown**.

The Interface Definition

The IDL file, **RefreshRate.idl**, has two **import** statements for the files **oaidl.idl** and **ocidl.idl** at the beginning. These add all the standard definitions for the interfaces supported by ATL. The file also contains two main definitions: a definition of the interface **IRefRate**, and a definition of what will go into the type library which records information about the COM component. In each case there's a set of attributes appearing between square brackets, followed by the details of the definition. The IDL code defining the **IRefRate** interface is:

```
[
        object,
        uuid(3A6DD1CF-1B63-11D2-B735-ADB796237F06),
        dual,
        helpstring("IRefRate Interface"),
        pointer_default(unique)
]
interface IRefRate : IDispatch
{
};
```

The **object** attribute indicates that this is a custom COM interface, and we'll be adding our own methods to this interface definition. The second attribute defines the UUID for the interface. This is the 128-bit universally unique ID we discussed in the previous chapter that identifies the interface, so the UUID you have in your version of the project will undoubtedly be different from the one here. The **dual** attribute determines that this is a dual interface, which as you know means that you can access functions directly through the vtable, or indirectly through **IDispatch::Invoke()**. **helpstring** can be used by applications that make use of the type library to describe the interface. The **pointer_default(unique)** dictates that if pointers to pointers are used as parameters in interface functions, they must each provide a unique access route to the data they point to — that is, to access any particular data item, only one pointer can be used. This enables the code that accesses the data to be simplified.

At the moment the interface contains no custom interface functions at all. We'll be adding ours between the braces following the **interface** statement. The basic COM requirement for **IUnknown** is taken care of with this, since **IRefRate** inherits from **IDispatch** which inherits from **IUnknown**.

The type library is specified with the following IDL code:

```
[
    uuid(3A6DD1C3-1B63-11D2-B735-ADB796237F06),
    version(1.0),
    helpstring("RefreshRate 1.0 Type Library")
]
library REFRESHRATELib
{
    importlib("stdole32.tlb");
    importlib("stdole2.tlb");

    [
        uuid(3A6DD1D0-1B63-11D2-B735-ADB796237F06),
        helpstring("RefRate Class")
    ]
    coclass RefRate
    {
        [default] interface IRefRate;
    };
};
```

The standard OLE type libraries are imported with the **importlib** statement. The **coclass** definition statement incorporates our custom interface **IRefRate** which was defined previously, so that this will be part of each instance of the COM component implemented by the C++ class **CRefRate**.

Extending the Interface

The basic function our component will perform is to calculate the refresh rate for a monitor, given the horizontal scan frequency. We will therefore need an interface function we can call **RefreshRate()** that will accept an argument specifying the horizontal scan frequency in kilohertz (of type **long**, say) and return the refresh rate in hertz as another **long** value. If we were declaring this as a regular C++ function, it would have a prototype something like

```
long RefreshRate(long HScan);
```

However, we're defining a COM interface function here, and there are some constraints. A COM interface function should return a value of type **HRESULT**. This is a 32-bit value containing fields indicating success or failure of the operation. This is necessary because of the diversity of contexts in which a component might be used. Bearing in mind that the client may be on a different machine from the COM server, a lot can go wrong in the general case, so the **HRESULT** return type provides a rich set of possible return codes.

A consequence of all this is that if you want to return a data value to the client, such as the refresh rate we plan to calculate, you must return it through a parameter to the function. This complicates the specification of interface function parameters somewhat. In addition to the constraint that they must be of a type supported by COM, we also have the requirement that you must indicate in the interface definition which parameters to a function are inputting data and which are outputting data. You must also specify which, if any, of the output parameters is passing a return value back to the client.

Because of all this, the definition of our interface function in the IDL file turns out to be:

```
HRESULT RefreshRate([in] long HScan, [out, retval] long* retval);
```

The return type is **HRESULT**, and each parameter is preceded by attributes defined between square brackets. A parameter will have the attribute **in** if a value is being passed by the client to the function, the attribute **out** if a value is being passed from the function to the client, and the attributes **out** and **retval** if a value is being passed from the function to the client as a return value. A parameter that is specified as **in** can also have the attribute **out** if the function will use the parameter to return a value. A parameter with the attribute **out** must always be specified as a pointer; this means that the memory for storing the value is owned by the client. A parameter with the attribute **retval** must also have the attribute **out**, and therefore must be a pointer. Note that a parameter with the attribute **retval** must also be named **retval**.

Since we'll need to obtain the current vertical display resolution in order to calculate the refresh rate, we might as well include functions to supply the horizontal and vertical resolution of the display independent of the refresh rate. You will therefore need to modify the interface definition in **RefreshRate.idl** by adding the following statements:

```
[
    object,
    uuid(3A6DD1CF-1B63-11D2-B735-ADB796237F06),
    dual,
    helpstring("IRefRate Interface"),
    pointer_default(unique)
]
interface IRefRate : IDispatch
{
    HRESULT RefreshRate([in] long HScan, [out, retval] long* retval);
    HRESULT GetVRes([out, retval] long* retval);
    HRESULT GetHRes([out, retval] long* retval);
};
```

Both the **GetVRes()** and **GetHRes()** functions have a single parameter that has the **retval** attribute. Since we'll get the values to be returned by using the Windows API, no input parameters are necessary.

Implementing the Interface Functions

We must first add the functions we have defined as part of the interface to the class definition for our COM object:

```
class ATL_NO_VTABLE CRefRate :
    public CComObjectRootEx<CComSingleThreadModel>,
    public CComCoClass<CRefRate, &CLSID_RefRate>,
    public IDispatchImpl<IRefRate, &IID_IRefRate, &LIBID_REFRESHRATELib>
{
public:
    CRefRate()
    {
    }

DECLARE_REGISTRY_RESOURCEID(IDR_REFRATE)

DECLARE_PROTECT_FINAL_CONSTRUCT()

BEGIN_COM_MAP(CRefRate)
    COM_INTERFACE_ENTRY(IRefRate)
    COM_INTERFACE_ENTRY(IDispatch)
END_COM_MAP()

// IRefRate
public:
    HRESULT __stdcall RefreshRate(long HScan, long* retval);
    HRESULT __stdcall GetVRes(long* retval);
    HRESULT __stdcall GetHRes(long* retval);
};
```

The **__stdcall** qualifier that appears in front of each function name specifies that the function uses the **WINAPI** (or **PASCAL**) calling convention. This prescribes how the parameters are handled when the function is called, and differs from the standard C++ calling convention. All COM interface functions with a fixed number of parameters use this. We must now add the implementations for these functions to the **RefRate.cpp** file. Let's implement **RefreshRate()** first:

```
// Calculate the refresh rate
HRESULT __stdcall CRefRate::RefreshRate(long HScan, long* retval)
{
    int ScreenY = GetSystemMetrics(SM_CYSCREEN);   // Get vertical
    ScreenY = static_cast<int>(1.04 * ScreenY);    // Allow for overscan areas
    *retval = HScan * 1000 / ScreenY;              // Return to client
    return S_OK;
}
```

Getting the current screen resolution is easy. We just call the Windows API function **GetSystemMetrics()** with an argument that specifies the kind of information we want. The argument value **SM_CXSCREEN** would give the number of pixels in the horizontal direction, and the argument we have used, **SM_CYSCREEN**, results in the number of pixels on the screen vertically being returned. This function can supply a large number of other items of information, on which you can find details by placing the cursor on the function name and pressing *F1*.

There is usually some time lost between ending one screen scan and starting the next, so we compensate for this by effectively increasing the number of screen pixels in the y direction by 4%. We then divide the result into the value for the horizontal scan frequency to get the refresh rate, the 1000 multiplier being necessary because the units are kilohertz. We need to dereference **retval** to store the result. When the function is called by a client, the value (rather than a pointer to the value) will be returned, as we shall see. Here we are storing the result in the location pointed to by the **retval** argument.

Finally, we return the **HRESULT** value **S_OK** to the COM environment. **HRESULT** is quite a complex value: packed into its 32 bits are four different fields indicating the status on return from the function. We don't need to get into the detail of these, since most of it is intended for the operating system. Returning **S_OK** indicates the function succeeded; **E_FAIL** indicates an unspecified failure. There are in fact a variety of return codes for success beginning with **S_**, and similarly a range of error return codes beginning with **E_**. Because there are multiple codes for success and failure, you should not test an **HRESULT** value by comparing it with specific return codes such as **S_OK** or **E_FAIL**. You should use the macro **SUCCEEDED()** to test for success and the macro **FAILED()** to test for failure. For example, if the **HRESULT** value returned is **hR**, you could write:

```
if(SUCCEEDED(hR))
    // Do something for success...
else
    // Oh dear, it didn't work...
```

Implementing the other two interface functions is very easy:

```
HRESULT __stdcall CRefRate::GetVRes(long* retval)
{
    *retval = GetSystemMetrics(SM_CYSCREEN); // Return horizontal resolution
    return S_OK;                             // Return to COM environment
}

HRESULT __stdcall CRefRate::GetHRes(long* retval)
{
    *retval = GetSystemMetrics(SM_CXSCREEN); // Return vertical resolution
    return S_OK;                             // Return to COM environment
}
```

They both work in the same way. Each stores the result to be returned to the client in the location pointed to by **retval**, and then returns the **S_OK** value.

Building the Component

Build the component in exactly the same way as any other project. First, the MIDL compiler will process the **.idl** file to produce the **.tlb** file containing the type library, then the C++ compiler will compile the C++ source, the link step will generate the **.dll**, and finally the component will be registered. This presumes, of course, that there are no errors in the code you have added.

If you look at the External Dependencies folder in FileView, you'll see that the MIDL compiler has produced three new files and included **RefreshRate.h** there as well:

File	Description
Basetsd.h	Contains definitions for the base types used by the IDL compiler
RefreshRate.tlb	Contains the type library for the program.
RefreshRate_i.c	Contains definitions for the IIDs for the IRefRate interface and the type library, and the CLSID for the COM component.

It has also added code to **RefreshRate.h**, which previously only contained a comment but now contains the code defining the virtual function table for our custom interface **IRefRate**. The virtual function table contains a pointer to each function in the interface. There's one version of the vtable that's selected if the symbol **__cplusplus** is defined (the C++ version), and one for when it isn't. In our context, the former applies.

You'll notice the macro **__RPC_FAR** applied to the type of the parameters in the pointer definitions for our interface functions in the virtual function table in **RefreshRate.h**. This macro only applies to 16-bit environments and is removed by the preprocessor in Windows 95 and other Win32 environments. That's why we didn't need it in our declarations in **CRefRate** class, but you should add it if you plan to compile the code for a 16-bit environment. The **STDMETHODCALLTYPE** macro that also appears is equivalent to the **__stdcall** specifier that we used in the **CRefRate** class and in the implementations of the functions.

If you're unsure what the prototypes in C++ for functions you have added to the interface in the **.idl** file are, you can always build the project to get the MIDL compiler to generate the **.h** file. There will be a lot of errors, since you won't have declared these functions in the component class, but you can copy the function declarations that appear in the interface definition in the **.h** file generated by the MIDL compiler. For example, if you look in the **RefreshRate.h** file you will see it has an interface entry for the **RefreshRate()** function as follows:

```
virtual HRESULT STDMETHODCALLTYPE RefreshRate(
        /* [in] */ long HScan,
        /* [retval][out] */ long __RPC_FAR *retval) = 0;
```

All you need to do is remove the **=0** at the end to get a declaration to put in your class:

```
virtual HRESULT STDMETHODCALLTYPE RefreshRate(
        /* [in] */ long HScan,
        /* [retval][out] */ long __RPC_FAR *retval);
```

You could then put this as the declaration in the class definition verbatim. The **STDMETHODCALLTYPE** is a macro that generates **__stdcall**, so you can leave that. The **__RPC_FAR** macro is for 16-bit environments and is ignored under Windows 95. The comments aren't particularly tidy, so you could remove those if you wanted to, but they don't do any harm.

Using the Component

Our component should be usable in any environment that supports COM. Using our COM component is easiest in Visual Basic, so let's give that a try first. After that, we'll see how we can incorporate **RefRate** into a C++ program. If you don't have or use Visual Basic, you can skip the next section and go straight to using **RefRate** in a C++ program.

Visual Basic Access to the COM Component

The first thing to establish, once you've started a new Visual Basic project, is that Visual Basic is aware of our COM component. Select the menu item References... in the Project menu to display the dialog shown here:

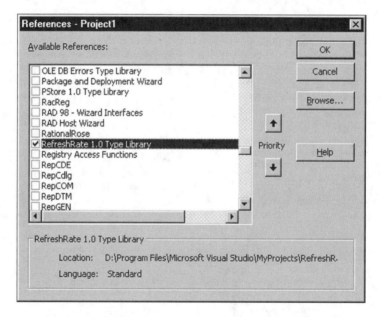

This lists the references that are identified in the system. All those checked are available to your Visual Basic program. If the type library for **RefreshRate** appears in the list, just click the check box and click on the OK button to make it available in your program. If it doesn't appear in the list, you can add it by clicking the Browse... button, going to the directory containing the **RefreshRate** code, and selecting the type library file, **RefreshRate.tlb**.

The first step is to design a form that we can use to exercise our COM component. All we need are some text boxes and a few labels, as shown:

Four text boxes have been added to the form. You can assign names to the text boxes in the property list that reflect their purpose. Running from top to bottom, I used the names **txtHScanMax**, **txtRRate**, **txtHRes** and **txtVRes** respectively. The last three are output only, so you could set the Locked property to **True** to prevent them from being edited. You could also clear the Text property so they appear empty. There is a label at the top with instructions, plus a label for each of the text boxes to identify them. All we need in addition to this is a small amount of code to handle the input.

You need to implement a subroutine to handle a **KeyPress** event for the **txtHScanMax** text box, as follows:

```
Private Sub txtHScanMax_KeyPress(KeyAscii As Integer)
    Dim objRefRate As New RefRate
    If (KeyAscii = 13) Then
        txtRRate.Text = objRefRate.RefreshRate(HScan:=Val(txtHScanMax.Text))
        txtHRes.Text = objRefRate.GetHRes
        txtVRes.Text = objRefRate.GetVRes
    End If
End Sub
```

The **Dim** statement declares an object variable, **objRefRate**, that's an instance of the **RefRate** component. We can use this variable to call the interface functions for the component. The **If** statement tests for the *Enter* key being pressed (code 13). If it is, it passes the value entered in the **txtHScanMax** text box as the argument to the interface function **RefreshRate()**. The refresh rate is then displayed in the text box **txtRRate**. In practice, it would be a good idea to verify that the **txtHScanMax** text box is not zero before passing the value to the COM interface function. We call the other two interface functions for the **RefRate** object and display the output in the appropriate text box.

As you may have already noticed, Visual Basic has the same intellisense features that Visual C++ does and will prompt you with the various member functions that an object has available to it. For example:

```
txtHRes.Text = objRefRate.GetHRes
txtVRes.Text = objRefRate.
                            GetHRes
                            GetVRes
                            RefreshRate
```

Visual Basic also provides you with an **Object Browser** which shows you every object and class that's available to you in your code, along with their properties, methods and events. Press the *F2* function key to display it. Once you've selected an object method, you can copy it to the clipboard by pressing 🗐 and then paste it into your code at your discretion.

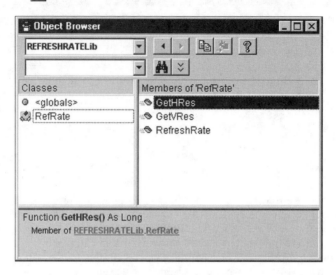

Running the program on my machine and typing in a value of 90 for the horizontal scan rate, I get this output:

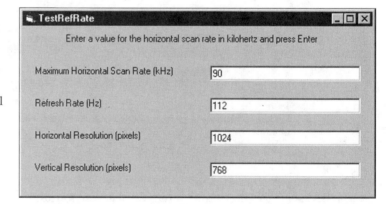

Using ATL-based COM objects in Visual Basic is very straightforward, once Visual Basic is aware of them. All you do is create a variable representing an instance of the component, and use the object variable to access the interface. What could be simpler than that?

Using the COM Component in C++

The simplest way we can explore the mechanics of using a COM component in Visual C++ is to create a project specifically to do this. Use **MFC AppWizard (exe)** to create a new project for an SDI program. I gave the project the name **UseRefRate**, but you can use whatever you want. You can leave the **ActiveX Controls** box on **Step 3** checked, and on **Step 6** change the base class for the view to **CFormView**. This will make it easy to set up some controls to operate the component.

The first thing we need to do is set up the dialog that's used in the view. Go to ResourceView and double-click on the dialog ID — with the name I assigned to the project it's **IDD_USEREFRATE_FORM**. We can set it up to look very similar to the Visual Basic form we had previously:

There are four edit boxes, each with a static text item alongside, and a static text item to indicate how to use the dialog. There's also a button labeled Calculate at the bottom. You can give the button the ID **IDC_CALCULATE**, and the edit boxes the IDs **IDC_HSCAN**, **IDC_REFRESH**, **IDC_HRES** and **IDC_VRES**. All the edit boxes should have the Number option checked on the Styles tab in the Properties dialog, and the bottom three should have the Read-only option checked as well.

Now we can add variables corresponding to the four edit boxes. You will recall that we can do this by double-clicking the edit box while holding down the *Ctrl* key. They should all be of type **long**, since each of the entries is an integer, and you can give them the names **m_lHScan**, **m_lRefresh**, **m_lHRes** and **m_lVRes**. They will be added to the view class definition and initialized in the constructor. You could change the default value set in the view class constructor for **m_lHScan** to 50, since this should always be non-zero. All the code necessary to pass data between the variables and the controls will already have been added to the **DoDataExchange()** function in the view class. We just need to add a handler for the button.

You can add the button handler in the same way as you added the variables for the edit boxes: just double-click the button in the dialog while holding down the *Ctrl* key. The **OnCalculate()** handler will do all of the work to call the COM component interface methods, but first we need to connect our program to an instance of the COM component. We'll need to do two basic things to make this happen: we must create an instance of the component, and we must implement a means of accessing the interface to the component. Since we get a lot of help from ClassWizard for the latter, let's do that first.

Creating the Interface

For the representation of the interface to the COM component, it's natural in C++ to think of a class. ClassWizard can create the class that we need automatically from the type library for the component.

Open the ClassWizard dialog by right clicking in the editor window and selecting from the context menu, and click on the Add Class... button. From the pop-up that appears, select the From a type library... option. You will then see this dialog:

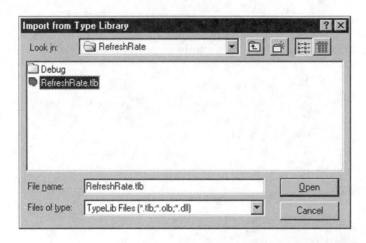

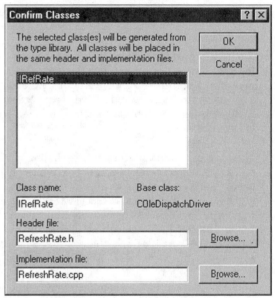

Navigate to the directory containing the type library for **RefreshRate**, select the file and click on Open. You will then see a dialog showing details of the class that will be created from the type library:

A class **IRefRate** will be derived from **COleDispatchDriver** to implement the interface defined in the type library file **RefreshRate.tlb**. Click on OK in the dialog to accept this, and then click on the OK button to close ClassWizard. If you look in ClassView you will see the class has been added to your project, and is defined as:

```
class IRefRate : public COleDispatchDriver
{
public:
    IRefRate() {}                  // Calls COleDispatchDriver default constructor
    IRefRate(LPDISPATCH pDispatch) : COleDispatchDriver(pDispatch) {}
    IRefRate(const IRefRate& dispatchSrc) : COleDispatchDriver(dispatchSrc) {}

// Attributes
public:
```

```
// Operations
public:
    long RefreshRate(long HScan);
    long GetVRes();
    long GetHRes();
};
```

The base class **COleDispatchDriver** enables COM interface functions to be called using the **IDispatch** interface. **COleDispatchDriver** has three constructors: one connects to a COM object by using an existing **COleDispatchDriver** object that has already established an interface to the COM object; one accepts a pointer to an **IDispatch** interface; the third is a default constructor that accepts no arguments. If you use the default constructor to create a **COleDispatchDriver**-derived object, you can use **CreateDispatch()** or **AttachDispatch()** to attach the dispatch interface to the object.

If you look in **RefreshRate.cpp**, you'll see how the interface functions have been implemented:

```
long IRefRate::RefreshRate(long HScan)
{
    long result;
    static BYTE parms[] = VTS_I4;
    InvokeHelper(0x60020000, DISPATCH_METHOD, VT_I4, (void*)&result,
                                                    parms, HScan);
    return result;
}

long IRefRate::GetVRes()
{
    long result;
    InvokeHelper(0x60020001, DISPATCH_METHOD, VT_I4, (void*)&result, NULL);
    return result;
}

long IRefRate::GetHRes()
{
    long result;
    InvokeHelper(0x60020002, DISPATCH_METHOD, VT_I4, (void*)&result, NULL);
    return result;
}
```

Each of the three functions calls the function **InvokeHelper()** that's inherited from the base class. This function packages the **Invoke()** function in the **IDispatch** interface and can accept five or more arguments, which we can use to find out how it works.

The first argument to **InvokeHelper()** is the DispID for the interface function that's to be called; the DispID was obtained from the type library for the component by ClassWizard. The second argument determines that a method is being called, rather than a property value being set or obtained. The third argument specifies the type of the return value — **VT_I4** corresponds to **long**. The types acceptable in the COM context are encoded so that they can be interpreted appropriately in any programming context, and there is a predefined set of symbols that correspond to these types. The fourth argument is a pointer to a variable that is to receive the return value from the interface function. This is the **retval** value, not the value of type **HRESULT** returned to COM. If the **HRESULT** value returned when the interface function is called indicates a failure, the **InvokeHelper()** function will throw an exception.

The fifth argument is a pointer to a string that indicates the type of each of the following arguments. If there are none, as is the case with **GetVRes()** and **GetHRes()**, this pointer is **NULL**. The types are specified in a language-neutral form similar to that for the return value. **VTS_I4** is used for **HScan**, which corresponds to **long**.

Once we've a created component object, we'll be able to access the interface functions for the **RefRate** component through the driver class, **IRefRate**, so add the following declaration to the **CUseRefRateView** class definition:

```
public:
    IRefRate* m_pRefRateDriver;    // Pointer to dispatch driver for RefRate
```

We'll be using this pointer in the button handler to call the interface functions for the component. You can also add an incomplete declaration for the **IRefRate** class immediately before the view class definition:

```
class IRefRate;                    // The RefRate dispatch driver class
```

Of course, we'll need the definition of the class **IRefRate** when we include the view class definition into the view implementation file, so add the following **#include** directive to the **UseRefRateView.cpp** file, just before the **#include** directive for **UseRefRateView.h**:

```
#include "RefreshRate.h"
```

You need to add the same **#include** directive to the **UseRefRate.cpp** file.

Using the COM Library

Before you can do anything with a COM component, even before constructing it, you need access to the **COM library** in your program. The COM library contains functions that enable you to create COM components, as well as a variety of other functions for working with COM objects. To make the COM library functions available to your program, you call a function **CoInitialize()**.

When you call this function, it requires an argument of **NULL** to be specified because the parameter is reserved for possible future use. Because it's a COM function, it returns a value of type **HRESULT**. The normal return value is **S_OK** if the COM library initialization was successful. **CoInitialize()** returns **S_FALSE** if the library was already initialized. Remember that you should not use an **if** to check for these values directly. Because there are several possible success or failure codes, you should use the macros **SUCCEEDED()** or **FAILED()** to test an **HRESULT** value.

Note that the COM library is part of the OLE library that's a prerequisite for OLE (ActiveX) controls. The OLE library is initialized by a call to **OleInitialize()**, which in turn calls **CoInitialize()**. If you think you'll need the full facilities of the OLE library at some point, you can call **OleInitialize()** instead of **CoInitialize()**. You must then call **OleUninitialize()** (rather than **CoUninitialize()**) when you're done. We only need COM in the present context, so we'll stick with that in our example.

All our usage of COM library facilities will be within the view class for our program. We can add the following statements to the constructor for the **CUseRefRateView** class, following the block of code bounded by the **AFX_DATA_INIT** comments:

```
    if(FAILED(CoInitialize(NULL)))                 // Initialize COM library
    {
      AfxMessageBox("COM Library init failed");
      AfxAbort();                                   // End the program
    }
```

This uses the **FAILED()** macro to test whether the **HRESULT** value returned indicates that the COM library was not initialized. If it wasn't, we can't proceed, so we display a message and end the program.

When you've finished with the library in your program, you should call the function **CoUninitialize()**, so add the following statement to the view class destructor:

```
    CoUninitialize();    // Uninitialize the COM library
```

With the COM library initialized, we are ready to create our first COM object.

Component Objects

A COM object is not a class object. Although we used a class to implement **RefRate**, doing so was a C++ convenience, nothing more. A COM component can be implemented without using classes at all. To create an instance of a COM component, you can call the COM library function **CoCreateInstance()**. This function will create the COM object by calling the **GetClassObject()** member of the **_Module** object in the component implementation, and supplying a pointer to the COM interface that you request. The function requires five arguments:

1 The CLSID for the component, of type **REFCLSID**.

2 A pointer of type **IUnknown**. If this is **NULL**, it indicates that the component isn't embedded in another component; a component incorporated into another component is said to be **aggregated**. If the component is aggregated, this pointer points to the **IUnknown** interface for the component that contains the component you want.

3 A value indicating the context in which the component is to run — this could be as an in-process server, as an out-of-process server, or as a remote server on a separate machine.

4 A reference to the ID for the interface to be used.

5 A pointer to a pointer to the required interface.

Luckily, **COleDispatchDriver** wraps up this function in a member function called **CreateDispatch()**. All that **CreateDispatch()** needs is a CLSID to be able to create an object and attach its **IDispatch** interface to the **COleDispatchDriver**-derived class. This is precisely what we need it to do, so let's investigate how we can get hold of the CLSID.

Obtaining the CLSID for a Component

There are several ways to get hold of a CLSID. The easy way out in this case would be to copy the definition of **CLSID_RefRate** from the **RefreshRate_i.c** file that was generated by the MIDL compiler when we compiled the code for the component. However, for other components, we can't be sure that this will always be available so we need a more general approach for the COM components you have on your system.

You can view information about **RefRate** and other COM components by using the **OLE/COM Object Viewer** (**Oleview.exe**) that you can access through the <u>T</u>ools menu. It runs as a completely independent program so you could execute it separately from Visual C++ if you wanted to.

To display information about our component using the OLE/COM Object Viewer, make sure <u>E</u>xpert Mode is checked in the <u>V</u>iew menu, and extend the **All Objects** folder in the left hand pane. You will then see a list of all the COM objects on your system in alphabetical order. You should find the **RefRate** entry in the list.

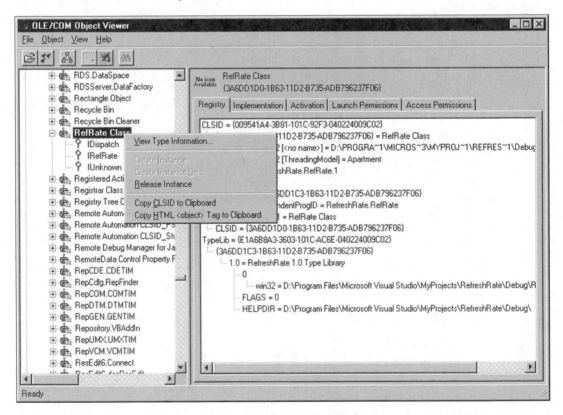

If you click on the entry to highlight it, the registry data will be displayed in the right hand window. Right clicking the entry will bring up a context menu, as shown, where you have an option to copy the CLSID to the clipboard. You will then be able to copy the CLSID from the clipboard into your program. However, there's a problem with that: the CLSID is actually a 128-bit binary number. When we copy the CLSID from the clipboard, we end up with a string of characters:

`{3A6DD1D0-1B63-11D2-B735-ADB796237F06}`

You need to convert this to the 16-*byte* numeric value for the CLSID for it to be of any use. Fortunately, the COM library provides a function called **CLSIDFromString()** that will do the conversion for you. You must supply two arguments to the function: a pointer to the string representation of the CLSID, and the address of a variable of type CLSID. You could therefore get the CLSID with the statements:

```
CLSID CLSID_RefRate;                                        // Object class ID
::CLSIDFromString(L"{3A6DD1D0-1B63-11D2-B735-ADB796237F06}", &CLSID_RefRate);
```

You'll have noticed the **L** preceding the first quote for the string representation of the CLSID. No, it isn't a typo! The **L** specifies the string constant as being a wide character string — of type **wchar_t**. The **L** is a cast to **long** which is the underlying type of **wchar_t**. With this type of string, each character requires 16 bits (two bytes), rather than the single byte for ASCII. You can just paste the string representation direct from the clipboard (including the braces), put quotes around it and add the initial **L**. In fact, it won't work if you remove the braces, so don't be tempted to delete them.

There's yet another way to get the CLSID. The registry contains a **ProgID** (a program ID) for each COM component. The ProgID is usually in the form **Program_Name.Component_Name.Version**. In our case, the program name is **RefreshRate**, the component name is **RefRate**, and the version is 1. If you look in the registry under **HKEY_CLASSES_ROOT**, you'll see a key for **RefreshRate.RefRate.1** which is the ProgID of our component. This key contains a subkey called **CLSID** that contains the CLSID for our component. Given that you've declared **CLSID_RefRate** as above, you can use the ProgID to produce the CLSID using the COM library function **CLSIDFromProgID()**, like this:

```
::CLSIDFromProgID(L"RefreshRate.RefRate.1",&CLSID_RefRate);
```

This is quite a nice way of getting a CLSID to use for creating an instance of a COM class, but it turns out that **COleDispatchDriver** provides an overloaded version of **CreateDispatch()** that accepts a string for the ProgID of the object to create, so we don't need to call **CLSIDFromProgID()** ourselves.

Creating an Instance of a Component

We can add the code to create an instance of **RefRate** to the view constructor:

```
CUseRefRateView::CUseRefRateView()
    : CFormView(CUseRefRateView::IDD)
{
    //{{AFX_DATA_INIT(CUseRefRateView)
    m_lHScan = 50;
    m_lRefresh = 0;
    m_lHRes = 0;
    m_lVRes = 0;
    //}}AFX_DATA_INIT
    // TODO: add construction code here

    if(FAILED(CoInitialize(NULL)))                      // Initialize COM Library
    {
        AfxMessageBox("COM library Init failed");
        AfxAbort();
    }                                                   // End the program
```

```
        // Create a new driver object to handle our COM object
        m_pRefRateDriver = new IRefRate;

        // Create an instance of the COM object using the ProgID
        // and attach the dispinterface to our OLEDispatchDriver-derived object
        m_pRefRateDriver->CreateDispatch(_T("RefreshRate.RefRate.1"));
    }
```

This is really just putting together what we've discussed. The only thing to notice is the **_T()** macro around the ProgID. If you've compiled your application for Unicode then the **CreateDispatch()** function accepts a wide string, but if you haven't then you must pass a standard string without prefixing it with an **L**. In our (non-Unicode) case we could get away with passing the string directly to the function, but it would be better if we wrapped the string up in a **_T()** macro. This macro is exactly the same as the **L** prefix if Unicode is used, but it means nothing if it isn't, so we're covered in either case. You'll see this macro used a lot in MFC itself.

Note that the pointer, **m_pRefRateDriver**, that we're using here is *not* a pointer to the **IDispatch** interface of the **RefRate** object. **m_pRefRateDriver** is a pointer to a **COleDispatchDriver**-derived class that implements functions corresponding to those in the **RefRate** dispatch interface. If you want to manipulate the dispatch interface directly, you can get a pointer to it from the public **m_lpDispatch** member of **COleDispatchDriver**.

Releasing the Component

The next thing we need to do is add code to the destructor to clean up the driver object that we've allocated with the **new** operator, so add the following statement to the **CUseRefRateView** class destructor:

```
CUseRefRateView::~CUseRefRateView()
{
    delete m_pRefRateDriver;
    CoUninitialize();   // Uninitialize the COM library
}
```

Note that the code must come *before* the call to **CoUninitialize()**. We can't uninitialize the COM library until all the COM objects that we've created have been released. Remember that each time you call **QueryInterface()** or **AddRef()** on an interface, you are increasing the reference count for that interface and that you need to call **Release()** when you've finished using the interface so that the reference count is decreased and the object can remove itself from memory when appropriate.

Although it doesn't look like we're calling **Release()** on the **IDispatch** interface that's wrapped up in the driver class, it is happening. The destructor for **COleDispatchDriver** calls **Release()** on the dispatch interface pointer that it has, as long as a member variable called **m_bAutoRelease** is set to **TRUE**. Since it is **TRUE** by default, the **delete** operation on **m_pRefRateDriver** does call **IDispatch::Release()** in our case.

Now we have an instance of the **RefRate** component and the interface is available to us, so we can implement the handler for the Calculate button.

Using Component Interface Functions

We're back on familiar ground now. We can use the functions in the **IRefRate** class object that connects to the COM object just like any other class member function. The implementation of the handler will be:

```
void CUseRefRateView::OnCalculate()
{
    UpdateData(TRUE);                    // Get m_lHScan from the dialog
    m_lRefresh = m_pRefRateDriver->RefreshRate(m_lHScan);
    m_lHRes = m_pRefRateDriver->GetHRes();
    m_lVRes = m_pRefRateDriver->GetVRes();
    UpdateData(FALSE);                   // Set the values in the dialog
}
```

We first call the **UpdateData()** member of our view class (inherited from **CWnd**) with the argument **TRUE**. This causes **DoDataExchange()** to be called to retrieve data from the form dialog controls — on this occasion, just the value entered for the scan rate. After calling the component interface functions to calculate the refresh rate and the screen resolution, we call **UpdateData()** with the argument **FALSE** to store these values back in the controls in the form dialog.

Our client for the component is complete. You can now build it and give it a whirl. You should get a dialog that looks like this one:

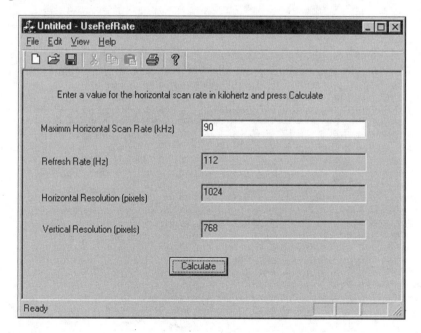

Using ATL to Create an ActiveX Control

Now that we've staggered through creating and using an elementary ATL-based COM object, we're ready for something a bit more challenging. We can see how to put together an ATL-based equivalent of the traffic signal control that we produced using MFC.

The first step is to create a project using the ATL COM AppWizard, exactly as before, but name the project **ATLSignal**. Once that's done you can add a COM object. Click on the button on the ATL toolbar, or select Insert | New ATL Object... from the menu.

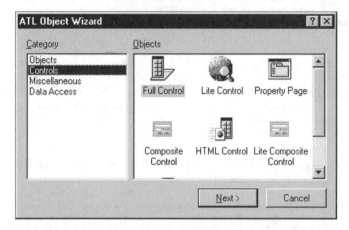

This time we want to insert a full ATL control from the Controls set of COM components, so make sure it's highlighted as shown, and click on Next >. You can enter **Signal** as the short name on the Names tab in the ATL Object Wizard Properties dialog:

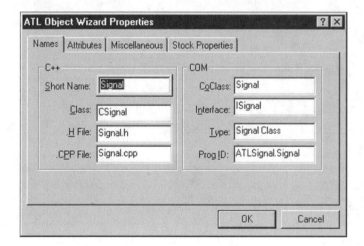

The Stock Properties tab enables you to add support for stock properties to the ATL control object that will be accessible from a client. If you look at the tab, you'll see that there are a greater variety of stock properties available here than through `COleControl` in MFC. However, we don't need to add any of these to our control. Take a look at the Attributes tab:

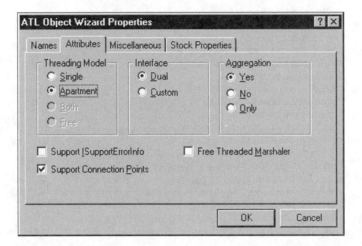

Check the box for Support Connection Points — this will be needed when we add the event to the control which signals the container when our traffic signal changes state. We had the capability in the MFC version to do this, so we should see how to implement it using ATL. Now take a look at the Miscellaneous tab:

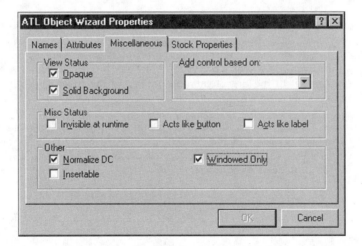

As you can see, this tab provides us with options to specify how we want our control to appear when it's being run. In this case, we'd like it to always appear in a window, so check the Windowed Only box.

That's all we need from the options, so just click on OK to add the files defining the control to our project. Let's take a look at what's been added.

The ATL Control Class

If you look at ClassView, you'll see that we have just one class added to our project, **CSignal**, and an interface, **ISignal**. If you look at the class definition though, there's some real meat here. Let's explore the interesting bits piecemeal:

```
class ATL_NO_VTABLE CSignal :
    public CComObjectRootEx<CComSingleThreadModel>,
    public IDispatchImpl<ISignal, &IID_ISignal, &LIBID_ATLSIGNALLib>,
    public CComControl<CSignal>,
    public IPersistStreamInitImpl<CSignal>,
    public IOleControlImpl<CSignal>,
    public IOleObjectImpl<CSignal>,
    public IOleInPlaceActiveObjectImpl<CSignal>,
    public IViewObjectExImpl<CSignal>,
    public IOleInPlaceObjectWindowlessImpl<CSignal>,
    public IConnectionPointContainerImpl<CSignal>,
    public IPersistStorageImpl<CSignal>,
    public ISpecifyPropertyPagesImpl<CSignal>,
    public IQuickActivateImpl<CSignal>,
    public IDataObjectImpl<CSignal>,
    public IProvideClassInfo2Impl<&CLSID_Signal,&DIID__ISignalEvents,
                                        &LIBID_ATLSIGNALLib>,
    public IPropertyNotifySinkCP<CSignal>,
    public CComCoClass<CSignal, &CLSID_Signal>
{
    // Details of the class definition...
};
```

Our class **CSignal** has no fewer than *seventeen* base classes, all of which are templates, so they're customized to fit with our class. Our class will inherit the functionality of all these classes, so you'd need to look into the members of all of them if you wanted to appreciate the full capabilities of **CSignal**. We won't be doing that here, but we will pick a few that are of interest to us. You can get to the documentation on any of the base classes by placing the cursor on the class name and pressing *F1*.

CComObjectRootEx, **CComCoClass**, **CComControl** and **IDispatchImpl** implement the basic COM capability that we discussed in the context of the previous COM example, so we won't repeat it here. We won't go through the others in detail, but a rough guide to the services that the other base classes provide is as follows:

Class Name	Purpose
`IProvideClassInfo2Impl`	Provides functions that make the type information for an object available.
`IPersistStreamInitImpl`	Provides a client interface to initiate saving and loading of the persistent data for an object in a stream.
`IPersistStorageImpl`	Provides a client interface to initiate saving and loading of the persistent data for an object in a structured form called a **storage** that can improve I/O performance with complex objects.
`IQuickActivateImpl`	Enables rapid loading of the control.
`IOleControlImpl`	Provides a default implementation of the **IOleControl** interface that supports signaling ambient property changes, among other things.
`IOleObjectImpl`	Provides a default implementation of **IOleObject** which provides the primary interface by which a container communicates with a control.
`IOleInPlaceActiveObjectImpl`	Provides a default implementation of the **IOleInPlaceActiveObject** interface which supports communications between a container and an in-place active control.
`IViewObjectExImpl`	Provides a default implementation of the **IViewObject** interface which enables a control to display itself in the container.
`IOleInPlaceObjectWindowlessImpl`	Provides an implementation of the **IOleInPlaceObjectWindowless** interface which enables a windowless control to receive Windows messages.
`IDataObjectImpl`	Provides an implementation of the **IDataObject** interface that supports the uniform data transfer which applies to transferring data via the clipboard and drag and drop operations.
`IConnectionPointContainerImpl`	Provides a container class for connection points which support events that are signaled from our control to the container.
`ISpecifyPropertyPagesImpl`	Provides an implementation of the **ISpecifyPropertyPages** interface which enables a container to obtain the CLSIDs for the property pages for a control.
`IPropertyNotifySinkCP`	Exposes the **IPropertyNotifySink** interface on a connection point for receiving notifications from the object that a property has changed

The COM AppWizard automatically deals with the registration of the control. The statement:

```
DECLARE_REGISTRY_RESOURCEID(IDR_SIGNAL)
```

is a macro that will generate the definition of a **static** function in the class that will register the control. The symbol **IDR_SIGNAL** is defined by the COM AppWizard and identifies the **.rgs** file containing the registry script.

This block of code in the class definition defines the COM map for the control:

```
BEGIN_COM_MAP(CSignal)
    COM_INTERFACE_ENTRY(ISignal)
    COM_INTERFACE_ENTRY(IDispatch)
    COM_INTERFACE_ENTRY(IViewObjectEx)
    COM_INTERFACE_ENTRY(IViewObject2)
    COM_INTERFACE_ENTRY(IViewObject)
    COM_INTERFACE_ENTRY(IOleInPlaceObjectWindowless)
    COM_INTERFACE_ENTRY(IOleInPlaceObject)
    COM_INTERFACE_ENTRY2(IOleWindow, IOleInPlaceObjectWindowless)
    COM_INTERFACE_ENTRY(IOleInPlaceActiveObject)
    COM_INTERFACE_ENTRY(IOleControl)
    COM_INTERFACE_ENTRY(IOleObject)
    COM_INTERFACE_ENTRY(IPersistStreamInit)
    COM_INTERFACE_ENTRY2(IPersist, IPersistStreamInit)
    COM_INTERFACE_ENTRY(IConnectionPointContainer)
    COM_INTERFACE_ENTRY(ISpecifyPropertyPages)
    COM_INTERFACE_ENTRY(IQuickActivate)
    COM_INTERFACE_ENTRY(IPersistStorage)
    COM_INTERFACE_ENTRY(IDataObject)
    COM_INTERFACE_ENTRY(IProvideClassInfo)
    COM_INTERFACE_ENTRY(IProvideClassInfo2)
END_COM_MAP()
```

Each entry is an interface which can be accessed by a container. All the functions that a container can call in the control will appear in one or other of the interfaces that appear here.

The property map defines the CLSIDs and other information relating to property pages supported by the control:

```
BEGIN_PROP_MAP(CSignal)
    PROP_DATA_ENTRY("_cx", m_sizeExtent.cx, VT_UI4)
    PROP_DATA_ENTRY("_cy", m_sizeExtent.cy, VT_UI4)
    // Example entries
    // PROP_ENTRY("Property Description", dispid, clsid)
    // PROP_PAGE(CLSID_StockColorPage)
END_PROP_MAP()
```

Next we have a connection point map:

```
BEGIN_CONNECTION_POINT_MAP(CSignal)
    CONNECTION_POINT_ENTRY(IID_IPropertyNotifySink)
END_CONNECTION_POINT_MAP()
```

This contains just the one point at the moment for receiving property changes, but you can add an entry here for each event that the control supports. Each event will be represented by a connection point that is specified in this map.

The message map defines the message handlers that the control provides:

```
BEGIN_MSG_MAP(CSignal)
    CHAIN_MSG_MAP(CComControl<CSignal>)
    DEFAULT_REFLECTION_HANDLER()
END_MSG_MAP()
```

The first entry defines where to find the message map of the base class for CSignal — which in this case in CComControl — and the second provides a default handler for the control that will receive reflected messages. We'll be adding further handlers to the message map a little later in the chapter.

The **DECLARE_VIEW_STATUS()** function specifies information to a container about whether the control has a solid background and is opaque or not. It will be called by a container when the view containing the control needs to be redrawn. This allows the container to make the drawing process more efficient, since items in the view that are covered by an opaque object with a solid background will not need to be redrawn.

At the end of the class definition there's a definition of the **OnDraw()** function which will draw the control in the container.

Before we can do much about drawing the control, however, we need to define a traffic signal. That means we need to add a class to the project.

Defining the Signal

We can implement the class to define the signal much as we did with the MFC-based version. However, we'll need to make a few changes because we no longer have MFC available to us.

Create a new class by selecting the Insert | New Class... menu item. Set the Class type to Generic in the New Class dialog and give the class the name **CTrafficSignal**, then click OK.

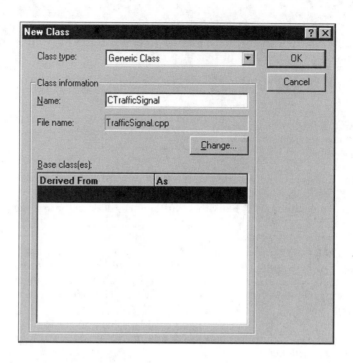

Now go to the class definition and add the following code:

```
#if !defined(AFX_TRAFFICSIGNAL_H__E21E34C2_1BC5_11D2_BA71_00600873394D__INCLUDED_)
#define AFX_TRAFFICSIGNAL_H__E21E34C2_1BC5_11D2_BA71_00600873394D__INCLUDED_

#if _MSC_VER > 1000
#pragma once
#endif // _MSC_VER > 1000

class CTrafficSignal
{
public:
    CTrafficSignal();
    virtual ~CTrafficSignal();
```

```
// Class interface
void SetPosition(int x, int y)
{
    m_ptPosition.x = x;
    m_ptPosition.y = y;
}

void SetHeight(int nHeight)
    { m_nHeight =nHeight; }
void SetState(int nState)
    { m_nState = nState; }
int NextState();                            // Change to the next state
void Draw(HDC& hDC);                         // Draw the traffic signal
```

```
private:
    POINT m_ptPosition;       // Bottom center of signal
    int m_nHeight;            // Height of signal
    int m_nState;             // State of signal
};

#endif
// !defined(AFX_TRAFFICSIGNAL_H__E21E34C2_1BC5_11D2_BA71_00600873394D__INCLUDED_)
```

This is almost the same as the definition we had in the MFC implementation in Chapter 23, but there are some differences you should note.

The **CPoint** class isn't available because we're not using MFC. To declare the member **m_ptPosition** to store the reference point for the signal we use the **POINT** structure which is defined for the Windows API. This has public members **x** and **y** storing the coordinates. The **SetPosition()** member of the original class accepted a **CPoint** argument; now it accepts two arguments of type **int**. We could use a **POINT** structure for the point here, but it will be easier to use the coordinates as arguments in this case.

The **Draw()** function has a different parameter type specified from the original version too. The **HDC** type is another Windows type defining a handle to a device context. A device context in Windows is a structure that you refer to with a variable of type **HDC**. All our drawing operations will need to use the Windows API, since we have no MFC facilities in our control, but it's not going to be that difficult, as you will see.

Implementing CTrafficSignal

In **TrafficSignal.cpp**, we need to implement three functions: the constructor, the **NextState()** function, and the **Draw()** function. We'll use the same constants that we used in the MFC version, so copy the **OurConstants.h** file to the current project directory. The contents are exactly as before:

```
//Definition of constants
#ifndef __OURCONSTANTS.H__
#define __OURCONSTANTS.H__

const int STOP          = 101;
const int GO            = 103;
const int READY_TO_STOP = 104;

const COLORREF RED    = RGB(255,0,0);
const COLORREF ORANGE = RGB(200,100,0);
const COLORREF GREEN  = RGB(0,255,0);
const COLORREF GRAY   = RGB(100,100,100);
```

We can implement the constructor for the **CTrafficSignal** class first, since that's the easiest function. The initial additions to **TrafficSignal.cpp** will be:

```
#include "stdafx.h"
#include "OurConstants.h"
#include "ATLSignal.h"
#include "TrafficSignal.h"

//////////////////////////////////////////////////////////////////////////
// Construction/Destruction
//////////////////////////////////////////////////////////////////////////
```

1045

```
CTrafficSignal::CTrafficSignal()
{
    m_ptPosition.x = m_ptPosition.y = 0;  // Set arbitrary position
    m_nHeight = 1000;                      // Set arbitrary height
    m_nState = STOP;                       // Set initial state to STOP
}
```

This just initializes the data members of the class to arbitrary values. The values for these data members will be set externally by the control.

We can implement the **NextState()** member function almost exactly as in the original version, so add the following code to **TrafficSignal.cpp**:

```
// Change the signal state to the next in sequence
int CTrafficSignal::NextState()
{
    switch (m_nState)
    {
        case STOP:                         // Next after STOP is GO
            m_nState = GO;
            break;
        case GO:                           // Next after GO is READY_TO_STOP
            m_nState = READY_TO_STOP;
            break;
        case READY_TO_STOP:                // Next after READY_TO_STOP is STOP
            m_nState = STOP;
            break;
        default:                           // We should never get to here
            m_nState = STOP;
            MessageBox(NULL, "Invalid signal state", "ATLSignal Error", MB_OK);
    }
    return m_nState;
}
```

However, note that the original call to **AfxMessageBox()** has to be replaced with a call to the Win32 **MessageBox()** function. The last function we need to implement in the **CTrafficSignal** class is **Draw()**.

Drawing the Signal

The visual representation of the signal is exactly the same as in the previous chapter. The reference point for describing the signal geometry is at the bottom center of the signal.

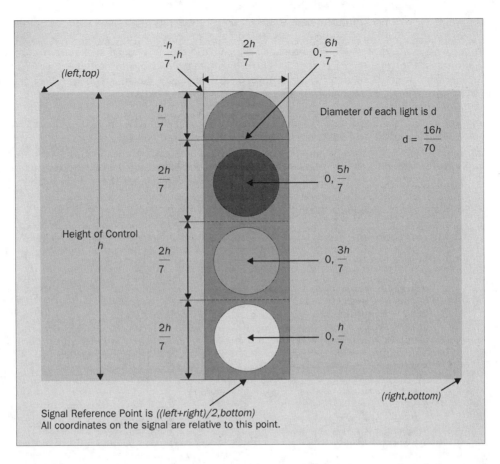

The dimensions for the signal are determined from the height of the control, and the signal will be drawn relative to the reference point. The reference point will be set by the control as being midway between the left and right boundaries of the control, on the bottom boundary.

Let's go through the code for the **Draw()** function step by step. There's quite a lot of it, although much will be essentially the same as the previous version in Chapter 23. We can start by setting up the brushes and pens we need to draw the traffic signal:

```
void CTrafficSignal::Draw(HDC& hDC)
{
    // Set the pen and brush to draw the signal
    HBRUSH hGrayBrush = (HBRUSH)GetStockObject(GRAY_BRUSH);
    HBRUSH hOldBrush = (HBRUSH)SelectObject(hDC, hGrayBrush);
    HPEN hBlackPen = (HPEN)GetStockObject(BLACK_PEN);
    HPEN hOldPen = (HPEN)SelectObject(hDC, hBlackPen);

    // Plus the rest of the code for the function...
}
```

The Windows API uses **HBRUSH** and **HPEN** types to specify brushes and pens to be used in a device context. These are handles — pointers to the structures representing those entities. Here we need a stock pen and a stock brush, so we can use the API function **GetStockObject()** to obtain them. The type of object that is returned is determined by the argument passed to the function. The object is returned as type **HGDIOBJ**, which is a generic type for all of the stock objects, so we must cast the handle returned to the type we want.

To select a pen or a brush into the device context, we call the API function **SelectObject()**. This works similarly to the **CDC** class member function (which in fact calls the API function eventually). Here we pass the handle to the device context as an argument, as well as the handle to the drawing object we want to select. Of course, we must save the handles to the pen and brush we displace in the device context so that we can restore them when we are done.

Next we can add the code to draw the basic outline of the signal:

```
void CTrafficSignal::Draw(HDC& hDC)
{
    // Set the pen and brush to draw the signal...

    // Define the main body of the signal
    int nLeft = m_ptPosition.x - m_nHeight/7;
    int nTop = m_ptPosition.y - (long)m_nHeight*6L/7L;
    int nRight = m_ptPosition.x + m_nHeight/7;
    int nBottom = m_ptPosition.y;

    Rectangle(hDC, nLeft, nTop, nRight, nBottom);       // Draw the body

    // Draw the semi-circular top of the signal
    Chord(hDC,                                          // Device context
        nLeft, nTop - m_nHeight/7,                      // Bounding rectangle top-left
        nRight, nTop + m_nHeight/7,                     // Bounding rectangle bottom-right
        nRight, nTop,                                   // Start point
        nLeft, nTop);                                   // End Point

    // Plus the rest of the code for the function...
}
```

The coordinates we need are calculated exactly as before. You should be able to relate them to the diagram. To draw the outline of the signal we call the **Rectangle()** and **Chord()** functions from the Windows API. The MFC functions are just wrappers for these functions, so the argument list is very similar. The only hardship we have to endure is to enter the coordinates for the bounding rectangle explicitly.

Next we can add the code to create the brushes we need to draw the lights:

```
void CTrafficSignal::Draw(HDC& hDC)
{
    // Set the pen and brush to draw the signal...

    // Define the main body of the signal...

    // Create brushes for the lights
    HBRUSH hbrStop;                     // A brush to fill the stop light
    HBRUSH hbrReady;                    // A brush to fill the ready light
    HBRUSH hbrGo;                       // A brush to fill the go light
```

1048

```
    switch (m_nState)
    {
      case STOP:                                          // Red only
        hbrStop = CreateSolidBrush(RED);
        hbrReady = CreateSolidBrush(GRAY);
        hbrGo = CreateSolidBrush(GRAY);
        break;
      case GO:                                            // Green only
        hbrStop = CreateSolidBrush(GRAY);
        hbrReady = CreateSolidBrush(GRAY);
        hbrGo = CreateSolidBrush(GREEN);
        break;
      case READY_TO_STOP:                                 // Orange only
        hbrStop = CreateSolidBrush(GRAY);
        hbrReady = CreateSolidBrush(ORANGE);
        hbrGo = CreateSolidBrush(GRAY);
        break;
      default:
        hbrStop = CreateSolidBrush(GRAY);
        hbrReady = CreateSolidBrush(GRAY);
        hbrGo = CreateSolidBrush(GRAY);
    }

    // Plus the rest of the code for the function...
}
```

To draw the lights, we must set up the appropriately colored brush that we'll use to fill each light, depending on the current signal state stored in the **m_nState** data member. We have a variable of type **HBRUSH** declared for each of the three lights. To create a brush, we can use the API function, **CreateSolidBrush()**. This will return a handle to a brush defined by the argument specified, which is of type **COLORREF**. Here we can use the symbols for the standard colors, but you can use the **RGB()** macro to specify the color if necessary. The overall logic here is exactly the same as before.

The last block of code we need to add will draw the lights using the brushes we have created:

```
void CTrafficSignal::Draw(HDC& hDC)
{
    // Set the pen and brush to draw the signal...

    // Define the main body of the signal...

    // Create brushes for the lights...

    // Define the rectangle bounding the stop light
    int nMargin = (long)m_nHeight * 2L/70L;              // Ten percent of the width
    nLeft += nMargin;                                     // Left side of stop light
    nTop += nMargin;                                      // Top of stop light
    nRight -= nMargin;                                    // Right side of stop light
    int nStep = (long)m_nHeight * 2L/7L;                 // Distance between lights
    nBottom = nTop + nStep - 2 * nMargin;                // Bottom of stop light

    // Draw the stop light
    SelectObject(hDC, hbrStop);
    Ellipse(hDC, nLeft, nTop, nRight, nBottom);
```

```
      // Set the position of the ready light
      nTop += nStep;
      nBottom += nStep;

      // Draw the ready light
      SelectObject(hDC, hbrReady);
      Ellipse(hDC, nLeft, nTop, nRight, nBottom);

      // Set the position of the go light
      nTop += nStep;
      nBottom += nStep;

      // Draw the go light
      SelectObject(hDC, hbrGo);
      Ellipse(hDC, nLeft, nTop, nRight, nBottom);

      SelectObject(hDC, hOldBrush);             // Put the old brush back
      SelectObject(hDC, hOldPen);               // Put the old pen back

      // Delete the brushes we have created
      DeleteObject(hbrStop);
      DeleteObject(hbrReady);
      DeleteObject(hbrGo);
  }
```

The main difference from the original code is that we call Windows API functions to select a brush, to do the drawing and to restore the original brush and pen. We also have to delete the brushes we create in the function. Using an MFC class, **CBrush**, in the previous chapter, the brush was deleted automatically when the **CBrush** object was destroyed. This would occur when the **Draw()** function exited. Here, if we don't delete the brushes, we will consume more and more GDI resources till we eventually run out and no programs will execute.

The names of the functions we use are the same as the equivalent **CDC** class members, so the basic logic is exactly the same. Only the arguments are a little different. Piece of cake, wasn't it?

Adding the Signal to the Control

Our control class **CSignal** will need an instance of **CTrafficSignal**, together with the data members that will keep track of the state of the signal. Add the following **private** members to the **CSignal** class definition:

```
  private:
     CTrafficSignal m_TrafficSignal;      // The traffic signal
     long m_1StopOrGoTime;                // Stop/Go duration in msecs
     BOOL m_bStartRed;                    // TRUE to start on red
     BOOL m_bSignalGo;                    // True to start the signal
     int m_nTimerID;                      // ID of timer controlling the signal
     int m_nChangeTime;                   // Time for READY_TO_STOP in msecs.
```

Because the class contains a member of type **CTrafficSignal**, we must add an **#include** directive for **TrafficSignal.h** to **Signal.cpp**, immediately preceding the one for **Signal.h**. Later, we'll be using the constants we've defined in **OurConstants.h**, so you can add an **#include** for this too while you're about it. Another place that needs access to the **CTrafficSignal** class that's easy to overlook is the **ATLSignal.cpp** file. This includes **Signal.h**, so you must add an **#include** directive for **TrafficSignal.h** before it does so.

Of course, we need to initialize the new data members in the constructor, which has its definition within the class definition:

```
public:
    CSignal()
    {
        m_bWindowOnly = TRUE;
        m_bSignalGo = FALSE;          // Not running initially
        m_bStartRed = TRUE;           // Start on red
        m_nTimerID = 100;             // Arbitrary ID for timer
        m_lStopOrGoTime = 5000L;      // Stop or go light on for 5 seconds
        m_nChangeTime = 2000;         // Orange light on for 2 seconds
    }
```

There's nothing new here; we can go straight on to drawing the control.

Drawing the Control

We already have an **OnDraw()** member implemented for us in the **CSignal** class by the ATL Object Wizard:

```
HRESULT OnDraw(ATL_DRAWINFO& di)
{
RECT& rc = *(RECT*)di.prcBounds;
Rectangle(di.hdcDraw, rc.left, rc.top, rc.right, rc.bottom);

SetTextAlign(di.hdcDraw, TA_CENTER|TA_BASELINE);
LPCTSTR pszText = _T("ATL 3.0 : Signal");
TextOut(di.hdcDraw,
        (rc.left + rc.right) / 2,
        (rc.top + rc.bottom) / 2,
        pszText,
        lstrlen(pszText));
return S_OK;
}
```

This is a COM function, so it returns a value of type **HRESULT**. The return value here is **S_OK,** but you can return other **HRESULT** values if you have a reason to do so. The parameter, **di**, that gets passed to the function is a reference to a structure of type **ATL_DRAWINFO**. This contains the information we need to implement drawing the control. It contains a member **prcBounds**, which is a pointer to the bounding rectangle for the control, and a member **hdcDraw**, which is a handle to a device context. The code here arbitrarily draws a rectangle around the boundary and displays some text. We'll replace this with our own code to draw the signal:

```
HRESULT OnDraw(ATL_DRAWINFO& di)
{
    RECT& rc = *(RECT*)di.prcBounds;               // Get control rectangle
    HDC hDC = di.hdcDraw;                           // Get the device context
    COLORREF clrBackGround;                         // Control background color
    OLE_COLOR clrClientBackColor;                   // Client background color

    // Get client backgound color and convert to COLORREF
    GetAmbientBackColor(clrClientBackColor);
    ::OleTranslateColor(clrClientBackColor,NULL,&clrBackGround);

    HBRUSH hbrBackground = CreateSolidBrush(clrBackGround);   // Create brush
    FillRect(hDC,&rc,hbrBackground);                          // Fill control area
```

```
        // Define position and height of the traffic signal
      m_TrafficSignal.SetPosition((rc.right+rc.left)/2,rc.bottom);
      m_TrafficSignal.SetHeight(rc.bottom-rc.top);

      m_TrafficSignal.Draw(hDC);                    // Draw the signal
      return S_OK;
  }
```

We get a **RECT** structure, **rc**, from the **prcBounds** member of **di** that corresponds to the rectangle bounding the control. The type **RECT** is a **struct** with members **left**, **top**, **right** and **bottom** corresponding to the *x* and *y* coordinates of the top-left and bottom-right corners of the rectangle. Since **prcBounds** is a pointer, we first cast it to type **RECT***, then dereference the result to get the rectangle. We also obtain a handle to the device context for the control which we store in **hDC**.

The ambient background color for the container is obtained by calling the **GetAmbientBackColor()** function inherited from the **CComControl** base class. The ambient background color is stored in the variable passed as an argument of type **OLE_COLOR**. Before we can use this value, we must convert it to a **COLORREF** value. This is done by the global function **OleTranslateColor()**, and the result is returned in the variable passed as the third argument, **clrBackground**. The second argument to the function gives you the opportunity of supplying a handle to a color palette to be used in the conversion.

To draw the background in the container background color, we create a brush corresponding to the background color and use the API function **FillRect()** to fill the rectangle **rc** with that color by using the brush we've created. The traffic signal will be drawn on top of this background.

To draw the traffic signal, we set the values for its position and height using the coordinates stored in the rectangle **rc**. We then call the **Draw()** function of the traffic signal object **m_TrafficSignal**.

Starting and Stopping the Signal

To start and stop the signal, we need to intercept mouse messages in our control. The **WM_LBUTTONDOWN** message is the one we want. We must first add our handler, **OnLButtonDown()** to the message map for the **CSignal** class. We need one extra line in the definition of the **CSignal** class:

```
BEGIN_MSG_MAP(CSignal)
    CHAIN_MSG_MAP(CComControl<CSignal>)
    DEFAULT_REFLECTION_HANDLER()
    MESSAGE_HANDLER(WM_LBUTTONDOWN, OnLButtonDown)
END_MSG_MAP()
```

With an MFC-based program we wouldn't meddle with the message map because ClassWizard would have managed it, but since we're using ATL here we don't have that support and must take care of the message map entries ourselves. Of course, we must also add the function **OnLButtonDown()** as a member of the class. You can add it as a **public** class member, following the declaration of the **OnDraw()** member:

```
public:
    HRESULT OnDraw(ATL_DRAWINFO& di);
    LRESULT OnLButtonDown(UINT uMsg, WPARAM wParam, LPARAM lParam, BOOL& bHandled);
```

In fact, all message handlers that are specified using the **MESSAGE_HANDLER()** macro must have the same prototype:

```
LRESULT MessageHandler(UINT uMsg, WPARAM wParam, LPARAM lParam, BOOL& bHandled);
```

The first parameter identifies the message, and the second and third parameters are standard parameter values passed to the handler by Windows that provide additional information about the message. The contents of both **wParam** and **lParam** depend on the message. For example, in the case of the **WM_LBUTTONDOWN** message, the **lParam** parameter contains the coordinates of the cursor when the button was clicked and the **wParam** parameter will indicate whether any of the mouse buttons, or the *Shift* or *Ctrl* keys were pressed. The *x* coordinate for the cursor position is retrieved from **lParam** by using the **LOWORD()** macro, and the *y* coordinate by using the **HIWORD()** macro. The last argument is set to **TRUE** before a handler is called. If you want the message to be handled elsewhere, you can set it to **FALSE** in your handler. The return value type is a 32-bit value used by Windows message handlers and callback functions.

We can implement the **WM_LBUTTONDOWN** message handler in **Signal.cpp** as:

```
LRESULT CSignal::OnLButtonDown(UINT uMsg, WPARAM wParam,
                               LPARAM lParam, BOOL& bHandled)
{
    // If the signal is stopped, start it
    // If the signal is running, stop it
    m_bSignalGo = !m_bSignalGo;
    if(m_bSignalGo)
        StartSignal();
    else
        StopSignal();
    return 0;
}
```

We're not interested in the cursor position. If the button is clicked we switch the running state of the signal — if it's stopped we start it, and if it's running we stop it. To make this work we need to add the **StartSignal()** and **StopSignal()** functions to the **CSignal** class. The declarations in the class definition will be:

```
public:
    HRESULT OnDraw(ATL_DRAWINFO& di);
    LRESULT OnLButtonDown(UINT uMsg, WPARAM wParam, LPARAM lParam,
                                                    BOOL& bHandled);
    void StartSignal();                 // Start the signal
    void StopSignal();                  // Stop the signal
```

We can implement these in **Signal.cpp** as:

```
// Start the signal
void CSignal::StartSignal()
{
    // Setup a timer with the required interval
    m_TrafficSignal.SetState(m_bStartRed ? STOP : GO);
    m_nTimerID = SetTimer(m_nTimerID, (UINT)m_lStopOrGoTime);
```

```
      if (!m_nTimerID)
         exit(1);                                 // No timer so exit

      Invalidate();                               // Get the control redrawn
   }

   // Stop the signal
   void CSignal::StopSignal()
   {
      KillTimer(m_nTimerID);                       // Destroy the timer
      Invalidate();                                // Redraw the control
   }
```

These work just like the versions we had in the last chapter. In **StartSignal()** we call the function **SetTimer()** to create a timer for the required interval; this function is inherited from the base class **CComControl**. The **SetTimer()** arguments are the timer ID and the time interval in milliseconds.

The **KillTimer()** function used in the **StopSignal()** function is also inherited from **CComControl** and it destroys the timer identified by the ID passed as an argument. To get the control redrawn we call the function **Invalidate()** which invalidates the whole area of the control, which will result in the **OnDraw()** member being called. **Invalidate()** is also inherited from the base class **CComControl**.

Controlling the Signal

To manage the operation of the signal in **CSignal** we use a timer, so we need to add a handler for **WM_TIMER** messages to the class. We do this in the same way as for the **WM_LBUTTONDOWN** message. First, add the message handler to the message map in the class definition:

```
BEGIN_MSG_MAP(CSignal)
    CHAIN_MSG_MAP(CComControl<CSignal>)
    DEFAULT_REFLECTION_HANDLER()
    MESSAGE_HANDLER(WM_LBUTTONDOWN, OnLButtonDown)
    MESSAGE_HANDLER(WM_TIMER, OnTimer)
END_MSG_MAP()
```

We also need to add a declaration for the handler function to the class definition:

```
public:
    HRESULT OnDraw(ATL_DRAWINFO& di);
    LRESULT OnLButtonDown(UINT uMsg, WPARAM wParam, LPARAM lParam, BOOL&
                                                            bHandled);
    void StartSignal();                              // Start the signal
    void StopSignal();                               // Stop the signal
    LRESULT OnTimer(UINT nIDEvent, WPARAM wParam, LPARAM lParam, BOOL& bHandled);
```

The declaration has the standard form for a handler specified in a **MESSAGE_HANDLER()** macro that we discussed earlier. In this case, the first parameter will be the ID of the timer. We can implement the handler by adding the following code to **Signal.cpp**:

```
LRESULT CSignal::OnTimer(UINT nIDEvent, WPARAM wParam,
                    LPARAM lParam, BOOL& bHandled)
```

```
{
   UINT nInterval = 0;                               // Interval in milliseconds

   // Step to the next signal state and set the time interval
   // based on the new state
   int nNewState = m_TrafficSignal.NextState();      // Go to next state

   switch (nNewState)
   {
      case STOP: case GO:
         nInterval = (UINT)m_lStopOrGoTime;          // Stop or Go interval
         break;

      default:
         nInterval = m_nChangeTime;                  // Transient interval
   }

   Invalidate();                                     // Redraw the signal
   KillTimer(m_nTimerID);                            // Make sure the old timer is dead

   // Set a new timer event
   m_nTimerID = SetTimer(m_nTimerID, nInterval);
   if (!m_nTimerID)                                  // No timer...
      exit(1);                                       // ...so end the program

   return 0;
}
```

This follows the same logic as in Chapter 23, so we don't need to go through it again.

Exercising the Control

If you build the control, you should be able to run it in the ActiveX Control Test Container that's available through the Tools menu. It will appear in the list of objects in the Insert Control dialog as Signal Class. Here are two copies running:

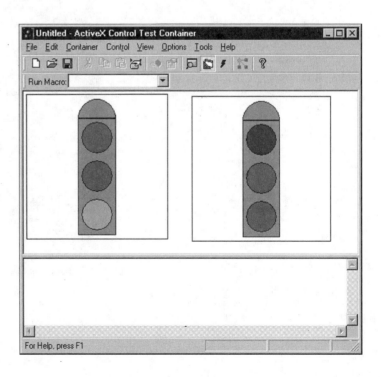

Our control will respond to the background color being set in the container, but we can't set the stop and go interval, or whether it starts on red or green. For that we need to add some properties to the control.

Adding Custom Properties

We add properties through the interface to the control. If you right-click on ISignal in ClassView, you'll see the context menu shown here:

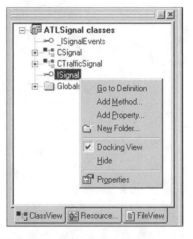

If you select Add Property... from the context menu, you'll be able to specify the property you want to add through the Add Property to Interface dialog:

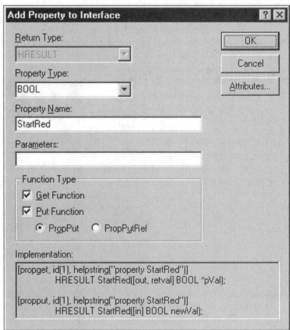

Select the type as BOOL and enter the name as **StartRed**. The information in the lower part of the dialog shown here appears when you click in, or tab to the Parameters edit box after entering the Property Type and Property Name data. This shows the **get** and **put** functions that will be added to the interface for retrieving and setting the property value. You should always select the property type from the drop down list, because only these are supported by COM. Click on the OK button to add the property to the interface.

If you look at the definition of **CSignal**, you'll see that the **get_StartRed()** and **put_StartRed()** functions for the property have been added, and there's a skeleton implementation in the file **Signal.cpp**. The implementations are trivial:

```
STDMETHODIMP CSignal::get_StartRed(BOOL *pVal)
{
    *pVal = m_bStartRed;                    // Return StartRed status
    return S_OK;
}


STDMETHODIMP CSignal::put_StartRed(BOOL newVal)
{
    m_bStartRed = newVal;                   // Store new StartRed status
    return S_OK;
}
```

The **get_StartRed()** function is passed a pointer to the location where the return value is to be stored, so we must dereference the parameter, **pVal**, to store the current value from **m_bStartRed**.

You can use the same procedure to add a property with the name **StopOrGoTime** of type **long** to the **ISignal** interface. The implementations of the **get** and **put** methods require just one extra line of code in each:

```
STDMETHODIMP CSignal::get_StopOrGoTime(long * pVal)
{
    *pVal = m_lStopOrGoTime;                // Return the current interval
    return S_OK;
}


STDMETHODIMP CSignal::put_StopOrGoTime(long newVal)
{
    m_lStopOrGoTime = newVal;               // Store the new interval
    return S_OK;
}
```

That's all we need for the container to be able to control these properties. We should do one more thing to match the functionality of the MFC-based control: add an event to signal the container when the light changes.

Adding Events

An event is a very different animal to the interface functions or properties, which are functions in the control that can be called by the container. An event puts the boot on the other foot: we want the control to be able to call a function in the container.

With the advent of Visual C++ 6, even more of the legwork has been taken out of adding an event to the control. The ATL AppWizard has automatically generated an event interface called **_ISignalEvents** for us in **ATLSignal.idl** so we declare our event there:

```
[
    uuid(E21E34B1-1BC5-11D2-BA71-00600873394D),
    version(1.0),
    helpstring("ATLSignal 1.0 Type Library")
]
library ATLSIGNALLib
{
    importlib("stdole32.tlb");
    importlib("stdole2.tlb");

    [
        uuid(E21E34BF-1BC5-11D2-BA71-00600873394D),
        helpstring("_ISignalEvents Interface")
    ]
    dispinterface _ISignalEvents
    {
        properties:
        methods:
            [id(1)] void SignalChanged([in]long lSignalState);
    };

    [
        uuid(E21E34BE-1BC5-11D2-BA71-00600873394D),
        helpstring("Signal Class")
    ]
    coclass Signal
    {
        [default] interface ISignal;
        [default, source] dispinterface _ISignalEvents;
    };
};
```

A **dispinterface** is just a dispatch interface. The interface name, **_ISignalEvents**, begins with an underscore. By COM convention, this indicates it's an outgoing interface — in other words, it's an interface that the control's container needs to implement.

Within the coclass definition, the attributes in square brackets define the nature of the interface. The **default** attribute indicates it's the default interface, and the **source** attribute specifies that it's outgoing from the control. To fire the event, you just call the function **Fire_SignalChanged()** with an argument specifying the current state of the signal. We need to do this in the **CSignal::OnTimer()** handler, so add the following statement immediately preceding the call to the **Invalidate()** function:

```
Fire_SignalChanged(nNewState);     // Signal the container
Invalidate();                      // Redraw the signal
KillTimer(m_nTimerID);             // Make sure the old timer is dead
```

Is that it, then? Unfortunately, no. We haven't defined how the container is going to connect to the interface. The **Fire_SignalChanged()** function needs to be implemented and must connect to a container in some way. After all, we're calling a container function here to communicate that the signal has changed. This is done through something called a **connection point**.

1058

Adding a Connection Point

A connection point on a control that represents an event is implemented through an interface called **IConnectionPoint**. It couldn't be anything else really, could it? Since we know nothing about any prospective container, the only way to communicate an event is through an outgoing interface. The connection point interface defines how the event will be communicated to the container. Because a control may have more than one connection point, something called a **connection point container** is used to contain however many connection points we need. A connection point container is implemented through an interface **IConnectionPointContainer**, which the container application will use to find out what connection points are supported. Conveniently, we already have a connection point container implemented in our control, courtesy of the ATL AppWizard.

We can get the code for the connection point generated automatically using the type library for our control. To get an up-to-date version of the type library, including the new event interface, we need to recompile the **.idl** file. We don't want to rebuild the whole project right now, as we'll get compiler errors — it isn't finished yet, after all. You can compile the **.idl** file alone by right-clicking it in FileView, and selecting <u>C</u>ompile ATLSignal.idl from the context menu.

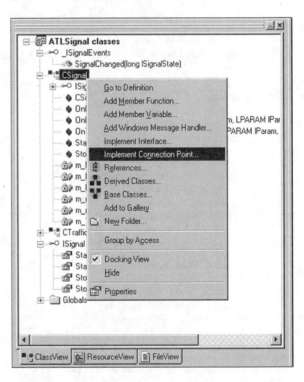

With the type library file generated we can add the **IConnectionPoint** interface. To do this, right click on CSignal and select Implement Connection Point....

In the Implement Connection Point dialog that's displayed, the wizard assumes we want to use the current project's type library for this implementation and names the tab ATLSIGNALLib accordingly. In the box beneath is a list of the outgoing interfaces we could generate a connection point for. Of course, **_ISignalEvents** is the only such interface here, so we check that and now press OK. The wizard will generate the code that will implement the **Fire_SignalChanged()** function so that it calls a container function through the connection point interface. On completion, this new code will be saved in **ATLSignalCP.h**.

A new class template, **CProxy_ISignalEvents<class T>**, will have appeared in the **1059**

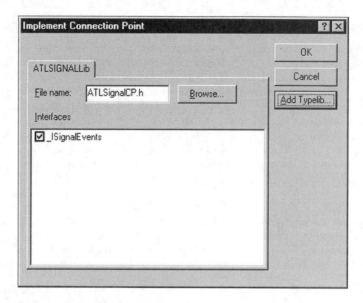

ClassView window. Double clicking on it will display its implementation. It's derived from **IConnectionPointImpl**, which implements a connection point.

The wizard has also added to the definition of our control class **CSignal** to incorporate the new template:

```
class ATL_NO_VTABLE CSignal :
    public CComObjectRootEx<CComSingleThreadModel>,
    public IDispatchImpl<ISignal, &IID_ISignal, &LIBID_ATLSIGNALLib>,
    public CComControl<CSignal>,
    public IPersistStreamInitImpl<CSignal>,
    public IOleControlImpl<CSignal>,
    public IOleObjectImpl<CSignal>,
    public IOleInPlaceActiveObjectImpl<CSignal>,
    public IViewObjectExImpl<CSignal>,
    public IOleInPlaceObjectWindowlessImpl<CSignal>,
    public IConnectionPointContainerImpl<CSignal>,
    public IPersistStorageImpl<CSignal>,
    public ISpecifyPropertyPagesImpl<CSignal>,
    public IQuickActivateImpl<CSignal>,
    public IDataObjectImpl<CSignal>,
    public IProvideClassInfo2Impl<&CLSID_Signal, &DIID__ISignalEvents,
                                              &LIBID_ATLSIGNALLib>,
    public IPropertyNotifySinkCP<CSignal>,
    public CComCoClass<CSignal, &CLSID_Signal>,
    public CProxy_ISignalEvents< CSignal >        // Added for event proxy

{
    // Detail of the class definition...
};
```

Note that the addition is a template class that requires **CSignal** as a parameter value. You'll note that an **#include** directive for **ATLSignalCP.h** was also added to **Signal.h**.

The **CProxy_ISignalEvents** class contains the **Fire_SignalChanged()** function that will communicate with the container. The **IConnectionPointContainerImpl** class that was added by the COM AppWizard implements an interface **IConnectionPointContainer** for the container to access the connection points on the control. This is re-iterated in the interface entry added to the COM map section of **Signal.h**.

```
BEGIN_COM_MAP(CSignal)
    COM_INTERFACE_ENTRY(ISignal)
    COM_INTERFACE_ENTRY(IDispatch)
    COM_INTERFACE_ENTRY(IViewObjectEx)
    COM_INTERFACE_ENTRY(IViewObject2)
    COM_INTERFACE_ENTRY(IViewObject)
    COM_INTERFACE_ENTRY(IOleInPlaceObjectWindowless)
    COM_INTERFACE_ENTRY(IOleInPlaceObject)
    COM_INTERFACE_ENTRY2(IOleWindow, IOleInPlaceObjectWindowless)
    COM_INTERFACE_ENTRY(IOleInPlaceActiveObject)
    COM_INTERFACE_ENTRY(IOleControl)
    COM_INTERFACE_ENTRY(IOleObject)
    COM_INTERFACE_ENTRY(IPersistStreamInit)
    COM_INTERFACE_ENTRY2(IPersist, IPersistStreamInit)
    COM_INTERFACE_ENTRY(IConnectionPointContainer)
    COM_INTERFACE_ENTRY(ISpecifyPropertyPages)
    COM_INTERFACE_ENTRY(IQuickActivate)
    COM_INTERFACE_ENTRY(IPersistStorage)
    COM_INTERFACE_ENTRY(IDataObject)
    COM_INTERFACE_ENTRY(IProvideClassInfo)
    COM_INTERFACE_ENTRY(IProvideClassInfo2)
    COM_INTERFACE_ENTRY_IMPL(IConnectionPointContainer)
END_COM_MAP()
```

Finally, just beneath the COM map, the wizard has made the connection point itself available to COM by adding an entry in the connection point map:

```
BEGIN_CONNECTION_POINT_MAP(CSignal)
    CONNECTION_POINT_ENTRY(IID_IPropertyNotifySink)
    CONNECTION_POINT_ENTRY(DIID__ISignalEvents)
END_CONNECTION_POINT_MAP()
```

All connection points for a control must appear in the connection point map. Each entry represents an outgoing interface from the control to the container, so there will be one entry here for each event interface that you define. Connection points are identified by their ID, which is generated by the MIDL compiler. We have just the one defined by the dispatch interface ID **DIID__ISignalEvents**. You will find that this has been defined in the file **ATLSignal_i.c** that appears in the External Dependencies folder in FileView.

If you've done everything correctly, the control is ready for another trial.

Running the Control

If you build the control once more, you can exercise it again using the ActiveX Test Container. You'll be able to trace the events being fired and change the properties.

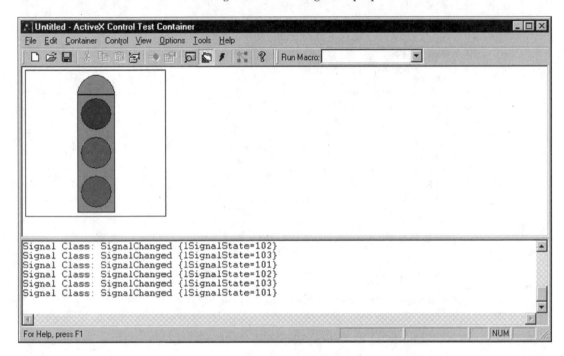

Note that to change the properties you need to use the **put** method. Remember that properties in COM use **get** and **put** methods to operate on property values. You can change the stop and go time interval and the starting condition. An event should fire each time the signal changes.

Summary

If you've made it this far without too much trouble, you have a solid understanding of C++ and you should have little difficulty progressing further into using Visual C++ on a wider basis and getting deeper into COM. We only scratched the surface of COM here because, as you will surely appreciate, it's a topic of above average complexity. You shouldn't find it particularly difficult; there's just rather a lot to it. I hope that you've found as much pleasure in getting to here as I have. Enjoy your programming!

Exercises

Ex24-1: 'Mission: Impossible?'
In this chapter, you've seen how to create a client for the **RefRate** ATL component. In fact, you've already created two versions of the client, one in Visual Basic and the other using MFC. Your final mission, should you choose to accept it, is to create yet another client for the **RefRate** component. This time, however, the only tool at your disposal is the Active Template Library. You'll need to prepare well for this expedition. Good luck!

Hints:
Use the documentation to help you learn more about ATL.
Start with an ATL executable project.
Discover how to use the compiler COM support, particularly the **#import** statement.

C++ Keywords

Keywords are words used for special purposes. You must not use these words as names of objects in your programs. The following is a list of Visual C++ keywords:

asm	auto	bool	break
case	catch	char	class
const	const_cast	continue	default
delete	do	double	dynamic_cast
else	enum	except	explicit
export	extern	false	finally
float	for	friend	goto
if	inline	int	long
mutable	namespace	new	operator
private	protected	public	register
reinterpret_cast	return	short	signed
sizeof	static	static_cast	struct
switch	template	this	throw
true	try	typedef	typeid
typename	union	unsigned	using
virtual	void	volatile	wchar_t
while			

The following is a list of Microsoft-specific keywords. In Microsoft C++, identifiers with two leading underscores are reserved for compiler implementations and cannot be used as identifier names. Those keywords without double underscores are special identifiers when used with __declspec; their use in other contexts is not restricted:

allocate	__inline	property
__asm	__int8	selectany
__based	__int16	__single_inheritance
__cdecl	__int32	__stdcall
__declspec	__int64	thread
dllexport	__leave	__try
dllimport	__multiple_inheritance	uuid
__except	naked	__uuidof
__fastcall	nothrow	__virtual_inheritance
__finally		

The C++ language is still evolving. There are a number of C++ keywords not at present supported in Visual C++, but they may well be in the future. Other compilers support at least some of them at the moment. You should therefore also avoid using these for your own identifiers. Accidental use of some of them is quite possible, as you can see from the list below:

and	bitand	compl	not_eq	or_eq	xor_eq
and_eq	bitor	not	or	xor	

The ASCII Table

The American Standard Code for Information Interchange or ASCII assigns values between 0 and 255 for upper and lower case letters, numeric digits, punctuation marks and other symbols. ASCII characters can be split into the following sections:

0 – 31   Control functions

32 – 127 Standard, implementation-independent characters

128 – 255 Special symbols, international character sets — generally
these are non-standard characters.

Since the latter 128 characters are implementation-dependent and have no fixed entry in the ASCII table, we shall only cover the first two groups in the following table:

ASCII Characters 0 - 31

Decimal	Hexadecimal	Character	Control
000	00	null	NUL
001	01	☺	SOH
002	02	●	STX
003	03	♥	ETX
004	04	♦	EOT
005	05	♣	ENQ
006	06	♠	ACK
007	07	•	BEL (Audible bell)
008	08		Backspace
009	09		HT
010	0A		LF (Line feed)
011	0B		VT (Vertical feed)
012	0C		FF (Form feed)
013	0D		CR (Carriage return)
014	0E		SO
015	0F	¤	SI
016	10		DLE
017	11		DC1

Decimal	Hexadecimal	Character	Control
018	12		DC2
019	13		DC3
020	14		DC4
021	15		NAK
022	16		SYN
023	17		ETB
024	18		CAN
025	19		EM
026	1A	→	SUB
027	1B	←	ESC (Escape)
028	1C	∟	FS
029	1D		GS
030	1E		RS
031	1F		US

ASCII Characters 32 - 127

Decimal	Hexadecimal	Character	Decimal	Hexadecimal	Character
032	20	space	060	3C	<
033	21	!	061	3D	=
034	22	"	062	3E	>
035	23	#	063	3F	?
036	24	$	064	40	@
037	25	%	065	41	A
038	26	&	066	42	B
039	27	'	067	43	C
040	28	(	068	44	D
041	29	)	069	45	E
042	2A	*	070	46	F
043	2B	+	071	47	G
044	2C	,	072	48	H
045	2D	-	073	49	I
046	2E	.	074	4A	J
047	2F	/	075	4B	K
048	30	0	076	4C	L
049	31	1	077	4D	M
050	32	2	078	4E	N
051	33	3	079	4F	O
052	34	4	080	50	P
053	35	5	081	51	Q
054	36	6	082	52	R
055	37	7	083	53	S
056	38	8	085	55	U
057	39	9	086	56	V
058	3A	:	087	57	W
059	3B	;	088	58	X

Decimal	Hexadecimal	Character	Decimal	Hexadecimal	Character
089	59	Y	109	6D	m
090	5A	Z	110	6E	n
091	5B	[	111	6F	o
092	5C	\	112	70	p
093	5D	]	113	71	q
094	5E	^	114	72	r
095	5F	_	115	73	s
096	60	´	116	74	t
097	61	a	117	75	u
098	62	b	118	76	v
099	63	c	119	77	w
100	64	d	120	78	x
101	65	e	121	79	y
102	66	f	122	7A	z
103	67	g	123	7B	{
104	68	h	124	7C	|
105	69	i	125	7D	}
106	6A	j	126	7E	~
107	6B	k	127	7F	delete
108	6C	l			

Solutions to Exercises

Chapter 1

Ex1-1: There are four direct ways to build a project:

- Press the Build button on the Build toolbar or on the Build Minibar toolbar
- Press the *F7* function key
- Choose the Build | Build menu item
- Click the right mouse button on the files item in the tree in the FileView pane, and select Build from the context menu

Ex1-2: The three files used to store information about a project are the **.dsp**, **.ncb** and **.dsw** files. The **.dsp** file stores information about the files that make up the project, the **.ncb** file stores 'browse information' used by several features in Visual C++, and the **.dsw** saves the IDE workspace settings.

Ex1-3: File types:

- **.obj** files hold the intermediate object code files produced by the compiler
- **.pch** files hold precompiled header information (more about this later!)
- **.pdb** files hold debugging information
- **.exe** files hold the final, executable program produced by the linker

Chapter 2

Ex2-1: [Prg1]

```cpp
#include <iostream>

using namespace std;

int main()
{
   int number = 0;

   cout << "Enter a number: ";
   cin >> number;
   cout << "\nThank you. Your number was " << number;
   cout << endl;

   return 0;
}
```

Ex2-2: Use of BIT operators to calculate a remainder:

```cpp
// Use the bitwise AND operator.  For example:
// 29 = (3x8)+5                    -14 = (-2x8)+2
// 29 = 0000 0000 0001 1101        -14 = 1111 1111 1111 0010
//  7 = 0000 0000 0000 0111          7 = 0000 0000 0000 0111
// ========================        ==========================
//      0000 0000 0000 0101 = rem 5   0000 0000 0000 0010 = rem 2

#include <iostream>

using namespace std;

int main()
{
int number1 = 0;
int seven = 0x7;

cout << "Type in an integer: ";
cin >> number1;

cout << endl
        << "The remainder when "
        << number1
        << " is divided by eight is "
        << (number1 & seven)
        << endl;

return 0;
}
```

Ex2-3: Precedence and associativity:

```cpp
(((1 + 2) + 3) + 4)

(((16 * 4) / 2) * 3)
```

```
(a > b) ? a : ((c > d) ? e : f)

(a & b) && (c & d)
```

Ex2-4: As it stands, the division will produce an integer result that is unlikely to be satisfactory. You need to cast one of the arguments to a **double** in order to force the division to be done correctly:

```
double aspect = static_cast<double>(width)/height;
```

Ex2-5: The value printed should be 2. Let's look at the statement:

```
int i = (s >> 4) & ~(~0 << 3);
```

What we're doing here is bit manipulation on **s**. The first clause, **(s >> 4)**, shifts **s** right by four bits; because 555 is 1000101011 in binary, a four-bit shift leaves it as 100010. In the second clause, **~0** is composed of all 1s, and it gets shifted left 3 bits, and then the second **~** complements all the bits to leave us with 111 in the bottom three bits. Doing a bitwise AND on 100010 and 111 gives 010, or 2, as the result.

Chapter 3

Ex3-1: The **while** version:

```
#include <iostream>

using namespace std;

int main()
{
    int val = 0;
    int total = 0;

    cout << "Enter numbers, one per line:\n";
    cin >> val;

    while (val != 0)
    {
        total += val;
        cin >> val;
    }

    cout << "\nThank you. The total was " << total;
    cout << endl;
    return 0;
}
```

The **do-while** version:

```
#include <iostream>

using namespace std;
```

```
int main()
{
   int val = 0;
   int total = 0;

   cout << "Enter numbers, one per line:\n";

   do
   {
      cin >> val;
      total += val;
   } while (val != 0);

   cout << "\nThank you. The total was " << total;
   cout << endl;
   return 0;
}
```

The **for** version:

```
#include <iostream>

using namespace std;

int main()
{
   int val = 0;
   int total = 0;

   cout << "Enter numbers, one per line:\n";
   cin >> val;

   // We don't need the initialization or increment expressions
   for (; val!=0;)
   {
      total += val;
      cin >> val;
   }

   cout << "Thank you. The total was " << total;
   cout << endl;
   return 0;
}
```

Ex3-2: Counting characters.

```
#include <iostream>

using namespace std;

int main()
{
   char c = ' ';
   int nVowels = 0;
   int nChars = 0;

   cout << "Type some characters and q or Q to stop counting followed by
```

```
ENTER.\n";

   for (;;)
   {
      cin >> c;

      if (c == 'q' || c == 'Q')
         break;

      switch(c)
      {
      case 'A': case 'a':
      case 'E': case 'e':
      case 'I': case 'i':
      case 'O': case 'o':
      case 'U': case 'u':
         nVowels++;

      default:
         nChars++;
      }
   }

   cout << "Total chars=" << nChars << ", vowels=" << nVowels;
   cout << endl;
   return 0;
}
```

Ex3-3: Multiplication tables.

```
#include <iostream>
#include <iomanip>

using namespace std;

int main()
{
   cout << "     2     3     4     5     6     7     8     9    10    11    12\n";
   cout << "-----------------------------------------------------------------------
--\n";
   for (int i=1; i<13; i++)         // rows
   {
      for (int j=2; j<13; j++)      // columns
      {
         cout << setw(6) << j*i;
      }
      cout << '\n';
   }
   return 0;
}
```

Ex3-4: Flags and bitwise operators.

```cpp
#include <iostream>

using namespace std;

const int text = 0x01;
const int binary = 0x02;

const int read = 0x10;
const int write = 0x20;
const int append = 0x40;

int main()
{
   int mode = text | append;

   if (mode & text)
      cout << "mode is (text,";
   else if (mode & binary)
      cout << "mode is (binary,";

   if (mode & read)
      cout << "read)\n";
   else if (mode & write)
      cout << "write)\n";
   else if (mode & append)
      cout << "append)\n";

   return 0;
}
```

Ex3-5: [Prg2]

```cpp
#include <iostream>

using namespace std;

int main()
{
   int number = 0;

   for (;;)
   {

   cout << "Enter a number: ";
   cin >> number;
   if (number == 0)
      break;
   cout << "Thank you. Your number was " << number << "\n";
   cout << endl ;
   }

   return 0;
}
```

Chapter 4

Ex4-1: The types of the expressions are:

a) `i`   `// int`
b) `j`   `// int`
c) `&i`   `// int*`
d) `pi`   `// int*`
e) `*pi`   `// int`
f) `array`   `// int*`
g) `*array` `// int`
h) `pi[3]`   `// int`
i) `pi+3`   `// int*`

Ex4-2: [Prg3]

```cpp
#include <iostream>

using namespace std;

int main()
{
    int number = 0;
    char name[15] = {'a'};

    for (;;)
    {

    cout << "Enter a number: ";
    cin >> number;
    if (number == 0)
        break;

    cout << "And a name: ";
    cin >> name;
    cout << "Thank you. Your number and name were " << number
            << " and '" << name << "'\n";
    }

    return 0;
}
```

Ex4-3: Character arrays:

```cpp
#include <iostream>
#include <cstring>

using namespace std;

int main()
{
    char str[] = "Doctor Livingstone, I presume?";
    cout << str << '\n';

    for (unsigned int i=0; i<strlen(str); i+=2)
    {
```

1079

```
            if (str[i] >= 'a' && str[i] <= 'z')
                str[i] -= 32;
        }

        cout << str << endl;
        return 0;
    }
```

Ex4-4: The statements produce:

a) `cout << c;`   `// hello world`
b) `cout << c[3]; // l`
c) `cout << pc;`   `// llo world`
d) `cout << *(pc-2);`   `// h`
e) `cout << *pc-2;`   `// 106`

Congratulations if you got the last one without trying it out first! The pointer expression `*pc-2` takes what `pc` is pointing to, the character `l` with ASCII code 108, and takes two from it in an integer subtraction operation (not a pointer operation), so the result is 106.

Ex4-5: In the declaration given, `ppi` is a 'pointer to a pointer to `int`', and gives two levels of indirect addressing. We can use it to construct a 2-D array dynamically by first creating a 'row vector' to hold pointers to the rows, and then creating arrays for each row and storing their addresses in the row vector. This gives us our two levels of addressing—row and column—and because of the equivalence of array and pointer notation, we can treat our two-level pointer as a 2-D array, as shown in the code below:

```
#include <iostream>

using namespace std;

const int ROWS = 4;
const int COLS = 4;

int main()
{
    int** ppi;

    // Create an array to hold the pointers to each row
    ppi = new int*[ROWS];

    // Create each row, and store it away
    for (int i=0; i<ROWS; i++)
        ppi[i] = new int[COLS];

    // Set all the elements to zero using a nested loop
    for (i=0; i<ROWS; i++)
        for (int j=0; j<COLS; j++)
            ppi[i][j] = 0;

    // Set ppi to the identity matrix, and print it out as a test
    ppi[0][0] = ppi[1][1] = ppi[2][2] = ppi[3][3] = 1;

    for (i=0; i<ROWS; i++)
    {
```

```
        for (int j=0; j<COLS; j++)
            cout << ppi[i][j] << ' ';
        cout << '\n';
    }

    // Delete it in reverse order...
    for (i=0; i<ROWS; i++)
        delete [] ppi[i];

    delete [] ppi;
    return 0;
}
```

Chapter 5

Ex5-1: Recursion. You could also add an **if** clause here to check that the number entered is greater than zero. This is left as a further exercise for you.

```
#include <iostream>

using namespace std;

long fact(long n)
{
    if (n == 1)
        return 1;
    else
        return n * fact(n-1);
}

int main()
{
    long val = 0;
    long result = 0;

    cout << "Give me a integer greater than 1: ";
    cin >> val;

    result = fact(val);
    cout << "\n" << val << "! = " << result << "\n";

    return 0;
}
```

Ex5-2: Swap two integers.

```
#include <iostream>

using namespace std;

void swap(int* pa, int* pb)
{
    int temp;

    cout << "Now we swap them.\n";
```

```
      temp = *pa;
      *pa = *pb;
      *pb = temp;
}

int main()
{
      int a=6;
      int b=4;

      cout << "Before: a= " << a << ", b= " << b << "\n";

      swap(&a, &b);

      cout << "After: a= " << a << ", b= " << b << "\n";
      return 0;
}
```

Ex5-3: Trig functions. There are 2*pi radians or 360 degrees in a circle. Thus the ratio between radians and degrees is 1:57.2957795.

```
#include <iostream>
#include <cmath>

using namespace std;

const double DEG_TO_RAD = 57.2957795;

double sind(double d)
{
      return sin(d/DEG_TO_RAD);
}

double cosd(double d)
{
      return cos(d/DEG_TO_RAD);
}

double tand(double d)
{
      return tan(d/DEG_TO_RAD);
}

int main()
{
      cout << "cos(30)=" << cosd(30.0) << "\n";
      cout << "sin(30)=" << sind(30.0) << "\n";
      cout << "tan(30)=" << tand(30.0) << "\n";

      return 0;
}
```

Ex5-4: [Prg4]

```cpp
#include <iostream>

using namespace std;

void GetData(int& number, char name[])
{
    cout << "Enter a number: ";
    cin >> number;
    if (number != 0)
    {
        cout << "And a name: ";
        cin >> name;
    }
}

void PutData(int number, char name[])
{
    cout << "Thank you. Your number and name were " << number
         << " and '" << name << "'\n";
}

int main()
{
    int number = 0;
    char name[15] = {' '};

    for (;;)
    {
        GetData(number, name);

        if (number == 0)
            break;

        PutData(number, name);
    }

    return 0;
}
```

Ex5-5: Parsing function.

```cpp
#include <iostream>
#include <cstring>

using namespace std;

char* parse(const char* str)
{
    static char* pStr = 0;
    static int len = 0;
    static int start = 0;
    int pos = 0;
    char* pReturn = 0;
```

```
      // First time through, save the string
      if (str)
      {
         delete pStr;    // in case it was allocated
         len = strlen(str);
         pStr = new char[len+1];
         strcpy(pStr,str);
      }

      if (start >= len)
         return 0;

      // Walk the string from 'start' till we find a blank or the end
      for (pos = start; pStr[pos] != ' ' && pStr[pos] != '\0'; pos++);

      // Copy the string if we've a word to return, otherwise return NULL
      if (pos != start)
      {
         pReturn = new char[pos - start + 1];
         int i=0;
         for (int j=start; j<pos; i++,j++)
            pReturn[i] = pStr[j];
         pReturn[i] = '\0';
         start = pos+1;
         return pReturn;
      }
      else
         return 0;
}

int main()
{
   char s1[] = "seventy-one fruit balls, please Doris";
   cout << "string is '" << s1 << "'\n\nParsing...\n";
   char* p = parse(s1);

   while (p)
   {
      cout << p << endl;
      delete p;
      p = parse(NULL);
   }

   return 0;
}
```

Chapter 6

Ex6-1: Calling function via a pointer.

```
#include <iostream>
#include <cstring>

using namespace std;
```

```
int ascVal(int i, const char* p)
{
   // print the ASCII value of the char
   if (!p || i > strlen(p))
       return -1;
   else
       return static_cast<int>(p[i]);
}

int main()
{
   char* str = "a bunch of bananas";
   int (*fp)(int, const char*);

   fp = ascVal;
   int i = (*fp)(3,str);

   cout << "value of '" << str[3] << "' is " << i << endl;

   return 0;
}
```

Ex6-2: Overloaded functions.

```
#include <iostream>
#include <cstring>

using namespace std;

bool equal(int a,int b)
{
   return (a==b) ? true : false;
}

bool equal(double a,double b)
{
   return (a==b) ? true : false;
}

bool equal(char a,char b)
{
   return (a==b) ? true : false;
}

bool equal(char* a,char* b)
{
   return (!strcmp(a,b)) ? true : false;
}

int main()
{
   int iA=3, iB=5;
   if (equal(iA,iB))
     cout << "iA and iB are the same" << endl;
   else
      cout << "iA and iB are different" << endl;
```

```
      char* pA = "hello";
      char* pB = "mickey";
      if (equal(pA,pB))
         cout << "pA and pB are the same" << endl;
      else
         cout << "pA and pB are different" << endl;

      char* pC = "mickey";
      if (equal(pB,pC))
         cout << "pB and pC are the same" << endl;
      else
         cout << "pB and pC are different" << endl;

      return 0;
   }
```

Ex6-3: Adding error reporting to the calculator.

```
   void error(char* str, int index);

double expr(char* str)
{
   // ...
   for(;;)
   {
      switch(*(str+index++))
      {
         case '\0':
            // ...
         case '+':
            // ...
         case '-':
            // ...
         default:
            cout << "Arrrgh!*#!! There's an error"
               << endl;
            error(str, index-1);
            exit(1);
      }
   }
}
```

```
   void error(char* str, int index)
   {
      cout << str << endl;
      for (int i=0; i<index; i++)
         cout << ' ';
      cout << '^' << endl;
   }
```

Ex6-4: Adding an exponentiation operator needs a simple extension to the **term()** function:

```
   #include <cmath>

double term(char* str, int& index)
{
   double value = 0;
```

```
      value = number(str, index);

   while((*(str+index)=='*') || (*(str+index)=='/') || (*(str+index)=='^'))
   {
      if (*(str+index)=='*')
         value *= number(str, ++index);
      if (*(str+index)=='/')
         value /= number(str, ++index);
      if (*(str+index)=='^')
         value = pow(value, number(str, ++index));
   }
   return value;
}
```

Notice the use of the `pow()` function from the math library. The limitation of this approach is that `^` should have higher precedence than `*` or `/`, but the calculator only gives us two levels: the plus-and-minus level, and the multiply-and-divide level. Without redesigning the calculator from the ground up, the best way to make exponentiation work properly is to always use parentheses, so that instead of `3*3^3`, you type `3*(3^3)`. This is what programmers call a 'feature'...

Ex6-5: Adding math functions. The place to do this is in the `number()` function, which currently checks whether the next item in the string is a number or an opening bracket. Since all math functions are going to be followed by an opening bracket, it is quite simple to collect alphabetic characters into a string until we hit an opening bracket, then process the contents of the brackets, and apply the operation on the way out. This version is pretty simple-minded, and errors (such as not putting the function argument in brackets) tend to get silently ignored.

```
double doOperation(char* op, double value);

double number(char* str, int& index)
{
   double value = 0.0;

   char op[6]={0};
   int ip = 0;
   while (isalpha(*(str+index)))
      op[ip++] = *(str+index++);
   op[ip] = '\0';

   if (*(str+index) == '(')
   {
      char* psubstr = 0;
      psubstr = extract(str, ++index);
      value = expr(psubstr);

      // If we have an operation saved, go and do it
      if (op[0])
         value = doOperation(op, value);

      delete [] psubstr;
      return value;
   }

   // the rest of the function is as before...
}
```

The **doOperation()** function is pretty simple:

```
const double degToRad = 57.295779;

double doOperation(char* op, double value)
{
   if (!stricmp(op, "sin"))
      return sin(value);
   else if (!stricmp(op, "sind"))
      return sin(value / degToRad);
   else if (!stricmp(op, "cos"))
      return cos(value);
   else if (!stricmp(op, "cosd"))
      return cos(value / degToRad);
   else if (!stricmp(op, "tan"))
      return tan(value);
   else if (!stricmp(op, "tand"))
      return tan(value / degToRad);
   else if (!stricmp(op, "sqrt"))
      return sqrt(value);
   else
   {
      cout << "Error: unknown operation '" << op << "'" << endl;
      exit(1);
   }
   return 0;
}
```

You could code this up in a more efficient way—maybe driven by a table—but this simple version shows how it works.

Chapter 7

Ex7-1: Simple structure:

```
#include <iostream>

using namespace std;

struct X
{
   int one;
   int two;
};

int main()
{
   X a;
   X b;

   a.one = 1;
   a.two = 2;

   cout << "a=(" << a.one << "," << a.two << ")\n";
```

```
    // b contains junk values. Dont worry when compiler gives warning
    cout << "b=(" << b.one << "," << b.two << ")\n";

    b = a;
    cout << "b=(" << b.one << "," << b.two << ")\n";

    return 0;
}
```

Ex7-2: Structure with **char*** member:

```
#include <iostream>
#include <cstring>

using namespace std;

struct X
{
    int one;
    int two;
    char* sptr;
};

int main()
{
    X a;
    X b;
    char s[] = "hello world!";

    a.one = 1;
    a.two = 2;
    a.sptr = s;

    cout << "a=(" << a.one << "," << a.two << "," << a.sptr << ")\n";

    b.one = a.one;
    b.two = a.two;
    b.sptr = new char[strlen(a.sptr)+1];
    strcpy(b.sptr,a.sptr);

    cout << "b=(" << b.one << "," << b.two << "," << b.sptr << ")\n";

    a.sptr[0] = 'H';

    cout << "a=(" << a.one << "," << a.two << "," << a.sptr << ")\n";
    cout << "b=(" << b.one << "," << b.two << "," << b.sptr << ")\n";

    delete [] b.sptr;

    return 0;
}
```

When you copy **b** into **a**, it is the pointer **sptr** which is copied, and not the string to which it points. Thus, both **a** and **b** are pointing to the same string, so when you modify it via **a.sptr**, you are also modifying **b**'s copy. To get around this, you need to manually make your own copy of the string and assign it to **b**. This sort of problem can be greatly eased by using classes instead of structs.

Ex7-3: Using pointers to structures.

```cpp
#include <iostream>
#include <cstring>

using namespace std;

struct X
{
   int one;
   int two;
   char* sptr;
};

void printX(X* pX)
{
   cout << pX->one << "," << pX->two << "," << pX->sptr;
}

int main()
{
   X a;
   X b;
   char s[] = "hello world!";

   a.one = 1;
   a.two = 2;
   a.sptr = s;

   cout << "a=("; printX(&a); cout << ")\n";

   b.one = a.one;
   b.two = a.two;
   b.sptr = new char[strlen(a.sptr)+1];
   strcpy(b.sptr,a.sptr);

   cout << "b=("; printX(&b); cout << ")\n";

   a.sptr[0] = 'H';

   cout << "a=("; printX(&a); cout << ")\n";
   cout << "b=("; printX(&b); cout << ")\n";

   delete [] b.sptr;

   return 0;
}
```

Ex7-4: [Prg5]

```cpp
#include <iostream>

using namespace std;

struct item
{
   int number;
```

```
      char name[15];
};


void GetData(item& r)
{
   cout << "Enter a number: ";
   cin >> r.number;

   if (r.number != 0)
   {
      cout << "And a name: ";
      cin >> r.name;
   }
}

void PutData(item r)
{
   cout << "Thank you. Your number and name were " << r.number
           << " and '" << r.name << "'\n";
}

int main()
{
   item rec;

   for (;;)
   {
      GetData(rec);

      if (rec.number == 0)
         break;

      PutData(rec);
   }
   return 0;
}
```

Ex7-5: The **GetSystemMetrics()** API call can be used to get the width and height of the screen in pixels, so you can use it to calculate the position and size of your window before you create it in **WinMain()**.

```
   int nXCenter = GetSystemMetrics(SM_CXSCREEN)/2;
   int nYCenter = GetSystemMetrics(SM_CYSCREEN)/2;
   int nWidth = 300;
   int nHeight = 200;

   hWnd = CreateWindow(
      szAppName,                        // The window class name
      "A Basic Window the Hard Way",    // The window title
      WS_OVERLAPPEDWINDOW,              // The window style
      nXCenter - nWidth/2,              // Upper-left x position
      nYCenter - nHeight/2,             // Upper-left y position
      nWidth,                           // The window width
      nHeight,                          // The window height
      0,                                // No parent window
      0,                                // No menu
```

```
        hInstance,                      // Program instance handle
        0                               // No window creation data
        );
```

Chapter 8

Ex8-1: List exercise—[Prg6]

```cpp
#include <iostream>

using namespace std;

class CRecord
{
private:
    int number;
    char name[15];
public:
    bool GetData();
    void PutData();
};

bool CRecord::GetData()
{
    cout << "Enter a number: ";
    cin >> number;

    if (number != 0)
    {
        cout << "And a name: ";
        cin >> name;
    return true;
    }
    else
    return false;
}

void CRecord::PutData()
{
    cout << "Thank you. Your number and name were " << number
         << " and '" << name << "'\n";
}

int main()
{
    CRecord rec;

    for (;;)
    {
        if (!rec.GetData())
            break;

        rec.PutData();
    }
```

```
      return 0;
   }
```

Ex8-2: **CTrace** class:

```cpp
#include <iostream>
#include <cstring>

using namespace std;

class CTrace
{
private:
   char* pstr;
public:
   CTrace(const char* str);
   ~CTrace();
};

CTrace::CTrace(const char* str)
{
   pstr = new char[strlen(str)+1];
   strcpy(pstr,str);
   cout << "Entry: " << pstr << endl;
}

CTrace::~CTrace()
{
   cout << "Exit: " << pstr << endl;
   delete pstr;
   pstr = NULL;
}

int main()
{
   CTrace t("Main routine");

   if (3 < 5)
   {
      CTrace t1("'if' block");
   }
   else
   {
      CTrace t2("'else' block");
   }

   return 0;
}
```

Ex8-3: Indenting the trace. You can do this using a **static** data member to hold the indentation level, so that every **CTrace** object increases the indentation level when it is created, and decreases it when it is destroyed, like this:

```cpp
#include <iostream>
#include <cstring>

using namespace std;
```

```cpp
class CTrace
{
private:
    char* pstr;
    static int indentLevel;
public:
    CTrace(const char* str);
    ~CTrace();
};

int CTrace::indentLevel = 0;

CTrace::CTrace(const char* str)
{
    indentLevel +=2;
    pstr = new char[strlen(str)+1];
    strcpy(pstr,str);

    for (int i=0; i<indentLevel; i++)
     cout << ' ';
    cout << "Entry: " << pstr << endl;
}

CTrace::~CTrace()
{
  for (int i=0; i<indentLevel; i++)
      cout << ' ';
    cout << "Exit: " << pstr << endl;
    delete pstr;
    pstr = NULL;
    indentLevel -=2;
}

int main()
{
    CTrace t("Main routine");

    if (3 < 5)
    {
        CTrace t1("'if' block");
    }
    else
    {
        CTrace t2("'else' block");
    }

    return 0;
}
```

Ex8-4: **CStack** class:

```cpp
#include <iostream>

using namespace std;

class CStack
{
```

```
private:
    int list[100];
    int next;
public:
    CStack() : next(0) {}
    void Push(int i);
    int Pop();
    void Print() const;
};

void CStack::Push(int i)
{
    if (next < 99)
        list[next++] = i;
}

int CStack::Pop()
{
    return list[--next];
}

void CStack::Print() const
{
    cout << '[';
    for (int i=next-1; i>=0; i--)
        cout << ' '<< list[i];
    cout << " ]\n";
}

int main()
{
    CStack s;

    s.Print();

    s.Push(5);
    s.Push(10);
    s.Push(8);

    s.Print();

    cout << "top of stack=" << s.Pop() << '\n';

    s.Print();

    return 0;
}
```

Ex8-5: Extending the **CStack** class. To guard against popping more items than there are on the stack (known as **stack underflow**) or storing more than you've got space for (**stack overflow**), you can print out an error message and return a 'safe' value, such as zero. In a real version of such a class, you'd probably use C++'s exception handling to trap this sort of error.

```
#include <iostream>

using namespace std;
```

```
class CStack
{
private:
   int list[100];
   int next;
public:
   CStack() : next(0) {}
   void Push(int i);
   int Pop();
   int Peek() const;
   void Print() const;
};

void CStack::Push(int i)
{
   if (next < 99)
      list[next++] = i;
   else
      cout << "Error! Stack Overflow\n";
}

int CStack::Pop()
{
   if (next==0)
   {
      cout << "Error! Stack Underflow\n";
      return 0;
   }
   else
      return list[--next];
}

int CStack::Peek() const
{
   if (next==0)
   {
      cout << "Error! Stack Underflow\n";
      return 0;
   }
   else
      return list[next-1];
}

void CStack::Print() const
{
   cout << '[';
   for (int i=next-1; i>=0; i--)
      cout << ' '<< list[i];
   cout << " ]\n";
}

int main()
{
   CStack s;

   s.Print();
```

```
    s.Push(5);
    s.Push(10);
    s.Push(8);

    s.Print();

    cout << "peek at top of stack=" << s.Peek() << '\n';

    s.Print();
    cout << "pop top of stack=" << s.Pop() << '\n';
    cout << "pop top of stack=" << s.Pop() << '\n';
    s.Print();
    cout << "pop top of stack=" << s.Pop() << '\n';
    cout << "pop top of stack=" << s.Pop() << '\n';

    return 0;
}
```

Chapter 9

Ex9-1: Estimated integer class:

```
#include <iostream>

using namespace std;

#define ESTIMATED true
#define EXACT false

class CEstInt
{
private:
    int val;
    bool bEst;

public:
    CEstInt(int i=0, bool e=EXACT) : val(i), bEst(e)
    {
    }

//   void SetEstimated(bool e)
//   {
//       bEst = (!e) ? EXACT : ESTIMATED;
//   }

    void Print();

    // Helper functions
    CEstInt Add(const CEstInt& b) const;
};

void CEstInt::Print()
{
    if (bEst)
        cout << 'E';
```

```
   cout << val;
}

CEstInt CEstInt::Add(const CEstInt& b) const
{
   CEstInt t(val+b.val);
   if (bEst || b.bEst)
      t.bEst = ESTIMATED;

   return t;
}

CEstInt operator+(const CEstInt& a, const CEstInt& b)
{
   return a.Add(b);
}

int main()
{
   CEstInt a=3, c;
   CEstInt b(5,ESTIMATED);

   cout << "a=";
   a.Print();
   cout << '\n';
   cout << "b=";
   b.Print();
   cout << '\n';

   c = a + b;
   cout << "c=";;
   c.Print();
   cout << '\n';

   return 0;
}
```

Ex9-2: Simple string class:

```
#include <iostream>
#include <cstring>

using namespace std;

class CSimpString
{
private:
   int len;
   char* buff;
public:
   CSimpString(const char* p = 0);
   CSimpString(const CSimpString& s);
   ~CSimpString();

   CSimpString& operator=(const CSimpString& rhs);
   void Print() const;
};
```

```cpp
CSimpString::CSimpString(const char* p) : len(0), buff(0)
{
   if (p != 0)
   {
      len = strlen(p);
      if (len > 0)
      {
         buff = new char[len+1];
         strcpy(buff,p);
      }
   }
}

CSimpString::CSimpString(const CSimpString& s)
{
   len = s.len;
   buff = new char[len+1];
   strcpy(buff,s.buff);
}

CSimpString::~CSimpString()
{
   delete [] buff;
}

CSimpString& CSimpString::operator=(const CSimpString& rhs)
{
   len = rhs.len;
   delete [] buff;
   buff = new char[len+1];
   strcpy(buff,rhs.buff);

   return *this;
}

void CSimpString::Print() const
{
   cout << buff;
}

int main()
{
   CSimpString s1 = "hello";
   CSimpString s2;

   s2 = s1;

   cout << "s1='";
   s1.Print();
   cout << "'\n";

   cout << "s2='";
   s2.Print();
   cout << "'\n";

   return 0;
}
```

Ex9-3: Extra constructors. Here are two suggestions—the first constructs a string from a repeated single character, while the second uses an integer.

```
#include <cstdlib>
#include <iostream>
#include <cstring>

class CSimpString
{
public:
    CSimpString(char c, int count=1);
    CSimpString(int i);
    // rest of class as before
};

CSimpString::CSimpString(char c, int count) : len(0), buff(0)
{
    len = count;
    if (len > 0)
    {
        buff = new char[len+1];
        memset(buff, c, len);
        buff[len] = '\0';
    }
}

CSimpString::CSimpString(int i) : len(0), buff(0)
{
    char sTmp[20];
    itoa(i, sTmp, 10);

    len = strlen(sTmp);
    if (len > 0)
    {
        buff = new char[len+1];
        strcpy(buff, sTmp);
    }
}
```

Ex9-4: As coded, our assignment operator won't cope with pathological cases such as **s1=s1**, because we delete the buffer before doing the copy. If we're trying to copy the same object, we'll have deleted the object's buffer before doing so. The simplest and easiest way around this is to check that the object isn't copying itself:

```
CSimpString& CSimpString::operator=(const CSimpString& rhs)
{
    if (&rhs != this)
    {
        len = rhs.len;
        delete buff;
        buff = new char[len+1];
        strcpy(buff,rhs.buff);
    }

    return *this;
}
```

Ex9-5: Overloading the **+** and **+=** operators for the simple string class. First, add these two functions to the **public** section class declaration:

```
CSimpString& operator+=(const CSimpString& rhs);
CSimpString Concat(const CSimpString& s2) const;
```

Here's their implementation. The **+=** operator is implemented as a member function, because it will always be called by a string object. The **+** operator, on the other hand, may be called upon to add string objects and string literals in any order, so it makes sense to make it a global operator function.

```
CSimpString& CSimpString::operator+=(const CSimpString& rhs)
{
    char* t = buff;
    buff = new char[len + rhs.len + 1];
    strcpy(buff,t);
    strcat(buff,rhs.buff);
    len += rhs.len;
    delete[] t;

    return *this;
}

CSimpString CSimpString::Concat(const CSimpString& s2) const
{
    char* tmp = new char[len + s2.len + 1];
    strcpy(tmp,buff);
    strcat(tmp,s2.buff);

    CSimpString t(tmp);
    delete [] tmp;
    return t;
}

CSimpString operator+(const CSimpString& s1, const CSimpString& s2)
{
    return s1.Concat(s2);
}
```

Ex9-6: When you dynamically allocate space for the stack, you'll need to provide a destructor to free the memory.

```
#include <iostream>

using namespace std;

class CStack
{
private:
    int* list;
    int size;
    int next;
public:
    CStack(int n = 10);
    ~CStack();
    void Push(int i);
```

```
        int Pop();
        int Peek() const;
        void Print() const;
};

CStack::CStack(int n) : next(0), size(n)
{
    list = new int[size];
}

CStack::~CStack()
{
    delete [] list;
}

void CStack::Push(int i)
{
    if (next < size-1)
        list[next++] = i;
    else
        cout << "Error! Stack overflow\n";
}

int CStack::Pop()
{
    if (next == 0)
    {
        cout << "Error! Stack underflow\n";
        return 0;
    }
    else
        return list[--next];
}

int CStack::Peek() const
{
    if (next == 0)
    {
        cout << "Error! Stack underflow\n";
        return 0;
    }
    else
        return list[next-1];
}

void CStack::Print() const
{
    cout << '[';
    for (int i=next-1; i>=0; i--)
        cout << ' '<< list[i];
    cout << " ]\n";
}

int main()
{
    CStack s(20);

    s.Print();
```

```
    s.Push(5);
    s.Push(10);
    s.Push(8);

    s.Print();

    cout << "peek at top of stack=" << s.Peek() << '\n';

    s.Print();
    cout << "pop top of stack=" << s.Pop() << '\n';
    cout << "pop top of stack=" << s.Pop() << '\n';
    s.Print();
    cout << "pop top of stack=" << s.Pop() << '\n';
    cout << "pop top of stack=" << s.Pop() << '\n';

    return 0;
}
```

Chapter 10

Ex10-1: The items in the initialization list will be processed in the 'wrong' order. In other words, **len** won't contain the length of the string in **p**, since **len** will be initialized before **p**. Remember that the members of a class are initialized in the order of their declaration, not in the order that they appear in the initialization list. For this reason, it's a good idea to ensure that your initialization lists are in the same order as the declarations.

Ex10-2: **COstrich** example. We were considering the **CBird** class:

```
class CBird
{
protected:
    int wingSpan;
    int eggSize;
    int airSpeed;
    int altitude;
public:
    virtual void fly() { altitude = 100; }
};
```

It's reasonable to derive a **CHawk** from this class, but not a **COstrich**. This is because the **fly()** function sets the altitude to 100, and (as we all know) ostriches can't fly. If we were to derive **COstrich** from **CBird**, we'd provide a **fly()** function which returned 0, and this might break existing code which relied on the altitude being 100.

A better derivation would be something like this:

```
class CAvian
{
protected:
    int wingSpan;
    int eggSize;
};
```

```
class CFlyingBird : public CAvian
{
protected:
   int airSpeed;
   int altitude;
public:
   virtual void fly() { altitude = 100; }
};

class CFlightlessBird : public CAvian
{
   // ...
};

class CHawk: public CFlyingBird
{
   // ...
};

class COstrich : public CFlightlessBird
{
   // ...
};
```

Now there's no reason for a user of the bird classes to suppose that an **COstrich** might be able to fly, and no need for us to bend the inheritance.

Ex10-3: Class **CBase** is an abstract base class, because it contains a pure virtual function. In order to derive a class from it, we need to provide a **Print()** method.

```
#include <iostream>

using namespace std;

class CBase
{
protected:
   int m_anInt;
public:
   CBase(int n) : m_anInt(n) { cout << "Base constructor\n"; }
   virtual void Print() const = 0;
};

class CDerived : public CBase
{
public:
   CDerived(int n) : CBase(n) { cout << "Derived constructor\n"; }
   void Print() const { cout << "value is " << m_anInt << '\n'; }
};

int main()
{
   CDerived d(3);

   d.Print();

   return 0;
}
```

Ex10-4: Multiple inheritance.

```cpp
#include <iostream>

using namespace std;

class CBase_A
{
public:
    void fA() const { cout << "This is CBase_A::fA" << endl; }
    void fCommon() const { cout << "This is CBase_A::fCommon" << endl; }
};

class CBase_B
{
public:
    void fB() const { cout << "This is CBase_B::fB" << endl; }
    void fCommon() const { cout << "This is CBase_B::fCommon" << endl; }
};

class CMulti : public CBase_A, public CBase_B
{
};

int main()
{
    CMulti t;

    t.fA();
    t.fB();
    t.CBase_A::fCommon();

    return 0;
}
```

Ex10-5: Changing the inheritance access level. The program doesn't work as it did before, because the functions that **CMulti** inherited from its base classes are no longer **public** in **CMulti**. In order to get at them, you'll have to provide **public** access functions in **CMulti**, as shown in the code below.

```cpp
#include <iostream>

using namespace std;

class CBase_A
{
public:
    void fA() const { cout << "This is CBase_A::fA" << endl; }
    void fCommon() const { cout << "This is CBase_A::fCommon" << endl; }
};

class CBase_B
{
public:
    void fB() const { cout << "This is CBase_B::fB" << endl; }
    void fCommon() const { cout << "This is CBase_B::fCommon" << endl; }
};
```

1105

```
class CMulti : private CBase_A, private CBase_B
{
public:
   void call_fA() const { fA(); }
   void call_fB() const { fB(); }
   void call_fCommon() const { CBase_A::fCommon(); }
};

int main()
{
   CMulti t;

   t.call_fA();
   t.call_fB();
   t.call_fCommon();

   return 0;
}
```

You might use this to provide a 'firewall' class. For instance, if you've created a hierarchy of classes, you might only want the class user to have access to the functions provided by certain 'interface' classes, and not to the functions provided by their base classes. Private inheritance will prevent use of inherited functionality, both directly and in further derived classes.

Chapter 11

Ex11-1: Adding an exponentiation operator. This operator fits in with the multiply and divide operators, rather than add and subtract, so you need to create a **CExp** class, modeled on the **CMultiply** class. The two new files you need to create are therefore very familiar. This is **Exp.h**:

```
// Exp.h: interface for the CExp class.
//
//////////////////////////////////////////////////////////////////////

#ifndef __EXP_H__
#define __EXP_H__

#include "Operation.h"

class CLogicUnit;

class CExp : public COperation
{
public:
   void DoOperation(CLogicUnit* pLogicUnit);
   CExp();
   virtual ~CExp();

};

#endif //__EXP_H__
```

The definition of the **CExp** class in **Exp.cpp** provides a suitable **DoOperation()** function to perform the exponentiation on the registers:

```
// Exp.cpp: implementation of the CExp class.
//
//////////////////////////////////////////////////////////////////////

#include "Register.h"
#include "LogicUnit.h"
#include "Exp.h"

//////////////////////////////////////////////////////////////////////
// Construction/Destruction
//////////////////////////////////////////////////////////////////////

CExp::CExp()
{

}

CExp::~CExp()
{

}

void CExp::DoOperation(CLogicUnit* pLogicUnit)
{
   pLogicUnit->m_MultiplyReg ^= pLogicUnit->m_DisplayReg;
   pLogicUnit->m_DisplayReg = pLogicUnit->m_MultiplyReg;
   return;
}
```

This will require a new **operator^=()** function in the **CRegister** base class, which will perform the real exponentiation. The easiest way to do this is to use the **pow()** function declared in the **<cmath>** header file (look in Help for details on how to use **pow()**). You'll need to add this line to **Register.h**:

```
   CRegister& operator^=(const CRegister& rhs);
```

and the following **#include** and function definition to **Register.cpp**:

```
// Register.cpp: implementation of the CRegister class.
//
//////////////////////////////////////////////////////////////////////

#include <cmath>
#include "Register.h"

// Rest of the function definitions as before...

// ^= operation
CRegister& CRegister::operator^=(const CRegister& rhs)
{
   m_Store = pow(m_Store, rhs.m_Store);
   return *this;
}
```

Then, add an **OnExp()** function to **CLogicUnit**:

```
public:
    void OnExp();
```

and a **case** to the **switch** statement in **CKeyboard::GetKey()** which calls this function when a ^ has been entered:

```
        case '^':
            pLogicUnit->OnExp();                // Send an exp message
            break;
```

Now implement **CLogicUnit::OnExp()** itself; it'll be almost identical to **CLogicUnit::OnMultiply()**, differing only in the fact that the new operation queued will be a **CExp** rather than a **CMultiply**:

```
// Process an exp message
void CLogicUnit::OnExp()
{
    if(m_pMultiplyDivide)                // Check for previous multiply/divide
    {
        m_pMultiplyDivide->DoOperation(this);       // If so, do it
        delete m_pMultiplyDivide;        // Now delete the operation object
    }
    else
        // No previous operation queued so save the display register
        m_MultiplyReg = m_DisplayReg;

    m_pMultiplyDivide = new CExp();      // Queue a new operation

    // Signal start of value in display
    m_DisplayReg.SetBeginValue();
    return;
}
```

The other things you'll need to remember are to put a **#include** for **Exp.h** in **LogicUnit.cpp**, and to make **CExp** a **friend** of the **CLogicUnit** class.

Ex11-2: Trapping divide by zero errors. The easiest method is to make changes to the **CDivide::DoOperation()** function. First of all, since we want to output a message, we need to **#include** another header file in **Divide.cpp**:

```
#include <iostream>
```

In **DoOperation()**, we check that the value in **pLogicUnit->m_DisplayReg** is not equal to 0 before performing the division, and outputs an error message if it is:

```
void CDivide::DoOperation(CLogicUnit* pLogicUnit)
{
    if ((pLogicUnit->m_DisplayReg.Get())!=0)
        pLogicUnit->m_MultiplyReg /= pLogicUnit->m_DisplayReg;
    else
    {
        cout << endl
             << "Divide-by-zero error detected. Operation skipped."
```

```
         << endl;
    }
   pLogicUnit->m_DisplayReg = pLogicUnit->m_MultiplyReg;
   return;
 }
```

This is hardly ideal since despite detecting the error, the calculation will carry on regardless. The offending operation is just passed over, but at least the calculator will keep going. The next exercise provides a rather more satisfactory solution.

Ex11-3: Arranging for divide-by-zero errors to terminate processing of the current line is actually quite tricky because a new calculator is created for every pair of parentheses, and you have to make sure all the instances are cleaned up correctly. We've already developed a method that 'rides out' a divide-by-zero error, so one method would be to extend it and add a global flag variable.

Change the **CDivide::DoOperation()** function to this:

```
void CDivide::DoOperation(CLogicUnit* pLogicUnit)
{
   if (pLogicUnit->m_DisplayReg.Get() != 0)
     pLogicUnit->m_MultiplyReg /= pLogicUnit->m_DisplayReg;
   else
     ZeroErrorFlag = true;
   pLogicUnit->m_DisplayReg = pLogicUnit->m_MultiplyReg;
   return;
}
```

This time, rather than produce the error message here, we raise an error flag. That means the header file we included in the last exercise is no longer required. We can now let the calculator continue on its way, just like last time, and catch the error when the time comes for output, which is in **CDisplay::ShowRegister()**:

```
void CDisplay::ShowRegister (CRegister& rReg)
{
   if (ZeroErrorFlag == true)
   {
     cout << endl << "Divide by zero error. Calculator reset." << endl;
     m_pCalc->GetLogicUnit()->Reset();
     ZeroErrorFlag = false;
   }

   cout << endl << setw(12) << rReg.Get() << endl;
   return;
}
```

The function now checks our error flag before outputting the result. If a divide-by-zero error has been detected, it produces an error message, resets the calculator and resets the flag. That just leaves the declarations required to make the flag available at global scope. The first comes in **Ex11_01.cpp**,

```
// EX11_01.CPP - the main() function
#include "Calculator.h"

bool ZeroErrorFlag = false;
```

1109

```
int main(void)
{
    CCalculator myCalculator;        // Create a calculator
    myCalculator.Run();              // ...then run it
    return 0;
}
```

and to make **ZeroErrorFlag** available to the **CDivide** and **CDisplay** classes, you need to add the line

```
extern bool ZeroErrorFlag;
```

after the **#include** statements in **Divide.cpp** and **Display.cpp**. The **extern** keyword forces the compiler to look outside the current source file for the definition of what follows it, and since we've declared **ZeroErrorFlag** at global scope, everything compiles as it should.

The problem with this method is the very fact that it uses global variables, which are rather inelegant and provide the opportunity for errors themselves—multiple definitions and the like—if used carelessly.

Chapter 13

Ex13-1: A document is a class which holds data for an application, while a view presents the data to the user in some form. There may be more than one type of view associated with a given document.

Ex13-2: The document template ties together the document, view and window types used by an application.

Ex13-3: You need to be careful when using AppWizard because you can't go back and modify your choices later! If you didn't select (say) database support when you generated the application, it can be hard to go back and manually edit in all the necessary code yourself.

Chapter 14

Ex14-1: Open the menu resource **IDR_SKETCHTYPE** in ResourceView, and add the item &Ellipse to the vacant position at the end of the Element pop-up. Assign the ID **ID_ELEMENT_ELLIPSE**. Add a prompt reading Draw an ellipse. Save the menu.

Ex14-2: Add a definition for **ELLIPSE** to **OurConstants.h**:

```
const WORD ELLIPSE = 105U;
```

Open ClassWizard and add a **COMMAND** handler and an **UPDATE_COMMAND_UI** handler to **CSketcherDoc,** corresponding to the ID **ID_ELEMENT_ELLIPSE**.

Implement the command handler as:

```
void CSketcherDoc::OnElementEllipse()
{
    m_Element = ELLIPSE; // Set element type as a ellipse
}
```

Add a command update handler as:

```
void CSketcherDoc::OnUpdateElementEllipse(CCmdUI* pCmdUI)
{
    // Set Checked if the current element is an ellipse
    pCmdUI->SetCheck(m_Element==ELLIPSE);
}
```

Ex14-3: Open the toolbar **IDR_MAINFRAME** in ResourceView. Draw a new toolbar button to represent an ellipse. Drag it to the group of buttons for elements types. Change its ID to that of the corresponding menu item, **ID_ELEMENT_ELLIPSE**. Save the toolbar.

Open the menu resource with the ID **IDR_SKETCHTYPE**. Open the properties box for the menu item Ellipse. Modify the prompt to include the tooltip.

Ex14-4: Use the **SetText()** member of the class **CCmdUI** to set the menu item text for each color to upper or lower case, depending on the current value of **m_Color**. A typical update handler will be modified as follows:

```
void CSketcherDoc::OnUpdateColorBlack(CCmdUI* pCmdUI)
{
    // Set menu item Checked if the current color is black
    pCmdUI->SetCheck(m_Color==BLACK);

    // Set upper case for a selected item, lower case otherwise
    if(m_Color == BLACK)
        pCmdUI->SetText("BLACK");
    else
        pCmdUI->SetText("black");
}
```

This modification does not affect the corresponding toolbar button.

Chapter 15

Ex15-1: The class definition should be:

```
// Class defining an ellipse object
class CEllipse: public CElement
{
    public:
        virtual void Draw(CDC* pDC) const;

        // Constructor for an ellipse
        CEllipse(const Cpoint& Start, const Cpoint& End, const COLORREF& Color);
```

```
     protected:
        CEllipse(){}                // Default constructor - should not be used
  };
```

The implementation of the **CEllipse** class constructor is:

```
// Constructor for an ellipse object
CEllipse:: CEllipse(const Cpoint& Start, const Cpoint& End, const COLORREF& Color)
{
   m_Color = Color;            // Set ellipse color
   m_Pen = 1;                  // Set pen width

   // Define the enclosing rectangle
   m_EnclosingRect = CRect(Start, End);
   m_EnclosingRect.NormalizeRect();
}
```

The implementation of the **Draw()** function for an ellipse object is:

```
// Draw an ellipse
void CEllipse::Draw(CDC* pDC) const
{
   // Create a pen for this object and
   // initialize it to the object color and line width of 1 pixel
   CPen aPen;
   if(!aPen.CreatePen(PS_SOLID, m_Pen, m_Color))
   {                                           // Pen creation failed
     AfxMessageBox("Pen creation failed drawing an ellipse", MB_OK);
     AfxAbort();
   }

   CPen* pOldPen = pDC->SelectObject(&aPen);  // Select the pen

   // Select a null brush
   CBrush* pOldBrush = static_cast<CBrush*>(pDC->SelectStockObject(NULL_BRUSH));

   // Now draw the ellipse
   pDC->Ellipse(m_EnclosingRect);

   pDC->SelectObject(pOldPen);                 // Restore the old pen
   pDC->SelectObject(pOldBrush);               // Restore the old brush
}
```

Ex15-2: Only the **CreateElement()** element function needs to be modified:

```
CElement* CSketcherView::CreateElement()
{
   // Get a pointer to the document for this view
   CSketcherDoc* pDoc = GetDocument();
   ASSERT_VALID(pDoc);                    // Verify the pointer is good

   // Now select the element using the type stored in the document
   switch(pDoc->GetElementType())
   {
      case RECTANGLE:
         return new CRectangle(m_FirstPoint, m_SecondPoint,
                                       pDoc->GetElementColor());
```

```
        case CIRCLE:
           return new CCircle(m_FirstPoint, m_SecondPoint,
                                           pDoc->GetElementColor());
        case CURVE:
           return new CCurve(pDoc->GetElementColor());

        case LINE:
           return new CLine(m_FirstPoint, m_SecondPoint,
                                         pDoc->GetElementColor());
        case ELLIPSE:
           return new CEllipse(m_FirstPoint, m_SecondPoint,
                                           pDoc->GetElementColor());

        default:                        // Something's gone wrong
           AfxMessageBox("Bad Element code", MB_OK);
           AfxAbort();
     }
  }
```

Ex15-3: Only the class constructor needs to be modified:

```
CEllipse:: CEllipse(const CPoint& Start, const CPoint& End, const COLORREF& Color)
{
   m_Color = Color;          // Set ellipse color
   m_Pen = 1;                // Set pen width

   // Define the enclosing rectangle
   m_EnclosingRect = CRect(Start - (End-Start), End);
   m_EnclosingRect.NormalizeRect();
}
```

The modified statement uses two different versions of the overloaded operator—in the **CPoint** class. The expression **(End-Start)** returns the difference between the two points as an object of class **CSize**. This object is then subtracted from the **CPoint** object **Start** to offset it by the **CSize** value.

Ex15-4: Open the menu **IDR_SKETCHTYPE** in ResourceView. Add a new pop-up to the menu bar, labeled P̲en Style. Add menu items to the pop-up for Solid, Dashed, Dotted, Dash-dotted, and Dash-dot-dotted lines. Save the resource.

Ex15-5: The following modifications are necessary:

▶ Add a protected member of type **int**, **m_PenStyle**, and a function to retrieve its value, to the **CSketcherDoc** class.

▶ Add initialization of **m_Penstyle** to **PS_SOLID** in the **CSketcherDoc** constructor.

▶ Add **COMMAND** and **UPDATE_COMMAND_UI** handlers for each of the new menu items.

▶ Add a protected member of type **int**, **m_PenStyle**, to the **CElement** class.

▶ Modify the constructors for each of the element classes to accept an argument of type **int** specifying the pen style.

▶ Modify the **CreateElement()** function member of **CSketcherView** to call the constructors using the additional parameter for pen style.

▶ Modify the **Draw()** functions in each of the element classes to draw using the pen style specified in the **m_PenStyle** member of each element class.

Ex15-6: The following line must be added to the protected section of the **CSketcherDoc** class definition:

```
int m_PenStyle;                    // Current pen style
```

Add the following function to retrieve the pen style from the document:

```
int GetPenStyle()                  // Get the pen style
   { return m_PenStyle; }
```

The following line should be added to the constructor, **CSketcherDoc()**:

```
m_PenStyle = PS_SOLID;             // Set initial style as solid
```

A typical **COMMAND** menu handler is:

```
void CSketcherDoc::OnPenstyleDashdotted()
{
   m_PenStyle = PS_DASHDOT;
}
```

A typical **UPDATE_COMMAND_UI** handler is:

```
void CSketcherDoc::OnUpdatePenstyleDashdotted(CCmdUI* pCmdUI)
{
   pCmdUI->SetCheck(m_PenStyle==PS_DASHDOT);
}
```

The following declaration should be added to the protected section of the **CElement** class:

```
int m_PenStyle;                              // Element pen style
```

The constructor declaration in each derived element class definition should be modified to add the extra parameter. The **CCircle** class is typical:

```
CCircle(const Cpoint& Start, const Cpoint& End, const COLORREF& Color,
                                                int aPenStyle);
```

The typical change to the constructor to support the pen style is:

```
CCircle::CCircle(const CPoint& Start, const CPoint& End,
                     const COLORREF& Color, int aPenStyle)
{
   // First calculate the radius
   // We use floating point because that is required by
   // the library function (in math.h) for calculating a square root.
   long Radius =
   static_cast<long>(sqrt(static_cast<double>((End.x-Start.x)*(End.x-Start.x)+
                                       (End.y-Start.y)*(End.y-Start.y))));


   // Now calculate the rectangle enclosing
   // the circle assuming the MM_TEXT mapping mode
   m_EnclosingRect = CRect(Start.x-Radius, Start.y-Radius,
                           Start.x+Radius, Start.y+Radius);
```

```
    m_Color = aColor;            // Set the color for the circle
    m_Pen = 1;                   // Set pen width to 1
    m_PenStyle = aPenStyle;      // Set the pen style
}
```

The **CreateElement()** member of **CSketcherView** is modified to:

```
CElement* CSketcherView::CreateElement()
{
    // Get a pointer to the document for this view
    CSketcherDoc* pDoc = GetDocument();
    ASSERT_VALID(pDoc);                     // Verify the pointer is good

    // Now select the element using the type stored in the document
    switch(pDoc->GetElementType())
    {
        case RECTANGLE:
            return new CRectangle(m_FirstPoint, m_SecondPoint,
                        pDoc->GetElementColor(), pDoc->GetPenStyle());
        case CIRCLE:
            return new CCircle(pDoc->GetElementColor(), pDoc->GetPenStyle());
        case CURVE:
            return new CCurve(m_FirstPoint, m_SecondPoint,
                        pDoc->GetElementColor(), pDoc->GetPenStyle());
        case LINE:
            return new CLine(m_FirstPoint, m_SecondPoint,
                        pDoc->GetElementColor(), pDoc->GetPenStyle());
        case ELLIPSE:
            return new CEllipse(m_FirstPoint, m_SecondPoint,
                        pDoc->GetElementColor(), pDoc->GetPenStyle());

        default:                    // Something's gone wrong
            AfxMessageBox("Bad Element code", MB_OK);
            AfxAbort();
            return NULL;
    }
}
```

The typical change to the implementation of the **Draw()** members of the element classes is:

```
void CCircle::Draw(CDC* pDC) const
{
    // Create a pen for this object and
    // initialize it to the object color and line width of 1 pixel
    CPen aPen;

    if(!aPen.CreatePen(m_PenStyle, m_Pen, m_Color))
    {                                       // Pen creation failed
        AfxMessageBox("Pen creation failed drawing a circle", MB_OK);
        AfxAbort();
    }

    CPen* pOldPen = pDC->SelectObject(&aPen);  // Select the pen

    // Select a null brush
    CBrush* pOldBrush = static_cast<CBrush*>(pDC->SelectStockObject(NULL_BRUSH));
```

```
        // Now draw the circle
        pDC->Ellipse(m_EnclosingRect);

        pDC->SelectObject(pOldPen);                  // Restore the old pen
        pDC->SelectObject(pOldBrush);                // Restore the old brush
    }
```

Chapter 16

Ex16-1: When the points are added to the head of the list, they will be in reverse order. We must modify the constructor and the **AddSegment()** function to add points to the head of the list, and change the **Draw()** function to process the points from the tail to the head.

The code for the constructor is:

```
    CCurve::CCurve(const CPoint& FirstPoint, const CPoint& SecondPoint,
                                                const COLORREF& Color)
    {
        m_PointList.AddHead(FirstPoint);        // Add the 1st point to the list
        m_PointList.AddHead(SecondPoint);       // Add the 2nd point to the list
        m_Color = Color;                        // Store the color
        m_Pen = 1;                              // Set the pen width
        m_PenStyle = aPenStyle;                 // Set the pen style

        // Construct the enclosing rectangle assuming MM_TEXT mode
        m_EnclosingRect = CRect(FirstPoint, SecondPoint);
        m_EnclosingRect.NormalizeRect();
    }
```

Here we just use the **AddHead()** function instead of **AddTail()**. The code for the **AddSegment()** member is:

```
    void CCurve::AddSegment(const CPoint& Point)
    {
        m_PointList.AddHead(Point);      // Add the point to the list

        // Modify the enclosing rectangle for the new point
        m_EnclosingRect = CRect( min(Point.x, m_EnclosingRect.left),
                                 min(Point.y, m_EnclosingRect.top),
                                 max(Point.x, m_EnclosingRect.right),
                                 max(Point.y, m_EnclosingRect.bottom) );
    }
```

Again, the change is just to use **AddHead()** in place of **AddTail()**. The code for the **Draw()** member function is:

```
    void CCurve::Draw(CDC* pDC, const CElement* pElement) const
    {
        // Create a pen for this object and
        // initialize it to the object color and line width of 1 pixel
        CPen aPen;
        COLORREF aColor = m_Color;               // Initialize with element color
        if(this == pElement)                     // This element selected?
```

```
        aColor = SELECT_COLOR;                     // Set highlight color
    if(!aPen.CreatePen(PS_SOLID, m_Pen, aColor))
    {
        // Pen creation failed. Close the program
        AfxMessageBox("Pen creation failed drawing a curve", MB_OK);
        AfxAbort();
    }

    CPen* pOldPen = pDC->SelectObject(&aPen);   // Select the pen

    // Now draw the curve
    // Get the position in the list of the first element
    POSITION aPosition = m_PointList.GetTailPosition();

    // As long as it's good, move to that point
    if(aPosition)
        pDC->MoveTo(m_PointList.GetPrev(aPosition));

    // Draw a segment for each of the following points
    while(aPosition)
        pDC->LineTo(m_PointList.GetPrev(aPosition));

    pDC->SelectObject(pOldPen);                         // Restore the old pen
}
```

The **GetTailPosition()** function returns the **POSITION** value for the last member of the list, which will correspond to the first point. We then step backwards through the list by using the **GetPrev()** function.

Ex16-2: The declaration in the **CCurve** class for the list should be changed to:

```
// Type safe point pointer list
CTypedPtrList<CPtrList, CPoint*> m_PointPtrList;
```

The constructor will now be implemented as:

```
CCurve::CCurve(const CPoint& FirstPoint, const CPoint& SecondPoint, const
COLORREF& Color)
{
    // Add the points to the list
    m_PointPtrList.AddTail(new CPoint(FirstPoint));
    m_PointPtrList.AddTail(new CPoint(SecondPoint));
    m_Color = Color;                            // Store the color
    m_Pen = 1;                                  // Set the pen width

    // Construct the enclosing rectangle assuming MM_TEXT mode
    m_EnclosingRect = CRect(FirstPoint, SecondPoint);
    m_EnclosingRect.NormalizeRect();
}
```

This now creates new points on the heap that are initialized with the points passed as arguments to the constructor, and passes their addresses to the **AddTail()** function.
Since we're using a pointer list, we need to implement the destructor for the **CCurve** class:

```
CCurve::~CCurve()
{
   POSITION aPos = m_PointPtrList.GetHeadPosition();
   while(aPos)
      delete m_PointPtrList.GetNext(aPos);   // Delete CPoint objects
   m_PointPtrList.RemoveAll();               // Delete the pointers
}
```

Don't forget to add a declaration for the destructor in **Elements.h**! The **AddSegment()** member of the **CCurve** class also needs to be modified:

```
void CCurve::AddSegment(const CPoint& Point)
{
   //Add the point to the end
   m_PointPtrList.AddTail(new CPoint(Point));

   // Modify the enclosing rectangle for the new point
   m_EnclosingRect = CRect( min(Point.x, m_EnclosingRect.left),
                            min(Point.y, m_EnclosingRect.top),
                            max(Point.x, m_EnclosingRect.right),
                            max(Point.y, m_EnclosingRect.bottom) );
}
```

The **Move()** member function is also affected:

```
void CCurve::Move(const CSize& aSize)
{
   m_EnclosingRect += aSize;                            // Move the rectangle

   // Get the 1st element position
   POSITION aPosition = m_PointPtrList.GetHeadPosition();

   while(aPosition)
      *m_PointPtrList.GetNext(aPosition)+= aSize;  // Move each point
}
```

Lastly, the **Draw()** function in the **CCurve** class must be changed:

```
void CCurve::Draw(CDC* pDC, const CElement* pElement) const
{
   // Create a pen for this object and
   // initialize it to the object color and line width of 1 pixel
   CPen aPen;
   COLORREF aColor = m_Color;              // Initialize with element color
   if(this == pElement)                    // This element selected?
      aColor = SELECT_COLOR;               // Set highlight color
   if(!aPen.CreatePen(PS_SOLID, m_Pen, aColor))
   {
      // Pen creation failed. Close the program
      AfxMessageBox("Pen creation failed drawing a curve", MB_OK);
      AfxAbort();
   }

   CPen* pOldPen = pDC->SelectObject(&aPen);  // Select the pen
```

```
    // Now draw the curve
    // Get the position in the list of the first element
    POSITION aPosition = m_PointPtrList.GetHeadPosition();

    // As long as it's good, move to that point
    if(aPosition)
      pDC->MoveTo(*m_PointPtrList.GetNext(aPosition));

    // Draw a segment for each of the following points
    while(aPosition)
      pDC->LineTo(*m_PointPtrList.GetNext(aPosition));

    pDC->SelectObject(pOldPen);                    // Restore the old pen
  }
```

Ex16-3: The declaration of the **CArray** data member in the **CCurve** class is:

```
    CArray<CPoint, const CPoint&> m_PointArray;        // Type safe point array
```

The second argument to the template specifies that arguments will be passed to function members of **m_PointArray** as references. Remember to delete the declaration of the **CList** data member in the **CCurve** class.

We can also add a protected data member to keep track of how many points we have in a curve:

```
    int m_nPoints;                              // Number of points
```

The constructor needs to be modified to:

```
    CCurve::CCurve(const CPoint& FirstPoint, const CPoint& SecondPoint,
                                            const COLORREF& Color)
    {
      m_PointArray.SetSize(10);
      m_PointArray[0] = FirstPoint;       // Add the 1st point to the array
      m_PointArray[1] = SecondPoint;      // Add the 2nd point to the array
      m_nPoints = 2;                      // Set the point count
      m_Color = Color;                    // Store the color
      m_Pen = 1;                          // Set the pen width

      // Construct the enclosing rectangle assuming MM_TEXT mode
      m_EnclosingRect = CRect(FirstPoint, SecondPoint);
      m_EnclosingRect.NormalizeRect();
    }
```

By setting the initial size of the array, we avoid unnecessary creation of array elements. The default situation allocates array elements one at a time. You can specify a second argument to the **SetSize()** function to define the number of additional elements to be created when it becomes necessary. If you omit the second argument, the framework will decide how many to create, based on the initial array size.

The **CArray** template provides overloading for **[]** so that you can use indexing to reference members of the array. The **AddSegment()** member of **CCurve** can be implemented as:

```
void CCurve::AddSegment(const CPoint& Point)
{
    //Add the point to the array and increment the count
    m_PointArray.SetAtGrow(m_nPoints++, Point);

    // Modify the enclosing rectangle for the new point
    m_EnclosingRect = CRect( min(Point.x, m_EnclosingRect.left),
                             min(Point.y, m_EnclosingRect.top),
                             max(Point.x, m_EnclosingRect.right),
                             max(Point.y, m_EnclosingRect.bottom) );
}
```

The **SetAtGrow()** member of **CArray** sets the array element specified by the first argument to the value passed as the second argument. If the first argument is beyond the extent of the array, the array will be automatically increased in size.

As in the previous exercises, we'll also need to modify the **Draw()** and **Move()** members. Here's the first of those two:

```
void CCurve::Draw(CDC* pDC, const CElement* pElement) const
{
    // Create a pen for this object and
    // initialize it to the object color and line width of 1 pixel
    CPen aPen;
    COLORREF aColor = m_Color;              // Initialize with element color
    if(this == pElement)                    // This element selected?
        aColor = SELECT_COLOR;              // Set highlight color
    if(!aPen.CreatePen(PS_SOLID, m_Pen, aColor))
    {
        // Pen creation failed. Close the program
        AfxMessageBox("Pen creation failed drawing a curve", MB_OK);
        AfxAbort();
    }

    CPen* pOldPen = pDC->SelectObject(&aPen);  // Select the pen

    // Now draw the curve
    // Set the position counter to the first element of the array
    int aPosition = 0;

    // Move to the first point in the curve
    pDC->MoveTo(m_PointArray[aPosition++]);

    // Draw a segment for each of the following points
    while(aPosition < m_nPoints)
        pDC->LineTo(m_PointArray[aPosition++]);

    pDC->SelectObject(pOldPen);                 // Restore the old pen
}
```

And these are the changes you need to make to **Move()**:

```
void CCurve::Move(const CSize& aSize)
{
    m_EnclosingRect += aSize;                // Move the rectangle
```

```
    // Set a counter to the 1st element
    int aPosition = 0;

    while(aPosition < m_nPoints)
       m_PointArray[aPosition++] += aSize; // Move each point in the array
}
```

Chapter 17

Ex17-1: Modify the scale dialog to appear as shown here:

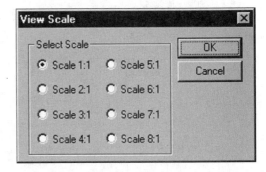

Make sure that each radio button has a unique ID, such as **IDC_SCALE1**, **IDC_SCALE2**, etc., then use ClassWizard to add functions to handle the **BN_CLICKED** message for each radio button. The implementations for these are all very similar. For example, the first two are:

```
void CScaleDialog::OnScale1()
{
   m_Scale = 1;
}

void CScaleDialog::OnScale2()
{
   m_Scale = 2;
}
```

Modify the **OnInitDialog()** member of **CScaleDialog** to check the appropriate radio button, based on the current scale, as follows:

```
BOOL CScaleDialog::OnInitDialog()
{
   CDialog::OnInitDialog();

   // Check the radio button corresponding to the scale
   switch(m_Scale)
   {
      case 1:
         CheckDlgButton(IDC_SCALE1,1);
         break;
      case 2:
         CheckDlgButton(IDC_SCALE2,1);
         break;
```

```
        case 3:
           CheckDlgButton(IDC_SCALE3,1);
           break;
        case 4:
           CheckDlgButton(IDC_SCALE4,1);
           break;
        case 5:
           CheckDlgButton(IDC_SCALE5,1);
           break;
        case 6:
           CheckDlgButton(IDC_SCALE6,1);
           break;
        case 7:
           CheckDlgButton(IDC_SCALE7,1);
           break;
        case 8:
           CheckDlgButton(IDC_SCALE8,1);
           break;
        default:
           CheckDlgButton(IDC_SCALE8,1);
           AfxMessageBox("Invalid scale set.");
   }

   return TRUE;  // return TRUE unless you set the focus to a control
                 // EXCEPTION: OCX Property Pages should return FALSE
}
```

Delete the code from the **DoDataExchange()** member of **CscaleDialog** that handled the previous version of the dialog controls, so it becomes:

```
void CScaleDialog::DoDataExchange(CDataExchange* pDX)
{
   CDialog::DoDataExchange(pDX);
   //{{AFX_DATA_MAP(CScaleDialog)
      // NOTE: the ClassWizard will add DDX and DDV calls here
   //}}AFX_DATA_MAP
}
```

If you changed Sketcher to work with the list box scale dialogue, rather than the original spin button control, there is an extra step to add to the solution. In the **CsketcherView::OnViewScale()** function, return the first line after the **DoModal()** call to its original state:

```
   m_Scale = aDlg.m_Scale;
```

That completes all the necessary modifications. Compile and run Sketcher as normal to see the new dialog in operation.

Ex17-2: Modify the pen width dialog box resource to the following:

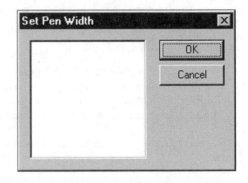

Assign a suitable ID, such as **IDC_PENWIDTH** to the list box, and make sure the <u>S</u>ort style is unchecked. Now delete the **m_PenWidth** data member of **CPenDialog** and the functions handling the previous **BN_CLICKED** messages for the radio buttons. Don't forget to delete them from the class definition, as well as from the message map in the implementation file. Save the two files so ClassWizard recognizes that the variable has been deleted.

Use ClassWizard to add a new variable for the dialog, **m_PenWidth**, of type **int** and corresponding to the list box ID, **IDC_PENWIDTH**. The variable will store the index to the selected list box item, and will also represent the pen width.

Modify the **OnInitDialog()** member of **CPenDialog** to add the strings to the list box, and highlight the string corresponding to the current pen width:

```
BOOL CPenDialog::OnInitDialog()
{
    CDialog::OnInitDialog();
// Initialize aBox
    CListBox* pLBox = static_cast<CListBox*>(GetDlgItem(IDC_PENWIDTH));
    pLBox->AddString("Pen Width 0");     // Add the strings to the box
    pLBox->AddString("Pen Width 1");
    pLBox->AddString("Pen Width 2");
    pLBox->AddString("Pen Width 3");
    pLBox->AddString("Pen Width 4");
    pLBox->AddString("Pen Width 5");
    pLBox->SetCurSel(m_PenWidth);        // Highlight the current pen width

    return TRUE;  // return TRUE unless you set the focus to a control
                  // EXCEPTION: OCX Property Pages should return FALSE
}
```

Ex17-3: Change the dialog again by removing the list box and replacing it by a combo box with the same ID. The dialog will look like this:

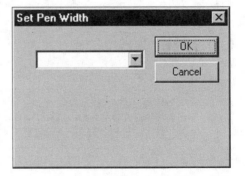

It's important to allow enough space in the dialog for the combo box to drop down, otherwise you will not see the complete list. Do this by clicking the down arrow and increasing the size of the area displayed.

You could delete the existing **m_PenWidth** member of **CPenDialog** and add it back as the variable to support the combo box, but because the differences are so slight the shortest way to implement the support for the combo box is to modify the existing code. The **DoDataExchange()** member of **CPenDialog** should be modified to:

```
void CPenDialog::DoDataExchange(CDataExchange* pDX)
{
    CDialog::DoDataExchange(pDX);
    //{{AFX_DATA_MAP(CPenDialog)
    DDX_CBIndex(pDX, IDC_PENWIDTH, m_PenWidth);
    //}}AFX_DATA_MAP
}
```

This calls **DDX_CBIndex()** instead of **DDX_LBIndex()**, because we're now using a combo box, not a list box. The only other modification necessary is to the **OnInitDialog()** member of **CPenDialog**:

```
BOOL CPenDialog::OnInitDialog()
{
    CDialog::OnInitDialog();

// Initialize aBox
    CComboBox* pCBox = static_cast<CComboBox*>(GetDlgItem(IDC_PENWIDTH));
    pCBox->AddString("Pen Width 0");     // Add the strings to the box
    pCBox->AddString("Pen Width 1");
    pCBox->AddString("Pen Width 2");
    pCBox->AddString("Pen Width 3");
    pCBox->AddString("Pen Width 4");
    pCBox->AddString("Pen Width 5");
    pCBox->SetCurSel(m_PenWidth);        // Highlight the current pen width

    return TRUE;  // return TRUE unless you set the focus to a control
                  // EXCEPTION: OCX Property Pages should return FALSE
}
```

The changed lines here are highlighted. The first statement creates a pointer to a **CComboBox** object instead of a pointer to a **CListBox** object, and casts the pointer returned by **GetDlgItem()** accordingly. You should also change the pointer name to **pCBox** for consistency. You also have to change all the succeeding statements which refer to it, of course.

Chapter 18

Ex18-1: Printing page numbers. These are the lines you need to add to **OnPrint()**:

```
...
// Output the document file name
    pDC->SetTextAlign(TA_CENTER);              // Center the following text
    pDC->TextOut(pInfo->m_rectDraw.right/2, -20, pPrintData->m_DocTitle);
```

```
    CString PageNum;
    PageNum.Format("Page %d", pInfo->m_nCurPage);
    pDC->TextOut(pInfo->m_rectDraw.right/2, -1050, PageNum);

    pDC->SetTextAlign(TA_LEFT);            // Left justify text
...
```

Using **CString**, it's easy! You create a string object, initialize it using the member function **Format()** with the **m_nCurPage** value we're already using elsewhere in **OnPrint()**, and output it just as we did with the document title (although in a different position, of course).

Ex18-2: Scaling text correctly is a matter of working out how and where to specify the font to be used. In fact, you need to do it twice: once in the **CText::Draw()** function, and then again in **CSketcherView::OnLButtonDown()**, to make sure that the text rectangle gets set up correctly. Here are the changes to **CText::Draw()**:

```
    void CText::Draw(CDC* pDC, CElement* pElement)
    {
        CFont aFont;
        aFont.CreatePointFont(100, "");
        CFont* pOldFont = pDC->SelectObject(&aFont);

        COLORREF Color(m_Color);              // Initialize with element color

        if(this==pElement)
            Color = SELECT_COLOR;             // Set selected color

        // Set the text color and output the text
        pDC->SetTextColor(Color);
        pDC->TextOut(m_StartPoint.x, m_StartPoint.y, m_String);
        pDC->SelectObject(pOldFont);
    }
```

The new code simply creates a new object of the **CFont** class, calls its member function **CreatePointFont()** to select a default 10 point font, selects it into the device context before the text is output, and selects it out again afterwards. Four very similar lines get added to **CSketcherView::OnLButtonDown()**:

```
        if(pDoc->GetElementType() == TEXT)
        {
            CTextDialog aDlg;
            if(aDlg.DoModal() == IDOK)
            {
                // Exit OK so create a text element
                CFont aFont;
                aFont.CreatePointFont(100, "");
                CFont* pOldFont = aDC.SelectObject(&aFont);

                CSize TextExtent = aDC.GetTextExtent(aDlg.m_TextString);

                // Get bottom right of text rectangle - MM_LOENGLISH
                CPoint BottomRt(point.x+TextExtent.cx, point.y-TextExtent.cy);
                CText* pTextElement = new CText(point, BottomRt,
                            aDlg.m_TextString, pDoc->GetElementColor());
```

```
                        // Add the element to the document
                        pDoc->AddElement(pTextElement);

                        // Get all views updated
                        pDoc->UpdateAllViews(0,0,pTextElement);

                        aDC.SelectObject(pOldFont);
                }
        return;
    }
```

Chapter 19

Ex19-1: Start off by using AppWizard to generate a new SDI application. You can turn off printer support if you like, and the name really isn't important. The files and classes here assume a project called SkView.

Copy the **DllImports.h** file into the project folder and add it to the project; insert **#include**s for this file into **SkView.cpp**, **SkViewDoc.cpp** and **SkViewView.cpp** , ensuring that you place them before the **#include**s for **SkViewDoc.h** and **SkViewView.h**. Just like in the chapter, amend the project settings so the **ExtDLLExample.lib** file is linked in, and don't forget to copy **ExtDLLExample.dll** to the **Debug** directory once that's been created. You'll also need to add a **#include** for **afxtempl.h** to **stdafx.h**.

To the document class definition, you need to add five member variables and three member functions, all of which you've used before:

```
// Attributes
protected:
    COLORREF m_Color;
    WORD m_Element;
    CTypedPtrList<CObList, CElement*> m_ElementList;
    int m_PenWidth;
    CSize m_DocSize;

// Operations
public:
    POSITION GetListHeadPosition()
        { return m_ElementList.GetHeadPosition(); }
    CElement* GetNext(POSITION &aPos)
        { return m_ElementList.GetNext(aPos); }
    CSize GetDocSize()
        { return m_DocSize; }
```

As for the implementation, since we're only dealing with documents held in files, we don't need to do any initialization in the constructor. However, we should add the code which deletes the element list cleanly to the destructor:

```
CSkViewDoc::~CSkViewDoc()
{
    POSITION aPosition = m_ElementList.GetHeadPosition();
    while(aPosition)
        delete m_ElementList.GetNext(aPosition);
```

```
      m_ElementList.RemoveAll();
}
```

The only other code to add to the document class is that required to enable serialization from a file. (Remember, we aren't worried about saving files because we never alter them in this application.) The **Serialize()** function looks like this:

```
void CSkViewDoc::Serialize(CArchive& ar)
{
   m_ElementList.Serialize(ar);

   if (ar.IsStoring())
   {
   }
   else
   {
      ar >> m_Color
         >> m_Element
         >> m_PenWidth
         >> m_DocSize;
   }
}
```

The view class requires a little more work, although not much. For a start, it doesn't need any new member variables, although you will need to use ClassWizard to add two new member functions: **OnPrepareDC()** and **OnOpenDocument()**. Once again, nothing needs adding to the constructor, and this time the destructor can be left empty as well. You should add some code to **OnDraw()**, but only the same as we had in Sketcher itself:

```
void CSkViewView::OnDraw(CDC* pDC)
{
   CSkViewDoc* pDoc = GetDocument();
   ASSERT_VALID(pDoc);

   POSITION aPos = pDoc->GetListHeadPosition();
   CElement* pElement = 0;
   while(aPos)
   {
      pElement = pDoc->GetNext(aPos);
      if(pDC->RectVisible(pElement->GetBoundRect()))
         pElement->Draw(pDC);
   }
}
```

OnPrepareDC() bears a little more inspection, and should look like this once you've created the handler and added the code:

```
void CSkViewView::OnPrepareDC(CDC* pDC, CPrintInfo* pInfo)
{
   CView::OnPrepareDC(pDC, pInfo);
   CSkViewDoc* pDoc = GetDocument();
   pDC->SetMapMode(MM_ANISOTROPIC);

   CSize DocSize = pDoc->GetDocSize();
   DocSize.cy = -DocSize.cy;
   pDC->SetWindowExt(DocSize);
```

```
    int xLogPixels = pDC->GetDeviceCaps(LOGPIXELSX);
    int yLogPixels = pDC->GetDeviceCaps(LOGPIXELSY);

    CRect WinRect;
    GetWindowRect(&WinRect);

    double xScale = (static_cast<double>(WinRect.right -
                            WinRect.left))/(DocSize.cx/100*xLogPixels);
    double yScale = -(static_cast<double>(WinRect.bottom -
                            WinRect.top))/(DocSize.cy/100*yLogPixels);

    long xExtent = static_cast<long>(DocSize.cx*xScale*xLogPixels/100L);
    long yExtent = static_cast<long>(DocSize.cy*yScale*yLogPixels/100L);

    pDC->SetViewportExt(static_cast<int>(xExtent), static_cast<int>(-yExtent));
}
```

The new lines here are the ones which handle the scaling. **GetWindowRect()** returns, in its argument, the coordinates in pixels of the view window. From these values, we contrive to produce two scaling factors (in general, they're different for the x and y directions) which map the document stored in **DocSize** to our view window — the expressions come down to (window width/document width) and (window height/document height), with all measurements in pixels.

You need to implement **OnOpenDocument()** in order that you have somewhere to delete the old document before opening a new one. If you don't do this, any new documents you open will just be superimposed on top of old ones, which is hardly ideal. The code you need to add is exactly the same as the code in the destructor:

```
BOOL CSkViewDoc::OnOpenDocument(LPCTSTR lpszPathName)
{
    POSITION aPosition = m_ElementList.GetHeadPosition();
    while(aPosition)
        delete m_ElementList.GetNext(aPosition);

    m_ElementList.RemoveAll();

    if (!CDocument::OnOpenDocument(lpszPathName))
        return FALSE;

    return TRUE;
}
```

That's everything required for the problem as specified, although you might like to include the text scaling we introduced in the last chapter's exercises, as the text is disproportionately large at these scales otherwise.

Chapter 20

Ex20-1: There are a number of things to do here. Start by adding a new button labeled something like Stock Info to the products dialog, and amend its ID appropriately. Implement a handler for it using ClassWizard and add this code:

```
void CProductView::OnStockinfo()
{
   ((CMainFrame*)GetParentFrame())->SelectView(STOCK_VIEW);
}
```

For this to work, you must also define a new constant in **OurConstants.h**

```
// Arbitrary constants to identify record views
const UINT PRODUCT_VIEW = 1U;
const UINT ORDER_VIEW = 2U;
const UINT CUSTOMER_VIEW = 3U;
const UINT STOCK_VIEW = 4U;
```

and add code to handle it in **CMainFrame::SelectView()**. The new class for the stock control dialog will be called **CStockView**:

```
if (pNewActiveView == NULL)
   {
      switch(ViewID)
      {
         case ORDER_VIEW:       // Create an Order view
            pNewActiveView = (CView*)new COrderView;
            break;
         case CUSTOMER_VIEW:    // Create a customer view
            pNewActiveView = (CView*)new CCustomerView;
            break;
         case STOCK_VIEW:       // Create a stock view
            pNewActiveView = (CView*)new CStockView;
            break;
```

Don't forget that you'll need to add a **#include** for **StockView.h** to **MainFrm.cpp**. Next, call up ClassWizard and use it to create a new class called **CStockSet**, with **CRecordset** as its base. Choose to use the **Products** table from the **Sample Data** database, and once you've done that, add a **public** member variable to the document class:

```
public:
   CStockSet    m_StockSet;
   CCustomerSet m_CustomerSet;
   COrderSet    m_OrderSet;
```

The next step is to add the dialog itself. Go to the ResourceView and insert a new dialog called **IDD_STOCK_FORM**. Make sure its Style and Border are set to Child and None respectively, delete the default controls and add new ones so it looks something like this:

After giving the important controls sensible IDs and ensuring that the tab order of the controls is such that each edit control immediately succeeds its partnering static text control, call up ClassWizard and create a new class called **CStockView**. Base this class on **CRecordView**, select **IDD_STOCK_FORM** as the dialog to be associated with it, and choose **CStockSet** as its recordset.

You can now *Ctrl*-double-click on all the edit controls to tie them to the recordset data members, and on the Products button so that you can implement the handler, which looks like this:

```
void CStockView::OnSkproducts()
{
    ((CMainFrame*)GetParentFrame())->SelectView(PRODUCT_VIEW);
}
```

Just three things remain: make the constructor for **CStockView** public, delete the code from the destructor, and add two **#include**s to **StockView.cpp**:

```
#include "stdafx.h"
#include "DBSample.h"
#include "OurConstants.h"
#include "Mainfrm.h"
#include "StockView.h"
```

Ex20-2: Add the **public** member variable **m_ProductIDparam**, of type **long**, to the definition of **CStockSet**. Initialize it and the parameter count **m_nParams** in the constructor in **StockSet.cpp**:

```
m_ProductIDparam = 0L;
m_nParams = 1;
```

Set up the parameter by adding a couple of lines to the **CStockSet::DoFieldExchange()** function:

```
void CStockSet::DoFieldExchange(CFieldExchange* pFX)
{
    //{{AFX_FIELD_MAP(CStockSet)
    pFX->SetFieldType(CFieldExchange::outputColumn);

    // Various RFX_... commands

    //}}AFX_FIELD_MAP
    pFX->SetFieldType(CFieldExchange::param);
    RFX_Long(pFX, _T("ProductIDparam"), m_ProductIDparam);
}
```

Next, you need to add code to define a filter in the `CStockView::OnInitialUpdate()` function:

```
void CStockView::OnInitialUpdate()
{
    BeginWaitCursor();

    CDBSampleDoc* pDoc = (CDBSampleDoc*)GetDocument();
    m_pSet = &pDoc->m_StockSet;  // Initialize the recordset pointer

    // Set the database for the recordset
    m_pSet->m_pDatabase = pDoc->m_productSet.m_pDatabase;

    // Set the current Product ID as the parameter
    m_pSet->m_ProductIDparam = pDoc->m_productSet.m_ProductID;

    // Filter on the Product ID field
    m_pSet->m_strFilter = "ProductID = ?";

    GetRecordset();
    CRecordView::OnInitialUpdate();
    if (m_pSet->IsOpen())
    {
        CString strTitle = m_pSet->m_pDatabase->GetDatabaseName();
        CString strTable = m_pSet->GetTableName();
        if (!strTable.IsEmpty())
            strTitle += _T(":") + strTable;
        GetDocument()->SetTitle(strTitle);
    }
    EndWaitCursor();
}
```

As in the chapter, you need to add an **OnActivateView()** handler to **CStockView**. Here's the code you need to insert:

```
void CStockView::OnActivateView(BOOL bActivate, CView* pActivateView,
                                                 CView* pDeactiveView)
{
    if(bActivate)
    {
        CDBSampleDoc* pDoc = (CDBSampleDoc*)GetDocument();

        // Set current Product ID as parameter and requery the database
        m_pSet->m_ProductIDparam = pDoc->m_productSet.m_ProductID;
        m_pSet->Requery();
        CRecordView::OnInitialUpdate();
    }
    CRecordView::OnActivateView(bActivate, pActivateView, pDeactiveView);
}
```

Finally, you should add **#include**s for **ProductSet.h** and **DBSampleDoc.h** to **StockView.cpp**.

Ex20-3: There are all kinds of ways you could approach this; here's a fairly easy method. Add a new edit control to the stock dialog and label it something like Stock Position. *Ctrl*-double-click on the edit box and add a new **CString** variable called **m_StockPosn**. Then you can simply add a few lines to **CStockView::DoDataExchange()**:

```
void CStockView::DoDataExchange(CDataExchange* pDX)
{
    CRecordView::DoDataExchange(pDX);

    m_StockPosn = "Situation normal";
    long StockBalance = m_pSet->m_UnitsInStock - m_pSet->m_ReorderLevel;

    if (m_pSet->m_ReorderLevel != 0)
    {
        if ((StockBalance > 0) && (StockBalance < 11))
            m_StockPosn = "*Warning: low stock*";
        if (StockBalance < 1)
            m_StockPosn = "**Urgent: reorder now**";
    }

    //{{AFX_DATA_MAP(CStockView)
    DDX_FieldText(pDX, IDC_SKPRODUCTNAME, m_pSet->m_ProductName, m_pSet);
    DDX_FieldText(pDX, IDC_SKPRODUCTID, m_pSet->m_ProductID, m_pSet);
    DDX_FieldText(pDX, IDC_SKUNITPRICE, m_pSet->m_UnitPrice, m_pSet);
    DDX_FieldText(pDX, IDC_SKUNITSINSTOCK, m_pSet->m_UnitsInStock, m_pSet);
    DDX_FieldText(pDX, IDC_SKREORDERLEVEL, m_pSet->m_ReorderLevel, m_pSet);
    DDX_Text(pDX, IDC_STOCKPOSN, m_StockPosn);
    //}}AFX_DATA_MAP
}
```

If all has gone well, you'll have a dialog which looks something like this:

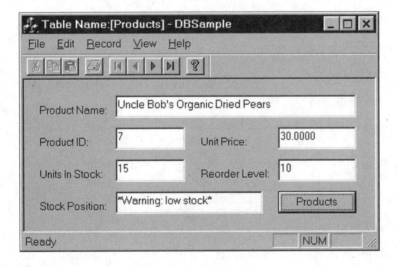

Chapter 21

Ex21-1: In order to display customers in alphabetical order, we need to change the **OnGetRecordSet()** method of the **CCustomerView** class:

```
CRecordset* CCustomerView::OnGetRecordset()
{
    if (m_pSet != NULL)
        return m_pSet;
```

```
        m_pSet = new CCustomerSet(NULL);

        // Sort by customer name
        m_pSet->m_strSort = "[CompanyName]";

        m_pSet->Open();

        return m_pSet;
    }
```

Then, to make sure that the dialog always displays the first customer when switching to the view, we need to alter the **SelectView()** member of the **CMainFrame** class:

```
    void CMainFrame::SelectView(int viewID)
    {
        ...

        if(viewID==NEWORDER_VIEW)
        {
            static_cast<CCustomerView*>(pNewActiveView)->SetNewOrderID();

            // Always move to the first record in the recordset
            static_cast<CCustomerView*>(pNewActiveView)->OnMove(ID_RECORD_FIRST);
        }
        else if(viewID == SELECTPRODUCT_VIEW)
            static_cast<CProductView*>(pNewActiveView)->InitializeView();

        ...

    }
```

Ex21-2: The **IDD_PRODUCT_FORM** dialog needs a couple of extra controls to display the total price. (Note that all the forms will need to be resized as you alter the size of **IDD_PRODUCT_FORM**):

We add a data member named **m_TotalValue** to **CProductView**, and associate this with the new edit control to display the total price.

Adding code to set **m_TotalValue** correctly, we need to modify the **InitializeView()** method of **CProductView**:

```
void CProductView::InitializeView()
{
   // Get a pointer to the document
   CDBSimpleUpdateDoc* pDoc = static_cast<CDBSimpleUpdateDoc*>(GetDocument());

   m_OrderID = pDoc->m_Order.m_OrderID;
   m_CompanyName = pDoc->m_Order.m_ShipName;
   m_Quantity = 1;                              // Must order at least 1
   m_Discount = 0;                              // No default discount
   m_TotalValue = 0.0;                          // Reset total value
   m_OrderAdded = false;                        // Order not added initially
   UpdateData(false);                           // Transfer data to controls
}
```

The **OnSelectproduct()** member of **CProductView** has additional code to accumulate and display the total price.

```
void CProductView::OnSelectproduct()
{
   ...

   if(m_OrderAdded)
   {
      pDoc->AddOrderDetails(m_pSet->m_ProductID,
                            m_pSet->m_UnitPrice,
                            m_Quantity,
                            m_Discount);

      // Copy and trim unit price string
      CString price = m_pSet->m_UnitPrice;    // Copy of unit price string
      price.TrimLeft();                        // Remove leading whitespace
      price.TrimRight();                       // Remove trailing whitespace

      // Convert price string to floating point value
      double priceValue = 0.0;                 // Nemeric value of unit price string
      int digitValue = 0;                      // Numeric value of digit character
      double factor = 10.0;                    // Multiplier in comnversion
      bool isPoint = false;                    // Indicates a decimal point found
      CString digits("0123456789");            // Legal digit characters

      for(int i = 0 ; i<price.GetLength(); i++)
      {
         if(price[i] == '.')                   // Decimal point?
         {
            isPoint = true;
            continue;
         }
         digitValue = digits.Find(price[i]); // Find index of digit
         if(digitValue<0)                      // No digit found?
         {
            AfxMessageBox("Invalid character in Unit Price string.");
            priceValue = 0.0;                  // reset price to zero
            break;
         }
```

```
            priceValue = isPoint ? priceValue+digitValue/factor :
                                   priceValue*factor+digitValue;
        }
        // Add price for current product quantity
        m_TotalValue += m_Quantity*priceValue*(1.0 - m_Discount);
```

```
        // Now reset the values in the quantity and discount controls

        ...

    }
}
```

Ex21.3: You need to use the ClassWizard add a new **CEmployeeSet** recordset class to retrieve employee data from sample database.

Next we need to modify the constructor to sort the records, as shown below:

```
CEmployeeSet::CEmployeeSet(CDatabase* pdb) : CRecordset(pdb)
{
    //{{AFX_FIELD_INIT(CEmployeeSet)
    m_EmployeeID = 0;
    m_LastName = _T("");
    m_FirstName = _T("");
    m_nFields = 3;
    //}}AFX_FIELD_INIT
    m_nDefaultType = snapshot;
```

```
    m_strSort = "LastName,FirstName"; // Sort records by name
}
```

Next, **#include** the **EmployeeSet.h** file in the document object, **CDBSimpleUpdateDoc**, and add a public member of type **CEmployeeSet** called **m_EmployeeSet**.

The **IDD_CUSTOMER_FORM** needs to provide an employee name selection facility, so add a listbox control, **IDC_EMPLOYEENAME**, to look like:

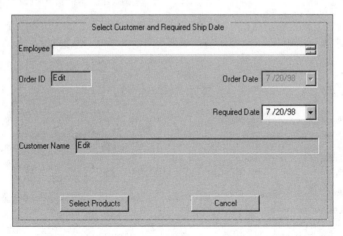

We need to add a constant to **OurConstants.h** to represent "no employee ID":

```
// Arbitrary constants to identify record views
const int ORDERDETAILS_VIEW = 1;
const int NEWORDER_VIEW = 2;
const int SELECTPRODUCT_VIEW = 3;
const long NO_EMPLOYEE_ID = 999999;
```

And we need a public data member, **m_pEmployeeID**, in **CCustomerView** to store the employee ID. To control the listbox, add another variable to **CCustomerView**:

```
class CCustomerView : public CRecordView
{
public:
    CCustomerView();            // protected constructor used by dynamic creation
    DECLARE_DYNCREATE(CCustomerView)

// Form Data
public:
    //{{AFX_DATA(CCustomerView)
    enum { IDD = IDD_CUSTOMER_FORM };
    CListBox    m_EmployeeCtrl;
    CCustomerSet* m_pSet;
    CTime    m_OrderDate;
    CTime    m_RequiredDate;
    long     m_NewOrderID;
    //}}AFX_DATA

    ...

// Operations
public:
    long m_EmployeeID;
    void SetNewOrderID();
    CCustomerSet* GetRecordset();
```

The **CEmployeeSet** object is used in **OnInitialUpdate()** method of **CCustomerView** to populate the listbox with employee names and IDs.

```
void CCustomerView::OnInitialUpdate()
{
    ...

    SetNewOrderID();                                        // Set up a a new order ID

    // Open employee recordset
    CEmployeeSet* pEmployeeSet = &static_cast<CDBSimpleUpdateDoc*>
                                        (GetDocument())->m_EmployeeSet;
    if(!pEmployeeSet->IsOpen())
        pEmployeeSet->Open(CRecordset::snapshot);

    // Set up employee control with names from the employee recordset
    int listIndex = 0;                                      // Index to listbox entries

    m_EmployeeCtrl.InsertString(listIndex, "Choose a name");    // First entry
    m_EmployeeCtrl.SetItemData(listIndex, NO_EMPLOYEE_ID);      // is not a name
```

```
      if(!pEmployeeSet->IsBOF())
         pEmployeeSet->MoveFirst();

      // Insert names in the listbox plus IDs
      while(!pEmployeeSet->IsEOF())
      {
         listIndex = m_EmployeeCtrl.InsertString(++listIndex,
                        pEmployeeSet->m_FirstName+ _T(" ") +
                        pEmployeeSet->m_LastName);
         m_EmployeeCtrl.SetItemData(listIndex,
                           static_cast<DWORD>(pEmployeeSet->m_EmployeeID));
         pEmployeeSet->MoveNext();
      }
      m_EmployeeID = NO_EMPLOYEE_ID;                       // No employee ID set
```

```
   EndWaitCursor();
   // Initialize time values
   SYSTEMTIME Now;
   GetLocalTime(&Now);                                // Get current time
   m_OrderDate = m_RequiredDate = CTime(Now);         // Set time as today
}
```

The **OnSelectproducts()** and **OnCancel()** handlers also need to be modified to deal with employee names:

```
void CCustomerView::OnSelectproducts()
{
```

```
   // Check employee has been selected - Exercise 3
   if(m_EmployeeID == NO_EMPLOYEE_ID)
   {
      AfxMessageBox("You must select the employee name.");
      return;
   }
```

```
   // Get a pointer to the document
   CDBSimpleUpdateDoc* pDoc = static_cast<CDBSimpleUpdateDoc*>(GetDocument());

   // Set up order field values from CCustomerSet object
   ...
```

```
   pDoc->m_Order.m_EmployeeID = m_EmployeeID;
```

```
   // Set up order field values from CCustomerView dialog input
   pDoc->m_Order.m_OrderID = m_NewOrderID;             // Generated new ID
   pDoc->m_Order.m_OrderDate = m_OrderDate;            // From order date control
   pDoc->m_Order.m_RequiredDate = m_RequiredDate;      // From required date control
```

```
   // Reset Employee Name listbox
   m_EmployeeCtrl.SetTopIndex(0);                      // Move to first item
   m_EmployeeID = NO_EMPLOYEE_ID;                      // Reset ID to no selection
```

```
   static_cast<CMainFrame*>(GetParentFrame())->SelectView(SELECTPRODUCT_VIEW);
}
```

```
void CCustomerView::OnCancel()
{
```

```
   // Reset Employee Name listbox
```

```
      m_EmployeeCtrl.SetTopIndex(0);                    // Move to first item in
   listbox
      m_EmployeeID = NO_EMPLOYEE_ID;                    // Reset ID to no selection

      static_cast<CMainFrame*>(GetParentFrame())->SelectView(ORDERDETAILS_VIEW);
   }
```

Lastly, the listbox handler we added to **CCustomerView** to receive the listbox select events needs the following code:

```
   void CCustomerView::OnSelchangeEmployeename()
   {
      m_EmployeeID = m_EmployeeCtrl.GetItemData(m_EmployeeCtrl.GetCurSel());
   }
```

Ex21-4: This is going to feel pretty familiar. First, add a **CShippersSet** recordset class added to retrieve shipping company data from database. Then modify the constructor to sort records:

```
   CShippersSet::CShippersSet(CDatabase* pdb) : CRecordset(pdb)
   {
      //{{AFX_FIELD_INIT(CShippersSet)
      m_ShipperID = 0;
      m_CompanyName = _T("");
      m_nFields = 2;
      //}}AFX_FIELD_INIT
      m_nDefaultType = snapshot;
      m_strSort = "CompanyName";  // Sort records by name
   }
```

Then we need to add the **CShippersSet** recordset object added to document object.

```
   #include "EmployeeSet.h"
   #include "ShippersSet.h"          // Added by ClassView

   class CDBSimpleUpdateDoc : public CDocument
   {
      ...

   // Implementation
   public:
      CShippersSet m_Shippers;
      ...
```

Add another listbox, **IDC_SHIPPERS**, to **IDD_CUSTOMER_FORM** to provide shipping company name selection facility:

OurConstants.h needs changing to represent "no shipping company ID":

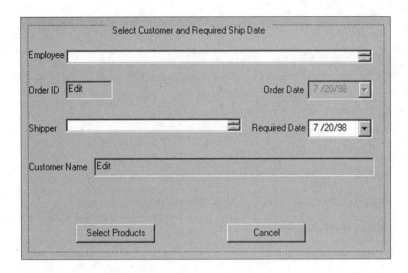

```
    const long NO_EMPLOYEE_ID = 999999;
    const long NO_SHIPPER_ID = 999998;
```

Next, we need to change **CCustomerView** to store the shipping company ID and add a variable for the listbox control:

```
public:
    //{{AFX_DATA(CCustomerView)
    enum { IDD = IDD_CUSTOMER_FORM };
    CListBox    m_ShippersCtrl;
    ...
    //}}AFX_DATA

...

// Operations
public:
    long m_ShipVia;
    long m_EmployeeID;
    ...
```

Turning our attention to the **OnInitialUpdate()** method of **CCustomerView**, we make the following changes to populate the listbox with shipping company names and IDs:

```
void CCustomerView::OnInitialUpdate()
{
    ...
    m_EmployeeID = NO_EMPLOYEE_ID;                              // No employee ID set

    // Open shippers recordset
    CShippersSet* pShippersSet = &static_cast<CDBSimpleUpdateDoc*>
                                         (GetDocument())->m_Shippers;
    if(!pShippersSet->IsOpen())
        pShippersSet->Open();
```

```
      // Set up shippers control with names from the shippers recordset - Exercise 4
      listIndex = 0;                                      // Index to listbox entries
      // First entry
      m_ShippersCtrl.InsertString(listIndex, "Choose a shipping company");
      m_ShippersCtrl.SetItemData(listIndex, NO_SHIPPER_ID);    // is not a shipper

      if(!pShippersSet->IsBOF())
         pShippersSet->MoveFirst();

      // Insert shippers in the listbox plus IDs - Exercise 3
      while(!pShippersSet->IsEOF())
      {
         listIndex = m_ShippersCtrl.InsertString(++listIndex,
                                            pShippersSet->m_CompanyName);
         m_ShippersCtrl.SetItemData(listIndex, static_cast<DWORD>
                                            (pShippersSet->m_ShipperID));
         pShippersSet->MoveNext();
      }
      m_ShipVia = NO_SHIPPER_ID;                           // No shipper ID set

   EndWaitCursor();
   // Initialize time values
   SYSTEMTIME Now;
   GetLocalTime(&Now);                                     // Get current time
   m_OrderDate = m_RequiredDate = CTime(Now);              // Set time as today
}
```

Similar changes are needed for the handlers **OnSelectproducts()** and **OnCancel()** to deal with shipping company names:

```
void CCustomerView::OnSelectproducts()
{
   // Check employee has been selected
   if(m_EmployeeID == NO_EMPLOYEE_ID)
   {
      AfxMessageBox("You must select the employee name.");
      return;
   }

   // Check shipper has been selected
   if(m_ShipVia == NO_SHIPPER_ID)
   {
      AfxMessageBox("You must select a shipping company.");
      return;
   }

   // Get a pointer to the document
   CDBSimpleUpdateDoc* pDoc = static_cast<CDBSimpleUpdateDoc*>(GetDocument());

   // Set up order field values from CCustomerSet object
   ...
   pDoc->m_Order.m_EmployeeID = m_EmployeeID;
   pDoc->m_Order.m_ShipVia = m_ShipVia;

   ...
```

```
    // Reset Employee Name listbox
    m_EmployeeCtrl.SetTopIndex(0);                        // Move to first item
    m_EmployeeID = NO_EMPLOYEE_ID;                        // Reset ID to no
selection

    // Reset Shippers listbox
    m_ShippersCtrl.SetTopIndex(0);
    m_ShipVia = NO_SHIPPER_ID;

    static_cast<CMainFrame*>(GetParentFrame())->SelectView(SELECTPRODUCT_VIEW);
}

void CCustomerView::OnCancel()
{
    // Reset Employee Name listbox - Exercise 3
    m_EmployeeCtrl.SetTopIndex(0);                        // Move to first item in
listbox
    m_EmployeeID = NO_EMPLOYEE_ID;                        // Reset ID to no
selection

    // Reset Shippers listbox - Exercise 4
    m_ShippersCtrl.SetTopIndex(0);
    m_ShipVia = NO_SHIPPER_ID;

    static_cast<CMainFrame*>(GetParentFrame())->SelectView(ORDERDETAILS_VIEW);
}
```

Finally, the listbox handler that the ClassWizard added to **CCustomerView** to receive listbox select events needs the following code:

```
void CCustomerView::OnSelchangeShippers()
{
    m_ShipVia = m_ShippersCtrl.GetItemData(m_ShippersCtrl.GetCurSel());
}
```

Chapter 22

Ex22-1: First, open the resource for the menu **IDR_WRXCONTYPE** and add a new menu item to the Edit menu with the properties shown below.

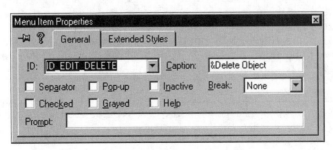

Ctrl-double-click on the new menu item to activate ClassWizard, then add **COMMAND** and **UPDATE_COMMAND_UI** handlers to the view class, **CWrxContainerView**. You can accept the default function names of **OnEditDelete()** and **OnUpdateEditDelete()**. Once the new handlers have been added, you can close ClassWizard and start adding some code to the new functions.

We need the new menu item to be enabled only when one of the items in the container is selected. We can determine whether an item is selected by looking at the **m_pSelection** member of the view class. Add the code shown to **OnUpdateEditDelete()**.

```
void CWrxContainerView::OnUpdateEditDelete(CCmdUI* pCmdUI)
{
    if (m_pSelection == NULL)
        pCmdUI->Enable(FALSE);
    else
        pCmdUI->Enable(TRUE);
}
```

This code enables the menu item when there's a valid pointer in **m_pSelection** and disables it when **m_pSelection** is **NULL**. This prevents the user of the container from trying to delete an item without first selecting one.

Deleting an item is simplicity itself — you can just call **COleClientItem::Delete()** to remove a client from a document. The code you should add to **OnEditDelete()** is shown below:

```
void CWrxContainerView::OnEditDelete()
{
    ASSERT(m_pSelection != NULL);
    if (m_pSelection != NULL)
    {
        CWrxContainerDoc* pDoc = GetDocument();
        m_pSelection->Delete();
        m_pSelection = NULL;
        pDoc->SetModifiedFlag();
        Invalidate();
    }
}
```

There's actually a bit more to this code than the single line that deletes the selected item because we need to ensure the integrity of our application. The first line uses the **ASSERT()** macro to alert us if **m_pSelection** is **NULL**. This also serves as documentation to show readers of this code that **m_pSelection** shouldn't be **NULL** when the function is called. We expect **m_pSelection** not to be **NULL** because of the way that we enable and disable the menu item, but this macro helps make doubly sure that **m_pSelection** is in the state we expect.

The **ASSERT()** macro is only active in debug builds so the **if** statement is also necessary to ensure that our code is robust in release builds. If **m_pSelection** does somehow turn out to be **NULL** when this function is called then we don't want to take any action in a release build.

If **m_pSelection** isn't **NULL**, we get a pointer to the document class, then delete the selected item. Next, we set **m_pSelection** to **NULL** because the selected item no longer exists. We need to let the framework know that the document has been modified so that it can save it when necessary, so we call **SetModifiedFlag()** through the document pointer. Finally, we **Invalidate()** the view so that it gets redrawn without the item that has just been deleted.

Chapter 23

Ex23-1: Limitations of the **StartRed** property. There are two main flaws:

1   It limits the starting state of the signal to one of two values: red or not red. This is a problem because there are more than two states that our signal can be in, and it seems unreasonable to exclude valid signal states from the possible start states. We should provide optimum flexibility to the users of our control.

2   Its name unnecessarily relates the state of the signal to a color. The interface of our control is inconsistent because we have one property (**StartRed**) that describes the state of the signal in terms of its color (red or not red) and another property (**StopOrGoTime**) and an event (**SignalChanged**) that describe the state of the signal in terms of the information it conveys (stop, go, or ready to stop). We should rationalize these inconsistencies and always describe the state of the signal in the same way. Since the signal is better defined in terms of the information it conveys than the colors it uses to convey that information, **StartRed** should be replaced or renamed.

To rectify the problems with **StartRed**, we could replace it with a property called **StartState**. This property could use the same enumeration for its possible values as we defined for the **SignalChanged** event. This means that we can provide greater flexibility to our control's users, and provide a consistent interface to our control.

Replacing **StartRed** with **StartState** would also allow us to alter the drawing code for the signal without worrying about whether the property name remained relevant to the control. If we wanted to provide a signal that used icons to represent the different states of the signal, all we would need to change would be the drawing code. The user of our control would be able to use the new version instantly without getting confused by our choice of property name.

Ex23-2: Implementing the **StartState** property. First, use ClassWizard to remove all traces of the **StartRed** property. Go to the Automation tab for the **CTrafficSignalCtrl** class, select **StartRed** and then click <u>D</u>elete. Follow the instructions you're given. Next, use ClassWizard again to add a new Automation property to **CTrafficSignalCtrl** using the settings shown in the screenshot:

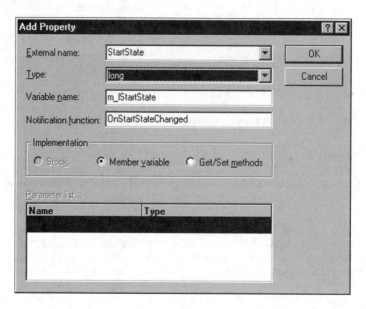

Add the following code to **CTrafficSignalCtrl::OnStartStateChanged()**:

```
void CTrafficSignalCtrl::OnStartStateChanged()
{
   // Stop the signal if necessary
   if (m_bSignalGo)
   {
      m_bSignalGo = FALSE;      // Set signal not running
      StopSignal();             // Stop the signal
   }
   // Set the signal object to the appropriate state
   m_pSignal->SetSignalState(m_lStartState);

   InvalidateControl();          // Get the control redrawn

   SetModifiedFlag();
}
```

Update the code in **CTrafficSignalCtrl::DoPropExchange()** as shown:

```
void CTrafficSignalCtrl::DoPropExchange(CPropExchange* pPX)
{
   ExchangeVersion(pPX, MAKELONG(_wVerMinor, _wVerMajor));
   COleControl::DoPropExchange(pPX);

   // TODO: Call PX_ functions for each persistent custom property.
   PX_Long(pPX, _T("StartState"), m_lStartState, STOP);
   PX_Long(pPX, _T("StopOrGoTime"), m_lStopOrGoTime, 5000);

   // Set the signal object to the appropriate state
   m_pSignal->SetSignalState(m_lStartState);
}
```

Update **CTrafficSignalCtrl::SetStopOrGoTime()** to use the new property notification function:

```
void CTrafficSignalCtrl::SetStopOrGoTime(long nNewValue)
{
   // Only alter the control if the value is different
   if (m_lStopOrGoTime != nNewValue)
   {
      m_lStopOrGoTime = nNewValue;          // Set the new stop or go time

      OnStartStateChanged();                // Set the initial state
      SetModifiedFlag();
   }
}
```

Update the **.odl** file as shown so that the new property uses the enumeration:

```
[id(2)] long StopOrGoTime;
[id(1)] SignalState StartState;
```

Ex23-3: Updating a control that has existing users needs to be handled sensitively if you want those users to upgrade to the new version. It can be quite tricky when you're just adding functionality, but that's as nothing compared with when you want to remove properties, methods or events from a control. Removing items from the public interface of a control is *not* something that should be done lightly, and you should try to avoid being in the position of wanting to remove something by carefully designing, implementing and testing your control *before* releasing it to the public.

In our case, we'll plan to remove the **StartRed** property in two stages which in the real world might be separated by months or even years. First, we'll release a control that retains the **StartRed** property and is completely compatible with the first version of the control. All code written to use the first version of the control will work fully with the new version. However, the new version of the control will discourage the use of the **StartRed** property so that in the future we may be able to release a version of the control that drops support for the **StartRed** property completely.

In fact, we may decide never to drop the **StartRed** property from our control because of the large amount of existing code that uses it. It might not be a problem with our simple traffic signal, but it's certainly a possibility for professionally produced ActiveX controls. With that in mind, the first thing that we'd do differently from the implementation of **StartState** in *Ex23-2* is not to delete the **StartRed** property!

> *When updating a control, make sure that you keep a clean backup copy of the source code for the existing control — you never know what might happen!*

We can add the **StartState** property to the control in the same way as before, but after doing so we need to make that it hasn't altered the DispIDs used for the existing methods and properties. It's a good idea to keep DispIDs consistent between versions of a control, even though it's quite unlikely for a client to be using the DispIDs directly. (It could be important if you distribute type libraries for the control separately from the control itself.)

1145

There are two places that you need to check the values of the DispIDs. Towards the end of `TrafficSignalCtl.h` you'll find the following:

```
enum {
//{{AFX_DISP_ID(CTrafficSignalCtrl)
dispidStartRed = 1L,
dispidStopOrGoTime = 3L,
dispidStartState = 2L,
eventidSignalChanged = 1L,
//}}AFX_DISP_ID
};
```

If you compare this with the original control, you may find that the DispID for the `StopOrGoTime` property has changed so change the code like this:

```
enum {
//{{AFX_DISP_ID(CTrafficSignalCtrl)
dispidStartRed = 1L,
dispidStopOrGoTime = 2L,
dispidStartState = 3L,
eventidSignalChanged = 1L,
//}}AFX_DISP_ID
};
```

You'll also need to change the values of the **id**s in the **.odl** file to corresponding values. Always make sure that the IDs for the properties and methods are unique, positive integers.

```
properties:
    // NOTE - ClassWizard will maintain property information here.
    //    Use extreme caution when editing this section.
    //{{AFX_ODL_PROP(CTrafficSignalCtrl)
    [id(DISPID_BACKCOLOR), bindable, requestedit] OLE_COLOR BackColor;
    [id(1)] boolean StartRed;
    [id(2)] long StopOrGoTime;
    [id(3)] SignalState StartState;
    //}}AFX_ODL_PROP
```

Note that we have changed the type of the **StartState** property so that it uses the enumeration, just as we did in *Ex23-2*.

If you change the DispIDs, the last area you'll need to change is the dispatch map itself, which you'll find in **TrafficSignalCtl.cpp**. The order of the entries in the map should match the DispIDs that you've assigned in the header and **.odl** files, so make sure that the code matches this:

```
BEGIN_DISPATCH_MAP(CTrafficSignalCtrl, COleControl)
    //{{AFX_DISPATCH_MAP(CTrafficSignalCtrl)
    DISP_PROPERTY_NOTIFY(CTrafficSignalCtrl, "StartRed",
                        m_bStartRed, OnStartRedChanged, VT_BOOL)
    DISP_PROPERTY_EX(CTrafficSignalCtrl, "StopOrGoTime",
                    GetStopOrGoTime, SetStopOrGoTime, VT_I4)
    DISP_PROPERTY_NOTIFY(CTrafficSignalCtrl, "StartState",
                        m_lStartState, OnStartStateChanged, VT_I4)
    DISP_STOCKPROP_BACKCOLOR()
    //}}AFX_DISPATCH_MAP
```

```
        DISP_FUNCTION_ID(CTrafficSignalCtrl, "AboutBox",
                         DISPID_ABOUTBOX, AboutBox, VT_EMPTY, VTS_NONE)
    END_DISPATCH_MAP()
```

> *As you've seen, ClassWizard provides DispIDs that match the alphabetical order of the properties you supply. This may be inappropriate if you're modifying a control that needs to maintain the DispIDs for its existing members. However, you can set the DispIDs of the properties manually by using the technique outlined above. Remember to match up the DispIDs in the control's header file, the .odl file and dispatch map.*

Now add the code for **OnStartStateChanged()**. The highlighted code shows up the differences between this version and *Ex23-2*, when we didn't have to worry about **StartRed**.

```
void CTrafficSignalCtrl::OnStartStateChanged()
{
    // Stop the signal if necessary
    if (m_bSignalGo)
    {
        m_bSignalGo = FALSE;  // Set signal not running
        StopSignal();         // Stop the signal
    }
    // Set the signal object to the appropriate state
    m_pSignal->SetSignalState(m_lStartState);

    // The following is only necessary if you are continuing
    // to support the StartRed property
    if (STOP == m_lStartState)
        m_bStartRed = TRUE;
    else
        m_bStartRed = FALSE;

    InvalidateControl();      // Get the control redrawn

    SetModifiedFlag();
}
```

Now change the code for **DoPropExchange()**. This is significantly different to the code we've had previously:

```
void CTrafficSignalCtrl::DoPropExchange(CPropExchange* pPX)
{
    ExchangeVersion(pPX, MAKELONG(_wVerMinor, _wVerMajor));
    COleControl::DoPropExchange(pPX);

    // TODO: Call PX_ functions for each persistent custom property.
    if (pPX->GetVersion() < MAKELONG(0, 2))
    {
        // If we are loading information from before version 2.0
        // then we know that StartRed will have been saved
        PX_Bool(pPX, _T("StartRed"), m_bStartRed, TRUE);
        PX_Long(pPX, _T("StopOrGoTime"), m_lStopOrGoTime, 5000);
```

1147

```
                // Set the signal object to the appropriate state
                if (m_bStartRed)
                {
                    m_pSignal->SetSignalState(STOP);
                    m_1StartState = STOP; // Added to support the new StartState property
                }
                else
                {
                    m_pSignal->SetSignalState(GO);
                    m_1StartState = GO; // Added to support the new StartState property
                }
            }
            else
            {
                // If we are loading/saving info from a version 2.0 or later file,
                // we don't have to worry about StartRed, we use StartState instead
                PX_Long(pPX, _T("StopOrGoTime"), m_1StopOrGoTime, 5000);
                PX_Long(pPX, _T("StartState"), m_1StartState, STOP);

                // Set the signal object to the appropriate state
                m_pSignal->SetSignalState(m_1StartState);

                // This is only necessary if you are continuing to support
                // the StartRed property
                if (STOP == m_1StartState)
                    m_bStartRed = TRUE;
                else
                    m_bStartRed = FALSE;
            }
        }
    }
```

Note the use of **CPropExchange::GetVersion()**. This function returns the version of the control, which is retrieved from the persistent data when loading properties and is taken from the values of the global constants **wVerMajor** and **wVerMinor** when saving properties. The function will save data in version 2.0 format just so long as we make sure that the control knows that it's a version 2.0 control. You can do this by changing the values of **wVerMajor** and **wVerMinor**, which you'll find at the top of **TrafficSignal.cpp**:

```
const WORD _wVerMajor = 2;
const WORD _wVerMinor = 0;
```

This code means that regardless of whether we load our properties from a version 1.0 or version 2.0 property store, they will always be saved in version 2.0 format. This means that we are already making a small step towards eliminating the use of the **StartRed** property.

If you want a way to save persistent properties using the same version format as they were loaded with, check out the documentation for ExchangeVersion().

The only thing left to do is to discourage the use of the **StartRed** property in new code. The best way to do this is to document the function as being out of date and point the programmer to the new **StartState** property. However, you can also hide the property from Visual Basic users by applying the **hidden** keyword to the property in the **.odl** file:

```
[id(DISPID_BACKCOLOR), bindable, requestedit] OLE_COLOR BackColor;
[id(1), hidden] boolean StartRed;
[id(2)] long StopOrGoTime;
```

This will tell Visual Basic (and other environments that respect this property) not to show the item to the user of your control. Thus **StartRed** will no longer appear in Visual Basic's Properties Window or the Object Browser. However, any code that uses **StartRed** will continue to work just as before.

Chapter 24

Ex24-1: To show you COM compiler support, we'll can create a Win32 Console Application, of type Simple Application, and add the following code to the **main()** function:

```
// Mytesting.cpp : Defines the entry point for the console application.
//

#include "stdafx.h"

int main(int argc, char* argv[])
{
    HRESULT hr = CoInitialize(NULL);          // Initialize COM
    if (FAILED(hr))                           // Check for failure
    {
        cout << "COM could not be initialized\n";
        return 0;
    }

    // If COM was successfully initialized, we can create the proper code
    // We wrap the code in a try block because the #import-generated wrappers
    // can throw _com_error exceptions on failure
    try
    {
        // Create the COM object and get a smart pointer to the IRefRate interface
        IRefRatePtr pRefRate(__uuidof(RefRate));

        // Get the horizontal and vertical resolutions
        long lHRes = pRefRate->GetHRes();
        long lVRes = pRefRate->GetVRes();

        //  Output the resolutions
        cout << "Horizontal resolution (pixels): " << lHRes << "\n";
        cout << "Vertical resolution (pixels): " << lVRes << "\n";

        while (true)                              // indefinite loop
        {
            cout << "\nEnter the maximum horizontal scan rate (kHz) or a negative
                    number to quit\n";
            long lHScan = -1;
            cin >> lHScan;

            if (lHScan < 0)                         // If the user wants to quit...
                throw "Application terminating...";  // ...terminate loop by throwing
                                                     // an exception
```

```
            long lRefresh = pRefRate->RefreshRate(lHScan);
            cout << "Refresh rate (Hz): " << lRefresh << "\n";
        }
    }
    // This error might be thrown by a wrapper class if something goes wrong
    catch (const _com_error& Err)
    {
        cout << Err.ErrorMessage() << "\n";
    }
    // We're expecting this error to be thrown when the user's had enough
    // It makes it easy to ensure that the smart pointer is finished with
    // by the time we call CoUninitialize()
    catch (const char* str)
    {
        cout << str << "\n";
    }

    CoUninitialize();   // Uninitialize COM
    return 0;
}
```

In **StdAfx.h**, add the following **#import** statements:

```
// #import generates smart pointer wrapper classes
// from the information contained in a type library
#import "..\RefreshRate\RefreshRate.tlb"
using namespace REFRESHRATELib;

// Use standard input and output
#include <iostream>
using std::cout;
using std::cin;
```

To implement the full ATL dialog-based application, start by creating a new project with the ATL COM AppWizard. Call it **CtrlClient** and select Executable (EXE) as the Server Type. Now add a dialog to the project by selecting Insert | New ATL Object..., and then Miscellaneous from the list in the ATL Object Wizard. Hit Next > and give the dialog a Short Name of **ClientDlg**. Then click OK.

Once the dialog class has been added to the project, we need to create an instance of the class when the executable starts. Open **CtrlClient.cpp** and add a **#include** statement for **ClientDlg.h** to the top of the file, just below the other **#include**s.

Now move down the file to the **_tWinMain()** function. This serves exactly the same purpose as the **WinMain()** function you saw back in Chapter 7, and acts as the entry point for the executable. (The **_t** prefix indicates that it will receive command line arguments as ASCII characters normally, or Unicode (wide) characters if **_UNICODE** is defined.)

The first half of the code provided by the Wizard for this function deals with parsing the command line arguments and registering or unregistering any components if the command line contains the **RegServer** or **UnregServer** switches. We don't need to worry about this because our client won't be exposing any COM objects. The code we're interested in will go in the second half of the function, after the **if (bRun)** check.

Add or modify the highlighted code shown below:

```
if (bRun)
    {
        hRes = _Module.RegisterClassObjects(CLSCTX_LOCAL_SERVER,
            REGCLS_MULTIPLEUSE);
        _ASSERTE(SUCCEEDED(hRes));

        CClientDlg* pdlgClient = new CClientDlg;
        pdlgClient->Create(NULL);
        pdlgClient->ShowWindow(SW_SHOW);

        MSG msg;
        while (GetMessage(&msg, 0, 0, 0) == TRUE)
        {
            TranslateMessage(&msg);      // Translate the message
            DispatchMessage(&msg);       // Dispatch the message
        }

        if (pdlgClient)
        {
            delete pdlgClient;
            pdlgClient = NULL;
        }

        _Module.RevokeClassObjects();
    }
```

The first section of code before the message loop just creates a new dialog object, then displays it to the user. Once the message loop exits (when it receives a **WM_CLOSE** message and **GetMessage()** returns zero), the dialog object is deleted to free the memory we used.

Now we have to make sure that that the application closes when the user closes the dialog. This means that we need to post a **WM_QUIT** message when the user clicks OK or Cancel on the dialog — for our purposes, both buttons perform the same action. If you look at the dialog class, you'll see that it already has functions (**OnOK()** and **OnCancel()**) to handle the buttons. The Wizard-produced code assumes that the dialog is modal, so it includes calls to **EndDialog()**. We're using a modeless dialog, so we need to replace this code with a call to **DestroyWindow()**.

Add the highlighted code shown below:

```
LRESULT CClientDlg::OnOK(WORD wNotifyCode, WORD wID, HWND hWndCtl, BOOL& bHandled)
{
    PostMessage(WM_QUIT);
    DestroyWindow();
    return 0;
}

LRESULT CClientDlg::OnCancel(WORD wNotifyCode, WORD wID, HWND hWndCtl, BOOL&
bHandled)
{
    PostMessage(WM_QUIT);
    DestroyWindow();
    return 0;
}
```

Now modify the dialog resource to include the controls necessary for the client. You can copy these controls from the existing dialog resource that you created for the MFC-based client. That done, the next step is to set up the variables that can be used to store the values associated with the controls, so add the following declarations to the **CClientDlg** class definition.

```
private:
    long m_lVRes;
    long m_lHRes;
    long m_lRefresh;
    long m_lHScan;
```

You should also initialize these variables in the class constructor. The top three can be initialized to zero, whereas **m_lHScan** should start at 50, just as it did in the MFC client.

Unfortunately, things get a little harder here. We can no longer use ClassWizard to add these variables, so you'll have to add them by hand. In addition, there's no ATL equivalent of the **UpdateData()** function so you'll need to write your own.

Add the function shown below to **CClientDlg** and give the single **bool** parameter a default value of **true**. This will work just like the **UpdateData()** member function in an MFC dialog.

```
void CClientDlg::UpdateData(bool bSave /* = true */)
{
  Exchange_Text(bSave, IDC_HSCAN, m_lHScan);
  Exchange_Text(bSave, IDC_REFRESH, m_lRefresh);
  Exchange_Text(bSave, IDC_HRES, m_lHRes);
  Exchange_Text(bSave, IDC_VRES, m_lVRes);
}
```

If you pass **true**, the **Exchange_Text()** function will take the strings stored in the control specified by the ID passed as the second parameter and convert their contents to a type compatible with the member variables passed as the third parameter. If you pass **false**, the **Exchange_Text()** function will take the values stored in the third parameter and display them in the control passed in the second parameter.

Your **Exchange_Text()** function should be added to **CClientDlg**, and could look something like this:

```
void CClientDlg::Exchange_Text(bool bSave, int nID, long& lValue)
{
  CComVariant converter = 0;
  if (bSave)
  {
    const int MAX_COUNT = 12;
    TCHAR strText[MAX_COUNT + 1] = {0};
    GetDlgItemText(nID, strText, MAX_COUNT);
    converter = strText;
    converter.ChangeType(VT_I4);
    lValue = converter.lVal;
  }
  else
  {
    USES_CONVERSION;
    converter = lValue;
    converter.ChangeType(VT_BSTR);
```

```
        LPCTSTR strText = OLE2T(converter.bstrVal);
        SetDlgItemText(nID, strText);
    }
}
```

This function is pretty rough-and-ready, but it does show how you might use a **VARIANT** (or the **CComVariant** wrapper class) to convert between a string and a **long**, and vice versa. It also demonstrates the use of the **OLE2T()** macro to convert from a **BSTR** to a **LPCTSTR**. In your own code, you'd probably want to provide something rather more robust.

Now we need to get hold of the server component so that we can use it to provide information about the refresh rate of our monitor. In contrast to the MFC client, we're going to use the compiler COM support to create a smart pointer class to wrap the **IRefRate** interface.

First, copy the type library for the RefreshRate component (**RefreshRate.tlb**) into the **CtrlClient** project directory. This is just so that we don't have to type a long path name into the **#import** statement for the library. Add **#import "RefreshRate.tlb" no_namespace** to the end of **StdAfx.h**.

Once you compile the project, this statement will produce two files in the output (**Debug** or **Release**) directory for the project, **RefreshRate.tlh** and **RefreshRate.tli**. These files contain class definitions for wrappers for the interfaces and classes contained in the type library. These output files are really for your reference (you don't need to include these files in your project explicitly since this is all handled by the **#import** statement), but it's worth taking a look at them to see what's available to you.

The smart pointer class that wraps the **IRefRate** interface is **typedef**'d to **IRefRatePtr**, so add a new member variable to the dialog class:

```
IRefRatePtr m_IRefRate;
```

Now we can use this member in **OnInitDialog()** and create an instance of the **RefRate** class:

```
LRESULT CClientDlg::OnInitDialog(UINT uMsg, WPARAM wParam, LPARAM lParam, BOOL&
bHandled)
{
    HRESULT hr = m_IRefRate.CreateInstance(__uuidof(RefRate));
    if SUCCEEDED(hr)
    {
        m_lVRes = m_IRefRate->GetVRes();
        m_lHRes = m_IRefRate->GetHRes();
        m_lRefresh = m_IRefRate.GetInterfacePtr()->RefreshRate(m_lHScan);
        UpdateData(false);
    }

    return 1;   // Let the system set the focus
}
```

Similarly, we can add code to respond to the Calculate button. You'll need to add an entry to the message map and a declaration for the **OnCalculate()** function to the **CClientDlg** class:

```
BEGIN_MSG_MAP(CClientDlg)
    MESSAGE_HANDLER(WM_INITDIALOG, OnInitDialog)
    COMMAND_ID_HANDLER(IDOK, OnOK)
```

1153

```
        COMMAND_ID_HANDLER(IDCANCEL, OnCancel)
        COMMAND_ID_HANDLER(IDC_CALCULATE, OnCalculate)
    END_MSG_MAP()
    // Handler prototypes:
    // LRESULT MessageHandler(UINT uMsg, WPARAM wParam, LPARAM lParam, BOOL&
    bHandled);
    // LRESULT CommandHandler(WORD wNotifyCode, WORD wID, HWND hWndCtl,
    //                         BOOL& bHandled);
    // LRESULT NotifyHandler(int idCtrl, LPNMHDR pnmh, BOOL& bHandled);
    LRESULT OnCalculate(WORD wNotifyCode, WORD wID, HWND hWndCtl, BOOL& bHandled);
```

The **OnCalculate()** function looks very similar to the **OnCalculate()** function in the MFC-based client:

```
    LRESULT CClientDlg::OnCalculate(WORD wNotifyCode, WORD wID, HWND hWndCtl, BOOL&
    bHandled)
    {
        UpdateData();
        m_lVRes = m_IRefRate.GetInterfacePtr()->GetVRes();
        m_lHRes = m_IRefRate.GetInterfacePtr()->GetHRes();
        m_lRefresh = m_IRefRate.GetInterfacePtr()->RefreshRate(m_lHScan);
        UpdateData(false);
        return 0;
    }
```

That's all there is to it. Now you can compile and run your ATL client just as you did with the MFC and Visual Basic clients. You don't need to worry about releasing the **IRefRate** pointer because it's all handled by the **IRefRatePtr** wrapper class.

Beginning
Visual C++ 6

Symbols

Case Study Exercise

By using our book, hope you have come to master many of the fundamnetal aspects of programming in Visual C++. It's now upto you to take your knowledge further by professionally programming in earnest.

To help you along the way we have designed a real-world "Case Study" that utilizes many of the lessons covered throughout the text. This short exercise in programming has been put together by Christophe Nasarre - an experienced Windows programmer and is available for download at our website :

www.wrox.com

...dial in and go to the *"Beginning Visual C++ 6"* book page, *"Source Code"* section - where you can download Christophe's complete explanation of the hows and whys behind a complete application.

You will need to be programming using the Windows NT4 Workstation (not Win95 / 98) as this Case Study uses files specific to the NT O/S.

Keep a lookout on the site for further case studies in the future.

Beginning ATL COM Programming

Authors: Various
ISBN: 1861000111
Price: $39.95 C$55.95 £36.99

This book is for fairly experienced C++ developers who want to get to grips with COM programming using the Active Template Library. The Beginning in the title of this book refers to COM and ATL. It does not refer to Programming.

We don't expect you to know anything about COM. The book explains the essentials of COM, how to use it, and how to get the most out of it. If you already know something about COM, that's a bonus. You'll still learn a lot about the way that ATL works, and you'll be one step ahead of the COM neophytes.

Neither do we expect you to know anything about ATL. ATL is the focus of the book. If you've never touched ATL, or if you've been using it for a short while, but still have many unanswered questions, this is the book for you.

Beginning MFC COM Programming

Author: Julian Templeman
ISBN: 1874416877
Price: $39.95 C$55.95 £36.99

This book is aimed at Visual C++ developers who have an understanding of MFC application programming, but have yet to make the leap into COM. To aid understanding, it introduces and describes the lower level of COM in broad terms, but this book certainly isn't for those seeking a reference to that subject.
Rather, it works through the excellent support that MFC provides to make it possible to write COM-enabled applications as efficiently as possible.
Beginning MFC COM Programming is an ideal second book for anyone who has read *Ivor Horton's Beginning Visual C++* and been intrigued by the introductory material on these subjects contained therein.

Beginning NT Programming

Author: Julian Templeman
ISBN: 1861000170
Price: $39.99 C$59.95 £36.99

This book is designed to lay bare the guts of NT programming. In order to do this, it concentrates on programming at a system level, using the Win32 API, rather than the Windows GUI. You'll learn about structured exception handling, how threads and processes work and how to deal with NT's filing system. You'll also learn about how to write NT Services, deal with the NT security system programmatically and implement inter-process communication.

If you're already familiar with C++, and are keen to take your first steps in writing NT system applications, or to add NT-specific features to your applications, then this is the book for you.

Beginning Java

Author: Ivor Horton
ISBN: 1861000278
Price: $36.00 C$50.40 £32.99

If you've enjoyed this book, you'll get a lot from Ivor's book, Beginning Java.

Beginning Java teaches Java 1.1 from scratch, taking in all the fundamental features of the Java language, along with practical applications of Java's extensive class libraries. While it assumes some familiarity with general programming concepts, Ivor takes time to cover the basics of the language in depth. He assumes no knowledge of object-oriented programming.

Ivor first introduces the essential bits of Java without which no program will run. Then he covers how Java handles data, and the syntax it uses to make decisions and control program flow. The essentials of object-oriented programming with Java are covered, and these concepts are reinforced throughout the book. Chapters on exceptions, threads and I/O follow, before Ivor turns to Java's graphics support and applet ability. Finally the book looks at JDBC and RMI, two additions to the Java 1.1 language which allow Java programs to communicate with databases and other Java programs.

Beginning Object Oriented Analysis and Design

Author: Jesse Liberty
ISBN: 1861001339
Price: $34.95 C$48.95 £32.49

Beginning Object-Oriented Analysis and Design is a tutorial about planning and designing a software product or project in a practical way, before getting involved with writing code. Using OOA&D, a programmer can develop a concrete blueprint or model of their software using the standard modeling language, UML. From the UML model, the programmer can successfully code the objects described. This can be done in any OO-capable language, although C++ is used as an example.

Going beyond the methodology and the modeling language, the book talks about the entire process of professional software development. *Beginning Object-Oriented Analysis and Design* is written in a straightforward manner that should be readily accessible to anyone developing software.

Instant UML

Authors: Pierre–Alain Muller
ISBN: 1861000871
Price: $34.95 C$48.95 £32.49

UML is the Unified Modeling Language. Modeling languages have come into vogue with the rise of object-oriented development, as they provide a means of communicating and recording every stage of the project. The results of the analysis and design phases are captured using the formal syntax of the modeling language, producing a clear model of the system to be implemented.

Instant UML offers not only a complete description of the notation and proper use of UML, but also an introduction to the theory of object-oriented programming, and the way to approach object-oriented application development. This is UML in context, not a list of the syntax without rhyme or reason.

This book is relevant to programmers of C++, VB, Java and other OO-capable languages, users of Visual Modeler (which comes with the Enterprise Edition of Microsoft's Visual Studio) and novice users of Rational Rose and similar UML-compliant tools.

COMDEVELOPER.COM

Microsoft's Component Object Model is the future of application development - a standard for creating software components in any language and using them on any platform. But with it comes the overhead of a whole new set of terms, types, interfaces and issues to confront and overcome. Whether you've been a COMHead for three years or three minutes, you'll find something of use here...

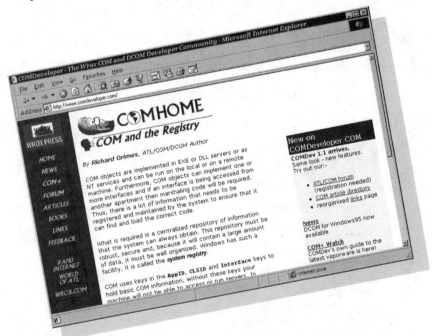

- · All the latest news on developments in the COM world
- · An up-to-date list of all the latest articles on COM around the web
- · Regular feature articles from noted COM authors and developers
- · Dedicated forum for COM and ATL queries and problems
- · Sample chapters from the complete series of WROX COM books
- · COM+ Watch - the first page of its kind which charts the progress of the next generation of the Component Object Model
- · Comprehensive listing of Other COM Websites

WROX PRESS INC.

Wrox writes books for you. Any suggestions, or
ideas about how you want information given in
your ideal book will be studied by our team.
Your comments are always valued at Wrox.

Free phone in USA 800-USE-WROX
Fax (312) 397 8990

UK Tel. (0121) 706 6826   Fax   (0121) 706 2967

Computer Book Publishers

NB. If you post the bounce back card below in the UK, please send it to:
Wrox Press Ltd. 30 Lincoln Road, Birmingham, B27 6PA